The SAGE
Handbook of

Personality Theory
and Assessment

Vol 1 Personality Theories and Models

The SAGE
Handbook of

Personality Theory
and Assessment

Vol 1 Personality Theories and Models

Edited by

Gregory J. Boyle
Gerald Matthews
Donald H. Saklofske

Los Angeles • London • New Delhi • Singapore

Chapter 1 Introduction and editorial arrangement © Gregory J. Boyle, Gerald Matthews and Donald H. Saklofske 2008

Chapter 2 © Robert M. Stelmack and Thomas H. Rammsayer 2008

Chapter 3 © Gerald Matthews 2008

Chapter 4 © Daniel Cervone 2008

Chapter 5 © Jens B. Asendorpf 2008

Chapter 6 © Chi-Yue Chiu, Young-Hoon Kim and Wendy W.N. Wan 2008

Chapter 7 © Andrew M. Johnson, Philip A. Vernon and Amanda R. Feiler 2008

Chapter 8 © Richard L. Michalski and Todd K. Shackelford 2008

Chapter 9 © John B. Campbell 2008

Chapter 10 © Kieron P. O'Connor 2008

Chapter 11 © Alan D. Pickering and Philip J. Corr 2008

Chapter 12 © Gregory J. Boyle 2008

Chapter 13 © In the Public Domain. Robert R. McCrae and Paul T. Costa, Jr. 2008

Chapter 14 © Gregory J. Boyle 2008

Chapter 15 © Andrew J. Elliot and Todd M. Thrash 2008

Chapter 16 © Marijn Lijffijt, Alan C. Swann and F. Gerard Moeller, 2008

Chapter 17 © David Rawlings and Sharon Dawe 2008

Chapter 18 © Marvin Zuckerman 2008

Chapter 19 © Melissa J. Green, Gregory J. Boyle and Adrian Raine 2008

Chapter 20 © Moshe Zeidner 2008

Chapter 21 © Herbert W. Marsh 2008

Chapter 22 © Rita Chang, Edward C. Chang, Lawrence J. Sanna and Robert L. Hatcher 2008

Chapter 23 © Jakob Smári Daníel Þór Ólason and Ragnar P. Ólafsson 2008

Chapter 24 © James D.A. Parker and Laura M. Wood 2008

Chapter 25 © Thomas A. Langens and Heinz-Dieter Schmalt 2008

Chapter 26 © Lazar Stankov and Sabina Kleitman 2008

Chapter 27 © Lazar Stankov and Jihyun Lee 2008

Chapter 28 © Elizabeth J. Austin, James D.A. Parker, K.V. Petrides and Donald H. Saklofske 2008

Chapter 29 © Mary L. Malik, Brynne E. Johannsen and Larry E. Beutler 2008

Chapter 30 © Gary Groth-Marnat, Elisa Gottheil, Weiling Liu, David A. Clinton and Larry E. Beutler 2008

Chapter 31 © Paula G. Williams, Timothy W. Smith and Matthew R. Cribbet 2008

Chapter 32 © Ephrem Fernandez and Robert D. Kerns 2008

Chapter 33 © Manuel I. Ibáñez, María A. Ruipérez, Helena Villa, Jorge Moya and Generós Ortet 2008

Chapter 34 © Donald G. Byrne and Jason Mazanov 2008

Chapter 35 © Robert P. Tett and Neil D. Christiansen 2008

First published 2008

SAGE Publications Ltd
1 Oliver's Yard
55 City Road
London EC1Y 1SP

SAGE Publications India Pvt Ltd
B 1/I 1 Mohan Cooperative Industrial Area
Mathura Road
New Delhi 110 044

SAGE Publications Inc.
2455 Teller Road
Thousand Oaks
California 91320

SAGE Publications Asia-Pacific Pte Ltd
33 Pekin Street #02-01
Far East Square
Singapore 048763

Library of Congress Control Number: 2007943494

British Library Cataloguing in Publication data
A catalogue record for this book is available from the British Library

ISBN 978-1-4129-4651-3

Typeset by Cepha Imaging Pvt. Ltd., Bangalore, India
Printed in Great Britain by The Cromwell Press Ltd, Trowbridge, Wiltshire
Printed on paper from sustainable resources

Dedications

Two of the greatest and most prolific contributors to the science of human personality during the 20th century were Raymond B. Cattell, PhD, DSc., and Hans J. Eysenck, PhD, DSc. While Professor Cattell pursued his academic career in prestigious USA universities (Harvard, Clark, Illinois), Professor Eysenck undertook his lifelong work at the Institute of Psychiatry, University of London. So prominent were these two men, that their work is now enshrined in the Cattellian and Eysenckian Schools of Psychology, respectively. Cattell concentrated on primary factors, while Eysenck focused on broader secondary dimensions. Indeed, at the second-order 16PF level, the degree of communality between the Eysenckian and Cattellian factors is striking!

'The Cattell and Eysenck constructs and theories should be seen, not as mutually contradictory, but as complementary and mutually supportive.'

Eysenck (1984). Cattell and the theory of Personality.
Multivariate Behavioral Research, 19(2–3): 323–336.

Both Ray Cattell and Hans Eysenck were our mentors and friends. Both men gave freely of their time, and their kindness and generosity was abundant. Our own academic careers were facilitated by the intellectual support and moral encouragement of both these great men who made a profound and lasting contribution to personality research and testing. Each was an exemplary scientist, humanitarian and mentor, qualities that all three editors respect and aspire to. We will remain forever indebted to both Ray Cattell and Hans Eysenck.

This book is also dedicated to:

My parents, my wife and family – GJB

Diana – GM

Frances and Harold, my parents – DHS

Contents

**Vol 2   Handbook of Personality Theory and Assessment:
          Personality Measurement and Testing**

Notes on Contributors

Jens Asendorpf is professor of psychology at Humboldt University, Berlin since 1994. He received his PhD from the University of Giessen, Germany in 1981. He studies transactions between personality and social relationships over the lifespan. Other interests include evolutionary approaches to personality and assessment of self-concept using the implicit association task. He is editor of the *European Journal of Personality*, and is author of more than 100 publications in the areas of personality and developmental psychology.

Elizabeth Austin is reader in psychology at the University of Edinburgh. She obtained her PhD from Oxford University in 1977. She studies how emotional intelligence can be fitted within the existing psychometric intelligence framework and associations among emotional intelligence, personality and health. Her other interests include the modelling of individual differences in responding to self-report scales. She is an associate editor of *Personality and Individual Differences* and the *British Journal of Psychology*.

Larry Beutler is distinguished professor at the Pacific Graduate School of Psychology. He received his PhD from the University of Nebraska-Lincoln in 1970. He is past editor of the *Journal of Clinical Psychology* and the *Journal of Consulting and Clinical Psychology*. He is a fellow of both the American Psychological Association and Association for Psychological Science. He is author of some 300 papers and book chapters, and has published 21 books on psychotherapy, psychopathology, depression, and drug abuse. He is co-author of the book *Treating Victims of Mass Disaster and Terrorism*, co-editor of *Rethinking the DSM: A Psychological Perspective*, as well as co-editor of the book, *Principles of Therapeutic Change that Work*.

Gregory Boyle is professor of psychology at Bond University, Australia. He earned separate PhDs from both the University of Delaware in 1983, and the University of Melbourne in 1985. He also received a DSc from the University of Queensland in 2006, for his research into personality and individual differences. He is a fellow of the Association for Psychological Science, and the Australian Psychological Society, and recipient of the Buros Institute of Mental Measurements Distinguished Reviewer Award in 2005. He is on a number of editorial boards including *Personality and Individual Differences*. He has over 200 publications, is co-author of a book on statistical methods, and co-editor of *Sage Benchmarks in Psychology: The Psychology of Individual Differences (4 Vols.)*. He is also co-editor of the current volumes.

Donald Byrne is professor of psychology at the Australian National University. He received his PhD from the University of Adelaide in 1975. He studies the roles of stress and behaviour in mediating risk of cardiovascular disease, adolescent stress and smoking behaviour. He has published over 130 papers and book chapters and is the author or editor of 13 books. He is co-author of *Health Psychology: Biopsychosocial Interactions – An Australian Perspective*, and co-editor of *Psycho-Neuro-Endocrino-Immunology*. He is a fellow of both the Academy of the Social Sciences in Australia and of the Australian Psychological Society.

John Campbell is professor of psychology at Franklin and Marshall College, Pennsylvania, where he has been on the faculty since 1984. He obtained his PhD from the University of Michigan in 1977. His major research interests are personality theory and measurement. Other interests include the origins of individual differences in subjective wellbeing, emotion regulation, and health. He is co-author of *Hall, Lindzey, and Campbell's Theories of Personality* (4th edition).

Daniel Cervone is professor of psychology at the University of Illinois, Chicago. He received his PhD from Stanford University in 1985. He has proposed the Knowledge-and-Appraisal Personality Architecture Model and has explored the contribution of social-cognitive structures to personality coherence. He is co-author of the books *Personality: Determinants, Dynamics, and Potentials,* and *Personality: Theory and Research*, and co-editor of *The Coherence of Personality*, and of *Advances in Personality Science*. He is an associate editor of the *Journal of Research in Personality*, and is on the editorial boards of *Psychological Review* and the *European Journal of Personality*.

Edward Chang is associate professor of psychology at the University of Michigan. He received his PhD from SUNY at Stony Brook. He has published on optimism and pessimism, perfectionism, social problem solving, and cultural influences on behaviour. He is co-editor of the book *Judgments Over Time: The Interplay of Thoughts, Feelings, and Behaviors*, and of the *Handbook of Mental Health in Racial/Ethnic Groups: Understanding Changes Across the Lifespan*. He is associate editor of the *Journal of Social and Clinical Psychology* and is on the editorial board of the *Journal of Personality and Social Psychology*.

Rita Chang is a doctoral candidate at the University of Michigan. Her research interests include the adaptive and maladaptive aspects of perfectionism and their relation to depressive symptoms, as well as risk and protective factors for suicide in Asian Americans. She has recent chapters published in the *Handbook of Asian American Psychology*, and in the book *Self-Criticism and Self-Enhancement: Theory, Research, and Clinical Implications*.

Chi-Yue Chiu is professor of psychology at the University of Illinois at Urbana-Champaign. He received his PhD from Columbia University in 1994. His major research interests are cultural processes, group processes, and intergroup relations. He is also interested in the dynamic interactions of cultural identification and cultural knowledge traditions, and their implications for cultural competence and intercultural relations. He has over 130 publications, and is author of several books, including *Social Psychology of Culture*. He is an associate editor of the *Journal of Personality, and the Journal of Cross-Cultural Psychology, and is on the editorial boards of the Journal of Personality and Social Psychology, and Social and Personality Psychology Compass*.

Neil Christiansen is professor of psychology at Central Michigan University. He obtained his PhD from Northern Illinois University in 1997. His major research interests concern the relationships between personality and work behaviour, applicant faking of personality measures, and improving methods of assessing personality in organisations. His publications are in the *Journal of Applied Psychology, Personnel Psychology, Journal of Organizational Behavior, Human Performance*, and the *International Journal of Selection and Assessment*.

David Clinton is a doctoral candidate at the Pacific Graduate School of Psychology. His major interest lies in the underlying factors of change that optimize psychotherapy across theoretical orientations, especially in regard to cultural applications and coping ability. Other interests include the effective application of psychotherapy with individuals suffering from severe and persistent psychopathology. He has several co-authored articles in journals such as, *Psychotherapy Research, Psychology and Psychotherapy: Theory, Research and Practice, the European Eating Disorders Review, and Psychotherapy and Psychosomatics*. He has contributed to three chapters on psychotherapy integration and empirical treatments as well as the examination of underlying factors of change that promote positive outcomes in therapy, the most recent appearing in the book, *The Art and Science of Psychotherapy*.

Philip Corr is professor of psychology at Swansea University. He obtained his PhD from the Institute of Psychiatry, London in 1994. His research centres around the behavioural, cognitive and affective neuroscience of emotion and personality, focusing on basic defensive systems of fear and anxiety, and the personality and psychopathology continuum. Other interests include schizophrenia spectrum research, focusing on laboratory markers of psychosis-proneness and actual psychosis. He has published extensively, and is author of the book *Understanding Biological Psychology*, and editor of *The Reinforcement Sensitivity Theory of Personality*.

Paul Costa, Jr. is chief of the Laboratory of Personality and Cognition, National Institute on Aging's Intramural Research Program and professor of psychiatry and behavioral sciences at the Johns Hopkins University School of Medicine. He obtained his PhD from the University of Chicago in 1970. His enduring interests are in the structure and measurement of personality and in lifespan development. He co-authored the NEO Personality Inventory-Revised and has actively developed the five-factor model of personality. He has published extensively in the area of personality assessment and he is co-editor of the book *Recent Advances in Psychology and Aging: Advances In Cell Aging and Gerontology* (Vol. 15).

Matthew Cribbet is a doctoral candidate in clinical health psychology at the University of Utah. His research interests are in the area of personality and health, with a particular focus on individual differences in psychophysiological responses to stress.

Sharon Dawe is professor of clinical psychology at Griffith University, Australia. She received her PhD from the Institute of Psychiatry, University of London in 1993 and moved to Australia in 1996. Her major interests are the study of substance abuse and personality, including treatment evaluations for illicit substance misuse and parenting. She has dozens of published articles and book chapters and is author of *Drug Use in the Family: Impacts and Implications for Children*. Also, she was an expert witness at the 2007 Australian Commonwealth Parliamentary Inquiry into the Impact of Illicit Drug on Families.

Andrew Elliot is professor of psychology at the University of Rochester, where he has been since receiving his PhD from the University of Wisconsin-Madison in 1994. His major interest is the study of approach and avoidance motivation. He has over 100 publications, and is an associate editor of the *Personality and Social Psychology Bulletin*, and editor of the emotion and motivation section of *Social and Personality Psychology Compass*. He is editor of the *Handbook of Approach and Avoidance Motivation*.

Amanda Feiler is in the final year of completing the Honours Psychology Program at the University of Western Ontario. She has collaborated on a meta-analysis of behaviour-genetic studies of personality factors and related traits. She plans to pursue graduate studies in industrial/organisational psychology.

Ephrem Fernandez is professor of clinical psychology at the University of Texas, San Antonio. Previously, he held faculty appointments at Southern Methodist University, and at the University Queensland, Australia. He received his PhD from Ohio State University in 1989. His research spans medical psychology and affect science, including the psychometric assessment and cognitive-behavioural management of pain, and assessment and integrative psychotherapy for maladaptive anger. He has numerous publications, and is author of the book *Anxiety, Depression, and Anger in Pain: Research Findings and Clinical Options* and co-editor of the *Handbook of Pain Syndromes: Biopsychosocial Approaches*. He has served on the editorial boards of *Headache* and the *Annals of Behavioral Medicine*. His research is funded by the US National Institutes of Health.

Elisa Gottheil is a psychologist at the Santa Barbara County Mental Health Care Services. She received her PhD in clinical psychology from Pacifica Graduate Institute. Her major area of interest has been developing improved service delivery to youth in treatment for addictions or to those who suffer from fetal alcohol syndrome. She also conducts research into adult spiritual growth, and provides psychological assessments of youth and adults on probation. She has published in the *California School Psychologist*.

Melissa Green is a research fellow at the School of Psychiatry and Black Dog Institute, University of New South Wales. She received her PhD from the University of Sydney in 2002. Her major research interests are in cognitive neuropsychiatry, with particular emphasis on cognitive and emotion processing disturbances in psychosis. Her recent research focuses on the delineation of cognitive markers of liability that may be shared among apparently distinct phenotypic expressions of affective and non-affective psychoses. She has published extensively, and received the Butters' Award for her research on social cognition from the International Neuropsychological Society in 2004.

Gary Groth-Marnat is professor of psychology at Pacifica Graduate Institute. He obtained his PhD from the California School of Professional Psychology in 1977. His interests include the psychological report, psychotherapy treatment planning, hypnosis, near-death experiences, metaphor in psychotherapy, computer-based test interpretation, and cross-cultural approaches to smoking cessation. He is author of the *Handbook of Psychological Assessment*, and of *Neuropsychological Assessment in Clinical Practice*. He is a fellow of the American Psychological Association, and the Society for Personality Assessment, and diplomat of the American Board of Professional Psychology, and of the American Board of Assessment Psychology.

Robert Hatcher is adjunct associate professor of psychology at the University of Michigan, where he received his PhD in 1971. His research interests include the therapeutic alliance and interpersonal processes in psychotherapy. His published articles appear in journals including *Psychotherapy* and *Psychotherapy Research*. He is on the editorial boards of the *Journal of Counseling Psychology*, and *Psychotherapy Research*, and is associate editor of *Training and Education in Professional Psychology*.

Manuel Ibáñez is a lecturer in psychology at Jaume I University of Castelló, Spain, where he obtained his PhD in 2001. His research and publications are focused on personality assessment, animal models of personality, behaviour genetics and personality influences on health-related behaviours. He is co-author of the Spanish version of the Eysenck Personality Questionnaire and has published in the journal, *Personality and Individual Differences*.

Brynne Johannsen is a doctoral candidate at the Pacific Graduate School of Psychology. Her major research interests include customising therapy based on patient predisposing characteristics. Other interests include providing effective therapy to forensic populations and the effectiveness of sex offender registration laws. She has co-authored two chapters on the principles of therapeutic change in *Evidence-Based Practices in Mental Health: Debate and Dialogue on the Fundamental Questions.*

Andrew Johnson is assistant professor in the Faculty of Health Sciences at the University of Western Ontario, where he has been on the faculty since receiving his PhD in 2001. His primary research interests include the study of individual differences in personality and mental abilities, focusing on behaviour genetics, information processing speed, and research methodology. He has also been active in the systematic evaluation of research evidence for clinical decision-making. He has authored dozens of articles and book chapters.

Robert Kerns is National Program Director for Pain Management of the Veterans Health Administration, Chief of the Psychology Service at the VA Connecticut Healthcare System, and Professor of Psychiatry, Neurology and Psychology at Yale University. He received his PhD from Southern Illinois University in 1980. His research interests include behavioural medicine and pain management. He has developed several pain assessment instruments, researched family health and illness issues, studied pain and emotional distress, and has developed cognitive-behavioural interventions for chronic pain. He has published over 150 articles, and is co-editor of the book, *Health, Illness, and Families: A Life-span Perspective,* and the book, *Behavioral and Psychopharmacological Therapeutics in Pain Management.* He is on several editorial boards including, *Pain Medicine, Cancer Pain and Palliative Care,* and the *Clinical Journal of Pain.*

Young-Hoon Kim is a doctoral student at the University of Illinois, Urbana- Champaign. His research interests are the cognitive and motivational aspects of self-enhancement and their implications for academic performance and psychological health. He also examines East-West differences in perspective taking and its influence on emotion, cognition, and behavior. He has published in journals such as *Self and Identity* and several book chapters in *Cultural processes: A Social psychological perspective.*

Sabina Kleitman is lecturer in psychology at the University of Sydney, where she received her PhD in 2003. Her major area of research is the study of metacognitive processes and their correlates. Other research interests include decision-making and developmental psychology. She has published in journals such as *Learning and Individual Differences, Personality and Individual Differences, Applied Cognitive Psychology, Harvard Educational Review, American Educational Research Journal, Journal of Applied Sport Psychology.*

Thomas Langens is a research fellow at the University of Wuppertal, Germany where he obtained his PhD in 2001. His research focuses on the effects of fantasy and daydreaming on motivation and emotion, emotion-regulation, illusions of control, assessment of implicit motives, and the relationship of implicit motives and goals. He has published in the *Journal of Personality, Personality and Individual Differences, Personality and Social Psychology Bulletin,* and *Motivation and Emotion.*

Jihyun Lee is associate research scientist in the Center for New Constructs at Educational Testing Service Princeton, New Jersey. She received her PhD from Columbia University in 2003. Her major research interests include non-cognitive measurement in large-scale assessments, and finding the link between cognitive and non-cognitive constructs. She is a co-author of several articles on culture, confidence, student engagement, and learning strategies, and co-author of *The Nation's Report Card: U.S. History*.

Marijn Lijffijt is a postdoctoral fellow in the Department of Psychiatry and Behavioral Sciences at the University of Texas, Houston. After completing his PhD at the University of Utrecht in 2004, he was a post-doctoral fellow for the late Dr Ernest Barratt at the University of Texas Medical Branch, Galveston. His research focuses on biological correlates of trait impulsivity and impulse related disorders. His publications appear in journals such as *Personality and Individual Differences,* the *Journal of Abnormal Psychology, Psychoneuroendocrinology, European Psychiatry, Clinical Neurophysiology, and the Journal of Cognitive Neuroscience.*

Weiling Liu is a doctoral candidate at the Pacific Graduate School of Psychology. She is the project coordinator for training initiatives and is involved with the Palo Alto Medical Reserve Corps. Her research interests include minority mental health, behavioural medicine, and telepsychiatry. Her co-authored publications include articles in the *Journal of Homeland Security, Psychiatric Services*, and the *Canadian Psychiatric Association Bulletin*, as well as chapters in books including *Ethnicity and the Dementias*, and in *Handbook of Clinical Geropsychology*.

Mary Malik is a private practice psychologist in San Luis Obispo, California. She earned a PhD in zoology from Duke University in 1996 and obtained her PhD in counseling/clinical/school psychology from the University of California, Santa Barbara in 2003. She has published over two-dozen articles on topics ranging from evolutionary biology to the treatment of anxiety disorders and psychotherapy outcome. She has a long-standing interest in diagnosis, and is co-editor of the book, *Rethinking the DSM: A Psychological Perspective*.

Herbert Marsh is professor of education at Oxford University, having spent much of his career in Sydney after completing his PhD at UCLA in 1974. He has widely published (370 articles in 70 journals, 60 chapters, 14 monographs, 350 conference papers) and co-edits the *International Advances in Self Research* monograph series. He is an "ISI highly cited researcher" (http://isihighlycited.com/) with 262 ISI publications, more than 10,000 citations, 52 articles with at least 52 citations (ISI-H-index = 52), and one article with over 1,000 citations. He founded the SELF Research Centre that has 450 members and satellite centres at leading Universities around the world (http://self.uws.edu.au/). He has been recognized as the most productive educational psychologist in the world, as one of the top 10 international researchers in Higher Education and in Social Psychology, and the 11th most productive researcher in the world across all disciplines of psychology.

Gerald Matthews is professor of psychology at the University of Cincinnati. He received his PhD from Cambridge University in 1984. His research interests include the effects of personality and stress on performance, information-processing models, applied personality research and emotional intelligence as well as the assessment of transient subjective states. He has over 200 publications and has co-authored the textbooks *Personality Traits* and *Human Performance: Cognition, Stress and Individual Differences*. He is editor of the book *Cognitive Science Perspectives on Personality and Emotion* and co-editor of *The Science of Emotional Intelligence: Knowns and Unknowns*. He is secretary-treasurer of the *International Society for the Study of Individual Differences,* and also is co-editor of the current volumes.

Jason Mazanov is a lecturer at the Australian Defence Force Academy, University of New South Wales. He obtained his PhD from the Australian National University in 2004.

He has published articles on adolescent substance use and is investigating performance enhancing substance use by athletes. Other research interests include the psychology of climate change. He has co-authored articles in journals such as the *British Journal of Health Psychology, the Australian Journal of Psychology, Personality and Individual Differences, and the Journal of Psychosomatic Research.*

Robert McCrae is a research psychologist in the Laboratory of Personality and Cognition at the National Institute on Aging. He received his PhD from Boston University in 1976. His research interests include personality structure, development and assessment, as well as cross-cultural studies. He has 300 publications and is co-author of the Revised NEO Personality Inventory, and *Personality in Adulthood: A Five-Factor Theory Perspective.* He is on the editorial boards of the *European Journal of Personality*, and *Psychological Assessment.* He is a fellow of the American Psychological Association, the Association for Psychological Science, the Gerontology Society of America, and the Society for Personality Assessment.

Richard Michalski is assistant professor of psychology at Hollins University since 2004. He received his PhD from Florida Atlantic University in 2005. His research interests in evolutionary psychology include the study of family and romantic relationships. He has published empirical papers and chapters on topics such as sibling relationships, grandparental relationships, jealousy, and sex differences in mating psychology. He is on the editorial board of *Evolutionary Psychology.*

Gerard Moeller is professor in the Department of Psychiatry and Behavioral Sciences at the University of Texas Health Science Center at Houston, where he received his MD in 1985. His research area is the clinical neurobiology of impulsivity as it relates to substance abuse. He is president of the International Society for Research on Impulsivity. He has funding from the US National Institute on Drug Abuse and has current and previous investigator-initiated projects on cocaine and MDMA abuse related to impulsivity. He has authored over 80 peer-reviewed papers as well as book chapters in the *Comprehensive Textbook of Psychiatry.*

Jorge Moya is a doctoral candidate at Jaume I University of Castelló, Spain. His major area of interest is personality and alcohol consumption. Other research interests include prospective longitudinal studies in adolescents and the genetics of personality. He has published articles on personality assessment and addiction in journals such as *Personality and Individual Differences*, and the *American Journal of Medical Genetics Part B: Neuropsychiatric Genetics.*

Kieron O'Connor is research professor in psychiatry at the University of Montreal, professor of psychology at Universitè du Quèbec en Outaouais, and researcher at the Fernand-Seguin Research Centre, Louis-H. Lafontaine Hospital. He received his PhD from the Institute of Psychiatry, United Kingdom, in 1984. His interests include applying individual differences theory to studies of the interaction of cognitive, psychophysiological, and behavioral factors in clinical problems, including smoking behavior, benzodiazepine dependence and obsessive compulsive disorders. He is the author or co-author of over 150 scientific publications. He is author of the book *Cognitive-Behavioral Management of Tic Disorders*, and co-author of *Beyond Reasonable Doubt: Reasoning Processes in Obsessive-Compulsive Disorder and Related Disorders.*

Ragnar Ólafsson is a psychologist at the Landspítali University Hospital in Iceland. He also lectures in clinical psychology in the Faculty of Social Sciences at the University of Iceland.

He received his MSc degree in psychology from the University of Amsterdam in 2003. His major research interest is anxiety disorders, especially repetitive thoughts and behaviours in generalised anxiety disorder and obsessive-compulsive disorder. He is editor of the *Icelandic Journal of Psychology*.

Daníel þór Ólason is assistant professor of psychology at the University of Iceland. He obtained his DPhil. from the University of York, UK in 2000. His main research interests are pathological gambling, individual differences, and psychometrics. He has been the research coordinator for the Icelandic Gambling Project and has co-authored articles in journals such as the *Scandinavian Journal of Psychology, Personality and Individual Differences, the Journal of Gambling Studies,* and *Current Psychology: Developmental, Learning, Personality, Social.* He is on the editorial board of the *Icelandic Journal of Psychology*.

Generós Ortet is reader in psychology at Jaume I University of Castelló, Spain. He received his PhD from the Autonomous University of Barcelona in 1990 and has been a visiting research associate at the Institute of Psychiatry (London). His major interests include personality and psychopathology. Other research interests include animal models of personality and behaviour genetics. He has published extensively on personality assessment, antisocial behaviour and addiction. He is co-author of the Eysenck Personality Questionnaire-Revised (Spanish version) and of the handbook, *Psychological Assessment* (in Spanish). He is on the editorial board of the *International Journal of Clinical and Health Psychology*.

James Parker is professor of psychology at Trent University and director of its Emotion and Health Research Laboratory. He obtained his PhD from York University in 1991. His research interests include emotional and social competency, coping and health, and predictors of academic success. He has published over 100 articles and chapters. He co-developed the Coping Inventory for Successful Situations (CISS). Also, he co-developed the youth version of the BarOn Emotional Quotient Inventory (EQ-i: YV). He is co-author of the book *Disorders of Affect Regulation: Alexithymia in Medical and Psychiatric Illness* and co-editor of the *Handbook of Emotional Intelligence*.

K.V. Petrides is reader in psychology and psychometrics at University College London, where he directs the trait emotional intelligence research program and is principal developer of the family of TEIQue instruments. He has contributed over three-dozen scientific articles in the field of individual differences. He is associate editor of *Personality and Individual Differences*, book review editor for the *British Journal of Mathematical and Statistical Psychology*, and is on the editorial board of the *European Journal of Personality*.

Alan Pickering is professor of psychology at Goldsmiths College, University of London. He received his PhD from the University of Manchester in 1987. His research studies reinforcement sensitivity theory and is focused on how learning may be mediated by reward, how personality traits may impact on this, using computational models to capture these effects. Other interests include addiction, schizophrenia, schizotypal personality, psychopharmacology, neuropsychology, and computational modelling. He is author/co-author of over 50 journal articles plus 10 chapters in edited books. He has served on the editorial board of *Perception and Psychophysics* and is associate editor of the journal, *Addiction*.

Adrian Raine is the Richard Perry University Professor of Criminology, Psychiatry, and Psychology at the University of Pennsylvania. Previously, he was the Robert G. Wright Professor of Psychology at the University of Southern California. He completed his undergraduate education at Oxford University and his DPhil at York University, UK in 1982. His interests include the biosocial bases of violence and schizotypal personality. He has 200 publications and has given over 200 invited talks throughout the world. He is co-editor of the book *Violence and Psychopathy* and editor of *Crime and Schizophrenia: Causes and Cures*. He has received several research excellence awards including from the British Psychological Society, and the US National Institute of Mental Health.

Thomas Rammsayer is professor of psychology at the University of Bern, Switzerland. He received his PhD from the University of Giessen, Germany in 1987. His research interests lie in experimental and biological psychology, including temporal information processing, psychopharmacology, the biological basis of individual differences, and research on intelligence. He has published over 100 scientific articles in journals such as *Biological Psychology, Cognitive Brain Research, International Journal of Neuroscience, Quarterly Journal of Experimental Psychology B: Comparative and Physiological Psychology,* and *Schizophrenia Research*. He is associate editor of the *Journal of Individual Differences* and is on the editorial board of the *Canadian Journal of Experimental Psychology*.

David Rawlings is a senior lecturer in psychology at the University of Melbourne. He obtained his DPhil from Oxford University in 1983. His research interests concern the interface between personality and psychopathology, focusing on psychoticism and schizotypy. His recent research has concerned the relationship of these constructs to phenomena such as creativity in the arts and sciences, aesthetic preference, humour creation and appreciation, and religious belief and experience. He has dozens of scientific articles published in journals including the *British Journal of Clinical Psychology, Personality and Individual Differences, Schizophrenia Research,* and the *Journal of Nervous and Mental Disease*.

María Ruipérez is reader in psychology at Jaume I University of Castelló, Spain. She received her PhD from the University of Valencia in 1994. Her main interests are clinical psychopathology and personality. Other research interests include quality of life and cultural framework of psychiatric disorders. She has published extensively on information processing and mood states, social phobia and psychotherapy. She is co-author of the handbook, *Mood and Anxiety Disorders: Case Analyses* (in Spanish).

Donald Saklofske is professor of applied psychology and associate dean of research at the University of Calgary. He received his PhD from the University of Calgary in 1973. His research interests include individual differences, personality, intelligence and emotional intelligence, cognition, and psychological assessment. He has co-authored and edited books on intelligence, the assessment of intelligence, individual differences and educational psychology. He is editor of *Journal of Psychoeducational Assessment* and the *Canadian Journal of School Psychology,* associate editor of *Personality and Individual Differences,* and a book series editor. He is a fellow of both the Canadian Psychological Association and the Association for Psychological Science and is also co-editor of the current volumes.

Lawrence Sanna is professor of social psychology at the University of North Carolina, Chapel Hill. He received his PhD from the Pennsylvania State University in 1991. His research interests are in social cognition, judgment, and decision-making, particularly people's judgments over time. In addition to numerous articles and book chapters, he is author of several books including *Judgments over Time: The Interplay of Thoughts, Feelings, and Behaviors,* and *Virtue, Vice,* *and Personality: The Complexity of Behavior*. He has also served on many editorial boards such as *Behavioral and Brain Sciences*; *European Journal of Social Psychology*; *Journal of Experimental Social Psychology*; *Journal of Social and Clinical Psychology*; and *Personality and Social Psychology Bulletin*.

Heinz-Dieter Schmalt is professor of psychology at the University of Wuppertal, Germany. He obtained his PhD at Ruhr-University in Bochum, Germany in 1974. His research interests include achievement motivation and motive assessment. Other research interests include power motivation and cognitive and emotional variables (attributions, intrinsic motivation, intentions) contributing to action regulation. He is co-author of the textbooks *Motivation* and *Achievement Motivation in Perspective*, and co-author of the 'grid technique' presented in this volume.

Todd Shackelford is professor of psychology at Florida Atlantic University. He received his PhD from the University of Texas at Austin in 1997. Much of his empirical and theoretical work focuses on conflict between men and women in intimate relationships. He has over 160 publications and several books including *Sperm Competition in Humans*, *Female Infidelity and Paternal Uncertainty*, *Evolutionary Cognitive Neuroscience*, *Family Relationships*, and *Evolutionary Forensic Psychology*. He is editor-in-chief of *Evolutionary Psychology* and an associate editor of *Personality and Individual Differences*, the *Journal of Personality*, and the *Human Ethology Bulletin*.

Jakob Smári is professor of psychology at the University of Iceland. He received his PhD from the University of Stockholm, Sweden in 1985. His major areas of interest are the study of individual differences in coping processes and obsessive-compulsive disorder and its cognitive aspects. Other research interests are autism and ADHD. He has contributed more than 60 articles to peer-reviewed international journals. He has co-edited two handbooks of psychology (*Handbook of Psychology*) and gerontology (*The Years after Sixty*) in Icelandic. He is on the editorial boards of *Cognitive Behaviour Therapy* and *La Revue Francophone de Clinique Comportementale et Cognitive* and is a national editor of the *Nordic Journal of Psychology*.

Timothy Smith is professor of clinical psychology at the University of Utah. He obtained his PhD from the University of Kansas in 1982. His research interests are personality and social risk factors for cardiovascular disease, and the application of interpersonal models to problems of physical health. He has over 180 publications. He has served as associate editor of *Annals of Behavioral Medicine*, *Health Psychology*, *Cognitive Therapy and Research*, *Journal of Social and Clinical Psychology*, *Journal of Consulting and Clinical Psychology*, and *American Psychologist*, and has been on numerous editorial boards. He is a past president of the Division of Health Psychology of the American Psychological Association, and recipient of the Distinguished Scientist Award from the Society of Behavioral Medicine.

Lazar Stankov is principal research scientist in the Center for New Constructs at Educational Testing Service, Princeton, New Jersey. He obtained his PhD from the University of Denver in 1971. Previously, he was professor of psychology at the University of Sydney, where he worked for over 30 years. His interests include the structure of cognitive abilities and the role of auditory processing, complexity manipulations and their effects on measures of intelligence, confidence, and meta-cognition, cross-cultural studies of personality, values, social attitudes and norms. He has over 100 publications and is editor of *Extending Intelligence: Enhancement and New Constructs*. He is on the editorial board of *Learning and Individual Differences*.

Robert Stelmack is an adjunct professor of psychology at the University of Ottawa, following his retirement in 2001. He obtained his PhD from the University of Ottawa in 1970. His research interests include the psychophysiology of personality and individual differences, notably extraversion and mental ability. He is a past president of the International Society for the Study of Individual Differences and is an associate editor of *Personality and Individual Differences*. His research is published in three edited volumes, including *The Psychobiology of Personality: Essays in Honor of Marvin Zuckerman*, 18 book chapters and over 60 journal articles. He is a fellow of the Canadian Psychological Association.

Alan Swann is Pat R. Rutherford Jr. professor in the Department of psychiatry and behavioral sciences and Vice Chair for Research at the University of Texas Medical School, Houston. He received his MD from the UT Southwestern Medical School at Dallas, in 1972. His research interests are clinical: prediction and measurable correlates of treatment response; preclinical: neurobiology of impulsivity and motivation; and basic: behavioural sensitisation to stimulants and stressors. He has published more than 200 peer-reviewed scientific papers on these topics.

Robert Tett is associate professor of psychology at the University of Tulsa. He received his PhD in 1995 from the University of Western Ontario. His research interests lie in personality testing and assessment centres as predictors of managerial and leadership performance, as well as personality trait expression and its value in work settings. He has published in the *Journal of Applied Psychology*, *Journal of Organizational Behavior*, *Personnel Psychology*, *Human Performance*, *Journal of Personality*, and *Personality and Social Psychology Bulletin*.

Todd Thrash is assistant professor of psychology at the College of William and Mary, Virginia. He received his PhD in social/personality psychology from the University of Rochester in 2003. His primary research interests include inspiration, creativity, congruence between implicit and explicit motives, and approach and avoidance components of motivation. His more recent focus has been on the biological basis of individual differences in temperament. He has published in journals such as the *Personality and Social Psychology Bulletin,* the *Journal of Personality and Social Psychology,* the *Journal of Personality,* and *Psychological Inquiry*.

Philip Vernon is professor of psychology at the University of Western Ontario. He received his PhD in 1981 from the University of California, Berkeley. His research interests include individual differences in personality and mental abilities and he has conducted and published numerous behaviour genetic studies. He is also interested in biological correlates of intelligence and mental abilities. He is a past president of the International Society for the Study of Individual Differences. He is currently on the editorial board of *Intelligence* and is co-editor-in-chief of *Personality and Individual Differences*.

Helena Villa is lecturer in psychology at Jaume I University of Castelló, Spain, where she received her PhD in 2005. Her main interest is biopsychosocial vulnerability to psychopathology. Other research interests include the relationship between personality and emotional and personality disorders. She is co-author of several articles and book chapters on assessment and psychological treatments for social phobia and panic disorder.

Wendy Wan is senior research fellow of Marketing and International Business at the City University of Hong Kong. Previously, she was assistant professor of psychology at Bond University, Gold Coast, Australia, after obtaining her PhD from the University of Hong Kong in 2002.

Currently, she is researching global and cultural influences on consumer behaviour. Her research has appeared in the *Journal of Personality and Social Psychology*, the *Journal of Cross Cultural Psychology*, *Personality and Individual Differences*, the *Journal of Creative Behavior*, and the *International Journal of Bank Marketing*.

Paula Williams is assistant professor of psychology at the University of Utah, where she obtained her Ph.D. in clinical health psychology in 1995. She also completed a pre-doctoral internship and post-doctoral fellowship in behavioural medicine at Duke University Medical Center. Her research focuses on individual differences in health, anxiety, and illness behaviour. She is on the editorial board of and has served as a guest editor of the *Annals of Behavioral Medicine*. She has published in journals such as the *Journal of Consulting and Clinical Psychology*, *Health Psychology*, and the *Personality and Social Psychology Bulletin*.

Laura Wood is research co-ordinator of the Emotion and Health Research Laboratory in the Psychology Department at Trent University, Canada. Her interests include the study of the relationship between emotional and social competency and success across the lifespan. Other research interests include scale development and assessment. She has published articles in journals such as *Personality and Individual Differences*, the *Journal of Individual Differences*, and *Psychotherapy and Psychosomatics*.

Moshe Zeidner is professor of educational psychology at Haifa University. He received his PhD from Hebrew University in 1983. His interests include personality and individual differences, the interface of personality and intelligence, emotional intelligence, stress and the coping process. He is the author or co-editor of 10 books and has 200 articles and book chapters. He is on the editorial boards of the *Journal of Educational Psychology; Anxiety, Stress and Coping: An International Journal; Emotion* and *Personality and Individual Differences*. He is co-editor of the series on *Human Exceptionality*. He received a lifetime achievement award from the Society for Stress and Anxiety Research.

Marvin Zuckerman is professor emeritus at the University of Delaware, where he taught and conducted research for 33 years. He obtained his PhD from New York University in 1954. His research has focused on sensation seeking, and the psychobiology of personality. He is author or co-author of well over 200 journal articles and book chapters. Recent books include *Sensation Seeking and Risky Behavior* and the *Psychobiology of Personality*. He is a past president of the International Society for the Study of Individual Differences and fellow of both the American Psychological Association and the Association for Psychological Science.

Personality Theories and Models: An Overview

Gregory J. Boyle, Gerald Matthews and Donald H. Saklofske

The thesis of these volumes is that the study of personality traits has advanced towards 'normal science' in the sense of a Kuhnian paradigm (cf. Eysenck, 1981; Kuhn, 1962). That is, most researchers in this area share a set of common core beliefs supported by empirical evidence. These include the relative stability of traits over time, a significant genetic and biological influence on personality, and relevance of traits to many areas of everyday life. Each one of these beliefs has been vigorously contested in the past, but the evidence in favour of each one is now overwhelming (Boyle and Saklofske, 2004; Matthews et al., 2003). At the same time, researchers do not subscribe to some crude biological determinism. The roles of gene–environment interaction in personality development and of person–situation interaction in determining behaviour are also well established. Within the overall paradigm, trait models have also stimulated important and unresolved debates, including the optimal measurement framework for traits, the mechanisms that transmit causal effects of traits on behaviour, as well as the roles of cultural and social factors in moderating the nature of traits.

The purpose of these handbooks is to review issues of both consensus and controversy. Contributors synthesize the state of the art of the research on the core tenets of trait theory, such as behaviour genetics and trait stability, and present perspectives on unresolved issues such as the important role of culture. In addition, trait theory is only *one* scientific paradigm for personality research. Although the focus here is on trait models, the handbooks also seek to explore key points of contact and differences with traditional approaches to personality (Campbell, Vol. 1) and with social-cognitive theory and methods (Cervone, Vol. 1; Zayas et al., Vol. 2).

In this introductory chapter, we will outline the case that the trait model of personality constitutes normal science, and compare the trait perspective with alternative scientific approaches. We will also set out the key criteria that must be satisfied to build a successful trait theory, subdivided into formal and often quantitative criteria such as test–retest stability, and criteria that relate to the psychological meaning and construct validity of traits. We will also discuss some of the challenges to trait theory, and the directions the field may take in addressing these challenges. We will conclude the chapter by introducing the various contributions to Vol. 1, related to the pivotal issues previously discussed.

TRAIT THEORY AS NORMAL SCIENCE

The basic tenets of modern trait theory are not new – indeed, their origins lie in antiquity (Stelmack and Stalikas, 1991). However, in their contemporary form, they owe much to three founding fathers of trait psychology: Gordon Allport, Raymond Cattell and Hans Eysenck. In his early career, Cattell was influenced by Allport, when both were faculty members at Harvard University. At the outset, Allport (1937) famously remarked, 'In everyday life, no-one, not even a psychologist, doubts that underlying the conduct of a mature person there are characteristic dispositions or traits.'

Allport defined a trait or disposition as 'a generalized neuropsychic structure (peculiar to the individual), with the capacity to render many stimuli functionally equivalent, and to initiate and guide consistent (equivalent) forms of adaptive and stylistic behaviour'. That is, a trait describes the filtering of experience through the self to impose a personal structure on the world, as for example, a trait-anxious person may interpret a miscellany of stimuli as threats. Furthermore, traits generate a consistency of response in the service of adaptive and expressive goals. These remain the central assumptions of contemporary trait theory. The phrase 'peculiar to the individual' is telling, in that it signals Allport's predominantly idiographic stance on traits. While this view has been cherished by much of social-cognitive personality psychology, trait theory has been dominated by nomothetic approaches that seek to identify traits that are meaningful for all individuals.

Nomothetic trait models owe much to Raymond Cattell (e.g. Cattell, 1973; Cattell and Kline, 1977: see Boyle, Vol. 1; Campbell,

Vol. 1), as the most articulate early proponent of the view that the main attributes of personality may be described by a number of discrete dimensions. Cattell's personality theory is inextricably linked to quantitative measurement models based on factor analysis of questionnaire responses and other sources of personality data (although known for the '16 Personality Factor Questionnaire' or 16PF, Cattell also identified several additional personality traits that were not amenable to questionnaire assessment). Cattell's formulation of trait models remains influential. Four attributes of these models stand out. First, the trait as a latent construct with causal force, the *source trait*, should be distinguished from superficial regularities in behaviour or *surface traits*. Second, personality models should be hierarchical; broad factors such as extraversion and anxiety are defined by groupings of more narrowly defined primary traits, such as in the case of extraversion – dominance, surgency and venturesomeness. Third, the personality sphere should be differentiated from other domains of individual differences, including ability, motivation and transient mood states. Fourth, the influence of traits on behaviour is moderated by situational factors. Controversies continue over whether numbers can ever capture human personality (see Pervin, 2002), and over the scaling and measurement assumptions inherent in assessment of traits (Barrett, 2005). Nevertheless, the four features of Cattellian theory listed here remain as key principles for most contemporary trait theorists.

The third figure in the trinity is Hans Eysenck (e.g. Eysenck, 1957, 1967; see O'Connor, Vol. 1). His debates with Cattell on the optimal number of factors (Eysenck focused on three broad dimensions: extraversion, neuroticism and psychoticism, as compared with the 16 primary factors and several secondary factors reported by Cattell) were a precursor to the number-of-factors issue that has embroiled the field ever since (e.g. see Boyle, 2006). However, this discrepancy was more apparent than real, since Eysenck and

Cattell were focusing on measurement at different levels within the hierarchical trait model. In fact, at the second-order 16PF level, communality between the Cattellian and Eysenckian factors was striking, so much so that 'the Cattell and Eysenck constructs and theories should be seen, not as mutually contradictory, but as complementary and mutually supportive' (Eysenck, 1984: 336).

We emphasize Eysenck's attempt to ground traits in heritable properties of the brain, so that extraversion, neuroticism and psychoticism were linked to specific brain systems. In addition, Eysenck pioneered the use of empirical studies to test the relationships between traits and behaviour – and the moderating role of situational factors – in rigorously controlled experiments. As O'Connor (Vol. 1) discusses, building causal models of individual differences requires both the matching of correlational and experimental methods, and the study of person *x* situation interaction. Also central to Eysenck's programme was empirical investigation of what these days are called *consequential outcomes* (Ozer and Benet-Martinez, 2006); the relevance of traits to real-life outcomes in relation to mental health, academic and work accomplishments and social relationships. Eysenck's specific hypotheses about the biological bases for personality remain open to debate (Matthews and Gilliland, 1999), but there is no serious argument among trait psychologists over the importance of the brain, the use of experimental methods and the investigation of real-life outcomes.

Basic assumptions and principles

Table 1.1 sets out some basic assumptions of trait theory, to which the great majority of researchers in the field would subscribe (cf. Matthews et al., 2003; Pervin, 2002). We suggest that many of the familiar, defining features of traits reflect four underlying principles, as shown in the table. The assumption that traits are relatively stable, continuous, dimensional qualities requires a psychometric basis for traits that meets standard criteria for reliability and validity. The internal consistency of major trait measures and their stability in the adult (e.g. Boyle, 1991; Asendorpf, Vol. 1; Terracciano et al., 2006) are not in question. Validity is a more complex issue that we can only touch upon at this point. The issue here is that traits possess criterion validity in correlating with a variety of quantitative external indices, including objective criteria, such as error rates during performance and amplitudes of physiological responses (Matthews et al., 2003; Stelmack and Rammsayer, Vol. 1). The multiplicity of traits requires a focus on a personality structure defined by latent factors. Multivariate methods including factor analysis (Cattell, 1978; Gorsuch, 1983) and structural equation modelling (Cuttance and Ecob, 1987) may be used to propose and test configurations of multiple dimensions that provide a comprehensive description of personality going beyond an arbitrary collection of single traits (see Boyle, 2006; & Vol.1 for a simplified psychometric model). A further consequence is that abnormality in personality may be defined statistically, in relation to the endpoints of each trait continuum. Whether abnormality is *pathological* is a distinct question, although in fact convergence between normal and abnormality in studies on personality structure (Costa and Widiger, 2002; Malik et al., Vol. 1) suggests a gradation from normal to abnormal personality. The contrary view, expressed by Cattell (see Cattell, 1995; Boyle, Vol. 1), is that pathology may need to be related to abnormal traits beyond the normal personality factor space.

The second principle of a genetic basis for the major traits has been supported by behavioural genetic and, increasingly, molecular genetic evidence (see Johnson et al., Vol. 1; Congden and Canli, Vol. 2). Historically, the heritability principle – especially when framed as a crude genetic determinism – clashed with the egalitarian ethos of the 1960s and the social science model of the time that denied any role to the genes (Pinker, 2002). The subsequent accumulation

Table 1.1   Core principles of trait theory

Stable quantitative dimensions	Reliability and validity	Traits may be assessed as numeric scales, evaluated against psychometric and external criteria
	Latent factor models	Multivariate methods indicate personality structure
	Abnormality	Pathology may correspond to the extremes of trait dimensions
Genetic basis	Behaviour genetics	Genetic influences are necessary to model effects of kinship on personality similarity
	Molecular genetics	DNA is linked to phenotypic personality
	Psychophysiology	Neuroscience models of traits generate testable predictions
	Universality	Traits correspond to individual differences in brain functioning evident in all cultures
Generality of trait expression	Cross-situational consistency	Traits are expressed in multiple situations and contexts
	Laboratory studies	Traits are expressed in controlled environments and psychological tasks
	Consequential outcomes	Traits are expressed in real-life contexts including health, work and relationships
	Pathology	Abnormal traits are sufficiently far-reaching to increase vulnerability to clinical disorder
Interactionism	Situational moderation	Situational factors moderate trait expression
	Dynamics of development	Personality development depends on the interplay between temperament and environment
	Applications	Traits may be matched against jobs, therapies and teaching styles, for example, to achieve real-world benefits

of evidence has been sufficiently persuasive that it is safe to say that the role of genetics is no longer controversial. As Plomin et al. (2001) noted, behaviour genetic studies also provide powerful evidence for the role of the environment in shaping personality (especially the 'non-familial' environment). The genetic assumption implies that traits can be understood within neuroscience models, supported by psychophysiological evidence. If personality is a 'window on the brain', it follows too that traits must be universal, in generalizing across the different cultures of *Homo sapiens*. The genetic basis for traits is also compatible with evolutionary accounts of personality.

The third principle listed in Table 1.1 is the generality of expression of traits. If, as Allport stated, traits work to render different stimuli equivalent, then the trait will encourage similar responses to different situations perceived as functionally equivalent. The point here is that a trait such as extraversion is not relevant to a single class of situations only – say, lively parties – but influences behaviour across a whole range of different contexts. This position depends on the evidence for cross-situational consistency in behaviour (e.g. Funder, 2006); without such consistency, traits could only describe behaviour in specific situations. Historically, cross-situational consistency has also been controversial, as exemplified by Mischel's (1968) famous (or notorious) 'situationist' critique of the personality trait field. As with genetics, accumulating evidence based on the important principle of aggregating data to provide reliable behavioural assessment

(Epstein, 1977) has persuaded many of the doubters. It follows too that the behavioural expression of traits may be studied in artificial laboratory situations. We are not obliged to study extraverted individuals only during naturalistic revelry; Eysenck's (1967) theory predicts the trait should influence laboratory tasks including conditioning, vigilance and memory, for example. Traits should also influence behaviour across a range of significant real-life contexts including the workplace, leisure pursuits, stressful encounters and intimate relationships (e.g. Furnham and Heaven, 1999).

The fourth principle is interactionism (Endler, 1983), necessary to accommodate the role of the situation evidenced in studies of cross-situational consistency. Most simply, traits may be switched on or off by situational factors; neuroticism might only be expressed in threatening or stressful situations, for example. More subtly, traits may correspond to parameters of key neural or psychological processes elicited by situational stimuli. For example, trait anxiety might correspond to the sensitivity to activation of a brain punishment system (Gray, 1991; Pickering and Corr, Vol. 1), or to the accessibility in the memory of a cognitive code representing threat (Wells and Matthews, 1994). The trait does not directly control behaviour but modulates processing. Some trait theorists (e.g. Eysenck, 1967; Gray, 1991) make explicit predictions about the processes thus modulated, such as reticulocortical activation in the case of Eysenck's theory (O'Connor, Vol. 1).

Over the extended timescale of personality development, the modulatory role of personality influences not just immediate behaviour but also feedback from the environment impacting on personality development (Asendorpf, Vol. 1; Caspi et al., 2005; Cattell and Nesselroade, 1988). For example, the risk-taking and the inhibited child are likely to experience rather different formative experiences. A final consequence of interactionism is that, given the resistance to change of adult traits, applied psychologists should address the congruence or compatibility of traits and environments. Examples include selecting job applicants whose personalities are congruent with job demands and tailoring therapies to the strengths and weaknesses conferred by traits; for example, a conscientious patient is more likely to follow programmes of 'homework' used in cognitive therapy (Bagby and Quilty, 2006; Miller, 1991). Interactionism generates no discernable controversy as a general principle; although naturally the specific theories are open to normal scientific criticism (e.g. Matthews and Gilliland, 1999).

Alternative strategies for personality science

The success of trait models as a scientific framework for studying personality does not preclude alternative strategies for scientific advance. A familiar point is that personality psychology is so wide-ranging that it needs multiple levels of explanation (Hettema and Deary, 1993; Matthews, 2000). Zuckerman refers to the ancient myth that the world rests on a stack of giant turtles. He states that 'Each turtle is a distinct creature to be studied at its own level, but for a complete understanding of any turtle one cannot ignore the next turtle down who forms its foundation' (1992: 681). Specifically, he lists seven turtles from the top down as traits, social behaviour, conditioning, physiology, biochemistry, neurology and genetics. Indeed, researchers working at different levels within this hierarchy propose different explanatory constructs ranging from DNA to high-level traits, such as E and N.

The differentiation of levels is uncontroversial, but two more difficult issues remain. The first is how to integrate the different theories relating to each individual level. The second is whether levels that reflect a 'natural science' approach to personality (Eysenck and Eysenck, 1985) are adequate to explain traditional concerns of personality psychology such as the nature of the self, social relationships and motives, and individuality. So far as integration of theories is concerned, there have been two broad strategies

(Matthews, 2000, 2004). The first is biological reductionism (occasionally, triumphalism) that seeks to explain all expressions of traits, including high-level social behaviours, in terms of brain functioning. The idea underlies the classic theories of Eysenck and Gray, in which individual differences in the brain (influenced by genetic variation) feed up the stack of 'turtles', progressively influencing integrative brain systems (e.g. Eysenck's reticulocortical circuit), learning and behaviour, and actual life outcomes. The strongest contemporary theory of this kind is Nyborg's (1994) view that the psychology of personality may be reduced entirely to biochemical explanations. However, a hard reductionism has been criticized on the basis that traits do not appear to be isomorphic with specific brain systems (Zuckerman, 2005). Traits may be seen as emergent, higher-order properties of self-organization that, while influenced by neural processes, do not directly map onto them.

The alternative strategy for accomplishing integration of theories at different levels is to accept that the various constructs used are equally valid as the basis for explanation. At the same time, it is important to explore how different types of explanation may be related to each other, for example by developing neural network models that may support parallel neurological and cognitive accounts of personality effects (Matthews and Harley, 1993). It has been proposed elsewhere that the 'classical' theory of cognitive science (Pylyshyn, 1984) provides a suitable framework of this kind (Matthews, 1997, 2000). It differentiates three forms of explanation, relating to the physical (brain) hardware, the virtual and symbolic software (information processing) and self-knowledge (motives, goals and intentions). The application of cognitive science to integrating different levels of trait theory is discussed further by Matthews (Vol. 1).

The second issue related to theory integration is that personality theory may need to accommodate models that are radically different to trait theory. Pervin (2002) lists

psychoanalytic theories originating with Freud and the social-cognitive theory associated with Bandura, Mischel and others as two major systems for understanding, which are at variance with trait theory in important respects. We will not dwell at length on the prospects of psychoanalysis and its successor theories as a basis for scientific understanding. It does not bode well that much of the debate on the scientific status of psychoanalysis hinges on whether it is fundamentally untestable, and outside the realm of science, or whether it is testable but disconfirmed by data (MacMillan, 1997). As Campbell (Vol. 1) discusses, psychodynamic theories may be important as sources of ideas. Some commentators, notably Westen (1999), have pointed out the re-emergence in scientific studies of some Freudian concepts, such as the importance of the unconscious and repression. However, we agree with Kihlstrom (1999) that the unconscious as revealed by experimental studies of implicit processes does not closely resemble the Freudian unconscious. More generally, whatever heuristic value there may be to Freud's insights, there is no evidence supporting the elaborate theoretical architecture of psychoanalysis.

Social cognitive theories are more deserving of attention as an alternative 'normal science'. One of the sustained minor chords of personality research has been of interest in the systematic study of individual lives expressed, for example, through research on personal constructs (Grice, 2004). Little and Chambers (2004: 65) highlight the 'personal projects' that 'range from the daily doings of say typical Thursdays (e.g. "put out the cat, quickly") to the self-defining passions of a lifetime (e.g. "transform Western thought, slowly")'. A more far-reaching approach is that of social-cognitive personality theory. Its antecedents include rigorous work on learning – both conditioning and social learning – and representations in memory of the self (the self-schema). Typically, social-cognitive approaches fuse a concern with general principles of psychological functioning with an emphasis on the individual as the appropriate unit of analysis for personality studies (Caprara and Cervone, 2000). A key question is the extent to which integration of trait theory and social cognitive theory is possible, or even desirable. The two forms of theory might be seen as fundamentally incommensurable (in the Kuhnian sense) and doomed to remain in mutual isolation. A different view (Matthews et al., 2003) is that while there are important differences in aims and assumptions, both approaches can learn from one another. Stable social knowledge, shaped by social learning, may contribute to traits, and the basic constructs of social-cognitive theory, including the self-concept, expectancies and motives, may not be immune to temperamental and trait influences. Various contributors to these handbooks integrate social-cognitive constructs into trait theories, most directly in the section on key self-regulative traits. Self-regulative theories may also serve to elucidate relationships between biologically based traits and cognitions of the self (Elliott and Thrash, Vol. 1). While the major focus of these volumes is on traits, the editors also considered it vital to present the essentials of social-cognitive theory (Cervone, Vol. 1) and methodologies (Zayas et al., Vol. 2).

PUSHING OUT THE FRONTIERS: KEY AREAS OF PROGRESS

The hallmark of a successful scientific paradigm is that it is 'progressive', in the sense of stimulating new and informative research (Lakatos, 1977). By contrast, degenerative programmes are more concerned with post hoc modifications to theory in order to explain away contradictory data. Personality trait models are open to progress (or degeneration) on two fronts. First, there is a 'syntax' of traits referring to their formal psychometric properties including the definition of reliable latent constructs, long-term stability and cross-situational generality. Second, there are 'semantics' of traits referring to construct

validity and an understanding of what traits actually mean in terms of psychological or biological theory. Matthews et al. (2003) identify four major areas of progress in recent trait research that support the scientific credibility of the enterprise. In addition to developments in psychometrics, progress in psychological understanding of traits is signalled by three important advances: a more sophisticated understanding of biological bases of traits, increasing integration of trait research with mainstream cognitive, social and developmental psychology, and the increasing applied value of assessment of traits.

In this section, we briefly review some of the sources of optimism among trait psychologists, covering both the psychometric 'syntax' and the theoretical 'semantics'. In the section that follows, we then turn to some of the emerging challenges to personality trait theories.

Psychometric advances

The question of how many basic factors are needed to describe human personality has, at times, seemed like asking: 'How many angels may dance on the end of a pin?' For a number of years, the issue appeared to founder on disagreements about factor-analytic techniques, sampling of personality data, and what constituted a 'basic' factor. However, recent years have seen signs of a growing convergence on psychometric accounts of broad, higher-order personality traits. Based on the work of McCrae and Costa (1997), Goldberg (1990) and others, the five-factor model (FFM) has risen into some prominence in some quarters as a putative framework for organizing personality trait data (McCrae and Costa, Vol. 1). At the second-stratum level, a somewhat different five-factor structure can also be derived from Cattell's personality questionnaires (Krug and Johns, 1986; see Boyle, Vol. 1). Furthermore, Zuckerman's version of the FFM with its emphasis on psychobiological underpinnings

(see Zuckerman, 1995), goes considerably beyond the simple trait descriptions postulated in the lexical FFM (see Fraley and Roberts, 2005). Thus, Zuckerman's FFM of personality structure in its incorporation of biological, comparative, experimental and trait approaches illustrates how descriptive accounts of personality may be integrated with sophisticated theory.

Clearly, consensus about the number of broad personality dimensions is not complete. Although the FFM has generated substantial empirical data spanning the various fields of psychology (McCrae and Costa, Vol. 1), substantive objections to the FFM have been raised in relation both to the validity of dimensional models in general (e.g. McAdams, 1992), and to the specific psychometric evidence supporting it (Block, 1995; Boyle, Vol. 1). There is also considerable current interest in adding additional major factors (e.g. Ashton and Lee, Vol. 2; Bond, 2000; Durrett and Trull, 2005). Indeed, as Eysenck (personal communication, 1996) pointed out, extraction of five factors is somewhat arbitrary. Presumably, the personality sphere can be divided into any number of factors, depending upon one's particular preference. It remains to be seen whether advances in psychometrics will eventually provide a universally accepted personality structure, akin to the periodic table of elements in chemistry.

Perhaps the most controversial element of the 'syntax' of traits has been their generality. Even if we accept that traits can be assessed reliably, and show temporal stability, we may question whether the construct assessed *generalizes* across different situations and different cultures. Indeed, an attack on the cross-situational generalization of behaviour was at the core of Mischel's (1968) critique of traits. He coined the term 'personality coefficient' to describe the typical correlation between trait measures and external criteria obtained using other methods (i.e. not further questionnaires). Mischel's claim was that the coefficient rarely exceeded 0.2–0.3, which he took as an argument for the triviality of traits.

However, as previously noted, we now know that Mischel's argument was over-stated, and convincing evidence for cross-situational consistency of behaviour is obtained when rigorous methods are used (e.g. Epstein, 1977; Eysenck and Eysenck, 1980; Funder, 2006). There is now a general consensus in favour of the interactionist position that both traits and situations are important influences on behaviour.

The issue of whether traits generalize across cultures has also been controversial (see Chiu et al., Vol. 1; Stankov and Lee, Vol. 1). If it is believed that personality is an expression of cultural values, there is no particular reason why personality structures found within different cultures should coincide. On the other hand, if traits reflect universal features of brain physiology – or, indeed, universal themes or challenges of human life – then the same traits should be observed in all cultures. As we have seen, this claim has been at the foundations of the argument for the FFM (Costa and McCrae, 1992). There appear to be different readings of the evidence on this issue. McCrae and Costa (Vol. 1) argue that the five-factor structure of traits has been confirmed in many studies conducted around the world. By contrast, psychologists working with indigenous personality constructs have identified what may be additional major traits such as those relating to 'Chinese traditions' (Bond, 2000). Of course, distributions of personality factors in different cultures may differ even if personality structure generalizes. Thus, cross-cultural differences in personality may actually explain some cultural differences in behaviour. Matsumoto (2006) found that differences in emotion regulation between Japanese and the US samples could be entirely explained by the higher neuroticism, and lower conscientiousness and extraversion, of the Japanese respondents.

To summarize, the psychometric criteria for traits refer to whether 'the numbers behave properly'. In fact, to a large extent, they do. Confirmatory factor analyses and structural equation modelling demonstrate reliable, and often corresponding, factor structures for leading instruments. Individual differences in behaviour correlate across situations, and relate predictably to personality traits. Personality structures also correlate across cultures, at least to some degree. New psychometric methods are expected to refine such investigations. At the same time, psychometrics also indicates some of the complexities and challenges which trait theory must accommodate, including the existence of alternate factor models, the powerful role of the situation as an influence on behaviour, and the existence of culture-specific traits. We will return to these challenges later in this chapter.

Towards a psychological understanding of traits

Psychometrics essentially provides a quantitative basis for understanding the network of relationships between various latent and manifest (measured) constructs. The approach was taken furthest by Cattell's notion (Cattell, 1973; Cattell et al., 2002) of the 'behavioural specification equation' that predicts some criteria from a linear equation including both trait and situational factors. A psychometric understanding can be pursued with only limited psychological theory. We can develop and validate empirically multiple-regression equations that afford prediction of, say, performance at some job, from traits and situational factors without asking whether trait influence is mediated by individual differences in brain functioning or in social learning.

There are several reasons why a purely psychometric understanding is insufficient (in addition to intellectual curiosity). First, quantitative assessment of situational factors is difficult; the lack of good measurement models for the situation is a familiar complaint in personality research. The issue is not just one of ignorance of how to measure the situation. Interactionist studies (e.g. King and Endler, 1990) suggest that it is the individual's appraisals and perceptions that

are critical, as much as objective qualities of the situation. The role of trait anxiety in governing behaviour depends on how much the person 'reads' threat into a situation that may or not be objectively dangerous. Threat appraisal itself may depend on trait anxiety, so that trait and situational influences become intertwined (cf. Endler and Kocovski, 2001).

A second, related issue is that empirical studies do, indeed, reveal that the influence of traits on behaviour is commonly – and sometimes, confusingly – dependent upon various moderator factors. Whether extraverted or introverted individuals perform better on laboratory tasks depends on whether performance is time-pressured, whether subjects have ingested caffeine, how well they have slept, whether they are rewarded or punished for performance, and even on the time of day of the study (e.g. Revelle et al., 1980). It seems unlikely that each moderator effect could be specified psychometrically on an empirical, actuarial basis. It would certainly be prohibitively expensive. A theory is needed that specifies *ante hoc* how moderator effects are to be understood. Indeed, Eysenck's (1967) personality theory sought just this aim, on the basis that the critical attribute of moderator factors was their impact on level of cortical arousal.

A third issue is that applications of personality science beyond the exercises in predictive validity that support occupational selection require theoretical understanding of mediating processes. In designing training programmes geared towards extraverted individuals and introverted individuals, we need to know whether the intervention should target brain functioning, information processing or social interactions. For example, neuroticism appears to predict poorer performance in police officers (Detrick and Chibnall, 2006). Should police departments then simply reject all high-N applicants, or should they train the 'talented-but-neurotic' in techniques for stress management? The answer depends upon the nature of the processes mediating stress vulnerability, and their amenability to change.

Finally, alternative approaches to personality have often been more concerned with semantics than syntax. Psychodynamic theories are exclusively concerned with finding the supposedly hidden meanings of an individual's behaviour and experience. In this case, neglect of measurement issues puts the approach beyond the scientific pale. Social-cognitive theory, by contrast, retains a strong focus on personal meaning, as expressed in the self, for example, but also incorporates quantitative behavioural measures, as in the assessment of the individual's 'behavioural signatures' (Mischel et al., 2002; Zayas et al., Vol. 2).

Matthews et al. (2003) single out three features of research that are increasingly contributing to psychological theories of traits, which we will now briefly review. These are the growing sophistication and power of biological theories, increasing integration of studies of traits with mainstream psychology and applications of research supported by studies of consequential outcomes.

Biological bases of personality

As already noted, Eysenck's (1957, 1967) contribution was remarkable in linking traits to neural processes that could be investigated experimentally, through behavioural and psychophysiological measures (O'Connor, Vol. 1). Eysenck's vision has been broadly substantiated by the ever-accumulating weight of evidence from behaviour genetics and an array of psychophysiological techniques (e.g. Johnson et al., Vol. 1; Stelmack and Rammsayer, Vol. 1; Zuckerman, 2005), although we may take issue with the specifics of the theory (Matthews and Gilliland, 1999).

Recent research advances are providing fresh impetus to biological approaches. Behaviour genetics is increasingly supplemented by molecular genetics that promises to relate traits to specific polymorphisms. Tracking down the genes involved may prove to be arduous (cf. Munafo et al., 2003), but the problem is now essentially a technical

one. Brain-imaging studies using fMRI (Congdon and Canli, Vol. 2) also promise to provide much more fine-grained mappings of traits onto specific brain structures than traditional psychophysiology afforded. Finally, evolutionary psychology, although typically directed towards species- rather than individual-level adaptations, may provide a deeper theoretical understanding of why individuals diverge in genotype and phenotype (Michalski and Shackelford, Vol. 1; Penke et al., 2007). Enthusiasm for the emerging new biology of traits should be tempered by an appreciation of its limitations (see Matthews, Vol. 1), but there are solid grounds for optimism that these parallel advances in psychobiology, which may inform one another, will in time give us increasingly powerful psychobiological theories of personality (Pickering and Corr, Vol. 1).

Integration with mainstream psychology

Traditionally, personality psychology has been a field somewhat set apart from other branches of psychology, with only sporadic points of contact, such as the integration of trait models and psychobiology effected by Eysenck and Gray. Recent trait research has been enriched by the growing adoption of process models from other areas of psychology to explain personality findings, notably developmental, cognitive and social psychology. There is extensive evidence that biologically based temperamental factors such as emotionality, inhibition and self-control provide a platform for adult personality development (Eisenberg et al., 2005; Rothbart and Bates, 2006). At a process level, there is growing interest in how interactions between caregivers and children influence, both brain development and social-emotional learning (Zeidner et al., 2003), and in the role of genetics in shaping interactions with the environment (Rutter et al., 2006).

Psychobiological accounts of trait effects on attention and performance have been increasingly complemented – or supplanted – by theories based on a cognitive psychological understanding of performance, using explanatory constructs including resource availability (Humphreys and Revelle, 1984), working memory (M.W. Eysenck et al., 2007) and spreading activation (Matthews and Harley, 1993). Social psychology has given trait theorists a better understanding of how agreeableness, for example, may influence interactions between people. For example, neuroticism may be related to the content of the social self, represented as a schema or schemas (Matthews et al., 2000b). Recent studies of agreeableness demonstrate its relationships with more positive and accepting social perceptions (e.g. Jensen-Campbell and Graziano, 2001), and with nonverbal behaviours that express greater attention and openness towards others (Berry and Sherman-Hansen, 2000).

Higher-level integrative accounts interrelated a personality and multiple fields of mainstream psychology. For example, cognitive neuroscience approaches (e.g. Derryberry and Reed, 2001; Matthews et al., 2000a) relate personality to both brain systems and the information processing those systems support. The emerging field of social neuroscience (Cacioppo and Berntson, 2004) offers an approach towards understanding how brain processes may control complex social processes (always a weakness of the traditional biological theories of personality). Matthews (Vol. 1) discusses how cognitive science provides an explanatory framework that may integrate – and, where appropriate, dissociate – biological, information processing and social-cognitive explanations for personality.

Integration is a two-way street. Not only is personality research enriched by the infusion of concepts and models from other fields; accommodating individual differences is also increasingly seen as an imperative for mainstream psychology (see Boyle and Saklofske, 2004). Not only is personality psychology becoming a mature science, but so too is psychology in general.

Consequences and applications

Trait psychologists have had to work hard to establish the relevance of traits to applied psychology. Clinical psychologists have typically been conflicted in their the one hand using abnormal trait such as the MMPI extensively, while other hand rejecting much of the theory makes sense of the traits. Eysenck's (e.g. 1994) jousts with the clinical profession illustrate the point. Although the use of personality measures in organizational psychology dates back to the 1900s (Kanfer et al., 1995), the modest effect sizes for traits as predictors of job performance have inspired scepticism. Some critics (e.g. Blinkhorn, 1997) have seen personality assessment as largely irrelevant to the needs of the practitioner. Many applied psychologists remain unenthused about the utility of trait assessments, but several factors have collaborated to increase acceptance. The most basic of these is the increasing evidence for traits as predictors of 'consequential outcomes' in diverse fields including health, work, interpersonal functioning, deviance and community involvement (Fisher and Boyle 1997; Ozer and Benet-Martinez, 2006). The final section in this volume illustrates some of these research areas. In addition, striking evidence for the predictive power of childhood temperament as a predictor of dysfunction in adults has emerged from longitudinal studies (Asendorpf, Vol. 1; Caspi et al., 2005). Somewhat similarly, while there has been a long-running debate over whether elevation of neuroticism and other traits is a cause or consequence of mental illness, recent evidence strongly supports an etiological role for traits (e.g. Harkness et al., 2002).

Some more subtle factors are also at work. In clinical psychology, there is increasing acceptance of dimensional models of abnormality, compatible with general trait models (Malik et al., Vol. 1; Widiger and Trull, 2007). The assumption incorporated into the various editions of the *American Psychiatric Association's Diagnostic and Statistical Manual* (DSM), that abnormal personality is represented by discrete all-or-nothing categories is simply not supported by the evidence for dimensional constructs. Factor analytic studies (e.g. Austin and Deary, 2000)

...ndences between ...imensions. Accep-...o eased by the ...psychology with ...used in clinical ...at the centre of ...apy (Clark et al., ...chema, attentional ...sfunctional coping, may readily be related to traits including neuroticism and its various facets (Matthews et al., 2000b; Wells and Matthews, 1994). Similarly, measurement of personality and temperament is an integral element of the spectrum of psychoeducational assessments of children (see Andrews et al., 2001).

An important finding from meta-analyses of traits and job performance is that effect sizes are larger for confirmatory studies with an *a priori* rationale for linking a specific trait to a specific job than for exploratory studies that are no more than 'fishing expeditions' (Tett and Burnett, 2003; Tett and Christiansen, Vol. 1). This empirical finding reinforces the need for good theories of traits that will support prediction on a reasoned basis, and this thinking appears to be gaining ground in organizational applications (cf. Hogan, 2005, 2006). For example, agreeableness may be an advantage in jobs requiring teamwork, but a hindrance when the individual must compete against others (Barrick et al., 1998). Another trend in industrial organization is the growing realization that it is not just overt job performance that makes an employee valuable. Contextual performance refers to those work behaviours that contribute more widely to the organization, such as supporting co-workers constructively, being a good organizational citizen, and being willing to volunteer (Motowidlo and Van Scotter, 1994). There has been a rapid accumulation of evidence that trait measures predict criteria of this kind (e.g. Judge et al., 2006); multiple correlations for occupational criteria in relation to personality dimensions may approach 0.5 (Ones et al., 2005).

Finally, trait psychology has proved to be in tune with contemporary zeitgeists in its focus on emotionality as a vital element of personality. Applied psychology has been both stirred and shaken by the new construct of 'emotional intelligence' (EI) (Austin et al., Vol. 1; Rivers et al., Vol. 2; Roberts et al., Vol. 2). It is widely believed that enhancing emotional competencies will prove pivotal for addressing deficiencies in provision of mental health services, education and criminal justice. Indeed, programmes directed towards various aspects of social-emotional learning in schools have proved effective in meta-analyses (Greenberg et al., 2003). We will note only briefly that existing measures of EI are of questionable construct validity (see Matthews et al. (2002) for a critique). The larger issue is that emotional competencies – and people's perceptions thereof – may define traits with wide-ranging real-life impacts.

CHALLENGES TO TRAIT MODELS

So far, we have presented the case for viewing personality research as a maturing science. Nevertheless, the field continues to face challenges that should be addressed. There is a somewhat standard critique of traits, typically offered by social psychologists, that is sufficiently familiar not to require repetition (e.g. Caprara and Cervone, 2000; Pervin, 2002). It refers to the validity of factor analysis as a means for uncovering personality structure, neglect of the individual in favour of group trends, neglect of dynamic and developmental processes in favour of static measurement structures, and the questionable cross-cultural generality of traits. To some degree, these are matters of the paradigm-defining assumptions that are adopted by researchers, which change (if they change at all) over generations of scientists. What is more germane here are the challenges which the researcher sympathetic to the trait approach should confront. A detailed critique is beyond the scope of this chapter, but we will offer some general remarks and differentiate some qualitatively different types of challenge. We will summarize these here.

Psychometric challenges

Traditionally, virtually all personality assessment instruments have comprised subjective self-report questionnaires (Q-data), or subjective reports (rating scales) of other people's personality characteristics (L-data). This approach, albeit economical and easy to apply, is nonetheless prone to the problems of item transparency and resultant motivational and response distortion, ranging all the way from deliberate dissimulation, to either conscious or unconscious faking (good or bad), to lack of adequate self-insight, and/or biased perceptions of others. If we consider the Freudian 'tip of the iceberg' analogy, it becomes readily apparent that much of human personality is at the unconscious level of the psyche, and therefore unavailable to conscious self-reports or to reports of others. In this light, most personality assessment instruments amount to subjective 'opinionnaires'. Whereas such introspective approaches would not be regarded as valid in the measurement of cognitive abilities, the current plethora of personality rating scales and questionnaires seems restricted by this fundamentally flawed methodology (see Boyle and Saklofske, 2004). One way forward would be to construct objective (T-data) tests of personality traits, wherein the respondent cannot detect what personality factors are being tapped by the various subtests, thereby alleviating the possibility of motivational and response distortion. Such an approach initially was advocated some 40 years ago by Cattell and Warburton (1967), and was actualized in the factor-analytic construction of the Objective Analytic Battery (OAB) by Cattell and Schuerger (1978), and Schuerger, (1986). However, little subsequent research has been undertaken into the construction of objective tests of personality. Clearly, construction of objective, computer-interactive T-data personality tests will require a major research effort in the years to come. This is the great challenge for personality assessment.

The vexations of normal science

As with any science in its early maturity, there are significant disputes among scientists who hold broadly similar views on the nature of personality. Critiques of trait theory (e.g. Block, 1995, 2001) make much of uncertainties over whether the FFM provides the optimum description of broad personality factors. The personality model outlined by Ashton and Lee (Vol. 2) posits a new factor of Honesty-Humility, and also makes some substantial modifications to the standard Big Five. However, finding additional broad factors that meet standard criteria (e.g. Gorsuch, 1983) does not threaten the trait approach (e.g. any more than the finding of additional solar planets threatens our understanding of the solar system).

Similarly, we should not be too disturbed that specific theories of traits have experienced vicissitudes. The pioneering psychobiological theories, in fact, transpired to show a spotty record of success in predicting psychophysiological and behavioural indices (Matthews and Gilliland, 1999). In response, researchers within this tradition have modified the theories (e.g. Corr, 2004; Pickering and Corr, Vol. 1), which still await large-scale testing. It is not surprising that building good, predictive theories is difficult; thus far, it does not appear that theory modifications are regressive.

Structure, process and causality

A more fundamental issue is how to progress from the structural descriptions of traits afforded by psychometric models to process-based models that specify causal agents. There is a danger that broad, process-based models of traits will degenerate into platitudes. Block (2001) criticizes theories that are expressed in terms solely of broad principles such as the interaction of trait and situational factors. Similarly, it is unclear what is the contribution of "systems theory" versions of interactionism that, in effect, state that everything interacts with everything else (cf. Cattell's (1980) VIDAS systems model). At the same time, there is a genuine theoretical challenge in that personality and environment do interact in a complex, bidirectional fashion (e.g. Caspi and Bem, 1990). Traits affect the environment that surrounds a person, and that environment, in turn, feeds back to influence personality – think, for example, of an adolescent whose life goes off the rail after falling in with bad company.

As Matthews (Vol. 1) argues, a particular challenge is the multiplicity of processes that may mediate the influence of traits. The hope of the early psychobiologists that we could find a small number of key neurological factors from which everything else would flow has proved to be forlorn (Matthews and Gilliland, 1999; Zuckerman, 2005). Traits are distributed across multiple processes; biological, cognitive and social. Suls (2001) aptly refers to the 'neurotic cascade' in referring to the multiple paths that link neuroticism to stress vulnerability. Thus, different mediating processes will emerge from different empirical paradigms, but no single process can bear the weight of fully explaining trait action. At the same time, as the contributors to these volumes demonstrate, good progress is being made in isolating specific mediating paths.

What do we do with a half-full glass?

Another source of frustration is that the data do not always provide unequivocal answers to the big questions. A case in point is the cross-cultural generality of traits (see Chui et al., Vol. 1); we often find factor structures roughly corresponding to the FFM in non-Western cultures, but these are not always a perfect match (however, see McCrae and Costa, Vol. 1). How concerned should we be? Is a rough correspondence sufficient to demonstrate some universality of personality traits? There are no criteria for deciding how large a discrepancy is tolerable for upholding the universality principle. Similar issues arise

in evaluating the mixed success of psychobiological theories, the modest effect sizes of traits as predictors of job performance, and discrepancies in self-ratings and other ratings of personality. The long-term answer is that we need more comprehensive theories that integrate trait and contextual effects on outcomes, but it may be hard to gauge the rate of progress towards this goal.

The unconscious

There is some force to the criticism that trait assessments may be biased through their typical basis in questionnaire measurement, and there is a worthy tradition within trait research of measuring response styles and differentiating them from more substantive traits (e.g. Paulhus, 2002). There are long-standing traditions of using objective tests, originating in Cattell's original work (Schuerger, Vol. 2), and the classical clinical projective tests (Blais and Baity, Vol. 2). The issue has gained impetus from recent research on implicit traits (see Langens and Schmalt, Vol. 1). A variety of novel behavioural techniques for assessing stable traits have emerged, such as the increasingly popular 'implicit activation test' (IAT: Schnabel et al., Vol. 2) and structured nonverbal tests (Hong and Paunonen, Vol. 2). It is still too early to say whether this work will support overarching structural models of 'unconscious' personality of similar scope to standard personality models. The impact of Cattell and Warburton's (1967), and Cattell and Schuerger's (1978) initial work on objective tests was limited by the excessive time taken to carry out such testing (e.g. administration of the OAB takes more than five hours), and by the limited convergence with subjective questionnaire and rating scale indices of personality. However, the potential importance of implicit personality is also signalled by the growing interest within social psychology in unconscious priming effects (Bargh and Williams, 2006).

Few would wish to return to the dark ages of psychoanalysis or the notion that conscious experience of the self is simply the froth on the surface of the true, unconscious structure of personality. Nevertheless, recent work on implicit processes challenges researchers to explore both the measurement and influence on behaviour of unconscious traits.

Setting the boundaries

A final challenge is the demarcation of those issues that trait psychology is apt to explain, and those features of personality that lie outside its boundaries. For example, limitations of the trait approach for understanding the individual person on an idiographic basis are generally accepted. Similarly, changes in personality through the adult lifespan may be difficult to capture within the trait model to the extent that change depends on idiographic processes such as the long-term pursuit of 'personal projects' (Little and Chambers, 2004).

Boundary issues are also relevant to an issue that Pervin (2002) flags as fundamental: what 'units of personality' we should adopt. He contrasts motivational units (e.g. needs) and cognitive units (e.g. self-referent beliefs) as alternatives to traits as units. Pervin does not do sufficient justice to the extent that contemporary trait psychology is in fact concerned with relating motives and cognitions to traits (e.g. Boyle et al., 1995), but the general point is valid. There may be some individual differences in motivation, such as traditional implicit achievement motivation, that should be separated from trait psychology (cf. Langens and Schmalt, Vol. 1). As noted earlier, the extent to which stable social cognitions may be accommodated within trait theory is also open to debate (Caprara and Cervone, 2000).

A recent article by McAdams and Pals (2006) makes some reasonable suggestions. As well as dispositional traits, they define two further levels of understanding of personality described as *characteristic adaptations* and *integrative life narratives*, both of which are more strongly influenced by culture than dispositional traits are. Characteristic adaptations refer to contextualized goals, values, coping strategies, relational patterns and so on, that fill in the details of individuality and describe everyday social functioning. Integrative life narratives refer to longer-term personal narratives and sources of identity that individuals construct to make sense of their place in the world and their contribution to it. The McAdams and Pals analysis is valuable in providing a sense of what expressions of personality trait models are well equipped or poorly equipped to explain. Although they do not make this point, we may also see characteristic adaptations as a halfway house between general trait dimensions and idiographic dispositions. There are successful research programmes on 'contextualized' traits such as test anxiety (Zeidner, 1998) and work self-efficacy (Judge et al., 2007) that may be assessed and investigated much as broader traits. As we narrow down the context, the trait becomes increasingly idiographic. Computer anxiety qualifies as a standard (contextualized trait); stress induced by a particular misbehaving machine is idiographic. In summary, it is unlikely that any single approach will attain hegemony over the entirety of personality research; instead, we may look forward to a multi-polar research world, in which there is a place for those varying perspectives that meet acceptable scientific standards.

STRUCTURE OF VOLUME 1

Explanatory models for personality

This first section of the book elaborates on the theoretical issues briefly introduced above, in reviewing and differentiating the key research strategies for investigating personality. How personality is studied depends on how it is conceptualized, and the chapters here serve to illustrate the range of explanatory models that may support a science of personality. Stelmack and Rammsayer review the biological bases of personality and individual differences, as revealed by over four decades of psychophysiological and neurochemical research. Their review focuses especially on the pivotal traits of extraversion, neuroticism and impulsive sensation seeking, and identifies several robust associations between these traits and electrocortical and biochemical responses. It also highlights the methodological challenges of work on these issues and inconsistencies requiring further work to resolve. Biological perspectives may be contrasted with the viewpoint from cognitive psychology. Matthews reviews studies that link traits to individual differences in information processing, using performance data. It is argued that these studies identify multiple processes that underpin the major dimensions of personality. The empirical data may be understood within a multi-levelled cognitive science framework that refers both to the neurological underpinnings of cognition and to high-level strategies for goal attainment. Traits are distributed across many component processes but derive functional unity as adaptive constructs.

Yet, another distinctive approach to understanding personality is provided by social-cognitive models, reviewed by Cervone. His review of the field includes an analysis of what such models should seek to explain, on the basis that mere prediction of behaviour is inadequate for understanding personality. Social-cognitive models are based on an intra-individual understanding of personality that finds coherence in the individual's construction of personal meaning. Cervone outlines the key contributions of Bandura and Mischel to personality theories built on social-cognitive principles. He also describes his KAPA (Knowledge-and-Appraisal Personality Architecture) model that – recapitulating the traditional distinction between structure and process – aims to specify the knowledge structures and appraisal processes that support personality coherence.

Understanding personality development requires a multi-levelled understanding of the interplay between maturation of the brain, and cognitive and social development. Asendorpf's survey of the major developmental issues for personality psychology arrives at three major principles for understanding stability and change. First, personality retains plasticity throughout life; it never becomes 'set like plaster'. Indeed, in line with a social psychological concern with the individual, plasticity can be demonstrated in individuals using the Q-sort technique. Second, the stability of inter-individual differences increases with age, because of several factors including genetic influence, dynamic person–environment interaction and the coherence conferred by stabilization of personal identity. Third, there is a synergy between person and environment in that the person's most characteristic traits interact most strongly with situational influences. Somewhat similar themes of dynamic interaction arise in the Chiu et al. (Vol. 1) account of personality and culture. A traditional assumption is a duality between nature (biology) and culture; in fact, personality research reveals the intricate interactions and interdependency of nature and social ecology. The authors propose an integrated framework that describes how culture influences personality, and personality influences culture. For example, culture may affect the knowledge structures that support the self, but personality shapes the strategies the individual uses to adapt to the cultural milieu. People are not pawns of their cultural programming.

The next two chapters in this section elaborate on the biological bases for personality. Johnson et al. (Vol. 1) present a comprehensive review of the many behaviour genetic studies that have investigated the contribution of genetic and environmental factors to both normal and abnormal personality traits. Beyond the familiar conclusion that both environmental and genetic factors are implicated, the authors identify some of the key methodological and theoretical issues in contemporary research. These include the role of the nonshared environment unique to each family member, correlations between genetic and environmental factors, and recent molecular genetic research which has attempted to identify specific polymorphisms that may influence personality development. Michalski and Shackelford set out the evolutionary psychology perspective on personality. Initially, they make the strong, potentially controversial claim that the evolutionary sciences provide the only scientifically viable framework for understanding the historical origins of human personality. They illustrate the contribution of evolutionary psychology to several areas of personality psychology including personality consistency, individual differences in personality, sex differences and similarities and contextual determinants of personality. It is necessary to understand both the many species-typical adaptations that characterize humans, and the place for individual differences in these mechanisms.

The final chapter, by Campbell, places modern explanatory models for personality in their historical context. Personality models have changed substantially from those proposed by the 'classic' personality theorists of the last century, including Allport, Murray and Lewin. Campbell traces the cultural evolution of personality from these theories to modern times. The classic models provide a direct or indirect basis for much contemporary research and application. Furthermore, their empirical utility is under-utilized; in particular, Cattell's multivariate approach has much to offer in predicting behavioural outcomes from personality data (Boyle, 2006 Cattell and Nesselroade, 1988). The chapter summarizes what has been lost and what has been gained as the theory has developed.

Comprehensive trait models

It follows naturally from the nomothetic trait approach that a comprehensive, universal description of the major personality dimensions may be determined. Indeed, like the periodic table of elements in chemistry, a comprehensive trait model may be a necessity for a true science of personality

(Cattell, 1973; Cattell and Kline, 1977). The idea also gains plausibility from the thesis that dimensions correspond to brain systems that influence personality in all cultures. At the same time, there are some obvious difficulties in making progress. Historically, the key question of how many dimensions to list has tended to degenerate into technical arguments over alternative factor solutions; confirmatory methods are stronger in this respect, but they remain vulnerable to variation in the initial sampling of data. Research also tends to proliferate minor traits of questionable generality; what criteria indicate whether a trait is truly universal, as opposed to being linked to a specific context? Hierarchical models in which a multiplicity of primary traits are overlaid by a smaller number of broad universal factors provide one answer to this issue. The assumption of a strong isomorphism between brain systems and basic traits is also open to question (Zuckerman, 2005). If traits are admitted to be indirectly rather than directly linked to the brain, the dimensionality of personality may in fact become rather more contingent, and the assumption of universality is thus undermined. A final difficulty is that progress has been slow. Although there may seem to be a partial consensus over the FFM, points of serious contention remain, as explored by contributors to this and other sections of Volume 1. Furthermore, there appears to be little progress towards any comprehensive description of primary traits.

The contributors to this section review the major comprehensive trait models that have shaped personality research. Hans Eysenck's model of individual differences, reviewed by O'Connor, is the most parsimonious of the major theories, in reducing personality to major dimensions of extraversion, neuroticism and psychoticism. O'Connor outlines the conceptual and methodological principles of Eysenck's individual difference paradigm, which has a good claim to introducing a Kuhnian revolution into personality research. O'Connor also addresses the translation of psychobiological theory into applied fields, illustrated by diverse examples related to education, drug addiction and psychotherapy. Eysenck's theory will always be paired with its major competitor, the reinforcement sensitivity theory (RST) developed by Jeffrey Gray, which is outlined by Pickering and Corr. RST shares many of the basic assumptions of Eysenck's theory but differs most sharply in attributing the major traits to motivational rather than generalized arousal systems. As Pickering and Corr discuss, personality reflects individual differences in processing reward and punishment stimuli. RST has evolved over time to meet the inevitable conceptual and empirical challenges that arise in a vigorous research programme. The chapter reviews these challenges, and the modifications to theory they have inspired, in order to set the course for future research. They point out that it is especially important to bring the neuroscience and personality wings of the theory into better alignment by capitalizing on methodological advances in biological psychology.

Raymond Cattell's work (see Boyle, 2006) was unparalleled in its dedication to developing a truly comprehensive model for individual differences, taking in not just orthodox personality dimensions, but also ability, abnormal personality, normal and abnormal moods and dynamic motivational traits. Boyle's chapter (Vol. 1) points out that the complexity and statistical sophistication of Cattell's programme may have impeded its general acceptance. He describes a programmatic series of psychometric studies directed towards uncovering higher-order factor structures that serve to simplify the Cattellian model, reducing 92 constructs to 30 broad factors that may jointly provide comprehensive coverage of 6 major domains of differential psychology. Boyle also emphasizes the importance of developing objective, interactive tests that counter the over-reliance of the field on subjective, self-report methodology.

The last two chapters in this section address the currently popular five-factor model (FFM). McCrae and Costa set out a case for the FFM that emphasizes its heritability, temporal stability and generalization across gender and cultures. Key issues here include the validity of alternate dimensional models, the optimal choice of lower-level personality facets and the taxing theoretical issue of how causation at the individual level can be understood by studying correlation at the group level. The last issue is central to social-cognitive critiques of trait theory (Cervone, Vol. 1), but McCrae and Costa counter that trait explanations provide abstract, high-level causal accounts that complement more fine-grained, mechanistic explanations for behaviour. Insightful critiques, including those of Cervone and Block, reject at least some of the core assumptions of nomothetic trait psychology. However, the FFM is also open to criticisms from within trait psychology. Boyle provides a critique of this kind. One line of questioning is psychometric in nature; re-examination of the empirical data suggests that the five-factor solution may not be optimal in view of the frequent application of less than adequate factor-analytic procedures (Boyle et al., 1995; Boyle and Saklofske, 2004). Furthermore, although proponents of the FFM claim there is a convergence between normal and abnormal personality dimensions, the FFM may not in fact provide adequate coverage of several major abnormal traits, including those related to psychoticism. A final source of difficulty is that a lack of underlying theory and a neglect of dynamic personality processes make the FFM less than ideal for predicting behaviour in applied fields including clinical and occupational psychology. Debate over the FFM is likely to continue; our hope is that the complementary chapters by McCrae and Costa, and by Boyle, will highlight the issues that are decisive for resolving its place as a comprehensive trait model.

Key traits: psychobiology

The search for comprehensive trait models occupies the conceptual high ground of personality research. By contrast, much of the daily grind of working to understand in detail the origins and consequences of traits is based on single traits. The next two sections of this book survey some of the key traits whose psychological significance is mapped by their relationships with other constructs. The painstaking exploration of these 'nomological networks' is essential for theory building in personality research. Indeed, given that single traits may be placed within more comprehensive trait models (see McCrae and Costa, Vol. 1), such work also serves to deepen understanding of the higher-level 'superfactors'. We have, somewhat arbitrarily, divided key traits into those for which research is guided by psychobiological theory, and those understood within the cognitive frameworks of self-regulation and stress theories. This distinction is made for convenience. As discussed previously (see also Matthews, Vol. 1), traits are typically multi-layered entities with both biological and cognitive expressions, and theory must integrate both aspects. Complementary sections in Volume 2 set out to cover the assessment of biological and self-regulative traits.

Thus far, we have highlighted Eysenck's arousal theory and Gray's RST as the leading comprehensive personality theories based on psychobiology. This section covers research that focuses more narrowly on specific traits rooted in brain functioning. It has something of a psychopathological flavour, in that much of this work reflects concerns with abnormalities in brain functioning that may contribute to personality disorders. Indeed, it may be seen as an outgrowth of Eysenck's and Gray's interests in the clinical significance of traits.

Zuckerman's work on sensation seeking may be seen as a paradigm for developing a theory of specific traits. It has generated a reliable and validated questionnaire, ample evidence for validity and a detailed model of the biological underpinnings of the trait. Furthermore, sensation seeking may be located within the more comprehensive personality model developed by Zuckerman (2006; see also Zuckerman, Vol. 2). The chapter reviews both behavioural expressions of sensation seeking across a wide range of risky behaviours, and also the biological

bases for the trait. The psychobiological account is supported by evidence from behaviour and molecular genetics, along with extensive psychophysiological and biochemical evidence. By contrast with Eysenck and Gray, Zuckerman sees phenotypic traits as emerging from multiple physiological processes; there is no isomorphism between the trait and any single biological system.

'Schizotypy' refers to a dimension of abnormal personality characterized by subclinical levels of oddities of belief and behaviour that resemble psychosis. The review by Green et al. (Vol. 1) of the trait illustrates a variety of themes in contemporary abnormal personality studies. Schizotypy can be assessed as a continuous trait in the normal population, grading increasingly into clinical symptoms at the top end of the scale. Subdimensions of schizotypy may be distinguished both psychometrically and in relation to etiology. Following Raine (2006), Green et al. distinguish a 'neuroschizotypy' that should be seen as a brain disorder from a 'pseudoschizotypy' that may be more dependent upon psychosocial factors. In both cases, the interplay between genetic and environmental factors is likely to be critical. Rawlings' chapter addresses some related issues in the context of the broader trait of psychoticism (P), and its relationship with impulsivity. The psychometric identification of P was motivated by Eysenck's interest in the diathesis for clinical psychosis. In fact, the evidence reviewed suggests that the P scale is inadequate as a measure of the essential elements of a classic psychotic disorder (to which schizotypy may be more relevant). P has greater validity as a measure of impulsive, antisocial forms of behaviour, and the chapter concludes with an account of the relationships between different forms of impulsivity and P.

Also discussed is the evidence relating aggression and impulsivity to personality traits and related neurophysiological mechanisms (see Lijffijt et al., Vol. 1). Underlying biological causes for higher trait impulsivity and emotional arousal in aggression could be related to suboptimal processing of errors, reward and punishment. Without checks and balances of either low neuroticism with high impulsivity, or low impulsivity with high neuroticism, it is less likely that stress can be countered effectively, thereby exacerbating pre-existing heightened levels of emotional arousal in aggressive individuals.

The final chapter in this section, Elliott and Thrash's account of approach and avoidance temperaments, bridges the somewhat artificial divide between psychobiological and self-regulative traits explicitly. Basic traits related to approach and avoidance motivations appear to have a biological basis conceptualized here in relation to Gray's RST (see Pickering and Corr, Vol. 1). Neurobiological sensitivity to reward is controlled by Gray's behaviour activation system (BAS); punishment sensitivity relates to the behaviour inhibition system (BIS). Elliott and Thrash go on to discuss the measurement of approach and avoidance temperaments, and provide evidence that these personality factors influence self-regulative processes such as adoption of goals for mastery and performance.

Key traits: self-regulation and stress

Self-regulative models of personality are built on the assumption that behaviour is controlled by a feedback loop that serves to reduce the discrepancy between ideal and desired behaviour, supported by various cognitive processes including goal setting, strategy choice and self-evaluation (Zeidner et al., 2000). Personality traits may relate both to the contents of stable self-knowledge that guides self-regulation, and to biases in specific information-processing components such as retrieval from memory and selective attention (Carver and Scheier, 1998; Matthews et al., 2000b). Self-regulative models are thus compatible with notions of approach and avoidance motivation (Elliott and Thrash, Vol. 1), with the transactional theory of stress (Lazarus, 1999), and with social-cognitive perspectives (Cervone, Vol. 1),

at least to the extent they lend themselves to nomothetic understanding of personality.

Contributions to this section illustrates the range and depth of personality theories of this kind. Several general issues are evident. First, there is a tension between general self-regulative trait models and contextualized models that differentiate multiple dimensions of self-regulation linked to specific situations or challenges. The former approach may add to understanding of general traits, for example, through exploring the role of low self-esteem in neuroticism. The second approach contributes to understanding what lies beyond standard traits for example, how research on evaluative anxieties complements general trait anxiety work (e.g. Endler and Kocovski, 2001). A second issue is whether research is directed towards the *content* of self-beliefs that guide self-regulation (e.g. self-concept, outcome expectancy) or towards specific self-regulative *processes* (e.g. self-directed attention, choice of coping strategy). Third, self-regulative models are intimately concerned with emotion and stress, and the interplay between negative affect and styles of self-regulation (Carver and Scheier, 1998). Dysfunctional self-regulation may contribute to clinical disorders so that therapeutic interventions may be usefully directed towards harmful content and process factors (Wells and Matthews, 1994).

Trait anxiety may relate to individual differences in strategies for self-preservation in threatening environments. Zeidner's review of trait and test anxiety points out that in modern times, the most salient threats are often social-evaluative in nature. The chapter reviews assessment issues, biological and environmental influences on anxiety and the behavioural expressions of anxiety revealed by performance studies. Evaluative anxieties may significantly interfere with personal goal attainment, causing test performance and job proficiency to fall short of actual competence. The chapter prefigures the applied issues that conclude Volume 1 by reviewing how psychological research supports interventions for excessive evaluative anxiety. Naturally, an understanding of the self-concept is central to self-regulative models of personality. Research on self-concept may also serve to integrate personality trait models with social-cognitive theory. In reviewing the field, Marsh describes a uni-dimensional conception of self-concept that focuses on global self-esteem. However, research shows that specific domains of self-concept are more useful than a general domain construct for understanding the self (cf. Boyle, 1994). In line with social-cognitive concerns about the context for behaviour, Marsh advocates a multi-dimensional approach to self-concept. Measurement of self-concept across different domains appears to provide better predictive validity for educational criteria than general self-esteem or standard personality traits. Domain-specific self-concepts may be reciprocally linked to personality traits through mutual causal effects.

Outcome expectancies also play a pivotal role in self-regulation. Optimists and pessimists appear to differ in these beliefs. Chang et al. define optimism and pessimism as generalized positive and negative outcome expectancies that directly or indirectly contribute to a variety of physical and psychological outcomes. They review several lines of research on these constructs, including alternate uni-dimensional and multi-dimensional measurement models, and the costs and benefits of the traits in dealing with stressful encounters. Optimism–pessimism research also adds to perspectives on cultural differences in personality (see Chiu et al., Vol. 1): the adaptive functions of optimism and pessimism may differ in Western and East Asian cultures.

Research on the contents of self-knowledge (e.g. self-concept) are complemented by studies of key self-referent processes that influence the availability and accessibility of self-knowledge. As Smári et al. discuss, an important family of constructs relates to self-consciousness. As traits, these constructs relate to the individual's style of attention to internal states and/or social personae. The distinction between public and private

self-consciousness has been especially influential, but other important dimensions also include rumination, mindfulness, self-monitoring and related traits. Smári et al. review the inter-relationships between different operationalizations of these traits. They suggest that advances in both psychometric and conceptual models are needed in order to resolve some theoretical ambiguities and empirical problems that have arisen from research on self-consciousness.

Process issues are also central to Parker and Wood's review of personality and coping. Growing out of earlier work on defence mechanisms, coping is now understood within an interactional model, such that due attention to both person and situation factors is essential. There is a considerable degree of consistency in individual differences in coping, supporting a role for personality traits as drivers of coping style. However, although various robust associations between standard traits and basic dimensions of coping have been established, the field has been held back by neglect of the intra-individual variation in coping that demonstrates situational influences. A truly interactionist perspective requires a more detailed examination of the interplay between personality and situational factors in determining coping.

New trait and dynamic trait constructs

As Boyle (Vol. 1) notes, operationalization of personality as a relatively small number of traits measured by questionnaire may fail to illuminate important aspects of the personality sphere. At any given time, there are always some personality psychologists who seek to add to the number of recognized traits by developing and validating new measures. Sometimes these efforts succeed; at other times, new traits lack validity or prove to be no more than old traits repackaged. At the lower end of the radicalism scale are those investigators who accept the broad validity of a questionnaire-based approach but seek to modify or extend canonical models such as the FFM. The chapters of Zuckerman, and Ashton and Lee in Vol. 2 represent such an approach. Rather more radical are attempts to redefine the scope of the personality domain, by identifying new kinds of content for personality questionnaires, such as culturally dependent belief structures. There may also be new traits to be found at the interface of personality and ability, such as meta-cognitions of task performance and 'emotional intelligence'. In such cases, the researcher must define both the overlaps and the distinctive features of the new traits, in relation to personality and intelligence. Developing psychometrically adequate measurement models that meet this goal may prove challenging, as the example of emotional intelligence shows (see Roberts et al., Vol. 2).

The greatest challenge to existing trait models derives from the recent resurgence of interest in implicit traits (i.e. those evident through behavioural consistency rather than from conscious experience and self-report). Interest in the unconscious, both looks back to psychoanalysis (see Campbell, Vol. 1), and looks sideways to modern experimental studies of implicit processes – although it is debatable whether the experimental findings support Freudian notions (Kihlstrom, 1999). Some researchers (e.g. Schmukle and Egloff, 2005) see explicit and implicit traits as representing largely different domains; we may have separate unconscious personalities that interact rather weakly with our explicit self-beliefs. On the other hand, psychobiological models imply – given that we are largely unaware of subcortical processes – that implicit neural processes provide the foundation for 'explicit' traits such as E and N. Thus (as with self-regulative approaches), work on implicit traits has the potential both for deepening our understanding of existing constructs, and adding novel dimensions to the personality sphere. Contributors to this section address some of the key principles that guide conceptualization of new explicit and implicit traits. Work concerned more directly with measurement of specific traits is covered in Vol. 2, including a

section devoted to implicit, projective and objective measures of personality.

Langens and Schmalt review the state of the art in the implicit measurement of human motives. Their approach builds on the earlier contributions of Cattell, in distinguishing dynamic traits from conventional personality traits (see Boyle, Vol. 1), and McClelland's use of the thematic apperception test (TAT) in measurement of basic needs. Implicit measures such as the TAT may provide a path towards motivational processes that instigate behaviour by means of unconscious affective processes, processes which are inaccessible to self-report. The authors' multi-motive grid (MMG) affords valid assessment of achievement, power and affiliation motives. It also differentiates implicit approach and avoidance components of these motives (compare the explicit measurement model reviewed by Elliott and Thrash, Vol. 1). Integrating the concept of motivational traits into the larger field of personality may cast light on the hidden forces that shape behaviour.

One contribution to new traits at the interface of ability and personality is provided by Stankov and Kleitman's account of confidence and its realism. A person's confidence in his/her performance may be measured separately from performance itself; that is, as an aspect of meta-cognition. The chapter shows that confidence can be assessed as a trait that is distinct – but meaningfully related to – cognate constructs, including performance accuracy, standard personality traits and questionnaire assessments of meta-cognition. A separate issue is the realism of judgements and confidence: can we find individuals who are systematically over- and under-confident? Stankov and Kleitman identify some psychometric difficulties in the measurement of realism, but also some application towards understanding group differences.

There is increasing interest in traits relating to standards and attitudes that are at least somewhat detached from conventional personality traits (e.g. Saucier, 2000). Stankov and Lee identify three trait domains distinct from the personality traits that describe broadly the way we 'think, feel or act'. These domains describe dealing with others (social attitudes), attaching meanings to long-term goals (values) and considering societal milieu (social norms). The authors describe empirical work supporting a factor model that may capture differences between a variety of different cultures. In addition to the domain factors already described, a further conservatism factor also emerges in the data. The factor model also serves to illuminate cultural dimensions in cognitive, gender and ethnic differences.

The last chapter in this section (Austin et al.) provides a second contribution to new directions in understanding the ability–personality interface, focusing on the new and sometimes controversial construct of emotional intelligence (EI: see also Roberts et al., Vol. 2). EI is broadly defined as a set of abilities for perceiving, understanding and managing emotions, but differing conceptualizations have emerged. 'Trait EI' refers to the construct operationalized as an explicit aspect of personality that can be measured by questionnaire. Alternatively, EI may be treated as a true ability that requires implicit assessment using objective tests (see Salovey et al., Vol. 2). Austin et al. review contemporary research based on trait and ability models for EI and the relevance of the construct to health, educational and occupational psychology.

Applications

On the basis that 'nothing is so practical as a good theory', it is expected that an increasingly rigorous science of personality should support a range of real-world applications. Growing evidence for the 'consequential validity' of personality traits (Ozer and Benet-Martinez, 2006), in particular, supports application. Indeed, there is a long tradition of using personality assessments as an aid to diagnosis and intervention in a variety of applied fields including organizational, clinical and educational psychology. The chapters in this section together provide a comprehensive survey of these principal applications of personality research; note that

educational issues are treated from an assessment perspective by Rowe et al. (Vol. 2).

In clinical practice, the two major applications are in diagnosis and treatment. As Malik et al. point out, the diagnosis of psychopathology has long been defined in the US by the *American Psychiatric Association's Diagnostic and Statistical Manual* (DSM). Their chapter reviews the relationship between this standard framework for diagnosis and abnormal personality traits. They identify various weakness of the DSM as a means for understanding personality disorder; weaknesses that may be remedied by use of dimensional models of abnormality. Such models may better fit the data than the categorical approach of DSM, and provide a better psychological understanding of disorders. Furthermore, dimensional models may provide guidance on the etiology and treatment of personality disorders, a topic further addressed by Groth-Marnat et al. These authors introduce the systematic treatment selection (STS) model which aims to optimize the *fit* between the client's personality and various strategies of psychotherapy. They discuss the application of STS to conditions including depression, substance abuse and trauma, and look forward to realizing the benefits of the approach.

Health psychology is a newer field than clinical psychology, but here too interest in personality traits is growing. Traits are relevant both to the medical patient's awareness and regulation of illness (e.g. complaining behaviours), and to the physiological processes that may contribute to objective pathology (e.g. stress-linked changes in immune system function). Williams et al. provide a general survey of the role of personality in health psychology, behavioural medicine and psychosomatics. Personality may be linked to a variety of physical health outcomes, including longevity and vulnerability to specific illnesses such as cardiovascular disease and cancer. The chapter reviews conceptual issues and methodological challenges, together with the main topics addressed by empirical studies. As Fernandez and Kerns discuss, medical illness is often accompanied by negative affect. Emotional disturbances may indeed become clinically significant. Their review of the field proposes that fear, sadness and anger should be identified as correlated, but functionally distinct aspects of negative affect. The chapter reviews the evidence on the medical significance of these components of emotion, including strategies for assessment and treatment.

Studies of substance abuse bring together practitioners of both clinical and health psychology. Two chapters here cover alcohol and nicotine abuse respectively. Given the damaging effects on health of these drugs, studies of personality may potentially make an important contribution to identifying and treating those individuals prone to substance abuse. Ibáñez et al. review the relationship between personality and individual differences in alcohol use and misuse. Traits including E, N and impulsivity/disinhibition are implicated in normal and pathological alcohol consumption. The authors caution that multiple mechanisms contribute to these behaviours, so that personality is only one piece in the complex puzzle of multiple biological, psychological and social variables. Their biopsychosocial model accommodates the role of personality traits by linking them to the biological trait models reviewed elsewhere in Volume 1 (Pickering and Corr; Zuckerman). Byrne and Mazanov likewise emphasize the multiple determinants of smoking behaviour: socio-demographic, environmental, behavioural and personal. Personality is related to smoking in cross-sectional studies of adolescents, but it has proved challenging to establish causal effects in longitudinal studies. There is better evidence for a causal effect of stress; personality may contribute to the onset of smoking behaviour by enhancing vulnerability to external stress or by undermining available coping strategies. The authors also indicate the need for better theories to guide the applied research in this area.

The chapter that concludes the section, Tett and Christiansen's review of personality assessment in organizations, covers one of the major applications of personality research. Their review of the literature on personality traits as predictors of job performance states that recent meta-analyses may underestimate the importance of traits by ignoring critical conditions favouring personality test use. They review essential methodological recommendations including the use of a formal job analysis to identify relevant personality factors, and generation of predictive directional hypotheses. Practical issues covered include the problem of faking, applicant reactions, alternative measurement strategies and legal issues. Tett and Christiansen also survey the importance of personality beyond the traditional concern of predicting performance. Personality information may be used not only in hiring, but for post-hire practices including worker motivation, team building and promotion.

CONCLUDING REMARKS

The editors believe that the contributions to these handbooks will speak for themselves in highlighting the strength, diversity and relevance to multiple fields of psychology of contemporary personality science. The integration of psychometrics and theory envisioned by Eysenck, Cattell and others provides a basis for exploring stable individual differences in a multitude of traits that permeate every area of life. The chapters also illustrate how the controversies that have historically divided personality researchers have in the end served to enhance the evidence for trait models. Moving on from debates over the stability, generality and heritability of traits has served to maintain the momentum of the field. The field is not free of controversy (and nor should it be). The biological basis of personality is evident, but it has sometimes seemed difficult to translate the general principle into theories that are effective in predicting behaviour. The challenge from social-psychological perspectives remains. Social-cognitive theory has inspired important self-regulative accounts of traits, but the idiographic focus of much of this work remains problematic. The Freudian unconscious is an historical relic for most researchers, but important questions about the role of conscious and unconscious processes in personality are still to be resolved. Given that validity coefficients in relation to real-life criteria are widespread but often modest in magnitude, it is still unclear how applied psychologists can best make use of personality assessment. Perhaps the most compelling sign of the vitality of personality research is that its most pressing problems are those that are critical to psychology in general. We look forward to future personality research helping to resolve the tension between biological and social psychological models, the impact of unconscious processes on behaviour and the application of psychological theory to real-world issues.

REFERENCES

Allport, G.W. (1937) *Personality: A Psychological Interpretation*. New York: Holt.

Andrews, J.J.W., Saklofske, D.H. and Janzen, H.L. (2001) (eds), *Handbook of Psychoeducational Assessment: Ability, Achievement, and Behavior in Children*. San Diego: Academic.

Austin, E.J. and Deary, I.J. (2000) 'The "four As": A common framework for normal and abnormal personality?', *Personality and Individual Differences*, 28(5): 977–95.

Bagby, R.M. and Quilty, C. (2006) 'Personality traits can predict best treatment for depression', *Directions in Psychiatry*, 26(4): 199–208.

Bargh, J.A. and Williams, L. (2006) 'The automaticity of social life', *Current Directions in Psychological Science*, 15(1): 1–4.

Barrett, P. (2005) 'What if there were no psychometrics?: Constructs, complexity, and measurement', *Journal of Personality Assessment*, 85(2): 134–40.

Barrick, M.R., Stewart, G.L., Neubert, M.J. and Mount, M.K. (1998) 'Relating member ability and personality to work-team processes and team effectiveness', *Journal of Applied Psychology*, 83(3): 377–91.

Berry, D.S. and Sherman-Hansen, J. (2000) 'Personality, nonverbal behavior, and interaction quality in female dyads', *Personality and Social Psychology Bulletin*, 26(3): 278–92.

Blinkhorn, S. (1997) 'Past imperfect, future conditional: Fifty years of test theory', *British Journal of Mathematical and Statistical Psychology*, 50(2): 175–86.

Block, J. (1995) 'A contrarian view of the five-factor approach to personality description', *Psychological Bulletin*, 117(2): 187–215.

Block, J. (2001) 'Millennial contrarianism: The five-factor approach to personality description 5 years later', *Journal of Research in Personality*, 35(1): 98–107.

Bond, M.H. (2000) 'Localizing the imperial outreach – The Big Five and more in Chinese culture', *American Behavioral Scientist*, 44(1): 63–72.

Boyle, G.J. (1991) 'Does item homogeneity indicate internal consistency or item redundancy in psychometric scales?' *Personality and Individual Differences*, 12(3): 291–4.

Boyle, G.J. (1994) 'Self-Description Questionnaire II', in D.J. Keyser and R.C. Sweetland (eds), *Test Critiques*, 10: 632–43.

Boyle, G.J. (2006) 'Scientific analysis of personality and individual differences', Doctor of Science thesis, University of Queensland.

Boyle, G.J. and Saklofske, D.H. (2004) (eds), *Sage Benchmarks in Psychology: The Psychology of Individual Differences* (Vols 1–4). London: Sage.

Boyle, G.J., Stankov, L. and Cattell, R.B. (1995) 'Measurement and statistical models in the study of personality and intelligence', in D.H. Saklofske and M. Zeidner (eds), *International Handbook of Personality and Intelligence*. New York: Plenum.

Cacioppo, J.T. and Berntson, G.G. (2004) 'Social neuroscience', in M.S. Gazzaniga (ed.), *The Cognitive Neurosciences* (3rd edn). Cambridge, MA: MIT Press. pp. 977–85.

Caprara, G.V. and Cervone, D. (2000) *Personality: Determinants, Dynamics, and Potentials*. Cambridge: Cambridge University Press.

Carver, C.S. and Scheier, M.F. (1998) *On the Self-Regulation of Behavior*. New York: Cambridge University Press.

Caspi, A. and Bem, D.J. (1990) 'Personality continuity and change across the life course', in L.A. Pervin (ed.), *Handbook of Personality: Theory and Research*. New York: Guilford, pp. 549–75.

Caspi, A., Roberts, B.W. and Shiner, R.L. (2005) 'Personality development: Stability and change', *Annual Review of Psychology*, 56: 453–84.

Cattell, R.B. (1973) *Personality and Mood by Questionnaire*. New York: Jossey Bass.

Cattell, R.B. (1978) *The Scientific Use of Factor Analysis in Behavioral and Life Sciences*. New York: Plenum.

Cattell, R.B. (1980) *Personality and Learning Theory, Vol. 2: A Systems Theory of Maturation and Learning*. New York: Springer.

Cattell, R.B. (1995) 'The fallacy of five factors in the personality sphere', *The Psychologist*, 8(5): 207–8.

Cattell, R.B., Boyle, G.J. and Chant, D. (2002) 'The enriched behavioral prediction equation and its impact on structured learning and the dynamic calculus', *Psychological Review*, 109(1): 202–5.

Cattell, R.B. and Kline, P. (1977) 'The Scientific Analysis of Personality and Motivation', New York: Academic.

Cattell, R.B. and Nesselroade, J.R. (1988) (eds), *Handbook of Multivariate Experimental Psychology* (rev. 2nd edn). New York: Plenum.

Cattell, R.B. and Schuerger, J.M. (1978) *Personality Theory in Action: Handbook for the Objective-Analytic (O-A) Test Kit*. Champaign, IL: Institute for Personality and Ability Testing.

Cattell, R.B. and Warburton, F.W. (1967) *Objective Personality and Motivation Tests: A Theoretical Introduction and Practical Compendium*. Champaign, IL: University of Illinois Press.

Clark, D.A., Beck, A.T. and Alford, B.A. (1999) *Scientific Foundations of Cognitive Theory and Therapy of Depression*. Hoboken, NJ: Wiley.

Corr, P.J. (2004) 'Reinforcement sensitivity theory and personality', *Neuroscience and Biobehavioral Reviews*, 28(3): 317–32.

Costa, P.T. Jr. and McCrae, R.R. (1992) 'Four ways five factors are basic', *Personality and Individual Differences*, 13(6): 653–65.

Costa, P.T. and Widiger, T.A. (2002) *Personality Disorders and the Five-Factor Model of Personality* (2nd edn). Washington, DC: American Psychological Association.

Cuttance, P. and Ecob, R. (1987) (eds), *Structural Modeling by Example: Applications in Educational, Sociological, and Behavioural Research*. New York: Cambridge University Press.

Derryberry, D. and Reed, M.A. (2001) 'A multidisciplinary perspective on attentional control', in C.L. Folk and B.S. Gibson (eds), *Attraction, Distraction and Action: Multiple Perspectives on Attentional Capture*. New York: Elsevier Science, pp. 325–47.

Detrick, P. and Chibnall, T. (2006) 'NEO PI-R personality characteristics of high-performing entry-level police officers', *Psychological Services*, 3(4): 274–85.

Durrett, C. and Trull, J. (2005) 'An evaluation of evaluative personality terms: A comparison of the Big Seven and Five-factor model in predicting psychopathology', *Psychological Assessment*, 17(3): 359–68.

Eisenberg, N., Sadovsky, A., Spinrad, T.L., Fabes, R.A., Losoya, S.H., Valiente, C., Reiser, M., Cumberland, A. and Shepard, S. (2005) 'The relations of problem behavior status to children's negative emotionality, effortful control, and impulsivity: Concurrent relations and prediction of change', *Developmental Psychology*, 41(1): 193–211.

Endler, N.S. (1983) 'Interactionism: A personality model but not yet a theory', in M.M. Page (ed.), *Nebraska Symposium on Motivation 1982: Personality – Current Theory and Research*. Lincoln, NE: University of Nebraska Press, pp. 155–200.

Endler, N.S. and Kocovski, N. L. (2001) 'State and trait anxiety revisited', *Journal of Anxiety Disorders*, 15(3): 231–45.

Epstein, S. (1977) 'Traits are alive and well', in D. Magnusson and N.S. Endler (eds), *Personality at the Crossroads*. Hillsdale, NJ: Erlbaum, pp. 83–98.

Eysenck, H.J. (1957) *The Dynamics of Anxiety and Hysteria*. London: Routledge and Kegan Paul.

Eysenck, H.J. (1967) *The Biological Basis of Personality*. Springfield, IL: Thomas.

Eysenck, H.J. (1981) 'General features of the model', in H.J. Eysenck (ed.), *A Model for Personality*. Berlin: Springer, pp. 1–37.

Eysenck, H.J. (1984) 'Cattell and the theory of personality', *Multivariate Behavioral Research*, 19(2–3): 323–36.

Eysenck, H.J. (1994) 'The outcome problem in psychotherapy: What have we learned?',

Behaviour Research and Therapy, 32(5): 477–95.

Eysenck, M.W. and Eysenck, H.J. (1980) 'Mischel and the concept of personality', *British Journal of Psychology*, 71(2): 191–204.

Eysenck, H.J. and Eysenck, M.W. (1985) *Personality and Individual Differences: A Natural Science Approach*. New York: Plenum.

Eysenck, M.W., Derakshan, N., Santos, R. and Calvo, M.G. (2007) 'Anxiety and cognitive performance: Attentional control theory', *Emotion*, 7(2): 336–53.

Fisher, C.D. and Boyle, G.J. (1997) 'Personality and employee selection: Credibility regained', *Asia Pacific Journal of Human Resources*, 35(2): 26–40.

Fraley, R.C. and Roberts, B.W. (2005) 'Patterns of continuity: A dynamic model for conceptualizing the stability of individual differences in psychological constructs across the life course', *Psychological Review*, 112(1): 60–74.

Funder, D.C. (2006) 'Towards a resolution of the personality triad: Persons, situations, and behaviors', *Journal of Research in Personality*, 40(1): 21–34.

Furnham, A. and Heaven, P. (1999) *Personality and Social Behaviour*. London: Arnold.

Gorsuch, R.L. (1983) *Factor Analysis* (rev. 2nd edn). Hillsdale, NJ: Erlbaum.

Goldberg, L.R. (1990) 'An alternative "Description of personality": The Big-Five factor structure', *Journal of Personality and Social Psychology*, 59(6): 1216–29.

Gray, J.A. (1991) 'Neural systems, emotion and personality', in J. Madden IV (ed.), *Neurobiology of Learning, Emotion and Affect*. New York: Raven, pp. 273–306.

Greenberg, M.T., Weissberg, R.P., O'Brien, M.U. and Zins, J.E. (2003) 'Enhancing school based prevention and youth development through coordinated social, emotional, and academic learning', *American Psychologist*, 58(6–7): 466–74.

Grice, J.W. (2004) 'Bridging the idiographic–nomothetic divide in ratings of self and others on the Big Five', *Journal of Personality*, 72(2): 203–42.

Harkness, K.L., Bagby, R.M., Joffe, R.T. and Levitt, A. (2002) 'Major depression, chronic minor depression, and the Five-Factor Model of Personality', *European Journal of Personality*, 16(4): 271–81.

Hettema, J. and Deary, I.J. (1993) 'Biological and social approaches to individuality: Towards a common paradigm', in J. Hettema and I.J. Deary (eds), *Foundations of Personality*. Dordrecht: Kluwer, pp. 1–14.

Hogan, R. (2005) 'In defense of personality measurement: New wine for old whiners', *Human Performance*, 18(4): 331–41.

Hogan, R. (2006) 'Who wants to be a psychologist?', *Journal of Personality Assessment*, 86(2): 119–30.

Humphreys, M.S. and Revelle, W. (1984) 'Personality, motivation and performance: A theory of the relationship between individual differences and information processing', *Psychological Review*, 91(2): 153–84.

Jensen-Campbell, L.A. and Graziano, W.G. (2001) 'Agreeableness as a moderator of interpersonal conflict', *Journal of Personality*, 69(2): 323–62.

Judge, T.A., Jackson, C.L., Shaw, J.C., Scott, B.A. and Rich, B.L. (2007) 'Self-efficacy and work-related performance: The integral role of individual differences', *Journal of Applied Psychology*, 92(1): 107–27.

Judge, T.A., LePine, J.A. and Rich, B.L. (2006) 'Loving yourself abundantly: Relationship of the narcissistic personality to self- and other perceptions of workplace deviance, leadership, and task and contextual performance', *Journal of Applied Psychology*, 91(4): 762–76.

Kanfer, R., Ackerman, P.L., Murtha, T. and Goff, M. (1995) 'Personality and intelligence in industrial and organisational psychology', in D.H. Saklofske and M. Zeidner (eds), *International Handbook of Personality and Intelligence*. New York: Plenum, pp. 577–602.

Kihlstrom, J.F. (1999) 'The psychological unconscious', in L.A. Pervin and O.P. John (eds), *Handbook of Personality: Theory and Research* (2nd edn). New York: Guilford, pp. 424–42.

King, P.R. and Endler, N.S. (1990) 'The trait anxiety x perception score: A composite predictor for state anxiety', *Journal of Personality and Social Psychology*, 58(4): 679–84.

Krug, S.E. and Johns, E.F. (1986) 'A large scale cross-validation of second-order personality structure defined by the 16PF', *Psychological Reports*, 59(2): 683–93.

Kuhn, T.S. (1962) *The Structure of Scientific Revolutions*. Chicago: University of Chicago Press.

Lakatos (1977) 'The methodology of scientific research programmes', *Philosophical Papers* (Vol. 1). Cambridge, UK: Cambridge University Press.

Lazarus, R.S. (1999) *Stress and Emotion: A New Synthesis*. New York: Springer.

Little, B.R. and Chambers, N.C. (2004) 'Personal project pursuit: On human doings and well-beings', in W.M. Cox and E. Klinger (eds), *Handbook of Motivational Counseling: Concepts, Approaches, and Assessment*. New York: Wiley, pp. 65–82.

McAdams, D.P. (1992) 'The five-factor model in personality: A critical appraisal', *Journal of Personality*, 60(2): 329–61.

McAdams, D.P. and Pals, J. (2006) A new Big Five: Fundamental principles for an integrative science of personality. *American Psychologist*, 61(3): 204–17.

McCrae, R.R. and Costa, P.T. Jr. (1997) 'Personality trait structure as a human universal', *American Psychologist*, 52(5): 509–16.

MacMillan, M. (1997) *Freud Evaluated: The Completed Arc*. Cambridge, MA: MIT Press.

Matsumoto, D. (2006) 'Are cultural differences in emotion regulation mediated by personality traits?', *Journal of Cross-Cultural Psychology*, 37(4): 421–37.

Matthews, G. (1997) 'An introduction to the cognitive science of personality and emotion', in G. Matthews (ed.), *Cognitive Science Perspectives on Personality and Emotion*. Amsterdam: Elsevier, pp. 3–30.

Matthews, G. (2000) 'A cognitive science critique of biological theories of personality traits', *History and Philosophy of Psychology*, 2(1): 1–17.

Matthews, G. (2004) 'Designing personality: Cognitive architectures and beyond', *Proceedings of the American Artificial Intelligence Society Symposium on Architectures for Modeling Emotion: Cross-Disciplinary Foundations*. Menlo Park, CA: AAIS, pp. 83–91.

Matthews, G., Deary, I.J. and Whiteman, M.C. (2003) *Personality Traits* (2nd edn). Cambridge: Cambridge University Press.

Matthews, G., Derryberry, D. and Siegle, G.J. (2000a) 'Personality and emotion: Cognitive science perspectives', in S.E. Hampson (ed.), *Advances in Personality Psychology (Vol. 1)*. London: Routledge, pp. 199–237.

Matthews, G. and Gilliland, K. (1999) 'The personality theories of H.J. Eysenck and J.A. Gray: A comparative review', *Personality and Individual Differences*, 26(4): 583–626.

Matthews, G. and Harley, T.A. (1993) 'Effects of extraversion and self-report arousal on semantic priming: a connectionist approach', *Journal of Personality and Social Psychology*, 65(4): 735–56.

Matthews, G., Schwean, V.L., Campbell, S.E., Saklofske, D.H. and Mohamed, A.A.R. (2000b) 'Personality, self-regulation and adaptation: A cognitive-social framework', in M. Boekarts, P.R. Pintrich and M. Zeidner (eds), *Handbook of Self-Regulation*. New York: Academic, pp. 171–207.

Matthews, G., Zeidner, M. and Roberts, R. (2002) *Emotional Intelligence: Science and Myth*. Cambridge, MA: MIT Press.

Miller, T. (1991) 'The psychotherapeutic utility of the five-factor model of personality: A clinician's experience', *Journal of Personality Assessment*, 57(3): 414–33.

Mischel, W. (1968) *Personality and Assessment*. New York: Wiley.

Mischel, W., Shoda, Y. and Mendoza-Denton, R. (2002) 'Situation-behavior profiles as a locus of consistency in personality', *Current Directions in Psychological Science*, 11(2): 50–4.

Motowidlo, S. J. and Van Scotter, R. (1994) 'Evidence that task performance should be distinguished from contextual performance', *Journal of Applied Psychology*, 79(4): 475–80.

Munafo, M.R, Clark, T.G., Moore, L.R., Payne, E., Walton, R. and Flint, J. (2003) 'Genetic polymorphisms and personality in healthy adults: A systematic review and meta-analysis', *Molecular Psychiatry*, 8(5): 471–84.

Nyborg, H. (1994) *Hormones, Sex, and Society: The Science of Physicology*. Westport, CT: Praeger.

Ones, D.S., Viswesvaran, C. and Dilchert, S. (2005) 'Personality at work: Raising awareness and correcting misconceptions', *Human Performance*, 18(4): 389–404.

Ozer, D.J. and Benet-Martinez, V. (2006) 'Personality and the prediction of consequential outcomes', *Annual Review of Psychology*, 57: 401–21.

Paulhus, D.L. (2002) 'Socially desirable responding: The evolution of a construct', in H.I. Braun and D.N. Jackson (eds), *The Role of Constructs in Psychological and Educational Measurement*. Mahwah, NJ: Erlbaum, pp. 49–69.

Penke, L., Denissen, J.J.A. and Miller, G.F. (2007) 'The evolutionary genetics of personality', *European Journal of Personality*, 21(5): 549–87.

Pervin, L.A. (2002) *Current Controversies and Issues in Personality* (3rd edn). New York: Guilford.

Pinker, S. (2002) *The Blank Slate: The Modern Denial of Human Nature*. New York: Penguin Putnam.

Plomin, R., Asbury, K. and Dunn, J. (2001) 'Why are children in the same family so different? Nonshared environment a decade later', *Canadian Journal of Psychiatry*, 46(3): 225–33.

Pylyshyn, Z.W. (1984) *Computation and Cognition: Toward a Foundation for Cognitive Science*. Cambridge, MA: MIT Press.

Raine, A. (2006) 'Schizotypal personality: Neurodevelopmental and psychosocial trajectories', *Annual Review of Clinical Psychology*, 2: 291–326.

Revelle, W., Humphreys, M.S., Simon, L. and Gilliland, K. (1980) 'The interactive effect of personality, time of day and caffeine: A test of the arousal model', *Journal of Experimental Psychology: General,* 109(1): 1–31.

Rothbart, M.K. and Bates, J.E. (2006) 'Temperament in children's development', in W. Damon, R. Lerner, and N. Eisenberg (eds), *Handbook of Child Psychology* (6th edn): *Vol. 3. Social, Emotional, and Personality Development*. New York: Wiley, pp. 99–166.

Rutter, M., Moffitt, T.E. and Caspi, A. (2006) 'Gene-environment interplay and psychopathology: Multiple varieties but real effects', *Journal of Child Psychology and Psychiatry*, 47(3–4): 226–61.

Saucier, G. (2000) 'Isms and the structure of social attitudes', *Journal of Personality and Social Psychology*, 78(2): 366–85.

Schmukle, S.C. and Egloff, B. (2005) 'A latent state-trait analysis of implicit and explicit personality measures', *European Journal of Psychological Assessment*, 21(2): 100–7.

Schuerger, J.M. (1986) 'Personality assessment by objective tests', in R.B. Cattell and R.C. Johnson (eds), *Functional Psychological Testing: Principles and Instruments*. New York: Brunner/Mazel.

Stelmack, R.M. and Stalikas, A. (1991) 'Galen and the humour theory of temperament', *Personality and Individual Differences*, 12(3): 255–63.

Suls, J. (2001) 'Affect, stress, and personality', in J.P. Forgas (ed.), *Handbook of Affect and Social Cognition*. Mahwah, NJ: Erlbaum. pp. 392–409.

Terracciano, A., Costa, P.T. and McCrae, R.R. (2006) 'Personality plasticity after age 30', *Personality and Social Psychology Bulletin*, 32(8): 999–1009.

Tett, R.P. and Burnett, D.D. (2003) 'A personality trait-based interactionist model of job performance', *Journal of Applied Psychology*, 88(3): 500–517.

Wells, A. and Matthews, G. (1994) *Attention and Emotion: A Clinical Perspective*. Hove: Erlbaum.

Westen, D. (1999) 'The scientific status of unconscious processes: Is Freud really dead?', *Journal of the American Psychoanalytic Association*, 47(4): 1061–106.

Widiger, T.A. and Trull, J. (2007) 'Plate tectonics in the classification of personality disorder: Shifting to a dimensional model', *American Psychologist*, 62(2): 71–83.

Zeidner, M. (1998) *Test Anxiety: The State of the Art*. New York: Plenum.

Zeidner, M., Boekaerts, M. and Pintrich, P.R. (2000) 'Self-regulation: Directions and challenges for future research', in M. Boekaerts, P.R. Pintrich and M. Zeidner (eds), *Handbook of Self-Regulation*. San Diego, CA: Academic, pp. 749–768.

Zeidner, M., Matthews, G., Roberts, R.D. and McCann, C. (2003) 'Development of emotional intelligence: Towards a multi-level investment model', *Human Development*, 46(2–3): 69–96.

Zuckerman, M. (1991) *Psychobiology of personality*. New York: Cambridge.

Zuckerman, M. (1992) 'What is a basic factor and which factors are basic? Turtles all the way down', *Personality and Individual Differences*, 13(6): 675–81.

Zuckerman, M. (1995) 'Good and bad humors: biochemical bases of personality and its disorders', *Psychological Science*, 6(6): 325–32.

Zuckerman, M. (2005) *Psychobiology of Personality* (2nd rev. edn). New York: Cambridge University Press.

PART I

Explanatory Models for Personality

2

Psychophysiological and Biochemical Correlates of Personality

Robert M. Stelmack and Thomas H. Rammsayer

The degree of activation, as shown by the writer in various publications (Duffy, 1962), appears to affect both sensory sensitivity and motor response, and is involved in those consistencies of behavior that we call personality characteristics. (Duffy, 1966: 281)

INTRODUCTION

Considering that these quoted words were written by Elizabeth Duffy 40 years ago, the view expressed was prescient indeed. There is considerable evidence today, from psychophysical, psychophysiological, and biochemical procedures (formerly considered measures of activation), establishing that the personality dimension of extraversion (E) is characterized by individual differences in sensitivity to simple physical stimulation and in the expression of motor responses. At the time when Duffy expressed her views, however, the association of personality with sensory sensitivity and motor processes was far from clear. In fact, in an assessment of the

personality literature, Duffy (1962: 273) concluded that 'Any survey of physiological studies of personality must recognize the surprising fact that relatively few investigators have reported relationships of any magnitude between physiological measures and measures of behavior within the normal population.' Since that time, however, there was considerable progress in delineating reliable relations between personality traits and physiological processes. This progress was abetted by the development of rigorous personality typologies; by compelling, large-scale projects determining the heritability of personality traits; by refinement and development of physiological measurement procedures; and by exploiting new paradigms for probing psychological processes such as sensation, attention, learning, and memory that are manifest in individual differences in personality. In this chapter, we mark this progress by assessing the current status of the psychophysiological and biochemical correlates of personality traits.

The nomenclatural framework for the present review consists of the three major personality dimensions of E, emotional stability–instability/neuroticism (N), and psychoticism (P)/impulsive sensation-seeking (ImpSS). These personality traits emerge as fundamental factors in most major personality typologies (e.g. Costa and McCrae, 1992; Eysenck and Eysenck, 1991; Zuckerman, 2002) and they capture the bulk of psychophysiological and biochemical research on individual differences in personality. An emphasis in this review is placed on electrocortical procedures (i.e. electroencephalography (EEG) and event-related potentials (ERPs)), and biochemical analyses (i.e. dopamine, serotonin, and cortisol), because these measurement procedures predominate in current research on personality. Conclusions drawn from earlier reviews of research on the biological bases of personality are briefly stated. An attempt is made to focus the functional significance of the biological procedures and paradigms on the social and behavioural expressions that characterize the personality dimensions, but the theoretical frameworks that inspired much of this research are left to other authors in this volume.

PSYCHOPHYSIOLOGICAL AND BIOCHEMICAL CORRELATES OF EXTRAVERSION

In previous reviews, it was concluded that there were fundamental differences between introverts and extraverts in their reaction to sensory stimulation and in their expression of motor activity (Matthews and Gilliland, 1999; Stelmack, 1997). There is compelling evidence from a range of measurement procedures indicating that introverts are more reactive or sensitive to simple sensory stimulation than are extraverts. Introverts display lower absolute auditory sensitivity (e.g. Stelmack and Campbell, 1974), lower pain thresholds (e.g. Barnes, 1975), lower noise thresholds (e.g. Dornic and Ekehammer, 1990), larger skin conductance responses to moderate intensity tones (e.g. Smith, 1983), and larger ERP amplitude to simple physical stimulation (e.g. Stelmack and Michaud-Achorn, 1985). Moreover, there was evidence from brainstem auditory evoked potentials indicating that these intensity effects are evident at the level of the auditory nerve (e.g. Stelmack and Wilson, 1982). These effects meld with the preference of introverts for quiet and solitude (Campbell and Hawley, 1982) and with their tendency towards withdrawal as a coping strategy in stressful social situations (Endler and Parker, 1990).

Introverts and extraverts differ in their expression of motor behaviour on a variety of tasks that require a simple motor response, with extraverts initiating faster and more frequent responses than introverts (e.g. Brebner and Flavell, 1978). These effects appear relevant to the disposition of extraverts to liveliness, activity, and talkativeness (Eysenck and Eysenck, 1975), involvement in athletic activities (Eysenck et al., 1982), restlessness in restricted environments (Gale, 1969), and preference for physical activity (Furnham, 1981). Moreover, there was evidence employing psychophysiological procedures that differences in motor activity between introverts and extraverts can be referred to peripheral nervous system processes (Stelmack and Pivik, 1996). There is good evidence that variation in dopaminergic activity (DA) is an important determinant of differences in E (e.g. Rammsayer et al., 1993). In general, more recent research on E and differences in sensory sensitivity and motor expression, using electrocortical and biochemical measurement procedures, endorse these findings.

Extraversion and the electroencephalograph

The electroencephalograph (EEG), recording electrical activity of the brain from small electrodes affixed to the scalp, was an important method for assessing cortical activity of the brain in the early study of the ascending reticular activating system (ARAS; Lindsley, 1951) and in exploring the role of the ARAS in attention, memory, and learning. The hypothesis that differences in E were determined by differences in cortical excitation and inhibition (Eysenck, 1957) and cortical arousal (Eysenck, 1967) fostered extensive analysis of E and the EEG. In early reviews (Gale, 1973; O'Gorman, 1977), support for the notion that introverts are characterized by higher levels of cortical arousal (indexed by lower EEG alpha wave activity) than extraverts was equivocal. These reviews did prompt improvements in design and recording techniques in subsequent research. Later reviews conceded that the direction of the results of these inquiries is towards higher levels of cortical activity for introverts (Matthews and Gilliland, 1999; Stelmack and Geen, 1992).

In more recent research, the ambiguous history of research on E using EEG recording is continued rather than clarified. The specific conditions under which reliable effects are replicated remain indeterminate. Tran et al. (2001) observed greater EEG activity in the 8–13 Hz (alpha) frequency range for extraverts than introverts but only at frontal electrode sites. This contrasts with other positive reports (e.g. O'Gorman and Lloyd, 1987) showing greater EEG activity at posterior electrode sites where alpha activity is maximal. In a project similar to Tran et al. (2001), higher E was associated with greater activity in low-frequency EEG bands (delta and theta) at temporal and parietal sites, and lower alpha activity at temporal and frontal sites (Knyazev et al., 2002). In another well-executed project, no EEG effects for E were observed (Schmidtke and Heller, 2004). Notably, the functional significance of the EEG effects in the studies cited here, when they are observed, is opaque. Typically, the EEG recordings were obtained while participants opened and closed their eyes. Without some experimental manipulation, few inferences of the functional significance

of the EEG can be made. An exception here is the work by Knyazev et al. (2002), where participants performed mental arithmetic during the EEG recording in an attempt to manipulate arousal level.

There was considerable interest in the claim that activation of right anterior cortical areas is associated with the expression of negative affect, whereas activation of left anterior cortical areas is associated with the expression of positive affect (Davidson and Fox, 1982). Investigation of these effects was drawn into the personality domain by Hagemann et al. (1999) who exploited the association of E with positive affect and N with negative affect (Tellegen, 1985). Contrary to expectations, higher negative affect scores were associated with greater activation at left anterior temporal cortical areas. As Hagemann et al. (1999) note, this result is typical of the mixed outcomes that plague EEG research on emotion and mood. No differences in EEG activity between introverts and extraverts were observed.

The line of inquiry initiated by Hagemann et al. (1999) was pursued by Gale et al. (2001). During EEG recording, participants were asked to empathise and rate photographs expressing positive and negative affect. Negative valence photographs elicited greater activation at left frontal cortical sites, an effect that endorses the sensitivity of the EEG measures to the affect manipulation. Robust effects were reported with extraverts exhibiting greater alpha activity at frontal, temporal and occipital sites.

Gale et al. (2001) state that their data accord with the view that extraverts are characterized by lower levels of tonic arousal as proposed by Eysenck (1967). Alternatively, one could argue that introverts were more reactive to the photographic stimuli than extraverts, a view concordant with an extensive literature showing the greater sensitivity of introverts to sensory stimulation in general (Stelmack, 1990). The positive and negative valence photographs did not exercise interactive effects on E; that is, one would suppose that the positive affect induction would favour the extraverts, resulting in greater frontal left hemisphere cortical areas. Overall, when EEG is recorded under resting conditions or with minimal or uncontrolled stimulation, the studies cited provide little consistent evidence associating E with greater alpha activation.

Extraversion and event-related potentials

Event-related potentials (ERPs) are records of the electrocortical activity in the brain that is evoked by physical stimuli and modulated by psychological processes such as attention, memory, and cognition. ERPs are derived by averaging ongoing EEG activity that is time-locked to specific stimulus events. It is assumed that random EEG activity emanating from neural sites that are not engaged in the repeated presentation of the stimulus is cancelled out in the averaging. What remains is a signature of the neural activity that occurred during the processing of the stimulus. This signature is a result of the initial activation of peripheral nerves and nuclei in the brainstem and of the subsequent sequence of neural activity along cortical projection pathways.

Extraversion and sensory ERPs

Early research on E and ERPs examined waveforms that were elicited by simple sensory stimuli such as brief light flashes or simple tones. Initially, inconsistent effects were reported that yielded to replicable results as the conditions for favourable findings became apparent. In ERP waveforms to tones, larger amplitude for introverts than extraverts is observed with some consistency for ERP waves that develop 100–200 ms following stimulation, notably when stimuli are (1) moderately intense, (2) lower frequency, and (3) presented in mixed serial order (Bruneau et al., 1984; Stelmack and Michaud-Achorn, 1985). These effects, which account for about 10% of the variation in E, are congruent with the greater response

to stimulation in introverts than in extraverts observed with psychophysical and autonomic system measures. Subsequently, there were few attempts to examine E and ERP using systematic changes in stimulus intensity or frequency. Occasionally, however, the enhanced response to auditory stimulation is observed incidentally (e.g. Doucet and Stelmack, 2000).

Extraversion and brainstem auditory evoked responses

A number of authors explored differences between introverts and extraverts by recording brainstem auditory evoked responses (BAER). BAER waveforms capture electrical activity along the auditory pathway that develops within the first 10 ms of acoustic stimulation. The neural generators of these waves, the auditory nerve (wave I), cochlear nucleus (wave II), lateral lemniscus and inferior colliculus (wave V), are well documented. The shorter BAER wave V latency for introverts than extraverts is the effect more consistently observed (Bullock and Gilliland, 1993; Stelmack and Wilson, 1982; Swickert and Gilliland, 1998). A recent report from Gilliland and colleagues is perhaps the most definitive (Cox-Fuenzalida and Gilliland, 2001). Introverts exhibited shorter wave V latency than extraverts, with correlations in several analyses ranging from $r = 0.23$ to 0.28. Gender effects, which are known to influence BAER latency, were not accounted for in these analyses. On the whole, the effect sizes were comparable to the marginally significant effects with smaller sample size reported by Stelmack et al. (1993a).

Although effect sizes tend to be modest, accounting for less than 10% of variation in E, the shorter wave V latency for introverts than extraverts is a reliable effect that is consistent with the greater reactivity to physical stimuli of introverts observed with other measures. The BAEP is exquisitely sensitive to changes in stimulus intensity with higher intensity stimulation evoking shorter latency and larger amplitude BAEP waves. Because collaterals from the auditory tracts ascending through the brainstem innervate the ARAS, the amygdala and the cortical centres, the BAEP effects do endorse the arousal hypothesis as noted by Matthews and Gilliland (1999), and also the view espoused by Woodward et al. (2001) concerning the role of the amygdala for highly reactive children. From a neurophysiological perspective, however, the inhibitory influence of the olivocochlear nucleus on brainstem nuclei is reduced or absent for intensities above 75 dB and these inhibitory effects are independent of the reticular system (Desmedt, 1975). Thus, the BAEP effects cannot be understood in terms of a corticoreticular loop as adopted by Eysenck as the basis for individual differences in E. The independence of BAEP waves from descending inhibitory effects is underscored functionally by the remarkable invariance of BAEP waves during different stages of sleep and arousal (Campbell and Bartoli, 1986) and even during metabolic coma (Chiappa, 1990). Similarly, the weight of the evidence indicates that BAEP waves are not influenced by directed attention (Connolly et al., 1989; Picton et al., 1981).

Extraversion and P3

The P3 wave is a positive ERP wave that develops maximum amplitude at about 300 ms in simple decision tasks. This wave is usefully exploited in cognitive psychology to study attention, memory and decision making. In general, the latency of the P3 is widely accepted as a measure of stimulus evaluation time that is independent of response selection and execution processes (Kutas et al., 1977). The P3 wave decreases in amplitude with increases in task difficulty and can be parsimoniously understood as an index of processing capacity (Kok, 2001). Several investigators examined individual differences in E during an auditory oddball task where a P3 wave develops to deviant stimuli presented among a series of standard stimuli. The most consistent effect is larger P3 amplitude for introverts than extraverts

(Brocke et al., 1996; Daruna et al., 1985; Ortiz and Maojo, 1993; Polich and Martin, 1992; Wilson and Languis, 1990). Similarly, smaller decrements in P3 amplitude across trial blocks for introverts were reported (Ditraglia and Polich, 1991), although opposite effects were subsequently observed (Cahill and Polich, 1992). Null effects were reported by Pritchard (1989). In early work, the larger P3 amplitude for introverts would be attributed to differences in the amount of resources allocated to the processing of the deviant stimuli. Other interpretations of the effects are possible, for example, differences in processing capacity or even differences in sensitivity to stimuli. There is some evidence that P3 is larger to more intense stimuli (e.g. Gonsalvez et al., 2007). The understanding of these P3 differences is hampered because the effects have not been put to the test of direct manipulation or concomitant behavioural evaluations.

Individual differences in E and P3 amplitude and latency were also explored in several decision-making paradigms. The outcomes of this work were equally varied. Introverts displayed larger P3 amplitude than extraverts during a difficult visual vigilance oddball task (Brocke et al., 1996). Brocke et al. (1997) subsequently observed this effect under quiet conditions, but extraverts exhibited larger amplitude than introverts when the task was performed during noisy conditions. A larger P3 amplitude for extraverts was also observed in a visual classification task (Stenberg, 1994). More recently, larger P3 amplitude for extraverts was observed to high intensity target tones in an auditory oddball task (Guerrera et al. 2001). No differences in P3 amplitude between introverts and extraverts were reported in several studies using a series of elementary cognitive tasks (Stelmack et al., 1993b), simple response and stimulus–response compatibility tasks (Doucet and Stelmack, 2000), or difficult target recognition tasks (De Pascalis, 1993).

The larger P3 amplitude for introverts than extraverts to moderate intensity target tones during auditory oddball tasks was observed with sufficient consistency to regard it as a valid effect that accounts for about 10% of variation in E. How the effect is interpreted and what it contributes to our understanding of E is not yet decided. In general, the effect is congruent with the greater electrodermal response amplitude for introverts observed in orienting response paradigms. These effects are regarded as intensity effects reflecting the greater sensitivity to stimulation of introverts. A systematic investigation of the effects of intensity on P3 is clearly desirable to assess that hypothesis. The larger P3 amplitude for extraverts observed in some studies is a puzzling effect that also requires more intensive investigation to disentangle sensory and motor contributions. There is little evidence linking E to differences in P3 amplitude on elementary cognitive tasks. Moreover, there is scant evidence of differences in P3 latency that would link E to differences in cognitive processing speed.

Extraversion and lateralized readiness potentials

There is a copious literature that implicates differences in the expression of motor behaviour as a fundamental determinant of differences in E (e.g. Doucet and Stelmack, 2000). These differences in motor expression were examined using simple response time (SRT) measures. Although faster and more frequent responding for extraverts was frequently observed, null effects were also reported often. Some progress in clarifying the disparities in this SRT work involved distinguishing between response decision time (DT), the time from stimulus onset to the release of the home button; and movement time (MT), the time from the release of a home button to the subsequent press of a target button.

In early research using response time measures with elementary cognitive tasks (Stelmack et al., 1993b), an association between E and individual differences in MT was observed, but not in DT. In subsequent work, MT was manipulated directly by varying the response button distance and by examining the interactive effects of stimulus and response compatibility (Doucet and Stelmack, 2000). Extraverts displayed faster MT than introverts under all conditions. The pattern of results also suggested that the effect reflected differences in the initiation of movement rather than in the acceleration of movement from the home button to the target response button. Because there were no individual differences in DT or P3 latency and amplitude, these effects implicate peripheral motor processes as determinants of E rather than central cortical mechanisms mediating sensory discrimination or stimulus evaluation. This question was explored in studies that employed an ERP measure termed the lateralized readiness potential (LRP).

The LRP is an ERP measure that permits direct assessment of movement initiation processes following stimulus-related processing. The LRP is derived by recording ERPs from electrodes placed over the motor areas of the left and right cortical hemispheres. Responses initiated by the left and right hand elicit greater electrical activity in the contralateral hemisphere. ERPs derived from the same side as the overt motor response are subtracted from the ERP of the contralateral hemisphere. When these difference waves are averaged across hands, they yield the LRP, reflecting pure hand-related ERP asymmetry. Analysis of the interval between the onset of the stimulus and the onset of the LRP (stimulus-linked LRP) is a measure for the duration of pre-motor activity, including stimulus analysis, response preparation and some aspects of response selection. In contrast, analysis of the interval between the onset of the LRP and the onset of the behavioural motor response (response-linked LRP) is a measure of the duration of motor activity independent of stimulus processing. There is a consensus that the LRP is generated in the primary motor cortex (Coles, 1989). A pattern of greater activity in the response-linked LRP for extraverts than introverts and no differences in stimulus-linked LRP or P300 latency and amplitude would confirm the involvement of primary cortical motor processes as relevant determinants of individual differences in E rather than central cortical mechanisms that are involved in sensory discrimination or stimulus evaluation.

Rammsayer and Stahl (2004) obtained LRPs in an auditory two-choice go/no-go task. With this task, longer response-linked LRP latencies were found for introverts than extraverts indicating faster speed of motor processing in extraverts than in introverts. There were no E differences, however, for stimulus-linked LRP latencies. The failure to demonstrate a difference in stimulus-linked LRP latencies was attributed to the low task demands induced by the auditory task. In a second study (Stahl and Rammsayer, 2004), a complex discrimination task was applied to increase pre-motor, cognitive task demands. With this condition, stimulus-linked LRP latencies were shorter for introverts than extraverts, indicating faster pre-motor information processing for introverts. However, there were no differences in response-linked LRP latencies, a failure attributed to the absence of a no-go condition (Stahl and Rammsayer, 2004).

Extraversion and dopamine

Dopaminergic (DA) projections from mesencephalic cell groups are divided into two functionally distinct systems, the mesostriatal and the mesolimbcortical (e.g. Robbins and Everitt, 1995). Mesolimbcortical DA is important in locomotor activity, active avoidance, incentive/reward motivation, associative learning and working memory (Kimberg et al. 1997; Müller et al., 1998; Robinson and Berridge, 2000; Salamone, 1994; Sokolowski et al., 1994; Tzschentke, 2001). Mesostriatal DA neurons serve to inhibit and modulate the striatum (Björklund and Lindvall, 1986), which in turn exerts a powerful inhibitory effect on the thalamus and the reticular formation (Carlsson and Carlsson, 1990). Any increase in mesostriatal DA activity counteracts the inhibitory effect of the striatum, resulting in increased reticular arousal and, for example, enhanced sensory sensitivity.

From this perspective, differences in DA brain mechanisms between introverts and extraverts may mediate the greater sensory sensitivity in introverts compared to extraverts (Rammsayer, 2004).

Rammsayer et al. (1993) addressed the question, 'Does pharmacologically induced decrease in brain DA activity differentially affect the transmission of sensory input into motor output in introverts and extraverts?' After pharmacological blockade of DA synthesis by means of alpha-methyl-para-tyrosine (AMPT), both DT and MT were markedly impaired in introverts but not in extraverts on a choice reaction time task. While DT indexes cognitive processes such as stimulus evaluation and response selection that are mediated by the mesolimbocortical DA system (Cohen and Servan-Schreiber, 1992; Rammsayer and Stahl, 2006), MT is a valid indicator of motor execution that is primarily mediated by mesostriatal DA activity (Amalric et al., 1993; Dunnett and Robbins, 1992; Salamone et al., 1993).

Because AMPT produced a non-specific decrease in DA activity, the D2 receptor blocker remoxipride was chosen in a subsequent study to selectively affect homeostasis of dopaminergic transmission (Rammsayer, 1998). Remoxipride primarily inhibits neurons of the mesolimbocortical DA system. In introverts, remoxipride caused a reliable increase in DT compared to extraverts, while MT was not affected in either group. Taken together, these findings indicate that introverts are more responsive to pharmacologically induced changes in D2 receptor activity than extraverts, irrespective of the specific DA system involved.

Although there are interactions between neurotransmitter systems, the observed differences between introverts and extraverts in the transmission of sensory input into motor output seem to be a clear function of DA modulation (Rammsayer, 2003). Depue and Collins (1999) argued that the mesolimbocortical DA system is the neurobiological substrate that mediates E and resulting in differences in incentive-facilitated behaviour.

Although their model is based on an integration of behaviour, affect and both cortical and subcortical neural mechanisms, it still lacks direct corroborative evidence from human pharmacopsychological studies (cf. Lawrence et al., 1999).

Following the model of Depue and Collins (1999), Wacker et al. (2006) combined behavioural and EEG measures with pharmacological treatment. As predicted, they found that the agency facet of E modulated the effect of 200 mg of sulpiride, a D2 receptor blocker, on behavioural and EEG measures. However, because dose-dependent pharmacological effects of sulpiride are unclear, (cf. Rammsayer, 1997), that effect is not definitive.

Using single photon emission tomography (SPECT), Gray et al. (1994) found no association between D2 receptor binding and E. In two subsequent PET studies (Breier et al., 1998a; Farde et al., 1997), a positive correlation was reported between D2 receptor density and E. Similar studies (Breier et al., 1998b; Kestler et al., 2000), however, failed to observe this relation. These inconclusive findings appear indicative of a complex relation between D2 receptor density and E.

In these PET studies, participants remained passive during the recording. Fischer et al. (1997), however, presented their subjects with videotaped scenes of individuals walking in a park during the PET recordings. Enhanced activity for introverts compared to extraverts in brain areas associated with the mesostriatal DA system was observed. This finding endorses DA as a basis for differences in E and accords with greater DA responsiveness for introverts than extraverts proposed by Rammsayer (1998, 2003; Rammsayer et al., 1993). For Fischer et al. (1997), the visual stimulation may have been the critical condition for eliciting increased mesostriatal DA activity for introverts. In the absence of experimental or pharmacological manipulation, mesostriatal DA activity for introverts and extraverts are within a similar range (Rammsayer et al., 1993) and thus no differences in E are expected under passive conditions.

Genetic factors that may influence E and cause variations in DA were also explored. Benjamin et al. (1996) and Ebstein et al. (1996) reported differences in E and the type-4 dopamine receptor (DRD4) gene. Numerous subsequent studies both supported (Benjamin et al., 2000; Ekelund et al., 1999; Noble et al., 1998; Okuyama et al., 2000; Ono et al., 1997; Strobel et al., 1999; Tomitaka et al., 1999) and failed (Burt et al., 2002; Ekelund et al., 2001; Gebhardt et al., 2000; Jönsson et al., 1997, 1998, 2002; Kuhn et al., 1999; Mitsuyasu et al., 2001; Persson et al., 2000; Pogue-Geile et al., 1998; Soyka et al., 2002; Strobel et al., 2002, 2003b; Vandenbergh et al., 1997) to support these findings.

The failures to replicate an association between DRD4 polymorphism and E was attributed to the use of different questionnaires for personality assessment, methods that inflate the potential for false positive results, lack of statistical power, lack of control for ethnic variability, or demographic differences among the studies participants (cf. Burt et al., 2002; Malhotra and Goldman, 2000; Strobel et al., 1999). None of these factors convincingly justify the failures to replicate the positive findings. Overall, the large number of null results challenges the significance of DRD4 polymorphism as a biological basis of E.

Although Noble et al. (1998) reported a positive association between the D2 dopamine receptor gene (DRD2) and high novelty seeking, other studies failed to show such an association (Burt et al., 2002; Cruz et al., 1995; de Brettes et al., 1998; Gebhardt et al., 2000).

Extraversion and cortisol

Cortisol is a corticosteroid hormone produced by the adrenal cortex with widespread actions that help to restore homeostasis after stress. Cortisol levels show a circadian rhythmicity, with peak values found in early morning and lower levels in the evening. Unlike N, E does not appear to be associated with variability in early morning salivary cortisol levels (Munafò et al., 2006b). There is also no evidence for a relationship between E and circadian cortisol rhythm or basal and stimulated free cortisol concentrations (Roy, 1996; Schommer et al., 1999; Zobel et al., 2004). However, a significant correlation between E and plasma levels of cortisol in the early afternoon was recently reported (LeBlanc and Ducharme, 2005).

PSYCHOPHYSIOLOGICAL AND BIOCHEMICAL CORRELATES OF NEUROTICISM

In personality classification schemas, such as the Eysenck Personality Questionnaire (Eysenck and Eysenck, 1991) or the NEO-PI (Costa and McCrae, 1992), N is an emotional stability–instability dimension that assesses differences in mood swings, negative affect, worry and tension. N is an important predictor of stress management, interpersonal effectiveness, and the development of clinical disorders involving anxiety, depression, and hostility (Zuckerman, 2005). Accordingly, N was the focus of intensive investigation with psychophysiological procedures and biochemical assays.

Many of the early psychophysiological studies that examined differences in E also examined differences in N. However, significant effects for N were seldom reported in studies where simple physical stimulation was the principal variable manipulated (Fahrenberg, 1987). Psychophysiological methods that record electrodermal, cardiac, and electrocortical activity are especially sensitive to changes in stimulus intensity. The dearth of psychophysiological effects of physical stimulation for N suggests that sensitivity to stimulation is not a determinant of differences in N. This view is endorsed by the paucity of evidence linking N to differences in sensory thresholds, pain thresholds or noise thresholds, and the psychological reports of those processes.

The vulnerability of N to negative valence stimulation and to stress (notably social stress such as ego threat) that was frequently demonstrated was confirmed with both psychophysiological methods and with biochemical assays.

Neuroticism and the EEG

In a 1981 review that spanned 45 years of research, Gale cited 29 EEG investigations of personality that assessed the relation of EEG indices to E. Overall, the conditions under which the recordings were made were benign. They were better suited to examine the psychophysiological bases of differences in attention and arousal that characterise E than hypotheses linking N to differences emanating from limbic activity. None of the studies cited in that review reported significant associations with N. Subsequent studies using improved technology to derive absolute indices of EEG power reported the same null effects for N (Matthews and Amelang, 1993; O'Gorman and Lloyd, 1987). However, Ivashenko et al. (1999) did associate higher N with greater beta activity in right temporal areas.

Stenberg (1992) manipulated affective demands with conditions involving neutral, pleasant and unpleasant imagery and examined absolute indices of EEG activity for individuals differing in N. Higher anxiety scorers (i.e. high N and low E) exhibited greater theta activity at right frontal sites than lower anxiety scorers across all conditions, an effect indicative of higher overall emotionality. The high anxiety group also exhibited greater beta activity in the temporal region during the unpleasant imagery condition. Similar effects were observed in a study that manipulated arousal level by engaging participants in a mental arithmetic task that is known to pose an ego threat (Knyazev, 2002). Higher N was characterized by higher beta and gamma activity in frontal regions, and lower delta and theta activity in temporal, parietal and left frontal areas.

Several authors explored the relationship between EEG asymmetry measures and N scales. Asymmetry measures are obtained by subtracting left hemisphere EEG power from right hemisphere EEG power. In the main, this work stemmed from research on emotion by Davidson (1993) and colleagues. In their schema, greater left frontal EEG asymmetry is implicated in the experience of positive affect and right frontal EEG asymmetry is implicated in the experience of negative affect. Given the association of N with negative affect, higher N may be characterized by greater right frontal asymmetry. Some support for this hypothesis was reported by Schmidt (1999) who observed greater relative right frontal EEG activity for individuals who scored higher on a shyness scale. EEG activity recorded under resting conditions observed that higher N was also associated with greater relative right posterior activity (Schmidtke and Heller, 2004) and with greater mid-frontal asymmetry variability (Minnix and Kline, 2004).

Neuroticism and dopamine

Because high N scores are indicative of emotional liability, vulnerability to stress, or proneness to anxiety (e.g. Bolger and Schilling, 1991), N can be viewed as a security measurement of potentially threatening environmental stimuli (Lee et al., 2005). Brain DA is involved in monitoring activities and also in cognitive and attentional processes (e.g. Saint-Cyr, 2003). From this perspective, high N may be characterized by higher levels of brain DA activity that enable more sensitive or intense reactions to perceived stressors.

Preliminary evidence does suggest a functional relationship between the DA neurotransmitter system and N-related personality traits (i.e. detached or avoidant behaviour). For example, subjects with the D2 receptor gene haplotype 1 exhibit a more neurotic and immature defence style compared with those without haplotype 1 (Comings et al., 1995). Two PET studies

(Breier et al., 1998a; Farde et al., 1997) revealed a negative association between D2 receptor density and individual detachment scores. Another study, using SPECT, yielded a positive correlation between striatal D2 receptor density and N (Lee et al., 2005). Similarly, Kestler et al. (2000) reported that the depression facet of NEO-PI N was associated with striatal DA receptor density measured by PET. However, Gray et al. (1994) failed to observe an association between N and D2 receptor binding in the basal ganglia. Additional support for the involvement of D2 receptor mechanisms in N is provided by a molecular genetic study where an association between a DRD2 promoter variant and measures of detachment and lack of assertiveness was reported (Jönsson et al., 2003).

Neuroticism and serotonin

N is an important liability factor for the development of anxiety and depressive disorders (e.g. Kendler et al., 1993). Because serotonin specific reuptake inhibitors are effective in the treatment of depression, neuronal mechanisms involved in pre-synaptic serotonin reuptake may be implicated in N. Serotonergic activity in the brain, which is involved in many affective disorders (Graeff et al., 1996), is mediated by the serotonin transporter gene (5-HTT). The principal function of 5-HTT is to remove serotonin from the synaptic cleft by returning it to the pre-synaptic neuron where the neurotransmitter can be stored for later re-release. 5-HTT expression is particularly abundant in cortical and limbic areas engaged in modulation of emotional aspects of behaviour (Westenberger et al., 1996). In humans, two common alleles, the short and long alleles, in a variable repeat sequence of the promoter region of 5-HTT were linked to N (e.g. Lesch et al., 1996; Sen et al., 2004b). N also mediated the association between 5-HTT polymorphism and lifetime major depression (Munafò et al., 2006a). Analysis of genotype–phenotype relations in healthy volunteers by means of imaging-genomics studies (Hariri and Weinberger, 2003) endorse an association between 5-HTT polymorphism and N; that is, increased responses of the amygdala as a function of the short allele in the linked promoter region of the 5-HTT (Hariri et al., 2005).

Numerous studies failed to confirm an association between 5-HTT polymorphism and N (e.g. Ball et al., 1997; Deary et al., 1999; Ebstein et al., 1997; Flory et al., 1999; Jorm et al., 1998; Mazzanti et al., 1998; Willis-Owen et al., 2005). Several possible explanations for these inconsistent results were proposed, namely a small sample size, different methods of personality assessment and phenotype ascertainment, or population stratification. Attempts to circumvent these methodological constraints, however, also failed to form a consensus. Five meta-analyses were also inconclusive (Munafò et al., 2005; Munafò et al., 2004; Munafò et al., 2003; Schinka et al., 2004; Sen et al., 2004a).

Animal research on the serotonin receptor subtype 5-HT$_{1A}$ provides converging evidence for serotonin as a biochemical correlate of N. Anxiety is more pronounced in mice lacking 5-HT$_{1A}$ receptors than controls (Parks et al., 1998; Ramboz et al., 1998). Further, 5-HT$_{1A}$ receptor agonists were effective in the treatment of anxiety (e.g. Sramek et al., 1997). A negative correlation between the anxiety facet of the NEO PI-N scale and cortical 5-HT$_{1A}$ receptor binding potential was also observed in a PET study of healthy volunteers (Tauscher et al., 2001); that is, high N is characterized by lower 5-HT$_{1A}$ receptor density. An association between HTR1A-1019 polymorphism and the NEO-PI-R N (Strobel et al., 2003a) also endorses a relation between allelic variation in the 5-HT$_{1A}$ receptor and the expression of the anxiety and depression aspects of N.

Neuroticism and cortisol

The hypothalamic–pituitary–adrenal (HPA) axis is a major part of the neuroendocrine system that controls reactions to stress and regulates mood. HPA dysregulation, as indicated by excess cortisol response after HPA stimulation, was identified as an indicator of depression (Pariante and Miller, 2001; Plotsky et al., 1998). Given that N is a powerful predictor of depression, an association between N and HPA dysregulation is plausible. Both N and HPA dysregulation operate as risk and vulnerability factors for depression (Holsboer, 2000). High N and HPA dysregulation are indicative of less effective coping with stress, critical life events, and psychological challenges. Several studies explored the relationship between these N and HPA.

McCleery and Goodwin (2001) were the first to demonstrate differences in HPA regulation as a function of N. Specifically, low N exhibited a stronger cortisol response than high N. This effect may be indicative of a down-regulated HPA axis for high N to prevent harmful over-activation. Subsequently, Zobel et al. (2004) observed the reverse pattern of cortisol response; that is, stronger cortisol responses were positively associated with N. Zobel et al. (2004) suggested that HPA dysregulation may provide a biochemical basis for N and depressive temperament. Higher cortisol levels for high N individuals without a previous history of depression (e.g. Bridges and Jones, 1968; Portella et al., 2005) provide additional evidence that high N is associated with altered HPA regulation. Overall, however, the relationship between N and HPA is not resolved.

PSYCHOPHYSIOLOGICAL AND BIOCHEMICAL CORRELATES OF IMPULSIVE SENSATION SEEKING

Research on impulsiveness is a challenge because it is a complex construct with multiple meanings. In the Eysenck three factor model, all three factors, E, N, and P, relate to some aspects of impulsiveness: venturesomeness is a feature of E, while narrow impulsiveness is a feature of P and N (Eysenck, 2004).

P also features prominently on an SS factor that is appropriately termed impulsive unsocialized sensation seeking (ImpSS) (Zuckerman et al., 1988). There is a substantial psychophysiological literature that explores individual differences in SS and the biochemical analysis of individual differences in ImpSS has flourished in recent years.

Psychophysiology of sensation seeking

From the psychophysiological literature, three conclusions can be drawn. First, there is little evidence of individual differences in base level of arousal between high and low scorers in SS using measures of skin conductance level, EEG desynchronization, or resting heart rate (Stelmack and Geen, 1992). These null effects negate the proposal that high SS is characterized by low tonic arousal (Zuckerman, 1979).

Second, there is good evidence that high SS scorers react more intensely to stimulation than low SS scorers under some conditions. High SS scorers exhibit larger skin conductance responses than low SS scorers to novel stimulus items that are relevant to the SS scale (SSS; Zuckerman, 1979), for example pictures of hang-gliding, marijuana smoking, mountain climbing, and sexual and violent stimuli (e.g. Smith et al., 1986). In general, these effects provide good support for the construct validity of the SSS, but provide little insight into the biological bases of SS.

Third, there are reliable individual differences in SS, accounting for about 10% of variation, that are observed in an augmenting-reducing paradigm with visual ERP changes to increases in the intensity of light flashes. Individuals with high scores on the disinhibition subscale of the SSS exhibit an increase in amplitude of an ERP wave (P1 N1) that develops at about 100 ms following stimulation. Low sensation seekers exhibit a decrease in amplitude with an increase in intensity of the light flashes whereas high sensation seekers exhibit an increase in

response amplitude (Buchsbaum, 1971; Lukas, 1987). More recent evidence from carefully executed studies endorses this view (e.g. Brocke et al., 1999).

The augmenting-reducing effect was considered as evidence supporting the view that high SS is characterized by lower tonic arousal, and that stimulation is amplified, or simple physical stimulation is experienced more intensely than in low SS scorers, in order to raise arousal to an optimal level (Zuckerman, 1979). Alternatively, in the absence of evidence indicative of differences in base levels of arousal, it can be argued that augmenting-reducing is an intensity effect in which high SS scorers are less sensitive to stimulation than low SS scorers and that low SS scorers initiate inhibitory, protective mechanisms in response to high intensity stimulation that result in smaller responses, (Smith et al., 1989). Coincidentally, it has been shown that a high ImpSS is characterized by greater pain tolerance, greater E, less hypochondriasis, higher absolute sensory thresholds (Goldman et al., 1983; Kohn et al., 1982) and smaller P3 amplitude to negative valence emotional stimuli (De Pascalis et al., 2004). This suggests that high SS scorers may engage in intense stimulating activities, not to achieve an optimum level of arousal, but because they can endure intense stimulation.

Impulsive sensation seeking and dopamine

Zuckerman (1994) proposed the construct of impulsive unsocialized sensation seeking (ImpSS) as an independent trait of personality, with Eysenck's P scale as its strongest marker (Zuckerman et al., 1988). According to Eysenck and Eysenck (1976), a continuum can be drawn from normal through psychopathic behaviour to psychotic states. In this view, the biological basis of P is continuous for healthy individuals and psychotic patients. Increased DA activity is a prominent hypothesis in neurochemical theories of schizophrenia (cf. Davis et al., 1991).

DA activity can also be expected to vary with P or ImpSS (Pickering and Gray, 2001; Zuckerman, 2005). Overall, there is good evidence associating DA activity with P

Although it is premature to determine whether E is more strongly related to brain DA than P/ImpSS, there are a number of DA-mediated effects related to P or psychosis proneness rather than to E, e.g. latent inhibition (e.g. Gibbon and Rammsayer, 1999; Lubow and Gewirtz, 1995), negative priming (e.g. Beech and Claridge, 1987; Swerdlow et al., 1995), and pre-pulse inhibition (e.g. Kumari et al., 1997; Simons and Giardina, 1992).

Netter and Rammsayer (1991) administered the DA antagonist haloperidol and the DA precursor L-dopa to normal subjects and tested them on a reaction time task. While high SS scorers tended to feel more relaxed and perform better after haloperidol, low SS scorers performed better after L-dopa, effects indicative of more responsive DA activity in high ImpSS scorers (Zuckerman, 1993). A negative relationship between P and D2 receptor binding in the basal ganglia was reported in a PET study by Gray et al. (1994). Because an increase in DA activity results in down-regulation of post-synaptic receptors, as indicated by a decrease in number of receptors or post-synaptic receptor sensitivity (Creese et al., 1977), the association between P and D2 binding is indicative of increased DA activity for P. Initially, this conclusion appears congruent with the hypothesis of increased brain DA in schizophrenia. However, DA hypothesis of schizophrenia predicts enhanced activity in the mesolimbocortical DA, whereas the Gray et al. (1994) finding referred to the functionally independent mesostriatal DA.

Impulsive sensation seeking and cortisol

An early study by Ballenger et al. (1983) reported that SS was characterized by low levels of free cortisol. Subsequent studies measuring cortisol baseline levels (Gerra et al., 1999) and cortisol response values (Gerra et al., 1998) failed to observe that negative relationship to ImpSS. More recently, a reliable inverse relation between cortisol and SS was reported for male, but not for female college students (Rosenblitt et al., 2001).

SUMMARY AND CONCLUSIONS

Overall, there was good progress in focusing the fundamental facts of the psychophysiological and biochemical correlates of personality. The greater sensory reactivity of introverts than extraverts to simple sensory stimulation observed with a wide range of psychophysical and psychophysiological procedures is well established. There is also good progress in demonstrating differences in motor expression between introverts and extraverts with psychophysiological procedures. The faster movement time for extraverts on simple response time tasks and the absence of P3 latency effects (an index of stimulus processing speed) do point to the involvement of peripheral and or/cortical motor processes as relevant determinants of individual differences in E rather than central cortical mechanisms that are involved in sensory discrimination or stimulus evaluation. The application of lateralized readiness potentials is a promising procedure for articulating the sensory and motor effects.

Biochemical analysis of the DA system, which is involved in the neuroregulation of sensory input and motor output, is proposed as a biochemical determinant of individual differences in E (Rammsayer, 2004). Although biochemical analyses revealed that DA turnover is the same in introverts and extraverts (Rammsayer et al., 1993), there is good evidence from different procedures for E differences in responsiveness to deviations from the physiological level of DA activity in the brain, with introverts more susceptible to changes in D2 receptor activity than extraverts.

The disappointing outcome of early psychophysiological research on N, using simple physical stimulation, has yielded more promising results with some EEG procedures. Although the effect is not conclusively established, the association of higher N with greater right frontal EEG activity was observed in several reports, notably under negative affect conditions.

Biochemical analyses of individual differences in N are equivocal. There is some evidence linking N and D2 receptor mechanisms, but this evidence is piecemeal. Analyses of the serotonergic system are inconclusive. Although there is good evidence relating depression to HPA dysfunction (as indexed by excess cortisol response following HPA stimulation) and although N is an important predictor of depression, no firm association betweeen N and HPA dysfunction is established.

With respect to ImpSS, psychophysiological research indicates: (1) no reliable individual differences in tonic levels of physiological activity; (2) greater response to highly novel, exciting or disturbing stimuli for higher SS; and (3) larger response (greater tolerance?) to higher intensity physical stimulation for higher SS. Although far from conclusive, there is increasing evidence relating P/ImpSS to increased or more reactive DA activity.

The review of psychophysiological and neurochemical research presented in this chapter aimed to focus the biological basis of personality and individual differences. The arousal construct was central to the early examination of personality from a physiological perspective. A distillation of that work is incorporated in this review. Over the past four decades, the neurosciences provided new findings, constructs, and models in an attempt to improve our understanding of the biological determinants of behaviour and individual differences, often without integration of previous effects that were reported. As Matthews and Gilliland (1999) suggested, this scenario may have lead, unintentionally, to an oversimplification of a number of neurophysiological processes. Both these considerations could contribute to the inconsistency of effects noted in this review. Clearly, future research must make an effort to exploit reliable effects and to incorporate them in a paradigm of personality that leads to a meaningful appreciation of how neural processes, neurotransmitters, and hormones contribute to individual differences in personality.

REFERENCES

Amalric, M., Berhow, M., Polis, I. and Koob, G.F. (1993) 'Selective effects of low-dose D2 dopamine receptor antagonism in a reaction-time task in rats', *Neuropsychopharmacology*, 8(3): 195–200.

Ball, D., Hill, L., Freeman, B., Eley, T.C., Strelau, J., Riemann, R., Spinath, F.M., Angleitner, A. and Plomin, R. (1997) 'The serotonin transporter gene and peer-rated neuroticism', *NeuroReport*, 8(5): 1301–4.

Ballenger, J.C., Post, R.M., Jimerson, D.C., Lake, C.R., Murphy, D.L., Zuckerman, M. and Cronin, C. (1983) 'Biochemical correlates of personality traits in normals: An exploratory study', *Personality and Individual Differences*, 4(6): 615–25.

Barnes, G. (1975) 'Extraversion and pain', *British Journal of Social and Clinical Psychology*, 14(3): 303–8.

Beech, A. and Claridge, G. (1987) 'Individual differences in negative priming: Relations with schizotypal personality traits', *British Journal of Psychology*, 78(3): 349–56.

Benjamin, J., Li, L., Patterson, C., Greenberg, B.D., Murphy, D.L. and Hamer, D.H. (1996) 'Population and familial association between the D4 dopamine receptor gene and measures of novelty seeking', *Nature Genetics*, 12(1): 81–4.

Benjamin, J., Osher, Y., Kotler, M., Gritsenko, I., Nemanov, L., Belmaker, R.H. and Ebstein, R.P. (2000) 'Association between tridimensional personality questionnaire (TPQ) and three functional polymorphisms: dopamine receptor D4 (DRD4), serotonin transporter promoter region (5-HTTLPR) and catechol O-methyltransferase (COMT)', *Molecular Psychiatry*, 5(1): 96–100.

Björklund, A. and Lindvall, O. (1986) 'Catecholaminergic brain stem regulatory systems', in American Physiological Society (ed.), *Handbook of Physiology. Section 1. The Nervous System. Vol. IV. Intrinsic Regulatory Systems of the Brain*. Bethesda: American Physiological Society, pp. 155–235.

Bolger, N. and Schilling, E.A. (1991) 'Personality and the problems of everyday life: The role of neuroticism in exposure and reactivity to daily stressors', *Journal of Personality*, 59(3): 355–86.

Brebner, J. and Flavell, R. (1978) 'The effect of catch-trials on speed and accuracy among introverts and extraverts in a simple RT task', *British Journal of Psychology*, 69(1): 9–15.

Breier, A., Adler, C.M., Weisenfeld, N., Su, T.P., Elman, I., Picken, L., Malhotra, A.K. and Pickar, D. (1998b) 'Effects of NMDA antagonism on striatal dopamine release in healthy subjects: application of a novel PET approach', *Synapse*, 29(2): 142–7.

Breier, A., Kestler, L., Adler, C., Elman, I., Wiesenfeld, N., Malhotra, A. and Pickar, D. (1998a) 'Dopamine D2 receptor density and personal detachment in healthy subjects', *American Journal of Psychiatry*, 155(10): 1440–2.

Bridges, P.K. and Jones, M.T. (1968) 'Relationship of personality and physique to plasma cortisol levels in response to anxiety', *Journal of Neurology, Neurosurgery, and Psychiatry*, 31(1): 57–60.

Brocke, B., Beauducel, A. and Tasche, K.G. (1999) 'Biopsychological bases and behavioral correlates of sensation seeking: Contributions to a multilevel validation', *Personality and Individual Differences*, 26(6): 1103–23.

Brocke, B., Tasche, K.G. and Beauducel, A. (1996) 'Biopsychological foundations of extraversion: Differential effort reactivity and the differential P300 effect', *Personality and Individual Differences*, 21(5): 727–38.

Brocke, B., Tasche, K.G. and Beauducel, A. (1997) 'Biopsychological foundations of extraversion: Differential effort reactivity and state control', *Personality and Individual Differences*, 22(4): 447–58.

Bruneau, W., Roux, S., Perse, J. and Lelord, G. (1984) 'Frontal evoked responses, stimulus intensity control, and the extraversion dimension', *Annals of the New York Academy of Sciences*, 425: 546–50.

Buchsbaum, M. (1971) 'Neural events and the psychophysical law', *Science*, 172(982): 502.

Bullock, W.A. and Gilliland, K. (1993) 'Eysenck's arousal theory of introversion-extraversion: A converging measures investigation', *Journal of Personality and Social Psychology*, 64(1): 113–23.

Burt, S.A., McGue, M., Iacono, W., Comings, D. and MacMurray, J. (2002) 'An examination of the association between DRD4 and DRD2 polymorphisms and personality traits', *Personality and Individual Differences*, 33(6): 849–59.

Cahill, J.M. and Polich, J. (1992) 'P300, probability and introverted/extroverted personality types', *Biological Psychology*, 33(6): 23–35.

Campbell, J.B. and Hawley, C.W. (1982) 'Study habits and Eysenck's theory of extraversion-introversion', *Journal of Research in Personality*, 16(2): 139–46.

Campbell, K.B. and Bartoli, E.A. (1986) 'Human auditory evoked potentials during sleep: The early components', *Electroencephalography and Clinical Neurophysiology*, 65(2): 142–9.

Carlsson, M. and Carlsson, A. (1990) 'Schizophrenia: A subcortical neurotransmitter imbalance syndrome?', *Schizophrenia Bulletin*, 16(3): 425–32.

Chiappa, K.H. (1990) *Evoked Potentials in Clinical Medicine*. Philadelphia: Lippincot-Raven.

Cohen, J.D. and Servan-Schreiber, D. (1992) 'Context, cortex, and dopamine: A connectionist approach to behavior and biology in schizophrenia', *Psychological Review*, 99(1): 45–77.

Coles, M.G.H. (1989) 'Modern mind-brain reading: Psychophysiology, physiology, and cognition', *Psychophysiology*, 26(3): 251–69.

Comings, D.E., MacMurray, J., Johnson, P., Dietz, G. and Muhleman, D. (1995) 'Dopamine D2 receptor gene (DRD2) haplotypes and the defense style questionnaire in substance abuse, Tourette syndrome, and controls', *Biological Psychiatry*, 37(11): 798–805.

Connolly, J.F., Aubry, K., McGillivary, N. and Scott D.W. (1989) 'Human brainstem evoked responses fail to provide evidence of efferent modulation of auditory input during attentional tasks', *Psychophysiology*, 26(3): 292–303.

Costa, P.T. Jr. and McCrae, R.R. (1992) *Revised NEO Personality Inventory and NEO*

Five-Factor Inventory. Odessa: Psychological Assessment Resources.

Cox-Fuenzalida, L. and Gilliland, K. (2001) 'Congruency of the relationship between extraversion and the brainstem auditory evoked response based on the EPI versus the EPQ', *Journal of Research in Personality*, 35(2): 117–26.

Creese, I., Burt, D.R. and Snyder, S.H. (1977) 'Dopamine receptor binding enhancement accompanies lesion-induced behavioral supersensitivity', *Science*, 197(4303): 596–8.

Cruz, C., Camarena, B., Mejia, J.M., Paez, F., Eroza, V. and Ramon de la Fuente, J. (1995) 'The dopamine D2 receptor gene *TaqI* A1 polymorphism and alcoholism in a Mexican population', *Archives of Medical Research*, 26(4): 421–6.

Daruna, J.H., Karrer, R. and Rosen, A.J. (1985) 'Introversion, attention and the late positive component of event-related potentials', *Biological Psychology*, 20(4): 249–59.

Davidson, R.J. (1993) 'The neuropsychology of emotion and affective style', in M. Lewis and J.M Haviland (eds), *Handbook of Emotion*. New York: Guilford Press, pp. 143–54.

Davidson, R.J. and Fox, N.A. (1982) 'Asymmetrical brain activity discriminates between positive and negative affective stimuli in infants', *Science*, 218(4578): 1235–7.

Davis, K.L., Kahn, R.S., Ko, G. and Davidson, M. (1991) 'Dopamine in schizophrenia: A review and reconceptualization', *American Journal of Psychiatry*, 148(11): 1474–86.

Deary, I.J., Battersby, S., Whiteman, M.C., Connor, J.M., Fowkes, F.G.R. and Harmar, A. (1999) 'Neuroticism and polymorphisms in the serotonin transporter gene', *Psychological Medicine*, 29(3): 735–9.

De Brettes, B., Laurent, C., Lepine, J.P., Mallet, J., Puech, A.J. and Berlin, I. (1998) 'The dopamine D2 receptor gene Taq I A polymorphism is not associated with novelty seeking, harm avoidance and reward dependence in healthy subjects', *European Psychiatry*, 13(8): 427–30.

De Pascalis, V. (1993) 'Hemispheric asymmetry, personality and temperament', *Personality and Individual Differences*, 14(6): 825–34.

De Pascalis,V., Strippoli, E., Riccardi, P. and Vergari, F. (2004) 'Personality, event-related potential (ERP) and heart rate (HR) in emotional word processing', *Personality and Individual Differences*, 36(4): 873–91.

Depue, R.A. and Collins, P.F. (1999) 'Neurobiology of the structure of personality: Dopamine, facilitation of incentive motivation, and extraversion', *Behavioral and Brain Sciences*, 22(3): 491–569.

Desmedt, J.E. (1975) 'Physiological studies of the efferent recurrent auditory system', in W.D. Keidel and W.D. Neff (eds), *Handbook of Sensory Physiology*, Vol. 5. Berlin: Springer, pp. 219–46.

Ditraglia, G.M. and Polich, J. (1991) 'P300 and introverted/extraverted personality types', *Psychophysiology*, 28(2): 177–84.

Dornic, S. and Ekehammar, B. (1990) 'Extraversion, neuroticism, and noise sensitivity', *Personality and Individual Differences*, 11(9): 989–92.

Doucet, C. and Stelmack, R.M. (2000) 'An event-related potential analysis of extraversion and individual differences in cognitive processing speed and response execution', *Journal of Personality and Social Psychology*, 78(5): 956–64.

Duffy, E. (1962) *Activation and Behavior*. New York: John Wiley & Sons.

Duffy, E. (1966) 'The nature and development of the concept of activation', in R.N. Haber (ed.), *Current Research in Motivation*. New York: Holt, Rinehart & Winston, pp. 278–82.

Dunnett, S.B. and Robbins, T.W. (1992) 'The functional role of the mesotelencephalic dopamine systems', *Biological Review*, 67(4): 491–518.

Ebstein, R.P., Gritsenko, I., Nemanov, L., Frisch, A., Osher, Y. and Belmaker, R.H. (1997) 'No association between the serotonin transporter gene regulatory region polymorphism and the Tridimensional Personality Questionnaire (TPQ) temperament of harm avoidance', *Molecular Psychiatry*, 2(3): 224–6.

Ebstein, R.P., Novick, O., Umansky, R., Priel, B., Osher, Y., Blaine, D., Bennett, E.R., Nemanov, L., Katz, M. and Belmaker, R.H. (1996) 'Dopamine D4 receptor (DRD4) exon III polymorphism associated with the human personality trait of novelty seeking', *Nature Genetics*, 12(1): 78–80.

Ekelund, J., Lichtermann, D., Jarvelin, M.R. and Peltonen, L. (1999) 'Association between novelty seeking and type 4-dopamine receptor gene in a large Finnish cohort sample', *American Journal of Psychiatry*, 156(9): 1453–5.

Ekelund, J., Suhonen, J., Järvelin, M.-R., Peltonen, L. and Lichtermann, D. (2001) 'No association of the -521C/T polymorphism in the promoter of DRD4 with novelty seeking', *Molecular Psychiatry*, 6(6): 618–19.

Endler, N.S. and Parker, J.D.A. (1990) 'Multidimensional assessment of coping: A critical evaluation', *Journal of Personality and Social Psychology*, 58(3): 844–54.

Eysenck, H.J. (1957) *The Dynamics of Anxiety and Hysteria*. London: Routledge & Kegan Paul.

Eysenck, H.J. (1967) *The Biological Basis of Personality*. Springfield: Thomas.

Eysenck, H.J. and Eysenck, S.B.G. (1975) *Manual of the Eysenck Personality Questionnaire*. London: Hodder & Stoughton Educational.

Eysenck, H.J. and Eysenck, S.B.G. (1976) *Psychoticism as a Dimension of Personality*. New York: Crane, Russak, & Co.

Eysenck, H.J. and Eysenck, S.B.G. (1991) *Manual of the Eysenck Personality Scales*. London: Hodder & Stoughton.

Eysenck, H.J., Nias, D.K.B. and Cox, D.N. (1982) 'Sport and personality', *Advances in Behavior Research and Therapy*, 4(1): 1–56.

Eysenck, S.B.G. (2004) 'How the impulsiveness and venturesomeness factors evolved', in R.M. Stelmack (ed.), *On the Psychobiology of Personality: Essays in Honor of Marvin Zuckerman*. Oxford: Elsevier, pp. 107–12.

Fahrenberg, J. (1987) 'Concepts of activation and arousal in the theory of emotionality (neuroticism)', in J. Strelau and H.J. Eysenck (eds), *Personality Dimensions and Arousal*. New York: Plenum Press, pp. 99–120.

Farde, L., Gustavsson, J.P. and Jönsson, E. (1997) 'D2 dopamine receptors and personality traits', *Nature*, 385(6617): 590.

Fischer, H., Wik, G. and Fredrikson, M. (1997) Extraversion, neuroticism and brain function: A PET study of personality. *Personality and Individual Differences*, 23(2): 345–52.

Flory, J.D., Manuck, S.B., Ferrell, R.E., Dent, K.M., Peters, D.G. and Muldoon, M.F. (1999) 'Neuroticism is not associated with the serotonin transporter (5-HTTLPR) polymorphism', *Molecular Psychiatry*, 4(1): 93–6.

Furnham, A. (1981) 'Personality and activity preference', *British Journal of Social Psychology*, 20(1): 57–68.

Gale, A. (1969) '"Stimulus hunger": Individual differences in operant strategy in a button-pressing task', *Behaviour Research and Therapy*, 7(3): 263–74.

Gale, A. (1973). 'The psychophysiology of individual differences: Studies of extraversion–introversion and the EEG', in P. Kline (ed.), *New Approaches in Psychological Measurement*. London: Wiley, pp. 211–56.

Gale, A., Edwards, J., Morris, P., Moore, R. and Forrester, D. (2001) 'Extraversion–introversion, neuroticism–stability, and EEG indicators of positive and negative empathic mood', *Personality and Individual Differences*, 30(3): 449–61.

Gebhardt, C., Schüssler, P., Fuchs, K., Stompe, T., Sieghart, W., Hornik, K., Kasper, S., Aschauer, H.N. and Leisch, F. (2000) 'Non-association of dopamine D4 and D2 receptor genes with personality in healthy individuals', *Psychiatric Genetics*, 10(4): 131–7.

Gerra, G., Avanzini, P., Zaimovic, A., Sartori, R., Bocchi, C., Timpano, M., Zambelli, U., Delsignore, R., Gardini, F., Talarico, E. and Brambilla, F. (1999) 'Neurotransmitters, neuroendocrine correlates of sensation-seeking temperament in normal humans', *Neuropsychobiology*, 39(4): 207–13.

Gerra, G., Zaimovic, A., Franchini, D., Palladino, M., Giucastro, G. and Reali, N. (1998) 'Neuroendocrine responses of healthy volunteers to "techno-music": Relationships with personality traits and emotional state', *International Journal of Psychophysiology*, 28(1): 99–111.

Gibbons, H. and Rammsayer, T.H. (1999) 'Differential effects of personality traits related to the P-ImpUSS dimension on latent inhibition in healthy female subjects', *Personality and Individual Differences*, 27(6): 1157–66.

Goldman, D., Kohn, P.M. and Hunt, R.W. (1983) 'Sensation seeking, augmenting reducing, and absolute auditory threshold: A strength of the nervous system perspective', *Journal of Personality and Social Psychology*, 45(2): 405–11.

Gonsalvez, C.J., Barry, R.J., Rushby, J.A. and Polich, J. (2007) 'Target-to-target interval, intensity, and P300 from an auditory single-stimulus task', *Psychophysiology*, 44(2): 245–50.

Graeff, F.G., Guimaraes, F.S., De Andrade, T.G. and Deakin, J.F. (1996) 'Role of 5-HT in stress, anxiety, and depression', *Pharmacology and Biochemical Behavior*, 54(1): 129–41.

Gray, N.S., Pickering, A.D. and Gray, J.A. (1994) 'Psychoticism and dopamine D2 binding in the basal ganglia using single photon emission tomography', *Personality and Individual Differences*, 17(3): 431–4.

Gurrera, R.J., O'Donnell, B.F., Nestor, P.G., Gainski, J. and McCarley, R.W. (2001) 'The P3 auditory event-related brain potential indexes major personality traits', *Biological Psychiatry*, 49(11): 922–9.

Hagemann, D., Naumann, E., Lürken, A., Becker, G., Maier, S. and Bartussek, D. (1999) 'EEG asymmetry, dispositional mood and personality', *Personality and Individual Differences*, 27(3): 541–68.

Hariri, A.R., Drabant, E.M., Munoz, K.E., Kolachana, B.S., Mattay, V.S., Egan, M.F. and Weinberger, D.R. (2005) 'A susceptibility gene for affective disorders and the response of the human amygdala', *Archives of General Psychiatry*, 62(2): 146–52.

Hariri, A.R. and Weinberger, D.R. (2003) 'Imaging genomics', *British Medical Bulletin*, 65(1): 259–70.

Holsboer, F. (2000) 'The corticosteroid receptor hypothesis of depression', *Neuropharmacology*, 23(5): 477–501.

Ivashenko, O.V., Berus, A.V., Zhuravlev, A.B. and Myamlim, V.V. (1999) 'Individual and typological features of basic personality traits in norms and their EEG correlates', *Human Physiology*, 25(2): 162–70.

Jönsson, E.G., Cichon, S., Gustavsson, J.P., Grunhage, F., Forslund, K., Mattila-Evenden, M., Rylander, G., Åsberg, M., Farde, L., Propping, P. and Nöthen, M.M. (2003). 'Association between a promoter dopamine D2 receptor gene variant and the personality trait detachment', *Biological Psychiatry*, 53(7): 577–84.

Jönsson, E.G. Ivo, R., Gustavsson, J.P., Geijer T., Forslund, K., Mattila-Evenden, M., Rylander, G., Cichon, S., Propping, P., Bergman, H., Åsberg, M. and Nöthen, M. (2002) 'No association between dopamine D4 receptor gene variants and novelty seeking', *Molecular Psychiatry*, 7(1): 18–20.

Jönsson, E.G., Nöthen, M.M., Gustavsson, J.P., Neidt, H., Brené, S., Tylec, A., Propping, P. and Sedvall, G.C. (1997) 'Lack of evidence for allelic association between personality traits and the dopamine D4 receptor gene polymorphisms', *American Journal of Psychiatry*, 154(5): 697–99.

Jönsson, E.G., Nöthen, M.M., Gustavsson, J.P., Neidt, H., Forslund, K., Mattila-Evenden, M., Rylander, G., Propping, P. and Asberg, M. (1998) 'Lack of association between dopamine D4 receptor gene and personality traits', *Psychological Medicine*, 28(4): 985–9.

Jorm, A.F., Henderson, A.S., Jacomb, P.A. Christensen, H., Korten, A.E., Rodgers, B., Tan, X. and Easteal, S. (1998) 'An association study of a functional polymorphism of the serotonin transporter gene with personality and psychiatric symptoms', *Molecular Psychiatry*, 3(5): 449–51.

Kendler, K.S., Neale, M.C., Kessler, R.C., Heath, A.C. and Eaves, L.J. (1993) 'A longitudinal twin study of personality and major depression in women', *Archives of General Psychiatry*, 50(11): 853–62.

Kestler, L.P., Malhotra, A.K., Finch, C., Adler, C. and Breier, A. (2000) 'The relation between dopamine D2 receptor density and personality: Preliminary evidence from the NEO Personality Inventory-Revised', *Neuropsychiatry, Neuropsychology, and Behavioral Neurology*, 13(1): 48–52.

Kimberg, D.Y., D'Esposito, M. and Farah, M.J. (1997) 'Effects of bromocriptine on human subjects depend on working memory capacity', *Neuroreport*, 8(16): 3581–5.

Knyazev, G.G., Slobodskaya, H.R. and Wilson, G.D. (2002) 'Psychophysiological correlates of behavioural inhibition and activation', *Personality and Individual Differences*, 33(4): 647–60.

Kohn, P.M., Hunt, R.W. and Hoffman, F.M. (1982) 'Aspects of experience seeking', *Canadian Journal of Behavioral Science*, 14(1): 13–23.

Kok, A. (2001) 'On the utility of P3 amplitude as a measure of processing capacity', *Psychophysiology*, 38(3): 557–77.

Kuhn, K.U., Meyer, K., Nöthen, M.M., Gansicke, M., Papassotiropoulos, A. and Maier, W. (1999) 'Allelic variants of dopamine receptor D4 (DRD4) and serotonin receptor 5-HT2C (HTR2C) and temperament factors: Replication tests', *American Journal of Medical Genetics*, 88(2): 168–72.

Kumari, V., Toone, B. and Gray, J.A. (1997) 'Habituation and prepulse inhibition of the acoustic startle reflex: Effects of smoking status and psychosis-proneness', *Personality and Individual Differences*, 23(2): 183–91.

Kutas, M., McCarthy, G. and Donchin, E. (1977) 'Augmenting mental chronometry: The P300 as a measure of stimulus evaluation time', *Science*, 197(4305): 792–5.

Lawrence, A.D., Koepp, M.J., Gunn, R.N., Cunningham, V.J. and Grasby, P.M. (1999) 'Steps to a neurochemistry of personality', *Behavioral and Brain Sciences*, 22(3): 528–9.

LeBlanc, J. and Ducharme, M.B. (2005) 'Influence of personality traits on plasma levels of cortisol and cholesterol', *Physiology and Behavior*, 84(5): 677–80.

Lee, I.H., Cheng, C.C., Yang, Y.K., Yeh, T.L., Chen, P.S. and Chiu, N.T. (2005) 'Correlation between striatal dopamine D2 receptor density and neuroticism in community volunteers', *Psychiatry Research: Neuroimaging*, 138(3): 259–64.

Lesch, K.-P., Bengel, D., Heils, A., Sabol, S.Z., Greenberg, B., Petri, S., Benjamin, J., Müller, C.R., Hamer, D.H. and Murphy, D.L. (1996) 'Association of anxiety-related traits with a polymorphism in the serotonin transporter gene regulatory region', *Science*, 274(5292): 1527–31.

Lindsley, D.B. (1951) 'Emotion', in S.S. Stevens (ed.), *Handbook of Experimental Psychology*. New York: Academic Press, pp. 473–516.

Lubow, R.E. and Gewirtz, J.C. (1995) 'Latent inhibition in humans: Data, theory and implications for schizophrenia', *Psychological Bulletin*, 117(1): 87–103.

Lukas, J.H. (1987) 'Visual evoked potential augmenting-reducing and personality: The vertex augmenter is a sensation seeker', *Personality and Individual Differences*, 8(3): 385–95.

Malhotra, A.K. and Goldman, D. (2000) 'The dopamine D-sub-4 receptor gene and novelty seeking', *American Journal of Psychiatry*, 157(11): 1885.

Matthews, G. and Amelang, M. (1993) 'Extraversion, arousal theory and performance: A study of individual differences in the EEG', *Personality and Individual Differences*, 14(2): 347–63.

Matthews, G. and Gilliland, K. (1999) 'The personality theories of H.J. Eysenck and J.A. Gray: A comparative review', *Personality and Individual Differences*, 26(4): 583–626.

Mazzanti, C.M., Lappalainen, J., Long, J.C., Bengel, D., Naukkarinen, H., Eggert, M., Virkkunen, M., Linnoila, M. and Goldman, D. (1998) 'Role of the serotonin transporter polymorphism in anxiety-related traits', *Archives of General Psychiatry*, 55(10): 936–40.

McCleery, J.M. and Goodwin, G.M. (2001) 'High and low neuroticism predict different cortisol responses to the combined dexamethasone-CRH test', *Biological Psychiatry*, 49(5): 410–15.

Minnix, J.A. and Kline, J.P. (2004) 'Neuroticism predicts resting frontal EEG asymmetry variability', *Personality and Individual Differences*, 36(4): 823–32.

Mitsuyasu, H., Hirata, N., Sakai, Y., Shibata, H., Takeda, K., Ninomiya, H., Kawasaki, H., Tashiro, N. and Fukumaki, Y. (2001) 'Association analysis of polymorphisms in the upstream region of the human dopamine D4 receptor gene (DRD4) with schizophrenia and personality traits', *Journal of Human Genetics*, 46(1): 26–31.

Müller, U., von Cramon, D.Y. and Pollmann, S. (1998) 'D1- versus D2-receptor modulation of visuospatial working memory in humans', *Journal of Neuroscience*, 18(7): 2720–8.

Munafò, M.R., Clark, T.G. and Flint, J. (2004) 'Are there sex differences in the association between the 5HHT gene and neuroticism? A meta-analysis', *Personality and Individual Differences*, 37(3): 621–6.

Munafò, M.R., Clark, T. and Flint, J. (2005) 'Does measurement instrument moderate the association between the serotonin transporter gene and anxiety-related personality traits? A meta-analysis', *Molecular Psychiatry*, 10(4): 415–9.

Munafò, M.R., Clark, T.G., Moore, L.R., Payne, E., Walton, R.T. and Flint, J. (2003) 'Genetic polymorphisms and personality: A systematic review and meta-analysis', *Molecular Psychiatry*, 8(5): 471–84.

Munafò, M.R., Clark, T.G., Roberts, K.H. and Johnstone, E.C. (2006a) 'Neuroticism mediates the association of the serotonin transporter gene with lifetime major depression', *Neuropsychobiology*, 53(1): 1–8.

Munafò, M.R., Lee, L., Ayres, R., Flint, J., Goodwin, G. and Harmer, C.J. (2006b) 'Early morning salivary cortisol is not associated with extraversion', *Personality and Individual Differences*, 40(2): 395–400.

Netter, P. and Rammsayer, T. (1991) 'Reactivity to dopaminergic drugs and aggression related personality traits', *Personality and Individual Differences*, 12(10): 1009–17.

Noble, E.P., Ozkaragoz, T.Z., Ritchie, T.L., Zhang, X., Belin, T.R. and Sparkes, R.S. (1998) 'D2 and D4 dopamine receptor polymorphisms and personality', *American Journal of Medical Genetics*, 81(3): 257–67.

O'Gorman, J.G. (1977) 'Individual differences in habituation of human physiological responses: A review of theory, method and findings in the study of personality correlates in non-clinical populations', *Biological Psychology*, 5(4): 257–318.

O'Gorman, J.G. and Lloyd, J.E. (1987) 'Extraversion, impulsiveness and EEG activity', *Personality and Individual Differences*, 8(2): 169–74.

Okuyama, Y., Ishiguro, H., Nankai, M., Shibuya, H., Watanabe, A. and Arinami, T. (2000) 'Identification of a polymorphism in the promoter region of DRD4 associated with the human novelty seeking personality trait', *Molecular Psychiatry*, 5(1): 64–9.

Ono, Y., Manki, H., Yoshimura, K., Muramatsu, T., Mizushima, H., Higuchi, S., Yagi, G., Kanba, S. and Asai, M. (1997) 'Association between dopamine D4 receptor (D4DR) exon III polymorphism and novelty seeking in Japanese subjects', *American Journal of Medical Genetics*, 74(5): 501–3.

Ortiz, T. and Maojo, V. (1993) 'Comparison of the P300 wave in introverts and extraverts', *Personality and Individual Differences*, 15(1): 109–12.

Pariante, C.M. and Miller, A.H. (2001) 'Glucocorticoid receptors in major depression: Relevance to pathophysiology and treatment', *Biological Psychiatry*, 49(5): 391–404.

Parks, C.L., Robinson, P.S., Sibille, E., Shenk, T. and Toth, M. (1998) 'Increased anxiety of mice lacking the serotonin 1A receptor', *Proceedings of the National Academy of Sciences*, 95(18): 10734–9.

Persson, M.L., Wasserman, D., Geijer, T., Frisch, A., Rockah, R., Michaelovski, E., Apter, A., Weizman, A., Joensson, E.G. and Bergman, H. (2000) 'Dopamine D4 receptor gene polymorphism and personality traits in healthy volunteers', *European Archives of Psychiatry and Clinical Neuroscience*, 250(4): 203–6.

Pickering, A.D. and Gray, J.A. (2001) 'Dopamine, appetitive reinforcement, and the neuropsychology of human learning: An individual differences approach', in A. Eliasz and A. Angleitner (eds), *Advances in Research on*

Temperament. Lengerich, Germany: Pabst Science Publishers, pp. 113–49.

Picton, T.W., Stapells, D. and Campbell, K.B. (1981) 'Auditory evoked potentials from the human cochlea and brainstem', *Journal of Otolaryngology*, supplement 9: 1–41.

Plotsky, P.M., Owen, M.J. and Nemeroff, C.B. (1998) 'Psychoneuroendocrinology of depression. Hypothalamic-pituitary-adrenal axis', *Psychiatric Clinics of North America*, 21(2): 293–307.

Pogue-Geile, M., Ferrell, R., Deka, R., Debski, T. and Manuck, S. (1998) 'Human novelty-seeking personality traits and dopamine D4 receptor polymorphisms: A twin and genetic association study', *American Journal of Medical Genetics*, 81(1): 44–8.

Polich, J. and Martin, S. (1992) 'P300, cognitive capability and personality: A correlational study of university undergraduates', *Personality and Individual Differences*, 13(5): 533–43.

Portella, M.J., Harmer, C.J., Flint, J., Cowen, P. and Goodwin, G.M. (2005) 'Enhanced early morning salivary cortisol in neuroticism', *American Journal of Psychiatry*, 162(4): 807–9.

Pritchard, W.S. (1989) 'P300 and EPQ/STP personality traits', *Personality and Individual Differences*, 10(1): 15–24.

Ramboz, S., Oosting, R., Amara, D.A., Kung, H.F., Blier, P., Mendelsohn, M., Mann, J.J., Brunner, D. and Hen, R. (1998) 'Serotonin receptor 1A knockout: An animal model of anxiety-related disorder', *Proceedings of the National Academy of Sciences*, 95(24): 14476–81.

Rammsayer, T. (1997) 'Are there dissociable roles of the mesostriatal and mesolimbo-cortical dopamine systems on temporal information processing in humans?', *Neuropsychobiology*, 35(1): 36–45.

Rammsayer, T.H. (1998). 'Extraversion and dopamine. Individual differences in response to changes in dopaminergic activity as a possible biological basis of extraversion', *European Psychologist*, 3(1): 37–50.

Rammsayer, T.H. (2003) 'NMDA receptor activity and the transmission of sensory input into motor output in introverts and extraverts', *Quarterly Journal of Experimental Psychology, Section B: Comparative and Physiological Psychology*, 56B(2): 207–21.

Rammsayer, T.H. (2004) 'Extraversion and the dopamine hypothesis', in R.M. Stelmack (ed.), *On the Psychobiology of Personality*. Amsterdam: Elsevier, pp. 411–29.

Rammsayer, T. and Stahl, J. (2004) 'Extraversion-related differences in response organization: Evidence from lateralized readiness potentials', *Biological Psychology*, 66(1): 35–49.

Rammsayer, T. and Stahl, J. (2006) 'Sensorimotor effects of pergolide, a dopamine agonist, in healthy subjects: A lateralized readiness potential study', *Psychopharmacology*, 187(1): 36–46.

Rammsayer, T.H., Netter, P. and Vogel, W.H. (1993) 'A neurochemical model underlying differences in reaction times between introverts and extraverts', *Personality and Individual Differences*, 14(5): 701–12.

Robbins, T.W. and Everitt, B.J. (1995) 'Arousal systems and attention', in M.S. Gazzaniga (ed.), *The Cognitive Neurosciences*. Cambridge, MA: MIT Press, pp. 703–20.

Robinson, T.E. and Berridge, K.C. (2000) 'The psychology and neurobiology of addiction: An incentive-sensitization view', *Addiction*, 95(suppl 2): 91–117.

Rosenblitt, J.C., Soler, H., Johnson, S.E. and Quadagno, D.M. (2001) 'Sensation seeking and hormones in men and women: Exploring the link', *Hormones and Behavior*, 40(3): 396–402.

Roy, A. (1996) 'HPA axis function and temperament in depression: A negative report', *Biological Psychiatry*, 39(5): 364–6.

Saint-Cyr, J.A. (2003) 'Frontal-striatal circuit functions: Context, sequence, and consequence', *Journal of the International Neuropsychological Society*, 9(1): 103–28.

Salamone, J.D. (1994) 'The involvement of nucleus accumbens dopamine in appetitive and aversive motivation', *Behavioural Brain Research*, 61(2): 117–33.

Salamone, J.D., Kurth, P.A., McCullough, L.D., Sokolowski, J.D. and Cousins, M.S. (1993) 'The role of brain dopamine in response initiation: effects of haloperidol and regionally-specific dopamine depletion on the local rate of instrumental responding', *Brain Research*, 628(1–2): 218–26.

Schinka, J.A., Busch, R.M. and Robichaux-Keene, N. (2004) 'A meta-analysis of the association between the serotonin transporter gene polymorphism (5-HTTLPR) and trait anxiety', *Molecular Psychiatry*, 9(2): 197–202.

Schmidt, L.A. (1999) 'Frontal brain activity in shyness and sociability', *Psychological Science*, 10(4): 316–20.

Schmidtke, J.I. and Heller, W. (2004) 'Personality, affect and EEG: Predicting patterns of regional brain activity related to extraversion and neuroticism', *Personality and Individual Differences*, 36(3): 717–32.

Schommer, N.C., Kudielka, B.M., Hellhammer, D.H. and Kirschbaum, C. (1999) 'No evidence for a close relationship between personality traits and circadian cortisol rhythm or a single cortisol stress response', *Psychological Reports*, 84(3, pt 1): 840–2.

Sen, S., Burmeister, M. and Ghosh, D. (2004a) 'Meta-analysis of the association between a serotonin transporter promoter polymorphism (5-HTTLPR) and anxiety-related personality traits', *American Journal of Medical Genetics*, 127B(1): 85–9.

Sen, S., Villafuerte, S., Nesse, R., Stoltenberg, S.F., Hopcian, J., Gleiberman, L., Weder, A. and Burmeister, M. (2004b) 'Serotonin transporter and GABA(A) alpha 6 receptor variants are associated with neuroticism', *Biological Psychiatry*, 55(3): 244–9.

Simons, R.F. and Giardina, B.D. (1992) 'Reflex modification in psychosis-prone young adults', *Psychophysiology*, 29(1): 8–16.

Smith, B.D. (1983) 'Extraversion and electrodermal activity: Arousability and the inverted-U', *Personality and Individual Differences*, 4(4): 411–19.

Smith, B.D., Davidson, R.A., Smith, D.L., Goldstein, H. and Perlstein, H.W. (1989) 'Sensation seeking and arousal: Effects of strong stimulation of electrodermal activation and memory task performance', *Personality and Individual Differences*, 10(6): 671–9.

Smith, B.D., Perlstein, W.M., Davidson, R.A. and Michael, K. (1986) 'Sensation seeking: Differential effects of relevant, novel stimulation on electrodermal activity', *Personality and Individual Differences*, 7(4): 445–52.

Sokolowski, J.D., McCullough, L.D. and Salamone, J.D. (1994) 'Effects of dopamine depletion in the medial prefrontal cortex on active avoidance and escape in the rat', *Brain Research*, 651(1–2): 293–9.

Soyka, M., Preuss, U.W., Koller, G., Zill, P. and Bondy, B. (2002) 'Dopamine D4 receptor gene polymorphism and extraversion revisited: Results from the Munich gene bank project for alcoholism', *Journal of Psychiatric Research*, 36(6): 429–35.

Sramek, J.J., Frackiewicz, E.J. and Cutler, N.R. (1997) Efficacy and safety of two dosing regimes of buspirone in the treatment of outpatients with persistent anxiety', *Clinical Therapeutics*, 19(3): 498–506.

Stahl, J. and Rammsayer, T. (2004) 'Differences in the transmission of sensory input into motor output between introverts and extraverts: Behavioral and psychophysiological analyses', *Brain and Cognition*, 56(3): 293–303.

Stelmack, R.M. (1990) 'The biological basis of extraversion: Psychophysiological evidence', *Journal of Personality*, 58(1): 293–311.

Stelmack, R.M. (1997) 'The psychophysics and psychophysiology of extraversion and arousal', in H. Nyborg (ed.), *The Scientific Study of Human Nature: Tribute to Hans J. Eysenck at Eighty*. London: Elsevier, pp. 488–503.

Stelmack, R.M. and Campbell, K.B. (1974) 'Extraversion and auditory sensitivity to high and low frequency', *Perceptual and Motor Skills*, 38(3): 875–9.

Stelmack, R.M., Campbell, K.B. and Bell, I. (1993a) 'Extraversion and brainstem auditory evoked potentials during sleep and wakefulness', *Personality and Individual Differences*, 14(3): 447–53.

Stelmack, R.M. and Geen, R.G. (1992) 'The psychophysiology of extraversion', in A. Gale and M.W. Eysenck (eds), *Handbook of Individual Differences: Biological Perspectives*. New York: Wiley, pp. 227–54.

Stelmack, R.M., Houlihan, M. and McGarry-Roberts, P.A. (1993b) 'Personality, reaction time, and event-related potentials', *Journal of Personality and Social Psychology*, 65(2): 399–409.

Stelmack, R.M. and Michaud-Achorn, A. (1985) 'Extraversion, attention, and habituation of the auditory evoked response', *Journal of Research in Personality*, 19(4): 416–28.

Stelmack, R.M. and Pivik, R.T. (1996) 'Extraversion and the effects of exercise on spinal motoneuronal excitability', *Personality and Individual Differences*, 21(1): 69–76.

Stelmack, R.M. and Wilson, K.G. (1982) 'Extraversion and the effects of frequency and intensity on the auditory brainstem evoked response', *Personality and Individual Differences*, 3: 373–80.

Stenberg, G. (1992) 'Personality and the EEG: Arousal and emotional arousability', *Personality and Individual Differences*, 13(10): 1097–113.

Stenberg, G. (1994) 'Extraversion and the P300 in a visual classification task', *Personality and Individual Differences*, 16(4): 543–60.

Strobel, A., Gutknecht, L., Rothe, C., Reif, A., Mossner, R., Zeng, Y., Brocke, B. and Lesch, K.P. (2003a) 'Allelic variation in 5-HT(1A) receptor expression is associated with anxiety- and depression-related personality traits', *Journal of Neural Transmission*, 110(12): 1445–53.

Strobel, A., Lesch, K.P., Hohenberger, K., Jatzke, S., Gutzeit, H.O., Anacker, K. and Brocke, B. (2002) 'No association between dopamine D4 receptor gene exon III and -512C/T polymorphism and novelty seeking', *Molecular Psychiatry*, 7(6): 537–8.

Strobel, A., Spinath, F.M., Angleitner, A., Riemann, R. and Lesch, K.P. (2003b) 'Lack of association between polymorphisms of the dopamine D4 receptor gene and personality', *Neuropsychobiology*, 47(11): 52–6.

Strobel, A., Wehr, A., Michel, A. and Brocke, B. (1999) 'Association between the dopamine D4 receptor (DRD4) exon III polymorphism and measures of novelty seeking in a German population', *Molecular Psychiatry*, 4(4): 378–84.

Swerdlow, N.R., Filion, D., Geyer, M.A. and Braff, D.L. (1995) '"Normal" personality correlates of sensorimotor, cognitive, and visuospatial gating', *Biological Psychiatry*, 37(5): 286–99.

Swickert, R.J. and Gilliland, K. (1998) 'Relationship between the brainstem auditory evoked response and extraversion, impulsivity, and sociability', *Journal of Research in Personality*, 32(3): 314–30.

Tauscher, J., Bagby, R.M., Javanmard, M., Christensen, B.K., Kasper, S. and Kapur, S. (2001) 'Inverse relationship between serotonin 5-HT1A receptor binding and anxiety: A [^{11}C]WAY-100635 PET investigation in healthy volunteers', *American Journal of Psychiatry*, 158(8): 1326–8.

Tellegen, A. (1985) 'Structure of mood and personality and their relevance to assessing anxiety, with an emphasis on self-report', in A.H. Tuma and J.D. Maser (eds), *Anxiety and the Anxiety Disorders*. Hillsdale, NJ: Erlbaum, pp. 681–706.

Tomitaka, M., Tomitaka, S., Otuka, Y., Kim, K., Matuki, H., Sakamoto, K. and Tanaka, A. (1999) 'Association between novelty seeking and dopamine receptor D4 (DRD4) exon III polymorphism in Japanese subjects', *American Journal of Medical Genetics*, 88(5): 469–71.

Tran, Y., Craig, A. and McIssac, P. (2001) 'Extraversion–introversion and 8–13 Hz waves in frontal cortical regions', *Personality and Individual Differences*, 30(2): 205–15.

Tzschentke, T.M. (2001) 'Pharmacology and behavioral pharmacology of the mesostriatal dopamine system', *Progress in Neurobiology*, 63(3): 241–320.

Vandenbergh, D.J., Zonderman, A.B., Wang, J., Uhl, G.R. and Costa, P.T. Jr. (1997) 'No association between novelty seeking and dopamine D4 receptor (D4DR) exon III seven repeat alleles in the Baltimore longitudinal study of aging participants', *Molecular Psychiatry*, 2(5): 417–19.

Wacker, J., Chavanon, M.-L. and Stemmler, G. (2006) 'Investigating the dopaminergic basis of extraversion in humans: A multilevel approach', *Journal of Personality and Social Psychology*, 91(1): 171–87.

Westenberger, H.G., Murphy, D.L. and den Boer, J.A. (1996) *Advances in the Neurobiology of Anxiety Disorders*. New York: Wiley.

Willis-Owen, S.A.G., Turri, M.G., Munafò, M.R., Surtees, P.G., Wainwright, N.W., Brixey, R.D. and Flint, J. (2005) 'The serotonin transporter length polymorphism, neuroticism, and depression: A comprehensive assessment of association', *Biological Psychiatry*, 58(6): 451–6.

Wilson, M.A. and Languis, M.L. (1990). 'A topographic study of differences in the P3 between introverts and extraverts', *Brain Topography*, 2(4): 269–74.

Woodward, S.A., McManis, M.H., Kagan, J., Deldin, P., Snidman, N., Lewis, M. and Kahn, V. (2001) Infant temperament and brainstem auditory evoked response in later childhood. *Developmental Psychology*, 37(4): 533–8.

Zobel, A., Barkow, K., Schulze-Rauschenbach, S., von Widdern, O., Metten, M., Pfeiffer, U., Schnell, S., Wagner, M. and Maier, W. (2004) 'High neuroticism and depressive temperament are associated with dysfunctional regulation of the hypothalamic-pituitary-adrenocortical system in healthy volunteers', *Acta Psychiatrica Scandinavica*, 109(5): 392–9.

Zuckerman, M. (1979) *Sensation Seeking: Beyond the Optimum Level of Arousal*. Hillsdale, NJ: Erlbaum.

Zuckerman, M. (1993) 'P-impulsive sensation seeking and its behavioural, psychophysiological and biochemical correlates', *Neuropsychobiology*, 28(1–2): 30–6.

Zuckerman, M. (1994) 'Impulsive unsocialized sensation seeking: The biological foundation of a basic dimension of personality', in J.E. Bates and T.D. Wachs (eds), *Temperament: Individual Differences at the Interface of Biology and Behavior*. Washington, DC: American Psychological Association, pp. 219–55.

Zuckerman, M. (2002) 'Zuckerman Kuhlman Personality Questionnaire (ZKPQ): An alternative five-factorial model', in B. De Raad and M. Perugini (eds), *Big Five Assessment*. Göttingen: Hogrefe & Huber, pp. 377–96.

Zuckerman, M. (2005) *Psychobiology of Personality* (2nd edn). New York: Cambridge University Press.

Zuckerman, M., Kuhlman, D.M. and Camac, C. (1988) 'What lies beyond E and N? Factor analyses of scales believed to measure basic dimensions of personality', *Journal of Personality and Social Psychology*, 54(1): 96–107.

3

Personality and Information Processing: A Cognitive-Adaptive Theory

Gerald Matthews

Personality traits correlate with a multitude of objective indices of information processing – but what do the correlations mean? This chapter aims to explore the implications of information-processing studies for personality theory. I will argue that the cognitive correlates of the major traits are distributed across many component mechanisms at different levels of abstraction from the brain. The distributed nature of traits raises the question of how the multiple components may support a unitary trait. My answer is that traits derive coherence from the functional commonalities of these component processes, which work to support common adaptive goals. The chapter is structured as follows. I will introduce the theoretical challenges raised by studies of information processing in a historical context. I will outline three principles necessary to meet the challenge: the distributed nature of traits, use of multiple levels of explanation and the key role of adaptation to environmental pressures

and affordances. I will present a cognitive science framework for capturing the richness of the multifarious components of traits, illustrated in relation to extraversion (E) and neuroticism (N). This descriptive scheme is the basis for the cognitive-adaptive theory of personality which links traits to the universal adaptive choices that human life mandates. I will finish with comments on how the theory illuminates some central issues in personality theory.

PERSONALITY AND INFORMATION PROCESSING: ACCOMPLISHMENTS AND CHALLENGES

Personality research woke up to the cognitive revolution rather late in the day. Pioneering psychobiological trait theorists, notably Hans Eysenck, introduced experiments that related traits to performance tasks requiring attention, memory and other cognitive functions. However, psychobiological theory treated cognition as an outcome of more fundamental neurological processes, rather than a causal influence on behavior. Carl Rogers and George Kelly highlighted the defining role of cognition in molding personality, but without computational models, such approaches lacked the rigor to build a systematic account of the major personality traits.

Several developments jump-started cognitive psychological accounts of traits. In *psychometrics*, researchers began to look beyond the traditional traits to identify dimensions that were defined by primarily cognitive qualities such as locus of control and dispositional focus of attention. In *clinical psychology*, Beck (1967) introduced the idea of the schema to explain depression, suggesting that personality reflects an organized, stable set of self-beliefs. In time, schema theory would help to explain traits linked to negative affectivity such as anxiety and neuroticism (Wells and Matthews, 1994). *Experimental psychology* provided new chronometric paradigms for relating traits to information processing. Michael Eysenck (1981), for example, reviewed studies relating extraversion to standard information-processing tasks such as attention, memory, speeded response, motor skills, problem-solving and strategy choice. Critically, such studies freed cognitive investigations from their reliance on self-report data, in favor of objective measures of speed and accuracy in performance. Humphreys and Revelle (1984) developed the first systematic account of how the major traits influenced a range of different tasks, mediated by individual differences in the availability of processing resources for attention and short-term memory.

Experimental studies became integrated with the clinical perspective through the studies relating clinical and trait anxiety to objective measures of bias in selective attention towards threat stimuli, using the emotional Stroop and other tasks (e.g. MacLeod and Mathews, 1988). Thus, in the mid-1980s (around the time I was completing my doctoral dissertation), the cognitive researcher could be quite sanguine about progress, despite some skepticism from an earlier generation of psychobiologists. However, the studies also raised some major challenges for applying cognitive theory to understanding personality.

Relevance to core attributes of the trait

By its nature, experimental cognitive psychology is concerned with very fine-grained mental processes, as simple as comparing two internal codes, or executing the press of a response key. By contrast, personality is a 'broad-sweep' domain, concerned with large-scale styles of behavior across all the major areas of life. Theories should not only make predictions in the laboratory, but also specify how individual differences in cognition and information processing impinge on real-life, consequential outcomes.

Small effect sizes

Correlations between traits and measures of information processing are generally of modest magnitude, falling short of those seen in intelligence research, and leading to difficulties in replication. The superiority of introverts at vigilance is one of the more reliable correlates of the trait, replicated in multiple studies. However, a meta-analysis of 53 studies (Koelega, 1992) showed that the effect size r for extraversion and target detection rate was only 0.07, although highly significant. Significant correlations in other paradigms rarely exceed 0.4. Koelega was less than optimistic about the future of the field; his article was arrestingly subtitled '30 years of inconsistency'.

Reconciliation with biological theory

The behavior-genetic evidence shows conclusively that the major personality traits have a substantial biological component (Johnson et al., Vol. 1), a view substantiated by psychophysiological research (Stelmack and Rammsayer, Vol. 1). However, cognitive processes cannot necessarily be reduced to neurological processes in any simple way (Matthews, 2000, 2004), although cognitive neuroscience is becoming increasingly important for personality research. At the least, theory needs to address the extent to which cognitive and biological explanations may be integrated – or must be separated.

Reconciliation with social-cognitive theory

Trait psychologists have tended to neglect the social learning processes identified by such theorists as Albert Bandura and Walter Mischel. Increasingly, research is showing that traits predict not just social behaviors, but measures of key social-psychological constructs such as self-efficacy, appraisals of the social self and scripts for social interaction (Matthews et al., 2003). Difficulties remain over the extent to which such constructs may be understood within the nomothetic framework of modern trait theory (Cervone, Vol. 1; Cervone et al., 2006). Again, we need to address the scope for integration of nomothetic information-processing models with social-cognitive theory.

Personality dynamics and interactionism

Trait theory acknowledges the importance of person–situation interaction over timescales of minutes (laboratory tasks), weeks (stressful encounters) and years (lifespan development). Cognitive theory must go beyond registering information-processing correlates of traits to exploring how processing functions may contribute to the interplay between person and environment.

MEETING THE CHALLENGES: THREE PRINCIPLES FOR COGNITIVE THEORY

The core of the problem is how to relate the cognitive correlates of traits to some broader theory of personality. The message of this chapter is that meeting the challenge requires attention to three key guiding principles that are often neglected in existing personality theory:

1 Traits relate to multifaceted cognitive patternings.
2 Cognitive science identifies multiple levels of explanation for performance effects.
3 Adaptation gives traits coherence.

Cognitive patterning of personality effects

There is a telling parallel between personality and stress research. Effects of stressors on performance cannot be attributed to any single mechanism, as assumed by traditional arousal theory. They reflect a *cognitive patterning* of facilitative and detrimental effects across multiple performance indicators (Hockey, 1984). As I will discuss, extraversion has multifarious performance correlates relating to attention, memory and speed–accuracy tradeoff (Matthews, 1992). Loss of the parsimony provided by arousal theory is a price that must be paid in order to characterize the data accurately. The effects of extraversion and other traits are *distributed* across multiple, qualitatively different mechanisms. Effect sizes across studies may be small because the studies mix tasks that draw upon different mechanisms haphazardly. Broad task categories such as 'vigilance' and 'reaction time' are cognitively heterogeneous in nature. Vigilance tasks (cf. Koelega, 1992) differ in the extent to which they require short-term memory, attentional resources, spatial scanning, use of cues and expectancies. If a trait such as extraversion maps differently onto different processing components, then we should expect inconsistencies across tasks that are not systematically designed to investigate the relevant components.

Matthews (1999) characterizes much of the relevant personality research as geared towards *cognitive mini-theories*; that is, accounts of personality effects within a specific task domain, such as divided attention or short-term memory. The challenge is to stitch together the mini-theories to obtain a more general account of the nature of the trait. The vector of performance change specified by the cognitive patterning is descriptive, not explanatory. To progress further, we need to consider what kinds of explanation are appropriate for data on personality and performance.

Multi-level explanations

Not only does task performance depend on multiple mechanisms, but these mechanisms are also themselves highly heterogeneous in nature. For example, explanations for vigilance decrement (e.g. Warm and Dember, 1998) variously refer to networks of right-brain structures implicated in neuroimaging studies, to abstracted qualities of processing such as resource availability or to high-level strategies related to motivation and effort. Extraversion effects on vigilance might be attributed to individual differences in any or all of these different – qualitatively different – processes.

No single type of explanation adequately integrates the evidence on different types of expression of personality (Matthews, 2000). Biological theories fail to specify how neural processes ultimately translate into higher order functions such as social cognition. Information-processing theories risk losing the defining features of traits in a morass of highly specific mini-theories. Both types

of theory offer a rather passive view of personality, as a consequence of biases in low-level neural or processing biases. Social-cognitive theories may do a better job of capturing the role of personality in the active management of interaction with the environment.

The solution to these difficulties is to develop multi-leveled conceptions of traits. Various multi-level theories have been applied to personality research. For example, Ortony et al. (2005) proposed that traits relate to parameters of a low-level reactive level, a routine level supporting automatic information processing, and a reflective level controlling higher-order cognition. Here, I will draw upon contemporary cognitive science (Pylyshyn, 1999), which provides three distinct levels of explanation relating, broadly, to the neurological 'hardware', the information-processing 'software', and the high-level design of the cognitive system for solving adaptive challenges. Any given task may potentially be understood at all three levels, but, in practice, one level will tend to provide a more tractable explanation for a given observation than the others.

Adaptation, cognition and skill

A third guiding principle is that theory must address the adaptive significance of cognitions. Here we have a decisive departure with earlier personality theories that see cognitive correlates of traits as merely an incidental by-product of more basic brain systems. Adaptation depends primarily on the acquired skills needed for specific tasks or environments (Ericsson and Charness, 1994). However, skills are built on a platform of individual differences in more basic neurological and information processes. The cognitive correlates of personality seen in the laboratory may be most important adaptively as *precursors* of skills that support adaptation to specific contexts. Of course, for many cognitive skills, general intelligence is the most reliable predictor, although personality factors may explain additional variance (Matthews, 1999). Personality may be especially relevant to acquiring social-emotional skills such as managing stress, self-regulation and control, and social skills. Such skills are often described as 'emotional intelligence' (EI), although there is actually a considerable overlap between EI and standard personality traits (Matthews et al., 2002).

Personality also relates critically to the quality of execution of skills, as well as to competence. Factors such as anxiety, lack of perceived self-efficacy or lack of motivation may cause the person to perform below their actual capabilities (Zeidner and Matthews, 2005). Thus, in line with some of the central concerns of social psychology (Bandura, 1997; Caprara and Cervone, 2000), adaptation depends not only on skill per se but also on cognitions about personal competence and external threats and affordances. Personality appears to influence both the objective skill and subjective self-relevant cognitions (Matthews et al., 2000). There is also a critical dynamic interplay between skill and self-knowledge: successful skill execution supports a virtuous circle of growing expertise, confidence and adaptive gains, whereas failures may lead to a vicious circle of negative beliefs and skill degradation (Wells and Matthews, 1994). Such processes may be the key to understanding person–situation interaction.

A final comment is that the primary concern is with immediate adaptation to the environment, the benefits and costs to the individual of the behaviors linked to personality traits. Such an analysis does not require any position on the respective roles of genes and environment as distal influences on adaptive behaviors. The heritability of traits begs the question of how they relate to adaptation in the Darwinian sense. Evolutionary analyses of personality are beyond the scope of this chapter, but they may well inform understanding of the proximal adaptive behaviors that are the current concern.

A COGNITIVE SCIENCE FRAMEWORK

Here, I set out a cognitive science framework that will provide a more formal basis for understanding and differentiating the various expressions of personality traits (Matthews, 2000). According to the 'classical theory' of cognitive science (Pylyshyn, 1999), cognitive phenomena are open to three complementary types of explanation (see Figure 3.1).

The first is the *biological* level, which refers to the neural 'hardware' supporting processing. Individual differences in performance might reflect variation in brain functioning, as proposed by biological personality theories (Corr, 2004). The second level of explanation is described by Pylyshyn (1999) as the *symbolic* level, referring to the computational operations affording symbolic processing, supported by facilities for real-time processing such as virtual memory space and communication channels. Individual differences in the parameters of this cognitive architecture may mediate personality effects on performance. The third level of explanation, the *semantic* level, refers to the personal meaning of the otherwise arbitrary processing codes. It is also called the *knowledge* level, because it refers to the person's knowledge of how to obtain personal goals. It explains personality on the basis of intentions, motivations and strategies for goal attainment.

The relationship between levels is a subject of ongoing debate, especially whether the more abstracted levels may be reduced to neurological explanations. There are various positions, including a 'hard reductionism' that states that the neurological level should assume primacy, and Pylyshyn's (1999) view that the levels are strongly autonomous from one another. I favor an explanatory pluralism that allows for alternate explanations of equal validity, coupled with efforts at co-evolution of theories at different levels to allow for some partial integration of concepts (Matthews, 2000). It is often useful to look to the interfaces between levels for

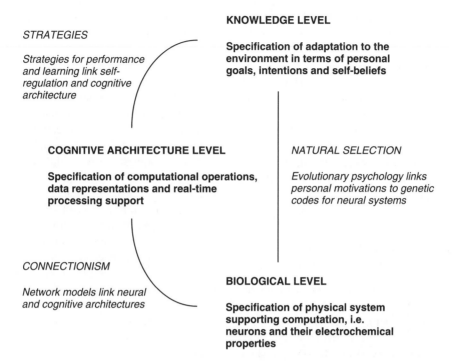

STRATEGIES

Strategies for performance and learning link self-regulation and cognitive architecture

KNOWLEDGE LEVEL

Specification of adaptation to the environment in terms of personal goals, intentions and self-beliefs

COGNITIVE ARCHITECTURE LEVEL

Specification of computational operations, data representations and real-time processing support

NATURAL SELECTION

Evolutionary psychology links personal motivations to genetic codes for neural systems

CONNECTIONISM

Network models link neural and cognitive architectures

BIOLOGICAL LEVEL

Specification of physical system supporting computation, i.e. neurons and their electrochemical properties

Figure 3.1   Levels of explanation from cognitive science for personality research

integrative explanations. Connectionist, neural net models (e.g. Matthews and Harley, 1993; Siegle and Hasselmo, 2002) provide a powerful means for integrating cognitive and biological explanations. At the interface of symbol-processing and knowledge levels, strategy choice is important for explaining features of performance such as speed–accuracy tradeoff. Such explanations require both a specification of the processing supporting the strategy (symbol-processing) and the self-knowledge that guides strategy choice (values attached to speed vs. accuracy). Figure 3.1 also suggests that we may complete the circle by placing evolutionary explanations at the interface of knowledge and biological explanations. The meaning the brain infers (explicitly or implicitly) from biologically significant stimuli is shaped by natural selection.

MULTIPLE LEVELS OF PATTERNING

In this section, I will draw out the implications of using multiple levels of explanation to understand the cognitive correlates of personality. I will review standard information-processing approaches, and then discuss the need to complement this perspective with those from neurobiological and knowledge levels.

Delineating the cognitive patterning approach of a stressor or trait requires a systematic investigation of tasks chosen to instantiate key information-processing mechanisms (Hockey, 1984). The exercise is only as good as the cognitive psychology harnessed for the purpose, and there are some methodological hazards. In particular, molar indices such as reaction times may reflect a variety of underlying processes, depending on task characteristics. (Cognitive psychology refers this issue as the identifiability problem – quite different models may give an equally good account of the same data.) Thus, information-processing analyses of personality effects should be seen as somewhat provisional, and it is essential to relate observed performance effects to theory-driven computational models. Next, I will summarize previous reviews (Matthews, 1997, 2004; Matthews et al., 2003) of performance data relating to extraversion and neuroticism/anxiety on this basis.

Cognitive patterning of extraversion–introversion

Extraversion–introversion research highlights some of the complexities of seeking to relate traits to information processing. Consistent with the cognitive approach (Hockey, 1984) extraversion–introversion differences show *task-dependence,* as shown in the outline cognitive patterning shown in Table 3.1.

(It is a convenient fiction to treat extraversion and introversion as discrete categories; the trait is continuous.) Extraverts show superiority in some tasks but perform poorly relative to introverts on others. Often, replicating these effects requires careful attention to task parameters; for example, Szymura and Necka (1998) replicated earlier findings of superior divided attention in extraverts only at the highest of several difficulty levels that they used. Some performance effects are qualitative in nature, such as the lower response criterion associated with extraversion in some studies. Extraversion may also interact with stimulus valence, so that processing of positive material is enhanced (Zelenski and Larsen, 2002), but such bias effects are better understood for anxiety, as discussed shortly. Some performance indices, including choice reaction time, show no consistent association with the trait across studies.

Table 3.1 sets out molar performance findings that may reflect various

Table 3.1   Outline cognitive patterning for extraversion–introversion

Cognitive function	Sample task	Result
Extravert superiority		
Divided attention	Memory search for single or multiple targets	Extraverts faster in dual-task versions conditions
Short-term memory	Free recall of video sequences	Extraverts better at immediate recall
Resisting distraction	Performing verbal tasks with background music	Extraverts less distracted by extraneous noise
Retrieval from semantic memory	Retrieval of semantic category instances	Extraverts faster at retrieving low dominance ('unusual') instances
Speed of movement	Choice reaction time?	Extraverts show faster response execution
Speech production	Conversation in a second language	Extraverts more fluent in speech production
Introvert superiority		
Visual vigilance	Detecting line signal	Introverts show higher detection rate
Long-term memory	Paired-associate learning	Introverts better at long-term recall
Problem solving	Problem-solving tasks requiring insight	Introverts faster and more accurate; extraverts finish impulsively
Qualitative performance differences		
Vigilance	Detection of brighter target stimulus	Extraverts adopt a lower response criterion
Response to stress and arousal	Serial choice reaction time	Extraverts are faster when high in arousal; introverts are faster when low in arousal (also depends on time of day)

Note. References for studies may be found in Matthews et al. (2003).

information-processing mechanisms. Identifying which specific components of the architecture are responsible for observed effects is difficult, and requires explicit hypothesis testing. For example, the Humphreys and Revelle (1984) theory proposes that extraverts, due to low arousal, should have depleted resources for sustained attention, contributing to poorer vigilance. Introvert superiority should then be most pronounced on higher workload tasks. This prediction was not confirmed in several studies (e.g. Matthews et al., 1990). Instead, extraversion tended to be detrimental to performance poorly on long-duration tasks placing high demands on visual perception, but the trait tended to facilitate performance on shorter duration tasks requiring symbolic processing. In a sense, the relationship between extraversion and vigilance was incidental to two different process correlates (Matthews, 1997). The Humphreys and Revelle (1984) theory successfully predicted facilitative effects of energetic arousal states in these studies; contrary to the theory, extraversion effects were not mediated by individual differences in arousal.

Extraversion effects are frequently *context-dependent*; the impact of the trait varies dramatically with factors such as external stressors. As Eysenck (1981), Revelle et al. (1980) and others showed, extraversion (and impulsivity) interacts systematically with level of arousal and time of day, across a range of tasks. This 'modal' extraversion × arousal interaction also illustrates the importance of probing underlying processing mechanisms with care. Within Eysenck's (1967) theory, the benefits of high arousal for extraverts were seen as an expression of the general efficiency of the cortex (see Matthews, 1992, for a refutation of conventional arousal theory). Humphreys and Revelle's (1984) analysis of resource utilization predicts that the modal interaction should affect only tasks that required both attentional and Short Term Memory resources, such as (in their formulation) solving intelligence test items. A series of

studies (e.g. Matthews et al., 1989, 1990) tested for interactive effects of extraversion and self-report arousal, as a more direct means for investigating arousal than using external stressors, whose effects may be complex. These studies failed to confirm that the interaction was found only for resource-limited tasks. In fact, *undemanding* tasks requiring rather routine encoding processes, such as detecting a single easily perceived letter stimulus, are most sensitive (Matthews, 1997). Similar findings are obtained when arousal is assessed using the electroencephalograph (EEG), rather than via self-report (Matthews and Amelang, 1993).

To investigate the mechanism for extraversion × arousal interactions, several studies (e.g. Matthews and Harley, 1993) investigated semantic priming in lexical decision. Recognition of a letter string as being a word rather than a non-word is speeded up by prior presentation of a semantically related prime. Depending on task parameters, there are multiple processes that contribute to priming effects, including an automatic spreading of activation between linked network units, expectancy-driven search and checking of decisions at a relatively late stage of processing. The studies showed that the extraversion effect could be switched on or off according to the choice of task parameters, data which helped to pinpoint the effect as dependent on automatic spreading activation, rather than a top-down search (Matthews, 1997).

Matthews and Harley (1993) proposed an 'activation-sensitization' hypothesis for this particular extraversion effect. Increasing cortical arousal tends to facilitate spreading activation in extraverts but inhibits activation within the semantic net in introverts. Matthews and Harley (1993) tested a connectionist model based on existing models of semantic priming, in which performance was controlled by various quantitative parameters of the network. Simulations showed that only one parameter – level of random noise – could be varied so as to produce outputs corresponding to the observed data, suggesting specific mechanism for the personality effect.

Whether or not the hypothesis is correct, the research shows how we can take a broad category of personality effects (extraversion × arousal interactions), and through systematic experimentation and simulation isolate a specific processing component that may be responsible. We have a well-specified cognitive mini-theory – but one that only explains a single feature of the cognitive patterning shown in Table 3.1.

Cognitive patterning of neuroticism/trait anxiety

A similar exercise may be performed for neuroticism and trait anxiety. (Here, I will not try to distinguish these traits, or distinguish trait from state anxiety effects.) Table 3.2 sketches some of the more reliable empirical findings (see Matthews et al., 2003;

Matthews, 2004). Effects of anxiety can be divided into those that concern overall efficiency of performance and those relating to bias in processing threat stimuli. Anxiety impairs performance of various demanding, high workload tasks, including both purely attentional tasks with no STM load and tasks whose mental load derives mainly from working memory. Anxiety also interacts with stress factors in disrupting performance, including evaluative stress (see Eysenck et al., in press), and cognitive stress factors such as an abrupt transition in workload (Cox-Fuenzalida et al., 2004). Anxiety also has motivational effects, including application of compensatory effort (Eysenck et al., in press), which may explain those instances where anxiety *enhances* performance of easy tasks (Zeidner, 1998).

Studies of cognitive bias (e.g. Mathews, 2004) suggest anxiety relates to involuntary

Table 3.2   Outline cognitive patterning for anxiety/neuroticism

Cognitive function	Sample task	Result
Processing efficiency effects		
Divided attention	Concurrent math and verbal memory	Anxiety leads to impairment in dual-task performance (especially on secondary tasks)
Working memory	Mental transformation of letter sequences	Anxiety-related impairment increases with memory load
Resisting distraction	Comprehending text with background speech	Anxiety relates to distraction by irrelevant speech
Verbal reasoning	Verifying accuracy of sentences	Anxiety relates to slower response time
Visual vigilance	Detecting line signal	Anxiety relates to lower detection rate
Cognitive bias effects		
Selective attention (single channel)	Emotional Stroop	Anxiety subjects are slow to name ink colors of threat words
Selective attention (multiple channel)	'Dot-probe' visual attention task	Anxious subjects respond more quickly to probe presented at location of threat
Disengagement from threat	Spatial orienting to cued and uncued locations	Anxious subjects are slow to disengage attention from a threatening cue
Semantic processing	Interpreting spoken homophones: e.g. 'die' vs. 'dye'	Anxious subjects biased towards selecting threatening interpretation
Predictive inference	Naming a word presented in a threatening or non-threatening context	Anxiety facilitates naming of threat words in threatening context
Qualitative performance differences		
Response to evaluative stress	Performance with evaluative instructions	Anxiety relates to performance impairment when evaluated
Memory strategies	Free recall of word lists	Anxiety relates to reduced strategic reorganization of words

Note. References for studies may be found in Matthews et al. (2003).

direction of selective attention towards sources of threat stimuli. Tasks used include the emotional Stroop – naming the ink colors of threatening and neutral words – and the dot-probe task that indicates how attention is allocated to threat and non-threat screen locations. Bias also occurs in later processing stages of assigning meaning to stimuli, such as making rapid predictive inferences of threat during reading (Calvo and Castillo, 2001).

Again, it is likely that anxiety/neuroticism biases multiple processes, and the specific processes supporting the observed findings are open to debate. Performance impairment in anxiety is broadly explained by diversion of attentional resources onto processing self-referent thoughts and preoccupations as the person worries (Zeidner, 1998). Eysenck et al. (in press) point out that attention allocation depends on multiple, executive processes, so that the resource explanation lacks precision. They propose that anxiety relates specifically to impairments in shifting attention between tasks and in inhibition of distracting stimuli.

Bias effects are also open to different interpretations. A central issue is whether bias relates to 'automatic' encoding processes or voluntary strategic control of attention (see reviews by Mathews, 2004; Matthews and Wells, 2000). Bias may sometimes be unconscious, demonstrated in studies of attention in which stimuli are masked to the point where they cannot be consciously perceived. However, unconscious processing is not entirely automatic, in that it remains sensitive to expectancies and efforts at executive control. There is considerable evidence that anxiety-related biases are moderated by 'top-down' influences of this kind (Matthews and Wells, 2000; Wells and Matthews, 1994). Again, explicit modeling of the processes is essential.

Matthews and Harley (1996) used a connectionist architecture capable of learning across trials to model bias on the emotional Stroop. Including network units representing top-down 'search for threat' as an explicit task simulated some major features of anxiety-related bias on the emotional Stroop. By contrast, the network was able to learn to compensate for automatic biases. The correspondence between the backpropagation network used by Matthews and Harley and the true cognitive architecture is open to question. However, the study shows how the broad mechanism proposed by Matthews and Wells (2000) – strategic search for threat – can be implemented within a formal computational model, as another instance of a cognitive mini-theory.

It is likely that multiple processes contribute to bias. Tasks typically used to index selective attention bias – emotional Stroop and dot-probe – are uncorrelated, implying they index different selective processes (Asmundson et al., 2005). Mathews and Mackintosh (1998) pointed out that the Matthews and Harley (1996) network model may unduly neglect evidence for automatic bias. They developed a two-process model in which anxiety may influence both an automatic threat evaluation system that modulates the parallel processing of multiple stimulus inputs and effortful control of stimulus priorities. Recent artificial intelligence (AI) work has also explored how anxiety may bias processing within a more elaborated architecture including multiple modules ranging from sensory preprocessing through more 'central' processes such as expectation generation to selecting goals and actions (Hudlicka, 2004). The simulation developed by Hudlicka (2004) shows how high-level biases in decision-making in dangerous environments may reflect the accumulation and interaction of multiple independent component biases.

Contribution of information-processing models

Information-processing analyses provide a metaphor for personality. Each person is 'tuned' a little differently across the range of processing components that make up the cognitive architecture (cf. Ortony et al., 2005). Plausibly, these sets of biases feed forward into more general personality attributes. Biases towards perceiving stimuli as threatening, diverting attention towards potential threats and retrieving unpleasant memories, may well serve to construct an anxious personality. To the extent that biases are unconscious, people inhabit different subjective worlds according to personality.

Like any metaphor, there are both advantages and limitations of information-processing models. On the positive side, we cannot build a science of personality and cognition without a detailed specification of component processes underpinning traits that influence performance and behavior. This approach is also highly compatible with the modularity evidenced by contemporary neuroscience. However, some expressions of personality cannot be readily linked to parameters of the cognitive architecture. Looking down a level from the architecture, we may discern non-symbolic neurological effects; looking up may reveal strategy choices requiring a knowledge-level analysis of goals and personal meanings. In the next section, I will look at how the additional levels of explanation are required to complement the perspective from cognitive architecture.

THE BIOLOGICAL LEVEL: TOWARDS A COGNITIVE NEUROSCIENCE OF PERSONALITY

There are compelling reasons for developing psychobiological theories of personality, including evolutionary continuity between humans and other mammals, the functional importance of brain reward and punishment systems, and the availability of sophisticated animal models. Nevertheless, there are some tensions between biological theory and information-processing models. Traditionally, biological theorists such as Hans Eysenck and Jeffrey Gray assumed that 'personality genes' coded for a small number of brain properties associated with broad arousal and

motivation systems, with far-reaching effects on behavior (see Corr, 2004; Pickering and Corr, Vol. 1).

A detailed critique of these theories is beyond the present scope (see Matthews and Gilliland, 1999). However, two aspects of the evidence are especially challenging to current biological theory. First, traits have multiple psychophysiological correlates relating to all levels of the central nervous system from brainstem to cortex, which cannot necessarily be reduced to only one or two neural mechanisms; traits are not neatly localized. Zuckerman (1991) criticizes the assumption of *isomorphism* between traits and brain systems made by both the Eysenck and Gray theories; traits may emerge from multiple brain systems. The psychophysiological evidence implies at least two distinct sets of correlates of extraversion, one set relating to sensitivity to stimulation ('reticulocortical E'), and a further set relating to activity of brain reward systems ('dopaminergic E'; Matthews and Gilliland, 1999). N may relate both to subcortical structures (Corr, 2004) and to cortically mediated modulation of motivation (Derryberry and Reed, 1997). Similarly, molecular genetic studies of personality suggest that each individual gene explains only a small part of the variance in the trait (Munafo et al., 2003).

Second, traditional biological theories are not very effective in predicting behavioral correlates of traits (Matthews and Gilliland, 1999). The Eysenck and Gray theories predict that trait effects should be moderated by level of stimulation and by presence of motivational signals respectively, but the evidence from performance studies is very mixed. Neither theory provides a strong basis for predicting the cognitive patterning of personality effects; that is, their dependence on the information-processing demands of the task. Anxiety research shows how traits may be linked to specific cortical systems. Using an established model of the neuroscience of attention, Derryberry and Reed (1997, 2002) related anxiety to specific attentional functions based on known neural circuits, such as difficulties disengaging attention from threat (linked to parietal cortex) and narrowing of attention (linked to left cingulate). This emerging cognitive neuroscience may be better suited to explaining the patterning of information processing than existing psychobiological theories.

Thus, brain hardware and cognitive software define partially overlapping sets of component processes. Traits are distributed across multiple brain systems that do not necessarily map onto cognitive functions in any simple way. Non-specific arousal and motivation systems may indeed provide influence behaviors, such as startle response and conditioning, which are not mediated by symbolic processing (Corr, 2004). Cognitive neuroscience offers the exciting prospect that, increasingly, complementary hardware and software explanations may be developed for information-processing correlates of personality. However, some emergent cognitive processes such as attentional resource utilization may be sufficiently difficult to map onto specific neural systems that the cognitive architecture will remain the primary basis for explanation and prediction.

THE KNOWLEDGE LEVEL AND SOCIAL COGNITION

Knowledge level explanations refer to the person's intentions, and their beliefs about how personal goals may be attained. For example, an individual's social behavior may be understood with reference to their social motivations, such as the need for affiliation, and the person's beliefs about which situations afford achievable opportunities for affiliation. Critical to such explanations is the meaning of the situation for the person. Knowledge-based explanation may also be a requisite for understanding inter-relationships between cognition, motivation and emotion. Examples are Bandura's (1997) work on self-efficacy, social learning and motivation, and Lazarus' (1999) transactional theory that

relates emotions to the meaning the person derives from events ('core relational themes'), supported by appraisals and efforts at coping. Lazarus also emphasizes dynamic person–situation interaction as the consequence of coping feeding back into changing appraisals of the situation.

Traditionally, such explanations were neglected by researchers working within a 'natural science' perspective. Social psychological approaches (see Cervone, Vol. 1) have often been seen as fundamentally incompatible with trait theory, but in recent years there have been signs of a partial rapprochement (Matthews et al., 2003). A critical insight is that the person's sense of self and identity may be supported by stable cognitive structures that organize key self-beliefs, such as the self-schema. Stable self-knowledge may plausibly influence traits; stable beliefs in one's social effectiveness may support extraversion and beliefs in personal vulnerability may contribute to neuroticism (Matthews et al., 2000). Schemas control how people interpret the world and their own place in it, producing wide-ranging consequences for social functioning and well-being (Caprara and Cervone, 2000). Furthermore, because situational factors influence whether items of self-knowledge are activated and accessible, schema theory provides a path towards understanding person–situation interaction.

Personality traits are readily found to be associated with knowledge-level constructs, including self-beliefs, appraisal and coping. Indeed, effect sizes often exceed those found with objective measures of information processing. Space limitations prevent adequate discussion of the data; see Matthews et al. (2000, 2003) for more detailed reviews. There are systematic differences between extraverts and introverts in their perceptions of themselves as social beings, in their appraisals of demanding events and in their preferred means of coping. Similarly, neuroticism/anxiety is characterized by a cluster of self-referent cognitions that refer to a sense of personal vulnerability and restricted personal control over potential hazards.

Given that theory separates these various correlates of traits – appraisal and coping are functionally distinct, for example (Lazarus, 1999) – traits are again distributed over multiple aspects of (social) cognition.

On the face of it, the knowledge-level perspective on personality is compatible with information-processing approaches. Developing cognitive architectures for self-regulation (e.g. Matthews and Wells, 2000; Wells and Matthews, 1994) should allow traits to be linked to specific parameters of those architectures, or to the contents of memory that influence memory. Wells and Matthews (1994) link neuroticism both to negative self-beliefs (represented within a stable schema) and to biases in attentional processes that prioritize processing and recycling of negative, self-referent information.

We should not celebrate the marriage of personality traits to social-cognitive theory prematurely. The key theorists in this area (e.g. Bandura, 1997; Mischel, 2004; Cervone et al., 2006) are at pains to point out some fundamental differences in assumptions. Social-cognitive theory is typically idiographic rather than nomothetic; Cervone et al. (2006) emphasize the importance of within-person analyses of personality structure and process variables. They state that constructs based on between-person analyses, such as the five-factor model (FFM), may not have much relevance to the cognition and behavior of individuals. Space limits further discussion of this important issue; my position is that traits correspond to emergent qualities of multiple social-cognitive processes, although they are not necessarily evident in fine-grained analyses of the individual. In addition, much social-cognitive theory is concerned with function rather than process; Cervone et al. (2006) point out that Bandura's account of self-regulation describes basic capabilities such as self-observation without reference to any particular mechanism for accomplishing the function. By contrast, the computational description of mechanisms is central to information-processing accounts. The functional accounts

provided by social-cognitive theory may redress some limitations of the information-processing metaphor noted by Caprara and Cervone (2000), including neglect of the tight connection of cognitive and affective processes, and the importance of self-directed agency in personality.

The information-processing perspective offers some complementary criticisms of typical social-cognitive theories. The prediction of individual differences in behavior often requires attention to mechanisms as well as to functions, as demonstrated by the 'cognitive patterning' data. Methodologically, social-cognitive research is over-reliant on verbal reports of beliefs and other cognitions. Research on, for example, chronometric studies of the self-schema and implicit, unconscious processing partially addresses this concern. Social-cognitive theory shares the concern of the cognitive psychologist in developing fine-grained models of mental processes (e.g. Cervone, 2004; Mischel, 2004; Shoda, Vol. 2), but typically lacks the computational models needed to predict performance data. Thus, information processing and social-cognitive models overlap, but only partially. Research on strategies, as constructs bridging the divide between knowledge and cognitive-architectural levels, may well inform both modes of understanding personality.

THE COGNITIVE-ADAPTIVE THEORY OF PERSONALITY TRAITS

At this point, the reader may ask for the real personality traits to stand up. Traits appear to be bewilderingly complex constructs that are distributed both within and between levels of explanation. No single level captures all the facets of the major traits, and even within levels, each trait relates to multiple independent processes and structures. Traits relate to multiple brain systems (both subcortical and cortical), to multiple elementary processing components (the cognitive patterning) and to multiple self-referent beliefs, social motivations and preferred strategies for attaining personal goals (Matthews and Gilliland, 1999; Matthews et al., 2000). Although the trio of levels provided by cognitive science (Pylyshyn, 1999) provides an organized and descriptively rich account of traits, it brings us no closer to understanding how the different facets of traits are inter-related, and to bringing unity and coherence to the disparate trait expressions.

Understanding trait coherence requires reference to the third major principle of cognitive-adaptive theory – that traits should be understood in relation to individual differences to adaptation. In this section, I will aim to pull the different threads of the argument together, by proposing that traits are matched to key environmental challenges. The interplay of genes and environment in childhood confers upon the adult a fairly stable set of biases in neuropsychological and cognitive functioning (Zeidner et al., 2003). It is these 'legacy' biases that are typically uncovered in laboratory studies of psychophysiology and information processing. However, the adaptive significance of these biases is typically indirect (except, perhaps, at the extreme of abnormal personality) in facilitating or hindering skill acquisition. Adaptation is mainly dependent upon acquired explicit and implicit skills geared to specific contexts, as described by skill theories (e.g. Ericsson and Charness, 1994). Skills cover not just overt control of behavior, but also skills for interpreting and regulating self-referent cognitions and emotions (Wells and Matthews, 1994).

Personality traits thus come to be associated with distinctive skill sets that support adaptation to specific environments. In parallel with acquiring skills, people also acquire self-knowledge that relates to those skills (Matthews, 1999). Acquiring actual social skills, such as being able to persuade other people to agree with one's opinions, occurs in tandem with acquiring confidence in one's social self-efficacy, and motivations to influence others. It is likely that actual skill and self-beliefs correlate, although subjective belief and objective reality may diverge, sharply in the case of mental disorder.

In the adult, personality dynamics are supported by the interplay of the *adaptive triangle* (Matthews et al., 2002). Objective skill and behavioral competence interact with context-relevant self-knowledge, and the adaptive outcome. Competence, self-confidence and positive outcomes will tend to be mutually reinforcing. Similarly, cycles of maladaptation may develop in which actual skill deficits, lack of self-confidence and unsuccessful outcomes are mutually reinforcing over time. Virtuous and vicious circles are extreme cases; more often all three vertices of the triangle include both adaptive and maladaptive elements so a variety of dynamic patterns may develop for example persevering with a task despite self-doubt, engaging with the task half-heartedly or seeking challenging situations in order to remedy deficiencies in skill. Also, outcomes typically are not universally beneficial or harmful; adaptive outcomes of real-life encounters are often a mixed bag of gains and costs that unfold over differing time periods (Zeidner and Saklofske, 1995).

Cognitive-adaptive theory proposes that traits correspond to differing modes of adaptation to the major, universal challenges of human life. The poles of each dimension represent adaptive specializations supporting contrary modes of adaptation to the challenge concerned. In the sections that follow, I will propose that extraversion and introversion correspond to adaptations for social overload and underload, respectively. Each type of adaptation requires specialized cognitive skills for coping with potentially overwhelming social information, and for perseverance without social support, respectively. Neuroticism represents the person's choice of strategy for adapting to threat. The high N person seeks to anticipate and pre-empt threat through maintaining awareness of danger, and supporting escape and avoidance strategies, whereas the low N person prefers to await the onset of threat and cope with it more directly. Overall, traits are adaptively neutral. The person at the extreme will find some environments where they flourish, and others with which their skills are not compatible. Those in the middle of the range are generalists that function adequately but not outstandingly in multiple environments.

Extraversion–introversion

Extraversion–introversion relates to a complex package of biases in neurological functioning, information processing and self-referent knowledge-level cognitions. Table 3.1 suggests some general cognitive themes, including: (1) a facility with verbal and symbolic material in relation to memory, attention and speech production; (2) temporal attributes of performance including behavioral impulsivity; and (3) handling arousing and stimulating environments. These separate processing characteristics, together with neurological arousal tolerance and reward sensitivity, provide a platform for developing skills for handling environments that are characterized by potential social

overload (Matthews, 1999). Extraverts famously enjoy lively parties; a social context which provides both affordances and threats. Success requires a skill set including: conversation skills, to impress and influence others; speed of response, to dominate a conversation and speak before others; and stress management skills, to maintain focus within a multitude of voices, and to handle any criticism or competition that social visibility may attract. The cognitive attributes of temperament are *invested* in contextualized skill acquisition (Zeidner et al., 2003). The child will more readily learn effective conversation skills to the extent that he or she has good divided attention, verbal STM, fluent speech production and tolerance of the stress and arousal likely to ensue in practicing those skills on unsympathetic peers and adults.

In the adult extravert, the component biases co-exist with learnt skills, social self-confidence and a history of mostly successful social outcomes. Figure 3.2 outlines a possible adaptive triangle for extraversion–introversion.

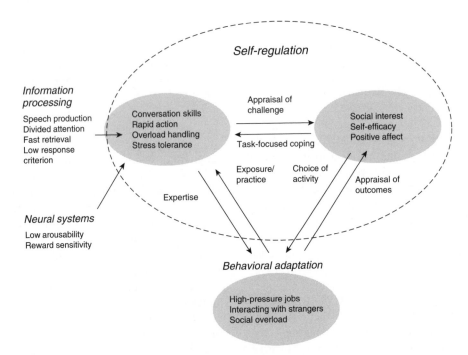

Figure 3.2   A cognitive-adaptive model of extraversion

Observational studies confirm that extraversion relate to social skills, especially verbal rather than non-verbal skills (Berry and Sherman Hansen, 2000). The role of cognitive factors was demonstrated by Lieberman and Rosenthal (2001). Extraversion related to better decoding skills only when task load was high, in a multi-tasking paradigm. These authors also reported data from a working memory task suggesting that extraversion became increasingly related to superior executive function with increasing task loads. Compared with introverts, extraverts perform better at industrial tasks requiring teamwork (Morgeson et al., 2005), manage verbal overload in applied settings more effectively (Matthews, 1999), and handle the novelty of job training better (e.g. Dean et al., 2006). Congruent with these skills are the knowledge-level correlates of extraversion including high self-efficacy, a greater likelihood of appraising situations as challenging, and employing direct, task-focused coping strategies (Matthews et al., 2000). Extraversion also correlates with elements of 'emotional intelligence' that relate to self-rated social skill and social self-confidence (Saklofske et al., 2003).

Skill and social self-confidence work together in supporting success in more demanding social environments such as high-pressure jobs and interacting with strangers. In such situations, the dynamic process may support a virtuous circle – indeed, two contra-rotating virtuous circles, as shown in Figure 3.2. Going clockwise around the triangle, actual social skills build positive self-beliefs and social self-efficacy, which encourages more engagement with socially demanding situations, which leads to greater exposure and opportunities to refine objective skill. Counterclockwise, social expertise generates more actual social success, which in turn leads to more positive outcome expectancies, increasing the likelihood and effectiveness of employing skills as strategies for coping with social pressures.

There is a social downside to extraversion also, including impulsivity, leading to greater accident involvement, promiscuity and narcissism (Matthews et al., 2002), and vulnerability to over-confidence during performance (Schaefer et al., 2004). At the other pole of the dimension, introversion comes with a different package of characteristic skills. Introverts' abilities to sustain attention in monotonous environments, to reflect productively during problem solving and to tolerate the stress of boredom support skills for sustaining work activities in the absence of immediate reward or help from others. Thus, scientists and writers tend to be more introverted than the average person (Matthews et al., 2003).

Neuroticism/anxiety

The conventional wisdom is that neuroticism reflects a maladaptive excess of negative emotionality. Cognitive-adaptive theory offers a different perspective. Negative affectivity is adaptive for anticipating threats that are not salient, but it is maladaptive for directly coping with threat. Figure 3.3 shows the adaptive triangle for anxiety. The neural and cognitive components intrinsic to anxiety build skills for recognition of threat and cautious, systematic decision-making. It is emphasized that threat detection is often an acquired skill rather than an innate sensitivity. Neuroticism relates especially to ego threat or social threat, and such threats differ in important ways from the spiders and snakes often treated as prototypical of threat in the anxiety literature. As Matthews (2004) discusses, social threats typically develop over extended time periods, often from someone with whom the person needs to maintain a functional relationship, such as a co-worker or family member. Furthermore, social threat is often complex and ambiguous, so that careful analysis of the situation and choice of coping strategy is needed.

In environments in which threats are disguised, the high N person remains vigilant and motivated to work to forestall potential harm (Matthews, 2004). The low N person is

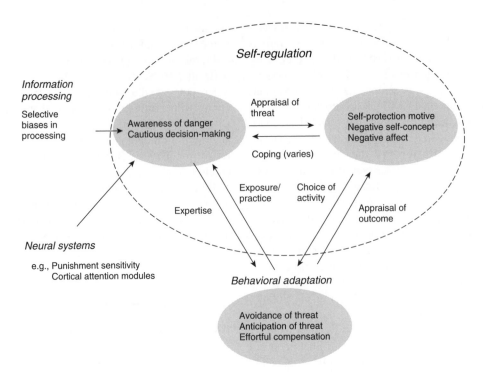

Figure 3.3   A cognitive-adaptive model of neuroticism / anxiety

vulnerable to complacency and lack of preparation. Threat detection skills interact with congruent elements of self-knowledge focused on the theme of personal vulnerability, leading to behavioral adaptation via avoidance of direct threat and assigning effort to compensatory strategies. Several lines of evidence support this analysis (see Matthews, 1999, 2004), including laboratory data showing that anxiety is linked to compensatory effort (Eysenck et al., in press). Negative affect may also encourage more thorough, systematic analysis in social-cognitive laboratory tasks (Forgas, 1995). In organizational settings, neuroticism relates to greater effort and sustained performance (Smillie et al., 2006). Negative affectivity relates to greater awareness of possible health problems and willingness to engage in adaptive, care-seeking behaviors such as visiting the doctor (Mayne, 1999).

The disadvantages of high N in coping with immediate stressors and pressures are well known and need little explication. Numerous studies of stress (see Matthews et al., 2003) show that neuroticism relates to overestimation of threats and underestimation of personal coping and personal agency, and to ineffective forms of emotion-focused coping such as self-criticism. Maladaptive response to stress is also fed by meta-cognitions that perpetuate awareness of negative self-beliefs, leading to perserverative and unproductive worry (Wells and Matthews, 1994). In the interpersonal realm, neuroticism appears to be linked to hostile appraisals of others, and 'reactive' aggression in the form of lashing out at others verbally. Such reactions to interpersonal stressors are damaging, and neuroticism relates to deteriorating relationship quality (Bouchard and Arseneault, 2005). The high N person is also vulnerable to dysfunctional cycles of person–situation interaction with others in stressful environments, such as social avoidance that leads to skill degradation and strengthening of overly negative self-beliefs (Wells and Matthews, 1994).

FURTHER THEORETICAL ISSUES

The previous section addressed the main purpose of this chapter, to link performance-based data on traits and information processing to a more general personality model. However, the cognitive-adaptive theory also has a number of further implications for personality theory, which I will here sketch very briefly (see also Matthews, 1997, 2000, 2004; Matthews and Zeidner, 2004; Zeidner and Matthews, 2000).

The five-factor model (FFM)

Strong claims have been made for the FFM as the defining paradigm for trait psychology (McCrae and Costa, 1997). Its merits are well known and need no defense here. The cognitive-adaptive model illuminates the adaptive basis for all five traits, although more research is needed on the elements necessary for an adaptive analysis of the traits additional to E and N; that is, their neurology, information-processing correlates, characteristic skills and self-knowledge. *Conscientiousness* pits sustained, systematic effort against opportunism. The trait is adaptive in social settings that reward sustained investment of effort, such as many organizational and educational environments. Low conscientiousness is matched to unstructured environments affording more opportunities for immediate gratification than for long-term planning, such as living in deprived conditions with poor future prospects. *Agreeableness* describes preferences for cooperation or competition as a strategy for adapting to social situations, supported, for example, by differing cognitive biases in whether others are appraised as helpful or antagonistic. *Openness* refers to the choice between relying on self-directed analysis of

the environment, as opposed to relying on the pragmatic, time-tested rules reflecting traditional wisdom (see Matthews et al., 2002, 2003, for further discussion).

Cognitive-adaptive theory also offers insights on how fundamental the FFM truly is. Goldberg (1990) links the Big Five to five universal challenges – power (E), emotion (N), work (C), love (A) and intellect (O). Extraversion is broadly universal because socially demanding situations calling for extraverted qualities are found in all cultures. Cross-cultural research has tended to provide a more nuanced picture (e.g. Bond, 2000) within which FFM traits identified in non-Western cultures match approximately but imperfectly the canonical Five. The cognitive-adaptive model implies that no truly universal trait model will be found, because social adaptation, while constrained by some universal human nature, remains culturally influenced. However, the skill sets required for establishing influence over others will vary, so that the elements of the adaptive triangle will possess their own local flavor within each culture. We will never have a 'periodic table of the elements' for personality, but rather a set of well-defined prototypes or schemas that play out somewhat differently in differing sociocultural environments. Culture-specific social challenges, such as the importance of honoring parents and maintaining social harmony in China, also generate culture-specific traits related to 'Chinese tradition' (Bond, 2000).

Contextualized traits

Traits linked to specific contexts are often the most predictive of consequential outcomes: compare trait anxiety with general anxiety, and work self-efficacy with general self-efficacy. Cognitive-adaptive theory informs their relationship to general personality models. Traits such as the FFM emerge as general because the situational challenges matched to the traits are broadly applicable. Adapting to potential threat, for example, is necessary in work, family and leisure contexts. More bounded threats such as test anxiety correspond to general anxiety in drawing in similar but context-specific cognitions and performance impairments into the dynamic adaptive process (Zeidner, 1998; Zeidner and Matthews, 2005).

In other domains, the environment itself places constraints on adaptation that correspondingly alter the nature of traits. For example, Matthews (2002) derived five factors of personality in the vehicle-driving context that only loosely correspond to the Big Five. Differences reflect the particular nature of the driving task. Driving is similar to life in general in being potentially threatening, and indeed a dislike-of-driving factor emerges that represents negative affectivity. Drivers high in this trait are more cautious in driving style (adaptive) but also more prone to worry under stress (maladaptive). However, social interactions in driving are very limited, and slanted towards aggression and confrontation as a means of coping with congestion. Thus, aggressiveness appears as a central trait, not (low) agreeableness. Likewise, sensation seeking, as also afforded by the driving environment, takes precedence over extraversion. The traits reflect the unique challenges of the vehicle-driving environment

Personality dynamics

The theory states that personality is not intrinsically a fixed set of biological or cognitive attributes, but emerges from the person–situation interactions described by the adaptive triangle. Nevertheless, it is important to explain trait stability evident over long durations (see Asendorpf, Vol. 1). An important source of stability is the largely fixed set of neurological and information-processing attributes of the trait which will continue to constrain skill acquisition throughout adult life. Another source is the dynamic patterning of interaction. The person with a distinctive set of skills and

self-beliefs will tend to gravitate towards the environments in which those personal attributes are useful, in turn reinforcing skill and self-knowledge. Stability in personality may in part reflect stability in environments generated by these dynamic processes. For example, academics typically create intellectually challenging environments for themselves that are likely to sustain the high levels of openness that contributed to the initial motivation to engage in scholarship and research.

We might also speculate on a more radical, 'ecological' personality theory in which traits escape from the head and reside in part in the surrounding physical and social environment. Such a view would match the folk psychology that we can infer individuals' personality from the state of their desk or the photos on their walls. In addition, the cognitive-adaptive theory is compatible with the evidence for adult personality change (e.g. Srivastava et al., 2003). Neuroticism may change appreciably during the course of mental illness and recovery (De Fruyt et al., 2006); major life disruptions may disrupt the normal stability of the adaptive triangle.

Implicit traits

The unconscious is once again thriving in personality research. Undoubtedly, recent work on objective methods for assessment of unconscious traits is important, and redresses over-reliance on self-report methods (see Schnabel et al., Vol. 2). However, the cognitive-adaptive perspective offers some cautions. It is assumed that traits such as anxiety can be broken down into largely separate, global explicit and implicit factors (e.g. Schmukle and Egloff, 2005). Do people possess largely independent conscious and unconscious personalities? Cognitive-adaptive theory suggests that, for example, both explicit and implicit anxiety traits may be functionally coherent, to the extent that they support the same strategy for managing threat. In addition, some implicit biases may the product of the proceduralization of explicit processes, as specified by theories of skill. The functional significance of specific implicit measures remains to be explored.

Also, it is wrong to equate the standard questionnaire-based scales for the major traits with no more than a conscious awareness of personality. Questionnaire measures of traits have proved to be remarkably successful in predicting (with modest effect sizes) a wide range of unconscious processes, as evidenced by psychophysiological and performance studies. Explicit traits correspond to adaptations supported by both conscious and unconscious processes (although there are legitimate issues relating to method factors in assessment). It is also unclear that implicit tests assess overarching constructs with as much range of application as standard trait measures. For example, performance tasks are sometimes used as implicit measures of anxiety and these tasks do not necessarily inter-correlate (Asmundson et al., 2005). Work on implicit tests is important and innovative, but much has to be done to put these new constructs on a par with established traits.

Personality and emotion

E is commonly identified with positive affectivity and N with negative affectivity. I have argued previously (e.g. Matthews et al., 2000) that this view is simplistic, and somewhat better supported for N than for E. Evidence against the affectivity hypothesis comes from the modest magnitudes of personality correlates of emotion in many controlled laboratory studies (Matthews and Gilliland, 1999), evidence in the variability of the associations across different real-world settings (Brandstätter, 1994), and psychometric evidence that sociability is closer to the core of extraversion than sociability (Ashton et al., 2002). At the same time, reinforcement sensitivity theory (Corr, 2004) together with recent brain-imaging studies (Gray et al., 2005) provide a rationale for treating emotionality as one of the multiple facets of E and N.

In fact, a multi-leveled perspective militates against a defining role of affectivity in personality. Like traits, emotional states integrate neurology, information processing and higher-level cognition, and are difficult to reduce to elementary components (see Matthews and Zeidner, 2004, for an adaptive treatment of states). However, it is reasonable to see the emotional attributes of E and N as supporting the overall adaptations. For example, neurological and cognitive sensitivity to negative affect serves to maintain vigilance for non-salient threats, but it is a liability in stressful situations.

Emotional intelligence

The recently developed construct of EI purports to define an ability that is essential for social adaptation (Mayer et al., 2004). In fact, research on EI has a number of deficiencies (see Matthews et al., 2002, for a critical account), not least the overlap of many published scales with established personality traits. As assessed by questionnaire, EI is mainly stable extraversion with a dash of conscientious and agreeableness. Cognitive-adaptive theory suggests that EI is unlikely to exist as an overarching personality trait in principle (ability-based definitions of EI may be more promising). Matthews et al. (2002) show that the various socialemotional competencies with which EI is typically associated are, in fact, linked to different personality traits, calling into question the unity of 'trait EI'. As we have seen, traits balance difference competencies against one another; agreeable individuals may appear as more emotionally intelligent in settings calling for teamwork and cooperation, but low agreeableness persons are better able to profit from competitive situations. Indeed, there is growing recognition of a 'dark side' to trait EI, related to qualities such as Machiavellianism, narcissism and inflated self-esteem (Matthews et al., 2002).

CONCLUSION

The cognitive-adaptive theory explains one of the more frustrating challenges of personality trait research. Despite the extensive evidence in favor of the predictive validity of traits in real-life settings (McCrae and Costa, 1997), the underlying component processes are elusive at all levels of data: molecular genetics (Munafo et al., 2003), psychophysiology (Matthews and Gilliland, 1999), information-processing (Zeidner and Matthews, 2000) and social behaviors (Caprara and Cervone, 2000). These observations should tell us that the decades-long search for single mechanisms isomorphic with traits has been informative but ultimately unrewarding. Instead, as cognitive-adaptive theory specifies, theory must accommodate the distributed nature of traits, both between and within the three levels of explanation provided by the classical theory of cognitive science. Traits have a coherence that is functional, not structural. A trait resembles a mosaic of separate tiles that must be viewed from a distance for the pattern to be apparent. Traits represent a higher level patterning or organization of many components, and no single component is decisive in shaping personality. The differing perspectives offered by neurology, information-processing studies and social cognition are all of value, but none are capable of providing a full description. Pragmatically, we can choose one or other perspective depending on the immediate research problem, but to understand the unity of traits, we must study how the multiplicity of processing components works together to adapt the person to the environment that matches the trait.

REFERENCES

Ashton, M.C., Lee, K. and Paunonen, S.V. (2002) 'What is the central feature of extraversion?: Social attention versus reward sensitivity', *Journal of Personality and Social Psychology*, 83(1): 245–51.

Asmundson, G.J.G., Wright, K.D. and Hadjistavropoulos, H.D. (2005) 'Hypervigilance and attentional fixedness in chronic musculoskeletal pain: Consistency of findings across modified stroop and dot-probe tasks', *Journal of Pain*, 6(8): 497–506.

Bandura, A. (1997) *Self-Efficacy: The Exercise of Control*. New York: Freeman.

Beck, A.T. (1967) *Depression: Causes and Treatment*. Philadelphia: University of Pennsylvania Press.

Berry, D.S. and Sherman Hansen, J. (2000) 'Personality, nonverbal behavior, and interaction quality in female dyads', *Personality and Social Psychology Bulletin*, 26(3): 278–92.

Bond, M.H. (2000) 'Localizing the imperial outreach: The Big Five and more in Chinese culture', *American Behavioral Scientist*, 44(1): 63–72.

Bouchard, G. and Arseneault, J. (2005) 'Length of union as a moderator of the relationship between personality and dyadic adjustment', *Personality and Individual Differences*, 39(8): 1407–17.

Brandstätter, H. (1994) 'Well-being and motivated person-environment fit: A time-sampling study of emotions', *European Journal of Personality*, 8(2): 75–94.

Calvo, M.G. and Castillo, M.D. (2001) 'Bias in predictive inferences during reading', *Discourse Processes*, 32(32): 43–71.

Caprara, G.V. and Cervone, D. (2000) *Personality: Determinants, Dynamics, and Potentials*. New York: Cambridge University Press.

Cervone, D. (2004) 'The architecture of personality', *Psychological Review*, 111(1): 183–204.

Cervone, D., Shadel, W.G., Smith, R.E. and Fiori, M. (2006) 'Self-regulation: Reminders and suggestions from personality science', *Applied Psychology: An International Review*, 55(3): 333–85.

Corr, P.J. (2004) 'Reinforcement sensitivity theory and personality', *Neuroscience and Biobehavioral Reviews*, 28(3): 317–32.

Cox-Fuenzalida, L., Swickert, R. and Hittner, J.B. (2004) 'Effects of neuroticism and workload history on performance', *Personality and Individual Differences*, 36(2): 447–56.

Dean, M.A., Conte, J.M. and Blankenhorn, T.R. (2006) 'Examination of the predictive validity of Big Five personality dimensions across training performance criteria', *Personality and Individual Differences*, 41(7): 1229–39.

De Fruyt, F., Van Leeuwen, K. and Bagby, R.M. (2006) 'Assessing and interpreting personality change and continuity in patients treated for major depression', *Psychological Assessment*, 18(1): 71–80.

Derryberry, D. and Reed, M.A. (1997) 'Motivational and attentional components of personality', in G. Matthews (ed.), *Cognitive Science Perspectives on Personality and Emotion*. Amsterdam: Elsevier, pp. 443–73.

Derryberry, D. and Reed, A. (2002) 'Anxiety-related attentional biases and their regulation by attentional control', *Journal of Abnormal Psychology*, 111(2): 225–36.

Ericsson, K.A. and Charness, N. (1994) 'Expert performance: Its structure and acquisition', *American Psychologist*, 49(8): 725–47.

Eysenck, H.J. (1967) *The Biological Basis of Personality*. Springfield, IL: Thomas, pp. 169–209.

Eysenck, M.W. (1981) 'Learning, memory and personality', in H.J. Eysenck (ed.), *A Model for Personality*. Berlin: Springer.

Eysenck, M.W., Derakshan, N., Santos, R. and Calvo, M.G. (2007) 'Anxiety and cognitive performance: Attentional control theory', *Emotion*, 7(2): 336–53.

Forgas, J.P. (1995) 'Mood and judgement: The affect infusion model (AIM)', *Psychological Bulletin*, 117(1): 39–66.

Goldberg, L.R. (1990) 'An alternative "description of personality": The Big-Five factor structure', *Journal of Personality and Social Psychology*, 59(6): 1216–29.

Gray, J.R., Burgess, G.C., Schaefer, A., Yarkoni, T., Larsen, R.J. and Braver, T.S. (2005) 'Affective personality differences in neural processing efficiency confirmed using fMRI', *Cognitive, Affective and Behavioral Neuroscience*, 5(2): 182–90.

Hockey, G.R.J. (1984) 'Varieties of attentional state: the effects of environment', in R. Parasuraman and D.R. Davies (eds), *Varieties of Attention*. London: Academic Press, pp. 449–83.

Hudlicka, E. (2004) 'Beyond cognition: Modeling emotion in cognitive architectures', in M. Lovett, C. Schunn, C. Lebiere and P. Munro (eds), *Proceedings of the Sixth International Conference on Cognitive Modeling: ICCCM 2004: Integrating Models*. Mahwah, NJ: Lawrence Erlbaum, pp. 118–23.

Humphreys, M.S. and Revelle, W. (1984) 'Personality, motivation and performance: A theory of the relationship between individual differences and information processing', *Psychological Review*, 91(2): 153–84.

Koelega, H.S. (1992) 'Extraversion and vigilance performance: 30 years of inconsistencies', *Psychological Bulletin*, 112(2): 239–58.

Lazarus, R.S. (1999) *Stress and Emotion: A New Synthesis*. New York: Springer.

Lieberman, M.D. and Rosenthal, R. (2001) 'Why introverts can't always tell who likes them: Multitasking and nonverbal decoding', *Journal of Personality and Social Psychology*, 80(2): 294–310.

MacLeod, C. and Mathews, A. (1988) 'Anxiety and the allocation of attention to threat', *Quarterly Journal of Experimental Psychology*, 38A(4–4): 659–70.

Mathews, A. (2004) 'On the malleability of emotional encoding', *Behaviour Research and Therapy*, 42(9): 1019–36.

Mathews, A. and Mackintosh, B. (1998) 'A cognitive model of selective processing in anxiety', *Cognitive Therapy and Research*, 22(6): 539–60.

Matthews, G. (1992) 'Extraversion', in A.P. Smith and D.M. Jones (eds), *Handbook of Human Performance. Vol. 3: State and Trait*. London: Academic, pp. 95–126.

Matthews, G. (1997) 'Extraversion, emotion and performance: A cognitive-adaptive model', in G. Matthews (ed.), *Cognitive Science Perspectives on Personality and Emotion*. Amsterdam: Elsevier, pp. 339–442.

Matthews, G. (1999) 'Personality and skill: A cognitive-adaptive framework', in P.L. Ackerman, P.C. Kyllonen and R.D. Roberts (eds), *The Future of Learning and Individual Differences Research: Processes, Traits, and Content*. Washington, DC: APA, pp. 251–70.

Matthews, G. (2000) 'A cognitive science critique of biological theories of personality traits', *History and Philosophy of Psychology*, 2(1): 1–17.

Matthews, G. (2002) 'Towards a transactional ergonomics for driver stress and fatigue', *Theoretical Issues in Ergonomics Science*, 3(2): 195–211.

Matthews, G. (2004) 'Neuroticism from the top down: Psychophysiology and negative emotionality', in R. Stelmack (ed.), *On the Psychobiology of Personality: Essays in Honor of Marvin Zuckerman*. Amsterdam: Elsevier Science, pp. 249–66.

Matthews, G. and Amelang, M. (1993) 'Extraversion, arousal theory and performance: A study of individual differences in the EEG', *Personality and Individual Differences*, 14(2): 347–64.

Matthews, G., Davies, D.R. and Lees, J.L. (1990) 'Arousal, extraversion, and individual differences in resource availability', *Journal of Personality and Social Psychology*, 59(1): 150–68.

Matthews, G., Deary, I.J. and Whiteman, M.C. (2003) *Personality Traits* (2nd edn). Cambridge: Cambridge University Press.

Matthews, G. and Gilliland, K. (1999) 'The personality theories of H.J. Eysenck and J.A. Gray: A comparative review', *Personality and Individual Differences*, 26(4): 583–626.

Matthews, G. and Harley, T.A. (1993) 'Effects of extraversion and self-report arousal on semantic priming: A connectionist approach', *Journal of Personality and Social Psychology*, 65(4): 735–56.

Matthews, G. and Harley, T.A. (1996) 'Connectionist models of emotional distress and attentional bias', *Cognition and Emotion*, 10(6): 561–600.

Matthews, G., Jones, D.M. and Chamberlain, A.G. (1989) 'Interactive effects of extraversion and arousal on attentional task performance: Multiple resources or encoding processes?', *Journal of Personality and Social Psychology*, 56(4): 629–39.

Matthews, G., Schwean, V.L., Campbell, S.E., Saklofske, D.H. and Mohamed, A.A.R. (2000) 'Personality, self-regulation and adaptation: A cognitive-social framework', in M. Boekarts, P.R. Pintrich and M. Zeidner (eds), *Handbook of Self-Regulation*. New York: Academic, pp. 171–207.

Matthews, G. and Wells, A. (2000) 'Attention, automaticity and affective disorder', *Behavior Modification*, 24(1): 69–93.

Matthews, G. and Zeidner, M. (2004) 'Traits, states and the trilogy of mind: An adaptive perspective on intellectual functioning', in D. Dai and R.J. Sternberg (eds), *Motivation, Emotion, and Cognition: Integrative Perspectives on Intellectual Functioning and Development*. Mahwah, NJ: Lawrence Erlbaum, pp. 143–74.

Matthews, G., Zeidner, M. and Roberts, R.D. (2002) *Emotional Intelligence: Science and Myth*. Cambridge, MA: MIT Press.

Mayer, J.D., Salovey, P. and Caruso, D.R. (2004) 'Emotional intelligence: Theory, findings, and implications', *Psychological Inquiry*, 15(3): 197–215.

Mayne, T.J. (1999) 'Negative affect and health: The importance of being earnest', *Cognition and Emotion*, 13(5): 601–35.

McCrae, R.R. and Costa, P.T. (1997) 'Personality trait structure as a human universal', *American Psychologist*, 52: 509–16.

Mischel, W. (2004) 'Toward an integrative science of the person', *Annual Review of Psychology*, 55: 1–22.

Morgeson, F.P., Reider, M.H. and Campion, M.A. (2005) 'Selecting individuals in team settings: The importance of social skills, personality characteristics, and teamwork knowledge', *Personnel Psychology*, 58(3): 583–611.

Munafo, M.R., Clark, T.G., Moore, L.R., Payne, E., Walton, R. and Flint, J. (2003) 'Genetic polymorphisms and personality in healthy adults: A systematic review and meta-analysis', *Molecular Psychiatry*, 8(5): 471–84.

Ortony, A., Norman, D.A. and Revelle, W. (2005) 'Affect and proto-affect in effective functioning', in J-M. Fellous and M.A. Arbib (eds), *Who Needs Emotions? The Brain Meets the Robot*. New York: Oxford University Press, pp. 173–202.

Pylyshyn, Z.W. (1999) 'What's in your mind?', in E. Lepore and Z.W. Pylyshyn (eds), *What is Cognitive Science?*. Oxford: Blackwell, pp. 1–25.

Revelle, W., Humphreys, M.S., Simon, L. and Gilliland, K. (1980) 'The interactive effect of personality, time of day and caffeine: A test of the arousal model', *Journal of Experimental Psychology: General*, 109(1): 1–31.

Saklofske, D.H., Austin, E.J. and Minski, P.S. (2003) 'Factor structure and validity of a trait emotional intelligence measure', *Personality and Individual Differences*, 34(4): 707–21.

Schaefer, P.S., Williams, C.C., Goodie, A.S. and Campbell, W.K. (2004) 'Overconfidence and the Big Five', *Journal of Research in Personality*, 38(5): 473–80.

Schmukle, S.C. and Egloff, B. (2005) 'A latent state–trait analysis of implicit and explicit personality measures', *European Journal of Psychological Assessment*, 21(2): 100–7.

Siegle, G.J. and Hasselmo, E. (2002) 'Using connectionist models to guide assessment of psychological disorder', *Psychological Assessment*, 14(3): 263–78.

Smillie, L.D., Yeo, G.B., Furnham, A.F. and Jackson, C.J. (2006) 'Benefits of all work and no play: The relationship between neuroticism and performance as a function of resource allocation', *Journal of Applied Psychology*, 91(1): 139–55.

Srivastava, S., John, O.P., Gosling, S.D. and Potter, J. (2003) 'Development of personality in early and middle adulthood: Set like plaster or persistent change?', *Journal of Personality and Social Psychology*, 84(5): 1041–53.

Szymura, B. and Necka, E. (1998) 'Visual selective attention and personality: An experimental verification of three models of extraversion', *Personality and Individual Differences*, 24(5): 713–29.

Warm, J.S. and Dember, W.N. (1998) 'Tests of vigilance taxonomy', in R.R. Hoffman, M.F. Sherrick and J.S. Warm (eds), *Viewing Psychology as a Whole: The Integrative Science of William N. Dember*. Washington, DC: APA, pp. 87–112.

Wells, A. and Matthews, G. (1994) *Attention and Emotion: A Clinical Perspective*. Hove, England: Lawrence Erlbaum.

Zelenski, J.M. and Larsen, J. (2002) 'Predicting the future: How affect-related personality traits influence likelihood judgments of future events', *Personality and Social Psychology Bulletin*, 28(7): 1000–10.

Zeidner, M. (1998) *Test Anxiety: The State of the Art*. New York: Plenum.

Zeidner, M. and Matthews, G. (2000) 'Personality and intelligence', in R.J. Sternberg (ed.), *Handbook of Human Intelligence* (2nd edn). Cambridge: Cambridge University Press, pp. 581–610.

Zeidner, M. and Matthews, G. (2005) 'Evaluation anxiety', in A.J. Elliot and C.S. Dweck (eds), *Handbook of Competence and Motivation*. New York: Guilford, pp. 141–63.

Zeidner, M., Matthews, G., Roberts, R.D. and McCann, C. (2003) 'Development of emotional intelligence: Towards a multi-level investment model', *Human Development*, 46(2–3): 69–96.

Zeidner, M. and Saklofske, D. (1995) 'Adaptive and maladaptive coping', in M. Zeidner and N.S. Endler (eds), *Handbook of Coping: Theory, Research, Applications*. New York: Wiley, pp. 505–31.

Zuckerman, M. (1991) *Psychobiology of Personality*. Cambridge: Cambridge University Press.

4

Explanatory Models of Personality: Social-Cognitive Theories and the Knowledge-and-Appraisal Model of Personality Architecture

Daniel Cervone

This is a chapter on the social-cognitive theories of personality, prepared for a section of the present handbook devoted to explanatory models of personality. This context for writing inherently raises three questions:

1 What is an explanatory model?
2 What needs to be explained (which roughly equates to 'What is personality?')
3 What are the social-cognitive theories, and in what sense are they explanatory models of personality?

We begin by considering these three questions in turn. The chapter then provides a broad overview of the social-cognitive approach by reviewing the landmark contributions of Bandura (1986, 2006) and Mischel (1973, 2004) and considering implications of the social-cognitive perspective for

the task of personality assessment. We turn next to a recent effort by the present author to formulate a system of social-cognitive personality variables and to apply that system to the identification and explanation of a phenomenon of enduring interest to the psychology of personality, namely cross-situational coherence in psychological response (Cervone, 2004).

A thesis of this chapter is that the social-cognitive approach to personality is best understood as one effort to model intra-individual personality architecture (Cervone, 2004, 2005; Cervone et al., 2004; cf. Cloninger, 2004; Kuhl et al., 2006; Matthews et al., 2000; Mischel, 2004). In the social-cognitive perspective, one explains personality by formulating and testing a conceptual model of the intra-individual mental architecture that underlies overt patterns of experience and action. This effort at theory construction inherently is interdisciplinary and integrative; theory and findings from throughout the psychological sciences inform the understanding of cognitive and affective mental architecture, and the personality psychologist endeavors to integrate this work into a coherent model of the whole person (Caprara and Cervone, 2000). One then seeks to build an 'integrative science of the person' (Mischel, 2004: 1) or a *personality science* (Cervone and Mischel, 2002; see also Bermudez, 2006; Duke, 1986; Little, 2005, 2006; Shadel, 2004).

The reader should then recognize that although the present chapter focuses on one particular theoretical tradition, the social-cognitive theories, the work to be presented is reflective of broader trends in the field. As Kuhl and colleagues explain, 'There exists a new breed of theories of *personality architecture*, which analyze the mental systems that shape the individual's enduring, distinctive patterns of experience and action' (Kuhl et al., 2006: 409).

SOCIAL-COGNITIVE THEORIES AS EXPLANATORY MODELS OF PERSONALITY

What is an explanatory model?

Science strives for explanation. Activities other than explanation – the description of entities and occurrences, the taxonomic classification of those entities and occurrences – are also on the scientists' 'to do' list. But the ultimate goal is to explain phenomena (Salmon, 1989). Our first question, then, is: What is a scientific explanation; that is, what are the qualities that are possessed by some statements[1] that lead us to recognize those statements as being explanations that are scientific.

A complete answer to this question is beyond not only the scope of this chapter, but the expertise of its author. Fully explicating

the nature of scientific explanation is a task for the philosopher of science (Woodward, 2003). However, a simple example illustrates that psychologists can come to basic agreement on the general form of statements that qualify as scientific explanations. Although there may remain nuances and complexities that are best left to professional philosophers, professional psychologists can identify and agree upon core principles of scientific explanation that can guide their theorizing and research.

The example is as follows. Suppose that one week in spring, your neighbor, Mr. Buonarroti, begins to spend his days chiseling on a large rock in front of his home. Imagine also that three other neighbors observing the scene say, respectively:

1　'That Mr. B, he banged on that rock 2416 times today. That's the same as yesterday and the day before – I counted 'em!'
2　'Mr. B's a Taurus; it's in the stars – they make him do this bull-headed stuff this time of year.'
3　'Mr. B has a lot of weird unconscious desires that he's not even aware of, and the form he is sculpting in the rock symbolically represents some aspect of these unconscious desires and thereby allows him to let off some pent up "mental steam".'

Everyone is likely to agree that the first statement is not a scientific explanation because it is not an explanation. It is merely a description of the events of the day (and the two days before). The description contains a quantification – the counting of a feature of Mr. B's behavior, the number of times he strikes the rock – but quantifying clearly does not convert the description into an explanation. Even if Mr. B's striking of the rock is so regular from day to day that one can predict his actions, a description of this regularity still is just that: a description, not an explanation.

Everyone is likely to agree that the second statement is not a scientific explanation because it is not scientific. It does seem to qualify as an explanation; that is, it has a logical form of statements that, intuitively, we call explanations.[2] The statement describes an entity that is said to influence causally the phenomenon to be explained. The purported causal entity has a feature that is necessary to scientific explanation: it does not possess the property that requires explanation (Hanson, 1961; Nozick, 1981; Salmon, 1989), as would be the case if one posited, for example, a chiseling motive or a trait of chiselingness. However, we still would not call the statement a *scientific* explanation. This is because it attributes to an entity a causal power that violates scientists' commonly accepted beliefs about how the world works. Science does recognize action at a distance, but it denies that there exists *this* action at *this* distance: a causal influence of stars on human action. When one evaluates its status as a scientific explanation, then, statement 2 succeeds logically but fails ontologically.

Most people likely would conclude that the third statement is, in fact, a scientific explanation; that is, the third statement at the very least has the general form of a scientific explanation. One might judge it to be a poor scientific explanation for any of a variety of reasons: the questionable quality of its substantive claims, the difficulty of verifying or disproving those claims, the availability of alternative scientific explanations that are superior with regard to substantive claims or the capacity to be tested. Nonetheless, the third statement does fit our standard conception of an explanation that is scientific. It makes reference to an entity that, in light of current scientific beliefs, plausibly may exist (unconscious desires) and plausibly may influence the phenomenon to be explained (the desires, even if they are outside of conscious awareness, may possibly underlie his sculpting).

The point of this example is the following. On the one hand, the formal study of scientific explanation is a technical area of investigation in which philosophers, to the present day, have not reached complete consensus (cf. Giere, 1999; Kitcher, 1985; Salmon, 1989; Woodward, 2003). However, this does not mean that personality psychologists

should throw up their hands and despair of ever claiming to have explained their phenomena of interest. Nor do the technicalities of contemporary philosophy imply that personality scientists have license to ignore principles of scientific explanation and merely to claim by fiat that their favorite constructs are explanatory. The fact that we can agree on the status – explanation or not, scientific or not – of the three statements above implies that we share beliefs about the nature of scientific explanation. These shared beliefs, which are sometimes merely implicit in discourse in personality psychology, have been made explicit in recent work in the philosophy of science.

Models

Much work in philosophy highlights the role in scientific explanation of models (Giere, 1999; Morgan and Morrison, 1999). The present discussion relies strongly on the explication of the role of explanatory models in psychological science that has been provided by Harré (2002). The basic idea is the following. Scientists explain events they observe by providing conceptual models of mechanisms and processes that may have generated those events.[3] The entities that are said to have generated the observed events commonly are not themselves observed or observable; the scientist infers the presence of both small (e.g. atoms) and large (e.g. tectonic plates) entities without directly observing them. This raises the question of how one can infer the existence of unseen events without engaging in unscientific flights of fancy. There are two considerations. First, accepted, pre-existing scientific knowledge constrains theorizing: one only infers the presence of entities that are generally consistent with accepted scientific knowledge. We recognized that our second statement above failed to quality as scientific because it included claims about a causal process that fell outside acceptable scientific belief. The second consideration is the question of how one creates the explanatory model within this space of constraints. This is generally done through an act of imagination; the scientist commonly imagines that the unseen structures and processes are analogous to some observable process that is already well understood. Darwin's explanation of evolution is a classic case of an explanatory model that rests on analogy. Darwin obviously could not observe the course of evolution and the pressures of natural selection that had shaped species in the distant past. But he could observe present-day farms. He posited that the evolutionary forces shaped species in the same general manner that farmers, through selective breeding, shape the populations of beings under their control. The evolutionary landscape was analogous to a farm. The farm, then, was the analogical grounding for an explanatory model of evolutionary forces.

An important implication of a model-based approach to explanation is one highlighted by the philosopher Giere (1999). It concerns the question of whether models are 'true' or 'false', and the related question of whether one should apply a falsifiability criterion when evaluating them (Popper, 1959). Giere explains that models are imperfect representations of the world. A model is imperfect in that it inevitably is incomplete; the world is sure to be more complex than the model. A model is successful if and when it provides understanding of aspects of the world that are important to a given scientific discipline. There will always be some additional aspects of the world that are not captured by a given model. Since this is inevitable, it is trivial to say that a given model is not fully true and thus is false in some respects. This, in turn, implies that it is counter-productive to apply a falsifiability criterion when deciding to accept versus reject scientific models. Since all models are incomplete, all could be rejected as 'false' in some regard. If one completely rejected an entire conceptual model whenever it could be shown to be false in some way, one inevitably would reject all conceptual models. As a result, one would lose the explanatory benefits those models provided (Proctor and Capaldi, 2001). One thus should not ask whether a model is 'true'

but whether it yields 'realism without truth' (Giere, 1999: 6); that is, whether the model provides a valuable representation of some important aspects of the really existent world.

Focusing on conceptual models as the source of scientific explanations brings another implication. It shifts one's focus from prediction to understanding. In the middle of the twentieth century, philosophy of science highlighted the role in scientific explanation of laws; nomothetic laws were said to correspond to regularities in the occurrence of events (see Salmon, 1989; Suppe, 1977). In a positivistic approach to science, one applied those laws in order to predict phenomena while making no claims about the hidden, unobservable structure of the entities whose behavior was being predicted. Positivistic thinking not only had a well-known direct impact on the psychological behaviorism of the early to mid-twentieth century, but also indirectly shaped the discourse of personality psychology in the second half of the century. Mischel's (1968) landmark critique of global dispositional constructs, for example, emphasized the predictive limitations of trait constructs more than their limitations for the task of explanation. Subsequent writers sometimes focused exclusively on prediction, completely ignoring the scientific task of explaining the behaviors they were trying to predict (e.g. Bem and Allen, 1974). Textbooks cast the field as being concerned centrally with predicting occurrences (Wiggins, 1973), with some claiming that 'in psychology, as in all science, *our major concern* is ... estimation or prediction' (Horst, 1966: 264–5, emphasis added). By the 1980s, wise commentators noted that the importance of behavioral prediction may have been overemphasized (Pervin, 1994). Yet even earlier, philosophers had explained that prediction is not science's central goal. Toulmin (1961) insightfully contrasted two cases from the ancient world. The Babylonians could predict astronomical events such as eclipses yet lacked 'any very original ideas about the physical nature of the heavenly bodies' (Toulmin, 1961: 28); they merely calculated from numerical tables that quantitatively described past occurrences. The Ionians, by contrast, developed explanatory conceptual models of the universe by imagining that it was analogous to objects they already understood. They suggested that earth resided in a tube surrounded by fire, with pinpricks in the tube being the light we called stars. They suggested that the moon did not generate light of its own but borrowed light from the sun. The Ionians failed to predict astronomical events with accuracy, yet they, not the Babylonians, were engaged in the fundamental task of scientific explanation (Toulmin, 1961: 30).

What needs to be explained in an explanatory model of personality?

The next question is what one needs to explain. Scientific disciplines generally are defined by their target of investigation, that is, by the entities and occurrences for which they seek to provide explanation. What, then, is the target of investigation in personality science (Cervone and Mischel, 2002)?

The personality of the individual

One can address this question by examining answers provided by founders of the field. Stern (1935) argued that personality psychology's target must be the whole, coherent individual: the unitas multiplex (see also Holt, 1962; Lamiell, 2003). Allport (1937) highlighted the intra-individual organization of psychological qualities and the potential idiosyncrasies of the individual. Proposition A.1. in Murray and colleagues' explorations was that the field's 'objects of study are individual organisms, not aggregates of organisms' (Murray, 1938: 38). Lewin's (1935) call for Galilean as opposed to Aristotelian modes of thought in personality psychology has a key corollary: it draws attention to the idiosyncrasies of the individual case (Cervone, 2006). In a mature Galilean science, Lewin explained, 'even a particular

case is ... assumed, without more ado, to be lawful' (Lewin, 1935: 26).

Founders of the field, then, clearly identified the target of inquiry: the individual person, in all his or her uniqueness. The study of 'the individual as an organized, dynamic, agentic system functioning in the social world' (Mischel, 2004: 2) is the centerpoint of the field's inquiry.

Some may disagree with Stern, Allport, Murray, Lewin, Mischel, and their ilk, and argue instead that the field's target phenomenon is inter-individual differences in the population. One could aim merely to describe between-person differences to determine whether measures of such differences predict outcomes of interest. Readers who prefer this tact should consider three points. First, the study of inter-individual differences will not lead one inexorably back to the study of intra-individual personality structure and coherence. Borsboom et al. (2003) explain that the latent variables that describe between-person variation in the population at large cannot be assumed to model psychological dynamics at the level of the individual case. The second point follows from the first. If the personality psychologist aimed solely to identify between-person differences in the population, psychological science would need some *other* discipline to pursue the lost phenomenon: intra-individual personality dynamics, structure, and functioning. Third, a focus on the individual is not in any way a rejection of the reality of individual differences and the necessity of explaining them. Stern, Lewin, and the others well recognized that individuals differ from one another systematically. Yet they surely also believed that a proper scientific understanding of the differences among individuals must be based on, and would follow naturally from, an understanding of intra-individual psychological systems.

Personality coherence

When one focuses on intra-individual personality systems, a main challenge is to explain these systems' coherence. The various grand theories of personality of the twentieth century (see Hall and Lindzey, 1957) all 'emphasize the consistency and coherence of normal personality and view the individual organism as an organized and complexly structured whole' (McAdams, 1997: 12).

The notion of personality coherence incorporates three closely inter-related issues (Cervone and Shoda, 1999a, 1999b). One is the coherent functional relations among distinct psychological processes. Even clearly distinct subsystems of personality, such as those involving mood and mental representations of oneself, commonly function as systems that are coherently linked (e.g. Cervone et al., 1994; Scott and Cervone, 2002; Tillema et al., 2001). A second issue is coherence in overt psychological response. Across circumstances and time, people exhibit patterns of behavior that are meaningly interconnected, or that 'cohere'. An explanatory model of personality clearly must explain cross-situational coherence in thought and action. Finally, personality coherence involves continuity in personal identity. Despite life transitions and a multiplicity of social roles, people generally develop a sense of identity that coheres.

In summary, a challenge for the personality psychologist is to develop explanatory models that provide understanding of these diverse aspects of personality coherence. One effort in this direction is the social-cognitive theories of personality.

What are the social-cognitive theories?

What, then, are the social-cognitive theories, and in what sense do they provide explanatory models of personality? We will overview this question here and then turn, in more depth, to the social-cognitive approach in the remainder of this chapter.

Social-cognitive theory represents one strategy for building an explanatory model of personality coherence. The strategy rests on a simple premise. It is that processes of meaning construction are so central to human experience that they must be placed front-and-center in any explanatory model of personality. People respond to personal meaning. Our flows of thinking, our emotional reactions and our plans for social action are based largely on our subjective interpretations of the events of our lives; on our conceptions of ourselves and of the people who are significant to us; and on our possibilities for the future. This insight of course is not unique to social-cognitive theory; it has been central to personality psychology since the work of Kelly (1955). It is the basic premise of cognitive analyses of emotion (Lazarus, 1991). It is a defining feature of efforts by anthropologists (Geertz, 1973) and cultural psychologists (Kitayama and Markus, 1999; Shweder and Sullivan, 1990) to understanding the socio-culturally embedded nature of persons.

There are other premises on which one could build an explanatory model of personality. One could, for example, center attention on the possible existence of a large number of evolved domain-specific mechanisms of mind that function in a relatively fixed, automatic manner when activated by evolutionarily relevant environmental cues (e.g. Buss, 1995; Hauser, 2006). Alternatively, one could posit a relatively small set of psychologically relevant neural systems that contribute to broad classes of action such as behavioral activation and inhibition (Gray, 1991). Even if one were to presume that such approaches are necessary to a full explanation of personality structure and functioning, they clearly are not sufficient. The activation of biologically based systems of affect and motivation rests, to a significant degree, on processes of meaning construction (Sander et al., 2005). Neural systems involved in the approach toward attainable goals and the avoidance of uncontrollable threats are activated when people interpret their circumstances as involving attainable challenges or unmanageable threats. In the everyday social world, the meaning of encounters is often ambiguous and cognitive structures of personality significantly shape their interpretation (Green and Sedikides, 2001). Past analyses have documented the role of cognitive processes in the activation of affective and motivational systems (e.g. Bandura, 1977). For example, Matthews and Gilliland's (1999) compelling review of evidence bearing on the neural bases of individual differences provided by Eysenck (1990) and Gray (1991) concluded that 'the human performance data challenge the centrality of neural explanations', and they suggest that 'cognitive constructs may be more appropriate than biological ones for explaining the majority of behaviors' (Matthews and Gilliland, 1999: 620).

THE SOCIAL-COGNITIVE THEORIES

The social-cognitive approach is a highly inter-related family of theoretical perspectives (Cervone and Shoda, 1999b). Different investigators naturally turn their attention to different scientific challenges. Nonetheless, there exists a highly coherent body of theory and research that, in summary, constitutes the social-cognitive approach. We consider first the contributions of two investigators whose work has been foundational: Albert Bandura and Walter Mischel.

Bandura's social-cognitive theory

Bandura's exceptionally comprehensive and impactful social-cognitive theory of personality (1986, 1999, 2006) is built on two central principles. Both have far-reaching implications for the understanding of personality and its assessment.

Reciprocal determinism

The first principle addresses our primary theme: the construction of an explanatory model of personality. Social cognitive theory rests on the explanatory principle of triadic reciprocal determinism (Bandura, 1978, 1986).

By 'triadic', Bandura suggests a distinction among three conceptually distinct classes of factors: (1) the physical and social environment, (2) the cognitive and affective systems that comprise the person, and (3) the individual's behavior as it occurs and is perceived in the social world. By 'determinism', Bandura refers to 'the production of effects by events' (Bandura, 1978: 345). This determinism may not be of a simple, inevitable, mechanistic variety. Social cognitive theory recognizes that, in the case of complex psychological functions, 'events produce effects probabilistically' (Bandura, 1978: 345) rather than inevitably (see Bandura, 1982).

The notion of reciprocity is perhaps the most important of the three concepts embedded in Bandura's notion of triadic reciprocal determinism. The idea is that when seeking to explain processes of personality functioning, it is generally wrong to ask: 'Which factor – the person, the environment, or the person's actions – was *the* cause?' These three factors are interlocking; each causally influences the others. The three elements, then, 'reciprocally determine' one another. The environments people experience commonly are ones that they choose to enter or that they alter upon their arrival. Belief systems that are central to personality functioning develop through transactions with the environment and reflections on one's own behavior.

Social cognitive theory of course is not unique in highlighting reciprocity. In contemporary psychology, principles of reciprocity are found in bioecological models of development (Bronfenbrenner, 2001). In the history of ideas, they are found at least as far back as the writings of Kant (Watkins, 2003). Bandura's achievement was not to devise the principle of reciprocity but to articulate its implications for explanation within the psychology of personality and socially situated action. Also of note is that biological analyses increasingly support principles of reciprocity. The structure and functioning of neural systems is partly determined by organisms' experiences with the world (Kolb and Whishaw, 1998). Genes are activated by environmental experience (Pennisi, 2001).

Personal determinants

A second defining feature of Bandura's social cognitive theory is the set of basic variables through which it conceptualizes persons. Bandura centers his theory on cognitive capabilities. The choice is critical. One could alternatively center a personality theory on dispositions (things that people tend to do), but this, to social cognitive theory, would portray persons in a manner that is too static. People possess cognitive capabilities that give them potentials for action and personal development that may not be apparent in their current behavior (cf. Caprara and Cervone, 2000).

Bandura (1986, 1999) delineates five basic capabilities around which he organizes his social cognitive theory. *Symbolizing capability* refers to people's cognitive capacity to think via symbols that represent features of the world – language of course being the most central of those symbol systems. *Vicarious capability* is the capacity to acquire knowledge and skills through observation rather than merely through direct experience. *Forethought capability* refers to the distinctly human capacity to anticipate future contingencies and to plan strategies for coping with events that have not yet arisen. *Self-regulatory capability* is the capacity to exert control over one's own actions and emotions by monitoring one's experiences, evaluating actions in relation to evaluative standards, and setting goals for the future. Finally, s*elf-reflective capability* refers to people's capacity to reflect not only on the world, but also on themselves. In particular, people's self-reflective beliefs about their own capabilities for performance, or self-efficacy beliefs (Bandura, 1997), are central to social-cognitive analyses of personality functioning. Extensive and converging lines of research document the impact of self-efficacy beliefs on human achievement (Bandura and Locke, 2003).

Mischel and Shoda's CAPS model

Processing dynamics

A complementary conception of personality structure and functioning is provided by Mischel and Shoda (1995, 1998; Mischel, 2004), who advanced the social-cognitive perspective by construing personality as a cognitive-affective processing system (CAPS). In their CAPS model, Mischel and Shoda do not posit a series of personality variables that are independent of one another. Instead, they construe personality in terms of a set of cognitive and affective processes that are highly interconnected – so much so that in total they function as a coherent system. It is not merely the case that people have goals, competencies, expectancies, etc. Instead, in the internal processing dynamics of personality, these conceptually distinct social-cognitive variables (Mischel, 1973) are functionally interconnected, and often are activated in parallel (cf. Rumelhart and McClelland, 1986).

An interesting implication of the CAPS perspective on personality dynamics is that particular constellations of cognitive-affective systems may appear recurrently. The cognitive-affective processing system, in other words, gives rise to recurrent personality profiles. Research has identified cognitive-affective profiles that are particularly consequential to well-being. A pattern of affect and future-oriented beliefs in romantic relationships produces a personality profile known as rejection sensitivity (Ayduk et al., 2002). A system of implicit beliefs, expectancies that are low and the goals that center on attaining positive evaluations from others produces 'helpless' patterns of achievement behavior (Grant and Dweck, 1999). By investigating the cognitive-affective dynamics, investigators are able not only to identify these personality profiles descriptively, but to explain them in terms of underlying social-cognitive processing dynamics.

In the CAPS model, internal personality processes function in interaction with features of the social environment.

Intra-individual personality structure and functioning, then, is inherently contextual. Different situational features activate different patterns of thinking that, in turn, have different affective and motivational implications (Mischel and Shoda, 1995). A challenge for researchers is that, even within the same general type of social circumstance, different situational features may be more salient and impactful for different individuals. Shoda and colleagues have developed paradigms to identify maximally relevant situational features at the level of the individual case (e.g. Shoda and LeeTiernan, 2002).

Contextually contingent behavioral expressions

The CAPS model of cognitive and affective dynamics has a crucial implication for the understanding of overt expressions of personality. It can be illustrated by a simple example. Suppose a person acts in a bold, assertive, outgoing manner in some situations but is shy and withdrawn in others. How are we to characterize the individual's personality? One possibility is to claim that all the behaviors (assertive acts; shy, withdrawn tendencies) are manifestations of a common high-level personality trait – for example, introversion – and to average together the different manifestations to obtain a single high-level trait score for the individual. In this example, the combinations of 'highs' and 'lows' might result in the person obtaining a mid-range score on introversion–extraversion. The job for an explanatory model of personality, then, would be to explain the person's mid-range behavioral tendencies. However, there quite obviously are two limitations to this procedure. The mid-range score – the statistical mean – is a mathematical abstraction that does not represent any of the person's concrete actions. The person, in this example, is never moderately introverted. A second limitation is evident if one imagines a different person who (1) is also assertive in some contexts and withdrawn in others, but (2) the contexts are the opposite of those that characterize the first person (i.e. where the

first person is, why the second is withdrawn and vice versa). The two individuals plainly differ, yet the computation of the mean equates them.

The point of the example, of course, is that one cannot jettison variability in action from the scope of inquiry. Variability in action needs to be explained. If personality is a dynamic cognitive-affective system that functions in interaction with social contexts, then there is every reason to expect that meaningful behavioral expressions of personality will include systematic variation in action as the person experiences different encounters. This variability must be assessed and, once it is, becomes a critical target phenomenon to be explained in any explanatory model of personality. In recent years, much research has documented that patterns of variability in action are enduring, distinctive 'signatures' of an individual's personality (reviewed in Mischel, 2004; Mischel and Shoda, 1995, 1998; Shoda, 1999). Numerous lines of research subsequent to the original studies of Mischel, Shoda, and colleagues document the existence of stable, meaningful profiles of variability in response across context (e.g. Shadel et al., 2000; Vansteelandt and Van Mechelen, 1998, 2004) and show that parameters of personality other than merely the mean are necessary to represent people's distinctive personality characteristics (Eid and Langeheine, 2003; Fleeson, 2001; Fleeson and Leicht, 2006; Moskowitz and Zuroff, 2005).

A social-cognitive theory of personality assessment

The social-cognitive models developed by Bandura, Mischel, and others have significant implications for how one construes the task of personality assessment. The goal of assessment no longer is merely to compare people in terms of what they do on average. Instead, one seeks to assess patterns of stability and variability overt personality functioning, as well as the contextualized personality structures and processes that contribute to these overt patterns. To address these challenges, Cervone et al. (2001) proposed a social-cognitive theory of personality assessment that featured five assessment principles:

1 *Distinguish between the assessment of internal personality structures and dynamics and overt behavioral tendencies.* Traditional assessment procedures commonly treat people's reports of their behavioral tendencies as an indicator of internal personality structures. This is problematic if only because different people may engage in the same overt actions for different reasons. In social-cognitive theory, one can distinguish two targets of assessment: (a) overt dispositional tendencies, which may be presented in any of a variety of ways that may prove useful to the assessor or assessee, and (b) internal personality structures and dynamics, whose assessment would be guided by a conceptual model of personality architecture.

2 *Assess personal determinants of action.* Social-cognitive is an agentic perspective that highlights people's capacity to contribute causally to their experiences and actions (Bandura, 2001, 2006; Caprara and Cervone, 2000, 2003). Personality assessments, then, should tap those competencies and self-regulatory systems (Cervone et al., 2006b) through which people contribute to their own development.

3 *Keep separate response systems separate.* McGrath (2005) has lamented that progress in psychology has been slowed by the tendency of psychological assessors to employ complex constructs; that is, constructs that incorporate a number of subconstructs, or facets, that are conceptually distinct. The third social-cognitive principle is one that accords with the ideas of McGrath. It is to keep separate response systems (cognition, affection, overt social action) separate. As a simple example, Bandura's self-efficacy theory (1977) is concerned with functional relations among self-referent beliefs, emotional arousal, and behavioral tendencies. In this theory, one would not combine measures of beliefs, emotion, and behavior into one complex construct. Aggregating data in this manner would forestall questions about the functional relations among distinct subsystems (Bandura, 1977).

4 *Employ assessments that are sensitive to individual idiosyncrasy.* The fourth principle, being sensitive to idiosyncrasy at the level of the individual case,

follows logically from arguments raised above. If the 'objects of study are individual organisms', then one's assessments must be sensitive to the idiosyncrasies of the individual. Multiple substantive considerations compel sensitivity to idiosyncrasy. People may differ idiosyncratically in the content of the cognitions that are most important to their interpretations of the world; the personal constructs through which people interpret ambiguous encounters sometimes exhibit little overlap from one person to another (Higgins et al.,1982). Even among people for employ semantically similar constructs, there is idiosyncrasy in the social situations in which those constructs come to mind (Cervone, 1997). A preference for formal psychometric measurement principles is no impediment to the pursuit of this principle, since measurement models that are sensitive to idiosyncrasy are available (Hamaker et al., 2007).

5 *Assess persons-in-context.* The fifth guideline calls attention to the contexts in which people live their lives. Social-cognitive theory indicates that a complete assessment of personality structure and dynamics must consider the contexts of persons lives (e.g. Zakriski et al., 2005). Contextualized assessment is required if one is assessing overt dispositional tendencies, since individual's distinctive tendencies include contextualized patterns of variability in response (Andersen and Chen, 2002; Ayduk et al., 2000). Attention to context is also required when assessing internal personality systems, since both cognitive personality structures (Cantor and Kihlstrom, 1987) and biologically based systems of temperament (Kagan, 2003) inherently function contextually.

THE KAPA (KNOWLEDGE-AND-APPRAISAL PERSONALITY ARCHITECTURE) MODEL AS AN EXPLANATORY MODEL OF PERSONALITY

Earlier, we noted that scientific explanation is grounded in explanatory models and that any such model is inevitably limited in some way; that is, any model is an imperfect representation of the world (Giere, 1999). An implication is that any model is, in principle, open to modifications or expansions.

The social-cognitive frameworks of Bandura and of Mischel are generative conceptions upon which one can build. One goal in building is to formulate a principled set of social-cognitive structures and process variables. The author (Cervone, 2004) recently has proposed such a system. It draws upon, and is complementary to, the work of prior investigators in addition to Bandura and Mischel (e.g. Cantor and Kihlstrom, 1987; Ingram and Kendall, 1986; Kreitler and Kreitler, 1976; Lazarus, 1991; Matthews et al., 2000; Smith and Lazarus, 1990).

A knowledge-and-appraisal personality architecture (KAPA)

The knowledge-and-appraisal personality architecture (KAPA) (Cervone, 2004) is designed to facilitate the goals discussed throughout this chapter. An overarching goal is to identify a system of cognitive and affective variables that are explanatory. The variables, then, should not be descriptors of overt dispositional tendencies but underlying psychological structures that contribute to the behavioral and emotional tendencies that one observes. The systems of variables should rest on a set of explicit principles that, in combination, yield a relatively comprehensive model of intra-individual personality architecture. One should be able to apply this model to the explanation of phenomena that are central to the psychology of personality, including cross-situational coherence in psychological response (Allport, 1937).

In the KAPA model, three distinctions are fundamental to modeling personality architecture. Each has foundations in an allied field of study. The individual distinctions, then, are not unique to the KAPA model; the model's uniqueness merely is in combining the distinctions and, then, turning the resulting conceptual framework to the questions of personality psychology.

The first distinction is found most prominently in the philosophy of the mind, where investigators recognize that mental contents

vary in whether they possess the quality of *intentionality*. Intentionality refers to a general property of mental life, namely that mental contents are directed beyond themselves to objects in the world (Searle, 1998). Consider, for example, the mental contents we call beliefs. It makes no sense to say: 'I am believing – not anything in particular, I'm just believing.' Beliefs, of their very nature, are directed outside themselves to some aspect of the world. Beliefs, in other words, have the quality of intentionality. Some mental contents do *not* have this quality. Core affective states (Russell, 2003) such as feeling tired or energetic are merely internal feelings. One necessary distinction in modeling personality architecture, then, differentiates mental contents that do versus those that do not have the quality of intentionality (Cervone, 2004).

The second principle pertains to those mental contents that are intentional. Searle (1983, 1998) proposes a distinction of utility to the personality scientist. It differentiates mental contents according to the principle of *direction of fit*. This term refers to the relation, or fit, between a proposition and the aspect of the world that it represents. Some propositions have a *mind-to-world* direction of fit. Such propositions are true (false) if, at the time they are held by the individual, they fit (or do not fit) an actually existing state of the world. Propositions that we label 'beliefs' have this property. Other propositions have a *world-to-mind* direction of fit. They are not true or false when formulated, but instead represent intentions to bring about a future state of the world that fulfils, or fits, the current mental content. The propositions we call goals (Pervin, 1989; Shah and Kruglanski, 2002) have this property. A third class of mental content is analytically distinct from the other two. These cognitions are criteria for judging the goodness or worth of an entity, or what one generally labels *evaluative standards*. Standards are distinct from beliefs in that they are not objectively true or false, and distinct from goals in that they do not necessarily entail a personal intention to attain a given future state (Cervone, 2004). Searle's (1983) principle of directions of fit, then, provides conceptual grounding for the traditional distinction among beliefs, goals, and standards.

The third principle (Cervone, 2004) captures personality psychology's traditional distinction between process and structure variables. It is derived from Lazarus and colleagues (1991; Smith and Lazarus, 1990), who distinguish between two aspects of cognition: knowledge and appraisal. Knowledge is 'our understanding of the way things are and work' (Lazarus, 1991: 144); that is, enduring mental representations of the attributes of entities. Appraisals, in contrast, are not stored facts about the world but dynamic evaluations of the meaning of encounters for oneself. Appraisals dynamically gauge 'the significance of what is happening for one's personal well-being' (Lazarus, 1991: 144).

Knowledge and appraisal mechanisms play qualitatively different roles in personality functioning. Knowledge is an enduring structural feature of personality. Appraisals are dynamic personality processes. People possess vast repertoires of knowledge, only a small subset of which is active, and thus potentially influential to appraisal processes, in a given setting (cf. Higgins, 1996; Markus and Wurf, 1987). An implication of the knowledge/appraisal distinction is that some traditional constructs, such as goals, fragment. Some of the mental contents that we call goals are enduring mental representations of personal aims. Others are dynamic, 'on line' appraisals.

These three principles comprise an intra-individual model labeled a 'knowledge-and-appraisal personality architecture' (KAPA) (Cervone, 2004). In this model, the knowledge/appraisal and directions-of-fit distinctions are cross-cutting (since both knowledge structures and appraisal processes are intentional cognitions); their combination yields six classes of cognitively based personality variables (Figure 4.1). Dispositional tendencies are treated, in this model, in the way that scientific theories usually treat dispositions (Harré, 2002), namely as observable phenomena to be explained, and *not* also as causal entities that figure into that scientific explanation (cf. Funder, 1991; McCrae and Costa, 1995).

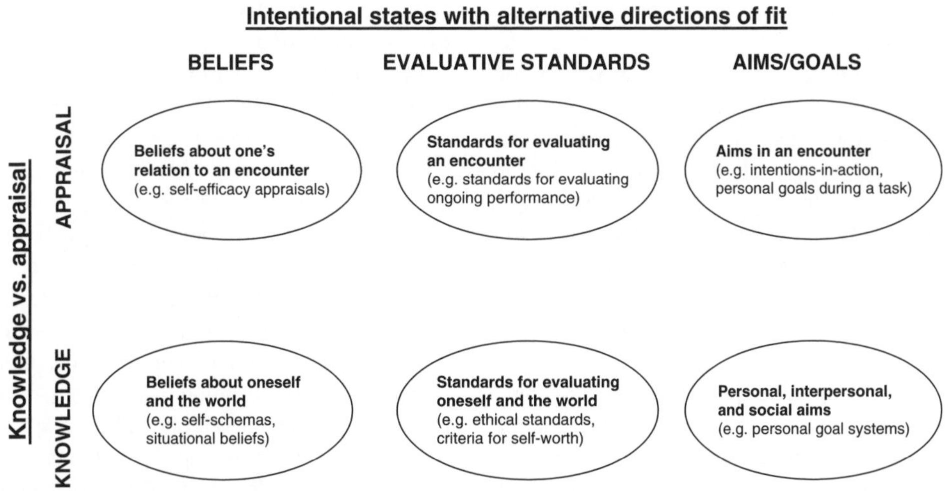

Figure 4.1 The KAPA system of social-cognitive personality variables. In the variable system, the distinction among beliefs, evaluative standards and aims holds at both the knowledge and the appraisal levels of the personality architecture, yielding six classes of social-cognitive variables.

The KAPA model is surely not sufficient for capturing all aspects of intra-individual personality structure and functioning; like all models, it can be improved. For example, in addition to delineating distinct affective systems, one might posit a distinct subsystem devoted to the automatic execution of simple behavioral routines (see Kuhl and Koole, 2004). Its goal is merely to delineate a simple set of necessary features in modeling personality structure and processes.

Using the KAPA model to explain cross-situational coherence in personality functioning

The KAPA distinctions yield an explanatory model of cross-situational coherence when they are combined with basic principles from the field of social cognition. Elements of knowledge naturally vary in the degree to which they chronically are mentally accessible (Higgins, 1996). In some domains, people may develop knowledge representations about the self that not only are highly accessible but also are particularly elaborate and information-rich; these generally are referred to as self-schemas (Markus, 1977). The KAPA model (Cervone, 2004) anticipates that a given schematic knowledge structure may contribute to appraisal processes across a variety of encounters. If so, the model predicts that the individual will display a relatively consistent pattern of appraisals in those schema-relevant encounters. Basic principles of knowledge accessibility and applicability (Higgins, 1996) explain how cross-situational coherence in response – a hallmark of 'personality' – is derived from basic processes of social cognition.

A challenge for personality assessment and research, then, is to identify the content of schematic knowledge structures and the situations in which this knowledge is most likely to become activated. We do this (Cervone, 1997, 2004; Cervone et al., in press; Shadel et al., 2004) by having participants take part in a series of assessment sessions. In a primary

paradigm (Cervone, 2004), an initial assessment session is designed to identify enduring elements of self-knowledge, or self-schemas, through the use of unstructured narratives in which participants describe positive and negative personal attributes of theirs. In a second session we assess situational knowledge, specifically, people's subjective beliefs about the relationships between personality characteristics and social settings. Participants complete in a categorization task in which they indicate the social contexts that, in their own view, are most relevant to a given feature of their personality – including the attributes identified in session 1 of our study. This enables us to identify particular subsets of situations that are relevant to positive and negative self-schemas for each individual. Finally, in a later assessment session, we assess one particular type of appraisal, namely appraisals of self-efficacy (Bandura, 1997). People appraise their capabilities to execute a wide variety of well-specified actions in concrete, specified contexts. The contexts employed are highly related to those of the situational beliefs task in session 2. This enables us to identify, based on the session 1 and 2 assessments, those subsets of situations within which the individual, in session 3, should display consistently high or low appraisals of self-efficacy.

Five aspects of our results are of note (Cervone, 1997, 2004). First, findings robustly confirm the prediction that people will form consistently high and low self-appraisals across situations that are linked to their positive and negative self-schemas, respectively. Self-efficacy perceptions are consistently higher when people appraise their efficacy for performance in circumstances in which positively valenced self-schemas were most likely to come to mind. Second, similar results are not obtained if one fails to consider idiosyncrasy in personal knowledge. For example, people do not display consistently high and low appraisals in situations that are of relevance to generic personality attributes, that is, attributes that the given participant does not see as highly relevant to himself or herself. Third, at the level of the individual the patterns of cross-situational coherence identified through our assessment procedures often violate the structure of traditional trait-based procedures. People commonly have idiosyncratic views of the meaning of a given trait term and the situations to which it applies. For example, one participant (see Cervone and Shoda, 1999a) indicated that four circumstances related to outgoing, extraverted social action were highly relevant to his beliefs about himself. The idiosyncrasy was that he did not see the four actions as manifestations of a single, uni-dimensional trait of extraversion. Instead, he divided the circumstances into two groups. This person indicated that his main personal weakness is that he is 'shy', and judged that two of the situations were relevant to his shyness. He further indicated that his main personal strength is that he is 'skilled at public relations', an attribute that he judged to be relevant to the other two circumstances. Fourth, the speed with which people appraise their efficacy for performance varies in schema-relevant versus schema-irrelevant circumstances. People respond more quickly to self-efficacy items when making appraisals in schema-relevant situations (Cervone et al., 2007; Shadel et al., 2004). The fifth feature is that experimentally priming material at the knowledge level of the KAPA architecture influences subsequent appraisals. Subtle priming procedures have been shown to raise the accessibility of one versus another aspect of self-knowledge, and thereby to influence the self-efficacy appraisals people subsequently form (Cervone et al., 2006; Shadel and Cervone, in press). In summary, the results converge to support the hypothesis that one source of cross-situational coherence in personality functioning is schematic self-knowledge. Self-schemas drive consistent patterns of appraisal. In studying self-efficacy appraisal, we are able to document that self-schemas drive appraisals that are already known to be strongly linked to emotional arousal, decision-making, and motivation (Bandura, 1997).

In summary, the KAPA system provides a model of social-cognitive structures and processes that underlie observed patterns of cross-situational coherence in psychological response. The model uniquely predicts idiosyncratic patterns of cross-situational coherence that might be overlooked in other approaches. It is uniquely able to predict contextual patterns of variability in the speed with which people appraise their capabilities, and it is open to experimental tests of its predictions about the influence of cognitive structures on appraisal processes. These attributes of the KAPA model surely are the sort of features one should desire in an explanatory model of personality.

FINAL CONSIDERATIONS AND CONCLUSIONS

To conclude, let us consider two topics not previously discussed. One is the role of genetics in the explanation of personality structure and functioning. Little was said about genetics because our topic was the social-cognitive theories of personality and these theories have not been engines of discovery in the study of personality and genetics. Metcalfe and Mischel's (1999) framework for studying self-control illustrates how one can incorporate biologically basic affective systems, whose functioning may be primarily determined by genetic factors, into a social-cognitive account. Yet, in general, the social-cognitive theories have emphasized the social foundations (Bandura, 1986) rather than the biological foundations of action.

A complete account of personality development and structure clearly requires more coverage of genetic factors than is found in this chapter. Nonetheless, two developments in the study of genetics and the developing organism are of particular note in the present context. One is mounting evidence that genetic mechanisms are activated by environmental experience. Organisms develop not as a result of fixed genetic 'programming' but through dynamic organism–environment interactions that occur throughout ontogenesis (Lickliter and Honeycutt, 2003; also see Gottlieb, 1998; Lewontin, 2000; Li, 2003). The ways in which environmental stressors influence gene expressions that have implications for social behavior are particularly well understood (Weaver et al., 2005). This work indicates, then, that not only social cognition but also the biology of the organism has its social foundations. A second development is the finding that in studies of inter-individual differences in global psychological characteristics, genetic effects are sometimes smaller than is commonly presupposed. Writers in personality science commonly claim that research findings show 'consistently' that 'at least half of the variability in trait scores' (McAdams and Pals, 2006) is due to genetics. It is true that this is a frequent result. However, exceptions to the general rule may be instructive, particularly when they involve large samples or samples that often are under-represented in research. For example, Pilia et al. (2006) report an exceptionally extensive study in which more than 6,000 residents of Sardinia completed measures including the complete NEO-PI-R, which assesses five primary global personality dispositions and facets of each. They 'estimated heritabilities of ... ~0.19 for personality factors and facets' (Pilia et al., 2006: 13). Across multiple measures of five-factor traits and facets, only one heritability estimate even reached 0.30: an estimate of 0.316 for conscientiousness measured among individuals 42 years of age and younger (the investigators provided separate estimates for younger and older adults; among older adults the estimated H^2 for conscientiousness was 0.107). Although there are multiple possibilities for the variability in results, one involves variation in the socio-economic conditions of participants. Grigorenko (2002) has reported relevant preliminary results from a family study conducted in Russia. Heritability estimates were found to be weaker in a sub-population that suffered from severe socio-economic stress, namely a criminal violation by at least one parent (Grigorenko, 2002).

In the study of IQ, a construct in which inter-individual differences are generally thought to be more highly heritable than inter-individual differences in global personality traits, it is similarly true that genetic factors frequently account for more than half the variability in scores. Yet sometimes they do not. Turkheimer et al. (2003) report a twin study in which genetic factors did explain the majority of variability in IQ among persons living in wealthy neighborhoods; however, among 'the most impoverished families, the modeled heritability of FSIQ [full-scale IQ] is essentially 0' (Turkmeimer et al., 2003: 626). A further consideration is one noted by Twenge (2002). Twin studies may underestimate the potential role of the environment by including populations who represent only one given historical period. Environmental factors that vary from one historical cohort to another generally are disregarded. Twenge finds that such cohort effects can be substantial; self-reported personality trait scores vary considerably across historical periods (Twenge, 2002, 2006). Once one considers this range of findings, it becomes clear that when one incorporates genetic factors into an explanatory model of personality, one must do so in a manner that is more sophisticated than the now-outdated notion that genes determine personality in a manner that is unaffected by the environment.

Finally, when evaluating any effort to develop an explanatory model of personality, one might ask how that model treats the personalities of individuals who obtain high versus low scores on global inter-individual difference dimensions. In principle, a social-cognitivist might try to identify those social-cognitive variables that are characteristic of people who obtain a given type (high or low) score on a given global trait dimension. One could, in other words, try to explicate the intra-individual dynamics that are linked to a given inter-individual difference factor. If one pursues this strategy, who surely will not obtain null results; people who obtain high and low scores on the inter-individual difference dimensions do differ from one another. However, this strategy was not pursued in the present paper, and for the following reason. Inter-individual difference dimensions such as those that comprise the five-factor model (Costa and McCrae, 1992) are explicitly multi-faceted. The factor of neuroticism, for example, encompasses facets including angry hostility, anxiety, and depression. The diversity of these factors inherently leaves open the possibility of equifinality: different individuals may obtain the same aggregate factor score for different underlying reasons. Equifinality implies that there may be no *consistent* explanation – no 'bridge principles' (Bennett and Hacker, 2003) – linking a single set of intra-individual causal dynamics to a given inter-individual factor score. For example, in the case of neuroticism, three people with the same relatively high N score may differ in that one primarily experiences anger, another anxiety and another depression. It is of course already established that different cognitive appraisals contribute to these different emotional experiences (Lazarus, 1991). There thus may be no singular 'social-cognitive dynamics of' the given NEO neuroticism score (Costa and McCrae, 1992). People who obtain that score cannot be assumed to be psychologically homogenous (cf. McGrath, 2005). This inconvenient fact complicates the life of personality scientists. Yet it is a fact of life if one aims for the target of investigation identified by Stern, Allport, Lewin, Murray, and Mischel.

NOTES

1 The word 'statement' here is used very broadly. Conceptions that qualify as explanations may include visual as well as verbal models (Giere, 1999).

2 The statements referred to as 'explanations' in this context are ones that provide an understanding of how some occurrence came about. The word 'explanation' can be used in other ways to which we are not referring here; for example, one may 'explain' to someone the meaning of a word.

3 Scientific models are of two types (we draw here directly from Harré, 2002). Analytical models represent observable features that are to be explained (e.g. a globe represents the shape and location of the continents). Explanatory models represent structures and processes that are thought to generate the observed phenomena described by the analytical

model; the structures and processes posited in the explanatory model commonly are not themselves directly observed (e.g. a model of plate tectonics explains the continents' shape, movement, and position).

REFERENCES

Allport, G.W. (1937) *Personality: A Psychological Interpretation*. New York: Holt.

Andersen, S.M. and Chen, S. (2002) 'The relational self: An interpersonal social-cognitive theory', *Psychological Review*, 109(1): 619–45.

Ayduk, O., Mendoza-Denton, R., Mischel, W., Downey, G., Peake, P. and Rodriguez, M. (2000) 'Regulating the interpersonal self: Strategic self-regulation for coping with rejection sensitivity', *Journal of Personality and Social Psychology*, 79(5): 776–92.

Ayduk, O., Mischel, W. and Downey, G. (2002) 'Attentional mechanisms linking rejection to hostile reactivity: The role of "hot" versus "cool" focus', *Psychological Science*, 13(5): 443–8.

Bandura, A. (1977) 'Self-efficacy: Toward a unifying theory of behavioral change', *Psychological Review*, 84(2): 191–215.

Bandura, A. (1978) 'The self system in reciprocal determinism', *American Psychologist*, 33(4): 344–58.

Bandura, A. (1982) 'The psychology of chance encounters and life paths', *American Psychologist*, 37(7): 747–75.

Bandura, A. (1997) *Self-Efficacy: The Exercise of Control*. New York: Freeman.

Bandura, A. (1986) *Social Foundations of Thought and Action*. Englewood Cliffs, NJ: Prentice Hall.

Bandura, A. (1999) 'Social cognitive theory of personality', in D. Cervone and Y. Shoda (eds), *The Coherence of Personality: Social-Cognitive Bases of Consistency, Variability, and Organization*. New York: Guilford, pp. 185–241.

Bandura, A. (2001) 'Social cognitive theory: An agentic perspective'. *Annual Review of Psychology*, 52: 1–26.

Bandura, A. (2006) 'Toward a psychology of human agency', *Perspectives on Psychological Science*, 1(2): 164–80.

Bandura, A. and Adams, N.E. (1977) 'Analysis of self-efficacy theory of behavioral change', *Cognitive Therapy and Research*, 1(4): 287–310.

Bandura, A., Adams, N.E. and Beyer, J. (1977) 'Cognitive processes mediating behavior change', *Journal of Personality and Social Psychology*, 35(3): 125–39.

Bandura, A. and Locke, E.A. (2003) 'Negative self-efficacy and goal effects revisited', *Journal of Applied Psychology*, 88(1): 87–99.

Bem, D.J. and Allen, A. (1974) 'Predicting some of the people some of the time: The search for cross-situational consistencies in behavior', *Psychological Review*, 81(6): 506–20.

Bennett, M.R. and Hacker, P.M.S. (2003) *Philosophical Foundations of Neuroscience*. Malden, MA: Blackwell.

Bermudez, J. (2006) 'Personality science, self-regulation, and health behavior', *Applied Psychology: An International Review*, 55(3): 386–96.

Berridge, K.C. and Robinson, T.E. (2003) 'Parsing reward', *Trends in Neuroscience*, 26(9): 507–13.

Borsboom, D., Mellenbergh, G.J. and van Heerden, J. (2003) 'The theoretical status of latent variables', *Psychological Review*, 110(2): 203–19.

Bronfenbrenner, U. (2001) 'The bioecological theory of human development', in N.J. Smelser and P.B. Baltes (eds), *International Encyclopedia of the Social and Behavioral Sciences*. Oxford: Elsevier, pp. 6963–70.

Buss, D.M. (1995) 'Evolutionary psychology: A new paradigm for psychological science', *Psychological Inquiry*, 6(1): 1–30.

Cantor, N. and Kihlstrom, J.F. (1987) *Personality and Social Intelligence*. Englewood Cliffs, NJ: Prentice-Hall.

Caprara, G.V. (1996) 'Structures and processes in personality psychology', *European Psychologist*, 1(1): 14–26.

Caprara, G.V. and Cervone, D. (2000) *Personality: Determinants, Dynamics, and Potentials*. New York: Cambridge University Press.

Caprara, G.V. and Cervone, D. (2003) 'A conception of personality for a psychology of human strengths: Personality as an agentic, self-regulating system', in L.G. Aspinwall and U.M. Staudinger (eds), *A Psychology of Human Strengths: Fundamental Questions and Future Directions for a Positive Psychology*. Washington, DC: American Psychological Association, pp. 61–74.

Cervone, D. (1985) 'Randomization tests to determine significance levels for microanalytic congruences between self-efficacy and

behavior', *Cognitive Therapy and Research*, 9(4): 357–65.

Cervone, D. (1997) 'Social-cognitive mechanisms and personality coherence: Self-knowledge, situational beliefs, and cross-situational coherence in perceived self-efficacy', *Psychological Science*, 8(1): 43–50.

Cervone, D. (2004) 'The architecture of personality', *Psychological Review*, 111(1): 183–204.

Cervone, D. (2005) 'Personality architecture: Within-person structures and processes', *Annual Review of Psychology*, 56: 423–52.

Cervone, D. (2006) 'Aristotelian and Galileian modes of thought in contemporary personality psychology: On the enduring importance of Kurt Lewin', in J. Trempala, A. Pepitone and B. Raven (eds), *Lewinian Psychology*. Bydgoszcz: Kazimierz Wielki University Press, pp. 69–85.

Cervone, D., Caldwell, T.L., Fiori, M., Orom, H., Shadel, W.G., Kassel, J. and Artistico, D. (in press) 'What underlies appraisals?: Experimentally testing a knowledge-and-appraisal model of personality architecture among smokers contemplating high-risk situations', *Journal of Personality*.

Cervone, D. and Caprara, G.V. (2001) 'Personality assessment', in N.J. Smelser and P.B. Baltes (eds), *International Encyclopedia of the Social and Behavioral Sciences*. Oxford: Elsevier, pp. 11281–7.

Cervone, D., Jencius, S. and Shadel, W.G. (2002) 'Personality assessment: Implications of a social-cognitive theory of personality', *Psychology: Journal of the Hellenic Psychological Association*, 9(2): 226–40.

Cervone, D., Kopp, D.A., Schaumann, L. and Scott, W.D. (1994) 'Mood, self-efficacy, and performance standards: Lower moods induce higher standards for performance', *Journal of Personality and Social Psychology*, 67(3): 499–512.

Cervone, D. and Mischel, W. (2002) (eds), *Advances in Personality Science*. New York: Guilford.

Cervone, D., Mor, N., Orom, H., Scott, W. and Shadel, W. (2004) 'Self-efficacy beliefs and the architecture of personality: On knowledge, appraisal, and self-regulation', in R.F. Baumeister and K.D. Vohs (eds), *Handbook of Self-Regulation: Research, Theory, and Applications*. New York: Guilford, pp. 188–210.

Cervone, D., Orom, H., Artistico, D., Shadel, W.G., and Kassel, J. (2007) 'Using a knowledge-and-appraisal model of personality architecture to understand consistency and variability in smokers' self-efficacy appraisals in high-risk situations', *Psychology of Addictive Behaviors*, 21(1): 44–54.

Cervone, D., Shadel, W.G. and Jencius, S. (2001) 'Social-cognitive theory of personality assessment', *Personality and Social Psychology Review*, 5(1): 33–51.

Cervone, D., Shadel, W.G., Smith, R.E. and Fiori, M. (2006b) 'Self-regulation: Reminders and suggestions from personality science', *Applied Psychology: An International Review*, 55(3): 333–85.

Cervone, D. and Shoda, Y. (1999a) 'Beyond traits in the study of personality coherence', *Current Directions in Psychological Science*, 8: 27–32.

Cervone, D. and Shoda, Y. (1999b) (eds), *The Coherence of Personality: Social-Cognitive Bases of Consistency, Variability, and Organization*. New York: Guilford.

Cloninger, C.R. (2003) 'Completing the psychobiological architecture of human personality development: Temperament, character and coherence', in U.M. Staudinger and U. Lindenberger (eds), *Understanding Human Development: Dialogues with Lifespan Psychology*. Dordrecht, Netherlands: Kluwer Academic Publishers, pp. 159–81.

Cloninger, C.R. (2004) *The Science of Well-Being*. New York: Oxford University Press.

Costa, P.T. and McCrae, R.R. (1992) *Revised NEO Personality Inventory (NEO-PI-R) and NEO Five-Factor Inventory (NEO-FFI) Professional Manual*. Odessa, FL: Psychological Assessment Resources.

Duke, M. (1986) 'Personality science: A proposal', *Journal of Personality and Social Psychology*, 50(2): 382–5.

Eid, M. and Langeheine, R. (2003) 'Separating stable from variable individuals in longitudinal studies by mixture distribution models', *Measurement: Interdisciplinary Research and Perspectives*, 1(3): 179–206.

Eysenck, H.J. (1990) 'Biological dimensions of personality', in L.A. Pervin (ed.), *Handbook of Personality: Theory and Research*. New York: Guilford, pp. 244–76.

Fleeson, W. (2001) 'Toward a structure- and process-integrated view of personality: Traits as density distributions of states', *Journal of Personality and Social Psychology*, 80(6): 1011–27.

Fleeson, W. and Leicht, C. (2006) 'On delineating and integrating the study of variability and stability in personality psychology: Interpersonal trust as illustration', *Journal of Research in Personality*, 40(1): 5–20.

Funder, D.C. (1991) 'Global traits: A neo-Allportian approach to personality', *Psychological Science*, 2(1): 31–9.

Geertz, C. (1973) *The Interpretation of Cultures*. New York: Basic Books.

Gergen, K.J. (1991) 'The saturated self: Dilemmas of identity in contemporary life', New York: Basic Books.

Giere, R.N. (1999) *Science Without Laws*. Chicago: University of Chicago Press.

Gottlieb, G. (1998) 'Normally occurring environmental and behavioral influences on gene activity: From central dogma to probabilistic epigenesis', *Psychological Review*, 105(4): 792–802.

Grant, H. and Dweck, C. (1999) 'A goal analysis of personality and personality coherence', in D. Cervone and Y. Shoda (eds), *The Coherence of Personality: Social-Cognitive Bases of Consistency, Variability, and Organization*. New York: Guilford, pp. 345–71.

Gray, J.A. (1991) 'Neural systems, emotion and personality', in J. Madden IV (ed.), *Neurobiology of Learning, Emotion and Affect*. New York: Raven Press.

Green, J.D. and Sedikides, C. (2001) 'When do self-schemas shape social perception? The role of descriptive ambiguity', *Motivation and Emotion*, 25(1): 67–83.

Grigorenko, E.L. (2002) 'In search of the genetic engram of personality', in D. Cervone and W. Mischel (eds), *Advances in Personality Science*. New York: Guilford, pp. 29–82.

Hall, C.S. and Lindzey, G. (1957) *Theories of Personality*. New York: Wiley.

Hamaker, E., Nesselroade, J.R. and Molenaar, P.C.M. (2007) 'The integrated trait-state model', *Journal of Research in Personality*, 41(2): 295–315.

Hanson, N.R. (1961) *Patterns of Discovery: An Inquiry into the Conceptual Foundations of*

Science. Cambridge: Cambridge University Press.

Harré, R. (2002) *Cognitive Science: A Philosophical Introduction*. London: Sage.

Hauser, M. (2006) *Moral Minds: How Nature Designed our Universal Sense of Right and Wrong*. New York: Ecco/Harper-Collins.

Higgins, E.T. (1996) 'Knowledge activation: Accessibility, applicability, and salience', in E.T. Higgins and A.W. Kruglanski (eds), *Social Psychology: Handbook of Basic Principles*. New York: Guilford, pp. 133–68.

Higgins, E.T., King, G.A. and Mavin, G.H. (1982) 'Individual construct accessibility and subjective impressions and recall', *Journal of Personality and Social Psychology*, 43(1): 35–47.

Holt, R.R. (1962) 'Individuality and generalization in the psychology of personality', *Journal of Personality*, 30(3): 377–404.

Horst, P. (1966) *Psychological Measurement and Prediction*. Belmont, CA: Wadsworth.

Ingram, R.E. and Kendall, P.C. (1986) 'Cognitive clinical psychology: Implications of an information processing perspective', in R.E. Ingram (ed.), *Information Processing Approaches to Clinical Psychology*. New York: Academic Press, pp. 3–21.

Kagan, J. (2003) 'Biology, context, and developmental inquiry', *Annual Review of Psychology*, 54: 1–23.

Kelly, G. (1955) *The Psychology of Personal Constructs*. New York: Norton.

Kitayama, S. and Markus, H.R. (1999) 'Yin and Yang of the Japanese self: The cultural psychology of personality coherence', in D. Cervone and Y. Shoda (eds), *The Coherence of Personality: Social-Cognitive Bases of Consistency, Variability, and Organization*. New York: Guilford, pp. 242–302.

Kitcher, P. (1985) 'Two approaches to explanation', *Journal of Philosophy*, 82(1): 632–9.

Kolb, B. and Whishaw, I.Q. (1998) 'Brain plasticity and behavior', *Annual Review of Psychology*, 49: 43–64.

Kreitler, S. and Kreitler, H. (1976) *Cognitive Orientation and Behavior*. New York: Springer.

Kuhl, J., Kazén, M. and Koole, S.L. (2006) 'Putting self-regulation theory into practice: A user's manual', *Applied Psychology: An International Review*, 55(3): 408–18.

Kuhl, J. and Koole, S.L. (2004) 'Workings of the will: A functional approach', in J. Greenberg, S.L. Koole and T. Pyszczynski (eds), *Handbook*

of Experimental Existential Psychology. New York: Guilford, pp. 411–30.

Lamiell, J.T. (2003) *Beyond Individual and Group Differences: Human Individuality, Scientific Psychology, and William Stern's Critical Personalism*. Thousand Oaks, CA: Sage.

Lazarus, R.S. (1991) *Emotion and Adaptation*. New York: Oxford University Press.

Lewin, K. (1935) *A Dynamic Theory of Personality*. New York: McGraw-Hill.

Lewontin, R. (2000) *The Triple Helix: Gene, Organism, and Environment*. Cambridge, MA: Harvard University Press.

Li, S. (2003) 'Biocultural orchestration of developmental plasticity across levels: The interplay of biology and culture in shaping the mind and behavior across the life span', *Psychological Bulletin*, 129(2): 171–94.

Lickliter, R. and Honeycutt, H. (2003) 'Developmental dynamics: Toward a biologically plausible evolutionary psychology', *Psychological Bulletin*, 129(6): 819–35.

Little, B.R. (2005) 'Personality science and personal projects: Six impossible things before breakfast', *Journal of Research in Personality*, 39(3): 4–21.

Little, B.R. (2006) 'Personality science and self-regulation: Personal projects as integrative units', *Applied Psychology: An International Review*, 55(3): 419–72.

Markus, H. (1977) 'Self-schemata and processing information about the self', *Journal of Personality and Social Psychology*, 35(2): 63–78.

Markus, H. and Wurf, E. (1987) 'The dynamic self-concept: A social psychological perspective', *Annual Review of Psychology*, 38: 299–337.

Matthews, G. and Gilliland, K. (1999) 'The personality theories of H.J. Eysenck and J.A. Gray: A comparative review', *Personality and Individual Differences*, 26(4): 583–626.

Matthews, G., Schwean, V.L., Campbell, S.E., Saklofske, D.H. and Mohamed A.A.R. (2000) 'Personality, self-regulation and adaptation: A cognitive-social framework', in M. Boekarts, P.R. Pintrich and M. Zeidner (eds), *Handbook of Self-Regulation*. New York: Academic, pp. 171–207.

McAdams, D.P. (1997) 'A conceptual history of personality psychology', in R. Hogan, J. Johnson, and S. Briggs (eds), *Handbook of Personality Psychology*. San Diego, CA: Academic Press, pp. 3–39.

McAdams, D.P. and Pals, J.L. (2006) 'A new big five: Fundamental principles for an integrative science of personality', *American Psychologist*, 61(3): 204–17.

McCrae, R.R. and Costa, P.T. (1995) 'Trait explanations in personality psychology', *European Journal of Personality*, 9(4): 231–52.

McCrae, R.R. and Costa, P.T. (1996) 'Toward a new generation of personality theories: theoretical contexts for the five-factor model', in J.S. Wiggins (ed.), *The Five-Factor Model of Personality: Theoretical Perspectives*. New York: Guilford, pp. 51–87.

McGrath, R.E. (2005) 'Conceptual complexity and construct validity', *Journal of Personality Assessment*, 85(2): 112–24.

Metcalfe, J. and Mischel, W. (1999) 'A hot/cool-system analysis of delay of gratification: Dynamics of willpower', *Psychological Review*, 106(1): 3–19.

Mischel, W. (1968) *Personality and Assessment*. New York: Wiley.

Mischel, W. (1973) 'Toward a cognitive social learning reconceptualization of personality', *Psychological Review*, 80(4): 252–83.

Mischel, W. (2004) 'Toward an integrative science of the person', *Annual Review of Psychology*, 55: 1–22.

Mischel, W. and Shoda, Y. (1995) 'A cognitive-affective system theory of personality: Reconceptualizing situations, dispositions, dynamics, and invariance in personality structure', *Psychological Review*, 102(2): 246–86.

Mischel, W. and Shoda, Y. (1998) 'Reconciling processing dynamics and personality dispositions', *Annual Review of Psychology*, 49: 229–58.

Morgan, M. and Morrison, M. (1999) (eds), *Models as Mediators*. New York: Cambridge University Press.

Moskowitz, D.S. and Zuroff, D.C. (2005) 'Robust predictors of flux, pulse, and spin', *Journal of Research in Personality*, 39(1): 130–147.

Murray, H.A. (1938) *Explorations in Personality*. New York: Oxford University Press.

Nozick, R. (1981) *Philosophical Explanations*. Cambridge, MA: Belknap Press of Harvard University Press.

Pennisi, E. (2001) 'Behind the scenes of gene expression', *Science*, 293(5532): 1064–7.

Pervin, L.A. (1989) (ed.) *Goal Concepts in Personality and Social Psychology*. Hillsdale, NJ: Erlbaum.

Pervin, L.A. (1994) 'A critical analysis of current trait theory', *Psychological Inquiry*, 5: 103–13.

Pilia, G., Chen, W.M., Scuteri, A., et al. (2006) 'Heritability of cardiovascular and personality traits in 6,148 Sardinians', *PLOS Genetics*, 2(8): e132.doi:10.1371/journal.pgen.0020132

Popper, K.R. (1959) *The Logic of Scientific Discovery*. London: Hutchinson.

Proctor, R.W. and Capaldi, E.J. (2001) 'Empirical evaluation and justification of methodologies in psychological science', *Psychological Bulletin*, 127: 759–72.

Rumelhart, D.E., McClelland, J.L. and PDP Research Group (1986) *Parallel Distributed Processing: Explorations in the Microstructure of Cognition: Vol. 1. Foundations*. Cambridge, MA: MIT Press.

Russell, J.A. (2003) 'Core affect and the psychological construction of emotion', *Psychological Review*, 110(1): 145–72.

Salmon, W.C. (1989) 'Four decades of scientific explanation', in P. Kitcher and W.C. Salmon (eds), *Minnesota Studies in the Philosophy of Science, Vol. XIII. Scientific Explanation*. Minneapolis: University of Minnesota Press, pp. 3–219.

Sander, D., Grandjean, D. and Scherer, K.R. (2005) 'A systems approach to appraisal mechanisms in emotion', *Neural Networks*, 18(4): 317–52.

Scott, W.D. and Cervone, D. (2002) 'The impact of negative affect on performance standards: Evidence for an affect-as-information mechanism', *Cognitive Therapy and Research*, 26(1): 19–37.

Searle, J.R. (1983) *Intentionality: An Essay in the Philosophy of Mind*. New York: Cambridge University Press.

Searle, J.R. (1998) *Mind, Language, and Society: Philosophy in the Real World*. New York: Basic Books.

Shadel, W.G. (2004) 'Applying personality science to cognitive-behavioral therapy and research [special series]', *Behavior Therapy*, 35 (1).

Shadel, W.G. and Cervone, D. (2006) 'Evaluating social cognitive mechanisms that regulate self-efficacy in response to provocative smoking cues: An experimental investigation', *Psychology of Addictive Behaviors*, 20(1): 91–6.

Shadel, W.G., Cervone, D., Niaura, R. and Abrams, D.B. (2004) 'Developing an integrative social-cognitive strategy for personality assessment at the level of the individual: An illustration with regular cigarette smokers', *Journal of Research in Personality*, 38(4): 394–419.

Shadel, W.G., Niaura, R. and Abrams, D. (2000) 'An idiographic approach to understanding personality structure and individual differences among smokers', *Cognitive Therapy and Research*, 24(3): 343–59.

Shah, J.Y. and Kruglanski, A. (2002) 'When opportunity knocks: Bottom-up priming of goals by means and its effects on self-regulation', *Journal of Personality and Social Psychology*, 84(6): 1109–22.

Shoda, Y. (1999) 'Behavioral expressions of a personality system: Generation and perception of behavioral signatures', in D. Cervone and Y. Shoda (eds), *The Coherence of Personality: Social-Cognitive Bases of Consistency, Variability, and Organization*. New York: Guilford, pp. 155–81.

Shoda, Y. and LeeTiernan, S. (2002) 'What remains invariant: Finding order within a person's thoughts, feelings, and behaviors across situations', in D. Cervone and W. Mischel (eds), *Advances in Personality Science*. New York: Guilford, pp. 241–70.

Shoda, Y., Mischel, W. and Wright, J.C. (1994) 'Intraindividual stability in the organization and patterning of behavior: Incorporating psychological situations into the idiographic analysis of personality', *Journal of Personality and Social Psychology*, 67(4): 674–87.

Shweder, R.A and Sullivan, M. (1990) 'The semiotic subject of cultural psychology', in L. Pervin (ed.), *Handbook of Personality*. New York: Guilford, pp. 399–416.

Smith, C.A. and Lazarus, R.S. (1990) 'Emotion and adaptation', in L.A. Pervin (ed.), *Handbook of Personality: Theory and Research*. New York: Guilford, pp. 609–37.

Stern, W. (1935) *Allgemeine Psychologie auf personalisticher grundlage*. Dordrecht: Nijoff.

Suppe, F. 'Afterword – 1977', in F. Suppe (ed.), *The Structure of Scientific Theories*. Urbana: University of Illinois Press, pp. 617–730.

Tillema, J., Cervone, D. and Scott, W.D. (2001) 'Dysphoric mood, perceived self-efficacy, and personal standards for performance: The effects of attributional cues on self-defeating patterns of cognition', *Cognitive Therapy and Research*, 25(5): 535–49.

Toulmin, S. (1961) *Foresight and Understanding: An Enquiry into the Aims of Science*. Bloomington: Indiana University Press.

Turkheimer, E., Haley, A., Waldron, M., D'Onofrio, B. and Gottesman, I. (2003) 'Socioeconomic status modifies heritability of IQ in young children', *Psychological Science*, 14(6): 623–8.

Twenge, J. (2002) 'Birth cohort, social change, and personality: The interplay of dysphoria and individualism in the 20th century', in D. Cervone and W. Mischel (eds), *Advances in Personality Science*. New York: Guilford, pp. 196–218.

Twenge, J. (2006) *Generation Me: Why Today's Young Americans Are More Confident, Assertive, Entitled – and More Miserable Than Ever Before*. New York: Free Press.

Vansteelandt, K. (1999) 'A formal model for the competency-demand hypothesis', *European Journal of Personality Psychology*, 13(5): 429–42.

Vansteelandt, K. and Van Mechelen, I. (1998) 'Individual differences in situation-behavior profiles: A triple typology model', *Journal of Personality and Social Psychology*, 75(3): 751–65.

Vansteelandt, K. and Van Mechelen, I. (2004) 'The personality triad in balance: Multidimensional individual differences in situation-behavior profiles', *Journal of Research in Personality*, 38(4): 367–93.

Watkins, E. (2003) 'Kant's philosophy of science', in E.N. Zalta (ed.), *The Stanford Encyclopedia of Philosophy* (Winter 2003 edn).

Weaver, I.C.G., Champagne, F.A., Brown, S.E., Dymov, S., Shakti, S. and Meaney, M.J. (2005) 'Reversal of maternal programming of stress responses in adult offspring through methyl supplementation: Altering epigenetic marking later in life', *The Journal of Neuroscience*, 25(47): 11045–54.

Wiggins, J.S. (1973) *Personality and Prediction: Principles of Personality Assessment*. Reading, MA: Addison-Wesley.

Woodward, J. (2003) 'Scientific explanation', in E.N. Zalta (ed.), *The Stanford Encyclopedia of Philosophy* (Winter 2003 edn).

Zakriski, A.L., Wright, J.C. and Underwood, M.K. (2005) 'Gender differences and similarities in social behavior: Finding personality in contextualized patterns of social adaptation', *Journal of Personality and Social Psychology*, 88(5): 844–55.

5

Developmental Perspectives

Jens B. Asendorpf

In this chapter I provide an overview of major developmental issues for personality psychology at the intersection of personality and developmental psychology. Whereas personologists have mainly focused on the long-term stability of personality and the long-term prediction of personality from antecedents at earlier ages such as socio-economic status or parenting styles, developmentalists have been more interested in personality change and the reasons thereof, and the prediction of major developmental outcomes such as social and emotional adaptation from personality at earlier ages. Answering any of these questions requires consideration of personality across developmental time, and conduction of *longitudinal studies* that follow a sample of individuals over a considerable period of time, including at least one assessment of personality and at least another assessment of personality, antecedents of personality, or consequences of personality.

Thus, considering personality from a developmental perspective is more than asking questions about stability and change of personality; it includes questions about the *context* of personality. Therefore I proceed in this chapter by discussing: (1) personality stability and change; (2) antecedents of adult personality in childhood; (3) consequences of childhood personality in adulthood; and (4) some principles of personality development. Thus, I illustrate the discussion of the developmental context of personality with questions that bridge childhood and adulthood, ignoring questions about the context of personality development during childhood and adolescence, and during adulthood. An additional discussion of the latter questions in some detail would not be possible within the space limitations of this chapter.

Before proceeding further, a conceptual note about personality is in order. The definition of personality advocated here for the purpose of this chapter includes at any age any social-emotional characteristic of an individual that shows some stability over shorter time periods such as a few weeks and that varies between individuals of the same culture (*personality trait*). This definition includes temperament (traits related to affect, arousal, and attention) but does not restrict early personality to temperament. It does exclude traits related to cognition such as general intelligence, in line with mainstream North American research, mainly because such traits are studied in a different research tradition, and including it would be difficult within the space limitations of this chapter.

STABILITY AND CHANGE OF PERSONALITY

In this section I discuss different concepts concerning the long-term stability and change of personality, and review relevant empirical findings.

Individual, average, and differential change

If people think about the personality development of an individual; that is, their own child, they usually take an individual perspective that contrasts this individual across age. For example, does the child grow in body size or aggressive tendencies between ages 10 and 14? *Individual change* (sometimes also called *ipsative change*) can be decomposed into two principally independent facets of change, namely *average change* of the agemates of the individual, and *differential change* of the individual, defined as the difference between individual change and average change (see Figure 5.1).

For example, is the observed increase in aggression age-typical (in this case it would be identical with the average change among

all agemates), stronger, or less strong? (In these latter cases, differential change has occurred.) It is important not to confuse these three facets of change. In the example illustrated in Figure 5.1, there was no individual change but there was a differential change due to an average increase in the trait.

Differential change is particularly important for personality psychology because it is directly linked with the stability of interindividual differences in a trait over time. If the interindividual differences in a trait remain the same across age in a sample of individuals, no differential changes occurred in the sample; if differential change occurs in at least one individual, the interindividual differences in the trait changed. The constancy of interindividual differences in a trait is commonly called the *stability of the trait*; thus, a trait is more stable the less that differential change occurs. Note that the stability of a trait is not a characteristic of an individual; it is a characteristic of a sample of individuals.

Confusion arises when 'stability' is used to refer to the absence of *average change*; that is, to the constancy of the mean level of the trait in a sample. The mean level can remain the same over age although many individuals changed in the trait; thus, a lot of differential

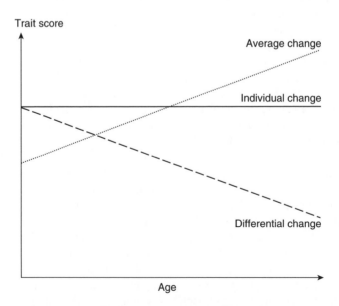

Figure 5.1 Individual, average and differential change

change occurred and the trait was not stable. This will be the case if the sum of the individual increases is the same as the sum of the individual decreases (see Figure 5.2).

To avoid such confusion, I will in the following use the term *stability* only for the constancy of interindividual differences in a sample of agemates (sometimes also called *normative stability* or *rank-order consistency* (see Roberts and DelVecchio, 2000), and the term *mean-level change* for the average change in a sample of agemates (see Roberts et al., 2006).

Interindividual differences can refer to psychological *states* that are not stable even over short periods of time such as hours or days (e.g. interindividual differences in emotional mood). Personality traits are assumed to show stability over longer time periods such as a few weeks, but that does not exclude the possibility, of course, that they are not very stable over many years. Therefore, long-term instability of personality traits does not violate the concept of stable personality traits.

Whether mean-level changes can occur in personality traits at all is more disputable; the answer depends on how personality is defined. I define here personality as consisting of traits that vary across individuals of the same culture. This definition allows for mean-level changes of traits. A more narrow definition of personality defines personality as consisting of traits that vary within agemates of the same culture. This definition excludes mean-level change because the mean level of a trait is constant across age by this definition. The more narrow definition corresponds more closely to the measurement of personality differences by contrasting an individual with a normative sample of agemates (e.g. when a personality trait is measured in terms of a z-score in a sample of agemates which is by definition zero).

The more narrow definition views personality as the individual deviation from age-typical patterns of cognition and behavior; in studies of personality ratings, it is consistent with instructions that ask raters to compare the target person with agemates. However, it cannot be avoided in such rating studies that raters' judgments will be influenced by their broader, less age-specific view; therefore, mean-level changes regularly occur even when the raters are asked to contrast each rated individual only with this individual's agemates.

The broader definition of personality in the present chapter allows for mean-level change in personality traits; in studies of personality ratings, it is consistent with instructions that ask raters to judge the individual behavior in terms of frequencies,

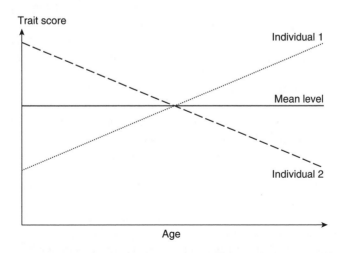

Figure 5.2 No mean-level change but strong differential change and instability

intensities, or saliencies. It should be noted, however, that raters in such judgment tasks will nevertheless intuitively adjust their judgments of an individual to the individual's broader age group. For example, if parents judge the aggressiveness of their 4-year-old, they will use their knowledge about aggressiveness of children for their judgment, not so much their knowledge about aggressiveness of adults. Consequently, rating studies of personality development necessarily *underestimate* the amount of developmental change, whatever the instruction is. I will come back to this issue once more in the section on the continuity of personality traits.

Mean-level change in personality traits

For many years most personality psychologists believed McCrae and Costa (1990), who assumed on the basis of insufficient data that personality trait ratings show little change after age 30. This was an assumption that continued to be present in their five-factor theory of personality, Postulate 1c: 'Traits develop through childhood and reach mature form in adulthood; thereafter they are stable in cognitively intact individuals' (McCrae and Costa, 1999: 145), assuming that maturity is reached by age 30. A commonly used metaphor for this pattern of change is that personality becomes 'set like plaster' by age 30 (Costa and McCrae, 1994; James, 1950). Whether this *plaster hypothesis* refers to individual change, differential change, or mean-level change has not always been clarified.

These authors were, however, also among the first to differentiate this hypothesis by revealing evidence for significant mean-level changes over adulthood in the five factors of their five-factor model of personality that were consistent across self- and acquaintance ratings and across many cultures: neuroticism, extraversion, and openness to experience decreased, and conscientiousness and

agreeableness increased over adulthood which rejects a mean-level version of the plaster hypothesis (e.g. McCrae et al., 2000; McCrae et al., 2005). This pattern was replicated and further differentiated in a large internet sample of adults ($n > 130,000$) aged 21–60 with a Big Five questionnaire (Srivastava et al., 2003). It was not clear from these cross-sectional studies, however, whether these age-related changes reflected developmental changes or historical changes due to differences between the different birth cohorts that were simultaneously tested. For example, the decrease in openness could be due to decreasing openness with increasing age, to increasing openness over historical time (e.g. adults born in 1950 are less open than adults born in 1975), or both.

Only longitudinal studies can help to distinguish developmental and historical effects. Roberts et al. (2006) conducted a meta-analysis of 92 longitudinal studies of mean-level change across the full life-course, comprising more than 50,000 participants born between 1898 and 1982. The traits in each study were then classified into the Big Five factors of personality. A particular feature of this study is that extraversion was differentiated into social vitality (a temperamental trait) and social dominance (reflecting more social status). The effect size d for a change in a trait was expressed as the raw score difference in the trait divided by the standard deviation of the raw scores at the first time point.

All six trait domains demonstrated significant changes past the age of 30, and four of them in middle or old age (see Figure 5.3). In young adulthood (age 20–40), social dominance, conscientiousness, and emotional stability increased (thus neuroticism decreased). In addition, social vitality and openness to experience increased in adolescence but then decreased in old age. Agreeableness increased significantly only between 50 and 60, and openness increased only up to age 22, and decreased after age 60. These data partly replicated the cross-sectional results for adulthood found earlier,

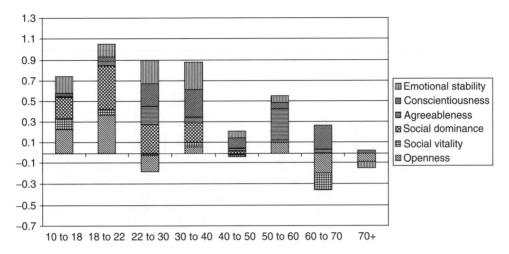

Figure 5.3   Summed mean-level changes in six personality trait domains across the life course (reprint of fig. 1 in Roberts et al., 2006, with permission of American Psychological Association)

particularly the increase in conscientiousness and the decrease in neuroticism. As Figure 5.3 indicates, the summed changes across the six trait domains were most marked between ages 18 and 30 but were substantial in the decades before and after. Between ages 40 and 50 there was less change, but after age 50 there was again substantial change. The change after age 70 should be considered with some reservation because of the small number of studies of that age range. These results clearly contradict a mean-level version of the plaster hypothesis; instead, they provide definitive evidence for a continued plasticity of traits after age 30.

Stability of interindividual differences

If we specify the plaster hypothesis to interindividual differences, it posits that there is little differential change after age 30. Because of the substantial plasticity of the Big Five trait domains in terms of mean-level changes after age 30 discussed in the preceding section, it would be surprising if the (rank-order) stability of interindividual differences in the Big Five trait domains would be continuously high after age 30. This could be the case only if nearly everyone would follow exactly the same normative pattern of age-related change (e.g. that nearly everyone would show the same increase in agreeableness between age 50 and 60, or the same decrease in social vitality after age 60).

Roberts and DelVecchio (2000) conducted a meta-analysis of 152 longitudinal studies of the rank-order stability of traits including more than 35,000 individuals. The average age difference between any two assessments of the same trait in the same sample was 6.8 years. Stability was measured by the correlation between two assessments of interindividual differences in the trait for the same sample (e.g. the correlation between neuroticism at age 18 and neuroticism at age 25 for a sample of 100 individuals). In contrast to the meta-analysis of mean-level changes, much more data was available for younger ages.

The results show an increasing stability from early childhood to age 50, and a continuously high stability thereafter (see Figure 5.4). During early childhood the stability is as

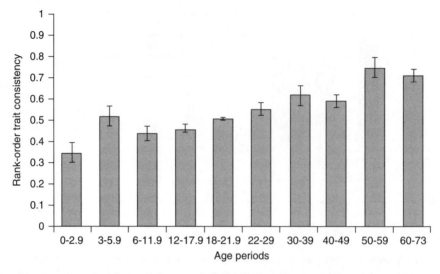

Figure 5.4   Mean seven-year rank-order stability of personality traits for different ages with 95% confidence interval around the estimated mean stability (reprint of fig. 1 in Roberts and DelVecchio, 2000, with permission of American Psychological Association)

low as 0.35 but reaches a moderate level of 0.52 already in middle childhood which continues into young adulthood. Subsequently, it increases until it reaches a level above 0.70 after age 50 which is not much lower than the mean reliability of 0.78 of the assessments at that age (interrater or interitem reliability in terms of Cronbach's alpha). This overall pattern of increasing stabilization of personality differences until age 50 did not vary markedly across the Big Five traits, by sex, or according to the assessment method. Thus, personality traits do not stabilize before age 50, which again contradicts a stability version of the plaster hypothesis; instead, these results again provide definitive evidence for a continued plasticity of traits after age 30.

Homotypic versus heterotypic stability

One reason for a low rank-order stability of personality traits over a long time can be that the validity of the assessment procedure changes over time because the functional meaning of the behaviors used for operationalizing the trait changes with age. For example, frequent crying in childhood certainly means something different than frequent crying in adulthood. Thus, if the individual frequency of crying is considered to be a trait, it might very well show a low stability between childhood and adulthood. In this case, it would be incorrect to infer from the low stability of frequency of crying that crying-related temperament is not stable between childhood and adulthood; instead, the trait assessed in childhood with frequency of crying may be better assessed with other behaviors for adulthood, and then may show a higher rank-order stability between childhood and adulthood.

Indeed, it is not always a good idea to assess the same trait at different ages with the same procedure, which leads to *homotypic stability*. As the example above shows, it can be sometimes better to use different *age-appropriate procedures*, which leads to *heterotypic stability* (Kagan, 1980). Sometimes it is not even possible to use the same procedure at different ages. Perhaps the best example is general intelligence which cannot be assessed with typical IQ testing procedures before age 2 because these procedures require verbal understanding. Nevertheless, procedures such as visual habituation have been developed that can be used to assess general intelligence even among infants, and this results in a substantial heterotypic stability between infancy and late childhood (Rose and Feldman, 1995).

Another example for heterotypic stability is the classic study of aggressiveness within and across generations by Huesmann et al. (1984). They studied aggressiveness at age 8 with judgments by classmates, and aggressiveness at age 30 of the same target individuals with judgments by self and, if available, spouses, finding a heterotypic stability of 0.46 (controlled for

unreliability of the assessments). They also studied at the first assessment with these age-appropriate procedures the aggressiveness of the target individuals' parents that were 30 years old on average, and 22 years later the aggressiveness of the target individuals' own children that were 8 years old on average. Thereby they could not only correlate aggressiveness between parents and their children at two time points 22 years apart but also aggressiveness across generations by correlating parents' aggressiveness with their children's aggressiveness 22 years later, and children's aggressiveness with the aggressiveness of their children in the next generation 22 years later (see Figure 5.5).

As Figure 5.5 indicates, these two cross-generation 'stabilities' were 0.58 and 0.65, thus higher than the within-generation stability of 0.46, which seems surprising because

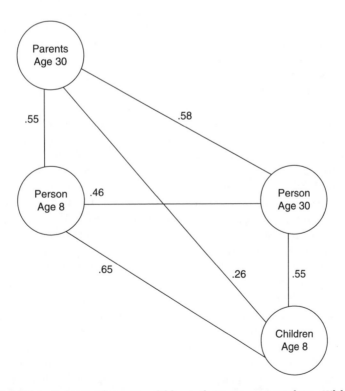

Figure 5.5 Stability of aggressiveness within and across generations. Within-generation stability is heterotypic; across-generation stability is homotypic

the former refers to different individuals. The reason for the higher cross-generation stabilities is that they are homotypic whereas the within-generation stability is heterotypic. Thus, the stability of aggressiveness of 0.46 seems to underestimate the 'true' stability at the construct level.

Stability of personality profiles

Mean-level change and rank-order stability refer to a trait variable as the unit of analysis; they are concepts within a *variable-centered approach* to personality (Magnusson, 2000; Mervielde and Asendorpf, 2000). However, personality consists of many traits and can be described in a first, rough approximation by an individual pattern, or profile, of traits. For example, the *intra*individual pattern of the Big Five traits could be determined for one individual, and then correlated for that individual between different ages, resulting in a coefficient of *profile stability* of the individual. The mean and the standard deviation of profile stability provides information about the overall stability of personality (rather than a specific trait) and about interindividual differences in the long-term stability of personality: some people are more stable than others. One advantage of this *person-centered approach* to personality (Magnusson, 2000; Mervielde and Asendorpf, 2000) is that stability and change are not conceptualized at the level of the sample (as in analyses of mean-level change and rank-order stability) but instead at the level of the individual person.

The individual profile stabilities are not particularly reliable in this case because each one refers to only five data points at each assessment. They are more reliable if they are based on much more than just five traits. Therefore, the Q-sort technique is particularly suited for this approach (see Block, 1971, for a first major application to personality development). Judges sort many (e.g. 100) different trait descriptions (the Q-set) into categories of increasing saliency for the target person (e.g. 10 categories). The stability of the resulting *Q-profiles* is more reliable because it is based on many data points (e.g. 100).

Asendorpf and van Aken (1991) and van Aken and Asendorpf (1999) used this technique to study the longitudinal stability of personality profiles over childhood, using a German version of the California Child Q-Set (Block and Block, 1980). A sample of children was assessed at ages 4 and 6 by their main preschool/kindergarten teacher, and once again at age 10 by their parents. The profile stabilities varied strongly between the children, from −0.44 to 0.88, with a mean stability of 0.43 between ages 4 and 6, and of 0.38 between ages 4 and 10 (despite the much greater age difference and the change in the type of judges). If one roughly estimates the stability of personality profiles by the average stability of the traits on which the profiles are based, these results are by and large consistent with the overall finding of moderate stability of personality traits over childhood (see Figure 5.4).

These authors were also able to explain the differences in the profile stabilities between the children to some extent by correlating the individual stabilities with personality characteristics at age 4 which were also assessed with the Q-sort method. The best predictor for these profile stabilities was children's *ego-resilience*, the tendency to respond flexibly rather than rigidly to changing situational demands, particularly stressful situations (Block and Block, 1980). Ego-resiliency at age 4 correlated 0.64 with the profile stability from age 4 to 6, and 0.49 with the profile stability from age 4 to 10.

Three different developmental mechanisms may contribute to these correlations between resiliency and stability. First, resilient children are better able to control the fit between their personality and their environment. Second, more stable environments very likely promote both ego-resiliency and stability of personality. And third, more stable personality leads to more consistent views of different judges of personality which, in turn, increases the predictability of the social environment of the child and thereby also ego-resiliency (see van Aken and Asendorpf, 1999, for empirical evidence). A similar effect of resilience is found in developmental studies of psychopathology that compare the stability of personality between pathological groups and normal controls: in most studies, the stability is higher in the control group (see Rutter, 1984, for example).

Integration: Plasticity of personality all over the life span

The empirical studies of mean-level change, rank-order stability and profile stability consistently show that, on average for mainly Western cultures, personality never reaches a point of (nearly) full stabilization. Even the high rank-order stability reached after age 50 (see Figure 5.4) does not exclude substantial differential change in many individuals, and the significant mean-level changes in agreeableness and openness to experience after age 50 (see Figure 5.3) even point to changes common to most individuals of that age. Thus, personality continues to change all over the life span in most individuals; contrary to the plaster hypothesis, personality is not set like plaster at any age.

The discussion of homotypic and heterotypic stability has shown that the moderate stability of personality over long time can be partly due to the fact that the assessment procedures are not fully age-appropriate. This can be the case if they remain the same over age (the case of homotypic stability), and even if they are changed over age to make them more age-appropriate (the case of heterotypic stability). This age-appropriateness problem is not only a measurement problem; it is a consequence of personality change and should therefore be rather considered as one indication for long-term personality change.

That personality changes at any age does not imply, of course, that personality is unstable and not predictable over long periods of time. Figures 5.3 and 5.4 show that personality differences are moderately stable from middle childhood onwards, and that the up and down of traits over the life course follow a systematic pattern too. Concerning long-term predictability, even early childhood personality can predict significantly personality and important developmental outcomes in adulthood as will be shown later in this chapter. Personality at any age does matter for further individual development!

In addition, it should be noticed that the overall findings reported in Figures 5.3 and 5.4 refer to averages in samples. It is important to note that an overall moderate stability of 0.50 can be due to moderate stability of personality in nearly everyone but also to high stability of personality in most people along with strong changes in a minority of individuals. Similarly, a significant mean-level change of $d = 0.25$ may very well go along with much stronger changes in one sub-sample, and no change at all in another sub-sample. Although studies of profile stability are still rare, the studies of interindividual differences in profile stability during childhood discussed above suggest the hypothesis that the stability of personality is higher in more competent, resilient individuals all over the life span. Thus, the overall plasticity of personality revealed in the meta-analyses by Roberts and colleagues may be more driven by less competent, less resilient people.

The plasticity of personality all over the life span is not necessarily due to environmental influences on the developing individual. As modern developmental genetics has shown (Rutter, 2006), genes are activated and deactivated all over the life span such that at least some of the mean-level changes, but also some of the differential changes, can be the result of age-related changes in gene activity that are shared by most people (leading to mean-level change) or that are shared only by people with particular alleles (gene variants that differ between individuals). Examples from psychopathology show that the activation even of a single gene can lead to dramatic changes in personality, for example the activation of the gene causing Huntington's chorea (Rutter, 2006). Multivariate behavioral genetic studies show that a substantial portion of the differential change in personality traits such as antisocial tendencies is due to genetic variance (O'Connor et al., 1998).

At the same time, these behavioral genetic studies also show that a substantial portion of the differential change in these personality traits is due to environmental influences. Environmental changes that are shared by most agemates can result in mean-level changes in personality, and environmental changes that occur in some people but not in others can lead to differential changes in personality. It is therefore a matter of empirical study, not of principal argument, to which extent observed changes in personality are due to genes or to the environment, and to which specific genes and to which specific environmental influences.

An example for environmental changes that influence personality is the impact of the first stable partnership on neuroticism and related traits. Neyer and Lehnart (2007) followed a fairly representative sample of young German adults from young adulthood over 8 years, with reassessments after 4 years and after 8 years. They asked them at every assessment whether they had already formed a first stable partnership. According to these reports, they could distinguish four groups: 253 early beginners who reported a partnership already at time 1, 38 timely beginners who reported it for the first time at time 2, 24 late beginners who reported it not before time 3, and 24 stable singles who had not formed any stable partnership up to time 3.

Stable singles did not significantly change in their moderate neuroticism, and the large group of early beginners continued to have the lowest neuroticism of all groups all over the study (see Figure 5.6). Particularly interesting in the present context are the two groups that formed a first stable partnership. Both started off with high neuroticism, and both decreased in neuroticism for the same amount after they established a stable partnership, but at different times. These data are

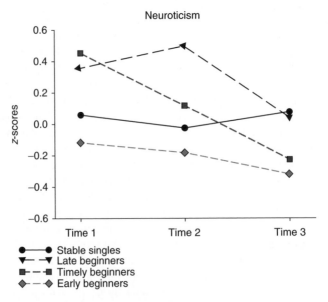

Figure 5.6   Impact of the first stable partnership on neuroticism (reprint of part of fig. 3 in Neyer and Lehnart, 2007 © Blackwell Publishing)

consistent with the interpretation based on attachment theory for adults (Mikulincer and Shaver, 2003) that the partner in a stable partnership functions as a secure base for coping with stress and anxieties and thus reduces neuroticism. Interestingly, dissolutions of a partnership did not increase neuroticism among these young adults; thus, engaging in a serious partnership is a game most people will only win (Neyer and Asendorpf, 2001).

This study nicely illustrates that an overall mean-level change can coexist with substantial differential change, and that *both* can be at least partly due to the same factor (in this case, forming a partnership). Forming a partnership decreased neuroticism, and because this is an environmental change experienced by the great majority of young adults, an overall mean-level change in neuroticism occurs over young adulthood (which is underestimated in this study because it occurred in the majority of the participants before time 1). But the environmental change occurred at different points in time, or not at all, leading to differential change. More generally, a mean-level change in personality at any age and for any trait will very likely go along with differential change for different subgroups, thus, with instability of personality. Therefore, strong mean-level changes are very likely accompanied by low rank-order stability, although mean-level change and rank-order stability are principally independent of one another.

ANTECEDENTS OF ADULT PERSONALITY

In general, adult personality is due to the interaction of genetic and environmental influences over prior development. Because these interactions are specific to specific traits, involving specific genes and specific environments, I illustrate the development of adult personality with two exemplary traits: shyness and aggressiveness. I choose these

traits because the developmental processes involved are relatively well studied.

Antecedents of adult shyness

Shyness in adulthood is a personality trait characterized by the tendency to react in a shy, inhibited, and anxious manner to three types of situations: confrontations with strangers, being in the center of attention of a large group, and anticipating negative or insufficiently positive evaluations by valued others (Asendorpf, 1989; Crozier, 2000). Individual differences in these three types of situations are moderately consistent in adulthood (Russell et al., 1986), which suggests a common underlying trait. Shyness 'cuts through' the two temperamental factors of the five-factor model of personality, extraversion and neuroticism, showing moderately positive correlations with both introversion and neuroticism. This close relation to the two temperamental factors of the Big Five suggests that we should view shyness as a dimension of temperament (Buss and Plomin, 1984).

A straightforward hypothesis is that adult shyness is rooted in early temperament. The importance of early temperament for later adult personality first became evident in the Fels longitudinal study (Kagan and Moss, 1962), where two measures of observed anxiety in unfamiliar social situations at ages 3–6 were both significantly correlated with social anxiety in adulthood, one of the few replicable significant predictions from this early age into adulthood. Much later, Kagan and associates took up this observation in their studies of *behavioral inhibition toward the unfamiliar*, which they defined as observed inhibited responses to both social and nonsocial unfamiliar situations (Kagan et al., 1984). They also studied the concurrent and predictive correlates of high versus low inhibition (often defined as the upper and lower 15% of the distribution of a normal sample) in considerable detail (see Kagan and Snidman, 2004, for a review).

However, it would be overly simplistic to reduce the antecedents of adult shyness to prior temperament. Asendorpf (1990) studied in preschool children the consistency of inhibited behavior across unfamiliar and familiar situations (confrontation with an adult stranger, dyadic play with an unfamiliar peer in the laboratory versus with a familiar peer in the familiar preschool setting, inhibition during free play over three years of preschool/kindergarten). Multiple measures within settings confirmed that inhibition was highly consistent between adult and peer strangers but less consistent with inhibition in the classroom, and not at all consistent with inhibition toward a familiar peer. Thus, other factors than inhibited temperament contributed to individual differences in shy, inhibited behavior.

Longitudinal analyses in the classroom showed an increasing influence of observed instances of peer neglect or rejection on inhibition in the classroom if inhibition toward strangers was controlled. Asendorpf (1990) interpreted this as the increasing influence of social-evaluative concerns on inhibition in the classroom. Follow-ups of extreme groups with stable inhibition toward strangers versus stable inhibition in the more familiar peer group in the second and third years in preschool revealed that stable high inhibition toward strangers was unrelated to self-esteem up to age 12, whereas stable high inhibition in the familiar peer group significantly predicted low social self-esteem between 8 and 12 years of age (Asendorpf and van Aken, 1994). Thus, inhibition in the familiar peer group which was probably due to social-evaluative concerns was a risk factor for internalizing problems over childhood but not inhibition toward the unfamiliar. In line with this finding, a more recent longitudinal study showed that teacher-assessed anxious solitude became associated with peer exclusion soon after entry into kindergarten, and that early peer exclusion increased the risk in anxious-solitary children of developing stable inhibition and depression (Gazelle and Ladd, 2003).

These findings suggest that inhibition in the peer group might be particularly important for the development of adult shyness because it can be due both to the temperamental factor of inhibition toward the unfamiliar and to negative experiences with peers, factors of individual differences that are partly independent of each other but which become easily associated later on. Because temperament is more likely stable than experiences of peer neglect or rejection across different peer groups, the consistency between inhibition toward the unfamiliar and social-evaluative anxiety is expected to increase with age. This hypothesis was confirmed in a longitudinal study by Gest (1997) who found that inhibition toward the unfamiliar was not correlated with negative peer relationships in late childhood (ages 8–11), but in early adulthood (ages 17–24).

Concerning parental influences, many studies rely on retrospective reports of shy adults about their parents' behavior in childhood which are highly questionable because later shyness may have biased childhood memories. Cross-sectional studies all over childhood consistently find that inhibition and shyness is positively associated with anxious-ambivalent attachment to the mother (e.g. Calkins and Fox, 1992) and with a parenting style characterized by either rejection of the child or overprotection of the child (Burgess et al., 2005).

Together, these findings suggest a developmental model for adult shyness as depicted in Figure 5.7. Genetic and early environmental risks lead to a 'slow-to-warm-up' temperament (Thomas and Chess, 1977) and to temperamental inhibition to the unfamiliar (see Kagan and Snidman, 2004, for a discussion of those risks). This early temperamental trait is a risk factor for anxious-ambivalent attachment to the mother and inadequate responses of the parents such as rejection or overprotection. If these risks coincide with risks on part of the parents, particularly parental insensitivity to children's needs (De Wolff and van IJzendoorn, 1997) or a rigid-authoritarian or overprotecting parenting

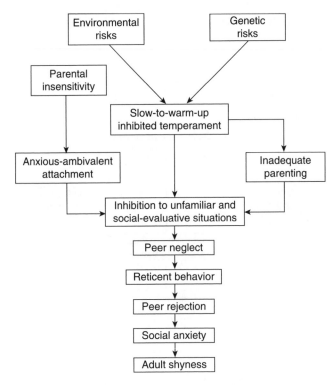

Figure 5.7   A developmental model for shyness (reprint of fig. 3 in Asendorpf, 2008 © Elsevier)

style (Baumrind, 1971), parents' behavior reinforces the children's inhibition tendencies.

When such children enter the unfamiliar social world of preschool, they face the risk of being ignored (but not rejected) by their peers which, in turn, leads to social withdrawal from the peers (Rubin et al., 1990). Beginning in grade 2, peers become more and more aware that the withdrawn children deviate from the age-appropriate pattern of social interaction, which increases the risk that they reject the withdrawn children (Younger et al., 1993). Such peer rejection, in turn, increases social-evaluative anxiety and social withdrawal of the formerly only inhibited children. If these children also face rejection by their potential dating and sexual partners later during adolescence, adult shyness likely results.

It is important to note that, in line with modern developmental psychology, this is a multifactor model of development where a single factor alone has little to no influence on development; what counts is the interaction between multiple risk factors. Also, personality traits such as early temperament alone are not sufficient for explaining later development; what counts is the transaction between personality and environment over age.

Antecedents of adult aggressiveness

Adult aggressiveness is correlated with educational underachievement, job instability, drug dependence, and antisocial behavior (Geen, 1998). As for shyness, aggressiveness can be traced back to early temperament, parental attachment, inadequate parenting, and peer rejection, although the specifics of the risk factors and their consequences on aggressiveness are different. The main developmental processes are depicted in Figure 5.8.

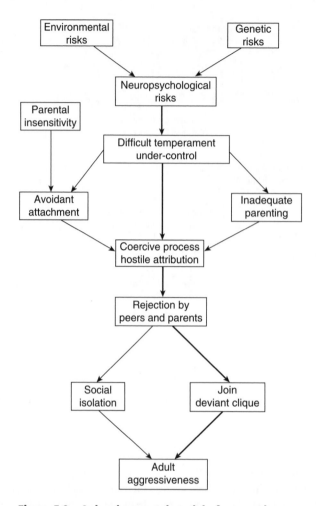

Figure 5.8   A developmental model of aggressiveness

Genetic and early environmental risks for adult aggressiveness are often visible in terms of minor physical anomalies (e.g. Paulhus and Martin, 1986). Aggressiveness in childhood is also correlated with perinatal problems such as oxygen starvation, and later with neuropsychological problems (Moffitt, 1993). These risks lead to a 'difficult temperament' (Thomas and Chess, 1977), characterized by irritability, distractibility, low soothability, and irregular biorhythms. A key feature of difficult temperament is *under-control* (Block and Block, 1980); that is, the inability to control emotional and motivational impulses, including low control of

emotional and motivational impulses, including restlessness, distractibility, and aggressiveness. Such children are difficult to handle by the parents and therefore run the risk of being rejected or maltreated by them. Also, parental insensitivity leads in this case to avoidant attachment (rather than anxious-ambivalent attachment as in the case of shy children). Avoidant attachment, in turn, increases the risk for later aggressiveness in school (Renken et al., 1989).

The parents of aggressive children often develop in early childhood a rigid authoritarian parenting style which is both the consequence of children's aggressive behavior and an antecedent of later aggressiveness (Lytton, 1990; Weiss et al., 1992). In addition, parental rejection and a laissez-faire parenting style (Baumrind, 1971) are also associated with childhood aggressiveness (Loeber and Stouthamer-Loeber, 1986).

Independent of the specific individual pattern of risks, families with an aggressive child are characterized by a *coercive process* (Patterson, 1982) consisting of a vicious circle of aggression and counter-aggression. The detailed behavioral observations of Patterson and colleagues showed that normal children's aggression can often be stopped by parental punishment and siblings' counter-aggression, whereas such social responses amplify rather than stop aggressive children's aggression. This coercive process is the key childhood risk factor for later aggressiveness. It includes not only family members but also peers.

The coercive process is maintained by a key social-cognitive factor: aggressive children's *hostile attribution bias* (Dodge, 1986). Whereas all children tend to react negatively to others' hostility that is clearly observable, aggressive children also respond with aggression to situations where others' behavior is ambiguous (i.e. might be due not only to hostile intention but also to other factors). In this case, they interpret this behavior as hostile whereas normal children would not do so. This hostile attribution bias increases their rate of aggression and leads to the reputation that they are non-predictable and inherently evil. This *bad reputation*, in turn, makes others suspicious, which again is often interpreted by the aggressive children as hostile, and is responded to with aggression.

Aggressive children's bad reputation among peers and among family members leads to rejection by most of these socialization agents. Important for the later development of aggressiveness is how consistently rejection occurs. In most cases, aggressive children join a deviant clique consisting of peers with similar aggressive and antisocial tendencies. If they become an accepted member of such a clique, their aggressiveness and self-esteem is stabilized, and rejection by others is devalued and without consequences (Dishion et al., 1991). If they do not join a deviant clique, aggressive children tend to become socially isolated and to develop negative social self-esteem and less direct forms of hostility. Thus, affiliation with a deviant clique functions as a 'developmental switch' that decides much about the future development of aggressiveness.

Again, this is a multifactor model of development where a single factor alone has little to no influence on development; what counts is the interaction between multiple risk factors. Also, personality traits such as early temperament alone are not sufficient for explaining later development; what counts is the transaction between personality and environment over age.

CONSEQUENCES OF CHILDHOOD PERSONALITY

The preceding section focused on adult personality and asked, looking backward, which antecedents lead to adult personality. In this section, I reverse the developmental perspective, focusing on childhood personality and asking, looking forward, which long-term consequences childhood personality has. Again, and for the same reasons as before, I use the exemplary traits of shyness and aggressiveness to illustrate the extent to which childhood personality predicts important developmental outcomes in adulthood.

Consequences of childhood shyness

As the model for the development of adult shyness suggests (see Figure 5.7), early individual differences in shy-inhibited behavior interact with parental and peer influences over development, and are therefore subject to differential developmental change. Therefore, a high stability from childhood into adulthood is not necessarily expected. Only a few longitudinal studies have followed shy-inhibited children from early or middle childhood into early or middle adulthood.

The earliest study was the Fels longitudinal study (Kagan and Moss, 1962), where two measures of observed anxiety in unfamiliar social situations at ages 3–6 were both significantly correlated with social anxiety in adulthood. Interestingly, the later extensive studies of temperamental inhibition by Kagan and associates (see earlier section on 'Antecedents of adult shyness') did not (yet) result in reports about significant predictions from early inhibition toward the unfamiliar to adulthood personality or social-emotional adaptation. The only significant prediction was so far reported by Schwartz et al. (2003) who found that observed high versus low inhibition at ages 2–3 predicted MRI-recorded high versus low responses to novel faces as compared to familiar faces at age 22. However, only a small number of children were followed into adulthood (e.g. the MRI data were based on only 22 participants) such that firm conclusions about non-predictions from early temperamental inhibition cannot be drawn. Another limitation of these studies by Kagan and associates is that they rely on comparisons between extremely inhibited and extremely uninhibited children (in most cases the upper and lower 15% of the distribution); therefore, it is not clear whether correlates of inhibition are mainly due to uninhibition or to inhibition.

Much better evidence for the long-term outcome of early inhibition is provided by the Dunedin longitudinal study, which follows a large, representative New Zealand birth cohort ($n = 1,037$) into adulthood (Caspi and Silva, 1995). Based on behavioral observations in various situations, 8% of the sample were classified as inhibited at age 3 and followed up until age 26. Compared to a control group of well-adjusted children (40% of the sample), the inhibited children reported more harm avoidance and less social potency and positive emotionality at

both ages 18 and 26, and at age 26 were described by informants as lower in extraversion but not higher in neuroticism (Caspi et al., 2003). The psychiatric interviews at age 21 showed that the inhibited children were not more likely to have anxiety disorders of various kinds, including social phobia, but were more often depressed and had more often attempted suicide (Caspi et al., 1996). Thus, the evidence for internalizing disorders in adulthood for formerly extremely inhibited children was mixed. Importantly, social phobia was not related to early inhibition, nor am I aware of any other prospective longitudinal study that has shown this, contrary to frequent claims in the clinical literature based on retrospective reports (e.g. Stemberger et al., 1995).

With regard to life-course sequelae of childhood inhibition, two longitudinal studies reported delays in social transitions for children classified as inhibited in middle childhood. In their reanalysis of the *Berkeley guidance study* (Macfarlane et al., 1954), Caspi et al. (1988) found such delays only for inhibited boys at ages 8–10 years. These inhibited boys married 3 years later, became fathers 4 years later, and entered a stable occupational career 3 years later than the remaining boys. No such delays were found for the inhibited girls; instead, these girls became women who spent less time in the labor force and married men with higher occupational status. This should not be attributed to instability of female inhibition because Q-sort ratings of inhibition based on two clinical interviews at ages 30 and 40 correlated significantly with both boys' and girls' inhibition. The strong sex difference in the outcomes can be attributed to the traditional gender roles for this 1928 birth cohort that required action and social contacts, particularly from men.

In an attempt to replicate these life-course patterns in a 1955–1958 Swedish cohort, Kerr et al. (1996) studied children that were rated as shy with unfamiliar people by their mothers at ages 8–10 years when they were 25 and 35 years old. Self-judgments of inhibition at age 35 correlated with childhood inhibition significantly for females but not at all for males. Inhibited boys married 4 years later than controls and became fathers 3 years later; shy girls were educational underachievers; that is, reached a lower educational level after controlling for IQ. No effects on the number of job changes or monthly income were observed. Thus, this study replicated the delays for inhibited boys regarding marriage and parenthood as well as the absence of this effect for girls; unfortunately, the age at beginning a stable career was not recorded.

In a recent follow-up of the Munich longitudinal study on the genesis of individual competencies (LOGIC) (Weinert and Schneider, 1999), Asendorpf et al. (in press) replicated the findings of delayed social transitions into adulthood not only for boys but also for girls, and also found a low stability of shyness between early childhood and adulthood. In this 19-year longitudinal study, the 15% most inhibited children at ages 4–6 years in a normal German sample were targeted by teacher Q-sort judgments, and were compared with controls who were below average in preschool inhibition. As adults, inhibited boys *and* girls were judged as shy by their parents and showed a delay in their first stable partnership and their first full-time job. This diminishing of a former sex difference was not unexpected for our sample, composed as it was of participants who grew up in a culture characterized by more egalitarian gender roles than one or two generations earlier. Only the upper 8% in terms of inhibition tended to show internalizing problems, including self-rated inhibition. This tendency was of a similar effect size as in the Dunedin longitudinal study but not significant because of the smaller longitudinal sample ($n = 147$).

Together, these longitudinal studies draw a consistent picture of the long-term consequences of early shyness. There is some stability of the core temperamental trait of inhibition toward unfamiliar situations. This temperamental trait makes it more difficult for inhibited persons to cope with *social life transitions* where they are confronted with unfamiliar people. They are 'slow-to-warm-up' (Thomas and Chess, 1977) in such situations, even as adults when they meet dating partners, enter new educational settings such as university, and apply for jobs, which results in delayed social development. For example, a short-term longitudinal study of the transition to university found that shy students learned to know new peers at a lower pace than their non-shy counterparts (Asendorpf and Wilpers, 1998; see Figure 5.9).

Shy students' peer network increased all the time during the 18 months of observation whereas the non-shy students did not any add more new peers to their network after 9 months than they lost. Because of their steadier network growth, the shy students had only slightly fewer peers in their network at the end of the study than the non-shy students (a non-significant difference). Thus, shyness led to a slower adaptation to the new social world of university, but in the long run to a peer network of similar size (if we had observed longer, the peer networks of shy and non-shy students may have been found to be equally large).

This early temperamental core of shyness is recognized by others (e.g. the parents of the adult participants of the LOGIC study) but interacts so strongly with parental and peer influences over development that it is detectable in adults' self-judgments only in cases of extremely high childhood inhibition. Besides, early shyness does not lead to any identified psychological problems in adulthood, particularly not to social phobia.

Consequences of childhood aggressiveness

As the model for the development of adult aggressiveness suggests (see Figure 5.8), early temperamental under-control interacts with parental and peer influences over development, and is therefore subject to differential developmental change. Therefore,

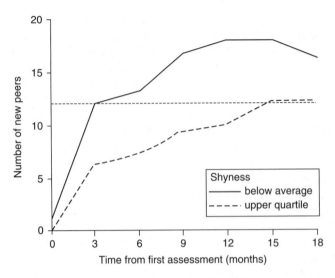

Figure 5.9   Change in the number of new peer relationships after entering university, by shyness (reprint of fig. 2 in Asendorpf and Wilpers, 1998, with permission of American Psychological Association)

a high stability from childhood into adulthood is not necessarily expected. However, numerous longitudinal studies exist that followed under-controlled or aggressive children into adulthood, and all found clear evidence for a substantial stability from childhood into adulthood (e.g. Robins, 1966; Huesmann et al., 1984; Tremblay, 2000).

Again, one of the best pieces of evidence for the long-term stability of this under-controlled pattern from early childhood into adulthood is the Dunedin longitudinal study (see previous section). Based on behavioral observations in various situations, 10% of the sample were classified as under-controlled at age 3. Compared to a control group of well-adjusted children (40% of the sample), the under-controlled children reported high negative emotionality at both ages 18 and 26, particularly feelings of being mistreated and betrayed by others, and at age 26 were described by knowledgeable informants as low in agreeableness, conscientiousness, and openness to experience, and high in neuroticism (Caspi et al., 2003). Psychiatric interviews and official crime records at age 21 showed that under-controlled children had

significantly increased risks for an antisocial personality disorder, convictions for a violent offense, a high variety of self-reported offenses, and suicide attempts (Caspi, 2000; Caspi et al., 1996).

With regard to life-course sequelae of childhood under-control even further into adulthood, Caspi et al. (1987) reanalyzed data from the Berkeley guidance study for boys and girls born in 1928 with a history of temper tantrums at ages 8–10 years. Interviews at ages 30 and 40 years revealed that under-controlled boys later experienced downward occupational mobility and erratic work lives, and were likely to be divorced; under-controlled girls later married men with lower occupational status, were likely to be divorced, and became ill-tempered mothers. Interestingly, the effect on men's erratic work lives was only partially mediated by their occupational status in midlife; thus, under-control in middle childhood directly contributed to later erratic work lives.

In the LOGIC study, Asendorpf et al. (in press) contrasted the 15% most aggressive children at ages 4–6 years (teacher Q-sort judgments) with controls who were below average in preschool aggression. Because nearly all aggressive children were male, sex differences could not be evaluated within this study. At age 23, they were judged by their parents to be more aggressive, less agreeable, less conscientious, lower in openness to experience, and more neurotic (particularly on items referring to impulsiveness). The aggressive group reported normal peer relationships at age 23; interpersonal conflict was perceived by themselves only in their relationship with the mother and, if available, their current romantic partner. It seems that at this age aggressiveness affected mainly close relationships that are not easily dissolved; later on, one might expect additional problems in close relationships at work (see Caspi et al., 1987). Furthermore, the aggressive children had reached a lower educational level by age 23. Their probability of finishing high school was only 33%, half of the probability for the control group. Their lower educational achievement can be partly attributed to their somewhat lower IQ at ages 4–6 although their IQ at age 23 was only slightly, and non-significantly, lower than the IQ of the control group. Statistical control for their lower IQ at either age did not change the picture; after this correction, 23% of the aggressive children but 62% of the controls were expected to finish high school. Thus, aggressive children were *educational underachievers* (Mandel, 1997). Their underachievement was present right from the beginning of primary school because many of the aggressive children started primary school a year later than expected for their birth cohort. This effect did not diminish during childhood and into adolescence but instead continued to show up in each grade until grade 11.

The aggressive children also turned into *occupational underachievers* who did not become as involved in full-time work as one would expect from their educational level. Interestingly, this effect of early aggressiveness was found only for the percentage of time in full-time employment, not for the latency to first full-time job. The discrepancy suggests that the aggressive group had problems with following a continuous

career after they had entered the job market. This result squares nicely with the more erratic work pattern found in the Berkeley guidance study (Caspi et al., 1987). It is notable that such an effect was already found early on in their working lives. Last but not least, the formerly aggressive children were at a 12-times higher risk of criminal charges after their eighteenth birthday than the controls. However, this impressive figure should be considered with caution because the delinquency rate was extremely low for the control children, and only a minority of the aggressive group reported criminal charges.

Together, these longitudinal studies of undercontrolled or aggressive children show a much higher stability of the personality pattern than the comparable analyses of shy-inhibited children, and more serious outcomes in adulthood. The main reason for this discrepancy in stability and predictability seems to be that personality effects on the social environment are strong and widespread for aggressiveness (Lytton, 1990), whereas they are less strong for shyness because shy individuals are more self-contained and interfere less with others.

CONCLUSION: THREE PRINCIPLES OF PERSONALITY DEVELOPMENT

I conclude this review by highlighting three principles of personality development (see Biesanz et al., 2003, for more methodology-related principles). The first principle is the *high plasticity* of personality all over the life span, which has already been discussed at some length earlier in the chapter.

The second principle is the *long-term stabilization* of personality. As the results for the rank-order stability of personality traits have shown (see Figure 5.4), the stability of interindividual differences continues to increase until at least age 50. This long-term stabilization seems to rely on at least four different processes (see, Caspi et al., 2005, for example).

First, multivariate behavior genetic studies suggest that much of the stability in adult personality is attributable to genetic factors (Rutter, 2006). The individual genetic make-up is stable over the life course after all, even though the genetic activity and hence genetic effects on personality can change (see the discussion of genetic influences on personality change earlier in the chapter).

Second, people select, modify, or create their own environment to some extent in line with their personality, and these 'niche-building processes' promote the stability of personality traits. For example, aggressive adolescents and young adults tend to join deviant groups, to drop out of school and work, and to create conflictual relationships with partners, which in turn stabilizes their aggressiveness (see sections on the consequences of childhood shyness and aggressiveness, earlier in the chapter). In other words, people partly create the environmental conditions for their own further development to be consistent with their personality. Once in a more personality-correlated environment, this environment can have causal effects of its own (e.g. the deviant clique, the conflictual partner relationship), promoting personality stability and cutting off opportunities for change.

Third, people develop, become committed to, and maintain a stable *personal identity* that provides a reference point for important life decisions. One's identity serves as a filter for life experiences and leads one to interpret new events in ways that are consistent with one's personality. Furthermore, this identity is perceived by others, and communicated to them, which evokes responses in line with one's personality. Identities become more and more stable all over adolescence and adulthood, and their stabilization promotes the stability of personality.

And fourth, as discussed earlier in the section on homotypic versus heterotypic stability, the stability of personality is linked to resiliency; that is, the ability to deal with environmental challenges. Because traits characteristic for resiliency such as emotional stability, conscientiousness, and agreeableness show a mean-level increase over adulthood (see section on mean-level change in personality traits), the resulting increase in resiliency leads to an increasing stability of personality.

A third principle of personality development has been more recently discovered in empirical studies of personality change and is called the *corresponsive principle* (Roberts et al., 2003). This principle links personality effects on the environment with environmental effects on personality across traits. The assumption is that those traits that select people into specific environments are the traits that are most influenced by these environments. For example, if people assume leadership positions because they are more dominant, they will become even more dominant through their leader position. Because of this principle, life experiences do not affect all traits of an individual equally strongly; instead, it is expected that the more characteristic traits of an individual are more affected than the less characteristic traits of that person because the life experiences are correlated with the more characteristic traits in the first place.

REFERENCES

Asendorpf, J.B. (1989) 'Shyness as a final common pathway for two different kinds of inhibition', *Journal of Personality and Social Psychology*, 57(3): 481–92.

Asendorpf, J.B. (1990) 'Development of inhibition during childhood: Evidence for situational specificity and a two-factor model', *Developmental Psychology*, 26(5): 721–30.

Asendorpf, J.B. (2008) 'Shyness', in M.M. Haith and J.B. Benson (eds), *Encyclopedia of Infant and Childhood Development*. Elsevier: San Diego, pp. 146–53.

Asendorpf, J.B., Denissen, J.J.A. and van Aken, M.A.G. (in press) 'Inhibited and aggressive preschool children at 23 years of age: Personality and social transitions into adulthood', *Developmental Psychology*.

Asendorpf, J.B. and van Aken, M.A.G. (1991) 'Correlates of the temporal consistency of personality patterns in childhood', *Journal of Personality*, 59(4): 689–703.

Asendorpf, J.B. and van Aken, M.A.G. (1994) 'Traits and relationship status', *Child Development*, 65(6): 1786–98.

Asendorpf, J.B. and Wilpers, S. (1998) 'Personality effects on social relationships', *Journal of Personality and Social Psychology*, 74(6): 1531–44.

Baumrind, D. (1971) 'Current patterns of parental authority', *Developmental Psychology Monographs*, 1: 1–103.

Biesanz, J.C., West, S.G. and Kwok, O.-M. (2003) 'Personality over time: Methodological approaches to the study of short-term and long-term development and change', *Journal of Personality*, 71(6): 905–41.

Block, J. (1971) *Lives Through Time*. Berkeley: Bancroft Books.

Block, J.H. and Block, J. (1980) 'The role of ego-control and ego-resiliency in the organization of behavior', in W.A. Collins (ed.), *Minnesota Symposium on Child Psychology*. Vol. 13. Hillsdale, NJ: Erlbaum, pp. 39–101.

Burgess, K.B., Rubin, K.H. and Cheah, C.S.L. (2005) 'Behavioral inhibition, social withdrawal, and parenting', in Crozier, W.R. and Alden, L.E. (eds), *The Essential Handbook of Social Anxiety for Clinicians*. New York: Wiley, pp. 99–120.

Buss, A.H. and Plomin, R. (1984) *Temperament: Early Developing Personality Traits*. Hillsdale, NJ: Erlbaum.

Calkins, S.D. and Fox, N.A. (1992) 'The relations among infant temperament, security of attachment, and behavioral inhibition at twenty-four months', *Child Development*, 63(6): 1456–72.

Caspi, A. (2000) 'The child is the father of the man: Personality continuities from childhood to adulthood', *Journal of Personality and Social Psychology*, 78(1): 158–72.

Caspi, A., Bem, D.J. and Elder, G.H. (1988) 'Moving away from the world: Life-course patterns of shy children', *Developmental Psychology*, 24(6): 824–31.

Caspi, A., Elder, G.H. and Bem, D.J. (1987) 'Moving against the world: Life-course patterns of explosive children', *Developmental Psychology*, 23(2): 308–13.

Caspi, A., Harrington, H., Milne, B., Amell, J.W., Theodore, R.F. and Moffitt, T.E. (2003) 'Children's behavioral styles at age 3 are linked to their adult personality traits at age 26', *Journal of Personality*, 71(4): 495–513.

Caspi, A., Moffitt, T.E., Newman, D.L. and Silva, P.A. (1996) 'Behavioral observations at age 3 years predict adult psychiatric disorders', *Archives of General Psychiatry*, 53(6): 1033–9.

Caspi, A., Roberts, B.W. and Shiner, R.L. (2005) 'Personality development: Stability and change', *Annual Review of Psychology*, 56: 453–84.

Caspi, A. and Silva, P.A. (1995) 'Temperamental qualities at age three predict personality traits in young adulthood: Longitudinal evidence from a birth cohort', *Child Development*, 66(2): 486–98.

Costa, P.T. Jr. and McCrae, R.R. (1994) 'Set like plaster: Evidence for the stability of adult personality', in T.F. Heatherton and J.L. Weinberger (eds), *Can Personality Change?* Washington, DC: American Psychological Association, pp. 21–40.

Crozier, W.R. (2000) (ed.), *Shyness: Development, Consolidation, and Change*. London: Routledge.

De Wolff, M.S. and van IJzendoorn, M.H. (1997) 'Sensitivity and attachment: A meta-analysis on parental antecedents of infant attachment', *Child Development*, 68(4): 571–91.

Dishion, T.J., Patterson, G.R., Stoolmiller, M. and Skinner, M.L. (1991) 'Family, school, and behavioral antecedents to early adolescent involvement with antisocial peers', *Developmental Psychology*, 27(1): 172–80.

Dodge, K.A. (1986) 'A social information processing model of social competence in children', in M. Perlmutter (ed.), *Minnesota Symposium on Child Psychology*. Vol. 18. Hillsdale, NJ: Erlbaum, pp. 77–125.

Gazelle, H. and Ladd, G.W. (2003) 'Anxious solitude and peer exclusion: A diathesis-stress model of internalizing trajectories in childhood', *Child Development*, 74(1): 257–78.

Geen, R.G. (1998) 'Aggression and antisocial behavior', in D.T. Gilbert, S.T. Fiske and G. Lindzey (eds), *The Handbook of Social Psychology*. Vol. 2 (4th edn). New York: McGraw-Hill, pp. 317–56.

Gest, S.D. (1997) 'Behavioral inhibition: Stability and associations with adaptation from childhood to early adulthood', *Journal of Personality and Social Psychology*, 72(2): 467–75.

Huesmann, L.R., Eron, L.D., Lefkowitz, M.M. and Walder, L.O. (1984) 'Stability of aggression over time and generations', *Developmental Psychology*, 20(6): 1120–34.

James, W. (1950) *The Principles of Psychology*. New York: Dover. (Original work published 1890).

Kagan, J. (1980) 'Perspectives on continuity', in O.G. Brim Jr. and J. Kagan (eds), *Constancy and Change in Human Development*. Cambridge, UK: Harvard University Press, pp. 26–74.

Kagan, J. and Snidman, N. (2004) *The Long Shadow of Temperament*. Cambridge, MA: Harvard University Press.

Kagan, J. and Moss, H.A. (1962) *Birth to Maturity: A Study of Psychological Development*. New York: Wiley.

Kagan, J., Reznick, J.S., Clarke, C., Snidman, N. and Garcia-Coll, C. (1984) 'Behavioral inhibition to the unfamiliar', *Child Development*, 55(6): 2212–25.

Kerr, M., Lambert, W.W. and Bem, D.J. (1996) 'Life course sequelae of childhood shyness in Sweden: Comparison with the United States', *Developmental Psychology*, 32(6): 1100–5.

Loeber, R. and Stouthamer-Loeber, M. (1998) 'Development of juvenile aggression and violence', *American Psychologist*, 53(2): 242–59.

Lytton, H. (1990) 'Child and parent effects in boys' conduct disorder: A reinterpretation', *Developmental Psychology*, 26(5): 683–97.

Magnusson, D. (2000) 'The individual as the organizing principle in psychological inquiry: A holistic approach', in L.R. Bergman, R.B. Cairns, L.-G. Nilsson and L. Nystedt (eds), *Developmental Science and the Holistic Approach*. Mahwah, NJ: Erlbaum, pp. 49–62.

MacFarlane, J.W., Allen, L. and Honzik, M.P. (1954) *A Developmental Study of the Behavior Problems of Normal Children Between Twenty-one Months and Fourteen Years*. Berkeley: University of California Press.

Mandel, H.P. (1997) *Conduct Disorder and Underachievement: Risk Factors, Assessment, Treatment, and Prevention*. New York: Wiley.

McCrae, R.R. and Costa, P.T. Jr. (1990) *Personality in Adulthood*. New York: Guilford Press.

McCrae, R.R. and Costa, P.T. Jr. (1999) 'A five-factor theory of personality', in L.A. Pervin and O.P. John (eds), *Handbook of Personality Theory and Research* (2nd edn). New York: Guilford, pp. 139–53.

McCrae, R.R., Costa, P.T. Jr., Ostendorf, F., Angleitner, A., Hrebickova, M., Avia, M.D., Sanz, J., Sanchez-Bernardoz. M.L., Kusdul, M.E., Woodfield, R. Saunders, P.R. and Smith, P.B. (2000) 'Nature over nurture: Temperament, personality, and life span development', *Journal of Personality and Social Psychology*, 78(1): 173–86.

McCrae, R.R., Terracciano, A. and 78 members of the Personality Profiles of Cultures Project (2005) 'Universal features of personality traits from the observer's perspective: Data from 50 cultures', *Journal of Personality and Social Psychology*, 88(3): 547–61.

Mervielde, I. and Asendorpf, J.B. (2000) 'Variable-centred and person-centred approaches to childhood personality', in S.E. Hampson (ed.), *Advances in Personality Psychology*. Vol. 1. East Sussex: Psychology Press, pp. 37–76.

Mikulincer, M. and Shaver, P.R. (2003) 'The attachment behavioral system in adulthood: Activation, psychodynamics, and interpersonal processes', in M.P. Zanna (ed.), *Advances in Experimental Social Psychology*. Vol. 35. New York: Academic Press, pp. 53–152.

Moffitt, T.E. (1993) 'Adolescence-limited and life-course-persistent antisocial behavior: A developmental taxonomy', *Psychological Review*, 100(4): 674–701.

Neyer, F.J. and Asendorpf, J.B. (2001) 'Personality-relationship transaction in young adulthood', *Journal of Personality and Social Psychology*, 81(6): 1190–204.

Neyer, F.J. and Lehnart, J. (2007) 'Relationships matter in personality development: Evidence from an 8-year longitudinal study across young adulthood', *Journal of Personality*, 75: 535–68.

O'Connor, T.G., Neiderhiser, J.M. and Reiss, D. (1998) 'Genetic contributions to continuity, change, and co-occurrence of antisocial and depressive symptoms in adolescence', *Journal of Child Psychology and Psychiatry*, 39(3): 323–36.

Patterson, G.R. (1982) *Coercive Family Process*. Eugene: Castalia.

Paulhus, D.L. and Martin, C.L. (1986) 'Predicting adult temperament from minor physical anomalies', *Journal of Personality and Social Psychology*, 50(6): 1235–9.

Renken, B., Egeland, B., Marvinney, D., Mangelsdorf, S. and Sroufe, L.A. (1989) 'Early childhood antecedents of aggression and passive-withdrawal in early elementary school', *Journal of Personality*, 57(2): 257–81.

Roberts, B.W., Caspi, A. and Moffitt, T.E. (2003) 'Work experiences and personality development in young adulthood', *Journal of Personality and Social Psychology*, 84(3): 582–93.

Roberts, B.W. and DelVecchio, W.F. (2000) 'The rank-order consistency of personality traits from childhood to old age: A quantitative review of longitudinal studies', *Psychological Bulletin*, 126(1): 3–25.

Roberts, B.W., Walton, K.E. and Viechtbauer, W. (2006) 'Patterns of mean-level change in personality traits across the life-course: A meta-analysis of longitudinal studies', *Psychological Bulletin*, 132(1): 1–25.

Robins, L.N. (1966) *Deviant Children Grown Up*. Baltimore: Williams & Wilkins.

Rose, S.A. and Feldman, J.F. (1995) 'Prediction of IQ and specific cognitive abilities at 11 years from infancy measures', *Developmental Psychology*, 31(4): 685–96.

Rubin, K.H., LeMare, L.J. and Lollis, S. (1990) 'Social withdrawal in childhood: Developmental pathways to peer rejection', in S.R. Asher and J.D. Coie (eds), *Peer Rejection in Childhood*. Cambridge, UK: Cambridge University Press, pp. 217–49.

Russell, D., Cutrona, C.E., and Jones, W.H. (1986) 'A trait-situational analysis of shyness', in W.H. Jones, J.M. Cheek and S.R. Briggs (eds), *Shyness: Perspectives on Research and Treatment*. New York: Plenum Press, pp. 239–49.

Rutter, M. (1984) 'Continuities and discontinuities in socioemotional development', in R.N. Emde and R.J. Harmon (eds), *Continuities and Discontinuities in Development*. New York: Plenum Press, pp. 41–68.

Rutter, M. (2006) *Genes and Behavior: Nature-Nurture Interplay Explained*. Malden, MA: Blackwell Publishing.

Schwartz, C.E., Wright, C.I., Shin, L.M., Kagan, J., and Rauch, S.L. (2003) 'Inhibited and uninhibited infants "grown up": Adult amygdalar response to novelty', *Science*, 300(5627): 1952–3.

Srivastava, S., John, O.P., Gosling, S. and Potter, J. (2003) Development of personality in early and middle adulthood: Set like plaster or persistent change? *Journal of Personality and Social Psychology*, 84(5): 1041–53.

Stemberger, R.T., Turner, S.M., Beidel, D.C. and Calhoun, K.S. (1995) Social phobia: An analysis of possible developmental factors. *Journal of Abnormal Psychology*, 104(3): 526–31.

Thomas, A. and Chess, S. (1977) *Temperament and Development*. New York: Brunner and Mazel.

Tremblay, R.E. (2000) 'The development of aggressive behavior during childhood: What have we learned in the past century?', *International Journal of Behavioral Development*, 24(2): 129–141.

van Aken, M.A.G. and Asendorpf J.B. (1999) 'A person-centered approach to development: The temporal consistency of personality and self-concept', in F.E. Weinert and W. Schneider (eds), *Individual Development from 3 to 12: Findings from a Longitudinal Study*. Cambridge, UK: Cambridge University Press, pp. 301–319

Weinert, F.E. and Schneider, W. (1999) 'Individual development from 3 to 12: Findings from the Munich Longitudinal Study', Cambridge, UK: Cambridge University Press.

Weiss, B., Dodge, K.A., Bates, J.E. and Pettit, G.S. (1992) 'Some consequences of early harsh discipline: Child aggression and a maladaptive social information processing style', *Child Development*, 63(6): 1321–35.

Younger, A., Gentile, C. and Burgess, K. (1993) 'Children's perceptions of social withdrawal: Changes across age', in K.H. Rubin and J.B. Asendorpf (eds), *Social Withdrawal, Inhibition, and Shyness in Childhood*. Hillsdale, NJ: Erlbaum, pp. 215–35.

6

Personality:
Cross-Cultural Perspectives

Chi-Yue Chiu, Young-Hoon Kim and Wendy W.N. Wan

CULTURE AND PERSONALITY STUDIES: THE HISTORICAL CONTEXT

The primary concern of culture and personality studies is to uncover the intimate connections between human nature and the knowledge traditions in different human groups. Culture and personality research reached its peak of interest in the social sciences when Kluckhohn and Murray published *Personality in Nature, Society, and Culture* in 1948. This edited volume sought to offer comprehensive frameworks for understanding the complex interactions of biology, society, culture, and personality. However, the field stumbled and crumbled just a decade after the publication of this volume when culture and personality research was associated with the controversial national character studies. National character researchers sought to understand the cultural patterns of nations (e.g. Japan, Russia) largely through indirect methods (e.g. interviewing immigrants) rather than by conducting fieldworks in those nations. National character studies invited skepticisms from the learned community and were

severely criticized for attributing an inordinate amount of homogeneity in a national group based on sparse and questionable evidence. Interest in culture and personality research declined quickly with the stigmatization of the field as a discipline that promotes national stereotypes (LeVine, 2001). According to LeVine (2001), in 1960, when Francis Hsu decided on the title of his handbook of culture and personality, he felt compelled to pick the title of *Psychological Anthropology* to avoid the association with the already stigmatized 'culture and personality studies'.

At the turn of the century, McCrae (2000) predicted that the advances in trait psychology will help to renew personality psychologists' interest in culture and personality studies. Unfortunately, this prophecy is not fulfilled. Of the 2901 articles published in five major journals in personality psychology (*Journal of Personality, Journal of Personality and Social Psychology, Journal of Research in Personality, Personality and Social Psychology Bulletin, Personality and Social Psychology Review*) between year 2000 and the date of a recent PsycINFO search (3 March, 2007), only 80 articles (2.8%) are indexed with a personality keyword ('personality', 'personality change', 'personality correlates', 'personality development', 'personality measures', or 'personality theory') *and* a culture keyword ('cross-cultural differences', 'culture', culture change', or 'culture shock'). Interestingly, of these 80 articles, 58 articles are indexed with the keyword 'cross-cultural differences'.

During the same period, a total of 764 articles were published in three major journals in culture and psychology (*Cultural Diversity and Ethnic Minority Psychology, Culture and Psychology, Journal of Cross-Cultural Psychology*). About 10% of them (79 articles) were indexed with a personality keyword *and* a culture keyword. Of these 79 articles, 69 (87.3%) were indexed with *cross-cultural differences*. These results support two conclusions. First, although the relationship of culture and personality is of considerable interest to culture researchers, it has received very little attention from personality psychologists. Second, in both culture research and personality psychology, cross-cultural differences have been the focal emphasis in the recent years.

The stigma associated with national character studies is still a reason why some personality psychologists avert their gaze from the relationship of culture and personality. In fact, when McCrae (2004) advocated for a trait psychology of culture, he was highly conscious of the risk that results concerning trait differences between ethnic groups can be misused as a basis of discrimination. Thus, he reminded culture and personality researchers to qualify their results with appropriate caveats: small effect size, low predictive relationship between traits and specific behaviors, the presence of variations within all cultural groups, limitations of the study, and availability of alternative interpretations.

Aside from the stigma attached to culture and personality studies, several conceptual issues have impeded the advances of the field. These issues include some misconceptions of culture, the oversold dualism of

personality versus culture, and the lack of an integrated theory of culture and personality (Church, 2000). To remove the intellectual obstacles in the field, the first step is to address each of these issues. Accordingly, our review of the contemporary research scholarships centers around the following themes: (a) defining what culture is; (b) the dualism of personality versus culture; and (c) theoretical pluralism in the field. Following the review, we will propose an integrated theoretical perspective to understand the nature of culture and personality and how they act on individual behaviors.

WHAT IS CULTURE?

Issues and controversies

There is a growing consensus among personality psychologists on what personality refers to. Although there are different theoretical perspectives in the discipline, most personality psychologists accept the assumption that there are stable individual differences. Moreover, an individual's characteristic patterns of cognitions, affects, motivations, and behaviors are assumed to reflect the dynamic organization of various psychological structures within the individual (Allport, 1961).

Personality psychologists differ in the relative emphasis they place on the different psychophysical systems. The five-factor model (FFM) assumes that biologically inheritable traits provide the foundational structures of human personality and treats the relatively proximal and the situationally flexible person variables (self-concept, goals, roles, schemas, scripts) as *characteristic adaptations*. In the FFM, traits and the environment jointly determine these characteristic adaptations (McCrae, 2004). Taking a social cognitive perspective, some personality psychologists focus on *how* biology and experiences (and the cognitive representations of these experiences) shape the development of personality structures and processes (Pervin, 1996). By comparison, in the social sciences, culture has been an elusive concept. As Lowell (1934: 115) puts it, trying to encompass the meaning of *culture* in words is like trying to seize air in the hand: 'It is everywhere but except within one's grasp.' In a classic review of the concept, Kroeber and Kluckhohn (1952) brought more than 160 definitions to light.

Influenced by symbolic anthropology, which was popular in American anthropology starting from the 1960s, in much current usage in cross-cultural and cultural psychology, culture is viewed as the specific meanings a certain human group assigns to objects, behaviors and emotions. In line with this definition of culture, in practice, many psychologists have studied the influence of culture by comparing national groups or ethnocultural groups residing in the same nation (e.g. Japanese, South Koreans, Hong Kong Chinese) (Chiu and Chen, 2004). As noted earlier, cross-cultural comparison is still a major research strategy in the culture and personality studies in psychology.

This research practice attributes culture to a specific *group* and has the undesirable consequence of giving *culture* the unwelcome connotation of being a bounded, homogenous, coherent, and stable entity. Some scholars have written against this usage of *culture*. In a disparaging tone, Keesing (1994: 302) wrote, 'Our conception of culture almost irresistibly leads us into reification and essentialism.' To a similar effect, Appadurai wrote:

> The noun *culture* appears to privilege the sort of sharing, agreeing, and bounding that fly in the face of the facts of unequal knowledge and the differential prestige of lifestyles, and to discourage attention to the worldviews and agency of those who are marginalized or dominated (1996: 12).

Culture as knowledge tradition

The debate on what culture is continues. However, there is a growing consensus among culture researchers (Barth, 2002; Brumann, 1999; Chiu and Chen, 2004; Chiu and Hong, 2006, 2007; Kashima, 2000; Keesing, 1974; Rohner, 1984; Shore, 1996, 2002; Sperber, 1996) that culture should be viewed as a knowledge tradition. A knowledge tradition refers to a loosely organized network of knowledge that is produced, distributed, and reproduced by a collection of interconnected individuals (Chiu and Hong, 2006).

Two important aspects of this definition should be emphasized. First, knowledge includes not only ideas; it consists of a cluster of common concepts, emotions, and practices that arise when people interact regularly (Barth, 2002; Brumann, 1999). These concepts, emotions, and practices exist not only in the mind of the individuals, but are also encoded in external carriers of culture (e.g. media) and institutionalized in shared practices (e.g. customs, rituals).

Second, this definition treats culture and society (a group of interconnected individuals) as separate theoretical entities. Every individual in a society has some, but probably nobody has perfect knowledge of his or her culture. Additionally, some knowledge is shared more in a society than other knowledge. The fact that at least some cultural knowledge is not perfectly shared in a society leaves room for cultural diversity within the society. Thus, by dissociating culture from a demarcated population, researchers avoid the criticism of reifying culture and attributing an inordinate amount of boundedness and homogeneity to a cultural group.

More important, by treating people and culture as separate theoretical entities, this definition permits researchers to describe the different ways people participate in and interact with culture. For example, investigators may examine how people create culture, use culture as guides for their social practices, reflect on the strengths and liabilities of a cultural tradition, identify with or dissociate themselves from a culture, use culture as a tool to attain their personal goals, reproduce culture (by spreading it to other territories and transmitting it to new generations), and change culture. Thus, people are not treated as passive recipients of cultural influence; they also express and actualize their agency via culture (Chiu and Chen, 2004).

THE DUALISM OF BIOLOGY VERSUS CULTURE

Culture and personality research can potentially reveal the intricate interactions and interdependence of nature and social ecology. A major intellectual obstacle in the field is the popularized dualism of nature versus culture or the assumption that what is cultural is not natural, and vice versa. This dualism is manifest in some early definitions of culture. For instance, Keesing (1958: 16) defined culture as 'the totality of *learned*, socially transmitted behavior', and Kroeber and Kluckhohn (1954: 283) referred to culture as 'the set of attributes and products of human societies, and therewith of mankind, which is *extrasomatic* and transmittable by mechanisms other than *biological heredity*' (emphases added).

The dualism of nature versus culture is also manifest in the five-factor theory (FFT) of culture and personality. For example, McCrae maintains that 'one distinctive feature of FFT is the postulate that the basis of traits is solely biological: there are no arrows connecting culture to personality traits' (2004: 5).

In our opinion, the dualism of nature versus culture is oversold. Before we elaborate on our position, it is important to distinguish the specific and generic senses of the word *culture*. The specific sense of culture refers to the knowledge tradition characteristic of a human population. This sense of culture distinguishes the culture of one society from that of another. The generic sense of culture refers to the uniquely human capability to create and cumulate shared knowledge. A certain culture (in the specific sense of the word) may develop in a certain society as a result of the interactions between individuals' fundamental social and psychological needs and the ecological constraints on the expression of these needs (Chiu and Hong, 2007). However, people in all societies are biologically prepared to create and cumulate human culture (in the generic sense of word). In this sense, all human cultures are biologically enabled.

Biological adaptations for culture

The ability to create culture or shared knowledge is not specific to humans. For years, researchers (van Schaik et al., 2003; Whiten et al., 1999) have observed chimpanzee behaviors in the rainforests of Africa and South Asia. In 1999, Whiten et al. provided a synthetic summary of the research findings from seven long-term studies that were conducted at seven research sites. Sixty-five different categories of behaviors were observed and recorded in seven chimpanzee populations. Most of these behaviors are related to chimpanzees' tool use, grooming, and courtship. Of the 65 behaviors, 39 have occurred in all or most able-bodied members of at least one age-sex class (e.g. female adults) or have occurred repeatedly in several individuals in some chimpanzee populations, an indication of some degree of social transmission, but are absent in others for no apparent ecological reason. The presence of local variations in learned behaviors among chimpanzees suggests that chimpanzees have culture; they transmit behaviors repeatedly through social and observational learning.

However, there is a fundamental difference between human and ape cultures: Human culture builds upon itself and ape culture does not. Some chimpanzees learned to build a cover on their nest during bright sunshine, but they do not pass this knowledge on to the next generation, and hence do not accumulate modifications of their invention over time. By comparison, human culture is cumulative. When humans discover a piece of knowledge, they start from there and go on. In human societies, once the wheel is invented, new generations do not have to invent it again. Instead, they build on it and invent the carriage, and then the motor vehicle. This uniquely human process is referred to as *ratcheting*, and is the engine for human cultures. Through ratcheting, sophisticated cultural knowledge and complex cultural practices *evolve* over time (Tomasello, 2001).

Cultural evolution is biologically enabled. Humans are biologically prepared for the rapid ratcheting of human culture and its evolution. For example, a cognitive adaptation for culture is the ability to voluntarily access past memories in the absence of the appropriate environmental cues. The great apes cannot self-trigger their memories of the skills they have learned, and therefore cannot voluntarily reflect on the skills they have acquired (Donald, 1993). Thus, the great apes will not voluntarily rehearse a learned behavioral sequence in order to teach a learned skill to their children and peers. In short, the limits of ape intelligence tie ape learning to the immediate environment, and forbid modifications of learned skills and ratcheting of ape cultures. In contrast, a hallmark of human intelligence is the ability to voluntarily retrieve, reflect on, and mentally manipulate acquired knowledge to generate new knowledge.

Non-human mammals (e.g. chimpanzees, gorillas) also have language (e.g. Premack, 1971; Rumbaugh, 1977; Savage-Rumbaugh et al., 1993): a chimpanzee can learn to communicate by pressing keys on a computer keyboard (Rumbaugh, 1997) and acquire a sign language (Savage-Rumbaugh et al., 1993). However, the ability to communicate rich ideas with spoken words is a unique human accomplishment. This cognitive accomplishment has important adaptive values. Unlike hand gestures and other body languages, spoken language works at a distance and in the dark, and does not interfere with other motor activities. These properties conferred important benefits to early humans who hunted in groups. Moreover, because humans can produce an infinite number of sound patterns, a vocal language can support a large

number of different words. As such, speech is much more efficient than hand gestures in conveying meanings (see Krauss and Chiu, 1998). More importantly, language facilitates creation of distributed knowledge and negotiation of meanings. As Bruner posits, 'Our culturally adapted way of life depends upon shared meanings and shared concepts depends as well upon shared modes of discourse for negotiating differences in meaning and interpretation' (1990: 13).

The evolution of human language is also biologically enabled. For example, the Broca's area in the brain controls speech in humans. In a recent study, Petrides et al. (2005) discovered a distinct brain region in macaque monkeys that controls jaw movements. This region is located in the same region and has the same anatomical characteristics as Broca's area and is connected with the brain area that is involved in the retrieval of information from memory. When this area in the monkey was electrically stimulated, the subject displayed jaw movement sequences. These results suggest that the evolution of human language is also built on a biological foundation.

Furthermore, the human brain is responsive to new demands from the cultural environment, as illustrated in the assignment of specific brain areas to handle the demand of information processing in a multicultural, multilingual environment. For example, bilingual individuals need effective mechanisms to minimize interference from one language while processing materials in the other. In a recent brain imaging study (Rodriguez-Fornells et al., 2002), bilingual individuals were instructed to press a button when presented with words in one language, while ignoring words in the other language. These participants were able to effectively avoid interference from the words of the non-target language by using an indirect phonological route to access the lexicon of the target language. Furthermore, functional magnetic resonance imaging (fMRI) results showed that the brain areas that are involved in this process are also implicated in phonological and pseudo-word processing control.

In summary, the dualism of culture versus nature is oversold. Humans are biologically prepared to construct a cultural tradition. Indeed, some evolutionary theorists hold that because culture adapts much more quickly to changing circumstances than biological or cognitive systems do, natural selection favored those who could develop cultural traditions (Dawkins, 1976).

Theoretical implications

The oversold dualism of culture versus nature can lead culture and personality investigators astray. For example, in the FFT, biological factors are assumed to be the sole determinants of an individual's trait levels and culture is assumed to be a proxy for shared environment (instead of distributed knowledge in a human group). As a result, trait theorists of culture often pit traits against culture and compare their relative explanatory force (Poortinga and van Hemert, 2001). Another objective is to explain 'culture' by reducing cultures to mean trait levels of a cultural group (McCrae, 2002; McCrae et al., 2005b).

Treating culture as a network of distributed knowledge affords a different view of the culture and personality relationship and suggests a very different agenda for culture and personality research. As illustrated in Figure 6.1, the joint actions of biology and ecology determine a person's genetic endowment as well as his or her trait levels. Early evolutionary processes involving the intimate interaction of biology and ecology are also responsible for the development of the facultative cognitive strategies that enable evolution of human culture. The interaction between variable environmental conditions and genetically developed cognitive mechanisms also produce variations across knowledge traditions, which are adaptive phenotypic variations (Boone and Smith, 1998). The dynamic interplay among

individuals' trait levels, the knowledge traditions that are currently available, and the situational features in the current context determines which person variables are activated. Finally, the activated person variables will call out their attendant behaviors in a concrete situation. According to this view, an important goal in culture and personality research is to uncover how individuals appropriate resources from their cultural traditions to further their life goals. Another important goal is to identify the basic psychological principles that underline the interplay of personality and cultural processes. This view may provide a unified framework for integrating the major theoretical perspectives on culture and personality. We will return to this after reviewing these major theoretical perspectives.

MAJOR THEORETICAL PERSPECTIVES ON CULTURE AND PERSONALITY

There are four alternative perspectives on culture and personality: pan-cultural approach, indigenous approach, evolutionary psychology and cultural psychology (Church, 2001a). As illustrated in Table 6.1, these approaches differ in whether universality of personality structures is assumed, how the culture and personality relationship is conceptualized, and the major explanatory constructs in the perspective. In this section, we provide a critical review of each approach's major theoretical insights and research achievements. In the next section, we will propose a general framework to integrate the theoretical insights from each perspective.

Pan-cultural approach

The pan-cultural approach seeks to explain cultural differences in terms of variations in the mean levels of different cultural groups on a small number of personality dimensions.

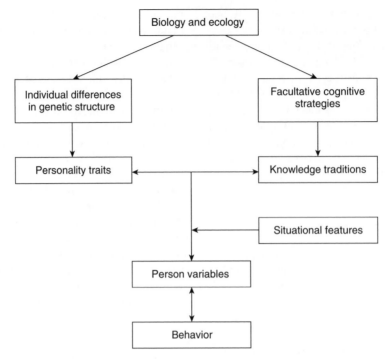

Figure 6.1   Nature, culture, and personality: some possible associations

Table 6.1   Four alternative theoretical approaches to culture and personality

	Pan-cultural approach	Indigenous psychology	Evolutionary approach	Cultural psychology
Universalism vs. cultural relativism	Universalism	Cultural relativism	Universalism	Cultural relativism
Culture–personality relationship	Personality shapes the character of a culture	Personality is a cultural construction	Personality traits are evolved mental structures and cultural differences in personality result from selective activation of numerous mental structures	Personality is a cultural construction
Major explanatory constructs	Universal traits	Indigenous personality constructs	Major domains of adaptive problems and their attendant evolved psychological structures	Cultural constructions of the self

The pan-cultural approach assumes that personality traits are similarly structured in different cultures; the same set of personality dimensions is found in all human cultures. This approach further assumes that personality traits are solely determined by biological factors; shared environmental factors have little impact on the levels of personality traits. If culture does not have any causal authority over personality, group differences in other cultural dimensions (e.g. individualism–collectivism) must be a result of group differences in personality (McCrae, 2004).

The pan-cultural approach has received some empirical support. First, results from multinational studies have provided consistent support for the universality of the FFM. The cross-cultural invariance of the FFM has been demonstrated in studies that used self-reported measures of personality (McCrae and Allik, 2002; McCrae and Costa, 1997; Yoon et al., 2002), observer trait ratings (McCrae et al., 2004, 2005a) and studies of trait terms in natural languages (Saucier and Goldberg, 2001). Additionally, similar gender and age differences in trait levels were obtained in several national groups (Costa et al., 2001; McCrae et al., 1999).

Second, comparisons of national (or regional) groups on mean trait levels have produced some consistent results across studies (McCrae, 2001, 2004; McCrae et al., 1998; McCrae et al., 2005a, 2005b). For example, individualist countries tend to have high scores on extraversion and openness to experience. High power distance countries tend to have low scores on extraversion. High uncertainty avoidance countries tend to have high scores on neuroticism. Recall that the pan-cultural approach assumes that personality can affect culture, but not vice versa. Thus, according to the pan-cultural perspective, a certain culture would emerge in a population when there is a high concentration of individuals with a certain person profile in it. For example, an individualist culture would emerge in countries where there is a high concentration of extraverts who are also open to experiences.

Despite the supportive findings, cross-cultural psychologists are skeptical of whether country differences in personality profiles are veridical. First, country differences in the mean levels of personality traits are difficult to interpret. Absence of cross-cultural equivalence in the meaning of the construct being measured, sampling, and measurement can threaten the validity of cross-cultural comparisons (Lalwani et al., 2006; Poortinga et al., 2002; Van De Vijver and Leung, 2001). Moreover, the effect size of country differences in personality is typically small; the amount of variance attributable to countries is considerably smaller than that attributable to persons (Poortinga and van Hemert, 2001).

Furthermore, the mean trait profile of a country does not resemble what individuals in the country believe the personality characteristics of a typical member in their own culture are like (Terracciano et al., 2005). Terraccinao et al. argue that perceptions of national character are based on unfounded stereotypes, which do not reflect mean personality trait levels. However, contrary to this argument, recent studies showed that perceived characteristics of typical members in one's cultural group, compared to individuals' actual characteristics, are more predictive of individuals' cultural identification (Wan et al., 2007a and 2007b).

Finally, results from recent studies on cultural frame switching challenge the assumption that culture cannot influence personality traits. Language encodes cultural meanings; thus, when individuals use language to express their thoughts, their thoughts and behaviors will be colored by the implicit cultural meanings embedded in their language (Chiu et al., 2007; Krauss and Chiu, 1998). For bilingual individuals, as they switch from one language to the other, they also switch cultural frames (Chiu and Chen, 2004; Chiu et al., 2007). Consistent with this idea, Earle (1969) reported that bilingual Hong Kong Chinese students have lower dogmatism scores when they respond to the dogmatism scale in English than when they answer the same scale translated into Chinese. This result provides the first evidence for the causal effect of culture on personality. In a more recent study (Ramirez-Esparza et al., 2006), the investigators first showed that compared to English-speaking Americans, Spanish-speaking Mexicans have higher scores on neuroticism and lower scores on extraversion, agreeableness, and conscientiousness. Next, they demonstrated that Spanish-English bilinguals (in Texas, California, and Mexico) had higher scores on extraversion, agreeableness, and conscientiousness, and lower scores on neuroticism when they responded to the Big Five inventory in English than when they did in Spanish. Again, this result challenges the assumption that culture cannot influence personality trait levels.

Indigenous psychology

The FFT acknowledges cultural variations in the expression of basic personality traits. For instance, in English, openness to experience is associated chiefly with traits related to intellectual interests or esthetic attitudes. However, in Castilian Spanish, openness to experience is associated with indigenous trait terms that characterize an unconventional lifestyle (Benet-Martinez and John, 1998, 2000). Despite these cultural variations, the FFM is assumed to represent the universal structure of personality.

Contrary to the FFT's claim, indigenous psychology holds that personality is a cultural construction and therefore rejects the idea that the FFM is a cultural universal (Ho et al., 2001). As Ho et al. put it, 'The generation of psychological knowledge is culture dependent: Both the conceptualization of psychological phenomena and the methodology employed to study them are informed by cultural values and presuppositions.' (2001: 931). Thus, indigenous psychologists maintain that investigators studying a cultural group's personality should use indigenous constructs and methods. The ultimate research goal of indigenous psychology is to develop an insider's perspective on culture and personality. For example, Guanzon-Lapena et al. (1998) attempted to construct an indigenous measure of traits in Filipino culture. They first asked 267 Filipino respondents to describe their own personality and the personality of somebody they liked and somebody they disliked. The respondents were also asked to briefly define each positive and negative trait used in the descriptions and to list a behavior that typified that trait. Based on these data, the investigators compiled 19 indigenous trait terms and 425 behavioral items. The item pool was pretested with a sample of 245 respondents and 220 items with the highest item–total correlations were retained in the final scale. The subscales have acceptable reliability and predict relevant behaviors. For example, the Pagkamalikhain (creativity) subscale predicted higher performance on tests of creativity (unusual uses, product improvement). The Pagkapalaibigan (sociability) subscale was positively correlated with the tendency to behave in a friendly manner while waiting for their turn to participate in an experiment.

The Chinese Personality Assessment Inventory (CPAI) (Cheung and Leung, 1998) provides another illustration of indigenous personality assessment. The investigators identified indigenous personality constructs in Chinese culture by reviewing classical and contemporary Chinese literatures, person descriptions used by Chinese people from different sectors, and recent personality research on the Chinese people. Next, psychologists from Hong Kong and mainland China were recruited to select the constructs for inclusion in the inventory. Indigenous constructs deemed to be of specific interest to the Chinese people (e.g. harmony, *renqing* or relationship orientation, thrift–extravagance, defensiveness, graciousness–meanness, face–family orientation) were also included (Cheung et al., 1996). A total of 22 subscales were constructed, and four factors were identified in a principal component analysis of the personality subscales in the CPAI: dependability, interpersonal relatedness, social potency, and individualism (Cheung and Leung, 1998).

According to indigenous psychology, indigenous personality dimensions identified in a culture may have relevance beyond the culture (Ho et al., 2001). For instance, when the CPAI was translated into English and tested with a sample of Chinese Singaporeans and Caucasian Americans, the factor structure of the English version of the CPAI was similar to that of the original Chinese version. Based on these results, the investigators concluded that the 'interpersonal relatedness' factor, which is not covered by the FFM, is also relevant to European American culture (Cheung et al., 2003).

In short, indigenous psychology assumes that personality is a cultural construction and rejects the notion of universal personality structures. Thus, indigenous psychologists strive to identify personality constructs and develop personality measures that are culturally sensitive by recruiting trait constructs from the indigenous cultural traditions. These indigenous constructs and measures are then exported to other cultures to assess its universal relevance.

Although indigenous psychologists aspire to develop indigenous personality inventories, many of the personality measures of local origins assess trait constructs that are familiar to Western psychologists. This is case probably because developers of indigenous tests also received inspirations from the Western research literature and Western personality instruments (Church, 2001b). The ultimate challenge of indigenous personality psychology is demonstrate that indigenous dimensions have incremental predictive utility beyond that of the FFM.

Evolutionary psychology

Evolutionary psychology rejects the idea that personality and culture are independent causal agents acting on human behaviors. It confirms the existence of universal traits, but views these traits as evolved psychological structures that serve the motive to replicate one's genes. Evolutionary psychology also recognizes the presence of cultural differences, but insists that culture does not explain these differences. Although cultural processes (culture production, evocation, transmission, and reception) are acknowledged within evolutionary psychology as real and important phenomena, these processes are understood within a broader evolutionary framework (Buss, 2001).

Evolutionary psychology attributes a universal motive to human nature – all humans are driven by the same fundamental motive to replicate their genes. Evolutionary psychology also assumes that that in all societies, individuals regularly encounter a set of recurrent problems that threaten successful reproduction of their genes. Thus, throughout evolution, humans have been designed by natural selection to apply a set of evolved psychological structures to solve the key problem areas regularly confronted by their ancestors (Kenrick et al., 2003). The key problem areas are self-protection, coalition formation, status seeking, mate choice, relationship maintenance, and offspring care (Kenrick et al., 2002). Each domain of adaptive problem (e.g. coalition formation) is associated with a fundamental goal (e.g. to protect the self and coalition members against threats to survival or reproduction), and numerous evolved psychological structures are available to achieve this goal. The objective of the evolutionary psychology research program is to explain how different psychological structures emerged in different problem areas (Kenrick et al., 2003).

This perspective has been applied to understand the universal structure of the FFM. According to evolutionary psychology, a certain trait emerged as a universal psychological structure because it recurrently contributes to successful solutions to a specific adaptive problem. For example, conscientiousness motivates individuals to monitor the environment for dangers and impending punishments and to persevere in pursuing valued long-range goals. Neuroticism or affect intensity increases arousal and mobilizes behavioral resources to cope with acutely demanding situations (MacDonald, 1998).

Regional differences in personality are explained within evolutionary psychology through selective activation of the numerous traits that have evolved in the long history of human evolution. When features of the social and physical ecology selectively activate a package of traits among individuals sharing the same environment, regional differences in personality emerged (Buss, 2001). Furthermore, some traits are more adaptive than others; the more adaptive ones are likely to be embodied in natural languages and reproduced in interpersonal communication.

Although evolutionary psychology provides an integrated framework for understanding the interaction of universal human nature and cultural variations in personality, it is the least influential perspective in culture and personality research (Church, 2001a). Nonetheless, evolutionary psychology has sparked an inquiry into how evolved fundamental goals unfold in social interaction and how the unfolding of these processes constrains the spread and reproduction of cultural ideas. For example, studies have been conducted to show that urban legends that arouse greater disgust (and so have greater immediate relevance to the self-protection goal) are more likely to be communicated between individuals, and consequently more likely to become part of the cultural mythology (Heath et al., 2001). In addition, Tesser (1993) found that attitudes with higher heritability (e.g. attitude toward death penalty for murder) are processed more efficiently, and are more resistant to conformity pressure, relative to attitudes with lower heritability. Finally, using computer simulation techniques, evolutionary psychologists have illustrated how different distributions of social norms might emerge when individuals negotiate the priorities of different fundamental goals in social interactions (Kenrick et al., 2003).

Cultural psychology

Like indigenous psychology, cultural psychology asserts that the construction of personality is culture-dependent. Thus, it also disbelieves in the universality of personality structure. However, unlike indigenous psychology that seeks to identify indigenous trait constructs and develop culture-sensitive measures of these constructs, cultural psychology rejects traits as the basic structural units in personality psychology and objective personality tests as universally valid measures of personality. Cultural psychology's critique of trait psychology is grounded in the premise that trait psychology is rooted in Western philosophical and religious assumptions about persons (Markus, 2004).

According to cultural psychology, what defines a person is a social and collective construction and is therefore culture-dependent by necessity. Trait psychology, originated in European American academia, reflects the conceptions of personhood that prevail in European American cultural contexts. These conceptions are rooted in a model of the person as a bounded entity independent of others; personality refers to the characteristic qualities that separate the self from other people (Markus, 2004). In contrast, in Asian cultures, personality is often experienced and understood in relation to others; individuals' characteristic patterns of relating to others in their social contexts are the individuals' behavioral signature of personality (Ho et al., 2001).

In summary, although cultural psychology acknowledges that in all human societies, there are marked individual variations in behaviors, the sources and patterns of these variations are dissimilar in different societies (Markus, 2004). Thus, objective measures of personality traits that are widely accepted as valid measures of individual differences in Western societies are ill-equipped to capture sources and patterns of individual differences in Asian societies. To cultural psychologists, 'a marriage between culture and [trait] psychology will never be a love match' (Markus, 2004: 75) – a union of culture and personality still needs to be arranged.

Not surprisingly, instead of mining cultural texts for indigenous trait constructs, cultural psychology has sought to achieve three research goals. The first goal is to articulate the markedly different conceptions of personality in different cultures (e.g. Eastern and Western cultures). In a recent study (Church et al., 2006a), participants from eight cultural groups (Americans, Anglo-Australians, Asian Australians, Chinese Australians, Filipinos, Japanese, Malays, and Mexicans) were asked to indicate their agreement and disagreement with trait beliefs (e.g. 'People who are quite industrious when they are students will probably be quite industrious in their jobs as adults,' 'An adolescent who is generally rebellious at home is probably also rebellious at school'); and contextual beliefs ('How arrogant a person is will tend to change a lot over time,' 'A person who is hotheaded at home might be calm and patient with friends.'). Consistent with the assumption that conceptions of personality traits are culture-bound, among the eight cultural groups, Americans and Anglo Australians agree most strongly with the trait beliefs and disagree mostly strongly with contextual beliefs. These two cultural groups are the only groups that agree much more strongly with trait beliefs than with contextual beliefs.

Another research goal in cultural psychology is to document how the divergent self-conceptions in Eastern and Western cultures are expressed in motivations, cognitions, emotions and behaviors (Markus and Kitayama, 1991, 2003). Research pursuing this goal has yielded fruitful results. It is beyond the scope of this chapter to review them here. Fortunately, contemporary reviews of this research literature are available (Chiu and Hong, 2006, 2007; Lehman et al., 2004; Wirtz and Chiu, 2008). Very briefly, the research evidence indicates that in Western cultural contexts, people spontaneously use internal dispositions to describe the self; people emphasize the independence of the self from others and are motivated to express and affirm their independence; people value self-direction and autonomy; behaviors are believed to be indicative of internal dispositions and/or personal preferences; and the self is viewed as an active agent acting on their physical and social environment. In contrast, in Asian contexts, a person's social relations and obligations define the self; others' regards for a person determine his or her social worth, and a person's characteristic ways of navigating social situations can affect his or her psychological well-being considerably.

The marked differences in self-processes across cultures do not imply that culture is a monolith. As noted, although cultural psychology emphasizes that personality is a social and collective construction, it also recognizes within-cultural heterogeneity in personality (Triandis, 2001). However, these individual differences are expected to have different patterns in different cultures. Therefore, the third research goal in cultural psychology is to demonstrate how culture influences the patterning of within-culture personality variation (Oishi, 2004). For example, in one study (Schimmack et al., 2002), the investigators found that there are individual differences in how frequently positive emotions are experienced in the United States and Japan. However, the frequency of positive emotion is highly correlated with life satisfaction in the United States only.

Despite the success of cultural psychology, some writers have questioned the strong cultural relativism assumption many cultural psychologists adhere to. For example, Rozin maintains that 'the differences between "cultures" seem bigger than the actual differences between the individuals in these same cultures' (2003: 274). To Rozin, the presence of cultural differences does not render cultural universalism indefensible. It is possible that there are universal human dispositions. What culture does is to push people in a direction other than the one to which they would naturally tend. For example, people have a natural motivation to self-enhance; self-enhancement is positively associated with better personal adjustment among North Americans and Asians (Church et al., 2006b). However, the norm of modesty in Asian contexts discourages people from presenting their favorable traits publicly (Kurman and Sriram, 2002). Oishi (2004) also submits that there is no contradiction in recognizing diverse cultural effects and universal personality dispositions; while individual variability in personality dispositions exists in every culture, culture constrains or amplifies how often and in what form these dispositions are expressed behaviorally.

While culture shapes the expression of personality, personality limits the effect of culture on individuals. Individuals are not pawns of their cultural programming. While some individuals prefer to adhere to their cultural tradition, others prefer to dissociate themselves from it. For instance, individuals who have a chronic motivation for certainty are more likely than those who do not to adhere to cultural norms (Chiu et al., 2000; Fu et al., 2007).

In short, cultural psychologists correctly point out that there is culture in personality and personality in culture. However, contrary to some radical claims in cultural psychology, there may be no contradiction between culture and personality. Indeed, culture and personality can be a love match.

Conclusion

The four perspectives on culture and personality reviewed above make different assumptions about cultural universalism and relativism. A major theme in this chapter is that the dualism of nature versus nurture is oversold. Our review of the conceptual and empirical issues in recent culture and personality research confirms that the interaction of biological and ecological factors can account for the universal structure of personality, as well as the presence of

between-culture and within-culture variations in behaviors. The evidence clearly suggests that there is personality in culture (within-culture heterogeneity in personality) and culture in personality (culture regulates the expression and patterning of personality in the culture).

The dualism of nature versus culture has created unnecessary tensions between the four perspectives and has hence impeded the development of an integrated theoretical framework on culture and personality, which is necessary for the progress of the field. This may explain the slow growth of culture and personality studies in personality psychology we noted at the beginning of this chapter.

Despite the four perspectives' differing theoretical commitments to universalism and cultural relativism, each perspective has inspired research that sheds light on the relationship of culture and psychology. The pan-cultural trait approach highlights possible cultural differences in broad personality dispositions. Evolutionary psychology explains why cultures differ in these broad personality dispositions. Indigenous psychology reveals some intellectual blind spots in Western trait theories by identifying new trait constructs from indigenous cultural traditions and studying the universal relevance of these indigenous traits. Cultural psychology reveals how the conception of personhood in a culture may influence the patterning of individual differences within a culture. In the next section, we borrow insights from the four perspectives to construct an integrated framework for culture and personality research.

THEORETICAL INTEGRATION

Cultural processes

The following summarizes the basic propositions of the proposed integrated framework of culture and personality.

Definition and nature of culture

- Culture is a network of distributed knowledge that is produced and reproduced by a group of interconnected individuals.
- Culture is biologically enabled.
- As a knowledge tradition, culture is encoded in external memory devices.

Cultural processes

Through extensive experiences in a culture, people acquire insider expertise in the culture. However, even individuals with insider expertise in the culture possess only a subset of the knowledge in their culture. Based on the subset of culture knowledge they have acquired, individuals develop a cognitive representation of the cultural tradition. When this representation is activated, its attendant cultural knowledge is activated. This is one mechanism through which culture influences behaviors.

Definition and nature of personality

Personality refers to an individual's characteristic patterns of cognitions, affects, motivations, and behaviors. These patterns are temporally stable and reflect the organization of the biological and psychological systems within the individual. Global personality traits are evolved psychological structures that have recurrently contributed to successful solutions to specific adaptive problems.

Personality processes

Global personality traits may influence person variables, which are acquired psychological structures for getting along in the world.

Personality–culture interactions

Culture on personality
- Culture may influence the way personality is conceptualized.
- Culture may influence the way individual differences within a culture are patterned.
- Culture may influence the way person variables such as the self-concept are constructed.

Personality on culture
- Individuals with certain personality traits may be attracted to a certain kind of ecology. Next, features in this type of ecology selectively activate and maintain these traits in the group, creating a culture with certain characteristic traits.
- Effects of culture on behaviors are particularly pronounced for individuals with a chronic need for certainty or firm answers.
- Personality traits can moderate the psychological benefits of multicultural experiences.

As noted, culture is a knowledge tradition; it is a network of distributed knowledge that is produced and reproduced by a group of interconnected individuals. As illustrated in Figure 6.1, culture is biologically enabled; the development of facultative strategies allows humans to create, cumulate, reproduce, and apply a knowledge tradition.

It is important to emphasize that as a knowledge tradition, culture is encoded in external memory devices. The Internet is an example of external memory devices. Other examples include videotapes, microfilms, photographs, books, paintings, and stone carvings. Encoding cultural knowledge in external memory devices enables rapid transmission and accumulation of cultural knowledge. If transmission of knowledge of knowledge relies exclusively on passing memory from one person to another, the rate of cultural knowledge reproduction and accumulation would have been slow. Technological developments create collective storage and retrieval systems of knowledge. Knowledge stored in these devices is relatively permanent. Whereas human memory is limited in capacity, external memory devices have virtually unlimited capacity. Whereas a single individual can access human memory, external memory devices usually have many retrieval paths and can be accessed by multiple users (Donald, 1993). The development of external memory devices modified the configuration of the human biological and cognitive systems. For example, the invention of written symbols has led to the development of brain areas that specialize in processing pictorial, phonetic, and ideographic symbols. It has also increased people's reliance on external devices to store, retrieve, reorganize, and edit a huge amount of information.

External memory devices give each of their users access to knowledge created by other individuals and knowledge accumulated over generations. Each user has at his or her disposal a huge amount and variety of knowledge for reflections and innovations. External memory devices also provide physical records of cultural histories. When new knowledge is created and stored into an external memory device, the new knowledge goes down in cultural history, is rendered public, and may be used as materials for further refinement and innovation. This iterative process enables cumulative modification of cultural knowledge to progress at an exponential rate.

Because of the vast amount of knowledge that has accumulated in a knowledge tradition, individuals in a culture typically do not have perfect knowledge of the culture. Through extensive experiences in a culture, people acquire insider expertise in the culture. However, even individuals with this expertise possess only a subset of the knowledge in their culture. Thus, culture is not perfectly shared. Based on the subset of cultural knowledge they have acquired, individuals develop a cognitive representation of the cultural tradition. When this representation is activated, its attendant cultural knowledge is also activated. This is one mechanism through which culture influences behaviors (Hong and Mallorie, 2004). Hong and her colleagues have provided convincing evidence for this idea. They studied individuals with extensive experiences in both American and Chinese cultures (highly Westernized Hong Kong Chinese university students, Chinese Americans). Because these participants have extensive experiences in both cultures, they have developed a cognitive representation of the Chinese cultural tradition and one of American cultural tradition. Among these bicultural individuals, when their representation of Chinese culture is activated (after they have been incidentally exposed to pictures of Chinese cultural icons), they apply knowledge in Chinese culture (Chinese cultural values, causal theories, decision rules) to grasp their experiences and guide their behavioral choices. However, when their representation of American culture is activated (after they have been incidentally exposed to pictures of American cultural icons), they apply knowledge in American culture (American cultural values, causal theories, decision rules) to grasp their experiences and guide their behavioral choices (Fu et al., 2007; Hong et al., 1997, 2000; Wong and Hong, 2005).

Personality processes

Personality refers to an individual's characteristic patterns of cognitions, affects, motivations, and behaviors. These patterns are temporally stable and reflect the organization of the biological and psychological systems within the individual. As evolutionary psychology maintains, global personality traits such as the Big Five factors are evolved psychological structures that have recurrently contributed to successful solutions to specific adaptive problems.

As illustrated in Figure 6.1, these psychological structures may influence the person variables, which are acquired psychological structures for getting along in the world. For example, people in the United States have the expectation that avoidance emotions (e.g. fear, worry) are useful for avoiding threats (Tamir et al., 2007). When individuals high in neuroticism anticipate a cognitively demanding task, they prefer to engage in activities that are likely to increase avoidance emotions before the task (Tamir, 2005).

Personality–culture interactions

Culture can influence personality in several ways. First, culture may influence the way personality is conceptualized. Compared to individuals in collectivist cultures, individuals in individualist cultures are more likely to subscribe to trait theories of personality and less likely to subscribe to contextualized theories (Church et al., 2006a). Second, culture may influence the way individual differences within a culture are patterned (Oishi, 2004). For example, in Asian cultures, subjective well-being is positively related to self-esteem and relationship harmony. In European-American culture, subjective well-being is positively related to self-esteem only (Kwan et al., 1997).

Culture also influences the way person variables such as the self-concept are constructed. For example, in one study, Hong Kong Chinese and European Americans were asked to describe themselves. When their cultural identity (being Chinese for Hong Kong Chinese and being American for European Americans) was made salient, compared to each other, Hong Kong Chinese were more likely to mention their interpersonal duties and European Americans were more likely to mention their rights. Moreover, in another study, Chinese Americans were asked to describe themselves. When these participants' Chinese (vs. American) identity was made salient, they were more likely to mention their obligations and less likely to mention their rights (Hong et al., 2001).

In another study, highly Westernized undergraduates in Beijing (China) were asked to describe themselves. Before they made their descriptions, they were incidentally exposed to pictures of Chinese cultural icons or American cultural icons. These participants mentioned more interdependent self-descriptors and fewer independent self-descriptors after having been reminded of the Chinese (vs. American) cultural tradition. A subsequent study showed that activating the Chinese (vs. American) cultural tradition makes these bilingual participants process information about themselves less elaborately and information about their mother more elaborately (Sui et al., 2007).

Personality also influences cultural processes. First, individuals with certain personality traits may be attracted to a certain kind of ecology. Next, features in this type of ecology selectively activate and maintain these traits in the group, creating a culture with certain characteristic traits. In a recent investigation of regional cultures in Japan (Kitayama et al., 2006), it was found that Hokkaido Japanese are more independent than mainland Japanese. Self-selection may account for this regional difference. Settlers from the rest of Japan moved to Hokkaido in the mid-nineteenth century in search of economic opportunities in the wilderness of Hokkaido. These settlers, who were motivated by economic opportunities, were more independent to begin with. The ecological features in the northern frontier foster the crystallization of a culture of independence in Hokkaido by selectively activating independent traits.

Second, people are not pawns of their cultural programming. Instead, culture is adaptive; it is an intellectual resource members of the culture appropriate to meet their needs and pursue their valued goals (Chiu and Hong, 2005). For example, individuals adhere to cultural norms because they provide consensually validated solutions to problems and hence reduce uncertainty. As noted, individuals with chronic motivations for certainty are particularly likely to follow cultural norms. As mentioned, effects of culture on behaviors are particularly pronounced for individuals with a chronic need for certainty or firm answers (Chiu et al., 2000; Fu et al., 2007).

As global connectivity increases, individuals are exposed to foreign cultures and are expected to perform in a culturally diverse environment. Personality traits can moderate how much individuals will benefit from their multicultural experiences. For example, openness to experience and flexibility are associated with receptiveness to new ideas from foreign cultures and better performance in culturally diverse work environment. Individuals who score higher on the flexibility subscale of the multicultural personality questionnaire have better performance in a culturally diverse work group (van der Zee et al., 2004).

CONCLUSION

Culture and personality studies fascinated social scientists in the first half of the twentieth century, because these studies may eventually reveal how biology, ecology, society, and culture act on individual behaviors within a certain cultural context. In this chapter, we identified three factors that might have contributed to the decline of the field: the concern that culture and personality research may reduce complex cultures to essences and hence promote cultural stereotypes; the oversold dualism of nature versus culture; and the lack of an integrated theory of culture and personality. As such, although some personality psychologists expressed optimism in the return of interest in the field at the turn of the century, culture and personality research continues to have low visibility in personality psychology.

In the present chapter, we offered a definition of culture as knowledge tradition. This definition dissociates culture from a demarcated population and does not treat culture as a reified entity with an inordinate amount of boundedness and homogeneity. Next, we debunked the dualism of nature versus culture and argue that culture, like personality, is biologically enabled. We then reviewed the state of theoretical pluralism in the field and discussed the conceptual and empirical issues each of the four major theoretical perspectives faces. Finally, drawing on the

insights from the four perspectives, we proposed an integrated model to understand the nature of culture and personality and how culture and personality act concertedly on individual behaviors. We hope these efforts will clear the way for the revival and rapid growth of the field in the coming decades.

REFERENCES

Allport, G.W. (1961) *Pattern and Growth in Personality*. New York: Holt, Rinehart, & Winston.

Appadurai, A. (1996) *Modernity at Large: Cultural Dimensions of Globalization*. Minneapolis, MN: University of Minnesota Press.

Barth, F. (2002) 'An anthropology of knowledge', *Current Anthropology*, 43(1): 1–18.

Benet-Martinez, V. and John, O.P. (1998) 'Los Cinco Grandes across cultures and ethnic groups: Multitrait multimethod analyses of the Big Five in Spanish and English', *Journal of Personality and Social Psychology*, 75(5): 729–50.

Benet-Martinez, V. and John O.P. (2000) 'Toward the development of quasi-indigenous personality constructs', *American Behavioral Scientist*, 44: 141–57.

Boone, J.L. and Smith, E.A. (1998) 'Is it evolution yet? A critique of evolutionary archaeology', *Current Anthropology*, 39: S141–57.

Brumann, C. (1999) 'Writing for culture: Why successful concept should not be discarded', *Current Anthropology*, 40: S1–27.

Bruner, J. (1990) *Act of Meaning*. Cambridge, MA: Harvard University Press.

Buss, D.M. (2001) 'Human nature and culture: An evolutionary psychological perspective', *Journal of Personality*, 69(6): 953–78.

Cheung, F.M. and Leung, K. (1998) 'Indigenous personality measures: Chinese examples', *Journal of Cross-Cultural Psychology*, 29(1): 233–48.

Cheung, F.M., Leung, K., Fan, R.M., Song, W.Z., Zhang, J.X. and Zhang, J.P. (1996) 'Development of the Chinese personality Assessment Inventory', *Journal of Cross-Cultural Psychology*, 27(2): 181–99.

Cheung, F.M., Leung, K., Ward, C. and Leong, F. (2003) 'The English version of the Chinese

Personality Assessment Inventory', *Journal of Cross-Cultural Psychology*, 34(4): 433–52.

Chiu, C-Y. and Chen, J. (2004) 'Symbols and interactions: Application of the CCC model to culture, language, and social identity', in S-H. Ng, C. Candlin and C-Y. Chiu (eds), *Language Matters: Communication, Culture, and Social Identity*. Hong Kong: City University of Hong Kong Press, pp. 155–82.

Chiu, C-Y. and Hong, Y. (2005) 'Cultural competence: Dynamic processes', in A. Elliot and C.S. Dweck (eds), *Handbook of Motivation and Competence*. New York: Guilford, pp. 489–505.

Chiu, C-Y. and Hong, Y. (2006) *Social Psychology of Culture*. New York: Psychology Press.

Chiu, C-Y. and Hong, Y-Y. (2007) 'Cultural processes: Basic principles', in E.T. Higgins, and A.E. Kruglanski (eds), *Social Psychology: Handbook of Basic Principles*. New York: Guilford, pp. 785–804.

Chiu, C-Y., Leung, A. and Kwan, L. (2007) 'Language, Cognition, and culture: Beyond the Whortian hypothesis', in S. Kitayama and D. Cohen (eds), *Handbook of Cultural Psychology*. New York: Guilford, pp. 668–88.

Chiu, C-Y., Morris, M., Hong, Y. and Menon, T. (2000) 'Motivated cultural cognition: The impact of implicit cultural theories on dispositional attribution varies as a function of need for closure', *Journal of Personality and Social Psychology*, 78(2): 247–59.

Church, A.T. (2000) 'Culture and personality: Toward an integrated cultural trait psychology', *Journal of Personality*, 68(4): 651–703.

Church, A.T. (2001a) 'Introduction', *Journal of Personality*, 69(6): 787–801.

Church, A.T. (2001b) 'Personality measurement in cross-cultural perspective', *Journal of Personality*, 69(6): 979–1006.

Church, A.T., Katigbak, M.S., del Prado, A.M., Mastor, K.A., Huarumi, Y., Tanaka-Matsumi et al. (2006a) 'Implicit theories and self-perceptions of traitedness across cultures: Toward integration of cultural and trait psychology perspectives', *Journal of Cross-Cultural Psychology*, 37(6): 694–716.

Church, A.T., Katigbak, M.S., del Prado, A.M., Valdez-Medina, J.L., Miramontes, L. G. and Ortiz, F.A. (2006b) 'A cross-cultural study of trait self-enhancement, explanatory variables, and adjustment', *Journal of Research in Personality*, 40(6): 1169–201.

Costa, P.T. Jr., Terracciano, A. and McCrae, R.R. (2001) 'Gender differences in personality traits across cultures: Robust and surprising findings', *Journal of Personality and Social Psychology*, 81(2): 322–31.

Dawkins, R. (1976) *The Selfish Gene*. Oxford: Oxford University Press.

Donald, M. (1993) 'Precis of "Origins of the modern mind: Three stages in the evolution of culture and cognition"', *Behavioral and Brain Sciences*, 16(4): 737–91.

Earle, M. (1969) 'A cross-cultural and cross-language comparison of dogmatism scores', *Journal of Social Psychology*, 79(1): 19–24.

Fu, H-Y., Chiu, C-Y., Morris, M.W. and Young, M. (2007) 'Spontaneous inferences from cultural cues: Varying responses of cultural insiders and outsiders', *Journal of Cross-Cultural Psychology*, 38(1): 58–75.

Fu, H-Y., Morris, M.W., Lee, S-L., Chao, M-C., Chiu, C-Y. and Hong, Y-Y. (2007) 'Epistemic motives and cultural conformity: Need for closure, culture, and context as determinants of conflict judgments', *Journal of Personality and Social Psychology*, 92(2): 191–207.

Guanzon-Lapena, M.A., Church, A.T., Carlota, A.J. and Katigbak, M.S. (1998) 'Indigenous personality measures: Philippine examples', *Journal of Cross-Cultural Psychology*, 29(1): 249–61.

Heath, C., Bell, C. and Sternberg, E. (2001) 'Emotional selection in memes: The case of urban legends', *Journal of Personality and Social Psychology*, 81(6): 1028–41.

Ho, D.Y.F., Peng, S., Lai, A.C. and Chan, S-F. (2001) Personality across cultural traditions', *Journal of Personality*, 69(6): 925–54.

Hong, Y., Chiu, C-Y. and Kung, M. (1997) 'Bringing culture out in front: Effects of cultural meaning system activation on social cognition', in K. Leung, Y. Kashima, U. Kim and S. Yamaguchi (eds), *Progress in Asian Social Psychology* (Vol. 1). Singapore: Wiley, pp. 139–49.

Hong, Y., Ip, G., Chiu, C-Y., Morris, M.W. and Menon, T. (2001) 'Cultural identity and the dynamic construction of the self: Collective duties and individual rights in Chinese and American cultures', *Social Cognition*, 19(3): 251–68.

Hong, Y., Morris, M., Chiu, C-Y. and Benet, V. (2000) 'Multicultural minds: A dynamic constructivist approach to culture and cognition', *American Psychologist*, 55(7): 709–20.

Hong, Y-Y. and Mallorie, L.M. (2004) 'A dynamic constructivist approach to culture: Lessons learned from personality psychology', *Journal of Research in Personality*, 38(1): 59–67.

Kashima, Y. (2000) 'Conceptions of culture and person for psychology', *Journal of Cross Cultural Psychology*, 31(1): 14–32.

Keesing, F.M. (1958) *Cultural Anthropology: The Science of Custom*. New York: Holt, Rinehart & Winston, pp. 301–12.

Keesing, R. M. (1974) 'Theory of culture', *Annual Review of Anthropology*, 3: 73–97.

Keesing, R.M. (1994) 'Theories of culture revisited', in R. Borofsky (ed.), *Assessing Cultural Anthropology*. New York: McGraw-Hill, pp. 301–10.

Kenrick, D.T., Li, M. and Butner, J. (2003) 'Dynamical evolutionary psychology: Individual decision rules and emergent social norms', *Psychological Review*, 110(1): 3–28.

Kenrick, D.T., Maner, J.K., Butner, J., Li, N.P., Becker, D.V. and Schaller, M. (2002) 'Dynamical evolutionary psychology: Mapping the domains of the new interactionist paradigm', *Personality and Social Psychology Review*, 6(4): 347–56.

Kitayama, S., Ishii, K., Imada, T., Takemura, K. and Ramaswamy, J. (2006) 'Voluntary settlement and the spirit of independence: Evidence from Japan's "Northern frontier"', *Journal of Personality and Social Psychology*, 91(3): 369–84.

Kluckhohn, C. and Murray, H.A. (1948) (eds), *Personality in Nature, Culture, and Society*. New York: Knopf.

Kluckhohn, K. (1954) 'Culture and behavior', in G. Lindzey (ed.), *Handbook of Social Psychology* (Vol. 2). Cambridge, MA: Addison-Wesley, pp. 921–76.

Krauss, R.M. and Chiu, C-Y. (1998) 'Language and social psychology', in D. Gilbert, S. Fiske-Emory and G. Lindzey (eds), *Handbook of Social Psychology* (4th edn, Vol. 2). New York: Guilford, pp. 41–88.

Kroeber, A.L. and Kluckhohn, C. (1952) *Culture: A Critical Review of Concepts and Definitions*. Cambridge, MA: Harvard University Press.

Kurman, J. and Sriram, N. (2002) 'Inter-relationships among vertical and horizontal collectivism, modesty, and self-enhancement', *Journal of Cross-Cultural Psychology*, 33(1): 71–86.

Kwan, V.S.Y., Bond, M.H. and Singelis, T.M. (1997) 'Pancultural explanations for life satisfaction: Adding relationship harmony to self-esteem', *Journal of Personality and Social Psychology*, 73(5): 1038–51.

Lalwani, A., Shavitt, S. and Johnson, T. 2006. 'What is the relation between cultural orientation and socially desirable responding?', *Journal of Personality and Social Psychology*, 90(1): 165–78.

Lehman, D., Chiu, C-Y. and Schaller, M. (2004) 'Culture and psychology', *Annual Review of Psychology*, 55: 689–714.

LeVine, R.A. (2001) 'Culture and personality studies, 1918–1960: Myth and history', *Journal of Personality*, 69(6): 803–18.

Lowell, A.L. (1934) *At War with Academic Traditions in America*. Cambridge, MA: Harvard University Press.

MacDonald, K. (1998) 'Evolution, culture, and the five-factor model', *Journal of Cross-Cultural Psychology*, 29(1): 119–49.

Markus, H.R. (2004) 'Culture and personality: Brief for an arranged marriage', *Journal of Research in Personality*, 38(1): 75–83.

Markus, H.R. and Kitayama S. (1991) 'Culture and the self: Implications for cognition, emotion, and motivation', *Psychological Review*, 98(2): 224–53.

Markus, H.R. and Kitayama, S. (1998) 'The cultural psychology of personality', *Journal of Cross-Cultural Psychology*, 29(1): 63–87.

Markus, H.R. and Kitayama, S. (2003) 'Culture, self and the reality of the social', *Psychological Inquiry*, 14(3–4): 277–83.

McCrae, R.R. (2000) 'Trait psychology and the revival of personality and culture studies', *American Behavioral Scientist*, 44(1): 10–31.

McCrae, R.R. (2001) 'Trait psychology and culture: Exploring intercultural comparisons', *Journal of Personality*, 69(6): 819–46.

McCrae, R.R. (2002) 'NEO-PI-R data from 36 cultures: Further intercultural comparisons', in R.R. McCrae and J. Allik (eds), *The Five-Factor Model of Personality and Culture*. New York: Kluwer Academic/Plenum, pp. 105–25.

McCrae, R.R. (2004) 'Human nature and culture: A trait perspective', *Journal of Research in Personality*, 38(1): 3–14.

McCrae, R.R. and Allik, J. (2002) (eds), *The Five-Factor Model of Personality and Culture*. New York: Kluwer Academic/Plenum.

McCrae, R.R. and Costa, P.T. Jr. (1997) 'Personality trait structure as a human universal', *American Psychologist*, 52(5): 509–16.

McCrae, R.R., Costa, P.T., Jr., Lima, M.P., Simoes, A., Ostendorf, F., Angleitner, A., Marusic, I., Bratko, D., Caprara, G.V., Barbaranelli, C., Chae, J.H. and Piedmont, R.L. (1999) 'Age differences in personality across the adult lifespan: Parallels in five cultures', *Developmental Psychology*, 35: 466–77.

McCrae, R.R., Costa, P.T. Jr., del Pilar, G.H., Rolland, J-P. and Parker, W.D. (1998) 'Cross-cultural assessment of the five-factor model: The revised NEO Personality Inventory', *Journal of Cross-Cultural Psychology*, 29(1): 171–89.

McCrae, R.R., Terracciano, A. and 78 Members of the Personality Profiles of Cultures Project (2005a) 'Universal features of personality traits from the observer's perspective. Data from 50 cultures', *Journal of Personality and Social Psychology*, 88(3): 547–61.

McCrae, R.R., Terracciano, A. and 79 Members of the Personality Profiles of Cultures Project (2005b) 'Personality profiles of cultures: Aggregate personality traits', *Journal of Personality and Social Psychology*, 89(3): 407–25.

Oishi, S. (2004) 'Personality in culture: A neo-Allportian view', *Journal of Research in Personality*, 38(1): 68–74.

Pervin, L.A. (1996) *The Science of Personality*. New York: Wiley.

Petrides, M., Cadoret, G. and Mackey, S. (2005) 'Orofacial somatomotor responses in the macaque monkey homologue of Broca's area', *Nature*, 435(7046): 1235–8.

Poortinga, Y.H., van De Vijver, F. and van Hemert, D.A. (2002) 'Cross-cultural equivalence of the Big Five: A tentative interpretation of the evidence', in R.R. McCrae and J. Allik (eds), *The Five-Factor Model of Personality and Culture*. New York: Kluwer Academic/Plenum, pp. 273–94.

Poortinga, Y.H. and van Hemert, D.A. (2001) 'Personality and culture: Demarcating between the common and the unique', *Journal of Personality*, 69(6): 1034–60.

Premack, D. (1971) 'Language in chimpanzees?', *Science*, 172(3985): 808–22.

Ramirez-Esparza, N., Gosling, S.D., Benet-Martinez, V., Potter, J.P. and Pennebaker, J.W. (2006) 'Do bilinguals have two personalities? A special case of cultural frame switching', *Journal of Research in Personality*, 40(2): 99–120.

Rodriguez-Fornells, A., Rotte, M., Heinze, H.J., Nosselt, T. and Munte, T.F. (2002) 'Brain potential and functional MRI evidence for how to handle two languages with one brain', *Nature*, 415 (6875): 1026–9.

Rohner, R.P. (1984) 'Toward a conception of culture for cross-cultural psychology', *Journal of Cross-Cultural Psychology*, 15(2): 111–38.

Rozin, P. (2003) 'Five potential principles for understanding cultural differences in relation to individual differences', *Journal of Research in Personality*, 37(4): 273–83.

Rumbaugh, D.M. (1977) (ed.), *Language Learning by a Chimpanzee: The Lana Project*. New York: Academic.

Saucier, G. and Goldberg, L.R. (2001) 'Lexical studies of indigenous personality factors: Premises, products, and prospects', *Journal of Personality*, 69(6): 847–79.

Savage-Rumbaugh, E.S., Murphy, J., Sevcik, R.A., Brakke, K.E., Williams, S.L. and Rumbaugh, D.M. (1993) 'Language comprehension in ape and child', *Monographs of the Society for Research in Child Development*, 58(3–4): 243–52.

Schimmack, U. Radhakrishnan, P., Oishi, S., Dzokoto, V. and Ahadi, S. (2002) 'Culture, personality, and subjective well-being: Integrating process models of life satisfaction', *Journal of Personality and Social Psychology*, 82(4): 582–93.

Shore, B. (1996) *Culture in Mind: Cognition, Culture, and the Problem of Meaning*. New York: Oxford University Press.

Shore, B. (2002) 'Taking culture seriously', *Human Development*, 45(4): 226–8.

Sperber, D. (1996) *Explaining Culture: A Naturalistic Approach*. Massachusetts: Blackwell.

Sui, J., Zhu, Y. and Chiu, C-Y. (2007) 'Bicultural mind, self-construal, and recognition memory: Cultural priming effects on self- and mother-reference effect', *Journal of Experimental Social Psychology*, 43(5): 818–24.

Tamir, M. (2005) 'Don't worry, be happy? Neuroticism, trait-consistent affect regulation, and performance', *Journal of Personality and Social Psychology*, 89(3): 449–61.

Tamir, M., Chiu, C-Y. and Gross, J.J. (2007) 'Business or pleasure? Utilitarian versus hedonic considerations in emotion regulation', *Emotion*, 7(3): 546–54.

Terracciano, A. and 86 Members of the Personality Profiles of Cultures Project (2005) 'National character does not reflect mean personality trait levels in 49 cultures', *Science*, 310(5745): 96–100.

Tesser, A. (1993) 'The importance of heritability in psychological research: The case of attitudes', *Psychological Review*, 100(1): 129–42.

Tomasello, M. (2001) 'Cultural transmission: A view from chimpanzees and human infants', *Journal of Cross-Cultural Psychology*, 32(2): 135–46.

Triandis, H.C. (2001) 'Individualism-collectivism and personality', *Journal of Personality*, 69(6): 901–24.

Van de Vijver, F. and Leung, K. (2001) 'Personality in cultural context: Methodological issues', *Journal of Personality*, 69(6): 1007–31.

Van Schaik, C.P., Ancrenaz, M., Borgen, G., Galdikas, B., Knott, C.D., Singleton, I., Suzuki, A., Utami, S.S. and Merrill, M. (2003) 'Orangutan cultures and the evolution of material culture', *Science*, 299(5603): 102–5.

Van dehZee, K., Atsma, N. and Brodbeck, F. (2004) 'The influence of social identity and personality on outcomes of cultural diversity in teams', *Journal of Cross-Cultural Psychology*, 35(3): 283–303.

Wan, C., Chiu, C-Y., Peng, S. and Tam, K-P. (2007a) 'Measuring cultures through intersubjective norms: Implications for predicting relative identification with two or more cultures' *Journal of Cross-Cultural Psychology*, 38(2): 213–26.

Wan, C., Chiu, C-Y., Tam, K-P., Lee, S-L., Lau, I. Y-M. and Peng, S-Q. (2007b) 'Perceived cultural importance and actual self-importance of values in cultural identification', *Journal of Personality and Social Psychology*, 92(2): 337–54.

Whiten, A., Goodall, J., McGrew W.C., Nishida, T., Reynolds, V., Sugiyama, Y., Tutin, C.E.G., Wrangham, R.W. and C. Boesch (1999) 'Cultures in chimpanzees', *Nature*, 399(6737): 682–5.

Wirtz, D. and Chiu, C-Y. (2008) 'Perspectives on the self in the East and West: Searching for the quiet ego', in H. Wayment and J. Bauer (eds), *Transcending Self-Interest: Psychological Explorations of the Quiet Ego*. Washington, DC: American Psychological Association.

Wong, R.Y-M. and Hong, Y. (2005) 'Dynamic influences of culture on cooperation in the Prisoner's Dilemma', *Psychological Science*, 16(6): 429–34.

Yoon, K., Schmidt, F. and Ilies, R. (2002) 'Cross-cultural construct validity of the Five-Factor Model of personality among Korean employees', *Journal of Cross-Cultural Psychology*, 33(3): 217–35.

7

Behavioral Genetic Studies of Personality: An Introduction and Review of the Results of 50+ Years of Research

Andrew M. Johnson, Philip A. Vernon and Amanda R. Feiler

INTRODUCTION

One of the longest-standing debates within psychology concerns the extent to which we can identify biological factors in the prediction of individual differences in personality. Factors may include 'acquired' states, such as disease (e.g. Balsis et al., 2005; Lyons et al., 2004; Menza et al., 1990; Netter and Rammsayer, 1991; Ogawa, 1981), drug use (e.g. Williamson et al., 1997) or brain injury (e.g. Max et al., 2006; Rush et al., 2006), or they may involve the co-variation of biological individual difference variables such as hormone (e.g. Edwards, 2006; Popma et al., 2006; van Bokhoven et al., 2006) or neurotransmitter levels (e.g. Benjamin et al., 2000; Delgado et al., 1990; Soyka et al., 2002; Zuckerman, 1995). By far the most commonly investigated biological predictor of personality is, however, genetics. Interestingly, studies of genetic precursors to

human personality and behavior are considered controversial (and even new), while studies of genetic precursors to medical disorders are considered more acceptable (and commonplace). Some of the earliest human genetic studies, however, involved the study of personality variables – in fact, the ubiquitous correlation coefficient was first described by Francis Galton in 1890, for the purpose of evaluating the extent to which monozygotic ('identical') and dizygotic ('fraternal' or 'sororal') twins differed in their expression of personality characteristics (Stigler, 1989).

Given that modern methods for quantifying genetic contributions to personality involve model-fitting and path analysis, power analysis for behavioral genetic (BG) studies tends to be quite complex. It is clear, however, that the precise estimation of genetic and environmental variance requires large sample sizes. Although exact numbers depend on the heritability of the variable, the effect of the shared environment, and the desired level of experimental error, one would need anywhere from 100 to 500 twin pairs in order to achieve 80% power (with 5% alpha), assuming that heritability accounted for 40–60% of the variability, and the shared environment accounted for 0–20% of the variability (Posthuma and Boomsma, 2000). Given that this is impractical for many laboratories to collect, exposition of the true genetic and environmental effects underlying commonly identified personality variables will require some form of effect size aggregation (i.e. meta-analysis). Fortunately, most published studies report the correlation coefficients associated with the twins used in their analyses, and this facilitates the estimation of overall heritability coefficients.

INTRODUCTION TO BEHAVIORAL GENETICS

Arguably the best-known genetic research was conducted by Gregor Mendel, from 1858 to 1866, when he carried out his seminal study on the genetic determinants of qualitative (i.e. categorical) phenotypic expressions. Despite the fact that he was studying pea plants, his research shares a number of important similarities with modern genetics, most notably his use of genetically informative data. Given the absence of advanced gene identification technology at the time, Mendel relied on the identification of 'true-breeding' plants (i.e. plants that always produced the same qualitative features in their offspring). By crossing such plants, Mendel was able to demonstrate the manner in which genetic information is transmitted between generations (Mendel, 1866).

Obviously, most heritable human characteristics are more complex than the skin texture of a seed from a pea plant. It is, for example, highly unlikely that individual differences in personality are determined

solely by the action of a single gene. Such traits are more likely to be subject to polygenic inheritance, where individual genes are inherited according to Mendel's laws of heritability, but the individual differences are caused by the manner in which the genes interact with each other or with the environment. The concept of polygenic inheritance gave rise to the study of quantitative genetics, a branch of genetics that forms the basis of most modern behavioral genetics research. Simply put, quantitative genetics proposes that a genetically determined quantitative (or continuous) trait will co-vary with increasing degrees of genetic relatedness. In other words, biological siblings should be more correlated on a quantitative trait than first cousins, who should be more correlated with each other than adopted siblings or random pairs of individuals within the population. Quantitative genetics is thus reliant on the collection of genetically informative data – which in most cases means that the data are collected within families, where inter-individual genetic relatedness is known. The most powerful studies are designed around the collection of twin pairs, ideally with roughly equal numbers of monozygotic and same-sex dizygotic twins.

In a behavioral genetic study, one is interested in determining the amount of variance that is attributable to genes and the amount of variance that is due to the environment. In twin studies, the dependent variables of interest are measured in a sample of monozygotic twins (MZ; twins sharing 100% of their genes) and dizygotic twins (DZ; twins sharing, on average, 50% of their genes in common). The phenotypic expression of this dependent variable may be expressed as: $P = G + E$, where G refers to the effect of genes and E refers to the effect of the environment.

Genes combine in two basic fashions: additively and non-additively. Additive effects occur when genes combine in a linear fashion for expression in the phenotype. Non-additive effects occur when genes do not combine in a simple linear fashion, with the most common form of non-additive genetic effect being classified as dominance effects. The term dominance is derived from Mendelian genetics, and refers to the interaction between alleles at corresponding loci on homologous chromosomes. The existence of dominance effects is indicated when an individual possessing different alleles for a given trait (heterozygote) is not exactly intermediate in the expression of the trait between individuals who possess matched pairs of alleles (homozygotes). This subdivision of genetic effects may be written algebraically as follows: G = A + D. Without direct access to actual genetic material, it is impossible to identify the exact nature of genetic effects within a particular construct. What is possible, however, is the construction of an expression that estimates the variance that is due to each source of variability. From the foregoing, we may express phenotypic effects as follows: P = A + D + E. Or in terms of variability, we could say that phenotypic variance is equal to the variance of the sum of additive genetic effects, dominance genetic effects, and environmental effects:

$$var\ (P) = var\ (A + D + E) \qquad (7.1)$$

Mathematically, we know that the variance of a sum may be expressed as:

$$var\ (x + y) = var\ (x) + var\ (y) \\ + 2Cov\ (x,\ y) \qquad (7.2)$$

We can thus generalize equation (6.2) to the sum of three variables, and expand equation (7.1) as follows:

$$var\ (P) = var\ (A) + var\ (D) \qquad (7.3) \\ + var\ (E) + 2Cov\ (A,\ D) \\ + 2Cov\ (A,\ E) + 2Cov\ (D,\ E)$$

Fortunately, equation (7.3) can be simplified somewhat, using our knowledge of genetic effects. The co-variation between additive and dominance genetic effects is equal to zero, as these effects are, by

definition, independent of one another. Genetic and environmental effects are also often considered to be independent, which would remove the remaining two co-variance terms from equation (7.3). Thus, we can consider

$$Cov\ (A,\ D) = Cov\ (A,\ E) = Cov\ (D,\ E) = 0$$

which leaves us with:

$$var\ (P) = var\ (A) + var\ (D) + var\ (E) \qquad (7.4)$$

We began the foregoing discussion by introducing the concept of genetically informative data, and the power of studying co-variation on quantitative variables among members of a family. In this context, therefore, we can begin to disentangle some of the effects of the environment. Although the effects of the environment are exceedingly complex (and likely more complex than the mechanism of genes), the use of genetically informative information within samples of twins and families allows us to roughly categorize environmental effects into two classes of predictors: those environmental predictors that are shared among family members (e.g. socio-economic status of the family, parental educational background, or geographic location of the family), and those environmental predictors that are unique to each individual (e.g. disease, injury, or non-shared peer relationships). Environmental predictors are intuitively labeled 'common environmental effects' and 'specific environmental effects'. These environmental effects are, however, somewhat confounded within most familial relationships. The predominant source of this confound is the age differential between the family members in question – for example, non-twin siblings that are separated by five years in age will (conceivably) have been exposed to different school teachers, different friends, different television shows, and so on. True control of the common environment variable is, therefore, only possible with MZ and DZ twins.

Based on what we know about the mechanisms through which twins are conceived (i.e. MZ twins are the result of post-fertilization mitosis, while DZ twins are the result of the simultaneous fertilization of two ova), we can draw conclusions about their genetic makeup. MZ twins share 100% of their genetic material, while DZ twins share 50% of their genetic material, on average. This means that MZ twins will share 100% of their additive genetic variation, while DZ twins will share only 50% of their additive genetic variation. Non-additive genetic variability is slightly more complex. For any given gene locus, there is a 50% chance that DZ and non-twin siblings will share the same maternal allele, and a 50% chance that they will share the same paternal allele. Therefore, there is a 25% (0.5×0.5) probability that they will share both maternal and paternal alleles. This leads to the conclusion that 25% of the variance that is attributable to dominance effects is shared among DZ and non-twin siblings. MZ twins are, however, genetically identical, and therefore share 100% of maternal and paternal alleles, meaning that they will share 100% of the variance that is attributable to dominance effects. Both sets of twins will share 100% of their common environment (provided that they have lived together since birth), owing to the fact that they have been raised in the same household at exactly the same time. Finally, as specific environmental effects are defined as factors that are not shared by other members of the family, both MZ and DZ twins will share 0% of their specific environmental effects.

Heritability that includes both additive and non-additive effects is often termed broad-sense heritability (narrow-sense heritability refers only to that heritability that is due to additive effects). Based on what we know about MZ and DZ twins, we can express correlations among twins on any given phenotypic expression as follows (where h^2 refers to narrow-sense heritability):

$$r_{MZ} = h^2 + c^2 \qquad (7.5)$$

$$r_{DZ} = \tfrac{1}{2} h^2 + c^2 \qquad (7.6)$$

Subtracting equation (7.6) from equation (7.5) yields:

$$r_{MZ} - r_{DZ} = h^2 + c^2 - (\tfrac{1}{2} h^2 + c^2)$$

$$r_{MZ} - r_{DZ} = \tfrac{1}{2} h^2$$

$$h^2 = 2(r_{MZ} - r_{DZ}) \qquad (7.7)$$

Furthermore, we can rearrange equation (7.5) to yield an estimate of c^2:

$$c^2 = r_{MZ} - h^2 \qquad (7.8)$$

Finally, we may consider h^2, c^2, and e^2 to be proportions of variance (given that they are squared variance estimates derived from correlations). Furthermore, we have presented the assumption that these three variance components will summate to represent all of the variability of the phenotype. Thus, these three variance components must sum to zero, and so:

$$c^2 + h^2 + e^2 = 1$$

$$r_{MZ} + e^2 = 1$$

$$e^2 = 1 - r_{MZ} \qquad (7.9)$$

Equations (7.7) to (7.9) represent the oldest method for estimating genetic and environmental effects using samples of twins, and are useful for deriving rough estimates of the extent to which genetic effects are important to the prediction of a quantitative trait. Modern behavioral genetics studies typically adopt a more sophisticated method for estimating genetic and environmental effects, termed 'model fitting'. Like equations (7.7) to (7.9), this technique leverages our knowledge of shared genes and environment in MZ and DZ twins. Figure 7.1a depicts a path diagram that

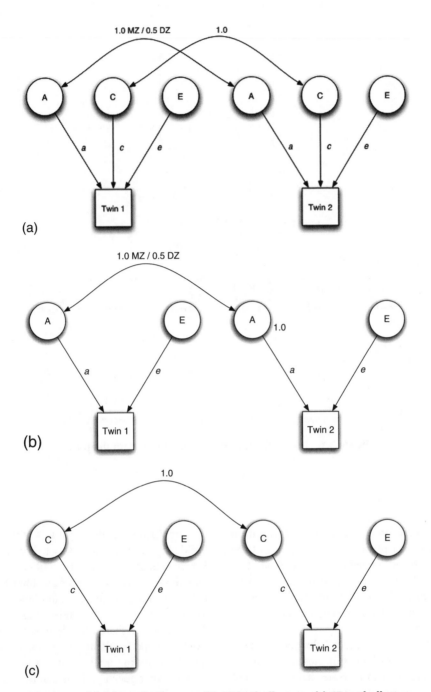

Figure 7.1 (a) ACE path diagram; (b) AE path diagram; (c) CE path diagram

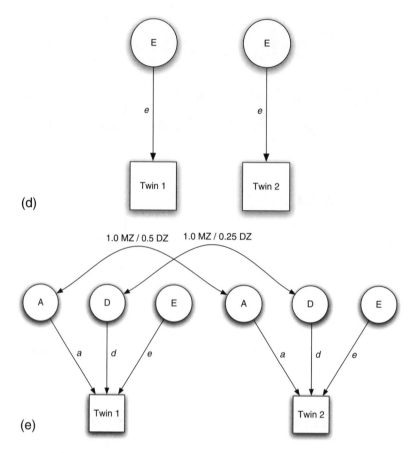

Figure 7.1   (d) E only path diagram; (e) ADE path diagram

shows that the phenotypic correlation between twin pairs (the curved lines at the top) can be accounted for by shared additive genes and shared environmental effects. This figure also shows that differences among twins are attributable to specific environmental factors.

In standard univariate behavioral-genetic model fitting, estimates of these A, C, and E effects are used to recreate the MZ and DZ variance/co-variance matrices of a particular variable and different models are compared in terms of the goodness-of-fit that they achieve to the observed variance/co-variance matrices that are obtained from the twins' actual data. Typically, a full ACE model

(Figure 7.1a) is applied first: this will always yield the best fit to the observed data. Reduced models can also be applied that systematically drop one or more of the parameters to identify more parsimonious models. Thus, an AE model can be fitted (Figure 7.1b), to see whether shared environmental factors can be dropped without a significant worsening of fit. Fitting a CE model (Figure 7.1c) tests whether genetic effects can be dropped, and an E only model (Figure 7.1d) is also frequently tested, if only to confirm that it results in a significantly poorer model than other models. Note that the E only model could only work if in fact there was no correlation between the twins. Finally, the

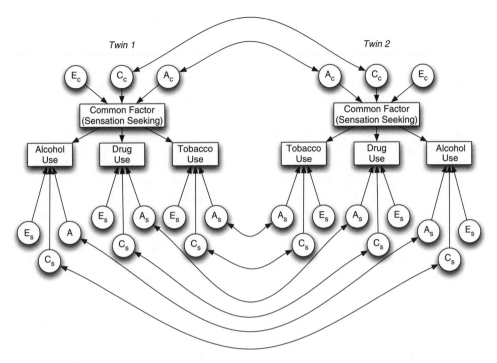

Figure 7.2   Common pathway model

presence of dominant genetic effects can also be investigated (although data from MZ and DZ twins raised together cannot simultaneously test for A, D, C, and E effects) by fitting an ADE model (Figure 7.1e) (Neale and Maes, 1998). Once a model has been selected, its effects are used to estimate the heritability (and/or environmentality) of the variable.

If a researcher is interested in understanding what the correlations between two or more variables are attributable to, a multivariate model such as appears in Figure 7.2 can be examined. Models such as this compute twin cross-correlations: the extent to which one twin's score on one variable correlates with his or her co-twin's score on another variable. Multivariate models also provide estimates of genetic and environmental correlations between variables; that is, the extent to which those genes or environmental factors that contribute to one of

the variables also contribute to the other variable. Perhaps the biggest advantage that multivariate behavior genetic analyses can bestow is that genetic and environmental correlations can exist even when there is no phenotypic correlation between two variables (Carey, 1988). Thus, a phenotypic correlation of zero between two variables may mean that the variables have no shared etiology; however, it is also possible that the variables in fact have sizeable genetic and environmental correlations, albeit of different signs, and therefore cancel each other out at the phenotypic level, and thus have shared etiologies of considerable interest. However, this could only be revealed in a multivariate behavior genetic study.

The multivariate model shown in Figure 7.2 is referred to as a common pathway model (Neale and Maes, 1998). This model is looking at three correlated domains – alcohol abuse, drug abuse, and tobacco abuse – and shows that the correlations between these variables can be attributed to the fact that common genetic and environmental factors (A_c, C_c, and E_c) impact on all three of them through a phenotypic latent variable (labeled 'Sensation Seeking' in this example). To the extent that the variables correlate less than perfectly, this is attributed to specific genetic and environmental factors (A_s, C_s, and E_s) that underlie each of them. As was the case with univariate model fitting, a full multivariate ACE model can be examined first and then compared to reduced models that drop one or more of these effects (Johnson and Vernon, 2004).

Genetically informative data, and behavior genetic techniques, are thus highly applicable to the identification of the structure of a disorder and the development of a robust model of personality. Behavior genetic analyses such as these cannot, however, generate information about specific genes (or allelic polymorphisms) that produce individual differences in personality, nor should a genetic correlation be interpreted as referring directly to molecular genetic information (e.g. the proportion of loci common between two variables) (Carey, 1988).

Genotype–environment effects

When we introduced methods for estimating genetic and environmental effects for quantitative variables, we presented the assumption that the effects of the environment are independent from the effects of genes. While this is a common assumption, there is increasing interest in the interplay between genes and the environment. We will discuss the three most common (and most powerful) of these effects: assortative mating, genotype–environment interaction, and genotype–environment correlation.

Assortative mating occurs when mate selection proceeds on the basis of phenotype, and the presence of this effect is thus indicated when there is a phenotypic correlation between mates on a given trait.

Positive assortment has been noted for variables such as education level, religion, attitudes, and socio-economic status, but is considered to be effectively random for most personality dimensions (Neale and Maes, 1998).

Genotype–environment interactions refer to a change in the phenotypic expression of a genotype, based on the environment in which an individual lives. Classically, genotype–environment interactions in personality are described with the diathesis-stress model, wherein a genetic predisposition interacts with life events and environmental factors to produce a phenotypic expression. The genotype is, therefore, a necessary but not sufficient condition for the expression of the trait – without the appropriate environmental triggers, the individual may never demonstrate the trait.

Genotype–environment correlations, on the other hand, occur when an individual's environment is 'selected' by their genotype, or when an individual is predisposed to a given environment by their genotype (Kendler and Eaves, 1986). Plomin et al. (2001) describe three forms of genotype–environment correlation: passive, evocative (or reactive), and active. Passive genotype–environment correlation occurs when children share both genetic and environmental factors with parents and other family members, and so they 'inherit' their environment. For example, a child who is born to parents who are gregarious and outgoing (i.e. who are high in 'extraversion') will likely be exposed to a higher-than-average number of social outings, which in turn may predict that the child will develop better-than-average social skills, and may engage in more independent social activities as he or she gets older. Evocative genotype–environment correlation refers to specific environmental experiences of children that are formed due to the reactions of others to the child's genetic characteristics. The child in the previous example might find it easier to make friends than children with more poorly developed social skills, and so he or she may have more opportunities for social activities.

Finally, active genotype–environment correlations occur when children seek out, or create, environments that are correlated with their genetic predispositions. The aforementioned 'naturally outgoing' child might, for example, select friends that are similarly extraverted.

Passive genotype–environment correlations can be detected by evaluating within-family correlations on measures assessing the impact of the shared environment. The hypothesized action of this type of correlation is that parental genotypes predict the type of home environment that children are exposed to, and so this mechanism would be suspected if the parent in a non-adoptive family demonstrated a personality trait that was correlated with both an environmental predictor of the trait and also with the child's trait level. A second source of evidence for genotype–environment correlations would be the trait correlation between a biological parent, and an environmental measure within the home of his or her adopted-away child. Such a correlation would suggest either an evocative or active genotype–environment correlation. Finally, one could apply the previously mentioned model-fitting techniques to perform a multivariate analysis investigating the genetic correlation between a trait measure and an environmental measure. A significant genetic correlation between the trait measure and the environmental measure would suggest a significant genotype–environment correlation (Plomin et al., 2001).

Genotype–environment correlations are potentially quite important to our understanding of the genetic determination of personality. Given that most twin studies assume a genotype–environment correlation of zero (i.e. that $2Cov (A, E) = 0$ in equation (7.3), the variance attributable to this effect will be rolled into either the environmental or the genetic variability. Given the foregoing information on genotype–environment correlations, one possible scenario is that very small genetic effects may be augmented by environments that are either inherited or manipulated by the action of the genotype.

Dickens and Flynn (2001) suggest that this is a possible explanation for the high heritabilities demonstrated by cognitive ability variables, and propose that this suggests that the heritabilities in this domain are overestimates of the true impact of genes.

REVIEW OF THE RESULTS OF 50+ YEARS OF BEHAVIORAL GENETIC RESEARCH ON PERSONALITY

Following the above brief introduction to behavior genetics, in this section we present the results of a review of over 50 years of twin and other kinship studies of personality. We began this review using library and online searches for any behavior genetic studies of the Big Five (openness-to-experience (O), conscientiousness (C), extraversion (E), agreeableness (A), and neuroticism (N)) and related personality traits (Costa and McCrae, 1992a; Tupes and Christal, 1992). To be included in this review, studies needed to indicate the number of MZ and DZ twins (or other kinships) sampled, report which personality scale(s) were used (which, in turn, needed to be a measure of one or more of the Big Five or related traits), and provide either twin or kinship correlations on these traits and/or to have reported h^2 estimates (computed by formulas such as equation (7.7)) or a^2, c^2, e^2 or d^2 estimates derived from model-fitting analyses. Starting with Cattell et al. (1955), who administered the Junior Cattell Personality Questionnaire to 134 pairs of MZ and DZ twins, we identified 145 studies through year 2006 that met these criteria. In total, these studies reported correlations or other statistics (h^2, etc.) computed from 85,640 pairs of MZ twins, 106,644 pairs of DZ twins, and 46,215 pairs of other non-twin kinships, ranging in age from 4 months to 96 years, who were administered a total of 83 different personality tests or questionnaires. Within studies, sample sizes for MZ twins ranged from 21 to 5,568 pairs, for DZ twins from

10 to 7,873 pairs, and for non-twin kinships from 20 to 7,823 pairs. A complete list of the 145 studies, the kinships investigated and their sample sizes, the type of report used (e.g. self-report or rating by another), the ages of the samples (where these were reported), and the specific tests or questionnaires administered appears in Table 7.1. Despite an extensive and careful search, we acknowledge the possibility that we may have overlooked some studies, but with samples as large as the ones we have included it is most unlikely that the pattern of results we observed and which we report below would change appreciably.

At the next stage, we went through the studies and extracted every pertinent piece of information that was reported: the kinships studied, their sample sizes, the tests used, the personality traits or variables that were measured and the statistics reported. Some studies reported a single statistic (e.g. one MZ correlation for one variable), others reported multiple statistics (e.g. MZ and DZ correlations and model-fitting analyses for all Big Five traits and all of their facets). Some studies used the NEO-PI-R or the NEO-FFI (Costa and McCrae, 1992b), which provide direct measures of the Big Five, or the Eysenck Personality Inventory or Questionnaire, which provide direct measures of E and N (Eysenck, 1947, 1967). In the five tables that follow (Tables 7.2–7.6), we refer to these scales as providing 'core' measures of the Big Five. As mentioned, across all studies a total of 83 different personality questionnaires were used. Those studies that did not use the NEO or an Eysenck questionnaire reported measuring a total of 127 personality variables that either they or we considered to be related to one or more of the Big Five. For example, one study might report twin correlations for variables labeled 'outgoing', 'sociable', or 'shy' which we classify as being related to extraversion (or introversion); another study might measure 'curious', 'idea-seeking', or 'imaginative': variables related to openness-to-experience. In addition to our own evaluations of which variables were related to the Big Five we also presented a list of over 130 variables to experts and had them categorize them as a measure of O, C, E, A, or N. Based on these ratings we removed a number of variables on which the experts either disagreed or stated were not associated with any of the Big Five (e.g. 'autonomous', 'dishonest', 'sophisticated'), leaving us with the 127 variables mentioned above. In Tables 7.7–7.11 we report results for these variables, which we refer to as being 'related to' each of the Big Five.

In the first column of Tables 7.2–7.11 we report all the kinships for which we found information for a given trait, listed in order of their genetic relatedness. Thus, all tables start with monozygotic twins raised together (MZT) or apart (MZA) and continue down through non-twin biological siblings, parents and their children, half-siblings, and so on, to genetically unrelated pairs such as spouses and adopted siblings. The other abbreviated kinships include dizygotic twins raised together (DZT) or apart (DZA) and opposite-sex dizygotic twins (DZO). All other kinships in these tables are written out fully. After each kinship we report (in parentheses) their degree of genetic relatedness (e.g. MZT = MZA = 1.0, biological siblings = 0.50, adopted siblings = 0, etc.)

In the second column of Tables 7.2–7.11 we report the total number of reported kinship correlations or other statistics that we found in the 145 studies we reviewed. Thus, for example, in the first row of Table 7.2 it can be seen that we found 19 reported MZT correlations for core openness. These reported correlations may or not have been extracted from different studies because some studies reported more than one MZT (or other kinship) correlation for two (or more) measures of the same variable. To help to clarify this, in column 3 of Tables 7.2–7.11 we report the *total* number of pairs of each kinship that the correlations are based on and in column 4 we report the number of *independent* pairs of each kinship obtained from different studies. If these

Table 7.1   Details of studies included in the review of behavioral genetic investigations of the Big 5 and related Personality traits

Study	Subjects (No. of pairs)	Type of measure	Ages	Measures
Cattell et al. (1955)	104 MZ, 30 DZ	Self-report	18–25	*Junior* Cattell Personality Questionnaire
Vandenberg (1962)	45 MZ, 37 DZ	Self-report	18–25	*Junior* Cattell Personality Questionnaire
Gottesman (1963)	34 MZ, 34 DZ	Self-report	18–25	*Junior* Cattell Personality Questionnaire
Scarr (1969)	24 MZ, 28 DZ	Maternal and observer rating	6–10	Gough's Adjective Check List (mother ratings) Fel's Child Behavior Scales (observer ratings)
Buss et al. (1973)	78 MZ, 50 DZ	Maternal rating	4 months– 16 years,	EASI Temperament Survey
Eaves and Eysenck (1975)	451 MZ, 257 DZ, 129 DZO	Self-report	Adults (18+)	Eysenck Personality Inventory
Eaves and Eysenck (1976)	253 MZ, 188 DZ	Self-report	Adults, 18+	Eysenck Personality Inventory Eysenck Personality Questionnaire
Horn et al. (1976)	99 MZ, 99 DZ	Self-report	45–55	California Psychological Inventory
Loehlin and Nichols (1976)	490 MZ, 317 DZ	Self-report	Young adults	California Psychological Inventory
Cohen et al. (1977)	181 MZ, 84 DZ	Parental rating	1–6	Child Personality Scale
Goldsmith and Gottesman (1977)	80 MZ, 68 DZ	Self-report	Adolescents	MMPI
Plomin and Rowe (1977)	36 MZ, 31 DZ, 24 DZO	Maternal rating	1–7	Colorado Childhood Temperament Inventory
Lykken et al. (1978)	231 MZ, 106 DZ	Self-report	Young Adults	Differential Personality Questionnaire
Rahe et al. (1978)	93 MZ, 97 DZ	Self-report	42–56	California Psychological Inventory Gough's Adjective Check List Jenkins Activity Survey Thurstone Temperament Schedule
Dworkin (1979)	54 MZ, 34 DZ	Self-report	m = 20.45, SD = 1.45	Self-Monitoring Scale (Snyder, 1974)
Floderus et al. (1980)	5025 MZ, 7873 DZ	Self-report	22–54	Eysenck Personality Inventory
Plomin and Foch (1980)	42 MZ, 29 DZ	Observer and video-based rating	m = 7.6, SD = 1.6	Bobo Clown and video observation
Eaves and Young (1981)	303 MZ, 172 DZ	Self-report	Adults (18+)	Eysenck Personality Questionnaire
Goldsmith and Gottesman (1981)	189 MZ, 315 DZ	Parental rating	Collected at ages: 8 months, 4 and 7 years	Bayley Infant Behavior Profile
Scarr et al. (1981)	Biological families: 120 families, 234 children adoptive families: 115 families, 194 children	Self-report	16–22	Activities Preference Questionnaire Differential Personality Questionnaire Eysenck Personality Inventory
Cattell et al. (1982)	237 biological siblings, 47 MZ, 63 DZ	Self-report	Young adults	Highschool Personality Questionnaire

Continued

Table 7.1   Details of studies included in the review of behavioral genetic investigations of the Big 5 and related Personality traits—cont'd

Study	Subjects (No. of pairs)	Type of measure	Ages	Measures
Loehlin (1982)	490 MZ, 317 DZ	Self-report	16	California Psychological Inventory Eysenck Personality Questionnaire
Miller and Rose (1982)	50 MZ, 59 DZ	Self-report and parental rating	10–72	Internal and External Locus of Control Scale
Price et al. (1982)	72 MZ, 264 parent-offspring, 71 co-twin-offspring, 75 sibling, and 54 cousins	Self-report	Adults	Eysenck Personality Questionnaire Thurstone Temperament Schedule
Koskenvuo et al. (1984)	1501 MZ, 3455 DZ	Self-report	18–69	Eysenck Personality Inventory
Langinvainio et al. (1984)	77 MZ, 230 DZ	Self-report	$m = 44.73$, $SD = 15$	Eysenck Personality Inventory (*short form*)
Loehlin (1985)	2 samples • National Merit Twin Study: 490 MZ, 317 DZ, 499 parent-adopted child pairs, 113 parent-biological child pairs, 120 adoptive-sibling pairs • Veterans Administration twin sample 99 MZ, 99 DZ	Self-report and parental rating	Adolescents and adults	California Psychological Inventory
Loehlin et al. (1985)	220 families: 299 adopted children, 62 biological children	Self-report	14–45	California Psychological Inventory Thurstone Temperament Schedule
Pogue-Geile and Rose (1985)	71 MZ, 62 DZ	Self-report	20–25	MMPI Welsh's A Scale Wiggins Social Maladjustment Scale
Stevenson and Fielding (1985)	219 MZ, 322 DZ	Parental rating	Birth–12 years	EASI Temperament Survey
Loehlin (1986)	4 samples: • Michigan twin sample: 45 MZ, 34 DZ • Veterans sample: 102 MZ, 119 DZ • Veterans sample with children: 44 MZ twin/ parent offspring pairs • Texas Adoption Study: 220 families with at least one adopted child	Self-report and parental rating	Adolescents and adults Michigan sample: high-school age Veterans sample: middle-age adult males Veterans sample with children: 18+ Texas Adoption Study: 14+	Thurstone Temperament Schedule
Martin and Jardine (1986)	1799 MZ, 1102 DZ	Self-report	Adults	Eysenck Personality Questionnaire
Neale et al. (1986)	326 MZ, 202 DZ, 99 DZO	Self-report	Adults	Eysenck Personality Questionnaire (90-item)
Rowe (1986)	168 MZ, 97 DZ	Self-report	$m = 17.5$, $SD = 1.5$	EASI-III Temperament Inventory
Rushton et al. (1986)	296 MZ, 179 DZ, 98 DZO	Self-report	19–60	Interpersonal Behavior Survey Personality Research Form (*Nurturance Scale*) Self-report Altruism Scale

Table 7.1   Details of studies included in the review of behavioral genetic investigations of the Big 5 and related Personality traits—cont'd

Study	Subjects (No. of pairs)	Type of measure	Ages	Measures
Martin et al. (1988)	1800 MZ, 1103 DZ	Self-report	18–69	Eysenck Personality Questionnaire
Pedersen et al. (1988)	99 MZA, 229 DZA, 160 MZT, 212 DZT	Self-report	$m = 58.6$, $SD = 13.6$	Eysenck Personality Inventory Karolinska Scales of Personality
Plomin et al. (1988)	99 MZA, 229 DZA, 160 MZT, 212 DZT	Self-report	27–80+	EAS Temperament Survey
Rose (1988)	228 MZ, 182 DZ	Self-report	14–34	MMPI
Rose et al. (1988)	2320 MZ, 4824 DZ	Self-report	24–49	Eysenck Personality Inventory
Tellegen et al. (1988)	217 MZT, 114 DZT, 44 MZA, 27 DZA	Self-report	Raised together $m = 21.7$, $SD = 7.7$ Raised apart $m = 40.9$, $SD = 11.65$	Multidimensional Personality Questionnaire
Neale and Stevenson (1989)	$n = 576$ families, 219 MZ, 322 DZ	Self-report, spouse, and parental rating	$m = 41.7$, $SD = 24.8$ months	EASI Temperament Scales
Pedersen et al. (1989a)	58 MZA, 103 MZT, 123 DZA, 124 DZT	Self-report	$m = 58.6$, $SD = 13.6$	Locus of Control Rotter Scale
Pedersen et al. (1989b)	160 MZT, 212 DZT, 99 MZA, 229 DZA	Self-report	$m = 58.6$, $SD = 13.6$	Cook-Medley Hostility Scale Framingham Type A Scale
Baker and Daniels (1990)	75 MZ, 29 DZ	Self-report	18–75	Eysenck Personality Questionnaire Self-Rating Depression Scale
Bouchard and McGue (1990)	45 MZA, 26 DZA	Self-report	19–68	California Psychological Inventory
Cyphers et al. (1990)	153 MZ, 153 DZ	Parental rating	1–4 years	Carey's Infant Temperament Questionnaire Toddler Temperament Scale
Tambs et al. (1991)	150 twin families: 133 MZ pairs, 226 twin-spouses, 221 co-twin-spouses, 97 spouses of co-twins, 524 parent-offspring, 284 twins with co-twins' offspring, 206 spouses with co-twins' offspring, 167 siblings, 235 half-sibs	Self-report	Ages 16+ Twins and spouses $m = 43.9$, $SD = 6.5$ Offspring $m = 21.9$, $SD = 4.6$	Eysenck Personality Questionnaire
Baker et al. (1992)	75 MZ, 30 DZ	Self-report	16–72	Affect Balance Scale (Bradburn, 1969)
Braungart et al. (1992)	85 MZ, 50 DZ, 95 pairs of non-adoptive siblings, 80 pairs of adoptive siblings	Parental rating	Collected at ages 1, 2 years	Bayley's Infant Behavior Record
Emde et al. (1992)	100 MZ, 100 DZ	Parental and observer rating	Collected at ages 14, 20, 24, 36 months	Bayley's Infant Behavior Record (observer ratings) Colorado Childhood Temperament Inventory (parental ratings)
Heath et al. (1992)	460 MZ, 366 DZ	Self-report and co-twin rating	21–57	Eysenck Personality Questionnaire

Continued

Table 7.1   Details of studies included in the review of behavioral genetic investigations of the Big 5 and related Personality traits—cont'd

Study	Subjects (No. of pairs)	Type of measure	Ages	Measures
Loehlin (1992)	44 MZA, 71 MZT, 97 DZA, 93 DZT	Self-report	Adults	Multidimensional Personality Questionnaire
Plomin et al. (1992)	72 MZA, 126 MZT, 178 DZA, 146 DZT	Self-report	$m = 60.7$, $SD = 13.1$	CES-D depression Questionnaire Cook-Medley Paranoid Hostility and Cynicism Scales Life Orientation Test of Optimism and Pessimism
Zahn-Waxler et al. (1992)	94 MZ, 90 DZ	Observer and maternal rating	Collected at ages 14 and 20 months	Video recordings for Prosocial and Empathetic behaviors during play episodes
Bergeman et al. (1993)	82 MZA, 132 MZT, 171 DZA, 167 DZT	Self-report	26–87	NEO-Personality Inventory (*shortened version*)
Coccaro et al. (1993)	71–74 MZA, 108–117 MZT 143–152 DZA, 135–157 DZT	Self-report	26–85	Cook-Medley Hostility Scale EAS Temperament Survey Eysenck Personality Questionnaire Karolinska Scales of Personality KNOX Psychosocial Work/Environment Scales Locus of Control Questionnaire NEO Personality Inventory OARS Mental Health Questionnaire Type A Behavior Questionnaire
Livesley et al. (1993)	90 MZ, 85 DZ	Self-report	16–71	Dimensional Assessment of Personality Pathology
Schulman et al. (1993)	115 MZ, 27 DZ	Self-report	12–65	Attributional Style Questionnaire Beck Depression Inventory
Bouchard (1994)	30 MZA, 23 DZA, 261 MZT, 204 DZT	Self-report	Adults	Multidimensional Personality Questionnaire
Heath et al. (1994)	1336 MZ, 757 DZ, 567 DZO	Self-report	18–88	Cloninger Tridimensional Personality Questionnaire Eysenck Personality Questionnaire
McGuire et al. (1994)	92 MZ, 97 DZ, 94 full-siblings 180 full-siblings, 109 half-siblings, 130 adopted-siblings from step (divorced) families	Self-report	10–18	EAS Temperament Survey Self-Perception Profile for Adolescents
Viken et al. (1994)	18–23 years cohort: 1039 MZ, 1334 DZ 24–29 years cohort: 813 MZ, 947 DZ 30–35 years cohort: 564 MZ, 639 twin pairs 36–41 years cohort: 444 MZ, 462 DZ	Self-report	18–53	Eysenck Personality Inventory (*short form*)

Table 7.1 **Details of studies included in the review of behavioral genetic investigations of the Big 5 and related Personality traits—cont'd**

Study	Subjects (No. of pairs)	Type of measure	Ages	Measures
	42–47 years cohort: 335 MZ, 379 DZ			
	48–53 years cohort: 219 MZ, 291 DZ			
Edelbrock et al. (1995)	99 MZ, 82 DZ	Parental rating	7–15	Child Behavior Check List
Hershberger et al. (1995)	58 MZT, 35 MZA, 81 DZT, 68 DZA	Self-report	26–87	Cook-Medley Hostility Scale
				EAS Temperament Survey
				Eysenck Personality Inventory (*short form*)
				Karolinska Scales of Impulsivity
				NEO (*Openness*) Personality Inventory
				Spielberger's State Anxiety Scale
Hur and Bouchard (1995)	58 MZA, 46 DZA	Self-report	$m = 41$, $SD = 13.4$	Family Environment Scale
Koopmans et al. (1995)	608 MZ, 534 DZ, 449 DZO	Self-report	12–24	Zuckerman Sensation-Seeking Scale
Roy et al. (1995)	Wave 1: 363 MZ, 238 DZ	Self-report	17–55	Rosenberg Self-Esteem Scale
	Wave 2: 430 MZ, 308 DZ			
Saudino et al. (1995)	93 MZ, 99 DZ, 95 full-siblings from non-divorced families, 182 full-siblings from divorced families, 109 half-siblings from divorced families, 130 adopted-siblings from divorced families	Parental rating	10–18	EAS Temperament Survey
Tambs et al. (1995)	1880 MZ, 1654 DZ, 1586 DZO	Self-report	18–25	Hopkins Symptom Checklist
DiLalla et al. (1996)	65 MZ, 38 DZ, 16 DZO	Self-report	18–77	3 MMPI scales
Jang et al. (1996)	123 MZ, 127 DZ	Self-report	16–68	NEO-PI-R
Stallings et al. (1996)	732 MZ, 348 DZ, 207 DZO	Self-report	50–96	Cloninger Tridimensional Personality Questionnaire
				Eysenck Personality Questionnaire
				Karolinska Scales of Personality
van den Oord et al. (1996)	446 MZ, 912 DZ	Parental rating	3 years	Child Behavior Check List
Coccaro et al. (1997)	182 MZ, 118 DZ	Self-report	36–54	Buss-Durkee Hostility Inventory
Finkel and McGue (1997)	626 MZ, 517 DZ, 114 DZO, 1690 spouses, 495 parents, 322 siblings, 535 offspring	Self-report, parental, spousal and sibling rating	27–64	Multidimensional Personality Questionnaire
Losoya et al. (1997)	63 MZ, 55 DZ, 20 adoptive siblings	Self-report and parental rating	Twins: 22–46 Adoptive siblings: 1–8 years	Inventory for Candid Self-Descriptions (a measure of the five-factor model of personality)
Riemann et al. (1997)	660 MZ, 200 DZ, 104 DZO	Self-report and peer rating	14–80	NEO Five Factory Inventory (*self-report and peer report versions*)
Saudino et al. (1997)	39 MZA, 80 MZT, 96 DZA, 105 DZT	Self-report	$m = 58.6$, $SD = 13.6$	Eysenck Personality Inventory
Vernon et al. (1997)	93 MZ, 50 DZ, 66 non-twin-siblings	Self-report	$m = 23.6$, $SD = 6.3$	Personality Research Form

Continued

Table 7.1   Details of studies included in the review of behavioral genetic investigations of the Big 5 and related Personality traits—cont'd

Study	Subjects (No. of pairs)	Type of measure	Ages	Measures
Beer et al. (1998)	181 families: 186 adopted children, 80 biological children, 150 adoptive Fathers, 148 adoptive mothers, 130 biological mothers	Self-report	Adopted Children $m = 17.7$ Biological Children $m = 20.2$	MMPI
Bouchard and Hur (1998)	61 MZA, 49 DZA, 92 spouses	Self-report and spouse rating	18–77	Myers-Briggs Type Indicator
Bouchard et al. (1998)	71 MZA, 53 DZA, 99 MZT, 99 DZT, 111 spouses of reared apart twins	Self-report and spouse rating	$m = 42.9$, $SD = 13.2$	California Psychological Inventory
Hur et al. (1998)	243 MZ, 164 DZ	Self-report	11–12	Piers-Harris Children's Self-Concept Scale
Jang et al. (1998a)	336 MZ, 249 DZ, 96 DZO	Self-report	16–84	Dimensional Assessment of Personality Pathology
Jang et al. (1998b)	Canadian sample: 183 MZ, 175 DZ German sample: 435 MZ, 205 DZ	Self-report	Canadian sample: 16–71 German sample: 15–67	NEO-PI-R
Kendler et al. (1998)	1359 MZ, 1014 DZ, 1420 DZO	Self-report	18–60	Rosenberg Self-Esteem Scale
Loehlin et al. (1998)	490 MZ and 317 DZ	Self-report	Young adults (18+)	California Psychological Inventory Gough and Heibrun's Adjective Checklist Trait Ratings Questionnaire
Plomin et al. (1998)	130–194 adoptive/biological and 149–219 non-adoptive parent-offspring pairs, 92 adoptive-siblings (on average), 101 non-adoptive-siblings (on average)	Self-report, sibling and parental rating	Collected at ages: 9–16	Colorado Childhood Temperament Inventory EASI Self-report Personality Questionnaire
Spinath and Angleitner (1998)	184 MZ, 109 DZ, 61 DZO	Parental rating	2–14	EAS Temperament Survey
DiLalla et al. (1999)	65 MZA, 54 DZA	Self-report	18–77	MMPI
Eley et al. (1999)	Swedish Sample: 336 MZ, 376 DZ, 310 DZO British Sample: 223 MZ, 173 DZ, 95 DZO	Parental rating	Swedish Sample: 7–9 years British Sample: 8–16 years	Child Behavior Check List
Saudino et al. (1999)	79 MZ, 51 DZ	Self-report	$m = 42.23$, $SD = 8.93$	Eysenck Personality Inventory Karolinska Scales of Personality
Seroczynski et al. (1999)	182 MZ, 118 DZ	Self-report	36–54	Barratt Impulsiveness Scale Buss-Durkee Hostility Inventory
Stein et al. (1999)	179 MZ, 158 DZ	Self-report	16–79	Anxiety Sensitivity Scale
Hudziak et al. (2000)	220 MZ, 272 DZ	Parental rating	8–12	Child Behavior Check List
Lake et al. (2000)	Australia sample: 4539 MZ, 2985 DZ, 2280 DZO, 3478 parents, 3632 siblings, 2419 spouses, 3353 aunt/uncles, 716 cousins	Self-report, parental, kin, and spousal rating	Adults (18+)	Eysenck Personality Questionnaire

Table 7.1   Details of studies included in the review of behavioral genetic investigations of the Big 5 and related Personality traits—cont'd

Study	Subjects (No. of pairs)	Type of measure	Ages	Measures
	USA sample: 5568 MZ, 3736 DZ, 2792 DZO, 2043 parents, 2720 Siblings, 3828 spouses, 7823 aunt/uncles, 1869 cousins			
Beatty et al. (2001)	62 MZ, 43 DZ	Self-report	$m = 41.76$	Communicative Adaptability Scale
Borkenau et al. (2001)	168 MZ, 132 DZ	Self-report and observer rating (video-based rating)	18–70	NEO-Five Factor Inventory
Coolidge et al. (2001)	70 MZ, 42 DZ	Parental rating	4–15	Coolidge Personality and Neuropsychological Inventory for Children
Jang et al. (2001)	Canadian sample: 253 MZ, 207 DZ German sample: 536 MZ, 269 DZ Japanese sample: 134 MZ, 86 DZ	Self-report	Canadian sample: 15–86 German sample: 14–80 Japanese sample: 15–27	NEO Personality Inventory
Krueger et al. (2001)	170 MZ, 106 DZ	Self-report	31–35	Clark Self-report List of Deviant Behavior Multidimensional Personality Questionnaire Seattle Self-report Instrument Short-Nye Self Report Delinquency Items
Lensvelt-Mulders and Hettema (2001)	57 MZ, 43 DZ	Self-report	18–47	TinSit Questionnaire (measuring the Big Five Personality traits)
Loehlin and Martin (2001)	2330 MZ, 1409 DZ, 1028 DZO	Self-report	17–90	Eysenck Personality Questionnaire
Olson et al. (2001)	195 MZ, 141 DZ	Self-report	$m = 30.4$	Personality Research Form
Valera and Berenbaum (2001)	45 MZ, 32 DZ	Self-report	16–62	Eysenck Personality Inventory
Zawadzki et al. (2001)	Polish sample: 317 MZ, 229 DZ, 2014 peer raters German sample: 732 MZ, 277 DZ, 4046 peer raters	Self-report and peer rating	Polish Sample: 17–64 German sample: 14–80	Formal Characteristics of Behavior- Temperament Inventory
Ando et al. (2002)	184 MZ, 77 DZ, 35 DZO	Self-report	14–29	Cloninger Temperament and Character Inventory (*Japanese Version*)
Fanous et al. (2002)	1369 MZ, 994 DZ, 1408 DZO	Self-report	28–68	Eysenck Personality Questionnaire
Jang et al. (2002)	Canadian sample: 253 MZ, 159 DZ, 48 DZO German sample: 526 MZ, 201 DZ, 68 DZO	Self-report	Canadian sample: 16–86 German sample: 14–80	NEO Personality Inventory (*Canadian and German versions*)
Roysamb et al. (2002)	941 MZ, 828 DZ, 793 DZO	Self-report	18–25	Subjective Well-being Scale
Torgersen and Janson (2002)	28 MZ	Self-report	29	NEO Personality Inventory

Continued

Table 7.1   Details of studies included in the review of behavioral genetic investigations of the Big 5 and related Personality traits—cont'd

Study	Subjects (No. of pairs)	Type of measure	Ages	Measures
Arseneault et al. (2003)	625 MZ, 491 DZ	Self-report, maternal, teacher, and observer rating	5	Berkeley Puppet Interview (child report) Child Behavior Check List (*maternal rating*) Dunedin Behavioral Observation Scale (*observer rating*) Teacher Report Form
Bartels et al. (2003)	598 MZ, 459 DZ, 424 DZO	Parental rating	12	Child Behavior Check List
Blonigen et al. (2003)	165 MZ, 106 DZ	Self-report	37–40 (*approx.*)	Psychopathic Personality Inventory
Constantino et al. (2003)	91 MZ, 128 DZ	Parental rating	7–15	Child Behavior Check List Social Responsiveness Scale
Eid et al. (2003)	169 MZ, 131 DZ	Self-report	18–68	NEO Five Factor Inventory (*German version*)
Gillespie et al. (2003)	1047 MZ, 1038 DZ	Self-report	$m = 61.9$, $SD = 8.9$	Cloninger Temperament and Character Inventory Cloninger Tri-dimensional Personality Questionnaire
Heiman et al. (2003)	577 MZ, 272 DZ	Self-report	50–89	Cloninger Tridimensional Personality Questionnaire
Hudziak et al. (2003)	3-year-old sample: 2258 MZ, 2047 DZ, 2131 DZO 7-year-old sample:1986 MZ, 1746 DZ, 1719 DZO 10-year-old sample: 1142 MZ, 925 DZ, 905 DZO	Parental and teacher rating	Collected at ages 3, 7, and 10	Child Behavior Check List Teacher Report Form
Krueger et al. (2003)	52 MZ, 28 DZ, 10 DZO	Self-report	$m = 42$, $SD = 13$	Multidimensional Personality Questionnaire
Oniszczenko et al. (2003)	Polish sample: 317 MZ, 229 DZ, 2014 peer raters German sample: 732 MZ, 277 DZ, 4036 peer raters	Self-report and peer rating	Polish sample: 17–64 German sample: 14–80	Dimensions of Temperament Survey EAS Temperament Survey Formal Characteristics of Behavior Temperament Inventory Pavlovian Temperament Survey
Van Beijsterveldt et al. (2003)	2281 MZ, 2063 DZ 2144 DZO	Parental rating	Collected at ages 3, 7, 10, and 12	Child Behavior Check List
Ando et al. (2004)	414 MZ, 131 DZ, 72 DZO	Self-report	15–30	Cloninger Temperament and Character Inventory (*Japanese Version*)
Angleitner et al. (2004)	225 MZ, 86 DZ, 27 DZO	Self-report and peer rating	21–75 years	NEO Personality Inventory Zuckerman-Kuhlman Personality Questionnaire Zuckerman Sensation Seeking Scale
DiLalla and Carey (2004)	88 MZ, 102 DZ, 101 DZO	Self-report	16–83	Multidimensional Personality Questionnaire
Gillespie et al. (2004)	12-year-old sample: 253 MZ, 225 DZ, 192 DZO	Self-report	Collected at ages 12, 14, and 16 years	Junior Eysenck Personality Questionnaire

Table 7.1 Details of studies included in the review of behavioral genetic investigations of the Big 5 and related Personality traits—cont'd

Study	Subjects (No. of pairs)	Type of measure	Ages	Measures
	14-year-old sample: 216 MZ, 192 DZ, 170 DZO 16-year-old sample: 249 MZ, 144 DZ, 152 DZO			
Heiman et al. (2004)	419 MZ, 295 DZ, 164 DZO	Self-report	11–18	Junior Temperament and Character Inventory Tridimensional Personality Questionnaire
Johnson and Krueger (2004)	315 MZ, 275 DZ	Self-report	25–74	NEO Personality Inventory
Johnson et al. (2004)	183 MZ, 64 DZ	Self-report	$m = 41.7$, $SD = 14.7$	Multifactor Leadership Questionnaire Personality Research Form
Vierikko et al. (2004)	556 MZ, 567 DZ, 513 DZO, 2488 teacher ratings, 2470 parental ratings	Parental and teacher rating	11–12	Multidimensional Peer Nomination Inventory
Wolf et al. (2004)	496 MZ, 181 DZ, 68 DZO	Self-report and peer rating	17–83	German Eysenck Personality Questionnaire
Wright and Martin (2004)	380 MZ, 662 DZ, 459 non-twin siblings	Self-report	10–25	Junior Eysenck Personality Questionnaire NEO Five Factor Inventory
Boomsma et al. (2005)	3558 MZ, 2188 DZ, 1848 DZO	Self-report	13–33	Young Adult Self-report Questionnaire
Kato and Pedersen (2005)	58 MZA, 101 MZT, 147 DZA, 140 DZT	Self-report	$m = 58.0$, $SD = 12.8$	Billings and Moos Coping Measure Eysenck Personality Inventory NEO-Personality Inventory (shortened version)
Keller et al. (2005)	2225 MZ, 2611 DZ, 3241 siblings	Self-report	18–90	Cloninger Temperament and Character Inventory Eysenck Personality Questionnaire
Ligthart et al. (2005)	2672 MZ, 2419 DZ, 2351 DZO	Maternal rating	7	Child Behavior Check List
Birley et al. (2006)	3808 twin pairs (not broken down by MZ and DZ)	Self-report	18–75 (approx.)	Eysenck Personality Questionnaire (12-item) Eysenck Personality Questionnaire (23-item)
Borkenau et al. (2006)	168 MZ and 132 DZ	Examiner-observer rating	18–70	Video-based Personality Rating Scale (based on the five-factor model of personality)
Luciano et al. (2006)	91 MZ, 95 DZ, 186 non-twin sibling pairs	Self-report	17–28	Eysenck Personality Questionnaire
Mackintosh et al. (2006)	1618 MZ, 2291 DZ	Self-report	55–74	Composite International Diagnostic Interview (shortened version based on DSM-III-R) Eysenck Personality Questionnaire (shortened version)
Read et al. (2006)	149 MZ and 202 DZ	Self-report	80+	Eysenck Personality Inventory
Rebollo and Boomsma (2006)	1050 MZ, 855 DZ, 759 DZO, 750 parent-offspring pairs (approx.)	Self-report and parental rating	12–25	Spielberger State-Trait Anger Scale
Rettew et al. (2006)	659 MZ, 497 DZ, 470 DZO	Self-report	12–18	Amsterdamse Biografische Vragenijst

numbers differ it indicates that at least one study reported two or more correlations or other statistics that we included in our review.

In the remaining columns of Tables 7.2–7.11, we report summary statistics for the kinship correlations and heritability and model-fitting estimates. These include the range of the reported values, their median, their unweighted mean (and standard deviation) and their mean weighted by the sample sizes. Note that when model-fitting results were provided, we included only those estimates that were actually reported. Thus, if a study only reported estimates of a^2 and e^2, we did not record values of zero for c^2 or d^2. The effect of this is that our average values for c^2 and d^2 in Tables 7.2–7.11 are overestimates; including those cases where unreported but implicit estimates of c^2 and d^2 are equal to zero reduces their average effect sizes close to zero.

What do the results in Tables 7.2–7.11 reveal? First, with few exceptions, the results obtained from different studies are remarkably consistent. For example, Table 7.4 shows that we found 47 reports of MZT correlations for core extraversion. The range of these correlations is large (0.20–0.88) but their standard deviation (around a mean of 0.52)

is only 0.13. Similarly, Table 7.6 shows that 46 reported MZT correlations for core neuroticism range from 0.21 to 0.59 and have a standard deviation of only 0.09. Given the very large variety of different variables included in Tables 7.7–7.11 we would expect to find a wider range of reported values and this is sometimes the case: 148 MZT correlations for variables related to extraversion (Table 7.9), for example, range from 0.08 to 0.89 but still have a standard deviation of just 0.15.

Second, again with few exceptions, the medians, unweighted means, and weighted means of the correlations are all so similar that they could essentially be used interchangeably. When differences between them do occur this can be attributed to one or two very-large-sample studies that reported an extreme value for a correlation – an event that occurred rarely. Given the similarity of these statistics we will base our following discussion of the results on the median values.

Overall, the correlations, formula-computed heritabilities, and model-fitting results reported in Tables 7.2–7.11 reveal a pronounced contribution of additive genetic and non-shared or unique environmental factors to individual differences in the Big Five

Table 7.2   Kinship correlations, heritabilities, and model-fitting results for core openness to experience

Kinship	No. of reported values	No. of pairs (total)	No. of pairs (independent)	Range	Median	Unweighted mean (SD)	Weighted mean
MZT (1.0)	19	5104	3464	0.18 to 0.69	0.49	0.48 (0.12)	0.47
MZA (1.0)	4	191	191	−0.08 to 0.57	0.43	0.34 (0.29)	0.36
DZT (0.5)	17	2861	2027	0.08 to 0.41	0.26	0.24 (0.10)	0.23
DZA (0.5)	2	239	239	0.05 to 0.23	0.14	0.14 (0.13)	0.18
DZO (0.5)	2	208	104	0.32	0.32	0.32 (0.00)	0.32
h^2	8	3371	3371	0.20 to 0.77	0.46	0.46 (0.17)	0.48
a^2	13	5894	5034	0.16 to 0.81	0.43	0.45 (0.19)	0.49
c^2	8	2251	2251	0.00 to 0.28	0.10	0.12 (0.12)	0.14
d^2	1	552	552	0.02	0.02	0.02 (0.00)	0.02
e^2	14	6136	5276	0.19 to 0.81	0.49	0.49 (0.17)	0.48

Table 7.3 Kinship correlations, heritabilities, and model-fitting results for core conscientiousness

Kinship	No. of reported values	No. of pairs (total)	No. of pairs (independent)	Range	Median	Unweighted mean (SD)	Weighted mean
MZT (1.0)	20	5156	4359	0.27 to 0.59	0.47	0.47 (0.08)	0.47
MZA (1.0)	3	157	157	0.19 to 0.54	0.25	0.33 (0.19)	0.27
DZT (0.5)	17	2757	2757	0.06 to 0.45	0.21	0.22 (0.10)	0.20
DZA (0.5)	2	194	194	0.07 to 0.10	0.09	0.09 (0.02)	0.10
DZO (0.5)	2	208	208	0.08 to 0.17	0.13	0.13 (0.06)	0.13
Biological (0.5) siblings	1	237	237	0.20	0.20	0.20 (0.00)	0.20
Adopted (0.0) siblings	1	20	20	0.11	0.11	0.11 (0.00)	0.11
h^2	6	2244	2244	0.29 to 0.78	0.47	0.49 (0.17)	0.47
a^2	12	4266	4266	0.00 to 0.53	0.41	0.37 (0.16)	0.38
c^2	6	1961	1961	0.02 to 0.25	0.11	0.11 (0.08)	0.12
d^2	1	553	553	0.29	0.29	0.29 (0.00)	0.29
e^2	12	4266	4266	0.00 to 0.86	0.52	0.48 (0.22)	0.49

Table 7.4 Kinship correlations, heritabilities, and model-fitting results for core extraversion

Kinship	No. of reported values	No. of pairs (total)	No. of pairs (independent)	Range	Median	Unweighted mean (SD)	Weighted mean
MZT (1.0)	47	22949	21352	0.20 to 0.88	0.50	0.52 (0.13)	0.50
MZA (1.0)	7	344	344	0.30 to 0.60	0.38	0.42 (0.13)	0.42
DZT (0.5)	44	24636	23721	−0.33 to 0.56	0.19	0.18 (0.16)	0.17
DZA (0.5)	6	490	490	−0.03 to 0.25	0.07	0.08 (0.10)	0.07
DZO (0.5)	9	3367	3367	0.11 to 0.28	0.15	0.16 (0.05)	0.14
Biological siblings (0.5)	6	3719	3719	0.06 to 0.33	0.18	0.19 (0.10)	0.19
Biological parent/ child (0.5)	5	1470	867	0.11 to 0.25	0.18	0.18 (0.05)	0.17
MZ twin/co-twin's child (0.5)	3	639	355	0.15 to 0.23	0.15	0.18 (0.05)	0.18
Adoptees/biological parent (0.5)	1	131	131	0.13	0.13	0.13 (0.00)	0.13
Biological half- siblings (0.25)	2	470	235	−0.01 to 0.05	0.02	0.02 (0.05)	0.02
First cousins (0.125)	1	54	54	0.13	0.13	0.13 (0.00)	0.13
Spouses (0.0)	1	92	92	0.10	0.10	0.10 (0.00)	0.10
Spouses of MZ twins (0.0)	1	97	97	0.06	0.06	0.06 (0.00)	0.06
MZ twin/co-twin's spouse (0.0)	1	221	221	0.11	0.11	0.11 (0.00)	0.11
Adopted siblings (0.0)	4	313	313	−0.21 to 0.07	−0.02	−0.05 (0.13)	0.00
Adoptees/adopted parents (0.0)	2	361	361	0.05 to 0.07	0.06	0.06 (0.02)	0.06
h^2	35	37207	37051	0.00 to 0.83	0.50	0.50 (0.19)	0.54
a^2	30	23181	23181	0.00 to 0.73	0.48	0.43 (0.21)	0.45
c^2	13	9672	9672	0.00 to 0.30	0.03	0.08 (0.10)	0.05
d^2	3	5188	5188	0.24 to 0.57	0.26	0.36 (0.19)	0.25
e^2	30	23181	23181	0.05 to 0.76	0.49	0.47 (0.15)	0.50

Table 7.5   Kinship correlations, heritabilities, and model-fitting results for core agreeableness

Kinship	No. of reported values	No. of pairs (total)	No. of pairs (independent)	Range	Median	Unweighted mean (SD)	Weighted mean
MZT (1.0)	17	4386	4259	0.23 to 0.61	0.41	0.42 (0.10)	0.40
MZA (1.0)	3	157	157	0.15 to 0.24	0.18	0.19 (0.05)	0.18
DZT (0.5)	16	2780	2439	0.06 to 0.47	0.23	0.23 (0.11)	0.22
DZA (0.5)	2	194	194	−0.03 to 0.09	0.03	0.03 (0.08)	−0.02
DZO (0.5)	2	208	208	0.12 to 0.19	0.16	0.16 (0.05)	0.16
h^2	7	2563	2563	0.24 to 0.78	0.35	0.43 (0.18)	0.49
a^2	12	5409	4715	0.00 to 0.51	0.37	0.30 (0.18)	0.29
c^2	6	1961	1961	0.09 to 0.27	0.17	0.17 (0.07)	0.18
d^2	1	553	553	0.12	0.12	0.12 (0.00)	0.12
e^2	12	5409	4715	0.04 to 0.86	0.54	0.49 (0.25)	0.57

Table 7.6   Kinship correlations, heritabilities, and model-fitting results for core neuroticism

Kinship	No. of reported values	No. of pairs (total)	No. of pairs (independent)	Range	Median	Unweighted mean (SD)	Weighted mean
MZT (1.0)	46	38698	36258	0.21 to 0.59	0.43	0.43 (0.09)	0.43
MZA (1.0)	5	238	238	0.25 to 0.49	0.25	0.31 (0.10)	0.29
DZT (0.5)	53	40890	37624	0.04 to 0.38	0.20	0.19 (0.08)	0.19
DZA (0.5)	4	415	415	0.09 to 0.44	0.20	0.23 (0.16)	0.22
DZO (0.5)	14	8400	8400	−0.08 to 0.19	0.12	0.10 (0.07)	0.13
Biological siblings (0.5)	7	10000	10000	0.12 to 0.28	0.16	0.18 (0.06)	0.15
Biological parent/child (0.5)	5	6833	6833	0.08 to 0.20	0.14	0.14 (0.05)	0.13
MZ twin/co-twin's child (0.5)	2	568	284	0.05 to 0.06	0.06	0.06 (0.01)	0.06
Adoptees/biological parent (0.5)	2	313	313	−0.01 to 0.13	0.06	0.06 (0.10)	0.05
Biological half-siblings (0.25)	2	470	235	0.03 to 0.04	0.04	0.04 (0.01)	0.04
Uncle (aunts)/nephews (nieces) (0.25)	2	11176	11176	0.03 to 0.11	0.07	0.07 (0.06)	0.05
First cousins (0.125)	3	2639	2639	0.05 to 0.16	0.07	0.09 (0.06)	0.06
Spouses (0.0)	2	6247	6247	0.03 to 0.14	0.08	0.08 (0.08)	0.10
Adopted siblings (0.0)	2	329	329	0.05 to 0.20	0.12	0.12 (0.10)	0.15
Adoptees/adopted parents (0.0)	1	179	179	0.05	0.05	0.05 (0.00)	0.05
h^2	42	69104	69104	0.00 to 0.86	0.41	0.41 (0.18)	0.43
a^2	32	43101	43101	0.03 to 0.66	0.41	0.38 (0.16)	0.40
c^2	18	17409	17409	0.00 to 0.26	0.06	0.08 (0.08)	0.06
d^2	2	5078	5078	0.12 to 0.31	0.22	0.22 (0.13)	0.13
e^2	32	43101	43101	0.01 to 0.97	0.59	0.53 (0.18)	0.57

Table 7.7   Kinship correlations, heritabilities, and model-fitting results for variables related to openness to experience

Kinship	No. of reported values	No. of pairs (total)	No. of pairs (independent)	Range	Median	Unweighted mean (SD)	Weighted Mean
MZT (1.0)	43	17057	9085	0.20 to 0.63	0.42	0.42 (0.11)	0.41
MZA (1.0)	4	222	177	0.10 to 0.51	0.36	0.33 (0.17)	0.34
DZT (0.5)	43	11918	6934	−0.27 to 0.42	0.18	0.19 (0.10)	0.17
DZA (0.5)	6	154	128	−0.02 to 0.34	0.11	0.12 (0.13)	0.17
DZO (0.5)	4	1744	1259	0.07 to 0.25	0.16	0.16 (0.10)	0.17
Biological siblings (0.5)	1	3241	3241	0.13	0.13	0.13 (0.00)	0.13
Biological parent/ child (0.5)	6	237	237	0.08 to 0.42	0.23	0.23 (0.13)	0.22
Spouses (0.0)	2	203	203	0.23 to 0.27	0.25	0.25 (0.03)	0.25
Adopted siblings (0.0)	3	120	120	0.06 to 0.37	0.24	0.22 (0.16)	0.13
Adoptees/adopted parents (0.0)	6	1097	1097	0.00 to 0.24	0.12	0.11 (0.08)	0.11
h^2	17	13055	8720	0.29 to 0.78	0.41	0.44 (0.11)	0.46
a^2	24	18197	13070	0.04 to 0.63	0.42	0.41 (0.14)	0.34
c^2	2	868	868	0.11 to 0.30	0.21	0.21 (0.13)	0.23
d^2	3	5494	5494	0.35 to 0.39	0.38	0.37 (0.02)	0.35
e^2	26	19065	13938	0.37 to 0.71	0.58	0.56 (0.09)	0.57

Table 7.8   Kinship correlations, heritabilities, and model-fitting results for variables related to conscientiousness

Kinship	No. of reported values	No. of pairs (total)	No. of pairs (independent)	Range	Median	Unweighted mean (SD)	Weighted mean
MZT (1.0)	93	29331	14343	0.14 to 0.85	0.40	0.42 (0.13)	0.42
MZA (1.0)	13	717	395	0.01 to 0.64	0.36	0.35 (0.21)	0.36
DZT (0.5)	93	20428	10589	−0.27 to 0.53	0.19	0.20 (0.14)	0.20
DZA (0.5)	14	795	471	−0.28 to 0.40	0.06	0.08 (0.20)	0.13
DZO (0.5)	8	1818	909	−0.03 to 0.57	0.26	0.27 (0.21)	0.34
Biological siblings (0.5)	7	4433	4111	−0.04 to 0.29	0.15	0.12 (0.12)	0.09
Biological parent/ child (0.5)	6	237	237	−0.07 to 0.07	−0.02	−0.02 (0.05)	−0.02
Biological half- siblings (0.25)	2	218	109	0.01 to 0.02	0.02	0.02 (0.01)	0.02
Spouses (0.0)	3	314	203	−0.15 to 0.31	0.00	0.05 (0.23)	0.07
Adopted siblings (0.0)	5	380	250	−0.14 to 0.12	0.02	0.00 (0.09)	0.01
Adoptees/adopted parents (0.0)	6	1097	1097	0.01 to 0.13	0.04	0.05 (0.05)	0.05
h^2	43	26529	18386	0.00 to 0.76	0.46	0.43 (0.18)	0.48
a^2	59	28954	16839	0.00 to 0.78	0.41	0.39 (0.18)	0.39
c^2	19	8459	3986	0.01 to 0.61	0.27	0.22 (0.16)	0.23
d^2	14	9602	7264	0.07 to 0.50	0.29	0.29 (0.15)	0.31
e^2	70	36890	23144	0.15 to 1.00	0.59	0.55 (0.18)	0.56

Table 7.9 Kinship correlations, heritabilities, and model-fitting results for variables related to extraversion

Kinship	No. of reported values	No. of pairs (total)	No. of pairs (independent)	Range	Median	Unweighted mean (SD)	Weighted mean
MZT (1.0)	148	32709	10832	0.08 to 0.89	0.49	0.49 (0.15)	0.47
MZA (1.0)	15	857	366	−0.15 to 0.53	0.21	0.22 (0.19)	0.24
DZT (0.5)	148	23868	8055	−0.28 to 0.63	0.20	0.21 (0.17)	0.21
DZA (0.5)	15	1258	569	−0.01 to 0.40	0.12	0.15 (0.13)	0.12
DZO (0.5)	10	3394	990	0.07 to 0.59	0.29	0.34 (0.19)	0.38
Biological siblings (0.5)	7	845	470	0.05 to 0.20	0.11	0.11 (0.05)	0.11
Biological parent/ child (0.5)	22	712	103	−0.02 to 0.62	0.30	0.22 (0.15)	0.24
Biological half- siblings (0.25)	2	218	109	0.03 to 0.04	0.04	0.04 (0.01)	0.04
Spouses (0.0)	2	222	111	0.05 to 0.22	0.14	0.14 (0.12)	0.14
Adopted siblings (0.0)	11	764	422	−0.45 to 0.59	−0.05	0.02 (0.33)	0.02
Adoptees/adopted parents (0.0)	22	4868	1142	−0.09 to 0.20	0.05	0.06 (0.08)	0.06
h^2	54	16296	8430	0.00 to 0.88	0.49	0.47 (0.18)	0.50
a^2	79	33313	14632	0.00 to 0.70	0.48	0.44 (0.16)	0.46
c^2	31	9572	4780	0.01 to 0.49	0.15	0.19 (0.15)	0.20
d^2	7	2616	1264	0.00 to 0.64	0.06	0.18 (0.23)	0.24
e^2	77	32586	14421	0.07 to 0.96	0.48	0.50 (0.17)	0.49

Table 7.10 Kinship correlations, heritabilities, and model-fitting results for variables related to agreeableness

Kinship	No. of reported values	No. of pairs (total)	No. of pairs (independent)	Range	Median	Unweighted mean (SD)	Weighted mean
MZT (1.0)	131	38956	18072	0.07 to 0.88	0.46	0.50 (0.20)	0.56
MZA (1.0)	10	614	446	0.16 to 0.55	0.33	0.34 (0.12)	0.32
DZT (0.5)	133	30284	14592	−0.14 to 0.58	0.23	0.27 (0.16)	0.33
DZA (0.5)	8	900	699	0.03 to 0.43	0.11	0.17 (0.16)	0.16
DZO (0.5)	19	12149	7453	0.09 to 0.58	0.45	0.40 (0.15)	0.46
Biological siblings (0.5)	3	596	596	0.01 to 0.12	0.10	0.08 (0.06)	0.05
Biological half- siblings (0.25)	1	109	109	0.03	0.03	0.03 (0.00)	0.03
Spouses (0.0)	1	111	111	0.25	0.25	0.25 (0.00)	0.25
Adopted siblings (0.0)	2	150	150	0.14	0.14	0.14 (0.00)	0.14
h^2	30	9440	5626	0.00 to 0.94	0.40	0.45 (0.22)	0.46
a^2	59	37089	25238	0.06 to 0.78	0.47	0.48 (0.19)	0.57
c^2	35	28569	20185	0.01 to 0.43	0.15	0.18 (0.11)	0.17
d^2	4	2479	2479	0.22 to 0.34	0.27	0.28 (0.05)	0.28
e^2	63	38568	26717	0.11 to 0.84	0.48	0.43 (0.23)	0.31

Table 7.11 Kinship correlations, heritabilities, and model-fitting results for variables related to neuroticism

Kinship	No. of reported values	No. of pairs (total)	No. of pairs (independent)	Range	Median	Unweighted mean (SD)	Weighted mean
MZT (1.0)	295	84663	37276	0.03 to 0.90	0.47	0.50 (0.18)	0.53
MZA (1.0)	36	2219	590	−0.06 to 0.62	0.34	0.34 (0.17)	0.34
DZT (0.5)	295	67601	31101	−0.18 to 0.78	0.22	0.23 (0.17)	0.28
DZA (0.5)	38	3726	1005	−0.26 to 0.46	0.11	0.12 (0.15)	0.09
DZO (0.5)	47	30197	18608	−0.07 to 0.58	0.32	0.30 (0.17)	0.36
Biological siblings (0.5)	17	6283	4485	−0.05 to 0.37	0.12	0.13 (0.13)	0.23
Biological parent/ child (0.5)	15	4482	1844	0.00 to 0.35	0.11	0.12 (0.11)	0.12
MZ twin/co-twin's child (0.5)	4	1136	284	−0.05 to 0.23	0.19	0.14 (0.13)	0.14
Adoptees/biological parent (0.5)	7	1041	293	−0.04 to 0.31	0.04	0.13 (0.14)	0.11
Biological half- siblings (0.25)	5	1049	344	−0.05 to 0.31	0.16	0.16 (0.13)	0.16
Spouses (0.0)	6	2052	1026	−0.01 to 0.23	0.07	0.09 (0.10)	0.08
MZ twin/co-twin's spouse (0.0)	2	442	221	0.08 to 0.13	0.10	0.10 (0.03)	0.10
Adopted siblings (0.0)	10	1612	668	−0.20 to 0.29	0.07	0.09 (0.14)	0.13
Adoptees/adopted parents (0.0)	7	1303	581	−0.01 to 0.19	0.07	0.05 (0.09)	0.05
MZ twin's spouse/ co-twin's child (0.0)	4	824	206	0.03 to 0.11	0.07	0.07 (0.04)	0.07
h^2	110	53136	29021	0.00 to 0.90	0.45	0.45 (0.16)	0.43
a^2	183	110584	59823	0.04 to 0.82	0.44	0.45 (0.18)	0.49
c^2	73	60918	33641	0.01 to 0.71	0.13	0.18 (0.14)	0.17
d^2	27	13524	4001	0.02 to 0.61	0.26	0.28 (0.15)	0.29
e^2	197	115115	60957	0.06 to 0.96	0.51	0.48 (0.21)	0.41

and related traits, and a small to negligible influence of dominant genetic and shared environmental factors. There are several ways in which the results convey this.

Evidence for the influence of genetic effects can be seen first by the fact that MZT correlations are consistently about two times greater than DZT correlations. Across all ten tables, the average (mean) of the MZT median correlations is 0.45 and the mean of the DZT correlations is 0.21. Putting these values into equation (7.7) yields an average heritability coefficient of 0.48. A second indication of the role of genetic factors is that MZA correlations – though smaller than

MZT correlations – are in all but one case greater than DZT correlations and are in all cases greater than correlations for adopted (genetically unrelated) siblings raised together. Across the ten tables, MZA median correlations average 0.31, a value which provides another estimate of heritability. For the eight tables where we report median correlations for adopted siblings, these average just 0.08. Third, computed heritabilities and model-fitting estimates of a^2 confirm the role of genetic factors: across the ten tables these average 0.44 and 0.43, respectively. Fourth, there is a close (positive) correspondence between the median correlations found for different kinships and the kinships' degree of genetic relatedness: for the core Big Five variables correlations between these are 0.87 for O, 0.75 for C, 0.85 for E, 0.62 for A, and 0.77 for N. For the variables related to the Big Five the corresponding correlations are 0.57 for O, 0.84 for C, 0.75 for E, 0.56 for A, and 0.79 for N. Clearly, as the degree of genetic relatedness between kinships becomes smaller so do the phenotypic correlations between them.

Evidence for the role of the non-shared environment comes first from the fact that the observed MZT and MZA phenotypic correlations are not 1.0. As reported above, these correlations average 0.45 and 0.31, respectively, and differences between MZ twins can almost entirely be attributed to non-shared environmental factors (including the unreliability of the measures). Thus (from equation (7.9)), the observed MZT and MZA correlations provide e^2 estimates of 0.55 and 0.69, respectively. Second, in ten out of ten cases MZA correlations are lower than the corresponding MZT correlations, and in nine out of ten cases, DZA correlations are lower than the corresponding DZT correlations (in the tenth case they are equal). The differences between these can be attributed to the greater differences that exist between the environments of the twins who were raised apart. Third, the model-fitting analyses yield substantial estimates for e^2 for all variables, averaging 0.53.

There is evidence for a small but not insignificant role for dominance genetic effects for at least some variables. In seven out of ten cases, for example, MZT correlations are more than twice as large as DZT correlations, and in eight out of ten cases MZA correlations are more than twice as large as DZA correlations: findings which suggest the presence of dominance. Model-fitting estimates of d^2 are also non-zero in a number of cases (although, as noted, this does not remain true after including non-reported but implicit values of zero), averaging 0.22 in Tables 7.2–7.11 but dropping to

zero after including zero estimates from studies which reported only ACE or AE models.

Finally, several lines of evidence suggest a negligible role for the shared environment. First, correlations between genetically unrelated adopted siblings are largely attributable to the environments they share and these correlations are typically low: ranging from −0.05 to 0.24 and averaging 0.08. In contrast, correlations between DZTs, DZOs, and non-twin biological siblings – who share both their common environments and 50% of their genes – are larger. Correlations between adopted children and their adoptive parents – again largely attributable to the shared environment – are also low: these range from 0.04 to 0.12 and average 0.07. These correlations can be compared to those between parents and the biological children that they raise which, with the exception of variables related to conscientiousness, are larger. Finally, model-fitting estimates of c^2 are small, averaging 0.14 in Tables 7.2–7.11, and dropping to 0.01 after including zero estimates from studies which reported only AE or ADE models.

A number of other interesting results are revealed in Tables 7.2–7.11. First, across the different variables in these tables, MZT and DZT correlations do not vary a great deal. MZT correlations, for example, range between just 0.40 (for variables related to conscientiousness) and 0.50 (for core extraversion); DZT correlations range between 0.18 (for variables related to openness) and 0.26 (for core openness). These results imply that there should be only small differences between the variables in the extent to which they are influenced by genetic and environmental factors and the model-fitting results largely support this: a^2 and e^2 estimates range between 0.37 and 0.48, and 0.48 and 0.59, respectively. Thus, although there is some indication that core extraversion and variables related to extraversion are the most highly heritable of the Big Five (each having a median a^2 of 0.48) and that core agreeableness is the least heritable (with a median a^2 of 0.37), overall the results suggest that the

Big Five and related personality traits are essentially quite equally heritable.

A second interesting result is the similarity in the heritabilities found for core measures of the Big Five as compared to those obtained for variables related to the Big Five. Given the very large number of different questionnaires that were used to assess the latter, it might not have been surprising if they had yielded somewhat different results. In the model-fitting analyses, however, the only substantial difference that appears is that between the a^2 estimate for core agreeableness (0.37) versus that for variables related to agreeableness (0.47). Median estimates of a^2 for the other Big Five traits show zero or trivial differences between core versus related variables. If nothing else, this result indicates that heritability estimates for the Big Five have very considerable generalizability across a large and diverse collection of measures.

Third, there is evidence in Tables 7.2–7.11 for assortative mating for some of those variables which reported spouse correlations. This occurred in seven of ten cases, for which median spouse correlations range from 0 (conscientiousness-related variables) to 0.25 (openness-related and agreeableness-related variables), averaging 0.13. For two variables (core extraversion and neuroticism-related variables) we found marginally significant correlations between MZ twins and their co-twin's spouses of 0.11 and 0.10, respectively, and for extraversion a non-significant correlation of 0.06 was found between the spouses of MZ twins. Overall, it appears that there is modest spousal-selection for openness (which may reflect the assortative mating that exists for intelligence) and for agreeableness, some evidence for selection for extraversion, while the evidence for neuroticism and conscientiousness is at best mixed (see the ranges in spouse correlations for these variables in Tables 7.6 and 7.8, respectively).

The summary of results that we report in Tables 7.2–7.11 – based on the largest sets of data ever previously examined – confirms what a large number of previous studies and

reviews have found; namely the overwhelming contributions of additive genetic and non-shared environmental factors to individual differences in the Big Five and related dimensions of personality. Our goal in undertaking this review was not so much to present new findings as to illustrate the extent to which information gathered from very large samples of twins, siblings, and other kinships, using a very diverse set of questionnaires which measured a large number of different (albeit related) variables, would converge. We hope that readers will agree that this goal has been achieved and that this chapter thereby makes a useful contribution to the body of behavioral genetic research on personality that precedes it.

REFERENCES

Balsis, S., Carpenter, B.D. and Storandt, M. (2005) 'Personality change precedes clinical diagnosis of dementia of the alzheimer type', *Journals of Gerontology: Series B: Psychological Sciences and Social Sciences*, 60(2): 98–101.

Benjamin, J., Osher, Y., Kotler, M., Gritsenko, I., Nemanov, L., Belmaker, R.H. et al. (2000) 'Association between tridimensional personality questionnaire (TPQ) traits and three functional polymorphisms: dopamine receptor D4 (DRD4), serotonin transporter promoter region (5-HTTLPR) and catechol O-methyltransferase (COMT)', *Molecular Psychiatry*, 5(1): 96–100.

Carey, G. (1988) 'Inference about genetic correlations', *Behavior Genetics*, 18(3): 329–38.

Cattell, R.B., Blewett, D.B. and Beloff, J.R. (1955) 'The inheritance of personality', *American Journal of Human Genetics*, 7(1): 122–46.

Costa, P.T. Jr. and McCrae, R.R. (1992a) 'Four ways five factors are basic', *Personality and Individual Differences*, 13(6): 653–65.

Costa, P.T. Jr. and McCrae, R.R. (1992b) *Revised NEO Personality Inventory (NEO-PI-R) and Five-Factor Inventory (NEO-FFI) Professional Manual*. Odessa, FL: Psychological Assessment Resources.

Delgado, P.L., Charney, D.S., Price, L.H., Aghajanian, G.K., Landis, H. and Heninger, G.R. (1990) 'Serotonin function and mechanism of antidepressant action: Reversal of antidepressant-induced remission by rapid depletion of plasma atryptophan', *Archives of General Psychiatry*, 47(5): 411–8.

Dickens, W.T. and Flynn, J.R. (2001) 'Heritability estimates versus large environmental effects: The IQ paradox resolved', *Psychological Review*: 108(2): 346–69.

Edwards, D.A. (2006) 'Competition and testosterone', *Hormones and Behavior*, 50(5): 681–3.

Eysenck, H.J. (1947) *Dimensions of Personality*. New York: Praeger.

Eysenck, H.J. (1967) *The Biological Basis of Personality*. Springfield, IL: Charles C. Thomas.

Johnson, A.M. and Vernon, P.A. (2004) 'The genetics of substance abuse: Mediating effects of sensation seeking', in R. Stelmack (ed.), *On the Psychobiology of Personality: Essays in Honor of Marvin Zuckerman*. London: Elsevier, pp. 147–68.

Kendler, K.S. and Eaves, L.J. (1986) 'Models for the joint effects of genotype and environment on liability to psychiatric illness', *American Journal of Psychiatry*, 143(3): 279–89.

Lyons, K.D., Tickle-Degnen, L., Henry, A. and Cohn, E. (2004) 'Impressions of personality in Parkinson's disease: Can rehabilitation practitioners see beyond the symptoms?', *Rehabilitation Psychology*, 49(4): 328–33.

Max, J.E., Levin, H.S., Schachar, R.J., Landis, J., Saunders, A.E., Ewing-Cobbs, L. et al. (2006) 'Predictors of personality change due to traumatic brain injury in children and adolescents six to twenty-four months after injury', *Journal of Neuropsychiatry and Clinical Neuroscience*, 18(1): 21–32.

Mendel, G.J. (1866) 'Versuche ueber Pflanzenhybriden', *Verhandlungen des Naturforschunden Vereines in Bruenn*, 4(1): 3–47.

Menza, M.A., Forman, N.E., Goldstein, H.S. and Golbe, L.I. (1990) 'Parkinson's disease, personality, and dopamine', *Journal of Neuropsychiatry and Clinical Neurosciences*, 2(3): 282–7.

Neale, M.C. and Maes, H.M. (1998) *Methodology for Genetic Studies of Twins and Families*. Dordrecht: Kluwer Academic.

Netter, P. and Rammsayer, T. (1991) 'Reactivity to dopaminergic drugs and aggression related personality traits', *Personality and Individual Differences*, 12(10): 1009–17.

Ogawa, T. (1981) 'Personality characteristics of Parkinson's disease', *Perceptual and Motor Skills*, 52(2): 375–8.

Plomin, R., DeFries, J.C., McClearn, G.E. and McGuffin, P. (2001) *Behavioral Genetics* (4th edn). New York: W.H. Freeman and Company.

Popma, A., Vermeiren, R., Geluk, C.A., Rinne, T., van den Brink, W., Knol, D.L. et al. (2006) 'Cortisol moderates the relationship between testosterone and aggression in delinquent male adolescents', *Biological Psychiatry*, 61(3): 405–11.

Posthuma, D. and Boomsma, D. I. (2000) 'A note on the statistical power in extended twin designs', *Behavior Genetics*, 30(2): 147–58.

Rush, B.K., Malec, J.F., Brown, A.W. and Moessner, A.M. (2006) 'Personality and functional outcome following traumatic brain injury', *Rehabilitation Psychology*, 51(3): 257–64.

Soyka, M., Preuss, U.W., Koller, G., Zill, P. and Bondy, B. (2002) 'Dopamine D4 receptor gene polymorphism and extraversion revisited: Results from the Munich gene bank project for alcoholism', *Journal of Psychiatric Research*, 36(6): 429–35.

Stigler, S.M. (1989) 'Francis Galton's account of the invention of correlation', *Statistical Science*, 4(2): 73–86.

Tupes, E.C. and Christal, R.E. (1992) 'Recurrent personality factors based on trait ratings', *Journal of Personality*, 60(2): 225–51.

van Bokhoven, I., van Goozen, S.H.M., van Engeland, H., Schaal, B., Arseneault, L., Seguin, J.R. et al. (2006) 'Salivary testosterone and aggression, delinquency, and social dominance in a population-based longitudinal study of adolescent males', *Hormones and Behavior*, 50(1): 118–25.

Williamson, S., Gossop, M., Powis, B., Griffiths, P., Fountain, J. and Strang, J. (1997) 'Adverse effects of stimulant drugs in a community sample of drug users', *Drug and Alcohol Dependence*, 44(2–3): 87–94.

Zuckerman, M. (1995) 'Good and bad humors: Biochemical bases of personality and its disorders', *Psychological Science*, 6(6): 325–32.

Figures 7.1 and 7.2, and accompanying text were originally published in Johnson, A.M. and Vernon, P.A. (2004), 'The genetics of substances abuse: Mediating effects of sensation seeking', in R.M. Stelmack (ed.), *On the Psychobiology of Personality: Essays in Honor of Marvin Zuckerman*. London: Elsevier Science, pp. 147–68. They are reproduced herein with the permission of Elsevier Science.

A full reference list for the studies cited in Table 6.1 could not be included due to space restrictions. These may instead be found at: http://publish.uwo.ca/~ajohnson/fifty-year-review/references.html

8

Evolutionary Perspectives on Personality Psychology

Richard L. Michalski and Todd K. Shackelford

INTRODUCTION AND BACKGROUND

In this chapter, we argue that the development, structure, and processes of human personality have been crafted over hundreds of thousands of generations by natural and sexual selection. We argue that there is no scientifically viable alternative framework for understanding the historical origins of human personality and that human personality is thus best conceptualized with the theoretical tools developed in the evolutionary sciences. Personality, from this perspective, represents a meta-category of the output of a suite of species-typical, relatively domain-specific, evolved psychological mechanisms designed in response to the social adaptive problems recurrently faced by our ancestors throughout human evolutionary history. This conceptualization of human personality provides for a novel and valuable reinterpretation of several areas of personality psychology including personality consistency, individual differences in personality, sex differences and similarities, and contextual determinants of personality. The reconceptualization of personality from an evolutionary perspective already has led to novel predictions about personality, including the function of social information conveyed through standings on the Big Five personality dimensions and in topics such as social anxiety, jealousy, altruism, aggression, psychopathology, mate preferences, desire for sexual variety, and father presence versus father absence in the development of sexual strategies. We argue that the limitations of the application of evolutionary theory to personality science are surmountable and that, despite these limitations, large strides have been made in anchoring personality science to the biological sciences by evolutionary scientists.

The ontogeny, structure, and processes of human personality and of human nature, more generally, have been crafted over hundreds of thousands of generations by natural and sexual selection. The meta-theory of evolution by natural and sexual selection (Darwin, 1859/1958; 1871) has been supported, at various theoretical levels, by thousands of investigations spanning the disciplines of, for example, biology, ecology, medicine, anthropology, psychology, and ethology (see for example Barkow et al., 1992; Daly and Wilson, 1983; Krebs and Davies, 1987; Smith and Winterhalder, 1992; Strickberger, 1990; Trivers, 1985). The efforts put forth to apply evolutionary theories in these disciplines have yielded insights into these fields lacking prior to the application of these theories. Personality psychology could be strengthened similarly by an integration of the evolutionary sciences with the personality sciences.

Human personality is often framed void of original considerations. Not only are the origins of personality often dismissed, so too are considerations of functionality dismissed regarding the development, structure, and processes of personality. Historically, we have been asked to accept the existence of personal constructs (Kelly, 1955), or needs (Freud, 1930/1949; Maslow, 1970; Murray, 1937, 1938), or traits (Allport, 1931, 1960), or factors (Eysenck, 1981; John, 1990), or drives (Freud, 1930/1949; Murray, 1936, 1938), or motives (Winter, 1973), or life tasks (Cantor, 1990), with little or no recourse to questions of adaptive design or functionality. Importantly, however, evolutionary processes are as relevant to humans as to every other life form with which we share the planet. There is no reason to expect that human nature or personality is exempt from natural or sexual selective pressures.

Human personality is thus best conceptualized within the framework of *evolutionary psychology* (see for example Barkow et al., 1992; Buss, 1990, 1991; Crawford et al., 1987; Daly and Wilson, 1983). Evolutionary psychology suggests that the way we think, feel, and behave today can be understood by considering which thoughts, feelings, and behaviors increased the relative survival and reproduction of our ancestors. Manifesting certain thoughts, feelings, and behaviors in certain contexts increased ancestral humans' abilities to out-survive and out-reproduce less successful conspecifics. These offspring had some positive probability of inheriting the genetic structure coding (in concert with

relevant environmental input) for the development of the psychological mechanisms that (in response to certain cues) produce that same pattern of thoughts, feelings and behaviors. The offspring, too, would be expected to be relatively more reproductively successful. And this would be true for *their* offspring. This process continues for hundreds of thousands of generations – for the span of human evolutionary history – such that today that pattern of thoughts, feelings, and behaviors guided by the particular psychological mechanisms is species-typical and encompasses what we call human nature.

Any comprehensive theory of personality should provide answers to the following questions: What is human nature? What underlies individual differences? Is personality age-graded? How many levels of personality should be considered? What supportive empirical evidence is there for the theory? Does the theory generate specific testable predictions, or is it based upon post hoc explanation of findings? In what ways are the sexes predicted to be different? In what ways are the sexes predicted to be similar? What causes these similarities and differences? What follows is a presentation of a developing theory of personality which aspires to answer each of these questions.

DARWINIAN CONCEPTS AND EVOLUTIONARY PRODUCTS

The observation that species change over time was known long before Charles Darwin's (1859) book *The Origin of Species*. Archeological evidence had revealed changes in morphology and had revealed structures of organisms that appeared well suited to the ecological niche occupied by the members of that species. What was lacking before publication of *The Origin of Species* was a causal mechanism to explain *how* species change over time. The theory of natural selection filled a gap in the explanatory framework which allowed researchers to explain changes in species over time. Darwin proposed natural selection as a solution to explain how variation in morphological (including psychological) characteristics better enabled organisms to survive and reproduce. Individuals that did not have the same morphology would have been out-reproduced by those individuals in ancestral environments that did. Through this process, successful variants would have become more frequently represented among organisms of a species and organisms with the less successful variants would have become less frequently represented.

The process of natural selection requires three key components. Darwin proposed that selection operates on characteristics of organisms that vary, that are heritable, and that are passed on to that organism's offspring. Variation, selection, and retention of mechanisms are the bases of natural selection. Among humans, for example, we vary along a wide variety of dimensions. We vary in morphological characteristics such as height and weight and we vary along psychological dimensions such as sexual orientation, sexual desire, and personality dimensions such as dominance, extraversion, and emotional stability. There are also a variety of characteristics along which humans do not vary. We do not vary, genetic mutations excluded, along characteristics such as number of fingers, the presence of navels, and number of eyes. From Darwin's perspective, it is only along those characteristics on which we vary that natural selection can operate. Once variation on a particular trait or feature exists, natural selection operates on those features best suited for survival in the environment. The operation of natural selection requires that those characteristics be heritable (although, at the time, Darwin was unaware of the mechanism by which characteristics of individuals could be passed to offspring). Individuals with characteristics that aided their survival and reproduction passed those characteristics to their offspring at greater frequency and those characteristics

became over-represented in members of the species over the course of evolutionary history. Darwin was puzzled by the characteristics of organisms that thwart survival and that are developmentally costly to produce. Reconciliation between observations of characteristics that impeded survival through increased predation, for example, was accomplished by Darwin with a second evolutionary theory – sexual selection theory (Darwin, 1871).

Darwin's (1871) theory of sexual selection was constructed to explain traits that seemingly reduced an organism's chances of survival by virtue of evolution by natural selection. A human male's greater aggression compared to human females comes at the cost of developing bodies capable of engaging in such conflicts (e.g. larger size, greater caloric intake necessary to grow and maintain such a body, maintaining higher testosterone levels). Sexual selection was proposed to explain how such features could be selected for (or at least not selected against) in ancestral environments. Darwin's theory suggests that those features of organisms that increase (a) the chances of being selected by the other sex for copulation; or (b) success in competition with the same sex for sexual access to the other, will be selected. These facets of sexual selection are called intersexual selection and intrasexual (epigamic) selection, respectively. For nearly a century after the publication of sexual selection theory, focus was placed on biological sex as the driving force behind sexual selection. Publication of Trivers' (1972) parental investment theory forced evolutionary biologists and, later, evolutionary psychologists to reformulate the impact of biological sex on sexual selection. Trivers proposed that it is not biological sex that drives sexual selection, but differences in the *minimum* obligatory parental investment. Parental investment is defined by Trivers as any investment that a parent makes in its offspring that increases that offspring's chances of survival at the expense of the parent's ability to invest in current or future offspring. This definition captures the metabolic costs of investing in offspring and all other forms of investment that benefit offspring. A key component of this theory is the minimum obligatory investment necessary in offspring. One well-supported prediction derived from this theory is that sexual selection operates more strongly on the sex that makes the smaller obligatory parental investment.

A critical test of this theory comes from parenting systems in which there is a sex role reversal in minimum obligatory parental investment. In such species, is there a reversal of patterns of competition among conspecifics for access to the other sex? Is there a reversal of patterns of mate selection? Trivers (1972) presented evidence that this is the case. Among several avian species, for example, females are the more brightly colored and compete for access to males. Parental investment by females in these species ends when fertilized eggs are laid, whereas male investment continues in the form of nest-tending and chick-feeding. Sexual selection theory was rendered silent when attempting to integrate such findings into existing theories. It is only when parental investment is considered can clear predictions be made about how the sexes will differ.

Among humans, females make the larger obligatory investment in their offspring (Clutton-Brock, 1991). Female sex cells are larger and metabolically more costly to produce than male sex cells. Additionally, fertilization occurs internally within females. As a result, females incur the costs of gestating an offspring, going through the process of birth, and potentially nursing an offspring for several years. A male's minimum obligatory investment can end with the placement of his sex cells in the reproductive tract of a female. Because the costs associated with parental investment are not isomorphic between the sexes, a suite of psychological characteristics are proposed to exist in human females that are not expected to exist in males. Following impregnation, a female's reproductive opportunities are constrained by the investment that must be made during pregnancy. A male's reproductive opportunities are not constrained in similar fashion. Males can continue investing mating effort in other fertile females. A female's reproductive success is limited by her ability to manufacture eggs and a male's reproductive success is limited by his ability to fertilize eggs. Reproductive variance is therefore greater among males than among females. For every man capable of successfully impregnating multiple females, another man is shut out of the reproductive game.

A feature of this theory reveals that there are trade-offs between mating effort and parenting effort that are magnified in comparative research between species with sexually asymmetric parental investment. Among humans, for example, a host of sex differences are expected to exist (Symons, 1979) that reflect investment differences that parents recurrently made in their offspring. These sex differences are expected to have arisen by processes of sexual selection that operated as a consequence of the difference between the sexes in parental investment in ancestral environments. Parental investment theory predicts that human females will be the more discriminating sex. Research has found consistently that females are less willing to engage in sex, desire fewer sexual partners, require greater time to pass prior to consenting to sex, have higher standards for sex partners, and report being more upset over emotional aspects of a partner's infidelity compared to sexual aspects of his infidelity (for a review see Buss and Schmitt, 1993). They also have, at all time ranges, lower mortality rates compared to males.

Cross-culturally, men invest substantially less than women do in their offspring (Geary, 2000). Even in cultures with relatively high paternal investment, maternal investment dwarfs the investments made by fathers. Parent investment theory generates expectations of many sex-differentiated psychological mechanisms. The investment asymmetry between the sexes sets the stage for the evolution of mechanisms to solve social dilemmas posed by other family members. Offspring, for example, would have been selected to not allow the expression of genes that signaled dissimilarity to a putative father. Fertilization, being internal to women, results in paternal uncertainty for men. If men have psychological mechanisms designed to detect dissimilarities (or similarities) between themselves and their putative offspring, then selection would operate to produce phenotypic anonymity in offspring. The simple fact is that if the sexes *did not* differ in their relative contributions to parenting then the platform for which additional adaptive problems selected for other psychological mechanisms would not exist.

Future research is necessary to understand the developmental trajectories of specific psychological mechanisms designed in response to the selection pressures hypothesized by parental investment theory. One avenue of sex-differentiated psychology not fully explored is the impact of early family experiences on later mating strategies. Research on attachment styles and mating strategies reveals that female mating strategies may be calibrated to anticipate certain mating environments later in life based on the availability of parents and expectations that others will invest earlier in life. This relationship does not hold as strongly for males. Future research is necessary to examine why some features of sexual psychology and behavior related to early childhood experiences are present for females (Belsky et al., 1991) and others emerge only for males (Michalski and Shackelford, 2002). Michalski and Shackelford, for example, found that men's desired sexual strategies later in life are related to their birth order. Similar relationships do not hold for women. Why might men's mating strategy be calibrated by their birth order and women's mating strategy be calibrated by the attachment they develop with their parents? To answer these questions it is necessary to understand the products of evolutionary processes.

The filtering processes of natural and sexual selection result in three products: adaptations, by-products of adaptations, and random variation or noise. Adaptations are the primary products of natural and sexual selection and can be defined as a 'reliably developing structure in the organism, which, because it meshes with the recurrent structure of the world, causes the solution to an adaptive problem' (Tooby and Cosmides, 1992: 104). Adaptive problems refer to recurrent features of ancestral environments that impeded successful survival or reproduction. Buss (2007) presents the example of a preference for sweet, highly caloric foods. In ancestral environments, when access to food was less reliable than it is today, selection favored adaptations in humans that functioned to increase immediate caloric content. The criteria utilized to identify adaptations are stringent (Williams, 1966). Adaptations must show features of special design, including efficiency, precision, and reliability.

By-products of adaptations include features or effects that are not considered to be adaptations but that tag along with or are related to an adaptation. In this sense, and as has been debated among evolutionary psychologists, rape may be an example of one such by-product (Thornhill and Palmer, 2000). Men, more often than women, are perpetrators of rape. Men, more than women, report a greater desire for sexual variety and for short-term sexual intercourse and a greater propensity to use physical violence to secure many different types of resources. Rape therefore might represent a phenomenon that is a by-product of adaptations that performed other functions for ancestral men (e.g. increased reproductive success in ancestral environments from pursuit of a short-term mating strategy and greater resource acquisition and reputation halo through physical aggression).

Random variation or noise refers to those characteristics that are selectively neutral or 'overlooked' by natural and sexual selection but that are produced through random mutation or developmental anomalies. In the design of certain physical characteristics, for example, the shape of one's navel serves no adaptive function but is a characteristic along which people do vary.

The focus of evolutionary psychologists has been on identification of specific classes of adaptive problems posed in ancestral environments and empirical verification of evolved solutions or evolved psychological mechanisms. The psychological adaptations are presumed to be relatively domain specific in nature. Domain-specific solutions to recurrent adaptive problems are theorized to incorporate a narrow slice of environmental input and to produce output specifically targeted toward a solution to the adaptive problem confronted in ancestral environments. Over the history of research on evolutionary theories of psychological phenomenon, confusion has surrounded and continues to surround whether invoking concepts such as domain-specific evolved psychological mechanisms implies reflexive triggering of that particular mechanism.

APPLICATIONS OF EVOLUTIONARY PSYCHOLOGY TO PERSONALITY PSYCHOLOGY

The marriage between concepts developed within evolutionary psychology and within personality psychology has a brief history. The historical divide between these two areas lies in the historical focus of each area. Evolutionary psychological accounts of human nature have focused largely on the similarities among people and the characteristics that all humans share that have evolved in response the problems of survival and reproduction faced by our ancestors. Personality psychology, in contrast, has been concerned largely with the ways in which humans differ. The divide between these two fields is obvious and raises questions that evolutionary psychologists need to address. If natural and sexual selection operates to filter less successful variants, why are stable,

heritable individual differences maintained? The first theoretical link between these two literatures and first attempt to reconcile this issue was provided by Buss (1984), who outlined four criteria according to which important sources of evolutionarily informed individual differences can be identified. These include heritability, inclusive fitness, sexual selection, and assortative mating. Each of these four criteria can be used to bridge the theoretical gap between evolutionary psychology and personality psychology.

Buss (1991) and Buss and Greiling (1999) propose that personality may not reflect evolutionary noise or represent by-products of other adaptations but may instead reflect the social landscape of adaptive strategies. Buss highlights that that there are at least four explanations for personality and individual differences in humans:

- Differences in personality are heritable alternative strategies.
- Differences in personality are calibrations to fluctuating strategies throughout development.
- Differences in personality are due to contextual differences and personality reflects those contexts.
- Personality differences emerge through calibration to various thresholds in development.

Appreciating that personality differences between individuals may reflect social landscapes, it is reasonable to question whether personality has an impact on shaping sexual desire, motivation, and attraction. Personality can be used as a source of information that answers some of the most important social dilemmas that humans have evolved to solve. Evolutionary psychologists have argued, for example, that the Big-Five personality characteristics summarize the most important facets of social landscapes. Perceiving, attending to, and acting upon differences in others likely would have yielded important benefits in ancestral environments. For example, openness/intellect of others can be used as a criterion for seeking out advice. Conscientiousness may be evaluated to assess whom to trust to complete important tasks. Agreeableness may be evaluated as an index of an individual's willingness to cooperate and to conform to group norms by suspending their individual concerns. Neuroticism may signify the inability to negotiate tasks effectively. Extraversion or surgency may be assessed as an index of who is likely to rise in the local status hierarchy.

From an evolutionary psychological perspective, human personality structure is comprised of a finite though numerous collection of species-typical, relatively domain-specific psychological mechanisms that have evolved over human evolutionary history because they solved the adaptive problems ancestral humans confronted. Personality is comprised of *psychological mechanisms*. Every theory of human personality – even the most environmentalistic – assumes that personality is at some basic level constructed of psychological mechanisms (Symons, 1987). If two members of a given species, or two members of two different species, are exposed to identical stimuli and respond in non-identical ways, we must infer the existence and operation of mechanisms internal to the organisms. These mechanisms can best be described as information-processing devices. These mechanisms take in certain classes of information, process that information according to a set of decision rules, and then generate output correlated with survival or reproductive success in ancestral environments. The information accepted for processing into the mechanism may come from other psychological mechanisms internal to the organism, or it may originate in the external environment – more often than not the particularly social environment comprised of other humans operating according to like mechanisms. The output generated by a psychological mechanism may be in the form of information which is channeled to and accepted by other psychological mechanisms internal to the organism. Or the output may be in the form of behavior, affect, or cognition enacted by the organism (Buss, 1991).

The psychological mechanisms underlying personality have *evolved over human evolutionary history because they solved the adaptive problems ancestral humans confronted*. Certain problems have been recurrently faced by ancestral humans. Consider the problem of which foods to ingest. To survive, certain nutrients had to be ingested (and, conversely, various toxins had to be avoided). This is a complicated problem when considered at the level of basic decision processes. Ancestral humans had to distinguish nutritive from non-nutritive goods; poisonous from non-poisonous fruits, vegetables, and organisms; higher caloric foods from less caloric foods, and so on. Those proto-humans who could not distinguish nutritive from non-nutritive foods are not our evolutionary ancestors, for they will have been out-survived and out-reproduced by their more discriminating conspecifics.

Personality is comprised of a *finite though numerous* collection of evolved psychological mechanisms. The adaptive problems our ancestors faced were many and varied in nature: from mate selection, to food ingestion, to forming successful reciprocal dyadic alliances (friendships). The solution to each of these problems has evolved as a circumscribed set of decision rules that guide human behavior, thought, and affect (in concert with relevant cues). The psychological mechanisms that evolved as solutions to adaptive problems will be as numerous and varied as the adaptive problems themselves. The fact that one might be quite successful in selecting a reproductively valuable mate has little or no direct bearing on whether one can successfully select and ingest the most nutritive foods available. Mate selection and food selection are qualitatively different adaptive problems that will have selected for qualitatively different sets of psychological mechanisms over human evolutionary history. Thus, the psychological mechanisms that comprise human personality structure will be as numerous as the adaptive problems that selected for those mechanisms. Relatedly, because the number of adaptive problems that confronted ancestral humans was finite though numerous, we expect that the number of mechanisms comprising the structure of personality are finite though numerous. Moreover, it follows that these finite though numerous mechanisms are *domain specific* – that is, they serve as evolved solutions to *specific* adaptive problems. Because ancestral humans did not confront a single 'survive and reproduce' adaptive problem, we have no reason to expect that personality is comprised of a single 'survive and reproduce successfully' psychological mechanism that evolved as a relatively domain-general adaptive solution (Buss, 1991; Symons, 1987; Tooby and Cosmides, 1990, 1992).

Finally, the basic structure of human personality is comprised of a *species-typical* collection of evolved psychological mechanisms. That is, the mechanisms that evolved as solutions to the adaptive problems confronting all ancestral humans over evolutionary history are presently characteristic of all representatives of the human species (with the exception of rare mutations and genetic drift). This is expected because all modern humans are, by definition, the evolutionary descendents of those ancestral humans who successfully solved the various adaptive problems they confronted. If it is the case then, that personality is comprised of a finite though numerous species-typical and domain-specific psychological mechanisms, does this mean that personality is stable or consistent from birth to death? Or might it be somehow dependent on the context or environment?

Evolutionary psychological theories do not imply the existence of adaptations that are incapable of change or are forever bound by our genome (Bjorklund and Pellegrini, 2002; Buss, 2004; Tooby and Cosmides, 1992). Few evolutionary psychologists actively present hypotheses and theories that stress the role that the environment has in shaping the expression of evolved modules of the mind, but these theories are nonetheless not deterministic theories. An examination of the arguments surrounding the claim that evolutionary psychology is a theory of

genetic determinism must start with an examination of what evolutionary psychologists *actually* propose. Tooby and Cosmides (1992) argue that developmental programs responsible for assembling an adaptation are also adaptations whose primary function is to reconstruct in offspring the design that enhanced reproduction in the preceding generation. They specifically note that it is useful to consider genes *together with* developmental programs as an integrated suite of adaptations. The reliable development of an organism's phenotypic features (including personality and sexual strategies) does not imply that these features are not modifiable. Developmental adaptations do not assemble an organism of fixed design but rather a set of expressed adaptations according to variables such as age, sex, and circumstance-dependent design specifications. Adaptive problems are often specific to particular life stages. Organisms must have the necessary adaptations for the particular stage regardless of whether they appear before they are necessary or continue after they are necessary. Tooby and Cosmides argue that every feature of every phenotype is *equally determined* by the interaction of that organism's genes and its ontogenetic environment. 'Biology', therefore, can be segregated to certain traits and not to others. In stressing the role of the environment, Tooby and Cosmides note that the 'developmentally relevant environment' refers to those features of the world that are rendered developmentally relevant by the evolved design of an organism's developmental adaptations. The assumption that genes are, therefore, the *only* target of natural selection is a misconception. Genes and developmentally relevant environments (species-typical environments) are both products of the evolutionary process. By selecting a developmental adaptation, for example, the evolutionary process is also selecting the triggers that the mechanisms will use to build an adaptation. Functional design is revealed as much by genes as it is by the environment that those genes use to construct an adaptation.

Evolution by natural and sexual selection is recognized as the origin of the many special-purpose and domain-specific cognitive decision rules (psychological mechanisms) according to which humans function. However, and crucial to this perspective, evolutionary psychology holds as a central goal to determine the historical, developmental, and situational forms of contextual input processed by the psychological mechanisms that guide human behavior. *Evolutionary psychologists are not 'genetic determinists'.* Rather, a key message of evolutionary psychology is that the complex architecture of species-typical, domain-specific psychological mechanisms allows for the impressive *context-dependant* flexibility of human behavior, cognition, and affect (Buss, 1991; DeKay and Buss, 1992). Modern evolutionary approaches aspire to understand – in addition to our species-typical, culturally differentiated, and sex-specific human nature – the ways that individuals differ within species, within cultures, and within sex.

Thus, the architectural unit of personality is the evolved psychological mechanism. But these mechanisms cannot and do not operate in a vacuum. The mechanisms are dependant for their activation on the contextual input for which they have evolved sensitivity. Personality is, therefore, relatively stable in the sense of being basically comprised of a finite (though numerous) collection of species-typical psychological mechanisms. At the level of the cognitive, affective, and behavioral *output* of these mechanisms, however, personality is better described as variable. The most accurate depiction of personality is that it is both consistent and variable – that it is comprised of a finite set of species-typical and domain-specific psychological mechanisms that depend for their activation on relevant contextual input. And because no two individual psychologies will receive and process identical input in an identical manner, there is room enough for individual differences. At the same time, we can expect base level similarities across a particular group of individuals, to the extent

that those individuals have historically faced similar classes of adaptive problems over evolutionary history. On these grounds, we expect sex-differentiated and age-differentiated personality structures, based on the evolved psychological architecture characteristic of the sex and of the age of the person. The issue of sex differences and similarities in evolutionary perspective will be taken up in a later section. Regarding the expected age-graded structure of human personality, different adaptive problems confronted ancestral humans at different ages or developmental stages, as is true of modern humans. Thus, for example, an adaptive problem of late infancy or early childhood, but presumably not of adolescence, or any stage of adulthood, is weaning. It is reasonable to suggest that as the lactating mother initiates the weaning process, the suckling infant or young child's personality is structured in part by mechanisms which are activated only in response to this very circumscribed conflict of interests. That is, we do not expect the personality of the typical young adult, for example, to be operative on those mechanisms which are specifically activated with the onset of weaning.

UNDERSTANDING INDIVIDUAL DIFFERENCES

There usually is not just one 'evolutionary approach' to a particular domain of human thought, behavior, and emotion. Rather, there are typically several competing or perhaps complementary evolutionary perspectives that are proposed to explain a given behavioral, cognitive, or affective phenomenon. This also is the case regarding attempts to explain the various manifestations of individual differences. There are currently at least four evolutionary approaches to the study of individual differences (Buss, 1991; DeKay and Buss, 1992). One approach is that of evolutionary developmental psychology. For example, Belsky et al. (1991) argue that individual differences in mating strategies are in part explicable in terms of whether the father was present or absent during the off-spring's childhood years. The general argument of this developmental approach is that mechanisms will be activated and operative only under certain developmental conditions or stages. Without input providing the appropriate developmental information, the mechanism presumably remains at or returns to an inactive or latent state.

A second evolutionary approach investigates the environment that is currently inhabited for an explanation of manifest individual differences. Thus, for example, Flinn (1988) finds that mate-guarding of Trinidadian females by males varies as a function of the reproductive status of the female: she is guarded against other males significantly more when she is fecund (impregnable) than when she is not fecund.

A third evolutionary approach to individual differences examines reactive individual differences. The general thesis is that there are evolved mechanisms which take as input a circumscribed class of anatomical data. Based on the processing of such information, the mechanisms guide the organism to adopt one strategy over an alternative in a given domain of behavior. For example, individuals who are small in stature and without physical size and strength will likely be most successful pursuing a strategy of diplomacy (rather than, say, aggressivity) in interacting with conspecifics. A person with a large, muscular build, on the other hand, may be anatomically and physiologically prepared to pursue an aggressive strategy in interactions with others (DeKay and Buss, 1992; Tooby and Cosmides, 1990).

A fourth evolutionary approach to explaining individual variation is exemplified by the work of Gangestad and Simpson (1990), who conceptualize the adoption of one of two general sexual strategies in terms of genetic differences arising through frequency-dependent selection. Gangestad and Simpson argue that individuals differ on the dimension of sociosexuality. Sociosexuality refers to an individual's willingness to engage in sexual intercourse with little or no emotional investment in or commitment to the relationship. Gangestad and Simpson present evidence supporting the proposal that two alternative sexual strategies (high and low sociosexuality) have been selected for, with the result of a bimodal distribution of these strategies in the current population. They suggest that the adoption of one of the strategies is heritable and that, moreover, a variety of personality characteristics co-vary with each strategy in a way that is consistent with evolutionary reasoning.

It is important to recognize that each of these approaches to understanding individual differences is complementary, rather than competing or mutually exclusive. Each perspective offers a different window through which to glimpse the structure of human personality. Application of each of these areas has profitably proceeded in the area of human sexual psychology.

PERSONALITY AND SEXUAL PSYCHOLOGY

Examinations of the relationships between personality and sexuality began in earnest with Eysenck (1976). Following from the guidance offered from an evolutionary perspective, we can attempt to couch our understanding of the relationships between personality and sexual psychology as a function of sexual selection. Parental investment theory (Trivers, 1972) predicts that human males will devote more resources to mating effort and that human females will devote more resources to parental investment by virtue of asymmetries in assurances of parentage. It is, therefore, not surprising that we observe differences in pursuit of social status, sensation seeking, extraversion, and risk-taking favoring men and that we observe differences in love/nurturance favoring women (MacDonald, 1998).

Linked with those characteristics that the sexes appear to differ on are characteristics that men and women view as desirable in a long-term partner. Surbey and Conohan (2000) found that female undergraduate students desired personality characteristics such as brightness, generosity, and having a sense of humor in a hypothetical partner with whom they would consider having sexual intercourse. Jensen-Campbell et al. (1995) report that females prefer as mates males high on altruism and agreeableness, with the highest ratings of attraction provided for agreeable and dominant males. Buss and Barnes (1986) report that women rank characteristics such as considerate, honest, dependable, kind, and understanding higher in a prospective mate than do men. Given that the obligatory parental investment costs are greater for women than for men, ancestral women with preferences that guided them toward prospective mates who were more likely to provide for them and their offspring would have been at a selective advantage relative to those women in ancestral environments that were indifferent to the personality characteristics linked with status and resources in men (Buss, 2003).

Research has revealed that personality plays a key role in human sexual psychology. Personality is a critical component of human mate choice (Buss, 2003) and is associated with the dissolution of relationships (Betzig, 1989). Figueredo et al. (2006), for example, report that men and women rate ideal romantic partners higher than themselves on the personality dimensions of extraversion, agreeableness, and conscientiousness, and lower than themselves on neuroticism. A significant difference between self-openness ratings and ideal partner openness ratings did not emerge in this study.

Sex differences are expected only in those domains of behavior, cognition, and affect for which males and females have historically to solve qualitatively different adaptive problems. Conversely, for those domains in which ancestral males and females confronted similar problems, there is no reason to expect that the related behavioral, cognitive, or affective output of the psychological mechanisms that evolved as solutions to these problems will be sex-differentiated. Here, we relate an example of the sort of sex differences and similarities that are expected, from research conducted on perceptions of relationship betrayal (see Shackelford and Buss, 1996).

Feelings of betrayal are expected when a relationship partner fails to provide, accept, or exchange benefits or resources expected in that relationship context. *Extra-relationship sexual involvement* will incite intense feelings of betrayal in the context of a committed, romantic, sexual relationship. This is expected to be true for both males and females: exclusive sexual access is a resource expected of and by both partners in a mateship (Buss et al.,1992; Buss and Schmitt, 1993; Wiederman and Allgeier, 1993; Wilson and Daly, 1992). Importantly, however, human reproduction is characterized by fertilization and gestation internal to the female. Consequently, males – but not females – over evolutionary history confronted the adaptive problem of uncertain parentage. A mate's sexual infidelity placed males at risk of investing in offspring to whom they were genetically unrelated. Those males who were indifferent to the sexual fidelity of their mates are thus not our ancestors, for they will have been out-reproduced by males who invested effort in and were sensitive to retaining exclusive sexual access to their mates. Feelings of betrayal incited in a male in response to the real or imagined sexual infidelity of his mate can thus be understood as a response to the threat of cuckoldry.

Although females have not faced the adaptive problem of uncertain parentage, the sexual infidelity of their mate likely served as a cue to the potential or current loss of other reproductively valuable and typically mateship-specific resources. That is, a woman may fear that the resources her mate contributes to their relationship (historically in the form of, for example, protection of her and their offspring from predation and hostile conspecifics; social and political support of her and their offspring; and basic provision of food, shelter, and related resources to her and their offspring) will be diverted to another woman and the other woman's offspring (Buss and Schmitt, 1993; Daly and Wilson, 1988). The ubiquitous phenomenon of female prostitution supports the observation – implied in the mated woman's concern over the sexual infidelity of her mate – that men often barter reproductively valuable resources for sexual access to females (Daly and Wilson, 1988). Feelings of betrayal incited in a woman in response to the real or imagined sexual infidelity of her mate can thus be understood as a response to the threatened loss of reproductively valuable resources (Buss et al., 1992; Buss and Schmitt, 1993).

Similarly, *extra-relationship romantic emotional involvement* will incite intense feelings of betrayal in the context of a mateship. This is true for both males and females (Buss et al., 1992; Buss and Schmitt, 1993; Wiederman and Allgeier, 1993; Wilson and Daly, 1992). Accordingly, a woman may fear that the resources her mate contributes to their relationship will be diverted to another woman and the other woman's offspring (Buss and Schmitt, 1993; Daly and Wilson, 1988). A man, on the other hand, may fear that the romantic emotional involvement of his mate with another male will escalate to sexual involvement, potentially rendering him a cuckold (see Buss, 2000, for a review of research).

Both sexes are predicted to feel betrayed by the sexual or romantic emotional infidelity of their long-term mate. Indeed, research paradigms that do not definitively disassociate sexual from romantic mate infidelity (reviewed in Wiederman and Allgeier, 1993) find no significant quantitative sex differences in what are effectively global measures of incited betrayal or jealousy. However, and consistent with the logic of evolutionary psychology, when the disassociation of sexual from romantic infidelity is made, men display greater psychological, physiological, and behavioral distress to a mate's sexual infidelity, whereas women display greater distress to a mate's romantic emotional infidelity (Buss et al., 1992; Buss et al. 1999; Buunk et al., 1996; DeSteno and Salovey, 1996; Geary et al., 1995; Harris, 2000; Harris and Christenfeld, 1996; Shackelford et al., 2002; Wiederman and Allgeier, 1993; Wiederman and Kendall, 1999; but see Harris, 2000, and Grice and Seely, 2000, for partial failures to replicate the sex difference using physiological measures). To reiterate, the pressing adaptive problem for mated men is the threat of cuckoldry – associated directly with a mate's *sexual* infidelity. The pressing adaptive problem for mated females is the threatened loss of reproductively valuable time and resources contributed by her mate – associated with her mate's *romantic emotional* involvement (and concomitant resource investment) in another woman and the other woman's offspring. That is, for the mated woman, the adaptive problem is not the sexual infidelity of her mate *per se*; rather, it is the threatened diversion of his time and resources to another woman in a bartering effort to gain (and perhaps retain) sexual access to her. Thus, assuming that the two types of infidelity are disassociated, men will experience more intense feelings of betrayal in response to their mate's sexual infidelity. Women, on the other hand, will experience more intense feelings of betrayal in response to the romantic emotional infidelity of their mate.

Evolution by natural and sexual selection is recognized as the origin of the many special-purpose and relatively domain-specific psychological mechanisms that comprise the structure of human personality. As noted earlier, however, these mechanisms are dependant for their activation on the appropriate contextual or environmental input. Only certain classes of information will be accepted and processed by a given psychological mechanism. Consider again the case of extra-relationship sexual involvement (see Shackelford and Buss, 1996).

Evolutionary logic suggests that the betrayal felt by *a mate's* extra-relationship sexual involvement will be most intense when it occurs with an enemy/rival of the mate's partner: Not only is exclusive sexual access (and perhaps various other forms of reproductively valuable resources) lost, in addition, it is lost to one's competitor. Similarly devastating would be the case where one's mate engages in sexual relations with one's close same-sex friend. Again, exclusive sexual access (and perhaps other forms of reproductively valuable resources) is lost; in addition, a close reciprocal alliance is disrupted in the process.

In the context of the typical close *same-sex friendship* or *same-sex coalition,* sexual involvement outside of the friendship or coalitional relationship will not generate feelings of betrayal, assuming otherwise appropriate relationship participation. Exclusive sexual access is not the (or even a) resource garnered from these relationships. If sexual involvement does occur, the relationship between the parties by definition is no longer *only* a friendship or coalitional relationship. The friendship or coalitional relationship may remain, but a new twist has been added, necessitating a reconsideration of the relational boundaries (Buss, 1990). However, if the sexual involvement of a close friend or fellow coalition member is with one's mate, feelings of betrayal are likely to arise. And if the extra-relationship sexual involvement is with a personal enemy of the other relationship member (in the friendship context), or with someone associated with an enemy/rival coalition (in the coalitional context) – another form of the 'double whammy', feelings of betrayal are likely to arise. In both relationship contexts, these feelings of betrayal will be greater when the sexual involvement is with the mate of the other relationship member, relative to when such involvement is with an enemy of the other relationship member. This is expected because loss of exclusive sexual access to a mate is likely to be far more (negatively) reproductively consequential than the loss associated with losing an alliance to a personal or coalitional enemy. Moreover, loss of exclusive sexual access and perhaps other forms of reproductively valuable resources to a mate is *direct* and *certain*. The benefit gained by a personal or coalitional enemy, however, is *indirect* and *uncertain*. That is, if indeed the close friendship or coalitional relationship is lost, this does not guarantee that a new alliance will be formed between the previous friend or coalition member and the personal or coalitional enemy.

Clearly then, an evolutionary perspective on human personality – and on human nature more generally – recognizes the relevance of context in attempting to understand the manifest behavioral, cognitive, and emotive output of the evolved psychological mechanisms that comprise the structure of human personality. Without input to the system, the mechanisms underlying personality can generate little in the way of output.

CONCLUDING COMMENTS

An evolutionary reconceptualization of the development, structure, and processes of human personality provides for a novel and valuable reinterpretation of several areas of personality psychology. These areas include the issue of personality consistency/variability, individual differences as well as a ubiquitous human nature, sex differences and similarities, age-graded and developmentally contingent personality phenomena, and the contextual determinants of personality. The scientific value of evolutionary theory offers guidance to areas that have largely operated outside of the evolutionary sciences. One such area is an understanding of psychopathology. An appreciation of the adaptive output of evolved psychological and physiological mechanisms can result in a richer and more strongly theoretically grounded understanding of psychopathology and personality disorders than what currently exists (Nesse and Williams, 1994;

Nesse, 2005). Applications of evolutionary theory to understanding human personality will improve the scope and viability of personality psychology. Inroads have already been made into developing a richer theoretical understanding of human personality and a more complete merging of evolutionary psychology and personality psychology, we believe, lies ahead.

REFERENCES

Allport, G.W. (1931) 'What is a trait of personality?', *Journal of Abnormal and Social Psychology*, 25(4): 368–72.

Allport, G.W. (1960) *Personality and Social Encounter*. Boston: Beacon.

Barkow, J., Cosmides, L. and Tooby, J. (1992) (eds), *The Adapted Mind*. New York: Oxford University.

Belsky, J., Steinberg, L. and Draper, P. (1991) 'Childhood experience, interpersonal development, and reproductive strategy: An evolutionary theory of socialization', *Child Development*, 62(4): 647–70.

Betzig, L. (1989) 'Causes of conjugal dissolution: A cross cultural study', *Current Anthropology*, 30(5): 654–76.

Bjorklund, D.F. and Pellegrini, A.D. (2002) *The Origins of Human Nature*. Washington, DC: American Psychological Association.

Buss, D.M. (1984) 'Evolutionary biology and personality psychology: Toward a conception of human nature and individual differences', *American Psychologist*, 39(10): 1135–47.

Buss, D.M. (1990) 'Evolutionary social psychology: Prospects and pitfalls', *Motivation and Emotion*, 14(4): 265–86.

Buss, D.M. (1991) 'Evolutionary personality psychology', *Annual Review of Psychology*, 42: 459–91.

Buss, D.M. (2000) *The Dangerous Passion*. New York: Free Press.

Buss, D.M. (2003) *The Evolution of Desire*. New York: Basic Books.

Buss, D.M. (2007) *Evolutionary Psychology: The New Science of the Mind*. Boston: Pearson.

Buss, D.M. and Barnes, M. (1986) 'Preferences in human mate selection', *Journal of Personality and Social Psychology*, 50(3): 559–70.

Buss, D.M. and Greiling, H. (1999) 'Adaptive individual differences', *Journal of Personality*, 67(2): 209–43.

Buss, D.M, Larsen, R.J., Westen, D. and Semmelroth, J. (1992) 'Sex differences in jealousy: Evolution, physiology, and psychology', *Psychological Science*, 3(4): 251–5.

Buss, D.M. and Schmitt, D.P. (1993) 'Sexual strategies theory: An evolutionary perspective on human mating', *Psychological Review*, 100(2): 204–32.

Buss, D.M., Shackelford, T.K., Kirkpatrick, L.A., Choe, J., Hang, K.L., Hasegawa, M., Hasegawa, T. and Bennett, K. (1999) 'Jealousy and the nature of beliefs about infidelity: Tests of competing hypotheses about sex differences in the United States, Korea, and Japan', *Personal Relationships*, 6(1): 125–50.

Buunk, B.P., Angleitner, A., Oubaid, V. and Buss, D.M. (1996) 'Sex differences in jealousy in evolutionary and cultural perspective: Tests from the Netherlands, Germany, and the United States', *Psychological Science*, 7(6): 359–63.

Cantor, N. (1990) 'From thought to behavior: "Having" and "doing" in the study of personality and cognition', *American Psychologist*, 45(6): 735–50.

Clutton-Brock, T.H. (1991) *The Evolution of Parental Care*. NJ: Princeton University

Crawford, C., Krebs, D. and Smith, M. (eds) (1987) *Sociobiology and Psychology*. Hillsdale, NJ: Erlbaum.

Daly, M. and Wilson, M. (1983) *Sex, Evolution, and Behavior* (2nd edn). Boston: Willard Grant.

Daly, M. and Wilson, M. (1988) *Homicide*. Hawthorne, NY: Aldine de Gruyter.

Daly, M., Wilson, M. and Weghorst, S.J. (1982) 'Male sexual jealousy', *Ethology and Sociobiology*, 3(1): 11–27.

Darwin, C. (1859/1958) *The Origins of Species by Means of Natural Selection or the Preservation of Favoured Races in the Struggle for Life*. New York: New American Library.

Darwin, C. (1871) *The Descent of Man and Selection in Relation to Sex*. London: Murray.

DeKay, W.T and Buss, D.M. (1992) 'Human nature, individual differences, and the importance context: Perspectives from evolutionary psychology', *Current Directions in Psychological Science*, 1(6): 184–9.

DeSteno, D.A. and Salovey, P. (1996) 'Evolutionary origins of sex differences in jealousy: Questioning the "fitness" of the model', *Psychological Science*, 7(6): 367–72.

Eysenck, H.J. (1976) *Sex and Personality*. London: England Open Books.

Eysenck, H.J. (1981) (ed.), *A Model for Personality*. New York: Springer-Verlag.

Figueredo, A.J., Sefcek, J. and Jones, D.N. (2006) 'The ideal romantic partner: Absolute or relative preferences in personality?', *Personality and Individual Differences*, 41(3): 431–44.

Flinn, M.V. (1988) 'Mate guarding in a Caribbean village', *Ethology and Sociobiology*, 9(1): 1–28.

Freud, S. (1930/1949) *Civilization and its Discontents*. London: Hogarth.

Gangestad, S.W. and Simpson, J.A. (1990) 'Toward an evolutionary history of female sociosexual variation', *Journal of Personality*, 58(1): 69–96.

Geary, D.C., Rumsey, M., Bow-Thomas, C.C. and Hoard, M.K. (1995) 'Sexual jealousy as a facultative trait: Evidence from the pattern of sex differences in adults from China and the United States', *Ethology and Sociobiology*, 16(5): 255–83.

Geary, D.C. (2000) 'Evolution and proximate expression of human paternal investment', *Psychological Bulletin*, 126(1): 55–77.

Grice, J.W. and Seely, E. (2000) 'The evolution of sex differences in jealousy: Failure to replicate previous results', *Journal of Research in Personality*, 34(3): 348–56.

Harris, C.R. (2000) 'Psychophysiological responses to imagined infidelity: The specific innate modular view of jealousy reconsidered', *Journal of Personality and Social Psychology*, 78(6): 1082–91.

Harris, C.R. and Christenfeld, N. (1996) 'Gender, jealousy, and reason', *Psychological Science*, 7(6): 364–7.

Jensen-Campbell, L.A., Graziano, W.G. and West, S.G. (1995) 'Dominance, prosocial orientation, and female preferences: Do nice guys really finish last?', *Journal of Personality and Social Psychology*, 68(3): 427–40.

John, O.P. (1990) 'The "big five" factor taxonomy: Dimensions of personality in the natural language and in questionnaires', in L. Pervin (ed.), *Handbook of Personality Theory and Research*. New York: Guilford.

Kelly, G.A. (1955) *The Psychology of Personal Constructs*. New York: Norton.

Krebs, J.R. and Davies, N.B. (1987) *An Introduction to Behavioral Ecology* (2nd edn). Boston: Blackwell.

MacDonald, K.B. (1998) 'Evolution, culture, and the five-factor model', *Journal of Cross-Cultural Psychology*, 29(1): 119–49.

Maslow, A.H. (1970) *Motivation and Personality* (2nd edn). New York: Harper & Row.

Michalski, R.L. and Shackelford, T.K. (2002) 'Birth order and sexual strategy', *Personality and Individual Differences*, 33(4): 661–7.

Michalski, R.L. and Shackelford, T.K. (2002) 'An attempted replication of the relationships between birth order and personality', *Journal of Research in Personality*, 36(2): 182–8.

Murray, H.A. (1937) 'Facts which support the concept of need or drive', *Journal of Psychology*, 3: 27–42. [Reprinted in D.C. McClelland and R.S. Steele (eds), *Human Motivation: A Book of Readings*. Morristown, NJ: General Learning, pp. 17–30.]

Murray, H.A. (1938) *Explorations in Human Personality*. New York: Oxford.

Nesse, R.M. (2005) 'Evolutionary psychology and mental health', in D.M. Buss (ed.), *The Handbook of Evolutionary Psychology*. Hoboken, NJ: Wiley, pp. 903–30.

Nesse, R.M. and Williams, G.C. (1994) *Why we Get Sick: The New Science of Darwinian Medicine*. New York: Vintage Books.

Smith, E.A. and Winterhalder, B. (1992) (eds), *Evolutionary Ecology and Human Behavior*. Hawthorne, NY: Aldine de Gruyter.

Shackelford, T.K. and Buss, D.M. (1996) 'Betrayal in mateships, friendships, and coalitions', *Personality and Social Psychology Bulletin*, 22(11): 1151–64.

Shackelford, T.K., Buss, D.M. and Bennett, K. (2002) 'Forgiveness or breakup: Sex differences in responses to a partner's infidelity', *Cognition and Emotion*, 16(2): 299–307.

Strickberger, M.W. (1990) *Evolution*. Boston: Jones and Bartlett.

Surbey, M.K. and Conohan, C.D. (2000) 'Willingness to engage in casual sex: The role of parental qualities and perceived risk of aggression', *Human Nature*, 11(4): 367–86.

Symons, D. (1979) *The Evolution of Human Sexuality*. New York: Oxford University Press.

Symons, D. (1987) 'If we're all Darwinians, what's the fuss about?', in C. Crawford, D. Krebs and M. Smith (eds), *Sociobiology and Psychology*. Hillsdale, NJ: Erlbaum, pp. 121–46.

Thornhill, R. and Palmer, C.T. (2000) *A Natural History of Rape*. Cambridge, MA: MIT Press.

Tooby, J. and Cosmides, L. (1990) 'On the universality of human nature and the uniqueness of the individual: The role of genetics and adaptation', *Journal of Personality*, 58(1): 17–68.

Tooby, J. and Cosmides, L. (1992) 'Psychological foundations of culture', in J. Barkow, L. Cosmides and J. Tooby (eds), *The Adapted Mind*. New York: Oxford University, pp. 19–136.

Trivers, R.L. (1972) 'Parental investment and sexual selection', in B. Campbell (ed.), *Sexual Selection and the Descent of Man*. Chicago: Aldine Publishing Company, pp. 136–79.

Trivers, R. (1985) *Social Evolution*. Menlo Park, CA: Benjamin/Cummings.

Wiederman, M.W. and Allgeier, E.R. (1993) 'Gender differences in sexual jealousy: Adaptationist or social learning explanation?', *Ethology and Sociobiology*, 14: 115–40.

Wiederman, M.W. and Kendall, E. (1999) 'Evolution, sex, and jealousy: Investigation with a sample from Sweden', *Evolution and Human Behavior*, 20(2): 121–8.

Williams, G.C. (1966) *Adaptation and Natural Selection*. New Jersey: Princeton University Press.

Wilson, M. and Daly, M. (1992) 'The man who mistook his wife for chattel', in J. Barkow, L. Cosmides and J. Tooby (eds), *The Adapted Mind*. New York: Oxford University. pp. 289–322.

Winter, D.G. (1973) *The Power Motive*. New York: Free.

9

Modern Personality Theories: What Have We Gained? What Have We Lost?

John B. Campbell

INTRODUCTION

My favorite among Stephen J. Gould's essays on natural history is 'The horn of Triton'. Gould described how his original expectation that rules of size and composition would determine the structure of planetary surfaces was disconfirmed by evidence sent back by Voyager 2 from Triton, Neptune's largest moon:

> I offer, as the most important lesson from Voyager, the principle of individuality for moons and planets. We anticipated greater regularity, but have learned that the surfaces of planets and moons cannot be predicted from a few general rules. To understand planetary surfaces, we must learn the particular history of each body as an individual object – the story of its collisions and catastrophes, more than its steady accumulations. The planets and moons are not a repetitive suite, formed under a few simple laws of nature. They are individual bodies with complex histories. And their major features are set by unique events – mostly catastrophic – that shape their surfaces. Planets are like organisms, not water molecules; they have irreducible personalities built by history. (1989: 18–26; my italics)

Every time I read these passages I am reminded of Gordon Allport's defining question for personality: 'How shall a psychological life history be written?' My task in this chapter is to frame what we have gained, as well as what we have lost sight of, during the progression of modern personality theories. I will approach that task from the perspectives of Gould and Allport on the reality and challenge of individual life histories.

I begin my review 107 years ago at the publication date for Freud's *The Interpretation of Dreams* (1900). I regard chapter VII in that text as the original core of psychoanalysis, and hence the most reasonable beginning for modern theories of personality. By modern theories, I reference cohesive frameworks for understanding the enduring tendencies that characterize individual human lives in their distinctive, unified, and evolving complexity. To frame these theories, I endorse the following propositions regarding personality theory from another landmark – Hall and Lindzey's (1957) *Theories of Personality*:

- 'An adequate understanding of human behavior will evolve only from the study of the whole person.' (1957: 6)
- The function of a theory is to serve 'as a kind of proposition mill, grinding out related empirical statements which can then be confirmed or rejected in the light of suitably controlled empirical data.' (1957: 13)
- A theory is evaluated based on verifiability, comprehensiveness, and heuristic influence, but most personality theories have been 'oriented toward after-the-fact explanation rather than toward the generation of new predictions concerning behavior.' (1957: 16)
- 'All matters of formal adequacy pale alongside the question of what empirical research is generated by the theory.' (1957: 20)
- '*Personality theory has occupied a dissident role in the development of psychology*' (1957: 4) and it is not clear whether progress toward a 'comprehensive and useful theory of human behavior' will benefit more from personality theories themselves or from a focus on relatively specific and delimited problems.

Recent essays on personality psychology also create a strategic context for the present work. For example, Mischel wrote,

> In the early history of psychology, the big, grand theories tried to spin de novo an all-encompassing brand new view of human nature in which a few antecedents – usually tucked away in early childhood or the unconscious – accounted for virtually everything. based on little data and cast so that they could not be disconfirmed. (2005: 19)

Mischel's analysis led him to advocate a bridge between personality and social psychology, reflecting the reality that person and situation are reciprocally interdependent, not independent, causes of behavior. And Mischel looked forward to 'a cumulative science [that] can flourish if many small but solidly data-based theories become integrated into bigger ones' (2005: 19).

In contrast, Smith (2005) proposed that Murray, Allport, Murphy, and Lewin did emphasize empirical science and had close linkages with emerging social psychology.

Smith also described factors that led personality psychology to 'go astray' from the empiricism, humanism, breadth of perspective, and relevance to social issues of its founders. First, World War II led to applied social psychology and a clinical psychology whose therapeutic goals 'over-shadowed' the agenda of Allport and Murray. Second, Mischel's (1968) persuasive empirical challenge to the consistency and relevance of global approaches to personality undermined the credibility and appeal of personality psychology, contributing to antagonism between personality and social psychology. Finally, the post-war system of federally funded grants, plus evolution of university promotion systems that rewarded rapid production of journal articles, worked against 'exploring personality the long way' (White, 1981) and fostered research that addressed variables rather than persons.

Similarly, Baumeister argued that personality and social psychologists can and must collaborate in exploring 'person by situation interaction [as] the only defensible model of human behavior' (1999: 367). In the process, they must move beyond their distinctive affinities for emphasizing independent variables (personality psychologists, with their reliance on a priori taxonomies) or dependent variables (social psychologists, with their reliance on ad hoc individual difference dimensions as correlates for behaviors of interest).

Pervin (1991) surveyed modern personality theory – the origin of the term I use as well. He highlighted Allport's and Murray's focus on the unity of the individual, and the taxonomic, factor analytic trait models of Cattell and Eysenck. Anticipating Smith, he noted three major impacts of World War II on personality: development of graduate programs of clinical psychology, and subsequent linkage of clinical and personality psychology; evolution of Murray's Office of Strategic Services into the Institute of Personality Assessment and Research; and social concerns that culminated in publication of *The Authoritarian Personality*.

Hogan noted that personality psychology alone 'takes the self-conscious evaluation of human nature as its central intellectual task' (1997: xxiii), thus accounting for 'the significance of personality psychology in modern social science' (see also Baumeister and Tice, 1996). Hogan attributed the comeback of personality during the 1980s and 1990s to social psychologists' discovery of the utility of individual differences, and industrial/organizational psychologists' discovery that well-constructed personality measures predict occupational performance as well as, but without the adverse impact of, cognitive tests.

McAdams (1997) addressed the evolution of personality theory during three periods. His first period emphasized Allport, Murray, and Cattell, who proposed multiple constructs that could be considered at varying levels of analysis. During the second period, 1950 to 1970, experimental social psychology flourished, but personality psychology floundered as it investigated specific constructs. The whole person was split into decontextualized dispositional constructs, and cognitive approaches to understanding the person were adopted. Finally, the period from 1970 to the present began with critiques of and uncertainty about personality psychology. McAdams aptly termed this period 'a decade of doubt', but he saw 'renewed optimism and vigor' in the late 1980s and 1990s.

I discuss this previous work to reflect my belief that recent personality psychology has suffered from a systematic disavowal of earlier theoretical positions. I disagree with Baumeister and Tice's suggestions that contemporary theorists need not be overly concerned with giving credit to 'some defunct speculator' (p. 368) and that the 'speculative theorizing' produced by prior generations should be ignored if it 'deter(s) modern theorizing' (1996: 369). Fair enough. But my concern is that contemporary personality psychologists *assume* there is nothing of value in these 'dusty mutterings', when in fact they *have not looked*. They *assume* that

there is no continuity, and therefore none can appear. They conclude that there has been no cumulative gain, in part because their lack of knowledge *precludes* any such possibility.

I agree with McAdams (1997) that historical essays tell a story highlighting broad conceptual trends. The central portion of this essay describes four cumulative *historical trends* that link and organize modern personality theories. At one level these trends are familiar; they echo Pervin's (2002) distinction among psychoanalytic models that relied on a clinical approach, trait models that relied on a correlational approach, and social cognitive theories that relied on an experimental approach. I, however, see more continuity within, and contributions from, these trends than most other commentators. The first trend focuses on personality dynamics, the second trend focuses on personality structure, the third trend describes the crisis when reactions against classic models produced a focus on individual differences, and the final trend describes an integrative resolution to the non-cumulative succession of theoretical positions that virtually every commentator has deplored.

HISTORICAL TRENDS

Trend 1: Personality dynamics

This first group of theorists is characterized by an emphasis on motivation, in particular motives not obvious to the person as a function of defensive dissociation. The primary representative is Freud, but I also include Carl Rogers. Theorists in this group articulated principles and structures that provide insight into the distinctive experience, behavior, and life trajectory of complex individuals. This orientation toward a within-person understanding anticipates Allport's commitment to finding general principles that account for individual uniqueness, as well as contemporary models whose goal is to characterize the individual.

Sigmund Freud

Freud developed the first systematic theory of personality; in many respects, all subsequent theories were reactions to his theory. For this reason alone, the story begins here. I stipulate that Freud's contributions are deeply flawed when evaluated as a source of disconfirmable hypotheses and operational definitions of measurable constructs, let alone supportive data that meet contemporary standards. Many of his propositions have the status of intellectual oatmeal – how are we to know when a cigar is just a cigar, and when it is not? And it is true that Freud's attitude toward experimental validation at best was one of indifference ('Still, [research] can do no harm,' he famously wrote to Saul Rosenzweig). Along with Meehl (1978, Addendum), however, I find substantial heuristic value in Freud's recognition that unaddressed conflicts and unrecognized impulses can affect thought and action in unintended ways.

The heart of Freud lies not in his psychosexual developmental stages or in 'metapsychological propositions' framed in terms of instincts or energy; rather, it is the 'clinical propositions' derived from the verbal and non-verbal behavior of patients, such as the relationship between conflictual wishes and psychopathology, that provide the essential core to his theory (Silverman, 1976). In particular, I emphasize Freud's dynamic model that conflict anxiety defense and compromise. Conflict arises because motives are incompatible with our childish moral prohibitions, and it festers in a repressed state if not resolved; this produces anxiety, which is resolved through some compromise brokered when the original, wished-for object is displaced by a substitute object that is similar (but not too similar) to the original object. Thus, behavior results from a nonconscious process of object choice that one alternatively could describe in learning terms. One can also describe the process in terms of a conflict between 'id' instincts and 'superego' prohibitions, where the 'ego' is the executive that negotiates the process, but these are terms for aspects of mental activity.

Westen (1998) argued that contemporary psychodynamic theory has evolved since Freud's death in 1939, reflecting the cognitive revolution that brought unconscious processes back into psychology. In addition, contemporary psychodynamic psychologists believe humans have multiple motives, many rooted in biology but nearly all modified by culture and experience. Westen assembled research to support five enduring psychodynamic propositions. First, much of mental life is unconscious, so people can behave in ways that are inexplicable to themselves. Second, mental processes operate in parallel; therefore, people can have conflicting feelings that motivate them in opposing ways and lead to compromise solutions. Third, stable personality patterns begin in childhood, and childhood experiences play an important role in personality development, especially forming social relationships. Fourth, mental representations guide our interactions. Finally, personality development involves not only learning to modify sexual and aggressive feelings, but also moving from immature and socially dependent states to mature and independent ones.

Jung and Adler rejected sexuality as the dominant dynamic and developmental theme, but Adler turned toward society, with his idea that social interest provides the 'barometer of mental health', and toward the environment, with his concept of superiority as a kind of competence or self-esteem. Jung, in contrast, turned even deeper into the collective unconscious. The growth tendency in Jung's model that maximizes potential by moving toward an integrative self was anticipated by Rogers. And Jung's proposal that the attitudes of extroversion–introversion, plus the functions of thinking–feeling and sensing–intuiting, guide an individual's ego functioning, although never intended as a taxonomic typology, provides a context for Kelly's construct theory, as well as contemporary emphases on cognition and apperception.

Robert White

In a now largely forgotten contribution, White addressed the Freudian psychosexual stages from the alternative perspective of the person's motivation to interact effectively with the environment. White (1960) argued that libido must be augmented by attention to growth in the child's sense of competence. That is, key aspects of development can be understood only from the perspective of changes in the child's actual and subjective sense of competence. In addition, he proposed that Freudian developmental prototypes (such as the infant at the breast), even when translated into interpersonal terms, provide inadequate models for development. White's competence model provides a link to Erikson's basic strength of Competence, Allport's principle of mastery and competence as one basis for functional autonomy, and Bandura's situationally specific constructs of efficacy (1999, 2000) and agency (2001, 2006).

Erik Erikson

Erikson often is considered essentially non-Freudian, in that he focused on lifespan development, emphasized historical and cultural contexts, replaced Freud's psychosexual stages with his own psychosocial stages, and emphasized identity concerns more than sexuality. But Erikson remained close to Freud. First, Erikson based his early developmental stages on zones, modes, and modalities, a model that remains true to Freud's erogenous zones and the non-conscious conversion of bodily modes into more general modalities. Second, Erikson's emphasis of identity over sexuality was not a repudiation of sexuality. Erikson wrote:

> The patient of today suffers most under the problem of what he should believe in and who he should – or, indeed, might – be or become; while the patient of early psychoanalysis suffered most under inhibitions which prevented him from being what and who he thought he knew he was.' (1963: 279)

His shift in conceptual emphasis was 'dictated by historical accident' rather than repudiation. Finally, Erikson's emphasis on cultural forces rather than instinctual urges needs to be understood within the Freudian model: 'Man's "inborn instincts" are drive fragments to be assembled, given meaning, and organized during a prolonged childhood by methods of child training and schooling which vary from culture to culture and are determined by tradition.' (1963: 95)

Despite these connections, Erikson has a different theoretical tone than Freud. Personality accrues as the developing person confronts and resolves a series of basic crises that are triggered not by inevitable physical maturation and intrapsychic conflict between impulse and prohibition, but by a series of conflicts that inevitably occur as the ego confronts demands from a predictable series of social agents. Furthermore, each basic crisis has its roots in earlier stages and its consequences in subsequent stages. A crisis is most salient during a particular stage, but it not absent at all other moments (Erikson, 1982).

Carl Rogers

I believe that Rogers fits best into this story line. He was a clinician who began with a theory of therapy, out of which he developed a theory of personality. Rogers, of course, rejected Freudian assumptions about human nature. He wrote, 'The basic nature of the human being, when functioning freely, is constructive and trustworthy. I have little sympathy with the rather prevalent concept that man is basically irrational. Man's behavior is exquisitely rational' (1961: 194). For Rogers, the central emphasis was on an 'actualizing tendency' that leads the person toward becoming 'that self which he truly is' (1961: 176). Moreover, despite the fact that Freud and Rogers had diametrically opposed assumptions about human nature, Freud aligning with Hobbes, and Rogers with Rousseau, they employed similar conflict models. For Rogers, conflict occurred between the individual's true nature and the distorted sense of self that results from conditions of worth, the external expectations or standards that the individual internalizes in order to preserve gratification of the need for positive regard. Subception of this incongruence leads to anxiety, which in turn prompts defense mechanisms whose function is to preserve the existing, inaccurate self. As perhaps the central statement of his personality theory, Rogers wrote:

> It is thus because of the distorted perceptions that arise from the conditions of worth that the individual departs from the integration which characterizes his infant state. This, as we see it, is the basic estrangement in man. He has not been true to himself but for the sake of preserving the positive regard of others has now come to falsify some of the values he experiences and to perceive them only in terms based upon their value to others. Yet this has not been a conscious choice, but a natural – and tragic – development in infancy. (1959: 226–7)

Unconscious conflict yet again, but for Rogers the inherent human nature is good and positive, and social pressures distort that nature. For Freud, in contrast, human nature is animalistic and dangerous, and the thin veneer of social morality controls these urges.

Trend 2: Personality structure

This trend differs in three important ways from the first one. First, there is a transition from the clinic to the laboratory, providing a foundation for therapeutic interventions to investigating behavioral tendencies that distinguish non-pathological individuals. Second, the orientation changes from personality dynamics and motivation to personality structure and taxonomies. Third, the dominant methodology changes from psychoanalysis and the inferences of depth psychology to factor analysis and issues related to reliability and validity of measurement. Central figures in this trend include Murray, Allport, Cattell, and Eysenck. The trend culminates in the contemporary Big Five synthesis.

Henry Murray

Murray's personology focused on developing a taxonomy of motivational tendencies in normal individuals. His emphasis on the necessity of conceptualizing behavior as an interaction between individual and environmental forces contradicts the many subsequent attempts to paint this generation of theorists as oblivious to environmental determinants of behavior. Murray also focused on a modified version of retained Freud's id–ego–superego framework. The id includes a person's basic energies, emotions, and needs, most of which are acceptable when expressed in a culturally approved manner. As a consequence, the role of the ego is not to suppress and defensively transform instinctual needs, so much as to schedule an appropriate time and manner to fulfill them. The superego refers to morality, but it develops in layers over time from many sources. Murray's version of Freud is less conflictual, but he retained Freudian concepts of depth psychology, defense, and childhood determinism. See, for example, Murray's 'highly speculative' proposal of infantile complexes from the child's preverbal period of development.

Murray's best known construct is the need, which

> stands for a force in the brain region, a force which organizes perception, apperception, intellection, conation and action in such a way as to transform in a certain direction an existing, unsatisfying situation. A need is sometimes provoked directly by internal processes of a certain kind but, more frequently (when in a state of readiness) by the occurrence of one of a few commonly effective press [or environmental forces]. Thus, it manifests itself by leading the organism to search for or to avoid encountering or, when encountered, to attend and to respond to certain kinds of press. (1938: 123–4)

Thus, Murray's need was defined as a person–situation interaction. Murray presented a list of 20 basic needs. Need was a general construct, but it had specific manifestations; he drew a distinction between need and aim, which represents the specific goal adopted by the person as an expression of the need. Furthermore, saying that someone has a strong need for aggression is an abstract statement that requires amplification, because it does not indicate how or toward what objects the need will be expressed.

Murray employed Freud's term cathexis to refer to the power of an object to evoke a positive or negative need in a person, and he claimed that personality is revealed in the objects that a person cathects. This allowed Murray to eliminate the dilemma of whether the focus should be on specific individual characteristics or general constructs. Adopting a sophisticated position regarding multiple levels of analysis, Murray wrote,

> The problem is to generalize for scientific purposes the nature of the cathected objects; for it does not seem that we can deal with concrete entities in their full particularity. [the cathected object] can have no scientific status until it is analysed and formulated as a compound of psychologically relevant attributes. The theory of press, we venture to hope, is a step in this direction. (1938: 107–8)

Murray knew that situations influence behavior, but he wanted a way to characterize situations in their own right, not in terms of the response that they evoked. He chose to classify situations in terms of the benefits, harms, and effects they have on the individual before he or she responds. 'Press' refers to a directional tendency that has an effect upon the person who encounters (alpha, or objective press) or perceives (beta or perceived press) the situation. Such subjective apperception results from past experiences that are triggered based on similarity to the present situation. Notice the similarity of this process to the encodings and expectancies that serve as cognitive–affective units in Mischel's 'cognitive affective personality system'. This analysis also sets the stage for contemporary work on person–environment fit (Harms et al., 2006).

Murray used thema, which he defined as a single need–press combination, to define behavioral episodes and to characterize individuals. One person might become physically abusive when insulted, whereas another person might respond to the same provocation by becoming apologetic. The first instance would be characterized as aggressive need following aggressive press, but the second would be described as deference need following aggressive press. Such episodes might be momentary, or they might recur as a characteristic response by the person to a particular press – a 'serial thema'. Murray believed, 'The biography of a man may be portrayed abstractly as an historic route of themas. Thus there is sameness (consistency) as well as change' (1938: 43). Note again that Murray's depiction of the individual in this manner is distinctly interactionist; personality is revealed in an individual's characteristic reaction to particular press, not a general behavioral tendency. In this sense, serial thema provides a clear historical antecedent to Mischel's if then signatures.

Gordon Allport

Allport also championed a shift from pathology to normal functioning. His emphases on rationality and unity of the personality, as well as his focus on the psychologically mature individual, make his the first non-Freudian model of personality. Allport addressed how mature one is, not how neurotic one is. And Allport provided a distinctly non-Freudian view of the self. Like Murray, Allport was concerned with personality structure, rather than embrace Murray's 'like all other men – like some other men – like no other man' orientation (Kluckhohn and Murray, 1953: 53). However, Allport was adamant that each person be understood as a 'system of patterned uniqueness' (1961: 9), not as the 'point of intersection' of a number of general dimensions. Allport adopted an idiographic focus on the idiosyncratic organization of the individual, rather than a nomothetic focus on between-person comparisons.

Allport specified two varieties of trait. A common trait, which refers to aspects of personality on which individuals can be compared, is 'a neuropsychic structure having the capacity to render many stimuli functionally equivalent, and to initiate and guide equivalent (meaningfully consistent) forms of adaptive and expressive behavior' (1961: 347). Personal dispositions are defined the same way, with the distinction that they are 'peculiar to the individual' (1961: 373). This distinction was central for Allport, who believed that individual lives are organized in a way that 'may not necessarily correspond at all well to any analytic scheme of common traits' (1961: 374).

Allport used 'functionally equivalent' situations to explain that 'transfer effects' (or cross-situational consistency) occur not because of objectively 'identical elements' in the two settings, but because of their perceived equivalence of meaning. Allport's usage seems remarkably similar to Mischel's if then behavioral signatures, especially given the mediating perceived meaning, as well as Cervone's (2004) reliance on self-schema and situational beliefs. For Allport, traits are loose tendencies whose expression varies in the face of differing determining conditions: 'Dispositions are never wholly consistent' (1961: 362).

Allport recognized the importance of a unifying sense of self: 'Whenever personal states are viewed as "peculiarly mine" the sense of self is present' (1961: 137). He organized seven aspects of selfhood as propriate functions under the rubric of proprium. Somewhat paradoxically, given his advocacy of an idiographic rather than a nomothetic approach, Allport also proposed six criteria for the mature personality: a widely extended sense of self; warm relations with others; emotional security and self-acceptance; realistic perceptions, thoughts, and actions; self-objectification, insight, and humor; and a unifying philosophy of life.

Allport agreed that psychology seeks general laws, but he drew 'special attention to those laws and principles that tell how uniqueness comes about' (1961: 572). His attempt to answer the question, 'How shall a psychological life history be written?' was guided by the belief that the patterned uniqueness of an individual's attributes is the central psychological reality. As a consequence, the central obligation for a psychological researcher is to bring insights 'back to the individual'.

Raymond Cattell

Cattell's contributions are not widely appreciated, due to the complexity of his models and the sophisticated mathematics required to comprehend them. Consistent with his training as a chemist, Cattell extended Murray's structural agenda by developing a periodic table of the personality elements. His multivariate approach maintained a focus on the whole person, rather than individual dimensions, and he included situational weightings as well as person variables in predicting behavior. He set the stage for the Big Five model and outlined a conceptual model for predicting individual behavior.

Cattell (1985, 1990; Cattell and Dreger, 1978) defined personality in terms of traits, or general relatively permanent reaction tendencies, and distinguished among ability traits, temperament or stylistic traits, and dynamic or motivational traits. He also distinguished between source traits, which are unitary building blocks of the personality, and surface traits, which are more specific aggregates of source traits. And finally, Cattell distinguished among three ways to collect information about personality: L-data, such as ratings of one person made by another person; Q-data, derived from self-report questionnaires; and T-data, or objective tests. Cattell's agenda was to identify the source traits of personality separately within each data type; if source traits identified using each data type converged, then he could have confidence that the structure of personality was not artifactually influenced by method variance. Relying on factor analyses plus a series of conceptual decisions, Cattell had reasonable success in this extraction and matching process (Cattell and Kline, 1977).

Cattell also followed Allport's dictum to 'come back to the person'. He developed the specification equation as a multivariate version of Lewin's B = f(P, E). A person's score on each source trait is multiplied by an empirically developed situational weight that indexes the relevance of that source trait to the specific behavior that is to be predicted in that particular situation. The full specification equation includes all ability, temperament, and dynamic (ergs and sentiments, see below) source traits, as well as roles, moods, and unpredictable specificity.

Cattell described three types of motivational traits. Ergs are biologically based, motivational source traits. Sentiments are motivational source traits acquired through experience and focused on some social object. Attitudes are motivational surface trait; they express source traits and indicate strength of intensity of a course of action toward a particular object. Dynamic traits are interrelated such that certain motivational units serve as means of expression for other more basic units. Cattell illustrated these multiple, overlapping pathways in the dynamic lattice, which serves as a snapshot of a section of an individual's motivational organization. This concept addresses Allport's goal of within-person organization, and is similar to Mischel's CAPS schematics.

Cattell repudiated the 'pre-scientific' approach of clinical theorists such as Freud, but many of the structures that he identified correspond to units previously identified by Freud's 'speculative' approach. For example, Cattell concluded that the first three components of attitudes resemble the Freudian id, ego, and superego. He distinguished between integrated or conscious and unintegrated or unconscious components of attitudes, and he suggested quantifying the amount of conflict a person feels about a particular action as the ratio of negative situational weights to positive situational weights in the specification equation for that attitude. Cattell also followed Freud's hydraulic model in his suggestion that sentiments allow us to drain off impulsive, ergic energy in socially sanctioned ways, as well as his belief that conscious goals and specific behaviors serve underlying innate ergic goals.

Finally, in contrast to other modern personality theorists, who address learning implicitly or in passing, Cattell (1979, 1980, 1983) developed an elaborate structured learning theory. Cattell (1982) also recog-

nized the heritability of personality and ability, and I do not have space to discuss his contributions to multivariate experimental psychology (Cattell and Nesselroade, 1988).

It has proven difficult for other researchers to replicate Cattell's personality structure. Furthermore, although Cattell's specification equation and dynamic lattice provide the best example of a structural approach to personality that uses complete information about the whole person to predict specific behaviors in particular contexts, this represents a pyrrhic victory because of their complexity. Despite these limitations, Cattell's dictum that 'science demands measurement' epitomizes the starting point for modern personality approaches to behavior. In addition, Cattell proposed different sets of variables to reference individual behavior (surface traits such as attitudes) and between-persons comparisons (source traits such as ergs and sentiments). He anticipated contemporary attempts to identify separate sets of variables for the two tasks of making interindividual comparisons and identifying intraindividual structure; Cattell, however, derived the latter from the former. In this final sense, Cattell can be understood as implementing Allport's pursuit of general law and principles that tell how uniqueness comes about.

Hans Eysenck

Eysenck proposed that personality can be summarized in terms of individual differences on three dimensions of temperament: introversion versus extraversion, neuroticism versus stability, and psychoticism versus non-psychoticism. Eysenck (1994a) recognized intelligence as an additional dimension that structures individual differences in the cognitive domain.

Eysenck proposed two explanatory models for his initial descriptive framework in terms of the orthogonal dimensions of extraversion and neuroticism. In his first model, Eysenck (1957) proposed that introverts have a low ratio of inhibitory to excitatory cortical processes and extraverts have a high ratio. Furthermore, if excitatory neural processes can be understood to facilitate the acquisition of conditioned responses, then a combination of Clark Hull's learning model and Eysenck's 1957 model predicts that introverts' nervous system permits them to condition more readily than extraverts.

In the second causal model, Eysenck (1967) related differences in introversion–extraversion to levels of activity in the ascending reticular activating system (ARAS). Because of greater ARAS activity, introverts have higher levels of and thresholds for cortical arousability than extraverts. Due to their higher arousability, introverts are more sensitive to external stimulation and more easily overstimulated than extraverts. The resulting tendency for introverts to avoid excessive stimulation and for extraverts to seek stimulation led Eysenck to designate introverts as 'stimulus shy' and extraverts as 'stimulus hungry' (although Eysenck qualified this general prediction in terms of transmarginal inhibition). Sensitivity to stimulation makes introverts avoid any source of intense stimulation. Other people can provide intense stimulation, leading introverts to avoid people; thus, low sociability is a derivative of the introvert's sensitivity to stimulation.

Individual differences in neuroticism depend on levels of limbic system activity, such that neurotics are characterized by higher levels and lower thresholds of activation. Eysenck and Eysenck (1976) subsequently introduced psychoticism as a third major personality type that addresses variability across people in aggressive, impulsive, and unsocialized behavior. Consistent with his general interest in behavior genetics, psychoticism and its constituent traits result from the additive effect of a number of genes. Eysenck (1994b) summarizes his position on biological foundations of personality.

Eysenck distinguished between trait, which refers to a set of related behaviors that repeatedly occur together, and type, which refers to a higher-order construct comprising a set of correlated traits (see Eysenck and Eysenck, 1985: 14–15, for schematic relationships between the three types and their defining traits). This distinction was part of Eysenck's (1981, 1988, 1990) hierarchical conception of behavior. The bottom level contains *specific responses*, such as talking before class on a single occasion. The second level contains *habitual responses*, such as talking before class on a regular basis. The third level contains *traits*, which are related sets of habitual responses. The highest level of generality contains *types* or related sets of traits. These alternative levels of analysis parallel Murray's distinction between need and aim, McCrae and Costa's distinction between Big Five traits and facets, and Cattell's distinctions among surface trait, source trait, and second-order factor.

Eysenck's theory is better in a formal sense than any other modern personality theory. The theory is subject to disconfirmation, and it has generated substantial experimentation. Eysenck's personality theory is also virtually unique in providing both descriptive or taxonomic and causal elements; it specifies a causal chain in which a biological substrate is responsible for individual differences on fundamental dimensions of personality. In a posthumous paper, Eysenck described this model in terms of distal antecedents that are expressed through proximal antecedents that are responsible for observed individual differences on the types. Understanding these relationships in turn permits deduction of proximal consequences, which Eysenck regarded as 'the most important aspects of any theory of personality' (1997: 1226). These in turn produce distal consequences (see figure 2 in Eysenck, 1997). With respect to extraversion, behavioral and molecular genetics are distal antecedents that explain the proximal antecedents of relatively lower cortical arousability of extraverts. This in turns produces the proximal consequence of lower sensitivity to stimulation in extraverts, which is responsible for distal consequences in learning and sociability.

The physiological causes Eysenck proposed are outdated, but he is right that an adequate personality theory must include a descriptive taxonomy and specify more fundamental biological mechanisms that explain observed differences on the descriptive dimensions. His hierarchical theory that specifies causal connections and from which testable hypotheses can be derived provides a model framework for personality theories. The major weakness of the theory is that it provided too little detail to account for individual behavior.

Gray and Zuckerman

Two related positions also merit attention. First, Jeffrey Gray's reinforcement sensitivity theory (1981, 1982) proposed that Eysenck's extraversion and neuroticism axes should be rotated 45 degrees (later 30 degrees). The two new resulting axes represent anxiety, which runs between Eysenck's stable extravert quadrant (low anxiety) and his neurotic introvert quadrant (high anxiety), and impulsivity, which runs from the stable introvert quadrant (low impulsivity) to the neurotic extravert quadrant (high impulsivity). From Gray's perspective, therefore, extraversion and neuroticism are secondary consequences of the interactions of anxiety and impulsivity.

Gray's model is similar to Eysenck's in its explanatory reliance on underlying physiological causes. A behavioral inhibition system (BIS) is the proximal antecedent of anxiety, and sensitivity to signals of punishment, non-reward, and novelty is the proximal consequence. A behavioral activation system (BAS) is the proximal antecedent of impulsivity, and increasing sensitivity to signals of reward and non-punishment is the proximal consequence. The BIS consists of 'an interacting set of structures comprising the septo-hippocampal system, its monoaminergic afferents from the brain stem and its neocortical projection in the frontal lobe' (Gray, 1981: 261), and the BAS is defined in terms of dopaminergic neurotransmission (see Fowles, 2006; Pickering and Gray, 1999).

Marvin Zuckerman (1979) developed a model of sensation seeking from his early work on sensory deprivation and optimal level of arousal. Sensation seeking correlates with Eysenck's measures of extraversion and psychoticism, but Zuckerman maintains that it cannot be subsumed by Eysenck's typology. Scores on sensation seeking have exhibited significant relationships with a variety of behaviors such as drug use, sexual activity, and participation in risky sports. Based on relationships among sensation seeking, augmenting versus reducing in cortical visually evoked potential, and monoamine oxidase, Zuckerman (1991) developed a psychobiological theory to account for individual differences in sensation seeking (see Fowles, 2006; Stelmack, 2004; Zuckerman, 2006).

The Big Five

The Big Five emerged in the 1980s following attempted replications of Cattell's factor structure (Goldberg, 1981; Norman, 1963; Tupes and Christal, 1961). A number of reviews (Digman, 1990; Goldberg, 1990, 1993; John, 1990; John and Srivastava, 1999) describe this evolution. A separate research program by McCrae and Costa (1987, 1990) identified neuroticism, extraversion, agreeableness, conscientiousness, and openness (OCEAN) by investigating personality questions rather than descriptive terms. Thus, there are two parallel sets of five-factor models: one from the lexical work and one from personality questionnaires. An important development in McCrae and Costa's approach was the specification of six specific facets that comprise each of the Big Five factors (Costa et al., 1991). Costa and McCrae thus echo Cattell and Eysenck in providing a hierarchical approach to personality structure, which serves as a basis for much contemporary work.

Cattell and Eysenck preferred their models to the Big Five. Other psychologists (see Carlson, 1992; Loevinger, 1994; Westen, 1995) objected to the Big Five on conceptual grounds, arguing that it is atheoretical, ignores behavior dynamics and change, excludes feelings and motives as well as situational contexts, and is not relevant for attempts to understand individual behavior and within-person organization. McAdams (1992, 1994) critiqued the Big Five as providing a 'psychology of the stranger'; that is, it provides a useful first approximation, but it cannot provide nuanced detail necessary to understand individual behavior. Similarly, Block (1995) objected that researchers should attend to intraindividual structure and functioning, adopting a broader set of conceptual and methodological orientations than afforded by the Big Five. Cervone (2005: 426) argued that the Big Five model addresses only between-person differences and cannot cast any light on within-person causal dynamics or capture the qualities of any individual person.

Partly in response to such criticisms, McCrae and Costa (1996, 1999) formulated the five-factor theory of personality. They proposed that the Big Five traits and their facets are universal, endogenous basic tendencies with (currently unspecified) biological bases. The concrete manifestations of the basic tendencies are characteristic adaptations, including a self-concept; these adaptations develop as reactions to the person's environment and demonstrate plasticity over time and place. The characteristic adaptations lead to and are influenced by an individual's objective biography as well as the external influences, through unspecified dynamic processes. McCrae and Costa noted parallels with McAdam's level 1 and level 2 personality variables (see below). The five-factor theory is also similar to Cattell's earlier proposal that attitudes emerge as expressions of underlying ergs and sentiments, and McCrae and Costa's (1999) figure 5.1 is conceptually similar to Cattell's dynamic lattice.

McCrae and Costa (1999: 149) noted that their model has 'nothing to say' about individual uniqueness and that 'personality profiles are more useful in understanding a life than in making specific predictions about what a person will do'. They also point out the remaining tasks to catalog characteristic adaptations, to specify the dynamic processes, and to detail the basic executive

mechanism in the system. Without these additional details, their theory remains descriptive and predictive, at which level it does have utility (see Ozer and Benet-Martinez, 2006; Paunonen, 2003).

Trend 3: Crisis – separate agendas on individual differences

This third period is often seen as the lost years in personality, resulting in fragmentation of the field. I prefer to think of it in Eriksonian terms as personality's identity crisis. In this sense, it was a period of confronting crises and developing consensus, to use Marcia's terms, and the field emerged with an invigorated sense of identity that reflects the achievements won in earlier developmental stages. The period was dominated by the 'debate' between persons and situations as the primary determinants of behavior. This debate framed an artificial distinction, as earlier theorists and numerous commentators made clear. Partly as a product of the debate, and partly due to the rise of social psychology, the field has moved from global models that focus on individuals as the unit of analysis to single dimensions derived ad hoc to account for individual differences on behaviors of interest. These variables do not represent theories of personality and are beyond my purview. Across these first three trends, we see a corresponding progression in data collection from psychoanalysis to factor analysis to analysis of variance. This trend was also the time when the neuropsychological and evolutionary perspectives that increasingly channel work in psychology as a whole grew in influence on personality psychology.

The person–situation debate

Publication of Mischel's (1968) *Personality and Assessment* was the landmark event in recent literature on personality, and it provoked a debate on the nature and validity of personality that dominated the next several decades. This controversy was not new, although Mischel framed it in a provocatively useful manner; Allport dealt with the first round of the debate when he rejected the concept of identical elements as the basis for cross-situational consistency (1937: chapter X; 1961: 319–24). Mischel (1968) issued an empirical challenge to advocates of global models to provide data demonstrating cross-situational consistency of personality. He claimed that the predictive utility of global traits of personality had not been established; furthermore, he argued that there was little evidence that behavior is cross-situationally consistent, as theories of personality as a set of trans-situational dispositions would seem to imply. His conclusion was that broad, situation-free traits and states obscure individual uniqueness and generate a 'grossly oversimplified view' that misses the richness, coherence, and organization of individuals' behavior.

Mischel's challenge provoked a number of responses. Funder and Ozer (1983) pointed out that the implicit alternative conclusion that situations must be strong determinants of behavior, if personality is a weak determinant, was in error. They demonstrated that the percentage of behavioral variance accounted for by such powerful situational forces as attitude change under forced compliance, bystander intervention, and obedience, when considered in terms of correlations rather than mean differences, did not exceed that acknowledged by Mischel for personality traits. Similarly, Bowers (1973) reported that the interaction of personality factors and situational forces, not main effects for either person variables or situational variables, had the greatest impact on behavior. Still other investigators reconceptualized the controversy. Epstein (1979) proposed that behavior is much more consistent when single behaviors have been aggregated into larger units. Similarly, Moskowitz (1982) demonstrated that broad and narrow trait constructs were characterized by different patterns of consistency. Regardless, Mischel's challenge to produce data that demonstrate cross-situational consistency persisted.

Bem and Allen (1974) offered perhaps the most influential response to Mischel. They noted an apparent paradox between our intuitions, which suggest that people display cross-situational consistency, and the empirical literature, which indicates that they do not. Echoing Allport, they argued that research demonstrates a nomothetic fallacy; that is, researchers implicitly have assumed that any trait dimension will be universally applicable to all persons. As a consequence, researchers may consider comparisons that make sense to them, but that do not necessarily exist in the phenomenology, equivalence classes, or behavior of their subjects. To the extent that this occurs, research will fail to find evidence of cross-situational consistency, not because it does not exist, but because it is being pursued in the wrong place. Bem and Allen wrote, 'The traditional verdict of inconsistency is in no way an inference about individuals; it is a statement about a disagreement between an investigator and a group of individuals and/or a disagreement among the individuals within the group' (1974: 510). They therefore expected to find consistency only for 'some of the people some of the time', and their data revealed greater cross-situational consistency for subjects who reported that they were consistent on the trait being studied than for subjects who reported that they were not consistent; that is, self-reported consistency served as a moderator variable for cross-situational consistency. The debate gradually faded during the 1980s, as the parties (re-) embraced an interactionist approach, with an associated emphasis on investigating correlates of isolated characteristics, particularly cognitive variables associated with social behavior (self-schemas, possible selves, explanatory styles and expectancies, etc.; see Leary, 2007; Mischel et al., 2004; Pervin et al., 2005), rather than comprehensive theories of personality.

Cognitive models

I next discuss two theorists – George Kelly and Julian Rotter – whose major works were published in the mid-1950s, and whose major influence today is largely indirect. This secondary status is unfortunate, as they anticipated the cognitive revolution in psychology and have important lessons to teach contemporary personality psychologists.

Kelly's (1955) approach was idiographic, with no taxonomy of enduring dispositions. Indeed, he believed that taxonomic labels reveal more about the person who uses them than the target who is rated with them. He rejected the concept of motivation, preferring to think of people as active by nature. He proposed that behavior reflects the way a person anticipates events, and a person anticipates events by 'construing their replications'; that is, individuals choose behavior based on what has happened before in situations that were appraised the same way. Appraisals are structured by relatively enduring bipolar tendencies called personal constructs. Like Allport, Kelly was interested in general principles that explain how uniqueness develops.

Kelly began with two assumptions. First, constructive alternativism reflected his belief that the fundamental difference among people is their alternative ways of construing the world; no way is right or wrong, but each way has different consequences. In addition, people can evolve different construct systems across time. Second, his analogy for understanding human behavior was the scientist. His 'man as scientist' assumption stated that people behave in their lives as scientists do in their labs; they formulate hypotheses about what will happen if they act a certain way, and the outcome provides data that support or disconfirm the prediction. A good scientist will revise hypotheses that are not supported, as will a healthy person; a neurotic person is like a bad scientist whose predictions are not validated but who is unwilling or unable to change them. Note the parallel with Piaget's contrast between assimilation and accommodation.

Kelly explained the nature and functioning of personal constructs in a fundamental postulate and eleven corollaries. For example, although the concept of dichotomous constructs seems not to conform to perception in gradations, Kelly described how dichotomous constructs could be used to form continuous scales. And his choice corollary states, 'A person chooses for himself that alternative in a dichotomized construct through which he anticipates the greater possibility for extension and definition (elaboration) of his system.' Confronting such 'elaborative choice', we are caught between a secure choice leading to a familiar action that minimally increases definition of the construct system, and an adventurous choice leading to substantial extension of the construct system.

Kelly's theory provided no apparent role for physiology, emotion, or the self. In addition, it is not clear to me how the experience and choice corollaries actually work or how we choose when we confront the dilemma of elaborative choice. Behavior is almost an afterthought – I am reminded of Guthrie's criticism that Tolman left the rat 'lost in thought' because he did not specify any relationship between expectancy and behavior. But there also are insights. For example, Kelly reconceptualized the unconscious in terms of a continuum of cognitive awareness: a person cannot be aware of preverbal constructs because they were formed before language with which to articulate the distinction was acquired, or one of the two poles that define a construct may be submerged. In contrast to Freud, it is structure rather than affect than leads to unawareness of material.

Kelly's constructs about change provide additional insight. For example, 'anxiety' occurs when one confronts an event that lies outside the range of convenience of the construct system, as with a traveler in a foreign country; anxiety occurs not when an event is traumatic, but when it is unknowable. But Kelly also caused confusion, as when he defined 'guilt' as the state that occurs when the self is dislodged from the person's core role structures; this is interesting, but paradoxical in the absence of any self-concept. Despite the omissions, Kelly's theory is provocative, as Walker and Winter (2007) demonstrate.

Rotter (1954) published the original cognitive social learning theory of personality.

His central concern was behavior potential: the probability that a person will engage in a particular behavior in a particular situation when a given reinforcer is available. He conceptualized this probability as a function of the person's expectancy that the behavior will lead to a particular reinforcer, plus the reinforcement value for that reinforcer. Furthermore, the situation is defined as the person perceives it, in terms of available cues and meanings (cf. Murray's beta press, Mischel's encodings and expectancies and beliefs, and Cervone's knowledge and appraisal beliefs).

Rotter also developed need potential to predict functionally related behaviors he called needs, such as dominance and independence. Need potential, or the likelihood of engaging in a set of related behaviors in a set of related situations for a set of reinforcers, was a function of the person's mean preference for a set of functionally related reinforcers (need value) plus the person's mean expectancy of obtaining positive satisfaction as a result of a set of related behaviors (freedom of movement). High freedom of movement thus means that a person believes behaviors will lead to desired outcomes in a particular domain. Note the similarity with Allport's definition of trait in terms of equivalent forms of behaviors that occur in functionally equivalent situations, as well as Bandura's self-efficacy expectations.

Rotter has important lessons to teach contemporary personality psychologists as they grapple with the relationship between generalized and specific personality constructs. He recognized that a person's overall expectancy combines specific expectancy in that particular situation plus relevant generalized expectancies. Furthermore, generalized expectancies are more important in novel or ambiguous situations where we have no available specific expectancies, and specific expectancies become more powerful the more experience we have in that specific instance. As a consequence, specific expectancies have greater predictive utility in the specific situation in which they apply, but they are useful only to the extent that we have experience in that situation; similarly, generalized expectancies have less predictive value in specific instances, but they are useful in a wide range of instances and apply when we lack relevant specific expectancies.

Walter Mischel's resolution

Mischel (1973, 1984) provided a conceptual response to his own challenge. He argued that what is stable and characteristic is not trait-linked behavior in general, but the person variables and resulting stable patterns of cross-situational variability that can be seen to characterize the individual only when behavior is examined in terms of the specific situations in which it occurs. Mischel thus shifted the focus from global, situation-free traits to situationally contingent dispositions. Echoing Allport, he expected consistent behavior across situations only to the extent that those situations are functionally equivalent in meaning. In the process, Mischel acknowledged his linkage with Allport's agenda of understanding the individual, although he did not emphasize the similarity between his if then signatures and Allport's definition of traits in terms of functional equivalence of situations based on perceived meaning (or Murray's serial thema).

Mischel noted the irony that personality psychologists reject the assumption, inherent in statistical tests of mean differences, that within-cell variability reflects only error variance; rather, they argue that between-subject variability on the dependent variable also reflects stable individual differences. When personality psychologists remove the situation by aggregating across situations, however, they make a parallel and equally problematic assumption. It is also ironic that classical psychometric theory assumes a true score that remains stable across items, but personality researchers employ correlations that ignore elevation and reflect only pattern covariation. Mischel argues that both elevation and shape of pattern profiles are important.

Mischel subsequently discovered a new paradox: people who report that they are consistent on a trait are seen by others as consistent, but their behavior is not cross-situationally consistent. Applying a cognitive prototype approach, Mischel and Peake (1982) proposed, 'The impression of consistency will derive not from average levels of consistency across all the possible features of the [trait] category but rather from the observation that some central features are reliably (stably) present' (Mischel, 1984: 357). That is, individuals' perception of cross-situational consistency is a mistaken generalization from the special case of temporal consistency on prototypic behaviors; therefore, Bem and Allen's self-reported consistency is seen as a dependent variable than a moderator variable. This work led Mischel and Shoda (1995, 1998, 1999; Mischel et al., 2002) to search for 'local consistencies' by proposing patterns of variability in terms of if then behavioral signatures of personality, as well as resulting unique and stable situation-behavior profiles, as the characteristic components of individual behavior.

Mischel proposed a cognitive-affective processing system (CAPS) as the framework of personality that accounts for if then signatures and the processes that produce them. The cognitive-affective units (CAUs), which 'include the person's construal and representations of the self, people, and situations, enduring goals, expectations-beliefs, and feeling states, as well as memories of people and past events' (2004: 11), are activated and organized by different psychological features of situations a person encounters. If then behavioral signatures are produced as the result. Furthermore, Mischel claimed,

Although cognitions and affects that are activated at a given time change, *how* they change, that is, the sequence and pattern of their activation, remains stable, reflecting the stable structure of the organization within the system. [The CAPS model] explicitly predicts, and can account for, the seeming inconsistencies in people's behaviors across situations that have so long been perplexing in the pursuit of the consistency of personality. (2004: 11)

This is a strong claim that at present remains a promissory note, similar to that implicit in Cattell's dynamic lattice and analogous to the currently unspecified dynamic processes in McCrae and Costa's five-factor theory.

Mischel also made the interesting suggestion that people use intuitive if then theories in impression formation; for example, rather than conclude that another is extraverted, they conclude that if someone needs to make a good impression, then that person acts friendly. Bem and Allen made the similar point that our intuitions 'operate on idiographic rather than nomothetic assumptions'. When asked to characterize another person, 'We do not first impose a trait term and then modify it by describing the instances which fail to fall into that equivalence class. Rather, we attempt first to organize his behavior into rational sets and only then to label them' (1974: 510). Mischel also wrote, 'The key for achieving generalizability is to identify psychological features of situations that play a functional role in the generation of behaviors' (2004: 15). This is a good point, which Murray addressed with the construct of press.

Mischel's CAPS model, along with the similar knowledge-and-appraisal personality architecture (KAPA) model proposed by Cervone (2004, 2005), provides a promising integration across contrasts that have often been seen as incompatible, such as structure versus dynamics and consistency versus variability. Cervone also makes a strong argument that within-person and between-person approaches require different variables. Murray addressed the same point, but he argued that thema and cathexes are related to needs and press; similarly, Cattell proposed that attitudes characterize individuals, but they express the ergs and sentiments that permit between-person comparisons. Regarding these two approaches as complementary rather than adversarial seems possible given Rotter's recognition that familiarity with a specific situation determines reliance on specific rather than generalized expectancies, as well as Moskowitz's (1982) demonstration of the trade-off between specific predictive accuracy and broad predictive utility. Finally, Mischel wrote that personality is the discipline charged to integrate findings that 'speak to the coherence and organization of the individual' (2004: 18). I agree that whatever theory (or theories) of personality ultimately emerge will incorporate this perspective.

Trend 4: Toward an integrative resolution

There has been cumulative progress within historical trends; in addition, personality psychology is moving toward integrative theories that address personality at multiple levels while incorporating (a) structure and dynamics; (b) stability and change; and (c) individual persons as well as between group differences, as complementary rather than inconsistent realities. But this emerging integration was made possible only as a result of what we have learned across the past 107 years. 'There was wisdom in the ancients', as Cervone (2005: 430) said in a different context, so we must continue to mine and acknowledge these valuable antecedents. Recent textbooks of personality (McAdams, 2006; Mischel et al., 2004) champion this integrative approach. Our challenge is to formulate a cohesive theory that provides an integrative framework for insights reached during the first three trends.

Dan McAdams

McAdams (1995, 1996a, 1996b, 1999) provides an excellent example of this integrative approach. He stipulated that the goal of personality psychology is to study individual persons, and he proposed that it is most useful to address individuality from three different vantage points. Level 1 entails dispositional traits that are non-conditional, decontextualized, and implicitly comparative dimensions, such as the Big Five. Traits are useful in providing a basic 'first read' of other people, in that they capture average tendencies across a range of settings, and they can be useful in making between-person distinctions. Traits, however, are not sufficient, because they fail to capture the temporal and spatial contingencies of individual behavior, or the integration and cohesion that flow from a person's sense of identity. Level 2, therefore, addresses personal concerns that are contextualized and contingent on time, place, or role. This level captures what individuals want and what strategies they employ; it includes motives, defenses, plans, and goals. The defining feature of such constructs is that they are specific rather than general – they depend on and systematically vary across circumstances. McAdams agrees that his person concerns are similar to McCrae and Costa's characteristic adaptations, but he makes the distinction that his level 2 variables are loosely related to but not necessarily derivatives of level 1 traits; they are 'conceptually and epistemologically independent' of traits (1995: 386), in contrast to the five-factor theory. There may be linkages, but McAdams argues that they should be 'established empirically rather than assumed' (1995: 380). Level 2 can subsume Mischel's if then behavioral signatures, intellectual ancestors such as Murray's thema, and the proliferation of specific dimensions.

Level 3 addresses identity as a narrative life story that synthesizes behavior and provides unity and purpose in a person's life. A life story is an adult's attempt to 'construe his or her life in narrative terms with the implicit goal of creating an internalized story of the self that binds together the reconstructed past, perceived present, and anticipated future in such a way as to confer upon adult life a sense of unity and purpose' (1999: 485). McAdams noted parallels with Erikson's identity, and he suggested that Erikson's 'eight psychosocial stages may be viewed as successive chapters in a generic story of human life' (1999: 483) with basic crises as plot lines. There also is similarity with the integrating function of Allport's proprium. And the model affords a home within levels 2 and 3 for personality dynamics and conflict characteristic of the first trend. The great strength of McAdams' model is that it provides a generic structure that can subsume many of the insights from earlier models while permitting both within-person understanding and between-person comparison.

GAINS, LOSSES, AND GOALS

Gains

What have we gained? Although personality psychology lost its comprehensive orientation and focus on the person during the 1970s, it gained a stronger empirical commitment and a wealth of information about specific dimensions. Furthermore, many of the controversies that earlier commentators such as Pervin (2002) identified now are moot or resolved: Personality psychologists use multiple motives and recognize that the proper question is not person versus situation, but how the two interact. We have genetic, evolutionary, and neuropsychological tools that might now permit Freud to continue to operate within neuroscience (see Kandel's, 2006, autobiography). Unconscious processes are studied across psychology, and psychoanalytic theory has evolved in terms of parallel processes, cultural forces, and broader motivational models. We have learned that specific tendencies are not incompatible with global or aggregate dimensions, but that the two serve different purposes and can be linked via the individual's experience in the specific situation. The idiographic – nomothetic dichotomy is seen as more a matter of levels of analysis and emphasis than incompatibility. We recognize that personality not only interacts with the environment but also structures our perceptions. The question of self and identity remains perplexing, but McAdams demonstrates that it can be incorporated into a cohesive theory.

Losses

What have we lost? We know more and more about smaller and smaller behaviors, but we have lost sight of how this knowledge fits together to explain the behavior of individuals, and we no longer care to know. We have little allegiance to Hall and Lindzey's principle that 'an adequate understanding of human behavior will evolve only from the study of the whole person' (1957: 6). We are assisting the rest of psychology to find individual differences on specific behaviors, but we have repudiated our original identity as the branch of psychology that focuses on the organism as a whole. We no longer care about the 'enduring themes and problems of human existence' (Monte and Sollod, 2003: 654), attention to which explains why interest in theorists in the first trend will not go away. Early theories 'raced far ahead of data' (Baumeister and Tice, 1996: 367), but we have lost their window on individual dynamics in the face of life's dilemmas. We are becoming increasingly unfamiliar with our intellectual ancestors and the insightful leads their work contains. We began with global, top-down global theories, then turned during the second half of the twentieth century to specific, bottom-up models. In the process, we have forgotten Murray's and Eysenck's lessons about levels of analysis and connections between the levels.

Goals

And how should we proceed? The unique challenge for personality psychology is to formulate a cohesive theory that provides a framework to understand individuals. Personality psychology has the difficult task of providing an integrated explanation for all three of Murray's levels – how the individual is like all other individuals (human nature and dynamic processes; trend 1), like some other individuals (taxonomy of between-person individual differences; trend 2), and like no one else (within-person structure;

trends 1, 2, and 3). It must accomplish all of this within a cohesive theory that explains origins of the various characteristics and specifies how the levels are related; in addition, its major propositions must be amenable to empirical disconfirmation.

McAdams (1997) made the similar point that Allport's and Murray's aspirations for personality psychology to provide a coherent understanding of individuals have not been realized. Early global theories 'have not proven adequate to the task, though they continue to provide insights and guidelines'. Personality psychology 'still suffers from the lack of a persuasive integrative framework for understanding the person as a differentiated and integrated dynamic whole living in a complex social context'. Until we generate candidates to replace the grand theories we have rejected, personality psychology 'will fall somewhat short of fulfilling the promise of its pioneers' (1997: 28–9).

Mischel, McCrae and Costa, and especially McAdams (e.g., McAdams and Pals, 2006) provide integrative frameworks that address different levels of personality and provide a framework for contributions from earlier theories and contemporary research. These theories are far from complete, but they offer promise for comprehensive personality theories that account for within-person organization as well as between-person comparison. Just as we now hold personality theories to rigorous standards of evidence, so we must also expect those who work with individual dimensions to identify not only effect sizes, but also causal chains, developmental processes, and correlates with established variables. Work on individual dimensions is an important part of personality psychology's larger agenda, but we must find ways to foster and reward integrative theorizing.

I end where I began, with Gould and Allport. The promise I see in this new brand of theory is that personality psychology will develop a framework to bring specific findings back to the person, in the process of describing how individual personalities are built by complex histories.

REFERENCES

Allport, G.W. (1937) *Personality: A Psychological Interpretation*. New York: Holt.

Allport, G.W. (1961) *Pattern and Growth in Personality*. New York: Holt, Rinehart & Winston.

Bandura, A. (1999) 'Social cognitive theory of personality', in L.A. Pervin and O.P. John (eds), *Handbook of Personality: Theory and Research* (2nd edn). New York: Guilford, pp. 154–96.

Bandura, A. (2000) 'Exercise of human agency through collective efficacy', *Current Directions in Psychological Science*, 9(3): 75–8.

Bandura, A. (2001) 'Social cognitive theory: An agentic perspective', *Annual Review of Psychology*, 52: 1–26.

Bandura, A. (2006) 'Toward a psychology of human agency', *Perspectives on Psychological Science*, 1(2): 164–80.

Baumeister, R. (1999) 'On the interface between personality and social psychology', in L.A. Pervin and O.P. John (eds), *Handbook of Personality* (2nd edn). New York: Guilford, pp. 367–77.

Baumeister, R. and Tice, D.M. (1996) 'Rethinking and reclaiming the interdisciplinary role of personality psychology: The science of human nature should be the center of the social sciences and humanities', *Journal of Research in Personality*, 30(3): 363–73.

Bem, D.J. and Allen, A. (1974) 'On predicting some of the people some of the time: The search for cross-situational consistencies in behavior', *Psychological Review*, 81(6): 506–20.

Block, J. (1995) 'A contrarian view of the five-factor approach to personality description', *Psychological Bulletin*, 117(2): 187–215.

Bowers, K.S. (1973) 'Situationism in psychology: An analysis and a critique', *Psychological Review*, 80(5): 307–36.

Carlson, R. (1992) 'Shrinking personality: One cheer for the Big Five', *Contemporary Psychology*, 37(7): 644–5.

Cattell, R.B. (1979) *Personality and Learning Theory, Vol. 1: The Structure of Personality in its Environment*. New York: Springer.

Cattell, R.B. (1980) *Personality and Learning Theory, Vol. 2: A Systems Theory of Maturation and Structured Learning*. New York: Springer.

Cattell, R.B. (1982) *The Inheritance of Personality and Ability: Research Methods and Findings*. New York: Academic.

Cattell, R.B. (1983) *Structured Personality-Learning Theory: A Wholistic Multivariate Research Approach*. New York: Praeger.

Cattell, R.B. (1985) *Human Motivation and the Dynamic Calculus*. New York: Praeger.

Cattell, R.B. (1990) 'Advances in Cattellian personality theory', in L.A. Pervin (ed.), *Handbook of Personality: Theory and Research*. New York: Guilford, pp. 101–10.

Cattell, R.B. and Dreger, R.M. (1978) (eds), *Handbook of Modern Personality Theory*. New York: Wiley.

Cattell, R.B. and Kline, P. (1977) *The Scientific Analysis of Personality and Motivation*. New York: Academic Press.

Cattell, R.B. and Nesselroade, J.R. (1988) (eds), *Handbook of Multivariate Experimental Psychology* (2nd edn). New York: Plenum.

Cervone, D. (2004) 'The architecture of personality', *Psychological Review*, 111(1): 183–204.

Cervone, D. (2005) 'Personality architecture: Within-person structures and processes', *Annual Review of Psychology*, 56: 423–52.

Costa, P.T. Jr., McCrae, R.R. and Dye, D.A. (1991) 'Facet scales for Agreeableness and Conscientiousness: A revision of the NEO Personality Inventory', *Personality and Individual Differences*, 12(9): 887–98.

Digman, J.M. (1990) 'Personality structure: Emergence of the five-factor model', *Annual Review of Psychology*, 41: 417–40.

Epstein, S. (1979) 'The stability of behavior: 1. On predicting most of the people much of the time', *Journal of Personality and Social Psychology*, 37(7): 1097–126.

Eysenck, H.J. (1967) *The Biological Basis of Personality*. Springfield, IL: Charles C. Thomas.

Erikson, E.H. (1963) *Childhood and Society* (2nd edn). New York: W.W. Norton & Co.

Erikson, E.H. (1982) *The Life Cycle Completed*. New York: W.W. Norton & Co.

Eysenck, H.J. (1957) *The Dynamics of Anxiety and Hysteria: An Experimental Application of Modern Learning Theory to Psychiatry*. London: Routledge & Kegan Paul.

Eysenck, H.J. (1981) 'General features of the model', in H.J. Eysenck (ed.), *A Model for Personality*. Berlin: Springer, pp. 1–37.

Eysenck, H.J. (1988) Dimensions of Personality. New Brunswick, NJ: Transaction Publishers.

Eysenck, H.J. (1990) 'Biological dimensions of personality', in L.A. Pervin (ed.), *Handbook of Personality: Theory and Research*. New York: Guilford, pp. 244–76.

Eysenck, H.J. (1994a) 'Personality and intelligence: Psychometric and experimental approaches', in R.J. Sternberg and P. Ruzgis (eds), Personality and Intelligence. New York: Cambridge University Press, pp. 3–31.

Eysenck, H.J. (1994b) 'Personality: Biological foundations', in P.A. Vernon (ed.), *The Neuropsychology of Individual Differences*. San Diego: Academic, pp. 151–207.

Eysenck, H.J. (1997) 'Personality and experimental psychology: The unification of psychology and the possibility of a paradigm', *Journal of Personality and Social Psychology*, 73(6): 1224–37.

Eysenck, H.J. and Eysenck, M.W. (1985) *Personality and Individual Differences: A Natural Science Approach*. New York: Plenum Press.

Eysenck, H.J. and Eysenck, S.B.G. (1976) *Psychoticism as a Dimension of Personality*. New York: Crane, Russak.

Fowles, D.C. (2006) 'Jeffrey Gray's contributions to theories of anxiety, personality, and psychopathology', in T. Canli (ed.), *Biology of Personality and Individual Differences*. New York: Guilford, pp. 7–34.

Freud, S. (1953) 'The interpretation of dreams', in J. Strachey (ed.), *The Standard Edition of the Complete Psychological Works* (Vols. 4 and 5). London: Hogarth. (First German edn, 1900).

Funder, D.C. and Ozer, D.J. (1983) 'Behavior as a function of the situation', *Journal of Personality and Social Psychology*, 44(1): 107–12.

Goldberg, L.R. (1981) 'Language and individual differences: The search for universals in personality lexicons', in L. Wheeler (ed.), *Review of Personality and Social Psychology* (Vol. 2). Beverly Hills, CA: Sage, pp. 141–65.

Goldberg, L.R. (1990) 'An alternative "description of personality": The Big-Five factor structure', *Journal of Personality and Social Psychology*, 59(6): 1216–29.

Goldberg, L.R. (1993) 'The structure of phenotypic personality traits', *American Psychologist*, 48(1): 26–34.

Gould, S.J. (1989) 'The horn of Triton', *Natural History*, December: 18–27.

Gray, J.A. (1981) 'A critique of Eysenck's theory of personality', in H.J. Eysenck (ed.), *A Model for Personality*. Berlin: Springer, pp. 246–76.

Gray, J.A. (1982) *The Neuropsychology of Anxiety: An Inquiry into the Functions of the Septal-Hippocampal System*. Oxford: Clarendon.

Hall, C.S. and Lindzey, G. (1957) *Theories of Personality*. New York: John Wiley & Sons, Inc.

Harms, P.D., Roberts, B.W. and Winter, D. (2006) 'Becoming the Harvard man: Person–environment fit, personality development, and academic success', *Personality and Social Psychology Bulletin*, 32(7): 851–65.

Hogan, R.T. (1997) 'Preface', in R. Hogan, J. Johnson and S. Briggs (eds), *Handbook of Personality Psychology*. San Diego: Academic Press, pp. xxiii–xxiv.

John, O.P. (1990) 'The "Big Five" factor taxonomy: Dimensions of personality in the natural language and in questionnaires', in L.A. Pervin (ed.), *Handbook of Personality: Theory and Research*. New York: Guilford, pp. 66–100.

John, O.P. and Srivastava, S. (1999) 'The Big Five taxonomy: History, measurement, and theoretical perspectives', in L.A. Pervin and O.P. John (eds), *Handbook of Personality: Theory and Research* (2nd edn). New York: Guilford, pp. 102–38.

Kandel, E.R. (2006) *In Search of Memory: The Emergence of a New Science of Mind*. New York: Norton.

Kelly, G.A. (1955) *The Psychology of Personal Constructs*. New York: Norton.

Kluckhohn, C. and Murray, H.A. (1953) 'Personality formation: The determinants', in C. Kluckhohn, H.A. Murray and D. Schneider (eds), *Personality in Nature, Society, and Culture* (2nd edn). New York: Alfred A. Knopf, pp. 53–67.

Leary, M.R. (2007) 'Motivational and emotional aspects of the self', *Annual Review of Psychology*, 58: 317–44.

Loevinger, J. (1994) 'Has psychology lost its conscience?' *Journal of Personality Assessment*, 62: 2–8.

McAdams, D.P. (1992) 'The five-factor model in personality: A critical appraisal', *Journal of Personality*, 60(2): 329–61.

McAdams, D.P. (1994) 'A psychology of the stranger', *Psychological Inquiry*, 5: 145–8.

McAdams, D.P. (1995) 'What do we know when we know a person?', *Journal of Personality*, 63(3): 365–96.

McAdams, D.P. (1996a) 'Personality, modernity, and the storied self: A contemporary framework for studying persons', *Psychological Inquiry*, 7(4): 295–321.

McAdams, D.P. (1996b) 'Alternative futures for the study of human individuality', *Journal of Research in Personality*, 30(3): 374–88.

McAdams, D.P. (1997) 'A conceptual history of personality psychology', in R. Hogan, J. Johnson and S. Briggs (eds), *Handbook of Personality Psychology*. San Diego: Academic Press, pp. 3–39.

McAdams D.P. (1999) 'Personal narratives and the life story', in L.A. Pervin and O.P. John (eds), *Handbook of Personality: Theory and Research* (2nd edn). New York: Guilford, pp. 478–500.

McAdams, D.P. (2006) *The Person: A New Introduction to Personality Psychology* (4th edn). New York: John Wiley & Sons.

McAdams, D.P. and Pals, J.L. (2006) 'A new Big Five: Fundamental principles for an integrative science of personality', *American Psychologist*, 61(3): 204–17.

McCrae, R.R. and Costa, P.T. Jr. (1987) 'Validation of the five-factor model of personality across instruments and observers', *Journal of Personality and Social Psychology*, 52(1): 81–90.

McCrae, R.R. and Costa, P.T. Jr. (1990) *Personality in Adulthood*. New York: Guilford.

McCrae, R.R. and Costa, P.T. Jr. (1996) 'Toward a new generation of personality theories: Theoretical contexts for the five-factor model', in J. Wiggins (ed.), *The Five-Factor Model of Personality: Theoretical Perspectives*. New York: Guilford, pp. 51–87.

McCrae, R.R. and Costa, P.T. Jr. (1999) 'A five-factor theory of personality', in L.A. Pervin and O.P. John (eds), *Handbook of Personality: Theory and Research* (2nd edn). New York: Guilford, pp. 139–53.

Meehl, P.E. (1978) 'Theoretical risks and tabular asterisks: Sir Karl, Sir Ronald, and the slow progress of soft psychology', *Journal of*

Consulting and Clinical Psychology, 46(4): 806–34.

Mischel, W. (1968) *Personality and Assessment*. New York: Wiley.

Mischel, W. (1973) 'Toward a cognitive social learning reconceptualization of personality', *Psychological Review*, 80(4): 252–83.

Mischel, W. (1984) 'Convergences and challenges in the search for consistency', *American Psychologist*, 39(4): 351–64.

Mischel, W. (2004) 'Toward an integrative science of the person', *Annual Review of Psychology*, 55: 1–22.

Mischel, W. (2005) 'Alternative futures for our science', *APS Observer*, 18(3): 15–19.

Mischel, W. and Peake, P.K. (1982) 'Beyond déjà vu in the search for cross-situational consistency', *Psychological Review*, 89(6): 730–55.

Mischel, W. and Shoda, Y. (1995) 'A cognitive-affective system theory of personality; Reconceptualizing situations, dispositions, dynamics, and invariance in personality structure', *Psychological Review*, 102(2): 246–68.

Mischel, W. and Shoda, Y. (1998) 'Reconciling processing dynamics and personality dispositions', *Annual Review of Psychology*, 49: 229–58.

Mischel, W. and Shoda, Y. (1999) 'Integrating dispositions and processing dynamics within a unified theory of personality: The cognitive-affective personality system', in L.A. Pervin and O.P. John (eds), *Handbook of Personality* (2nd edn). New York: Guilford, pp. 197–218.

Mischel, W., Shoda, Y. and Mendoza-Denton, R. (2002) 'Situation-behavior profiles as a locus of consistency in personality', *Current Directions in Psychological Science*, 11(2): 50–4.

Mischel, W., Shoda, Y. and Smith, R.E. (2004) *Introduction to Personality: Toward an Integration* (7th edn). New York: John Wiley & Sons.

Monte, C.F. and Sollod, R.N. (2003) *Beneath the Mask: An Introduction to Theories of Personality* (7th edn). New York: John Wiley & Sons.

Moskowitz, D.S. (1982) 'Coherence and cross-situational generality in personality: A new analysis of old problems', *Journal of Personality and Social Psychology*, 43(4): 754–68.

Murray, H.A. (and collaborators) (1938) *Explorations in Personality*. New York: Oxford University Press.

Norman, W.T. (1963) 'Toward an adequate taxonomy of personality attributes: Replicated factor structure in peer nomination personality ratings', *Journal of Abnormal and Social Psychology*, 66(6): 574–83.

Ozer, D.J. and Benet-Martinez, V. (2006) 'Personality and the prediction of consequential outcomes', *Annual Review of Psychology*, 57: 401–21.

Paunonen, S.V. (2003) 'Big Five factors of personality and replicated predictions of behavior', *Journal of Personality and Social Psychology*, 84(2): 411–22.

Pervin, L.A. (1991) 'A brief history of modern personality theory', in L.A. Pervin (ed.), *Handbook of Personality: Theory and Research*. New York: Guilford, pp. 3–18.

Pervin, L.A. (2002) *Current Controversies and Issues in Personality* (3rd edn). New York: John Wiley & Sons.

Pervin, L.A., Cervone, D. and John, O.P. (2005) *Personality: Theory and Research* (9th edn). New York: John Wiley & Sons.

Pickering, A.D. and Gray, J.A. (1999) 'The neuroscience of personality', in L.A. Pervin and O.P. John (eds), *Handbook of Personality* (2nd edn). New York: Guilford, pp. 277–99.

Rogers, C.R. (1959) 'A theory of therapy personality, and interpersonal relationships, as developed in the client-centered framework', in S. Koch (ed.), *Psychology: A Study of a Science* (Vol. 3). New York: McGraw-Hill, pp. 184–256.

Rogers, C.R. (1961). *On Becoming a Person*. Boston: Houghton Mifflin.

Rotter, J.B. (1954) *Social Learning and Clinical Psychology*. Englewood Cliffs, NJ: Prentice-Hall.

Silverman, L.H. (1976) 'Psychoanalytic theory: "The reports of my death are greatly exaggerated"', *American Psychologist*, 31(9): 621–37.

Smith, M.B. (2005) '"Personality and social psychology": Retrospections and aspirations', *Personality and Social Psychology Review*, 9(4): 334–40.

Stelmack, R.M. (2004) (ed.), *On the Psychobiology of Personality: Essays in Honor of Marvin Zuckerman*. Oxford: Elsevier.

Tupes, E.C. and Christal, R.E. (1961) Recurrent personality factors based on trait ratings', USAF ASD Tech. Rep. No. 61-97. Lackland Air Force Base, TX: US Air Force. (Reprinted in *Journal of Personality*, 1992, 60(2): 225–51.)

Walker, B.M. and Winter, D.A. (2007) 'The elaboration of personality construct psychology', *Annual Review of Psychology*, 58: 453–77.

Westen, D. (1995) 'A clinical-empirical model of personality: Life after the Mischellian Ice Age and the Neolithic era', *Journal of Personality*, 63(3): 495–524.

Westen, D. (1998) 'The scientific legacy of Sigmund Freud: Toward a psychodynamically informed psychological science', *Psychological Bulletin*, 124(3): 333–71.

White, R.W. (1960) 'Competence and the psychosexual stages of development', *The Nebraska Symposium on Motivation*, 8: 97–141.

White, R.W. (1981) 'Exploring personality the long way: The study of lives', in A.L. Rabin, J. Aronoff, A.M. Barclay and R.A. Rucker (eds), *Further Explorations in Personality*. New York: Wiley, pp. 3–19.

Zuckerman, M. (1979) *Sensation Seeking: Beyond the Optimal Level of Arousal*. Hillsdale, NJ: Erlbaum.

Zuckerman, M. (1991) *Psychobiology of Personality*. Cambridge, UK: Cambridge University Press.

Zuckerman, M. (2006) 'Biological bases of sensation seeking', in T. Canli (ed.), *Biology of Personality and Individual Differences*. New York: Guilford, pp. 37–59.

PART II

Comprehensive Trait Models

10

Eysenck's Model of Individual Differences

Kieron P. O'Connor

INTRODUCTION

Hans Eysenck made many pioneering contributions to clinical, experimental, social, political, criminal, developmental, genetic, health and aesthetic psychology, although his best-known work was in personality psychology. These rich diverse contributions are clearly testament to his extensive intellect and enquiring mind, but a closer look at his writings reveals a consistent and systematic approach to unravelling behaviour in all these domains and which I shall term the individual difference paradigm (IDP). There are three pillars to this paradigm. First, adoption of a dimensional approach to quantifying individual characteristics; second, that a sufficient understanding requires a matching of correlational and experimental methods to be complete; and third, that accounting for person–situation variation is the key to building causal models of behaviour. Each of these three pillars may require a different emphasis depending on the maturity of the subject area but the principle IDP message is that methods of observation and quantification should be set up to accommodate individual differences and where this is not

explicitly done, valuable information and predictive power will be lost (see Figure 10.1).

In the initial part of this chapter I will focus on support for the main principles of the IDP and selectively chart its evolution and application in diverse areas, initially drawing principally on Eysenck and co-workers' own work. I will then discuss more recent methodological issues in IDP research and the development of new constructs. I will focus on how the IDP facilitates translational research between theory and practice, research and clinic with particular reference to Eysenck's concern for the IDP to move between correlational and experimental areas. Finally, I will end with recommendations for future application of the IDP, particularly with respect to exploring non-traditional methods of analysis more suitable to unravelling individual differences.

THE PERSON AS A DIMENSION

Eysenck's early ambition was to place psychology on an empirical footing and for him this was synonymous with developing

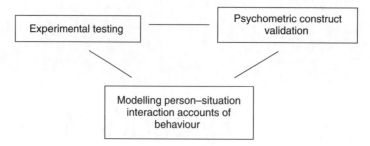

Figure 10.1   Three arms of the individual difference paradigm

quantitative methods that allowed observed variations to be assessed with robust statistical procedures (Eysenck, 1952a). Use of empirical methods has since become a distinguishing hallmark in the advance of scientific psychology.

Based on the observable fact that human physical attributes (height, weight, etc.) are normally distributed, psychological traits, if they existed in different degrees in different people, should also be normally distributed. Hence any meaningful psychological construct could be formally operationalized in dimensional terms, if it was to be successfully quantifiable. Invariant characteristics were either uninformative or awaiting finer scrutiny. Operationalizing variables along quantifiable dimensions groups together disparate characteristics as different expressions of a single continuum. (Eysenck, 1947,1998) first book, *Dimensions of Personality,* elaborated the use of factor analysis to look for communalities that might parsimoniously explain disparate performance in terms of more general personality factors. Factor analysis groups scores that represent identifiably distinct groupings along a quantitative dimension. Typically, measures will have some characteristics in common and others unique (Cattell, 1952, 1978). If the same factor covers all variables, it is a general factor. A common factor is a factor shared by at least two variables. A group factor is a factor common to a specific group of variables, and a unique factor is unique to one variable. Factor analysis hence permits a set of

variables or people to be grouped together to share common and general associations while retaining their individuality – a bit like an ideal society!

Of course, the person is multidimensional, and it is unusual that one factor will account for complex behaviours. But knowing that an underlying pattern of behaviour is typical of one person but not another, and that this pattern may influence a range of abilities, is key to understanding individual differences. But these person variables are not static. In viewing the person as the fundamental unit and starting point for psychology, the IDP provides a firm basis for understanding the many diverse and dynamic, even contradictory behaviours a person may perform over time and situation. Since behind all the variable actions and reactions there is always a person, and a person–world interaction.

THE DIMENSION AS A CONSTRUCT

The notion of a dimension forces a finite range of scores within a theoretical and empirically sound construct. But there are procedures to follow to ensure a dimension is correctly identified. Whereas physical dimensions (height, weight, etc) may be directly observable, psychological characteristics along the same psychological construct may manifest themselves in distinctive ways. Eysenck adopted the method of taking disparate performance measures and looking for communalities that might parsimoniously explain common underlying latent factors. Although there are different schools of thought on optimal factor extraction, using orthogonal rotation optimizes factor interpretation, and it is important that a factor represents enough items on an explicit as well as an implicit pole by containing negative and positive loadings. However, in this case the opposite pole must make logical and empirical sense and not just be intuitively meaningful. On an anecdotal level, I well remember debates at dinner with Hans Eysenck concerning his dissatisfaction with the sweet–dry dimension of white wine which he would insist should be replaced by the more logical sweet–sour dimension, much to the consternation of the wine waiter.

A construct dimension once identified need not be unidimensional in the strict statistical sense of possessing a unit rank matrix. Indeed Eysenck recognized that for a dimension to form a strong construct, it needed to be composed of lesser-order primary factors, rather as intelligence (g) was a second-order factor in Guilford's original analysis (Eysenck, 1977a) since this gave the construct the application over distinct domains. A higher-order construct necessarily has lower-order constructs applicable to distinct behaviours. For example, extraversion may be divided into sociability and impulsive components. The impulsive dimension (Eysenck and Eysenck, 1985) itself may be further subdivided into narrow impulsiveness, venturousness and empathy subcomponents. These subcomponents in turn are likely to relate differentially to motor and cognitive functions (Miller et al., 2003).

There are of course pitfalls to factor analysis which have been ably outlined by Kline (1992). One objection to the factor analysis method is that there is no test of significance for factors. Rotational procedures are just convenient algorithms, not scientific formulae. Confirmatory analysis using model fitting has partly alleviated this problem but chi-square estimates are biased by sample size and it is sometimes difficult to define a target matrix. Also, different factors may emerge across samples simply because there may be more variance in traits with one or another sample.

GROUPING DIMENSIONAL SCORES

A dimensional approach is compatible with a categorical grouping of scores into separate identifiable groups. This approach is useful for testing specific hypotheses concerning different performance between groups, but it can also serve to reduce variance in order to enhance effect size. Such grouping is particularly useful to test experimental manipulation and converting dimensions into groups is usually achieved by one of four methods.

The first method was that proposed by Eysenck (1950) himself in what he considered his only major statistical contribution (and he was proud of it!). The statistical method was 'criterion analysis' and in this method a quantitative psychometric dimension is considered alongside a criterion for, say, clinical classification. Eysenck's suggestion for deriving a unique invariant and psychologically meaningful solution was to rotate the first factor analytic centroid factor into a position of maximum correlation with the criterion column. People included in the analysis are given scores according to which group they belong, and the criterion variable is biserially correlated with other continuous experimentally derived measures. According to Cattell (1952, 1978), criterion analyses should be more properly called criterion rotation as it is a form of peripheral validation which gives additional meaning to an established factor. Criterion analysis also allows the option of including several experimental measures, thereby establishing their factor composition. Indeed, rotation may reveal several criterion factors collinear with the group variable.

A second alternative to permit subtyping of group membership is the use of cluster analysis. The cluster analysis may reveal distinct groups of participants. This method has been used extensively in the subtyping of clinical groups within a dimension. For example, Calamari et al. (2004) have shown how qualitatively distinct groupings can emerge from symptomatology. However, a limitation is that the relationship between correlationally derived clusters is not always clear and some clusters may represent several factors.

However, a more satisfactory method of classification for groups is taxonometric analysis developed by Paul Meehl and associates and termed 'the coherent cut kinetics method' (Meehl, 2001; Waller and Meehl, 1998). This method tests whether a construct exists as a discrete class versus a continuum. The basic premises of the coherent cut method is that if true classes exist, indicators of the groupings should be correlated only when the sample contains all groupings since indices of group differences will not be correlated within just one group. The key here is to identify at least two indicator variables which are related only due to their discrimination of the two latent classes. Hence the point of 'cut-off' of one variable on the other that consistently yields the largest mean difference is the point which separates the sample into distinct groups. The approach has been applied to investigate a number of clinical, social and personality groups since it reliably indicates taxonicity when there are classes of variables, but not where there is dimensionality (for a review see Arnau et al., 2003).

The fourth and (least satisfactory) way to group continuous scores is by mid-point (median; mean) split. The problem here is that the cut-off may include a middle group qualitatively distinct from the two outlying groups. For example, ambiverts show distinct responses to extraverts and introverts on various measures and so a median split on this personality measure may easily mask differences between groups. As a case in point, Luciano et al. (2006) reported distinct arousal and intelligence relationships in

ambiverts as opposed to introverts and extraverts. Obviously in the absence of other criteria, a median split may be acceptable or the sample could be divided on the basis of three or more percentile cut-off points.

Comparison of group types will not necessarily yield the same results or the same significance obtained using correlational analysis. Correlational analysis, particularly on large numbers, is likely to inflate relationships, whereas a more accurate picture of the relationship might come from group comparison. Conversely, typologies may oversimplify the relation between a construct and a criterion (Pittenger, 2004). As a good illustration, a recent study by Julien et al. (2006) looking at the relationship between belief domains and obsessional symptomatology, showed that correlational and categorical approaches yielded different results. Furthermore, a process relationship between dimensions does not establish this process as a difference attributable to types. Again, in the Julien et al. (2006) study, the finding that perfectionism correlated with severity of obsessional checking symptoms did not imply that overall those in the checking subtype were more perfectionist than normal. The safest route to ensure a smooth passage from correlational grouping to subtype grouping lies through establishing a robust construct with empirically derived attributes underlying the grouping.

DIMENSIONAL VERSUS CATEGORICAL THINKING

Much current psychological thinking is now associated with dimensional approaches where behaviour is considered a continuum. It is hard to think back now to a time when such approaches were revolutionary and very much against the grain of categorical and sometimes dogmatic classification. One can still catch the flavour of such a categorical approach in the diagnostic and statistical manual (e.g. DSM-IV) (APA, 2000) of psychiatric diagnostic nosology. Here one clearly sees the loss of information in trying to categorize a person into a solitary standalone slot when the problem should be viewed multidimensionally. For example, some symptoms of depressive disorder (e.g. lack of self-worth, anhedonia, hopelessness) are themselves dimensional constructs and could, in different degrees, reflect distinct clinical states. Such behavioural or psychological dimensions can show an explanatory power greater than diagnostic category. For example, the dimensional trait of neuroticism cuts across the diagnostic boundaries and accounts for distress and adaptation more reliably than nosological classification (Stewart et al., 2005). Ambwani et al. (2006) showed that neuroticism fully mediates the relationship between borderline personality features and bulimic symptomatology. Clarke (2004) has shown how neuroticism partially mediates the relationship between loss of control and depression. Our own studies have indicated that neuroticism better predicts withdrawal distress than psychiatric diagnoses (O'Connor et al., 1999).

In recent years, the construct of neuroticism has been shown to partially or fully mediate:

1 cognitive abilities including attention, control (Muris et al., 2004), attentional bias, error detection (Schell et al., 2005), intelligence (Moutafi et al., 2006), cognitive failure (Wallace, 2004), marital satisfaction (Bouchard et al., 1999), goal directedness, general knowledge (Chamonro-Premuzic et al., 2006), procedural learning (Corr, 2003);
2 pathological states such as depression (Chioqueta and Stiles, 2005), fantasy proneness (Sanchez-Bernardos and Avia, 2004), sadness (Stewart et al., 2005), well-being (Austin, 2005), loss of control (Clarke, 2004), difficulty coping, smoking dependence (Munafo et al., 2004), alexithymia (De Gucht et al., 2004), anxiety (Gomez and Francis, 2003), test anxiety (Moutafi et al., 2006), rumination (Muris et al., 2004).

Neuroticism has also been consistently related to central psychophysiological markers such as regional brain activity (Minnix and Kline, 2004), alpha rhythms (Knyazev et al., 2004) and event-related cortical potentials (De Pascalis et al., 2004). To the author's knowledge there is no diagnostic categorical variable that can boast such a powerful and comprehensive predictive value.

The importance of a dimensional approach is firstly that it forces the clinician to specify criteria for deciding that a phenomenon is both necessary and sufficient to characterize a disorder and is present in what degree. Second, a dimensional approach leads readily to understanding the processes involved in producing, say, anxiety, since the problem is viewed as a more extreme form of a 'normal' phenomenon. This view not only 'normalizes' the phenomenon for the clinician and the patient, but it encourages the researcher to consider 'analogue' experimental studies which test hypotheses about events or contexts which might 'abnormalize' the normal experience; in other words increase degree to a pathological level. Excessive responsibility and exaggeration of threat are important characteristics of obsessional behaviour. Several experimental studies manipulating responsibility have shown how beliefs about being responsible increase obsessional checking behaviour. For example, manipulating conditions of responsibility for blame encourages repeated checking in non-OCD participants (Radomsky et al., 2006).

As Eysenck (1985) himself concluded, the DSM nosology is based on foundations that are insecure, lacking in scientific support and contrary to facts, and the use of DSM criteria may be justified only in terms of social need or pressures. He would be heartened to know that his dimensional approach continues to challenge such committee decisions. Increasingly, psychological studies are showing that the so-called abnormal phenomenon, contrary to received psychiatric wisdom, is indeed dimensional and prevalent, to a lesser degree, among the normal population. And I speak here not only of anxiety, but of other pathologies such as obsessional ruminations, hallucinations, delusions and depersonalization.

Gordon Claridge, following Eysenck, (see Claridge, 2006, for a review) has long championed a fully dimensional view of schizotypy, that it is a trait and holds out the possibility at one end of the dimension of a functioning healthy type of schizotypy (McCreery and Claridge, 2002). Recently, Goulding (2004), for example, following Paul Meehl, provided further evidence for a dimensional model of schizophrenia which views schizotypy as a milder form of schizophrenia. Eysenck also made the connection between psychoticism and creativity. Eysenck (2003) postulated a continuum between convergent and divergent thinking referring to the relative steepness of an associative gradient, thereby claiming that discussion of thinking and thinking disorder in categorical terms is redundant. Recent developments of diagnostic benchmark measures are beginning to discover the benefits of adding dimensional rating scales, although these fall short of multidimensional prototypic practice. For example, the dimensional Yale-Brown Obsessive Compulsive Scale (Y-BOCS) (Rosario-Campos et al., 2006), the gold standard for assessing obsessive compulsive symptoms, has recently shown its utility as a more compatible research instrument than the categorical Y-BOCS.

MATCHING CORRELATIONAL AND EXPERIMENTAL METHODS (THE TWO PSYCHOLOGIES)

Eysenck (1977a) was clear that a viable construct for IDP research could not arise from correlational analysis alone. He set out four criteria that need to be met to make up a robust construct. The first criterion for a construct is that it should meet psychometric criteria and find support in factor analytic studies. But this is a necessary, not sufficient criterion. A second criterion is a link to genetic determination. The third criterion is a theoretical underpinning in the biological

factors underlying individual differences, established either directly or indirectly through laboratory investigations. The fourth requirement is some associations between the construct dimensions of personality and important social factors or events. These relations in turn require theoretical deduction from prior hypotheses relating to the nature and biological substructure of the factors in question. A simple atheoretical collection of correlational statistics is clearly unsatisfactory to define a construct.

Eysenck appealed in several of his writings to the distinction Cronbach made in his 1952 American Psychological Association (APA) address between experimental and correlational methods or the two psychologies and how they should work in tandem (e.g. Eysenck, 1997). Eysenck understood very well the importance of matching correlational with experimental methods, particularly for exposing biological concomitants and/or determinants of behaviour. He realized correlational methods were imprecise and could be unstable. For example, sources of error in psychometrics are very different to those in experimental manipulation and may arise due to unreliable instruments, response bias, extraneous influences and insensitivity. Eysenck (1997) considered that traditional correlational approaches to personality and intelligence had not yielded much of value since they are too theoretical and heuristic, whereas experimental methods are much more productive. What he meant by this was that there are more interesting relationships between personality and intelligence than mere correlations. Different personalities might have different profiles on subsets of cognitive batteries, personality variables might interact with performance on cognitive tests, personality might affect compliance, cognitive set or achievement motivation differentially and at different stages in development from childhood (e.g. Eysenck, 1977b).

Eysenck (1967) even proposed that psychological theorists may have arrived at different laws of learning as a consequence of personality differences among their choice of emotional versus non-emotional rat populations: Tolman using emotional rats; Hull and Spence, non-emotional rats!

PERSON–SITUATION EFFECTS: MEDIATION OR MODERATION

As Eysenck and Eysenck (1980) have pointed out, if one looks at the effect of a single independent variable on a single behavioural measure, say stress on task performance, then a model of a single functional relationship suffices. However, in practice two points mitigate against this simplistic solution. First, frequently without a third contributing individual difference variable, the main effects portion of the total variance may be small and the error variance inflated. Second, where there is more than one separate functional relationship with different measures, a unifying intervening variable will improve efficiency. A trait construct then can explain the diverse effects of several independent variables and do so by mediating or moderating the effect.

Correlational studies reveal that a wealth of variables moderate or mediate performance effects. Situational variables may mediate an effect but personality factors may moderate the situational effect. Bowers (1973) reported over 11 studies where person factors accounted for 11%, situations 10%, and the interaction between them 20–77%.

A mediation model seeks to identify the variable underlying correlations between a independent and dependent variables via a third intervening variable, so that the independent variable causes the mediator variable, which in turn causes the dependent variable. The importance of moderator/mediation analysis is that it pinpoints influential variables for further manipulation. There are direct and indirect effects. A direct effect changes with mediation added to the model. The mediation effect is complete when the direct effect between the independent and

dependent variable is zero after controlling for the mediation effects, or of course the effect can be partial. If the mediation effect is negative, then controlling for mediation may increase the direct effects.

Four specific criteria need to be met for mediation analyses: (1) all variables must be correlated; (2) there must be significant variance available to be explained; (3) the effects must be reliable; (4) there is no outside causal factor. The standard four-step procedure for establishing mediation (Baron and Kenny, 1986) usually involves a series of multiple regression testing: (1) direct effects of A→C; (2) mediational effect of A→B mediator variable; (3) effect of A + B→C through entering A and B into a regression equation predicting C; and (4) calculation of the effect of the mediational model by Sobel test statistics. Partial correlation, if requirement for mediation or moderation are not met, can also examine contributing variables. Part correlation is a way of indicating the unique contribution of a variable when sources of variance have been accounted for. Structural equation modelling path analysis and hierarchical regression are ways to order the contribution of mediating variables into a comprehensive sequence of events.

Individual differences affect every level of functioning and is not just an interaction between static terms but often a synergy creating its own unique variable. Personality can mediate not only specific behavioural cognitive and physiological reactions to stress, but also what type of demand and how much of it is defined as stress (Besser and Shackelford, 2007). Personality can mediate affect (Karlsson and Archer, 2007), it mediates the relationship between worry and negative affect (Rammstedt, 2007) and subsequent pathological behaviour (Gladstone et al., 2005), and emotional processing (Rusting, 1998). Personality further mediates metacognition and the way we evaluate our thoughts and worries (Zhiqiang, 1999) and performance (Washburn et al., 2005) and our self-concept (Bhattacharya et al., 2006). Personality mediates transient motivational

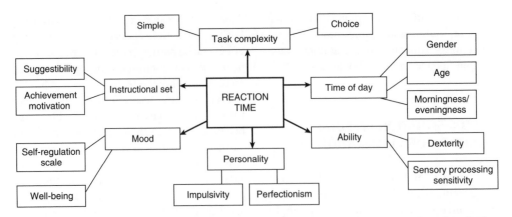

Figure 10.2   Potential first- and second-order moderating factors on reaction time (RT)

states (Code and Langan-Fox, 2001), personal ideology (de St-Aubin, 1999), subjective well-being (Gutiérrez et al., 2005), social well-being (Roysamb, 2006), spiritual well-being (Ramanaiah et al., 2001), emotional well-being (Bono and Vey, 2007), and sense of humour (Kazarian and Martin, 2006), which in turn can moderate health (Boyle and Joss-Reid, 2004) and quality of life (Francis and Jackson, 2003) and happiness (Chan and Joseph, 2000).

When we begin to construct a diagram representing molecular and molar levels of these moderating and mediating effects, we begin to see the complexity of the profile confronting the experimentalist. An example of the complexity is given in Figure 10.2 which illustrates how the apparently straightforward measure of reaction time (RT) may be influenced by a diversity of individual difference effects at multiple levels. The figure illustrates only the first- and second-order interaction variables which might be considered in a hierarchical model explaining RT. Every time we try to arrive at a straightforward effect, we find individual differences in process in play. Behaviour is likely moderated by individual differences in motor performance. It is also likely modulated by cognitive attentional factors. It is mediated by task demand and also moderated by meta-cognitive processes such as suggestibility and persuasiveness, which will

affect the response to the instructional set. Beyond all this may be a wider set of personal beliefs about performance ability.

MEDIATION TO MANIPULATION

On the face of it, identifying key moderator and mediator variables should facilitate translation to experimental paradigms, where variables are manipulated. Moderator variables are particularly important to the IDP because specific factors such as context information are often assumed to influence the effect of specific independent variables on specific dependent variable responses. The moderator effect represents the interaction between a major independent variable and a factor that specifies conditions for its operation.

A key factor in the many debates with situational theorists such as Mischel was in understanding the essential interactive and synergistic nature of person–situation interactions, and how such interactions took as much account of transient cognitive states as enduring trans-situational consistencies. According to Eysenck and Eysenck (1980), traits and states are intervening or mediating variables that are useful in explaining individual differences in behaviour to the extent that they are incorporated into an appropriate theoretical framework. The interactive influence of traits and situations produces transient internal conditions termed 'states'. The relationship between 'traits' or 'states' and behaviour is typically indirect, being affected or moderated by the interaction between dependent and independent variables.

Much of the early work establishing these interactions relied heavily on analysis of variance (ANOVA), and first- and second-order interaction effects. However, relying on these effects is not only suboptimal, it is wasteful and potentially illegitimate. The problem with ANOVA, and to some extent top-heavy hypothetico-deductive methods for IDP, is their espousal of binary hypotheses in keeping with binary probability models. In other words, strictly speaking the only effect to be tested in such a model is the main effect (null hypothesis). Any interactive effects, far from being informative, instead simply indicate confounds to the main effect and effectively indicate that no firm conclusions can be drawn.

Although a first-order interaction effect in ANOVA may permit further comparison of its main effect according to further group subdivision, the ensuing power will be low. When, however, considering second- and third-order interaction effects, the power of any inference is sorely stretched since the appearance of any non-linear trend looks more like the result of random activity and badly controlled procedures. The researcher faced with a complicated nth-order interaction is likely to abandon the thesis about individual differences as a factor on performance, ironically in the face of too much evidence rather than too little. Yet it is just such interactions which preoccupy the IDP. The ANOVA model seeks change due to one factor, be it an extrinsic factor (e.g. stimulus value) or intrinsic factor (e.g. drug state), but in the IDP such a model is uninformative. The effect of either an intrinsic or extrinsic stimulus parameter is nuanced by personality and situation. The effects, for example, of a drug on state depends on stimulus, personality, dosage, time of day and impulsiveness (Eysenck, 1983; Revelle et al., 1980). In the ANOVA model, one is supposed to control for these

factors, but such control ends up excluding key sources of variance and creating an artificial situation with little external validity, and furthermore such control does not give us access to process. Of course, individual differences may be diminished under extreme stimulus conditions. Exposing people to extreme stimulus intensity to ensure everybody jumps at the same time may flatten individual variation in response but tells us nothing about habitual processing demands.

As an illustration of how individual interactions can sabotage a unitary effect model, we need to only look at individual difference in diurnal variation interacting with caffeine, personality, task performance and mood. Humphreys et al. (1980) reported that digit span performance was moderated at one level by attention and short-term memory, but these in turn linked back to arousal, task effort and anxiety on the one hand, and time-of-day effects, caffeine dose and distraction moderated by impulsivity on the other hand. Humphreys et al. (1980) tried to accommodate the curvilinear relations to performance within a monotonic relationship with information processing constructs whereas Eysenck and Folkard (1980) argued that the model required three arousal constructs for diurnal rhythms, impulsivity and environmental factors. The issue here is whether a unitary model of effects (e.g. on arousal or anxiety) should be imposed from the top down and applied to all contexts and measures rather than accepting that person–behaviour situation differences may well interact to produce a contextual activation.

CONTEXT AND CONSTRUCT

The difficulty in applying ANOVA techniques to experimental parts of the IDP concerns the defining role of context in individual difference research. I say 'defining' rather than 'moderating' or 'mediating' since it is the person–situation interaction which defines the IDP unit to be explained. As noted previously, effects in ANOVA relate to a hypothetical binary probability distribution testing one null hypothesis. Complexity of effects is therefore not welcome. Interaction effects not only play havoc with statistical inference, they also compromise construct validity. Eysenck was aware of the limitations of relying on interaction effect, to test significance with its corresponding low power and proposed the solution of a programmatic approach to research whereby consecutive experiments would cumulatively build up an IDP construct. The hallmark of a robust construct is that it is defined in terms of lower-order elements, but obviously these elements must converge. The easiest way to ensure convergence is to operationalize the elements as an interaction effect of the higher-order construct. Rather as we saw earlier with impulsivity where first-order constructs give rise to the second-order construct. Here the distinct second-order constructs supply diversity to the application of the first-order construct but do not undermine its coherence. However, this is problematic in ANOVA where a construct needs to be operationalized uniformly to predict a uniform effect and any qualification of the effect by interaction is likely to weaken the initial construct.

A good example of how a unitary construct leads to difficulties in accommodating divergent findings and weakness in the theory is the construct of 'arousal'. This construct, and in particular its curvilinear relationship with performance, has figured widely in explaining individual differences to stimulation. In particular, introverts are hypothesized to experience high arousal and are likely to show a paradoxical tranquilizing effect to stimulation compared to extraverts who, with low arousal, will be activated by extrinsic or interoceptive stimulation (Eysenck, 1981).

A key problem in testing predictions from a unitary arousal model was the difficulty in operationalizing arousal and agreeing on its measurement in cognitive, behavioural and physiological systems. The construct could validly be applied to say, sensory arousal, motor arousal, behavioural arousal and emotional arousal, and divergent findings led to a theoretical paradox where one could

seemingly be aroused and not aroused at the same time depending on the system measured.

Lang (1968, 1978), in his tripartite model, offered a way of operationalizing arousal in terms of three separate systems: a physiological, behavioural and subjective system. Lang's notion was that much of the divergence in reports spring from the variable relationship between these three systems of arousal, which might co-vary, but might also vary inversely or show no relationship at all. At first sight, the tripartite model seemed an ingenious way of accounting for the wide variation in association between measures of behaviour and indices of arousal, while still maintaining a coherent arousal model. A wealth of early studies did report a lack of association between avoidance behaviour, subjective distress and physiological responses to anxiety. However, only 10 of 32 studies (Sallis et al., 1980) reported an association between these systems, and these were mostly in clinical case studies. In fact, a meta-review reported overwhelmingly a complete lack of association or 'fractionation' between these distinct systems (Feldman et al., 1999). But far from supporting a coherent model of anxiety, such fractionation demonstrated instead that arousal was not a unitary construct (Bellack and Lombardo, 1984). The tripartite model also has little or no predictive clinical validity or indeed outcome validity. Is someone with anxiety whose physiological arousal remains high, but who avoids less events, improved compared to someone whose somatic arousal is lower but who continues to avoid? Are there alternatives to arousal as an explanatory construct?

DIMENSIONS OF ACTIVATION

Arousal was not well defined as a unitary dimensional process in the first place (contrary to IDP principles) rather its sense derived from common sense observation of behaviour

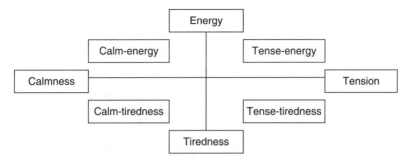

Figure 10.3   Thayer's energy-tension model of state regulation

(people can appear to be in distinct states of alertness) which it was assumed translated linearly to other systems. H.J. Eysenck (pers. comm.) was never completely at ease with the concept of arousal and arousability, and was often searching for a substitute. Two candidate constructs which seem to offer more validity from the IDP perspective are Thayer's (1996) construct of 'energy' and O'Connor's (1989a, 1989b) constructs of 'preparation-adaptation'.

Thayer (1996) in his seminal work on the regulation of mood noted that there are wide individual differences in the way people regulate their state. For example, the strategies used to change a bad mood can vary enormously from taking a shower to going shopping. However, the strategies nearly all relate to modifying energy or tension. He suggested that moods are best considered along two activation continuums: energy and tension. This leads to four quadrants: calm-energy, calm-tiredness, tense-energy, tense-tiredness. Thayer found that the quadrants formed by these two dimensions (see Figure 10.3) were adequate to predict state and self-regulating behaviour. So, for example, depression represents a mixed pattern of low energy and moderately high tension whereas a bored person is likely to be slightly tensed and tired. Such states are more likely to lead to substance abuse to regulate mood. A calm-energy state is more likely to lead to activities to increase positive state, such as

exercise or sexual activity. Conversely, calm-tiredness might lead to reading or listening to music while a tense-energy state would likely lead to a more aggressive competitive way of regulating state.

The relationship between energy and tension is complex, and as tension increases, so energy will increase, but only to a certain point after which it will decrease and tense-tiredness will develop. But ironically, as energy increases from low to moderate levels, tension also increases, and at higher levels of energy tension decreases and calm-energy is the result. An important part of Thayers' construct of energy-tension is that he views it as an action system in concordance with the flow of behaviour, fine-tuned to the daily cycles of everyday life, with different degrees operating within individuals as well as identifying different habitual styles of action. The construct then can be operationalized as observable behaviour, measured through a psychometrically valid questionnaire designed to identify the mood quadrants and predictive of individual differences in mood regulation.

Several psychophysiological investigators have long considered psychophysiological activation as a physiological support for behaviour; that is, an element of behaviour rather than a response. Malmo (1957, 1959, 1965) has shown, in a series of studies, how physiological activation depends exclusively on what a person is doing rather than a general level of arousal. In short, there is no general level of activation or arousal; rather what system is activated depends on task demand, and fractionation is the norm, but such fractionation specifically depends on the nature of *preparation*.

Following on from Malmo's original observations, research by O'Connor (1989a) supports the claim that the concept of preparation has greater predictive power in explaining psychophysiological activation than arousal. Preparation is guided by goal-directed intention, which is reflected directly in physiological activation, and such preparation reflects a gradient of activation proportionally related to the progress of the task (e.g. Malmo and Malmo, 2000). The key parameters emerging from this preparation model are: (1) the intention (that is, the goal directing action driving the preparation to act; (2) the conflict experienced between preparation and action in situ; and (3) the effort of *adaptation* needed to overcome conflict and adapt to the ongoing situation. The preparation-adaptation model predicts that where preparation to act is restricted to a fixed intention and there is conflict between intended and actual goals, the more the flow of action will be interrupted, possibly to the point where it will be impeded. Obviously, if there is no conflict, there will be more continuity in the flow of action, and where preparation is flexible, the adaptation required under conflict or no conflict will be similar, requiring more effort under conflict and more targeted adaptation under goal continuity. A low to medium level of intention will require a greater or lesser degree of adaptation under conflict whereas a highly invested intention may lead to a demobilization of effort, a kind of 'freezing' in the face of extreme conflict. Type and degree of psychophysiological activation during task performance is hence a function of type of adaptation. (see Figure 10.4)

O'Connor (1989a, 1989b) applied the model to individual differences in the psychophysiological effects of smoking, and hypothesized that individual differences in

degree of cortical activation in smokers would depend on whether the smoker wished to maintain a goal-directed activity or adapt to a novel task in the face of conflict. In the latter case, more effortful adaptation was linked with greater inhalation of nicotine. In other applications of the model, O'Connor (2002) also specified how motor conflict may produce inappropriate activation in redundant muscles, leading to tic responses as a way of reducing motor conflict. A preparation-adaptation model of tic onset is coherent with other neurophysiological theories of neural relays of excitation and inhibition producing excessive tension (O'Connor, 2005). The preparation model has also been applied to explain how the muscle tension in generalized anxiety disorder can be operationalized as preparation for worry, and indeed preparation for alternative scenarios can reduce muscle activity in generalized anxiety (O'Connor et al., 1999).

A recent study testing the preparation model (Roy, 2006) has shown during an interpersonal discussion that socially anxious individuals, compared to other groups, are characterized by a high level of preparation of action oriented towards self-protection. Further analyses revealed that a greater proportion of the socially anxious were characterized by intentional preparation towards 'avoidance' and 'performance/ dissimulation', compared to a control group. These 'preparation of action' categories differed on the subjective units of distress during the discussion and differed on physiological measures of heart rate. The categories also differed regarding the effort of adaptation under conflict.

The preparation-adaptation model, unlike the inverted U-shaped or other arousal models, relates physiological parameters directly and linearly to activity. It does not rely on the role of curvilinear hypothetical processes producing contradictory effects which may hamper predictions. For example, restructuring style of action and redistributing tension can help relieve generalized anxiety without necessarily reducing level of activation, and the tension

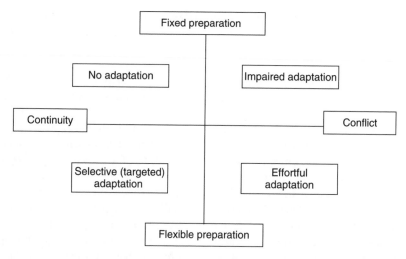

Figure 10.4 O'Connor's preparation-adaptation model of psychophysiological activation as a function of adaptation of preparation in the face of conflict between intended and actual goal

distribution is a function of this activity restructuring (O'Connor et al., 1999).

The preparation-adaptation model then not only explains differential activation among physiological systems (according to type of preparation), but also makes predictions about the type of activation characterizing different disorders. For example, chronic muscle contraction during generalized worry might reflect anticipation of distant events, and conversely the autonomic activity in social anxiety might reflect preparation for a more immediate interpersonal threat.

In both Thayer's and O'Connor's two-dimensional models, the constructs are built up on the basis of observed individual differences in response. The complex interactive nature of the construct aids simplicity in theory, whereas striving for a unitary construct is likely to lead to complications in the theory when unpredicted interactions arise. The development of these alternative constructs to arousal brings us back to a wider consideration of construct and theory in IDP which is germane to choice of statistical method.

CONSTRUCT VALIDITY IN THE IDP

Divergent findings should not compromise a construct's validity, rather they should enrich it. It is the ability to accommodate both divergent and convergent findings in elaborating theory which defines a strong construct (Shawyer, 1977). The answer is to ground constructs in empirically strong observations and build theory from the bottom-up rather than imposing overgeneral constructs. As Springer (1990) notes, there seems a fear among practitioners that unless their theories are abstract they will be redundant on observation to the extent they are situation specific. But generality comes from diversity and to do this theories must be able to lay down principles that apply to a variety of particular and diverse instances.

The importance of specifying context in IDP might appear to bring it into conflict with the aim of generalizing findings to a larger population of contexts and people. But from the IDP point of view, in experimental terms, we are interested in the specific way a person variable operates over a series of well-defined contexts. If we return to the diagram depicting the intervening variables on RT in Figure 10.2, the IDP question would be likely to take the form: which is the RT more typical of a population who have high achievement motivation performing a choice RT in the morning: an RT of 150 ms or one of 250 ms? My knowledge might allow me to quote these alternative RT outcomes within 10 ms of each other or only within 100 ms of each other. I may for example be able to attribute a higher probability to the person's RT being between 100 and 200 ms than between 200 and 400 ms if I know the person's extravert? But if I know also they are high on impulsivity and disinhibition scales the probability may become higher. Further knowledge about mood and motor dexterity may allow the predicted outcome to become more precise, say, between 100 and 150 ms versus 150–200 ms. So the goal is to arrive at an inference about the choice RT performance of an extraverted, impulsive, disinhibited sportsman, with high achievement motivation during the morning. The conclusion here is very different from the typical conclusion about a random sample showing a significant main effect. In the IDP the goal effectively is to identify the performance of a unique population, not a random sample. The aim is to achieve as much precision as possible. One moves from a general trait classification of personality to the specific first- and second-order attributes this trait entails.

These and subsequent predictions are nested within related contexts. The contexts are linked by their relationship to first- and second-order factors. For example, my knowledge of, say, extraverted performance under simple RT conditions under stress provides a parameter space for predicting choice RT performance under stress in the same population.

ALTERNATIVE DESIGNS FOR THE IDP

Alternative statistical approaches to ANOVA can be helpful to IDP experimentation and one alternative is conditional probability,

Bayesian or likelihood approaches. The advantage of these methods is that they are not tied to binary hypotheses. Many alternative outcomes can be proposed and prior probability derived from previous knowledge of person–context effects can be factored into significance testing.

Bayesian likelihood approaches are one of a set of procedures which 'personalize' (in the words of L.J. Savage, 1962) statistical inference. In other words, they ground statistical inference, on the one hand, in understanding of the process itself and also in the intentions of the experimenter in measuring this process. As such they end up giving more credible information on the defining 'typicality' of the process (e.g. compatibilities, boundaries and equivalence). There are key differences in design that spring from this difference in inference. Principally, the Bayesian is not bound by formal statistical constraints in dealing with independence of observations, dealing with interaction of measures, in comparing/combining separate measures, in defining sample space and in generalizing findings. The conditional probability approach also allows for individual differences among researchers in experience and purpose to be quantified.

It is not the intention here to provide a full account of Bayesian and other alternative methods to behavioural research, which are described in detail elsewhere (Kline, 2005; O'Connor, 1992; Pole et al., 1994). The advantage of the Bayesian approach to the IDP is that the research is not limited to a single-hypothesis. In fact, one can hypothesize several effects with different probabilities at the same time. Furthermore, probabilities are conditional on the original specification of the variables, and can be updated as knowledge of different contexts becomes known. Finally, because prior knowledge of the sample is the basis for the estimate of likelihood, so individual differences among scientists' personal beliefs and knowledge can become a part of the analysis.

The Bayesian analysis encourages a bottom-up approach to operationalize a construct in detail. So to describe an experimental context as the recording of reaction time (RT) in extraverts who score high on impulsivity after ingestion of caffeine during the morning provides no greater difficulty for the Bayesian than defining the context as recording reaction time within a group of extraverts, period. In both cases any specific interactions or subdivisions of personality are welcome as marking the particular idiosyncrasy of this context and hence giving decisions on outcome a more precise and relative (hence individually meaningful) applicability.

According to Bayes' theorem, the probability of an event can be divided into prior and posterior probability. The a posteriori probability of an event is thus the combination of its a priori probability (derived from previous experience) and its observed probability in the present case. The relations are expressed simply as:

$$P(E/O) = \frac{P(O/E) \times P(E)}{P(O)}$$

where P(E) is the expected or prior probability; P(O) the actual observed probability. P(E/O) is the expected probability given the observed probability and P(O/E) is the probability of the observation given the expected probability. So this formula permits probability estimates from distinct data sets and conditions to be compared and for posteriori probabilities to be updated and refined depending on the experimental context. For example, an estimate of the probability of an RT under 150 msec may be low for a group of extraverts during a choice but high during a simple paradigm. Distinct a priori estimates of RT may specify mood states or degrees of motivation.

The probability calculation can usefully be modified to contain conditional probability; that is instead of an absolute probability we can talk of a conditional probability estimate of alternative probabilities. In other words, the relative probability of event A over event B. The extent to which the probability of

estimate A is supported over estimate B leads to a likelihood distribution of how likely A is relative to B for any given data and is expressed similarly to Bayes theorem as $L(P_a/P_o)/L(P_b/P_o)$ where L is the likelihood and P_a and P_b are respectively the probabilities of each hypothesis given the observed data (P_o). The higher the odds, the stronger the evidence in favour of one model (Dixon and O'Reilly, 1999; Edwards, 1972).

Likelihood ratios of two probabilities can be expressed as odds in favour of one probability versus another and can be multiplied together on independent data sets. The most likely probability given alternative probabilities is termed the maximum likelihood. Other probabilities will fall either side of this maximum to form a likelihood distribution. O'Connor (1992) has illustrated the use of likelihood ratios to identify which among alternative psychophysiological processes is more probably associated with specific behavioural dimensions.

The Bayesian and other approaches are very appropriate for looking at conditional effects and arriving at conditional probabilistic estimates. The Bayesian approach also uses fiducial or credibility limits rather than significance level (Rouanet and Lecoutre, 1983). Such credibility limits accord a credible range of response values to an individual or group, so emphasizing that a specific response pattern is typical of a particular person–situation interaction.

PASSING FROM THEORY TO PRACTICE: APPLICATIONS OF IDP IN TRANSLATIONAL RESEARCH

The practical applied and clinical implications of IDP were ably outlined by Eysenck in several texts. For example, Eysenck (1988) argued that difficulties in education may be due to lack of use of discoveries about the influence of personality and learning curves on the acquisition of knowledge. Extraverted children benefit from teaching by discovery learning while introverted children benefit from receptive learning. The lack of overall effect between methods hides the interaction effect. Eysenck (1997) proposed an individual difference model of learning which explained incubation as well as extinction effects in learning predicted by precise relations between personality and conditionability in neurosis. He explored the differences in the mental and metabolic effects of vitamins and minerals, suggesting individual differences should dictate intake and metabolism. Eysenck (1997) viewed personality as an essential construct to any theory of criminality and antisocial behaviour, and provided a taxonomy including antisocial and aggressive traits. A crime is committed by a person in a certain situation; individual differences are responsible for the fact that in a similar situation, one person will commit a crime, another will not. A recent study reported that the interaction of Eysenckian personality traits (P,E,L) predicted self-reported anti-social behavior (Center et al., 2005). Personal traits are indicators of criminal propensity and differentiate between violent and non-violent people and distal and proximal antecedents.

The synergistic interaction of smoking and neuroticism plays an important role in predicting heart disease and also as a risk factor in smoking and cancer (Eysenck, 2000; Marusic and Eysenck, 2001). The so-called addictive behaviour fits into a psychological resource model in which the habits in question are acquired because they serve a useful function for the individual, and the nature of the functions they fulfil is related to the personality profile of the 'addict'. For some people this resource function develops into a form of addiction, and it is suggested that the reason this occurs is related to excessive dopamine functioning. This, in turn, is used to suggest the nature of the addictive personality. Excessive dopamine functioning is related to the personality dimension of psychoticism, and there is evidence that psychoticism is closely related to a large number of addictions. The precise reasons for the addictive effects of dopamine are still undebated, but clearly

personality and biological factors link together in the production of addictive behaviour. Eysenck himself together with Grossarth-Maticek (1991) developed 'creative novation' behaviour therapy, and demonstrated the positive effect of a stress-management-oriented 'creative novation' behaviour therapy on cancer and coronary heart disease outcomes. This latter finding needs further replication, but indicates the far-reaching implications of the role of individual differences in determining psychological and physical health.

Translational research involves carrying knowledge of basic processes through to practical application, and has become a priority in clinical settings (Whittal, 2006). Such a link is embedded in the IDP as it moves from correlational to experimental to real-life application of individual differences. Examples of such translational research come from Eysenck and O'Connor's (1979) work on individual differences in smoker behaviour. This work began from some previous observations on the situational profile of smokers based on Chris Frith's (1971) earlier work on high and low arousal smokers. Nicotine is a stimulant but produces paradoxical effects. The traditional arousal model of nicotine's paradox, following the Yerkes-Dodson law, is the inverted U-shape arousal curve which predicts that at a certain level of arousal, nicotine will have a paradoxical effect and reduce arousal, so explaining the often subjectively calming effects reported by smokers. O'Connor (1985, 1989a, 1989b, 1989c) established not only that situational preference to smoke was often a function of type of task engagement, but further physiological effects were mediated by type of task, often interacting with type of personality and motor activity. These situational factors were reduced to a four-factor questionnaire which divided smoking cues into high and low emotional, and high and low attentional (O'Connor and Langlois, 1991). The distinction was experimentally validated by looking at individual differences in physiological effects and the smoker's regulation of smoking under attentional and emotional conditions.

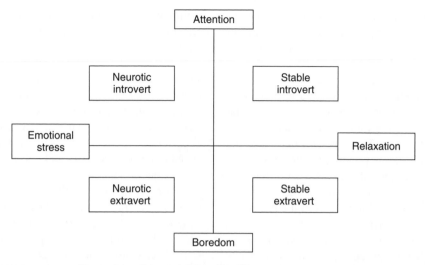

Figure 10.5   Personality and smoking activity classified according to the two cognitive and emotional smoking motivations (from O'Connor, 1985)

Introverts and extraverts not only inhaled different amounts of nicotine but experienced different physiological and mood and behavioural effects as a function of smoking situation. Introverted smokers tended to inhale little, using the cigarette more for sensorimotor stimulation, and smoked to aid concentration and skilled performance (see Figure 10.5). Extraverted smokers inhaled deeply and tended to be more motorically and autonomically activated by smoking. The clinical implications of these findings for behaviour therapy led to the design of a smoking treatment programme based on our predictions of individual differences in state-situation interaction, and the use of appropriately tailored behavioural substitutions to help smokers perform tasks without smoking (O'Connor, 1989b). For example, physical exercise could be an aid to cessation in extraverted but not introverted smokers.

CONCLUSION AND RECOMMENDATIONS

The evidence is now so overwhelming for the contribution of individual differences to most areas of psychological life that it seems naïve to carry out experiments or studies ignoring this source of variance. It seems important to study individual differences from both a correlational and experimental effect. Indeed in terms of construct validity, it seems essential to combine both to be sure that, for example, mediational variables are correctly defined in experimental terms. A convincing path analysis requires input from both psychologies. In the IDP, the two psychologies may need to complement each other. Whereas correlational studies provide an initial rich construct, experimental studies may need to explicitly develop methods which give priority to explaining effects in a specific context before over-generalizing to a wider population.

Bayesian and conditional probability methods may offer appropriate statistical inference procedures both for IDP experimental interaction effects and for studying longitudinal effects. In such designs, time points can be ordered as event spaces and variables can be conditional on one another's occurrence regardless of time of occurrence (O'Connor et al., 2001, Careau et al., 2003). Applying such methods permits the study of individual differences in longitudinal temporal sequences of behaviour, where conventional time series analyses are inappropriate (Grenier et al., 2008).

The link between correlational and experimental methods in elucidating the source of individual difference permits a clear translational route between theory and practice, product and process. The constant back and forth between psychometric and experimental methods pays dividends when discussing the specific factors to modify when changing a person by situation effect in a clinical setting. Clearly there is still more room for the development of sound dimensions to classify a number of psychological traits. Eysenck (1987) felt in particular that clinical cognitive constructs currently in vogue merited such validation.

One of the major existing development areas for the IDP is moving beyond situation–trait interaction into synergistic interaction approach. In a synergistic model, functionally equivalent situation and person factors amplify or suppress each other's effects on behaviour in a dynamic and reciprocal way. This synergy moves beyond an additive interaction model to propose that behaviour is a joint function of both person and situation (Endler, 1997; Schmidtke and Heller, 2004). So, for example, vulnerability to stress may depend on personality and degree of perceived strain, but a positive coping attitude may decrease the degree of perceived strain. Yet this ability to decrease perceived strain may itself vary as a function of personality. The synergistic interaction hypothesis can be tested using moderated regression analysis (Aiken and West, 1991). For example, Schmidtke and Heller (2004), using this synergistic model, showed that reactions to injustice varied as a function of attitude to equality.

Drug and placebo effects likewise could benefit from further applications of IDP. Eysenck (1983) suggested that anxiolytics were more likely to affect the degree of neuroticism while stimulants and depressants would affect degree of extroversion. But the effect of the drug and its dose would depend on the client's personality. Stimulants, for example, stimulate extraverts but show a paradoxical effect on introverts. Eysenck also listed a whole range of subtle factors that would affect drug response such as present state, physical health, time of day, previous experience, mode of administration and social environment (Eysenck, 1983). The dimension of neuroticism, for example, is clearly a predictor not only of drug effects, but of successful withdrawal from anxiolytic dependence (Bélanger et al., 1998). This finding ties in with Eysenck' previous studies of personality and successful smoking cessation (Eysenck, 1980b). Willhelm Janke (1983) in his work on individual differences in response to tranquillizers and stimulants noted the continued absence of the systematic consideration of individual differences in mainstream psychopharmacology practice.

One of Eysenck's most important theoretical contributions was his outline of a conditioning model of placebo effects and his subsequent insistence on criteria for the controlled testing and evaluation of clinical versus placebo effects (Eysenck, 1987). He noted that a whole class of influences needs to be considered to constitute a credible placebo condition. The person must have faith in the treatment, a convincing rationale, perceive the therapist and the place as credible; be appropriately engaged in the therapy; be optimistic and confident. He suggested that few placebo conditions were so stringent but even so the effect size of psychotherapy compared to placebo was negligible (Eysenck, 1980a, 1982). So Hans Eysenck never saw any reason to revise his 1952 view of the effectiveness of psychotherapy as 'not proven' even 40 years later (Eysenck, 1952b/1992).

The IDP as we have seen in this chapter has the potential to transform our approach to research in most areas of psychology stretching from social behaviour to psychosomatics and psychophysiology.

By its nature the IDP is, in the Kuhnian sense, a revolutionary scientific paradigm requiring that we rethink our assumptions not only about our subject matter but about the very way we do human science. Perhaps for this reason the IDP is still some way from universal application in many areas of psychology where it could play a valuable role and offer parsimonious explanations for divergent findings.

REFERENCES

Aiken, L.S. and West, S.G. (1991) *Multiple Regression: Testing and Interpreting Interactions*. Newbury Park: Sage.

American Psychiatric Association (APA) (2000) *Diagnostic and Statistical Manual of Mental Disorders* (4th edn, text rev.). Washington, DC: APA.

Ambwani, S., Clarke, A., Stoner, J. and Hopwood, C. (2006) 'Neuroticism fully mediates the relationship between borderline personality features and bulimic symptomatology', Presentation at the 40th Annual Convention of the ABCT, Chicago, November 16–19.

Arnau, R.C., Green, B.A., Rosen, D.H., Gleaves, D.H. and Melancon, J.G. (2003) 'Are Jungian preferences really categorical?: An empirical investigation using taxometric analysis', *Personality and Individual Differences*, 34(2): 233–51.

Austin, E.J. (2005) 'Personality correlates of the broader autism phenotype as assessed by the Autism Spectrum Quotient (AQ)', *Personality and Individual Differences*, 38(2): 451–60.

Baron, R.M. and Kenny, D.A. (1986) 'The moderator-mediator variable distinction in social psychological research: Conceptual, strategic and statistical considerations', *Journal of Personality and Social Psychology*, 51(6): 1173–82.

Bhattacharya, T., Singh, V. and Ravinder, K. (2006) 'Judgment of subjective *well-being*: Influences of *personality* and affect.' *Psychological Studies. Special Issue: Psychology of Health and Well-Being*, 51(2–3): 132–8.

Bélanger, L., O'Connor, K.P., Marchand, A., Dupuis, G. and Elie, R. (1998) 'Psychological distress and quality of life experiences during discontinuation of benzodiazepines', Annual Convention, Canadian Psychological Association, Edmonton, Alberta, June 4–6.

Bellack, A.S. and Lombardo, T.W. (1984) 'Measurement of anxiety', in S.M. Turner (ed.), *Behavioral Theories and Treatment of Anxiety*. New York: Plenum Press, pp. 51–89.

Besser, A. and Shackelford, T.K. (2007) 'Mediation of the effects of the big five personality dimensions on negative mood and confirmed affective expectations by perceived situational stress: A quasi-field study of vacationers', *Personality and Individual Differences*, 42(7): 1333–46.

Bono, J.E. and Vey, M.A. (2007) 'Personality and emotional performance: Extraversion, neuroticism, and self-monitoring', *Journal of Occupational Health Psychology*, 12(2): 177–92.

Boyle, G.F. and Joss-Reid, J.M. (2004) 'Relationship of humour to health: A psychometric investigation', *British Journal of Health Psychology*, 9(1): 51–66.

Bouchard, G., Lussier, Y. and Sabourin, S. (1999) 'Personality and marital adjustment: Utility of the five-factor model of personality', *Journal of Marriage and the Family*, 61(3): 651–60.

Bowers, K.S. (1973) 'Situationism in psychology: An analysis and a critique', *Psychological Review*, 80(5): 307–36.

Calamari, J.E., Wiegartz, P.S., Riemann, B.C. and Cohen, R.J. (2004) 'Obsessive-compulsive disorder subtypes: An attempted replication and extension of a symptom-based taxonomy', *Behaviour Research and Therapy*, 42(6): 647–60.

Careau, Y., O'Connor, K.P. and Turgeon, L. (2003) 'Mood stages and interpretations of thoughts in an OCD subject', Poster, 37th Annual Convention, Association for Advancement of Behavior Therapy (AABT), Boston, MA, November 20–23.

Cattell, R.B. (1952) *Factor Analysis*. New York: Harper.

Cattell, R.B. (1978) *The Scientific Use of Factor Analysis in Behavioral and Life Sciences*. New York: Plenum.

Center, D.B., Jackson, N. and Kemp, D. (2005) 'A test of Eysenck's antisocial behaviour hypothesis employing 11–15-year-old students dichotomous for PEN and L', *Personality and Individual Differences*, 38(2), 395–412.

Chamonro-Premuzic, T., Furnham, A. and Ackerman, P.L. (2006) 'Ability and personality correlates of general knowledge', *Personality and Individual Differences*, 41(3), 419–29.

Chan, R. and Joseph, S. (2000) 'Dimensions of personality, domains of aspiration, and subjective well-being', *Personality and Individual Differences*, 28(2): 347–54.

Chioqueta, A.P. and Stiles, T.C. (2005) 'Personality traits and the development of depression, hopelessness, and suicide ideation', *Personality and Individual Differences*, 38(6): 1283–91.

Claridge, G. (2006) 'Divided selves as nervous types', *The Psychologist*, 19(11): 656–8.

Clarke, D. (2004) 'Neuroticism: Moderator or mediator in the relation between locus of control and depression?', *Personality and Individual Differences*, 37(2): 245–58.

Code, S. and Langan-Fox, J. (2001) 'Motivation, cognition and traits: Predicting occupational health, well-being and performance', *Stress and Health: Journal of the International Society for the Investigation of Stress*, 17(3): 159–74.

Corr, P.J. (2003) 'Personality and dual-task processing: Disruption of procedural learning by declarative processing', *Personality and Individual Differences*, 34(7), 1245–69.

De Gucht, V., Fischler, B. and Heiser, W. (2004) 'Neuroticism, alexithymia, negative affect, and positive affect as determinants of medically unexplained symptoms', *Personality and Individual Differences*, 36(7): 1655–67.

De Pascalis, V., Stippoli, E., Riccardi, P. and Vergari, F. (2004) 'Personality, event-related potential and heart rate in emotional word processing', *Personality and Individual Differences*, 36(4): 873–91.

de St. Aubin, E. (1999) 'Personal ideology: The intersection of personality and religious beliefs', *Journal of Personality*, 67(6): 1105–39.

Dixon, P. and O'Reilly, T. (1999) 'Scientific versus statistical inference', *Canadian Journal of Experimental Psychology*, 53(2): 133–49.

Edwards, A.W.F. (1972) (ed.), *Likelihood. An Account of the Statistical Concept of Likelihood and its Application to Scientific Inference*. New York, NY: Cambridge University Press.

Endler, N.S. (1997) 'Stress, anxiety, and coping: the multidimensional interaction model', *Canadian Psychology*, 38(August): 136–53.

Eysenck, H.J. (1950) 'Criterion analysis on application of the hypothetico-deductive method to factor analysis', *Psychological Review*, 57(1): 38–53.

Eysenck, H.J. (1947,1998) *Dimensions of personality*. London, UK: Transaction Publishers.

Eysenck, H.J. (1952a) *The Scientific Study of Personality*. New York: Praeger.

Eysenck, H.J. (1952b, 1992) 'The effects of psychotherapy', *Journal of Consulting and Clinical Psychology*, 60(5), 659–63.

Eysenck, H.J. (1967) *The Biological Basis of Personality*. Springfield, IL: C.C. Thomas.

Eysenck, H.J. (1977a) 'Personality and factor analysis: A reply to Guilford', *Psychological Bulletin*, 84(3): 405–11.

Eysenck, H.J.(1977b) *Human Memory: Theory, Research and Individual Differences*. Oxford: Pergamon.

Eysenck, H.J. (1980a) 'The biosocial nature of man', *Journal of Social and Biological Structure*, 3(2): 125–34.

Eysenck, H.J. (1980b) *The Causes and Effects of Smoking*. London: Temple Smith.

Eysenck, H.J. (1981) 'Personality and psychosomatic diseases', *Activitas Nervosa Superior (Praha)*, 23(2): 112–29.

Eysenck, H.J. (1982) 'Why do conditioned responses show incrementation, while unconditioned responses show habituation?', *Behavioral Psychotherapy*, 10(3): 217–20.

Eysenck, H.J. (1983) 'Drugs as research tools in psychology: Experiments with drugs in personality research', *Neuropsychobiology*, 10(1): 29–43.

Eysenck, H.J. (1985) 'Behaviorism and clinical psychiatry', *International Journal of Clinical Psychiatry*, 31(3): 163–9.

Eysenck, H.J. (1987) 'What does "cognitive" add to behavior therapy?', *Southern Psychologist*, 3(2), 5–11.

Eysenck, H.J. (1988) 'Skinner, Skinnerism, and the Skinnerian Psychology', *Counselling Psychology Quarterly*, 1–3: 299–301.

Eysenck, H.J. (1997) 'Personality and experimental psychology: The unification of psychology and the possibility of a paradigm', *Journal of Personality and Social Psychology*, 73(6): 1224–37.

Eysenck, H.J. (2000) 'Personality as a risk factor in cancer and coronary heart disease', in D. Kenny, J. Carlson and F.J. McGuigan (eds), *Stress and Health: Research and Clinical Applications*. Amsterdam: Harwood Academic Publishers, pp. 291–318.

Eysenck, H.J. (2003) 'Creativity, personality and the convergent-divergent continuum', in: *Critical Creative Processes*. Cresskill, NJ: Hampton Press.

Eysenck, H.J. and Eysenck, M.W. (1985) *Personality and Individual Differences: A Natural Science Approach*. New York: Plenum Press.

Eysenck, H.J. and Grossarth-Maticek, R. (1991) 'Creative novation behaviour therapy as a prophylactic treatment of cancer and coronary heart disease: effects of treatment', *Behaviour Research Therapy*, 29(1): 17–31.

Eysenck, H.J. and O'Connor, K.P. (1979) 'Smoking personality and arousal', in A. Remond (ed.), *Electrophysiological Effects of Nicotine*. Amsterdam: Elsevier, pp. 147–57.

Eysenck, M.W. and Eysenck, H.J. (1980) 'Mischel and the concept of personality', *British Journal of Psychology*, 71(2): 191–204.

Eysenck, M.W. and Folkard, S. (1980) 'Personality, time, of day and caffeine: some theoretical and conceptual problems', in Revelle (ed.), *Journal of Experimental Psychology*, 109(1): 32–41.

Feldman, P.D., Cohen, S., Lepore, S.J., Matthews, K.A., Kamarck, T.W. and Marsland, A.L. (1999) 'Negative emotions and acute physiological responses to stress', *Annals of Behavioral Medicine*, 21(3): 216–22.

Francis, L.J. and Jackson, C.J. (2003) 'Eysenck's dimensional model of personality and religion: are religious people more neurotic?' *Mental Health, Religion & Culture*, 6(1): 87–100.

Frith, C.D. (1971) 'Smoking behaviour and its relation to the smoker's immediate experience', *British Journal of Social and Clinical Psychology*, 10(1): 73–8.

Gladstone, G.L., Parker, G.B., Mitchell, P.B., Malhi, G.S., Wilhelm, K.A. and Austin, M.P. (2005) 'A brief measure of worry severity (BMWS): Personality and clinical correlates of severe worriers', *Journal of Anxiety Disorders*, 19(8): 877–92.

Gomez, R. and Francis, L. (2003) 'Generalized anxiety disorder: Relationship with Eysenck's, Gray's and Newman's theories', *Personality and Individual Differences*, 34(1): 3–17.

Goulding, A. (2004) 'Schizotypy models in relation to subjective health and paranormal beliefs and experiences', *Personality and Individual Differences*, 37(1): 157–67.

Gutiérrez, J.L.G., Jiménez, B.M., Hernández, E.G. and Puente, C.P. (2005) 'Personality and subjective well-being: Big five correlates and demographic variables', *Personality and Individual Differences*, 38(7): 1561–9.

Humphreys, M.S., Revelle, W., Simon, L. and Gilliland, K. (1980) 'Individual differences in diurnal rhythms and multiple activation states: A reply of M.W. Eysenck and Folkard', *Journal of Experimental Psychology: General*, 109(1): 42–8.

Janke, W. (1983) *Response Variability Of Psychotropic Drugs*. London: Pergamon Press.

Julien, D., O'Connor, K.P., Aardema, F. and Todorov, C. (2006) 'The specificity of belief domains in obsessive-compulsive symptom subtypes', *Personality and Individual Differences*, 41(7): 1205–16.

Karlsson, E. and Archer, T. (2007) 'Relationship between personality characteristics and affect: Gender and affective personality', *Individual Differences Research*, 5(1): 44–58.

Kazarian, S.S. and Martin, R.A. (2006) 'Humor styles, culture-related personality, well-being, and family adjustment among Armenians in Lebanon', *Humor: International Journal of Humor Research*, 19(4): 405–23.

Kline, P. (1992) 'The factor structure in the fields of personality and ability', in A. Gale and M. Eysenck (eds), *Handbook of Individual Differences: Biological Perspectives*. Chichester: John Wiley & Sons, pp. 141–55.

Kline, R.B. (2005) *Beyond Significance Testing*. Washington, DC: American Psychological Association.

Knyazev, G.G., Belopolsky, V.I., Bodunov, M.V. and Wilson, G.D. (2004) 'Impulsivity as a predictor of smoking and alcohol consumption',

Personality and Individual Differences, 37(8): 1681–92.

Lang, P.J. (1968) 'Fear reduction and fear behavior: Problems in treating a construct', in J.M. Shlien, H.F. Hunt, J.D. Matarazzo and C. Savage (eds), *Research in Psychotherapy* (Vol. III). Washington, DC: American Psychological Association, pp. 90–102.

Lang, P.J. (1978) 'Anxiety: Toward a psychophysiological definition', in H.S. Akiskal and W.L. Webb (eds), *Psychiatric Diagnosis: Exploration of Biological Predictors*. New York: Spectrum, pp. 365–89.

Luciano, M., Wainwright, M.A., Wright, N. and Martin, N. (2006) 'The heritability of conscientiousness facets and their relationship to IQ and academic achievement', *Personality and Individual Differences*, 40(6): 1189–99.

Malmo, R.B. (1957) 'Anxiety and behavioral arousal', *Psychological Review*, 64(5): 276–87.

Malmo, R.B. (1959) 'Activation: A neuropsychological dimension', *Psychological Review*, 66(6): 367–86.

Malmo, R.B. (1965) 'Physiological gradients and behaviour', *Psychological Bulletin*, 64(4): 225–34.

Malmo, R.B. and Malmo, H.P. (2000) 'On electromyographic (EMG) gradients and movement-related brain activity: Significance for motor control, cognitive functions, and certain psychopathologies', *International Journal of Psychophysiology*, 38(2): 145–209.

Marusic, A. and Eysenck, H.J. (2001) 'Synergistic interaction of smoking and neuroticism as a risk factor in ischaemic heart disease: Case-control study', *Personality and Individual Differences*, 30(1): 47–57.

McCreery, C. and Claridge, G. (2002) 'Healthy schizotypy: The case of out-of-the-body experiences', *Personality and Individual Differences*, 32(1): 141–54.

Meehl, P.E. (2001) 'Comorbidity and taxometrics', *Clinical Psychology: Science and Practice*, 8(4): 507–19.

Miller, E., Joseph, S. and Tudway, J. (2003) 'Assessing the component structure of four self-report measures of impulsivity', *Personality and Individual Differences*, 37(2): 349–58.

Minnix, J. and Kline, J.P. (2004) 'Neuroticism predicts resting frontal EEG asymmetry variability', *Personality and Individual Differences*, 36(4): 823–32.

Moutafi, J., Furnham, A. and Paltiel, L. (2006) 'Can personality factors predict intelligence?', *Personality and Individual Differences*, 38(5): 1021–33.

Munafo, M.R., Clark, T.G. and Flint, J. (2004) 'Are there sex differences in the association between the 5HTT gene and neuroticism? A meta-analysis', *Personality and Individual Differences*, 37(3): 621–6.

Muris, P., de Jong, P.J. and Engelen, S. (2004) 'Relationships between neuroticism, attentional control, and anxiety disorders symptoms in non-clinical children', *Personality and Individual Differences*, 47(4): 789–97.

O'Connor, K.P. (1985) 'A model of situational preference amongst smokers', *Personality and Individual Differences*, 6(2): 151–60.

O'Connor, K.P. (1989a) 'A motor psychophysiological model of smoking and personality', *Personality and Individual Differences*, 19(8): 889–903.

O'Connor, K.P. (1989b) 'Individual differences and motor systems', in T. Ney and A. Gale (eds), *Smoking and Human Behaviour*. Chichester: Wiley, pp. 141–70.

O'Connor, K.P. (1989c) 'Psychophysiology and skilled behaviour', *Journal of Psychophysiology*, 3(4): 219–24.

O'Connor, K.P. (1992) 'Design and analysis in individual difference research', in A. Gale and M. Eysenck (eds), *Handbook of Individual Differences: Biological Perspectives*. Chichester: Wiley, pp. 45–79.

O'Connor, K.P. (2002) 'A cognitive behavioural/psychophysiological model of tic disorders', *Behavior Research and Therapy*, 40(10): 1113–42.

O'Connor, K.P. (2005) *Cognitive Behavioural Management of Tic Disorder*. Chichester: Wiley.

O'Connor, K.P. and Langlois, R. (1991) 'Smoking types or smoker types profiles of craving amongst smokers', *Personality and Individual Differences*, 12(2): 189–94.

O'Connor, K.P., Gareau, D., Gaudette, G. and Robillard, S. (1999) 'Relaxation and the treatment of generalized anxiety disorder', Presentation at the Association for the Advancement of Behavior Therapy, Toronto, November 11–14.

O'Connor, K.P., Aardema, F. and Freeston, M. (2001) 'A Bayesian approach to modelling continuous self-report data: Transforming time into space', Poster, World Congress of Behavioural and Cognitive Therapies (WCBCT), Vancouver, July 17–21.

Pittenger, D.J. (2004) 'The limitations of extracting typologies from trait measures of personality', *Personality and Individual Differences*, 37(4): 779–87.

Pole, A., West, M. and Harrison, J. (1994) *Applied Bayesian Forecasting and Time Series Analysis*. New York: Chapman Hall.

Radomsky, A., Lavoie, S. and Douglas, M. (2006) 'Ecological valid manipulations of cognitive factors in compulsive checking: from clinic to laboratory and back again', Paper presented at the 40th Annual Convention of the ABCT, Chicago, November 16–19.

Ramanaiah, N.V., Rielage, J.K. and Sharpe, J.P. (2001) 'Spiritual well-being and personality', *Psychological Reports*, 89(3): 662–8.

Rammstedt, B. (2007) 'Who worries and who is happy? Explaining individual differences in worries and satisfaction by personality', *Personality and Individual Differences*, 43(6): 1626–34.

Revelle, W. and Humphreys, M. (1980) 'The interactive effect of personality, time of day, and caffeine: A test of the arousal model', *Journal of Experimental Psychology (General)*, 109(1): 1–31.

Rosario-Campos, M.C., Miguel, E.C., Quatrano, S., Chacon, P., Ferrao, Y., Findley, D., Katsovich, L., Scahill, L., King, R.A., Woody, S.R., Tolin, D., Hollander, E., Kano, Y. and Leckman, J.F. (2006) 'The dimensional Yale-Brown Obsessive-Compulsive Scale (DY-BOCS): An instrument for assessing obsessive-compulsive symptom dimensions', *Molecular Psychiatry*, 11(5): 495–504.

Rouanet, H. and Lecoutre, B. (1983) 'Specific reference in ANOVA: Form significance tests to Bayesian procedures', *British Journal of Mathematical and Statistical Psychology*, 36: 252–68.

Roy, C. (2006) 'A comparison of anxiety and preparation as explanations of social phobia', Unpublished PhD dissertation, University of Montréal, Montréal.

Roysamb, E. (2006) 'Personality and well-being', in M.E. Vollrath (ed.), *Handbook of Personality and Health*. New York, NY: John Wiley & Sons Ltd, pp. 115–34.

Rusting, C.L. (1998) 'Personality, mood, and cognitive processing of emotional information: Three conceptual frameworks', *Psychological Bulletin*, 124(2): 165–96.

Sallis, J.F., Lichstein, K.L. and McGlynn, F.D. (1980) 'Anxiety response patterns: A comparison of clinical and analogue populations', *Journal of Behavior Therapy and Experimental Psychiatry*, 11(3): 179–83.

Sanchez-Bernardos, M.L. and Avia, M.D. (2004) 'Personality correlates of fantasy proneness among adolescents', *Personality and Individual Differences*, 37(5): 1069–79.

Savage, L.J. (1962) *The Foundations of Statistical Inference*. London: Methuen.

Schell, K., Woodruff, G., Corbin, B. and Melton, E. (2005) 'Trait and State predictors of error detection accuracy in a simulated quality control task', *Personality and Individual Differences*, 39(1): 47–60.

Schmidtke, J.I. and Heller, W. (2004) 'Personality, affect, EEG: Predicting patterns of regional brain activity related to extraversion and neuroticism', *Personality and Individual Differences*, 36(3): 717–32.

Shawyer, L. (1977) 'Research variables in psychology and the logic of their creation', *Psychiatry*, 40(1): 1–16.

Springer, K. (1990) 'In defense of theories', *Cognition*, 35(3): 293–8.

Stewart, M., Ebmeier, K. and Deary, I. (2005) 'Personality correlates of happiness and sadness: EPQ-R and TPQ compared', *Personality and Individual Differences*, 38(5): 1085–96.

Thayer, R.E. (1996) *The Origin of Everyday Moods. Managing Energy, Tension, and Stress*. New York: Oxford University Press.

Wallace, J.C. (2004) 'Confirmatory factor analysis of the cognitive failures questionnaire: Evidence for dimensionality and construct validity', *Personality and Individual Differences*, 37(2): 307–24.

Waller, N.G. and Meehl, P.E. (1998) *Multivariate Taxometric Procedures: Distinguishing Types From Continua*. Newberry Park, CA: Sage.

Washburn, D.A., Smith, J.D. and Taglialatela, L.A. (2005) 'Individual differences in metacognitive responsiveness: Cognitive and personality correlates', *Journal of General Psychology*, 132(4): 446–61.

Whittal, M. (2006) 'Message from the program chair', 40th Annual Convention of the of Association of Behavioral and Cognitive Therapies (ABCT), Chicago, November 16–19.

Zhiqiang, Y. (1999) 'The relationship between metacognition and five major personality factors.' *Psychological Science (China)*, 22(1): 85–7.

11

J.A. Gray's Reinforcement Sensitivity Theory (RST) of Personality

Alan D. Pickering and Philip J. Corr

Jeffrey Gray's (1976, 1982) behavioural inhibition system (BIS) theory of anxiety has stood well the test of time. This theory of personality – which is now widely known as *reinforcement sensitivity theory* (RST) – has gradually evolved over the past 30 years, seeing its major revision in 2000 by Gray and McNaughton, and even further elaborations and refinements subsequently (McNaughton and Corr, 2004, 2008; Corr and McNaughton, 2008). However, recent data that have strengthened the general foundations of the neural basis of the theory have also forced significant modifications of, and additions to, its superstructure. These changes are not inconsequential; as such, predictions cannot now be based on prior knowledge of the 1982 version. These changes, we contend, have the potential to lead to confusion. A major purpose of this chapter is to review the current scientific status of Gray's RST and draw out some of its major implications for future research.

RST is built upon a *state* description of neural systems and associated, relatively short-term, emotions and behaviours, which, according to the theory, give rise to longer-term *trait* dispositions of emotion and behaviour. This theory argues that statistically defined personality factors are sources of variation that are stable over time and that derive from underlying properties of an individual; it is these, and current changes in the environment, that comprise the neuropsychological foundations of 'personality'. This assertion is demanded by the fact that personality traits account for behavioural differences between individuals presented with identical environments; also, behavioural differences show consistency across time. Thus, the ultimate goal of personality research is to identify the relatively static (underlying) biological variables that determine the (superficial) factor structure measured in behaviour. It would, of course, be a mistake to deny the relevance of the environment in controlling behaviour, but to produce consistent long-term effects, environmental influences must be mediated by, and instantiated in, biological systems.

Gray's approach to the biological basis of personality followed a particular pattern: (a) first identify the fundamental properties of brain-behavioural systems that might be involved in the important sources of variation observed in human behaviour and (b) then relate variations in these systems to known measures of personality. Central to this approach is the assumption that the variation observed in the functioning of these brain-behavioural systems comprise what we term 'personality'. As discussed below, relating (a) to (b) has proved the major challenge to RST researchers.

Now, most RST studies have tested the unrevised (pre-2000) version of RST. But, as we shall see, in many crucial respects, the revised Gray and NcNaughton (2000) theory of the underlying neural systems and their function is very different, leading to the formulation of new personality hypotheses, some of which stand in opposition to those generated from the unrevised theory (for more detailed discussion of these matters, see Corr, 2004, 2008; Corr and McNaughton, 2008; McNaughton and Corr, 2004, 2008).

'CLASSIC' (1970–2000) AND REVISED (2000–) REINFORCEMENT SENSITIVITY THEORY

Today, in personality research, it is common to relate personality factors to emotion and motivational systems, but this consensus did not prevail before the time of Gray's original work. It is a mark of achievement that Gray's (1970, 1982) approach is today so widely accepted, and the emergence of a *neuroscience of personality* can be seen to be largely shaped by his work. In a similar vein to Hans Eysenck's (1957, 1967) theories before him, Gray's innovation was to put together the existing pieces of the scientific jigsaw in order to provide the foundations of a general theory of personality. Gray, like Pavlov (1927) before him, advocated a twin-track approach: the *conceptual nervous*

system (cns), and the *central nervous system* (CNS) (cf. Hebb, 1955). That is, the cns components of personality (e.g. learning theory; see Gray, 1975) and the component brain systems underlying systematic variations in behaviour (ex hypothesi, personality). As noted by Gray (1972a), these two levels of explanation *must* be compatible, but given a state of imperfect knowledge it would be unwise to abandon one approach in favour of the other. Gray used the language of cybernetics, in the form of cns–CNS bridge, to show how the flow of information and control of outputs is achieved (e.g. the Gray and Smith, 1969, 'arousal-decision' model).

Theoretical origins of RST

In contrast to Gray's bottom-up general approach, Hans Eysenck adopted a very different 'top-down' method. His search for causal systems was determined by the structure of statistically derived personality factors/dimensions. In an important respect, Eysenck's approach was viable: this was to understand the causal bases of *observed* personality structure, defined as a unitary whole (e.g. extraversion and neuroticism). For this very reason, it is perhaps not surprising to learn that Eysenck's causal systems never developed beyond the postulation of a small number of very general brain processes, principally the ascending reticular activating system (ARAS), underlying the dimension of introversion–extraversion and cortical arousal (for a summary see Corr, 2004). A second dimension, neuroticism (N), was related to activation of the limbic system and emotional instability (see Eysenck and Eysenck, 1985). Taken together, Gray's and Eysenck's approaches are complementary, tackling important problems at different levels of analysis.

Eysenck's (1967) arousal theory of extraversion hypothesized that introverts and extraverts differ with respect to the sensitivity of their cortical arousal system; and this is in

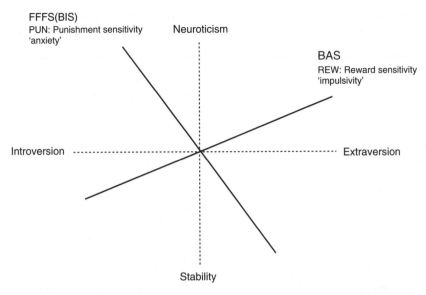

Figure 11.1   Position in factor space of the fundamental punishment sensitivity and reward sensitivity (unbroken lines) and the emergent *surface expressions* of these sensitivities, viz. extraversion (E) and neuroticism (N) (broken lines). The current working hypothesis is that 'punishment sensitivity' – which, in the unrevised model, was labelled 'anxiety – relates to both the FFFS and BIS'

consequence of differences in response thresholds of their ARAS. According to this theory, compared with extraverts, introverts have lower response thresholds and thus higher cortical arousal. In general, introverts were said to be more cortically aroused and more arousable when faced with sensory stimulation. However, the extraversion-arousal champions marched under a banner upon which was blazoned an inverted-U symbol – chosen, in large measure, by virtue of the Pavlovian notion of transmarginal inhibition (TMI; a protective mechanism that breaks the link between increasing stimuli intensity and behaviour at high intensity levels – in the Hullian learning literature this effect went under the name of 'stimulus intensity dynamism'). It was against this theoretical backdrop that RST developed.

Gray's (1970, 1972b, 1981) modification of Eysenck's theory proposed changes: (a) to the position of extraversion (E) and neuroticism

(N) in Eysenckian factor space; and (b) to their neuropsychological bases. Gray argued that E and N should be rotated by approximately 30 degrees to form the more causally efficient axes of 'punishment sensitivity', reflecting anxiety (Anx), and 'reward sensitivity', reflecting impulsivity (Imp) (Figure 11.1; see Pickering et al., 1999).

This modification stated that Imp+ individuals are more sensitive to *signals* of reward, relative to Imp– individuals, and Anx+ individuals are more sensitive to *signals* of punishment, relative to Anx– individuals. The proposed independence of the axes suggested that (a) responses to reward should be the same at all levels of Anx and (b) responses to punishment should be the same at all levels of Imp – this position was dubbed the 'separable subsystems hypothesis' by Corr (2001, 2002). According to RST, Eysenck's E and N dimensions are derivative secondary factors of these more fundamental punishment and reward sensitivities: E reflects the balance of punishment and reward sensitivities; N reflects their joint strengths (Gray, 1981).

Clinical neurosis

Eysenck's taxonomic model of personality was based on the factor analysis of the symptoms of war 'neurotics' (1944, 1947), and his 1957 and 1967 causal theories were designed to explain the genesis of these neuroses; it is, thus, on these grounds that the theory is critically tested. In brief, Eysenck postulated that introverts are more prone to suffer from anxiety disorders by virtue of their greater conditionability, especially of emotional responses. This theory was later elaborated to include the notion of incubation effects in conditioning (Eysenck, 1979), in order to account for the 'neurotic paradox' (i.e. the failure of extinction with continued non-reinforcement of the CS). Coupled with emotional instability, reflected in N, this made the introverted neurotic (E−/N+) particularly prone to anxiety disorders.

However, from the very beginning of this arousal-based theory of personality, a number of problems refused to be silenced. For one, introverts show *weaker* classical conditioning under conditions conducive to high arousal (which, we must assume, is also induced by aversive UCSs), as seen in eyeblink conditioning studies (Eysenck and Levey, 1967). This finding supports Eysenck's *own* theory that introverts are transmarginally inhibited by high arousal, but *at the very same moment* fails to explain adequately the genesis of clinical neurosis. Other problems also screamed out to be heard. For example, impulsivity (inclined into the N plane; see Figure 11.1), not sociability (defining the extraversion axis), is often found to be associated with conditioning effects (Eysenck and Levey, 1972), but this places high arousability, and thus high

conditionability, along an axis that is orthogonal to the one which has its high pole in the neurotic-introvert quadrant where clinical neurosis is located. Thus, Eysenck's *own* theory seems unable to explain the development of anxiety in neurotic-introverts. Time-of-day effects further undermine the central postulates of Eysenck's personality theory of clinical neurosis (see Gray, 1981).

In addition to the above problems, Gray cited a further reason to prefer a non-conditioning explanation (Corr, 2008). Now, classical conditioning theory states that as a result of the conditioned stimulus (CS) and unconditioned stimulus (UCS) being systematically paired, the CS comes to take on many of the eliciting properties of the UCS. That is, when presented alone after conditioning, the CS produces a response (i.e. the conditioned response, CR) that resembles the unconditioned response (UCR) elicited by the UCS. However, the CR *does not* substitute for the UCR – in several important respects, the CR does not even resemble the UCR. For example, a pain UCS will elicit a wide variety of reactions (e.g. vocalization and behavioural excitement) which are quite different to those elicited by a CS *signalling* pain, which consists of a quite different set of behaviours (e.g. quietness and behavioural inhibition). We thus have a theory that does not seem fit for purpose: classical conditioning cannot explain the pathogenesis or phenomenology of neurosis, although it can explain how initially neutral stimuli (CSs) acquire the motivational power to elicit this state. Gray asked the crucial question: if classical conditioning does not account for the generation of the negative emotional state that characterises neurosis, then what does? His answer – based upon extensive animal research (e.g. behavioural, pharmacological, lesion, and electrical stimulation studies) – was an innate mechanism, namely the *behavioural inhibition system* (BIS; Gray, 1976, 1982).

Three systems of 'classic' RST

RST gradually developed over the years to include three major systems of emotion:

1 The *behavioural inhibition system* (BIS) was postulated to be sensitive to *conditioned* aversive stimuli (i.e. signals of both punishment and the omission/termination of reward) relating to Anx, but also to extreme novelty, high-intensity stimuli, and innate fear stimuli (e.g. snakes, blood), which are more related to fear.

In addition, two other systems were postulated:

2 The *fight/flight system* (FFS) was postulated to be sensitive to *unconditioned* aversive stimuli (i.e. innately painful stimuli), mediating the emotions of rage and panic. This system was related to the state of negative affect (NA) (associated with pain) and speculatively associated by Gray with Eysenck's trait of psychoticism.
3 The *behavioural approach system* (BAS) was postulated to be sensitive to *conditioned* appetitive stimuli, forming a positive feedback loop, activated by the presentation of stimuli associated with reward and the termination/omission of signals of punishment. This system was related to the state of positive affect (PA) and the trait of Imp.

The BIS was modelled on the detailed pattern of behavioural effects of classes of drugs known to affect anxiety in human beings. By this route, Gray argued, anxiety could be operationally specified as those behaviours changed by anxiolytic drugs. Of course, there exists here the danger of circularity of argument; this was avoided by the postulation that anxiolytic drugs do not simply reduce anxiety (itself a vacuous tautology), but could be shown to have a number of behavioural effects in typical animal learning paradigms. Experimental evidence showed that anti-anxiety drugs affected responses to conditioned aversive stimuli, the omission of expected reward and conditioned frustration, all of which Gray postulated were mediated by a BIS, which was responsible for suppressing ongoing operant behaviour in the face of threat, as well as enhancing information processing and vigilance. (We shall see that in this revised theory, these effects can be reclassified as *conflict* effects.) Later, the BAS was added to account for behavioural reactions to rewarding stimuli – these were largely unaffected by anti-anxiety drugs. The danger of a circularity of argument was further reduced by the behavioural profile of the newer classes of anxiolytics which, it turned out, had the same behavioural effects and acted on the same neural systems as the older class of drugs, despite the fact that they had different psychopharmacological modes of action and side-effects (Gray and McNaughton, 2000).

Revised (2000–) RST

The Gray and McNaughton (2000) revised theory updates and extends the 'classic' version. These changes are, in parts, substantial: but, in other parts, more a clarification of the 1982 theory. Revised RST postulates three systems.

1 The *fight–flight–freeze system* (FFFS) is responsible for mediating reactions to aversive stimuli of all kinds, conditioned *and* unconditioned. It further proposes that there exists a hierarchical array of neural modules, responsible for avoidance and escape behaviours. Now, the FFFS mediates the emotion of fear, not anxiety. The associated personality factor comprises fear-proneness and avoidance, which is clinically mapped onto such disorders as phobia and panic.
2 The BAS mediates reactions to *all* appetitive stimuli, conditioned and unconditioned. This system generates the appetitively hopeful emotion of 'anticipatory pleasure', and hope itself. The associated personality comprises optimism, reward-orientation and impulsiveness, which clinically maps onto addictive behaviours (e.g. pathological gambling) and various varieties of high-risk, impulsive behaviour, and possibly the appetitive component of mania. The BAS is largely unchanged in the revised Gray and McNaughton version of RST.

3   The BIS is responsible, not, as in the 1982 version, for mediating reactions to conditioned aversive stimuli and the special class of innate fear stimuli, but for the resolution of *goal conflict* in general (e.g. between BAS-approach and FFFS-avoidance, as in foraging situations – but it is also involved in BAS–BAS and FFFS–FFFS conflicts). The BIS generates the emotion of anxiety, which entails the inhibition of prepotent conflicting behaviours, the engagement of risk assessment processes, and the scanning of memory and the environment to help resolve concurrent goal conflict.

The BIS resolves conflicts by increasing, through recursive loops, the negative valence of stimuli (these are adequate inputs into the FFFS), until behavioural resolution occurs in favour of approach or avoidance. Subjectively, this state is experienced as worry and rumination. The associated personality comprises worry-proneness and anxious rumination, leading to being constantly on the look-out for possible signs of danger, which map clinically onto such conditions as generalized anxiety and obsessional-compulsive disorder (OCD). There is an optimal level of BIS activation: too little leads to risk seeking (e.g. psychopathy) and too much to risk aversion (generalized anxiety), both reflecting suboptimal conflict resolution.

NEUROPSYCHOLOGICAL STRUCTURE OF THE REVISED THEORY

Revised RST agrees with the classical version in its assertion that substantive affective events fall into just two distinct major classes: positive and negative (Gray, 1975; Gray, 1982; Gray and McNaughton, 2000). Rewards and punishments are the obvious exemplars of positive and negative events, respectively. But, importantly for human experiments, the absence of an expected positive event is functionally the same as the presence of a negative event and vice-versa (Gray, 1975). Omission of expected reward is thus punishing. Similarly, the absence of an

expected negative event is functionally the same as the presence of a positive event. Omission of punishment is rewarding. This basic scheme gives rise to a two-dimensional model of the neuropsychology of emotion, motivation, and personality that simplifies the theory, as well as serving as a point of unification of the otherwise complex arrangement of the separate neural modules underlying behaviour (McNaughton and Corr, 2004).

Fear and anxiety – defensive direction

The first dimension, 'defensive direction', is categorical. It rests on a functional distinction between behaviours that remove an animal from a source of danger (FFFS-mediated) and those that allow it cautiously to approach a source of potential danger (BIS-mediated). These functions are ethologically and pharmacologically distinct and, on each of these separate grounds, can be identified with fear and anxiety, respectively. The revised theory treats fear and anxiety as not only quite distinct but also, in a sense, as opposites. The categorical separation of fear from anxiety as classes of defensive responses has been demonstrated by Robert and Caroline Blanchard (Blanchard and Blanchard, 1988, 1990; Blanchard et al., 1997).

The Blanchards used 'ethoexperimental analysis' of the innate reactions of rats to cats to determine the functions of specific classes of behaviour. One class of behaviours was elicited by the immediate presence of a predator. This class could clearly be attributed to a state of fear. The behaviours, grouped into the class on purely ethological grounds, were sensitive to panicolytic drugs but not to drugs that are specifically anxiolytic. This is consistent with the insensitivity to anxiolytic drugs of active avoidance in a wide variety of species, and phobia in humans is also insensitive to anxiolytic drug treatment (Sartory et al., 1990). A second, quite distinct, class of behaviours (including 'risk assessment') was elicited by the potential presence of a predator.

This class of behaviours was sensitive to anxiolytic drugs. Both functionally and pharmacologically, this class was distinct from the behaviours attributed to fear and could be attributed to a state of anxiety.

Fear and anxiety – defensive distance

The second dimension, 'defensive distance', is graded: it rests on a functional hierarchy that determines appropriate behaviour in relation to defensive distance (i.e. perceived distance from threat). This second dimension applies equally to fear and anxiety but is instantiated separately in each.

Defensive distance equates with real distance; but in a more dangerous situation, the perceived defensive distance is shortened. In other words, defensive behaviour (e.g. active avoidance) will be elicited at a longer (objective) distance with a highly dangerous stimulus (which shortens *perceived* defensive distance), as compared to the elicitation of defensive behaviour by a less dangerous stimulus. According to the theory, certain individuals have a much shorter perceived defensive distance for a given threat stimulus, and thus react more intensively to relatively innocuous (in real distance terms) stimuli.

McNaughton and Corr (2004) view individual differences in defensive distance for a fixed real distance as a reflection of the personality dimension underlying 'punishment sensitivity', or 'threat perception'. They suggest that the high pole of this dimension is neurotic-introversion and the low pole is stable-extraversion. This personality dimension affects the FFFS-mediated behaviours directly, but affects those mediated by the BIS only indirectly (e.g. via FFFS-BAS goal conflict). Anxiolytic drugs are argued to alter (internally perceived) defensive distance relative to actual external threat. They *do not* affect defensive behaviour directly, but rather operate to shift behaviour along the defensive axis, often leading to the output of a different behaviour (e.g. risk-assessment to pre-threat behaviour).

An important conclusion of this theory, which goes to show the subtlety of revised RST, is the claim that the comparison of individuals on a single measure of performance at only a single level of threat may produce results that are difficult to interpret. For example, for an objectively defined defensive distance, one person may be in a state of panic and so cease moving, while another may actively avoid and so increase their movement. That is, highly sensitive and insensitive fearful individuals will show *different* behaviours *at the same level of threat* (defined in objective terms), as indeed will trait-identical individuals at different levels of threat. Thus moving people along this axis of defensive distance (by drugs or by experimental means) will not simply affect the strength or probability of a given behaviour, but is expected to result in different behaviours (which, themselves, may be in opposition). As we can see, at the core of the revised theory are ethological factors, relating specific behaviours to specific threats and environmental conditions.

Conflict

Revised RST defines anxiety in terms of defensive approach. However, this notion contains something more fundamental about anxiety, namely, *conflict*. An animal approaches a threat only if there is some possibility of a positive outcome (e.g. food when foraging in an unsafe field). But threats are not the only sources of aversion and avoidance encountered. In principle, approach–approach and avoidance–avoidance conflicts also involve activation of the same system and have essentially the same effects as classic approach–avoidance. It turns out that the conditioned stimuli to which the unrevised version of the BIS was said to be sensitive are, according to this formulation, specific examples of conflict stimuli. Thus, the new BIS theory reclassifies conditioned stimuli and expands the type of stimuli processed by the BIS. All of these now fall under the common rubric of goal conflict. This reformulation also helps tidy-up the rag-bag of other eliciting stimuli of the BIS (i.e. innate stimuli and high-intensity noise): in their non-conflict form, they now belong with the FFFS.

NEURAL SYSTEMS OF FEAR AND ANXIETY

Revised RST combines a large number of brain structures ranging from the prefrontal cortex, at the highest level, to the periaqueductal grey, at the lowest level, assigning to each structure: (a) a specific place in the theory; (b) a specific fundamental class of function; and (c) a specific class of mental disorder (McNaughton and Corr, 2008). Thus, the most fundamental change to the old view of the BIS is that it is *distributed* among a number of neural structures.

General architecture

The concepts of defensive direction and defensive distance provide a two-dimensional schema within which all defensive behaviours can be described. The theory translates this two-dimensional psychological schema into a matching two-dimensional neurological one. In particular, the categorical distinction *between* defensive approach and defensive avoidance is translated into two distinct parallel streams of neural structures; and the dimension of defensive distance is translated into the levels of a hierarchy of structures *within* each of the parallel streams (Figure 11.2).

The neural mapping of defensive distance into the two hierarchies is rendered simple by two architectural features. First, smaller defensive distances map to more caudal, subcortical neural structures while larger defensive distances map to more rostral, cortical

neural structures with intermediate structures arranged in caudo-rostral order in between. Second, this mapping occurs in a symmetrical fashion with matching structures located within each of the parallel streams (this often involves subdivisions, or nuclei, of the same named area).

THE BEHAVIOURAL APPROACH SYSTEM (BAS)

We now have an outline of the FFFS and the matching components of the BIS. Revised RST theory also has a central place for the BAS. It must be borne in mind that, although the BIS would be activated with the simultaneous activation of the FFFS and the BAS (e.g. in the case of approach–avoidance conflict), it remains the case that the BAS is conceptually distinct from both the BIS and the FFFS.

Neural organization of the BAS

There are tensions in attempts to map the BAS onto brain systems and functions. As with the BIS and the FFFS, the BAS can be viewed as hierarchically organized. Gray (Gray and McNaughton, 1996; Gray et al., 1991) has described the BAS as having a 'caudate' component and an 'accumbens' component. However, he also made clear that 'accumbens holds a list of subgoals making up a given motor program and is able to switch through the list in an appropriate order, but to retrieve the specific content of each step, it needs to call up the appropriate subroutine by way of its connections to the [caudate] system' (Gray and McNaughton, 1996). Such caudate motor command subroutines are quite distinct from the affect-laden goals that are the subject of the FFFS, BAS and BIS (Gray and McNaughton, 2000).

On the other hand, as with the FFFS, the hierarchical organization of the BAS makes

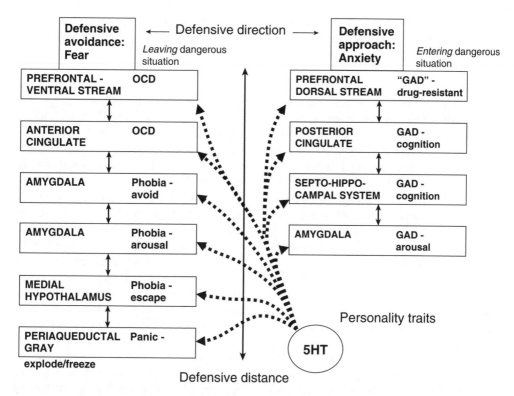

Figure 11.2   The two-dimensional defence system of fear and anxiety. On either side are defensive avoidance and defensive approach, respectively (this is a categorical dimension of 'defensive direction'). Each system is divided into a number of hierarchical levels (corresponding to the second dimension of 'defensive distance'). These are ordered from high to low (top to bottom) both with respect to neural level (and cytoarchitectonic complexity) and to functional level. Each level is associated with specific classes of behaviour and so symptom and syndrome (as shown). General monoamine modulation is shown as the putative 'personality' influence that provides unity to each system

it difficult for any part of it to control overall BAS sensitivity. Where a personality factor is thought to alter such sensitivity generally, we should probably look for appropriate modulatory systems. The neuromodulator that is probably of primary importance in BAS functioning is dopamine (DA; Depue and Collins, 1999; Pickering and Gray, 1999). The accumbens and caudate separation, alluded to by Gray, is reflected in the distinction between the so-called mesolimbic and nigrostriatal projection pathways of dopaminergic cells (these project to accumbens and caudate respectively, along with

other structures). However, many influences (e.g. genes), which could generate individual differences in dopaminergic neurotransmission, may well express their effects on more than one dopaminergic projection system (Depue and Collins, 1999). Moreover, the structures innervated by these distinct dopaminergic systems act cooperatively to deliver behavioural responses thought of as being under BAS control.

In the neuroscience literature, over the last 15 years or so, a strong consensus has emerged over the functional significance of firing of dopaminergic cells in the midbrain

(Arbuthnott and Wickens, 2007; Schultz, 1998). The view is that DA cell firing reflects a 'reward prediction error' (RPE) signal. Specifically, in primates, increased bursts of DA cell firing result when an unexpected (under-predicted) reward occurs. Decreases in DA cell firing are observed when an expected reward does not occur (see Schultz, 1998, for details). Neuroimaging evidence in humans has also emerged which is consistent with this view (e.g. Abler et al., 2006). As argued elsewhere (Pickering and Gray, 1999, 2001; Pickering and Smillie, 2008), a proper neuroscientific understanding of the BAS will need to incorporate this RPE conceptualization of DA cell firing.

Of great interest in this area, the RPE view of DA cell firing is consistent with classic computational models of reinforcement learning (e.g. Dayan and Abbott, 2001). Learning in these models is hypothetically controlled by an RPE signal: a positive RPE (caused by an unexpected reward) is used to strengthen learning in the neural pathways which generated the behaviour leading to the reward; a large negative RPE (caused by a non-occurring expected reward) is used to extinguish learning in the neural pathways which generated the behaviour leading to the reward. When the RPE is close to zero (i.e. the level of reward is accurately predicted), then little learning takes place. The observations that DA cells fire in a fashion closely resembling an RPE signal was seen as providing a neural validation of these models. Moreover, the dopaminergic projection pathways release dopamine at sites very close to synapses on the dendritic spines of caudate and accumbens cells; these synapses are at the terminals of cortical inputs to the striatum. This synaptic arrangement, and the dendritic spines themselves, have a number of neurophysiological features (Wickens and Kotter, 1995) which enables an incoming burst of dopaminergic firing to operate effectively as a reinforcement/RPE signal and control learning at those cortico-striatal synapses.

The RPE conceptualization of dopamine cell firing in projections to BAS structures (caudate, accumbens, etc.) has strong resonances with the Gray and Smith (1969) cybernetic model of the functional interactions between the reward and punishment systems. In this model, the reward system had a comparator within it which determined whether the level of reward received matched the level expected. It was proposed that the results of this comparison process were fed back appropriately as inputs to the reward and punishment systems, although the detailed way in which this controlled learning of responses was not specified. The RPE account outlined above suggests how this learning may be accomplished. The Gray and Smith (1969) model proposed a general framework for choosing between responses leading to rewarding versus punishing behavioural consequences. Recent theoretical models of potential BAS structures in the basal ganglia have formalized the way that they may allow efficient decision-making of this kind (for an overview and references, see Bogacz, 2007).

Previously, accounts have been offered to begin to incorporate the neuroscience of dopamine cells and the basal ganglia into our understanding of the BAS (Pickering and Gray, 1999, 2001; see also Pickering and Smillie, 2008). This research is proceeding apace, and the final details have yet to be worked out. A challenge will be able to find an appropriate level of modelling which is able to distinguish between alternative neurally based accounts of the BAS.

What personality trait is linked to the BAS?

What broad personality trait might correspond to variations in the functioning of the BAS? Gray's original decision to call it 'impulsivity' was entirely ad hoc, as he repeatedly admitted. He used the ancient circular model of the humours (popularized by Eysenck) and drew a line between the types 'anxious' and 'carefree' (being confident that the BIS subserved trait anxiety). The line at right angles to the anxiety dimension (he assumed the BAS and BIS traits were orthogonal) approximately joins the labels of 'impulsive' and 'thoughtful' (although he might as easily have chosen 'optimistic' and 'careful' on these geometric grounds!). Thus, the impulsivity dimension was born; although Gray also had to decide which way round to place the dimension (high BAS types were assigned to the impulsive end of the dimension, on grounds of plausibility). This decision was further reinforced by the two components of extraversion in Eysenck's model, namely sociability and impulsivity, as well as experimental work showing impulsivity related to classical conditioning effects (see above).

On a related matter, Corr (2008) has drawn attention to the inadequate conceptualization of the BAS, especially as it relates to impulsivity. On evolutionary grounds, the BAS may be thought to be more complex than the FFFS, or indeed the BIS. The *primary* function of the BAS is to move the animal up the temporo-spatial gradient to the final biological reinforcer. This primary function is supported by a number of *secondary* processes, comprising perhaps simple approach, perhaps with BIS activation exerting behavioural caution at critical points, designed to reduce the distance between current and desired appetitive state (e.g. as seen in foraging behaviour in a densely vegetated field). However, in human behaviour, this depiction of BAS-controlled approach behaviour may be oversimplified.

First, it is helpful to distinguish the *incentive* motivation component and the *consummatory* component of reactions to appetitive stimuli. The neural machinery controlling reactions to unconditioned (innate) stimuli, and its associated emotion, must be different from that controlling the behaviour and emotion associated with *approach*, signalled by conditioned stimuli, to such stimuli. Thus, while

the BAS responds to all appetitive stimuli, it is concerned specifically with the appetitive-approach aspects that move the animals towards the final biological reinforcer; at this point, non-BAS consummatory mechanisms, specific to the particular reinforcer concerned, are activated, e.g. the eating of food.

Second, moving to approach proper, we can discern a number of relatively separate, albeit overlapping, processes. At the simplest level, there seems an obvious difference between the 'interest' and 'drive' that characterizes the early stages of approach, and the behavioural and emotional excitement as the animal reaches the final biological reinforcer. Emotion in the former case may be termed 'anticipatory pleasure' (or 'hope'); in the latter, 'excitement'. There is evidence that, at the psychometric level, the BAS is multidimensional. For example, the Carver and White (1994) BIS/BAS scales measure three aspects of BAS: *reward responsiveness*, *drive,* and *fun-seeking*. It may be speculated that *drive* is concerned with actively pursing desired goals, *reward-responsiveness* is concerned with excitement at doing things well and winning, and *fun-seeking* is concerned with the impulsivity aspect of the BAS (which is especially appropriate for the capture of the final biological reinforcer).

Subgoal scaffolding

As discussed in detail by Corr (2008), BAS behaviour may best be seen as involving a series of appetitively motivated subgoals. That is, in order to move along the temporo-spatial gradient to the final primary biological reinforcer, it is necessary to engage in *subgoal scaffolding*. This process has several stages: (a) identification of the biological reinforcer; (b) planning behaviour; and (c) executing the plan. Important in this regard is the following: complex approach behaviour entails a series of behavioural processes, some of which oppose each other. For example, behaviour *restraint* and *planning* are often demanded to achieve BAS goals, but not at the final point of *capture* of the biological reinforcer, where non-planning and fast reactions (i.e. impulsivity) are more appropriate. Being a highly impulsive person – that is, acting fast without thinking and not planning – would not be appropriate BAS behaviour in anything other than very simple situations. Indeed, such behaviour would often move the animal *away* from their desired goal. For this reason, and others mentioned above, 'impulsivity' is not the most appropriate term for the personality factor corresponding to the full range of processes entailed by the BAS.

Therefore, given such a weak basis for Gray's initial labelling of the BAS, as well its apparent complexity, it is somewhat surprising that the BAS has been equated with impulsivity for so long. The first serious contradictory views came many years later. Depue and Collins (1999) argued that extraversion (and in particular its agentic aspects) better captured the nature of the BAS-related personality trait. Their argument drew on detailed support from the animal neurophysiological literature but was, in essence, a simple one. First, they suggested that the BAS was closely linked to dopaminergic neurotransmission. Second, they argued that the extant evidence pointed to a link between extraversion and dopaminergic neurotransmission which was stronger than the link for any other major personality trait. We (Corr, 1999; Pickering, 1999; Pickering and Gray, 1999) cautioned that the evidential basis for part two of their argument rested on a tiny body of data, mostly from Depue and colleagues' own laboratory. In addition, we suggested that Depue and Collins had ignored an equally small body of data which pointed to links between dopaminergic neurotransmission and a cluster of traits we have termed impulsive antisocial sensation seeking (ImpASS), rather than extraversion. At that time we felt that the jury could not reach as clear a verdict as that reached by Depue and Collins and argued that (aspects of) the ImpASS trait cluster might correspond to the BAS trait. Subsequent neuroscience data has emerged

that is broadly in line with Depue and Collins' thesis (e.g. Cohen et al., 2005; Wacker et al., 2006). However, there are also psychometric and behavioural data (see Smillie et al., 2006, for a review) which we feel now tip the scales more strongly in favour of the idea that extraversion might be the BAS trait. But, further data are needed, especially ones relating specific psychometric measures of the revised RST's systems to extraversion.

INTERACTIONS OF THE BAS, FFFS, AND BIS: IMPLICATIONS FOR TRAIT MEASUREMENT

The old description of RST supposed that each system had a reactivity/sensitivity to its key inputs, which we can denote w_A, w_I, and w_F for the sensitivity of the BAS, BIS, and FFFS, respectively. Interindividual variations in w_A, w_I, and w_F are assumed to follow a normal distribution with each sensitivity independent of (uncorrelated with) the others. The trait of anxiety, Anx, was taken to reflect variation in w_I and another trait ('the BAS trait') was taken to reflect variation in w_A.

Elsewhere we (Corr, 2002; Pickering, 1997) argued that the effects of such systems on behaviour would generally not be independent of one another even though the sensitivities were themselves independent – although, under certain conditions, they would (specified by Corr, 2002). Thus, for example, a behaviour controlled by reward reinforcers would not only be influenced by the BAS personality trait (i.e. w_A) but could also often be influenced by Anx. Corr (2002) dubbed this the *joint subsystems hypothesis* in contrast to an earlier view that behaviour controlled by reward would depend selectively upon w_A (the *separable subsystems hypothesis*).

Recently, Smillie et al. (2006) took this view further. They argued that self-report questionnaire responses, used to measure personality traits, are likely to reflect subjective estimates of the functional *outcomes* rather than latent properties of the individual neural systems. A functional outcome of the BAS might be its mean output level across a range of situations, whereas a latent property would be its sensitivity (w_A). They suggested that the functional outcome will be available for introspection (and hence self-report) whereas a sensitivity will not, although the sensitivities will clearly have a direct influence on the observable functional outcome (someone with a higher value of w_A will, all other things being equal, have a higher mean BAS output level than a person with lower w_A). Looking at the item content of various possible BAS personality trait measures, Pickering (2008) concluded that such questionnaires might well reflect functional BAS outcomes (such as mean output level).

This viewpoint leads to some potentially striking conclusions. The functional outcomes of each system are, as for other reinforcer-controlled behaviours, likely to be susceptible to the joint influences of the various interacting systems. Smillie et al. (2006) report the results of simulation studies which illustrate this point. For one particular plausible set of interactions between the BIS, BAS and FFFS (in line with the revised Gray and McNaughton, 2000, model) they simulated functional outcomes (in this case mean output) across 200 randomly sampled and widely varying combinations of reinforcers. The mean BAS output across simulated individuals was predicted ($R^2 = 0.89$) by the following regression equation:

$$Mean\ BAS\ output = (\beta_A \times w_A) - (\beta_F \times w_F) - (\beta_I \times w_I)$$

where the βs are positive-valued regression coefficients. The same model showed that mean BIS output was predicted ($R^2 = 0.85$) by:

$$(\beta'_A \times w_A) + (\beta'_F \times w_F) + (\beta'_I \times w_I)$$

By contrast, it is interesting to note that the mean FFFS output was predicted ($R^2 = 0.82$) only by the sensitivity of the FFFS.

Assuming some trait questionnaires do reflect functional outcomes of specific systems then these simulations raise important and paradoxical results. For example, the 'BAS-related' trait measures is BAS-related because it is defined by the functional outcome of the BAS and yet it is influenced by the sensitivities of all three interacting systems (w_A, w_F and w_I). Thus, if one were to develop a new BAS trait measure then one should not consider it invalidated if it correlated negatively with anxiety (BIS trait) measures; the simulations predict that such trait correlations should be observed. These predictions occur, it is worth reiterating, even though w_A and w_I (the underlying system sensitivities) are independent of one another. The description of the 'reinforcement sensitivity' theory of personality has implied a one-to-one mapping of traits (e.g. anxiety) onto the sensitivities of single systems (e.g. the BIS). The simulations show that this need not be the case and trait measures may be jointly determined by the sensitivities of all three interacting systems. It remains sensible, however, to talk of the theory as 'reinforcement sensitivity' theory, as the resulting personality traits are determined by the sensitivities of reinforcement-dependent systems; however, the one-to-one mapping of traits onto sensitivities is now being questioned.

In a speculative footnote to this section, we consider whether there might be some trait measures which line up more directly with underlying sensitivities rather than functional outcomes? The simulations suggested that, for traits related to FFFS functioning, the two bases (sensitivities, functional outcomes) may sometimes be more or less interchangeable. This fits well with the account proposed by McNaughton and Corr (2004, 2008) in which the trait of fearfulness (neurotic-introversion to stable-introversion) maps directly onto underlying punishment sensitivity.

However, one might also imagine a situation in which a trait measure, *T*, had items which reflected the functional outcome of one system along with other items which reflected the functional outcome of another system (we finesse here the question of whether such a trait measure could ever emerge in a factor analytic approach to trait measure development). Imagine such a measure was based on a mixture of BAS and BIS functional outcomes. The final trait measure (from the results of the simulations presented earlier) would be given by a summation of the two earlier regression equations:

$$T = (\beta_A \times w_A) - (\beta_F \times w_F) - (\beta_I \times w_I) + (\beta'_A \times w_A) + (\beta'_F \times w_F) + (\beta'_I \times w_I)$$

Assuming the values of β_I and β'_I, and β_F and β'_F, were broadly similar then the above equation would approximately reduce to

$$T = (\beta_A + \beta'_A) \times w_A$$

In this scenario, the trait measure T would directly reflect the sensitivity of a single underlying system (the BAS in this example).

High scores on such a trait measure would be found in people who had higher BAS functional outcomes (e.g. higher mean BAS outputs) *and* higher BIS functional outcomes (e.g. higher mean BIS outputs) across a range of situations. Is such a trait measure likely? Do any existing trait measures plausibly satisfy such conditions? We do not think this is likely. It might be suggested that extraversion questionnaires might be candidates for traits like T above. The EPQ extraversion scale, for example, has several items about enjoying social situations (e.g. Do you enjoy meeting new people? Would you enjoy yourself at a lively party?); these can plausibly be viewed by indexing mean BAS output in these contexts. However, under Gray and McNaughton's (2000) reformulation of RST, and based on the description of the action of the BIS, someone with a high mean BIS output would often be rather cautious and deliberate, tending to seek extra information when situations are ambiguous or when motivations are conflicting, and so on. Such

a person might be described as low impulsive and deliberate. Items addressing these behavioural aspects might be found on some extraversion scales, and items addressing these behaviours on other scales would be very likely to correlate moderately with traditional extraversion items. However the correlation would be the opposite way round to that required for a trait measure such as T above; in our view, a trait measure like T therefore seems very unlikely to exist.

In summary, the main message of this section remains: the role of underlying reinforcement sensitivities in our revised understanding of RST seems likely to be more complex than has been hitherto suggested. With the possible exception of the punishment/fear system, variations in the sensitivities of the underlying systems to their characteristic inputs may not have one-to-one mappings onto observable personality traits.

PERSONALITY AND PSYCHOPATHOLOGY

How does personality relate to psychological conditions (e.g. anxiety). No doubt, the details of RST shall continue to undergo continual refinement and change – that is in the nature of any scientific theory – but we believe that 'defensive distance' and 'defensive direction' shall continue to play a pivotal role as they map onto a series of distinct neural modules, to each of which can be attributed a particular class of function, and so generation of a particular symptomatology (e.g. panic, phobia, obsession). As noted by McNaughton and Corr (2004, 2008), these 'symptoms' may be generated in several different ways:

1   as a normally adaptive reaction to specific (mild) eliciting stimuli (e.g. mild anxiety just before an exam);
2   as excessive activation of a related structure by its specific (strong) eliciting stimuli, but where the 'symptoms' are not excessive given the level

of input from the related structure (e.g. panic when crossing a railway line at the sight of a rapidly oncoming train);

3 at maladaptive intensity, as a result of excessive sensitivity to their specific eliciting stimuli (e.g. fearful avoidance as a result of seeing a harmless spider) – this would be a pathological reaction.

In addition, pathologically excessive (BIS) anxiety could generate (FFFS) panic with the latter being entirely appropriate to the level of apprehension experienced. Conversely, pathological panic could, with repeated experience, condition anxiety with the level of the latter being appropriate to the panic experienced. This modular view of the defence system, separated into distinct syndrome and symptom-specific, components was developed largely on the basis of animal experiments. In addition, the linking of this view to terms such as panic, phobia, and obsession is also justified by the clinical effects of drugs when taken together as a class. (All drugs have common and unique effects, and it is only their common effects that interest us here.) RST may provide a satisfactory explanation of the variety of clinical 'neurotic' phenomena observed, yet at the same time, may appear to destroy the very unity of an underlying personality trait.

However, this problem seems worse than it is. For rescue, we need only appeal to the fact that, based on quantitative genetic studies, there is a common fundamental predisposition to the plethora of clinical neurotic conditions observed, even though that predisposition manifests differently in different individuals (Kendler et al., 2003). Indeed, the action of many clinically effective drugs is best viewed as an interaction with more global modulatory systems. For example, 5HT neurons innervate virtually the entire defence system; and drugs such as imipramine or specific serotonin reuptake inhibitors (SSRIs), have a general effect on 5HT synapses. Such drugs affect anxiety, depression and panic because they increase the levels of 5HT in the different parts of the system controlling each.

Therefore, comparison of drug classes can be used to dissect out different parts of the defence system. But this comparison must involve several different drugs within each class if specific conclusions are to be drawn about specific brain systems. Conversely, the systems as a joint whole, and each system individually, may be globally susceptible to modulation controlled by the biological substrates underlying personality. In detail, then, the system underlying clinical drug action consists of two sets of parallel, interconnected modules dealing with defensive avoidance and defensive approach, respectively. Superimposed on these specialized modules are general modulatory systems.

It should be expected that if these modulatory systems are crucial for personality, there is also a conceptual need for general control. Certainly with the BIS, anxiolytics clearly alter defensive distance: they alter at whatever point of the neural hierarchy is in control given progressive variations in the external situation, and they do so in a lawful manner. Assuming that the control of fear by the monoamines operates in a similar manner to the control of anxiety by anxiolytic drugs, we should expect the personality factor related directly to 'punishment sensitivity' would be the one that alters the internal defensive distance in relation to any particular real distance. Put another way, a personality factor of fearfulness multiplies the quantum of fear inherent in a particular stimulus, producing many different levels (across different individuals) with the same stimulus.

CONCLUSIONS

There remains some considerable uncertainty as the best way to relate fundamental systems of emotion and motivation to personality factors, yet we contend that considerable progress has already been made. This chapter has illustrated that there is a lot of new theorizing which has substantially reformulated a popular theory of personality. As yet, however, this new thinking has not stimulated many new empirical findings. We hope that this situation will change in the near future. In relation to this issue, Smillie et al. (2006: 320) note that although RST is most often seen as a theory of anxiety and impulsivity, it is 'more accurately identified as a neuropsychology of emotion, motivation and learning. In fact, RST was born of basic animal learning research, initially not at all concerned with personality.' They go on to remark, 'RST did not develop as a theory *of* specific traits, but as a theory of specific biological systems which were later suggested to relate, *inter alia*, to personality' (2006: 321).

There is a related reason why basic emotion and motivation systems do not map neatly onto personality factors: basic emotion and motivation theory has extended beyond the point at which Gray suggested that the BIS and BAS relate to anxiety and impulsivity, respectively. Furthermore, RST personality researchers have developed scales to measure the BIS and BAS that were influenced by Gray's original thinking but which do not reflect more recent developments in the basic theory. Thus, RST research represents two distinct bodies of knowledge, the first concerned with neural systems and processes, the second with personality and its measurement. One of our purposes in writing this chapter is to encourage other researchers to work to bring these two aspects into closer alignment. Nonetheless, the Janus-faced nature of RST has also been a strength, making it a dynamically evolving theory, but it also poses obvious problems for, at any given time, specifying a consensual model agreed by researchers.

REFERENCES

Abler, B., Walter, H., Erk, S., Kammerer, H. and Spitzer, M. (2006) 'Prediction error as a linear function of reward probability is coded in human nucleus accumbens', *NeuroImage*, 31(2): 790–5.

Arbuthnott, G.W. and Wickens, J. (2007) 'Space, time and dopamine', *Trends in Neurosciences*, 30(2): 62–9.

Blanchard, D.C. and Blanchard, R.J. (1988) 'Ethoexperimental approaches to the biology of emotion', *Annual Review of Psychology*, 39: 43–68.

Blanchard, R.J. and Blanchard, D.C. (1990) 'An ethoexperimental analysis of defense, fear and anxiety', in N. McNaughton and G. Andrews (eds), *Anxiety*. Dunedin: Otago University Press, pp. 12–133.

Blanchard, R.J., Griebel, G., Henrie, J.A. and Blanchard, D.C. (1997) 'Differentiation of anxiolytic and panicolytic drugs by effects on rat and mouse defense test batteries', *Neuroscience and Biobehavioral Reviews*, 21(6): 783–9.

Bogacz, R. (2007) 'Optimal decision-making theories: Linking neurobiology with behaviour', *Trends in Cognitive Sciences*, 11(3): 118–25.

Carver, C.S. and White, T.L. (1994) 'Behavioral inhibition, behavioral activation, and affective responses to impending reward and punishment: The BIS/BAS scales', *Journal of Personality and Social Psychology*, 67(2): 319–33.

Cohen, M.X., Young, J., Baek, J.M., Kessler, C. and Ranganath, C. (2005) 'Individual differences in extraversion and dopamine genetics reflect reactivity of neural reward circuitry', *Cognitive Brain Research*, 25(3): 851–61.

Corr, P.J. (1999) 'Does extraversion predict positive incentive motivation?', *Behavioral and Brain Sciences*, 22(3): 520–1.

Corr, P.J. (2001) 'Testing problems in J.A. Gray's personality theory: A commentary on Matthews and Gilliland (1999)', *Personal Individual Differences*, 30(2): 333–52.

Corr, P.J. (2002) 'J.A. Gray's reinforcement sensitivity theory: Tests of the joint subsystem hypothesis of anxiety and impulsivity', *Personality and Individual Differences*, 33(4): 511–32.

Corr, P.J. (2004) 'Reinforcement sensitivity theory and personality', *Neuroscience and Biobehavioral Reviews*, 28(3): 317–32.

Corr, P.J. (2008) 'Reinforcement sensitivity theory (RST): Introduction', in P.J. Corr (ed.)

The Reinforcement Sensitivity Theory of Personality. Cambridge: Cambridge University Press, pp. 1–43.

Corr, P.J. and McNaughton, N. (2008). 'Reinforcement sensitivity theory and personality', in P.J. Corr (ed.), *The Reinforcement Sensitivity Theory of Personality*. Cambridge: Cambridge University Press, pp. 155–87.

Dayan, P. and Abbott, L.F. (2001) *Theoretical Neuroscience: Computational and Mathematical Modeling of Neural Systems*. Cambridge, MA: MIT Press.

Depue, R.A. and Collins, P.F. (1999) 'Neurobiology of the structure of personality: Dopamine, facilitation of incentive motivation, and extraversion', *Behavioral and Brain Sciences*, 22(3): 491–517.

Eysenck, H.J. (1944) 'Types of personality: A factorial study of 700 neurotics', *Journal of Mental Science*, 90: 859–61.

Eysenck, H.J. (1947) *Dimensions of Personality*. London: K. Paul, Trench Trubner.

Eysenck, H.J. (1957) *The Dynamics of Anxiety and Hysteria*. New York: Preger.

Eysenck, H.J. (1967) *The Biological Basis of Personality*. Springfield, IL: Thomas.

Eysenck, H.J. (1979) 'The conditioning model of neurosis', *Behavioural and Brain Sciences*, 2(2): 155–99.

Eysenck, H.J. and Eysenck, M.W. (1985) *Personality and Individual Differences: A Natural Science Approach*. New York: Plenum Press.

Eysenck, H.J. and Levey, A. (1972) 'Conditioning, introversion–extraversion and the strength of the nervous system', in V.D. Nebylitsyn and J.A. Gray (eds), *The Biological Bases of Individual Behaviour*. London: Academic Press, pp. 206–20.

Gray, J.A. (1970) 'The psychophysiological basis of introversion–extraversion', *Behaviour Research and Therapy*, 8(3): 249–66.

Gray, J.A. (1972a) 'Learning theory, the conceptual nervous system and personality', in V.D. Nebylitsyn and J.A. Gray (eds), *The Biological Bases of Individual Behaviour*. New York: Academic Press, pp. 372–99

Gray, J.A. (1972b) 'The psychophysiological nature of introversion–extraversion: A modification of Eysenck's theory', in V.D. Nebylitsyn and J.A. Gray (eds), *The Biological Bases of Individual Behaviour*. New York: Academic Press, pp. 182–205.

Gray, J.A. (1975) *Elements of a Two-Process Theory of Learning*. London: Academic Press.

Gray, J.A. (1976) 'The behavioural inhibition system: A possible substrate for anxiety', in M.P. Feldman and A.M. Broadhurst (eds), *Theoretical and Experimental Bases of Behaviour Modification*. London: Wiley, pp. 3–41.

Gray, J.A. (1981) 'A critique of Eysenck's theory of personality', in H.J. Eysenck (ed.), *A Model for Personality*. Berlin: Springer, pp. 246–76.

Gray, J.A. (1982) *The Neuropsychology of Anxiety: An Enquiry into the Functions of the Septo-Hippocampal System*. Oxford: Oxford University Press.

Gray, J.A., Feldon, J., Rawlins, J.N.P., Hemsley, D.R. and Smith, A.D. (1991) 'The neuropsychology of schizophrenia', *Behavioral and Brain Sciences*, 14(1): 1–84.

Gray, J.A. and McNaughton, N. (1996) 'The neuropsychology of anxiety: Reprise', in D.A. Hope (ed.), *Perspectives on Anxiety, Panic and Fear*. Nebraska: University of Nebraska Press, pp. 61–134.

Gray, J.A. and McNaughton, N. (2000) *The Neuropsychology of Anxiety: An Enquiry into the Functions of the Septo-Hippocampal System*. Oxford: Oxford University Press.

Gray, J.A. and Smith, P.T. (1969) 'An arousal decision model for partial reinforcement and discrimination learning', in R.M. Gilbert and N.S. Sutherland (eds), *Animal Discrimination Learning*. London: Academic Press, pp. 243–72.

Hebb, D.O. (1955) 'Drives and the C.N.S. (Conceptual Nervous System)', *Psychological Review*, 62(4): 243–54.

Kendler, K.S., Prescott, C.A., Myers, J. and Neale, M.C. (2003) 'The structure of genetic and environmental risk factors for common psychiatric and substance use disorders in men and women', *Archives of General Psychiatry*, 60(9): 929–37.

McNaughton, N. and Corr, P.J. (2004). 'A two-dimensional neuropsychology of defense: Fear/anxiety and defensive distance', *Neuroscience and Biobehavioral Reviews*, 28(3): 285–305.

McNaughton, N. and Corr, P.J. (2008). 'The neuropsychology of fear and anxiety: A foundation for reinforcement sensitivity theory', in P.J. Corr (ed.), *The Reinforcement*

Sensitivity Theory of Personality. Cambridge: Cambridge University Press, pp. 44–94.

Pavlov, I.P. (1927) *Reflexes: An Investigation of the Physiological Activity of the Cerebral Cortex.* Oxford: Oxford University Press. (Translated and edited by G.V. Anrep.)

Pickering, A.D. (1997) 'The conceptual nervous system and personality: From Pavlov to neural networks', *European Psychologist*, 2(2): 139–63.

Pickering, A.D. (1999) 'Personality correlates of the dopaminergic facilitation of incentive motivation: Impulsive sensation seeking rather than extraversion?', *Behavioural and Brain Sciences*, 22(3): 534–5.

Pickering, A.D. (2008) 'Formal and computational models of reinforcement sensitivity theory', in P.J. Corr (ed.), *The Reinforcement Sensitivity Theory of Personality.* Cambridge: Cambridge University Press, pp. 453–81.

Pickering, A.D., Corr, P.J. and Gray, J.A. (1999) 'Interactions and reinforcement sensitivity theory: A theoretical analysis of Rusting and Larsen (1997)', *Personality and Individual Differences*, 26(2): 357–65.

Pickering, A.D. and Gray, J.A. (1999) 'The neuroscience of personality', in L. Pervin and O. John (eds), *Handbook of Personality* (2nd edn). New York: Guilford, pp. 277–99.

Pickering, A.D. and Gray, J.A. (2001) 'Dopamine, appetitive reinforcement, and the neuropsychology of human learning: An individual differences approach', in A. Eliasz and A. Angleitner (eds), *Advances in Individual Differences Research*. Lengerich, Germany: PABST Science Publishers, pp. 113–49

Pickering, A.D. and Smillie, L.D. (2008) 'The behavioural activation system: Challenges and opportunities', in P.J. Corr (ed.), *The Reinforcement Sensitivity Theory of Personality*. Cambridge: Cambridge University Press, pp. 120–54.

Sartory, G., MacDonald, R. and Gray, J.A. (1990) 'Effects of diazepam on approach, self-reported fear and psychophysiological responses in snake phobics', *Behaviour Research and Therapy*, 28(4): 273–82.

Schultz, W. (1998) 'Predictive reward signal of dopamine neurons', *Journal of Neurophysiology*, 80(1): 1–27.

Smillie, L.D., Pickering, A.D. and Jackson, C.J. (2006) 'The new reinforcement sensitivity theory: Implications for personality measurement', *Personality and Social Psychology Review*, 10(4): 320–35.

Wacker, J., Chavanon, M. and Stemmler, G. (2006) 'Investigating the dopaminergic basis of extraversion in humans: A multilevel approach', *Journal of Personality and Social Psychology*, 91(1): 171–87.

Wickens, J. and Kotter, R. (1995) 'Cellular models of reinforcement', in J.C. Houk, J.L. Davis and D.G. Beiser (eds), *Models of Information Processing in the Basal Ganglia*. London: MIT Press, pp. 189–214.

12

Simplifying the Cattellian Psychometric Model

Gregory J. Boyle

This chapter concerns the scientific analysis of individual differences in human psychological functioning including personality structure, undertaken by the author over a 30-year period (Boyle, 2006b). A key aspect of this programmatic work has been the taxonomic delineation of psychological constructs relating to cognitive abilities, personality traits (both normal and abnormal), dynamic (motivation) traits and transitory (emotional/mood) states within the framework of the *Cattellian psychometric model* (e.g. see Cattell, 1973, 1979, 1980a, 1980b, 1982a, 1983, 1984, 1986a, 1986b, 1986c, 1986d, 1986e, 1986f, 1986g, 1988a, 1988b, 1988c, 1990a, 1990b, 1990c, 1995; 1996, Cattell and Child, 1975; Cattell and Horn, 1982; Cattell and Kline, 1977; Cattell and Nesselroade, 1988; Cattell et al., 2002). This extensive body of taxonomic psychometric research has been empirical and measurement oriented, using a combination of multi-variate experimental and quasi-experimental designs (e.g. Boyle, 1988c; Boyle et al., 1995; Cattell, 1988b, 1988c, 1988e) although some critical reviews and integrative position papers have also been generated (e.g. Boyle, 1985b; Boyle and Cattell, 1987; Boyle and Smári, 2002; Boyle et al., 1995).

Raymond B. Cattell was a prodigious, psychometrically oriented behavioural scientist, listed among the top ten most highly cited psychologists of the twentieth century (Haggbloom et al., 2002: 142). Cattell led a team of internationally visible researchers in undertaking a programmatic series of innovative psychometric research studies into the structure and assessment of human personality and individual differences (e.g. see Cattell, 1980a, 1980b). The Cattellian School contributed significantly to the contemporary understanding of human personality constructs, and made numerous psychometric advances, including several technical refinements to exploratory factor-analytic methodology as well as being responsible for the construction of a wide range of factor-analytically derived measurement instruments. Cattell was the recipient of several prestigious awards and prizes, including, for example, the Wenner Gren Prize of the New York Academy of Sciences, Distinguished Honorary membership of the British Psychological Society, the Darwin Fellowship, and inaugural president of the Society of Multivariate Experimental Psychology (SMEP), which he founded (see Cattell, 1990b). Cattell also was involved in founding the Institute for Personality and Ability Testing (IPAT) which is recognised internationally as a major publisher of a wide range of factor-analytically based psychological tests and measurement instruments.

Nevertheless, the report by Haggbloom et al. (2002) confirms that even though both Cattell and Eysenck were listed as among the ten most highly cited psychologists in the published journal literature (attesting to their vast empirical outputs), the number of citations of their work in general psychology textbooks and in a survey of American Psychological Society (now Association for Psychological Science) members was disproportionately lower. In Cattell's case, part of the difficulty may reside in the complex mathematical models underpinning the Cattellian psychometric model, thereby making his writings difficult to comprehend. Moreover, the Cattellian psychometric model was unnecessarily complicated, including no fewer than 92 primary factors – far too many for practical utility. Simplifying the overly large taxonomy of Cattellian psychological constructs was demonstrably needed. Accordingly, a sustained, programmatic sequence of exploratory and confirmatory factor-analytic studies was conducted over several years with the goal of elucidating a reduced number of broad factors that would have greater utility for psychological measurement, test construction and professional practice. Other multivariate statistical procedures such as canonical correlation analysis, multiple regression analysis, discriminant function analysis, multidimensional scaling, multivariate analysis of variance, and structural equation modelling were employed as required (cf. Boyle, 1991a; Nesselroade and Cattell, 1988). As a result of this programmatic research, the 92 primary Cattellian psychometric model factors were reduced down to just 29 broad factors (a 68% reduction) – that is, 30 broad factors with addition of the separate factor-analytically elucidated curiosity construct (see Boyle,

1983a, 1989a). The resultant *Boyle psychometric model* is not only more concise, but also retains the specificity needed for detailed measurement across several psychological domains including both the normal and abnormal personality spheres (cf. Boyle et al., 2001; Boyle and Smári, 2002).

Thus, a major reduction in number of taxonomic psychological constructs has been achieved through the systematic factor analysis of the primary factor intercorrelations measured in the Cattellian psychometric instruments (see descriptions of instruments in Cattell, 1973, 1988d; Cattell and Schuerger, 1978; Cattell and Johnson, 1986; Curran and Cattell, 1976; Krug, 1980; Schuerger, 1986; Smith, 1988; Sweney et al., 1986). In regard to exploratory factor analytic methodology (see Cattell, 1978; Gorsuch, 1983), an empirical study (Boyle and Stanley, 1986) demonstrated that the simple structure of factor-pattern solutions (cf. Child, 1990) can be maximised by applying a topological rotation in addition to analytical rotation alone (e.g. via the Statistical Package for the Social Sciences, SPSS). Nevertheless, the actual increase in simple structure (measured via the $\pm$ 0.10 hyperplane count – see Cattell, 1978) was only about 6%, making it hard to justify all the extra effort required. On the other hand, a critical review of factor-analytic methodology (Boyle, 1993b) appears to have preceded new enhancements being incorporated into the SPSS exploratory factor-analytic programs (e.g. inclusion of the psychometric Scree test – see Cattell, 1988d), increasing the efficiency and practical utility of the current SPSS factor-analytic programs.

In these studies (see Boyle, 2006b), the specific factor-analytic methodology used, mostly employed either an iterative maximum-likelihood or a principal-factoring procedure, together with factor extraction number estimated via careful application of the psychometric Scree test (Cattell, 1978, 1988d). In several empirical investigations (e.g. Cattell and Vogelmann, 1977; Hakstian et al., 1982), the psychometric Scree test had been shown to be considerably more accurate than Kaiser's 'eigenvalues greater than 1.0' rule (which underestimated the number of factors when there were fewer than about 20 variables, and seriously overestimated the number of factors when there were more than about 40 variables in the analysis). In addition, oblique rotation (either direct Oblimin or Promax) was employed throughout, in the search for maximum simple-structure factor solutions, as indexed via the ± 0.10 hyperplane count (cf. Boyle, 1993b; Cattell, 1978, 1988d; Child, 1990; McArdle, 1984; McArdle and Cattell, 1994). In future work, it is planned to construct a comprehensive set of modern neo-Cattellian psychometric instruments based on the reduced set of broad factors that now has been elucidated. Specifically, the focus will be on the construction of (T-data) objective test measures, thereby avoiding the serious drawback of item-transparent, self-report (subjective) questionnaires, currently so prevalent within the personality assessment field (cf. Boyle, 1985b; Cattell, 1979: 123; Schuerger, 1986; Smith, 1988). Accordingly, this chapter not only summarises an extensive body of past empirical research efforts, but also provides the point of departure for significant future works, based on improved psychometric test construction principles.

A concise taxonomy of psychological constructs (akin to the periodic table in chemistry) is yet to be formulated. Within the framework of the general psychometric model (Kline, 1979, 1980), the initial task is the empirical (factor-analytic) delineation of psychological constructs including cognitive/intellectual abilities, relatively stable personality traits (both normal and abnormal), less stable dynamic (motivational) traits and transitory, situationally sensitive mood states. In line with the dictum that measurement is the *sine qua non* of any scientific enterprise, so too, psychological science depends on valid and reliable psychometric instruments that measure inferred psychological (including personality) constructs. Aside from the empirical elucidation and quantitative

measurement of psychological constructs, *per se*, psychological science also involves differential empirical studies, and hypothesis testing experimentation (e.g. via functional psychological testing (Cattell, 1986d, 1986e; Cattell and Johnson, 1986; see Boyle, 1989f, for a review). In line with Cronbach's (1957) historic call for combining the 'two disciplines' of scientific psychology, the published research collated in this chapter has attempted to meld both correlational and experimental approaches within the context of the Cattellian framework (cf. Eysenck, 1997), adopting wherever possible a distinctly multivariate-experimental perspective (Boyle, 1988c, 1991b).

Use of exploratory factor-analytic procedures in the construction of personality instruments has produced somewhat conflicting outcomes. Thus, Eysenck reported three higher-stratum personality dimensions, as measured, for example, in the Eysenck Personality Questionnaire Revised or EPQ-R that were labelled *extraversion, neuroticism* and *psychoticism* (e.g. see Eysenck and Eysenck, 1985), whereas Cattell reported 16 normal personality trait factors (Birkett-Cattell, 1989; Krug, 1981; see Boyle, 1990a, for a review of the Sixteen Personality Factor Questionnaire (16PF) and Clinical Analysis Questionnaire (CAQ) personality trait instruments). Despite being rather unwieldy, the Cattellian psychometric model has enabled comprehensive measurement of cognitive abilities alongside normal and abnormal personality traits, dynamic (motivational) traits and situationally sensitive mood states (cf. Cattell, 1982b, 1988a; Eysenck, 1984). Thus, a key research focus has been the discovery, through use of exploratory factor-analytic methods, of a reduced set of higher-stratum factors within the Cattellian framework (Boyle, 2006b). In these studies, many non-Cattellian psychometric instruments have also been utilized both specifically and generically, not only for the purpose of validating or verifying their factor structure, but more importantly, to enable comparisons with instruments constructed within the framework of the Cattellian psychometric model, and in relation to the more concise, simplified Boyle psychometric model, subsequently elucidated.

Source traits delineated factor-analytically have been incorporated by the Institute for Personality and Ability Testing (IPAT) into several multidimensional measurement instruments including:

- Sixteen Personality Factor Questionnaire (16PF)
- Clinical Analysis Questionnaire (CAQ)
- Motivation Analysis Test (MAT)
- School Motivation Analysis Test (SMAT)
- Children's Motivation Analysis Test (CMAT)
- Eight State Questionnaire (8SQ)
- Objective-Analytic Battery (OAB)
- Culture Fair Intelligence Tests (CFIT)
- Comprehensive Ability Battery (CAB).

Despite Cattell's enormous productivity, the complexity of his 'all-inclusive' psychometric approach has tended to be rather problematic, serving as an ongoing source of frustration for many psychological researchers and practitioners alike. Indeed, as stated above, Cattell had elucidated no fewer than 92 primary factors, including 20 cognitive ability factors, 16 normal personality trait dimensions (including 16PF Factor B, intelligence), 12 abnormal personality traits, 20 integrated/unintegrated dynamic traits, 12 normal mood states and 12 abnormal mood states (derived from dR-factor analyses of Clinical Analysis Questionnaire subscale intercorrelations), which was too unwieldy for practical utility. It was evident that a reduction in number of taxonomic constructs was urgently needed (Kline, 1979, 1980), and the Cattellian psychometric model with its emphasis on numerous primary factors provided a logical starting point for elucidating a reduced set of pertinent higher-stratum constructs. In contrast, the Eysenckian psychometric model (EPM) was too minimalist, accounting for only a small fraction of the known personality trait variance (cf. Boyle et al., 1995; Cattell, 1986g, 1995). Thus, the Eysenckian factors provided an inadequate account of the dimensionality of abnormal personality structure (i.e. the unitary psychoticism scale is problematic in light of the several varieties and subtypes of psychopathology documented in the DSM-IV-TR or ICD-10 psychodiagnostic classification manuals, respectively). Additional goals (Boyle, 2006b) also included the clarification and refinement of methodological issues relating to exploratory factor analysis, as well as undertaking empirical studies into personality within various applied settings.

Several of the studies presented in this chapter were published either in *Multivariate Experimental Clinical Research* or in *Personality and Individual Differences*, in order to disseminate the research findings to the comparatively small but select target audience interested in multivariate psychometric research related to personality and individual differences within the Cattellian framework. In contrast to more subjective test construction approaches, the empirical use of factor analysis was used to map out the important underlying psychological constructs, and the derived factors guided subsequent construction of measurement instruments (e.g. Boyle, 1992, 1999). Importantly, since each of the Cattellian instruments including the Sixteen Personality Factor Questionnaire or 16PF (Cattell et al., 1970; Krug, 1981), the Motivation Analysis Test or MAT (Cattell, 1985; Cattell and Child, 1975; Sweney et al., 1986), and the Eight State Questionnaire or 8SQ (Curran and Cattell, 1976) measured essentially discrete variance (see Boyle, 1988c; Boyle et al., 1995), and in light of relevant psychometric principles (Boyle, 1985b), the search for higher-stratum factors within each intrapersonal psychological domain appeared especially promising. Accordingly, the sustained program of multivariate research studies presented here comprised many factor analyses of empirical data derived mostly from large samples that cumulatively involved psychometric assessment of many thousands of individuals.

Boyle (1989e) and Fisher and Boyle (1997) reported the higher-stratum factor structure of normal personality traits measured in the

Sixteen Personality Factor Questionnaire (cf. Cattell, 1994, 1995; Cattell and Krug, 1986; Krug and Johns, 1986), thereby providing support for a simplified and more practical structure of five broad personality dimensions (a 69% reduction). In a factor analysis of the subscale intercorrelations of the 16PF/MAT/8SQ instruments (the first ever such combined study), Boyle (1988c) also reported three additional normal personality dimensions, thereby enabling measurement of a substantially greater proportion of the personality trait variance than that provided by the Eysenkian factors. Previously published data for the 16PF, the Comrey Personality Scales and the Eysenck Personality Inventory (an early version of the Eysenck Personality Questionnaire or EPQ) was subjected to close scrutiny (Boyle 1989e) using methodologically sound factor-analytic procedures (see Boyle, 1985b, 1988c, 1993b; Boyle and Stanley, 1986; and Boyle et al., 1995, for specification of the factor-analytic methodology employed). Results of this well-cited reanalysis confirmed the work of Krug and Johns (1986) that there are at least five broad normal personality factors labelled extraversion, anxiety-neuroticism, tough poise, independence, and control. These five second-stratum factors have made a substantial impact, having been incorporated, for example, into the revised 16PF (5th edition or 16PF5; see H.E.P. Cattell, 2001, 2004; R.B. Cattell and H.E.P. Cattell, 1995; H.E.P. Cattell and Schuerger, 2003). These higher-stratum 16PF5 factors were shown to compare more than favourably with other models of personality structure such as the currently popular five-factor model (FFM) (see Boyle, 2006a; Fisher and Boyle, 1997), and were found to correspond with primary T-data factors measured in the objective-analytic battery (OAB) (Cattell and Birkett, 1980).

Boyle et al. (1995) in their chapter in the *International Handbook of Personality and Intelligence* provided a detailed technical critique of the exploratory factor-analytic research leading to development of both the 16PF and the currently popular FFM

(cf. Boyle, 2006a; H.E.P. Cattell, 1993). Importantly, simple structure for the 16PF second-stratum factor solution (measured via the ± 0.10 hyperplane count (see Cattell, 1978) was significantly greater than that observed for the FFM (Boyle et al., 1995; Boyle and Saklofske, 2004; Boyle and Smári, 1997, 1998, 2002; Krug and Johns, 1986), suggesting that the 16PF second-stratum factors provide a more satisfactory structuring of the normal personality trait domain than the popular FFM. However, since the second-stratum factor QIII (tough poise), calculated via the algorithm provided in the 16PF handbook produced spurious results, Boyle and Robertson (1989) recommended that previous studies involving the computation of second-stratum 16PF factors should be reanalysed in light of the new corrected algorithm. Since historically, the 16PF has been the most highly cited psychometric measure of normal personality, the potential impact of correcting this computational error was considerable.

Parenthetically, we had demonstrated (Cattell et al., 2002) that personality traits are susceptible to modification as a function of life experience, indicative of substantial 'structural learning' (see Cattell, 1983; Cattell et al., 2002; Roberts et al., 2006a, 2006b). This finding casts doubt on the adequacy of 'static' models of personality structure such as the FFM, thereby providing an advance in our understanding of the structuring of human personality. This new knowledge that personality traits are not fixed, immutable dispositions, but rather are only relatively stable dispositions that are subject to structural change (e.g. as a result of learning and enculturation) undoubtedly will impact greatly on the future construction of personality measurement instruments.

Boyle (1987a) also reported a number of second-stratum factors within the abnormal personality trait domain. The 12 abnormal (psychopathological) trait dimensions measured in the Clinical Analysis Questionnaire or CAQ (Krug, 1980) were reduced down to just six second-stratum factors (a 50% reduction) that were labelled: depressive schizophrenia, psychopathic dominance, psychotic inadequacy, paranoid depression, helpless depression and anxious depression, thereby providing a much greater economy of measurement. Furthermore, the seven primary Clinical Analysis Questionnaire depression factors were reduced down to just four broad depression factors, having greater practical, conceptual and measurement utility for researchers and professional psychologists alike (cf. Boyle and Comer, 1990). It is to be hoped that the impact of these findings will likely be realised with future construction of more efficient measures of abnormal personality, based on broad second-stratum dimensions, rather than focusing on a plethora of narrow primary trait factors.

Turning to the dynamic (motivation) trait domain (e.g. see Barton et al., 1986; Cattell, 1981, 1985; 1992; Cattell and Child, 1975; Cattell and Kline, 1977; Kline, 1979) several publications (e.g. Boyle, 1985a, 1988c, 1989b; Boyle and Start, 1988, 1989a; and Boyle et al., 1989a) examined the higher-stratum factor structure of objective motivation tests (T-data measures avoid the problematic item transparency and associated response distortion that plagues Q-data self-report personality questionnaires). While objective tests of cognitive abilities have been used for decades, the use of objective motivation tests has been less prominent. A notable exception has been the Cattellian work with its incorporation of objective T-data tests into the Motivation Analysis Test (MAT) and its downward extensions, the School Motivation Analysis Test (SMAT) and Children's Motivation Analysis Test (CMAT), respectively (Boyle et al., 1988; Cattell, 1985, 1992; Cattell and Child, 1975; Cattell and Warburton, 1967).

Some early work (e.g. Boyle and Cattell, 1984) had examined the MAT construct and predictive validity. It was found that presentation of a stressful stimulus induced significant elevations in several dynamic traits (especially fear), lending confidence that factor-analytic refinements would be efficacious (parenthetically, the empirical findings obtained by Boyle and Cattell also suggested that fear appeals, in the absence of positive instructions, are likely to be ineffective in promoting safer driving behaviours). An earlier factor analysis of the subscale intercorrelations of the MAT/8SQ instruments was subsequently revised (Boyle, 1985a) using more methodologically sound factor-analytic procedures, resulting in reduction of the 20 integrated/conscious (I) and unintegrated/unconscious (U) primary MAT dimensions down to just seven second-stratum factors (a 65% reduction). The broad dynamic trait factors delineated were labelled: home orientation, pugnacity, narcism (narcissism), career orientation, fear, self-sentiment, and superego (specific factor-analytic procedures were provided in Boyle, 1993b). Accordingly, an updated, simplified MAT, constructed to measure the above higher-stratum factors, would make the instrument more useful as a measure of dynamic traits. The impact of such a revised addition to the psychometric armamentarium would likely be considerable, since objective T-data tests of motivation are rare.

Boyle (1989b) also investigated higher-stratum factors in the SMAT (version used with adolescents). The 20 (U and I) primary factors were reduced down to just five second-stratum factors (a 75% reduction). In line with the recent verification that personality structure can be modified somewhat as a result of experience (Cattell et al., 2002), so too, reduction in second-stratum factors (five SMAT factors versus seven MAT factors) pointed to the developmental nature of motivational structure. In Boyle et al. (1989a), evidence for a possible sixth second-stratum SMAT factor was obtained. However, variation in factor pattern solutions suggested that, as with the objective MAT, further psychometric refinement of the SMAT was also required (cf. Boyle et al., 1989a, 1989b). Hopefully, such a revised objective T-data instrument would enable the valid measurement of factor-analytically elucidated dynamic traits among adolescents.

In addition, Boyle and Start (1988) reported broad second-stratum CMAT factors (version used with primary school children). The four factors that emerged (an 80% reduction) were labelled: superego, narcism (narcissism), play, and self-sentiment. It was noted that school orientation (second-stratum SMAT factor) was not included among the CMAT second-stratum factors, suggesting perhaps that primary school children have not yet developed a strong motivational focus on school activities (cf. Boyle and Houndoulesi, 1993). This finding is consistent with the observation that motivational structure itself is partly a product of experiential learning, wherein sentiments are culturally acquired. In a comparison of gender differences in motivation (Boyle and Start, 1989a, 1989b), the second-stratum factor loadings for primary school boys and girls differed appreciably, suggesting general differences in interests and motivational structure. Girls reported significantly higher mean scores on fear, pugnacity, and curiosity, whereas boys reported significantly higher scores on play. Theoretically, at least, if these observed gender differences in motivation were taken into account and explicitly capitalised upon with the aim of producing enhanced educational outcomes, the impact of this finding could be considerable.

A research note (Boyle (1989c) reported the first available normative data for the (unpublished) CMAT. Provision of this normative data was useful, establishing an objective basis for comparing children's CMAT scores. In a study that manipulated curiosity and boredom states, Boyle et al. (1993) provided some predictive validity for the instrument. Four of the 20 (U and I) CMAT factors exhibited significant changes in mean scores following experimental interventions (decreases were observed in I-assertiveness and I-fear; increases were observed in U-narcism and U-pugnacity). These findings (cf. Boyle and Cattell, 1984) provided further evidence of the situational sensitivity of the dynamic trait factors. It was observed also that superego and self-sentiment

appeared to emerge factor analytically as 'master sentiments' for all three MAT/SMAT/CMAT instruments. Finally, Boyle (1988c) – in the *Handbook of Multivariate Experimental Psychology* – summarised the psychometric findings from several empirical studies carried out conjointly into the MAT/SMAT/CMAT instruments. While some evidence of predictive or discriminative validity was observed in each case, it was also apparent that these instruments need extensive psychometric revision, not only to simplify their factor structure, but also to bring them up to date for contemporary use.

Turning to the mood-state domain, both canonical correlation analyses and multiple regression analyses, as well as several exploratory factor analyses, were undertaken in an attempt to quantify the measurement overlap (in terms of percentage of common measurement variance) across the 8SQ/DES-IV (differential emotions scale) instruments (Boyle, 1986, 1989d). Results demonstrated that only a small number of the DES-IV subscales predicted most of the 8SQ variance, and vice-versa, showing that the Eight State Questionnaire (8SQ) alone does not provide comprehensive assessment of the mood-state domain. Redundancy analyses of the 8SQ/POMS instruments (cf. Boyle, 1987b) demonstrated that the Eight State Questionnaire and Profile of Mood States (POMS) instruments measured considerable discrete variance, supporting the search for higher-stratum state factors from factor analyses of all three 8SQ/POMS/DES-IV mood-state instruments.

Accordingly, several factor-analytic studies (Boyle, 1987d, 1988a, 1989d, 1991c) sought higher-stratum mood state factors from the 8SQ/POMS/DES-IV instruments (while Cattell had delineated 12 mood-state factors, only the first 8 were incorporated into the 8SQ). The outcome of these studies was a significant reduction from 12 primary factors down to just four broad mood-state factors (a 67% reduction) that were labelled state extraversion, state neuroticism, state hostility, and arousal-fatigue, respectively. In addition, a differential (dR) scale factoring of the Clinical Analysis Questionnaire (Boyle, 1987a) provided evidence for two abnormal mood-state factors (an 83% reduction) that were labelled paranoid state and psychopathic dominance state, respectively (cf. Cattell and Kameoka, 1985). Taken together, these findings provided justification for the construction of new simplified scales that focused on broad second-stratum dimensions. In Boyle and Katz (1991), multidimensional scaling (MDS) of 8SQ/DES-IV data also revealed that most DES-IV subscales were aligned in close proximity to each other, suggesting inadequate separation, and therefore suggesting the need for psychometric refinement of the DES-IV. In contrast, separate factor analyses of the POMS/8SQ (see Boyle, 1988a) confirmed the purported factor structure for each instrument.

In regard to the taxonomic structure of cognitive abilities, a hierarchical model comprising broad higher-stratum factors, several primary factors, and numerous specific abilities also had been postulated within the Cattellian psychometric model (e.g. Cattell, 1982a, 1986f, 1986g, 1987a; Cattell and Cattell, 1977). Boyle (1988b, 1995) reported that both fluid (G_f) and crystallised (G_c) intelligence factors are accompanied by a number of important second-stratum ability factors labelled: memory capacity (G_m), perceptual speed (G_{ps}), retrieval capacity (G_r), visualisation capacity (G_v), and auditory organisation (G_a). This reduced number of ability factors, as compared with say the 20 primary factors measured in the Cognitive Ability Battery (CAB), would appear to have greater practical utility (a 75% reduction). While these higher-stratum cognitive ability factors have been incorporated to some extent into existing ability measures there appears to be room for construction of a new, simplified intelligence test that simultaneously measures each of the higher-stratum factors and builds on well-established instruments such as the Stanford–Binet Intelligence Scale (SB-IV) and the Wechsler Intelligence Scales. Boyle (1990b) and Bernard et al. (1990) reported

exploratory, congeneric and confirmatory factor analyses of SB-IV data that supported the four putative area dimensions (verbal reasoning, quantitative reasoning, abstract-visual reasoning, and short-term memory). Boyle (1993a, 1995) as well as Boyle et al. (1995) and Stankov et al. (1995) examined the covariation between personality and cognitive ability measures. Their findings revealed only slight measurement overlap, suggesting that personality and ability factors measure essentially discrete psychological domains.

Other psychometric studies, either arising from or benefiting research into the Cattellian psychometric model, contributed new insights relating to:

1. Use of change scores in canonical-redundancy analyses of multidimensional mood-state instruments, thereby avoiding 'trait contamination variance' (Boyle, 1987e). This study demonstrated that neither the Eight State Questionnaire nor the Differential Emotions Scale provided comprehensive coverage of the mood-state domain, highlighting the need to include additional scales in factor analyses of mood-state data.

2. Desirable levels of item homogeneity in psychometric scales (Boyle, 1991d). This highly cited study demonstrated that to achieve greater breadth of measurement, item homogeneity (e.g. as measured via the Cronbach alpha coefficient) should be moderate rather than maximal.

3. Validity of meta-analytic procedures (Fernandez and Boyle, 1996). This paper highlighted the importance of framing hypotheses in a rigorous operational manner, making adjustments and taking sample size into account in estimating effect sizes.

4. Test validity as a function of method of administration (Grossarth-Maticek et al., 1995). This study demonstrated that the outcomes of psychological investigations may depend greatly on the particular test administration method employed.

Taken together, these and other methodological papers have clarified several important psychometric issues, serving as an essential prerequisite for improved psychological test construction. In addition, substantive advances have included calculation of measurement redundancy across different instruments via canonical correlation analyses (e.g. 16PF/MAT), derivation of multiple regression prediction equations for translating scores across different measures (e.g. 8SQ/POMS/DES-IV), as well as elucidation of higher-stratum factors for both normal and abnormal (psychopathological) personality traits (16PF/CAQ), dynamic (motivation) traits (MAT/SMAT/CMAT), and transitory mood states (8SQ), respectively.

This sustained research program has also culminated in a number of integrative technical reviews and position papers (e.g. Boyle, 1987c; Boyle and Smári, 2002; Boyle et al., 2001; Fisher and Boyle, 1997), some of which were published in foreign-language peer-reviewed journals (Norwegian, Spanish, French, plus some abstracts in German and Japanese), thereby increasing international visibility and dissemination of the findings. Finally, Boyle and Saklofske (2004) provided a comprehensive and relatively up-to-date integrative overview of research findings within the field of personality and individual differences.

SUMMARY OF MAJOR OUTCOMES OF THIS RESEARCH

- Justification of the search for higher-stratum factors, since 16PF/MAT/8SQ measured substantial discrete variance;
- Support for reduction of 16PF primary factors down to *at least* five broad factors (69% reduction);
- Demonstration of significantly greater simple structure for the 16PF second-stratum factors than for the FFM;
- Reduction of 12 CAQ abnormal personality trait dimensions down to six broad factors (50% reduction);
- Reduction of 20 (U and I) MAT factors down to seven broad factors (65% reduction);
- Reduction of 20 (U and I) SMAT factors down to five broad factors (75% reduction);
- Reduction of 20 (U and I) CMAT factors down to just four broad factors (80% reduction);

- Demonstration that superego and self-sentiment emerged as 'master sentiments' for all three MAT/SMAT/CMAT instruments;
- Reduction of 12 (8SQ/POMS/DES-IV) primary mood-state factors down to just four broad factors (67% reduction);
- Elucidation of two abnormal CAQ mood-state dimensions (83% reduction);
- Support for *at least* five broad reporting of five broad ability factors (75% reduction);
- Reduction of 92 Cattellian psychometric model primary factors (ability, personality, motivation, and mood-state domains) down to 29 broad factors. (68% reduction);
- Production of a simplified Boyle psychometric model (30 broad factors with inclusion of the curiosity construct).

Methodological recommendations

- Evaluate item homogeneity in terms of *both* internal consistency *and* item redundancy and to enhance breadth of measurement by including greater diversity of items in psychometric scales;
- Use *objective personality tests* rather than subjective, item-transparent self-report scales (to avoid motivational/response distortion);
- Measure reliability via immediate and longer-term test-retest (*dependability* vs. *stability*) estimates for state-trait measures;
- Use methodologically sound exploratory factor-analytic (EFA) methods;
- Demonstrated that *method of test administration* significantly influences predictive validity of psychometric tests.

SUMMARY AND CONCLUSIONS

This sustained body of empirical research (Boyle, 2006b) has pinpointed a number of limitations in the psychometric assessment of personality and individual differences within the framework of the Cattellian psychometric model. It has identified several important questions needing to be addressed, and has included many experimental and/or empirical studies, providing a set of more practical taxonomic constructs for effective use by the psychological, medical, educational and commercial communities. The extensive body of taxonomic research provides a practical solution to the extreme/conflicting positions adopted by earlier investigators (e.g. Cattell's comprehensive approach versus Eysenck's minimalist approach). Over many years, through the sustained application of methodologically sound factor analysis, a simplified version of the Cattellian psychometric model has been produced, resulting in a 68% reduction from 92 factors down to 29 broad factors. With inclusion of the 'state curiosity' dimension (also elucidated factor analytically— Boyle, 1983a, 1989a), the Boyle psychometric model comprises 30 broad factors that taken together cover the intrapersonal psychological domains of cognitive abilities, personality traits, dynamic traits, and transitory mood states, respectively (see Table 12.1).

The next sequential step will be to construct a wide range of modern neo-Cattellian multidimensional psychometric instruments, incorporating the reduced number of higher-stratum factors into objective test measures (rather than relying on item-transparent questionnaires with their inherently flawed self-report methodology). The plethora of so-called 'personality tests' has exploded in recent years. Many of these are relatively simple rating scales (ratings of others or L-data; self ratings or Q-data). Aside from response sets, and superficial reporting, a major problem with subjective L-data and Q-data rating scales of personality/motivation is that they depend upon transparent, face valid items. Item transparency is extremely problematic, inviting response/motivational distortion, such that virtually all current 'personality testing' is essentially based on subjective methodology. Correction scales can go only so far, and in some cases (e.g. the Minnesota Multiphasic Personality Inventory or MMPI K-scale) application of the proposed modification may produce 'corrected' scores that are no more accurate than the 'uncorrected' ones.

What is needed are truly *objective interactive tests* of personality traits and motivational dynamic traits (with computer implementation, and stimulus items individualised for each respondent). Indeed, Cattell and Warburton (1967) had produced a compendium comprising more than 2000 objective T-data personality tests, several of which were subsequently incorporated into the OAB (Cattell and Schuerger, 1978). Evidently, the field of personality measurement needs to be transformed out of its present quagmire (based predominantly on subjective self-report methodology) and lifted onto an altogether more technologically advanced level of objective-interactive testing (Schuerger, 1986).

Table 12.1   *Reduced Set of 30 Broad Factors – Boyle Psychometric Model (BPM)*

Normal Personality: (five factors)
   Extraversion, Neuroticism, Tough Poise, Independence, Control

Abnormal Personality: (six factors)
   Depressive Schizophrenia, Psychopathic Dominance, Psychotic Inadequacy, Paranoid Depression, Helpless Depression, Anxious Depression

Motivation: (adult–seven factors)
   Home Orientation, Pugnacity, Narcism (narcissism), Career Orientation, Fear, Self-sentiment, Superego

Normal Mood States: (four factors + State Curiosity)
   State Extraversion, State Neuroticism, State Hostility, State Curiosity; Arousal-Fatigue

Abnormal Mood States: (two factors)
   Paranoid State, Psychopathic Dominance State

Cognitive Abilities: (five factors)
   Memory Capacity, Perceptual Speed, Retrieval Capacity, Visualisation Capacity, Auditory Organisation

Hopefully, neo-Cattellian instruments constructed to measure the higher-stratum factors delineated in the Boyle psychometric model should take approximately 70% less time to administer than is currently required for all 92 Cattellian psychometric model primary factors using the currently available spectrum of Cattellian instruments (Boyle, 2006b). Such a major saving in testing time should have a considerable beneficial impact for various areas of psychological research and professional practice. Thus, the work presented in this chapter is more than just a summary of past research efforts. It also provides a rich source of hypotheses, and lays the very foundations for challenging and rewarding future works and directions in personality test construction.

REFERENCES

Barton, K., Dielman, T.E. and Cattell, R.B. (1986) 'Prediction of objective child motivation test scores from parents' reports of child-rearing practices', *Psychological Reports*, 59(2): 343–52.

Bernard, M.E., Boyle, G.J. and Jackling, B.F. (1990) 'Sex-role identity and mental ability', *Personality and Individual Differences*, 11(3): 213–7.

Birkett-Cattell, H. (1989) *The 16PF: Personality in Depth*. Champaign, IL: Institute for Personality and Ability Testing.

Boyle, G.J. (1983a) 'Critical review of state–trait curiosity test development', *Motivation and Emotion*, 7(4): 377–97.

Boyle, G.J. (1983b) 'Effects on academic learning of manipulating emotional states and motivational dynamics', *British Journal of Educational Psychology*, 53(3): 347–57.

Boyle, G.J. (1985a) 'A reanalysis of the higher-order factor structure of the Motivation Analysis Test and the Eight State Questionnaire', *Personality and Individual Differences*, 6(3): 367–74.

Boyle, G.J. (1985b) 'Self-report measures of depression: Some psychometric considerations', *British Journal of Clinical Psychology*, 24(1): 45–59.

Boyle, G.J. (1986) 'Estimation of measurement redundancy across the Eight State Questionnaire and the Differential Emotions Scale', *New Zealand Journal of Psychology*, 15(2): 54–61.

Boyle, G.J. (1987a) 'Psychopathological depression superfactors in the Clinical Analysis Questionnaire', *Personality and Individual Differences*, 8(5): 609–14.

Boyle, G.J. (1987b) 'Quantitative and qualitative intersections between the Eight State Questionnaire and the Profile of Mood States', *Educational and Psychological Measurement*, 47(2): 437–43.

Boyle, G.J. (1987c) 'The role of intrapersonal psychological variables in academic school learning', *Journal of School Psychology*, 25(4): 389–92.

Boyle, G.J. (1987d) 'Typological mood-state factors measured in the Eight State Questionnaire', *Personality and Individual Differences*, 8(1): 137–40.

Boyle, G.J. (1987e) 'Use of change scores in redundancy analyses of multivariate psychological inventories', *Personality and Individual Differences*, 8(6): 845–54.

Boyle, G.J. (1988a) 'Central clinical states: An examination of the Profile of Mood States and the Eight State Questionnaire', *Journal of Psychopathology and Behavioral Assessment*, 10(3): 205–15.

Boyle, G.J. (1988b) 'Contribution of Cattellian psychometrics to the elucidation of human intellectual structure', *Multivariate Experimental Clinical Research*, 8(3): 267–73.

Boyle, G.J. (1988c) 'Elucidation of motivation structure by dynamic calculus', in J.R. Nesselroade and R.B. Cattell (eds), *Handbook of Multivariate Experimental Psychology* (2nd edn). New York: Plenum, pp. 737–87.

Boyle, G.J. (1989a) 'Breadth-depth or state–trait curiosity? A factor analysis of state–trait curiosity and state anxiety scales', *Personality and Individual Differences*, 10(2): 175–83.

Boyle, G.J. (1989b) 'Central dynamic traits measured in the School Motivation Analysis Test', *Multivariate Experimental Clinical Research*, 9(1): 11–26.

Boyle, G.J. (1989c) 'Children's Motivation Analysis Test (CMAT): Normative data', *Psychological Reports*, 65(3): 920–2.

Boyle, G.J. (1989d) 'Factor structure of the Differential Emotions Scale and the Eight State Questionnaire revisited', *Irish Journal of Psychology*, 10(1): 56–66.

Boyle, G.J. (1989e) 'Re-examination of the major personality-type factors in the Cattell, Comrey and Eysenck scales: Were the factor solutions by Noller et al. optimal?', *Personality and Individual Differences*, 10(12): 1289–99.

Boyle, G.J. (1989f) 'Review of R.B. Cattell and R.C. Johnson's (1986) "Functional psychological testing: Principles and instruments"', *Multivariate Experimental Clinical Research*, 9(1): 41–3.

Boyle, G.J. (1989g) 'Sex differences in reported mood states', *Personality and Individual Differences*, 10(11): 1179–83.

Boyle, G.J. (1990a) 'A review of the factor structure of the Sixteen Personality Factor Questionnaire and the Clinical Analysis Questionnaire', *Psychological Test Bulletin*, 3(1): 40–5.

Boyle, G.J. (1990b) 'Stanford-Binet IV Intelligence Scale: Is its structure supported by LISREL congeneric factor analyses?', *Personality and Individual Differences*, 11(11): 1175–81.

Boyle, G.J. (1991a) 'Experimental psychology does require a multivariate perspective', *Contemporary Psychology*, 36(4): 350–1.

Boyle, G.J. (1991b) 'Interset relationships between the Eight State Questionnaire and the Menstrual Distress Questionnaire', *Personality and Individual Differences*, 12(7): 703–11.

Boyle, G.J. (1991c) 'Item analysis of the subscales in the Eight State Questionnaire (8SQ): Exploratory and confirmatory factor analyses', *Multivariate Experimental Clinical Research*, 10(1): 37–65.

Boyle, G.J. (1991d) 'Does item homogeneity indicate internal consistency or item redundancy in psychometric scales?', *Personality and Individual Differences*, 12(3): 291–4.

Boyle, G.J. (1992) 'Multidimensional Mood State Inventory (MMSI)', Unpublished manuscript, Department of Psychology, University of Queensland.

Boyle, G.J. (1993a) 'Intelligence and personality measurement within the Cattellian psychometric model', in G.L. Van Heck, P. Bonaiuto, I. J. Deary, and W. Nowack (eds), *Personality Psychology in Europe* (Vol. 4). Tilburg: Tilburg University Press, pp. 183–201.

Boyle, G.J. (1993b) 'Evaluation of the exploratory factor analysis programs provided in SPSSX and SPSS/PC+', *Multivariate Experimental Clinical Research*, 10(2): 129–35.

Boyle, G.J. (1995) 'Measurement of intelligence and personality within the Cattellian psychometric model', *Multivariate Experimental Clinical Research*, 11(1): 47–59.

Boyle, G.J. (1999) 'Pavlovian Temperament Survey (PTS): Australian normative data', in J. Strelau, A. Angleitner, and B.H. Newberry. *The Pavlovian Temperament Survey (PTS): An International Handbook*. Seattle, WA: Hogrefe & Huber, pp. 78–84.

Boyle, G.J. (2006a) 'Five Factor Model of personality structure', in D. Westen, L. Burton and R. Kowalski (eds), *Psychology* (Australian and New Zealand edn). Milton, Queensland: Wiley, p. 443.

Boyle, G.J. (2006b) 'Scientific analysis of personality and individual differences', DSc thesis, University of Queensland, St. Lucia, Queensland.

Boyle, G.J. and Cattell, R.B. (1984) 'Proof of situational sensitivity of mood states and dynamic traits – ergs and sentiments – to disturbing stimuli', *Personality and Individual Differences*, 5(5): 541–8.

Boyle, G.J. and Cattell, R.B. (1987) 'A first survey of the similarity of personality and motivation prediction of "in situ" and experimentally controlled learning, by structured learning theory', *Australian Psychologist*, 22(2): 189–96.

Boyle, G.J. and Comer, P.G. (1990) 'Personality characteristics of direct-service personnel in community residential units', *Australia and New Zealand Journal of Developmental Disabilities*, 16(2): 125–31.

Boyle, G.J. and Houndoulesi, V. (1993) 'Utility of the School Motivation Analysis Test in predicting second language acquisition', *British Journal of Educational Psychology*, 63(3): 500–12.

Boyle, G.J. and Katz, I. (1991) 'Multidimensional scaling of the Eight State Questionnaire and the Differential Emotions Scale', *Personality and Individual Differences*, 12(6): 565–74.

Boyle, G.J., Ortet, G. and Ibáñez, M.I. (2001) 'Evaluación de la personalidad y la inteligencia: Una perspectiva cattelliana [Evaluation of personality and intelligence: A Cattellian perspective]', *Universitas Tarraconensis Revista de Psicología*, 23(1–2): 73–92.

Boyle, G.J., Richards, L.M. and Baglioni, Jr. A.J. (1993) 'Children's Motivation Analysis Test (CMAT): An experimental manipulation of curiosity and boredom', *Personality and Individual Differences*, 15(6): 637–43.

Boyle, G.J. and Robertson, J.M. (1989) 'Anomaly in equation for calculating 16PF second-order factor QIII', *Personality and Individual Differences*, 10(9): 1007–8.

Boyle, G.J. and Saklofske, D.H. (2004) (eds), 'Editors' Introduction', in *Sage Benchmarks in Psychology: The Psychology of Individual Differences*. London: Sage, pp. xix–lvi.

Boyle, G.J. and Smári, J. (1997) 'De fem stora och personlighetspsykologins matningsproblem [The big five and measurement problems in personality psychology]', *Nordisk Psykologi* [*Nordic Psychology*], 49(1): 12–21.

Boyle, G.J. and Smári, J. (1998) 'Statiska femfaktorpersonlighets-modeller-Svar till Engvik [Static five-factor models of personality: A reply to Engvik]', *Nordisk Psykologi* [*Nordic Psychology*], 50(3): 216–22.

Boyle, G.J. and Smári, J. (2002) 'Vers une simplification du modèle cattellien de la personnalité', *Bulletin de Psychologie*, 55(6): 635–43.

Boyle, G.J., Stankov, L. and Cattell, R.B. (1995) 'Measurement and statistical models in the study of personality and intelligence', in D.H. Saklofske and M. Zeidner (eds), *International Handbook of Personality and Intelligence*. New York: Plenum, pp. 417–46.

Boyle, G.J. and Stanley, G.V. (1986) 'Application of factor analysis in psychological research: Improvement of simple structure by computer-assisted graphic oblique transformation', *Multivariate Experimental Clinical Research*, 8(1): 175–82.

Boyle, G.J., Stanley, G.V. and Start, K.B. (1985) 'Canonical/redundancy analyses of the Sixteen Personality Factor Questionnaire, the Motivation Analysis Test, and the Eight State Questionnaire', *Multivariate Experimental Clinical Research*, 7(3): 113–22.

Boyle, G.J. and Start, K.B. (1988) 'A first delineation of higher-order factors in the Children's Motivation Analysis Test (CMAT)', *Psychologische Beiträge*, 30(4): 556–67.

Boyle, G.J. and Start, K.B. (1989a) 'Comparison of higher-order motivational factors across sexes using the Children's Motivation Analysis Test', *Personality and Individual Differences*, 10(4): 483–7.

Boyle, G.J. and Start, K.B. (1989b) 'Sex differences in the prediction of academic achievement using the Children's Motivation Analysis Test', *British Journal of Educational Psychology*, 59(2): 245–52.

Boyle, G.J., Start, K.B. and Hall, E.J. (1988) 'Comparison of Australian and American normative data for the School Motivation Analysis Test', *Psychological Test Bulletin*, 1(1): 24–7.

Boyle, G.J., Start, K.B. and Hall, E.J. (1989a) 'Dimensions of adolescent motivation as measured by higher-order factors in the School Motivation Analysis Test', *Journal of School Psychology*, 27(1): 27–33.

Boyle, G.J., Start, K.B. and Hall, E.J. (1989b) 'Prediction of academic achievement using the School Motivation Analysis Test', *British Journal of Educational Psychology*, 59(1): 92–9.

Cattell, H.E.P. (1993) 'The structure of phenotypic personality traits: Comment', *American Psychologist*, 48(12): 1302–3.

Cattell, H.E.P. (2001) 'The Sixteen Personality Factor (16PF) Questionnaire', in W.I. Dorfman, and M. Hersen (eds), *Understanding Psychological Assessment*. Dordrecht, Netherlands: Kluwer Academic, pp. 187–215.

Cattell, H.E.P. (2004) 'The Sixteen Personality Factor (16PF) Questionnaire', in M.J. Hilsenroth, and D.L. Segal (eds), *Comprehensive Handbook of Psychological Assessment (Vol. 2): Personality Assessment*. Hoboken, NJ: Wiley, pp. 39–49.

Cattell, H.E.P. and Schuerger, J.M. (2003) *Essentials of 16PF Assessment*. Hoboken, NJ: Wiley.

Cattell, R.B. (1973) *Personality and Mood by Questionnaire*. San Francisco: Jossey-Bass.

Cattell, R.B. (1978) *The Scientific Use of Factor Analysis in Behavioral and Life Sciences*. New York: Plenum.

Cattell, R.B. (1979) *Personality and Learning Theory, Vol. 1: The Structure of Personality in its Environment*. New York: Springer.

Cattell, R.B. (1980a) *Personality and Learning Theory, Vol. 2: A Systems Theory of Maturation and Structured Learning*. New York: Springer.

Cattell, R.B. (1980b) 'Personality theory derived from quantitative experiment (Vol. 1)', in H.I. Kaplan, A.M. Freeman, and B.J. Sadock (eds), *Comprehensive Textbook of Psychiatry* (3rd edn). Baltimore, MD: Williams & Wilkin, pp. 848–68.

Cattell, R.B. (1981) 'Where next in human motivation research? Some possible crucial experiments', in R. Lynn (ed.), *Dimensions of Personality: Papers in Honour of H.J. Eysenck*. Oxford: Pergamon, pp. 53–77.

Cattell, R.B. (1982a) 'The development of Cattellian structured systems theory of personality: The VIDAS model', *Zeitschrift fur Differentielle und Diagnostische Psychologie*, 3(1): 7–25.

Cattell, R.B. (1982b) 'The psychometry of objective motivation measurement: A response to the critique of Cooper and Kline', *British Journal of Educational Psychology*, 52(2): 234–41.

Cattell, R.B. (1983) *Structured Personality-Learning Theory: A Wholistic Multivariate Research Approach*. New York: Praeger.

Cattell, R.B. (1984) 'Personality as a scientifically based concept', in J. Kuper and M. Kuper (eds), *The Social Science Encyclopedia*. London: Routledge & Kegan Paul, pp. 10–37.

Cattell, R.B. (1985) *Human Motivation and the Dynamic Calculus*. New York: Praeger.

Cattell, R.B. (1986a) 'Dodging the third error source: Psychological interpretation and use of given scores', in R.B. Cattell and R.C. Johnson (eds), *Functional Psychological Testing: Principles and Instruments*. New York: Brunner/Mazel, pp. 496–543.

Cattell, R.B. (1986b) 'General principles across the media of assessment', in R.B. Cattell and R.C. Johnson (eds), *Functional Psychological Testing: Principles and Instruments*. New York: Brunner/Mazel, pp. 15–32.

Cattell, R.B. (1986c) 'Selecting, administering, scoring, recording, and using tests in assessment', in R.B. Cattell and R.C. *Johnson* (eds), *Functional Psychological Testing: Principles and Instruments*. New York: Brunner/Mazel, pp. 105–26.

Cattell, R.B. (1986d) 'Structured tests and functional diagnoses', in R.B. Cattell and R.C. Johnson (eds), *Functional Psychological Testing: Principles and Instruments*. New York: Brunner/Mazel, pp. 3–14.

Cattell, R.B. (1986e) 'The actual trait, state, and situation structures important in functional testing', in R.B. Cattell and R.C. Johnson (eds), *Functional Psychological Testing: Principles*

and Instruments. New York: Brunner/Mazel, pp. 33–53.

Cattell, R.B. (1986f) 'The psychometric properties of tests: Consistency, validity, and efficiency', in R.B. Cattell and R.C. Johnson (eds), *Functional Psychological Testing: Principles and Instruments*. New York: Brunner/Mazel, pp. 54–78.

Cattell, R.B. (1986g) 'The 16PF personality structure and Dr. Eysenck', *Journal of Social Behavior and Personality*, 1(2): 153–60.

Cattell, R.B. (1987) *Intelligence: Its Structure, Growth and Action*. Amsterdam: North Holland.

Cattell, R.B. (1988a) 'Handling prediction from psychological states and roles by modulation theory', in S.G. Cole, R.G. Demaree and W. Curtis (eds), *Applications of Interactionist Psychology: Essays in Honor of Saul B. Sells*. Hillsdale, NJ: Erlbaum, pp. 189–210.

Cattell, R.B. (1988b) 'Psychological theory and scientific method', in J.R. Nesselroade and R.B. Cattell (eds), *Handbook of Multivariate Experimental Psychology* (2nd edn). New York: Plenum, pp. 3–20.

Cattell, R.B. (1988c) 'The data box: Its ordering of total resources in terms of possible relational systems', in J.R. Nesselroade and R.B. Cattell (eds), *Handbook of Multivariate Experimental Psychology* (2nd edn). New York: Plenum, pp. 69–130.

Cattell, R.B. (1988d) 'The meaning and strategic use of factor analysis', in J.R. Nesselroade and R.B. Cattell (eds), *Handbook of Multivariate Experimental Psychology* (2nd edn). New York: Plenum, pp. 131–203.

Cattell, R.B. (1988e) 'The principles of experimental design and analysis in relation to theory building', in J.R. Nesselroade and R.B. Cattell (eds), *Handbook of Multivariate Experimental Psychology* (2nd edn). New York: Plenum, pp. 21–67.

Cattell, R.B. (1990a) 'Advances in Cattellian personality theory', in L.A. Pervin (ed.), *Handbook of Personality: Theory and Action*. New York: Guilford, pp. 101–10.

Cattell, R.B. (1990b) 'The birth of the Society of Multivariate Experimental Psychology', *Journal of the History of the Behavioral Sciences*, 26(1): 48–57.

Cattell, R.B. (1990c) 'The experimental testing of the Vidas systems theory', *Journal of Mathematical Psychology*, 34(1): 109–15.

Cattell, R.B. (1992) 'Human motivation objectively, experimentally analysed', *British Journal of Medical Psychology*, 65(3): 237–43.

Cattell, R.B. (1994) 'Constancy of global, second-order personality factors over a twenty-year-plus period', *Psychological Reports*, 75(1): 3–9.

Cattell, R.B. (1995) 'The fallacy of five factors in the personality sphere', *The Psychologist*, 8(5): 207–8.

Cattell, R.B. (1996) 'What is structured learning theory?', *British Journal of Educational Psychology*, 66(3): 411–3.

Cattell, R.B. and Birkett, H. (1980) 'The known personality factors found aligned between first order T-data and second order Q-data factors, with new evidence on the inhibitory control, independence and regression traits', *Personality and Individual Differences*, 1(3): 229–38.

Cattell, R.B., Boyle, G.J. and Chant, D. (2002) 'The enriched behavioral prediction equation and its impact on structured learning and the dynamic calculus', *Psychological Review*, 109(1): 202–5.

Cattell, R.B. and Cattell, A.K.S. (1977) *Measuring Intelligence with the Culture Fair Tests*. Champaign, IL: Institute for Personality and Ability Testing.

Cattell, R.B. and Cattell, H.E.P. (1995) 'Personality structure and the new fifth edition of the 16PF', *Educational and Psychological Measurement*, 55(6): 926–37.

Cattell, R.B. and Child, D. (1975) *Motivation and Dynamic Structure*. London: Holt, Rinehart & Winston.

Cattell, R.B., Eber, H.W. and Tatsuoka, M.M. (1970) *Handbook for the Sixteen Personality Factor Questionnaire*. Champaign, IL: Institute for Personality and Ability Testing.

Cattell, R.B. and Horn, J.L. (1982) 'Whimsy and misunderstanding of Gf-Gc theory: A comment on Guilford', *Psychological Bulletin*, 91(3): 621–33.

Cattell, R.B. and Johnson, R.C. (1986) (eds), *Functional Psychological Testing: Principles and Instruments*. New York: Brunner/Mazel.

Cattell, R.B. and Kameoka, V.A. (1985) 'Psychological states measured in the Clinical Analysis Questionnaire (CAQ)', *Multivariate Experimental Clinical Research*, 7(2): 69–87.

Cattell, R.B. and Kline, P. (1977) *The Scientific Analysis of Personality and Motivation*. New York: Academic.

Cattell, R.B. and Krug, S.E. (1986) 'The number of factors in the 16PF: A review of the evidence with special emphasis on methodological problems', *Educational and Psychological Measurement*, 46(3): 509–22.

Cattell, R.B. and Nesselroade, J.R. (1988) (eds), *Handbook of Multivariate Experimental Psychology* (2nd edn). New York: Plenum.

Cattell, R.B. and Schuerger, J.M. (1978) *Personality Theory in Action: Handbook for the Objective-Analytic (O-A) Test Kit*. Champaign, IL: Institute for Personality and Ability Testing.

Cattell, R.B. and Vogelmann, S. (1977) 'A comprehensive trial for the scree and KG criteria for determining the number of factors', *Multivariate Behavioral Research*, 12(3): 289–325.

Cattell, R.B. and Warburton, F.W. (1967) *Objective Personality and Motivation Tests: A Theoretical Introduction and Practical Compendium*. Champaign, IL: University of Illinois Press.

Child, D. (1990) *The Essentials of Factor Analysis* (2nd edn). London: Cassell.

Cronbach, L.J. (1957) 'The two disciplines of scientific psychology', *American Psychologist*, 12(11): 671–84.

Curran, J.P. and Cattell, R.B. (1976) *Manual for the Eight State Questionnaire*. Champaign, IL: Institute for Personality and Ability Testing.

Eysenck, H.J. (1984) 'Cattell and the theory of personality', *Multivariate Behavioral Research*, 19(2–3): 323–36.

Eysenck, H.J. (1997) 'Personality and experimental psychology: The unification of psychology and the possibility of a paradigm', *Journal of Personality and Social Psychology*, 73(6): 1224–37.

Eysenck, H.J. and Eysenck, M.W. (1985) *Personality and Individual Differences: A Natural Science Approach*. New York: Plenum.

Fernandez, E. and Boyle, G.J. (1996) 'Meta-analytic procedure and interpretation of treatment outcome and test validity for the practitioner psychologist', in M. Smith and V. Sutherland (eds), *International Review of Professional Issues in Selection and Assessment* (Vol. 2). New York: Wiley, pp. 109–25.

Fisher, C.D. and Boyle, G.J. (1997) 'Personality and employee selection: Credibility regained', *Asia Pacific Journal of Human Resources*, 35(2): 26–40.

Gorsuch, R.L. (1983) *Factor Analysis* (2nd edn). Hillsdale, NJ: Erlbaum.

Grossarth-Maticek, R., Eysenck, H.J. and Boyle, G.J. (1995) 'Method of test administration as a factor in test validity: The use of a personality questionnaire in the prediction of cancer and coronary heart disease', *Behaviour Research and Therapy*, 33(6): 705–10.

Haggbloom, S.J., Warnick, R., Warnick, J.E., Jones, V.K., Yarbrough, G.L., Russell, T.M., Borecky, C.M., McGahhey, R., Powell III, J.L., Beavers, J. and Monte, E. (2002) 'The 100 most eminent psychologists of the 20th century', *Review of General Psychology*, 6(2): 139–52.

Hakstian, A.R. and Cattell, R.B. (1982) *Manual for the Comprehensive Ability Battery*. Champaign, IL: Institute for Personality and Ability Testing.

Hakstian, A.R., Rogers, W.T. and Cattell, R.B. (1982) 'The behavior of number-of-factors rules with simulated data', *Multivariate Behavioral Research,* 17(2): 193–219.

Kline, P. (1979) *Psychometrics and Psychology*. London: Academic.

Kline, P. (1980) 'The psychometric model', in A.J. Chapman and D.M. Jones (eds), *Models of Man*. Leicester: British Psychological Society, pp. 322–28.

Krug, S.E. (1980) *Clinical Analysis Questionnaire Manual*. Champaign, IL: Institute for Personality and Ability Testing.

Krug, S.E. (1981) *Interpreting 16PF Profile Patterns*. Champaign, IL, Institute for Personality and Ability Testing.

Krug, S.E. and Johns, E.F. (1986) 'A large scale cross-validation of second-order personality structure defined by the 16PF', *Psychological Reports*, 59(2): 683–93.

McArdle, J.J. (1984) 'On the madness in his method: R.B. Cattell's contributions to Structural Equation Modelling', *Multivariate Behavioral Research*, 19(2): 245–67.

McArdle, J.J. and Cattell, R.B. (1994) 'Structural equation models of factorial invariance in parallel proportional profiles and oblique confactor problems', *Multivariate Behavioral Research*, 29(1): 63–113.

Nesselroade, J.R. and Cattell, R.B. (1988) (eds), *Handbook of Multivariate Experimental Psychology* (2nd edn). New York: Plenum.

Roberts, B.W., Walton, K.E. and Viechtbauer, W. (2006a) 'Patterns of mean-level change in personality traits across the life course: A meta-analysis of longitudinal studies', *Psychological Bulletin*, 132(1): 1–25.

Roberts, B.W., Walton, K.E. and Viechtbauer, W. (2006b) 'Personality traits change in adulthood: Reply to Costa and McCrae (2006)', *Psychological Bulletin*, 132(1): 29–32.

Schuerger, J.M. (1986) 'Personality assessment by objective tests', in R.B. Cattell and R.C. Johnson (eds), *Functional Psychological Testing: Principles and Instruments*. New York: Brunner/Mazel, pp. 260–287.

Smith, B.D. (1988) 'Personality: Multivariate systems theory and research', in J.R. Nesselroade and R.B. Cattell (eds), *Handbook of Multivariate Experimental Psychology* (2nd edn). New York: Plenum.

Stankov, L., Boyle, G.J. and Cattell, R.B. (1995) 'Models and paradigms in personality and intelligence research', in D.H. Saklofske and M. Zeidner (eds), *International Handbook of Personality and Intelligence*. New York: Plenum, pp. 15–43.

Sweney, A.R., Anton and Cattell, R.B. (1986) 'Evaluating motivation structure, conflict, and adjustment', in R.B. Cattell and R.C. Johnson (eds), *Functional Psychological Testing: Principles and Instruments*. New York: Brunner/Mazel, pp. 288–315.

13

Empirical and Theoretical Status of the Five-Factor Model of Personality Traits

Robert R. McCrae and Paul T. Costa, Jr.

Progress sometimes seems elusive in psychology, where old methods such as the Rorschach endure despite decades of criticism (Costa and McCrae, 2005), and where new research is often based on passing fads (Fiske and Leyens, 1997) rather than cumulative findings. It is remarkable, therefore, when clear progress is made, and there are few more dramatic examples than the rise to dominance of the Five-Factor Model (FFM) of personality traits in the past quarter century. Before that time, trait psychology had endured a Thirty Years' War of competing trait models, with Guilford, Cattell, and Eysenck only the most illustrious of the combatants. The discovery of the FFM by Tupes and Christal (1961/1992) in the midst of that war was largely ignored, but its rediscovery 20 years later quickly led to a growing acceptance. Today it is the default model of personality structure, guiding not only personality psychologists, but increasingly, developmentalists (Kohnstamm et al., 1998), cross-cultural psychologists (McCrae and Allik, 2002), industrial/organizational psychologists (Judge et al., 1999), and clinicians (J.A. Singer, 2005).

This chapter has two parts. The first is an overview of the FFM and associated research findings, and may appeal primarily to the general reader. The second half, 'Challenges to the FFM', contains more detailed and technical accounts of current controversies, and is addressed chiefly to personality researchers.

ORIGINS AND ACCOMPLISHMENTS OF THE FFM

The FFM is the most widely accepted solution to the problem of describing trait structure – that is, finding a simple and effective way to understand relations among traits. Trait adjectives (such as *nervous, energetic, original, accommodating*, and *careful*) describe individual differences that usually show a bell-shaped distribution: For example, a few people are very energetic, most people are somewhat energetic, and a few are lethargic. There are thousands of such terms in the English language, and many other traits have been identified by psychologists (such as ego strength, tolerance of ambiguity, and need for achievement). It was recognized long ago that these traits overlap: Someone who is described as nervous is also likely to be described as worried, jittery, anxious, apprehensive, and fearful. Beyond semantic similarity, psychologists realized that some classes of traits were closely related. For example, there is a clear difference between being sad and being scared, but people who are frequently sad are also frequently scared.

To summarize trait information in a manageable number of constructs, psychologists used factor analysis, a statistical technique that in effect sorts variables into groups of related traits that are more or less independent of the other groups. For example, *sad* and *scared* would define the high pole of a factor (or dimension) called 'neuroticism' (N), because it was first observed in psychiatric patients diagnosed with a neurosis. The opposite pole of the same dimension would be defined by traits such as *calm* and *stable*. A completely different factor, 'extraversion' (E), contrasts *warm, outgoing*, and *cheerful* with *reserved, solitary*, and *somber*. Just as any place on Earth can be specified by the three dimensions of latitude, longitude, and altitude, so anyone's personality can be characterized in terms of the five dimensions of the FFM.

N and E factors have been familiar to psychologists since the mid-twentieth century. The former is central to many forms of mental disorder, and thus well known to clinical psychologists and psychiatrists. The latter is the most easily observed factor, and 'extravert' has long been part of popular speech. The remaining factors are 'openness to experience' (O; also called 'intellect', or 'openness vs. closedness'), which describes imaginative, curious, and exploratory tendencies as opposed to rigid, practical, and traditional tendencies; 'agreeableness'

(A), which contrasts generosity, honesty, and modesty with selfishness, aggression, and arrogance; and 'conscientiousness' (C; or 'dependability', 'constraint', or 'will to achieve'), which characterizes people who are hardworking, purposeful, and disciplined rather than laid-back, unambitious, and weak-willed.

Psychologists took several decades to identify the FFM, chiefly because they differed in their ideas of what variables should be included in their factor analyses. Many approaches were offered, but the breakthrough came from lexical researchers, who argued that traits are so important in daily life that people will have invented names for all the important ones. A search of an unabridged dictionary should yield an exhaustive list of traits, and it was in analyses of such traits that the FFM was discovered. Although there had been previous indications that five factors were necessary and sufficient, the case was clearly made for the first time by two Air Force psychologists, Ernest Tupes and Ray Christal, who published a technical report in 1961. It was known to a few personality psychologists but had little influence until researchers returned to the lexical approach around 1980, again searching the dictionary and again finding five factors (Goldberg, 1983). Researchers who work in the lexical tradition, focusing on lay trait vocabularies in different languages, generally call the factors the 'Big Five' and distinguish them from the dimensions of the FFM, which are not based on lay terminology. These labels, however, are used interchangeably by many psychologists.

Lexical researchers initially had a limited impact on the field as a whole because most psychologists relied on questionnaires that measured traits (and related concepts like preferences and needs). Most of these questionnaires had been developed to operationalize particular theories of personality and were thought to be more scientific than lay terms. For example, Jung's (1923/1971) theory of psychological types was the basis of the Myers-Briggs Type

Indicator (MBTI; Myers and McCaulley, 1985), a widely used measure of four dimensions, from which introvert versus extravert, sensing versus intuiting, thinking versus feeling and perceiving versus judging preferences were scored.

The dominance of the FFM came as a result of empirical studies showing that the traits assessed by psychological questionnaires were closely related to the lexical Big Five factors (McCrae, 1989). It is not surprising that the 'introvert versus extravert' dimension of the MBTI corresponded to the lexical E factor, but it was very revealing that 'sensing versus intuiting' was in fact O, 'thinking versus feeling' was A, and 'perceiving versus judging' was C (McCrae and Costa, 1989a). Scales from many other questionnaires were also found to match up with lexical factors, and it became clear that in creating their scientific questionnaires, personality psychologists had rediscovered and formalized what had long been implicit in lay conceptions of personality.

Research accomplishments

The widespread acceptance of the FFM in the 1990s led to systematic research on a variety of topics, allowing important advances in our understanding of personality trait psychology. One of the first issues resolved by research on the FFM concerned consensual validation. As a result of influential critiques (e.g. Mischel, 1968), it was widely believed in the 1970s that personality traits were cognitive fictions – beliefs people held about themselves and others around them that had no basis in fact. Because traits assessed by personality tests were relatively poor predictors of specific behaviors in laboratory tests, some researchers concluded that all trait attributions were illusory. However, single behaviors in the artificial setting of a psychological laboratory are not very meaningful criteria for judging the reality of traits. Much more important criteria are provided by the views of significant others in

one's life. If there is substantial agreement across different raters, and if raters agree with self-reports, it is likely that the agreement is based on the common perception of real psychological characteristics in the target.

This was a crucial issue in the early 1980s, especially because two of the five factors, A and C, are highly evaluative. It was easy to argue that rating someone as being high on these factors merely meant that one liked them; rating oneself as high on A and C could be nothing more than socially desirable responding. However, studies in which self-reports were compared to peer and spouse ratings showed moderately high agreement on all five factors (Funder et al., 1995; McCrae and Costa, 1987), suggesting that all reflected real characteristics of the individual.

The reality of traits was also demonstrated by studies of their heritability (Bouchard and Loehlin, 2001). Identical twins, who share all their genes, resemble each other much more than fraternal twins do, whether or not they were raised in the same family. About half the observed variation in trait scores appears to be genetically based, and this is true for all five factors (Jang et al., 1996). Recent work has shown that the five-factor structure itself is genetically based (Yamagata et al., 2006), presumably meaning that traits like orderliness and deliberation go together because they are both influenced in part by the same genes. So far the actual genes involved have not been identified, probably because a large number of genes affect each trait, so the effect of any single gene is very small and correspondingly hard to detect.

Longitudinal studies, in which personality is assessed twice many years apart, show that individual differences are very stable (Roberts and DelVecchio, 2000). A person who is artistically sensitive, intellectually curious, and politically liberal at age 30 is likely to be artistically sensitive, intellectually curious, and politically liberal – relative to his or her age peers – at age 80. There is strong evidence for stability over periods as long as 40 years; all five factors are roughly equally stable; and both self-reports and observer ratings show stability (Costa and McCrae, 1992b; Terracciano et al., 2006). Although rank-order is stable, there are gradual changes in the mean level of traits from adolescence to old age. People in general decrease in N, E, and O, and increase in A and C as they age (Terracciano et al., 2005). Thus, older men and women tend to be less active and adventurous than their grandchildren, but more emotionally stable and mature.

Cross-cultural studies once required researchers to travel to foreign lands and master new languages in order to gather personality data, and consequently they were rare. Today, almost every nation in the world has psychologists who speak English and are trained in modern methods of psychological research, and email makes it possible to collaborate from the convenience of one's own office. As a result, there has been a surge of cross-cultural research on personality (e.g. Schmitt et al., 2007). The first questionnaire designed to operationalize the FFM, the Revised NEO Personality Inventory (NEO-PI-R; Costa and McCrae, 1992a), has been translated into over 40 languages and used to assess personality in countries around the world, from the Congo to Iceland to Iran. This research was based on the assumption that the traits assessed by the NEO-PI-R would be found everywhere, and that assumption has been supported by dozens of studies. In country after country, factor analysis of the NEO-PI-R has yielded the five factors familiar to American psychologists (McCrae et al., 2005c). The FFM appears to be a universal aspect of human nature, probably because it is genetically based, and all human beings share the same human genome.

Many other properties of traits have also been shown to be universal. Some psychologists have argued that traits are less important than relationships in collectivistic countries like Japan, and consequently trait ratings would be less reliable and valid. But studies of cross-observer agreement in collectivistic

cultures show correlations as high as those in the United States (McCrae et al., 2004). So far, there are no longitudinal studies of personality in non-Western nations, so we cannot determine whether traits are equally stable around the world. However, cross-sectional studies of age differences show the same trends everywhere: N, E, and O decline, and A and C increase as people age (McCrae et al., 1999). In the United States, women score a little higher than men on measures of N and A, and the same is true of women in Malaysia, Peru, and Burkina Faso (McCrae et al., 2005c).

Long before the FFM was formulated, psychologists studied personality traits because they were useful in predicting important outcomes (Ozer and Benet-Martínez, 2006). It is true that traits are usually poor predictors of any single behavior; otherwise, people would be automatons. But traits endure over long periods of time, and the small influence they exert on single behaviors is compounded across a lifetime. Traits are good predictors of patterns of behavior (McCrae and Costa, 2003).

The most important outcomes of N are those related to well-being and mental health. Individuals high in N tend to be unhappy, regardless of their life situation, and they are more susceptible than others to psychiatric disorders such as depression (Bagby et al., 1997) and many of the personality disorders (Trull and McCrae, 2002). E is associated with popularity and social success, with enterprising self-promotion, and ultimately, with higher lifetime income (Soldz and Vaillant, 1999). Extraverts are also likely to be happier than introverts. O is a predictor of creative achievement, whereas closedness predicts political conservatism and religious fundamentalism (McCrae, 1996). Agreeable people are more likely to be desired as mates (Buss and Barnes, 1986) and have better marital relations (Donnellan et al., 2004), whereas antagonistic men and women are more likely to commit crimes and abuse drugs (Brooner et al., 2002). C is the most consistent predictor of job performance

(Barrick and Mount, 1991); it is not surprising that employees who are punctual, hard-working, and systematic are usually more productive. C is also associated with a number of positive health habits, like safe driving, exercise, and a sensible diet; in consequence, conscientious people are more likely to be healthy and live longer (Weiss and Costa, 2005).

Clinical utility

Most instruments that assess the FFM are intended for use in personality research, but the NEO-PI-R and the structured interview for the five-factor model (SIFFM; Trull and Widiger, 1997) were also designed to be used in clinical practice. The NEO-PI-R, which offers norms, profile sheets, and computer administration and interpretation, has been widely adopted by clinical psychologists and psychiatrists and is becoming a standard part of routine clinical assessment (see Archer and Smith, in press; Weiner and Greene, 2008).

By 1991, Miller had identified a number of ways in which the NEO-PI-R could be used to facilitate clinical practice: It can provide a rapid understanding of the client and thus foster rapport; it can help the clinician anticipate potential problems (such as resistance and poor motivation to change); it can help in the selection of optimal forms of treatment; it can predict likely treatment outcomes. Singer (2005) has updated this list, showing how feedback to the client can help raise self-awareness, and how the joint interpretation of personality profiles from couples can help them understand each other.

There has been extensive research on personality disorders and the FFM (Costa and Widiger, 2002), and that, too, has clinical applications. NEO-PI-R computer software (Costa et al., 1994) can compare a client's profile to personality disorder prototypes and formulate hypotheses about which disorders might characterize the client. For example, a client who scores high on N2: angry hostility

and low on A1: trust, A2: straightforwardness, and A4: compliance, might warrant a diagnosis of paranoid personality disorder. The clinician would, of course, need to confirm this diagnosis by evaluating *DSM-IV* criteria.

A new approach to personality disorder diagnosis has also been proposed (McCrae et al., 2005a) in which clinicians proceed from the personality profile directly to an assessment of problems in living. After assessing FFM traits, clinicians would consult a list of problems relevant to the traits that characterize the client, and determine if they are in fact problematic for this client. For example, an individual high in agreeableness may be gullible and easily taken advantage of. If so, and if the clinician believes that this causes clinically significant personal distress or impairment, then a diagnosis of high agreeableness-related personality disorder would be appropriate.

Theoretical context

The FFM is a model of the structure of traits, and thus a basis for organizing research findings. But it is not a theory of personality; it does not explain how traits function in daily life, or how individuals understand themselves, or how people adapt to the cultures in which they find themselves. The wealth of new findings about traits has inspired a number of personality psychologists to formulate new theories of personality. In 1996, Wiggins edited a book in which he invited prominent FFM researchers to put their findings in theoretical contexts, from evolutionary to socio-analytic. Other views have since been offered as part of a new generation of personality theories (Cervone, 2004a; Mayer, 2005; McAdams and Pals, 2006; Sheldon, 2004).

Five-factor theory (FFT; McCrae and Costa, 1996, in press) shares features with many of these models, and has proven particularly useful in understanding the functioning of traits across cultures. The major

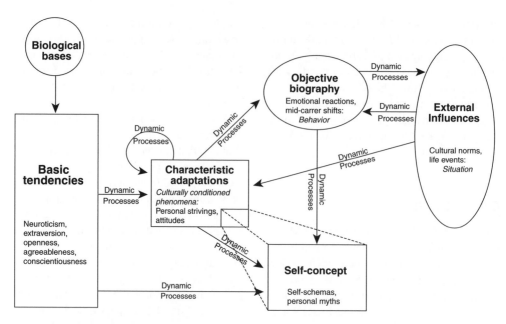

Figure 13.1 A schematic representation of the personality system. 'Biological bases' (such as genes) and 'external influences' (such as cultural norms) are inputs to the system. Personality traits are found in the category of 'basic tendencies', which are influenced by biological bases, but not external influences. Causal paths are indicated by arrows, and show that, over time, traits interact with the environment to produce 'characteristic adaptations' (such as attitudes), and these in turn interact with the situation to produce the output of the system, the 'objective biography'. The 'self-concept' is a subset of characteristic adaptations of particular importance to self theorists. Adapted from McCrae and Costa (1996)

components in the theory are represented schematically in Figure 13.1. The central elements, in rectangles, are *basic tendencies* and *characteristic adaptations* (of which the *self-concept* is a part). The distinction between these two is central to the theory; it holds that personality traits (as well as other characteristics such as intelligence and musical ability) are biologically based properties of the individual that affect the rest of the personality system, but are not themselves affected by it. Personality traits are thus conceptualized in the tradition of temperaments (McCrae et al., 2000).

In contrast, *characteristic adaptations* are acquired from the interaction of the individual's *basic tendencies* and a range of *external influences*. A man may speak Hindi because he was born with the capacity for

human speech and grew up in India; in the same way, a woman may smile at strangers because she was born agreeable and raised in America, where smiling at strangers is appropriate behavior. Characteristic adaptations include a vast range of psychological mechanisms: habits, interests, values, skills, knowledge, beliefs, attitudes, and the internalized aspect of roles and relationships. All of these are thought to be shaped to some extent by basic personality traits, and it is because of this pervasive influence that traits are correlates of so many psychological characteristics. At the same time, all these features depend on learning and experience in particular social and cultural environments, so the specific ways in which traits are expressed is likely to vary across cultures. In Saudi Arabia, women do not speak to men who are not close relations (Cole, 2001), so Saudi women who are extraverted are likely to be especially talkative among their female friends.

Although in principle it might seem that cultures could dictate any sort of behavior as the appropriate way to express traits, in fact the range of variation is fairly circumscribed (cf. Baumeister, 2005). Antagonistic behavior, for example, is recognizable anywhere. As a result, fairly direct translations of personality questionnaires yield serviceable measures that retain most of the psychometric properties of the original (Schmitt et al., 2007). One fortunate consequence of this fact is that it makes possible an important test of FFT. According to FFT, personality traits reflect only biological bases; because all humans share the same genome, FFT predicts that the structure of personality should be the same everywhere. That prediction, which would have evoked profound skepticism from a generation of personality-and-culture researchers (M Singer, 1961), has now been strongly supported at both the phenotypic (McCrae et al., 2005c) and genotypic (Yamagata et al., 2006) levels. This is powerful evidence in favor of FFT.

The most controversial aspects of FFT concern two postulates about the origin and development of traits. As the arrows in Figure 13.1 suggest, FFT asserts that traits are influenced only by biology (which includes genetics, but also physical disease, malnutrition, intrauterine hormonal environment, etc.). Neither life experiences nor culture are supposed to affect traits, a radical position that is supported mostly by a conspicuous lack of compelling evidence for environmental effects (McCrae and Costa, in press). For example, Roberts et al. (2002) reported that divorce led to decreases in dominance in women, whereas Costa et al. (2000) found that among women divorce led to *increases* in E, which includes dominance. Without replication is it difficult to trust either of these findings.

FFT acknowledges that trait levels change over lifespan, but attributes the change to intrinsic maturation rather than life experience.

If that account is correct, then the same pattern of personality change should be seen in different cultures, and the same pattern of age differences should be seen in nations with very different recent histories. In one study we compared Chinese, many of whom had lived through the Cultural Revolution and other social upheavals, with Americans of the same birth cohorts. Despite the profound differences in life history of these two groups, the pattern of age differences was remarkably similar (Yang et al., 1998).

Although this finding is consistent with FFT, it is susceptible to alternative explanations. Roberts et al. (2005b) have proposed social investment theory as a way to account for similar patterns of personality development. Higher levels of A and C are useful attributes for responsible adults to have, whereas E and O are not as important after the individual has found his or her way into the adult world. Consequently, they argued, societies everywhere encourage high A and C and discourage high E and O in adults. Members of each culture invest in this social vision and change their traits accordingly. That is certainly a possibility; what are needed are designs that would allow researchers to compare conflicting predictions from these two theories to see which better accounts for the facts.

CHALLENGES TO THE FFM

The success of the FFM as a description of personality trait structure does not mean that it has gone unchallenged. In fact, its prominence has made it the target of numerous critiques, some from those who advocate alternative structures (Ashton et al., 2004; De Raad and Peabody, 2005), some from those who see limitations in any factor model (Block, 2001; Cervone, 2004a). We have addressed the issue of alternative structures elsewhere (McCrae and Costa, in press); briefly, we argued that six-factor models added nothing that could not be subsumed by the FFM. In the remainder of this chapter, we consider three other current controversies about the FFM: the nature of higher-order factors, the specification of facets, and the status of trait explanations.

Higher-order factors

The *structure* postulate of FFT states that personality trait structure is hierarchical, and that the five factors 'constitute the highest level of the hierarchy' (McCrae and Costa, 2003: 190). Yet in 1997, Digman showed that in many global measures of the FFM, the five factors were not independent, but co-varied to define two very broad factors, which he called α (or socialization) and β (or personal growth). α contrasted N with A and C, whereas β combined E and O. Such factors can be found in the NEO-PI-R if domain scores are factored, and they also appear in larger samples of personality instruments (Markon et al., 2005). These factors have attracted sporadic interest in the past decade. DeYoung et al. (2002) proposed a neurobiological model for β, which they called plasticity, and Jang and colleagues (Jang et al., 2006) presented evidence that α and β are heritable.

There are two substantive explanations for associations among the five factors. One is that there are shared causal structures that influence different factors. For example, a set of genes or a neurological structure might have effects on both E- and O-related traits in general. This interpretation is the basis of the work of DeYoung and colleagues (2002) and Jang and colleagues (2006). Less interesting, but also possible, is that the associations reflect the particular choice of facets to define each factor. For example, the NEO-PI-R N domain includes N5: impulsiveness, which reflects an inability to control impulses, and which is, not surprisingly, also related to low C. The NEO-PI-R does not have a perfectionism scale, but such a scale would probably be related to N and high C (cf. Hill et al., 1997). The negative correlation between

NEO-PI-R N and C would be decreased, perhaps substantially, by substituting a perfectionism facet for the impulsiveness facet. Although the selection of facets surely is one influence on the correlation among domain scales, the fact that different instruments, with different item and subscale compositions, often yield higher order factors akin to α and β (Digman, 1997; Markon et al., 2005) suggests the need for a deeper explanation.

That explanation, however, need not be substantive. McCrae and Costa (in press) have argued that α and β may be evaluative biases, akin to the (low) *negative valence* and *positive valence* factors identified by Tellegen and Waller (1987). People who are prone to describe themselves (or others) in highly positive terms such as *remarkable, flawless,* and *outstanding* are also more likely to describe themselves (or others) as higher in E and in O. Thus, β might result from a positive valence bias. Such a bias would probably not be shared by others, so multimethod assessments would yield uncorrelated E and O factors. This is precisely what Biesanz and West (2004) found in a study of self-reports and peer – and parent ratings. They concluded that 'observed correlations among Big Five traits are the product of informant-specific effects' (2004: 870) and that 'theoretical frameworks that integrate these traits as facets of a broader construct may need to be reexamined' (2004: 871).

Yet some studies do show significant cross-observer correlations among domains. For example, McCrae and Costa (1987) reported a correlation of $r = 0.25$, $p < 0.001$, between self-reported O and peer-rated E. One way to integrate this small body of literature is by assuming that there are both substantive and artifactual explanations for the intercorrelations among domains, substance predominating in some studies and instruments, artifact in others.

This argument assumes that agreement across observers is necessary and sufficient to infer substantive causes. That is a very attractive argument, the basis of claims that personality traits show consensual validation

(Woodruffe, 1985). But alternative interpretations are possible. Two raters may agree about a target because both subscribe to the same unfounded stereotype; indeed, researchers in social perception often distinguish between mere consensus and true accuracy (Funder and West, 1993). One stereotype that observers may share is that extraverts are open to experience. Then raters who correctly perceived a target to be high in E might inflate their estimates of O; across raters, this would generate a positive correlation between these two factors that might be mistaken for consensual validation.

Multimethod assessments are thus not foolproof as ways of separating substance from artifact, but they are far more informative than mono-method assessment. One way to analyze cross-observer data is by examining the joint factor structure (cf. McCrae and Costa, 1983), and for this chapter we conducted new analyses that compared factor structures for substantive and artifactual models of α and β.

We factored data from 532 adults for whom both self-reports and observer ratings were available on the NEO-PI-3 (McCrae et al., 2005b), a slightly simplified version of the NEO-PI-R. When analyzed separately, parallel analysis indicated five factors, and the familiar structure was seen in both self-reports and observer ratings. When analyzed jointly, however, parallel analysis indicated ten factors, suggesting that there is considerable method variance in scores. We first examined a five-factor solution, rotating the factors toward maximal alignment with a 60×5 target matrix formed by doubling the normative structure (see McCrae et al., 1996). The results showed acceptable fit for N, E, A, and C factors (factor congruence coefficients = 0.89 to 0.98), but not for O (congruence coefficient = 0.71), which was poorly defined in the observer rating facets.

We next tested a seven-factor model, adding two columns to the target matrix reflecting a substantive interpretation of α and β. In these models, each facet would be expected to have its primary loading on a joint N, E, O, A, or C factor, and a secondary loading on a joint α or β factor. If α and β are substantive factors, they should affect both self-reports and observer ratings and be jointly defined. For this analysis we created a new, 60×7 target matrix in which the first five columns were unchanged from the previous analysis. In the sixth column we entered -0.5 for the 12 N facets and $+0.5$ for the 24 A and C facets to define a sixth factor, α; in the seventh column we entered $+0.5$ for the 24 E and O facets to define the seventh factor, β. We extracted seven factors and rotated them to best fit the new target. This improved the fit for the five original factors, giving congruence coefficients of 0.90–0.94. However, neither α nor β were well defined, with congruence coefficients of only 0.76 and 0.82. Despite Procrustes rotation, which finds the best possible fit to the target, a was defined exclusively by observer rating facets; the largest loading from any self-report facet was 0.22. β was defined by ten observer rating facets (loadings = 0.34–0.63) and, weakly, by three self-report facets (loadings = 0.30–0.35). Thus, α and β do not appear as cross-method factors when seven factors are extracted.

Finally, Table 13.1 shows the results of a model in which (low) negative valence and positive valence artifacts were targeted within method. Target loadings for these factors were defined as for α and β, except that only self-report facets were targeted in the sixth and seventh factors, and only observer ratings were targeted in the eighth and ninth factors. All five joint substantive factors are well defined in this solution, and although the factor congruence coefficients for negative and positive valence are not high (probably because many of the untargeted facets have real non-zero loadings on the factors), the informant-specific factors are clearly recognizable. These analyses suggest that it is primarily within-method artifact that contributes to the emergence of higher-order α and β factors. The 'FFT structure' postulate withstands this test.

Table 13.1   Loadings for substantive and method factors in a joint analysis of NEO-PI-3 self-reports and observer ratings

NEO-PI-3 facet	Substantive factor					Method factor				
	N	E	O	A	C	NV_S	PV_S	NV_R	PV_R	VC
Self-Reports										
N1: Anxiety	**0.71**	−0.04	−0.10	−0.00	−0.00	***−0.33***	0.05	0.13	0.06	0.96
N2: Angry hostility	**0.51**	0.01	−0.01	**−0.47**	0.01	***−0.40***	−0.17	−0.03	−0.14	0.95
N3: Depression	**0.65**	−0.09	−0.03	0.04	−0.18	***−0.44***	−0.09	−0.05	−0.06	0.98
N4: Self-consciousness	**0.59**	−0.28	−0.03	0.17	−0.09	***−0.36***	−0.15	0.08	0.01	0.94
N5: Impulsiveness	0.37	0.32	0.05	−0.08	−0.22	***−0.49***	0.03	−0.06	−0.09	0.97
N6: Vulnerability	**0.59**	−0.08	−0.16	0.14	−0.28	***−0.48***	0.06	−0.03	0.15	0.96
E1: Warmth	−0.11	**0.66**	0.08	0.38	0.04	0.19	***0.30***	−0.02	−0.03	0.95
E2: Gregariousness	−0.09	**0.57**	−0.09	0.14	−0.08	−0.09	***0.45***	−0.15	0.21	0.92
E3: Assertiveness	−0.24	0.38	0.19	**−0.46**	0.21	0.08	0.18	−0.06	0.04	0.90
E4: Activity	−0.04	**0.42**	0.02	−0.29	0.39	0.06	0.29	−0.08	0.06	0.95
E5: Excitement seeking	−0.07	0.38	0.11	−0.39	−0.10	−0.14	***0.35***	−0.00	0.15	0.93
E6: Positive emotions	−0.10	**0.53**	0.19	0.13	0.11	0.24	***0.49***	−0.02	−0.03	0.94
O1: Fantasy	0.22	0.07	**0.47**	−0.12	−0.24	−0.03	***0.41***	0.11	−0.03	0.98
O2: Aesthetics	0.09	0.04	**0.55**	0.22	0.05	0.05	***0.44***	−0.08	0.03	0.98
O3: Feelings	0.27	**0.41**	**0.42**	0.04	0.17	0.15	***0.35***	0.06	−0.16	0.94
O4: Actions	−0.36	0.13	**0.45**	0.10	0.02	−0.03	***0.32***	−0.22	0.09	0.88
O5: Ideas	−0.09	−0.06	**0.67**	−0.09	0.11	0.15	***0.34***	0.06	0.04	0.97
O6: Values	−0.08	0.13	**0.51**	0.12	0.04	−0.02	0.24	0.03	−0.10	0.84
A1: Trust	−0.31	0.18	0.12	**0.63**	0.09	0.12	0.17	−0.16	−0.02	0.85
A2: Straightforwardness	0.01	−0.08	0.05	**0.63**	0.22	0.28	−0.23	−0.11	−0.10	0.90
A3: Altruism	−0.00	**0.43**	0.12	**0.49**	0.19	***0.38***	0.06	0.09	−0.08	0.96
A4: Compliance	−0.18	−0.18	−0.09	**0.71**	−0.09	0.23	0.08	0.00	0.12	0.93
A5: Modesty	0.09	−0.10	0.05	**0.67**	0.09	−0.04	***−0.32***	−0.15	−0.11	0.60
A6: Tender-mindedness	0.10	0.27	0.24	**0.53**	0.11	0.03	0.15	−0.14	−0.28	0.71
C1: Competence	−0.28	0.15	0.20	−0.13	**0.47**	***0.63***	0.04	0.07	−0.09	0.94
C2: Order	0.05	−0.05	−0.27	−0.07	**0.64**	0.18	0.21	−0.12	0.15	0.85
C3: Dutifulness	−0.04	0.08	0.08	0.19	**0.53**	***0.52***	−0.14	0.09	−0.09	0.93
C4: Achievement striving	−0.05	0.15	0.06	−0.27	**0.56**	***0.41***	0.21	0.09	0.02	0.93
C5: Self-discipline	−0.19	0.01	−0.06	−0.02	**0.63**	***0.49***	0.08	0.01	0.06	0.97
C6: Deliberation	−0.07	−0.27	−0.03	0.08	**0.38**	***0.60***	0.03	0.13	0.07	0.92
Observer Ratings										
N1: Anxiety	**0.79**	−0.03	−0.04	0.07	0.00	0.06	0.06	−0.15	0.11	0.91
N2: Angry hostility	**0.45**	0.09	0.08	−0.37	0.11	−0.06	−0.18	***−0.57***	−0.18	0.90
N3: Depression	**0.70**	−0.14	0.01	0.01	−0.17	0.07	−0.05	***−0.37***	0.07	0.98
N4: Self-consciousness	**0.66**	−0.28	−0.10	0.08	−0.15	0.07	0.16	−0.25	0.06	0.93
N5: Impulsiveness	0.35	0.28	0.06	−0.28	−0.29	0.02	−0.14	***−0.50***	0.05	0.97
N6: Vulnerability	**0.64**	−0.07	−0.09	−0.03	−0.33	0.10	0.19	***−0.39***	0.10	0.95
E1: Warmth	−0.09	**0.65**	0.07	0.34	−0.04	0.08	−0.05	**0.36**	0.24	0.85
E2: Gregariousness	−0.03	**0.65**	−0.03	0.06	−0.17	−0.09	0.15	0.01	***0.39***	0.93
E3: Assertiveness	−0.28	**0.46**	0.25	−0.29	0.29	−0.18	−0.19	−0.06	0.09	0.84
E4: Activity	−0.04	**0.44**	0.05	−0.11	**0.50**	−0.22	0.02	−0.08	0.25	0.89
E5: Excitement seeking	−0.09	0.34	0.09	**−0.43**	−0.14	−0.05	0.11	−0.07	***0.42***	0.93
E6: Positive emotions	−0.00	**0.57**	0.16	0.11	0.05	0.05	0.06	0.28	***0.45***	0.93
O1: Fantasy	0.17	0.10	0.32	−0.06	−0.32	0.13	0.14	−0.03	***0.53***	0.92
O2: Aesthetics	0.18	−0.07	**0.57**	0.25	0.08	−0.03	0.17	−0.12	***0.43***	0.94
O3: Feelings	0.33	**0.49**	0.35	0.10	0.18	0.11	−0.11	0.05	***0.32***	0.94
O4: Actions	−0.29	0.07	0.38	−0.01	−0.01	−0.14	0.00	−0.08	***0.58***	0.92
O5: Ideas	−0.09	−0.14	**0.67**	−0.03	0.18	0.06	0.01	0.13	0.29	0.95
O6: Values	−0.10	0.07	**0.44**	0.08	−0.02	0.00	−0.03	0.22	0.26	0.85

Table 13.1 Loadings for substantive and method factors in a joint analysis of NEO-PI-3 self-reports and observer ratings—cont'd

NEO-PI-3 facet	Substantive factor					Method factor				
	N	E	O	A	C	NV_S	PV_S	NV_R	PV_R	VC
A1: Trust	−0.25	0.22	0.00	**0.55**	−0.10	0.01	0.03	*0.34*	0.24	0.91
A2: Straightforwardness	0.01	−0.07	−0.05	**0.50**	0.09	0.11	−0.06	*0.55*	−0.12	0.94
A3: Altruism	0.00	**0.40**	0.15	**0.45**	0.11	0.15	−0.09	*0.58*	0.10	0.92
A4: Compliance	−0.17	−0.18	−0.11	**0.52**	−0.19	0.15	0.17	*0.51*	0.20	0.87
A5: Modesty	0.14	−0.10	0.00	**0.57**	0.03	0.08	−0.21	*0.36*	−0.01	0.91
A6: Tender-mindedness	0.18	0.31	0.21	**0.56**	0.10	0.05	−0.09	0.17	0.14	0.87
C1: Competence	−0.26	0.12	0.21	0.11	**0.59**	−0.03	−0.14	*0.51*	−0.06	0.96
C2: Order	0.08	−0.03	−0.24	0.04	**0.70**	−0.19	0.13	0.01	0.20	0.75
C3: Dutifulness	−0.06	0.07	0.01	0.24	**0.61**	−0.03	−0.07	*0.47*	−0.04	0.97
C4: Achievement striving	−0.14	0.14	0.12	−0.10	**0.69**	−0.14	−0.02	0.29	0.15	0.95
C5: Self-discipline	−0.14	0.08	−0.06	0.13	**0.74**	−0.15	−0.01	*0.35*	0.09	0.95
C6: Deliberation	−0.20	−0.26	−0.02	0.23	**0.48**	0.02	0.05	*0.48*	−0.07	0.99
Factor congruence										
Five-factor solution	0.98	0.89	0.71	0.96	0.97					0.91
Seven-factor solution	0.93	0.94	0.90	0.94	0.93	0.76	0.82			0.89
Nine-factor solution	0.97	0.97	0.94	0.96	0.96	0.82	0.78	0.85	0.80	0.92

Note n = 532. These are Procrustes-rotated principal components. The last lines report congruences with the target matrix for factors and total matrix. Joint factor loadings over 0.40 in absolute magnitude are given in boldface. Method factor loadings over 0.30 in absolute magnitude are given in boldface italic. NV_S = self-report negative valence (reflected). PV_S = self-report positive valence. NV_R = observer rating negative valence (reflected). PV_R = observer rating positive valence. VC = variable congruence coefficient. Data from McCrae, et al. (2005b).

A system of facets

As Digman and Inouye noted, 'If a large number of rating scales is used and if the scope of the scales is very broad, the domain of personality descriptors is almost completely accounted for by five robust factors' (1986: 116). At one level, this is good news, because it means that the FFM is robust and does not depend on the particular selection of traits one uses to assess it. At another level this is bad news, because it means the FFM offers little guidance about which facets should be included in a comprehensive assessment of personality. There is growing evidence that facet scales offer incremental validity over the five factors in predicting a variety of criteria (Paunonen and Ashton, 2001; Reynolds and Clark, 2001) and that facets within a domain may show different developmental trajectories (Terracciano et al., 2005). Thus, a full understanding of personality traits requires a system in which the most important facet-level traits are assessed. As yet, however, there is no consensus on which specific traits should be included in this system, or even how we should go about identifying them.

Facets for the NEO-PI-R were selected based on reviews of the literature and on a series of item analyses (Costa and McCrae, 1995). Our goal was to include traits that reflected the variables that psychologists have considered important in describing people and predicting behavior, and that were minimally redundant. A rather similar rational approach was taken by Watson and Clark (1997) for the E domain. They also identified six facets on the basis of a review of existing personality inventories. Four of these corresponded to four NEO-PI-R E facets: ascendance to E3: Assertiveness, energy to E4: Activity, venturesomeness to E5: Excitement Seeking (and Openness to Actions), and positive affectivity to E6: Positive Emotions. Their affiliation facet combined E1: Warmth and E2: Gregariousness. To this set they added ambition, which 'plays an important role in Tellegen's and Hogan's models, [but] is omitted from all of the others'

(1997: 775). In the NEO-PI-R, the construct of ambition is included as C4: Achievement Striving, a definer of C with a small (0.23) secondary loading on E (Costa and McCrae, 1992a).

More recently, Roberts and colleagues have made systematic empirical attempts to map the facets of C. In a study of trait-descriptive adjectives, they began with a list of adjectives that were related either solely or primarily to the lexical C factor, but which might also have secondary loadings on other factors (Roberts et al., 2004). This broad selection strategy led to the identification of eight factors, five of which correspond conceptually to NEO-PI-R C facets: reliability (≈NEO-PI-R C3: Dutifulness), orderliness (C2: Order), impulse control (C6: Deliberation), decisiveness (C1: Competence), and industriousness (C4: Achievement Striving). Their remaining factors were punctuality, formalness, and conventionality; these had the lowest correlations with the overall lexical C factor ($r = 0.34$–0.39), and, as the authors noted, formalness and conventionality 'may be more strongly related to ... openness to experience', (2004: 175), with formalness a form of high O and conventionality a form of low openness to values.

In a subsequent study they factored scales from seven personality inventories, including the NEO-PI-R (Roberts et al., 2005a). They identified 36 scales conceptually related to C and interpreted six factors. Here the correspondence with the NEO-PI-R system was less clear. Their order factor was defined by C2: Order, and their self-control factor was defined by C6: Deliberation, but their industriousness factor had loadings on all four remaining NEO-PI-R C facets, and their responsibility, traditionalism, and virtue scales were not defined by any NEO-PI-R variables. They interpreted this to mean that the NEO-PI-R definition of C (like those of other inventories) was too narrow.

That study, however, had limitations. The personality instruments were administered on different occasions over a period of years, so correlations within instrument may have been inflated relative to correlations across instru-

ments by time-of-measurement effects. That might account for the clumping of NEO-PI-R scales on the industriousness factor. Some scales were taken from the California Psychological Inventory (CPI; Gough, 1987), where item overlap between scales makes factor analysis inappropriate. The responsibility and virtue factors were defined chiefly by CPI scales, and may represent little more than item overlap. Finally, this study illustrates the dangers of attempting to define the facets of any single domain in isolation, because the resulting factors had serious problems of discriminant validity. Traditionalism had almost as strong a relation to O ($r = -0.42$) as to C ($r = 0.44$), and virtue was more strongly related to both A ($r = 0.54$) and N ($r = -0.59$) than to C ($r = 0.51$). It is hard to justify its designation as a facet of C.

We are not aware of attempts by other investigators to define facets for O or A, but Endler et al. (1997) reported item factor analyses of NEO-PI-R N items suggesting that a different set of facets might better be scored from this item pool. They found factors corresponding to N1: Anxiety, N2: Angry Hostility, and N5: Impulsiveness, but the remaining three factors distributed items from the other facets into new combinations. McCrae et al. (2001) attempted to replicate Endler and colleagues' findings and to determine whether they were attributable to acquiescence, which tends to create factors with items keyed in one direction. After controlling for acquiescence, McCrae and colleagues found that varimax-rotated item factors showed a one-to-one correspondence with the a priori scales, with correlations ranging from 0.68 to 0.92. It thus appeared that the division of NEO-PI-R N items into the established facets was justified.

The issue that Endler and colleagues (1997) raised warrants more attention than it has so far been given. McCrae and colleagues (2001) also examined the factor structure of A items, and Costa and McCrae (1998) factored C items, but there have been no recent item analyses of E and O. To address these issues, we conducted new analyses on two data sets. The first ($n = 1,135$)

is from a study of adolescents aged 14–20 and adults aged 21–90 who completed the NEO-PI-3 (McCrae et al., 2005b); both self-report and observer-rating data were available. The second ($n = 12,156$) is from a study of observer ratings of personality conducted in 51 cultures (McCrae et al., 2005d) using translations of the NEO-PI-R into over 20 languages.

The first question that might be asked is if the items have been assigned to the correct domain. To test this, we factored the 240 items, extracting five varimax-rotated factors, and correlated the resulting factor scores with the a priori domain scales. Note that no attempt was made to control for effects of acquiescence, because the distinctions between domains should be sufficiently strong to override them. Convergent correlations ranged from 0.87 to 0.94 for the NEO-PI-3 data; the largest discriminant correlation was 0.32. In the international sample, convergent correlations ranged from 0.84 to 0.95; the largest discriminant correlation was 0.33. The item factors in the NEO-PI-R and NEO-PI-3 thus correspond very closely to the five domains.

Similar analyses, conducted separately for sets of 48 items within domain, are reported in Table 13.2. Here, the first three data columns show correlations between facets and varimax-rotated factor scores. With a few exceptions (e.g. N4: Self-consciousness in form S data; A6: Tender-mindedness in the international data), item factors could be clearly matched to a corresponding facet. However, the distinction between some facets is relatively subtle, and acquiescent responding can distort results. A more accurate account is provided by orthogonal validimax rotation (McCrae and Costa, 1989b), in which the factors are rotated to maximize convergent and discriminant validity with the facet scales. The last three data columns in Table 13.2 report these correlations; the smallest convergent correlation in each domain is larger that the largest discriminant correlation, and the median convergent correlation is a substantial 0.84. It is clear that, across samples, methods of measurement, and languages of administration, the conceptual distinctions drawn among NEO-PI-R facets are reflected in the empirical structure of the items.

This small literature on studies that have attempted to articulate facets for FFM domains suggests to us that the system used in the NEO-PI-R is reasonable, with similar facets identified in rational analyses by other investigators and in empirical studies of adjectives and (to a lesser extent) of questionnaire scales. It is clearly not the case that these 30 scales exhaust the full range of traits related to each of the factors; punctuality is a good example of a marker of C that is not included. But an analysis of personality that incorporates NEO-PI-R facets and their combinations can lead to detailed information that goes far beyond the five factors.

One major contribution of the FFM is that it has become a common framework for research by psychologists from many fields, with the result that information can be readily shared and cumulative progress can be made: The developmentalist interested in impulse control can learn from the I/O psychologist studying job performance, because both understand the connection of their constructs to C. The advantages of a common framework would of course apply also to studies conducted at the facet level, so in an ideal world, all psychologists and psychiatrists would utilize the same set of facet constructs. The NEO-PI-R facet system provides one such set, and there are as yet no real alternatives that cover the full FFM. We already know a great deal about the NEO-PI-R facets: their discriminant validity (McCrae and Costa, 1992), heritability (Jang et al., 1998), longitudinal stability and developmental course (Terracciano et al., 2005; Terracciano et al., 2006), consensual validity (McCrae et al., 2005b), universality (McCrae et al., 2005c), and utility in understanding Axis I (Quirk et al., 2003) and Axis II (Widiger and Costa, 2002) mental disorders. Personality research must move beyond the broad factors of the FFM, and the facets of the NEO-PI-R provide a proven system for doing so (see Costa and McCrae, Vol. 2).

Table 13.2 Convergent and discriminant validity of within-domain item factors

	Varimax factor			Validimax factor		
Facet Scale	Form S[a]	Form R[a]	Form R[b]	Form S[a]	Form R[a]	Form R[b]
N1: Anxiety	0.78	0.90	0.80	0.79	0.85	0.80
N2: Angry hostility	0.86	0.94	0.94	0.89	0.90	0.91
N3: Depression	0.85	0.76	0.84	0.69	0.75	0.80
N4: Self-consciousness	0.07	0.74	0.51	0.55	0.74	0.67
N5: Impulsiveness	0.68	0.76	0.91	0.79	0.83	0.92
N6: Vulnerability	0.62	0.65	0.76	0.72	0.72	0.77
Largest ADC	*0.77*	*0.38*	*0.44*	*0.48*	*0.35*	*0.30*
Mdn ADC	*0.20*	*0.19*	*0.19*	*0.22*	*0.25*	*0.20*
E1: Warmth	0.26	0.86	0.83	0.75	0.85	0.78
E2: Gregariousness	0.89	0.82	0.73	0.83	0.83	0.80
E3: Assertiveness	0.92	0.94	0.93	0.90	0.92	0.91
E4: Activity	0.71	0.79	0.69	0.83	0.86	0.85
E5: Excitement seeking	0.90	0.93	0.92	0.90	0.92	0.87
E6: Positive emotions	0.91	0.88	0.72	0.77	0.88	0.76
Largest ADC	*0.70*	*0.35*	*0.50*	*0.42*	*0.31*	*0.38*
Mdn ADC	*0.13*	*0.14*	*0.10*	*0.15*	*0.13*	*0.11*
O1: Fantasy	0.92	0.92	0.90	0.92	0.90	0.88
O2: Aesthetics	0.89	0.82	0.82	0.87	0.85	0.80
O3: Feelings	0.84	0.90	0.59	0.86	0.91	0.73
O4: Actions	0.57	0.81	0.82	0.52	0.84	0.86
O5: Ideas	0.83	0.93	0.93	0.86	0.92	0.93
O6: Values	0.74	0.93	0.64	0.83	0.93	0.74
Largest ADC	*0.49*	*0.30*	*0.42*	*0.35*	*0.26*	*0.32*
Mdn ADC	*0.16*	*0.12*	*0.15*	*0.17*	*0.10*	*0.14*
A1: Trust	0.91	0.91	0.82	0.90	0.90	0.89
A2: Straightforwardness	0.82	0.77	0.84	0.84	0.82	0.84
A3: Altruism	0.86	0.80	0.75	0.84	0.79	0.65
A4: Compliance	0.83	0.79	0.84	0.88	0.82	0.84
A5: Modesty	0.92	0.90	0.87	0.92	0.90	0.88
A6: Tender-mindedness	0.88	0.92	0.12	0.87	0.90	0.57
Largest ADC	*0.31*	*0.42*	*0.71*	*0.25*	*0.31*	*0.47*
Mdn ADC	*0.14*	*0.19*	*0.21*	*0.15*	*0.20*	*0.20*
C1: Competence	0.60	0.65	0.05	00.69	0.70	0.63
C2: Order	0.89	0.92	0.84	0.89	0.90	0.85
C3: Dutifulness	0.75	0.68	0.77	0.77	0.67	0.72
C4: Achievement striving	0.86	0.75	0.69	0.84	0.82	0.73
C5: Self-discipline	0.67	0.12	0.57	0.66	0.64	0.61
C6: Deliberation	0.86	0.85	0.87	0.85	0.80	0.84
Largest ADC	*0.41*	*0.66*	*0.62*	*0.37*	*0.40*	*0.38*
Mdn ADC	0.22	0.23	0.24	0.26	0.26	0.26

Note Tabled values are correlations between facets and best matched item factors. ADC = absolute discriminant correlation.
[a]NEO-PI-3 data from McCrae, Martin, & Costa, 2005, $n = 1,135$. [b]NEO-PI-R data from McCrae et al. (2005d), $n = 12,156$.

Causal explanation

We turn at this point from data to philosophy of science, returning to an issue we have addressed earlier (McCrae and Costa, 1995). Proponents of the social-cognitive approach to personality have long disputed the claim that traits provide causal explanations (Mischel and Shoda, 1994). A common statement is that trait explanations are circular: We observe sociable behavior, infer a trait of sociability, and 'explain' the behavior by the trait. If that were the end of the story, trait explanations would indeed be circular and trivial. But there is a vast literature showing that when we have assessed sociability (ideally from much more than a single act), we have learned something from which we can make novel predictions about, for example, the person's cheerfulness a year from now, and the sociability of her identical twin. These are non-trivial and non-circular predictions that suggest that traits have real causal status (McCrae and Costa, 1995).

Recently, however, Cervone (2004a, 2004b) has advanced a new critique of trait explanations, based on a philosophical analysis of the latent variables that are central to structural equation modeling, confirmatory factor analysis, and several other statistical methods (Borsboom et al., 2003). The authors of that article were deeply versed in both the statistical and the philosophical literature on this topic and offered a thoughtful analysis. They came to two major conclusions. The first was that latent variables, such as the factors of the FFM, imply a realist ontology – that is, they are based on the assumption that there is something real in the world that gives rise to individual differences in observed variables; they are not mere fictions or social constructions. That is entirely in keeping with FFT, which postulates real basic tendencies underlying personality development and expression.

Their second major conclusion is odd. They argued that latent variables have causal standing when construed as between-subjects accounts: extraversion, for example, can apparently explain why Americans are more likely to make new friends than Koreans (Allik and McCrae, 2004). But Borsboom and colleagues (2003) denied that traits can provide causal explanations for the behavior of individuals. Cervone (2004b) interpreted this to mean that traits, although useful for making some kinds of predictions, do not explain the behavior of individuals; they are at best descriptive.

In brief, the argument of Borsboom and colleagues (2003) is that causation, by definition, implies that the cause, x, and the effect, y, must co-vary. Such co-variation can be observed across individuals, but on any one occasion cannot be observed in a single individual, because the individual does not vary.

No variation, no co-variation, no causation. Borsboom and colleagues admitted that some individual difference variables, such as height, can be considered causes of individuals' behavior, but claim that assuming that the same will hold for variables like extraversion is 'little more than an article of faith; the standard measurement model [for latent variables] has virtually nothing to say about characteristics of individuals' (2003: 206).

To the trait psychologist, Borsboom and colleagues's (2003) conclusion is counterintuitive. The statement that John went to a party because he was an extravert may or may not be correct, but it does not seem to be nonsensical, which is the implication of their argument. Where, then, did their argument go wrong? Borsboom and colleagues argued that causation means the co-variation of cause and effect, but that definition confounds the evidence of causation with the phenomenon itself. Intuitively, causation means that one circumstance or event made a later event occur. In order to *demonstrate* that there is a causal connection, there must be co-variation – indeed, in the absence of experimental manipulation even co-variation is weak evidence of causation. But a cause does not cease to exist merely because it cannot be shown to be a cause. Merely observing that John is an extravert and that John goes to a party does not in itself prove that he went to the party because he was an extravert, but it certainly does not preclude that possibility.

McCrae and Costa (1999: 146–147) explored the relation of co-variation to causation in a thought experiment in which a new utopia was peopled with clones of an adjusted extravert. If traits were 100% heritable, there would be no individual differences among its residents, differences in personality scores would be entirely due to error, and it would be impossible to demonstrate with the usual correlational studies the stability or behavioral consequences of traits. Yet the clones would still talk loudly, laugh often, and otherwise act like adjusted extraverts, because their basic tendencies (indirectly) cause this kind of behavior.

Borsboom and colleagues (2003) suggested that causal attributions at the level of the individual might be justified by evidence that there is a corresponding within-subject latent variable, seen, for example, in intraindividual factor analyses conducted within individuals across occasions. Can personality states (Fleeson, 2001) be characterized by the FFM? This is an intriguing question, and some empirical efforts have been made to answer it (e.g. Borkenau and Ostendorf, 1998). They show only limited evidence of a similar structure for personality states when analyzed at the level of the individual.

However, a moment's reflection shows that the structure, and thus the causes, of state perturbation in personality is irrelevant to the causes of personality traits. FFM traits are very largely heritable (Jang et al., 1996), meaning that they are themselves caused by genes (their biological basis). It is most unlikely that these same genes would be the cause of transient variations in personality states. Thus, even evidence that the intraindividual structure of states perfectly paralleled the FFM would not speak to the causal source of behavior. The mechanisms that account for fluctuation in personality are surely different from those that account for stable individual differences.

Borsboom and colleagues noted that their conclusion is not surprising in view of the fact that 'the within-subjects causal interpretation of between-subjects latent variables rests on a logical fallacy' (2003: 212), a charge raised by Lamiell (1987) and repeated by Rorer, who asserted, 'There is no way to get from the relation between two traits or characteristics in the population to the relation between those traits within an individual' (1990: 711). This is a troubling prospect to the trait psychologist until it is recognized that there is actually no fallacy in trait explanations, because in trait explanations, characteristics of the group are not being attributed to individuals. This is obscured by the term 'relation' in Rorer's quote, which seems to refer to the same thing at two levels. It does not. The relation at the level of the population is one of correlation, whereas the relation at the level of the individual is one of causation.

How does one get from correlation at the group level to causation at the individual level? By scientific inference. The logic is straightforward: if E causes party-going in individuals, then in the general population, people who are more extraverted should go to more parties. They do. Therefore, E may cause party-going in individuals. This is an inductive, not a rigorous deductive argument, so it may be incorrect, but that is a fate it shares with all scientific propositions, and one that scientists have learned to deal with by testing alternatives and seeking corroborating evidence.

Thus, the study of associations at the group level can assuredly tell us about characteristics of individuals, and does provide a legitimate basis for trait explanations (McCrae and Costa, 1995). A trait explanation is, however, a very abstract explanation, admitted by Borsboom and colleagues (2003) as an 'elliptical explanation' in which 'the position on the latent variable is shorthand for whatever process leads to person's response' (2003: 214), a position they consider 'uninformative'. That is surely a value judgment, and one not shared by many clinicians (J.A. Singer, 2005) and their clients (Mutén, 1991), who find that trait explanations are an important first step in understanding the origins of problems in living.

Borsboom and colleagues (2003) and Cervone (2004b) are correct in implying that the five-factor structure of personality is not to be found in the mind (or brain) of any individual. 'Personality structure' is an ambiguous term that can be applied within or across people, but with very different meanings (McCrae, 2005). They are also correct in asserting that if one wishes to understand the processes that lead to the flow of behavior and experience in individual persons, trait psychology is a limited guide. McCrae and Costa (in press) also recognized this, and offered FFT as a schematic representation of what goes on. FFT is not a detailed account of any particular behavior, but it provides an outline of where one ought to look for detailed explanations. For example, if FFT is correct, then the search for the origins of traits (and trait-related behavior) should neglect non-shared environmental influences (Reiss et al., 2000) and concentrate perhaps on molecular genetics.

Following Borsboom and colleagues (2003), Cervone (2004b) argued that FFT cannot in principle be a useful framework for explaining behavior because the whole category of basic tendencies offer mere descriptions rather than causal explanations, and so cannot be a legitimate link in a causal chain. But if Borsboom and colleagues are wrong in their argument, so is Cervone. The distinction he wishes to draw between explanation and description is better seen as a distinction between promixal and distal causes, and thus between mechanistic and trait explanations.

In a French-language article, Cervone (2006) offered an analogy: If a car breaks down, one might attribute this either to the unreliability of that model or to the failure of a fuel pump. The latter is clearly a more useful explanation at the moment, because it points directly to an intervention. But Cervone wished to argue that 'unreliability' cannot be a cause of breakdown, because 'it does not make reference to anything in the car that causally contributed to the car's breaking down' (English version courtesy D. Cervone). It can only be a description of a class of cars, useful as a buying guide perhaps, but not explanatory.

In fact, unreliability can be seen under the hood, if one knows where to look. It is seen in the poor design, in the shoddy workmanship, in the flimsy materials used to construct the car. Any good mechanic could point these out, even without knowing the performance history of that model. Unreliability is an elliptical explanation, pointing to unspecified features that provide a more mechanistic explanation, but it is no less an explanation for being abstract. The two kinds of explanations are not in competition; they are different levels of explanation, useful in

different circumstances. FFT was intended to indicate, at least roughly, how they work together. The work of social-cognitive personality psychologists may be most helpful in filling in the details.

ACKNOWLEDGEMENT

This research was supported by the Intramural Research Program of the NIH, National Institute on Aging. Robert R. McCrae and Paul T. Costa, Jr., receive royalties from the Revised NEO Personality Inventory.

REFERENCES

Allik, J. and McCrae, R.R. (2004) 'Toward a geography of personality traits: Patterns of profiles across 36 cultures', *Journal of Cross-Cultural Psychology*, 35(1): 13–28.

Archer, R.P. and Smith, S.R. (in press) (eds), *A Guide to Personality Assessment: Evaluation, Application, and Integration*. Mahwah, NJ: Erlbaum.

Ashton, M.C., Lee, K., Perugini, M., Szarota, P., De Vries, R.E., Di Blass, L., Boies, K. and De Raad, B. (2004) 'A six-factor structure of personality descriptive adjectives: Solutions from psycholexical studies in seven languages', *Journal of Personality and Social Psychology*, 86(2): 356–66.

Bagby, R.M., Bindseil, K., Schuller, D.R., Rector, N.A., Young, L.T., Cooke, R.G., Seeman, M.V., McCay, E.A. and Joffe, R.T. (1997) 'Relationship between the Five-Factor Model of personality and unipolar, bipolar and schizophrenic patients', *Psychiatry Research*, 70(2): 83–94.

Barrick, M.R. and Mount, M.K. (1991) 'The Big Five personality dimensions and job performance: A meta-analysis', *Personnel Psychology*, 44(1): 1–26.

Baumeister, R.F. (2005) *The Cultural Animal: Human Nature, Meaning, and Social Life*. New York: Oxford University Press.

Biesanz, J.C. and West, S.G. (2004) 'Towards understanding assessments of the Big Five: Multitrait-multimethod analyses of convergent and discriminant validity across measurement occasion and type of observer', *Journal of Personality*, 72(4): 845–76.

Block, J. (2001) 'Millennial contrarianism: The five-factor approach to personality description 5 years later', *Journal of Research in Personality*, 35(1): 98–107.

Borkenau, P. and Ostendorf, F. (1998) 'The Big Five as states: How useful is the Five-Factor Model to describe intraindividual variations over time?', *Journal of Research in Personality*, 32(2): 202–21.

Borsboom, D., Mellenbergh, G.J. and van Heerden, J. (2003) 'The theoretical status of latent variables', *Psychological Review*, 110(2): 203–19.

Bouchard, T.J. and Loehlin, J.C. (2001) 'Genes, evolution, and personality', *Behavior Genetics*, 31(3): 243–73.

Brooner, R.K., Schmidt, C.W. and Herbst, J.H. (2002) 'Personality trait characteristics of opioid abusers with and without comorbid personality disorders', in P.T. Costa Jr. and T.A. Widiger (eds), *Personality Disorders and the Five-Factor Model of Personality* (2nd edn). Washington, DC: American Psychological Association, pp. 249–68.

Buss, D.M. and Barnes, M. (1986) 'Preferences in human mate selection', *Journal of Personality and Social Psychology*, 50(3): 559–70.

Cervone, D. (2004a) 'The architecture of personality', *Psychological Review*, 111(1): 183–204.

Cervone, D. (2004b) 'Personality assessment: Tapping the social-cognitive architecture of personality', *Behavior Therapy*, 35(1): 113–29.

Cervone, D. (2006) 'Systèms de personnalité au niveau de l'individu: ver uns évaluation de l'architecture sociocogntivie de la personnalité [Personality systems at the level of the individual: assessing social-cognitive personality architecture]', *Psychologie Française*, 51(3): 357–76.

Cole, D.P. (2001) 'Saudi Arabia', in M. Ember and C.R. Ember (eds), *Countries and their Cultures* (Vol. 4). New York: Macmillan, pp. 1927–39.

Costa, P.T. Jr., Herbst, J.H., McCrae, R.R. and Siegler, I.C. (2000) 'Personality at midlife: Stability, intrinsic maturation, and response to life events', *Assessment*, 7(4): 365–78.

Costa, P.T. Jr. and McCrae, R.R. (1992a) *Revised NEO Personality Inventory (NEO-PI-R) and NEO Five-Factor Inventory (NEO-FFI) Professional Manual*. Odessa, FL: Psychological Assessment Resources.

Costa, P.T. Jr. and McCrae, R.R. (1992b) 'Trait psychology comes of age', in T.B. Sonderegger (ed.), *Nebraska Symposium on Motivation: Psychology and aging*. Lincoln, NE: University of Nebraska Press, pp. 169–204.

Costa, P.T. Jr. and McCrae, R.R. (1995) 'Domains and facets: Hierarchical personality assessment using the Revised NEO Personality Inventory', *Journal of Personality Assessment*, 64(1): 21–50.

Costa, P.T. Jr. and McCrae, R.R. (1998) 'Six approaches to the explication of facet-level traits: Examples from Conscientiousness', *European Journal of Personality*, 12(2): 117–34.

Costa, P.T. Jr. and McCrae, R.R. (2005) 'A Five-Factor Theory perspective on the Rorschach', *Rorschachiana*, 27: 80–100.

Costa, P.T. Jr., McCrae, R.R. and PAR Staff. (1994) *NEO Software System [Computer Software]*. Odessa, FL: Psychological Assessment Resources.

Costa, P.T. Jr. and Widiger, T.A. (2002) (eds), *Personality Disorders and the Five-Factor Model of Personality* (2nd edn). Washington, DC: American Psychological Association.

De Raad, B. and Peabody, D. (2005) 'Cross-culturally recurrent personality factors: Analyses of three factors', *European Journal of Personality*, 19(6): 451–74.

DeYoung, C.G., Peterson, J.B. and Higgins, D.M. (2002) 'Higher-order factors of the Big Five predict conformity: Are there neuroses of health?', *Personality and Individual Differences*, 33(4): 533–52.

Digman, J.M. (1997) 'Higher-order factors of the Big Five', *Journal of Personality and Social Psychology*, 73(6): 1246–56.

Digman, J.M. and Inouye, J. (1986) 'Further specification of the five robust factors of personality', *Journal of Personality and Social Psychology*, 50(1): 116–23.

Donnellan, M.B., Conger, R. and Bryant, C.M. (2004) 'The Big Five and enduring marriages', *Journal of Research in Personality*, 38(5): 481–504.

Endler, N.S., Rutherford, A. and Denisoff, E. (1997) 'Neuroticism: How does one slice the PI(e)?', *European Journal of Personality*, 11(2): 133–45.

Fiske, S.T. and Leyens, J.-P. (1997) 'Let social psychology be faddish or, at least, heterogeneous', in C. McGarty and S.A. Haslam (eds), *The Message of Social Psychology: Perspectives on Mind in Society*. Malden, MA: Blackwell Publishing, pp. 92–112.

Fleeson, W. (2001) 'Toward a structure- and process-integrated view of personality: Traits as density distributions of states', *Journal of Personality and Social Psychology*, 80(6): 1011–27.

Funder, D.C., Kolar, D.C. and Blackman, M.C. (1995) 'Agreement among judges of personality: Interpersonal relations, similarity, and acquaintanceship', *Journal of Personality and Social Psychology*, 69(4): 656–72.

Funder, D.C. and West, S.G. (1993) (eds), 'Viewpoints on personality: Consensus, self-other agreement and accuracy in personality judgment', *Journal of Personality*, 61(4): 457–76.

Goldberg, L.R. (1983) 'The magical number five, plus or minus two: Some considerations on the dimensionality of personality descriptors', Paper presented at a Research Seminar, Gerontology Research Center, Baltimore, MD.

Gough, H.G. (1987) *California Psychological Inventory Administrator's Guide*. Palo Alto, CA: Consulting Psychologists Press.

Hill, R.W., McIntire, K. and Bacharach, V.R. (1997) 'Perfectionism and the Big Five factors', *Journal of Social Behavior and Personality*, 12(1): 257–70.

Jang, K.L., Livesley, W.J., Ando, J., Yamagata, S., Suzuki, A., Angleitner, A., Ostendorf, F. Riemann, R. and Spinath, F. (2006) 'Behavioral genetics of the higher-order factors of the Big Five', *Personality and Individual Differences*, 41(2): 261–72.

Jang, K.L., Livesley, W.J. and Vernon, P.A. (1996) 'Heritability of the Big Five personality dimensions and their facets: A twin study', *Journal of Personality*, 64(3): 575–91.

Jang, K.L., McCrae, R.R., Angleitner, A., Riemann, R. and Livesley, W.J. (1998) 'Heritability of facet-level traits in a cross-cultural twin sample: Support for a hierarchical model of personality', *Journal of Personality and Social Psychology*, 74(6): 1556–65.

Judge, T.A., Higgins, C.A., Thoresen, C.J. and Barrick, M.R. (1999) 'The Big Five personality traits, general mental ability, and career success across the life span', *Personnel Psychology*, 52(3): 621–52.

Jung, C.G. (1971) *Psychological Types*, (H.G. Baynes, trans., revised by R.F.C. Hull) Princeton, NJ: Princeton University Press. (Original work published 1923).

Kohnstamm, G.A., Halverson, C.F. Jr. Mervielde, I. and Havill, V.L. (1998) (eds), *Parental Descriptions of Child Personality: Developmental Antecedents of the Big Five?* Mahwah, NJ: Lawrence Erlbaum Associates.

Lamiell, J.T. (1987) *The Psychology of Personality: An Epistemological Inquiry*. New York: Columbia University Press.

Markon, K.E., Krueger, R.F. and Watson, D. (2005) 'Delineating the structure of normal and abnormal personality: An integrative hierarchical approach', *Journal of Personality and Social Psychology*, 88(1): 139–57.

Mayer, J.D. (2005) 'A tale of two visions: Can a new view of personality help integrate psychology?', *American Psychologist*, 60(4): 294–307.

McAdams, D.P. and Pals, J.L. (2006) 'A new Big Five: Fundamental principles for an integrative science of personality', *American Psychologist*, 61(3): 204–17.

McCrae, R.R. (1989) 'Why I advocate the Five-Factor Model: Joint analyses of the NEO-PI and other instruments', in D.M. Buss and N. Cantor (eds), *Personality Psychology: Recent Trends and Emerging Directions*. New York: Springer-Verlag, pp. 237–45.

McCrae, R.R. (1996) 'Social consequences of experiential openness', *Psychological Bulletin*, 120(3): 323–37.

McCrae, R.R. (2005) 'Personality structure', in V.J. Derlega, B.A. Winstead and W.H. Jones (eds), *Personality: Contemporary Theory and Research* (3rd edn). Belmont, CA: Wadsworth Group, pp. 192–216.

McCrae, R.R. and Allik, J. (2002) (eds), *The Five-Factor Model of Personality Across Cultures*. New York: Kluwer Academic/ Plenum Publishers.

McCrae, R.R. and Costa, P.T. Jr. (1983) 'Joint factors in self-reports and ratings: Neuroticism, Extraversion, and Openness to Experience', *Personality and Individual Differences*, 4(3): 245–55.

McCrae, R.R. and Costa, P.T. Jr. (1987) 'Validation of the Five-Factor Model of personality across instruments and observers', *Journal of Personality and Social Psychology*, 52(1): 81–90.

McCrae, R.R. and Costa, P.T. Jr. (1989a) 'Reinterpreting the Myers-Briggs Type Indicator from the perspective of the Five-Factor Model of personality', *Journal of Personality*, 57(1): 17–40.

McCrae, R.R. and Costa, P.T. Jr. (1989b) 'Rotation to maximize the construct validity of factors in the NEO Personality Inventory', *Multivariate Behavioral Research*, 24(1): 107–24.

McCrae, R.R. and Costa, P.T. Jr. (1992) 'Discriminant validity of NEO-PI-R facets', *Educational and Psychological Measurement*, 52(1): 229–37.

McCrae, R.R. and Costa, P.T. Jr. (1995) 'Trait explanations in personality psychology', *European Journal of Personality*, 9(4): 231–52.

McCrae, R.R. and Costa, P.T. Jr. (1996) 'Toward a new generation of personality theories: Theoretical contexts for the Five-Factor Model', in J.S. Wiggins (ed.), *The Five-Factor Model of Personality: Theoretical Perspectives*. New York: Guilford, pp. 51–87.

McCrae, R.R. and Costa, P.T. Jr. (2003) *Personality in Adulthood: A Five-Factor Theory Perspective* (2nd edn). New York: Guilford.

McCrae, R.R. and Costa, P.T. Jr. (in press) 'The Five-Factor Theory of personality', in O.P. John, R.W. Robins and L.A. Pervin (eds), *Handbook of Personality: Theory and Research* (3rd edn). New York: Guilford.

McCrae, R.R., Costa, P.T. Jr., Lima, M. P., Simões, A., Ostendorf, F., Angleitner, A., Marušić, I., Bratko, D., Caprara, G.V., Barbaranelli, C., Chae, J-H. and Piedmont, R.L. (1999) 'Age differences in personality across the adult life span: Parallels in five cultures', *Developmental Psychology*, 35(2): 466–77.

McCrae, R.R., Costa, P.T. Jr., Martin, T.A., Oryol, V.E., Rukavishnikov, A.A., Senin, I.G., Hřebíčková, M. and Urbánek, T. (2004) 'Consensual validation of personality traits across cultures', *Journal of Research in Personality*, 38(2): 179–201.

McCrae, R.R., Costa, P.T. Jr., Ostendorf, F., Angleitner, A., Hřebíčková, M., Avia, M.D., Sanz, J., Sánchez-Bernardos, M.L., Kusdil, M.E., Woodfield, R., Saunders, P.R. and Smith, P.B. (2000) 'Nature over nurture: Temperament, personality and lifespan development', *Journal of Personality and Social Psychology*, 78(1): 173–86.

McCrae, R.R., Herbst, J.H. and Costa, P.T. Jr. (2001) 'Effects of acquiescence on personality factor structures', in R. Riemann, F. Ostendorf and F. Spinath (eds), *Personality and Temperament: Genetics, Evolution, and Structure*. Berlin: Pabst Science Publishers, pp. 217–31.

McCrae, R.R., Löckenhoff, C.E. and Costa, P.T. Jr. (2005a) 'A step towards *DSM-V*: Cataloging personality-related problems in living', *European Journal of Personality*, 19(4): 269–86.

McCrae, R.R., Martin, T.A. and Costa, P.T. Jr. (2005b) 'Age trends and age norms for the NEO Personality Inventory-3 in adolescents and adults', *Assessment*, 12(4): 363–73.

McCrae, R.R., Terracciano, A. and 78 Members of the Personality Profiles of Cultures Project. (2005c) 'Universal features of personality traits from the observer's perspective: Data from 50 cultures', *Journal of Personality and Social Psychology*, 88(3): 547–61.

McCrae, R.R., Terracciano, A. and 79 Members of the Personality Profiles of Cultures Project. (2005d) 'Personality profiles of cultures: Aggregate personality traits', *Journal of Personality and Social Psychology*, 89(3): 407–25.

McCrae, R.R., Zonderman, A.B., Costa, P.T. Jr., Bond, M.H. and Paunonen, S.V. (1996) 'Evaluating replicability of factors in the Revised NEO Personality Inventory: Confirmatory factor analysis versus Procrustes rotation', *Journal of Personality and Social Psychology*, 70(3): 552–66.

Miller, T. (1991) 'The psychotherapeutic utility of the Five-Factor Model of personality: A clinician's experience', *Journal of Personality Assessment*, 57(3): 415–33.

Mischel, W. (1968) *Personality and Assessment*. New York: Wiley.

Mischel, W. and Shoda, Y. (1994) 'Personality psychology has two goals: Must it be two fields?', *Psychological Inquiry*, 5(2): 156–8.

Mutén, E. (1991) 'Self-reports, spouse ratings, and psychophysiological assessment in a behavioral medicine program: An application of the Five-Factor Model', *Journal of Personality Assessment*, 57(3): 449–64.

Myers, I.B. and McCaulley, M.H. (1985) *Manual: A Guide to the Development and Use of the Myers-Briggs Type Indicator*. Palo Alto: Consulting Psychologists Press.

Ozer, D.J. and Benet-Martínez, V. (2006) 'Personality and the prediction of consequential outcomes', *Annual Review of Psychology*, 57: 401–21.

Paunonen, S.V. and Ashton, M.C. (2001) 'Big Five factors and facets and the prediction of behavior', *Journal of Personality and Social Psychology*, 81(3): 524–39.

Quirk, S.W., Christiansen, N.D., Wagner, S.H. and McNulty, J.L. (2003) 'On the usefulness of measures of normal personality for clinical assessment: Evidence of the incremental validity of the Revised NEO Personality Inventory', *Psychological Assessment*, 15(3): 311–25.

Reiss, D., Neiderhiser, J.M., Hetherington, E.M. and Plomin, R. (2000) *The Relationship Code: Deciphering Genetic and Social Influences on Adolescent Development*. Cambridge, MA: Harvard University Press.

Reynolds, S.K. and Clark, L.A. (2001) 'Predicting dimensions of personality disorder from domains and facets of the Five-Factor Model', *Journal of Personality*, 69(2): 199–222.

Roberts, B.W., Bogg, T., Walton, K.E., Chernyshenko, O.S. and Stark, S.E. (2004) 'A lexical investigation of the lower-order structure of Conscientiousness', *Journal of Research in Personality*, 38(1): 164–78.

Roberts, B.W., Chernyshenko, O.S., Stark, S.E. and Goldberg, L.R. (2005a) 'The structure of Conscientiousness: An empirical investigation based on seven major personality questionnaires', *Personnel Psychology*, 58(1): 103–39.

Roberts, B.W. and DelVecchio, W.F. (2000) 'The rank-order consistency of personality traits from childhood to old age: A quantitative review of longitudinal studies', *Psychological Bulletin*, 126(1): 3–25.

Roberts, B.W., Helson, R. and Klohnen, E.C. (2002) 'Personality development and growth in women across 30 years: Three perspectives', *Journal of Personality*, 70(1): 79–102.

Roberts, B.W., Wood, D. and Smith, J.L. (2005b) 'Evaluating Five-Factor Theory and social investment perspectives on personality trait development', *Journal of Research in Personality*, 39(1): 166–84.

Rorer, L.G. (1990) 'Personality assessment: A conceptual survey', in L.A. Pervin (ed.), *Handbook of Personality: Theory and Research*. New York: Guilford, pp. 693–720.

Schmitt, D.P., Allik, J., McCrae, R.R., Benet-Martínez, V., Alcalay, L., Ault, L. et al. (2007) 'The geographic distribution of Big Five personality traits: Patterns and profiles of human self-description across 56 nations', *Journal of Cross-Cultural Psychology*, 38(2): 173–212.

Sheldon, K.M. (2004) *Optimal Human Being: An Integrated Multi-Level Perspective*. Mahwah, NJ: Erlbaum.

Singer, J.A. (2005) *Personality and Psychotherapy: Treating the Whole Person*. New York: Guilford.

Singer, M. (1961) 'A survey of culture and personality theory and research', in B. Kaplan (ed.), *Studying Personality Cross-Culturally*. Evanston, IL: Row, Peterson, pp. 9–90.

Soldz, S. and Vaillant, G.E. (1999) 'The Big Five personality traits and the life course: A 45-year longitudinal study', *Journal of Research in Personality*, 33(2): 208–32.

Tellegen, A. and Waller, N.G. (1987, August). '*Reexamining basic dimensions of natural language trait descriptors*', Paper presented at the Annual Convention of the American Psychological Association, New York.

Terracciano, A., Costa, P.T. Jr. and McCrae, R.R. (2006) 'Personality plasticity after age 30', *Personality and Social Psychology Bulletin*, 32(8): 999–1009.

Terracciano, A., McCrae, R.R., Brant, L.J. and Costa, P.T. Jr. (2005) 'Hierarchical linear modeling analyses of NEO-PI-R scales in the Baltimore Longitudinal Study of Aging', *Psychology and Aging*, 20(3): 493–506.

Trull, T. J. and McCrae, R.R. (2002) 'A five-factor perspective on personality disorder research', in P.T. Costa Jr. and T.A. Widiger (eds), *Personality Disorders and the Five-Factor Model of Personality* (2nd edn). Washington, DC: American Psychological Association, pp. 45–57.

Trull, T.J. and Widiger, T.A. (1997) *Structured Interview for the Five-Factor Model of Personality (SIFFM): Professional Manual*. Odessa, FL: Psychological Assessment Resources.

Tupes, E.C. and Christal, R.E. (1992) 'Recurrent personality factors based on trait ratings', *Journal of Personality*, 60(2): 225–51. (Original work published 1961).

Watson, D. and Clark, L.A. (1997) 'Extraversion and its positive emotional core', in R. Hogan, J. Johnson and S.R. Briggs (eds), *Handbook of Personality Psychology*. New York: Academic Press, pp. 767–93.

Weiner, I.B. and Greene, R.L. (2008) *Handbook of Personality Assessment*. New York: John Wiley.

Weiss, A. and Costa, P.T. Jr. (2005) 'Domain and facet personality predictors of all cause mortality among Medicare patients aged 65 to 100', *Psychosomatic Medicine*, 67(5): 724–33.

Widiger, T.A. and Costa, P.T. Jr. (2002) 'Five-Factor Model personality disorder research', in P.T. Costa Jr. and T.A. Widiger (eds), *Personality Disorders and the Five-Factor Model of Personality* (2nd edn). Washington, DC: American Psychological Association, pp. 59–87.

Wiggins, J.S. (1996) (ed.), *The Five-Factor Model of Personality: Theoretical Perspectives*. New York: Guilford.

Woodruffe, C. (1985) 'Consensual validation of personality traits: Additional evidence and individual differences', *Journal of Personality and Social Psychology*, 48(5): 1240–52.

Yamagata, S., Suzuki, A., Ando, J., Ono, Y., Kijima, N., Yoshimura, K., Ostendorf, F., Angleitner, A., Riemann, R., Spinath, F.M., Livesley, W.J. and Jang, K.L. (2006) 'Is the genetic structure of human personality universal? A cross-cultural twin study from North America, Europe, and Asia', *Journal of Personality and Social Psychology*, 90(6): 987–98.

Yang, J., McCrae, R.R. and Costa, P.T. Jr. (1998) 'Adult age differences in personality traits in the United States and the People's Republic of China', *Journal of Gerontology: Psychological Sciences*, 53B(6): P375–83.

14

Critique of the Five-Factor Model of Personality

Gregory J. Boyle

INTRODUCTION: LEXICAL COVERAGE OF THE PERSONALITY TRAIT SPHERE

Assuming that most aspects of human personality structure are represented in the trait lexicon (i.e. that the personality sphere is encompassed by trait-descriptive words – see Ashton et al., 2004; Saucier and Goldberg, 2001), Allport and Odbert's (1936) list of more than 4,000 English trait descriptors was reduced down to some 35+ clusters of trait synonyms (e.g. see Cattell, 1986). Raymond B. Cattell (who, along with Freud, Piaget, and Eysenck, was listed among the ten most highly cited psychologists of the twentieth.century – Haggbloom et al., 2002: 142), attempted.a comprehensive sampling of the trait lexicon, on the further assumption that the most important attributes of human personality are encoded in the English language (cf. John, 1990; Peabody and de Raad, 2002). It was Cattell's early pioneering work that served as the starting point for the subsequent lexically based development of the popular five-factor model (FFM) of personality structure which includes dimensions

(traits) labelled neuroticism (N), extraversion (E), openness to experience–intellectance (O), agreeableness (A), and conscientiousness (C). The FFM dimensions were derived from various factor analytic studies of self-report and peer reports of adjectival (e.g. Goldberg's, 1992, 'Big Five') and questionnaire personality-related data (e.g. Costa and McCrae's, 1992, FFM). However, it is important to note that some significant aspects of this factor-analytic work leading to the current FFM have been methodologically flawed (Boyle et al., 1995; Boyle and Saklofske, 2004). Although the Big Five (e.g. Goldberg, 1993) and the FFM (e.g. Costa and McCrae, 1992) dimensions technically are considered to be conceptually distinct constructs, in this chapter, for ease of presentation, these terms are used interchangeably.

Contemporary personality research generally adopts an interactionist model, whereby traits and situationally sensitive states interact in influencing behavioural outcomes. However, some support for the causal nature of the Big Five has been forthcoming (Paunonen and Ashton, 2001). For example, it has been argued that individuals vary on each of these five trait dimensions in line with a normal curve distribution and that the factors are at least partially genetically pre-determined (Jang et al., 2002; Loehlin et al., 1998). Furthermore, research within the framework of evolutionary psychology has also provided some evidence that these five personality dimensions may have influenced social adaptation and natural selection (Buss, 1996), although similar claims could probably be made about any putative set of personality trait dimensions.

While the two largest factors (anxiety/neuroticism and extraversion) appear to have been universally accepted (e.g. in the pioneering factor-analytic work of R.B. Cattell, H.J. Eysenck, J.P. Guilford, and A.L. Comrey), the present critique suggests, nevertheless, that the FFM provides a less than optimal account of human personality structure. Saucier and Goldberg (2001) reported many difficulties with the proposed Big Five personality dimensions, and indeed Saucier (2002: 1) concluded, 'It is not yet clear that this is the "optimal" model. An optimal model will be replicable across methods, cross-culturally generalizable, comprehensive, and high in utility' (cf. de Raad and Perugini, 2002). Furthermore, in analyses of adjectival data, Paunonen and Jackson (2000) provided hard evidence that many personality traits lie beyond the putative Big Five dimensions (such as conservativeness, honesty, deceptiveness, conceit, masculinity–femininity, thriftiness, humorousness, sensuality, and religiosity). Moreover, as indicated above, in a critique of the empirical factor-analytic work leading to delineation of the FFM, Boyle et al. (1995) pointed to some questionable methodological decisions, including Costa and McCrae's (1992) use of procrustean factor-analytic techniques to ensure that factors supporting their Big Five model would be extracted (Block, 1995; Boyle, 1997).

In addition, the FFM provides a rather *static* account of personality (Terracciano et al., 2006). According to McCrae and

Costa (1999: 145), personality traits develop throughout the childhood years and from around 30 years of age onwards remain relatively stable in otherwise healthy individuals. Soldz and Vaillant (1999) reported some significant test–retest correlations for some of the Big Five dimensions (neuroticism, extraversion, and openness), but failed to find significant correlations for other traits (agreeableness and conscientiousness) across the 45-year test–retest period. The significant test–retest correlations accounted for only a small proportion of the variance, suggesting that the Big Five personality traits are subject to considerable change across the adult years. Actually, the great minds of personality psychology (Cattell, Allport, and Murray) all thought that personality dispositions changed, leading to the inference that the FFM model may be an anachronism of the present generation (B.W. Roberts, pers. comm., 21 OCT., 2006). Indeed, there is now mounting empirical evidence that ongoing changes to personality structure occur across the whole lifespan (e.g. see Cattell et al., 2002; Fraley and Roberts, 2005; Roberts et al., 2006a, 2006b; Srivastava et al., 2003). In light of this empirical evidence, McCrae and Terracciano (2005) have acknowledged that there are discernible increases in agreeableness and conscientiousness over the adult years, along with decreases in extraversion, neuroticism, and openness to experience (cf. Srivastava et al., 2003). In a large meta-analytic study of nearly 100 longitudinal studies into the stability of personality traits (Roberts et al., 2006a, 2006b), significant changes in mean trait levels were found right across the lifespan, including even among the elderly. While many such changes were linear, some changes were curvilinear (e.g. it was found that openness to experience increased during adolescence but decreased in old age). Evidently, the modification of personality traits (personality learning) continues throughout the adult years confirming Cattell's contentions regarding structured-personality-learning theory (e.g. Cattell, 1983, 1996; Cattell et al., 2002). Clearly, the 'set in plaster' hypothesis put forward by McCrae and Costa (1999) that personality learning virtually ceases at around 30 years of age is not supported by the mounting empirical research evidence to the contrary.

As a hierarchical model, the FFM potentially provides a useful structure for understanding the organization of personality constructs, at least within the normal trait sphere. While some evidence supports the cross-cultural replicability of the Big Five (e.g. Egger et al., 2003), the fact that each of the broad dimensions has multiple underlying environmental and genetic determinants, raises concerns about construct validity (Jang et al., 2002: 99). For example, as Saucier (2002: 1) pointed out, empirical evidence shows that the Big Five dimensions are not always orthogonal in marker sets. Furthermore, Toomela (2003: 723) reported that a coherent FFM personality structure emerged only among samples of individuals who had received extensive formal education, thereby raising doubts as to the genetic determination of the postulated Big Five personality dimensions (cf. Roberts et al., 2006a, 2006b). Despite the popularity of the FFM in recent years, its construct validity has been queried (e.g. see Block, 1995; Boyle, 1997, Boyle and Smári, 1997, 1998; Boyle et al., 1995; Cattell, 1995; Eysenck, 1991, 1992, 1994).

The present critique further reviews the empirical research evidence (see the meta-analytic review by Saulsman and Page, 2004) pertaining to the putative Big Five dimensions, including examination of work in applied areas such as clinical psychological assessment and occupational selection. Issues.considered include (1) the FFM in relation to other trait taxonomies; (2) the adequacy of the trait lexicon in covering the total personality domain (including normal, abnormal, and dynamic trait dimensions); (3) the adequacy of the factor-analytic methodology used in the derivation of the FFM structure, as measured by the NEO-PI-R and 16PF instruments; and finally, (4) utility of the FFM in various applied areas of

psychological practice (including clinical and occupational psychology).

THE FFM VERSUS OTHER PERSONALITY TRAIT MODELS

Even though the FFM is based on an atheoretical taxonomy of trait descriptors, it has nevertheless received wide general acceptance (O'Connor, 2002). As already stated above, two factors (extraversion and neuroticism) appear to be universally accepted and they appear in all major contemporary models of broad personality traits. However, interpretation of the remaining three Big Five dimensions (openness to experience-intellectance, agreeableness, and conscientiousness) continues to remain controversial. Indeed, various alternative dimensions have been put forward (e.g. see Block, 1995, 2001; Boyle and Smári, 1997, 1998; Boyle et al., 1995; Cattell, 1995; Eysenck, 1991, 1992, 1993; Hough, 1992; McAdams, 1992; McKenzie, 1998; Zuckerman, 2002; Zuckerman et al., 1993). Taken together, these findings raise concerns about the adequacy of the proposed FFM.

Measures of the three broad personality dimensions extraversion, neuroticism, and psychoticism (which have psychobiological underpinnings) were incorporated into the Eysenck Personality Questionnaire and its revised version (EPQ-R). Eysenck (1991, 1992) asserted that Costa and McCrae's reported criteria for accepting the FFM were insufficient for determining the dimensions of personality structure. He argued that agreeableness and conscientiousness are primary facets/traits (of the EPQ-R psychoticism factor). In any event, it is possible that the three Eysenckian personality factors (E, N, P) and the Big Five dimensions reflect different levels of description of hierarchically arranged personality traits (Boyle, 1989).

Any detailed consideration of the FFM requires an understanding of the historical development of the model and associated psychometric measures. Several Big Five self-report and adjectival rating scales have been devised (see Matthews et al., 2003), including the Big-Five Inventory (Benet-Martínez and John, 1998; John and Srivastava, 1999); Goldberg's 100-trait Adjective Rating Checklist (Goldberg, 1992) and short-form (Saucier, 1994) as well as the Big Five Questionnaire and the Big Five Observer (Caprara et al., 1994),. More recently, Gosling et al. (2003) constructed a brief 10-item measure, while Paunonen (2003; Paunonen et al., 2001) constructed the Five-Factor Nonverbal Personality Questionnaire. Arrival of the NEO Personality Inventory and the revised NEO-PI-R (Costa and McCrae, 1992; McCrae and Costa, 2004) has greatly bolstered FFM studies. In addition, a short 60-item form of the NEO-PI-R (the Five Factor Inventory or NEO-FFI) has been administered in many studies involving pre-adolescents (e.g. Markey et al., 2003; Scholte and de Bruyn, 2004).

Of these FFM instruments, the NEO-PI-R appears to have received the most attention over recent years. In addition to measuring the putative Big Five personality dimensions, the NEO-PI-R also comprises 30 facet scales which appear to vary in levels of heritability (Jang et al., 2002), highlighting the importance of primary factors (or facet dimensions), in addition to second-stratum dimensions. Indeed, Mershon and Gorsuch (1988) demonstrated that higher stratum models such as the FFM account for a considerably lower proportion of the predictive validity than do first-stratum (primary) factors such as those measured in the 16PF. Thus, there is little doubt that primary factors (including the NEO-PI-R facet sub-scales) measure a significantly greater proportion of the personality trait variance over and above that represented in their respective higher-stratum domains (Quirk et al., 2003).

The NEO PI-R has been utilized considerably in empirical research into the relationship between broad personality dimensions and various external criteria (e.g., see Angleitner and Ostendorf, 1994; Barbaranelli and Caprara, 2000; Deary, 1996; Deary and Matthews, 1993; Jang et al., 2002; John, 1990; Marusic et al., 1996; McKenzie, 1998; Miller et al., 2004; Piedmont and Chae, 1997; Trull et al., 1998). In addition, reservations have been raised about the susceptibility to motivational response distortion of the NEO-PI-R and the shortened NEO-FFI instruments. While there have been attempts to devise validity scales (e.g. Schinka et al., 1997; Scandell, 2000), their utility remains to be determined. Furthermore, Egan et al. (2000) in their study using the NEO-FFI reported that neuroticism, agreeableness, and conscientiousness were found to exhibit greater reliability than the openness and extraversion dimensions.

Even though some investigators (e.g. Angleitner and Ostendorf, 1994) have sought evidence of concurrent validity, the empirical data suggest that the FFM accounts for less than 60% of the known personality trait variance (see Boyle et al., 1995). Evidently, the FFM as measured in the NEO-PI-R instrument provides only a partial description of the actual complexity of human personality structure (cf. Aluja et al., 2004; Shafer, 2001; Schmitt and Buss, 2000).

Claims that the Big Five factors are robust (Goldberg, 1993) and basic (Costa and McCrae, 1992) have also been queried. It is important to note that openness to experience has not been found in lexical analyses. In addition, both lexical and psychophysiological approaches have suggested factor structures other than the Big Five (see Boyle et al., 1995; McKenzie et al., 1997). Apparently, Costa and McCrae's initial three-dimensional (NEO) solution was derived from a cluster analysis of the Cattellian personality trait intercorrelations (cf. McKenzie, 1998: 479). However, cluster analysis cannot detect underlying source traits, and instead can only reveal superficial syndrome groupings. Nevertheless, while some factor-analytically oriented personality researchers (e.g. Cattell, 1995; Comrey, 1993) have proposed additional trait dimensions, tentative support for the FFM has been provided in studies by

Hofstee et al. (1992) and Marusik et al. (1996) as well as by Piedmont and Chae (1997) Also there have been replications of the FFM using representative adjective samples from various languages (cf. Goldberg, 1992; McCrae and Allik, 2002; McCrae et al., 2004).

The empirical evidence shows that openness and conscientiousness dimensions appear to differ from one study to another (e.g. Hofstee et al., 1992; Johnson and Ostendorf, 1993; Stumpf, 1993). Also, several investigators, despite having factor analyzed FFM markers, have not been able to reproduce the popular Big Five structure (e.g. Church and Burke, 1994; Livneh and Livneh, 1989; Schmit and Ryan, 1993). Even though these studies have sometimes used non-representative item samples and small sample sizes, it nevertheless appears that the FFM cannot be reproduced reliably across different samples (Block, 1995: 200; Waller, 1995).

The study by McKenzie et al. (1997) did not support the FFM dimensions labelled agreeableness, conscientiousness, and openness to experience. However, since McKenzie et al. based their analyses on Cattellian and Eysenckian measures (neither of which has good openness-to-experience markers), it is not altogether surprising that their factor solution differed from that of the FFM. In fact, Eysenck (1991: 667) had previously suggested that these three dimensions are correlated primaries which coalesce into a single higher stratum psychoticism (P) factor. On the other hand, Egan et al. (2000) subjected NEO-FFI data derived from a large sample ($n = 1,025$) to both exploratory and confirmatory factor analysis, but obtained support for only three dimensions (neuroticism, agreeableness, and conscientiousness). In addition, Saucier and Goldberg (2001) found that three factors emerged from a larger range of languages than did all Big Five dimensions, raising further concerns about the construct validity of the FFM. The apparent dynamic complexity of human personality structure and its developmental characteristics across the human lifespan, as highlighted via Cattellian structured

personality-learning, would seem to necessitate a model other than the static Big Five approach (cf. Block, 1995; Boyle, 1993; Cattell et al., 2002; Romney and Bynner, 1992; Hough and Schneider, 1996; Schneider et al., 1996). To shed further light on this problem, the methodological strategies utilised in the derivation of the FFM are next examined in some detail.

FACTOR ANALYTIC METHODOLOGY: NEO-PI-R AND 16PF MEASURES

The issue of factor-analytic methodology is critically important in the derivation of the Big Five personality dimensions. Costa and McCrae's (1992) NEO-PI-R factors were delineated using a 'top-down' approach, wherein the predetermined FFM theoretical model was 'verified' by manipulating exploratory factor-analytic methods in a rather idiosyncratic, and procrustean manner (Roberts et al., 2006a, 2006b; Saucier, 2002). However, the extraction of a restricted number of factors together with orthogonal rotation has been extensively critiqued (e.g. Boyle et al., 1995; McDonald, 1985) since it often precludes simple-structure solutions (see Child, 1990). Determination of the appropriate number of factors should be based on accepted criteria such as the well-established Scree test (Cattell, 1988). Simple-structure factor solutions facilitate substantive interpretation (Gorsuch, 1988). Adequate simple structure is suggested when the ± 0.10 hyperplane count (i.e. proportion of trivial ≤ 0.10 factor loadings) is maximized (cf. Boyle et al., 1995: 421). It is noteworthy that the studies conducted by Costa and McCrae (1992) appear not to have tested the simple structure of their factor analytic solutions. Likewise, Goldberg (1992), who subsequently subjected his adjectival rating data to oblique rotation, provided no quantitative evidence on hyperplane counts (cf. Cattell, 1995: 207).

When observer data is added to self-report data, the overlap among factors decreases substantially, a strategy adopted by Costa and McCrae (1992) in deriving validimax factors for the NEO-PI-R. It appears that their self-report data was weighted so as to create factors with reduced correlations (Costa and McCrae's preference for procrustean rotation has been queried – see Block, 1995). Thus, in constructing the NEO-PI-R instrument, it appears that Costa and McCrae's analyses, rather than being empirically data-driven, were unduly influenced and moulded specifically to accord with the popular Big Five dimensions (Block, 1995). It is not surprising, therefore, that the NEO-PI-R facet subscales have not received universal support (e.g. Glisky et al., 1991; Goldberg, 1993; Hahn and Comrey, 1994; Tellegen, 1993; Zuckerman et al., 1993). Interestingly, oblique simple structure rotations of adjectival ratings in large samples have led to a new method for representing the FFM structure called the AB5C (Hofstee, 1994).

Costa and McCrae maintained that their observed factor intercorrelations resulted from correlated method error related to self-report data. However, there is little reason to expect, a priori, that the Big Five factors should necessarily be orthogonal. Furthermore, McCrae et al. (1996) argued that confirmatory factor analysis is too restrictive (see Mulaik, 1988; Vassend and Skrondal, 1997, for a discussion of some of these issues). For example, McCrae and Allik (2002) pointed to a number of confirmatory factor-analytic studies that had been undertaken cross-culturally with mixed outcomes.

Other factor-analytically derived models of personality structure have also appeared, such as the second-stratum 16PF factors (Boyle, 1989; Boyle and Smári, 2002; Boyle et al., 2001; Cattell and Nichols, 1972; Gorsuch and Cattell, 1967; Krug and Johns, 1986), Hogan's six personality factors (e.g. Hogan et al., 1996), the eight personality trait factors which Comrey (1993) reported, and the three broad, higher stratum factors elucidated by Eysenck (e.g. 1994)

(see also Byravan and Ramanaiah, 1996; H.E.P. Cattell, 1996; McKenzie et al., 1997; Ormerod et al., 1996; Russell and Karol, 1994). However, at least the first two dimensions of the Big Five (neuroticism and extraversion) appear to have emerged from the separate factor-analytic investigations carried out by Cattell, Comrey, and Eysenck (see Boyle, 1989; Caprara et al., 2001).

Krug and Johns (1986) carried out a large-scale factoring of the 16PF and reported at least five second-stratum personality factors labelled 'extraversion', 'anxiety/neuroticism', 'tough poise', 'independence', and 'control', plus an intelligence factor (cf. Smith, 1988). Krug and Johns based their large-scale factor analyses on the intercorrelations of Cattell's 16PF primary trait factors; they utilized simple structure factor-analytic procedures, and they checked (cross-validated) the validity of their factor-pattern solutions across separate large samples of 9,222 males and 8,159 females, providing strong evidence of the robustness of their factor solutions.

Nonetheless, Cattell (1995) in his position statement ('The fallacy of five factors in the personality sphere') had been critical of the Krug and Johns (1986) study, claiming that they had extracted an insufficient number of second-stratum factors. Even so, the large-scale factor analysis of 16PF data, conducted by Krug and Johns on a combined sample of 17,381 participants, yielded a ± 0.10 hyperplane count of 71%. In contrast, Costa and McCrae's (1992) FFM solution resulted in a ± 0.10 hyperplane count of only 31%, suggesting that their factor solution failed to satisfy simple-structure criteria (cf. Deary, 1996: 992). In addition to the extraversion and neuroticism dimensions, Zuckerman (2002), and Zuckerman et al. (1993) had also identified traits of aggression-hostility and impulsive sensation-seeking, providing yet further evidence of the limitations of the popular FFM. Clearly, the five-factor Zuckerman–Kuhlman Personality Questionnaire (ZKPQ, in its incorporation of biological, comparative, experimental, and trait approaches, is more sophisticated than the popular, but rather descriptive Big Five model which serves as the basis for the NEO-PI-R and NEO-FFI instruments. As Zuckerman (1991: 17) pointed out, the popularity of the FFM over recent years probably reflects a compromise between the minimalist three Eysenckian typological factors (e.g. Eysenck, 1994, 1997) and the far more numerous Cattellian 16PF primary factors (e.g. Cattell and Cattell, 1995; H.E.P. Cattell, 1993, 1995, 1996a, 1996b). Nevertheless, the predictive validity of a smaller number of higher order factors is necessarily reduced as compared with measurement based on primary factors (Boyle et al., 1995; Cattell, 1995: 208; Mershon and Gorsuch, 1988).

Rossier et al. (2004) asserted that the NEO-PI-R is more internally reliable than the 16PF, but as Boyle (1991) has pointed out, high item homogeneity (as measured via Cronbach alpha coefficients) may also reflect item redundancy and narrow measurement of a construct. Indeed, the Cattellian psychometric instruments have been constructed specifically to minimize item redundancy and to increase their breadth of measurement (e.g. see Cattell, 1992). As Boyle (1991) argued, moderate rather than maximum item homogeneity is psychometrically desirable. Since Rossier et al. did not report any test–retest consistency data, their conclusions about the reliability of the respective instruments were evidently misguided. However, putting aside such technical psychometric issues, some applications of the popular FFM are now considered, including applications within clinical and occupational contexts.

THE FFM AND ABNORMAL PERSONALITY STRUCTURE

Several studies have attempted to locate abnormal personality traits within the FFM factor space (see O'Connor and Dyce, 2001).

While the FFM has been shown to exhibit correlations with Axis II clinical constructs (e.g. Costa and Widiger, 2002; Widiger et al., 2002), in practice, such correlations are typically observed even between quite unrelated psychometric measures, and are of little psychological importance, being attributable largely to overlapping media of measurement variance (e.g. intercorrelations between unrelated self-report scales). Similarly, Quirk et al. (2003) examined the incremental validity of the NEO-PI-R in the prediction of Axis I and II disorders, and found that the instrument accounted for some additional diagnostic variance over and above that explained by the MMPI-2 inventory. However, such 'incremental validity' may well have resulted primarily from contamination due to method variance.

Based on previous research suggesting a link between procrastination and lack of consideration for others, Lay et al. (1998) developed self-report scales to assess procrastination and the FFM dimension (conscientiousness) in school children. They found the expected negative relationship between the two constructs. In a study of Dutch university students, Schouwenburg and Lay (1995) used the NEO-PI-R to assess conscientiousness which was also found to be inversely related to procrastinatory behaviour as suggested by self-descriptive adjectives. In contrast, perfectionism was correlated positively with conscientiousness (Hill et al., 1997). When perfectionism was self-oriented, it was also positively associated with the FFM 'agreeableness' dimension, but when perfectionism was expected of others, it was negatively associated with agreeableness. Moral reasoning has been shown to be related not to the FFM dimension (conscientiousness) but to the FFM 'openness to experience-intellectance' dimension (Dollinger and LaMartina, 1998) (openness to values and feelings, respectively). Emotional intelligence was also found to relate more to the FFM 'openness to experience-intellectance' dimension than to the other four FFM dimensions (Schutte et al., 1998).

The studies reviewed here suggest some applicability of the FFM in the multifactorial classification of abnormal personality traits. One problem is the possible oversimplification of some of the FFM traits. For example, it has been argued that openness to experience-intellectance embodies at least three different features, namely absorption, intellectance, and liberalism (Glisky and Kihlstrom, 1993), while conscientiousness has been disaggregated into six facets (Schouwenberg and Lay, 1995). Trull and Widiger developed a structured interview (SIFFM) to assess personality disorders using the NEO-PI-R as a guiding principle (see Trull et al., 1998).

Schroeder et al. (1992) found a general convergence of various measures of personality disorders with four of the FFM dimensions. Neuroticism was most related, while openness to experience-intellectance was least related to personality disorders. Since there are various tried and tested tools for assessing neuroticism, the incremental validity of the FFM in clinical diagnosis needs to be determined. Also, the behavioural aspects of personality disorders are not sufficiently accessed by the FFM (Schroeder et al., 1992). A review of several studies of personality disorder symptomatology found that number of symptoms correlated with scores on FFM measures (Duijsens and Diekstra, 1996). The evidence suggests that the FFM does explain substantial parts of the variance in abnormal personality dimensions (e.g. Bagby et al., 1999, replicated the five-factor NEO-PR-R structure in a sample of psychiatric patients), although it seems evident that additional trait dimensions are required. Furthermore, as would be expected, there is considerable overlap between FFM measures and Minnesota Multiphasic Personality Inventory (MMPI) scales (Costa and Widiger, 2002). In addition, there are empirical links between FFM measures and DSM-IV Axis I disorders, such as the link between neuroticism and other FFM dimensions and anxiety disorders (Trull et al., 1998).

The idea of differentiating various DSM-IV-defined personality disorders in terms of the FFM was discussed by Widiger et al. (2002), who reported, for example, that borderline personality disorder correlated highly with the 'neuroticism' dimension, that schizotypal personality disorder correlated highly with introversion, and that histrionic personality correlated with extraversion. In addition, Ignjatovic and Svrakic (2003) investigated the utility of both the FFM and the Cloninger seven-factor model (Cloninger et al., 1999) in relation to Axis I and II mental disorders (depression, psychoses, anxiety, and personality disorder) among Yugoslav psychiatric patients. Their empirical findings supported the applicability of both psychometric models. However, since the FFM does not provide specific coverage of the abnormal trait domain, as measured for example in the MMPI, the Clinical Analysis Questionnaire (CAQ), or the Personality Assessment Inventory (PAI), this leaves the FFM quite a way from the clinical objective of differential diagnosis of personality disorders and Axis I mental disorders (Waller, 1995), and highlights the need to consider abnormal personality trait dimensions, in addition to normal trait dimensions alone.

Thus, despite having some utility in assessing personality disorders (Costa and Widiger, 2002; Soldz et al., 1993), the FFM does not appear to be directly helpful in psychiatric diagnosis (Clark, 1993; Waller, 1995), since it relates primarily to normal personality structure, rather than to the psychopathological trait domain. Normal personality trait dimensions may be useful in clinical applications in ways other than assisting diagnosis. For example, normal traits might capture important heterogeneity that exists within diagnostic categories. As shown in Table 14.1, the FFM does not appear to provide adequate coverage of the major psychoticism traits. Still, it would seem advantageous to consider simultaneously both specific and broad personality traits in evaluating clinical psychotherapeutic outcomes (e.g. see Cattell, 1987).

Parenthetically, studies have also emerged relating the FFM to somatic health. In one

Table 14.1 Comparison of Major Personality Trait Models

FFM (NEO-PI-R)	Eysenck (EPQ-R)	Cattell (16PF5)	Cattell (CAQ)	Brand	Hogan (HPI)	Comrey (CPS)	Hough
Extraversion	Extraversion	Extraversion	Extraversion	1. Energy 2. Affection	Sociability	1. Extraversion 2. Activity	Affiliation
Neuroticism	Neuroticism	Anxiety/Neuroticism	Anxiety/Neuroticism	Neuroticism	Adjustment	Emotional Stability	Adjustment
Conscientiousness		Superego/Control	Superego/Control	Conscientiousness	1. Prudence 2. Ambition	Orderliness	Dependability
Agreeableness		Independence	Independence	Will	Likeability	1. Trust 2. Empathy	1. Agreeableness 2. Locus of Control
Openness to Experience (Intellectance/Culture)		Intelligence	Intelligence	Intelligence	Intellectance		Intellectance
		Tough Poise	Tough Poise			Masculinity	1. Rugged Individualism 2. Masculinity
			Socialization			Social Conformity	
	Psychoticism		Psychoticism				
			Depression				

Notes. 1. Where more than one trait dimension overlaps with a particular FFM dimension, these are numbered sequentially. 2. Comrey's (CPS) Activity factor is not close enough to the FFM Extraversion to represent any kind of match although they are correlated to some degree. 3. FFM Openness appears to be an idiosyncratic complex of relatively independent factors, including some relationship to CPS Social Conformity vs. Rebelliousness, but not high enough to consider them to be matched to any substantial degree. 4. Some of the factors are negatively related (e.g. Neuroticism vs. Emotional Stability; Adjustment vs. Neuroticism; Independence vs. Agreeableness; Will vs. Agreeableness; Internal Locus of Control vs. Neuroticism). 5. Psychoticism is conventionally attributed to a combination of low Agreeableness and low Conscientiousness, although it also has elements of schizotypal personality that don't fit well with the FFM (or the Big Five, more generally). It is, of course, a rather heterogeneous dimension that is hard to match up with others in a clean way (G. Matthews, pers. comm., 15 May, 2008). 6. Cattell's (16PF/CAQ) higher-stratum Tough Poise factor, for example, also overlaps with low Agreeableness and low Openness, while Hogan's Ambition factor also appears to overlap with Extraversion, highlighting the difficulty of arriving at precise alignments between dimensions from different personality models.

study of more than 1,000 undergraduate students (Lemos-Giraldez and Fidalgo-Aliste, 1997), conscientiousness and agreeableness were found to be predictive of smoking, drinking alcohol, exercise, diet, and stress. Courneya and Hellsten (1998) reported that particular motives, barriers, and preferences involved in exercise behaviour related to the FFM in the expected direction, with neuroticism and lack of conscientiousness predicting exercise barriers. This line of investigation can be extended to shed light on health behaviour change which has become the subject of much interest in health psychology.

USE OF FFM IN PERSONNEL SELECTION

In recent years, the FFM has attracted considerable attention in employee selection (cf. Noty, 1986). Major contributing influences have been influential meta-analytic studies; adoption of a framework for categorizing trait measures (Fisher and Boyle, 1997) and economic and labour market changes (Mount and Barrick, 1995). For example, Hurtz and Donovan conducted a meta-analysis of scales designed to measure FFM constructs. Their findings (2000: 875) supported the work of Barrick et al. (2001), and Mount and Barrick (1995), that conscientiousness exhibited the highest validity of the FFM dimensions in relation to predicting job performance. As for conscientiousness, Hurtz and Donovan (2000: 875–876) concluded that the validity estimates reported by Salgado (1997) may have been overestimates. The actual predictive variance accounted for was only around 4%, raising doubts as to the utility of the FFM measures in making valid predictions of occupational performance.

While the FFM has remained popular, it is evident that additional broad dimensions are needed (Hogan and Roberts, 1996). For example, Hough (1992) added locus of control and masculinity to the list of constructs needed to predict occupational performance. Ozer and Reise (1994) pointed out that the FFM does not include a dimension relating to self-control, despite its importance in work environments. Nevertheless, use of the FFM was supported by Ones and Viswesvaran (1996), arguing that occupational performance criteria are broad constructs. However, reliance on only five factors necessarily restricts predictive validity (see Hogan et al., 1996; Mershon and Gorsuch, 1988). In addition, Schneider et al. (1996) acknowledged that more specific trait dimensions are more predictive of occupational performance criteria (cf. Church and Burke, 1994; Hofstee et al., 1992). Evidently, predictive validity is enhanced when specific traits are matched to specific occupational performance criteria, and broad traits are matched to broad occupational performance criteria (Hogan and Roberts, 1996).

CONCLUSIONS

In summary, several problems with the currently popular FFM are apparent. For example, the FFM does not provide adequate coverage of the normal personality trait domain (let alone the abnormal personality trait domain); it is unable to be replicated consistently in different samples; it is not linked to underlying physiological mechanisms or to neurochemical brain processes; it postulates heterogeneous broad traits which are too few in number to enable highly accurate predictions; it provides a static account of regularities in behaviour; and a major difficulty with the FFM is that it has no established theoretical basis. What are the underlying biochemical, neuroanatomical, neuropharmacological, and genetic substrates of the so-called Big Five dimensions? Also, it appears that FFM personality instruments fail to detect significant sex differences in personality structure (Poropat, 2002: 1198). Evidently, the Big Five dimensions are too broad and heterogeneous, and lack the specificity to make accurate predictions in many real-life settings. Johnson and Kreuger (2004) examined multivariate models of genetic and environmental influences on adjectives describing the Big Five dimensions. It was found that each domain was aetiologically complex, raising fundamental questions about the conceptual and empirical adequacy of the FFM.

It has been asserted by Costa and McCrae (e.g. 1997, 2006) that studies of personality development have shown little maturational change for the FFM dimensions in adulthood. Nevertheless, since personality structure is constantly undergoing developmental change in response to experiential learning (Cattell et al., 2002; Roberts et al., 2006a, 2006b; Srivastava et al., 2003), it is important to recognize that adoption of more dynamic models that take into account personality-learning processes (Cattell, 1983; Cattell et al., 2002) necessarily precludes simple models of static trait dimensions such as those proposed in the FFM. Instead of representing a conceptual framework for outlining the developmental and dynamic aspects of personality traits within a larger psychological structure, the FFM tends merely to provide a descriptive account of presumed regularities in behaviour, and to view personality structure as a set of static dimensional tendencies not readily influenced by social learning experience and enculturation during childhood development. Indeed, as Rothbart et al. (2000: 130) pointed out, 'Purely descriptive models of personality do not readily lend themselves to making predictions about interactions ... they tend to reinforce a simple trait-based model of personality'. In conclusion, it appears that the currently popular FFM should be replaced with an expanded and altogether more inclusive model of *dynamic* personality structure.

NOTES

This chapter was written at the behest of Hans J. Eysenck, PhD, DSc (Lond.) - (dec. Sept. 4, 1997) in a personal meeting with him in Brisbane during his last visit to Australia in late 1996. Based on his empirical factor analytic research, Professor Eysenck argued strongly against the notion of five personality dimensions.

Likewise, Raymond B. Cattell, PhD, DSc. (Lond.) – (dec. Feb. 2, 1998) had also pointed out in 1995 that the empirical factor analytic evidence that was based on methodologically sound simple structure procedures did not strongly support the FFM or "Big Five" notion.

REFERENCES

Allport, G.W. and Odbert, H.S. (1936) 'Trait names: A psycho-lexical study', *Psychological Monographs*, 47(Whole No. 211): 177–220.

Aluja, A., Garcia, O. and Garcia, L.F. (2004) 'Replicability of the three, four and five Zuckerman's personality super-factors: Exploratory and confirmatory factor analysis of the EPQ-RS, ZKPQ and NEO-PI-R', *Personality and Individual Differences*, 36(5): 1093–108.

Angleitner, A. and Ostendorf, F. (1994) 'Temperament and the Big Five factors of personality', in C.F. Halverson Jr., G.A. Kohnstamm and R.P. Martin (eds), *The Developing Structure of Temperament and Personality from Infancy to Adulthood*. Hillsdale, NJ: Erlbaum, pp. 69–90.

Ashton, M.C., Lee, K., Perugini, M., Szarota, P., de Vries, R.E., Di Blas, L., Boies, K. and De Raad, B. (2004) 'A six-factor structure of personality-descriptive adjectives: Solutions from psycholexical studies in seven languages', *Journal of Personality and Social Psychology*, 86(2): 356–66.

Bagby, R.M., Costa, P.T. Jr., McCrae, R.R., Livesley, W.J., Kennedy, S.H., Levitan, R.D., Levitt, A.J., Joffe, R.T. and Young, L.T. (1999) 'Replicating the five factor model of personality in a psychiatric sample', *Personality and Individual Differences*, 27(6): 1135–9.

Barbaranelli, C. and Caprara, G.V. (2000) 'Measuring the Big Five in self-report and other ratings: A multitrait-multimethod study', *European Journal of Psychological Assessment*, 16(1): 31–43.

Barrick, M.R., Mount, M.K. and Judge, T.A. (2001) 'Personality and performance at the beginning of the new millennium: What do we know and where do we go next?', *International Journal of Selection and Assessment,* 9(1–2): 9–30.

Benet-Martínez, V. and John, O.P. (1998) '"Los Cinco Grandes" across cultures and ethnic groups: Multitrait-Multimethod analyses of the Big Five in Spanish and English', *Journal of Personality and Social Psychology,* 75(3): 729–50.

Block, J. (1995) 'A contrarian view of the five-factor approach to personality description', *Psychological Bulletin,* 117(2): 187–229.

Block, J. (2001) 'Millenial contrarianism: The five factor approach to personality description 5 years later', *Journal of Research in Personality,* 35(1): 98–107.

Boyle, G.J. (1989) 'Re-examination of the major personality-type factors in the Cattell, Comrey, and Eysenck scales: Were the factor solutions by Noller et al. optimal?', *Personality and Individual Differences,* 10(12): 1289–9.

Boyle, G.J. (1991) 'Does item homogeneity indicate internal consistency or item redundancy in psychometric scales?', *Personality and Individual Differences,* 12(3): 291–4.

Boyle, G.J. (1993) 'Review of D.M. Romney and J.M. Bynner (1992) "The Structure of Personal Characteristics"', *Contemporary Psychology,* 38(10): 1080–1.

Boyle, G.J. (1997) 'Crisis in traditional personality assessment: Implications for military testing', Proceedings of the 39th Annual Conference of the International Military Testing Association, Sydney, October 14–16, pp. 61–6.

Boyle, G.J., Ortet, G. and Ibáñez, M.I. (2001) 'Evaluación de la personalidad y la inteligencia: Una perspectiva cattelliana', *Universitas Tarraconensis Revista de Psicología,* 23(1–2): 73–92.

Boyle, G.J. and Saklofske, D.H. (2004) (eds), *Sage Benchmarks in Psychology: The Psychology of Individual Differences* (4 Vols). London: Sage.

Boyle, G.J. and Smári, J. (1997) 'De fem stora och personlighetspsykologins matningsproblem [Big Five and the problem of measurement in the psychology of personality]', *Nordisk Psykologi,* 49(1): 12–21.

Boyle, G.J. and Smári, J. (1998) 'Statiska femfaktorpersonlighets-modeller-Svar till Engvik [Static five-factor models of personality: A reply to Engvik]', *Nordisk Psykologi,* 50(3): 216–22.

Boyle, G.J. and Smári, J. (2002) 'Vers une simplification du modèle cattellien de la personnalité', *Bulletin de Psychologie,* 55(6): 635–43.

Boyle, G.J., Stankov, L. and Cattell, R.B. (1995) 'Measurement and statistical models in the study of personality and intelligence', in D.H. Saklofske and M. Zeidner (eds), *International Handbook of Personality and Intelligence.* New York: Plenum, pp. 417–46.

Buss, D.M. (1996) 'Social adaptation and five major factors of personality', in J.S. Wiggins (ed.), *The Five-Factor Model of Personality: Theoretical Perspectives.* New York: Guilford, pp. 180–207.

Byravan, A. and Ramanaiah, N.V. (1996) 'Study of the structure of the 16PF fifth edition from the perspective of the five-factor model – reply', *Psychological Reports,* 79(1): 123–6.

Caprara, G.V., Barbaranelli, C., Hahan, R. and Comrey, A.L. (2001) 'Factor analyses of the NEO-PI-R inventory and the Comrey personality scales in Italy and the United States', *Personality and Individual Differences,* 30(2): 217–28.

Caprara, G.V., Barbaranelli, C. and Borgogni, L. (1994) *BFO: Big Five Observer Manual.* Firenze: Organizzazioni Speciali.

Cattell, H.E.P. (1993) 'The structure of phenotypic personality traits: comment', *American Psychologist,* 48(12): 1302–3.

Cattell, H.E.P. (1995) 'Some comments on a factor analysis of the 16PF and NEO Personality Inventory – revised', *Psychological Reports,* 77(3): 1307–11.

Cattell, H.E.P. (1996) 'The original big five: An historical perspective', *Revue Européenne de Psychologie Appliquée,* 46(1): 5–14.

Cattell, R.B. (1983) *Structured Personality-Learning Theory: A Wholistic Multivariate Research Approach.* New York: Praeger.

Cattell, R.B. (1986) 'The 16PF personality structure and Dr. Eysenck', *Journal of Social Behavior and Personality,* 1(2): 153–60.

Cattell, R.B. (1987) *Psychotherapy by Structured Learning Theory.* New York: Springer.

Cattell, R.B. (1988) 'The meaning and strategic use of factor analysis', in J.R. Nesselroade and R.B. Cattell (eds), *Handbook of Multivariate Experimental Psychology* (2nd edn). New York: Plenum, pp.131–203.

Cattell, R.B. (1992) 'Human motivation objectively, experimentally analysed', *British Journal of Medical Psychology*, 65(3): 237–43.

Cattell, R.B. (1995) 'The fallacy of five factors in the personality sphere', *Psychologist*, 8(5): 207–8.

Cattell, R.B. (1996) 'Personality and structured learning', *European Review of Applied Psychology*, 46(1): 73–5.

Cattell, R.B., Boyle, G.J. and Chant, D. (2002) 'Enriched behavioral prediction equation and its impact on structured learning and the dynamic calculus', *Psychological Review*, 109(1): 202–5.

Cattell, R.B. and Cattell, H.E.P. (1995) 'Personality structure and the new fifth edition of the 16PF', *Educational and Psychological Measurement*, 55(6): 926–37.

Cattell, R.B. and Nichols, K.E. (1972) 'An improved definition, from 10 researches, of second order personality factors in Q-data (with cross-cultural checks)', *Journal of Social Psychology*, 86(2): 187–203.

Child, D. (1990) *The Essentials of Factor Analysis* (2nd edn). London: Cassell.

Church, A.T. and Burke, P.J. (1994) 'Exploratory and confirmatory tests of the Big Five and Tellegen's three- and four-dimensional models', *Journal of Personality and Social Psychology*, 66(1): 93–114.

Clark, L.A. (1993) 'Personality disorder diagnosis: Limitations of the five-factor model', *Psychological Inquiry*, 4(2): 100–4.

Cloninger, C.R., Svrakic, D.M., Bayon, C. and Przybeck, T.R. (1999) 'Measurement of psychopathology as variants of personality', in C.R. Cloninger (ed.), *Personality and Psychopathology*. Washington, DC: American Psychiatric Association, pp. 33–65.

Comrey, A.L. (1993) *Revised Manual and Handbook of Interpretation for the Comrey Personality Scales*. San Diego: Educational and Industrial Testing Service.

Costa, P.T. Jr. and McCrae, R.R. (1992) *Revised NEO Personality Inventory and NEO Five-Factor Inventory: Professional Manual*. Odessa, FL: Psychological Assessment Resources.

Costa, P.T. Jr. and McCrae, R.R. (1997) 'Longitudinal stability of adult personality', in R. Hogan, J.A. Johnson and S.R. Briggs (eds), *Handbook of Personality Psychology*. Orlando: Academic, pp. 269–90.

Costa, P.T. Jr. and McCrae, R.R. (2006) 'Age changes in personality and their origins: Comment on Roberts, Walton, and Viechtbauer (2006)', *Psychological Bulletin*, 132(1): 26–8.

Costa, P.T. Jr. and Widiger, T.A. (2002) (eds), *Personality Disorders and the Five-Factor Model of Personality* (2nd edn). Washington, DC: American Psychological Association.

Courneya, K.S. and Hellsten, L.A. (1998) 'Personality correlates of exercise behaviour, motives, barriers and preferences: An application of the five-factor model', *Personality and Individual Differences*, 24(5): 625–33.

Deary, I.J. (1996) 'A (latent) Big Five personality model in 1915? A reanalysis of Webb's data', *Journal of Personality and Social Psychology*, 71(5): 992–1005.

Deary, I.J. and Matthews, G. (1993) 'Personality traits are alive and well', *Psychologist*, 6(7): 299–311.

de Raad, B. and Perugini, M. (2002) *Big Five Assessment*. Seattle: Hogrefe and Huber.

Dollinger, S.J. and LaMartina, A.K. (1998) 'A note on moral reasoning and the five-factor model', *Journal of Social Behavior and Personality*, 13(2): 349–58.

Duijsens, I.J. and Diekstra, R.F.W. (1996) 'DSM-III-R and ICD-10 personality disorders and their relationship with the Big Five dimensions of personality', *Personality and Individual Differences*, 21(1): 119–33.

Egan, V., Deary, I. and Austin, E. (2000) 'The NEO-FFI: Emerging British norms and an item level analysis suggest N, A and C are more reliable than O and E', *Personality and Individual Differences*, 29(5): 907–20.

Egger, J.I.M., De Mey, H.R.A., Derksen, J.J.L. and van der Staak, C.P.F. (2003) 'Cross-cultural replication of the Five Factor Model and comparison of the NEO-PI-R and MMPI-2 PSY-5 scales in a Dutch psychiatric sample', *Psychological Assessment*, 15(1): 81–8.

Eysenck, H.J. (1991) 'Dimensions of personality: 16, 5, 3?: Criteria for a taxonomic paradigm', *Personality and Individual Differences*, 12:(8) 773–90.

Eysenck, H.J. (1992) 'Four ways five factors are not basic', *Personality and Individual Differences*, 13(6): 667–73.

Eysenck, H.J. (1993) 'Comment on Goldberg', *American Psychologist*, 48(12): 1299–300.

Eysenck, H.J. (1994) 'The Big Five or giant three: Criteria for a paradigm', in C.F. Halverson, G.A. Kohnstamm and R.P. Martin (eds), *The Developing Structure of Temperament and Personality from Infancy to Adulthood.* Hillsdale, NJ: Erlbaum, pp. 37–51.

Eysenck, H.J. (1997) 'Personality and experimental psychology: The unification of psychology and the possibility of a paradigm', *Journal of Personality and Social Psychology*, 73(6): 1224–37.

Fisher, C.D. and Boyle, G.J. (1997) 'Personality and employee selection: Credibility regained', *Asia Pacific Journal of Human Resources*, 35(2): 26–40.

Fraley, R.C. and Roberts, B.W. (2005) 'Patterns of continuity: A dynamic model for conceptualizing the stability of individual differences in psychological constructs across the life course', *Psychological Review*, 112(1): 60–74.

Glisky, M.L. and Kihlstrom, J.F. (1993) 'Hypnotizability and facets of openness', *International Journal of Clinical and Experimental Hypnosis*, 41(2): 112–23.

Glisky, M.L., Tataryn, D.J., Tobias, B.A., Kihlstrom, J.F. and McConkey, K.M. (1991) 'Absorption, openness to experience, and hypnotizability', *Journal of Personality and Social Psychology*, 60(2): 263–72.

Goldberg, L.R. (1992) 'The development of markers for the Big Five factor structure', *Psychological Assessment*, 4(1): 26–42.

Goldberg, L.R. (1993) 'The structure of phenotypic personality traits', *American Psychologist*, 48(1): 26–34.

Gorsuch, R.L. (1988) 'Exploratory factor analysis', in J.R. Nesselroade and R.B. Cattell (eds), *Handbook of Multivariate Experimental Psychology* (2nd edn). New York: Plenum, pp. 231–58.

Gorsuch, R.L. and Cattell, R.B. (1967) 'Second stratum personality factors defined in the questionnaire realm by the 16PF', *Multivariate Behavioral Research*, 2(2): 211–24.

Gosling, S.D., Rentfrow, P.J. and Swann, W.B. Jr. (2003) 'A very brief measure of the big-five personality domains', *Journal of Research in Personality*, 37(6): 504–28.

Haggbloom, S.J., Warnick, R., Warnick, J.E., Jones, V.K., Yarbrough, G.L., Russell, T.M., Borecky, C.M., McGahhey, R., Powell III, J.L.,

Beavers, J. and Monte, E. (2002) The 100 most eminent psychologists of the 20th centur, *Review of General Psychology*, 6(2): 139–52.

Hahn, R. and Comrey, A.L. (1994) 'Factor analysis of the NEO-PI and the Comrey Personality Scales', *Psychological Reports*, 75(1–2): 355–65.

Hill, R.W., McIntire, K. and Bacharach, V.R. (1997) 'Perfectionism and the big five factors,' *Journal of Social Behavior and Personality,* 12(1): 257–70.

Hofstee, W.K.B. (1994) 'The abridged Big Five circumplex (AB5C) model of trait structure: Heymans' cube, Kiesler's circle and Peabody and Goldberg's double cone model', *European Review of Applied Psychology*, 44(1): 27–33.

Hofstee, W.K.B., Raad, de B. and Goldberg, L.R. (1992) 'Integration of the Big Five and circumplex approaches to trait structure', *Journal of Personality and Social Psychology*, 63(1): 146–63.

Hogan, R., Hogan, J. and Roberts, B.W. (1996) 'Personality measurement and employment decisions', *American Psychologist*, 51(5): 469–77.

Hogan, J. and Roberts, B.W. (1996) 'Issues and non-issues in the fidelity-bandwidth trade-off', *Journal of Organizational Behavior*, 17(6): 627–37.

Hough, L.M. (1992) 'The Big Five personality variables–construct confusion: Description versus prediction', *Human Performance*, 5(1–2): 139–55.

Hough, L.M. and Schneider, R.J. (1996) 'Personality traits, taxonomies, and applications in organizations', in K.R Murphy (ed.), *Individual Differences and Behavior in Organizations*. San Francisco: Jossey-Bass, pp. 31–87.

Hurtz, G.M. and Donovan, J.J. (2000) 'Personality and job performance: The big five revisited', *Journal of Applied Psychology*, 85(6): 869–79.

Ignjatovic, T.D. and Svrakic, D. (2003) Western personality models applied in Eastern Europe: Yugoslav data. *Comprehensive Psychiatry*, 44(1): 51–9.

Jang, K.L., Livesley, W.J., Angleitner, A., Riemann, R., and Vernon, P.A. (2002) 'Genetic and environmental influences on the covariance of facets defining the domains of the five factor model of personality', *Personality and Individual Differences*, 33(1): 83–101.

John, O.P. (1990) 'The Big Five factor taxonomy: Dimensions of personality in the natural language and in questionnaires', in L. Pervin (ed.), *Handbook of Personality Theory and Research*. New York: Guilford, pp. 66–100.

John, O.P. and Srivastava, S. (1999) 'The Big Five trait taxonomy: History, measurement, and theoretical perspectives', in L.A. Pervin and O.P. John (eds), *Handbook of Personality: Theory and Research*. New York: Guilford, pp. 102–38.

Johnson, J.A. and Ostendorf, F. (1993) 'Clarification of the five-factor model with the abridged big five dimensional circumplex', *Journal of Personality and Social Psychology*, 65(3): 563–76.

Johnson, W. and Krueger, R.F. (2004) 'Genetic and environmental structure of adjectives describing the domains of the Big Five Model of personality: A nationwide US twin study', *Journal of Research in Personality*, 38(5): 448–72.

Krug, S.E. and Johns, E.F. (1986) 'A large scale cross-validation of second-order personality structure defined by the 16PF', *Psychological Reports*, 59(2): 683–93.

Lay, C., Kovacs, A. and Danto, D. (1998) 'The relation of trait procrastination to the big-five factor conscientiousness: An assessment with primary junior school children based on self-report scales', *Personality and Individual Differences*, 25(2): 187–93.

Lemos-Giraldez, S. and Fidalgo-Aliste, A.M. (1997) 'Personality dispositions and health-related habits and attitudes: A cross-sectional study', *European Journal of Personality*, 11(3): 197–209.

Livneh, H. and Livneh, C. (1989) 'The five-factor model of personality: Is evidence of its cross-measure validity premature?', *Personality and Individual Differences*, 10(1): 75–80.

Loehlin, J.C., McCrae, R.R., Costa, P.T. Jr. and John, O.P. (1998) 'Heritabilities of common and measure-specific components of the Big Five personality factors', *Journal of Research in Personality*, 32(4): 431–53.

Markey, C.N., Markey, P.M. and Tinsley, B.J. (2003) 'Personality, puberty, and preadolescent girls' risky behaviours: Examining the predictive value of the five-factor model of personality', *Journal of Research in Personality*, 37(5): 405–19.

Marusic, I., Bratko, D. and Eterovic, H. (1996) 'A contribution to the cross-cultural replicability of the five-factor personality model', *Review of Psychology*, 3(1–2): 23–35.

Matthews, G., Deary, I.J. and Whiteman, M.C. (2003) *Personality Traits* (2nd edn). New York: Cambridge.

McAdams, D.P. (1992) 'The five-factor model in personality: A critical appraisal', *Journal of Personality*, 60(2): 329–61.

McCrae, R.R. and Allik, J. (2002) (eds), *The Five-Factor Model of Personality Across Cultures*. New York: Kluwer/Plenum.

McCrae, R.R. and Costa, P.T., Jr. (1999) 'A five-factor theory of personality', in L.A. Pervin and O.P. Johns (eds), *Handbook of Personality Theory and Research* (2nd edn). New York: Guilford, pp. 139–53.

McCrae, R.R. and Costa, P.T. Jr. (2004) 'A contemplated revision of the NEO Five Factor Inventory', *Personality and Individual Differences*, 36(3): 587–96.

McCrae, R.R., Costa Jr. P.T., Martin, T.A., Oryol, V.E., Rukavishnikov, A.A., Senin, I.G. Hrebickova, M. and Urbanek, T. (2004) 'Consensual validation of personality traits across cultures', *Journal of Research in Personality*, 38(2): 179–201.

McCrae, R.R. and Terracciano, A. (2005) 'Universal features of personality traits from the observer's perspective: Data from 50 cultures', *Journal of Personality and Social Psychology*, 88(3): 547–61.

McCrae, R.R., Zonderman, A.B., Costa, P.T. Jr., Bond, M.H. and Paunonen, S.V. (1996) 'Evaluating replicability of factors in the Revised NEO Personality Inventory: Confirmatory factor analysis and Procrustes rotation', *Journal of Personality and Social Psychology*, 70(3): 552–66.

McDonald, R.P. (1985) *Factor Analysis and Related Methods*. Hillsdale, NJ: Erlbaum.

McKenzie, J. (1998) 'Fundamental flaws in the five factor model: A re-analysis of the seminal correlation matrix from which the "openness-to-experience" factor was extracted', *Personality and Individual Differences*, 24(4): 475–80.

McKenzie, J., Tindell, G. and French, J. (1997) 'The great triumvirate: Agreement between lexically and psycho-physiologically based models of personality', *Personality and Individual Differences*, 22(2): 269–77.

Mershon, B. and Gorsuch, R.L. (1988) 'Number of factors in the personality sphere: Does increase in factors increase predictability of real-life criteria?', *Journal of Personality and Social Psychology*, 55(4): 675–80.

Miller, J.D., Lynam, D., Zimmerman, R.S., Logan, T.K., Leukefeld, C. and Clayton, R. (2004) The utility of the Five Factor Model in understanding risky sexual behavior, *Personality and Individual Differences*, 36(7): 1611–26.

Mount, M.K. and Barrick, M.R. (1995) 'The big five personality dimensions: Implications for research and practice in human resource management', *Research in Personnel and Human Resource Management*, 13(2): 153–200.

Mulaik, S.A. (1988) 'Confirmatory factor analysis', in J.R. Nesselroade and R.B. Cattell (eds), *Handbook of Multivariate Experimental Psychology* (2nd edn). New York: Plenum, pp. 259–88.

Noty, C. (1986) 'Industrial and vocational selection' in R.B. Cattell and R.C. Johnson (eds), *Functional Psychological Testing: Principles and Instruments*. New York: Brunner/Mazel, pp. 425–46.

O'Connor, B.P. (2002) 'A quantitative review of the comprehensiveness of the five-factor model in relation to popular personality inventories', *Assessment*, 9(2): 188–203.

O'Connor, B.P. and Dyce, J.A. (2001) 'Rigid and extreme: A geometric representation of personality disorders in five-factor model space', *Journal of Personality and Social Psychology*, 81(6): 1119–30.

Ones, D.S. and Viswesvaran, C. (1996) 'Bandwidth-fidelity dilemma in personality measurement for personnel selection', *Journal of Organizational Behavior*, 17(6): 609–26.

Ormerod, M.B., McKenzie, J. and Woods, A. (1995) 'Final report on research relating to the concept of five separate dimensions of personality – or six including intelligence', *Personality and Individual Differences*, 18(4): 451–61.

Ozer, D.J. and Reise, S.P. (1994) 'Personality assessment', *Annual Review of Psychology*, 45: 357–88.

Paunonen, S.V. (2003) 'Big five factors of personality and replicated predictions of

behaviour', *Journal of Personality and Social Psychology*, 84(2): 411–24.

Paunonen, S.V. and Ashton, M.C. (2001) 'Big Five factors and facets and the prediction of behaviour', *Journal of Personality and Social Psychology*, 81(3): 524–39.

Paunonen, S.V., Ashton, M.C. and Jackson, D.N. (2001) 'Nonverbal assessment of the Big Five personality factors', *European Journal of Personality*, 15(1): 3–18.

Paunonen S.V. and Jackson, D.N. (2000) 'What is beyond the Big Five? Plenty!,' *Journal of Personality*, 68(4): 821–35.

Peabody, D. and De Raad, B. (2002) 'The substantive nature of psycholexical personality factors: A comparison across languages', *Journal of Personality and Social Psychology*, 83(4): 983–97.

Piedmont, R.L. and Chae, J.H. (1997) 'Cross-cultural generalizability of the five-factor model of personality: Development and validation of the NEO-PI-R for Koreans', *Journal of Cross-Cultural Psychology*, 28(2): 131–55.

Poropat, A. (2002) 'The relationship between atrributional style, gender and the Five-Factor Model of personality', *Personality and Individual Differences*, 33(7): 1185–201.

Quirk, S.W., Christiansen, N.D., Wagner, S.H. and McNulty, J.L. (2003) 'On the usefulness of measures of normal personality for clinical assessment: Evidence of the incremental validity of the Revised NEO Personality Inventory', *Psychological Assessment*, 15(3): 311–25.

Roberts, B.W., Walton, K.E. and Viechtbauer, W. (2006a) 'Patterns of mean-level change in personality traits across the life course: A meta-analysis of longitudinal studies', *Psychological Bulletin*, 132(1): 1–25.

Roberts, B.W., Walton, K.E. and Viechtbauer, W. (2006b) 'Personality traits change in adulthood: Reply to Costa and McCrae (2006)', *Psychological Bulletin*, 132(1): 29–32.

Romney, D.M. and Bynner, J.M. (1992) *The Structure of Personal Characteristics*. Westport, CT: Praeger.

Rossier, J., de Stadelhofen, F.M. and Berthoud, S. (2004) 'The hierarchical structures of the NEO-PI-R and 16 PF 5', *European Journal of Psychological Assessment*, 20(1): 27–38.

Rothbart, M.K., Ahadi, S.A. and Evans, D.E. (2000) 'Temperament and personality: Origins and outcomes', *Journal of Personality and Social Psychology*, 78(1): 122–35.

Russell, M.T. and Karol, D.L. (1994) *The 16PF Fifth Edition Administrator's Manual*. Champaign, IL: IPAT.

Salgado, J.F. (1997) 'The five factor model of personality and job performance in the European community', *Journal of Applied Psychology*, 82(1): 30–43.

Saucier, G. (1994) 'Mini-markers: A brief version of Goldberg's unipolar Big-Five markers', *Journal of Personality Assessment*, 63(3): 506–16.

Saucier, G. (2002) 'Orthogonal markers for orthogonal factors: The case of the Big Five', *Journal of Research in Personality*, 36(1): 1–31.

Saucier, G. and Goldberg, L.R. (2001) 'Lexical studies of indigenous personality factors: Premises, products and prospects', *Journal of Personality*, 69(6): 847–79.

Saulsman, L.M. and Page, A.C. (2004) 'The five-factor model and personality disorder empirical literature: A meta-analytic review', *Clinical Psychology Review*, 23(8): 1055–85.

Scandell, D.J. (2000) 'Development and initial validation scales for the NEO-Five Factor Inventory', *Personality and Individual Differences*, 29(10): 1153–62.

Schmitt, D.P. and Buss, D.M. (2000) 'Sexual dimensions of person description: Beyond or subsumed by the big five?', *Journal of Research in Personality*, 34(2): 141–77.

Schmit, M.J. and Ryan, A.M. (1993) 'The big five in personnel selection: Factor structure in applicant and nonapplicant populations', *Journal of Applied Psychology*, 78(6): 966–74.

Schneider, R.J., Hough, L.M. and Dunnette, M.D. (1996) 'Broadsided by broad traits: How to sink science in five dimensions or less', *Journal of Organizational Behavior*, 17(6): 639–55.

Schinka, J.A., Kinder, B.N. and Kremer, T. (1997) 'Research validity scales for the NEO PI-R: Development and initial validation', *Journal of Personality Assessment*, 68(1): 127–38.

Scholte, R.H.J. and de Bruyn, E.E.J. (2004) 'Comparison of the giant three and the big five in early adolescents', *Personality and Individual Differences*, 36(6): 1353–71.

Schouwenberg, H.C. and Lay, C.H. (1995) 'Trait procrastination and the Big Five factors of personality', *Personality and Individual Differences*, 18(4): 481–90.

Schroeder, M.L., Wormworth, J.A. and Livesley, W.J. (1992) 'Dimensions of personality disorder and their relationships to the Big Five dimensions of personality', *Psychological Assessment*, 4(1): 47–53.

Schutte, N.S., Malouff, J.M., Hall, L.E., Haggerty, D.J., Cooper, J.T., Golden, C.J. and Dornheim, L. (1998) 'Development and validation of a measure of emotional intelligence', *Personality and Individual Differences*, 25(2): 167–77.

Shafer, A.B. (2001) 'The big five and sexuality trait terms as predictors of relationships and sex', *Journal of Research in Personality*, 35(3): 313–38.

Smith, B.D. (1988) 'Personality: Multivariate systems theory and research', in J.R. Nesselroade and R.B. Cattell (eds), *Handbook of Multivariate Experimental Psychology* (2nd edn). New York: Plenum, pp. 687–736.

Soldz, S., Budman, S., Demby, A. and Merry, J. (1993) 'Representation of personality disorders in circumplex and five-factor space: Explorations with a clinical sample', *Psychological Assessment*, 5(1): 41–52.

Soldz, S. and Vaillant, G.E. (1999) 'The Big Five personality traits and the life course: A 45-year longitudinal study', *Journal of Research in Personality*, 33(2): 208–32.

Spinath, B., Spinath, F.M., Riemann, R. and Angleitner, A. (2003) 'Implicit theories about personality and intelligence and their relationship to actual personality and intelligence', *Personality and Individual Differences*, 35(4): 939–51.

Srivastava, S., John, O.P., Gosling, S. and Potter, J. (2003) 'Development of personality in early and middle adulthood: Set like plaster or persistent change?', *Journal of Personality and Social Psychology*, 84(5): 1041–53.

Stumpf, H. (1993) 'The factor structure of the Personality Research Form: A cross-national evaluation', *Journal of Personality*, 61(1): 27–48.

Tellegen, A. (1993) 'Folk concepts and psychological concepts of personality and personality disorder', *Psychological Inquiry*, 4(2): 122–30.

Terracciano, A., Costa, P.T Jr. and McCrae, R.R. (2006) 'Personality plasticity after age 30.', *Personality and Social Psychology Bulletin*, 32(8): 999–1009.

Toomela, A. (2003) 'Relationships between personality structure, structure of word meaning, and cognitive ability: A study of cultural mechanisms of personality', *Journal of Personality and Social Psychology*, 85(4): 723–35.

Trull, T.J., Widiger, T.A., Useda, J.D., Holcomb, J., Doan, B-T., Axelrod, S.R., Stern, B.L. and Gershuny, B.S. (1998) 'A structured interview for the assessment of the Five-Factor Model of Personality', *Psychological Assessment*, 10(3): 229–40.

Vassend, O. and Skrondal, A. (1997) 'Validation of the NEO Personality Inventory and the five-factor model. Can findings from exploratory and confirmatory factor analysis be reconciled?', *European Journal of Personality*, 11(2): 147–66.

Waller, N.G. (1995) 'Evaluating the structure of personality', in R. Cloninger (ed.), *Personality and Psychopathology*. Washington, DC: American Psychiatric Association, pp. 155–97.

Widiger, T.A., Costa, P.T. Jr. and McCrae, R.R. (2002) 'A proposal for Axis II: Diagnosing personality disorders using the five-factor model', in P.T. Costa Jr. and T.A. Widiger (eds), *Personality Disorders and the Five-Factor Model of Personality* (2nd edn). Washington, DC: American Psychological Association, pp. 431–56.

Zuckerman, M. (1991) *Psychobiology of Personality*. New York: Cambridge.

Zuckerman, M. (2002) 'Zuckerman–Kuhlman Personality Questionnaire (ZKPQ): An alternative five-factorial model', in B. De Raad and M. Perugini (eds), *Big Five Assessment*. Ashland, OH: Hogrefe and Huber, pp. 376–92.

Zuckerman, M., Kuhlman, D.M., Joireman, J., Teta, P. and Kraft, M. (1993) 'A comparison of three structural models for personality: The big three, the big five, and the alternative five', *Journal of Personality and Social Psychology*, 65(4): 757–68.

Key Traits: Psychobiology

15

Approach and Avoidance Temperaments

Andrew J. Elliot and Todd M. Thrash

INTRODUCTION

The search for basic building blocks of personality is an old enterprise, formally commencing with Galen's typological conceptualization based on humors. Contemporary models of personality structure primarily focus on continuous dimensions rather than discrete typologies. Regardless of whether they are discrete or dimensional, these portraits of personality seek to uncover the core dispositions that are responsible for consistency in human behavior.

Three popular approaches to the search for basic components of personality are the trait adjective approach, the affective disposition approach, and the motivational system approach. Each of these three approaches has made important contributions to the personality psychology literature, but there has been little attempt, to date, to examine the degree of convergence or overlap among them. Herein we contend, on the basis of our recent conceptual and empirical work, that these three approaches share fundamental similarities, both in terms of the general nature of the constructs they proffer and in terms of the specific content of these constructs. In short, we propose that the central constructs of the trait adjective, affective disposition, and motivational system approaches to personality are grounded in even more basic and fundamental dispositions, namely approach and avoidance temperaments.

In this chapter, we begin by making the case for the approach–avoidance distinction in conceptualizations of personality structure. We then overview the three aforementioned approaches with an eye toward convergence and overlap. Next we introduce the approach and avoidance temperament constructs and review research that links these temperaments to the constructs from the other three approaches. We also review research that links these temperaments to goal constructs, which are at the heart of the self-regulatory process, and to affect and inspiration in daily experience. Finally, we describe our most recent research that is designed to create a measure of approach and avoidance temperaments.

APPROACH AND AVOIDANCE MOTIVATION AS FUNDAMENTAL AND BASIC

The approach–avoidance motivational distinction is one of the oldest conceptual distinctions in the history of psychological thinking about human beings. Indeed, it is well over two millennia old, having made its initial appearance in the writings of the ancient Greek philosopher Democritus (460–370 BC). Democritus postulated approach–avoidance as an ethical prescription in which the immediate pursuit of pleasure and avoidance of pain were viewed as the obligatory guides for human action (see also the writings of Socrates's pupil Aristippus (435–356 BC) and Epicurus (342–270 BC)). Many years later, but still within the realm of philosophy, Jeremy Bentham (1748–1832) moved from ethical prescription to psychologically relevant description by stating: 'Nature has placed mankind under the governance of two sovereign masters, pain and pleasure. It is for them alone to point out what we ought to do, as well as to determine what we shall do' (Bentham, 1779/1879: 1). Within the field of scientific psychology, the approach–avoidance distinction was utilized from the beginning. For example, William James, in his foundational *Principles of Psychology*, described pleasure and pain as 'springs of action' (1890: 549–559, Vol. 2) that reinforce and inhibit behavior, respectively, and even offered rudimentary thoughts regarding the neural mechanisms that produce approach and avoidance behavioral tendencies. Many of the most prominent contributors to scientific psychology since the time of James have explicitly incorporated the approach–avoidance distinction into their theorizing. This is the case across theoretical and meta-theoretical perspectives (see Elliot, 1999; Elliot and Covington, 2001, for reviews).

Use of the approach–avoidance distinction at the theoretical level has been paralleled by use of this distinction in empirical work across many different substantive areas of inquiry. Approach and avoidance concepts, principles, and constructs have been empirically validated in the following literatures (and beyond): animal learning (Gray, 1982; Overmier and Archer, 1989), attitudes (Cacioppo and Berntson, 1994; Tesser and Martin, 1996), cognitive appraisal (Lazarus, 1991; Tomaka and Blaskovich, 1994), coping (Moos and Schaeffer, 1993; Roth and Cohen, 1986), emotion (Higgins et al., 1997; Roseman, 1984), decision making (Kahneman and Tversky, 1979; Messick and McClintock, 1968), goals (Carver and Scheier, 1998; Elliot and Sheldon, 1998), health behavior (Rogers, 1975; Rothman and Salovey, 1997), memory (Förster and Strack, 1996; Kuiper and Derry, 1982), mental control (Newman et al., 1980; Wegner, 1994), motives (McClelland et al., 1953; Birney et al., 1969), perception-attention (Derryberry, 1991; Dixon, 1981), psychobiology (Davidson, 1993; Depue and Iacono, 1989), psycholinguistics (Clark, 1974; Just and Carpenter, 1971), psychopathology (Fowles, 1988; Newman, 1987), self-regulation (Baumeister et al., 1989; Wood et al., 1994), and social interaction (Arkin, 1981; Tedeschi and Norman, 1985).

The approach-avoidance distinction is based in positive–negative valences and their accompanying forces (see Lewin, 1926, 1935). Approach motivation may be defined as the energization of behavior by, or the direction of behavior toward, positive stimuli (objects, events, possibilities), whereas avoidance motivation may be defined as the energization of behavior by, or the direction of behavior away from, negative stimuli (objects, events, possibilities). The etymological root of 'motivation' is 'to move', and the concept of physical or psychological movement is inherent in the approach-avoidance distinction. Positively evaluated stimuli are inherently associated with an approach orientation to bring or keep the stimuli close to the organism (literally or figuratively), whereas negatively evaluated stimuli are inherently associated with an avoidance orientation to push or keep the stimuli away from the organism (literally or figuratively).

A great deal of evidence points to the fundamental nature of approach–avoidance motivation, not only in humans, but also in organisms of varying degrees of complexity. Approach–avoidance processes are present in monkeys (Suomi, 1983), cats (Adamec, 1991), dogs (Goddard and Beilharz, 1985), wolves (MacDonald, 1983), cows (Fordyce et al., 1982), goats (Lyons et al., 1988), marmots (Armitage, 1986), rats (Garcia-Sevilla, 1984), mice (see Kagan, 1998), birds (Verbeek et al., 1994), snakes (Herzog and Burghardt, 1988), fish (Wilson et al., 1993), octopuses (Mather and Anderson, 1993), crustaceans (see Wilson et al., 1994), and even single cell amoebae (Schneirla, 1959; see Elliot and Covington, 2001; Jones and Gosling, in press, for reviews). Approach and avoidance processes are essential for successful adaptation to the environment. Some (Davidson, 1992; Tooby and Cosmides, 1990) characterize approach–avoidance behavioral decisions as the most critical adaptive judgments that organisms have had to make in the evolutionary past. Indeed, it is the adaptive function of approach–avoidance processes – approach processes move the organism toward potentially beneficial stimuli, whereas avoidance processes move the organism away from potentially harmful stimuli – that is presumed to be the reason for the ubiquity of such processes across phyla (Schneirla, 1959).

It is not just the organism's ability to discern between hospitable and hostile stimuli that is central to survival, but also the speed with which such discriminations are made (Berntson et al., 1993; Orians and Heerwagen, 1992). Approach–avoidance evaluative decisions appear to be the primary and most elemental reaction that organisms have to stimuli they encounter in their environment (Zajonc, 1998). These approach–avoidance evaluations take place immediately and without intention or awareness (Bargh, 1997). Indeed, there is some evidence that such automatic evaluations may represent direct responses to stimuli that are unmediated by any higher order cognitive processing (LeDoux, 1987; Shizgal, 1999). At minimum,

it is clear that positively and negatively evaluated stimuli produce a physiological and somatic preparedness for physical movement toward and away from the stimuli, respectively (Chen and Bargh, 1999; Solorz, 1960). These behavioral predispositions may or may not be translated directly into observable behavior (Elliot, 2006; Lang et al., 1997).

In short, the approach-avoidance distinction has a long and rich history in philosophical and psychological thinking about organisms, is present throughout the broad spectrum of animate life, and represents an immediate and automatic reaction to stimuli that has direct behavioral implications. As such, we think that the approach-avoidance distinction is an ideal lens through which to examine the structure of personality.

BASIC PERSONALITY DISPOSITIONS

As noted earlier, three popular approaches to the study of basic dispositions are the trait adjective approach, the affective disposition approach, and the motivational system approach. Of these approaches, the trait adjective approach has attracted the most theoretical and empirical attention. Two trait adjective models have dominated this approach: the 'Big Five' model and the 'Big Three' model. The Big Five model is comprised of neuroticism, extraversion, conscientiousness, agreeableness, and openness to experience (McCrae and Costa, 1987; see Digman, 1990; Goldberg, 1993; John, 1990 for reviews and alternative labels), whereas the Big Three model is comprised of neuroticism, extraversion, and psychoticism (Eysenck, 1985). There is consensual agreement in the literature that the neuroticism and extraversion constructs in the Big Five model correspond directly to the constructs of the same name in the Big Three model (Costa and McCrae, 1992; Eysenck, 1992; Pervin and John, 1999). Obviously there is no agreement between proponents of the Big Five and Big Three on the number of additional constructs needed to account for the basic structure of personality; less obviously, there is only a moderate degree of agreement, both within and between the Big Five and Big Three traditions, on precisely how the agreed-upon 'Big Two' (Wiggins, 1968) constructs should be conceptualized. For the present purposes, it is sufficient to state that neuroticism is typically defined using characteristics such as worry-prone, emotionally unstable, and insecure, whereas extraversion is typically defined using characteristics such as sociable, active, and optimistic.

With regard to the second popular approach, the affective disposition approach, two primary models have emerged. One model, proposed by Tellegen (1985), comprises positive emotionality, negative emotionality, and constraint; and the other model, proposed by Watson and Clark (1993), comprises positive temperament, negative temperament, and disinhibition. These models have focused primarily on the positive emotionality/temperament and negative emotionality/temperament dimensions, and the dimensions of like valence in these models (positive emotionality and positive temperament; negative emotionality and negative temperament) are widely regarded as directly analogous to each other (Clark and Watson, 1999). Positive emotionality and positive temperament (hereby referred to as positive emotionality) are conceptualized as a broad tendency to experience positive emotion and to engage life in a positive manner; negative emotionality and negative temperament (hereby referred to as negative emotionality) are conceptualized as a broad tendency to experience negative emotion and to engage life in a negative manner (Tellegen, 1985; Watson and Clark, 1993). These constructs are similar to the respective trait positive affect and trait negative affect constructs (Watson et al., 1988) that are also quite popular in personality research, except that the positive emotionality and negative emotionality constructs are broader in scope.

With regard to the third popular approach, the motivational system approach, many theorists over the years have proffered that there are two basic, valenced systems that are responsible for energizing affect and behavior. One is an appetitive system that generates positive affect and facilitates behavior, and the other is an aversive system that generates negative affect and inhibits behavior (Cacioppo and Berntson, 1994; Dickinson and Dearing, 1979; Konorski, 1967; Lang et al., 1990; Macintosh, 1983; Panksepp, 1982; Schneirla, 1959; Solomon and Corbitt, 1974). The model that has received the most attention in this area is that offered by Gray (1970). In this model, two conceptual nervous systems are proposed, a behavioral activation system (BAS) that produces positive affect and facilitates behavior, and a behavior inhibition system (BIS) that produces negative affect and inhibits behavior. Several other theorists have proposed constructs that map rather closely onto one or both of the constructs offered by Gray (see Cloninger, 1987; Depue and Collins, 1999; Newman, 1987; Zuckerman, 1991). For simplicity, we will refer to this class of models using the BAS and BIS rubrics.

The trait adjective, affective disposition, and motivational system approaches clearly offer distinct models of the structure of personality with different foci and emphases. However, it is possible to identify areas of convergence among these different approaches, both in terms of the general nature of the basic constructs they propose and in terms of the specific content of these constructs. Regarding the general nature of the proposed constructs, the theorists from each approach describe their constructs as biologically based. An emphasis on biology has been a part of the affective disposition (Tellegen, 1985; Watson and Clark, 1993) and motivational system (Gray, 1970; Konorski, 1967; Schneirla, 1959) approaches since their inception. The same is true of Eysenck's (1967) model. In recent years, advocates of the Big Five model have also begun to focus on and offer speculation about the biological basis of their trait dimensions (McCrae and Costa, 1999). In addition to convergence regarding the biological basis of basic personality constructs, there also seems to be an emerging consensus that these basic constructs are heritable, present in early childhood, relatively stable across the lifespan, and include an affective element. These characteristics are commonly viewed as aspects of temperament (see Buss and Plomin, 1984), and proponents of each of the three approaches have used the term temperament in describing the nature of their proposed constructs (Clark and Watson, 1999; Cloninger, 1987; Eysenck, 1970; Gray, 1982; McRae et al., 2000; Tellegen, 1985; Zuckerman, 1991).

Regarding the specific content of the basic constructs of personality, a number of theorists have speculated about possible conceptual links among different pairs of like-valenced constructs. Some have focused on possible links between the extraversion/neuroticism and positive emotionality/negative emotionality constructs (see Carver et al., 2000; Clark and Watson, 1999; Tellegen, 1985; Watson and Clark, 1993), others have focused on possible links between the positive emotionality/negative emotionality and BAS/BIS constructs (see Clark and Watson, 1999; Tellegen, 1985; Watson, 2000), and still others have focused on possible links between the extraversion/neuroticism and BAS/BIS constructs (indeed it is this link that has been of particular interest to theorists; see Carver et al., 2000; Cloninger, 1987; Depue and Collins, 1999; Gray, 1987; Larsen and Ketelaar, 1991; Lucas et al., 2000; Newman, 1987; Watson, 2000; Zuckerman, 1991). Several researchers have conducted correlational and factor analytic studies designed to examine the proposed associations. This research has tended to yield supportive data in the form of positive relationships among and similar factor loadings for the following variables: extraversion and positive emotionality (Clark and Watson, 1999; Watson and Clark, 1993), neuroticism and negative emotionality

(Clark and Watson, 1999; Watson and Clark, 1993; Zelenksi and Larsen, 1999), positive emotionality and BAS (Carver and White, 1994; Quilty and Oakman, 2004), negative emotionality and BIS (Carver and White, 1994), extraversion and BAS (Ball and Zuckerman, 1991; Carver and White, 1994; Caseras et al., 2003; Corr et al., 1997; Corulla, 1987; Diaz and Pickering, 1993; Fruyt et al., 2000; Gomez et al., 2000; Gomez and Gomez, 2005; Jorm et al., 1999; Muris et al., 2005; Smits and Boeck, 2006; Stallings et al., 1996; Torrubia et al., 2001; Zelenski and Larsen, 1999), and neuroticism and BIS (Ball and Zuckerman, 1991; Caseras et al., 2003; Corr et al., 1997; Diaz and Pickering, 1993; Fruyt et al., 2000; Gomez et al., 2000; Gomez and Gomez, 2005; Heubeck et al., 1998; Jorm et al., 1999; MacAndrew and Steele, 1991; Muris et al., 2005; Smits and Boeck, 2006; Stallings et al., 1996; Torrubia et al., 2001; Torrubia and Tobena, 1984; Zelenski and Larsen, 1999).

Clearly, there are strong reasons to conclude that there is convergence in the like-valenced constructs that have been proposed by the trait adjective, affective disposition, and motivational system approaches to personality. The key question is: What accounts for the shared variance among these constructs?

APPROACH AND AVOIDANCE TEMPERAMENTS CONCEPTUALIZED

It is our contention that the shared variance among the constructs under consideration is best explained by positing the existence of underlying approach and avoidance temperaments. This conceptual move is primarily based on a recognition of the deep, functional nature of approach and avoidance motivation in human behavior. However, it is also more concretely based on a careful inspection of the items commonly used to assess extraversion/neuroticism, positive/negative emotionality, and BAS/BIS; most of these items are explicitly valenced, and many additionally contain reference to the energizing and/or orienting of behavior.

Approach temperament is defined as a general neurobiological sensitivity to positive (i.e. reward) stimuli (present or imagined) that is accompanied by a perceptual vigilance for, an affective reactivity to, and a behavioral predisposition toward such stimuli. Avoidance temperament is defined as a general neurobiological sensitivity to negative (i.e. punishment) stimuli (present or imagined) that is accompanied by a perceptual vigilance for, an affective reactivity to, and a behavioral predisposition toward such stimuli. We use the approach and avoidance labels because the constructs represent motivated reactions to valenced stimuli. We use the temperament label because the constructs represent foundational elements of personality that are presumed to possess the primary characteristics of temperament noted earlier – that is, they are heritable, emerge in early childhood, are stable across the lifespan, and are affective in nature.

Approach and avoidance temperaments naturally emerge from the operation of a broad network of neuroanatomical structures and neurochemical/neuroendocrinological processes. Phylogenetically early approach-avoidance mechanisms are simple and straightforward, and afford low-level responding to concrete environmental stimuli (Schneirla, 1959). Over our lengthy evolutionary history, more complex approach-avoidance mechanisms have emerged in addition to, rather than in place of, these rudimentary mechanisms to afford more sophisticated responding to a broader range of stimuli. Approach and avoidance mechanisms are operative in the spinal chord (Berntson et al., 1993; Lang, 1995), the brainstem (Berridge and Pecina, 1995; Panksepp, 1998), and the cortex (Davidson, 1993; Heller, 1993), as well as in neurotransmitter and hormonal activity (Berridge, 2000; Matthews and Gilland, 2001; Zuckerman, 1995). Interindividual variation

in each of these processes is presumed to contribute to approach and avoidance temperaments; the phylogenetically later mechanisms undoubtedly manifest more variation and therefore contribute disproportionately to approach and avoidance temperaments. In short, human functioning involves a complex, partially redundant, partially independent array of approach-avoidance mechanisms that are perpetually active across the neuraxis (Cacioppo and Berntson, 2001; Stellar and Stellar, 1985; Zuckerman, 1995). The joint operation of these mechanisms produces a net neurobiological sensitivity to valenced stimuli that we label approach and avoidance temperaments.

Functionally, approach and avoidance temperaments are construed as energizers and instigators of valence-based propensities; they are responsible for immediate affective, cognitive, and behavioral reactions to encountered or imagined stimuli. Although humans share approach and avoidance temperaments with lower animals (Jones and Gosling, in press; Schneirla, 1959), human functioning is distinct from the functioning of lower animals in that human behavior often emerges from self-regulatory processes, as well as direct temperamental proclivities per se. That is, human behavior is flexible in that persons may adopt goals (and other forms of self-regulation) that are congruent with and give precise direction to their underlying temperaments, but they may also adopt goals (and other forms of self-regulation) that are incongruent with and override their underlying temperaments (Elliot, 2006; Elliot and Niesta, in press).

Of the three focal approaches to personality structure, our approach and avoidance temperament constructs are most similar to the constructs proposed by motivational system theorists, particularly the BAS and BIS constructs proposed by Gray. In some respects, approach and avoidance temperaments may be seen as extensions of Gray's specific BAS and BIS constructs, which are grounded in a constrained set of neuroanatomical structures and neurophysiological processes (see Gray, 1990). We agree that the motivational systems discussed by Gray are important, and view such systems as integral components of our temperament constructs. It is possible that these motivational systems even serve as central integrators of or operating centers for our temperament constructs. However, we contend that there are other important approach and avoidance mechanisms distributed across the central nervous system that must be considered to fully represent approach and avoidance temperaments. Our knowledge regarding the neurobiology of approach and avoidance processes is still in its infancy, and history has shown a tendency for theorists to underestimate the multiplicity of the biological sources of personality. As such, we believe that it is best, at present, to be tentative in creating biologically based conceptual models, and to realize that the neural substrates and operations implicated in appetitive and aversive processes are likely to be more widely distributed and complex than one might initially anticipate (Panksepp, 1998).

We should add that our approach and avoidance temperament constructs differ from Gray's BAS and BIS constructs in other ways as well. First, Gray portrays BAS as sensitive to stimuli representing reward and non-punishment, and BIS as sensitive to stimuli representing punishment, non-reward, and novelty. In contrast, we view approach temperament as sensitive to reward stimuli per se (absence or presence), and avoidance temperament as sensitive to punishment stimuli per se (absence or presence; see also Carver and Scheier, 1998). Furthermore, we believe that the two temperaments are sensitive to different types of novel stimuli, with approach temperament being sensitive to new stimuli that are interesting and optimally complex (Berlyne, 1960), and avoidance temperament being sensitive to new stimuli that possess characteristics found in inherently engrained fear stimuli (Öhman et al., 2001). Second, Gray characterizes the BAS and BIS

constructs in terms of sensitivity to conditioned stimuli alone. In contrast, we construe the approach and avoidance temperament constructs in terms of sensitivity to both conditioned and unconditioned stimuli (see also Panksepp, 1998). Third, Gray portrays BAS and BIS as having direct effects on behavior. In contrast, we contend that approach and avoidance temperament *can* have a direct effect on behavior, but that they can also influence behavior indirectly as a function of the self-regulation process (see also Elliot and Church, 1997).

In summary, we posit that the extraversion, positive emotionality, and BAS constructs all share the same basic core: approach temperament, whereas neuroticism, negative emotionality, and BIS also share the same basic core: avoidance temperament. That is, approach temperament is posited to underlie the positive characteristics assessed by measures of extraversion (Lucas et al., 2000; Watson and Clark, 1997), the positive affective orientation assessed by measures of positive emotionality (Tellegen, 1985), and the behavioral facilitation and impulsivity assessed by measures of BAS (Depue and Collins, 1999), whereas avoidance temperament is posited to underlie the negative characteristics assessed by measures of neuroticism (Carver et al., 2000; Larsen and Ketelaar, 1991), the negative affective orientation assessed by measures of negative emotionality (Watson, 2000), and the behavioral inhibition and anxiety assessed by measures of BIS (Gray, 1982). Measures of each of these constructs are presumed to emphasize a particular aspect of their corresponding temperament, along with additional aspects of personality that are conceptually unrelated to approach and avoidance temperaments. As such, we do not think that the existing constructs and our temperament constructs are isomorphic, but we do think that much can be gained from interpreting the literatures that have developed around each of the existing constructs through the lens of approach and avoidance temperaments.

EMPIRICAL SUPPORT FOR APPROACH AND AVOIDANCE TEMPERAMENTS

Our extant research designed to empirically validate the approach and avoidance temperament constructs has primarily used exploratory and confirmatory factor analysis (EFA and CFA, respectively) to examine the deep structure of the constructs associated with the trait adjective, affective disposition, and motivational system approaches to personality. These studies have sought to demonstrate that like-valenced representations of each of these three approaches load together on the same underlying factor or latent variable. Furthermore, some of our studies have examined whether the proposed two-factor model is robust when controlling for a variety of response biases and whether this model fits better than alternative models. We have also investigated the link between temperaments and self-regulation in the form of goal adoption, as well as links between approach temperament and aspects of daily experience (e.g. positive affect).

Elliot and Thrash (2002: study 1) assessed the following variables in a sample of university undergraduates: extraversion and neuroticism (using Costa and McCrae's, 1992, NEO five-factor inventory (NEO-FFI)), positive and negative temperament (using Watson and Clark's, 1993, general temperament survey (GTS)), and BAS and BIS (using Carver and White's, 1994, measure). An EFA using principal components analysis with varimax rotation yielded a two-factor solution that accounted for 75.4% of the variance in scores. All variables loaded 0.80 or above on their hypothesized factor, and no cross-loading variables were revealed (all loaded less than 0.30 on the secondary factor). This same pattern of results was obtained by Gable et al., (2003: study 1) in research with university undergraduates using a somewhat different set of constructs (e.g. trait positive and negative affect, instead of positive and negative temperament) and measures (e.g. the Eysenck Personality Questionnaire – Revised

(EPQ-R, Eysenck et al., 1985), instead of the NEO-FFI to assess extraversion and neuroticism).

Having obtained the hypothesized two-factor structure using EFA, Elliot and Thrash (2002: study 2) moved to CFA. Again, a university sample was used and the constructs and measures for the study were the same as those used in the first study. The fit of the two-factor model was examined using covariance matrices as input, and solutions were generated on the basis of maximum likelihood estimation. Both absolute and incremental fit indices revealed that the two-factor model was a good fit to the data. All latent variable variances and factor loadings were strong and highly significant. This same pattern of results was obtained in a later study in Elliot and Thrash (2002: study 6), and by Gable et al. (2003: study 2), who used a somewhat different set of constructs (e.g. trait positive and negative affect, instead of positive and negative temperament in the Gable et al. study) and measures (e.g. the EPQ-R, instead of the NEO-FFI in the Elliot and Thrash study). Both studies used undergraduate samples.

In addition to obtaining support for the two-factor model using CFA, Elliot and Thrash (2002: study 2) also used scores from Paulhus' (1991) balanced inventory of socially desirable responding (BIDR) to examine whether the obtained results were simply due to various forms of response biases. The primary analyses used unique variables derived from the BIDR, specifically self-enhancement response bias and self-protection response bias. Self-enhancement response bias represents a tendency to agree with positive statements about oneself that are uncommon, whereas self-protection response bias represents a tendency to disagree with negative statements about oneself that are common. In a first analysis, self-enhancement response bias scores were residualized out of each of the three approach temperament indicators, self-protection response bias scores were residualized out of each of the three avoidance temperament indicators, and the initial two-factor CFA was repeated with these resid-ualized variables. As in the initial analysis, both absolute and incremental fit indices revealed that the two-factor model was a good fit to the data, and all latent variable variances and factor loadings were strong and highly significant. In a second analysis, a four-factor model was examined in which approach temperament, avoidance temperament, self-enhancement response bias, and self-protection response bias were all modeled as separate latent variables. This model also yielded a good fit to the data and produced strong and highly significant latent variable variances and factor loadings. Furthermore, the four-factor model fit significantly better than a two-factor model created by collapsing approach temperament and self-enhancement response bias into one factor, and avoidance temperament and self-protection response bias into a second factor. In a set of secondary analyses, a number of variants of the afore-mentioned analyses were conducted using the impression management and self-deceptive enhancement indexes of the BIDR. As with the self-enhancement and self-protection response bias analyses, each of these ancillary analyses yielded a good fit to the data, and produced strong and highly significant latent variable variances and factor loadings.

Gable et al. (2003: study 2) further exam-ined the robustness of the two-factor model by examining the viability of two alternative models. The first alternative model was a one-factor model based on the premise that approach and avoidance temperament are opposite sides of the same coin, so to speak, and that indicators of approach temperament would therefore load on one end of a unidi-mensional continuum while indicators of avoidance temperament would load on the opposite end of this continuum. This model fit the data poorly, and the fit was shown to be significantly worse than the fit of the two-factor model. The second alternative model was a three-factor model based on the premise that the structure of the data might simply represent method variance alone,

and that each of the pairs of variables assessed using the same instrument would therefore load together on the same factor. As with the first alternative model, this model fit the data poorly, and the fit was shown to be sig-nificantly worse than the fit of the two-factor model.

Elliot and Thrash (2002: study 6) examined the link between approach and avoidance temperaments and approach and avoidance goal adoption. Three indicators of approach and avoidance temperament were assessed (see the above description for details) and approach and avoidance goals in the achieve-ment domain were assessed, specifically, mastery-approach, performance-approach, and performance-avoidance goals (see Elliot and Harackiewicz, 1996; Elliot and Church, 1997, for details on these goal constructs). An initial set of analyses tested whether approach and avoidance temperaments were empiri-cally distinguishable from approach and avoidance achievement goals. The fit of a five-factor model (two temperament and three goal latent variables) was examined, and both absolute and incremental fit indices revealed that the five-factor model was a good fit to the data; all latent variable variances and factor loadings were strong and highly significant. An alternative model, in which the approach temperament and goal variables formed one latent variable, and the avoidance tempera-ment and goal constructs formed a second latent variable, was rejected based on unac-ceptably low factor loadings for the achieve-ment goals. A full structural equation model then tested approach and avoidance tempera-ments as antecedents of achievement goals. As predicted, approach temperament was shown to be a significant positive predictor of mastery-approach and performance-approach goals, whereas avoidance temperament was shown to be a significant positive predictor of performance-avoidance and performance-approach goals. This pattern of temperament-goal relations represents both valence symmetry (approach in order to approach) and valence override (approach in order to avoid) processes (Elliot, 2006).

Additional evidence of the validity of approach temperament comes from a study by Thrash and Elliot (2004: study 3), in which university undergraduates were participants. The aim of this study was to discriminate the constructs of positive affect and inspiration by showing that they are predicted distally by different traits (approach temperament and openness, respectively) and proximally by different triggering events (reward salience and illumination, respectively). Two findings from this study are particularly relevant to the present chapter. First, a principal component EFA of three approach-temperament-related traits (extraversion, positive emotionality, and BAS) and three openness-related traits (openness to aesthetics, absorption, and self-forgetfulness) yielded a two-factor solution that accounted for 71.3% of the variance in scores. All variables loaded 0.65 or above on the hypothesized factor, and no cross-loading variables were revealed (all loaded 0.31 or less on the secondary factor). Whereas the studies reviewed above indicate that approach temperament is factorially distinct from self-enhancement biases and from achievement goals, this study was the first to show that approach temperament is factorially distinct from another basic, as well as desirable, trait dimension. Moreover, it is particularly noteworthy that approach temperament is distinct from openness-related traits, because, from the perspective of the Big Five approach, openness to experience is the trait dimension that tends to be most strongly related to extraversion (Digman, 1997), and therefore is most in need of discrimination from approach temperament.

The second relevant finding from Thrash and Elliot (2004: study 3) is that composite indexes of approach temperament and openness were linked to different daily outcomes and mediating processes during the course of a two-week diary study. Individuals higher in approach temperament were found to be more prone to positive affect than inspiration, whereas individuals higher in openness were more prone to inspiration than positive affect. These effects were mediated by different triggering events to which individuals high in approach temperament and openness were prone. Individuals higher in approach temperament experienced higher mean levels of reward salience, which in turn predicted positive affect more strongly than inspiration. Individuals higher in openness experienced higher means levels of illumination, which in turn predicted inspiration more strongly than positive affect. Although approach temperament did not predispose individuals to become inspired, it predicted the strength of individuals' approach motivation once they had become inspired. These findings are important because they directly link approach temperament to a theoretically central outcome (i.e. daily positive affect) and mediating process (i.e. reward salience). Moreover, they suggest that approach temperament, which has ancient evolutionary roots, is implicated even in one of the highest and most uniquely human forms of approach motivation (i.e. inspiration).

Thus, the results of the aforementioned studies nicely support the proposition that approach and avoidance temperaments underlie the like-valanced variables commonly used as representations of the trait adjective, affective disposition, and motivational system approaches to personality. Not only was the proposed two-factor solution consistently found to be a good fit to the data, but this two-factor solution withstood the challenge of several plausible alternative solutions. Approach and avoidance were shown to be distinguishable from, but systematically linked to, approach and avoidance goals. Finally, approach temperament was discriminated from openness-related traits and linked to reward salience, positive affect, and inspiration.

A MEASURE OF APPROACH AND AVOIDANCE TEMPERAMENTS

The research reviewed to this point has utilized latent variables or composites created from other constructs to represent approach and avoidance temperaments. This was an important step in our research program, because it allowed us to establish deep connections to the existing literature on personality structure. However, approach and avoidance temperaments are conceptualized as variables in their own right, not simply as foundations of trait adjective, affective disposition, and motivational system variables. Furthermore, assessing approach and avoidance temperaments in the manner that we have in the aforementioned research is quite unwieldy, in that it requires the use of three measures for each temperament construct. As such, an important additional step in our research program has been to create measures that directly assess the approach and avoidance temperament constructs. We (Elliot and Thrash, in prep.) have recently completed four studies designed to take this next step; these studies, all with university undergraduate samples, are overviewed in the following.

As a precursor to the four main studies, a series of pilot studies was conducted to examine a broad sampling of candidate items that covered the content universe under consideration. From these candidates, twelve items were culled, six representing approach temperament and six representing avoidance temperament. In study 1, participants completed these twelve items and the data were submitted to an EFA with principal components extraction and varimax rotation. The analysis yielded two factors with eigenvalues exceeding unity. The first factor accounted for 31.78% of the variance and consisted of the six approach temperament variables, and the second factor accounted for an additional 18.70% of the variance and consisted of the six avoidance temperament variables. For approach temperament, the factor loadings on the primary factor ranged from 0.75 to 0.65, and the factor loadings on the secondary factor ranged from 0.03 to −0.36. For avoidance temperament, the factor loadings on the primary factor ranged from 0.82 to 0.53, and the factor loadings on the secondary factor ranged from 0.10 to −0.24. The internal consistency of both the approach and avoidance temperament measures far exceeded the widely held 0.70 standard, and the correlation between the two measures was −0.27. Thus, the results from this study clearly supported a two-factor structure representing relatively independent approach and avoidance temperament constructs.

The items that comprise this Approach-Avoidance Temperament Questionnaire (ATQ), as well as the participant instructions and response options for the measure, are presented in Appendix A. Two features of this measure are worthy of note. First, approach and avoidance temperament are each posited to be accompanied by a perceptual vigilance for, an affective reactivity to, and a behavioral inclination with regard to valenced stimuli, and each temperament measure includes at least one representative item from each of these three categories. That is, the approach temperament measure includes the item 'I'm always on the lookout for positive opportunities and experiences' to assess perceptual vigilance, 'When good things happen to me, it affects me very strongly' to assess affective reactivity, and 'When I want something, I feel a strong desire to go after it' to assess behavioral inclination. Likewise, the avoidance temperament measure includes the item 'It is easy for me to imagine bad things that might happen to me' to assess perceptual vigilance, 'I react very strongly to bad experiences' to assess affective reactivity, and 'When it looks like something bad could happen, I have a strong urge to escape' to assess behavioral inclination. Second, given the centrality of affect in temperament, each of the temperament measures is weighted toward affective reactivity.

In study 2, participants completed the ATQ, as well as the BIDR to examine both the structure of the ATQ using CFA, and to examine whether the observed patterns were contaminated by various forms of response bias. The two-factor CFA using covariance matrices as input and solutions generated on the basis of maximum likelihood estimation confirmed the EFA results. Both absolute and incremental fit indices revealed that the two-factor model was a good fit to the data, and all latent variable variances and factor loadings were strong and highly significant. The same set of response bias analyses used in Elliot and Thrash (2002: study 2) were examined in this study (self-enhancement response bias, self-protection response bias, impression management, and self-deceptive enhancement). Each model that was tested yielded a good fit to the data, and produced strong and highly significant latent variable variances and factor loadings. Clearly, the ATQ is capturing systematic variance that is independent of response bias.

In study 3, participants completed the ATQ and established indicators of the trait adjective, affective disposition, and motivational system approaches to personality: extraversion and neuroticism (using the EPQ-R), trait positive and negative affect (using the positive affect/negative affect schedule (Watson et al., 1988)), and BAS and BIS (using Carver and White's, 1994, measure). They also completed the BIDR. In an initial analysis, structural equation modeling was used to test a model in which an approach temperament latent variable (as indicated by the ATQ approach temperament items) underlies extraversion, trait positive affect, and BAS latent variables, and an avoidance temperament latent variable (as indicated by the ATQ avoidance temperament items) underlies neuroticism, trait negative affect, and BIS latent variables. Both absolute and incremental fit indices revealed that the two-factor model was a good fit to the data, and all latent variable variances and factor loadings were strong and highly significant. Additional analyses were then conducted to test for the same set of response biases examined in study 2. Each of these models also yielded a good fit to the data and produced strong and highly significant latent variable variances and factor loadings. These results support the notion that approach temperament underlies extraversion, trait positive affect, and BAS, that avoidance temperament underlies neuroticism, trait negative affect, BIS, and that these patterns are not a mere function of response bias.

In study 4, participants completed the ATQ and a measure of approach and avoidance achievement goals. Four achievement goals were assessed with Elliot and McGregor's (2001) Achievement Goal Questionnaire, specifically, the three goals examined in Elliot and Thrash (2002: study 6) – mastery-approach, performance-approach, and performance avoidance – as well as mastery-avoidance goals (see Elliot, 1999; Elliot and McGregor, 2001; for details on the mastery-avoidance goal construct). Grade point average (GPA) and exam performance data were also acquired in this study. An initial set of analyses analogous to those used in Elliot and Thrash (2002: study 6) tested whether approach and avoidance temperaments were empirically distinguishable from approach and avoidance achievement goals. A six-factor model comprised of the two temperament latent variables and the four goal latent variables provided a good fit to the data, and all latent variable variances and factor loadings were strong and highly significant. An alternative model in which the approach temperament and approach goal variables formed one latent variable, and the avoidance temperament and avoidance goal constructs formed a second latent variable, was rejected based on unacceptably low factor loadings for the achievement goals. A structural model then tested approach and avoidance temperaments as predictors of achievement goals. As predicted, approach temperament was shown to be a significant positive predictor of mastery-approach and performance-approach goals, whereas avoidance temperament was shown to be a significant positive predictor of mastery-avoidance and performance-avoidance. The only proposed path that did not receive support was that between avoidance temperament and performance-approach goals. A path model was then tested in which the aforementioned model was supplemented with GPA and exam performance variables. In line with prior research (see Elliot, 2005, for a review), performance-approach goals were expected to positively predict exam performance, whereas performance-avoidance goals were expected to negatively predict exam performance (both controlling for GPA).

Approach and avoidance temperaments were expected to lead to achievement goal adoption, but to have no proximal direct influence on exam performance. The data confirmed each of these predictions. Thus, this study demonstrates that temperaments are not only structurally distinct from goals, but also have a different functional role in the prediction of important outcomes.

SUMMARY AND FINAL WORDS

In this chapter, we have laid out the conceptual rationale for considering approach and avoidance temperaments as basic constructs that serve as the common foundation for variables emerging from the popular trait adjective, affective disposition, and motivational system approaches to personality structure. We have also overviewed published and ongoing research supporting the idea of approach and avoidance temperaments, and highlighting the links between these temperament constructs, goals, and real-world outcomes. Approach and avoidance temperaments indeed appear to represent foundational, core components of personality that play an important role in the production of affect, cognition, and behavior.

Identifying approach and avoidance temperaments as the 'deep structure' underlying other dispositions is yet another example of the utility of the approach-avoidance distinction. This distinction is neither new, nor provocative in and of itself, but both the breadth of its reach in explaining and predicting psychological functioning in humans (and lower organisms) is nothing short of astounding. Certainly theoretical conceptualizations of human functioning require (much) more than the approach–avoidance distinction to sufficiently account for affect, cognition, and behavior. However, the present chapter highlights the fact that it is not only necessary to attend to this distinction in our theoretical models, it is foundationally necessary.

REFERENCES

Adamec, R. (1991) 'Anxious personality in the cat', in B. Carroll and J. Barrett (eds), *Psychopathology and the Brain*. New York: Raven Press, pp. 153–68.

Arkin, R. (1981) 'Self-presentation styles', in J. Tedeschi (ed.), *Impression Management Theory and Social Psychological Research*. New York: Academic Press, pp. 311–33.

Armitage, K. (1986), Individuality, Social Behavior, and Reproductive Success in Yellow-Bellied Marmots Kenneth B. Armitage Ecology, 67(5): 1186–93.

Ball, S.A. and Zuckerman, M. (1991) 'Sensation seeking, Eysenck's personality dimensions and reinforcement sensitivity in concept formation', *Personality and Individual Differences*, 11(2): 343–53.

Bargh, J. (1997) 'The automaticity of everyday life', *Advances in Social Cognition*, 20–7.

Baumeister, R., Tice, D. and Hutton, D. (1989) 'Self-presentational motivations and personality differences in self-esteem', *Journal of Personality*, 57(4): 547–79.

Bentham, J. (1779/1879) *Introduction to the Principles of Morals and Legislation*. Oxford: Clarendon Press.

Berlyne, D.E. (1960) *Conflict, Arousal, and Curiosity*. New York: McGraw-Hill.

Bernston, G.G., Boyson, S.T. and Cacioppo, J.T. (1993) 'Neurobehavioral organization and the cardinal principle of evaluative bivalence', *Annals of the New York Academy of Sciences*, 702(11): 75–102.

Berridge, K. (2000) 'Irrational pursuit: Hyperincentives from a visceral brain', in I. Brocas and J. Carrillo (eds), *Psychology and Economics*. Oxford: Oxford University Press.

Berridge, K. and Pecina, S. (1995) Benzodiazepines, appetite, and taste palatability. *Neuroscience and Biobehavioral Reviews*, 19(1): 121–31.

Birney, R., Burdick, H. and Teevan, R. (1969) *Fear of Failure*. New York: Van Norstrand-Reinhold Co.

Buss, A. and Plomin, R. (1984) *Temperament: Early Developing Personality Traits*. Hillsdale, NJ: Erlbaum.

Cacioppo, J. and Bernston, G. (1994) Relationship between attitudes and evaluative space: A critical review, with emphasis on the separability of positive and negative substrates, *Psychological Bulletin*, 115(3): 401–22.

Cacioppo, J.J. and Berntson, G.G. (2001) 'The affect system and racial prejudice', in J. Bargh and D. Apsley (eds), *Unraveling the Complexities of Social Life: A Festschrift in Honor of Robert B. Zajonc*. Washington, DC: American Psychological Association, pp. 95–110.

Carver, C. and Scheier, M. (1998) *On the Self-Regulation of Behavior*. New York: Cambridge University Press.

Carver, C.S., Sutton, S.K. and Scheier, M.F. (2000) 'Action, emotion, and personality: Emerging conceptual integration', *Personality and Social Psychology Bulletin*, 26(6): 741–51.

Carver, C.S. and White, T.L. (1994) 'Behavioral inhibition, behavioral activation, and affective responses to impending reward and punishment: The BIS/BAS scales', *Journal of Personality and Social Psychology*, 67(2): 319–33.

Caseras, X., Avila, C. and Torrubia, R. (2003) 'The measurement of individual differences in Behavioral Inhibition and Behavioral Activation Systems: A comparison of personality scales', *Personality and Individual Differences*, 34(6): 999–1013.

Chen, M. and Bargh, J. (1999) 'Consequences of automatic evaluation: Immediate behavioral predispositions to approach or avoid the stimulus', *Personality and Social Psychology Bulletin*, 25(2): 215–234.

Clark, H. (1974) 'Semantics and comprehension', in T. Seebok (ed.), *Current Trends in Linguistics* (Vol. 12). Lisse: Mouton & Co., pp. 1291–428.

Clark, L.A. and Watson, D. (1999) 'Temperament: A new paradigm for trait psychology', in L. Pervin and O. John (eds), *Handbook of Personality: Theory and Research*. New York: Guilford, pp. 399–423.

Cloninger, C.R. (1987) 'A systematic method for clinical description and classification of personality variants', *Archives of General Psychiatry*, 44(3): 573–88.

Corr, P.J., Pickering, A.D. and Gray, J.A. (1997) 'Personality, punishment, and procedural learning: A test of J.A. Gray's anxiety theory', *Journal of Personality and Social Psychology*, 73: 337–44.

Corulla, W.J. (1987) 'A psychometric investigation of the Eysenck Personality Questionnaire (Revised) and its relationship to the Impulsiveness Questionnaire', *Personality and Individual Differences*, 8(5): 651–8.

Costa, P.T. and McCrae, R.R. (1992) *Revised NEO Personality Inventory (NEOPI-R) and Five Factor Inventory (NEO-FFI) Professional Manual*. Odessa, FL: Psychological Assessment Resources.

Davidson, R. (1992) 'Prolegomenon to the structure of emotion: Gleanings from neuropsychology', *Cognition and Emotion*, 6(2): 245–68.

Davidson, R. (1993) 'Cerebral asymmetry and emotion: conceptual and methodological conundrums', *Cognition and Emotion*, 7(1): 115–38

Depue, R. and Collins, P.F. (1999) 'Neurobiology of the structure of personality: Dopamine, facilitation of incentive motivation, and extraversion', *Behavioral and Brain Sciences*, 22(3): 491–569.

Depue, R. and Iacono, W. (1989) 'Neurobehavioral aspects of affective disorders', *Annual Review of Psychology*, 40(1): 457–92.

Derryberry, D. (1991) 'The immediate effects of positive and negative feedback signals', *Journal of Personality and Social Psychology*, 61(2): 267–78.

Diaz, A. and Pickering, A.D. (1993) 'The relationship between Gray's and Eysenck's personality spaces', *Personality and Individual Differences*, 15(3): 297–305.

Dickinson, A. and Dearing, M. (1979) 'Appetitive-aversive interactions and inhibitory processes', in A. Dickinson and R. Boakes (eds), *Mechanisms of Learning and Motivation*. Hillsdale, NJ: LEA, pp. 203–31.

Digman, J. (1990) 'Personality structure: Emergence of the five-factor model', *Annual Review of Psychology*, 41(1): 417–40.

Digman, J. (1997) 'Higher-order factors of the Big Five', *Journal of Personality and Social Psychology*, 73(6): 1246–56.

Dixon, N. (1981) *Preconscious Processing*. New York: Wiley.

Elliot, A. (1999) 'Approach and avoidance motivation and achievement goals', *Educational Psychologist*, 34(3): 169–89.

Elliot, A.J. (2005) 'A conceptual history of the achievement goal construct', in A. Elliot and

C. Dweck (eds), *Handbook of Competence and Motivation*. New York: Guilford, pp. 52–72.

Elliot, A.J. (2006) 'The hierarchical model of approach-avoidance motivation', *Motivation and Emotion*, 30(2): 111–6.

Elliot, A.J. and Church, M.A. (1997) 'A hierarchical model of approach and avoidance achievement motivation', *Journal of Personality and Social Psychology*, 72(1): 218–32.

Elliot, A.J. and Covington, M.V. (2001) 'Approach and avoidance motivation', *Educational Psychology Review*, 13(2): 73–92.

Elliot, A.J. and Harackiewicz, J.M. (1996) 'Approach and avoidance achievement goals and intrinsic motivation: A mediational analysis', *Journal of Personality and Social Psychology*, 70(3): 461–75.

Elliot, A.J. and McGregor, H.A. (2001) 'A 2 x 2 achievement goal framework, *Journal of Personality and Social Psychology*, 80(3): 501–19.

Elliot, A.J. and Niesta, D. (in press) 'Goals in the context of the hierarchical model of approach-avoidance motivation', in G. Moskowitz and H. Grant (eds), *Goals.* New York: Guilford.

Elliot, A. and Sheldon, K. (1998) 'Avoidance personal goals and the personality-illness relationship', *Journal of Personality and Social Psychology*, 75(5): 1282–99.

Elliot, A.J. and Thrash, T.M. (2002) 'Approach-avoidance motivation in personality: Approach and avoidance temperaments and goals. *Journal of Personality and Social Psychology*, 82(5): 804–18.

Elliot, A.J. and Thrash, T.M. (in preparation) 'Approach and avoidance temperaments: Measurement and predictive utility'.

Eysenck, H.J. (1992) 'A reply to Costa and McCrae: P or A and C – the role of theory', *Personality and Individual Differences*, 13(8): 867–8.

Eysenck, H.J. (1967) *The Biological Basis of Personality*. Springfield, IL: Charles C. Thomas.

Eysenck, H.J. (1970) *The Structure of Human Personality* (3rd edn.) London: Methuen.

Eysenck, H.J. and Eysenck, M.W. (1985) *Personality and Individual Differences: A Natural Science Approach*. New York: Plenum.

Eysenck, S.B.G., Eysenck, H.J. and Barret, P. (1985) 'A revised version of the psychoticism scale', *Personality and Individual Differences*, 6: 21–9.

Fordyce, G., Goddard, M. and Seifert, G. (1982) 'The measurement of temperament in cattle and the effect of experience and genotype', *Proceedings of the Australian Society of Animal Production*, 14(3): 329–32.

Förster, J. and Strack, F. (1996) 'Influence of overt head movements on memory for valenced words: A case of conceptual-motor compatibility', *Journal of Personality and Social Psychology*, 71(3): 421–30.

Fowles, D. (1988) 'Psychophysiology and psychopathology: A motivational approach', *Psychophysiology*, 25(3): 373–91.

Fruyt, F., Van De Wiele, L. and Van Heeringen, C. (2000) Cloninger's psychobiological model of temperament and character and the Five-Factor model of personality', *Personality and Individual Differences*, 29(3): 441–52.

Gable, S., Reis, H. and Elliot, A.J. (2003) 'Evidence for bivariate systems: An empirical test of appetition and aversion across domains', *Journal of Research in Personality*, 37(5): 349–72.

Garcia-Sevilla, L. (1984) 'Extraversion and neuroticism in rats', *Personality and Individual Differences*, 5(5): 511–32.

Goddard, M. and Beilharz, R. (1985) 'A multivariate analysis of the fearfulness potential in potential guide dogs', *Behavioral Genetics*, 15(1): 69–89.

Goldberg, L.R. (1993) 'The structure of phenotypic personality traits', *American Psychologist*, 48(1): 26–34.

Gomez, R., Cooper, A. and Gomez, A. (2000) 'Susceptibility to positive and negative mood states: Test of Eysenck's, Gray's, and Newman's theories', *Personality and Individual Differences*, 29(2): 351–65.

Gomez, R. and Gomez, A. (2005) 'Convergent, discriminant, and concurrent validities of measures of behavioral approach and behavioral inhibition systems: Confirmatory factor analytic approach', *Personality and Individual Differences*, 38(1): 87–102.

Gray, J.A. (1970) 'The psychophysiological basis of introversion-extroversion', *Behavior Research and Therapy*, 8(3): 249–66.

Gray, J. (1982) *The Neuropsychology of Anxiety*. New York: Oxford University Press.

Gray, J.A. (1987) *The Psychology of Fear and Stress* (2nd edn). New York: Cambridge.

Gray, J.A. (1990) 'Brain systems that mediate both emotion and cognition', *Cognition and Emotion*, 4: 269–88.

Heller, W. (1993) 'Neurophyschological mechanisms of individual differences in emotion, personality, and arousal', *Neuropsychology*, 7(4): 476–89.

Herzog, H.A. Jr. and Burghardt, G.M. (1988) 'Development of antipredator responses in snakes', *Ethology*, 77(2): 250–8.

Heubeck, B.G., Wilkinson, R.B. and Cologon, J. (1998) 'A second look at Carver and White's (1994) BIS/BAS scales', *Personality and Individual Differences*, 25(4): 785–800.

Higgins, E.T. (1997) 'Beyond pleasure and pain', *American Psychologist*, 52(12): 1280–300.

Higgins, E.T., Shah, J.Y. and Friedman, R. (1997) 'Emotional responses to goal attainment: Strength of regulatory focus as moderator', *Journal of Personality and Social Psychology*, 72(3): 515–25.

James, W. (1890) *The Principles of Psychology* (Vol. 2). New York: Holt.

John, O.P. (1990) 'The "Big Five" factor taxonomy: Dimensions of personality in the natural language and in questionnaires', in L. Pervin (ed.) *Handbook of Personality: Theory and Research*. New York: Guilford, pp. 66–100.

Jones, A.C. and Gosling, S.D. (in press) 'Individual differences in approach and avoidance motivation in animals', in A. Elliot (ed.), *Handbook of Approach and Avoidance Motivation*. Mahwah, NJ: Erlbaum.

Jorm, A.F., Christensen, H., Henderson, A.S., Jacomb, P.A., Korten, A.E. and Rodgers, B. (1998) 'Using the BIS/BAS scales to measure behavioral inhibition and behavioral activation: Factor structure, validity and norms in a large community sample', *Personality and Individual Differences*, 26(1): 49–58.

Just, M. and Carpenter, P. (1971) 'Comprehension of negation with quantification', *Journal of Verbal Learning and Verbal Behavior*, 12(1): 21–31.

Kagan, J. (1998) 'Biology and the child', in N. Eisenberg (ed.), *Handbook of Child Psychology*. New York: John Wiley & Sons.

Kahneman, D. and Tversky, A. (1979) 'Prospect theory: An analysis of decision under risk', *Econometrica*, 47(2): 263–91.

Konorski, J. (1967) *Integrative Activity of the Brain: An Interdisciplinary Approach*. Chicago, IL: University of Chicago Press.

Kuiper, N. and Derry, P. (1982) 'Depressed and nondepressed content self-reference in mild depression', *Journal of Personality*, 50(1): 67–79.

Lang, P. (1995) 'Studies of motivation and attention', *American Psychologist*, 50(5): 372–85.

Lang, P.J., Bradley, M.M. and Cuthbert, B.N. (1990) 'Emotion, attention, and the startle', *Psychological Review*, 97(3): 377–95.

Lang, P.J., Bradley, M.M. and Cuthbert, B.N. (1997) 'Motivated attention: Affect, activation, and action', in P. Lang, R. Simmons and M. Balaban (eds), *Attention and Orienting: Sensory and Motivational Processes*. Mahwah, NJ: Erlbaum, pp. 97–135.

Larsen, R.J. and Ketelaar, T. (1991) 'Personality and susceptibility to positive and negative emotional states', *Journal of Personality and Social Psychology*, 61(1): 132–40.

Lazarus, R. (1991) *Emotion and Adaption*. New York: Oxford University Press.

LeDoux, J. (1987) 'Emotion', in F. Plum (ed.), *Handbook of Physiology* (Vol. 5). Bethesda, MD: American Physiological Society, pp. 419–54.

Lewin, K. (1926). Untersuchungen zur Handlungs- und Affektpsychologie: I. Vorbemerkungen über die psychischen Kräfte und Energien und über die Struktur der Seele [in German]. *Psychologische Forschung*, 7: 294–329.

Lewin, K. (1935) *A Dynamic Theory of Personality*. New York: McGraw-Hill.

Lucas, R.E., Diener, E., Grob, A., Suh, M.E. and Shao, L. (2000) 'Cross-cultural evidence for the fundamental features of extraversion', *Journal of Personality and Social Psychology*, 79(3): 452–68.

Lyons, D., Price, E. and Moberg, G. (1988) 'Individual differences in temperament of domestic dairy goats: Constancy and change', *Animal Behavior*, 36(5): 1323–33.

MacAndrew, C. and Steele, T. (1991) 'Gray's behavioral inhibition system: A psychometric examination', *Personality and Individual Differences*, 12(2): 157–71.

MacDonald, K. (1983) 'Stability and individual differences in behavior in a litter of wolf cubs (canis lupus)', *Journal of Comparative Psychology*, 97(2): 99–106.

Macintosh, N.J. (1983) *Conditioning and Associative Learning*. Oxford: Clarendon Press.

Mather, J. and Anderson, R. (1993) 'Personalities of octopuses (octopus robescens)', *Journal of Comparative Psychology*, 107(3): 336–40.

Matthews, G. and Gilliland, K. (2001) 'Personality, biology and cognitive science: A reply to Corr', *Personality and Individual Differences*, 30(2): 353–62.

McClelland, D.C., Atkinson, J.W., Clark, R.A. and Lowell, E.L. (1953) *The Achievement Motive*. New York: Appleton-Century-Crofts.

McCrae, R.R. and Costa, P.T. (1987) 'Validation of the five-factor model of personality across instruments and observers', *Journal of Personality and Social Psychology*, 52(1): 81–90.

McCrae, R.R. and Costa, P.T. (1999) 'A five-factor theory of personality', in L. Pervin and O. John (eds), *Handbook of Personality: Theory and Research* (2nd edn). New York: Guilford, pp. 139–53.

McCrae, R.R., Costa, P.T., Ostendorf, F., Angleitner, A., Hrebickova, M., Avia, M.D. et al. (2000) 'Nature over nurture: Temperament, personality and lifespan development', *Journal of Personality and Social Psychology*, 78(1): 173–86.

Messick, D. and McClintock, C. (1968) 'Motivational bases of choice in experimental games', *Journal of Experimental Social Psychology*, 4(1): 1–25.

Moos, R. and Schaefer, J. (1993) 'Coping resources and processes: Current concepts and measures', in L. Goldberger and S. Brenznitz (eds), *Handbook of Stress: Theoretical and Clinical Aspects* (2nd edn). New York: Free Press, pp. 234–57.

Muris, P., Meesters, C., de Kanter, E., Timmerman, P.E. (2005) 'Behavioral inhibition and behavioral activation system scales for children: relationships with Eysenck's personality traits and psychopathological symptoms', *Personality and Individual Differences*, 38(4): 831–41.

Newman, J. (1987) 'Reaction to punishment in extraverts and psychopaths: Implications for the impulsive behavior of disinhibited individuals', *Journal of Research in Personality*, 21(4): 464–80.

Newman, J., Wolff, W. and Hearst, E. (1980) 'The feature-positive effect in adult human subjects', *Journal of Experimental Psychology: Human Learning and Memory*, 6(5): 630–50.

Öhman, A. (1997) 'As fast as the blink of an eye: evolutionary preparedness for preattentive processing of threat', in P. Lang, R. Simmons and M. Balaban (eds), *Attention and Orienting: Sensory and Motivational Processes*. Florida: Lawrence Erlbaum Associates, pp. 87–135.

Öhman, A., Flykt, A. and Esteves, F. (2001) 'Emotion drives attention: Detecting the snake in the grass', *Journal of Experimental Psychology: General*, 130(3): 466–78.

Orians, G. and Heerwagen, J. (1992) 'Evolved responses to landscapes', in J. Barkow, L. Cosmides, and J. Tooby (eds), *The Adapted Mind*. New York: Oxford University Press, pp. 555–79.

Overmeir, J. and Archer, T. (1989) 'Historical perspectives on the study of aversively motivated behavior: History and new look', in T. Archer and L. Nilsson (eds), *Aversion, Avoidance, and Anxiety: Perspectives on Aversively Motivated Behavior*. Mahwah, NJ: LEA, pp. 3–39.

Panksepp, J. (1982) Toward a general psychobiological theory of emotions. *Behavioral and Brain Sciences*, 5(4): 407–67.

Panksepp, J. (1998) *Affective Neuroscience: The Foundations of Human and Animal Emotions*. New York: Oxford University Press.

Paulhus, D.L. (1991) 'Measurement and control of response bias', in J. Robinson, P. Shaver, and L.S. Wrightsman (eds), *Measures of Personality and Social Psychological Attitudes*. New York: Academic Press, pp. 1–59.

Pervin, L.A. and John, O.P. (1999) *Handbook of Personality: Theory and Research* (2nd edn). New York: Guilford.

Quilty, L.C. and Oakman, J.M. (2004) 'The assessment of behavioral activation – The relationship between positive emotionality and the Behavioral Activation System', *European Journal of Personality*, 18(7): 557–71.

Rogers, R. (1975) 'A protection motivation theory of fear appeals and attitude change', *Journal of Psychology*, 91(1): 93–114.

Roseman, I. (1984) 'Cognitive determinants of emotions: A structural theory', in P. Shaver (ed.), *Review of Personality and Social Psychology* (Vol. 5). Beverly Hills, CA: Sage, pp. 11–36.

Roth, S. and Cohen, L. (1986) 'Approach, avoidance, and coping with stress', *American Psychologist*, 41(7): 813–9.

Rothman, A. and Salovey, P. (1997) 'Shaping perceptions to motivate healthy behavior: The role of message framing', *Psychological Bulletin*, 121(1): 3–19.

Schneirla, T.C. (1959) 'An evolutionary and developmental theory of biphasic processes underlying approach and withdrawal', in M. Jones (ed.), *Nebraska Symposium on Motivation*. Lincoln: University of Nebraska Press, pp. 1–42.

Shizgal, P. (1999) 'On the neural computation of utility: Implications from studies of brain stimulation reward', in D. Kahneman, E. Diener and N. Schwarz (eds), *Wellbeing: The Foundations of Hedonic Psychology*. New York: Russell Sage Foundation, pp. 500–24.

Smits, D.J. and Boeck, P.D. (2006) 'From BIS/BAS to the Big Five', *European Journal of Personality*, 20(2): 255–70.

Solomon, R. and Corbit, J. (1974) 'An opponent-process theory of motivation: I. Temporal dynamics of affect', *Psychological Review*, 81(2):119–45.

Solorz, A. (1960) 'Latency of instrumental responses as a function of compatibility with the meaning of eliciting verbal signs', *Journal of Experimental Psychology*, 59(2): 239–45.

Stallings, M.C., Hewitt, J.K., Cloninger, C.R., Heath, A.C. and Eaves, L.J. (1996) 'Genetic and environmental structure of the Tridimensional Personality Questionnaire: Three or four temperament dimensions', *Journal of Personality and Social Psychology*, 70(1): 127–40.

Stellar, J.R. and Stellar, E. (1985) *The Neurobiology of Motivation and Reward*. New York: Springer-Verlag.

Suomi, S. (1983) 'Social development in rhesus monkeys: Consideration of individuals differences', in A. Oliverio and M. Zappella (eds), *The Behavior of Human Infants*. New York: Plenum Press, pp. 71–92.

Tedechsi, J. and Norman, N. (1985) 'Social power, self-presentation, and the self', in B. Schlenker (ed.), *The Self and Social Life*. New York: McGraw-Hill, pp. 293–322.

Tellegen, A. (1985) 'Structures of mood and personality and their relevance to assessing anxiety, with an emphasis on self-report', in A. Tuma and J. Maser (eds), *Anxiety and the Anxiety Disorders*. Hillsdale, NJ: Erlbaum.

Tesser, A. and Martin, L. (1996) 'The psychology of evaluation', in E.T. Higgins and A. Kruglanski (eds), *Social Psychology: Handbook of Basic Principles*. New York: Guilford, pp. 400–32.

Thrash, T.M. and Elliot, A.J. (2004) 'Inspiration: Core characteristics, component processes, antecedents, and function', *Journal of Personality and Social Psychology*, 87(6): 957–73.

Tomaka, J. and Blascovich, J. (1994) 'Effects of justice beliefs on cognitive appraisal of, and subjective, physiological, and behavioral responses to, potential stress', *Journal of Personality and Social Psychology*, 67(4): 732–40.

Tooby, J. and Cosmides, L. (1990) 'The past explains the present: Emotional adaptations and the structure of ancestral environments', *Ethology and Sociobiology*, 11(4): 375–424.

Torrubia, R., Avila, C., Molto, J. and Caseras, X. (2001) 'The Sensitivity to Punishment and Sensitivity to Reward questionnaire (SPSRQ) as a measure of Gray's anxiety and impulsivity dimensions', *Personality and Individual Differences*, 31(6): 837–62.

Torrubia, R. and Tobena, A. (1984) 'A scale for the assessment of "susceptibility to punishment" as a measure of anxiety: Preliminary results', *Personality and Individual Differences*, 5(3): 371–5.

Verbeek, M., Drent, P. and Wiepkema, P. (1994) 'Consistent individual differences in early exploratory behavior of male great tits', *Animal Behavior*, 48(5): 1113–21.

Watson, D. (2000) *Mood and Temperament*. New York: Guilford.

Watson, D. and Clark, L.A. (1993) 'Behavioral disinhibition versus constraint: A dispositional perspective', in D.M. Wegner and J.W. Pennebaker (eds), *Handbook of Mental Control*. New York: Prentice Hall, pp. 506–27.

Watson, D. and Clark, L.A. (1997) 'Extraversion and its positive emotional core', in R. Hogan, J. Johnson, and S. Briggs (eds), *Handbook of*

Personality Psychology. San Diego: Academic Press, pp. 767–93.

Watson, D., Clark, L.A. and Tellegen, A. (1988) 'Development and validation of brief measures of positive and negative affect: The PANAS scales', *Journal of Personality and Social Psychology*, 54(6): 1063–70.

Wegner, D. (1994) 'Ironic processes of mental control', *Psychological Review*, 101(1): 34–52.

Wiggins, J.S. (1968) 'Personality structure', *Annual Review of Psychology*, 19(1): 293–350.

Wilson, D., Clark, A., Coleman, K. and Dearstyne, T. (1994) 'Shyness and boldness in humans and other animals', *Trends in Ecology and Evolution*, 9(11): 442–6.

Wilson, D., Coleman, K., Clark, A. and Biederman, L. (1993) 'Shy-bold continuum in pumpkin-seed sunfish (Lepomis gibbosus): An ecological study of a psychological trait', *Journal of Comparative Psychology*, 107(3): 250–60.

Winter, D.G., John, O.P., Stewart, A.J., Klohnen, E.C. and Duncan, L. (1998) 'Traits and motives: Toward and integration of two traditions in personality research. *Psychological Review*, 105(2): 230–50.

Wood, J.V., Giordano-Beach, M., Taylor, K.L., Michela, J.L. and Gaus, B. (1994) 'Strategies of social comparison among people with low self-esteem: Self-protection and self-enhancement', *Journal of Personality and Social Psychology*, 67(4): 713–31.

Zajonc, R. (1998) 'Emotion', in D. Gilbert, S. Fiske and G. Lindzey (eds), *The Handbook of Social Psychology* (4th edn). New York: McGraw-Hill, pp. 591–632.

Zelenski, J.M., and Larsen, R.J. (1999) 'Susceptibility to affect: A comparison of three personality taxonomies', *Journal of Personality*, 67(5): 761–92.

Zuckerman, M. (1991) *Psychology of Personality*. Cambridge: Cambridge University Press.

Zuckerman, M. (1995) 'Good and bad humors: Biochemical bases of personality and its disorders', *Psychological Science*, 6(6): 325–32.

APPENDIX A

Please indicate how much you agree or disagree with each of the following statements by writing a number in the space provided. All of your responses are anonymous and confidential. Please select numbers according to the following scale:

1	2	3	4	5	6	7
Strongly disagree			Neither agree nor disagree			Strongly agree

1 By nature, I am a very nervous person.
2 Thinking about the things I want really energizes me.
3 It doesn't take much to make me worry.
4 When I see an opportunity for something I like, I immediately get excited.
5 It doesn't take a lot to get me excited and motivated.
6 I feel anxiety and fear very deeply.
7 I react very strongly to bad experiences.
8 I'm always on the lookout for positive opportunities and experiences.
9 When it looks like something bad could happen, I have a strong urge to escape.
10 When good things happen to me, it affects me very strongly.
11 When I want something, I feel a strong desire to go after it.
12 It is easy for me to imagine bad things that might happen to me.

Scoring key

Approach temperament = item 2 + item 4 + item 5 + item 8 + item 10 + item 11

Avoidance temperament = item 1 + item 3 + item 6 + item 7 + item 9 + item 12

16

Biological Substrate of Personality Traits Associated with Aggression

Marijn Lijffijt, Alan C. Swann and F. Gerard Moeller

INTRODUCTION

Despite a major decrease during the last decade in aggressive and violent offences, countering a surge during the early 1990s (see Figure 16.1), interpersonal aggression and violence remain a huge problem for society at large as well as a major political and scientific challenge. At the start of the twenty-first century, 1.3 to 1.4 million violent crimes were reported to the police, approximately one violent act per 200 citizens. Arrest rates followed the trend in crime rate (see Figure 16.1). Approximately 600,000 arrests per year are being made for violent offences alone, solving 40–50% of these crimes.

Aggressive and violent behaviour is also a common phenomenon in individuals meeting criteria for DSM-IV axis-I and axis-II diagnoses, such as schizophrenia, bipolar disorder, substance abuse, borderline personality disorder, and antisocial personality disorder (Moeller et al., 2001; Swann, 2003). The same has been reported for psychiatric disorders in children and adolescents, such as paediatric bipolar disorder, autism, and attention deficit hyperactivity disorder (Jensen et al., 2007). This was reason for a group of patients and family advocates, clinicians, researchers, the Food and Drug Administration (FDA), the National Institute of Mental Health (NIMH), and the pharmaceutical industry to issue a consensus report advising to include aggression as a separate symptom across the several psychiatric diagnoses in childhood and adolescence (Jensen et al., 2007). Thus, violent behaviour is not incidental in our

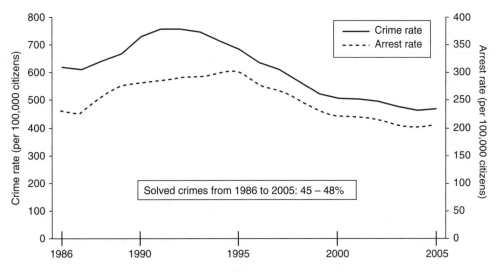

Figure 16.1 Crime and arrest rates in the US between 1986 and 2005. The vertical bar on the left side of the graph represents crime rate, and the vertical bar on the right side of the graph represents arrest rate. Note the difference in scaling for both rates.
Source: Federal Bureau of Investigation Uniform Crime Reports, 2006

society, and warrants continuous aggressive research into predictors and causes for aggression and violence in the society at large and within specific patient groups.

A large number of studies has investigated aggressive behaviour by asking aggressors to report how they thought, felt, and behaved. These reports generally focus on a consistent pattern of behaviour across several years, or on mood states and thoughts just moments before an aggressive act was committed. These self-report measures revealed potential markers in the personality of the aggressor, which can be combined with the literature on the influence of biological and environmental factors on aggression. In this chapter we will discuss aggressive and violent behaviour from the standpoint of personality traits.

Studying differences in personality traits between aggressive and non-aggressive individuals can provide opportunities to narrow down the scope which aspects researchers can focus on in understanding aggression and violence. First, we briefly present three influential models of personality traits. Two of the models specifically involve

self-report and observations, while the third approach integrates measures from different disciplines. Next, we discuss different types of aggression, and the importance of making a distinction between the types. This is followed by exploring personality traits associated with aggressive and violent behaviour, including traits that overlap or differentiate between the different types of aggression. Finally, we discuss underlying biological factors of the traits that are involved in aggressive and violent behaviour.

TRAIT THEORY OF PERSONALITY

Reviews on the history of personality often begin by highlighting the inferences made by Greek philosophers. They suggested a handful of personality traits that can combine to describe an individual. Then the authors of those reviews continue by focusing on work of philosophers who lived during the middle ages, before reaching the modern era when personality became a topic for research that used new methods enabling to categorize observations systematically and statistically, and test hypotheses empirically (e.g. Allport, 1946; Cattell, 1957; Digman, 1990, 1994; Eysenck, 1953; Eysenck and Eysenck, 1976). Applying the new empirical approach revealed that early philosophers were right in one thing: there are a few basic personality types. The early philosophers were, however, incorrect in their inferences on what the specific types were.

Personality traits are based on a pattern of behaviour that is more or less stable across situations and time (Eysenck, 1953: 2). In the early age of the empirical approach to personality it became clear that some traits tend to cluster together, whereas other traits formed other clusters, independent from the first cluster. These independent clusters were regarded as basic personality types (e.g. Allport, 1946; Cattell, 1957; Costa and Widiger, 1994; Eysenck, 1953; Eysenck and Eysenck, 1976; Matthews and Deary, 1998). Although the conclusions of different research groups were consistent on that observation, they differed in the number of independent types that could be extracted from the data.

The two most influential models of personality are the 'Big Three' and 'Big Five'. The Big Three has been championed by Hans J. and Sybil B.G. Eysenck, who based their model on observation, clinical experience, and factor analysis of responses on self-report questionnaires. They proposed that all individuals could be described by predispositions towards extraversion, neuroticism, and psychoticism (Eysenck and Eysenck, 1976). They also argued that every individual could occupy any position on a hypothetical axis of the three types. The Eysencks developed a scale that could reliably and validly assess the position of every individual on the three types: the Eysenck Personality Questionnaire (EPQ) (Eysenck and Eysenck, 1975). The second model, which has strongly influenced research on DSM-IV axis II diagnoses (e.g. Miller et al., 2005a) and could have predictive value for axis-II diagnoses (Bagby et al., 2005;

Miller et al., 2005b), contains five personality types. The Big Five solution for personality was proposed by Goldberg (1981) and developed further by McCrae and Costa, who developed the neuroticism-extraversion-openness personality inventory (NEO-PI) (Digman, 1990, 1994). The NEO-PI consists of five types and 30 lower-level factors by which individuals can be described. The five types are extraversion, neuroticism, openness, agreeableness, and conscientiousness (e.g. Costa and Widiger, 1994).

Despite extensive research devoted to identify basic personality types, which model represents the best abstraction of the reality has yet to be resolved, as results of empirical studies are inconclusive. Several studies showed a major overlap between the three- and five-factor models in terms of both extraversion and neuroticism scales (Draycott and Kline, 1995). Furthermore, an overlap between psychoticism and conscientiousness has been replicated in numerous studies (e.g. Aluja et al., 2002; Draycott and Kline, 1995; Zuckerman et al., 1993), independent of whether a three-, or five-factor solution is accepted. If the scales assessing the three- and five-factor model are forced into a three-factor model, agreeableness is loading on the same factor as psychoticism and conscientiousness; if a four factor model is accepted, this type loads on a separate factor that may relate to psychoticism (i.e. agreeableness loads together with aggression-hostility) (Aluja et al. 2002; Zuckerman et al. 1993). This suggests at least three stable big factors, probably with one or two factors that are smaller. This is consistent with the conclusion from a review on personality in externalizing disorders where three factors were found: extraversion, neuroticism, and psychoticism/ impulsivity/disinhibition (Sher and Trull, 1994). We will frequently refer to these three factors in discussing personality in aggression.

The late Ernest S. Barratt has proposed another approach to personality. He proposed a general systems model to define personality beyond assessing general types through self-report (Barratt, 1985, 1991; Barratt et al., 2000; Barratt and Slaughter, 1998). In his general systems model, Barratt defined four categories that basically align with different disciplines in social and medical sciences. These four categories are biology, cognition, environment, and behaviour. To study behaviour, a personality type, or even a single personality trait, measures should be chosen from all of the four disciplines, tapping into behaviour, a type, or a trait from different points of view. As these measures do not necessarily tap into the same aspect of behaviour, all measures together provide a more complete picture of the behaviour than one measure alone. An additional advantage of research based on the general systems model is that if a study only relies on self-reports, no inferences can be made about underlying causes of differences in types or in traits among different groups of individuals (Barratt, 1985, 1991; Barratt et al., 2000; Barratt and Slaughter, 1998). The advantage of using this systems model will be illustrated in our discussion of trait impulsivity (see below), a complex, multifactorial construct that can only be measured reliably by using measures from more than one discipline.

In this chapter, and for personality research in general, we intend to promote the use of self-report personality questionnaires combined with other measures assessing behaviour. Research that relies only (or primarily) on personality types obtained through self-report questionnaires may lead a researcher or clinician to circular conclusions (Matthews and Deary, 1998). For example, one could argue that someone is aggressive because the person is impulsive, whereas being impulsive is derived partly from behaviour that is reflected in aspects of aggressive behaviour itself! Thus, self-report data on personality cannot explain the reasons for aggressive behaviour, but can describe the spectrum of behaviours that constitute aggression: certainly very important, but hardly the ultimate goal. Using measures of one or more of the four disciplines laid out in the general systems model of personality can generate results that go beyond describing behaviour, providing insights into potential

underlying causes of a behaviour or trait. In this chapter we will focus on biological correlates of personality types and traits associated with the predisposition to commit aggressive and violent acts. First, we will discuss studies focusing on personality types of aggressive and violent individuals, focusing the window of research towards more specific personality traits.

PERSONALITY CORRELATES OF INTERPERSONAL AGGRESSION AND VIOLENCE

Definitions and types of aggression

In everyday life aggression and violence are considered as synonymous, although there may be a vague feeling that the two terms could refer to slightly different concepts. However, in the justice system, clinics, and for research the two terms are defined very specifically, in which the intensity of an act determines in what category a person's aggressive act is classified. Aggression is behaviour with the direct intent to harm another person, and in which a victim is motivated to avoid the situation and the aggressor. Violence is a more extreme form of aggression with an aggressor intended to seriously harm a victim (Anderson and Bushman, 2002). Violent acts are homicide, forcible rape, aggravated assault, and robbery.

However, aggressive acts classified by intent would suggest that aggression is more or less a unified construct where intent is needed to harm another person. The implication would be that all aggressive acts are premeditated (however short the planning may take). Recently, Ramírez and Andreu (2006) questioned the definition of aggression provided by Anderson and Bushman, particularly the *intent* aspect of it. Ramírez and Andreu argued to define aggression instead simply as any behaviour that harms a target, regardless of intent. This definition integrates the premeditated and impulsive types of aggression that are observed in clinical and research settings.

Premeditated aggression (also referred to as predatory, instrumental, or proactive aggression) refers to aggressive acts that are committed to obtain a goal (e.g. money), are planned in advance, and are not followed by a feeling of remorse. Impulsive aggression (also referred to as affective or reactive aggression) refers to an uncontrolled type of aggression exacerbated by an emotional state (usually anger or irritability) in which aggressors react with more aggression than is called for by the situation, and for which the aggressor shows remorse after the act is completed (Barratt et al., 1999).

The majority of aggressors commit a combination of premeditated and impulsive acts (Barratt et al., 1999; Stanford et al., 2003a), with an estimated 90% being predominantly impulsive aggressive, and 10% being predominantly premeditated aggressive (Stanford et al., 2003a). Determining whether aggressive acts are premeditated or impulsive is important, for it can directly influence decisions made by the courts (Barratt and Felthous, 2003). More importantly, however, for the aggressor and the society at large, individuals who are predominantly impulsive aggressive could benefit from pharmacological interventions, whereas subjects with predominantly premeditated aggression may not (Barratt et al., 1997a).

The importance of distinguishing between impulsive and premeditated acts and determining which type of aggression dominates in a person warrants standardized and reliable measures. A recent meta-analysis on

measures differentiating impulsive and premeditated aggression in children and adolescents showed that the best measures were based on observation of behaviour and on self-reports (Polman et al., 2007), which are relatively easy to assess.

Measures of aggression

More than 70 self-report measures and (semi-structured) interviews have been published to assess aggression, or behaviour closely related to it, such as anger, impulsivity, and hostility. A comprehensive overview of aggression measures developed prior to 2002 was provided by Suris et al. (2004). Their paper can serve as an excellent source for investigators interested in aggression and violence to choose a measure that will serve their need. A comprehensive overview of clinical measures has been provided by Bech (1993). For differentiating between premeditated and impulsive aggression special questionnaires (see Table 16.1) have been developed assessing feelings and the context before and during the aggressive act. These measures have been validated in students, aggressive males, and several patient groups and can be used in adolescent and adult populations (Barratt et al., 1999; Mathias et al., 2007; Raine et al., 2006; Stanford, 2003a).

Personality traits of aggressive and violent behaviour

Self-report questionnaires can be used to assess the type of aggression, and the level or

Table 16.1 Specialized measures to assess premeditated and impulsive aggression in adolescent and adult populations

Name of measure	Specifics	Population	Reference
Aggressive Acts Questionnaire (AAQ)	22-item, self-report	Adolescent and adult	Barratt et al., 1999
Reactive-Proactive Aggression Questionnaire (RPQ)	23-item, self-report	Adolescent	Raine et al., 2006
Impulsive/Premeditated Aggression Scale (IPAS)	30-item, self-report	Adolescent and adult	Stanford et al., 2003a

intensity of aggressive behaviour, but they give no information that could provide opportunities for intervention. Properly designed assessment of specific behaviours, or of personality types and traits, can provide opportunities for intervention, especially when underlying biological and environmental causes are known. Further, defining personality traits of people who commit violent acts could provide information on what defines a person as being violent, possibly contributing to identifying individuals who may need additional attention.

In the past 60 years, many studies have been devoted to determining what makes a violent individual violent. Results of all these studies can be summarized in a meaningful quantifier with meta-analytic techniques: the effect size. In a meta-analysis effect sizes can be calculated is two ways. First, as a difference between samples (e.g. non-violent versus violent) divided by the standard deviation of one of the two groups or pooled across the two groups. This generates a difference between groups expressed as a standard deviation difference (d). Secondly, correlation coefficients (Pearsons's r) between variables (e.g. neuroticism and reported violence) can be used, expressing the strength of the association between variables. As numerous studies are included in a meta-analysis, this will generate an average d or r. The strength of this technique is that it will provide a result across several hundreds or even thousands of participants instead of 20 or 30 used in individual studies, optimizing the reliability of the outcome. Furthermore, potential moderator variables can be defined (e.g. age) that could influence the variation of the results across studies. For the interpretation of outcomes, differences or associations can be considered to be weak, moderate, or strong (see Table 16.2). For a more elaborate overview and a comprehensive introduction into meta-analysis, see Lipsey and Wilson (2001).

Recently, Cale (2006) conducted a meta-analysis of studies carried out between 1976 and 2001 investigating the relationship

Table 16.2 Interpretation of strength in difference (d) and association (Pearson's r) measures obtained in meta-analyses

Measure	Weak	Moderate	Strong
r at least	0.10	0.25	0.40
d at least	0.20	0.50	0.80

Note Statistical significance of the associations depends on sample size. Source: Lipsey and Wilson, 2001.

between the Big Three and antisocial behaviour. The author used the three factors described by Sher and Trull (1994): extraversion, neuroticism, and impulsivity/disinhibition. Cale included 52 studies describing results obtained in 97 samples that assessed personality measures and antisocial behaviour in over 15,000 subjects. The association between antisocial behaviour and personality type was weakest for extraversion ($r = 0.10$) and neuroticism ($r = 0.18$), although the association for the latter type became stronger if studies were conducted in older samples. The association was strongest ($r = 0.37$) between antisocial behaviour and impulsivity/disinhibition, although this effect was weaker in older samples. Unfortunately, Cale did not differentiate between different forms of antisocial behaviour, leaving unanswered the specific question of this chapter: the association between personality type and violent behaviour. However, we will show that the same pattern emerges when focusing on violence only.

In his 1977 book *Crime and Personality*, Eysenck discussed findings from his laboratory and work by Maclean (which has never been published) showing high extraversion, neuroticism, and psychoticism scores in samples of criminals compared to controls (1977: 58–61). Furthermore, he discussed a difference that his lab found between violent offenders and those who were incarcerated for destroying property. Both groups scored high on psychoticism, but the two groups scored relatively low (within the total population of criminals) on neuroticism. The difference between violent and property offenders was the higher extraversion score in the violent group compared to the property group. Based on these results, Eysenck argued that individuals are predisposed to behave aggressively or violently through an interaction of processes associated with scoring high on all of the Big Three factors: extraversion, neuroticism, and psychoticism (i.e. impulsivity/disinhibition).

However, findings from other groups are less clear-cut. For the three-factor model assessed by the EPQ, Rushton and Chrisjohn (1990) reported positive correlations between self-reported delinquency with extraversion and psychoticism, but not with neuroticism. Similarly, Walker and Gudjonsson (2006) reported a positive correlation between self-reported offending and psychoticism (see also Chico and Ferrando, 1995, who only used the psychoticism scale of the EPQ), and a weak correlation with offending and extraversion in males only. A study employing the Big Five model revealed results consistent with the previous studies showing a negative correlation between conscientiousness (which we previously showed formed one factor with psychoticism) and a precursor for aggression or anger. In a situation in which a non-existent participant rated an essay of the subject as negative (precursor), the subject, when provided the opportunity, gave the non-existent participant a drink that the subject knew the non-existent participant disliked. This response in reaction to the negative evaluation was considered an act of aggression (Jensen-Campbell et al., 2007).

Unfortunately, the above-mentioned studies relied on healthy populations, which are likely to show less variance in neuroticism scores, obscuring any correlation between neuroticism and aggression. For example, even if healthy participants score relatively high on self-reported delinquency, they are clearly not in jail. Even if these participants have high scores on psychoticism (or impulsivity/disinhibition), or on extraversion, a low neuroticism score may prevent breakthroughs of heavy aggressive or violent acts, which would certainly attract attention of the law. Research with groups who show violence so

frequently and/or so severely that they encountered social or legal consequences of their actions may provide an answer to the question whether neuroticism is involved in aggression.

Men who were violent within their relationship had higher levels of psychoticism, and experienced more anxiety and depression (Gavazzi et al., 1996), suggesting higher levels of neuroticism. In physically aggressive men scores on the IPAS correlated positively with psychoticism and neuroticism, and negatively with extraversion. Furthermore, moderately strong correlations (an r between 0.25 and 0.53) were reported between IPAS score and feelings and expressions of anger (Stanford et al., 2003a). Comparable findings were reported in adolescents with conduct disorder (Mathias et al., 2007). Dåderman (1999) also showed, both in her study and in analyses of three other samples, that between 20 and 45% of violent offenders had high scores on psychoticism and on neuroticism. Extraversion did not play a significant role in this scenario. In contrast, if scores on psychoticism were lower, the majority of the violent offenders had high neuroticism and high extraversion scores. Thus, in samples of adult males and adolescents with known aggressive behaviour, both psychoticism and neuroticism play a role, confirming the results obtained by Eysenck's group (1977). This illustrates the importance of data from subjects going beyond healthy controls or students.

Thus, aggression could be related to specific traits constituting psychoticism/impulsivity/disinhibition and neuroticism. This is in agreement with a recent meta-analysis across 63 studies showing that aggressive behaviour in both neutral and provoking conditions was associated with trait aggression and trait irritability (Bettencourt et al., 2006), which could be features of psychoticism and neuroticism, respectively. This same study revealed that personality aspects associated with aggressive behaviour under provocation only were anger, emotional susceptibility (possibly related to neuroticism), type A personality, and impulsivity (possibly related to psychoticism). It must be stressed that the authors did not focus on personality types, but on trait-like features only, of which it is rather unclear to what types they could belong. However, a picture emerges showing that aspects of both psychoticism and neuroticism are important in aggression, especially impulsivity, anger, and irritability. These aspects will be discussed in more detail below. Moreover, the differentiation should still be made between personalities of individuals primarily committing premeditated or impulsive aggressive acts, an often-neglected topic that is important regarding outcomes for treatment and underlying biological correlates.

Aggression, impulsivity, and anger

Trait impulsivity reflects the ability to control behaviours and thoughts. Impulsivity itself is not regarded as a simple trait, but a complex one which constitutes several lower-level subtraits, and can be assessed with a multitude of self-report scales and laboratory tasks (Evenden, 1999; Moeller et al., 2001). The complexity of trait impulsivity had been acknowledged by an influential researcher in the field of trait impulsivity, who showed that trait impulsivity has at least three partly dependent lower-level subtraits: motor impulsiveness (acting without thinking), non-planning impulsiveness (a lack to regard the future and a focus towards the present), and attention or cognitive impulsiveness (an intolerance for cognitive complexity and making quick cognitive decisions), which can be assessed with the Barratt impulsiveness scale, eleventh version (BIS-11) (Patton et al., 1995; Barratt, 1965, 1994).

Impulsivity is not necessarily dysfunctional, but can be functional depending on the situation, as measured with the Dickman impulsiveness scale (DIS) (Dickman, 1990). However, trait impulsivity assessed with the measures frequently used in research reflects dysfunctional, and not functional, impulsivity.

Using an impulsivity questionnaire that they developed (the I-7), Eysenck et al. (1985) showed that the I-7 impulsiveness subscale, but not the venturesomeness (sensation-seeking) subscale, correlated significantly with EPQ psychoticism and neuroticism, a finding that was replicated by O'Boyle and Barratt (1993) in an inpatient population of substance abusing patients. Stronger evidence that trait impulsivity assessed with the I-7 and the BIS-11 reflected a pathological aspect of behaviour was provided by Miller et al. (2004), who showed that the three BIS-11 scales load on one factor with the I-7 impulsivity scale and the DIS dysfunctional impulsiveness scale, constituting one factor that Miller et al. labelled 'non-planning dysfunctional', and which we will simply refer to as 'impulsivity' in this chapter. This outcome is certainly in agreement with the previously mentioned association between higher levels of impulsivity with higher scores on psychoticism and neuroticism reported by Eysenck et al. (1985). The pathological and dysfunctional aspects of impulsivity are further illustrated by a positive correlation between self-reported impulsivity scores and the number of psychiatric disorders diagnosed in inmates (Stanford and Barratt, 1992), and between impulsivity and the number of substances that substance abusers were using (McCown, 1988; O'Boyle and Barratt, 1993).

Aggression and impulsivity

Regarding aggression and violence, trait impulsivity was higher in aggressive compared to non-aggressive individuals (e.g. Apter et al., 1990; Barratt et al., 1997b; Dåderman, 1999; Fehon et al., 2005; Stanford et al., 1995, 2003b; Wang and Diamond, 1999), irrespective of whether an aggressor committed predominantly premeditated or impulsive aggressive acts (Barratt et al., 1997b; Stanford et al., 2003b). Moreover, higher levels of impulsivity during childhood were associated with delinquent behaviour that persisted from childhood into early adolescence (White et al., 1994).

A positive correlation was found between BIS score and the number of impulsive aggressive acts committed one month prior to testing (Stanford et al., 1995). Trait impulsivity correlated significantly stronger with premeditated aggression ($r = 0.38$) than with impulsive aggression ($r = 0.21$) (Stanford et al., 2003a). However, this difference may be explained by a less reliable score in the premeditated group which consisted of 10 subjects, compared to the impulsive group consisting of 87 subjects. In adolescents trait impulsivity correlated more strongly with aggression in the predominantly impulsive aggressive group than with aggression in the predominantly premeditated aggressive group (Mathias et al., 2007; Raine et al., 2006), suggesting an effect of aging on the relationship between aggression, and impulsive and premeditated aggression. The different correlations between impulsive aggressive behaviour and impulsivity, and between premeditated aggressive behaviour and impulsivity was enhanced dramatically if only groups with pure impulsive or premeditated aggression were taken into account. The group of adolescent males who only committed impulsive aggressive acts had a significant positive correlation between aggression and impulsivity ($r = 0.19$), whereas the pure premeditated aggression group had a correlation between aggression and impulsivity close to zero ($r = 0.01$). As no information was provided on the sample size of the pure groups, we could not with certainly conclude that the correlation coefficients are significantly different between the two types of aggression.

Aggression and anger

As for neuroticism, numerous studies showed that aggressive behaviour correlated with higher scores on self-reported anger (Barratt et al., 1997b; Cornell et al., 1999; Mathias et al., 2007; Stanford et al., 2003a, 2003b), irritability (Stanford et al., 1995), or other emotions (Fehon et al., 2005;

Loeber et al., 2005; Raine et al., 2006). As we previously reported for impulsivity, anger, and irritability were high in both premeditated and impulsive aggressors (Barratt et al., 1997b; Stanford et al., 1995, 2003b), without a significant difference for trait impulsivity or anger between aggressive and premeditated aggressors (Barratt et al., 1997b). Furthermore, higher scores on anger related to higher aggression scores on the IPAS for both types of aggression (Mathias et al., 2007; Stanford et al., 2003a). Interestingly, however, neuroticism did differentiate between participants who were predominantly impulsive aggressive versus those who were predominantly premeditated aggressive (Mathias et al., 2007; Miller and Lynam, 2006), suggesting that anger and irritability could be distinguished from neuroticism. This is consistent with a significant positive correlation between anxiety and impulsive aggression in adolescents ($r = 0.15$), whereas the correlation between these two variables is not significant for adolescents involved in premeditated aggression ($r = -0.09$) (Raine et al., 2006). Again, no certainty can be provided whether the correlations differed between the two types. Not differentiated between impulsive and premeditated aggression, but still an interesting finding, is a higher incidence of depressed mood in violent offenders (Loeber et al., 2005). Finally, Coccaro et al. (2007) reported higher anger and depression scores in ten subjects diagnosed with intermittent explosive disorder (i.e. impulsive aggression) compared to healthy controls. These results suggest that in addition to anger, anxiety and depression could also be involved in aggressive behaviour, and that the role that the emotions play may be similar in impulsive and premeditated aggression, at least for anger and irritability.

Aggression, stress, and coping

Higher emotional arousal could function as a drive. Anger has been argued to prepare an individual for aggressive behaviour

(Martínez and Andrue, 2006), and stress may lead to an increased chance of an aggressive reaction. Stress increased an aggressive reaction in healthy subjects, especially males (Verona and Kilmer, 2007), but this reaction to stress may be exacerbated in individuals already high on anger and impulsivity (Bettencourt et al., 2006), which would be consistent with the theory put forward by Davidson et al. (2000). They theorized that impulsive aggression could be related to diminished regulation of emotions. Everyday events may evoke stress and subsequent emotions, and need to be coped with and regulated, otherwise a minor event may induce a considerable amount of stress (Lazarus, 1999). One of the suggested mechanisms to regulate stress and emotions is by consciously appraising stressful events (Lazarus, 1999). This suggests that coping with stress involves higher-order functions, such as language, that could be used in the appraisal process. Higher-order functions are frequently studied with neuropsychological tests, revealing a significant impairment in impulsive aggressive individuals on planning, and language (Barratt et al., 1997b; Stanford et al., 1997). Results in premeditated aggressive individuals are less consistent, although in the worse case scenario non-impulsive aggressive individuals may also be impaired on these functions, but to a significantly lesser extent, especially on language ability (Barratt et al., 1997b). In the best-case scenario, individuals committing premeditated aggression do not differ from healthy control subjects on any executive function (Stanford et al., 2003a). The difference in executive functions may help premeditated aggressors, but not impulsive aggressors, to cope with stress, thus inhibiting their anger and aggression and aiding in the process of planning. Of course, much more research is needed to confirm and extent these findings. Next, we will discuss the relation between brain and aggression, especially brain areas involved in higher-order functioning and regulation of behaviour and emotion.

AGGRESSION, IMPULSIVITY, AND ANGER: A BIOLOGICAL APPROACH

The results discussed so far imply the involvement of trait impulsivity and emotions in aggressive behaviour, confirming suggestions of an association between violence and the personality types of psychoticism and neuroticism. However, trait impulsivity and anger are present in both premeditated and impulsive aggression, suggesting that other mechanisms may be involved in a difference in modulation of the effects of impulsivity and anger in the two types of aggression. One of the mechanisms that could differentiate the two types is a better executive functioning. To examine other possible mechanisms, we will now focus on correlates of brain activity underlying trait impulsivity and anger, and aggression per se. The relationship between brain and behaviour can be investigated with neuroimaging and electrophysiological techniques, allowing study of the integrity of brain networks in processing information and regulating behaviour and emotions.

A rich literature exists with strong evidence that aggression relates to deficient functioning of prefrontal cortical structures (e.g. Amen et al., 1996; Blair, 2004; Brower and Price, 2001; Bufkin and Cuttrell, 2005; Juhasz et al., 2001; Raine et al., 1998; Soloff et al., 2003). Miller and Cohen (2001) recently proposed a 'biased competition' theory for the functioning of the prefrontal cortex. In this theory the authors argue that the prefrontal cortex is responsible for controlling cognition and behaviour by monitoring the internal or external environments (i.e. bodily and environmental changes, respectively) and comparing that continuously with internal representations of goals. If a discrepancy is detected between environment and goal, the prefrontal cortex shows an increase in activity and signals other brain areas to process information differently thus biasing weak representations of thoughts and behaviour over strong ones, so that goals will be met in the near future. Thus, if a representation is weak (e.g. if someone has to respond with behaviour normally not applied by that individual) the prefrontal cortex comes into action by modulating attention, response selection, and other behavioural and emotional processes. If someone has to react with a response that is frequently applied, in this model the prefrontal cortex would not come into action. If the prefrontal cortex is not working properly, weak representations are less likely to overcome highly learned or reflexive ones. For aggression this suggest that the probability of reflexive reaction to a stressful situation (i.e. fight or flight), is higher than that of appraising or reflecting on the situation and walking away. We will now discuss the relationship between deficient functioning of selected areas of the prefrontal cortex as underlying biological causes of impulsivity and anger, and how it can predispose some individuals towards being aggressive.

Controlling behaviour and emotion: the prefrontal cortex

Bechara (2004) described a cortical network that is involved in regulating behaviour, thought, and emotion. This network included amongst other areas the amygdala, the lateral orbitofrontal cortex, the dorsolateral prefrontal cortex, and the anterior cingulate cortex (ACC). Studies showed the involvement of the orbitofrontal cortex in inhibiting an aggressive response through modulation of limbic activity, especially that of the amygdala (e.g. Davidson et al., 2000). Regarding the orbitofrontal cortex, imaging studies revealed diminished activity of this prefrontal structure in individuals with impulsive aggression, (Coccaro et al., 2007; New et al., 2002; Raine et al., 1998; for a review see Blair, 2004), and excessive activation of the amygdala (Coccaro et al. 2007; Raine et al., 1998). Interestingly, although activity of the amygdala did not differentiate impulsive from premeditated aggressors, premeditated

aggressors showed patterns of prefrontal activity intermediate to controls and impulsive aggressors (Raine et al., 1998), suggesting a somewhat better ability to regulate emotions by individuals predominantly involved in premeditated aggression.

Of the neural network proposed by Bechara (2004), the anterior cingulate cortex is involved in monitoring behaviour by detecting errors and response conflict, and detecting deviances between reward prediction and actual outcome. Neuroimaging studies, most notably functional magnetic resonance imaging (fMRI) and positron emission tomography (PET), showed that activity of the anterior cingulate cortex increases if individuals make an error compared to if they make a correct response, if they expect an award which is not delivered, and if an individual encounters situations with conflicting information (for timely reviews and meta-analyses on this topic, see Bush et al., 1998, and Ridderinkhof et al., 2004a, 2004b). Moreover, a meta-analysis of fMRI studies showed that ACC could be divided into at least two functionally different areas: cognitive and emotional/affective areas (Bush et al., 1998), although this division needs replication and is issue of debate (Ridderinkhof et al., 2004a). It seems certain, however, that the ACC is involved in processing both cognitive and emotional information (Davis et al., 2005). Behaviour and cognitive processes could be regulated through modulating response tendencies (Devinsky et al., 1995); emotional states could be regulated through interactions with the amygdala and orbitofrontal cortex (Phillips et al., 2003).

The functioning of the ACC can also be studied with electrophysiological techniques, like the event-related potential (ERP) (Gehring et al., 1993). An ERP is a derivate of the electroencephalogram (EEG) that measures cortical activity on the scalp. If a stimulus is presented, numerous cortical neurons fire at the same time, eliciting a peak in activity measured on the scalp (Coles and Rugg, 1995: 1–7). Because the activity is evoked by a specific stimulus (event), the part of the EEG relative to the stimulus is referred to as ERP. Because information on stimulus processing can be assessed on a millisecond-to-millisecond basis, this technique makes it possible to study how the brain processes information in time, what the functional significance of processes may be, and (with advanced techniques to estimate where in the brain a neural source underlying activity measured on the scalp is located) which cortical area may be involved in the process.

To study the integrity of the functioning of the ACC, a task is selected in which participants encounter conditions with conflicting information, for example the Stroop task or the Eriksen flanker task. In the Stroop task participants have to name a colour of a conflicting colour word (e.g. name 'red' if the word 'yellow' is printed in red), creating a conflict to overcome the more automated response to read the name of the colour word (i.e. yellow). In the Eriksen flanker task strings of five letters are presented in which participants must respond to the central letter of the string. The condition is easy if the flanking letters and the central letter are the same; the condition is difficult and error prone if the central letter is flanked by letters that require an opposite response (e.g. respond with the right hand to the letter H and with the left hand to the letter S; the situation is difficult if the participants perceive the conflicting stimulus SSHSS). In case of a conflicting stimulus, or an error, the ACC becomes activated and an increase in EEG activity can be measured at the scalp. After approximately 200 ms following a conflicting stimulus, activity of the ACC evokes a negativity in the ERP that is referred to as the N200 (or N2) (Yeung et al., 2004). If an individual makes an error, the increase in ACC activity can be measured in the ERP as a more pronounced negativity between 50 and 100 ms following an error (all activity in the ERP, whether negative or positive, signifies activation of a large cluster of neurons), referred to as the error-related negativity (ERN).

Individuals who commit aggressive acts have higher impulsivity (psychoticism) and anger/irritability (neuroticism). This, and the pattern of violence committed by both types of offenders, suggests a disturbance in regulation of behaviour and emotion, possibly not at the level of the orbitofrontal cortex, but at the level of the ACC. Impulsivity relates to a mechanism of control of behaviour; emotionality relates to coping mechanisms, and thus also to a mechanism of control but at a different level of abstraction. This implies that high-impulse individuals and highly neurotic individuals could show less activity of the ACC, especially if both high impulsivity and neuroticism combine in aggressive individuals.

Our hypothesis has indeed been confirmed in groups of participants whose aggressive behaviour was predominantly impulsive. Recent neuroimaging studies (Frankle et al., 2005; New et al., 2002) demonstrated that impulsive aggression is associated with less activity of the ACC. Similar findings were also reported in the ERP literature with a smaller N2 amplitude in male inmates who had committed an impulsive aggressive offence versus inmates who had committed a non-impulsive aggressive offence (Chen et al., 2005). Could this effect be attributed to trait impulsivity or to neuroticism?

If the ACC plays a role in impulsivity, we would expect lower ACC activity following an error in high compared to low impulsive individuals, reflected as a smaller ERN in the ERP in the high impulsive group. Moreover, a negative correlation is expected between trait impulsivity and the strength of activation of the ACC (i.e. a positive correlation between impulsivity score and ERN amplitude, indicating a smaller ERN with higher impulsivity). If neuroticism is involved, we should expect a smaller ERN amplitude with an increase in neuroticism.

Several studies have reported results consistent with these hypotheses (Dikman and Allen, 2000; Lijffijt and Barratt, 2005; Pailing and Segalowitz, 2004; Potts et al., 2006; Ruchsow et al., 2005; Santesso et al., 2005). These studies showed a smaller ERN for healthy participants who could be considered high on impulsivity compared to those participants who could be considered low on impulsivity (groups were made by the median-split approach on scales of conscientiousness, socialization, agreeableness, and the BIS-11). Pailing and Segalowitz (2004) further showed a negative correlation between ERN amplitude and scores on the NEO-PI conscientiousness scale, confirming our hypothesis that the ERN becomes smaller if impulsivity is increased (impulsivity is a component of psychoticism; psychoticism and conscientiousness correlate negatively).

Lijffijt and Barratt (2005) replicated these findings in healthy volunteers who were divided by a median-split approach into a group of subjects who had relatively high BIS-11 scores ($n = 8$) and a group who had relatively low BIS-11 scores ($n = 8$). Subjects performed an Eriksen flanker task in a relatively simple condition in which subjects were requested to respond within 400 ms (well before the mean reaction time of most healthy subjects performing a moderately complex reaction time task), and a relatively hard condition where subjects were requested to respond within 300 ms. The high impulsive group had a significantly lower ERN amplitude than the low impulsive group for both conditions (see Figure 16.2). In addition, this study demonstrated a significant positive correlation between the ERN amplitude and the total BIS-11 score across the total sample of subjects (i.e. a smaller ERN with higher impulsivity). Moreover, this correlation was more pronounced in the 300 ms condition (Pearson's $r = 0.67$, $p = 0.005$) (right panel of Figure 16.3) than in the 400 ms condition ($r = 0.47$, $p = 0.07$) (left panel of Figure 16.3). As expected, the ERN is smaller in subjects reporting higher levels of impulsivity, especially in a more stressful condition where subjects had to respond very rapidly. These results confirmed that trait impulsivity can be related to activity of the ACC, and is thus related directly to a behavioural control mechanism.

In a different approach, Potts et al. (2006) rewarded or punished participants depending on their performance on an Eriksen flanker task. Participants were divided into a low- and high-impulsive groups based on a median-split approach. Low-impulsive participants showed a more pronounced ERN after punishment than after a reward, signifying a stronger signal for regulation to avoid errors on subsequent trials. High-impulsive individuals, however, showed a reversed pattern, with reward evoking a more pronounced ERN than punishment. As with the other studies mentioned above, Potts et al. used healthy controls – mostly students. Research in subjects with known aggression may reveal even more pronounced differences between processing reward and punishment. The results obtained in the studies on the relationship between ACC functioning and impulsivity are in direct agreement with the hypothesis of Eysenck (1977), who argued that individuals scoring high on trait impulsivity had lower levels of cortical arousal, resulting in a lower ability to be conditioned, as conditioning benefited from higher levels of cortical arousal (Eysenck and Eysenck, 1985: 237–288). Errors and punishment result in lower ERN activity in high-impulsive compared to low-impulsive individuals, potentially reflecting less regulation of behaviour towards goals of making fewer errors. Neuroticism may have a same influence as impulsivity in this group. Pailing and Segalowitz (2004) showed a positive correlation between the NEO-PI neuroticism score and the ERN amplitude, indicating lower ERN amplitudes if participants score higher on neuroticism.

The results discussed above showed that both impulsivity and neuroticism are related to activity of the ACC, with an increase in the traits leading to a smaller ERN suggesting less reactivity of the ACC and a smaller signal to other areas of the brain to improve performance. Unfortunately, to our knowledge no studies have been devoted to tease apart the relationship of premeditated and impulsive aggression on the functioning of the ACC. We may hypothesize, however, that with similar results for impulsivity and anger in

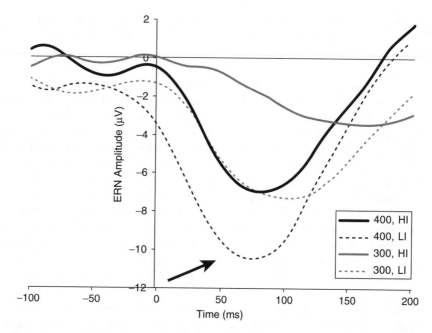

Figure 16.2   Error processing negativity (ERN) in a sample of low ($n = 8$) (LI) and high ($n = 8$) (HI) impulsive participants performing an Eriksen flanker task with pressure to respond within 400 ms (400) and 300 ms (300). LI have consistently more pronounced amplitudes than HI

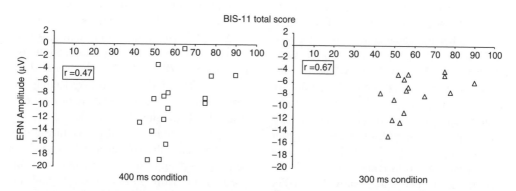

Figure 16.3   The relationship between ERN amplitude and trait impulsivity obtained with the Barratt impulsiveness scale (BIS-11). The correlations show a decrease in ERN amplitude with an increase in trait impulsivity score, which was slightly stronger in the 300 ms condition compared to the 400 ms condition

both types of aggression, functioning of the ACC may also not differentiate between impulsive and premeditated aggression. If so, lower ACC activity could still have different effects in impulsive versus premeditated aggression. Aggression may be perceived by the impulsive aggressor as punishment or potential source of punishment because of direct feelings of guilt (Barratt et al., 1999); individuals who are primarily involved in premeditated aggressive acts are of course rewarded, or at least anticipate reward, for their act. As the ACC could be more sensitive to reward than to punishment in impulsive individuals, the premeditated aggressor may be motivated to aggress again, whereas low ACC activity for the impulsive aggressor may reduce the ability to learn from consequences of an aggressive act, even when the consequence is perceived as punishment.

BOTTOM-UP PROCESSING AND TOP-DOWN CONTROL: DIFFERENTIATING IMPULSIVE AND PREMEDITATED AGGRESSORS?

Aggression, impulsivity, and neuroticism (especially anger) may, like deficient regulation of behaviour and emotions, be associated with deficiencies in information processing at other levels. ERPs make it possible to investigate both instruction-induced (top-down), and sensory related (bottom-up) processes. Bottom-up processes frequently occur relatively early after stimulus presentation (prior to 200 ms post-stimulus), possibly reflecting early selection and filtering of sensory information. A recent study showed smaller P100 (P1) and larger N100 (N1) amplitudes for adult impulsive aggressive individuals compared to healthy controls (Houston and Stanford, 2001). The authors suggested that the smaller P1 could reflect inefficient filtering of sensory information, whereas the larger N1 could reflect stronger orientation towards the stimulus. This is consistent with a recent finding reporting on the relationship between impulsivity and automatically directing attention towards new information. Franken et al. (2005) showed a negative correlation between dysfunctional impulsivity assessed with the DIS and the mismatch negativity (MMN). The MMN is thought to reflect a signal for directing attentional resources towards new information, resulting from the detection of a mismatch between a new stimulus and a frequently presented stimulus (Näätänen, 1992). However, the findings on the P1 and N1 were not replicated in a study with aggressive inmates, non-aggressive inmates, and healthy controls (Barratt et al., 1997b), whereas a larger P1 amplitude was found in aggressive adolescents (Bars et al., 2001). Once again, however, even though early bottom-up processing of information may be involved in aggression, we know of only limited information about whether it differentiates between the different types of aggression.

Top-down processes can be induced by specific task instructions, and reflect higher-order processing of information. A classic paradigm in ERP research is the 'oddball task', in which subjects are instructed to distinguish between frequently and rarely presented stimuli, most often by pressing a button when subjects see the rare stimulus. In the ERP, rare stimuli elicit more positive activity 250–500 ms after presentation of the stimulus (P300 ERP component) than frequent stimuli do, possibly reflecting an increase in attentional capacity to process the task salient stimulus (Kok, 2001).

Numerous studies have appeared measuring the P300 in healthy volunteers who varied on self-reported impulsivity and aggression, in participants with antisocial traits, and in aggressive inmates. The amplitude of the P300 to the rare stimulus was smaller in adolescents who had an externalizing disorder (e.g. conduct disorder, drug abuse) compared to adolescents who did not (Iacono et al., 2002; Patrick et al., 2006). A smaller amplitude was also reported in students who had had several aggressive encounters that were considered impulsive (Gerstle et al., 1998; Mathias and Stanford, 1999). These authors also reported a delay in peak latency of the P300 (Mathias and Stanford, 1999). In 18 men convicted of abuse of their spouse/partner, the P300 amplitude was significantly lower than for controls (Stanford et al., 2007). Finally, the P300 amplitude was lower in inmates convicted for violent crimes compared to those convicted for non-violent crimes (Bernat et al., 2007). Smaller and prolonged P300 peaks were found for adult inmates with aggressive infractions compared to inmates with no infractions (Drake et al., 1988). We partly replicated this finding in a small sample of juvenile offenders who performed an auditory oddball task in which they had to respond to an infrequent target stimulus. Juvenile inmates who had committed aggressive infractions ($n = 11$) had a significantly smaller P300 amplitude following the

rare as well as the frequent stimulus than non-aggressive juvenile inmates ($n = 8$) (F(1,17 = 5.40, $p = 0.03$) (Lijffijt et al., 2005) (see Figure 16.4).

Interestingly, the P300 also differentiated between individuals who had committed predominantly impulsive versus premeditated aggressive acts. Barratt et al. (1997b) showed smaller P300 amplitudes in inmates who committed impulsive aggressive acts while being incarcerated compared to control subjects. The P300 was enhanced in inmates who had committed premeditated aggressive infraction, although the difference in amplitude was not significant compared to the impulsive aggressive inmate group. However, in a slightly different oddball task containing not only frequent non-target and rare target stimuli, but also rare unexpected stimuli of which the subjects received no information prior to the test, the P300

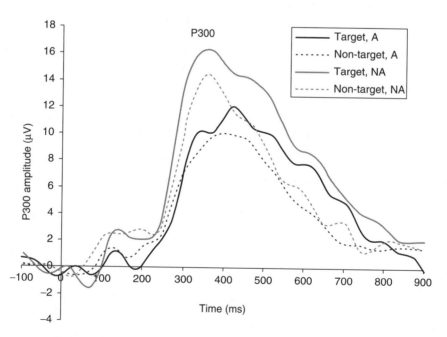

Figure 16.4   P300 peak amplitudes obtained with an auditory oddball task for juvenile inmates who committed aggressive infractions during incarceration (designated A) ($n = 11$) compared to juvenile inmates who did not commit infractions (designated NA) ($n = 8$). The groups differ on the amplitude for both the salient target and the non-salient non-target stimulus. The P300 was smaller in the aggressive group, irrespective whether the stimulus was a target or non-target

amplitude compared to control subjects was smaller for impulsive but not premeditated aggressive inmates when processing the new and unexpected stimulus. For this condition, the P300 did not differ between inmates who had committed premeditated aggressive acts and normal controls. Stanford et al. (2003b) found a comparable effect. In a group of predominantly premeditated aggressors the P300 amplitude was not significantly different from the P300 obtained in a healthy control sample.

Thus, the P300 has been shown consistently to be smaller in individuals displaying aggression, and is potentially related to impulsivity. Scores on the BIS correlated negatively with the amplitude of the P300 in children diagnosed with an externalizing disorder (r ranged between −0.25 and −0.46, depending on the lead the P300 was scored on and the specific task that was used) (Harmon-Jones et al., 1997), and in adults with a substance abuse disorder ($r = −0.44$) (Moeller et al., 2004). Moeller et al. found no significant correlation between BIS scores and the P300 in a sample of healthy controls. These results suggest that trait impulsivity and P300 amplitude share common variance (up to about 16%).

These results are consistent with the possibility that new stimuli are processed with adequate resources in individuals who commit predominantly premeditated aggression, whereas new stimuli are not processed adequately in those who commit predominantly impulsive aggressive acts. To us this suggests that inappropriate processing of new stimuli could lead to an incorrect interpretation of the stimulus, which may then be perceived as a possible thread, and become a stressor that warranted action. Because of the predisposition for an aggressive response due to high anger, and a poor control mechanism due to high impulsivity, the disturbance in processing everyday stimuli could push someone with high anger and high impulsivity over the edge to committing an aggressive act. By contrast, individuals with premeditated aggression tend to benefit from processing new stimuli in a manner similar to the way healthy individuals do.

CONCLUSION

In this chapter we have discussed evidence relating aggression and impulsivity to personality traits and to relevant neurophysiological mechanisms (see Table 16.3 for general conclusions). Aggression, in general, is associated with a higher score on psychoticism.

Table 16.3   General conclusions on aggression and personality

	Aggressive individuals vs. controls	Impulsive aggression vs. premeditated aggression*
Trait impulsivity	A higher than C	I similar to P
Emotional arousal	A higher than C	I similar to P
Executive functioning	A worse than C	I worse than P
Neuroimaging and electrophysiology		
Amygdala	A more activity than C	I similar to P
Orbitofrontal cortex	A lower activity than C	I lower activity than P
Anterior cingulate cortex	A lower activity than C	No information
N2/ERN	A smaller than C	No information
P300	A smaller than C	I smaller than P

Note Aggressive individuals are contrasted with healthy controls, and individuals with impulsive aggression are contrasted with individuals with premeditated aggression. Emotional arousal includes anger, irritability, anxiety, and depression.
A = aggressive individuals; C = healthy controls; I = Individuals committing predominantly impulsive aggressive acts; P = Individuals committing predominantly premeditated aggressive acts.
* The conclusions should be interpreted with caution on the difference between impulsive and premeditated aggression and results need replication.

If neuroticism was high, subjects were likely to show a maladaptive, pathological form of aggression. Among lower-order personality characteristics, trait impulsivity and anger were higher in aggressors than in controls. These characteristics did not differentiate impulsive and premeditated aggressors. In contrast to individuals committing impulsive aggressive acts, those who used predominantly premeditated aggression may benefit from better executive functioning and better information processing, possibly reducing the impact of impulsivity and anger on behaviour. Underlying biological causes for higher trait impulsivity and emotional arousal in aggression could be related to suboptimal processing of errors, reward, and punishment. Furthermore, aggression has been associated with a multitude of differences in information processing assessed with ERPs, both bottom-up and top-down. Top-down control measured with the P300 to salient stimuli differentiated premeditated and impulsive aggression. In aggression, the higher drive and reactivity to stress (anger) and the lower control mechanism converge. Without check and balances potentially provided by either low neuroticism with high impulsivity, or low impulsivity with high neuroticism, an individual is less likely to counter stress effectively, thus modulating the already high level of emotional arousal in aggressive individuals. This is exacerbated in the impulsive aggressor because of poor information processing, leading to behaviour (including aggression) that is inappropriate to the situation. Because impulsive individuals are also less sensitive to punishment than individuals low on impulsivity, and more sensitive to reward, the impulsive aggressor, even though experiencing negative feedback because of guilt and remorse, may not learn from mistakes, whereas for the premeditated aggressor the result of the aggressive act is seen as rewarding, stimulating the aggressor to commit more acts. Impulsive and non-impulsive aggression therefore have contrasting implications for behavioural and pharmacological management.

ACKNOWLEDGEMENT

This paper is dedicated to the memory of Ernest S. Barratt, PhD (1925–2005), Marie B. Gale Centennial Professor in Psychiatry. Data presented in this chapter was collected through sponsorship by the Dreyfus Health Foundation; Rogosin Institute, affiliated with New York-Presbyterian Hospital; and Weill Medical College of Cornell University. This chapter was supported in part by the Pat R. Rutherford, Jr. Chair in Psychiatry (ACS), and by NIH grants RO1-MH69944 (ACS), RO1-DA08425 (FGM), and KO2-DA00403 (FGM).

REFERENCES

Allport, G.W. (1946) *Personality: A Psychological Interpretation*. New York: Holt.

Aluja, A., García, Ó. and García, L.F. (2002) 'A comparative study of Zuckerman's three structural models for personality through the NEO-PI-R, ZKPQ-III-R, EPQ-RS and Goldberg's 50-bipolar adjectives', *Personality and Individual Differences*, 33(5): 713–25.

Amen, D.G., Stubblefield, M., Carmicheal, B. and Thisted, R. (1996) 'Brain SPECT findings and aggressiveness', *Annals of Clinical Psychiatry*, 8(3): 129–37.

Anderson, C.A. and Bushman, B.J. (2002) 'Human aggression', *Annual Review of Psychology*, 53: 27–51.

Apter, A., van Praag, H.M., Plutchik, R., Sevy, S., Korn, M. and Brown, S. (1990) 'Interrelationships among anxiety, aggression, impulsivity, and mood: A serotonergically linked cluster?', *Psychiatry Research*, 32(2): 191–9.

Bagby, R.M., Costa, P.T., Widiger, T.A., Ryder, A.G. and Marshall, M. (2005) 'DSM-IV personality disorders and the five-factor model of personality: A multi-method examination of domain- and facet-level predictions', *European Journal of Personality*, 19(4): 307–24.

Barratt, E.S. (1965) 'Factor analysis of some psychometric measures of impulsiveness and anxiety', *Psychological Reports*, 16: 547–54.

Barratt, E.S. (1985) 'Impulsiveness defined within a systems model of personality', in C.D. Spielberger and J.N. Butcher (eds), *Advances in Personality Assessment*. Hillsdale, NJ: Erlbaum.

Barratt, E.S. (1991) 'Measuring and predicting aggression within the context of a personality theory', *Journal of Neuropsychiatry*, 3: S35–9.

Barratt, E.S. (1994) 'Impulsiveness and aggression', in J. Monohan and H.J. Steadman (eds), *Violence and Mental Disorder*. Chicago: University of Chicago Press, pp. 61–79.

Barratt, E.S. and Slaugther, L. (1998) 'Defining, measuring, and predicting impulsive aggression: A heuristic model', *Behavioral Sciences and the Law*, 16(3): 285–302.

Barratt, E.S. and Felthous, A.R. (2003) 'Impulsive versus premeditated aggression: Implications for mens rea decisions', *Behavioral Sciences and the Law*, 21: 619–30.

Barratt, E.S., Felthous, A., Kent, T., Liebman, M.J. and Coates, D.D. (2000) 'Criterion measures of aggression – impulsive versus premeditated aggression', in D.H. Fishbein (ed.), *The Science, Treatment, and Prevention of Antisocial Behaviors: Application to the Criminal Justice System*. Kingston, NY: Civic Research Institute, pp. 4-1–4-18.

Barratt, E.S., Stanford, M.S., Dowdy, L., Liebman, M.J. and Kent, T.A. (1999) 'Impulsive and premeditated aggression: A factor analysis of self-reported acts', *Psychiatry Research*, 86(2): 163–73.

Barratt, E.S., Stanford, M.S., Felthous, A.R. and Kent, T.A. (1997a) 'The effects of phenytoin on impulsive and premeditated aggression: A controlled study', *Journal of Clinical Psychopharmacology*, 17(5): 341–9.

Barratt, E.S., Stanford, M.S., Kent, T.A. and Felthous, A. (1997b) 'Neuropsychological and cognitive psychophysiological substrates of impulsive aggression', *Biological Psychiatry*, 41(10): 1045–61.

Bars, D.R., Heyrend, F. La M., Simpson, C.D. and Munger, J.C. (2001) 'Use of visual evoked-potential studies and EEG data to classify aggressive, explosive behavior in youths', *Psychiatric Services*, 52(1): 81–6.

Bech, P. (1993) 'The clinical measurement of aggression', in C. Thompson and P. Cowen (eds), *Violence: Basic and Clinical Science*. Oxford, UK: Butterworth-Heinemann, pp. 186–96.

Bechara, A. (2004) 'Performance monitoring, decision making, and cognitive control', in M. Ullsperger and M. Falkenstein (eds), *Errors, Conflict, and the Brain: Current Opinions on Performance Monitoring*. Dortmund, Germany: Max Planck Institute for Human Cognitive and Brain Sciences, Leipzig-Munchen, pp. 55–63.

Bernat, E.M., Hall., J.R., Steffen, B.V. and Patrick, C.J. (2007) 'Violent offending predicts P300 amplitude', *International Journal of Psychophysiology*, 66(2): 161–7.

Bettencourt, B.A., Talley, A., Benjamin, A.J. and Valentine, J. (2006) 'Personality and aggressive behavior under provoking and neutral conditions: A meta-analysis', *Psychological Bulletin*, 132(5): 751–77.

Blair, R.J. (2004). The roles of orbital frontal cortex in the modulation of antisocial behavior. *Brain and Cognition,* 55 (1), 198–208.

Brower, M.C. and Price, B.H. (2001) 'Neuropsychiatry of frontal lobe dysfunction in violent and criminal behavior: A critical review', *Journal of Neurology and Neurosurgical Psychiatry*, 71: 720–6.

Bufkin, J.L. and Cuttrell, V.R. (2005) 'Neuroimaging studies of aggressive and violent behavior: Current findings and implications for criminology and criminal justice', *Trauma, Violence and Abuse*, 6(2): 176–91.

Bush, G., Whalen, P.J., Rosen, B.R., Jenike, M.A., McInerney, S.C. and Rauch, S.L. (1998) 'The counting stroop: An interference task specialized for functional neuroimaging – validation study with functional MRI', *Human Brain Mapping*, 6(4): 270–82.

Cale, E.M. (2006) 'A quantitative review of the relations between the "Big 3" higher order personality dimensions and antisocial behavior', *Journal of Research in Personality*, 40(3): 250–84.

Cattell, R.B. (1957) *Personality and Motivation: Structure and Measurement*. New York: World Book Co.

Chen, C., Tien, Y., Juan, C., Tzeng, O.J.L. and Hung, D.L. (2005) 'Neural correlates of impulsive-violent behavior: An event-related potential study', *NeuroReport*, 16(11): 1213–16.

Chico, E. and Ferrando, P.J. (1995) 'A psychometric evaluation of the revised P scale in delinquent and non-delinquent Spanish samples', *Personality and Individual Differences*, 18(3): 331–7.

Coccaro, E.F., McCloskey, M.S., Fitzgerald, D.A. and Phan, K.L. (2007) 'Amygdala and orbitofrontal reactivity to social threat in individuals with impulsive aggression', *Biological Psychiatry*, 62(2): 168–78.

Coles, M.G.H. and Rugg, M.D. (1995) 'Event-related brain potentials: am introduction', in M.D. Rugg and M.G.H. Coles (eds), *Electrophysiology of Mind: Event-related Brain Potentials and Cognition*. Oxford, UK: Oxford University Press, pp. 1–39.

Cornell, D.G., Peterson, C.S. and Richards, H. (1999) 'Anger as a predictor of aggression among incarcerated adolescents', *Journal of Consulting and Clinical Psychology*, 67(1): 108–15.

Costa, P.T. and Widiger, T.A. (1994) 'Introduction: Personality disorders and the five-factor model of personality', in P.T. Costa and T.A. Widiger (eds), *Personality Disorders and the Five-factor Model of Personality*. Washington, DC: American Psychological Association, pp. 1–10.

Dāderman, A.M. (1999) 'Differences between severely conduct-disordered juvenile males and normal juvenile males: The study of personality trait', *Personality and Individual Differences*, 26(5): 827–45.

Davidson, R.J., Putman, K.M. and Larson, C.L. (2000) 'Dysfunction in the neural circuitry of emotion regulation – a possible prelude to violence', *Science*, 289(5479): 591–94.

Davis, K.D., Taylor, K.S., Hutchison, W.D., Dostrovsky, J.O., McAndrews, M.P., Richter, E.O. and Lozano, A.M. (2005) 'Human anterior cingulate cortex neurons encode cognitive and emotional demands', *Journal of Neuroscience*, 25(37): 8402–6.

Devinsky, O., Morrell, M.J. and Vogt, B.A. (1995) 'Contributions of anterior cingulate cortex to behaviour', *Brain*, 118(1): 279–306.

Dickman, S.J. (1990) 'Functional and dysfunctional impulsivity: Personality and Cognitive correlates', *Journal of Personality and Social Psychology*, 58(1): 95–102.

Digman, J.M. (1990) 'Personality structure: emergence of the five-factor model', *Annual Review of Psychology*, 41: 417–40.

Digman, J.M. (1994) 'Historical antecedents of the five-factor model', in P.T. Costa and T.A. Widiger (eds), *Personality Disorders and the Five-factor Model of Personality*. Washington, DC: American Psychological Association, pp. 13–18.

Dikman, Z.V. and Allen, J.J.B. (2000) 'Error monitoring during reward and avoidance learning in high- and low-socialized individuals', *Psychophysiology*, 37(1): 43–54.

Drake, M.E., Pakalnis, A., Brown, M.E. and Hietter, S.A. (1988) 'Auditory event related potentials in violent and nonviolent prisoners', *European Archives of Psychiatry and Neurological Sciences*, 238(1): 7–10.

Draycott, S.G. and Kline, P. (1995) 'The big three or the big five – the EPQ-R vs the NEO-PI: A research note, replication and elaboration', *Personality and Individual Differences*, 18(6): 801–4.

Evenden, J.L. (1999) 'Varieties of impulsivity', *Psychopharmacology*, 146(4): 348–61.

Eysenck, H.J. (1953) *The Structure of Human Personality*. New York: Wiley.

Eysenck, H.J. (1977) *Crime and Personality*. London: Routledge & Kegan Paul.

Eysenck, H.J. and Eysenck, M.W. (1985) *Personality and Individual Differences: A Natural Science Approach*. New York: Plenum.

Eysenck, H.J. and Eysenck, S.B.G. (1975) *The Eysenck Personality Questionnaire Manual*. London: Hodder & Stoughton.

Eysenck, H.J. and Eysenck, S.B.G. (1976) *Psychoticism as a Dimension of Personality*. London: Hodder & Stoughton.

Eysenck, S.B.G., Pearson, P.R., Easting, G. and Allsopp, J.F. (1985) 'Age norms for impulsiveness, venturesomeness, and empathy in adults', *Personality and Individual Differences*, 6(5): 613–19.

Fehon, D.C., Grilo, C.M. and Lipschitz, D.S. (2005) 'A comparison of adolescent inpatients with and without a history of violence perpetration: Impulsivity, PTSD, and violence risk', *Journal of Nervous and Mental Disease*, 193(6): 405–11.

Franken, I.H.A., Nijs, I. and Van Strien, J.W. (2005) 'Impulsivity affects mismatch negativity (MMN) measures of preattentive auditory processing', *Biological Psychology*, 70(5): 161–7.

Frankle, W.G., Lombardo, I., New, A.S., Goodman, M., Talbot, P.S., Haung, D. et al. (2005) 'Brain serotonin transporter distribution in subjects with impulsive aggressivity: a positron emission study with [11C]mcn 5652', *American Journal of Psychiatry*, 162(5): 915–23

Gavazzi, S.M., Julian, T.W. and McKenry, P.C. (1996) 'Utilization of the brief symptom inventory to discriminate between violent and nonviolent male relationship partners', *Psychological Reports*, 79: 1047–56.

Gehring, W.J., Goss, B., Coles, M.G.H., Meyer, D.E. and Donchin, E. (1993) 'A neural system for error detection and compensation', *Psychological Science*, 4(6): 385–90.

Gerstle, J.E., Mathias, C.W. and Stanford, M.S. (1998) 'Auditory P300 and self-reported impulsive aggression', *Progress in Neuro-Psychopharmacology and Biological Psychiatry*, 22(4): 575–83.

Goldberg, L.R. (1981) 'Language and individual differences: The search for universals in personality lexicons', in L. Wheeler (ed.), *Review of Personality and Social Psychology* (Vol. 2). Beverly Hills, CA: Sage, pp. 141–65.

Harmon-Jones, E., Barratt, E.S. and Wigg, C. (1997) 'Impulsiveness, aggression, reading, and the P300 of the event-related *potential'*, *Personality and Individual Differences*, 22(4): 439–45.

Houston, R.J. and Stanford, M.S. (2001) 'Mid-latency evoked potentials in self-reported impulsive aggression', *International Journal of Psychophysiology*, 40(1): 1–15.

Iacono, W.G., Carlson, S.R., Malone, S.M. and McGue, M. (2002) 'P3 event-related potential amplitude and the risk for disinhibitory disorders in adolescent boys', *Archives of General Psychiatry*, 59(8): 750–57.

Jensen, P.S., Youngstrom, E.A., Steiner, H., Findling, R.L., Meyer, R.E., Malone, R.P. et al. (2007) 'Consensus report on impulsive aggression as a symptom across diagnostic categories in child psychiatry: Implications for medication studies', *Journal of the American Academy of Child and Adolescent Psychiatry*, 46(3): 309–22.

Jensen-Campbell, L.A., Knack, J.M., Waldrip, A.M. and Campbell, S.D. (2007) 'Do big five personality traits associated with self-control influence the regulation of anger and aggression?', *Journal of Research in Personality*, 41(2): 403–24.

Juhasz, C., Behen, M.E., Muzik, O., Chugani, D.C. and Chugani, H.T. (2001), 'Bilateral medial prefrontal and temporal neocortical hypometabolism in children with epilepsy and aggression', *Epilepsia*, 42(8): 991–1001.

Kok, A. (2001) 'On the utility of P3 amplitude as a measure of processing capacity', *Psychophysiology*, 38(3): 557–77.

Lazarus, R.S. (1999) *Stress and Emotion: A New Synthesis*. New York: Springer.

Lijffijt, M. and Barratt, E.S. (2005) 'ERP and performance measures of error processing in low and high impulsive subjects', Poster presented at the meeting of the International Society for Research on Impulsivity and Impulse Related Disorders, November, Washington, DC.

Lijffijt, M., Coates, D.D. and Barratt, E.S. (2005) 'EEG band power and event related potentials in aggressive and non-aggressive male youthful offenders', Poster presented at the annual meeting of the Society for Neuroscience, November, Washington, DC.

Lipsey, M.W. and Wilson, D.B. (2001) *Practical Meta-analysis*. Thousand Oaks, CA: Sage.

Loeber, R., Pardini, D., Homish, D.L., Wei, E.H., Crawford, A.M., Farrington, D.P. et al. (2005) 'The prediction of violence and homicide in young men', *Journal of Consulting and Clinical Psychology*, 73(6): 1074–88.

Martínez, J.M. and Andrue, J.M. (2006) 'Aggression, and some related psychological constructs (anger, hostility, and impulsivity): Some comments from a research project', *Neuroscience and Biobehavioral Reviews*, 30(3): 276–91.

Matthews, G. and Deary, I.J. (1998) *Personality Traits*. Cambridge, UK: Cambridge University Press.

Mathias, C.W. and Stanford, M.S. (1999) 'P300 under standard and surprise conditions in self-reported impulsive aggression', *Progress in Neuro-Psychopharmacology and Biological Psychiatry*, 23(6): 1037–51.

Mathias, C.W., Stanford, M.S., Marsh, D.M., Frick, P.J., Moeller, F.G., Swann, A.C. et al. (2007) 'Characterizing aggressive behavior with the impulsive/premeditated aggression scale among adolescents with conduct disorder', *Psychiatry Research*, 151(3): 231–42.

McCown, W.G. (1988) 'Multi-impulsive personality disorder and multi substance abuse: Evidence from members of self-help groups', *British Journal of Addiction*, 83(4): 431–2.

Miller, J.D., Bagby, R.M. and Pilkonis, P.A. (2005a) 'A comparison of the validity of the five-factor model (FFM) personality disorder prototypes using FFM self-report and interview measures', *Psychological Assessment*, 17(4): 497–500.

Miller, E.K. and Cohen, J.D. (2001) 'An integrative theory of prefrontal cortex function', *Annual Review of Neuroscience*, 24: 267–202.

Miller, E., Joseph, S. and Tudway, J. (2004) 'Assessing the component structure of four self-report measures of impulsivity', *Personality and Individual Differences*, 37(2): 349–58.

Miller, J.D. and Lynam, D.R. (2006) 'Reactive and proactive aggression: Similarities and differences', *Personality and Individual Differences*, 41(8): 1469–80.

Miller, J.D., Pilkonis, P.A. and Clifton, A. (2005b) 'Self- and other-reports of traits from the five factor model: Relations to personality disorders', *Journal of Personality Disorder*, 19(4): 400–19.

Moeller, F.G., Barratt, E.S., Dougherty, D.M., Schmitz, J.M. and Swann, A.C. (2001) 'Psychiatric aspects of impulsivity', *American Journal of Psychiatry*, 158(11): 1783–93.

Moeller, F.G., Barratt, E.S., Fischer, C.J., Dougherty, D.M., Reilly, E.L., Mathias, C.W. et al. (2004) 'P300 event-related potential amplitude and impulsivity in cocaine-dependent subjects', *Neuropsychobiology*, 50(2): 167–73.

Näätänen, R. (1992) *Attention and Brain Function*. Hillsdale, NJ: Erlbaum.

New, A.S., Hazlett, E.A., Buchsbaum, M.S., Goodman, M., Reynolds, D., Mitropoulou, V. et al. (2002) 'Blunted prefrontal cortical 18Fluorodeoxyglucose positron emission tomography response to meta-chloro-phenylpiperazine in impulsive aggression', *Archives of General Psychiatry*, 59(7): 621–9.

O'Boyle, M. and Barratt, E.S. (1993) 'Impulsivity and DSM-III-R personality disorders', *Personality and Individual Differences*, 14(4): 609–11.

Pailing, P.E. and Segalowitz, S.J. (2004) 'The error-related negativity as a state and trait measure: Motivation, personality, and ERPs in response to errors', *Psychophysiology*, 41(1): 84–95.

Patrick, C.J., Bernat, E.M., Malone, S.M., Iacono, W.G., Krueger, R.F. and McGue, M. (2006) 'P300 amplitude as an indicator of externalizing in adolescent males', *Psychophysiology*, 43(1): 84–92.

Patton, J.H., Stanford, M.S. and Barratt, E.S. (1995) 'Factor structure of the Barratt impulsiveness scale', *Journal of Clinical Psychology*, 51(6): 768–74.

Phillips, M.L., Drevets, W.C., Rauch, S.L. and Lane, R. (2003) 'Neurobiology of emotion perception II: Implications for major psychiatric disorders', *Biological Psychiatry*, 54(5): 515–28.

Polman, H., Orobio de Castro, B., Koops, W., van Boxtel, H.W. and Merk, W.W. (2007) 'A meta-analysis of the distinction between reactive and proactive aggression in children and adolescents', *Journal of Abnormal Child Psychology*, 35(4): 522–35.

Potts, G.F., George, M.R.M., Martin, L.E. and Barratt, E.S. (2006) 'Reduced punishment sensitivity in neural systems of behaviour monitoring in impulsive individuals', *Neuroscience Letters*, 397(1–2): 130–4.

Raine, A., Dodge, K., Loeber, R. Gatzke-Kopp, L., Lynam, D., Reynolds, C. et al. (2006) 'The reactive-proactive aggression questionnaire: Differential correlates of reactive and proactive aggression in adolescent boys', *Aggressive Behavior*, 32(2): 159–71.

Raine, A., Meloy, J.R., Bihrle, S., Stoddard, J., LaCasse, L. and Buchsbaum, M.S. (1998) 'Reduced prefrontal and increased subcortical brain functioning assessed using positron emission tomography in predatory and affective murderers', *Behavioral Sciences and the Law*, 16(3): 319–32.

Ramìrez, J.M. and Andreu, J.M. (2006). 'Aggression, and some related psychological constructs (anger, hostility, and impulsivity); some comments from a research project', *Neuroscience and Biobehavioral Reviews*, 30(3): 276–91.

Ridderinkhof, K.R., Ullsperger, K., Crone, E.A. and Nieuwenhuis, S. (2004a) 'The role of the medial frontal cortex in cognitive control', *Science*, 306(5695): 443–7.

Ridderinkhof, K.R., van den Wildenberg, W.P.M., Segalowitz, S.J. and Carter, C.S. (2004b) 'Neurocognitive mechanisms of cognitive control: The role of prefrontal cortex in action selection, response inhibition, performance monitoring, and reward-based learning', *Brain and Cognition*, 56(2): 129–40.

Ruchsow, M., Spitzer, M., Grön, G., Grothe, J. and Kiefer, M. (2005) 'Error processing and impulsiveness in normals: Evidence from event-related potentials', *Cognitive Brain Research*, 24(2): 317–25.

Rushton, J.P. and Chrisjohn, R.D. (1990) 'Extraversion, neuroticism, psychoticism and self-reported delinquency: Evidence from eight separate samples', in N.Z. Hilton, M.A. Jackson and C.D. Webster (eds), *Clinical Criminology: Theory, Research and Practice*. Toronto: Canada: Canadian Scholars' Press, pp. 100–111.

Santesso, D.L., Segalowitz, S.J. and Schmidt, L.A. (2005) 'ERP correlates of error monitoring in 10-year olds are related to socialization', *Biological Psychology*, 70(2): 79–87.

Sher, K.J. and Trull, T.J. (1994) 'Personality and disinhibitory psychopathology: Alcoholism and antisocial personality disorder', *Journal of Abnormal Psychology*, 103(1): 92–102.

Soloff, P.H., Meltzer, C.C., Becker, C., Greer, P.J., Kelly, T.M. and Constantine, D. (2003) 'Impulsivity and prefrontal hypometabolism in borderline personality disorder', *Psychiatry Research*, 123(3): 153–63.

Stanford, M.S. and Barratt, E.S. (1992) 'Impulsivity and the multi-impulsive personality disorder', *Personality and Individual Differences*, 13(7): 831–4.

Stanford, M.S., Conklin, S.M., Helfritz, L.E. and Kockler, T.R. (2007) 'P3 amplitude reduction and executive function deficits in men convicted of spousal/partner abuse', *Personality and Individual Differences*, 43(2): 365–75.

Stanford, M.S., Greve, K.W. and Dickens Jr, T.J. (1995) 'Irritability and impulsiveness: Relationship to self-reported impulsive aggression', *Personality and Individual Differences*, 19(5): 757–60.

Stanford, M.S., Greve, K.W. and Gerstle, J.E. (1997) 'Neuropsychological correlates of self-reported impulsive aggression in a college sample', *Personality and Individual Differences*, 23(6): 961–5.

Stanford, M.S., Houston, R.J., Mathias, C.W., Villemarette-Pittman, N.R., Helfritz, L.E. and Conklin, S.M. (2003a) 'Characterizing aggressive behavior', *Assessment*, 10(2): 183–90.

Stanford, M.S., Houston, R.J., Villemarette-Pittman, N.R. and Greve, K.W. (2003b) 'Premeditated aggression: Clinical assessment and cognitive psychophysiology', *Personality and Individual Differences*, 34(5): 773–81.

Suris, A., Lind, L., Emmett, G., Borman, P.D., Kashner, M. and Barratt, E.S. (2004) 'Measures of aggressive behavior: Overview of clinical and research instruments', *Aggression and Violent Behavior*, 9(2): 165–227.

Swann, A.C. (2003) 'Neuroreceptor mechanisms of aggression and its treatment', *Journal of Clinical Psychiatry*, 64(54): 26–35.

Verona, E. and Kilmer, A. (2007) 'Stress exposure and affective modulation of aggressive behavior in men and women', *Journal of Abnormal Psychology*, 116(2): 410–21.

Walker, J.S. and Gudjonsson, G.H. (2006) 'The Maudsley Violence Questionnaire: Relationship to personality and self-reported offending', *Personality and Individual Differences*, 40(4): 795–806.

Wang, E.W. and Diamond, P.M. (1999) 'Empirically identifying factors related to violence risk in corrections', *Behavioral Sciences and the Law*, 17(3): 377–89.

White, J.L., Moffitt, T.E., Caspi, A., Bartusch, D.J., Needles, D.J. and Stouthammer-Loeber, M. (1994) 'Measuring impulsivity and examining its relationship to delinquency', *Journal of Abnormal Psychology*, 103(2): 192–205.

Yeung, N., Botvinick, M.M. and Cohen, J.D. (2004) 'The neural basis of error detection: conflict monitoring and the error-related negativity', *Psychological Review*, 111(4): 931–59.

Zuckerman, M., Huhlman, D.M., Joireman, J., Teta, P. and Kraft, M. (1993) 'A comparison of the three structural models for personality: The big three, the big five, and the alternative five', *Journal of Personality and Social Psychology*, 65(4): 575–768.

17

Psychoticism and Impulsivity

David Rawlings and Sharon Dawe

The present chapter focuses on psychoticism and the related construct of impulsivity. The chapter begins with a discussion of the history of the concept, psychoticism, its measurement, its correlates in a wide range of areas, and a brief evaluation. In a shorter section, the concept of impulsivity is discussed and is related to the psychoticism construct.

PSYCHOTICISM

The term 'psychoticism' is employed almost exclusively in personality psychology to refer to a specific dimension within H.J. Eysenck's 'PEN' theory of personality, and it is in this sense that we shall use it for most of the present chapter. In Eysenck's theory, comprising the three continuous dimensions of psychoticism (P), extraversion (E), and neuroticism (N), the concept represents individual differences in the personality dimension believed to underlie the development of psychosis.

The term first appeared in Eysenck's writings in his second book, *The Scientific Study of Personality* (1952), where it received a definition not unlike more recent conceptualisations. Several early studies employed the construct as a latent variable, usually within a clinical context, and early self-report measures began to appear in the late 1960s. Substantial exploration of the concept followed the appearance at around the same time of the first well-developed questionnaire, the Eysenck Personality Questionnaire (H.J. Eysenck and S.B.G. Eysenck, 1975), and the seminal monograph, *Psychoticism as a Dimension of Personality* (H.J. Eysenck and S.B.G Eysenck, 1976). Psychoticism was now considered by the Eysencks to be a dimension of personality approaching equal importance to E and N.

It is of interest that the word 'psychoticism' has at various times been substituted by Eysenck or other authors in the field, mostly in an effort to remove its pathological implications. Alternative names for the dimension have included 'tough-mindedness/tender-mindedness', 'adventurousness/caution', and 'social nonconformity/conformity'. In addition, the low end of the dimension, while initially named 'normality', has been labelled at various times 'superego functioning', 'superego control' or 'impulse control'.

Eysenck's conceptualisation of the psychoticism construct grew out of his consideration of some of the major debates in psychiatry as they appeared at that time

(H.J. Eysenck, 1992a). Two issues were of particular importance and will be briefly discussed.

Psychoticism as a dimension of personality

In forming his opinion on the dimensionality of psychoticism, Eysenck set himself firmly against the traditional view of psychiatric illness which was based on the ideas of the early German psychiatrist, Emil Kraepelin, and envisaged a clear distinction between the normal and the pathological. Kraepelin argued that schizophrenia, called *dementia praecox* (premature deterioration), is an organic disease. While recognising the presence of premorbid abnormality, Kraepelin emphasised that people either suffer from mental illness or do not, an assumption which still underlies contemporary psychiatric conceptualisations of the functional disorders, as exemplified by the DSM-IV-TR.

Early critics of Kraepelin's view included the Swiss psychiatrist, Eugene Bleuler, and the German psychiatrist, Ernst Kretschmer. The latter was particularly influential on Eysenck's theorising. Kretschmer argued that the endogenous psychoses were simply accentuations of normal temperament types, and proposed a continuum from schizophrenia through schizoid behaviour to dystonic (normal introverted) behaviour, then through syntonic (normal extraverted) behaviour, cycloid and finally manic-depressive disorder. H.J. Eysenck and S.B.G. Eysenck (1976) recognised the importance of this schizothymia–cyclothymia continuum, but noted that it implied a second dimension of *severity* which cuts across that continuum. This second dimension was, they argued, psychoticism.

For Eysenck, psychoticism exemplified the diathesis-stress model of disease, representing a continuous dimension of genetic predisposition which, when appearing in appropriate environmental circumstances, leads to a continuum of observable behavioural traits.

The continuum of overt behaviour could be measured within the normal population, and extended at the high end into 'psychotic' mental illness. In fact, the term 'psychoticism' appears in Eysenck's writings with a number of meanings.

1. It sometimes stands for individual differences in genetic predisposition. Here it is a biological construct.
2. It represents individual differences in behavioural traits: aggressive, cold, egocentric, impersonal, impulsive, antisocial, unempathic, creative, tough-minded. Here it is a continuum of normal personality, which can be measured using, among other things, self-report questionnaires.
3. It may also represent individual differences in abnormal behaviour; that is, in the symptoms of disorder. This point is illustrated by the appearance of a continuum of severity in several of Eysenck's writings (e.g. H.J. Eysenck, 1992a) extending from empathy, altruism and conformity (at one extreme) through criminal, hostile, aggressive, alcoholic, schizoid, psychopathic, unipolar depressive, manic-depressive, and schizoaffective to schizophrenia (at the other extreme). Thus, both normal traits and abnormal conditions appear on this list, such that the break between normal and abnormal is substantially arbitrary.
4. Finally, it sometimes refers to the overall personality system representing both predisposition and behaviour – both normal and abnormal; in other words, to all three of the previous dimensions.

It is noted, with respect to point 3 above, that Claridge (1990) suggested a modification to Eysenck's view which retains the spirit of the original conceptualisation. Claridge argues that some physical diseases do include elements of both genuine continuity and discontinuity, and may provide a useful metaphor for the consideration of mental disorder. Blood pressure/hypertension is used as an example. Level of blood pressure represents a continuum of disease proneness which may or may not produce disease. However, the predisposition may, when accompanied by environmental stressors, produce clear discontinuities of functioning involving such hypertensive conditions as stroke or heart disease.

Likewise, a person high on the continuous predisposition to psychosis may, when placed in an appropriately stressful environment, begin to develop the functional discontinuities represented by the more florid symptoms of schizophrenia.

The breadth of the psychoticism concept

The word 'psychosis' provided the starting point for the formulation of the new word 'psychoticism'. An early task for Eysenck was to establish the difference between the psychoses and the other major group of mental disorders, the neuroses. One could either take the view of Freud that there was a single continuum from normality, through neurosis, to psychosis; or, alternatively, postulate two separate dimensions, the one leading from normality to neurosis and the other from normality to psychosis. H.J. Eysenck and S.B.G. Eysenck (1976) describe several studies dating from the 1950s which provide strong support for a clear differentiation into separate dimensions, labelled 'neuroticism' and 'psychoticism'.

Having shown that psychosis was different from neurosis, Eysenck attempted to establish whether the various forms of psychosis reflected a single underlying phenomenon or were, in fact, quite distinct. The former view involved the early concept of the *Einheitpsychose*, or unitary psychosis. The basis of the latter view was a major distinction put forward by Kraepelin between the affective, manic-depressive forms of psychotic illness and *dementia praecox*, which forms the basis for the contemporary psychiatric viewpoint on the issue.

On the one hand, Eysenck's view of psychoticism clearly reflects the unitary psychosis viewpoint. As H.J. Eysenck and S.B.G. Eysenck (1976) point out, if there is no common ground among the functional varieties of psychosis, the concepts of psychoticism and psychosis become meaningless, and several writers point to the

similarity of symptomatology in schizophrenia and affective psychosis (e.g. Kendell, 1991). On the other hand, not all reviews of the genetic evidence support the unitary psychosis position (e.g. Gottesman and Bertelsen, 1991) and evidence from other areas, such as the differential effects of medication, support Kraepelin's view that specific types of psychosis may be usefully differentiated. In formulating his view of the nature of psychosis, Eysenck summarised the arguments for both sides of the debate and came to the conclusion that

> It would not be reasonable to stress either line to the exclusion of the other; psychoticism is a reality, but so is the distinction between schizophrenia ... and manic-depression ... clearly there is no victory in all these studies for either rigid Kraepelinian distinctions or for the ancient *Einheitpsychose* (1995: 217).

In its simplest form, Eysenck's position was a combination of the *Einheitpsychose* view and Kretschmer's bipolar dimension. Psychoticism, representing the predisposition to psychosis, was conceptualised as substantially independent of the other two personality dimensions, but the nature of the psychosis which developed in the highly psychosis-prone individual was partly determined by the person's degree of extraversion. Introverts were more likely to suffer from schizophrenia or paranoid disorders, extraverts from affective psychoses (Verma and Eysenck, 1973).

However, Eysenck did not stop at the two major psychotic disorders when deciding the breadth of his concepts of psychosis and psychoticism. Criminal behaviour comprised part of the broad conceptualisation, where psychopathy was believed to result from high scores on all three personality dimensions (H.J. Eysenck and S.B.G. Eysenck, 1978). Also incorporated were the various 'schizophrenia spectrum disorders' identified by writers such as Reich (1976), which included disorders labelled 'schizoid' or 'schizotypal' and frequently referred to minor manifestations of schizophrenia. In light of such conceptual breadth it was difficult to maintain the neat differentiation proposed by Verma and Eysenck (1973).

Psychoticism, then, is the personality dimension underlying the development of psychosis, as broadly defined by Eysenck to include not only such classic psychoses as schizophrenia, affective psychosis and paranoid psychosis, but criminal and antisocial behaviour as well. Because it is a continuum, it also includes minor manifestations of these disorders. Eysenck's view is a somewhat broadened conceptualisation of the (already broad) *Einheitpsychose* position.

Measuring psychoticism

Questionnaire measures of extraversion and neuroticism appeared fairly early in Eysenck's research career. His earliest questionnaire measure, the Maudsley Medical Questionnaire (measuring neuroticism), dates from 1952; extraversion was introduced in the Maudsley Personality Inventory of 1959; while the Eysenck Personality Inventory (EPI) appeared in 1964 and included modified, more clearly orthogonal measures of both E and N. The inventory added a dissimulation or 'lie' scale, and included two parallel forms.

The Eysenck Personality Questionnaire (EPQ) (H.J. Eysenck and S.B.G. Eysenck, 1975) was the first commercially published questionnaire to include a psychoticism scale; however, several prototype P scales were developed much earlier (e.g. H.J. Eysenck and S.B.G. Eysenck, 1968; S.B.G. Eysenck and H.J. Eysenck 1968). These prototype scales typically had high positive skew and showed moderate correlation with N; revisions aimed at overcoming these problems led to the EPQ. A 'junior' version of the scale, suitable for the older primary and early adolescent years, was introduced as an updated form of the earlier Junior EPI. A major modification to the P scale was carried out in a revision of the EPQ in 1985, which produced the EPQ Revised (EPQ-R) (S.B.G. Eysenck et al., 1985). The other three scales of the original EPQ remained effectively unchanged. A short form of the

EPQ-R, in which 12 items measured each of the 4 scales, was also published in the original article.

As the most recent Eysenck inventory in the public domain, the EPQ-R remains a popular measure of Eysenck's personality dimensions. Several subsequent investigators have examined its psychometric properties and produced a junior form of the questionnaire, including a junior short form with 12 items per scale (Corulla, 1990), and 'abbreviated' (6 items per scale) measures aimed at both adult (Francis et al., 1992) and junior (Francis, 1996) samples. While the original 32-item P scale produced alpha coefficients of 0.73 and 0.81 for females and males respectively, and comparable reliabilities were reported in subsequent studies (e.g. Corulla, 1987), the reduced forms of the EPQ-R P scale show widely varying, and often quite inadequate, reliability. Thus, S.B.G. Eysenck et al. (1985) reported alpha coefficients for their 12-item scale of 0.68 and 0.62 for males, and 0.51 and 0.61 for females, in two separate samples in their original study. However, Francis et al. (1992) reported coefficients between 0.52 and 0.33 for the 12-item version and Shevlin et al. (2002) review several studies showing reliabilities between 0.74 and 0.28 for the 6-item version. Slightly higher coefficients have been reported for the reduced junior versions (Corulla, 1990; Francis, 1996).

The various versions of the Eysenck Personality Profiler, dating originally from 1988, comprise the most recently developed instruments (e.g. H.J. Eysenck and Wilson, 1999; H.J. Eysenck et al., 1999). These vary in length from 630 to 200 items, and psychoticism is now generally labelled 'adventurousness' or 'adventurousness/caution'. The most distinctive feature of these measures is the appearance of correlated subscales or 'primary' scales making up the three super-factors. For psychoticism (adventurousness), the seven primary scales are:

- P1: risk-taking
- P2: impulsiveness

- P3: irresponsibility
- P4: manipulativeness
- P5: sensation-seeking
- P6: tough-mindedness
- P7: practicality.

Responses are made on three-category response scales ('yes', 'no', 'can't decide') rather than the two-category scales in earlier Eysenck questionnaires. Using the 420-item version of the inventory, Jackson et al. (2000) reported reliabilities on the various primary scales in three large studies. They noted high consistencies in quoted alphas across studies, though with levels occasionally falling below 0.6.

Empirical correlates of the psychoticism scale

As noted above, H.J. Eysenck and S.B.G. Eysenck (1976) reported a number of empirical connections to P. Many early studies employed prototype versions of the P-scale which were highly correlated with N and quite different in content to the 1975 and later versions. Thus, Rawlings (1983) compared the P-scales from the EPQ and the PEN, an early measure of P. The two scales have only eight common items and produced very different patterns of correlation with a wide range of questionnaire and behavioural variables. In this brief review of empirical studies we shall subsequently refer only to studies employing the EPQ and later versions of the scale, and will focus on more recent studies.

We first note that the P-scale is consistently higher in some groups than others. Males score significantly higher than females; young participants (particularly young males) higher than old participants. Lynn and Martin (1995) report cross-national differences in P, indicating that the highest scores were obtained by the inhabitants of Czechoslovakia, India, Yugoslavia, Hong Kong and Australia, and the lowest by persons living in Norway, Portugal, The Netherlands,

Spain and the United States; though sampling considerations make it necessary to treat such generalisations with caution.

Psychotics score higher on the scale than do non-clinical normal individuals, but the highest scores are typically obtained by substance abusers, alcoholics and prisoners. The strong relationship between P and drug dependence has been replicated several times (e.g. Doherty and Matthews, 1988), and extends to the use of legal, socially accepted drugs such as alcohol and tobacco (Gilbert, 1988; Golding et al., 1983); and while the relationship between criminality and P appears consistently in the literature (Furnham and Thompson, 1991; Romero et al., 2001), the relationship is not always a simple one. For example, Heaven et al. (2004) note that while the P scale appears to predict most delinquent behaviours among younger adolescents, it predicts more serious delinquent behaviours in adults, while van Dam et al. (2005) found that the scale predicted self-reported, but not officially recorded, recidivism.

The P-scale has been correlated with a wide range of self-report measures, including Machiavellianism (Allsopp et al., 1991), externalising behaviour (Center et al., 2005), violent and non-violent offending (Walker and Gudjonsson, 2006), social psychopathy (Edelmann and Vivian, 1988), and 'reducing' on Vanda's reducer–augmenter scale (Dragutinovich, 1987). O'Boyle and Holzer (1992) found links between P and measures of antisocial and schizotypal personality disorder; using the MMPI-2 personality disorder scales. Hendricks (2005) supported these correlations, and found additional positive correlations with borderline, histrionic, passive aggressive, and narcissistic; and a negative correlation with schizoid, personality disorder types in a normal population. Correlations with measures of impulsivity are reported later.

Many behavioural measures have been related to P in correlational or quasi-experimental studies. In studies of visual perception, high P scorers report seeing more complex objects in computer-generated random dot patterns (Jakes and Hemsley, 1986); and require longer stimulus duration to identify a stimulus (Badcock et al., 1988).

Robinson and Zahn (1985) manipulated *arousal* by requiring participants to recline or stand. High P individuals displayed lower autonomic arousability in the reclining (low activation) condition. Clark et al. (1987) reported lower autonomic, particularly cardiac, activity in high P scorers, while Mecacci et al. (1986) found that evening types had significantly higher P scores. However, whereas Wilson (1990) confirmed this latter finding, he also discovered that apparently lower skin conductance levels in high P scorers than low scorers disappeared when age-correction was applied to the data. Glicksohn and Naftuliev (2005) reported *greater* responsivity/arousability in high P scorers using an EEG-based index.

Inconsistent results have been found in studies of *hemisphere laterality*. In an eye-movement task of Christie and Raine (1988), fewer rightward eye-movements (suggesting left hemisphere underactivation) were reported in high P individuals. This result is consistent with the dichotic listening study of Rawlings and Borge (1987), in which high P individuals failed to show the normal right ear/left hemisphere superiority for verbal material, and parallels an earlier study of Hare and McPherson (1984) employing criminal psychopaths. However, Rawlings and Borge (1987) report a second study in which the above effect was not found, and refer to several other studies in which P showed no significant relationship with hemisphere functioning.

The area of *learning*, broadly defined, has been frequently given prominence by Eysenck as providing among the more adequate methods for testing his theory. Two learning paradigms given particular prominence in theorising about psychoticism have been latent inhibition and negative priming; both paradigms provide evidence pointing to the low cognitive inhibition presumed by Eysenck to underlie P. *Latent inhibition*, referring to the retardation in learning which occurs following repeated non-reinforced presentation (pre-exposure) of the conditioned stimulus, has been negatively associated both with acute schizophrenia (Baruch et al., 1988a) and eminent creative achievement (Carson et al., 2003). The effect has also been shown in high P scorers (Baruch et al., 1988b; Lubow et al., 1992), but tends to be weak and inconsistent (cf. Peterson and Carson, 2000; Wuthrich and Bates, 2001).

The words *negative priming* were used by Tipper (1985) to refer to the increased delay in responding to a target object when that object has previously served as a distracting stimulus which was to be ignored. Reduced negative priming has been found in schizophrenics (Beech et al., 1989) and in high P scorers (Stavridou and Furnham, 1996). However, Beech and Claridge (1987) found that P (non-significantly) correlated with negative priming in the direction opposite to prediction, while Kwiatkowski et al. (1999) report no correlations between negative priming and P.

The area of *aesthetic preference* was among the earliest concepts studied by Eysenck (e.g. H.J. Eysenck, 1941), though his initial focus was on its connection to extraversion. H.J. Eysenck (1993b) and Cox and Leon (1999) both found a positive relationship between P and preference for more complex figures on the Barron-Welsh art scale, which measures liking for abstract line drawings. Rawlings et al. (1995) found that high P scorers enjoyed hard rock and heavy metal music more, and easy listening music less, than low P scorers. Psychoticism was also associated with a relative preference for discords compared to consonant (major or minor) chords played on a piano. More recently, Rawlings and Leow (in press) found a tendency for high P individuals to show a relative preference for music that is typically classified as 'unpleasant' (disturbing or boring); while Rawlings and Bastian (2002) and Rawlings (2003) found a relationship between P and liking for violent and unpleasant paintings.

Numerous studies have correlated P with psychometric tests of *creativity*, such as word association, where high P individuals tend to make more unique and fewer common responses than low P participants (H.J. Eysenck, 1994; Ward et al., 1991). Quite strong correlations have sometimes been found using *divergent thinking* tasks, such as the Kogan–Wallach battery of creativity tests, though results have varied widely. Woody and Claridge (1977) produced correlations between P and each of the five sub-scales of above 0.6, a result that was substantially replicated by Stavridou and Furnham (1996). Several studies have found no relationship at all between divergent thinking measures and P, though these have sometimes employed number ('fluency') of responses as their criterion measure of creativity (Kwiatkowski et al., 1999; McCrae, 1987), have employed a criterion less stringent than the selection of truly unique responses (Wuthrich and Bates, 2001), or have capped the number of possible responses to each item (Cox and Leon, 1999). In fact, the very strong correlations tend to appear in studies providing relaxing, untimed conditions and individual (as opposed to group) testing, though weak correlations have been reported in some studies which specifically provided such conditions (e.g. Asgari, 2000; Rawlings, 1984). Rawlings and Toogood (1997) found support for the view that the relationship between P and divergent thinking may be at least partly due to participants' willingness to make mildly antisocial responses in addition to their tendency to show unusual thinking. It could be argued that face-to-face contact (in contrast to anonymity) would increase the importance of interpersonal variables, providing an explanation of the very high correlations in studies where participants were tested individually.

A number of studies have related P to *achievement creativity*, particularly in the arts, with higher P obtained by artists than non-artists across a number of artistic types (Booker et al., 2001; Gotz and Gotz, 1979; Hu and Gong, 1990; Merten and Fischer, 1999; Mohan and Tiwana, 1987). Rushton (1990) found relatively high P scores among more successful academic psychologists. Abraham et al. (2005) differentiated the 'originality' from the 'practicality' aspects of creative cognition, finding that P was related to the former rather than the latter.

A wide range of *social phenomena* have been related to P. An early review by Wilson (1981) described a number of studies relating personality to social behaviour, including conflict, socio-political attitudes, sexual behaviour, and pathology. Subsequent studies in the area of sexual behaviour have indicated that high P-scoring males are more likely to be curious about morbid and sexual events, and to be aroused by depictions of rape, than are low scorers (Zuckerman and Litle, 1986; Barnes et al., 1984; but cf. Malamuth, 1986). Measures of traditional religiosity have been associated with low P scores in several studies, though the association is often weak (see Egan et al., 2004). In a large study by Jorm and Christensen (2004), the typical negative relationship was found in younger participants, but the relationship became curvilinear in middle or older participants such that high P scores were associated with the lowest and highest quartiles.

Explanatory models for psychoticism

As with his other dimensions, Eysenck saw psychoticism as a personality dimension with a strong genetic and biological basis. In their early conceptualisation of the psychoticism dimension, H.J. Eysenck and S.B.G. Eysenck (1976) tentatively considered two biologically oriented theories which held promise for providing a theoretical framework for the dimension. Using an early prototype P scale, Claridge (1972) postulated a breakdown in the homeostatic relations between a 'tonic arousal system' and an 'arousal modulation system', which was evidenced by the reversal in schizophrenia, and high P (Claridge and Chappa, 1973), of the normal inverted-U shaped relationship between experimental measures of autonomic arousal and attention. Using the EPQ version of the scale, Robinson and Zahn (1979) failed to replicate the above pattern, a finding believed by Claridge (1987) to evidence the weakness of the EPQ scale.

An alternative view was based on the tendency for males to typically obtain higher scores than females on the P-scale. J.A. Gray (1973) put forward the 'maleness' hypothesis, suggesting that P reflects the tendency to an excessive degree of intra-specific aggressive behaviour in response to unconditioned punishment or frustrative non-reward, and is possibly facilitated by some aspect of male sexuality. Interestingly, Zuckerman (1989) argued that P is more clearly associated with 'irritable aggression' in animals, or the type 'which does not seem to be tied to obvious survival or competitive motives'.

The above models reflect the two major orientations to theorising about the nature of P. On the one hand are models which reflect the belief that P is clearly linked to psychotic predisposition, an orientation adopted most obviously by Eysenck. In particular, Eysenck's later theorising was influenced by the attempts of Gray and his colleagues to link psychoticism to neurotransmitter function in line with developing evidence for the importance of neurotransmitters, particularly dopamine, in schizophrenia (e.g. J.A. Gray et al., 1991; N.S. Gray et al., 1994). Thus, in his most fully developed integration of the various components of his theory of psychoticism, Eysenck concluded: 'It seems likely that dopaminergic over-activity and serotogenic under-activity jointly and severally constitute the basic causes of schizophreniform cognition' (1995: 265). Together these lead to low levels of cognitive inhibition in the psychotic or high P individual, producing the loose, 'overinclusive' thinking that characterises both psychotic thought disorder and the creative thinking of the artist or scientist (cf. H.J. Eysenck, 1995, figure 8.1).

A second major approach to the conceptualisation of P is based on the assumption that it is clearly linked to impulsive and antisocial behaviour. Zuckerman (2005) conceived psychoticism as part of a broad personality dimension referred to as P-impulsive-unsocialised-sensation-seeking. High scorers were particularly characterised by lack of behavioural restraint or disinhibition. While the serotonin system is particularly associated with disinhibition, Zuckerman (e.g. 1989) emphasised its complex interaction with a number of other biochemical systems in producing the personality dimension. Such interaction involved the catecholamines noradrenalin (producing weak arousability) and dopamine (producing strong approach to novelty), the sex hormone testosterone, and the enzyme monoamine oxidase (MOA). A link between serotonin and P was specifically established in a study by Pritchard (1991), while Hennig (2004) has reviewed recent research on the links between personality and the serotonin system. Also focusing on the antisocial/impulsive aspects of psychoticism-related measures, Pickering (2004) has critically reviewed and evaluated the research into the relationship of dopamine activity to these measures, arguing that hippocampal function may more adequately explain the variance associated with P. This area is further examined in the later section on impulsivity.

Genetic research has tended to support Eysenck's emphasis on heredity in the determination of the major personality dimensions. A review of 15 twin studies using the P scale by Eaves et al. (1989) found a mean MZ twin correlation of 0.46 and DZ correlation of 0.23, with a mean heritability of 0.49 and no evidence of shared environment. Several other studies using measures with conceptual or empirical links to P have provided indirect evidence for the heritability of the dimension, including 'conscientiousness' and 'agreeableness' from the five-factor model of personality and 'constraint' from Tellegen's model (Bouchard and McGue, 2003), and measures of impulsivity and sensation-seeking (Zuckerman, 2005).

However, other studies sound a note of caution. Using the EPQ P-scale, Heath and Martin (1990) found that the genetic factor structure of the scale differed considerably from the environmental structure; while Loehlin and Martin (2001) found a heritability for P of only 0.28, possibly because they used the short, unreliable form of the EPQ-R P scale. Recently, Pergadia et al. (2006) have suggested that shared family environment may play a more important role than previously thought when extreme personality characteristics are defined categorically.

In the relatively new area of molecular genetics, the data can provide no more than suggestive evidence and has centred around the genes underlying neurotransmitter functioning. Thus, early studies linking the dopamine D4 (D4DR) receptor exon III polymorphism with novelty-seeking (Ebstein et al., 1996) and the short form of the serotonin transporter genotype (5-HTTLPR) with neuroticism (Lesch et al., 1996) led to numerous attempts at replication, some of which were successful and some not. Zuckerman (2005) reviews several of these and related studies, suggesting links between the genes involved in the dopaminergic system and the 'approach' behaviour found in both normal extraverted behaviour and antisocial personality; and between low levels of serotonin and both lack of anxiety and violent, aggressive acts of hostility (cf. Hennig et al., 2005). There remains widespread, and substantial, disagreement in this area.

Not all molecular genetic studies have focused on neurotransmitters. An Australian study by Turakulov et al. (2004) suggested, in the tradition of Gray's (1973) 'maleness' hypothesis, a possible link between P and the X-linked androgen receptor gene CAG polymorphism in males and, less strongly, in females. Using a different Australian sample, Loehlin et al. (2005) attempted to replicate the result, concluding that CAG sequence length could, at best, account for a very small proportion of the variance of P.

Critique and an alternative: schizotypy and psychosis proneness

In psychoticism, Eysenck gave the field of personality a concept of extraordinary breadth.

As was typical of Eysenck as a theorist, he painted with a broad brush, elaborating a dimension with links to genetics and biology and with correlates in diverse areas. In the defining area of clinical diagnosis, psychoticism included not only the concepts of schizophrenia and affective disorder, but psychopathy, schizotypy, and schizoid conditions, and indeed much of what has come to be called the personality disorders.

In attempting to operationalise the broad psychoticism construct, however, Eysenck produced a scale which measured just one, relatively narrow area of the broad domain of behaviour covered by the construct. While early prototype versions may have been more satisfactory (Claridge, 1981, 1987), it has been argued that EPQ and later versions of the scale sampled aspects of behaviour quite marginal to the area of psychosis, as generally understood, or even outside that area altogether. A typical criticism was Block's (1977) comment that 'the P items directly imply an aggressive, impulsive, unconscientious individual who can be expected to be frequently represented in criminal or psychopathic populations' (1977: 434).

A number of writers attempted to produce alternative measures of psychotic behaviour appropriate to normal populations, frequently focusing on just one or a few aspects of psychotic symptomatology. Many of these are based on very similar assumptions to the P scale, and may well have been called measures of 'psychoticism' had the term not already been used by Eysenck. In fact, they tend to be referred to as measures of 'schizotypy' or 'psychosis proneness'.[1] Mason et al. (1997) list several such measures and note that, when factor analyses of the various scales are carried out, a three or four factor structure tends to occur: One factor reflects the 'positive' symptoms of schizophrenia, including items related to magical thinking and mild hallucinatory experience; a second factor reflects 'negative' schizophrenic symptoms such as anhedonia and introverted withdrawal; a third factor measures aspects of social anxiety, attentional disturbance and disorganised thinking. Finally, a factor is sometimes produced which loads on P, on the Lie-scale, and on the impulsive nonconformity scale of L.J. Chapman et al. (1984).

It is noteworthy that many of the empirical results reported above for psychoticism, including many with substantial theoretical importance, have been replicated using self-report indices of 'positive' schizotypy. These studies comprise a body of literature which present a genuine alternative to the P scale as providing measures of psychotic predisposition (see Claridge, 1997, for reviews of research in several areas). Furthermore, the limited evidence available suggests that they are at least as adequate as the P scale in the prediction of psychotic breakdown (cf. L.J. Chapman et al., 1994; J.P. Chapman et al., 1994).

Not surprisingly, although Eysenck (e.g. 1995) used many validation studies of the various schizotypy scales to support the validity of the P scale, he was highly critical of the concept, noting that its various measures were correlated with neuroticism (H.J. Eysenck and Barrett, 1993). In reply, proponents of the schizotypy viewpoint might argue that factorial purity need not be regarded as of overriding importance in making a decision on the usefulness of the schizotypy concept, and in any case several of the more recent measures of positive schizotypy have relatively small correlations with N (around 0.25).

It would seem reasonable to conclude that the very broad psychoticism construct identified by Eysenck is inadequately sampled by the P-scale, and several views on the possible relationship between the scale and the broad domain of psychotic disorder have been put forward. The fact that the scale continues to show some degree of correlation with the various measures of positive schizotypy implies some overlap in meaning, and one view is that it measures one component of the broad, multi-faceted construct representing psychotic predisposition (e.g. Mason et al., 1995). Other theorists exclude the scale entirely, arguing that the relationship is an 'historical accident' (Pickering, 2004), and identifying it with a totally different domain

of personality and psychopathology; a domain built around concepts such as 'impulsivity'. The concept of impulsivity, and its relation to P, is the focus of the remainder of the chapter.

IMPULSIVITY

Unlike psychoticism, where the focus has been around a single theoretical framework, approaches to the study of impulsivity within personality research have emerged from a wide range of theoretical perspectives and methodological approaches. In the remainder of the chapter, we briefly describe these models and associated instruments, suggest their integration around two major dimensions, and relate the concepts of impulsivity and psychoticism.

Models of impulsivity

Eysenck's view of impulsivity

Impulsivity was never considered by Eysenck to be a fundamental, higher-order factor in his three-factor model of personality but rather one of a number of primary traits that are correlated to form the higher-order dimensions. As a primary trait related to both P and E, Eysenck proposed that impulsivity was related to low cortical arousal, which in turn is related to poor functioning of the reticular activating system. In addition, the strong evidence on disinhibited behaviour linked to damage to the right hemisphere frontal lobes and to the orbitofrontal area led Eysenck to propose that these brain areas were also involved in impulsive behaviour. These findings are consistent with the general proposition that low levels of serotonergic activity and altered dopamine functioning, as evidenced by studies showing low levels of MAO, are characteristic of those who have high P, high E and high impulsiveness scores (H.J. Eysenck, 1993).

The I_7 Adult Impulsivity Questionnaire (H.J. Eysenck and S.B.G. Eysenck, 1992) is one of the most widely used measures of impulsiveness. It consists of three scales: impulsiveness, a measure of rash, unplanned impulsive behaviour that is related to psychoticism; venturesomeness, a measure of impulsive acts in which consequences have been weighed and considered acceptable risks, that is related to extraversion; and empathy, as a source of filler items.

Zuckerman and sensation-seeking

Zuckerman views sensation-seeking as a trait with a biological basis resulting in an increased tendency to seek out intense, novel forms of sensation and experience accompanied by a willingness to seek such experiences regardless of the risks involved. One widely used measure of Zuckerman's sensation-seeking is the sensation-seeking scale, form V (SSS-V). This 40-item self-report measure is made up of four subscales of ten items each: thrill- and adventure-seeking (SSS-TAS), experience-seeking (SSS-ES), disinhibition (SSS-DIS), and boredom susceptibility (SSS-BS). The broad-based Zuckerman–Kuhlman Personality Questionnaire (ZKPQ; Zuckerman et al., 1993) includes a measure of impulsive sensation-seeking (ImpSS), in addition to four scales measuring other aspects of personality. This scale, whose two highly correlated components (impulsivity and sensation-seeking) may be used separately or singly, has been proposed to measure, in part, features related to Eysenck's P construct (Pickering, 2004).

As noted in relation to Zuckerman's view of psychoticism, the biological basis of sensation-seeking is particularly related to activity in serotonergic and dopaminergic pathways. In relation to the latter, Zuckerman proposes that it is the enzyme monoamine oxidase (MAO) that is sensitive to sensation-seeking (Zuckerman, 1994) with levels of MAO inversely and significantly related to scores on the SSS. There is also a substantial body of evidence supporting a relationship between low MOA levels and psychopathologies characterised by disorders of impulse such as substance abuse and gambling (Af Klinteberg et al., 2004). Zuckerman

proposed that much of what drives these particular psychopathologies is 'impulsive sensation-seeking' (Zuckerman, 2005).

Cloninger and novelty-seeking

Cloninger's personality taxonomy, as operationalised in his Temperament and Character Inventory, consists of four higher order temperament traits with three additional character dimensions. The four temperament dimensions are: novelty-seeking (NS), describing individuals who are excitable, curious, and keen to engage in rewarding activities; harm avoidance (HA), describing individuals who tend to be cautious, careful apprehensive, and nervous; reward dependence (RD), describing individuals who tend to be highly sociable, warm, and tender hearted; and persistence (P), describing individuals in terms of eagerness of effort (Cloninger et al., 1994). NS is related to both dopaminergic and noradrenergic processes (Cloninger, 2000) while HA is associated with individual differences in serotonergic function.

Dickman's distinction between functional and dysfunctional impulsivity

According to Dickman, individuals high in functional impulsivity are energetic, adventurous, risk-takers whose volume of output is sufficient to outweigh the negative consequences of non-reflection. Dysfunctional impulsivity reflects individual differences in the attentional domain (as opposed to arousal or cognitive tempo/rapidity of thought). Both intensity and sustainability of focused attention are purported to be deficient in dysfunctional impulsivity, such that impulsive individuals may have trouble ignoring irrelevant stimuli or staying on task for a prolonged period (Dickman, 1993, 2000). The Dickman Impulsivity Inventory (DII) (Dickman, 1990) was developed to measure these two facets of impulsivity consisting of directed impulsive behaviour (functional impulsivity) and reckless or undirected impulsive behaviour (dysfunctional impulsivity). Although both scales load on separate factors they are nonetheless correlated with one another (0.22) (Dickman, 1990).

Gray's reinforcement sensitivity theory (RST)

RST (Gray and McNaughton, 2000; Corr, 2004) proposes three biologically mediated motivational systems: (i) the behavioural approach system (BAS), which underpins individual differences in sensitivity to reward; (ii) the fight, flight, freeze system (FFFS), which is sensitive to threat (conditioned or unconditioned); and (iii) the behavioural inhibition system (BIS), which is sensitive to goal conflict. Focusing on the BAS, it is noted that while Gray originally proposed that the trait manifestation of the BAS was impulsivity, there has been considerable discussion regarding the use of this term with some writers suggesting a more appropriate title is in fact 'reward sensitivity'. Indeed the label 'impulsivity' was assigned, 'on a rather ad hoc basis initially' by Gray (Diaz and Pickering, 1993: 298). The neural substrate of BAS involves the dopaminergic systems, particularly the mesolimbic dopaminergic pathways. These pathways are responsive to cues of reward that produce positive incentive motivational behaviour and to aversive stimuli that require goal-directed behaviour (see Pickering and Gray, 1999). Thus, those with high BAS sensitivity are more likely to engage in approach and active avoidance behaviour, and to experience greater positive affect in situations containing cues for reward.

Several measures have been developed to assess Gray's trait impulsivity or reward sensitivity. The BIS/BAS scale developed by Carver and White (1994), a 20-item self-report questionnaire consisting of one subscale measuring BIS and three BAS subscales: drive (BAS-D), reward responsiveness (BAS-RR), and fun-seeking (BAS-FS). A second questionnaire which has also received some empirical support as a measure of Gray's RST is the Sensitivity to Punishment and Sensitivity to Reward Questionnaire (SPSRQ). Finally, a recent 20-item scale developed by Jackson and colleagues (Jackson and Smillie, 2004) as a measure of Gray's RST includes items measuring behavioural activation and motivation to approach potentially rewarding stimuli and situations.

Convergence amongst measures of impulsivity and P

There are literally hundreds of studies investigating the relationships between the measures described above. From the outset it was clear that all of the measures were tapping related constructs, as would be predicted from Eysenck's original proposal that impulsivity was a primary trait related to higher-order dimensions of E and P. Early studies on the I_7 reported correlations between EPQ-R P and I_7 (impulsiveness) of 0.46 while a somewhat lower correlation of 0.22 was obtained for I_7 (venturesomeness). Similar correlations were found between EPQ-R E and I_7 (impulsiveness) and E and I_7 (venturesomeness; 0.39 and 0.37 for males; 0.22 and 0.44 for females respectively) (H.J. Eysenck and S.B.G. Eysenck, 1992). More recently, Caseras et al. (2003) reported a correlation of 0.43 between P and I_7 (impulsiveness) and 0.32 between E and I_7 (impulsiveness). In relation to other measures of impulsivity the I_7 (impulsiveness) also correlates with the Barratt Impulsiveness Scale BIS-11 ($r = 0.69$) whilst I_7 (venturesomeness) did not ($r = 0.16$) (Marsh et al., 2002).

It is notable that there are also strong correlations between other measures of impulsiveness and P. ImpSS from the ZKPQ-III-R correlated with EPQ-P at 0.56 while the correlation between ImpSS and NEO-conscientiousness was -0.50, replicating the earlier study by Zuckerman (Aluja et al., 2003). Brunas-Wagstaff et al. (1994) found that dysfunctional impulsivity correlated only with extraversion (0.44), whilst functional impulsivity correlated positively with extraversion (0.35) and psychoticism (0.37), and negatively with neuroticism (-0.37). The findings from this study are surprising, as dysfunctional rather than functional impulsivity would seem on the surface to have more in common with Eysenck's measure of psychoticism. In a later study, Chico et al. (2003) found a significant correlation between psychoticism and both dysfunctional and functional impulsivity (0.39 and 0.32 respectively), and suggested that the relationship between functional impulsivity and P may reflect the goal-focused component of the functional impulsivity scale, whereby those people high on P may be prepared to carry out behaviours that are of benefit to them but not to wider society.

A two-dimensional view of impulsivity

There is now widespread agreement that impulsivity is a multidimensional construct that consists of a number of related dimensions. Currently, there is reasonable evidence for a two-factor model with the two factors reflecting, respectively, approach tendencies/reward sensitivity and cognitive disinhibition/impulsivity (Dawe and Loxton, 2004;

De Wit and Richards, 2004). Specifically, measures of Gray's BAS construct, such as the BIS/BAS scales (Carver and White, 1994), functional impulsivity (Dickman, 1990), Eysenck's I_7 (venturesomeness) and the appetitive motivation scale (Smillie and Jackson, 2006), have been found to load on a separate factor from scales such as Eysenck's I_7 (impulsiveness), Cloninger's NS scale, Zuckerman's sensation-seeking scale and Barratt's BIS11 (see Table 17.1).

It is notable that many recent studies using a range of behavioural tasks support the proposal that impulsiveness is, at least, a two-dimensional construct relating to reward drive and impulsiveness/disinhibition. A study of Smillie and Jackson (2006) is of particular relevance here. Using a go/no-go discrimination task as a behavioural measure of reward reactivity, they found that FI, appetitive motivation and BAS (Carver and White, 1994), predicted the development of a response bias in favour of reward while DI did not. Other recent studies have also found that high scorers on self-report measures of reward responsivity but not impulsiveness perform better on behavioural tasks involving explicit reward for particular behaviours; for example, faster

Table 17.1 Results of factor analytic studies

Author	Impulsiveness	Reward sensitivity
Eysenck	I_7 (Impulsiveness)[abc]	I_7 (Venturesomeness)[c]
	Psychoticism[g]	2E + N[d (1)]
	EPP sensation-seeking[g]	Extraversion[aeg]
Cloninger	TPQ novelty-seeking (NS)[abf]	TPQ reward dependence[f]
Barratt	Motor impulsiveness[c]	
Zuckerman	Non-planning impulsiveness[c]	
	Cognitive impulsiveness[c]	
	BIS-11 (total)[d]	
	Sensation-seeking scale form V[d]	
Carver and White	BAS fun-seeking (BAS-FS)[acf]	BAS fun-seeking (BAS-FS)[abcf]
		BAS drive (BAS-drive)[abcf]
		BAS reward responsiveness (BAS-RR)[abcfg]
		BAS (total)[deg]
Dickman	Dysfunctional impulsivity[cefg]	Functional impulsivity[cefg]
Torrubia et al.	Sensitivity to reward (SR)[defg]	Sensitivity to reward (SR)[bdefg]
Jackson		Appetitive motivation scale[eg]

[(1)]2E + N = EPQ-R extraversion (X2) + neuroticism
[a]Zelenski and Larsen (1999); [b]Caseras et al. (2003); [c]Miller et al. (2004); [d]Quilty and Oakman (2004); [e]Smillie et al. (2006); [f]Franken and Muris (2006); [g]Smillie and Jackson (2005)

card sorting. (e.g. Kambouropoulos and Staiger, 2004). On the other hand, individuals high in measures referred to as 'rash impulsiveness' by Dawe et al. (2004), have greater difficulty inhibiting previously rewarded responses (e.g. cannot stop pressing a computer key) when making a response resulting in loss of points/money (Marsh et al., 2002; Swann et al., 2002; Vigil-Colet and Codorniu, 2004). Thus, there is growing evidence supporting at least two distinct impulsivity dimensions with some evidence indicating that P is more closely aligned with rash impulsiveness than reward drive.

It is widely accepted that the neurobiological basis of personality systems, involving appetitive motivation, approach behaviour, and perhaps novelty-seeking, involve dopaminergic systems, particularly the mesolimbic dopaminergic pathways. This system is most clearly articulated by Gray and colleagues in relation to the BAS (Corr, 2004) although both Depue and Collins (1999) and Cloninger et al. (1994) acknowledge the importance of dopamine in incentive motivation. Finally, there is strong evidence that extraversion is also linked to dopamine mechanisms (Rammsayer, 2004). This does not really present any problems with the view that dopamine underlies reward sensitivity as extraversion is a measure that is related to the propensity to seek out enjoyable social activities (Pickering, 2004). As reviewed above, there is also a strong body of literature supporting the role of serotonin in the behaviours that have been referred to in the latter part of this chapter as rash impulsivity (Hennig, 2004). Serotonergic neurons project from the raphe throughout the brain to diverse regions including the hippocampus, orbitofrontal cortex and amygdala (Kreek, 2005). There have been a series of investigations demonstrating that individuals with damage to the orbitofrontal cortex show impairment in decision-making, in particular on tasks that tap 'impulsive behaviour' (e.g. Bechara, 2005). Neuroimaging studies have also demonstrated frontal cortical dysfunction as a core component of response disinhibition (Horn et al., 2003). Thus, there is converging

evidence that rash impulsive behaviour is linked to low levels of serotonin in nonclinical groups and that this becomes even more apparent in clinical populations where there has been clear evidence of serotonergic dysfunction.

CONCLUDING COMMENT: PSYCHOTICISM AND IMPULSIVITY

There is considerable agreement among researchers that the P scale is, at best, a quite inadequate measure of the essential elements of classic psychotic disorders, while being a much more adequate measure of impulsive, antisocial forms of behaviour. How then does the scale overlap with the impulsivity construct? We have argued above that impulsivity may be divided into two dimensions, a dimension representing reward sensitivity which is most clearly associated with Gray's conceptualisation of behavioural approach, and a dimension representing rash responding without due consideration to the consequences of one's actions, which is more closely aligned to the classic view of impulsivity. This differentiation is supported (though not universally) by the correlational and empirical evidence. Furthermore, while emphasising the complex interactions between the various biological systems argued by writers such as Zuckerman, and noting the substantial disagreement in the area, the neuropsychological evidence appears to link the former more clearly to the dopamine system and the latter to the serotonin system. It is argued that it is the latter type of impulsivity, called 'rash impulsivity' (Dawe et al., 2004), impulsive unsocialised sensation-seeking (Zuckerman, 2005) or impulsive antisocial sensation-seeking (Pickering, 2004), which is more clearly related to P. Reward sensitivity is, on the other hand, more closely linked to E.

A further issue concerns the unitary nature of the rash impulsivity/psychoticism dimension. Several decades of lexical research (L.R. Goldberg, 1993) accompanied by considerable research within the framework of the five-factor model of personality (Costa and McCrae, 1992) have led many writers to the conclusion that the factors of conscientiousness and agreeableness should be separated at the most basic level of personality structure. These two factors, which may be construed to represent respectively the low ends of impulsive, undisciplined behaviour and unempathic, antisocial behaviour, both correlate negatively with the P scale (McCrae and Costa, 1985). Zuckerman's own research suggests that P and IUSS both load on conscientiousness, but that P also shows a substantial cross-loading on agreeableness (Zuckerman et al., 1993).

Neurobiologically oriented writers such as Eysenck, Zuckerman, and Pickering argue strongly for a single dimension. H.J. Eysenck (1992b), for example, argued that agreeableness and conscientiousness should be seen as 'primaries' at a lower hierarchical level than P. On the other hand, the consistent differentiation of the two dimensions in factor analytic and cross-validation studies holds more weight for the five-factor theorists. Goldberg (1993) suggests that the person able to solve this problem merits a Nobel Prize! Further research from genetic, biological, behavioural, and psychometric perspectives will indicate where the lines may be most fruitfully drawn in the differentiation of psychoticism, impulsivity, and related constructs.

NOTES

1 We note that a scale developed by Harkness et al. (2002) from the MMPI-2 item pool does use the label 'psychoticism'. In terms of content, this scale fits with the various 'schizotypy' measures described in the text, and its authors clearly differentiate it from Eysenck's P scale.

REFERENCES

Abraham, A., Windmann, S., Daum, I., Gunturkun, O. (2005) 'Conceptual expansion and creative imagery as a function and psychoticism', *Consciousness and Cognition*, 14(3): 520–34.

Af Klinteberg, B., von Knorring, L. and Oreland, L. (2004) 'On the psychobiology of impulsivity', in R. Stelmack (ed.), *Essays in Honor of Marvin Zuckerman*. Amsterdam: Pergamon Press, pp. 429–51.

Allsopp, J., Eysenck, H.J. and Eysenck, S.B.G. (1991) 'Machiavellianism as a component in psychoticism and extraversion', *Personality and Individual Differences*, 12(1): 29–41.

Aluja, A., Garcia, O. and Garcia, L.F. (2003) 'Psychometric properties of the Zuckerman–Kuhlman personality questionnaire (ZKPQ-III-R): A study of a shortened form', *Personality and Individual Differences*, 34(7): 1083–97.

Asgari, F. (2000) 'The role of psychoticism and openness to experience as contributing factors to trait creativity', Unpublished Honours Thesis, University of Melbourne.

Badcock, J.C., Smith, G.A. and Rawlings, D. (1988) 'Temporal processing and psychosis proneness', *Personality and Individual Differences*, 9(4): 709–19.

Barnes, G.E., Malamuth, N.M. and Check, J.V.P. (1984) 'Psychoticism and sexual arousal to rape depictions', *Personality and Individual Differences*, 5(3): 273–9.

Baruch, I., Hemsley, D.R. and Gray, J.A. (1988a) 'Differential performance of acute and chronic schizophrenics in a latent inhibition task', *Journal of Nervous and Mental Disease*, 176(10): 598–606.

Baruch, I., Hemsley, D.R. and Gray, J.A. (1988b) 'Latent inhibition and "psychotic proneness" in normal subjects', *Personality and Individual Differences*, 9(4): 777–83.

Bechara, A. (2005) 'Decision making, impulse control and loss of willpower to resist drugs: a neurocognitive perspective', *Nature Neuroscience*, 8(11): 1458–63.

Beech, A. and Claridge, G. (1987) 'Individual differences in negative priming: Relations with schizotypal personality traits', *British Journal of Psychology*, 78(3): 349–56.

Beech, A., Powell, T., McWilliam, H. and Claridge, G. (1989) 'Evidence of reduced "cognitive inhibition" in schizophrenia', *British Journal of Clinical Psychology*, 28(2): 109–16.

Bleuler, E. (1911) *Dementia Praecox or the Group of Schizophrenias* (trans. J. Zinkin). New York: International Universities Press.

Block, J. (1977) 'P scale and psychosis: Continued concerns', *Journal of Abnormal Psychology*, 86(4): 431–4.

Booker, B.B., Fearn, M. and Francis, L.J. (2001) 'The personality profile of artists', *Irish Journal of Psychology*, 22(3–4): 277–81.

Bouchard, T.P. and McGue, M. (2003) 'Genetic and environmental influences on human psychological differences', *Journal of Neurobiology*, 54(1): 4–45.

Brunas-Wagstaff, J., Bergquist, A. and Wagstaff, G.F. (1994) 'Cognitive correlates of functional and dysfunctional impulsivity', *Personality and Individual Differences*, 17(2): 289–92.

Carson, S.H., Peterson, J.B. and Higgins, D.M. (2003) 'Decreased latent inhibition is associated with increased creative achievement in high-functioning individuals', *Journal of Personality and Social Psychology*, 85(3): 499–506.

Carver, C.S. and White, T.L. (1994) 'Behavioral inhibition, behavioral activation and affective responses to impending reward and punishment: The BIS/BAS scales', *Journal of Personality and Social Psychology*, 67(2): 319–33.

Caseras, X., Avila, C. and Torrubia, R. (2003) 'The measurement of individual differences in behavioural inhibition and behavioural activation systems: A comparison of personality scales', *Personality and Individual Differences*, 34(6): 999–1013.

Center, D.B., Jackson, N. and Kemp, D. (2005) 'A test of Eysenck's antisocial behavior hypothesis employing 11–15-year-old students dichotomous for PEN and L', *Personality and Individual Differences*, 38(2): 395–402.

Chapman, J.P., Chapman, L.J. and Kwapil, T.R. (1994) 'Does the Eysenck Psychoticism scale predict psychosis? A ten year longitudinal study', *Personality and Individual Differences*, 17(3): 369–75.

Chapman, L.J., Chapman, J.P., Eckblad, M. and Kwapil, T.R. (1984) 'Impulsive nonconformity as a trait contributing to the prediction of psychotic-like and schizotypal symptoms', *Journal of Nervous and Mental Disease*, 172(11): 681–91.

Chapman, L.J., Chapman, J.P., Kwapil, T.R., Eckblad, M. and Zinser, M.C. (1994) 'Putatively psychosis-prone subjects 10 years later', *Journal of Abnormal Psychology*, 103(2): 171–83.

Chico, E., Tous, J.M., Lorenzo-Seva, U. and Vigil-Colet, A. (2003) 'Spanish adaptation of Dickman's Impulsivity Inventory, its relationship to Eysenck's Personality Questionnaire', *Personality and Individual Differences*, 35(8): 1883–92.

Christie, M. and Raine, A. (1988) 'Lateralized hemisphere activity in relation to personality and degree course', *Personality and Individual Differences*, 9(6): 957–64.

Claridge, G. (1972) 'The schizophrenias as nervous types', *British Journal of Psychiatry*, 112(560): 1–17.

Claridge, G. (1981) 'Psychoticism', in R. Lynn (ed.), *Dimensions of Personality: Papers in Honour of H.J. Eysenck*. Oxford: Pergamon Press.

Claridge, G. (1987) 'Psychoticism and arousal, in J. Strelau and H.J. Eysenck (eds), *Personality Dimensions and Arousal*. New York: Plenum Press, pp. 133–150.

Claridge, G. (1997) *Schizotypy: Implications for Illness and Health*. Oxford: Oxford University Press.

Claridge, G. (1990) 'Can a disease model of schizophrenia survive', in R.P. Bentall (ed.), *Reconstructing Schizophrenia*. London: Routledge, pp. 157–83.

Claridge, G. and Chappa, H.J. (1973) 'Psychoticism: A study of its biological basis in normal subjects', *British Journal of Social and Clinical Psychology*, 12(2): 175–87.

Clark, D.A., Hemsley, D.R. and Nason-Clark, N. (1987) 'Personality and sex differences in emotional responsiveness to positive and negative cognitive stimuli', *Personality and Individual Differences*, 8(1): 1–7.

Cloninger, C.R. (2000) 'Biology of personality dimensions', *Current Opinions in Psychiatry*, 13(6): 611–16.

Cloninger, C.R., Przybeck, T.R., Svrakic, D.M. and Wetzel, R.D. (1994) *The Temperament and Character Inventory (TCI): A Guide to its Development and Use*. St. Louis, MO: Center for Psychobiology of Personality.

Corr, P.J. (2004) 'Reinforcement sensitivity theory and personality', *Neuroscience and Biobehavioral Reviews*, 28(3): 317–32.

Corulla, W.J. (1987) 'A psychometric investigation of the Eysenck Personality Questionnaire (revised) and its relationship to the I.7 Impulsiveness Questionnaire', *Personality and Individual Differences*, 8(5): 651–8.

Corulla, W.J. (1990) 'A revised version of the psychoticism scale for children', *Personality and Individual Differences*, 11(1): 65–76.

Costa, P.T. and McCrae, R.R. (1992) *The Revised NEO Personality Inventory Manual*. Odessa, FL: Psychological Assessment Resources.

Cox, A.J. and Leon, J.L. (1999) 'Negative schizotypal traits in the relation of creativity to psychopathology', *Creativity Research Journal*, 12(1): 25–36.

Dawe, S. and Loxton, N.J. (2004) 'The role of impulsivity in the development of substance use and eating disorders', *Neuroscience and Biobehavioural Reviews*, 28(3): 343–51.

Dawe, S., Gullo, M.J. and Loxton, N.J. (2004) 'Reward drive and rash impulsiveness as dimensions of impulsivity: Implications for substance misuse', *Addictive Behaviors*, 29(7): 1389–405.

Depue, R.A. and Collins, P.F. (1999) 'Neurobiology of the structure of personality: Dopamine, facilitation of incentive motivation, and extraversion', *Behavioral and Brain Sciences*, 22(3): 491–569.

De Wit, H. and Richards, J.B. (2004) 'Dual determinants of drug use in humans: Reward and impulsivity', in R.A. Bevins and M.T. Bardo (eds), *Motivational Factors in the Etiology of Drug Abuse*. Lincoln, Nebraska: University of Nebraska Press, pp. 19–55.

Diaz, A. and Pickering, A.D. (1993) 'The relationship between Gray's and Eysenck's personality spaces', *Personality and Individual Differences*, 15(3): 297–305.

Dickman, S.J. (1990) 'Functional and dysfunctional impulsivity: Personality and cognitive correlates', *Journal of Personality and Social Personality*, 58(1): 95–102.

Dickman, S.J. (1993) 'Impulsivity and information processing', in W.G. McCown, J.L. Johnson and M.B. Shure (eds), *The Impulsive Client: Theory, Research and Treatment*. Washington: American Psychological Association, pp. 57–70.

Dickman, S.J. (2000) 'Impulsivity, arousal and attention', *Personality and Individual Differences*, 28(3): 563–81.

Doherty, O. and Matthews, G. (1988) 'Personality characteristics of opiate addicts', *Personality and Individual Differences*, 9(1): 171–2.

Dragutinovich, S. (1987) 'Stimulus intensity reducers: Are they sensation seekers, extraverts and strong nervous types?', *Personality and Individual Differences*, 8(5): 693–704.

Eaves, L.J., Eysenck, H.J. and Martin, N.G. (1989) *Genes, Culture and Personality*. London: Academic Press.

Ebstein, R.P., Novick, O., Umansky, R., Priel, B., Osher, Y., Blaine, D., Bennett, E.R. Nemanov, L., Katz, M. and Belmakers, R.H. (1996) 'Dopamine D4 receptor (D4DR) exon III polymorphism associated with the human personality trait of novelty seeking', *Nature Genetics*, 12(1): 78–80.

Edelmann, R.J. and Vivian, S.E. (1988) 'Further analysis of the Social Psychopathy Scale', *Personality and Individual Differences*, 9(3): 581–7.

Egan, E., Kroll, J., Carey, K., Johnson, M. and Erickson, P. (2004) 'Eysenck personality scales and religiosity in a US outpatient sample', *Personality and Individual Differences*, 37(5): 1023–31.

Eysenck, H.J. (1941) '"Type" factors in aesthetic judgments', *British Journal of Psychology*, 31: 262–70.

Eysenck, H.J. (1952) *The Scientific Study of Personality*. London: Routledge & Kegan Paul.

Eysenck, H.J. (1992a) 'The definition and measurement of psychoticism', *Personality and Individual Differences*, 13(7): 757–85.

Eysenck, H.J. (1992b) 'Four ways five factors are *not* basic', *Personality and Individual Differences*, 13(6): 667–73.

Eysenck, H.J. (1993) 'The nature of impulsivity', in W.G. McCown, J.L. Johnson and M.B. Shure (eds), *The Impulsive Client: Theory, Research and Treatment*. Washington: American Psychological Association, pp. 57–70.

Eysenck, H.J. (1994) 'Creativity and personality: Word association, origence and psychoticism', *Creativity Research Journal*, 7(2): 209–16,

Eysenck, H.J. (1995) *Genius: The Natural History of Creativity*. Cambridge: Cambridge University Press.

Eysenck, H.J. and Barrett, P. (1993) 'The nature of schizotypy', *Psychological Reports*, 73(1): 59–63.

Eysenck, H.J. and Eysenck, S.B.G. (1968) 'A factorial study of psychoticism as a dimension of personality', *Multivariate Behavioural Research*, 3(All-Clinical Special Issue): 15–31.

Eysenck, H.J. and Eysenck, S.B.G. (1975) *Manual of the Eysenck Personality Questionnaire*. London: Hodder & Stoughton.

Eysenck, H.J. and Eysenck, S.B.G. (1976) *Psychoticism as a Dimension of Personality*. London: Hodder & Stoughton.

Eysenck, H.J. and Eysenck, S.B.G. (1978) 'Psychopathy, personality and genetics', in R. Hare and D. Schalling (eds), *Psychopathic Behaviour*. London: Wiley, pp. 197–223.

Eysenck, H.J. and Eysenck, S.B.G. (1992) *Manual of the EPQ-R and the Impulsiveness, Venturesomeness and Empathy Scales*. London: Hodder & Stoughton.

Eysenck, H.J. and Wilson, G. (1999) *The Eysenck Personality Profiler* (2nd edn). Guildford: Psi-Press.

Eysenck, H.J., Wilson, G. and Jackson, C. (1999) *The Eysenck Personality Profiler (short)* (2nd edn). Guildford: Psi-Press.

Eysenck, S.B.G. and Eysenck, H.J. (1968) 'The measurement of psychoticism: A study of factor stability and reliability', *British Journal of Social and Clinical Psychology*, 7(4): 286–94.

Eysenck, S.B.G., Eysenck, H.J. and Barrett, P. (1985) 'A revised version of the psychoticism scale', *Personality and Individual Differences*, 6(1): 21–9.

Franken, I.H.A. and Muris, P. (2006) 'Gray's impulsivity dimension: A distinction between reward sensitivity versus rash impulsiveness', *Personality and Individual Differences*, 40(7): 1337–47.

Francis, L.J. (1996) 'The development of an abbreviated form of the Revised Junior Eysenck Personality Questionnaire (JEPQR-A) among 13–15 year olds', *Personality and Individual Differences*, 21(6): 835–44.

Francis, L.J., Brown, L.B. and Philipchalk, R. (1992) 'The development of an abbreviated form of the Revised Eysenck Personality Questionnaire (EPQR-A): Its use among students in England, Canada, the USA and Australia', *Personality and Individual Differences*, 13(4): 443–9.

Furnham, A. and Thompson, J. (1991) 'Personality and self-reported delinquency', *Personality and Individual Differences*, 12(6): 585–93.

Gilbert, D.G. (1988) 'EEG and personality differences between smokers and non-smokers', *Personality and Individual Differences*, 9(3): 659–65.

Glicksohn, J. and Naftuliev, Y. (2005) 'In search of an electrophysiological index for psychoticism', *Personality and Individual Differences*, 39(6): 1083–92.

Goldberg, L.R. (1993) 'The structure of phenotypic personality traits', *American Psychologist*, 48(1): 26–34.

Golding, J.F., Harpur, T. and Brent-Smith, H. (1983) 'Personality, drinking and drug-taking correlates of cigarette smoking', *Personality and Individual Differences*, 4(6): 703–6.

Gottesman, I.I. and Bertelsen, A. (1991) 'Schizophrenia: Classical approaches with new twists and provocative results', in P. McGuffin and R. Murray (eds), *The New Genetics of Mental Illness*. London: Butteworth-Heinemann, pp. 85–97.

Gotz, K.O. and Gotz, K. (1979) 'Personality characteristics of successful artists', *Perceptual Motor Skills*, 49(3): 919–24.

Gray, J.A. (1973) 'Causal theories of personality and how to test them', in J.R. Royce (ed.), *Multivariate Analysis and Psychological Theory*. London: Academic Press.

Gray, J.A., Feldon, J., Rawlins, J.P., Hemsley, D.R. and Smith, A.D. (1991) 'The neuropsychology of schizophrenia', *Behavioral and Brain Sciences*, 14(1): 1–84.

Gray, J.A. and McNaughton, N. (2000) *The Neuropsychology of Anxiety: An Enquiry into the Functions of the Septo-hippocampal System* (2nd edn). New York: Oxford University Press.

Gray, N.S., Pickering, A. and Gray, J. (1994) 'Psychoticism and dopamine D2 binding in the basal ganglia using SPET', *Personality and Individual Differences*, 17(3): 431–4.

Hare, R.D. and McPherson, L.M. (1984) 'Psychopathy and perceptual asymmetry during verbal dichotic listening', *Journal of Abnormal Psychology*, 93(2): 141–9.

Harkness, A.R., McNutty, J.L., Ben-Porath, Y.S. and Graham, J.G. (2002) *The Personality Psychopathology Five (PSY-5) Scales*. Minneapolis: University of Minnesota Press.

Heath, A.C. and Martin, N.G. (1990) 'Psychoticism as a dimension of personality:

A multivariate genetic test of Eysenck and Eysenck's psychoticism construct', *Journal of Personality and Social Psychology*, 58(1): 111–21.

Heaven, P., Newbury, K. and Wilson, V. (2004) 'The Eysenck psychoticism dimension and delinquent behaviours among non-criminals: Changes across the lifespan?', *Personality and Individual Differences*, 36(8): 1817–25.

Hendricks, K. (2005) 'The relationship between creativity, dimensions of normal personality and scales of personality disorder among artists and nonartists', Unpublished PhD thesis, University of Melbourne.

Hennig, J. (2004) 'Personality, serotonin and noradrenaline', in R. Stelmack (ed.), *Essays in Honor of Marvin Zuckerman*. Amsterdam: Pergamon Press, pp. 379–408.

Hennig, J., Reuter, M., Netter, P., Burk, C. and Landt, O. (2005) 'Two types of aggression are differentially related to serotonergic activity and the A779C TPH polymorphism', *Behavioral Neuroscience*, 119(1): 16–25.

Horn, N., Dolan, M., Elliott, R., Deakin, J. and Woodruff, P. (2003) 'Response inhibition and impulsivity: An fMRI study', *Neuropsychologia*, 41(14): 1959–66.

Hu, C. and Gong, Y. (1990) 'Personality differences between writers and mathematicians on the EPQ', *Personality and Individual Differences*, 11(6): 637–8.

Jackson, C.J., Furnham, A., Forde, L. and Cotter, T. (2000) 'The structure of the Eysenck Personality Profiler', *British Journal of Psychology*, 91(2): 223–39.

Jackson, C.J. and Smillie, L.D. (2004) 'Appetitive motivation predicts the majority of personality and an ability measure: a comparison of BAS measures and a re-evaluation of the importance of RST', *Personality and Individual Differences*, 36(7): 1627–36.

Jakes, S. and Hemsley, D. (1986) 'Individual differences in reaction to brief exposure to unpatterned visual stimulation', *Personality and Individual Differences*, 7(1): 121–3.

Jorm, A.F. and Christensen, H. (2004) 'Religiosity and personality: Evidence for non-linear associations', *Personality and Individual Differences*, 36(6): 1433–41.

Kambouropoulos, N. and Staiger, P.K. (2004) 'Personality and responses to appetitive and aversive stimuli: The joint influence of behavioural approach and behavioural inhibition

systems', *Personality and Individual Differences*, 37(6): 1153–65.

Kendell, R.E. (1991) 'The major functional psychoses: Are they independent entities or part of a continuum? Philosophical and conceptual issues underlying the debate', in A. Kerr and H. McClelland (eds), *Concepts of Mental Disorder: A Continuing Debate*. London: Gaskell, pp. 1–16.

Kreek, M.J., Nielsen, D.A., Butelman, E.R. and LaForge, K.S. (2005) 'Genetic influences on impulsivity, risk taking, stress responsivity and vulnerability to drug abuse and addiction', *Nature Neuroscience*, 8(11): 1450–7.

Kwiatkowski, J., Vartanian, O. and Martindale, C. (1999) 'Creativity and speed of mental processing', *Empirical Studies of the Arts*, 17(2): 187–96.

Lesch, K.P., Bengel, D., Heils, A., Sabol, S.Z., Greenberg, B.D., Petri, S., Benjamin, J., Muller, C.R., Hamer, D.H. and Murphy, D.L. (1996) 'Association of anxiety-related traits with a polymorphism in the serotonin transporter gene regulation region', *Science*, 274(5292): 1527–31.

Loehlin, J.C. and Martin, N.G. (2001) 'Age changes in personality traits and their heritabilities during the adult years: Evidence from Australian twin registry samples', *Personality and Individual Differences*, 30(7): 1147–60.

Loehlin, J.C., Medland, S.E., Montgomery, G.W. and Martin, N.G. (2005) 'Eysenck's Psychoticism and the X-linked androgen receptor gene CAG polymorphism in additional Australian samples', *Personality and Individual Differences*, 39(3): 661–7.

Lubow, R.E., Ingberg-Sachs, Y., Zalstein-Orda, N. and Gewirtz, J.C. (1992) 'Latent inhibition in low and high "psychotic-prone" normal subjects', *Personality and Individual Differences*, 13(5): 563–72.

Lynn, R. and Martin, T. (1995) 'National differences in thirty-seven nations in extraversion, neuroticism, psychoticism and economic, demographic and other correlates', *Personality and Individual Differences*, 19(3): 403–6.

Malamuth, N.M. (1986) 'Predictors of naturalistic sexual aggression', *Journal of Personality and Social Psychology*, 50(5): 953–62.

Marsh, D.M., Dougherty, D.M., Mathias, C.W., Moeller, F.G. and Hicks, L.R. (2002)

'Comparisons of women with high and low trait impulsivity using behavioral models of response-disinhibition and reward-choice', *Personality and Individual Differences*, 33(8): 1291–310.

Mason, O., Claridge, G. and Jackson, M. (1995) 'New scales for the assessment of schizotypy', *Personality and Individual Differences*, 18(1): 7–13.

Mason, O., Claridge, G. and Williams, L. (1997) 'Questionnaire measurement', in G. Claridge (ed.), *Schizotypy: Implications for Illness and Health*. Oxford: Oxford University Press, pp. 17–37.

McCrae, R.R. (1987) 'Creativity, divergent thinking and openness to experience', *Journal of Personality and Social Psychology*, 52(6): 1258–65.

McCrae, R.R. and Costa, P.T. (1985) 'Comparison of EPI and psychoticism scales with measures of the five-factor model of personality', *Personality and Individual Differences*, 6(5): 587–97.

Mecacci, L., Zani, A., Rocchetti, G. and Lucioli, R. (1986) 'The relationship between morningness-eveningness, ageing and personality', *Personality and Individual Differences*, 7(6): 911–3.

Merten, T. and Fischer, I. (1999) 'Creativity, personality and word association responses: Associative behaviour in forty supposedly creative persons', *Personality and Individual Differences*, 27(5): 933–42.

Miller, E., Joseph, S. and Tudway, J. (2004) 'Assessing the component structure of four self-report measures of impulsivity', *Personality and Individual Differences*, 37(2): 349–58.

Mohan, J. and Tiwana, M. (1987) 'Personality and alienation of creative writers: A brief report', *Personality and Individual Differences*, 8(3): 449.

O'Boyle, M. and Holzer, C. (1992) 'DSM-III-R personality disorders and Eysenck's personality dimensions', *Personality and Individual Differences*, 13(10): 1157–9.

Pergadia, M.L., Madden, P.A.F., Lessov, C.N., Todorov, A.A., Bucholz, K.K., Martin, N.G. and Heath, A.C. (2006) 'Genetic and environmental influences on extreme personality dispositions in adolescent female twins', *Journal of Child Psychology and Psychiatry*, 47(9): 902–9.

Peterson, J.B. and Carson, S. (2000) 'Latent inhibition and openness to experience in a high-achieving student population', *Personality and Individual Differences*, 28(2): 323–32.

Pickering, A.D. (2004) 'The neuropsychology of impulsive antisocial sensation seeking personality traits: From dopamine to hippocampal function?', in R. Stelmack (ed.), *Essays in Honor of Marvin Zuckerman*. Amsterdam: Pergamon Press, pp. 455–78.

Pickering, A.D. and Gray, J.A. (1999) 'The neuroscience of personality', in L.A. Pervin (ed.), *Handbook of Personality: Theory and Research* (2nd edn). New York: Guilford, pp. 277–99.

Pritchard, W.S. (1991) 'The link between cigarette smoking and P: A serotonergic hypothesis', *Personality and Individual Differences*, 12(11): 1187–204.

Quilty, L.C. and Oakman, J.M. (2004) 'The assessment of behavioural activation – the relationship between impulsivity and behavioural activation', *Personality and Individual Differences*, 37(2): 429–42.

Rammsayer, T.H. (2004) 'Extraversion and the dopamine hypothesis', in R. Stelmack (ed.), *On the Psychobiology of Personality: Essays in Honor of Marvin Zuckerman*. Amsterdam: Pergamon Press, pp. 409–28.

Rawlings, D. (1983) 'An inquiry into the nature of psychoticism as a personality dimension', Unpublished DPhil thesis, Oxford University.

Rawlings, D. (1984) 'The correlation of EPQ psychoticism with two behavioural measures of impulsivity', *Personality and Individual Differences*, 5(5): 591–4.

Rawlings, D. (2003) 'Personality correlates of liking for "unpleasant" paintings and photographs', *Personality and Individual Differences*, 34(3): 395–410.

Rawlings, D. and Bastian, B. (2002) 'Painting preference and personality, with particular reference to Gray's behavioral inhibition and behavioral approach systems', *Empirical Studies of the Arts*, 20(2): 177–93.

Rawlings, D. and Borge, A. (1987) 'Personality and hemisphere functions: Two experiments using the dichotic shadowing technique', *Personality and Individual Differences*, 8(4): 483–8.

Rawlings, D., Hodge, M., Sherr, D. and Dempsey, A. (1995) 'Toughmindedness and preference for musical excerpts, categories and triads', *Psychology of Music*, 23(1): 63–80.

Rawlings, D. and Leow, S.H. (in press) 'Investigating the role of psychoticism and sensation seeking in predicting emotional reactions to music', *Psychology of Music*.

Rawlings, D. and Toogood, A. (1997) 'Using a "taboo response" measure to examine the relationship between divergent thinking and psychoticism', *Personality and Individual Differences*, 22(1): 61–8.

Reich, W. (1976) 'The schizophrenia spectrum: A genetic concept', *The Journal of Nervous and Mental Disease*, 162(1): 3–12.

Robinson, T.N. and Zahn, T.P. (1979) 'Co-variation of two-flash threshold and autonomic arousal for high and low scores on a measure of psychoticism', *British Journal of Social and Clinical Psychology*, 18(4): 431–41.

Robinson, T.N. and Zahn, T.P. (1985) 'Psychoticism and arousal: Possible evidence for a linkage of P and Psychopathy', *Personality and Individual Differences*, 6(1): 47–66.

Romero, E., Luengo, M.A. and Sobral, J. (2001) 'Personality and antisocial behaviour: Study of temperamental dimensions', *Personality and Individual Differences*, 31(3): 329–48.

Rushton, J.P. (1990) 'Creativity, intelligence and psychoticism', *Personality and Individual Differences*, 11(12): 1291–8.

Shevlin, M., Bailey, F. and Adamson, G. (2002) 'Examining the factor structure and sources of differential functioning of the Eysenck Personality Questionnaire Revised – Abbreviated', *Personality and Individual Differences*, 32(3): 479–87.

Smillie, L.D. and Jackson, C.J. (2005) 'The appetitive motivation scale and other BAS measures in the prediction of approach and active avoidance', *Personality and Individual Differences*, 38(4): 981–94.

Smillie, L.D. and Jackson, C.J. (2006) 'Functional impulsivity and reinforcement sensitivity theory', *Journal of Personality*, 74(1): 47–84.

Smillie, L.D., Jackson, C.J. and Dalgleish, L.I. (2006) 'Conceptual distinctions among Carver and White's (1994) BAS scales: A reward-reactivity versus trait impulsivity perspective', *Personality and Individual Differences*, 40(5): 1039–50.

Stavridou, A. and Furnham, A. (1996) 'The relationship between psychoticism, trait

creativity and the attention mechanism of cognitive inhibition', *Personality and Individual Differences*, 21(1): 143–53.

Swann, A.C., Bjork, J.M., Moeller, F.G. and Dougherty, D.M. (2002) 'Two models of impulsivity: Relationship to personality traits and psychopathology', *Biological Psychiatry*, 51(12): 988–94.

Tipper, S.P. (1985) 'The negative priming effect: Inhibitory priming by ignored objects', *Quarterly Journal of Experimental Psychology: Human Experimental Psychology*, 37A(4): 571–90.

Torrubia, R., Avila, C., Molto, J. and Caseras, X. (2001) 'The Sensitivity to Punishment and Sensitivity to Reward Questionnaire (SPSRQ) as a measure of Gray's anxiety and impulsivity dimensions', *Personality and Individual Differences*, 31(6): 837–62.

Turakulov, R., Jorm, A.F., Jacomb, P.A., Tan, X. and Easteal, S. (2004) 'Association of dopamine-beta-hydroxylase and androgen receptor gene polymorphisms with Eysenck's P and other personality traits', *Personality and Individual Differences*, 37(1): 191–202.

van Dam, C., Janssens, J.M.A.M. and Bruyn, E.E.J. (2005) 'PEN, Big Five, juvenile delinquency and criminal recidivism', *Personality and Individual Differences*, 39(1): 7–19.

Verma, R.M. and Eysenck, H.J. (1973) 'Severity and type of psychotic illness as a function of personality', *British Journal of Psychiatry*, 122(570): 573–85.

Vigil-Colet, A. and Codorniu, M.J. (2004) 'Aggression and inhibition deficits, the role of functional and dysfunctional impulsivity', *Personality and Individual Differences*, 37(7): 1431–40.

Walker, J.S. and Gudjonsson, G.H. (2006) 'The Maudsley Violence Questionnaire: Relationship to personality and self-reported offending', *Personality and Individual Differences*, 40(4): 795–806.

Ward, P.B., McConaghy, N. and Catts, S.V. (1991) 'Word association and measures of psychosis-proneness in university students', *Personality and Individual Differences*, 12(5): 473–80.

Wilson, G.D. (1990) 'Personality, time of day and arousal', *Personality and Individual Differences*, 11(2): 153–68.

Wilson, G.D. (1981) 'Personality and social behaviour', in H.J. Eysenck (ed.), *A Model for*

Personality. Berlin: Springer-Verlag, pp. 210–45.

Woody, E. and Claridge, G. (1977) 'Psychoticism and thinking', *British Journal of Social and Clinical Psychology*, 16(3): 241–8.

Wuthrich, V. and Bates, T.C. (2001) 'Schizotypy and latent inhibition: Non-linear linkage between psychometric and cognitive markers', *Personality and Individual Differences*, 30(5): 783–98.

Zelenski, J.M. and Larsen, R.J. (1999) 'Susceptibility to affect: A comparison of three personality taxonomies', *Journal of Personality*, 67(5): 761–91.

Zuckerman, M. (1987) 'A critical look at three arousal constructs in personality theories: Optimal levels of arousal, strength of the nervous system, and sensitivities to signals of reward and punishment', in J. Strelau and H.J. Eysenck (eds), *Personality Dimensions and Arousal*. New York: Plenum Press, pp. 217–31.

Zuckerman, M. (1989) 'Personality in the third dimension: A psychobiological approach',

Personality and Individual Differences, 10(4): 391–418.

Zuckerman, M. (1994) *Behavioural Expressions and Biosocial Bases of Sensation Seeking*. New York: Cambridge University Press.

Zuckerman, M. (2005) *Psychobiology of Personality* (2nd edn). Cambridge: Cambridge University Press.

Zuckerman, M., Juhlman, D.M., Teta, P., Joireman, J. and Kraft, M. (1993) 'A comparison of three structural models of personality: the big three, the big five and the alternative five', *Journal of Personality and Social Psychology*, 65(4): 757–68.

Zuckerman, M., Kuhlman, M., Joireman, J., Teta, P. and Kraft, M. (1993) 'A comparison of three structural models for personality', *Journal of Personality and Social Psychology*, 65(4): 757–68.

Zuckerman, M. and Litle, P. (1986) 'Personality and curiosity about morbid and sexual events', *Personality and Individual Differences*, 7: 49–56.

18

Personality and Sensation Seeking

Marvin Zuckerman

We regard sensation seeking as a major dimension of personality within an 'alternative five-factor' model of personality (Zuckerman, 1991). Although invited to write a chapter on the larger model itself I declined to do so because I assume that much of the research supporting the biosocial theory will be contained in the chapter by Stelmack and Rammsayer entitled 'Psychophysiological and Biochemical Perspectives on Personality'. Furthermore, the research on the personality test developed to define the model is described in Vol. 2. However, interested readers can find the alternative five-factor theory used as a model for the psychobiology of personality in two books (Zuckerman, 1991, 2005), while books dedicated to the specific topic of sensation seeking are also available (Zuckerman, 1979a, 1994, 2007).

ORIGINS OF THE CONSTRUCT

The first sensation-seeking scale was developed as part of a program of research on sensory deprivation during the 1960s (Zubek, 1969). The optimal level of stimulation and arousal (OLS, OLA) is an old theory first developed by Wundt (1893) and even postulated by Freud in his earliest writing. The constancy principle of Breuer and Freud (1895/1955) suggested that there is a tendency to maintain an optimal level of 'intracerebral excitement' and that levels of arousal above and below this optimal level are unpleasant and lead to attempts to reduce overarousal or increase underarousal. Both Wundt and Freud conceived of the source of arousal as stimulus intensity and therefore an optimal level of stimulation determined the optimal level of arousal. Later theorists recognized that novelty of stimulation was also a source of arousal. Sixty years later Hebb (1955) reformulated this theory in terms of cortical physiology using the reticulocortical activating systems as the source of arousal function.

The OLS/OLA theory was a general theory of performance but it furnished a possible basis for individual differences in response to the experimental situation of sensory deprivation (Zuckerman, 1969). The first sensation-seeking scale was developed to measure differences in the need for stimulation and arousal as a potential predictor of reactions to sensory deprivation. It did predict some reactions to sensory deprivation and also the tendency to volunteer for such experiments (Zuckerman, 1979a). The fact that sensation seekers were over-represented in volunteers for sensory deprivation seemed a paradox until we discovered that they volunteered because they expected to hallucinate and experience other novel mental effects as a consequence of the procedure. We realized then that sensation seekers can seek novel internal as well as external stimulation through exciting activities.

DEVELOPMENT OF SENSATION-SEEKING SCALES

Cronbach and Meehl (1955) defined 'construct validity' as the development of tests from empirical observations guided by theory. In first devising a test around a construct one must write items derived from little more than an inferential sense of what a person is like who is a prototype for either extreme of the trait. For the first form of the sensation-seeking scale (SSS-form II) we did this in the form of forced choice items representing the likely option for either a high- or a low-sensation seeker. The forced choice form was used in an attempt to control both social desirability and acquiescence response sets. The social desirability was controlled by making either choice seem equally rational, rather than deviant or abnormal. A general scale was developed from item analyses of the initial form (Zuckerman et al., 1964).

Factor analyses of this early form indicated that there might be more than one factor involved in the broader factor, but there were not enough items to define these subfactors with any clarity. New experimental items were written and factor analyses were done to develop a new form containing the previous general scale and four intercorrelated subfactors (Zuckerman, 1971).

Defined in terms of their content the four factors were:

1. Thrill and adventure seeking (TAS), or the intent or desire to engage in physical activities or sports involving unusual sensations as in speed, or falling, or new experiences, as in exploring the underwater world in scuba diving;
2. Experience-seeking (ES), or the intent or desire to have new sensations and experiences through the mind and senses as in music, travel, and an unconventional lifestyle;
3. Disinhibition (Dis), seeking excitement through other people in parties, sex, and alcohol;
4. Boredom susceptibility (BS), an aversion to sameness and routine in activities and people, and a restlessness when little variety is present.

All four factors were moderately intercorrelated but the general score was used rather than a total score to measure the general factor. Four scores were reliable as measured by coefficients of internal consistency (the BS score somewhat less than the others) and retest reliabilities.

Form V was developed in England and America in an attempt to provide shorter ten-item scales for each factor that were reliably similar in factor reliability in both countries and between both genders (Zuckerman et al., 1978). Some attempt was made to select items loading primarily on their own factors, and as a consequence correlations among the factors were somewhat reduced compared to form IV but they were still significant. A highly reliable total score was produced by the simple addition of scores on all four factors and this was substituted for the general scale from earlier versions of the SSS.

Form VI of the SSS was developed to separate items representing actual experience in sensation seeking activities from items expressing only an intention or desire to engage in such activities (Zuckerman, 1984). It contains experience and intention subscales, for TAS. Dis, for both. The SSS VI was designed to measure the discrepancies between experience and intentions for either of these two types of activities. It has not been widely used.

The impulsive sensation-seeking scale (ImpSS) was developed as the outcome of our factor analyses of many different personality scales and ultimately a factor analyses of items selected from these scales in terms of a five-factor model (Zuckerman, 1994, 2002a). ImpSS was one of the five major factors emerging from factor analyses of both scales and items. It combines items reflecting a non-planning, spontaneous type of impulsivity and sensation-seeking items reflecting a general need for excitement and change without any specific types of activities included in the content of the items.

Others have developed scales closely related to the SSS, although giving them different names. Most notable is the novelty-seeking scale developed by Cloninger (1987a) which is one of the major factors in his system of personality description. This scale correlates very highly with the ImpSS scale (Zuckerman and Cloninger, 1996).

PHENOMENAL CORRELATES OF SENSATION SEEKING

Definition

The broad construct of sensation seeking has guided the areas of investigation of life activities and experimental variables investigated. The definition in turn has been somewhat expanded by the empirical findings. The current definition of the trait is, 'The seeking of varied novel, complex, and intense sensations and experiences, and the willingness to take physical, social, legal, and financial risks for the sake of such experience' (Zuckerman, 1994: 27).

Not all sensation-seeking activities are risky, therefore it is incorrect to identify sensation seekers as risk seekers. Risk is not the point of what they do, although they tend to underestimate it and have confidence in good outcomes. However they are willing to accept risk as the price for experiencing the sensations they enjoy. Low sensation seekers are not generally fearful but see no sense in taking risks that might cause harm or anxiety to themselves.

Volunteering

As previously mentioned, high sensation seekers tended to volunteer for sensory deprivation experiments for the sake of experiencing unusual mental effects which low sensation seekers saw as dangerous. We explored the general volunteering phenomena and found that sensation seeking was related to volunteering for experiments offering unusual types of experience; for example, hypnosis, extrasensory perception, encounter groups, transcendental meditation, and viewing pornography, but not for experiments in learning or social psychology. The volunteering could be predicted by a higher gradient of anticipated anxiety in low sensation seekers and a relatively higher gradient of anticipated pleasant excitement in high sensation seekers as a function of the perceived riskiness of experiments (Zuckerman, 1979b).

Sensation seeking was also related to volunteering for risky missions in soldiers in the US Army (Jobe et al., 1983) and the Israeli Army (Hobfoll et al., 1989). In Israel, volunteers for risky security jobs were also high sensation seekers (Montag and Birenbaum, 1986).

Sex

Sexual behavior is a primary area for sensation seeking. The needs for intensity, variety, and novelty were expected to manifest themselves in sexual experience in terms of activities and number of partners. Early studies of self-reported sexual behavior in college students confirmed these hypotheses (Zuckerman et al., 1972; Zuckerman et al., 1976). The number of types of heterosexual activities and the number of partners in sexual experience correlated positively with the general scale and all of the subscales of the SSS IV in males but primarily with ES and Dis in females. From the content of the subscales we might have expected the correlations to be primarily with the Dis subscale, but in males sexual experience correlated nearly equally with all of the subscales indicating that sexual experience is a function of a general trait of sensation seeking rather than confined to one subtrait.

With the advent of the AIDS pandemic the emphasis in research has been on risky sex, defined as number of partners, unprotected sex (condom use), and high-risk sexual encounters with strangers. In gay men unprotected anal sex is a particular risky form of sexual activity. Hoyle et al. (2000) reviewed all studies up to 1999 relating major personality traits to sexual risk taking. Sensation seeking proved to be the personality trait most consistently related to risky sex. The results were consistent in 38 studies involving sensation-seeking scales, but the effect sizes were modest, 0.25 for number of partners and 0.19 for overall sexual risk taking. The effect sizes for risky sex were higher among college students (0.24) and gay men (0.27) than in non-college populations, but still modest.

Zuckerman (2007) reviewed sexual risk taking in studies done between 1999 and 2006. The results continue to show significant relationships between sensation seeking and risky sex in high school, college, community, and gay populations. The likelihood of all types of sexual risk taking is increased by the use of alcohol and drugs prior to sexual activity. These substances have disinhibiting effects on behavior and the stimulant types intensify the sexual arousal. They also reduce anxiety from anticipations of negative effects like HIV infection and unwanted pregnancy in women. Sensation seeking is also related to heavy drinking and drug use.

Kalichman and Rompa (1995) developed a sexual sensation-seeking scale (SSSS), with items specifically addressed to novelty, excitement, and intensity of sexual experience, and a non-sexual experience-seeking scale (NSES), which is heavily loaded with TAS-type items. Both the SSSS and NSES are highly correlated and both correlate equally with drug and alcohol use before sex, number of sexual partners, and unprotected anal intercourse in gay men.

Relationships

Sensation seeking is inversely related to relationship satisfaction of self and partner in unmarried college couples (Thornquist et al., 1991). Discrepancies between sensation-seeking scores of cohabiting or marital partners is inversely related to relationship satisfaction (Schroth, 1991), and the correlation between scores of partners is higher in happily married couples than in couples entering marital therapy. Overall, married couples have relatively high correlations for sensation seeking, a phenomenon called 'assortative mating', a result not found for other personality traits where the correlations are close to zero. Divorced persons have higher SSS scores than married persons (Zuckerman and Neeb, 1980). Divorced men are also higher on the SSS than single men.

It is clear that sensation seeking is a crucial factor in the stability of relationships. The more satisfied and enduring relationships are between two low sensation seekers. The discrepancy between sensation-seeking levels in partners is a problem. Two high sensation seekers, although initially compatible, often run into problems when their need for variety drives them in different directions.

Smoking, drinking, and drugs

A study of risk taking in several areas shows that the most tightly correlated areas are smoking, drinking, drugs, and sex (Zuckerman and Kuhlman, 2000). Risky driving and gambling are more peripherally related to the central core of risk taking. Sex and the role of drinking and drugs in disinhibiton have already been discussed. The idea of an 'addictive personality' is supported by the correlations between risk taking in these areas.

Even sex can assume addictive qualities in some people.

A study of smoking in college students conducted in the early 1970s showed a strong relationship to smoking among males with 67% of the high, 47% of the medium, and 18% of the low sensation seekers smoking (Zuckerman et al., 1972). A second study at the same university was conducted in the mid-1980s (Zuckerman et al., 1990). During the intervening years there was a dramatic reduction in smoking among male students but little reduction in incidence of female smokers. Still, the relationship was significant with 20% of the high, 12% of the medium and 19% of the low sensation seekers still smoking. Combining past and present smokers the percentages were 43%, 32%, and 22% for high, medium, and low sensation seekers respectively.

Similar relationships between smoking were found during the 1980s in the general American population, high school students, the general Swiss male population, Norwegian army recruits and high school students, the Dutch general population, and Israeli adolescents (Zuckerman, 1994, 2007, for summaries). The association between smoking and sensation seeking continues into the next two decades (Carton et al., 1994; Zuckerman and Kuhlman, 2000). Zuckerman and Kuhlman found the relationship using the ImpSS.

In our first studies of college students, drug use correlated with the general and all of the SSS subscales in females and all of the subscales except Dis in males (Zuckerman et al., 1972). In contrast, the extent of drinking alcohol correlated specifically with Dis and additionally with only one other subscale (TAS in males and ES in females). There is some confounding of experience scale items in the SSS with drinking for Dis and drugs for ES. Later studies however have eliminated those items from the SSS and still found the relationships with drinking and drug use. Segal et al. (1980), for instance, found that modified ES and Dis scales were related to drinking and drug use in large samples of college students and naval personnel

of both genders. Other personality scales failed to discriminate between abstainer, alcohol only, marijuana only, and multidrug users.

More recent studies have attempted to identify the mediating mechanisms accounting for the relationship between sensation seeking and drinking. Sensation seeking not only correlates with alcohol consumption but is also related to perceived benefits and risks and outcome expectancies from drinking (Fromme et al., 1993; Hampson et al., 2001). Katz et al. (2000), however, found that although sensation seeking was related to positive expectancies for drinking it was also directly related to alcohol consumption without mediation by expectancies. Stacy (1997) found that both sensation seeking, as measured by the ImpSS, and positive expectancies were related to alcohol use in college students. Zuckerman and Kuhlman (2000) also found the ZKPQ ImpSS scale related to heavy drinking in college students. The ImpSS contains no item content relating to drinking or drug use. They also found that the aggression and sociability scales were related to heavy drinking in both males and females. In contrast, drug use was related only to ImpSS and sociability in males and only to ImpSS in females.

Cloninger (1987b) described two types of alcoholics: type 1 has a relatively late onset, loss of control over drinking, and guilt or fear about their dependence; type 2 has a relatively early age of onset and a pattern of antisocial behavior, involving fighting and arrests, that worsens when they are drinking. Type 2s are high on novelty seeking (Cloninger, 1987b) and sensation seeking (Sannibale and Hall, 1998, 2001; Varma et al., 1994).

Numerous studies during the 1970s and 1980s showed that sensation seeking was related to drug use among the youth (Zuckerman, 1994). The step from drinking only to marijuana is related to higher scores on sensation seeking, and there is another increment in sensation seeking going from marijuana to other more potent drugs

(Segal et al., 1980). Sensation seeking is related to all types of drug use whether stimulants, like cocaine, amphetamine, marijuana, and LSD; or depressants, like barbiturates or heroin (Andrucci et al., 1989, Zuckerman, 1979a). Most drugs of abuse produce euphoria through activation of the mesolimbic dopamine system although at different loci along the system; stimulant drugs at the nucleus accumbens and opiates at the ventral tegmental end (Bozarth, 1987). Experience seekers are curious about many types of drugs. Sometimes stimulants and depressants are used together or in sequence. Within the drug-using population sensation seeking is related to the number of different drugs used rather than to any specific drug use (Kaestner et al., 1977; Kern et al., 1986; Moorman et al., 1989).

Sensation seeking in young adolescents predicts later alcohol and drug use (Bates et al., 1985; Cloninger et al., 1988; Teichman et al., 1989). Ball (1995) used the ZKPQ to predict responses to treatment in cocaine addicts. High scores on ImpSS, Agg-Host, and N-Anx were found in those who continued to use drugs during the program as indicated by a high percentage of 'dirty' urine tests. Those high on ImpSS kept fewer treatment appointments and were less likely to stay in treatment for one month or complete treatment. In another cocaine treatment study, Patkar et al. (2004) found that the SSS total score and all subscales predicted days in treatment, drop-outs, and dirty urines.

Risky driving, sports, and other activities

Not many persons, even high sensation seekers, actually engage in risky sports like sky-diving, but many find an outlet for their need for physical thrills in daily driving. Risky driving includes driving at high speeds far above the legal speed limits, driving while intoxicated or high, following other cars too closely at high speeds ('tail-gating'), frequent and abrupt lane changes in order to maintain maximum speeds in crowded

traffic, and generally reckless and aggressive driving. Such behavior usually results in a relatively high rate of citations for traffic violations, but not necessarily accidents, suggesting that the sensation-seeking drivers are also skillful (or just lucky) (Zuckerman, 2007). However, aggression is related to accident involvement so accidents may be a combination of sensation seeking and aggression ('road rage'), often associated with antisocial behavior.

Jonah (1997) summarizing a review of 40 studies of the role of sensation seeking in risky driving concluded that 'the vast majority' of studies showed moderate correlations between trait and behavior. The first study showing a direct relationship between sensation seeking and reported speed of driving was done by Zuckerman and Neeb (1980). These results have been replicated many times as described in Zuckerman (2007). The relationships with speeding and other kinds of reckless driving found using self-reports have also been confirmed using behavioral observations in laboratory simulations or in real driving (Heino et al., 1996; Rosenbloom and Wolf, 2002; Thiffault and Bergeron, 2003; Versey and Zaidel, 2000). Studies have reported relationships between sensation seeking and records for convictions for speeding and driving while intoxicated (Burns and Wilde, 1995; Donovan et al., 1985; Jonah, 1997).

Sports are the rule-limited extensions of the physical play of children, particularly young males. Mock fighting and hunting is apparent in the play of the young of many other species. Sensation seeking, however, is a characteristic correlate of exceptional, often risky, sports involving defiance of gravity, speed, and unusual experiences in unfamiliar environments. The analog in animals is explorativeness in novel environments or approach reactions to novel stimuli including strangers of the same species.

Zuckerman (1983) reviewed the studies of sports at that time and found that sensation seeking was high in participants in high-risk sports, somewhat higher in those engaging in medium-risk sports, but not at all related to participation in low-risk sports. Later reviews by Jack and Ronan (1998) and Gomà-i-Freixanet (2004) reached the same conclusion: sensation seeking is related to the riskiness of the sports. There are exceptions to this generalization. Gymnastics is probably more risky in the sense of injuries than parachuting, but when a parachute fails the risk is for the ultimate consequence, loss of life.

I will not cite all of the studies relating sensation seeking to specific sports (see Zuckerman, 1994, 2007). Sensation seeking is high in participants in: skydiving, hanggliding, airplane or glider-flying, scubadiving, white-water canoeing, mountain and rock climbing, downhill skiing, and surfing. Intermediate levels are found in participants in automobile racing, swimming, karate, icehockey, and other competitive sports. When sports are confined to one activity, low levels of sensation seeking tend to characterize long-distance or marathon runners, bowlers, golfers, and volleyball players.

Within riskier sports, sensation seeking is higher in those who participate more often in the sport or engage in riskier forms of the sport. For instance expedition mountain climbers, experienced parachutists, volunteer salvage divers, ski instructors, and skiers who use the more challenging, steeper slopes tend to be higher on sensation seeking than less risk-taking participants in their sports.

There are sports or activities with little or no risk that attract high sensation seekers for reasons unknown including pool, target shooting, modern dancing (Rowland et al., 1986), and even something as cerebral as chess (Joireman et al., 2002). Risk is not the point of most sensation seeking but, as the definition of the trait suggests, sensation seekers are more willing to accept risk if the activity promises some other kind of reward.

Vocations

Military service alone is not necessarily an example of sensation seeking. Recruits may enlist during a time of peace and may be motivated by the security and benefits of service. However, volunteering for special risky services within the military is more likely to be motivated by high sensation seeking. Breivik (1991) found that Norwegian paratroopers were higher than ordinary recruits but did not differ from civilian parachutists on sensation seeking. Similarly, Swedish airforce pilots were higher than army draftees (Hallman et al., 1990, unpublished). Israeli soldiers who received medals for bravery in combat were higher than those who engaged in combat in the same war but did not receive decorations for bravery (Neria et al., 2000). Applicants for risky security-related jobs in Israel were higher on sensation seeking than those applying for less risky jobs (Montag and Birenbaum, 1986).

Gomà-i-Freixanet (1995, 2001) compared men and women engaged in prosocial occupations, like firemen, policemen, security guards, ambulance drivers and lifeguards with controls. This heterogeneous group only exceeded the control group in sensation seeking on the TAS subscale, and only in men. However, Gomà-i-Freixanet et al. (1988) found that Spanish firemen were higher than student controls on the total SSS, and TAS and ES subscales.

Policemen in general are not higher on sensation seeking than the norms from the general population (Gomà-i-Freixanet and Wismeijer; 2002; Homant et al., 1994), but risky behavior within the group may be influenced by sensation seeking. Self-reports and official records of high-speed pursuits by patrol officers correlated with sensation seeking (Hormant et al., 1994).

Some jobs are not personally risky but stressful in terms of risk to others. Air-traffic controllers, for instance, have the fate of many passengers in their hands and at times the monitoring of flights can become very stressful. In fact, air-traffic controller is rated as second only to test-pilot in rankings of jobs for riskiness (Musolino and Hershenson, 1977). In comparison with groups of civil servants and students, air-traffic controllers scored significantly higher on the SSS general and all of the subscales.

The emergency room (ER) in an urban setting is often a stressful environment in terms of emergency cases needing immediate attention. Physicians, nurses, psychologists, and paraprofessionals who volunteered for ER duty scored higher on all of the SSS subscales than physicians working in traditional medical settings (Irey, 1974). Similarly, rape crisis counselors scored higher than pediatric nurses matched for age and education on the Dis and ES subscales of the SSS (Best and Kilpatrick, 1977).

Media and entertainment preferences

Sensation seeking is not confined to risky behaviors but also affects risk-free entertainments (Zuckerman, 2006). Although sensation seekers prefer direct experiences (as at parties, nightclubs, rock concerts, etc.) they also seek vicarious experiences as in dramatics in television and movies. Tastes in music and art are also characteristic of high and low sensation seekers.

High sensation seekers are interested in portrayals of explicit sex in TV, movies, magazines, or elsewhere (Brown et al., 1974; Schierman and Rowland, 1985; Zuckerman and Litle, 1986; Zuckerman, 2006). They also attend and enjoy movies featuring violence and sadism as in horror movies (Lawrence and Palmgreen, 1996; Rowland et al., 1989; Zuckerman, 2006; Zuckerman and Litle, l986). They also like fast-moving action-adventure films and TV (Schierman and Rowland, 1985; Slater, 2003; Aluja and Torrubia, 1998). Low sensation seekers prefer musical and romantic movies. The need for change and susceptibility to boredom is expressed in TV channel-switching when given free choice of program options (Schierman and Rowland, 1985; Perse, 1996). They also tend to engage in other activities while watching TV.

Musical preferences vary with age and education. Litle and Zuckerman (1986) devised a musical preference scale with a wide variety of musical styles. Sensation seeking in general correlated with a liking for rock music, particularly hard rock. However, the ES subscale correlated with a wider variety of musical preferences such as jazz, rhythm and blues, new age, folk-ethnic, and even classical music. Carpenter et al. (2003) included more modern rock and hip-hop music selected for its edgy sound and hostile, rebellious lyrics. High scorers on the disinhibition subscale of the SSS particularly liked such defiant music as judged by self-selected exposure to it.

Art and photographic preferences

The art preferences of high sensation seekers include relatively high liking for expressionist, surreal, abstract, and pop art (Furnham and Walker, 2001a, 2001b; Zuckerman et al., 1993). They like art with tension in the painting expressed in content or style, or both. Violent or sexual content is of interest to high sensation seekers (Rawlings et al., 2000). This attraction to the morbid and violent extends to photographs (Rawlings, 2003; Zaleski, 1984). It should be emphasized that sensation seeking and aggression are distinctly different traits which are uncorrelated but may be combined. The attraction for the morbid in film or art is a function of the higher arousal value of such portrayals, not an indication of morbid or sadistic tendencies. The widespread attraction of horror films is not an indication of an aggressive instinct in humans, but a special outlet for those seeking arousal through empathic fear (Lawrence and Palmgreen, 1996).

PSYCHOBIOLOGY OF SENSATION SEEKING

This review of the phenomenal correlates of the sensation-seeking trait has shown the broad generality of the latent trait in behavioral expressions and preferences. However this 'nomological network' does not answer the question of causation. Whatever underlies the trait has some tenuous claim to explain the behavior in which the trait is involved, disregarding other factors. My approach is a psychobiological one. I assume that personality arises from an interaction of genetically influenced differences in nervous system function and environmental models and reinforcements (Zuckerman, 2005). The learning/motivation theory and research will not be described to any extent in this chapter (see Pickering, 2004). Genetics is a good place to begin.

Biometric genetics

The classical biometric twin method contrasts the similarities of or differences between identical or monozygotic (MZ), and fraternal or dizygotic (DZ) twins to estimate the proportion of variance that can be attributed to genetic factors: heritability. The remaining variance is divided into that attributable to shared environment, growing up in the same family and social environment, and non-shared environment, due to influences outside of the family and specific to each member of the family such as peers and non-related authority figures. The latter is a residual factor that also contains the error variance in measurement of the trait itself.

The genetics of sensation seeking is reviewed in a chapter (Zuckerman, 2002b). The first twin study of sensation seeking found a relatively high heritability (58%) for the SSS total score (Fulker et al., 1980). The remainder of the variance was due to non-shared environment and error of measurement. A study of twins separated at birth and raised in different families confirmed this heritability and the lack of influence of shared environment (D.T. Lykken, pers. comm., 1992).

Eysenck (1983) analyzed the data on the subscales in the Fulker et al. study, Hur and Bouchard (1997) analyzed the subscales in the separated twin study, and Koopmans et al. (1995) analyzed the subscales in a new study in the Netherlands. Heritabilities for three of the subscales were high in all three studies with mean heritabilities of 0.57 for ES, 0.54 for TAS, and 0.50 for Dis. The heritability for BS (0.43) was somewhat lower, probably because of the lower reliability of this subscale.

The broad heritability for the SSS Total is at the high end of heritabilities found for Eysenck's three major personality factors and the Big Five factors which are in the 0.40 to 0.60 range with a mean of 0.48 (Bouchard and Loehlin, 2001). Significant shared environmental effects are rarely found in these studies. However in most studies the shared environment is not measured directly but its influence is inferred by the degree to which DZ twin correlations approach those for MZ twins, on the assumption that shared environment is equal for both.

In the Koopmans et al. (1995) study, the analysis from twin data in the total sample indicated a strong genetic effect with no effect of shared environment for any of the subscales. This was a large study of nearly 2,000 twin pairs. The twin sample was divided into those who were raised in religious homes (about 60%) and those raised in non-religious homes (about 40%). The disinhibition subscale showed the largest difference between the two types of home so the biometric analyses were done separately for religious and non-religious homes. For twins raised in non-religious homes the heritabilities were high (61% for females and 49% for males) with no significant effects of shared environment for either (0% for females, 11% for males). However, analyses of twins raised in religious homes showed no genetic effect for males and only a weak one for females (37%). The shared environment effect for males was 62% for males and a lower but significant 25% for females. This phenotype by environment interaction suggests that the traditional biometric method may conceal genotype by environment interactions and that we should make some attempt to look for these by assessing environmental differences directly rather than by inference.

Family studies involving parent–child or sibling correlations assess additive genetic variance only, in contrast to twin studies which assess a broad type of genetic variance, including effects due to dominance or epistasis as well as additive genetic influences. The correlations between the average of mothers' and fathers' scores and the trait in their children represent the heritability due to additive genetic variance. These correlations were only 0.28 in the study by Kish and Donnenwerth (1972) and 0.31 in one by Bratko and Butkovic (2003). These heritabilities are only half of those found in twin studies. This contrast between heritabilities obtained from twin and family studies is common for other personality traits (Bouchard and Loehlin, 2001). One inference is that non-additive genetic mechanisms may also be involved in personality traits.

Older theories of personality attributed a large role to parental behavior and attitudes, particularly affection, punishment, rejection, and control. Correlations between childrens' personalities and parental behaviors and attitudes, as perceived or recalled by children, could be a function of selective memory bias by children or shared genetic factors in parents and children. However the absence of any correlation does not support an influence of parental treatment (at least in the normal range) and personality regardless of source. Kraft and Zuckerman (1999) found that the ImpSS score of adolescents from intact families did not correlate with any descriptions of parental treatment on a scale measuring perceived parental love, punishment/rejection, and control. There were no significant differences between intact families and families with one step-parent on ImpSS or any of the other personality traits in the ZKPQ or EPQ.

Assortative mating

Assortative mating is the selection of mates based on similarity in phenotype. Despite assumptions that 'like attracts like'

or 'opposites attract' there is very little evidence of assortative mating for personality traits, with spousal correlations on the major traits close to zero (Bouchard and Loehlin, 2001). Sensation seeking, however, is an exception. Summarizing such studies, Zuckerman (1994) reported substantial correlations between spouses on sensation seeking. More recently, Bratko and Butkovic (2003) reported a spousal correlation of 0.44 between husbands and wives on the SSS total scale.

As previously discussed, resemblance in sensation seeking is an important factor in premarital and marital relationship satisfaction. Divorce is heritable (McGue and Lykken, 1992) and this genetic effect is in part mediated by the genetic factors in personalities of the spousal partners (Jocklin et al., 1996). But beyond this assortative mating implies an evolutionary significance for the trait. Assortative mating could inflate additive-type heritability although it does not appear to do so for sensation-seeking judging from parent–child correlations.

Molecular genetics

Molecular genetics allows for the identification of specific genes associated with personality traits or disorders. The first such gene, the dopamine receptor 4 (DRD4), was found to be associated with the trait of novelty seeking in two independent studies, one in Israel (Ebstein et al., 1996) and the other in America (Benjamin et al., 1996). The DRD4 has two primary alleles (alternate gene forms) in Israeli and Western populations, a short form with four repeats of the base sequence and a long form with seven repeats. The long form is associated with higher scores on novelty seeking or similar scales. Recently it has been discovered that the short form is associated with altruism or selflessness (Bachner-Melman et al., 2005).

Many replication attempts followed these initial studies, some successful but some with negative findings. The most recent count shows 12 replications with 13 non-replications (Ebstein et al., 2003). However these findings cannot be established by merely counting. We must understand why some studies find a relationship and others do not. Population differences and differences in methods used to assess the personality trait are obvious sources of differences. Personality traits are all polygenic and any one gene only accounts for a small part of the variance in the trait. The relative effect of the gene determines the ability to detect associations and many genes may have effects that are too small to be detected. Furthermore, there is increasing evidence of gene interactions and gene–environment interactions in determining traits or disorders.

What is encouraging is the finding of DRD4 associations with behavioral phenomena and disorders that are also associated with sensation seeking (Ebstein, 2006). In mice with the DRD4 knocked out there is a reduction in exploration of new environments. In horses the gene alleles were related to curiosity, and in dogs to aggression. In humans the long forms of the gene are associated with heroin and alcohol abuse (in some but not all studies), pathological gambling, and attention deficit/hyperactivity disorder (Ebstein and Kotler, 2002). The seven-repeat form of the DRD4 has been linked to attention deficit hyperactivity disorder (ADHD) in a metanalysis of fourteen studies (Faraone et al., 2001). The DRD4 and several polymorphisms have been associated with sexual desire, function, and arousal (Ben Zion et al., 2006). This association suggests an evolutionary explanation for the relatively recent emergence of the seven-repeat form of the DRD4 in the Paleolithic era about 40,000–50,000 years ago when our species of humanoid came out of Africa to explore and settle around the earth (Ebstein, 2006). Mating proclivity and exploration may be adaptive traits linked to the DRD4-7. However, the older DRD4-4, related to altruism, still characterized the majority of the population. A society needs many cooperators and a minority of risk-taking explorers.

Psychophysiology

The early theory of sensation seeking was based on an 'optimal level of arousal' idea, with 'arousal' referring to cortical arousal. It was therefore natural to turn to psychophysiological studies to test the theory. We began with studies of the orienting reflex (OR) as measured by the arousal produced by a novel stimulus, a measure of attention and interest. The prediction was that high sensation seekers would be more aroused than lows by a novel stimulus but would habituate quickly when the same stimulus was repeated. The first study using a simple tone and visual stimuli showed this effect (Neary and Zuckerman, 1976). There were no differences in basal levels of arousal as measured by the skin conductance level, but high sensation seekers had a higher amplitude of skin conductance response (SCR) to the first presentation of a stimulus which quickly habituated on subsequent trials repeating the same stimulus. Replication results were mixed. However, Smith and his colleagues found that the content and emotional intensity of the stimulus enhanced the SCR OR in high sensation seekers relative to those lower in the trait (Smith et al., 1986, 1989).

Phasic changes in heart rate (HR) in response to stimuli have also revealed stronger ORs to novel stimuli in high sensation seekers. A decelerating HR is characteristic of an OR. Several studies found that HR change in reaction to a novel stimulus of moderately high intensity elicits a stronger OR in high than in low sensation seekers (Orlebeke and Feij, 1979; Ridgeway and Hare, 1981; Zuckerman et al., 1988). Low sensation seekers tend to show a stronger defensive reflex (DR) to a stimulus of high intensity.

Autonomic measures are of interest as surrogates for brain responses but the latter are more directly related to the optimal level theory. The relationship between stimulus intensities and the amplitudes of cortical evoked potentials (EPs) has proven to be a fruitful way of exploring individual differences, sensation seeking in particular. Buchsbaum (1971) developed a method using the slope of the relationship between stimulus intensity and EPs as a measure of cortical 'augmenting/reducing'. Those who show a high slope with EPs increasing substantially with increases in stimulus intensity are called 'augmenters' and those who show minimal increase and even a reduction in EPs at the highest intensities are described as 'reducers'. Although described in terms of type extremes the actual distribution of slopes is normal.

Zuckerman et al. (1974) found a direct relationship between the Dis subscale of the SSS and the visual EP. Since then a number of studies have replicated this finding and many more have replicated the relationship between Dis or SSS Total scores and the auditory EP (Brocke, 2004; Zuckerman, 1990). The visual EP studies have mostly used the P1N1 component of the EP and the auditory EP studies have generally used either the slopes of N1/P2 or P2 alone in relation to stimulus intensities. The N1 is a negative peak at about 80–90 ms and the P2 is a positive peak at about 170 ms after the stimulus. The N1/P2 complex is generated at the auditory cortex in the temporal lobe. The slopes based on N1/P2 and P2 alone are the most reliable over time of the early auditory EP slopes (Brocke, 2004), and therefore the most likely source for individual differences.

EP augmenting/reducing in humans is also related to impulsivity (Barratt et al., 1987). In cats selected on the basis of visual EP augmenting, the augmenter cats were superior on a bar-pressing task for food based on a fixed interval reinforcement schedule (Saxton et al., 1987). However, when the schedule was shifted to reinforcement for a low rate of response (DRL) the reducer cats were superior because the augmenter cats could not restrain responding. The augmenter cats are more approaching and aggressive and the reducer cats more inhibited when confronted with novel stimuli and in reactions to humans. A subspecies of rats characterized by EP augmenting is more exploratory and aggressive than another strain, characterized by EP reducing, which is more fearful in a novel environment (Siegel et al., 1993). Differences between the two strains in brain self-stimulation and neurotransmitter and hormone responses to stress are suggestive of physiological and biochemical sources of differences in sensation seeking in humans.

BIOCHEMICAL STUDIES

Monoamine oxidase (MAO) is an enzyme that catabolizes the oxidative deamination of monoamines in brain. There are two forms of MAO in human brain, MAO A type and MAO B type. MAO-A preferentially oxidizes serotonin and norepinephrine, whereas in human and primate brain, dopamine is primarily oxidized by MAO-B (Shih et al., 1999). In humans MAO-B is obtained from blood platelets. In nine of thirteen studies of MAO-B and sensation-seeking there was a significant negative correlation between the two. In other words high sensation seekers tend to have low levels of MAO-B (Zuckerman, 1994).

Low MAO levels are also found in persons with clinical disorders characterized by impulsivity and sensation seeking, including ADHD, antisocial and borderline personality disorders, alcoholism and drug abuse, and bipolar mood disorder (see table 5-13 in Zuckerman, 2005). Low levels of the enzyme are also found in the relatives of alcoholics and those with bipolar disorder suggesting a genetic linkage of the biological trait with the behavioral one. Apart from the extreme of clinical disorders, low MAO-B levels are found in those who smoke, drink heavily, and use drugs. It is also associated with convictions for felony offenses in male college students (Coursey et al., 1979).

The preferential regulation of the neurotransmitter dopamine by MAO-B would suggest that dopamine may be higher or more reactive to stimulation in high sensation seeking. Netter (2006) has reviewed a number of studies of dopamine challenge tests that indicate this hypothesis might be valid. Those scoring high on the novelty-seeking scale tend to have a lower density of D-2 receptors in the right insula part of brain. Density of receptors is inversely related to activity in neurotransmitters so that the inference is that there is a higher level of dopamine activity in novelty seekers. Netter compared subjects with early versus late responses to a dopamine stimulant. The quick responders were high on several measures of sensation seeking and impulsivity including the disinhibition subscales of the SSS, the exploratory excitability of Cloninger's (1987) TPQ and the fun-seeking and behavioral activation scales of the Carver and White (1994) behavioral activation scale. Scales of shyness, inhibition, and constraint were related to the absence of an early peak in dopamine reactivity. The euphoria and increased drive in patients in manic states is reduced by dopamine antagonists.

In contrast to dopamine, which is associated with drive, activity, sexuality, and exploration in animals, serotonin in the limbic system is generally associated with behavioral inhibition (Soubrié, 1986). Sensation seeking has been shown to be negatively correlated with response to serotonin stimulants (Depue, 1995; Netter et al., 1996). This would make sense in terms of the link between impulsivity and sensation-seeking.

Little research has been done with the third monoamine in the brain, norepinephrine, because blood or urine measures are largely from peripheral nervous system sources. However, norepinephrine in the cerebrospinal fluid (CSF) may have a closer relationship to brain norepinephrine. Ballenger et al. (1983) found a high negative correlation between CSF norepinephrine and sensation seeking. Noone has as yet attempted to replicate this association. Norepinephrine in brain regulates general cortical arousal so this finding could indicate that high sensation seekers are underaroused. No evidence for low cortical arousal in basal levels has been found for sensation seeking.

My psychopharmacological model for impulsive sensation seeking suggests that activity in all three monoamines interact to produce the behavioral and personality trait: dopaminergic reactivity in the tendency to approach novel or potentially rewarding stimuli; a lack of serotonergic reactivity to inhibition by conflicting expectancies of punishment, and a lack of noradrenergic reactivity or low arousability by such expectancies (Zuckerman, 1994, 1995, 2005). Ebstein and Auerbach (2002) have postulated a similar approach-inhibition conflict and relate dopaminergic and serotonergic reactivity traits to genetic sources in the DRD4 and serotonin transporter general variants.

Gonadal hormones, particularly testosterone, are also involved in the sensation-seeking motive. Plasma testosterone in males is associated with sensation seeking, particularly disinhibition, and impulsivity, as well as extraversion-related traits like sociability, activity, and assertiveness (Aluja-Fabregat and Torrubia, 2004; Daitzman and Zuckerman, 1980). This hormone is also related to number of sexual partners (Bogaert and Fisher, 1995; Dabbs, 2000; Daitzman and Zuckerman, 1980) and antisocial behavior (Aluja and Garcia, 2005; Dabbs, 2000). The sex differences and age curves on testosterone and sensation seeking are quite similar. Males are higher than females on testosterone and sensation seeking and both variables peak in late adolescence and decline with age thereafter.

CONCLUSION

Sensation seeking is both a personality trait and a motive. As a trait it is involved in a wide variety of behaviors. The common element is an appetite for sensation and experience that is exciting either through novelty or intensity. This motivates a search for change and an aversive state of boredom when sensations and experiences are too constant or familiar. The sensation seeker is an explorer in either outer space or inner space. The sensation seeker is an adventurer in risky physical activities or has a readiness to engage in risky experiences as in drugs and sex. It can be expressed in prosocial or antisocial behavior. It has both an evolutionary advantage and disadvantage.

There is a strong genetic component in this trait and the environmental contributions may come more from the world outside of the early family than from family examples and interactions. The brain of a high sensation seeker is reactive to novel and intense stimuli but not to repetitious or too-familiar stimuli. The basis of this may lie in the reactivity of biochemical systems in the brain and hormonal systems as determined by genetic differences. Much remains to be done in testing the postulated biological framework on which the trait is constructed. Unlike simpler one gene, one neurotransmitter, one behavioral mechanism models, interactions are suggested at all levels, genes, neurotransmitters, and behavioral traits. The neat separation of traits by factor analysis is based on a messier complex interaction of underlying behavioral and biological mechanisms.

As Wilson asserts: 'Complexity is what interests scientists in the end, not simplicity. Reductionism is the way to understand it. The love of complexity without reductionism makes art; the love of complexity with reductionism makes science.' (1998: 58–59).

REFERENCES

Aluja, A. and Garcia, L.F. (2005) 'Sensation seeking, sexual curiosity and testosterone in inmates', *Neuropsychobiology*, 51(1): 28–33.

Aluja, A. and Torrubia, B.F. (1998) 'Viewing of mass media violence, perception of violence, personality, and academic achievement', *Personality and Individual Differences*, 25(5): 973–89.

Aluja-Fabregat, A. and Torrubia, R. (2004) 'Hostility-aggressiveness, sensation seeking, and sexual hormones in men: Reexploring their relationship', *Neuropsychobiology*, 50(1): 102–7.

Andrucci, G.L., Archer, R.P., Pancoast, D.L. and Gordon, R.A. (1989) 'The relationship of MMPI and sensation seeking scales to adolescent drug use', *Journal of Personality Assessment*, 53(2): 253–66.

Bachner-Melman, R., Gritsenko, I., Nemanov, L., Zohar, A.H., Dina, C. and Ebstein, R.P. (2005) 'Dopaminergic polymorphisms associated with self-report measures of human altruism: A fresh phenotype for the dopamine D4 receptor', *Molecular Psychiatry*, 10(x): 333–5.

Ball, S.A. (1995) 'The validity of an alternative five-factor measure of personality in cocaine abusers', *Psychological Assessment*, 7(2): 148–54.

Ballenger, J.C., Post, R.M., Jimerson, D.C., Lake, C.R., Murphy, D.L., Zuckerman, M. and Cronin, C. (1983) 'Biochemical correlates of personality traits in normals: An exploratory study', *Personality and Individual Differences*, 4(6): 615–25.

Barratt, E.S., Pritchard, W.S., Faulki, D.M. and Brandt, M.E. (1987) 'The relationship between impulsiveness subtraits, trait anxiety, and visual N100-augmenting–reducing: A topographic analysis', *Personality and Individual Differences*, 8(1): 43–51.

Bates, M.E., Labourie, E.W. and White, H.R. (1985) 'A longitudinal study of sensation seeking needs and drug use', Paper presented at the 93rd Annual Convention of the American Psychological Association, August, Los Angeles, 1985.

Ben Zion, I.Z., Tessler, R., Cohen, L., Lerer, E., Raz, Y., Bachner-Melman, R. et al. (2006) 'Polymorphisms in the dopamine D4 receptor gene (DRD4) contribute to individual differences in human sexual behavior: Desire, arousal, and sexual function', *Molecular Psychiatry*, 11(8): 782–6.

Benjamin, J., Li, L., Patterson, C., Greenberg, B.D., Murphy, D.L. and Hamer, D.H. (1996) 'Population and familial association between the D4 dopamine receptor gene and measures of sensation seeking', *Nature Genetics*, 12(Jan): 81–4.

Best, C.L. and Kilpatrick, D.G. (1977) 'Psychological profiles of rape crisis counselors', *Psychological Reports*, 40(3, pt. 2): 1127–34.

Bogaert, A.F. and Fisher, W.A. (1995) 'Predictors of university men's number of sexual partners', *Journal of Sex Research*, 32(2): 119–30.

Bouchard, T.J., Jr. and Loehlin, J.C. (2001) 'Genes, evolution, and personality', *Behavior Genetics*, 31(3): 243–73.

Bozarth, M.A. (1987) 'Ventral tegmental reward system', in J. Engel, L. Oreland, B. Pernov, S. Rossner and L.A. Pelhorn (eds), *Brain Reward Systems and Abuse*. New York: Raven, pp. 1–17.

Bratko, D. and Butkovic, A. (2003) 'Family study of sensation seeking', *Personality and Individual Differences*, 35: 1559–70.

Breivik, G. (1991) 'Personality and sensation seeking in risk sport: A summary', Unpublished manuscript.

Breuer, J. and Freud, S. (1955) *Studies on Hysteria*, (J. Strachey and A. Freud, trans.). London: Hogarth. (Original work published 1895.)

Brocke, B. (2004) 'The multilevel approach in sensation seeking: Potentials and findings of a four level research program', in R.M. Stelmack (ed.), *On the Psychobiology of Personality: Essays in Honor of Marvin Zuckerman*. Amsterdam: Elsevier, pp. 267–93.

Brown, L.T., Ruder, V.G., Ruder, J.H. and Young, S.D. (1974) 'Stimulation seeking and the Change Seeker Index', *Journal of Consulting and Clinical Psychology*, 42(2): 311.

Buchsbaum, M.S. (1971) 'Neural events and psychophysical law', *Science*, 172(April): 502.

Burns, P.C. and Wilde, G.J.S. (1995) 'Risk taking in male taxi drivers: Relationships among personality, observational data, and driver records', *Personality and Individual Differences*, 18: 267–78.

Carpenter, F.D., Knoblock, S. and Zellman, D. (2003) 'Rock, rap, and rebellion: Comparisons of traits predicting selective exposure to defiant music', *Personality and Individual Differences*, 35(7): 1643–55.

Carton, S., Jouvent, R. and Widlocecher, D. (1994) 'Sensation seeking, nicotine dependence and smoking motivation in female and male smokers', *Addictive Behaviors*, 19(3): 219–27.

Carver, C.S. and White, T.L. (1994) 'Behavioral inhibition, behavioral activation, and affective responses to impending reward and punishments: The BIS/BAS scales', *Journal of Personality and Social Psychology*, 67(2): 319–33.

Cloninger, C.R. (1987a) 'A systematic method for clinical description and classification of personality variants', *Archives of General Psychiatry*, 44(6): 573–88.

Cloninger, C.R. (1987b) 'Neurogenic adaptive mechanisms in alcoholism', *Science*, 236(4800): 410–16.

Cloninger, C.R., Sigvardsson, S. and Bohman, M. (1988) 'Childhood personality predicts alcohol abuse in young adults', *Alcoholism: Clinical and Experimental Research*, 12(4): 494–505.

Coursey, R.D., Buchsbaum, M.S. and Murphy, D.L. (1979) 'Platelet MAO activity and evoked potentials in the identification of subjects biologically at risk for psychiatric disorders', *British Journal of Psychiatry*, 134(April): 372–81.

Cronbach, L.J. and Meehl, P.E. (1955) 'Construct validity in psychological tests', *Pychologica1 Bulletin*, 52(4): 281–302.

Dabbs, J.M. (2000) *Heroes, Rogues and Lovers*. New York: McGraw-Hill.

Daitzman, R.J. and Zuckerman, M. (1980) 'Personality, disinhibitory sensation seeking and gonadal hormones', *Personality and Individual Differences*, 1(2): 103–10.

Depue, R.A. (1995) 'Neurobiological factors in personality and depression', *European Journal of Personality*, 9(5): 413–39.

Donovan, D.M., Queisser, H.R., Salzberg, P.M. and Umlauf, R.L. (1985) 'Intoxicated and bad drivers: Subgroups within the same population of high-risk men drivers', *Journal of Studies on Alcohol*, 46(5): 375–82.

Ebstein, R.P. (2006) 'The molecular genetic architecture of human personality: Beyond self-report questionnaires', *Molecular Psychiatry*, 11(5): 427–45.

Ebstein, R.P. and Auerbach, J.G. (2002) 'Dopamine D4 receptor and serotonin transporter promoter polymorphisms and temperament in early childhood', in J. Benjamin, R.P. Ebstein and R.H. Belmaker (eds), *Molecular Genetics and the Human Personality*. Washington, DC: American Psychiatric Publishing, pp. 137–49.

Ebstein, R.P., Benjamin, J. and Belmaker, R.H. (2003) 'Behavioral genetics, genomics, and personality', in R. Plomin, J.C. De Fries, I.W. Gaig and P. McGuffin (eds), *Behavioral Genetics in the Postgenomic Era*. Washington, DC: American Psychological Association, pp. 365–88.

Ebstein, R.P. and Kotler, M. (2002) 'Personality, substance abuse, and genes', in J. Benjamin., R.P. Ebstein and R.H. Belmaker (eds), *Molecular Genetics and the Human*

Personality. Washington, DC: American Psychiatric Publishers, pp. 151–63.

Ebstein, R.P., Novick, O., Umanshy, R., Priel, B., Osher, Y., Blaine, D. et al. (1996) 'Dopamine D4 receptor (D4DR) exon III polymorphism associated with the human personality trait of novelty seeking', *Nature Genetics*, 12: 78–80.

Eysenck, H.J. (1983) 'A biometrical genetical analysis of impulsive and sensation seeking behavior', in M. Zuckerman (ed.), *Biological Bases of Sensation Seeking, Impulsivity, and Anxiety*. Hillsdale, NJ: Erlbaum, pp. 1–27.

Faraone, S.V., Doyle, A.E., Mick, E. and Biederman, J. (2001) 'Meta-analysis of the association between the 7-repeat allele of the dopamine D(4) receptor gene and attention deficit hyperactivity disorder', *American Journal of Psychiatry*, 158(7): 1052–7.

Fromme, K., Stroot, E. and Kaplan, D. (1993) 'Comprehensive effects of alcohol: Development and psychometric assessment of a new expectancy questionnaire', *Psychological Assessment*, 5(1): 19–26.

Fulker, D.W., Eysenck, S.B.G. and Zuckerman, M. (1980) 'A genetic and environmental analysis of sensation seeking', *Journal of Research in Personality*, 14(2): 261–81.

Furnham, A. and Walker, J. (2001a) 'Personality and judgments of abstract, pop art, and representational paintings', *European Journal of Personality*, 15(1): 57–72.

Furnham, A. and Walker, J. (2001b) 'The influence of personality traits, previous experiences of art, and demographic variables on artistic preferences', *Personality and Individual Differences*, 31(6): 997–1017.

Gomà-i-Freixanet, M. (1995) 'Prosocial and antisocial aspects of personality', *Personality and Individual Differences*, 19(2): 125–34.

Gomà-i-Freixanet, M. (2001) 'Prosocial and antisocial aspects of personality in women: A replication study', *Personality and Individual Differences*, 30(8): 1401–11.

Gomà-i-Freixanet, M. (2004) 'Sensation seeking and participation in physical risk sports', in R.M. Stelmack (ed.), *On the Psychobiology of Personality: Essays in Honor of Marvin Zuckerman*. New York: Elsevier, pp. 185–201.

Gomà-i-Freixanet, M., Perez, J. and Torrubia, R. (1988) 'Personality variables in antisocial and prosocial behavior', in T.E. Moffitt and S.A. Mednick (eds), *Biological Contributions to Crime Causation*. Dordrecht, The Netherlands: Martinus Nijhoff, pp. 211–22

Gomà-i-Freixanet, M. and Wismeijer, A.J. (2002) 'Applying personality theory to a group of police bodyguards: A physically risky prosocial prototype?', *Psicothema*, 14(2): 387–92.

Hallman, J., Klinteberg, B., Oreland, L., Wirsen, A., Levander, S.E. and Schalling, D. (1990) 'Personality, neuropsychological and biochemical characteristics of air force pilots', Unpublished manuscript.

Hampson, S.E., Severson, H.H., Burns, W.J., Slovik, P. and Fisher, K.J. (2001) 'Risk perception, personality factors and alcohol use among adolescents', *Personality and Individual Differences*, 30(1): 167–81.

Hebb, D.O. (1955) 'Drives and the C.N.S. (conceptual nervous system)', *Psychological Review*, 62(4): 243–54.

Heino, A., van der-Molen, H. and Wilde, G.J.S. (1996) 'Differences in risk experience between sensation avoiders and sensation seekers', *Personality and Individual Differences*, 20(1): 71–9.

Hobfoll, S.E., Rom, T. and Segal, B. (1989) 'Sensation seeking, anxiety, and risk-taking in the Israeli context', in S. Ebstein (ed.), *Drugs and Alcohol Use: Issues and Facts*. New York: Plenum, pp. 53–9.

Hormant, R.J., Kennedy, D.B. and Howton, J.D. (1994) 'Risk taking and police pursuit', *Journal of Social Psychology*, 134(2): 213–21.

Hoyle, R., Fejfar, M.C. and Miller, J.D. (2000) 'Personality and sexual risk-taking: A quantitative review', *Journal of Personality*, 68(6): 1203–31.

Hur, Y.-M. and Bouchard, T.J. Jr. (1997) 'The genetic correlation between impulsivity and sensation seeking traits', *Behavior Genetics*, 27(5): 455–63.

Irey, P.A. (1974) 'Personality dimensions of crisis intervenors vs. academic psychologists, traditional clinicians and paraprofessionals', Unpublished PhD dissertation, Southern Illinois University, Carbondale.

Jack, S.J. and Ronan, K.R. (1998) 'Sensation seeking among high- and low risk sports participants', *Personality and Individual Differences*, 25(6): 1063–83.

Jobe, J.B., Holgate, S.H. and Spransky, T.A. (1983) 'Risk taking as motivation for volunteering for a hazardous experiment', *Journal of Personality*, 51(1): 95–107.

Jocklin, V., McGue, M. and Lykken, D.T. (1996) 'Personality and divorce: A genetic analysis', *Journal of Personality and Social Psychology*, 71(2): 288–99.

Joireman, J.A., Fick, C.S. and Anderson, J.W. (2002) 'Sensation seeking and involvement in chess', *Personality and Individual Differences*, 32(3): 509–15.

Jonah, B.A. (1997) 'Sensation seeking and risky driving: A review and synthesis of the literature', *Accident Analysis and Prevention*, 29(5): 651–65.

Kaestner, E., Rosen, L. and Apel, P. (1977) 'Patterns of drug abuse: Relationships with ethnicity, sensation seeking, and anxiety', *Journal of Consulting and Clinical Psychology*, 45(3): 462–8.

Kalichman, S.C. and Rompa, D. (1995) 'Sexual sensation seeking and sexual compulsivity scales: Reliability, validity, and predicting HIV risk behavior', *Journal of Personality Assessment*, 65(3): 586–601.

Katz, E.C., Fromme, K. and D'Amico, E.J. (2000) 'Effects of outcome expectancies and personality of young adults' illicit drug use, heavy drinking, and risky sexual behavior', *Cognitive Therapy and Research*, 24(6): 1–22.

Kern, M.F., Kenkel, M.B., Templer, D.I. and Newell, T.G. (1986) 'Drug preference as a function of arousal and stimulus screening', *International Journal of the Addictions*, 21(2): 255–65.

Kish, G.B. and Donnenwerth, G.V. (1972) 'Sex differences in the correlates of stimulus seeking', *Journal of Consulting and Clinical Psychology*, 38(1): 42–49.

Koopmans, J.R., Boomsma, D.I., Heath, A.C. and Lorenz, J.P.D. (1995) 'A multivariate genetic analysis of sensation seeking', *Behavior Genetics*, 25(3): 349–56.

Kraft, M.R., Jr. and Zuckerman, M. (1999) 'Parental behaviors and attitudes of their parents reported by young adults from intact and stepparent families and relationships between perceived parenting and personality', *Personality and Individual Differences*, 27(3): 453–76.

Lawrence, P.A. and Palmgreen, P.C. (1996) 'A uses and gratification analysis of horror', in J.B. Weaver III and R. Tamborini (eds), *Horror Films: Current Research on Audience Preferences and Reactions*. Mahwah, NJ: Erlbaum, pp. 161–78.

Litle, P. and Zuckerman, M. (1986) 'Sensation seeking and music preferences', *Personality and Individual Differences*, 7(4): 575–7.

McGue, M. and Lykken, D.T. (1992) 'Genetic influence on risk of divorce', *Psychological Science*, 7(6): 368–73.

Montag, I. and Birenbaum, M. (1986) 'Psychopathological factors and sensation seeking', *Journal of Research in Personality*, 20(3): 338–48.

Moorman, P.P., de Cocq van Delwijnen, H., van Wessel, K. and Bauer, H. (1989) 'Personality characteristics of drug addicts in the Netherlands', Leiden Psychological Reports LPR-PP02-89, Leiden: Leiden University, Department of Psychology.

Musolino, R.F. and Hershenson, D.B. (1977) 'Avocational sensation seeking in high and low risk-taking occupations', *Journal of Vocational Behavior*, 10(3): 358–65.

Neary, R.S. and Zuckerman, M. (1976) 'Sensation seeking, trait and state anxiety, and the electrodermal orienting reflex', *Psychophysiology*, 13(3): 205–11.

Neria, Y., Solomon, Z., Ginzburg, K. and Dekel, R. (2000) 'Sensation seeking, wartime performance, and long-term adjustment among Israeli war veterans', *Personality and Individual Differences*, 29(5): 921–32.

Netter, P. (2006) 'Dopamine challenge tests as an indicator of psychological traits', *Human Psychopharmacology: Clinical and Experimental*, 21(2): 91–9.

Netter, P., Hennig, J. and Roed, I.S. (1996) 'Serotonin and dopamine as mediators of sensation seeking behavior', *Neuropsychobiology*, 34(3): 155–65.

Orlebeke, J.F. and Feij, J.A. (1979) 'The orienting reflex as a personality correlate', in E.H. van Holst and J.F. Orlebeke (eds), *The Orienting Reflex in Humans*. Hillsdale, NJ: Erlbaum, pp. 567–85.

Patkar, A.A., Murray, H.W., Mannelli, P., Gottheil, E., Weinstein, S.P. and Vergare, M.J. (2004) 'Pre-treatment measures of impulsivity, aggression and sensation seeking are associated with treatment outcome for African-American cocaine-dependent patients', *Journal of Addictive Diseases*, 23(1): 109–22.

Perse, E.M. (1996) 'Sensation seeking and the use of television for arousal', *Communication Reports*, 9(1): 37–48.

Pickering, A.D. (2004) 'The neuropsychology of impulsive antisocial sensation seeking personality traits: From dopamine to hippocampal function?', in R.M. Stelmack (ed.), *On the Psychobiology of Personality: Essays in Honor of Marvin Zuckerman*. Oxford: Elsevier, pp. 453–76.

Rawlings, D. (2003) 'Personality correlates of liking for "unpleasant" paintings and photographs', *Personality and Individual Differences*, 34(3): 395–410

Rawlings, D., Barrantes i Vidal, N. and Furnham, A. (2000) 'Personality and aesthetic preference in Spain and England: Two studies relating sensation seeking and openness to experience to liking for paintings and music', *European Journal of Personality*, 14(6): 553–76.

Ridgeway, D. and Hare, R.D. (1981) 'Sensation seeking and psychophysiological responses to auditory stimulation', *Psychophysiology*, 18(6): 613–18.

Rosenbloom, T. and Wolf, Y. (2002) 'Signal detection in conditions of everyday life traffic dilemmas', *Accident Analysis and Prevention*, 34(6): 763–72.

Rowland, G.L., Fouts, G. and Heatherton, T. (1989) 'Television viewing and sensation seeking: Uses, preferences, and attitudes', *Personality and Individual Differences*, 10(9): 1003–6.

Rowland, G.L., Franken, R.E. and Harrison, K. (1986) 'Sensation seeking and participating in sporting activities', *Journal of Sport Psychology*, 8(3): 212–20.

Sannibale, C. and Hall, W. (1998) 'An evaluation of Cloninger's typology of alcohol abuse', *Addiction*, 93: 1241–9.

Sannibale, C. and Hall, W. (2001) 'Gender related problems and correlates of alcohol dependence among men and women with a lifetime diagnosis of alcohol-use disorders', *Drug and Alcohol Review*, 20(4): 369–83.

Saxton, P.M., Siegel, J. and Lukas, J.H. (1987) 'Visual evoked potential augmenting/reducing slopes in cats-2. Correlations with behavior', *Personality and Individual Differences*, 8(4): 511–19.

Schierman, M.J. and Rowland, G.L. (1985) 'Sensation seeking and selection of entertainment', *Personality and Individual Differences*, 5(5): 599–603.

Schroth, M.L. (1991) 'Dyadic adjustment and sensation seeking compatibility', *Personality and Individual Differences*, 12(5): 467–71.

Segal, B.S., Huba, G.J. and Singer, J.F. (1980) *Drugs, Daydreaming and Personality: Studies of College Youth*. Hillsdale, NJ: Erlbaum.

Shih, J.C., Chen, K. and Ridd, M.J. (1999) 'Monoamine oxidase: From genes to behavior', *Annual Review of Neuroscience*, 22: 197–217.

Siegel, J., Sisson, D.F. and Driscoll, P. (1993) 'Augmenting and reducing of visual evoked potentials in Roman high- and low-avoidance rats', *Physiology and Behavior*, 54(4): 707–11.

Slater, M.D. (2003) 'Alienation, aggression, and sensation seeking as predictors of adolescent use of violent film, computer, and website content', *Journal of Communication*, 53(1): 105–21.

Smith, B.D., Davidson, R.A., Smith, D.L., Goldstein, H. and Perlstein, W. (1989) 'Sensation seeking and arousal: Effects of strong stimulation on electrodermal activation and memory task performance', *Personality and Individual Differences*, 10(6): 671–9.

Smith, B.D., Perlstein, W.M., Davidson, R.A. and Michael, K. (1986) 'Sensation seeking: Differential effects of relevant novel stimulation on electrodermal activity', *Personality and Individual Differences*, 7(4): 445–52.

Soubrié, P. (1986) 'Reconciling the role of central serotonin neurons in human and animal behavior', *Behavioral and Brain Sciences*, 9(2): 319–64.

Stacy, A.W. (1997) 'Memory activation and expectancy as prospective predictors of alcohol and marijuana use', *Journal of Abnormal Psychology*, 106(1): 61–73.

Teichman, M., Barnes, Z. and Rahav, G. (1989) 'Sensation seeking, state and trait anxiety and depressive mood in adolescent substances users', *International Journal of the Addictions*, 24(2): 87–9.

Thiffault, P. and Bergeron, J. (2003) 'Fatigue and individual differences in monotonous simulated driving', *Personality and Individual Differences*, 34(1): 159–76.

Thornquist, M.H., Zuckerman, M. and Exline, R.V. (1991) 'Loving, liking, looking, and sensation seeking in unmarried college couples', *Personality and Individual Differences*, 12(1): 1283–92.

Varma, V.K., Basu, D., Malhotra, A. and Sharma, A. (1994) 'Correlates of early- and late-onset alcohol dependence', *Addictive Behaviors*, 19(6): 609–19.

Versey, W.B. and Zaidel, D.M. (2000) 'Predicting drowsiness accidents from personal attributes, eyeblinks and ongoing driving behavior', *Personality and Individual Differences*, 28(1): 123–42.

Wilson, E.O. (1998) *Consilience: The Unity of Knowledge*. New York: Vintage Books.

Wundt, W.M. (1893) *Grundzüge der Physiologischen Psychologie*. Leipzig, Germany: Engleman.

Zaleski, Z. (1984) 'Sensation seeking and preference for emotional visual stimuli', *Personality and Individual Differences*, 5(5): 609–11.

Zubek, J.P. (1969) *Sensory Deprivation: Fifteen Years of Research*. New York: Appleton-Century-Crofts.

Zuckerman, M. (1969) 'Theoretical formulations: I', in J.P. Zubek (ed.), *Sensory Deprivation: Fifteen Years of Research*. New York: Appleton-Century-Crofts, pp. 407–32.

Zuckerman, M. (1971) 'Dimensions of sensation seeking', *Journal of Consulting and Clinical Psychology*, 36(1): 45–52.

Zuckerman, M. (1979a) *Sensation Seeking: Beyond the Optimal Level of Arousal*. Hillsdale, NJ: Erlbaum.

Zuckerman, M. (1979b) 'Sensation seeking and risk taking', in C.E. Izard (ed.), *Emotions in Personality and Psychopathology*. New York: Plenum, pp. 163–97.

Zuckerman, M. (1983) 'Sensation seeking and sports', *Personality and Individual Differences*, 4(3): 285–92.

Zuckerman, M. (1984) 'Experience and desire: A new format for sensation seeking scales', *Journal of Behavioral Assessment*, 6(2): 101–14.

Zuckerman, M. (1990) 'The psychophysiology of sensation seeking', *Journal of Personality*, 58(1): 313–45.

Zuckerman, M. (1991) *Psychobiology of Personality*. Cambridge, UK: Cambridge University Press.

Zuckerman, M. (1994) *Behavioral Expressions and Biosocial Bases of Sensation Seeking*. New York: Cambridge University Press.

Zuckerman, M. (1995) 'Good and bad humors: Biochemical bases of personality and its disorders', *Psychological Science*, 6(6): 325–32.

Zuckerman, M. (2002a) 'Zuckerman-Kuhlman Personality Questionnaire (ZKPQ): An alternative five-factorial model', in B. DeRaad and M. Perugini (eds), *Big Five Assessment*. Seattle, WA: Hogrefe & Huber, pp. 377–96.

Zuckerman, M. (2002b) 'Genetics of sensation seeking', in J. Benjamin, R.P. Epstein and R.H. Belmaker (eds), *Molecular Genetics and the Human Personality*. Washington, DC: American Psychiatric Publishing, pp. 193–210.

Zuckerman, M. (2005) *Psychobiology of Personality* (2nd edn). New York: Cambridge University Press.

Zuckerman, M. (2006) 'Sensation seeking in entertainment', in J. Bryant and P. Vorderer (eds), *Psychology of Entertainment*. Mahwah, NJ: Erlbaum, pp. 367–87.

Zuckerman, M. (2007) *Sensation Seeking and Risky Behavior*. Washington, DC: American Psychological Association.

Zuckerman, M., Ball, S. and Black, J. (1990) 'Influence of sensation seeking, gender, risk appraisal and situational motivation on smoking', *Addictive Behaviors*, 15(3): 209–20.

Zuckerman, M., Bone, R.N., Neary, R., Mangelsdorf, D. and Brustman, B. (1972) 'What is the sensation seeker? Personality trait and experience correlates of the Sensation Seeking Scales', *Journal of Consulting and Clinical Psychology*, 39(2): 308–21.

Zuckerman, M. and Cloninger, C.R. (1996) 'Relationships between Cloninger's, Zuckerman's, and Eysenck's dimensions of personality', *Personality and Individual Differences*, 21(2): 283–5.

Zuckerman, M., Eysenck, S.B.G. and Eysenck, H.J. (1978) 'Sensation seeking in England and America: Cross-cultural, age, and sex comparisons', *Journal of Consulting and Clinical Psychology*, 46(1): 139–49.

Zuckerman, M., Kolin, I., Price, L. and Zoob, I. (1964) 'Development of a sensation seeking scale', *Journal of Consulting Psychology*, 28: 477–82.

Zuckerman, M. and Kuhlman, D.M. (2000) 'Personality and risk-taking: Common biosocial factors', *Journal of Personality*, 68(6): 999–1029.

Zuckerman, M. and Litle, P. (1986) 'Personality and curiosity about morbid and sexual events', *Personality and Individual Differences*, 7(1): 49–56.

Zuckerman, M., Murtaugh, T.T. and Siegel, J. (1974) 'Sensation seeking and cortical augmenting-reducing', *Psychophysiology*, 11(5): 535–42.

Zuckerman, M. and Neeb, M. (1980) 'Demographic influences in sensation seeking and expressions of sensation seeking in religion, smoking, and driving habits', *Personality and Individual Differences*, 1(3): 197–206.

Zuckerman, M., Simons, R.F. and Como, P.G. (1988) 'Sensation seeking and stimulus intensity as modulators of cortical, cardiovascular and electrodermal response: A cross-modality study', *Personality and Individual Differences*, 9(2): 361–72.

Zuckerman, M., Tushup, R. and Finner, S. (1976) 'Sexual attitudes and experience: Attitude and personality correlates and changes produced by a course in sexuality', *Journal of Consulting and Clinical Psychology*, 44(1): 7–19.

Zuckerman, M., Ulrich, R.S. and McLaughlin, J. (1993) 'Sensation seeking and reactions to nature paintings', *Personality and Individual Differences*, 15(5): 563–76.

19

Schizotypal Personality Models

Melissa J. Green, Gregory J. Boyle and Adrian Raine

'Schizotypy' is a multidimensional construct referring to a range of biologically determined personality factors, reflected in cognitive style and perceptual experiences that manifest as subclinical levels of psychotic-like behaviours in otherwise psychologically healthy individuals (Claridge, 1985). Recent epidemiological studies provide support for the continuity of psychotic experience in the general population (see Hanssen et al., 2005; Johns and van Os, 2001; van Os et al., 2000, 2001), observed as oddities of belief, behaviour, eccentricities, idiosyncratic speech, peculiar ideas, and social awkwardness or aversion (Siever et al., 1993).While these schizotypal personality features may represent a dimensional susceptibility to clinically psychotic behaviour, the precise relationship of schizotypy with clinical disorders such as schizophrenia and schizotypal personality disorder (SPD) is a matter of continuing debate. This chapter will provide an outline of the historical development of the schizotypy construct, highlighting subtle theoretical differences in its conceptualisation, and related issues of measurement, factor structure, and the association with other dimensions of personality. The development of schizotypal personality models and their relationship with clinical disorders will be discussed in light of several decades of research in neurocognition, psychophysiology, and psychosocial risk factors, from which the current conceptualisation of schizotypy within a biosocial neurodevelopmental framework has emerged.

Empirical evidence for the continuity of psychosis has emerged from research into the genetics (Gottesman and Shields, 1972), psychophysiology (Raine et al., 1995), and neuropsychology of schizophrenia (Rosa et al., 2000), supporting the idea that multiple genes contribute to the inheritance of personality traits that define one's psychotic disposition (Claridge, 1985). This view acknowledges the potential interplay between the proposed genetic predisposition to schizophrenia (diathesis) and the combined effects of certain life experiences (stress) in accounting for an individual's decompensation to clinical schizophrenia (cf. Grossarth-Maticek et al., 1994). The involvement of both genetic and environmental factors has been inferred from the less than perfect monozygotic concordance rate of approximately 50–60%, for the development of schizophrenia (Kender and Diehl, 1993), this being over 50 times greater than the lifetime morbidity risk of 1% (Hamilton, 1984; Warner, 1985), and four to five times greater than the same-sex dizygotic concordance (Gottesman and Shields, 1972; Lytton et al., 1988).

THEORETICAL MODELS OF SCHIZOTYPY

Models of schizotypal personality have developed in recent decades in line with a conceptual shift in thinking about psychosis from a continuum perspective (cf. Claridge, 1985, 1997; Eysenck and Eysenck, 1977; Meehl, 1962, 1990; Ortet et al., 1999; Raine, 2006; Raine et al., 1995). Within this framework, there have been three major theoretical models of schizotypal personality: the *quasi-dimensional* (or disease) model (Meehl, 1962; Rado, 1953) which places the schizotypy–schizophrenia continuum within the realm of illness; the *totally* dimensional view (Eysenck, 1947; Eysenck and Eysenck, 1977), based in personality theory, which makes no distinction between enduring personality traits and signs of abnormality; and the *fully* dimensional model (Claridge, 1997), based also in personality theory, but which proposes that some discontinuity of function must demarcate the line between psychological health and abnormality or disease. It is important to distinguish the tenants of each of these models at the outset.

The quasi-dimensional model endorsed by Meehl (1962, 1990), following initial formulations by Rado (1953), represents a categorical approach to schizophrenic aetiology by presupposing a qualitative distinction between signs of health and those of disorder, consistent with orthodox psychiatry. Within this neurodevelopmental model, schizotypy refers to a *typology* of behaviours expressed by a discrete class of individuals with a common defective genotype (Meehl, 1962, 1989, 1990). According to this view, schizotypal personality traits arise due to the presence of the genetically determined integrative neural defect (termed *hypokrisia*) that is hypothesised to affect neural functioning throughout the brain. The effects of hypokrisia on the brain are characterised by an 'insufficiency of separation, differentiation, or discrimination' in neural transmission that amounts to a ubiquitous anomaly of synaptic control within the central nervous system (CNS), termed *schizotaxia*, and this brain organisation is argued to represent the genetically determined predisposition to schizophrenia (Meehl, 1990). The essential element of the integrative neural defect that produces the schizotaxic nervous system (i.e. neuronal 'slippage') is thus conceived as more than a simple inhibitory deficit or basic sensory abnormality, and can be seen to map directly onto schizophrenic symptomatology such as associative loosening and cognitive-affective dysregulation. Indeed, modern incarnations of these ideas are evident in contemporary models of schizophrenia such as those proposing aberrant neuronal connectivity under the guise of new terminology, such as cognitive dysmetria (Andreasen et al., 1998; Dolan et al., 1999; Friston, 1998).

Further elaboration of Meehl's model (1990) predicts that the transition from schizotaxia to schizophrenia should involve the interaction of other factors such as environmental influences (e.g. social learning experiences) and a range of genetically determined personality dimensions (independent of schizotaxia) referred to as *polygenic potentiators*. A potentiator was defined as any genetic factor which, given the presence of the schizogene, had the potential to raise the probability of schizotypal decompensation. Potentiators thus included personality dimensions of social introversion, anxiety proneness, aggressivity, anhedonia (among others) that did not literally modify the expression of the putative schizogene, but instead interacted with the established schizotypal personality organisation and the social environment to either facilitate or depotentiate the development of overt psychotic symptoms. The interaction between schizotaxia and social learning experiences was therefore also hypothesised to contribute directly to the development and expression of *schizotypal* personality organisation. The term 'schizotype' was used by Meehl to denote an individual displaying schizotypal behaviours or experiences as a result of this interplay.

In review, Meehl's concept of schizotypy refers to the personality organisation resulting from the interaction of an inherited schizotaxic brain with other polygenetically determined personality traits and random environmental influences, and ultimately represents the phenotypic expression of vulnerability to schizophrenia. Meehl's model represents a quasi-dimensional account because of the clear demarcation proposed to exist between the healthy and schizotaxic brain; that is, the abnormal brain state (schizotaxia) is taken as a reference point, and dimensions of the spectrum of schizophrenia-like (schizotypal) behaviours are construed as degrees of expression of disorder, with the ultimate end-point of decompensation being schizophrenia. While this model does not imply that all schizotypes will develop schizophrenia (a common misperception of Meehl's theoretical views – see Lenzenweger, 2006), Meehl did contend that nearly all individuals with a schizotaxic brain would develop schizotypal personality on the basis of social learning regimes. Regardless of the level of decompensation, the descriptors of dysfunction along the schizotaxia–schizotypy–schizophrenia continuum consisted of overt signs of abnormality, ranging from subclinical levels of deviance detectable on laboratory measures (e.g. psychometric or neurocognitive measures) to full-blown schizophrenia or other schizotypic psychopathology (e.g. schizotypal or paranoid personality disorder). As such, this quasi-dimensional model places the continuity of function within the schizophrenia spectrum completely in the abnormal/illness domain. On this view, outstanding issues for debate include those of nosological relevance, such as how to differentiate factors contributing to the development of schizophrenia versus SPD.

In contrast to Meehl's quasi-dimensional model of schizotypy, both the totally and fully dimensional models endorsed by Eysenck (1947, 1977) and Claridge (1985, 1997)

respectively, place the starting point of schizotypal continuity within the normal/healthy domain of functioning. Historically, these models emerged from studies of personality and temperament within experimental psychology. As an opponent of the disease concept in psychiatry, Eysenck's (1960) influential personality theory saw the placement of psychotic illness at the extreme end of a continuously variable personality dimension, couched within naturally occurring variation in CNS functioning. This proposed biological origin of personality dimensions was historically derived from the Pavlovian concept of 'nervous types', wherein variations in personality or temperament are seen to reflect the underlying capacity of the CNS to endure or tolerate the action of very strong stimulation, reflecting a combination of weakness or strength of excitatory and inhibitory capacity of the CNS (Pavlov, 1928; cf. Boyle, 1992). At the time, Eysenck's (1960) proposal of an inextricable connection between normal and abnormal personality along with the assumption of biological causation dissected many issues within the ongoing debate between psychiatry and the sociologically minded anti-psychiatry movement. The development of the biological personality paradigm burgeoned a new perspective on mental illness that neither accepted the orthodox organic view nor the exclusively sociological, non-biological view, but instead attempted an integration of both.

As such, the *fully* dimensional model of schizotypy endorsed by Claridge (1985, 1997) took the normality of health, or more precisely, normal variation in personality, as the starting point of the schizotypal spectrum (Claridge and Beech, 1995). According to Claridge (1985), schizotypy denotes a range of enduring personality traits, reflected in cognitive style and perceptual experiences, arising from a combination of polygenetic and environmental determinants, which are normally distributed within the general population. Claridge's model of schizotypy drew parallels between psychiatric illness and systemic diseases of the body, using the example of hypertension (in which sustained high blood pressure brings about irreversible signs of disease evidenced in multiple physiological systems), as a template for understanding the origins of mental illness. Claridge (1985) argued that both systemic and mental diseases could be seen to arise from a breakdown in the otherwise normal functioning of a biological system, rather than an affliction imposed on the body. A second shared quality could be seen in the continuity between adaptive and maladaptive functioning of the system, given arbitrary cut-off points for determining abnormal functioning. Thirdly, both systemic and mental diseases may have multiple causes; in the case of hypertension, a number of environmental factors such as smoking, lack of exercise, diet, obesity, and stress may contribute to aberrant and sustained high blood pressure. Similarly, a variety of factors including genetic, psychosocial, and adverse life experiences may contribute to psychological ill health. In summary, Claridge (1985: 11) argued that 'the genetically influenced variations in brain organisation which underlie temperamental and personality differences . . . can be construed as dispositions to varying forms of mental disorder; and that the emergence of such disorder is, in essence, a transformation of these biological dispositions into signs of illness . . . It is only at the extremes that the disease "entities" of psychiatry become clearly definable'.

An important distinction between the fully dimensional model proposed by Claridge (1985/1997) and Eysenck's 'totally dimensional' model is that the former proposes a distinct boundary between health and illness along the schizotypal–schizophrenia continuum, where signs of discontinuity of function are used to denote disorder. For Claridge, schizotypal traits comprise dual properties insofar as they represent adaptive variation in personality but also comprise the potential for maladaptive psychological functioning. Consistent with Meehl (1990), Claridge contended that the transformation from schizotypy to clinically defined schizophrenia may

occur for a variety of reasons with protective factors including a relative weakness of the predisposing personality factors, the degree to which modifying experiences throughout life have afforded protection against severe disorder, and/or an absence of external triggers in the individual's life experiences. The fully dimensional model of schizotypy can therefore be seen to encompass both the quasi- and totally dimensional accounts described above: the continuity of schizotypal behaviours and experiences are regarded as inherent in normal personality variation and are recognised as representing only a *predisposition* to disorder within a spectrum of schizophrenic psychiatric illness (see DSM-IV criteria for schizophrenia, SPD, schizoaffective disorder, and paranoid personality disorder–APA, 1994), while decompensation to the disorder must involve a disintegration of functioning into the abnormal domain.

Despite these subtle theoretical distinctions, considerable effort has been directed towards the development of psychometric indices of schizotypy and the investigation of psychophysiological correlates of schizotypal personality organisation. Variability in the expression of schizotypy may reflect the severity of decompensation towards psychosis, and/or the type of schizotypal and other potentially protective personality traits present on the endophenotype. Schizotypal personality may thus manifest in mild thought disorder, excessive social anxiety, or in aberrant perceptual experiences that may not be objectively observable. In other cases, manifestations of schizotypy may be detectable only via laboratory measures of psychophysiological responding (such as eye-tracking dysfunction, sustained attention deficits, psychomotor impairment).

PSYCHOMETRIC MEASUREMENT OF SCHIZOTYPY

The measurement of schizotypal traits and the investigation of their psychophysiological correlates has become an increasingly popular strategy for research into the aetiology of schizophrenia spectrum disorders. This approach removes all potential confounds due to illness factors (such as the long-term impact of multiple hospitalisations and/or the use of psychotropic medications), and may enable detection of individuals 'at risk' for developing psychosis, thereby allowing possible preventative action to be taken (see Boyle, 1998a, 1998b; Claridge, 1994, 1997; Claridge and Beech, 1996; Claridge et al., 1996; Lenzenweger, 1994; Raine et al., 1995; Tyrka et al., 1995; Vollema and van den Bosch, 1995). While the medical model of schizophrenia has not been entirely jettisoned by this endeavour, increasing focus upon the psychotic continuum may reflect scepticism regarding the past century of research that has not yet elucidated the causal factors of schizophrenia as a categorical entity.

There are two strategies for assessing schizotypy in the general population: one 'high risk' approach involves the study of biological relatives of individuals with schizophrenia, since schizotypal traits should be found more commonly among those with a diagnosed schizophrenic as a blood relative (Claridge, 1985); another approach involves the investigation of members of the general population who score highly on psychometric indices of schizotypy, regardless of familial history of illness. Individuals reporting high levels of schizotypy have shown similar patterns of performance as schizophrenia patients in several cognitive, psychophysiological, and neuropsychological domains (Claridge, 1997; Raine et al., 1995). These findings are reviewed in a later section.

Several attempts have been made to measure schizotypal personality traits by administering self-report scales to samples drawn from the general adult population. The content and style of psychometric measures of schizotypal personality traits has varied according to the investigators' aims and theoretical standing. The earliest schizotypy scales focused on the measurement of vulnerability

for specific symptoms of schizophrenia, including perceptual aberration (Chapman et al., 1978), magical ideation (Eckblad and Chapman, 1983), physical and social anhedonia (Chapman et al., 1976), hypomanic personality traits (Eckblad and Chapman, 1986), predisposition to hallucination (Launay and Slade, 1981), and more recently for delusions (Peters et al., 1999), paranoia (Rawlings and Freeman, 1996) and schizotypal cognitions (Rust, 1988). Other psychometric scales have been formulated on the basis of psychiatric classification systems for 'schizotypal personality' (Raine, 1991) and/or 'borderline' personality disorders (Claridge and Broks, 1984), or by assuming the existence of fundamental components such as the asocial element of 'psychoticism' proposed by Eysenck and Eysenck (1977). In contrast, the recent development of psychometric scales tapping the general schizotypy construct has been based upon the empirically observed factor structure of schizotypal traits (Mason and Claridge, 2006; Mason et al., 1995; 2005; Rawlings and MacFarlane, 1994).

Factor analytic studies have supported the existence of up to four psychometrically distinct schizotypal dimensions depending on the range and content of the scales included in the analyses of schizotypal personality traits in the general population (Bentall et al., 1989; Boyle 2003; Boyle and Baxter, 2004a 2004b, 2006; Chen et al., 1997; Claridge et al., 1996; Fossati et al., 2003; Hewitt and Claridge, 1989; Kelley and Coursey, 1992; Kendler and Hewitt, 1992; Mason et al., 1997; Montag and Levin, 1992; Raine and Allbutt, 1989; Raine et al., 1994; Venables and Rector, 2000). Evidence of distinct schizotypal trait dimensions also comes from the biological relatives of schizophrenic patients (Calkins et al., 2004), clinical patients with schizophrenia (Arndt et al., 1991; Bentall et al., 1989; Bergman et al., 2000; Liddle, 1987; Mason, 1995; Peralta et al., 1997; Thompson and Meltzer, 1993), and schizotypal personality disorder (Axelrod et al., 2001; Battaglia et al., 1997). The three-factor version of schizotypal trait dimensions parallels Liddle's three 'syndromes' of schizophrenia represented by the factors of 'reality distortion', 'disorganisation', and 'psychomotor poverty'. Furthermore, this factor structure appears to be invariant to gender, ethnicity, religion, and social background (Reynolds et al., 2000), and may be seen to support the fully dimensional model of schizotypy (Goulding, 2004).

Possibly the most comprehensive measure of schizotypal personality – the Combined Schizotypal Traits Questionnaire (CSTQ) – was constructed by Claridge et al. (1996) to comprise 18 self-report scales (altogether there were 420 dichotomously scored items) including the following:

- Schizotypy Questionnaire (STQ) – STA and STB scales (Claridge and Broks, 1984)
- Physical (PhA) and social anhedonia (SoA) scales (Chapman et al., 1976)
- Perceptual aberration (PAb) scale (Chapman et al., 1980)
- Magical ideation (MgI) scale (Eckblad and Chapman, 1983)
- Hypomanic personality (HoP) scale (Eckblad and Chapman, 1986)
- Launay–Slade hallucination scale (Launay and Slade, 1981)
- Schizophrenism (NP) scale (Nielsen and Petersen (1976)
- MMPI schizoidia scale (Golden and Meehl, 1979)
- Delusions symptoms (grandeur; disintegration; persecution; contrition) (Foulds and Bedford, 1975)
- E, N, P, L (EPQ) scales (Eysenck and Eysenck, 1975)

Using a large sample of 1,095 individuals, an iterative maximum-likelihood exploratory factor analysis of the CSTQ scale intercorrelations (excluding the Foulds and Bedford (1975) delusional scales which were markedly skewed) was undertaken together with oblique simple-structure rotation (Claridge et al., 1996). Four schizotypal factors were reported, reflecting 'perceptual aberration', 'cognitive disorganisation', 'introverted anhedonia', and 'impulsive nonconformity'. The first factor was represented by aberrant perceptual experiences and paranormal beliefs and cognition (including

magical thinking, ideas of reference, paranoid ideation), thus reflecting subclinical forms of psychotic delusions and hallucinations. The second factor referred to subclinical forms of cognitive disorganisation, reflected in thought-blocking, disorganised speech, attentional difficulties (e.g. distractibility), as well as mild forms of worry and social anxiety. The third factor tapped subclinical experiences of social withdrawal and the inability to experience pleasure. Finally, the fourth factor referred to subclinical asocial behaviours such as drug-taking, violence, and deception, more typically associated with antisocial or psychopathic personality disorders. The Claridge et al. four-factor solution attained a ± 0.10 hyperplane count (i.e. the proportion of factor loadings ≤ 0.10 in magnitude) of 35.7%, suggesting only moderate approximation to simple structure criteria (cf. Cattell, 1978; Child, 1990).

Subsequently, Boyle (1998b) reanalysed the CSTQ data, using a slightly smaller, but more refined sample ($n = 1,021$), this time including the Foulds and Bedford (1975) delusional scales (following application of a square root transformation to reduce their skewness). An iterative maximum-likelihood procedure was undertaken, with factor number estimated via the Scree test (Cattell, 1978), followed by oblique simple structure rotation (Child, 1990). Five factors were extracted, relating to 'positive schizotypy', 'extraverted personality', 'neurotic personality', 'negative schizotypy', and 'psychopathic personality'. Positive schizotypal traits related to symptoms such as magical ideation, perceptual aberration, hallucinations, and delusions. Negative schizotypal traits related to symptoms such as lack of logical thought, lack of appropriate affect, as well as physical and social anhedonia. The factor loadings obtained for each of the five CSTQ factors are shown in Table 19.1. (This table is adapted from a more comprehensive report of these findings (Boyle, 1998b: 116).

The ± 0.10 hyperplane count obtained for the five-factor solution was 48.9%, suggesting a better approximation to simple structure

Table 19.1 Loadings for five CSTQ factors

Psychometric scales	CSTQ factor loadings				
	Factor 1	Factor 2	Factor 3	Factor 4	Factor 5
Claridge STA	0.59	—	−0.48	—	—
Claridge STB	—	—	−0.58	—	−0.37
Magical Ideation	0.86	—	—	—	—
Perceptual Aberration	0.81	—	—	—	—
Delusions of Persecution	0.38	—	—	—	—
Delusions of Grandeur	0.45	—	—	—	—
Delusions of Disintegration	0.82	—	—	—	—
Hypomanic Personality	0.42	−0.47	—	—	—
Social Anhedonia	—	0.41	—	0.38	—
Physical Anhedonia	—	—	—	0.59	—
Schizophrenism Scale	—	—	−0.73	—	—
MMPI schizoidia Scale	—	—	−0.42	—	—
Neuroticism	—	—	−0.96	—	—
Extraversion	—	−0.83	—	—	—
Psychoticism	—	—	—	—	−0.60
EPQ lie scale	—	—	—	—	0.65

criteria than that obtained in the Claridge et al. (1996) study (i.e. a 13.2% improvement in the hyperplane count). In addition, a LISREL confirmatory factor analysis (cf. Cuttance and Ecob, 1987) revealed that the five-factor solution provided a better fit to the empirical data than the corresponding four-factor solution. These findings extended those of Claridge et al. and highlighted the distinction between positive and negative schizotypal traits, which were shown to be distinct from general (Eysenckian) personality dimensions. Furthermore, the positive schizotypal factor also loaded strongly on measures of delusions (especially on 'delusions of disintegration'), suggesting that delusional cognition does play an important role in schizotypal personality.

Another psychometric instrument (the Schizotypal Personality Questionnaire or SPQ) was designed by Raine (1991) specifically to measure all nine schizotypal personality traits as listed in the DSM-III-R diagnostic criteria for schizotypal personality disorder (see also DSM-IV, section 301.22). Thus, as compared with the CSTQ (Claridge et al., 1996), which resulted from an attempt to comprehensively measure all major aspects of schizotypy and related constructs (including the Eysenckian personality

dimensions), use of the SPQ with its focus on specific diagnostic criteria provides a very different approach to the measurement of schizotypal traits. In order to further elucidate the factor structure of schizotypal traits, Boyle and Baxter (2004a, 2004b, 2006) performed a series of maximum-likelihood factor analyses with oblique simple-structure rotation of the SPQ subscale intercorrelations. A two-factor solution (presented in Table 19.2) clearly emerged which separated positive from negative schizotypal traits. A three-factor solution demonstrated that the positive

Table 19.2 Loadings for a two-factor solution for the SPQ

SPQ subscales	Factor loadings	
	SPQ Factor 1	SPQ Factor 2
Ideas of reference	0.73	—
Odd beliefs/magical thinking	0.64	—
Unusual perceptual experiences	0.80	—
Odd thinking and speech	0.55	—
Suspiciousness/paranoid ideation	0.52	—
Inappropriate/constricted affect	—	−0.74
Odd/eccentric/peculiar behaviour	0.49	—
Lack of close friends	—	0.90
Excessive social anxiety	—	0.52

schizotypy factor can be split into two additional factors. Unusual Perceptual Experiences (.98), and Odd Beliefs/Magical Thinking (.59) vs. Ideas of Reference (.78), Odd/Eccentric/Peculiar Behaviour (.43), Odd Thinking and Speech (.51), and Suspiciousness/Paranoid Ideation (.85). Finally, a four-factor solution demonstrated that the second of these positive schizotypy factors can be further split into two additional factors. Ideas of Reference (.77), and Suspiciousness/Paranoid Ideation (.55) vs. Odd/Eccentric/Peculiar Behaviour (.76), and Odd Thinking and Speech (.60).

These factor analytic findings confirmed that there are both positive and negative schizotypy factors, and that positive schizotypy can be further subdivided into: (1) perceptual aberration/magical thinking; (2) ideas of reference/paranoia; and (3) odd/eccentric behaviour/speech.

SCHIZOTYPY MEASURES: IMPLICATIONS FOR DISORDER

If schizotypy reflects the phenotypic expression of a genetic predisposition to schizophrenia, a significant proportion of individuals exhibiting schizotypal personality traits would be expected to develop schizophrenia. Schizotypal characteristics in clinical samples have been associated with breakdown rates of 40% over a 15-year follow-up (Fenton and McGlashan, 1989) and 25% over 2 years (Schultz and Soloff, 1987). Additionally, 7.6% of children with schizotypal-like diagnoses at age 10 years received a diagnosis of schizophrenia by age 27 years (Wolff et al., 1991). Studies of individuals in the prodromal phase of schizophrenia with schizotypal features have documented relatively high rates of breakdown for psychosis, for example, 40.8% over one year (Yung et al., 2003). Others have estimated the breakdown from adolescent schizotypy to schizophrenia to be in the order of 20–40% (Walker et al., 2004).

Reported rates of breakdown for psychotic disorders in undergraduates showing extreme scores on schizotypal personality are generally much lower. There is mixed evidence as to whether cognitive-perceptual or interpersonal factors of schizotypy are better at predicting later psychosis: one study suggests that physical anhedonia is not predictive (Chapman et al., 1994), while another (Gooding et al., 2005) reports a significantly higher rate of schizophrenia-spectrum disorders in those with high social anhedonia scores (15.6%), but failed to observe any breakdown in a high-scoring perceptual aberration – magical ideation group (3.4%). This suggests that interpersonal but not cognitive features may be more predictive of later schizophrenia-related disorders.

RELATIONSHIP OF SCHIZOTYPY WITH THE PUTATIVE 'BIG FIVE' FACTORS OF PERSONALITY

Studies of the static five-factor model of personality (the so-called 'Big Five': neuroticism, extraversion, openness to experience, agreeableness, and conscientiousness) in relation to schizotypy, SPD, and schizophrenia have produced inconsistent results, potentially because the Big Five model does not specifically include a dimension related to maladaptive cognition (Costa and McCrae, 1992). Perhaps the most controversial factor is the status of 'openness to experience' in relation to schizotypal personality traits. In SPD patients, one study has found that openness was elevated (Morey et al., 2002), while other studies report no such relationship (Blais, 1997; Trull, 1992). In studies of psychometrically defined schizotypy, high scores have most commonly been positively associated with neuroticism and openness to experience in undergraduate students (Coolidge et al., 1994; Wiggins and Pincus, 1989, and negatively associated with extraversion and agreeableness (Dyce and O'Connor, 1998); however, Tien et al. (1992)

reported that openness to experience was negatively correlated with schizotypy in a community sample, and others have reported no association with openness to experience depending upon the type of measure used to define schizotypy (Costa and McCrae, 1990). Finally, lower levels of openness to experience have been reported in studies of schizophrenic patients (Camisa et al., 2005; Gurrera et al., 2005) and their first-degree relatives (Yeung et al., 1993).

Generally, those studies reporting a positive association between schizotypy and openness to experience have sampled university undergraduates, while those suggesting a negative association between these constructs have utilised clinical populations (Ross et al., 2002). In clinical populations, elevated schizotypy is most commonly associated with elevated neuroticism and lower levels of extraversion, agreeableness and conscientiousness, with the exception of Yeung et al. (1993) who found no relationship with extraversion; Tien (1992) who found no association with agreeableness or conscientiousness; and Trull (1992), Blais (1997) and Dyce and O'Connor (1998) who found no relationship with conscientiousness. Evidently the Big Five personality dimensions (five-factor model) fail to provide adequate coverage of aberrant traits reflected in the schizotypal domain (including schizotypal traits). Indeed, Boyle et al. (1995) demonstrated empirically that the Big Five dimensions account for less than 60% of the known trait variance within the normal personality sphere alone. Part of the difficulty may also reside in the fact that the Big Five dimensions are premised on a relatively outmoded and unduly restrictive static conceptualisation of personality structure. Recent empirical studies (e.g. Cattell et al., 2002; Roberts et al., 2006b) suggest that personality structure is subject to learning and substantial developmental change across the entire lifespan (Fraley and Roberts, 2005; Roberts et al., 2006a), such that personality traits may not represent stable, enduring dispositions as historically thought.

NEUROCOGNITION AND PSYCHOPHYSIOLOGY

Studies of cognitive and psychophysiological impairments in schizotypy provide overwhelming evidence for replicable neurocognitive impairments that are common to both individuals with clinical psychotic disorder, and ostensibly healthy individuals exhibiting schizotypal personality traits. A relatively wide range of neurocognitive abilities and psychophysiological processes are impacted, with the strongest evidence for impairment in the areas of executive functions, sustained attention, working memory, verbal and spatial learning and memory, latent inhibition, negative priming, hemisphere asymmetry, and motor ability. In general, performance in schizotypy tends to be intermediate between those reporting few or no schizotypal personality traits, and schizophrenia patients (see Raine, 2006).

Specifically, heightened levels of psychometrically defined schizotypy have been associated with perceptual aberrations (Lenzenweger, 1994) and mild cognitive deficits in sustained (Gooding et al., 2006; Obiols et al., 1999) and selective attention (Moritz and Mass, 1997; Williams, 1995), disrupted latent inhibition (Tsakanikos et al., 2003), poor executive functioning (Lyons et al., 1991; Moritz et al., 1999; Wilkins and Venables, 1992), working memory deficits (Tallent and Gooding, 1999), impaired visual context processing (Uhlhaas et al., 2004), semantic activation deficits (Evans, 1997), as well as aberrant cerebral asymmetry (Goodarzi et al., 2000; Gruzelier et al., 1995; Jutai, 1989; Luh and Gooding, 1999; Mason and Claridge, 1999).

The alternative 'high risk' strategy of studying correlates of schizotypy within biological relatives of schizophrenia patients has also shown that family members demonstrate a greater frequency of perceptual aberration (Clementz et al., 1991), attentional disturbance (Balogh and Merritt, 1985; Laurent et al., 1999; Steinhauer et al., 1991), eye-tracking impairments (Blackwood et al., 1991; Waldo and

Freedman, 1999), and electrodermal responding (Claridge et al., 1983), with biologically high-risk children showing a similar psychophysiological profile to their schizophrenic parent (Gruzelier, 1999; Mednick and Schulsinger, 1968).

Additional psychophysiological similarities between schizophrenia and schizotypy include reduced attentional modulation (Abel et al., 2004; Cadenhead et al., 1993, 2000; Evans et al., 2005; Hazlett et al., 1997; Schell et al., 1995), abnormal electrodermal correlates of the human orienting response (Dawson and Nuechterlein, 1984), dysfunctions in smooth-pursuit eye-movements (Gooding, 1999; Holahan and O'Driscoll, 2005; Larrison et al., 2000; Lee and Williams, 2000; Smyrnis et al., 2003), slowed habituation of gamma and beta neural oscillations (Vernon et al., 2005). Behavioural studies within interpersonal domains have also revealed impaired communication (Martin and Chapman, 1982) and reduced social competence (Haberman et al., 1979; Numbers and Chapman, 1982) in relation to high levels of schizotypy in the general population.

There has been relatively little study of social-emotional information processing in schizotypy, despite considerable evidence for impaired facial emotion perception in schizophrenia (Edwards et al., 2002; Green et al., 2005) alongside initial findings of poor facial emotion processing in SPD (Mikhailova et al., 1996; Waldeck and Miller, 2000).

Those studies that have examined social information processing in schizotypy report evidence of poor facial emotion processing (Poreh et al., 1994; van Wout et al., 2004) and increased sensitivity to threat-related stimuli, evident in psychophysiological responses of psychometrically defined schizotypal individuals (Green et al., 2001, 2003; Raine et al., 2002). Initial reports on mentalising also indicate that those high on schizotypy show impaired processing of information related to self (Platek et al., 2005), others (i.e. 'theory of mind') (Langdon and Coltheart, 1999), and perspective taking skills (Langdon and Coltheart, 2001).

Finally, despite these impairments, some neurocognitive functions appear to be spared or even enhanced in schizotypy. For example, there are no reported IQ deficits in schizotypy. More specifically, several studies suggest enhanced creativity in schizotypy in association with superior verbal fluency (Duchene et al., 1998; Green and Williams, 1999), and increased right hemisphere functioning (Fisher et al., 2004; Weinstein and Graves, 2002). Indeed, it has been argued that cognitive inhibitory impairments in schizotypy may paradoxically enhance ability to form broad, unusual associations that favour cognitive flexibility and creativity (e.g. Green and Williams 1999).

PSYCHOSOCIAL RISK FACTORS

Prevailing evidence does not support Meehl's (1989) hypothesis that schizotypal personality (as opposed to schizophrenia) is not influenced by environmental stressors (such as negative child-rearing practices and maternal rejection), and instead gives rise to the counter-hypothesis that negative psychosocial influences are significant risk factors for the development of schizotypal personality, and in particular, cognitive-perceptual features. For example, initial studies suggest *increased* child abuse and early trauma in schizotypal individuals compared with controls. Multiple forms of abuse (physical, sexual, emotional, neglect) and posttraumatic stress symptomatology are associated with both higher self-report schizotypy and clinician-assessed symptoms of SPD (Berenbaum et al., 2003). Similar findings have been observed for child abuse and dissociative experiences in high schizotypy scorers (Irwin, 2001; Irwin et al., 1999) and those with high cognitive disorganisation scores (Startup, 1999). Furthermore, individuals with SPD (in addition to borderline patients) suffer more types of trauma exposure compared to other personality disordered groups and depressed patients (Yen et al., 2002). Child maltreatment (physical, sexual, emotional) has been associated with increased perceptual aberration and magical ideation scores (Berenbaum, 1999). Similarly, a large-scale community study of 4,045 adults reported a 3.6-fold increase in subclinical positive symptoms in those reporting broad-based child abuse (Janssen et al., 2004).

Disturbances in early parental bonding are also associated with schizotypal personality. Anxious attachment has been found to be associated with higher positive schizotypy, while avoidant attachment has been associated with both positive and negative symptom schizotypy (Wilson and Costanzo, 1996). Berenbaum (2003) found neglect to be a particularly salient form of maltreatment in those with schizotypal symptoms, but another study found neglect only non-significantly raised in patients with SPD (85%) compared to a depressed control group (68%) (Battle et al., 2004).

Limitations of the above studies include reliance on self-report measures of abuse, neglect, and schizotypy, the lack of official records of neglect, co-morbidity of SPD with other disorders, selected populations, and potential demographic confounds. Overcoming all of these limitations, one study of 738 randomly sampled youths from the community demonstrated that both prospectively collected maternal reports and official state-verified documentation of both emotional and physical forms of neglect were associated with increased diagnostically assessed schizotypal symptoms during late adolescence/early adulthood, even after controlling for other personality disorder symptoms, past physical and sexual abuse, and demographic factors (Johnson et al., 2000). Particularly striking was a 4.9-fold increase in SPD in those with physical neglect.

Broader measures of psychosocial adversity and stress in relation to occupational, recreational, and social spheres have also been linked to schizotypy. Two studies controlling for multiple confounds (e.g. IQ) have found increased cognitive-perceptual features of schizotypy to be associated with

urban-living (Stefanis et al., 2004). One study observed significantly fewer positive life events, and in particular, an increase in negative life events related to criminal or legal activities in association with SPD (Pagano et al., 2004). These findings suggest a pernicious cycle whereby early stress results in schizotypal symptoms that increase social and occupational dysfunction, resulting in further sustained life stress and long-term schizotypal symptomatology.

The notion that schizotypy is associated with a benign psychosocial environment (Meehl, 1989) thus no longer seems tenable: schizotypal individuals have significantly impaired family environments. This highlights an unusual point for departure from the tendency for schizotypal individuals to share risk factors in common with schizophrenia as there is little evidence favouring abuse and neglect in the development of schizophrenia. Findings raise the possibility of two subgroups of schizotypy with differing aetiologies: one in whom the genetic liability for schizophrenia accounts for schizotypal symptoms, and another in whom psychosocial adversity contributes to symptomatology (Raine, 2006). One implication for future research is that genetic and neurobiological links to schizotypy may be stronger and more consistent in those schizotypal individuals *lacking* psychosocial risk factors of abuse and neglect.

Future studies need to both further test the hypothesis of psychosocial risk factors for schizotypy and address the causal question of *why* psychosocial factors should result in schizotypal features. One working hypothesis is that early abuse, neglect, and stress results in the structural and functional brain impairments that in turn give rise to schizotypal symptoms. Significant stress during a critical period is thought to result in neurodevelopmental reorganisation of the brain (Teicher et al., 2004) and could in part account for structural and functional brain abnormalities associated with schizotypal personality features (see below). Early trauma and stress has also been associated with alterations in glucocorticoid release and increased dopamine levels (Glaser, 2000). Since abuse appears to be somewhat more associated with cognitive-perceptual schizotypy features, abuse could partly account for the hypothesised link between these schizotypal features and increased dopamine (Siever, 1995).

Finally, social ramifications of early trauma or neglect should be considered alongside neurobiological explanations. For example, lack of social trust and security resulting from experiencing child abuse could directly predispose to paranoid attributional style, social anxiety, lack of close friends, and more hypersensitive, self-referential thinking (Raine, 2006). That this is a feasible causal hypothesis is suggested by the fact that individuals at baseline who lack any lifetime psychotic-like experience but who go on to experience discrimination show an increased rate of clinically assessed delusional ideation three years later (Janssen et al., 2004). Similarly, disrupted attachment and bonding early in life could result in social-emotional impairments that disrupt normal interpersonal behaviour and predispose to the schizotypal features of a lack of close friends, constricted affect, and odd social behaviour.

A BIOSOCIAL NEURODEVELOPMENTAL MODEL OF SCHIZOTYPAL PERSONALITY

Raine's (2006) recent model of schizotypy incorporates a neurodevelopmental framework, the operation of psychosocial risk factors, a three-factor conceptualisation of schizotypy, and two forms of schizotypy with different aetiological paths. In this model, one form of schizotypal personality is termed 'neuro-schizotypy', and is proposed to have origins predominantly (though not exclusively) in the genetic, neurodevelopmental, and neurobiological processes that are shared with schizophrenia, and which predominantly

give rise to interpersonal and disorganised features. In contrast, environmental influences largely give rise to 'pseudo-schizotypy', a phenocopy of neuro-schizotypy, in which cognitive-perceptual features predominate. The differential aetiological pathways to the two forms of schizotypy are relative rather than absolute; both forms present with clinical features from all three domains, and both likely have contributions from both genes and the environment. Nevertheless, schizophrenia or SPD will only be an outcome for neuro-schizotypy, and only when critical protective factors are lacking. These conjectures may be seen to clarify and extend the model of schizotypy originally proposed by Meehl (1989), yet differ in the extent that early environmental factors are not excluded from contributing to either form of schizotypy.

According to Raine (2006), neuro-schizotypy is viewed fundamentally as a brain disorder (evident as SPD) with its origins in genetics, early prenatal environmental processes, and early postnatal influences. Genetic factors and prenatal environmental insults are proposed to precipitate structural and functional brain changes that unfold throughout development in frontal, temporal, and limbic regions, which in turn give rise to psychological abnormalities in cognition and affect. At the same time, postnatal environmental influences (e.g. physical abuse, neglect, poor bonding, discrimination) contribute to further brain impairment, and also directly result in cognitive and affective disturbances. At the level of personality, while cognitive disturbances primarily shape cognitive-perceptual (e.g. unusual perceptual experiences) and disorganised features (e.g. odd speech), affective disturbances (both CNS and ANS) give rise predominantly to interpersonal deficits (e.g. blunted affect). In addition, both cognitive and affective processes contribute in more limited ways to all three domains of schizotypal symptomatology.

While the basic elements of this model are empirically sound in terms of incorporating current evidence for genetic and environmental processes, cognitive impairments, three factors of schizotypy, and linkage to schizo-phrenia, other elements (e.g. prenatal and postnatal environment, psychosocial risk factors, neurodevelopmental processes) require further empirical scrutiny. For example, empirical support is required for the following proposals.

1. Neuro-schizotypy has a relatively stronger genetic and neurobiological basis; an early onset; presents with predominantly interpersonal, disorganised features; is influenced by affective as well as cognitive basic processes; is not associated with significant psychosocial adversity; demonstrates greater symptom stability; is more responsive to psychopharmacological treatments; and presents higher risk for schizophrenia.
2. Pseudo-schizotypy has a relatively weaker genetic and neurobiological basis; is an outcome of predominantly postnatal environmental and psychosocial influences; presents predominantly with cognitive-perceptual features; may have either an early or late onset; does not progress to schizophrenia; shows symptom fluctuation over time; is less responsive to neurobiological treatment programmes; and is more responsive to psychological interventions.

Although the two hypothesised forms of schizotypy cannot be definitively assessed at initial assessment, approximations and alternative strategies to test this model are feasible. Subjects presenting with predominantly interpersonal and disorganised features (though not meeting full DSM-IV criteria for SPD or schizophrenia) may be delineated as putative neuro-schizotypes, while those presenting with predominantly (or even solely) cognitive features may be delineated as putative pseudo-schizotypes. A similar delineation can be taken with questionnaire assessments of schizotypy. Alternatively, schizotypal patients or psychometrically defined schizotypal individuals could be provisionally delineated as pseudo-schizotypals on the basis of a history of significant psychosocial adversity, while neurodevelopmental schizotypy assignment could be based on a family history of schizophrenia or presence of neurodevelopmental markers.

Group differences on symptom stability, estimated age of onset, neurocognitive markers, candidate gene linkage, treatment efficacy, antisocial behaviour, and symptom presentation could then be tested.

While pseudo-schizotypy is postulated to 'mimic' the clinical features of neurodevelopmental schizotypy, its status as a true disorder is not questioned, such that it may be no less debilitating. The key difference is that pseudo-schizotypy has a somewhat different aetiology, involving more psychosocial influences (cf. Jackson, Vol. 2) and possibly accounting for higher schizotypy in minority groups and co-morbidity for antisocial behaviour. Nevertheless, neurobiological processes likely play some supporting aetiological role in pseudo-schizotypy as most of those who experience early bonding, abuse, discrimination, and other psychosocial adversity do not succumb to decompensation into SPD or schizophrenia.

REFERENCES

Abel, K., Jolley, S., Hemsley, D. and Geyer, M. (2004) 'The influence of schizotypy traits on prepulse inhibition in young healthy controls', *Journal of Psychopharmacology*, 18(2): 181–8.

American Psychiatric Association (1994) *Diagnostic and Statistical Manual of Mental Disorders* (4th edn). Washington, DC: American Psychiatric Association.

Andreasen, N.C., Paradiso, S. and O'Leary, D.S. (1998) '"Cognitive dysmetria" as an integrative theory of schizophrenia: A dysfunction in cortical-subcortical-cerebellar circuitry?', *Schizophrenia Bulletin*, 24(2): 203–18.

Arndt, S., Alliger, R.J. and Andreasen, N.C. (1991) 'The distinction of positive and negative symptoms: The failure of a two-dimensional model', *British Journal of Psychiatry*, 158(3): 317–22.

Axelrod, S.R., Grilo, C.M., Sanislow, C. and McGlashan, T.H. (2001) 'Schizotypal personality questionnaire-brief: Factor structure and convergent validity in inpatient adolescents', *Journal of Personality Disorders*, 15(2): 168–79.

Balogh, D.W. and Merritt, R.D. (1985) 'Susceptibility to type a backward pattern masking among hypothetically psychosis-prone college students', *Journal of Abnormal Psychology*, 94(3): 377–83.

Battle, C.L., Shea, MT., Johnson, D.M., Yen, S., Zlotnick, C., Zanarini, M.C., Sanislow, C.A., Skodol, A.E., Gunderson, J.G., Grilo, C.M., McGlashan, T.H., Morey, L.C. (2004) 'Childhood maltreatment associated with adult personality disorders: Findings from the collaborative longitudinal personality disorders study', *Journal of Personality Disorders*, 18(2): 193–211.

Battaglia, M., Cavallini, M.C., Macciardi, F. and Bellodi, L. (1997) 'The structure of DSM-III-R schizotypal personality disorder diagnosed by direct interviews', *Schizophrenia Bulletin*, 23(1): 83–92.

Bentall, R.P., Claridge, G.S. and Slade, P.D. (1989) 'The multidimensional nature of schizotypal traits: A factor analytic study with normal subjects', *British Journal of Clinical Psychology*, 28(4): 363–75.

Berenbaum, H. (1999) 'Peculiarity and reported childhood maltreatment', *Psychiatry: Interpersonal and Biological Processes*, 62(1): 21–35.

Berenbaum, H., Valera, E.M. and Kerns, J.G. (2003) 'Psychological trauma and schizotypal symptoms', *Schizophrenia Bulletin*, 29(1): 143–52.

Bergman, A.J., Silverman, J.M., Harvey, P.D., Smith, C.J. and Siever, L.J. (2000) 'Schizotypal symptoms in the relatives of schizophrenia patients: An empirical analysis of the factor structure', *Schizophrenia Bulletin*, 26(3): 577–86.

Blackwood, D.H., St. Clair, D.M., Muir, W.J. and Duffy, J.C. (1991) 'Auditory p300 and eye tracking dysfunction in schizophrenic pedigrees', *Archives of General Psychiatry*, 48(10): 899–909.

Blais, M.A. (1997) 'Clinician ratings of the five-factor model of personality and the dsm-iv personality disorders', *Journal of Nervous and Mental Disease*, 185(6): 388–93.

Boyle, G.J. (1992) 'Pavlovian Temperament Survey (PTS): Australian normative data', in J. Strelau, A. Angleitner and B.H. Newberry (1999) *The Pavlovian Temperament Survey (PTS): An International Handbook*. Seattle: Hogrefe & Huber, pp. 78–84.

Boyle, G.J. (1998a) 'Review of the rust inventory of schizotypal cognitions', in J. Impara and B. Plake (eds), *The Thirteenth Mental Measurements Yearbook*. Lincoln, NE: Buros Institute of Mental Measurements, pp. 860–61.

Boyle, G.J. (1998b) 'Schizotypal personality traits: An extension of previous psychometric investigations', *Australian Journal of Psychology*, 50(2): 114–18.

Boyle, G.J. (2003) 'Schizotypal personality traits: Factor structure', Paper presented at the 17th World Congress on Psychosomatic Medicine, August 23–28, Waikoloa, Hawaii.

Boyle, G.J. and Baxter, T.C. (2004a) 'Redefining the factor structure of schizotypal personality traits', Paper presented at the 16th Annual Convention, American Psychological Society, May 27–30, Chicago.

Boyle, G.J. and Baxter, T.C. (2004b) 'Factor structure of the Schizotypal Personality Questionnaire (SPQ)', Paper presented at the 28th International Congress of Psychology, August 8–14, Beijing.

Boyle, G.J. and Baxter, T.C. (2006) 'Factor structure of schizotypal personality traits', Paper presented at the 9th International Congress of Behavioral Medicine, November 29–December 2, Bangkok.

Boyle, G.J., Stankov, L. and Cattell, R.B. (1995) 'Measurement and statistical models in the study of personality and intelligence', in D.H. Saklofske and M. Zeidner (eds), *International Handbook of Personality and Intelligence*. New York: Plenum, pp. 281–329.

Cadenhead, K.S., Geyer, M.A. and Braff, D.L. (1993) 'Impaired startle prepulse inhibition and habituation in patients with schizotypal personality disorder', *American Journal of Psychiatry*, 150(12): 1862–7.

Cadenhead, K.S., Light, G.A., Geyer, M.A. and Braff, D.L. (2000) 'Sensory gating deficits assessed by the p50 event-related potential in subjects with schizotypal personality disorder', *American Journal of Psychiatry*, 157(1): 55–9.

Calkins, M.E., Curtis, C.E., Grove, W.M. and Lacono, W.G. (2004) 'Multiple dimensions of schizotypy in first degree biological relatives of schizophrenia patients', *Schizophrenia Bulletin*, 30(2): 317–25.

Camisa, K.M., Bockbrader, M.A., Lysaker, P., Rae, L.L., Brenner, C.A. and O'Donnell, B.F. (2005) 'Personality traits in schizophrenia and related personality disorders', *Psychiatry Research*, 133(1): 23–33.

Cattell, R.B. (1978) *The Scientific Use of Factor Analysis in Behavioral and Life Sciences*. New York: Plenum.

Cattell, R.B., Boyle, G.J. and Chant, D. (2002) 'Enriched behavioral prediction equation and its impact on structured learning and the dynamic calculus', *Psychological Review*, 109(1): 202–5.

Chapman, L.J., Chapman, J.P., Kwapil, T.R. and Eckblad, M. (1994) 'Putatively psychosis-prone subjects 10 years later', *Journal of Abnormal Psychology*, 103(2): 171–83.

Chapman, L.J., Chapman, J.P. and Raulin, M.L. (1976) 'Scales for physical and social anhedonia', *Journal of Abnormal Psychology*, 85(4), 374–82.

Chapman, L.J., Chapman, J.P. and Raulin, M.L. (1978) 'Body-image aberration in schizophrenia', *Journal of Abnormal Psychology*, 87(4): 399–407.

Chapman, L.J., Edell, W.S. and Chapman, J.P. (1980) 'Physical anhedonia, perceptual aberration, and psychosis proneness', *Schizophrenia Bulletin*, 6(4): 639–53.

Chen, W.J., Hsiao, C.K. and Lin, C.C.H. (1997) 'Schizotypy in community samples: The three-factor structure and correlation with sustained attention', *Journal of Abnormal Psychology*, 106(4): 649–54.

Child, D. (1990) *The Essentials of Factor Analysis* (revised 2nd edn). London: Cassell.

Claridge, G.S. (1985) *Origins of Mental Illness*. Oxford: Blackwell.

Claridge, G.S. (1994) 'Single indicator of risk for schizophrenia: Probable fact or likely myth?', *Schizophrenia Bulletin*, 20(1): 151–68.

Claridge, G.S. (1997) *Schizotypy: Implications for Illness and Health*. Oxford: Oxford University Press.

Claridge, G.S. and Beech, A. (1995) 'Fully and quasi-dimensional constructions of schizotypy', in A. Raine and T. Lencz (eds), *Schizotypal Personality*. New York: Cambridge University Press, pp. 192–216.

Claridge, G.S. and Beech, A. (1996) 'Schizotypy and lateralised negative priming in schizophrenics' and neurotics' relatives', *Personality and Individual Differences*, 20(2): 193–9.

Claridge, G.S. and Broks, P. (1984) 'Schizotypy and hemisphere function: I. Theoretical considerations and the measurement of schizotypy', *Personality and Individual Differences*, 5(6): 633–48.

Claridge, G.S., McCreery, C., Mason, O., Bentall, R., Boyle, G.J., Slade, P. and Popplewell, D. (1996) 'The factor structure of "schizotypal" traits: A large replication study', *British Journal of Clinical Psychology*, 35(1): 103–15.

Claridge, G.S., Robinson, D.L. and Birchall, P. (1983) 'Characteristics of schizophrenics' and neurotics' relatives', *Personality and Individual Differences*, 4(6): 651–64.

Clementz, B.A., Grove, W.M., Katsanis, J. and Iacono, W.G. (1991) 'Psychometric detection of schizotypy: Perceptual aberration and physical anhedonia in relatives of schizophrenics', *Journal of Abnormal Psychology*, 100(4): 607–12.

Coolidge, F.L., Becker, L.A., DiRito, D.C., Durham, R.L., Kinlaw, M.M. and Philbrick, P.B. (1994) 'On the relationship of the five-factor personality model to personality disorders: Four reservations', *Psychological Reports*, 75(1): 11–21.

Costa, P.T. and McCrae, R.R. (1990) 'Personality disorders and the five-factor model of personality', *Journal of Personality Disorders*, 4(4): 362–71.

Costa, P.T. and McCrae, R.R. (1992) 'The five-factor model of personality and its relevance to personality disorders', *Journal of Personality Disorders*, 6(4): 343–59.

Cuttance, P. and Ecob, R. (1987) (eds), *Structural Modeling by Example: Applications in Educational, Sociological, and Behavioral Research*. New York: Cambridge University Press.

Dawson, M.E. and Nuechterlein, K.H. (1984) 'Psychophysiological dysfunctions in the developmental course of schizophrenic disorders', *Schizophrenia Bulletin*, 10(2): 204–32.

Dolan, R.J., Fletcher, P.C., McKenna, P., Friston, K. J. and Frith, C.D. (1999) 'Abnormal neural integration related to cognition in schizophrenia', *Acta Psychiatrica Scandinavica*, 99(Suppl 395): 58–67.

Duchene, A., Graves, R.E. and Brugger, P. (1998) 'Schizotypal thinking and associative processing: A response commonality analysis of verbal fluency', *Journal of Psychiatry and Neuroscience*, 23(1): 56–60.

Dyce, J.A. and O'Connor, B.P. (1998) 'Personality disorders and the five-factor model: A test of facet-level predictions', *Journal of Personality Disorders*, 12(1): 31–45.

Eckblad, M. and Chapman, L.J. (1983) 'Magical ideation as an indicator of schizotypy', *Journal of Consulting and Clinical Psychology*, 51(2): 215–25.

Eckblad, M. and Chapman, L.J. (1986) 'Development and validation of a scale for hypomanic personality', *Journal of Abnormal Psychology*, 95(3): 214–22.

Edwards, J., Jackson, H.J. and Pattison, P.E. (2002) 'Emotion recognition via facial expression and affective prosody in schizophrenia: A methodological review', *Clinical Psychology Review*, 22(6): 789–832.

Evans, J.L. (1997) 'Semantic activation and preconscious processing in schizophrenia and schizotypy', in G.S. Claridge (ed.), *Schizotypy: Implications for illness and Health*. Oxford: Oxford University Press, pp. 80–97.

Evans, L.H., Gray, N.S. and Snowden, R.J. (2005) 'Prepulse inhibition of startle and its moderation by schizotypy and smoking', *Psychophysiology*, 42(2): 223–31.

Eysenck, H.J. (1947) *Dimensions of Personality*. London: Kegan Paul.

Eysenck, H.J. (1960) 'Classification and the problem of diagnosis', in H.J. Eysenck (ed.), *Handbook of Abnormal Psychology*. London: Pitman.

Eysenck, H.J. and Eysenck, S.B.G. (1975) *Manual of the Eysenck Personality Questionnaire*. London: Hodder & Stoughton.

Eysenck, H.J. and Eysenck, S.B.G. (1977) *Psychoticism as a Dimension of Personality*. New York: Carne & Russak.

Fenton, W.S. and McGlashan, T.H. (1989) 'Risk of schizophrenia in character disordered patients', *American Journal of Psychiatry*, 146(10): 1280–4.

Fisher, J.E., Mohanty, A., Herrington, J.D., Koven, N.S., Miller, G.A. and Heller, W. (2004) 'Neuropsychological evidence for dimensional schizotypy: Implications for creativity and psychopathology', *Journal of Research in Personality*, 38(1): 24–31.

Fossati, A., Raine, A., Carretta, I., Leonardi, B. and Maffei, C. (2003) 'The three-factor model of schizotypal personality: Invariance across age and gender. *Personality and Individual Differences*, 35(5): 1007–19.

Foulds, G.A. and Bedford, A. (1975) 'Hierarchy of classes of personal illness', *Psychological Medicine*, 5(2): 181–92.

Fraley, R.C. and Roberts, B.W. (2005) 'Patterns of continuity: A dynamic model for conceptualizing the stability of individual differences on psychological constructs across the life course', *Psychological Review*, 112(1): 60–74.

Friston, K.J. (1998) 'The disconnection hypothesis', *Schizophrenia Research*, 30(2): 115–25.

Glaser, D. (2000) 'Child abuse and neglect and the brain – a review', *Journal of Child Psychology and Psychiatry*, 41(1): 97–116.

Golden, R.R. and Meehl, P.E. (1979) 'Detection of the schizoid taxon with MMPI indicators', *Journal of Abnormal Psychology*, 88(3): 217–233.

Goodarzi, M.A., Wykes, T. and Hemsley, D.R. (2000) 'Cerebral lateralization of global-local processing in people with schizotypy', *Schizophrenia Research*, 45(1–2): 115–21.

Gooding, D.C. (1999) 'Antisaccade task performance in questionnaire-identified schizotypes', *Schizophrenia Research*, 35(2): 157–66.

Gooding, D.C., Matts, C.W. and Rollmann, E.A. (2006) 'Sustained attention deficits in relation to psychometrically identified schizotypy: Evaluating a potential endophenotypic marker', *Schizophrenia Research*, 82(1): 27–37.

Gooding, D.C., Tallent, K.A. and Matts, C.W. (2005) 'Clinical status of at-risk individuals 5 years later: Further validation of the psychometric high-risk strategy', *Journal of Abnormal Psychology*, 114(1): 170–5.

Goulding, A. (2004) 'Schizotypy models in relation to subjective health and paranormal beliefs and experiences', *Personality and Individual Differences*, 37(1): 157–67.

Gottesman, I.I. and Shields, J. (1972) *Schizophrenia and Genetics: A Twin Study Vantage Point*. New York: Academic.

Green, M.J., Uhlhaas, P.J. and Coltheart, M. (2005) 'Context processing and social cognition in schizophrenia', *Current Psychiatry Reviews*, 1(1): 11–21.

Green, M.J. and Williams, L.M. (1999) 'Schizotypy and creativity as effects of reduced cognitive inhibition', *Personality and Individual Differences*, 27(2): 263–76.

Green, M.J., Williams, L.M. and Davidson, D.J. (2001) 'Processing of threat-related affect is delayed in delusion-prone individuals', *British Journal of Clinical Psychology*, 40(2): 157–65.

Green, M.J., Williams, L.M. and Davidson, D. (2003) 'Visual scanpaths and facial affect recognition in delusion-prone individuals: Increased sensitivity to threat?', *Cognitive Neuropsychiatry*, 8(1): 19–41.

Grossarth-Maticek, R., Eysenck, H.J. and Boyle, G.J. (1994) 'An empirical study of the diathesis-stress theory of disease', *International Journal of Stress Management*, 1(1): 3–18.

Gruzelier, J. (1999) 'Implications of early sensory processing and subcortical involvement for cognitive dysfunction in schizophrenia', in C.A. Tamminga (ed.), *Schizophrenia in a Molecular Age. Review of Psychiatry Series*. Washington, DC: American Psychiatric Press, pp. 29–75.

Gruzelier, J., Burgess, A., Stygall, J., Irving, G. and Raine, A. (1995) 'Patterns of cognitive asymmetry and syndromes of schizotypal personality', *Psychiatry Research*, 56(1): 71–9.

Gurrera, R.J., Dickey, C.C., Niznikiewicz, M.A., Voglmaier, M.M., Shenton, M.E. and McCarley, R.W. (2005) 'The five-factor model in schizotypal personality disorder', *Schizophrenia Research*, 80(2–3): 243–51.

Haberman, M.C., Chapman, L.J., Numbers, J.S. and McFall, R.M. (1979) 'Relation of social competence to scores on two scales of psychosis proneness', *Journal of Abnormal Psychology*, 88(6): 675–7.

Hamilton, M. (1984). *Fish's Schizophrenia* (3rd edn). Bristol: Wright.

Hanssen, M., Bak, M., Bijl, R., Vollebergh, W. and van Os, J. (2005) 'The incidence and outcome of subclinical psychotic experiences in the general population', *British Journal of Clinical Psychology*, 44(2): 181–91.

Hazlett, E.A., Dawson, M.E., Filion, D.L., Schell, A.M. and Nuechterlein, K.H. (1997) 'Autonomic orienting and the allocation of processing resources in schizophrenia patients and putatively at-risk individuals', *Journal of Abnormal Psychology*, 106(2): 171–81.

Hewitt, J.K. and Claridge, G. (1989) 'The factor structure of schizotypy in a normal population', *Personality and Individual Differences*, 10(3): 323–9.

Holahan, A.-L.V. and O'Driscoll, G.A. (2005) 'Antisaccade and smooth pursuit performance in positive- and negative-symptom schizotypy', *Schizophrenia Research*, 76(1): 43–54.

Irwin, H.J. (2001) 'The relationship between dissociative tendencies and schizotypy: An artifact of childhood trauma?', *Journal of Clinical Psychology*, 57(3): 331–42.

Irwin, H.J., Green, M.J. and Marsh, P.J. (1999) 'Dysfunction in smooth pursuit eye movements and history of childhood trauma', *Perceptual and Motor Skills*, 89(3): (Pt 2), 1230–6.

Janssen, I., Krabbendam, L., Bak, M., Hanssen, M., Vollebergh, W., de Graaf, R., van Os J. (2004) 'Childhood abuse as a risk factor for psychotic experiences', *Acta Psychiatrica Scandinavica*, 109(1): 38–45.

Johns, L.C. and van Os, J. (2001) 'The continuity of psychotic experiences in the general population', *Clinical Psychology Review*, 21(8): 1125–41.

Johnson, J.J., Smailes, E.M., Cohen, P., Brown, J. and Bernstein, D.P. (2000) 'Associations between four types of childhood neglect and personality disorder symptoms during adolescence and early adulthood: Findings of a community-based longitudinal study', *Journal of Personality Disorders*, 14(2): 171–87.

Jutai, J.W. (1989) 'Spatial attention in hypothetically psychosis-prone college students', *Psychiatry Research*, 27(2): 207–15.

Kelley, M.P. and Coursey, R.D. (1992) 'Factor structure of schizotypy scales', *Personality and Individual Differences*, 13(6): 723–31.

Kender, K.S. and Diehl, S.R. (1993) 'The genetics of schizophrenia: A current genetic-epidemiologic perspective', *Schizophrenia Bulletin*, 19(2): 261–85.

Kendler, K.S. and Hewitt, J. (1992) 'The structure of self-report schizotypy in twins', *Journal of Personality Disorders*, 6(1): 1–17.

Langdon, R. and Coltheart, M. (1999) 'Mentalising, schizotypy, and schizophrenia', *Cognition*, 71(1): 43–71.

Langdon, R. and Coltheart, M. (2001) 'Visual perspective-taking and schizotypy: Evidence for a simulation-based account of mentalising in normal adults', *Cognition*, 82(1): 1–26.

Larrison, A.L., Ferrante, C.F., Briand, K.A. and Sereno, A.B. (2000) 'Schizotypal traits, attention and eye movements', *Progress in Neuro-Psychopharmacology and Biological Psychiatry*, 24(3): 357–72.

Launay, G. and Slade, P.D. (1981) 'The measurement of hallucinatory predisposition in male and female prisoners', *Personality and Individual Differences*, 2(3): 221–34.

Laurent, A., Saoud, M., Bougerol, T., d'Amato, T., Anchisi, A.M., Biloa-Tang, M., Dalery, J., Rochet, T. (1999) 'Attentional deficits in patients with schizophrenia and in their non-psychotic first-degree relatives', *Psychiatry Research*, 89(3): 147–59.

Lee, K.-H. and Williams, L.M. (2000) 'Eye movement dysfunction as a biological marker of risk for *schizophrenia*', *Australian and New Zealand Journal of Psychiatry*, 34(Suppl): S91–S100.

Lenzenweger, M.F. (1994) 'Psychometric high-risk paradigm, perceptual aberrations, and schizotypy: An update', *Schizophrenia Bulletin*, 20(1): 121–35.

Lenzenweger, M.F. (2006) 'Schizotaxia, schizotypy, and schizophrenia: Paul e. Meehl's blueprint for the experimental psychopathology and genetics of schizophrenia', *Journal of Abnormal Psychology*, 115(2): 195–200.

Liddle, P.F. (1987) 'The symptoms of chronic schizophrenia: A re-examination of the positive and negative dichotomy', *British Journal of Psychiatry*, 151(8): 145–51.

Luh, K.E. and Gooding, D.C. (1999) 'Perceptual biases in psychosis-prone individuals', *Journal of Abnormal Psychology*, 108(2): 283–9.

Lyons, M.J., Merla, M.E., Young, L. and Kremen, W.S. (1991) 'Impaired neuropsychological functioning in symptomatic volunteers with schizotypy: Preliminary findings', *Biological Psychiatry*, 30(4): 424–6.

Lytton, H., Watts, D. and Dunn, B.E. (1988) 'Stability of genetic determination: From age 2 to age 9: A longitudinal twin study', *Social Biology*, 35(1–2): 62–73.

Martin, E.M. and Chapman, L.J. (1982) 'Communication effectiveness in psychosis-prone college students', *Journal of Abnormal Psychology*, 91(6): 420–25.

Mason, O. (1995) 'A confirmatory factor analysis of the structure of schizotypy', *European Journal of Personality*, 9(4): 271–81.

Mason, O. and Claridge, G. (1999) 'Individual differences in schizotypy and reduced asymmetry using the chimeric faces task', *Cognitive Neuropsychiatry*, 4(4): 289–301.

Mason, O. and Claridge, G. (2006) 'The Oxford–Liverpool inventory of feelings and experiences (O-LIFE): Further description and extended norms', *Schizophrenia Research*, 82(2–3): 203–11.

Mason, O., Claridge, G. and Jackson, M. (1995) 'New scales for the assessment of schizotypy', *Personality and Individual Differences*, 18(1): 7–13.

Mason, O., Claridge, G. and Williams, L. (1997) 'Questionnaire measurement', in G. Claridge (ed.), *Schizotypy: Implications for Illness and Health*. Oxford: Oxford University Press, pp. 19–37.

Mason, O., Linney, Y. and Claridge, G. (2005) 'Short scales for measuring schizotypy', *Schizophrenia Research*, 78(2–3): 293–6.

Mednick, S.A. and Schulsinger, F. (1968) 'Some premorbid characteristics related to breakdown in children wirh schizophrenic mothers', in D. Rosenthal and S.S. Kety (eds), *The Transmission of Schizophrenia*. Oxford: Pergamon.

Meehl, P.E. (1962) 'Schizotaxia, schizotypy, schizophrenia', *American Psychologist*, 17(12): 827–38.

Meehl, P.E. (1989) 'Schizotaxia revisited', *Archives of General Psychiatry*, 46(10): 935–44.

Meehl, P.E. (1990) 'Toward an integrated theory of schizotaxia, schizotypy, and schizophrenia', *Journal of Personality Disorders*, 4(1): 1–99.

Mikhailova, E.S., Vladimirova, T.V., Iznak, A.F., Tsusulkovskaya, E.J., Sushko, N.V. (1996) 'Abnormal recognition of facial expression of emotions in depressed patients with major depression disorder and schizotypal personality disorder', *Biological Psychiatry*, 40(8): 697–705.

Montag, I. and Levin, J. (1992) 'Personality correlates of schizotypy factors', *Personality and Individual Differences*, 13(5): 545–8.

Morey, L.C., Gunderson, J.G ., Quigley, B.D., Shea, M.T., Skodol, A.E., McGlashan, T.H., Stout, R.L., Zanarini, M.C. (2002) 'The representation of borderline, avoidant, obsessive-compulsive, and schizotypal personality disorders by the five-factor model', *Journal of Personality Disorders*, 16(3): 215–34.

Moritz, S., Andresen, B., Naber, D., Krausz, M. and Probsthein, E. (1999) 'Neuropsychological correlates of schizotypal disorganisation', *Cognitive Neuropsychiatry*, 4(4): 343–9.

Moritz, S. and Mass, R. (1997) 'Reduced cognitive inhibition in schizotypy', *British Journal of Clinical Psychology*, 36(3): 365–76.

Nielsen, T.C. and Petersen, K.E. (1976) 'Electrodermal correlates of extraversion, trait anxiety, and schizophrenism', *Scandinavian Journal of Psychology*, 17(2): 73–80.

Numbers, J.S. and Chapman, L.J. (1982) 'Social deficits in hypothetically psychosis-prone college women', *Journal of Abnormal Psychology*, 91(4): 255–60.

Obiols, J.E., Serrano, F., Caparros, B., Subira, S. and Barrantes, N. (1999) 'Neurological soft signs in adolescents with poor performance on the continuous performance test: Markers of liability for schizophrenia spectrum disorders?', *Psychiatry Research*, 86(3): 217–28.

Ortet, G., Ibáñez, M.I., Moro, M., Silva, F. and Boyle, G.J. (1999) 'Psychometric appraisal of Eysenck's revised Psychoticism scale: A cross-cultural study', *Personality and Individual Differences*, 27(6): 1209–19.

Pagano, M.E., Skodol, A.E., Stout, R.L., Shea, M.T., Yen, S., Grilo, C.M., Sanislow, C.A., Bender, D.S., McGlashan, T.H., Zanarini, M.C. and Gunderson, J.G. (2004) 'Stressful life events as predictors of functioning: Findings from the collaborative longitudinal personality disorders study', *Acta Psychiatrica Scandinavica*, 110(6): 421–9.

Pavlov, I.P. (1928) *Lectures on Conditioned Reflexes*. New York: Liveright.

Peralta, V., Cuesta, M.J. and Farre, C. (1997) 'Factor structure of symptoms in functional psychoses', *Biological Psychiatry*, 42(9): 806–15.

Peters, E.R., Joseph, S.A. and Garety, P.A. (1999) 'Measurement of delusional ideation in the normal population: Introducing the PDI (Peters et al. Delusions Inventory)', *Schizophrenia Bulletin*, 25(3): 553–76.

Platek, S.M., Fonteyn, L.C., Izzetoglu, M., Myers, T.E., Ayaz, H., Li, C. and Chance, B. (2005) 'Functional near infrared spectroscopy reveals differences in self-other processing as a function of schizotypal personality traits', *Schizophrenia Research*, 73(1): 125–7.

Poreh, A.M., Whitman, R.D., Weber, M. and Ross, T. (1994) 'Facial recognition in hypothetically schizotypic college students: The role of generalized poor performance', *Journal of Nervous and Mental Disease*, 182(9): 503–7.

Rado, S. (1953) 'Dynamics and classification of disordered behavior', *American Journal of Psychiatry*, 110(6): 406–26.

Raine, A. (1991) 'The SPQ: A scale for the assessment of schizotypal personality based on DSM-III-R criteria', *Schizophrenia Bulletin*, 17(4), 555–64.

Raine, A. (2006) 'Schizotypal personality: Neurodevelopmental and psychosocial trajectories', *Annual Review of Clinical Psychology*, 2: 291–326.

Raine, A. and Allbutt, J. (1989) 'Factors of schizoid personality', *British Journal of Clinical Psychology*, 28(1): 31–40.

Raine, A., Lencz, T., Mednick, S.A. and Sarnoff, A. (1995) (eds), *Schizotypal Personality*. New York: Cambridge University Press.

Raine, A., Reynolds, C., Lencz, T., Scerbo, A., Triphon, N. and Kim, D. (1994) 'Cognitive-perceptual, interpersonal, and disorganized features of schizotypal personality', *Schizophrenia Bulletin*, 20(1): 191–201.

Raine, A., Venables, P.H., Mednick, S. and Mellingen, K. (2002) 'Increased psychophysiological arousal and orienting at ages 3 and 11 years in persistently schizotypal adults', *Schizophrenia Research*, 54(1–2): 77–85.

Rawlings, D. and Freeman, J.L. (1996) 'A questionnaire for the measurement of paranoia/suspiciousness', *British Journal of Clinical Psychology*, 35(3): 451–61.

Rawlings, D. and MacFarlane, C. (1994) 'A multidimensional schizotypal traits questionnaire for young adolescents', *Personality and Individual Differences*, 17(4): 489–96.

Reynolds, C.A., Raine, A., Mellingen, K., Venables, P.H. and Mednick, S.A. (2000) 'Three-factor model of schizotypal personality: Invariance across culture, gender, religious affiliation, family adversity, and psychopathology', *Schizophrenia Bulletin*, 26(3): 603–18.

Roberts, B.W., Walton, K.E. and Viechtbauer, W. (2006a) 'Patterns of mean-level change in personality traits across the life course: A meta-analysis of longitudinal studies', *Psychological Bulletin*, 132(1): 1–25.

Roberts, B.W., Walton, K.E. and Viechtbauer, W. (2006b) 'Personality traits change in adulthood: Reply to Costa and McCrae (2006)', *Psychological Bulletin*, 132(1): 29–32.

Rosa, A., van Os, J., Fananas, L., Barrantes, N., Caparros, B., Gutierrez, B. and Obiols, J. (2000) 'Developmental instability and schizotypy', *Schizophrenia Research*, 43(2–3): 125–34.

Ross, S.R., Lutz, C.J. and Bailley, S.E. (2002) 'Positive and negative symptoms of schizotypy and the five-factor model: A domain and facet level analysis', *Journal of Personality Assessment*, 79(1): 53–72.

Rust, J. (1988) 'The rust inventory of schizotypal cognitions (RISC)', *Schizophrenia Bulletin*, 14(2): 317–22.

Schell, A.M., Dawson, M.E., Hazlett, E.A. and Filion, D.L. (1995) 'Attentional modulation of startle in psychosis-prone college students', *Psychophysiology*, 32(3): 266–73.

Schultz, S.C. and Soloff, P.H. (1987) 'Still borderline after all these years', Paper presented at the 140th Annual Meeting of the American Psychiatric Association, Chicago, IL May12, 1987, New York.

Siever, L.J. (1995) 'Brain structure/function and the dopamine system in schizotypal personality disorder', in A. Raine, T. Lencz and S.A. Mednick (eds), *Schizotypal Personality*. New York: Cambridge University Press, pp. 272–86.

Siever, L.J., Kalus, O.F. and Keefe, R.S. (1993) 'The boundaries of schizophrenia', *Psychiatric Clinics of North America*, 16(2): 217–44.

Smyrnis, N., Evdokimidis, I., Stefanis, N.C., Avramopoulos, D., Constantinidis, T.S., Stavropoulos, A. and Stefanis, C.N. (2003) 'Antisaccade performance of 1,273 men: Effects of schizotypy, anxiety, and depression', *Journal of Abnormal Psychology*, 112(3): 403–14.

Startup, M. (1999) 'Schizotypy, dissociative experiences and childhood abuse: Relationships among self-report measures', *British Journal of Clinical Psychology*, 38(4): 333–44.

Stefanis, N.C., Delespaul, P., Smyrnis, N., Lembesi, A., Avramopoulos, D.A., Evdokimidis, I.K., Stefanis, C.N., van Os, J. (2004) 'Is the excess risk of psychosis-like experiences in urban areas attributable to altered cognitive development?', *Social Psychiatry and Psychiatric Epidemiology*, 39(5): 364–8.

Steinhauer, S.R., Zubin, J., Condray, R., Shaw, D.B., Peters, J.L. and van Kammen, D.P. (1991) 'Electrophysiological and behavioral signs of attentional disturbance in schizophrenics and their siblings', in C.A. Tamminga and C.S. Schulz (eds), *Schizophrenia Research. Advances in Neuropsychiatry and Psychopharmacology* (Vol. 1). New York: Raven, pp. 169–78.

Tallent, K.A. and Gooding, D.C. (1999) 'Working memory and Wisconsin card sorting test performance in schizotypic individuals: A replication and extension', *Psychiatry Research*, 89(3): 161–70.

Teicher, M.H., Dumont, N.L., Ito, Y., Vaituzis, C., Giedd, J.N. and Andersen, S.L. (2004) 'Childhood neglect is associated with reduced corpus callosum area', *Biological Psychiatry*, 56(2): 80–5.

Thompson, P.A. and Meltzer, H.Y. (1993) 'Positive, negative, and disorganisation factors from the schedule for affective disorders and schizophrenia and the present state examination: A three-factor solution', *British Journal of Psychiatry*, 163(9): 344–51.

Tien, A.Y., Costa, P.T. and Eaton, W.W. (1992) 'Covariance of personality, neurocognition, and schizophrenia spectrum traits in the community', *Schizophrenia Research*, 7(2): 149–58.

Trull, T.J. (1992) 'DSM-III-R personality disorders and the five-factor model of personality: An empirical comparison', *Journal of Abnormal Psychology*, 101(3): 553–60.

Tsakanikos, E., Sverdrup-Thygenson, L. and Reed, P. (2003) 'Latent inhibition and psychosis-proneness: Visual search as a function of pre-exposure to the target and schizotypy level', *Personality and Individual Differences*, 34(4): 575–89.

Tyrka, A.R., Cannon, T.D., Haslam, N., Mednick, S.A., Schulsinger, F., Schulsinger, H., Parnas, J. (1995) 'The latent structure of schizotypy: I. Premorbid indicators of a taxon of individuals at risk for schizophrenia-spectrum disorders', *Journal of Abnormal Psychology*, 104(1): 173–83.

Uhlhaas, P.J., Silverstein, S.M., Phillips, W.A. and Lovell, P.G. (2004) 'Evidence for impaired visual context processing in schizotypy with thought disorder', *Schizophrenia Research*, 68(2–3): 249–60.

Van Os, J., Hanssen, M., Bijl, R.V. and Ravelli, A. (2000) 'Strauss (1969) revisited: A psychosis continuum in the general population?', *Schizophrenia Research*, 45(1–2): 11–20.

Van Os, J., Hanssen, M., Bijl, R.V. and Vollebergh, W. (2001) 'Prevalence of psychotic disorder and community level of psychotic symptoms – an urban-rural comparison', *Archives of General Psychiatry*, 58(7): 663–8.

Van Wout, M., Aleman, A., Kessels, R.P., Laroi, F. and Kahn, R.S. (2004) 'Emotional processing in a non-clinical psychosis-prone sample', *Schizophrenia Research*, 68(2–3): 271–81.

Venables, P.H. and Rector, N.A. (2000) 'The content and structure of schizotypy: A study using confirmatory factor analysis', *Schizophrenia Bulletin*, 26(3): 587–602.

Vernon, D., Haenschel, C., Dwivedi, P. and Gruzelier, J. (2005) 'Slow habituation of induced gamma and beta oscillations in association with unreality experiences in schizotypy', *International Journal of Psychophysiology*, 56(1): 15–24.

Vollema, M.G. and van den Bosch, R.J. (1995) 'The multidimensionality of schizotypy', *Schizophrenia Bulletin*, 21(1): 19–31.

Waldeck, T.L. and Miller, L. (2000) 'Social skills deficits in schizotypal personality disorder', *Psychiatry Research*, 93(3): 237–46.

Waldo, M.C. and Freedman, R. (1999) 'Neurobiological abnormalities in the relatives of schizophrenics', *Journal of Psychiatric Research*, 33(6): 491–5.

Walker, E., Kestler, L., Bollini, A. and Hochman, K.M. (2004) 'Schizophrenia: Etiology and course', *Annual Review of Psychology*, 55: 401–30.

Warner, R. (1985). *Recovery from Schizophrenia*. London: Routledge & Kegan Paul.

Weinstein, S. and Graves, R.E. (2002) 'Are creativity and schizotypy products of a right hemisphere bias?', *Brain and Cognition*, 49(1): 138–51.

Wiggins, J.S. and Pincus, A.L. (1989) 'Conceptions of personality disorders and dimensions of personality', *Psychological Assessment*, 1(4): 305–16.

Wilkins, S. and Venables, P.H. (1992) 'Disorder of attention in individuals with schizotypal personality', *Schizophrenia Bulletin*, 18(4): 717–23.

Williams, L.M. (1995) 'Further evidence for a multidimensional personality disposition to schizophrenia in terms of cognitive inhibition', *British Journal of Clinical Psychology*, 34(2): 193–213.

Wilson, J.S. and Costanzo, P.R. (1996) 'A preliminary study of attachment, attention, and schizotypy in early adulthood', *Journal of Social and Clinical Psychology*, 15(2): 231–60.

Wolff, S., Townshend, R., McGuire, R.J. and Weeks, D.J. (1991) '"Schizoid" personality in childhood and adult life. II: Adult adjustment and the continuity with schizotypal personality disorder', *British Journal of Psychiatry*, 159(11): 620–29.

Yen, S., Shea, M.T., Battle, C.L., Johnson, D.M., Zlotnick, C.. Dolan-Sewell, R., Skodol, A.E., Grilo, C.M., Gunderson, J.G., Sanislow, C.A., Zanarini, M.C., Bender, D.S., Rettew, J.B., McGlashan, T.H. (2002) 'Traumatic exposure and posttraumatic stress disorder in borderline, schizotypal, avoidant and obsessive-compulsive personality disorders: Findings from the collaborative longitudinal personality disorders study', *Journal of Nervous and Mental Disease*, 190(8): 510–18.

Yeung, A.S., Lyons, M.J., Waternaux, C.M., Faraone, S.V. and Tsuang, M.T. (1993) 'The relationship between DSMII personality disorders and the five-factor model of personality', *Comprehensive Psychiatry*, 34(4): 227–34.

Yung, A.R., Phillips, L.J., Yuen, H.P., Francey, S.M., McFarlane, C.A., Hallgren, M. and McGorry, P.D. (2003) 'Psychosis prediction: 12-month follow up of a high-risk ("prodromal") group', *Schizophrenia Research*, 60(1): 21–32.

PART IV

Key Traits: Self-Regulation and Stress

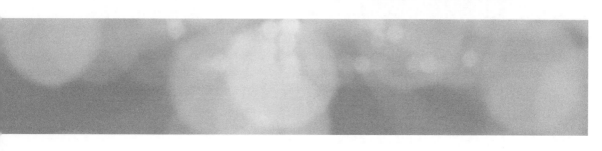

20

Anxiety Revisited: Theory, Research, Applications

Moshe Zeidner

OVERVIEW

'To a man who is afraid, everything rustles.' (Sophocles)

Anxiety has figured prominently in the literature as a ubiquitous and disturbing human emotion and one of the most prevalent reactions to psychological stress experienced by mankind (Sarason and Sarason, 1990). Anxiety is evoked when a person perceives a particular situation or event as threatening, dangerous, or harmful (Spielberger et al., 1976). The emotional reactions characteristic of anxiety are characterized by unpleasant feelings of tension and apprehension; worrisome thoughts and self-ruminative cognitions; and perceived emotional arousal, accompanied by heightened activity of the autonomic nervous system (palpitations, sweat, muscle tension, etc.).

Anxiety affords intriguing data for individual differences and clinical research for a number of reasons. First, anxiety is a pervasive phenomenon, with about 15% of the adult population suffering from some form of anxiety disorder; anxiety reactions are co-morbid with most forms of psychopathology,

including depression; and it is an intriguing and complex phenomena, involving the interplay of cognitions (attention, perception, reasoning, memory), subjective feelings, and behavioral tendencies of avoidance and escape.

Anxiety may result in crucial real-life consequences for many individuals in modern society and play an important role in a wide array of domains, ranging from social relations, work satisfaction, personal trauma and community disaster situations (Zeidner and Matthews, 2005). For example, social anxiety relates to various difficulties in occupational adjustment, presumably because of deficits in social behaviors or skills (Bruch et al., 2003). Thus, the loss to society of the full contribution of potentially capable people through anxiety-related distress and somatic ailments, underachievement and failure at school, or performance decrements in occupational or sports settings, constitutes an important mental health problem in society. When anxiety goes awry, it can develop into a serious debilitating psychological disorder, causing untold suffering and serious psychosocial dysfunction to many.

Chapter goals and structure

This chapter discusses current and recurrent thinking and research on anxiety, primarily when conceptualized as a normative individual difference variable and emotional state. Following an overview of conceptual distinctions, I move on to address measurement and assessment issues, with a focus on both self-report and alternative assessment procedures. I briefly discuss the biological and environmental determinants of anxiety, focusing on socialization and learning issues. I then assess the anxiety–performance interface, pointing out key moderating and mediating factors. I conclude with a discussion of clinical parameters, including a brief discussion of anxiety disorders, intervention principles, and selected intervention techniques designed to alleviate the distressing and debilitating effects of anxiety – both normal and pathological.

CONCEPTUAL ISSUES

Anxiety, as a basic human emotion, refers to a loosely coupled ensemble of cognitive, affective, somatic arousal, and behavioral components, evoked in response to mental representations of future threat or danger in the environment. The DSM-IV (1994) defines anxiety as 'apprehensive anticipation of future danger or misfortune accompanied by a feeling of dysphoria or somatic symptoms of tension' (1994: 764). Anxiety is typically characterized by the following five criterial attributes (Tyrer, 1999): an emotional state of apprehension, unpleasantness, uneasiness directed towards the future, exaggerated reaction to the objective threat, subjective and objective bodily systems. According to Sarason (1978), psychological stress is intrinsic to the *interpretation* of a specific situation, whereas anxiety is commonly conceptualized as a *reaction* to a perceived threat. Anxiety is often brought about by a sense of difficulty or perceived inefficacy to cope with the situational challenge or threat in a satisfactory way (Sarason, 1978). An anxious person feels he or she cannot meet the demands of this call for action (Sarason, 1978, 1984).

In contrast to early mechanistic views of anxiety as a unified construct, anxiety is currently construed as a complex multi-dimensional construct embodying a series of inter-related cognitive, affective, and behavioral components and reactions. The fact that anxiety is such a complex construct, encompassing as it does both worry and self-preoccupation, physical upset, disruptive feelings, and maladaptive behaviors, makes it particularly difficult for researchers to sort out all these components. In fact, there has been wide disagreement about its exact definition as well as its criterial attributes and there is currently no universally accepted definition of anxiety (Barlow, 2002). Thus, anxiety has been variously conceptualized as an antecedent stimulus condition, as a latent mediating process (e.g. as a probability of a harmful future outcome), and as a response (physiological, affective, behavioral, etc.) to a stressful condition.

CONCEPTUAL ADVANCES

Although fear has been of interest since ancient times, anxiety was not fully recognized as a distinct human condition until shortly before the beginning of the century (Spielberger, 1983). It was the founder of psychoanalysis, Sigmund Freud, who first proposed a critical role for anxiety in personality theory and in the etiology of psychoneurotic and psychosomatic disorders. According to Freud's psychoanalytic thinking, anxiety was both the 'fundamental phenomenon and the central problem of neurosis' (1936: 85). Anxiety, for Freud, was something a person experienced or felt – a specific unpleasant emotional state or condition of the human organism that included physiological, subjective, and behavioral components.

Prior to the early 1950s there was relatively little empirical research on anxiety. Among the factors contributing to the scant research on anxiety were: the complexity and multidimensionality of the phenomena; the ambiguity and vagueness in theoretical conceptions of anxiety; the lack of appropriate measuring instruments; and ethical problems associated with inducing anxiety in laboratory settings. Since the 1950s, studies of human anxiety have appeared in the psychological, psychiatric, and psychoanalytic literature with increasing regularity. The anxiety construct was dramatically advanced by a number of important conceptual distinctions, which helped refine thinking and research in the area.

One useful distinction, advanced by Charles Spielberger (1966, 1972) differentiates between anxiety as a relatively stable personality *trait* and anxiety as a more transitory *state* reaction to specific ego-threatening situations. Thus, state anxiety is a palpable, temporary reaction to a stressful event characterized by subjective feelings of tension, apprehension, nervousness, and worry, and by activation or arousal of the nervous system. Although anxiety state reactions are transitory, they can recur when evoked by appropriate stimuli and they may endure over time when the evoking situation persists. Trait-anxiety, by contrast, refers to relatively stable individual differences in anxiety-proneness; that is, to differences between people in the tendency to perceive stressful situations as dangerous and threatening and to respond to these situations with varying amounts of state anxiety. Trait anxiety may be regarded as a temporal cross-section in the stream-of-life of a person, with specific anxiety reactions construed as expressions of trait anxiety. Whether or not people who differ in trait anxiety will show corresponding differences in state anxiety depends on the extent to which each of them perceives a specific situation as psychologically dangerous or threatening and this is influenced by each individual's constitution and past experiences.

Another important conceptual and methodological contribution to the test anxiety literature is the distinction made by Alpert and Haber (1960) between *facilitating* and *debilitating* anxiety. Accordingly, facilitating and debilitating anxiety, respectively, are claimed to lead to task-related and task-irrelevant behaviors during evaluative ego-threatening situations. A particularly useful conceptual distinction was advanced by Liebert and Morris (1967), differentiating between *worry* and *emotionality* components of anxiety. This distinction proved to be instrumental in shifting anxiety theory and research, mainly in the area of evaluative anxiety research, toward a more cognitive orientation. Specifically, the cognitive component of anxiety (i.e. worry) was viewed primarily as a cognitive concern about the consequences of the stressful situation. By contrast, the affective component of anxiety (i.e., emotionality) was construed as perceptions of autonomic reactions evoked by stress. These two components are revealed to be empirically distinct, though correlated, and worry relates more strongly to cognitive performance than emotionality does.

Lazarus's transactional theory of stress and coping (Lazarus and Folkman, 1984; Lazarus, 1991, 1999) provided a fundamental conceptual framework for the analysis of stress, anxiety, and coping. According to this framework, stress and emotions are primarily about person–environment relationships (1991, 1993). Thus, the quality or intensity of an emotion are products of actual or anticipated adaptational encounters with the environment, which are appraised by the individual as having either positive or negative significance for wellbeing. Underlying each emotion are core themes, which refer to personal meanings attributed to events (e.g. harm, loss, threat, benefit). Any evoked emotion reflects a high-level synthesis of several appraisals relating to the individual's adaptational status in the current environment. The core theme in anxiety is danger or threat to ego or self-esteem, especially when a person is facing an uncertain, existential threat. Emotions, such as anxiety, tell us something of a person's goal hierarchy and belief system and how events in the immediate environment are appraised by the anxious person. Thus, the very presence of anxiety in an evaluative encounter is informative because it tells us that an existential threat has not been controlled very well, thus providing the researcher and clinician with critical diagnostic information.

A plethora of conceptual models of anxiety (psychodynamic, developmental, motivational, cognitive-attentional, self-merit, self-regulation) have been proposed in the literature to account for the phenomenology of anxiety, its antecedents and cognitive and behavioral consequences. Among the most promising of these models is Endler and Parkers' *interactional* model of stress and anxiety (Endler and Parker, 1990). This model assumes that the dynamic interaction among personal traits (i.e. trait anxiety) and the characteristics of situations (i.e. social-evaluative) determine situational anxiety in a particular context. The interactional model identifies four different potentially stressful environmental contexts (daily routine, social evaluation, ambiguous, and physical danger) as sources of stress. Comparably, this model identifies four isomorphic facets of trait anxiety (daily routine, social evaluation, ambiguous, physical danger). Furthermore, two facets of state anxiety, namely worry and emotionality, are distinguished.

The *differential hypothesis* of the interactional model (cf. Endler and Parker, 1991) postulates that state anxiety will be experienced in a given situation when there is a congruency or fit between the nature of a person's vulnerability (e.g. high physical danger trait anxiety) and the nature of the situation (e.g. an intrusive medical procedure or an imminent parachute jump off a plane).

In summary, no single theoretical perspective on anxiety can readily account for the complex and multifaceted nature of anxiety, including: phenomenology, developmental antecedents, correlates and consequences, and therapeutic interventions. Current explanatory models seem capable of subsuming only parts of available research, but no one model is capable of encompassing all of current research. Given the multivariate nature of anxiety, its various channels of expression, and its myriad causes, and consequences, it is reasonable to assume that not one, but several conceptual models and mechanisms are needed to account for modern multi-faceted conceptions of anxiety.

MEASUREMENT AND ASSESSMENT ISSUES

As a scientific construct, anxiety is useful to the extent that it can be measured objectively. Although a wide variety of observational procedures may be used to assess anxiety, we focus our discussion on the most prevalent methods of operationalizing the anxiety construct.

Subjective self-report measures

Subjective self-report instruments are by far the most popular observational procedure for mapping out the phenomenology of anxiety. Subjective reports include any direct report by the person regarding his or her own anxiety experience and responses, usually elicited via questionnaires, single-item rating scales, 'think aloud' procedures, or interviews before, during, or after an important stressful event.

Self-report instruments have become popular because they are considered to provide the most direct access to a person's subjective experiences in ego-threatening situations, possess good psychometric properties, are relatively inexpensive to produce, and are simple to administer and score (Zeidner, 1998). Self-report paper and pencil questionnaire measures of *state* anxiety ask individuals to report which of the relevant symptoms of anxiety they are currently experiencing in a particular situation, whereas *trait* measures ask subjects to report symptoms they typically or generally experience in a particular class of situations (e.g. public speaking, classroom exam, social interaction, sports competition, hospital invasive procedure, parachuting). Unfortunately, many studies use self-report data exclusively, without any attempt to measure salient behavior (e.g. through observational procedures), thus either under- or over-estimating the anxiety levels.

A wide array of measures have been constructed using conventional psychometric test construction procedures, including: State-Trait Anxiety Inventory (Spielberger, 1983), Endler Multidimensional Anxiety Scale (Endler et al., 1991), Beck Anxiety Inventory (Beck and Steer, 1990), Anxiety Status Inventory (Zung, 1971), Hamilton's Anxiety Scale (Hamilton, 1959), and Taylor's Manifest Anxiety Scale (Taylor, 1953). Among the many scales available to assess anxiety, the State-Trait Anxiety Inventory (STAI, Spielberger, 1983) has become the uncontested standard in the field, standing out as the most cited and frequently used scale in anxiety research worldwide over the last three decades.

By and large, these standardized anxiety instruments are highly practical: they do not require a great deal of expensive professional time, are relatively inexpensive to produce, and are easily administered and scored. A good number of the scales (e.g. State-Trait Anxiety Inventory, Endler Multidimensional Anxiety Inventory) have been factorially derived and validated and have demonstrated strong convergent, and discriminant reliability coefficients. Rather fortunately, most popular anxiety inventories have satisfactory reliability coefficients, typically in the high 0.80s to low 0.90s. Among the factors influencing reliability are test length, test–retest interval, variability of scores, and variation within test situation. It is of note that recent years have seen more sophisticated methods being used in validating anxiety scales and in decomposing the effects of person and occasion, such as latent state-trait theory (e.g. Schermelleh-Engel et al., 2004). Clearly, some of the threats that adhere to self-report measures plague anxiety measures (e.g. response bias, defensiveness, social desirability), which may serve as a source of systematic error in the assessment of the construct.

Alternative assessment procedures

Although self-report inventories remain the most popular assessment tools, a variety of less frequently used assessments have been employed, including 'think-aloud' procedures (e.g. 'Please list as many thoughts and feelings as you can recall having during the job interview'), physiological measures designed to gauge changes in somatic activity believed to accompany the phenomenological and behavioral components of anxiety (e.g. pulse, heart rate, respiration rate, skin resistance level), trace measures (e.g. accretion levels of corticosteroids, adrenaline products, free fatty acids), and performance measures (e.g. job placement test scores, semester grade point averages, latency and errors in recall of stress-relevant stimulus materials), and unobtrusive observations of specific behaviors reflective of anxiety in a specific stressful situation (perspiration, excessive body movement, chewing on nails or pencil, hand wringing, 'fidgety' trunk movements, and inappropriate laughter in social interactions). Despite some important advantages, these alternative indices often suffer from a number of formidable methodological problems, including questionable construct validity, poor reliability, and low practicality in naturalistic field settings (see Zeidner, 1998).

Overall, the assessment of anxiety has not kept pace with the theoretical advances in conceptualizing the construct (Zeidner, 2007). Thus, much of the construct domain (e.g. task irrelevant thinking, off-task thoughts, and poor academic self-concept) is under-represented in current measures of anxiety. Stressful situations would typically have effects on various response systems (i.e. verbal, physiological, cognitive/performance), and each measurement method possesses unique functions in anxiety assessment as well as is characterized by specific and unique limitations. It is desirable to obtain measures from a number of systems and 'triangulate' any observed effects by means of converging operations (Allen et al., 1980).

BIOLOGICAL AND ENVIRONMENTAL DETERMINANTS AND FACETS

This section will briefly summarize what we currently know about the origins and antecedents of anxiety. For the purposes of our discussion, it is useful to distinguish between *distal* and *proximal* antecedents of anxiety (Phillips et al., 1972). *Distal* factors would include biological givens and environmental factors (e.g. specific patterns of the parent–child relationship, preschool and early school experiences, cumulative success and failure experiences, etc.), which contribute more indirectly to anxiety reactions as responses to stressful or threatening conditions. They are indirect in the sense that they are the factors which have their major initial impact as antecedents of anxiety in the early years of life, although their influence continues to be felt throughout life.

By contrast, *proximal* antecedents are those factors which are specific to the stressful situation and directly responsible for anxiety reactions in specific settings. For example, the intensity of the threat, its scope, degree of preparation for the stressor and its controllability may be proximal antecedents of anxiety in community disaster situations, whereas contextual factors (test atmosphere, task difficulty, time pressure, etc.) would appear to be proximal factors in the development of evaluative anxiety. This section focuses mainly on the role of *distal* factors, the biological constitution and primary socialization practices, in the development of anxiety.

Biological perspectives

From an evolutionary perspective, anxiety is viewed as absolutely functional to survival and adaptation, facilitating the detection of threat or danger in a potentially hazardous environment. According to Panskepp (1998), the potential for fear and anxiety is genetically ingrained into the nervous system because an organism's ability to perceive and detect danger is of such importance that evolution could not simply have left it to the vagaries of individual learning. The neural substrates mediating anxiety were developed during evolution to help orchestrate and co-ordinate the perceptual, physiological, cognitive, and behavior tendency changes that promote survival in the face of danger and threat.

As noted by LeDoux (1996), when a person encounters a suspicious object on the side of the road, it is better to have treated the stick as a snake than not to have responded in a safe manner to a possible snake. Individuals confronted with an imminent threat appear to have a wired-in bias to favor type I errors (i.e. responding with anxiety when no danger is present) relative to type II errors (i.e. failing to respond to danger when danger is present). In decision-theoretic terms, *false negatives* (i.e. failing to respond with anxiety and elicit defensive behavior to potentially hazardous stimuli) are more costly from an evolutionary perspective than false positives (i.e. evoking anxiety and eliciting defensive response to stimuli that is harmless). In fact, it is less costly to abort falsely initialized defense responses than fail to elicit defense when threat is real, as this can cost one his or her life. Furthermore, anxious people tend to be hypervigilant (Eysenck, 1992b), and they tend to overpredict both the danger and their own anxiety in a given situation. This may be adaptive in the short run in that it helps them avoid threatening situations (Rachman, 2004).

Research points to a meaningful genetic component underlying the development of trait anxiety, with heredity shown to contribute about half of the variance in explaining individual differences in the major personality factor of neuroticism, or its mid-level trait expression, trait anxiety (cf. Eysenck and Eysenck, 1985; Eysenck, 1992a). Overall, twin/kinship studies actually report a very small effect of the shared environment on, for example, neuroticism, and a very large effect of the non-shared environment (see, for example, Table 6.6 in the chapter by Johnson et al.).

It is a plausible hypothesis that individuals are born with a basic 'wired in' propensity to react with increased arousal and elevated worry when confronted with stressful conditions. Accordingly, anxiety may serve to facilitate the detection of threat in important contexts in modern society, allowing individuals to prepare for and adequately cope with impending threats. However, this process may go awry and become maladaptive for persons who are 'hypervigilant'; that is, perceive an exaggerated number of evaluative threats in their surroundings or magnify the severity or consequences of such threats.

Just over a century ago, Freud lamented that we know practically nothing about the creation of anxiety in the brain (Panskepp, 1998). Fortunately, the past few decades have seen dramatic progress in research on the neurobiological substrates of anxiety and fear. This progress may be responsible, in part, for the renaissance of interest of emotion within both psychology and neurosciences (LeDoux, 2006). Current research suggests that anxiety is not localized in one specific brain structure. Instead, several cortico-limbic neural structures working in a parallel and holistic manner subserve the experience of normal anxiety and support the neural circuits underlying the pathophysiology of anxiety disorders. These include the amygdala (LeDoux, 1996; Panskepp, 1998), the septo-hippocampal circuit (Gray and McNaughton, 2003), the insula (Morris, 2002), the interior and medial hypothalamus (Panskepp, 1998), and cingulum (Eysenck, 1967).

Furthermore, Panskepp (1998) has posited the existence of a separate FEAR circuit of the brain mediating fear and anxiety, coursing between the central amygala, the periaqueductal gray and mesolimbic system (Panskepp, 1998). More specifically, this system extends from the temporal lobe (central and lateral amygdala), through the anterior and medial hypothalamus. It projects to the lower brainstem, through periventriuclar

gray (PVG) substrata of the diencephalon and mesencephalon. It then continues down to specific autonomic and behavioral output components of the lower brainstem and spinal chord. These systems control the physical symptoms of fear (e.g. increased blood pressure, heart rate, startle response, and perspiration). Minor tranquillizers may exert their anti-anxiety effects by decreasing arousal in this system.

It stands to reason that high trait anxious persons have lower activity thresholds in these cortico-limbic brain areas when compared to their low trait-anxious counterparts. It is the amygdala, it appears, that has received the lion's share of interest and systematic research on the neural underpinnings of anxiety (LeDoux, 1996). One of the key functions of the amygdala is to interrupt ongoing activity in order to induce quick responses to dangerous situations. Thus, the brain, via the neural circuits of the amygdala, is able to detect and respond to danger quickly and efficiently, interrupting whatever one is doing or attending to, in order to trigger a rapid bodily reaction. Another function of the amygdala is to enhance the perception of potentially dangerous stimuli. This structure not only helps us survive in extreme conditions but also sets priorities in the comparative safety of different environmental contexts. The amygdala is responsible for unconscious emotional learning, which is automatic and impulsive, as opposed to more conscious processing and memories, which are processed in the hippocampus and parts of the prefrontal cortex. Furthermore, the amygdala stores emotion memories and may modulate memories in other areas as well, and helps retrieve them rapidly and efficiently in time of need. This turns out to be critical to survival.

Research in LeDoux's lab demonstrated that there is both a *high road* and a *low road* to processing of incoming sensory stimuli, providing an outline of the fear reaction system. The amygdala, through parallel transmission, receives both low-level inputs from sensory-specific regions (sensory, acoustic, etc.) of the thalamus as well as higher-level information from sensory-specific cortex, and still higher-level information about the general situation from the hippocampus. Through such connections, the amygdala is able to process the emotional significance of individual stimuli as well as complex situations.

Consider, for example, a person crossing a busy highway and suddenly hearing a loud screech. In a highly simplified depiction of the 'high road' neural circuits involved, this acoustic signal is picked up by special receptors in the person's ear and is transmitted into the brain by way of the auditory nerve, which terminates in the auditory brainstem nuclei. Axons from these regions mostly cross over to the other side of the brain and ascend to the inferior colliculus of the midbrain. From there, the signal is transmitted to the auditory thalamic relay nucleus (medial geniculate body), which provides the auditory input to the cortex (auditory association area) for cognitive processing. The cortex then transmit the information to the amygdala for emotional processing and regulation of the expression of fear responses by way of projections to brainstem areas and appropriate response (behavior, autonomic, hormonal, etc.).

In the parallel 'low road' circuits, the acoustic stimulus reaches the amygdala by way of direct pathways form the thalamus. This direct thalamo-amygdal path is a shorter and faster transmission route than the pathway from the thalamus through the cortex to the amygdala. The direct pathway allows one to begin to respond to potentially dangerous stimuli before we fully know what the stimulus is. Its utility requires that the cortical pathway be able to over-ride the direct pathway. In the parallel low road thalamo-amygdala circuit, the thalamus short-circuits the cortical areas and projects directly to the amygdala, which in turn reacts and hopefully sends signals to the striate muscles to act to avoid the imminent danger.

In his work with rodents, LeDoux demonstrated that the direct thalamo-amygdala path is a shorter and thus faster transmission route than the pathway from the thalamus through the cortex to the amygdala. The direct pathways allow a person to begin to respond to potentially dangerous stimuli before one fully knows what the stimulus is, and this is very useful in dangerous situations. Because the direct thalamo-amygdala pathway bypasses the cortex, it is unable to benefit from cortical processing. The thalamic-amygdala pathway is relatively fast, taking about 12 ms, compared to 40 ms for the high road circuit. Although this quick circuit cannot tell the amygdala exactly what is out there (truck, car, horse, train), it can provide a fast signal that warns that something dangerous may be there. Thus, it is 'a quick and dirty processing system.' The neural circuits for the parallel pathways are schematically presented in Figure 20.1.

In addition, recent research suggests that the amygdala may mediate the effects of genetic expression of the S allele on chromosome 17 and vulnerability to anxiety. Thus, a recent review by Hariri and Holmes (2006) has reported an association between the 5-HTTLPR S allele on chromosome 17 – associated with relative loss of 5-HTT gene function (presynaptically located serotonin, which returns 5-HT for recycling or metabolic degradation), and anxiety in normal populations. Hariri and Holmes report that three independent meta-analyses have demonstrated a significant association between the S allele and increased trait anxiety (N) or harm avoidance. Their review suggests that this allele not only biases toward increased anxiety but also exerts a negative influence on the capacity to cope with stress in normal populations. Functional imaging studies pinpointed the amygdala as a brain region with exaggerated reactivity to emotional provocative stimuli in S allele carriers, paving the way for future research to elucidate the precise neural mechanisms underlying the behavioral abnormalities associated with this gene variant. Overall, a single gene variant such as the 5-HTTLPR would be expected to contribute only a small amount of the overall inter-individual variance within the milieu of other genetic and environmental influences.

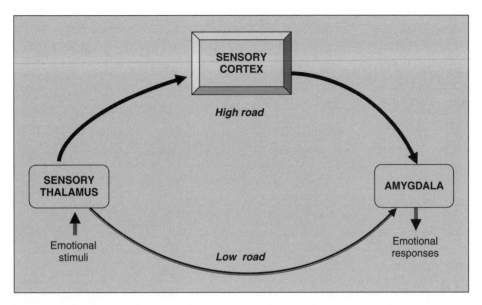

Figure 20.1   Parallel circuits in processing emotional information: low and high roads (adapted from LeDoux, 1996)

Gray's neuropsychological model of anxiety (Gray and McNaughton, 2003) diverges from the current 'amygdalocentric orthodoxy' in anxiety research by implicating the septo-hippocamal system as the major player in the neurobiology of anxiety. Gray (Gray and McNaughton, 2003) regards anxiety as a central state that mediates behavioral responses to stimuli that signal either punishment or non-reward. Based on a formidable assembly of scores of studies generating psychopharmacological, ethological, and physiological data, Gray implicated the septo-hippocampal system in anxiety. However, in man, the brain structures mediating anxiety can be affected by neocortical influences, particularly those that originate in prefrontal and cingulated regions.

The major system mediating anxiety is the behavioral inhibition system (BIS) of the brain. The BIS is posited to control the inhibition of ongoing behavior, the increase in vigilance, and the increase in arousal. It is designed to resolve conflicts between similarly and highly attractive concurrent goals – and in many cases to reduce the effects of interference. Thus, when a person is thrust into a conflict between competing goals the BIS is evoked. The BIS achieves a resolution to the conflict by increasing the valence of affectively negative association of those goals. These outputs of the system can be produced by stimuli associated with pain, punishment, failure, loss of reward, novelty, or uncertainty.

Four major types of stimuli activate the BIS and serve as primary inputs to the BIS system (Gray, and McNaughton, 2003). These are: (a) signals of punishment, (b) signals of non-reward, (c) novel stimuli, and (d) evolutionary salient innate fears (loud noise, heights, insects, rodents, and reptilian) and threatening social encounters of stimuli (Gray and McNaughton, 2003). It is virtually axiomatic that humans and lower organisms are motivated to seek out rewards and avoid punishment (Rolls, 1999), and therefore may suffer anxiety when punishments are presented to them or when rewards are omitted or unexpectedly terminated. This explains the inclusion of the first two inputs in Gray's model. As for the inclusion of novel stimuli,

Gray posits that novel stimuli produce a cognitive discrepancy or mismatch, identified by the comparator of the system, and between what is presented to the system and what is expected. More specifically, the comparator receives information about the current state of the world, along with the prediction what the state should be. Armed with this information it decides whether there is a match or mismatch between predictors and actual events. As for innate fear stimuli, these include stimuli associated with specific dangers and aversive emotional stimuli in social interactions (e.g. contempt or disgust in facial expression of significant other). According to Gray's theory, these stimuli are basically functionally equivalent, in that they each activate the BIS and evoke anxiety. The outputs of the system involve various forms of conflict resolution, including: (a) behavioral inhibition, where all ongoing behavior, whether innate or instrumental or classically conditioned, is inhibited; (b) orienting response; and (c) elevated arousal and

increased attention. This model is presented in Figure 20.2

Gray's model has generally been accepted as a solid animal model of fear and anxiety, with researchers less sanguine in accepting its generalizability to humans or its validity as a solid theoretical framework for anxiety research. As aptly pointed out by M. Eysenck (1992b), any realistic model of anxiety would need to consider the complex, independent functioning of cognitive, physiological, and behavioral systems, and not rely on neurobiological systems alone. Gray's model is also found wanting in the specification of cognitive processes preceding the activation of the BIS as well as in the delineation of moderating factors impacting the association between inputs and outputs. Thus, Gray's model appears to be more successful at identifying the brain structures and processes mediating anxiety than it is at specifying the cognitive processes which determine whether or not these structures and processes are activated. In addition, as aptly pointed out

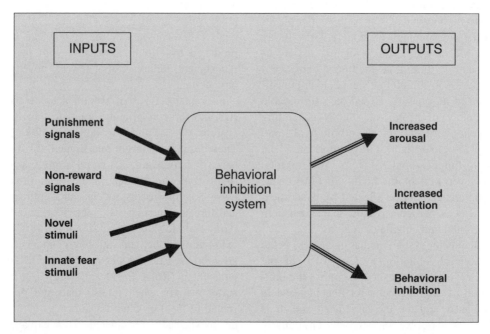

Figure 20.2   Gray's behavioral inhibition model of anxiety (adapted from Gray and McNaughton, 2003)

in a recent review by G. Matthews (in press), psychophysiological data provide only weak support for Gray's model. Moderator effects of motivational factors on associations between anxiety, arousal responses, and conditioning are inconsistent, and vary across different experimental paradigms. It is also unclear how the model may accommodate the cognitive aspects of anxiety, which are critical for its effects on performance, and for understanding how anxiety relates to distorted perceptions of the self and environmental threats. Overall, in agreement with M. Eysenck and G. Matthews, it seems reasonable to conclude that a complete understanding of anxiety as an individual difference trait will require a detailed analysis of individual differences in cognitive processes that precede the activation of proposed mediating system, such as the BIS.

Family environment

Researchers who have applied the developmental approach to the study of anxiety over the years have emphasized the importance of interpersonal and family influences in understanding the developmental background of children's disposition to experience anxiety, particularly in evaluative situations (Teichman and Ziv, 1994). Family climate and parental socialization practices have been claimed to bear important influences on the development of children's emotional and social behaviors, including anxiety (Hill, 1972; Krohne, 1992). Although more research is clearly desirable, current theory and research provides us with a preliminary and tentative foundation from which to begin sketching the origins and developmental course of anxiety.

Krohne's (1992) two-process model traces the development of trait anxiety to a unique configuration of specific parental child-rearing styles and practices. The model assumes that one's social learning history, primarily the residuals of past experiences

and acquired behavioral tendencies, largely determines whether a person responds to a danger cue with state anxiety or adequate coping strategies. The experiences a child encounters within the family, particularly parental child-rearing styles, are postulated to shape certain competencies and cognitive structures in children (i.e. perceived competencies and expectancies), which in turn are hypothesized to impact upon the development of anxiety. Parental punishment of the child and inconsistency may be important factors in the child's development of anxiety responses.

In addition, based on learning theoretic principles, a child may acquire anxious response tendencies as a result of the cumulative effects of various learning processes over time (Hill, 1972; Pekrun, 1985). Thus, scientific principles and models of human learning (modeling of anxious behavior in adults and peers, classical conditioning, reinforcement, etc.) may account for the acquisition of anxiety response tendencies and their maintenance at home, school, and in social settings

ANXIETY AND COGNITIVE PERFORMANCE

A virtual flood of studies have probed the pattern of relationships between anxiety and a wide array of cognitive performances. The studies have converged in showing that specific types of anxiety (e.g. test, math, sport, computer, social; see Zeidner and Matthews, 2005) have been found to interfere with competence in true-to-life situations (school, collegiate, sport, social, military, occupational). Furthermore, numerous lab-based studies indicate that various processing deficits are related to anxiety, including general impairments of attention and working memory, together with more subtle performance changes, such as failure to organize semantic information effectively (Zeidner, 1998).

Hembree's (1988) meta-analytic study, based on 562 North American studies, demonstrated that test anxiety correlated negatively, though modestly, with a wide array of conventional measures of school achievement and ability at both high school and college level, although the correlation was typically about −0.2. Data collected on students from upper elementary school level through high school show that anxiety scores (trait, state, and test scores) were significantly related to grades in various subjects. Overall, evaluative anxiety appears to account for about 4% of the performance variance in a variety of evaluative settings, including math performance, sports, occupational, and social settings (Zeidner and Matthews, 2005). A second meta-analysis by Hembree (1990), focusing on math anxiety and math performance, found mean correlations between math anxiety and various indices of math achievement (e.g. pre-college math achievement scores, high school math grades, college math grades) ranging between −0.27 and −0.31.

Deficits related to anxiety have been identified at various stages of information processing (input, cognitive processing, output), suggesting some general impairment in attention and/or working memory (Zeidner, 1998). These various performance deficits are often attributed to high levels of worry and cognitive interference (Cassady and Johnson, 2002; Sarason et al., 1995), or to loss of functional working memory (Ashcraft and Kirk, 2001). Cognitive interference has also been implicated in detrimental effects of computer anxiety (Rosen and Maguire, 1990), math anxiety (Ashcraft and Ridley, 2005), social anxiety (Sarason et al., 1990), and sports anxiety (Smith, 1996).

Current theory, particularly focusing on the test anxiety–performance interface, is heavily influenced by a 'cognitive-attentional' or 'interference' perspective (Culler and Holahan, 1980; Wine, 1980; Sarason, 1980; Zeidner, 1998). Accordingly, in stressful situations, individual differences in anxiety, in interactions with the stressful evaluative context, determine the tendency in certain individuals to engage in dysfunctional cognitive activity,

and this heightened self-preoccupation interferes with task performance (Sarason, 1980; Sarason et al., 1990; Sarason et al., 1984). More specifically, highly anxious persons are likely to become extremely self-focused when placed in a social evaluation or test setting.

Biases related to anxiety have been found at later stages of processing also. In several studies, Calvo (e.g. Calvo et al., 1997) has shown that when subjects read ambiguous sentences, high anxious persons show a bias towards inferring threatening meanings. Careful analyses of the time-course of reading suggest that bias in inference operates relatively late in processing, following lexical access. Biasing effects of anxiety on memory are generally less robust than for selective attention. However, Ingram et al. (1987) demonstrated that high test anxiety facilitated incidental recall for threat-related trait adjectives. In a recent study of math anxiety, Hopko et al. (2002) failed to demonstrate any bias associated with a 'Stroop' test requiring naming the ink color of math-related words. The study did show that math anxious undergraduates were impaired on a Stroop-like task requiring counting of numerals printed on cards. Bias in math anxiety may be expressed in attention to the structure of numeric stimuli, rather than to words.

Overall, it appears that anxious subjects may suffer from varying degrees of deficits and interference at all three stages of information processing (i.e. intake, processing, and retrieval performance) (Tobias, 1980). These deficits are not independent, but may be related in a cumulative fashion. More research is needed detailing how anxiety influences specific cognitive structures and processes, including: scanning behavior, breadth of stimuli utilization, various facets of judgment and decision making, long-term memory, inductive and deductive processes, ideation, and creative behavior. Research is also needed in the area of remediation of specific deficits in encoding, processing, and rehearsal, although some progress had been made in this area (Tobias, 1992).

CLINICAL PARAMETERS

This section looks at various clinical parameters of anxiety, focusing primarily on anxiety disorders and psychological intervention techniques. As noted, anxiety has considerable survival utility. Thus, the rapid and early detection of warning signs of danger in the immediate surroundings enables the individual to avoid, prepare for, and cope more effectively with future threatening encounters (Eysenck, 1992a). In fact, a reasonable amount of anxiety experienced by an individual in response to a potentially dangerous or threatening situation is viewed as a normal reaction to stress, frequently helping one cope with the stressful situation (e.g. remaining focused on task at work or studying harder for an upcoming exam). Indeed, when an individual enters a new or novel situation, or one that is unfamiliar and has a history of threat and danger, the early detection of threat and appropriate anxiety has considerable functional utility and survival value (Rachman, 2004). However, some anxious individuals may have such inborn or highly developed danger detection processes that they may grossly exaggerate the number and severity of threatening or dangerous events in their surroundings.

When anxiety goes awry

When anxiety goes awry and becomes excessive, irrational, or leads to a dread of daily routine situations or events, it can cause untold psychic pain and discomfort and develop into a host of disabling and costly anxiety disorders (panic attacks, generalized anxiety disorders, obsessive behaviors, social phobia, PTSD, etc.). Anxiety is frequently co-morbid with many psychological problems, including those formerly called 'neuroses'. Regular (normal) levels of anxiety may be distinguished from abnormal or pathological levels by a number of criteria, including appropriateness of reaction, persistence, recurrence, and effects on coping and functioning (see Table 20.1). Specifically, when compared to normal anxiety reactions to threatening events, anxiety disorders tend to manifest greater intensity, are recurrent and persistent, show relatively diminished coping capability and seriously impede daily functioning.

Anxiety disorders are found to be among the most common forms of psychopathology (Achenbach et al., 1995). According to a recent review by Mineka and Zinbarg (2006), approximately 29% of the US population is estimated to have or have had one or more diagnosable anxiety disorders at some point in their lives. These disorders generally maintain a chronic course when untreated and result in substantial impairment across the lifetime. (Feldner et al., 2004). A large-scale survey conducted in the US has concluded that anxiety disorders constitute the single largest mental health problem in the US (Barlow, 2002). Taken together, this suggests that anxiety disorders are the most common

Table 20.1 Criteria differentiating normal and abnormal levels of anxiety

Criteria	Normal	Abnormal
Intensity	Appropriate levels of anxiety, given impending stress or objective threat	Inappropriate and excessive levels of anxiety, given impending stress or threat
Persistance	Relatively short bouts of anxiety	Relatively longer periods of severe anxiety
Recurrence	Anxiety reactions usually do not repeat themselves without specific stress	Anxiety reactions tend to be recurrent even in absence of objective stress
Ego resiliency	Ego functioning remains intact and person generally successful in coping with the anxiety	Anxiety tends to paralyze the individual and person finds it difficult to cope with the anxiety
Effects on behavior	Minimal to moderate effects on social and behavioral functioning	Seriously impedes psychosocial and behavioral/somatic functioning, with frequent breakdown in social functioning

category of diagnoses in the DSM-IV (1994). About 20 million Americans suffer from various anxiety disorders, leading to an estimated economic cost of more than $50 billion per year in loss of work productivity, health care, hospitalization, etc. (LeDoux, 2006). Furthermore, it is estimated that about 50% of the visits Americans make to mental health professional are anxiety related.

There has been a steep increase in research and public interest in anxiety and its disorders, not only because it is one of the most pervasive and distressing of emotions, but because the American Psychiatric Association committee responsible for preparing a new diagnostic system for mental disorders, decided to create a separate category for anxiety disorders and to introduce clear definitions and criteria for diagnosing anxiety disorders (Barlow, 2002; Norton et al., 1995). The introduction of this classification system – *The Diagnostic and Statistical Manual of Mental Disorders* – was a major advance on the chaos that prevailed before

1980. The DSM (1994) is in its fourth revision at present. Unfortunately, a major shortcoming of this classification is that it encourages the mistaken notion that all anxiety problems are indeed mental disorders (Rachman, 2004). Some experts think that a dimensional system, rather than a categorical system, with respect to anxiety may have been preferable. The major categories of anxiety disorders identified in the DSM appear in Table 20.2. At any rate, given the multifaceted nature of these disorders, a multifaceted approach is needed to effectively address the mental health problem of anxiety-related psychopathologies.

Figure 20.3 depicts various forms of anxiety reactions to increasing stress. As shown in Figure 20.3, when stress is low and anxiety is low, most people will not show symptoms of anxiety or distress. When stress is high and anxiety is high, the outcome is diagnosed as an adjustment or stress disorder. However, when stress is low to moderate, and anxiety is excessive, persistent, and inhibits daily

Table 20.2   Brief description of anxiety disorders (adapted from Rachman, 2004)

Disorders	Brief description
• Generalized anxiety disorder (GAD)	Persistent, excessive, unrealistic anxiety about possible misfortunes, such as ill health, possible death, financial loss, welfare of family members, or combination of these misfortunes.
• Specific phobia	Intense, persistent and circumscribed fear of specific objects (e.g. snakes or spiders) or places (tall buildings)
• Panic disorder	Repeated episodes of intense fear of rapid onset, often unexpected, often accompanied by avoidance behavior (in case of panic and agoraphobia).
• Agoraphobia (without history of panics)	Fear of being in public places or fear of coming to harm when alone at home; avoidance of unsafe places, either specific or very generalized; some fear going out of house and remain housebound.
• Obsessive-compulsive disorder (OCD)	Repetitive, intentional, stereotyped, acts (e.g. compulsive walking on sidewalk cracks or checking if door is locked) or repetitive unwanted intrusive thoughts (repeating names of all people encountered during past week or list of things to do) of an unacceptable nature or repugnant quality that the affected person resists.
• Social phobia/anxiety	Intense persistent anxiety about social situations, particularly when evaluated or scrutinized by others.
• Post-traumatic stress disorder (PTSD) or acute stress disorder (ASD)	Syndrome following unusually stressful encounter (violent terror attack, battle, rape, car collision, natural disaster, etc.). Symptoms include anxiety, disturbances of memory, elevated arousal, avoidance, and fear or horror. Symptoms persist for prolonged period after event and are accompanied by involuntary recall or re-experience of event, flashbacks, and nightmares, along with strong tendencies to avoid people or places associated with the original stress.

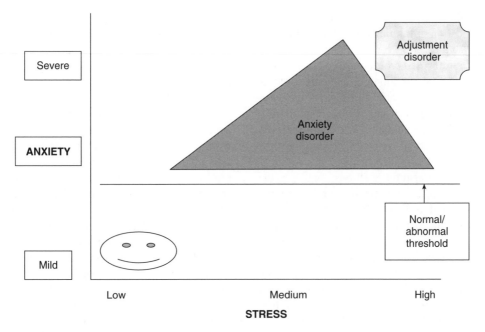

Figure 20.3   Stress and anxiety relationship distinguishing different categories of anxiety (based on Tyrer, 1999)

functioning, this suggests the emergence of a fully blown anxiety disorder.

Clinical interventions

A bewildering array of anxiety treatment programs have been developed and evaluated over the past three decades for normative, subclinical, as well as clinical forms of anxiety. Treatment fashions and orientations have swayed sharply from the clinical to the behavioral, and more recently to the cognitive perspective – essentially mirroring the evolution of the behavior therapies. There is no simple organizing principle with which to categorize the plethora of therapeutic techniques and approaches that have proliferated over the past few decades. Current attempts have typically focused either on treatments directed toward the emotional, cognitive, or behavioral facets of anxiety. Thus, treatment programs typically include both 'emotion-focused' treatments, designed largely to alleviate negative emotional affect experienced by anxious persons, 'cognitive-focused' treatments, designed to help the anxious client cope with worry and task-irrelevant thinking, and skills training, designed to improve various skills (social, athletic, motor, study, test-taking skills) and enhance their performance.

Emotion-focused interventions

Emotionally oriented therapies aim primarily at reducing the arousal and heightened emotional reactions of anxious persons when faced with stressful situations. Based on the assumption that anxiety comprises a physiological component, attempts to alleviate anxiety symptoms should prove successful, in part, if they focus on reducing levels of arousal or on altering ways in which people appraise their arousal in threatening situations.

The basic strategy in these treatments is directed to teach the client certain skills (mainly relaxational) so that when confronted by stress-inducing situations in the future, he or she will be able to handle them adequately.

The therapies also provide opportunities for application of training either within the therapy setting or in real-life situations. These emotion-focused procedures typically include a number of common components, such as: theoretical explanations of anxiety as a conditioned response and the 'deconditioning' rationale for treatment; instructions in specific methods for reducing anxiety, such as relaxation and guided imagery; guided practice in therapeutic methods; and practice (homework, in vivo practice). By and large, these emotion-focused treatments rely on key behavioral learning principles (counter conditioning, reciprocal inhibition, extinction, observational and coping skill learning, etc.) And also draw from an arsenal of behavioral techniques, such as deep muscle relaxation, guided imagery, and graduated hierarchies. For example, relaxation and guided imagery is not unique to a particular anxiety behavioral intervention method, but is employed in several methods, including relaxation as self-control, systematic desensitization, and anxiety management training.

Procedures designed to reduce emotionality, while clearly useful in modifying subjectively experienced anxiety, appear to have little effect on cognitive performance. Overall, emotion-focused treatments appear to be relatively ineffective in reducing anxiety unless these treatments contain cognitive elements. It may therefore be necessary to combine such approaches with therapy modes focusing specifically on cognitive change in order to reliably elicit improvement in cognitive performance.

Cognitive-focused interventions

Recent years have witnessed a proliferation of cognitively oriented intervention programs that emphasize the mediating role of cognitive processes in sustaining or eliminating anxiety. In part, the documented failure of emotionally oriented behavioral therapies to markedly improve the academic performance of anxious clients, coupled with the inconsistent relation reported between emotional arousal and performance, has led to a greater emphasis on cognitive factors, particularly in anxiety intervention. Indeed, reviews of the literature conclude that cognitively based treatment strategies are more powerful than direct behavioral therapies in effecting anxiety and performance changes.

'Cognitive therapy' is a generic term that refers to a wide array of therapeutic approaches directed toward modifying the worry and irrational thought patterns of anxious clients. Broadly speaking, cognitively oriented approaches to anxiety intervention are quite similar in assuming that cognitive processes are determining factors in anxiety, although they differ in terms of actual intervention procedures. A fundamental assumption shared by contemporary cognitive models of anxiety is that cognitive processes mediate the person's emotional and behavioral responses to stressful evaluative situations. It follows that in order to modify the negative emotional reactions of anxious clients to evaluative situations, therapy needs to be directed at reshaping the faulty premises, assumptions, and negative attitudes underlying maladaptive cognitions of test anxious subjects. Given their multiple emphasis on modifying emotional processes, irrational thoughts and cognitions, and behavioral deficits, this results in a powerful approach that merges emotionally oriented, cognitively oriented, and behaviorally oriented techniques to alleviate clients' test anxiety and enhance their test performance.

The distinction between the various treatment orientations is quite fuzzy, and these approaches are becoming increasingly difficult to distinguish. Although there may be highly specific interventions, which have an affective (e.g. relaxation therapy) or cognitive (e.g. rational emotive therapy) orientation, most methods are normally embedded in a multidimensional context. At present, a combination of procedures (whether combined in a truly integrative manner or in the stance of technical eclecticism) seems to best represent the true nature of the anxiety intervention process.

Anti-anxiety drugs

Biological psychiatry has repeatedly demonstrated the effectiveness of a number of different drug groups in alleviating anxiety. Although a systematic treatment of the pharmacology of anxiety is beyond the scope of this chapter, we would like to make a number of brief comments. First, neuropharmacological research has demonstrated the effectiveness of a number of commonly prescribed anti-anxiety drugs. Primarily, these include sedatives and hypnotics (e.g. benzodiazepines such as valium), monoamine oxidase inhibitors (MAOs) (e.g. phenelzine), betablocking drugs (e.g. propranolol), azospirodecanediones (e.g. buspirone), antihistamines (e.g. promethazine), tricyclic antidepressants (e.g. chlomipramine), and serotonin reuptake inhibitors (SSRIs) (e.g. paroxetine). Benzodiazepines promote calmness by promoting GABA-mediated inhibition of the fear system (Panskepp, 1998). Whereas propranalol has been shown to be particularly congenial for treating panic attacks and physical symptoms of anxiety, MAO inhibitors (e.g. phenalzine) have effective control of social phobias. It has been suggested that anxiety may be quelled by modern anti-anxiety drugs by the hyperpolarization of neuronal elements that pass anxiety messages through the neuroaxis (Panskepp, 1998).

Until the development of modern anti-anxiety drugs the only drugs that could successfully control anxiety were opiods, alcohol, and barbiturates – all which had many negative side-effects. Quite fortunately for victims of anxiety, benzodiazepines such as valium, in particular, seem to produce no apparent physical effects and have greater specificity and better safety margins than some of the other drugs on the market. The major problem with this class of drugs is the dependency developed by clients during long-term use. Most current drugs can be very useful as adjuncts to psychotherapeutic treatment (Tyrer, 1999).

Clinical considerations

The following considerations should be held in mind by both researchers and practitioners when developing, implementing, or evaluating test-anxiety intervention programs.

1 *Performing careful diagnosis of client's problem.* In order to tailor treatment programs to meet the specific needs and problems of the client, a logical first step is a careful diagnostic assessment and analysis of the nature of the anxious person's affective and cognitive problem(s). For some anxious subjects, provision of skills training may be the treatment of choice, whereas for others it would involve building up of self-confidence in a particular content area (e.g. math), or teaching relaxation skills. Information about the following aspects of the client's problem might be particularly useful: the nature of the problem as experienced and defined by the anxious client, perceived severity and generality of the problem, duration and extent of anxiety, perceived origins of anxiety, situation-specific factors which intensify or alleviate anxiety reactions, specific consequences of anxiety for the client, and suggested changes the client views as potentially helpful. A careful diagnostic assessment may suggest factors other than anxiety proper that underlie one's heightened emotional reactions in threatening situations.

2 *Meeting pre-conditions for therapeutic effectiveness.* In order for an anxiety intervention program to work, a number of preconditions need to be met. First, anxious individuals ought to possess certain relevant skills in their behavioral repertoire (e.g. problem-solving, relaxation, study/test taking skills) to apply under appropriate evaluative circumstances. Second, anxious clients must be sufficiently motivated to deal directly with stressful situations and have the wherewithal and self-efficacy to efficiently implement the coping skills they have at their disposal. Third, anxious persons must be provided with an adequate amount of practice and experience in applying various coping skills in true-to-life stressful situations in order to insure transfer of therapy from the treatment environment to the real world.

3 *Adjusting treatment to the needs of particular 'types' of anxious individuals.* Interventions and therapeutic techniques would be most effective if they could be adjusted to suit the needs of different types of

anxious persons. Because there are different types of high anxious individuals, each characterized by different problems and concerns (e.g. failure in meeting personal or social expectations, low feelings of self-efficacy and failure acceptance, poor study skills, etc.), no single treatment program would be expected to be equally effective across the board. Thus, for some highly perfectionist test anxious students, therapy may focus on lowering socially prescribed performance expectations, whereas for other 'failure accepting' students therapy may consist of raising performance expectancies and enhancing perceived self-efficacy. Comparably, persons high in social anxiety with sound social skills should profit from behavioral treatment focusing on anxiety reduction. By contrast, those with defective social skills and high anxiety in social situations would profit from a combined intervention program to improve their social skills as well as decrease anxiety.

4 *Basing treatment on the broader diagnostic picture and specific goals of therapy.* The choice of which therapy to use will be influenced not only by the diagnosis of the specific nature of the client's problem and type of anxiety but by the broader diagnostic picture, the immediate and long-term goals of treatment, and the therapeutic orientation adopted. For example, although relaxation may not increase the performance of test anxious students with study-skill deficits, it may be prescribed by the therapist in order to help the student achieve the immediate goal of achieving control over test anxiety – as a first step toward academic problem-solving. Thus, once the anxiety that interferes with learning new study skills is removed, the next step would then be training the student in efficient study skills. Furthermore, there are different ways that a therapist may view her anxious clients' problem (distorted thinking styles, poor problem-solving skills, etc.) and each of these views may give rise to different treatment procedures.

5 *Consideration of individual differences.* Before implementing a particular treatment one needs to determine to what extent the treatment may interact with particular client characteristics. For example, some interventions may reduce anxiety or successfully increase the performance of high-anxious individuals, only to have a negative effect on the anxiety performance of others who are low in anxiety. Another case in point: Whereas some people might considerably benefit from relaxation training, experiencing a substantial decrease in anxiety, some have difficulty in acquiring relaxation skills and benefit little from relaxation training. Some clients may even experience relaxation-induced anxiety during relaxation training!

6 *Addressing multiple modalities and loci of therapeutic impact.* One important consideration is that the various components of anxiety must be dealt with if the anxiety experienced in various ego-threatening situations is to be reduced and improved performance is to occur as a result of treatment. It is important to have interventions sufficiently complex to deal with the major facets (cognitive, affective, and behavioral) of the anxiety experience. Indeed, a treatment would be expected to be most effective if it impacts upon the entire range of components and chain of events leading to anxious manifestations in evaluative situations (arousal, worry, meaning system, internal dialogue, behavioral acts, etc.), rather than focusing on only one aspect of the process.

7 *Interaction among components of anxiety.* A basic consideration is that anxiety is more than a combination of physiological arousal, negative self-preoccupation, and a deficit in stress-related coping skills, and poor study habits. It is the complex interaction among these diverse components that seems to define anxiety. Because the cognitive, affective, and behavioral components of anxiety interweave in contributing to the problem of anxiety and its treatment, it is predicted that an induced change in one system would generally be followed by a change in the other. Thus therapeutic approaches, which emphasize cognition often, extend to the emotional life too and vice versa. For example, it is likely that emotion-focused training

Table 20.3   Some focal anxiety intervention techniques

Treatment	Description	Effectiveness
I. Emotion-focused interventions		
Biofeedback	Use of instrumentation (e.g. a physiograph) to provide a person with immediate and continuous information about one or more physiological processes (e.g. skin conductance, temperature, heart rate, blood volume pulse, respiration, electromyograph). Biofeedback teaches high test anxious persons to monitor and modify the physiological processes associated with their emotional reactions.	A large body of literature supports the notion of increased physiological control when using physiological feedback and self-regulation. However, biofeedback alone is not effective in reducing anxiety (nor does the addition of biofeedback training improves the efficacy of other forms of treatment). Given the potential cost and inconvenience of using biofeedback training, it many not be the treatment of choice for anxiety intervention.
Relaxation training	Recommended on the premise that maintaining a relaxed state, via deep breathing and muscle relaxation exercises, would counteract a person's aroused state. Presumably, if a person knows when and how to apply relaxation, it will be applied directly as a counter-response to anxiety.	Meta-analytic research tends to support the effectiveness of relaxation therapy. However, the effects on performance tend to be negligible.
Systematic desensitization	Situation-specific anxiety is viewed as a classically emotional reaction resulting from a person's aversive experiences in aversive situations. Systematic desensitization proposes that anxiety reactions to threatening situations may also be unlearned through specific counter-conditioning procedures. The anxious client is typically trained in a deep muscle relaxation procedure and, while relaxed, instructed to visualize an ordered series of increasingly stressful scenes (an 'anxiety hierarchy'). The client imaginally proceeds up the hierarchy until he or she is able to visualize the most stressful scenes on the list without experiencing anxiety. Through repeated pairings of imaginal representations of threatening evaluative situations with deep relaxation, the bond between the threatening evaluative scenes and anxiety is expected to be weakened.	Meta-analytic data lends support to the effectiveness of systematic desensitization in reducing anxiety, particularly test anxiety, in school children, and college students. It is shown to be as effective, if not more effective, in reducing test anxiety than a variety of other treatments, including: relaxation training, hypnosis, and skills training. However, systematic desensitization fares less well when cognitive performance (e.g. academic achievement) is the criterion or outcome being assessed.
Anxiety management	Teaches highly anxious subjects to recognize their situation-specific-related arousal responses as they are building, and then to use them as cues for initiating the coping response of relaxation in threatening situations.	A body of research supports the effectiveness of this technique in reducing anxiety. Thus, anxiety management training appears to be as robust and effective, if not more so, than related interventions. Reductions in debilitating anxiety were maintained for follow-up periods ranging several week to several months.
Modeling	Involves the live or symbolic (e.g. through videotape) demonstration of desired coping behaviors in a stressful situation such that they can be subsequently imitated by the anxious person. It is assumed that exposure to models displaying adaptive behavior may play a positive role in facilitating performance. Clients are instructed to vividly imagine the stressful evaluative scene and to focus on the anxiety and associated response-produced cues (e.g. racing heart, neck and shoulder tensing, dryness of the mouth, and catastrophic thoughts). Clients are then trained to use these cues to prompt adaptive coping skills to actively relax away tension, and reduce anxiety before it mounts too severely	A body of research lends support to the effectiveness of modeling in treating anxiety. In particular, exposure to models who are task-oriented and provide attention-directing cognitive structuring clues is beneficial to the performance of anxious persons. Of additional benefit is evidence in the behavior of the model that he or she is successfully coping with the worry and tension associated with anxiety.

Continued

Table 20.3 Some focal anxiety intervention techniques—cont'd

Treatment	Description	Effectiveness
II. Cognitive-focused interventions		
Cognitive-attentional training	Cognitive attentional training provides specific training in the redirection of attention to task-focused thinking and emphasizes the inhibition of task-irrelevant thinking and nonproductive worry. The cognitive attentional approach relates performance decrements to the diversion of attention to self-focused thinking, coupled with the cognitive overload caused by the Worry component of anxiety. By redirecting attention to the task and reducing worry and task-irrelevant thinking, cognitive resources are freed, and when redirected to the task, performance is improved. Attentional training programs traditionally provide clients with instructions to attend fully to the task and to inhibit self-relevant thinking while working on a variety of academic tasks.	The beneficial effects of attentional instruction on the anxiety and cognitive performance of high anxious students is supported by some empirical research. Task instructions that provide examinees with information about appropriate problem-solving strategies, and away from self-preoccupied worry, may be particularly helpful to the anxious individual's cognitive functioning
Cognitive restructuring	The rationale is that anxious persons will be able to master their anxiety by learning to control task-irrelevant cognitions that generate their anxiety and direct attention from their task-directed performance. The two most prominent cognitive therapeutic methods in test anxiety intervention are rational emotive therapy and systematic rational restructuring. Both forms of treatments are based on the premise that anxiety or emotional disturbance is a result of illogical or 'irrational' thinking. Two key irrational beliefs that maintain anxiety is that one must succeed at all cost, and that success is equivalent to self-worth. Anxious individuals are taught how to recognize, vigorously challenge, question, and dispute their irrational beliefs, and replace their maladaptive internal dialogue with more rational structures and beliefs. Presumably, by modifying irrational beliefs and schemas, negative emotional reactions will be reduced, and performance improved. Systematic rational restructuring aims at helping test anxious clients to discover the worrisome task-irrelevant thoughts they entertain, to eclipse such thoughts, and to substitute positive self-statements that redirect their attention to the task at hand.	Research indicates that whereas cognitive restructuring reduces anxiety, there is no concomitant improvement in performance. A number of studies provide evidence showing that these technique may be effective in reducing anxiety. However, concomitant improvements in cognitive performance are observed with far less consistency.
Cognitive behavioral modification	A multifaceted program merging both cognitively focused and emotionally focused techniques (as well as skill training in many cases), thus offering the test anxious client the best of many worlds, so to speak. This multimodal treatment attempts to deal with the multiple manifestations of anxiety, including negative motivational or affective tendencies, irrational thought patterns, and skills deficits, and emphasizes the application, and transferring of acquired coping skills to in vivo test situations. Given its dual emphasis on modifying both emotional processes and irrational thoughts and cognitions, this results in a powerful approach that merges emotionally oriented and cognitively oriented techniques to alleviate clients' anxiety and enhance their performance. This procedure is based on the premise that reducing a person's level of anxiety involves both anxiety reduction training as well as detailed cognitive restructuring of certain faulty beliefs or misconceptions	'Multimodal' treatment packages, such as cognitive-behavior modification, are most likely to be effective by their support for the inclusion of multiple domains related to anxiety. These procedures are relatively effective in reducing self-reported levels of debilitating anxiety, and are equally effective, more or less, in reducing both cognitive and affective components of anxiety. These procedures increase test performance, on average, by about half a standard deviation in school-aged samples, and elevates grade point average by close to three quarters of a standard deviation

(e.g. progressive relaxation) may make the client less anxious and result in a decrease in anxiety-focused, task-irrelevant ideation. By the same token, some forms of cognitive therapy may provide anxious subjects with an increased sense of perceived control, which might spill over into the emotional domain and result in lower emotional arousal in a stressful situation.

Because anxiety has many facets, including arousal, subjective feeling of dread, worry cognitions, and escape tendencies, there is frequently a loose coupling among the components in intervention. Thus, the components of anxiety may show some asynchrony or different rates of change in response to treatment (Rachman, 2004). For example, cognitive-behavioral therapy aims first at the client's maladaptive cognitions, whereas behavioral therapy regularly aims at the client's behavior, with the first possibly occurring earlier in the chain.

A brief summary of key emotion-focused, and cognitive-focused psychological treatment techniques and methods, and their reported effectiveness, targeted for normative anxiety states, are presented in Table 20.3. These interventions have been offered for the entire spectrum of anxiety states, from mild through severe and pathological.

CONCLUSION

As LeDoux (2006) recently commented with respect to the positive psychology zeitgeist, placing primary emphasis on happiness and wellbeing: 'The brain evolved to stay alive, not be happy.' Fear and anxiety are a function of the brain's fear system and the product of evolution, allowing the person to handle danger. Because anxiety has functional utility, we do not want to make people apathetic or cause them to fail to respond to threat. If we could control or alleviate anxiety levels in the population, we would have the potential for improved health, happiness, and economic wellbeing, both as individuals and societies.

Clearly, we want to train people to accurately assess the threat value of stimuli and respond appropriately. In controlling fear and anxiety we need to be aware that these functions exist in the brain for a reason – sometimes they are needed to serve the useful purpose of ensuring survival and/or wellbeing. Future research on brain mechanisms of fear and anxiety may give us clues about how these normally function, what changes in the brain when they malfunction, and how specific malfunctions might be most effectively treated.

REFERENCES

Achenbach, T.M., Howell, C.T., McConnaughy, S.H. and Stanger, C. (1995) 'Six-year predictors of problems in a national sample of children and youth: I. Cross-informant syndromes', *Journal of the American Academy of Child and Adolescent Psychiatry*, 34(7): 336–47.

Allen, G.J., Elias, M.J. and Zlotlow, S.F. (1980) 'Behavioral interventions for alleviating test anxiety: A methodological overview of current therapeutic practices', in I.G. Sarason (ed.), *Test Anxiety: Theory, Research and Applications*. Hillsdale, NJ: Erlbaum, pp. 155–85.

Alpert, R. and Haber, R.N. (1960) 'Anxiety in academic achievement situations', *Journal of Abnormal and Social Psychology*, 61(2): 207–15.

American Psychiatric Association (2004). *Diagnostic and Statistical Manual of Mental Disorders* (DSM IV-R) (4th edn). American Washington, D.C., US. Psychiatric Association.

Ashcraft, M.H. and Kirk, E.P. (2001) 'The relationships among working memory, math anxiety, and performance', *Journal of Experimental Psychology: General*, 130(2): 224–237.

Ashcraft, M.H. and Ridley, K.S. (2005) 'Math anxiety and its cognitive consequences: A tutorial review', in J.I.D. Campbell (ed.), *Handbook of Mathematical Cognition*. New York: Psychology Press, pp. 315–27.

Barlow, D.H. (2002) *Anxiety and its Disorders: The Nature and Treatment of Anxiety and Panic* (2nd edn). New York: Guilford.

Beck, A.T. and Steer, R.A. (1990) '*A Manual for the Beck Anxiety Inventory*', San Antonio: Psychological Corporation.

Bruch, M.A., Fallon, M. and Heimberg, R.G. (2003) 'Social Phobia and difficulties in occupational adjustment', *Journal of Counseling Psychology*, 50(1): 109–17.

Calvo, M.G., Eysenck, M.W. and Castillo, M.D. (1997) 'Interpretation bias in test anxiety: The time course of predictive inferences', *Cognition and Emotion*, 11(1): 43–63.

Cassady, J.C. and Johnson, R.E. (2002) 'Cognitive test anxiety and academic performance', *Contemporary Educational Psychology*, 27(2): 270–95.

Culler, R.E. and Holahan, C.J. (1980) 'Test anxiety and academic performance: The effects of study-related behaviors', *Journal of Educational Psychology*, 72(1): 16–20.

Endler, N.S., Edwards, J.M. and Vitelli, R. (1991) *Endler Multidimensional Anxiety Scales*. Los Angeles: Western Psychological Services.

Endler, N.S. and Parker, J.D.A. (1990) 'Stress and anxiety: Conceptual and assessment issues', *Stress Medicine*, 6(3): 243–8.

Eysenck, H.J. (1967) *The Biological Basis of Personality*. Springfield, IL: C.C. Thomas.

Eysenck, H.J. and Eysenck, M.W. (1985) *Personality and Individual Differences*. New York: Plenum Press

Eysenck, M.W. (1992a) *Anxiety: The Cognitive Perspective*. Hove: Erlbaum.

Eysenck, M.W. (1992b). 'The nature of anxiety', in A. Gayle and M.W. Eysenck, *Handbook of Individual Differences: Biological Perspectives*. Chichester: Wiley, pp. 157–78.

Feldner, M.T., Zvolensky and Schmidt, N.B. (2004). Prevention of anxiety psychopathology: A critical review of the empirical literature, *Clinical Psychology: Science and Practice*, 11(4): 405–23.

Freud, S. (1936) *The Problem of Anxiety*. New York: Norton.

Gray, J.A. and McNaughton, N. (2003) *The Neuropsychology of Anxiety*. New York: Oxford University Press.

Hamilton, M. (1959) 'The assessment of anxiety states by rating', *British Journal of Medical Psychology*, 32(1): 50–5.

Hariri, A.R. and Holmes, A. (2006) 'Genetics of emotional regulation: The role of the serotonin transporter in neural function', *Trends in Cognitive Sciences*, 10(4): 182–91.

Hembree, R. (1988) 'Correlates, causes, effects, and treatment of test anxiety', *Review of Educational Research*, 58(1): 7–77.

Hembree, R. (1990) 'The nature, effects, and relief of mathematics anxiety', *Journal for Research in Mathematics Education*, 21(1): 33–46.

Hill, K.T. (1972) 'Anxiety in the evaluative context', in W. Hartup (ed.), *The Young Child* (Vol. 2). Washington, DC: National Association for the Education of Young Children, pp. 225–63.

Hopko, D.R., McNeil, D.W., Gleason, P.J and Rabalais, A.E. (2002) 'The emotional Stroop paradigm: Performance as a function of stimulus properties and self-reported mathematics anxiety', *Cognitive Therapy and Research*, 26(2): 157–66.

Ingram, R.E., Kendall, P.C., Smith, T.W. and Donnell, C. (1987) 'Cognitive specificity in emotional distress', *Journal of Personality and Social Psychology*, 53(4): 734–42.

Krohne, H.W. (1992) 'Developmental conditions of anxiety and coping: A two-process model of child-rearing effects', in K.A. Hagtvet and B.T. Johnsen (eds), *Advances in Test Anxiety Research* (Vol. 7). Lisse, Netherlands: Swets and Zeitlinger, pp. 143–55.

Lazarus, R.S. (1991) *Emotion and Adaptation*. New York: Oxford University Press.

Lazarus, R.S. (1999) *Stress and Emotion: A New Synthesis*. New York: Springer.

Lazarus R.S. and Folkman, S. (1984) *Stress, Appraisal, and Coping*. New York: Springer.

LeDoux, J.E. (1996) The Emotional Brain: *The Mysterious Underpinnings of Emotional Life*. New York: Simon & Schuster.

LeDoux, J. (2006) 'Why is it hard to be happy: The fearful brain is the problem and the solution. Frontiers of Consciousness', Chichele Lectures, 4 May, All Souls College, Oxford.

Liebert, R.M. and Morris, L.W. (1967) 'Cognitive and emotional components of test anxiety: A distinction and some initial data', *Psychological Reports*, 20(3): 975–8.

Mineka, S. and Zinbarg, R. (2006) 'A contemporary learning theory perspective on the etiology of anxiety disorders: It's not what you thought it was', *American Psychologist*, 61(1): 10–26.

Morris, J.S. (2002). 'How do you feel?', *Trends in Cognitive Sciences*, 6(8): 317–19.

Norton, R., Cox, B., Asmundson, G. and Maser, J. (1995) 'The growth of research on anxiety disorders during the 1980's', *Journal of Anxiety Disorders*, 9(1): 75–85.

Panksepp, J. (1998) *Affective Neuroscience: The Foundations of Human and Animal Emotions*. New York: Oxford University Press.

Pekrun, R. (1985) 'Classroom climate and test anxiety: Developmental validity of expectancy-value theory of anxiety', in H.M. Van der Ploeg, R. Schwarzer and C.D. Spielberger (eds), *Advances in Test Anxiety Research* (Vol. 4). Lisse: Swets & Zeitlinger, pp. 147–58.

Phillips, B.N., Martin, R.P. and Meyers, J. (1972) 'Interventions in relation to anxiety in school', in C.D. Spielberger (ed.), *Anxiety: Current Trends in Theory and Research* (Vol. 2). New York: Academic Press, pp. 410–64.

Rachman, S. (2004). *Anxiety* (2nd edn). Oxford: Blackwell.

Rolls, E.T. (1999) *The Brain and Emotion*. New York: Oxford University Press.

Rosen, L.D. and Maguire, P. (1990) 'Myths and realities of computerphobia: A meta-analysis', *Anxiety Research*, 3: 175–91.

Sarason, I.G. (1978) 'The Test Anxiety scale: Concept and research', in C.D. Spielberger and I.G. Sarason (eds), *Stress and Anxiety* (Vol. 5). Washington, DC: Hemisphere, pp. 193–216.

Sarason, I.G. (1980) 'Introduction to the study of test anxiety', in I.G. Sarason (ed.), *Test Anxiety: Theory, Research and Applications*. Hillsdale NJ: Erlbaum, pp. 3–14.

Sarason, I.G. (1984) 'Stress, anxiety, and cognitive interference: Reactions to tests', *Journal of Personality and Social Psychology*, 46(1): 929–38.

Sarason, I.G. and Sarason, B.R. (1990) 'Test anxiety', in H. Leitenberg (ed.), *Handbook of Social and Evaluative Anxiety*. New York: Plenum Press, pp. 475–96.

Sarason, I.G., Sarason, B.R. and Pierce, G.R. (1990) 'Anxiety, cognitive interference, and performance', *Journal of Social Behavior and Personality*, 5(2): 1–18.

Sarason, I.G., Sarason, B.R. and Pierce, G.R. (1995) 'Cognitive interference: At the intelligence–personality crossroads', in D. Saklofske and M. Zeidner (eds), *International Handbook of Personality and Intelligence*. New York: Plenum, pp. 285–96.

Sarason, I.G., Sarason, B.R., Keefe, D.E., Hayes, B.E. and Shearin, E.N. (1984)

'Cognitive interference: Situational determinants and trait-like characteristics. *Journal of Personality and Social Psychology*, 51(1): 215–26.

Schermelleh-Engel, K., Keith, N., Moosbrugger, H. and Hodapp, V. (2004) 'Decomposing person and occasion-specific effects: An extension of latent state-trait (LST) theory to hierarchical structures', *Psychological Methods*, 9(2): 198–219.

Smith, R.E. (1996) 'Performance anxiety, cognitive interference, and concentration enhancement strategies in sports', in Sarason, I.G., Pierce, G.R. and Sarason, B.R. (eds), *Cognitive Interference: Theories, Methods, and Findings*. Hillsdale: Lawrence Erlbaum Associates, pp. 261–83.

Spielberger, C.D. (1966) 'Theory and research on anxiety', in C.D. Spielberger (ed.), *Anxiety and Behavior*. New York: Academic Press, pp. 3–20.

Spielberger, C.D. (1972) *Anxiety: Current Trends in Theory and Research: I*. Oxford: Academic Press.

Spielberger, C.D. (1983) *Manual for the State-Trait Anxiety Inventory (STAI)*. PaloAlto, CA: Consulting Psychologists Press,

Spielberger, C.D., Anton, W.D. and Bedell, J. (1976) 'The nature and treatment of test anxiety', in M. Zuckerman and C.D. Spielberger (eds), *Emotions and Anxiety: New Concepts, Methods, and Applications*. New York: LEA/Wiley, pp. 317–44.

Taylor, J.A. (1953). 'A personality scale of manifest anxiety', *Journal of Abnormal and Social Psychology*, 48(2): 285–90

Teichman, Y. and Ziv, R. (1994) 'Characteristics of extended family and children's trait anxiety', *Anxiety, Stress, and Coping: An International Journal*, 7: 291–303.

Tobias, S. (1977) 'Anxiety and instructional methods: An introduction', in J.E. Sierra, H.F. O'Neil Jr. and S. Tobias (eds), *Anxiety, Learning and Instruction*. Hillsdale, NJ: Erlbaum, pp. 73–86.

Tobias, S. (1992) 'The impact of test anxiety on cognition in school learning', in K.A. Hagtvet and B.T. Johnsen (eds), *Advances in Test Anxiety Research* (Vol. 7). Lisse, Netherlands: Swets and Zeitlinger, pp. 18–31.

Tryer, P. (1999) *Anxiety: A Multidisciplinary Review*. London: World Scientific Publications.

Wine, J.D. (1980) 'Cognitive-attentional theory of test-anxiety', in I.G. Sarason, (ed.), *Test*

Anxiety: Theory, Research, and Applications. Hillsdale, NJ: Erlbaum, pp. 349–85.

Zeidner, M. (1998) *Test Anxiety: The State of the Art.* New York: Plenum Press.

Zeidner, M. (2007) 'Test anxiety: Conceptions, findings, conclusions', in P. Schutz and R. Pekrun (eds), *Emotions in Education.* Beverly Hills, CA: Sage, pp.165–84.

Zeidner, M. and Matthews, G. (2005) 'Evaluation anxiety: Current theory and research', in Elliot, A.J. and Dweck, C.S. (eds), *Handbook of Competence and Motivation.* New York, Guilford Publications, pp. 141–63.

Zung, W.W.K. (1971) 'A rating instrument for anxiety disorders', *Psychosomatics*, 129(6): 371–9.

21

A Multidimensional, Hierarchical Model of Self-Concept: An Important Facet of Personality

Herbert W. Marsh

INTRODUCTION

Self-concept is one of the oldest and most important constructs in the social sciences. In this chapter, I distinguish between: (a) an older, *unidimensional perspective* of self-concept that focuses on global self-esteem and (b) the more recent, *multidimensional perspective* of self-concept that is based on a hierarchical model of self-concept. In support of the multidimensional perspective, I review research showing that specific domains of self-concept are more useful than a general domain for understanding the complexity of the self in different contexts, predicting a wide variety of behaviors, providing outcome measures for diverse interventions, and relating self-concept to other constructs in a variety of disciplines. Particularly strong support for the multidimensionality of self-concept comes from academic self-concept research, where diverse academic outcomes are systematically related to academic self-concept but

almost unrelated to global self-esteem, from longitudinal studies showing that prior academic self-concept and achievement are reciprocally related – each being both a cause and an effect of the other, and from frame-of-reference models based on social comparison theory, which show that school-average ability has negative effects on academic self-concept.

Increasingly, there is support for the multidimensional perspective across diverse disciplines of psychology. Personality research, however, still relies largely on unidimensional measures of self-esteem rather than on multiple dimensions of self-concept, despite clear support for well-defined multivariate patterns of relations between multiple dimensions of self-concept, personality, well-being, and academic criteria. This highly differentiated pattern of relations between self-concept and personality factors argues against the unidimensional perspective of self-concept still prevalent in personality research and augurs well for further research that more fully maps the complex nature of relations between multiple dimensions of self-concept and multiple dimensions of personality.

SIGNIFICANCE OF SELF-CONCEPT

Self-concept, self-worth, and self-esteem are highly relevant to important individual and societal problems that stem from low self-concept. Nathaniel Branden, an eminent philosopher and psychologist, attests to the significance of the self-concept/self-esteem construct and outcomes:

> I cannot think of a single psychological problem – from anxiety to depression, to under-achievement at school or at work, to fear of intimacy, happiness or success, to alcohol or drug abuse, to spouse battering or child molestation, to co-dependency and sexual disorders, to passivity and chronic aim-lessness, to suicide and crimes of violence – that is not traceable, at least in part, to the problem of deficient self-esteem. (1994: xv)

In his review of personality and social psychological research, Greenwald emphasized the central importance of self 'because it is a major (perhaps the major) structure of personality' (1988: 30). In support of this claim, he asserted, '(a) that the search for self-worth is one of the strongest motivating forces in the adolescent and adult human behavior, and (b) that differences between persons in their manner of, and effectiveness in, establishing self-worth are fundamental to personality' (1988: 37). More generally, the importance of self-concept and related constructs is high-lighted by the regularity and consistency with which self-concept enhancement is identified as a major focus in diverse settings and disciplines. Self-concept is also an important medi-ating factor that facilitates the attainment of other desirable psychological and behavioral outcomes. Hence, the need to think and feel positively about oneself, and the likely bene-fits of positive cognitions on choice, planning, and subsequent accomplishments transcend traditional disciplinary barriers, and are cen-tral to goals in many social policy areas.

THE HIERARCHICAL MULTIDIMENSIONAL MODEL OF SELF-CONCEPT

Self-concept has a long, controversial his-tory. In the first introductory textbook in psy-chology, William James (1890) laid a foundation for the study of self and intro-duced many issues still of relevance today. Despite the rich beginning provided by James, advances in theory, research, and measurement of self-concept were slow, par-ticularly during the heyday of behaviorism. Thus, reviewers in that era noted the poor quality both of theoretical models and self-concept measurement instruments (e.g. Shavelson et al., 1976; Wells and Marwell, 1976; Wylie, 1979), leading Hattie (1992) to describe this period as one of 'dustbowl empiricism' in which the predominant research design in self-concept studies was 'throw it in and see what happens'. Thus, in her review of past, present, and future self-concept research, Byrne concluded:

> Without question, the most profound happening in self-concept research during the past century was the wake-up call sounded regarding the sorry state of its reported findings, which was followed by a conscious effort on the part of methodologi-cally oriented researchers to rectify the situation. (2002: 898)

Although a multidimensional conception of self-concept was already evident in William James' (1890/1963) pioneering work, early self-concept research was dominated by a unidimensional perspective in which self-concept was typically represented by a single score (e.g. Coopersmith, 1967), variously referred to as general self-concept, global self-worth, or self-esteem. As used in this chapter, *self-esteem* is inferred from responses to a relatively unidimensional self-concept scale that refers to a separate, distin-guishable facet comprising characteristics such as self-confidence and self-competence, which are superordinate, but not specific, to any particular self-concept domain. Typical items include: 'On the whole, I am satisfied with myself'. Rosenberg (1979) recognized the importance of domain-specific evaluations but, wishing to avoid such complexities, opted to measure global self-esteem directly by assessing general perceptions that were not specific to any particular domain. Self-esteem may be inferred from stand-alone instruments (e.g. the Rosenberg self-esteem measure) or from a self-esteem scale that is part of a multidimensional self-concept instrument such as the Self-Description Questionnaires (Marsh, 1990b, 1993, 2007). Rosenberg's approach finessed many of the complexities in measuring esteem, but it also loses potentially important information in specific components of self-concept (see Rosenberg et al., 1995).

In their classic review of self-concept research, theory, and measurement, Shavelson et al. (1976) developed a multidimensional, hierarchical model of self-concept that fundamentally impacted on self-concept research (Marsh and Hattie, 1996). Self-concept, broadly defined by Shavelson et al. (1976), is a person's self-perceptions formed through experience with and interpretations of one's environment. They are influenced especially by evaluations by significant others, reinforcements, and attributions for one's own behavior. Self-concept is not an entity within the person, but a hypothetical construct that is potentially useful in explaining and predicting how a person acts. Shavelson et al. noted that self-concept is important both as an outcome and as a mediating variable that helps to explain other outcomes. Self-perceptions influence the way one acts and behaviors in turn influence one's self-perceptions.

Shavelson et al. (1976) represented their model pictorially as a hierarchical organization in which general self-concept at the apex is divided into academic and non-academic components of self-concept (see Figure 21.1). The academic component is divided into self-concepts specific to general school subjects and non-academic self-concept is divided into physical, social, and emotional components. This multidimensional model integrates the unidimensional perspective,

which focuses on the global component of the self-concept hierarchy, and the multidimensional perspective, which focuses on the increasingly domain-specific components of self-concept near the base of the hierarchy.

A new generation of self-concept instruments stimulated in part by the Shavelson et al. (1976) model has provided overwhelming support for the multidimensionality of self-concept. There are several widely used inventories for measuring multiple dimensions of self-concept that, to some extent, differ in the self-concept dimensions included (e.g. Bracken, 1996; Harter, 1998; Marsh, 1990b; see review by Byrne, 1996a). Typically, however, these instruments include at least one or more factors representing the specific academic (e.g. math and verbal self-concept), social (e.g. relations with friends, relations with parents), physical (e.g. physical competence, attractiveness), and emotional domains of self-concept, and a global self-esteem scale as posited in the Shavelson et al. (1976) model. Among the various instruments, external reviews (see Boyle, 1994; Byrne, 1996b; Hattie, 1992; Wylie, 1989) suggest that the Self-Description Questionnaire (SDQ) instruments are the strongest multidimensional self-concept instruments for children (SDQI), adolescents (SDQII), and young adults (SDQIII).

A CONSTRUCT VALIDITY APPROACH TO TESTING UNIDIMENSIONAL VERSUS MULTIDIMENSIONAL PERSPECTIVES IN DIFFERENT PSYCHOLOGICAL DISCIPLINES

Over the last 25 years, influenced by the Shavelson model (see reviews by Byrne, 1996a; 1996b; Marsh and Hattie, 1996; Marsh and Craven, 2006), many disciplines of psychology have shifted from primary reliance on global self-esteem to the multidimensional perspective, with domain-specific assessments of self-concept in

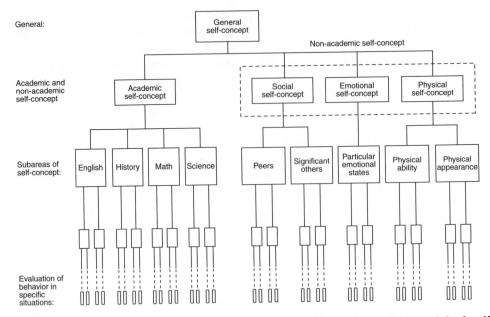

Figure 21.1 Pictorial representation of the multidimensional, hierarchical model of self-concept posited by Shavelson et al. (1976) and Marsh and Shavelson (1985)

addition to – or instead of – global self-esteem. This research has consistently shown that the proposed hierarchy is weaker than anticipated by Shavelson et al. (1976) and that the specific components of self-concept (e.g. social, academic, physical, emotional) are highly differentiated (Marsh and Craven, 1997; also see Harter, 1998). Marsh (1993; Marsh and Craven, 1997) argued logically – and demonstrated empirically – that if specific components of self-concept are highly differentiated, then there is much variation in the specific components that cannot be explained in terms of a single global component such as self-esteem. Following from this, they proposed a multidimensional perspective on self-concept in which specific components of self-concept most logically related to the aims of the research will typically be more useful – more strongly related to important criteria, more influenced by interventions, and more predictive of future behavior – than a single, global component of self-concept that is intended to provide an overall index of self-concept.

Educational psychology

The strongest support for the multidimensional perspective comes from educational psychology research, where many important academic outcomes (e.g. academic achievement, coursework selection, educational aspirations) are substantially related to academic self-concept but relatively unrelated to self-esteem and other non-academic components of self-concept (e.g. Byrne, 1996a; Marsh, 1993; Marsh and Craven, 1997, 2006). In an early meta-analysis of the correlations between academic achievement and self-concept, Hansford and Hattie (1982) found that measures of academic ability and performance correlated about 0.20 with self-esteem and undifferentiated measures of general self-concept, but about 0.40 with measures of academic self-concept. Similarly, Shavelson and Bolus (1982) found that grades in English, mathematics, and science were correlated more highly with matching areas of academic self-concept than with global self-esteem. In her review of studies relating self-concept to academic achievement, Byrne (1996a, 2002) also found that nearly all studies report that self-concept and self-esteem are correlated positively to achievement, but that most find achievement correlated more strongly with academic self-concept than with global self-esteem.

Research reviewed by Marsh and Craven (1997; see also Marsh, 1993) provided even stronger support for the convergent and discriminant validity of academic self-concept responses in different domains in relation to corresponding measures of achievement. Thus, for example, Marsh and O'Neill (1984) related mathematics and English achievement to responses by high school students to the SDQIII instrument. Math achievement correlated 0.58, 0.27, and 0.11 with math, general academic, and verbal self-concepts, respectively, whereas English achievement correlated 0.42, 0.24 and 0.19 with verbal, general academic, and math self-concepts. Remarkably, none of the nine non-academic scales – including global self-esteem – was significantly related to either of the achievement scores. Demonstrating the generalizability of these effects, Marsh et al. (1988) found that correlations between math and English self-concepts based on each of three different instruments were close to zero, that math achievement was substantially correlated with math self-concept but not English self-concept, and that English achievement is substantially correlated with English self-concept but not math self-concept.

Marsh (1992) extended these earlier studies by evaluating relations between specific components of academic self-concept (based on responses to a newly developed Academic Self-Description Questionnaire, or ASDQ) and school performance in eight core school subjects. Consistent with predictions and the logic of construct validation, he found that correlations between matching areas of achievement and self-concept were substantial for all eight content areas (r's varied from 0.45 to 0.70; mean = 0.57) and substantially less than correlations between non-matching

areas of academic self-concept and achievement. In contrast, self-esteem was nearly uncorrelated with school grades in all the school subjects, indicating that it had no validity in relation to this criterion.

In summary, there is considerable research showing that academic achievement and associated academic outcomes are substantially correlated with academic self-concept but relatively uncorrelated with non-academic components of self-concept and with global self-esteem. These correlational studies demonstrate the domain specificity of self-concept that supports a multidimensional perspective of self-concept and undermines support for a unidimensional perspective that focuses solely on global self-esteem.

Sport/exercise psychology

In a review of early self-concept measures, Marsh (1997, 2002) concluded that most either ignored physical self-concept completely or treated it as a relatively unidimensional domain incorporating characteristics as diverse as fitness, health, appearance, grooming, sporting competence, body image, sexuality, and physical activity into a single score. Concerns such as these led researchers to develop multidimensional measures of physical self-concept (Fox and Corbin, 1989; Marsh, 1997, 2002) such as the Physical Self-Description Questionnaire (PSDQ; Marsh et al., 1994). In support of the instrument (see Marsh, 1997; 2002), PSDQ factors demonstrate good internal consistency, short- and long-term test–retest stability, and convergent and discriminant validity in relation to other physical self-concept instruments and to external validity criteria (reflecting body composition, physical activity, and other components of physical fitness). Marsh (1996) related PSDQ responses to 23 external validity criteria: measures of body composition, physical activity, endurance, strength, and flexibility. Each criterion was predicted to be most highly correlated to one of the PSDQ scales. In support of convergent validity, every predicted correlation was significant. In support of discriminant validity, most predicted correlations were larger than other correlations involving the same criterion. In summary, a growing body of sport psychology research, which demonstrated physical self-concept, is more appropriately represented from a multidimensional perspective than a unidimensional one.

Developmental psychology

Developmental and early-childhood researchers perceive self-concept as 'the cornerstone of both social and emotional development' (Kagen et al., 1995: 18; see also Marsh et al., 2005a). Many authors argue that self-concept is developed very early in childhood and that, once established, it is enduring (e.g. Eder and Mangelsdorf, 1997). The development of self-concept is therefore emphasized in many early childhood programs (e.g. Head Start).

Recent research in developmental psychology research provides clear support for a multidimensional perspective of self-concept. Theoretical research from cognitive psychology argues that even young children should be able to differentiate between multiple dimensions of self-concept (Marsh et al., 2005a). Whereas early research did not provide strong support for a clearly differentiated structure of multiple dimensions of self-concept, critical reviews and subsequent empirical research suggested that this was due to limitations in the instrument, methodology, and the data collection strategies (Marsh et al., 1991, 1998). More recent research demonstrates that responses by children to appropriate instruments support a well-differentiated, multidimensional structure of self-concept at younger ages than previously thought possible (Marsh et al., 2005a). This differentiation between multiple dimensions of self-concept improves systematically during early childhood and preadolescent ages.

Mental health

In mental health research, Marsh et al. (2004a, 2004b) demonstrated that relations between 11 self-concept factors and seven mental health problems varied substantially (+0.11 to −0.83; mean $r = -0.35$) and formed an a priori multivariate pattern of relations that supported a multidimensional perspective. Support for the multidimensional perspective was particularly strong for the externalizing (e.g. delinquent and aggressive behavior) problems. This externalizing factor was modestly negatively correlated with self-esteem ($r = -0.34$), substantially negatively correlated with some specific components of self-concept (e.g. parent relations, $r = -0.70$), and nearly uncorrelated or even positively correlated with physical, appearance, same-sex, and opposite-sex self-concepts. Self-esteem was able to uniquely explain only 3% of the covariation between mental health and self-concept factors, whereas specific components of self-concept explained 97% of this covariation. Based on higher-order factor analyses, Marsh et al. noted that single higher-order factors could not explain relations among the self-concept factors, among the mental health factors, or between the self-concept and mental health factors. These results attest to the explanatory power of specific facets of self-concept to influence and explain relations among a wide range of constructs of practical significance that serve to inform mental health theory and practice, enhance understanding of difficult social problems, and are useful for intervention. On this basis, they concluded that a unidimensional perspective was not viable in mental health research.

Social psychology: self–other agreement

Particularly in sociology and in social psychology there is a rich theoretical literature, stemming from a symbolic interactionist perspective, about agreement between self-ratings and ratings by significant others. More generally, self-concept ratings inferred by others are used to determine how accurately external observers can infer self-concept, validate interpretations of responses to self-concept instruments, and test theoretical hypotheses. However, in a widely cited review of early research, Shrauger and Schoeneman (1979) concluded that there was no consistent agreement between people's self-perceptions and how they were actually viewed by others, calling into question the validity of self-concept ratings. Subsequent research, however, demonstrated that such conclusions were overly pessimistic, apparently reflecting the poor methodology of these early studies.

When multiple dimensions of self-concept are represented by both self-ratings and inferred-ratings, MTMM analysis (Campbell and Fiske, 1959) provides an important analytical tool for testing the construct validity of the responses. *Convergent validity* is inferred from substantial correlations between self-ratings and inferred-ratings on matching self-concept traits. *Discriminant* validity provides a test of the distinctiveness of self–other agreement and of the multidimensionality of the self-concept facets; it is inferred from the lack of correlation between non-matching traits. In eight MTMM studies, Marsh (1990b, 1993) demonstrated significant agreement between multiple self-concepts inferred by primary school teachers and student responses to the SDQI; the mean of the 56 convergent validities (self–other agreement on matching scales) was 0.30, and was reasonably specific to each area of self-concept. Student–teacher agreement was strongest where the teachers could most easily make relevant observations (math, 0.37; reading, 0.37; school, 0.33; physical ability, 0.38; and, perhaps, peer relations 0.29). Student–teacher agreement was lower on relations with parents (0.17) and physical appearance (0.16). These studies demonstrate that external observers can infer self-concepts in many areas with modest accuracy and support the construct validity of SDQI responses.

Much stronger results were found in two MTMM studies with young adults. In Australian (Marsh and O'Neill, 1984) and Canadian (Marsh and Byrne, 1993) studies, university students completed the SDQIII and asked the 'person in the world who knew them best' to complete the SDQIII as if they were that person (significant others typically were family members, boy/girl friends). Factor analyses of self-ratings and responses by others each identified all 13 SDQIII scales in both studies. Self–other agreement was very high (mean $r = 0.57$), and four of the scales had self–other correlations over 0.75. Both the traditional Campbell and Fiske guidelines and the new CFA models of the MTMM data provided strong support for the convergent and discriminant validity of the ratings. The results in both studies were remarkably similar, thus supporting the replicability of the results. In support of a multidimensional perspective of self-concept, the average correlation among the 13 SDQIII factors was only 0.09. Hence, a single global dimension of self-concept cannot adequately account for the agreement specific scales.

Of particular relevance to comparisons of multidimensional and unidimensional perspectives, Shavelson et al. (1976) predicted that self–other agreement would be lower on general dimensions of self-concept, near the apex of their hierarchy, than dimensions closer to the base of their hierarchy, which are more directly related to observable behavior. Marsh and Byrne (1993) also reported that self–other agreement was lower for self-esteem than for any other SDQIII scale. Based on their review of self–other agreement in personality research, McCrae and Costa (1987, 1988) also suggested that agreement would be higher on traits that are more observable.

Marsh and Byrne (1993) argued that self–other agreement was so high in their studies because (1) the participants were older and thus knew themselves better, (2) both participants and significant others made their responses on the same well-developed, multi-item self-concept instrument, and (3) self–other agreement was for specific characteristics rather than for broad, ambiguous characteristics or general esteem. More generally, research on self–other agreement on multiple dimensions of self-concept provides convincing evidence for the convergent and discriminant validity of multidimensional self-concept ratings, and for the construct validity of a multidimensional perspective of self-concept.

Gender studies

The richness of gender differences in self-concept cannot be understood from a unidimensional perspective. Although gender differences in self-esteem are very small (Wylie, 1979), differences favoring boys grow larger through high school and then decline in adulthood (Kling et al., 1999). However, these small gender differences in self-esteem mask larger, counterbalancing gender-stereotypic differences in specific components of self-concept (e.g. boys have high math self-concepts, girls have higher verbal self-concept) and this pattern of gender differences is reasonably consistent from early childhood to adulthood (e.g. Eccles et al., 1993; Marsh, 1989, 1993).

The research on gender differences in multiple dimensions of self-concept is also relevant to androgyny research. Central postulates in androgyny research (e.g. Marsh and Myers, 1986; Marsh and Byrne, 1991) are that masculinity (M) and femininity (F) both contribute to self-concept, but most research has shown that F is not related to self-esteem after controlling for the effects of M. Marsh and Byrne, however, demonstrated that this apparent lack of support for F was due in part to an over-reliance on a unidimensional perspective of self-concept, and global self-esteem measures that emphasize stereotypically masculine characteristics such as self-confidence, assertiveness, and a sense of agency. When measures of M and F were related to multidimensional self-concept measures, there was support for a logical a priori pattern of relations leading to the development of the differentiated additive androgyny model. Consistent with this model, the relative contributions of M and F varied substantially for different areas of self-concept and F contributed more positively than M for self-concept domains that were more stereotypically feminine. Marsh and Byrne found that support for the model was consistent across responses by males and females, across self-responses and responses by significant others, and across age groups. This research demonstrates that relations between self-concept, M, and F, cannot be adequately understood if the multidimensionality of self-concept is ignored.

Intervention studies: A multidimensional perspective on construct validation

According to a multidimensional perspective of self-concept, interventions should impact in ways that map onto specific, relevant dimensions of the self-concept. Hence, intervention studies provide a strong test of the construct validity of a multidimensional perspective of self-concept. To the extent that an intervention has the predicted pattern of effects on multiple dimensions of self-concept, there is even stronger support for the construct validity of interpretations of the intervention.

Physical fitness enhancement
Marsh and Peart (1988) randomly assigned high school students to competitive, cooperative, and control groups. The cooperative group completed exercises in pairs and feedback emphasized individual improvement. The competitive/social comparison group completed individual exercises and feedback emphasized comparisons with whoever did best on each exercise. Consistent with a priori predictions, it was found that the cooperative intervention increased physical fitness and physical self-concept; the competitive intervention increased physical fitness but decreased physical self-concept. Important for a multidimensional perspective,

the intervention effects were specific to physical components of self-concept, while global self-esteem and other non-physical components of self-concept were unaffected.

'Outward Bound' studies

The construct validity approach was demonstrated in a series of studies based on the Outward Bound program, which encourages individuals to recognize and understand their own weaknesses, strengths, and resources, and thus find within themselves the wherewithal to master the difficult and unfamiliar. The Outward Bound standard course is a 26-day residential program based on physically and mentally demanding outdoor activities (Marsh et al., 1986a, 1986b). The authors evaluated short- and long-term effects of participation in the Outward Bound program using the SDQIII. Prior to the start of the study, the program director rated the relevance of each of the 13 SDQIII scales to the goals of the program. Results were consistent with the primarily non-academic goals of the Outward Bound standard course: (a) gains were significantly larger for the SDQIII scales predicted a priori to be most relevant to the goals of the program, (b) the effect sizes were consistent across 27 different Outward Bound groups run by different instructors at different times and in different locations, and (c) the size and pattern of the gains were maintained over an 18-month follow-up period.

In contrast to the Outward Bound standard course, the Outward Bound bridging course is a 6-week residential program designed to produce significant gains in the academic domain for underachieving adolescent males through an integrated program of remedial teaching, normal schoolwork, and experiences likely to influence academic self-concept (Marsh and Richards, 1988). Consistent with the primarily academic goals of the Outward Bound bridging course: (a) academic self-concept effects were substantial and significantly larger than non-academic self-concept effects and (b) there were corresponding effects on reading and math achievement.

The juxtaposition of these two interventions and support for their contrasting predictions provides a powerful demonstration of the importance of a multidimensional perspective of self-concept. If self-esteem only had been measured, both interventions would have been judged much weaker, and a rich understanding of the match between specific intended goals and actual outcomes would have been lost.

Meta-analyses of intervention studies

In a meta-analysis of self-concept intervention studies, Haney and Durlak (1998) found modest – but significantly positive – effect sizes. However, reflecting the prevailing unidimensional perspective of many studies included in their meta-analysis, they considered only one effect size per intervention – the mean effect size averaged across different self-concept dimensions, where more than one had been considered. In contrast, O'Mara et al. (2006) updated and extended this meta-analysis to embrace a multidimensional perspective, by coding the nature of the self-concept outcomes in relation to the intervention. Effect sizes were consistent with a multidimensional perspective, being substantially larger for specific components of self-concept logically related to intended outcomes of the intervention than for other less relevant components of self-concept. Importantly, studies designed to enhance global self-esteem were not very successful, compared to studies that focused on more specific components of self-concept that were most relevant to goals of the intervention. These results support the usefulness of a multidimensional perspective of self-concept in intervention research.

SUMMARY AND IMPLICATIONS: MULTIDIMENSIONAL VERSUS UNIDIMENSIONAL PERSPECTIVES

In the research reviewed here, unidimensional and multidimensional perspectives have been integrated into a multidimensional, hierarchical model of self-concept. However, appropriately selected specific domains of self-concept are more useful than self-esteem in most research settings. Clearly it follows that a multidimensional perspective that incorporates specific components of self-concept and self-esteem is more useful than a unidimensional perspective, which relies solely on self-esteem. Self-esteem is ephemeral in that it is more affected by short-term response biases, situation-specific context effects, short-term mood fluctuations, and other short-term, time-specific influences. Self-esteem apparently cannot adequately reflect the diversity of specific self-domains. Indeed, as emphasized by Marsh and Yeung (1998, 1999), it is worrisome that a construct so central to the self seems to be so easily influenced by apparently trivial laboratory manipulations, bogus feedback, and short-term mood fluctuations. In fact, according to modern ethical requirements, such manipulations would probably be unethical if they did have lasting effects on self-esteem. Despite the overwhelming empirical support for a multidimensional perspective on self-concept, I am not arguing that researchers should abandon the self-esteem measures that have been used so widely. Indeed, self-esteem is one of the scales in each of the SDQI, SDQII, and SDQIII instruments, the basis of much of the research considered here. Rather, researchers should be encouraged to consider multiple dimensions of self-concept particularly relevant to the concerns of their research – supplemented, perhaps, by self-esteem responses.

Analogous debates reverberate across different psychological disciplines, where researchers are increasingly recognizing the value of multidimensional perspectives (e.g. multiple intelligences versus a global measure of IQ to characterize a profile of intellectual abilities). The case for a multidimensional self-concept perspective is particularly strong because the multiple dimensions of self-concept are so distinct that they cannot be explained in terms of a single global component and because they display dramatically different patterns of relations with different background variables, outcomes, and experimental manipulations. Although support for this perspective is evident in many areas of psychological research, it is particularly strong in educational research, where academic outcomes are substantially related to academic self-concept but nearly unrelated to global measures of self-esteem. This emphasis on a multidimensional perspective on relations between self-concept and academic achievement is critical to studies attempting to establish the causal ordering of self-concept and achievement in longitudinal panel studies.

THE RECIPROCAL EFFECTS MODEL OF CAUSAL ORDERING

Do changes in self-concept lead to changes in subsequent performance? This question has important theoretical and practical implications, and has been the focus of considerable research, particularly in the academic domain. Byrne (1996a) emphasized that much of the interest in the academic self-concept/achievement relationship stems from the belief that academic self-concept has motivational properties such that will lead to changes in subsequent academic achievement. Calsyn and Kenny (1977) contrasted self-enhancement (i.e. self-concept causes achievement) and skill development (i.e. achievement causes self-concept) model of this relation. However, based on more advanced statistical tools, empirical results, and self-concept theory, Marsh (1990a; Marsh et al., 1999; Marsh and Craven, 2006) argued that a more realistic compromise between the self-enhancement and skill-development models was a *reciprocal effects model* (REM), in which prior self-concept affects subsequent achievement *and* prior achievement affects subsequent self-concept.

Because self-concept and academic achievement are not readily amenable to experimental manipulations, most research relies on longitudinal panel data, in which both self-concept and achievement performance are measured on at least two occasions (i.e., a two-wave design) and preferably three (see Figure 21.2). The critical predictions distinguishing three theoretical models are the cross-paths relating prior self-concept (SC) to subsequent achievement performance (PERF) and prior PERF to subsequent SC (Figure 21.2). The basic REM model is very flexible and can be extended in many different ways to include more (or fewer) waves of data, to control for the effects of background variables (e.g. gender, age, and their interaction), or to include different performance or self-belief constructs (see Marsh et al., 2005b).

Marsh (1990a) tested the causal ordering of academic self-concept and academic achievement with data from the large, nationally representative Youth in Transition study, considering data from times 1 (early tenth grade), 2 (late eleventh grade), 3 (late twelfth Grade), and 4 (one year after normal high-school graduation). Three latent constructs were considered: academic ability (T1 only) inferred on the basis of four standardized test scores, academic self-concept (T1, T2, and T4), and school achievement (T1, T2, T3). At T2, academic self-concept was influenced by academic ability and T1 academic self-concept, but not T1 school achievement. At T2

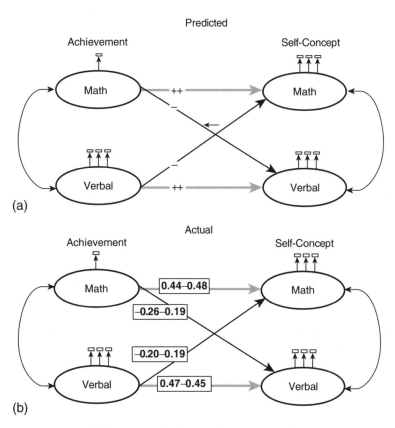

Figure 21.2   Predicted (A) and actual (B) results based on the I/E model. In A, the horizontal (positive) paths are predicted to be substantial and positive (++), whereas the cross (negative) paths are predicted to be smaller and negative (–). In B, the actual results for the total group analysis are based on responses from 15-year-olds from 26 countries and the corresponding results from multiple group analysis in which each country was considered separately (Marsh and Hau, 2004)

school achievement was influenced both by T1 academic self-concept and by T1 school achievement. Similarly, school achievement at T3 was influenced significantly both by T2 academic self-concept and by T2 achievement. Academic self-concept at T4 was influenced significantly by prior academic self-concept but not by T3 school achievement. Particularly since the results were replicated across two different time intervals, the findings provide strong support for the effect of prior self-concept on subsequent academic achievement. This study was important because it was one of the first to demonstrate the effect of prior academic self-concept on subsequent academic achievement and because it was apparently methodologically stronger than previous research.

In their review of causal-ordering research, Marsh et al. (1999) concluded that there was not a sufficiently strong basis for evaluating the generality of the REM for young children. Taking up this challenge, Guay et al. (2003) tested causal ordering between academic self-concept and academic achievement in a multicohort–multioccasion design (i.e. three age cohorts, each with three measurement waves) with students in grades 2, 3, and 4. They found that as children grew older, their academic self-concept responses became more reliable, more stable, and more strongly correlated with academic achievement. However, these differences were not large. The results of this study provided strong support for the REM for all three age cohorts, and support for a self-enhancement model was stronger than for a skill development model. Parameter estimates were invariant over the three age groups, demonstrating the generalizability of support for the REM. Because this study is apparently the methodologically strongest test of the causal ordering of academic self-concept differences for young children, it provides important new support for the REM.

Whereas the research reviewed here has focused specifically on academic self-concept research, recent meta-analytic research has considered self-belief constructs more generally (Valentine et al., 2004), and has found that the effect of prior self-beliefs on subsequent achievement after controlling for the effects of prior achievement was highly significant overall and positive in 90% of the studies in their meta-analysis. Furthermore, they found that the effects of prior self-beliefs were significantly stronger when the measure of self-belief was based on a domain-specific measure of self-concept rather than on global measures such as self-esteem, and when the self-concept and achievement measures were matched in terms of subject area (e.g. mathematics achievement and math self-concept). In particular, Valentine et al. (2004) reported little evidence of effects of global or generalized self-beliefs on academic achievement.

Generalizability to the physical domain

More recent research has tested the generalizability of the REM in the physical domain. Marsh et al. (2006a) demonstrated support for the REM in relation to gymnastics performance based upon expert judges' independent evaluations of videotaped performances on a standardized gymnastics performance test. Even after controlling for the effects of gender and age, the effect of T1 gymnastics self-concept on T2 gymnastics performance (0.20) and the effect of T1 gymnastics performance on T2 gymnastics self-concept (0.14) were both highly significant. Multiple group structural equation models indicated that support for the reciprocal effect model generalized over responses by boys and girls and by younger and older students.

Physical inactivity and sedentary lifestyles – leading to poor physical fitness, obesity, and a multitude of related health problems – constitute a worldwide health problem for which traditional preventive medicine interventions have had limited success. Marsh et al. (2006b) adapted the reciprocal effects model in a study of the causal ordering of physical self-concept and exercise behavior. Based on a large sample of Greek physical education classes (2,786 students, 200 classes, 67 teachers) tested early (T1) and late (T2) in the school year, results supported a REM in which prior (T1) physical self-concept and exercise behavior each influenced subsequent (T2) physical self-concept and exercise behavior.

Marsh and Perry (2005) extended REM research, testing the effect of self-concept on subsequent performance for a large sample of many of the best swimmers in the world, who competed in the Pan Pacific Swimming Championships in Australia and the World Short Course Championships in Greece (270 elite swimmers from 30 countries). Whereas subsequent championship performance was highly related to prior personal best performances ($r = 0.90$), structural equation models demonstrated that prior elite athlete self-concept contributed significantly to the prediction of subsequent championship performance, explaining approximately 10% of the residual variance after controlling for personal best performances. Furthermore, for swimmers who competed in two events, results based on the first event were replicated by results in the second event. The results show that elite athlete self-concept has an effect on the subsequent championship performances of elite swimmers beyond that which can be explained in terms of personal best performances. A positive self-concept contributes to winning gold medals.

Implications for practice

The direction of causality posited in the REM has important practical implications for mentors (e.g. teachers, coaches, counselors, and parents). If the direction of causality were from self-concept to performance (the self-enhancement model), then mentors might be justified in putting more effort into enhancing self-concepts rather than fostering skills and performance. On the other hand, if the

direction of causality were from performance to self-concept (the skill development model), then mentors should focus primarily on improving skills and performance as the best way to improve self-concept. In contrast to both these apparently overly simplistic (either–or) models, the reciprocal effects model implies that self-concept and performance are reciprocally related and mutually reinforcing. Improved self-concepts will lead to better performance *and* improved performance will lead to better self-concepts. For example, if mentors enhance self-concepts without improving underlying skills and performance, then the gains in self-concept are likely to be short-lived. However, if mentors improve performances and skills without also fostering self-beliefs in their capabilities, then the performance gains also are unlikely to be long lasting. If mentors focus on either one of these constructs to the exclusion of the other, then both are likely to suffer. Hence, according to the REM, mentors should strive to improve both self-concept and performance simultaneously.

Baumeister et al. (2003, 2005) claim to have exploded the self-esteem myth and to have shown that self-esteem has no benefits beyond 'seductive pleasure', and may even be detrimental to subsequent performance. These authors interpret their widely cited results to conflict with REM results, but Marsh and Craven (2006) disputed these interpretations; they demonstrate that the older, *unidimensional perspectives* that focus on global self-esteem underpin the Baumeister et al. study, whereas *multidimensional perspectives* that focus on specific components of self-concept are the basis of REM research. Thus, Baumeister et al. (2003, 2005) simply demonstrate that self-esteem has little or no positive effect on academic outcomes, and lend support to Marsh and Craven's use of the multidimensional perspective. Marsh and Craven's claim that academic self-concept has positive effects on subsequent achievement and accomplishments – whereas self-esteem does not – is also supported by the Valentine et al. (2004) meta-analysis. Hence, Marsh and Craven's review provides a constructive integration between what might superficially appear to be contradictory conclusions by Baumeister et al. (2003, 2005) and REM research.

FRAME OF REFERENCE EFFECTS IN THE FORMATION OF ACADEMIC SELF-CONCEPTS

Self-concept cannot be adequately understood if the role of frames of reference is ignored. The same objective characteristics and accomplishments can lead to disparate self-concepts depending on the frame of reference or standards of comparison that individuals use to evaluate themselves. Here I summarize research on two theoretical models of frame-of-reference effects.

Frame of reference and the big-fish-little-pond effect (BFLPE)

Does attending a school with exceptionally bright students increase or decrease academic self-concept? Do the effects of these academically selective schools vary for students differing in academic ability? Psychologists from the time of William James (1890/1963) have recognized that objective accomplishments are evaluated in relation to frames of reference. Thus James indicated, 'We have the paradox of a man shamed to death because he is only the second pugilist or the second oarsman in the world' (1890/1963: 310). The historical, theoretical underpinnings of this research (see review by Marsh, 2005, 2007; Marsh and Craven, 2002) derive from research in psychophysical judgment, social judgment, sociology, social comparison theory, and the theory of relative deprivation.

In an educational context, Marsh (1984, 2005; Marsh and Craven, 2002; Marsh and Parker, 1984; see also Byrne, 2002; Diener and Fujita, 1997) proposed a frame-of-reference model called the big-fish-little-pond effect (BFLPE) to encapsulate frame-of-reference effects posited in social comparison theory. In this model, Marsh hypothesized that individuals compare their abilities with the abilities of their classmates and use this social comparison impression as one basis for forming their own self-concept. A negative BFLPE occurs when equally able students have lower academic self-concepts when they compare themselves to more able classmates, and higher academic self-concepts when they compare themselves with less able classmates. According to this BFLPE model, academic self-concept is positively affected by individual achievement (more able students have higher self-concepts), but negatively affected by class-average average achievement (the same student will have a lower academic self-concept when class-average ability is high).

The BFLPE in academic settings is specific to academic self-concept. Marsh and Parker (1984) and Marsh (1987) showed that there were large negative BFLPEs for academic self-concept, but little or no BFLPEs for self-esteem. Marsh et al. (1995) reported two studies of the effects of participation in gifted and talented programs on different components of self-concept over time, and in relation to a matched comparison group. There was clear evidence for negative BFLPEs, in that academic self-concept in the gifted and talented programs declined over time and in relation to control groups. These BFLPEs were consistently large for math, verbal, and academic self-concepts, but were small and largely non-significant for physical, appearance, peer relationships, and parent relationships self-concepts, and for global self-esteem. Demonstrating the generalizability of the results, Marsh (1991, 1994) reported that the effects of school-average achievement were negative in two very large US studies, each based on nationally representative samples of more than 1,000 US high schools. In support of the BFLPE, Marsh and Craven (2002) summarized results from a diverse range of studies using different samples and methodological approaches, showing that: (a) educationally disadvantaged students have higher academic self-concepts in special education classes than in regular mixed-ability (mainstreamed) classes, whereas (b) academically gifted students have higher academic self-concepts in regular, mixed-ability classes than in specialized education settings for gifted students.

Support for the cross-cultural generalizability of the BFLPE comes from (a) a comparison of East and West German students' self-concepts following the fall of the Berlin Wall (West German students' choice of school was largely based on their academic ability, whereas East German schools were based on mixed ability) (Marsh et al., 2001) and (b) an evaluation of BFLPEs on attending academically selective Hong Kong high schools (Marsh et al., 2000). Marsh and Hau (2003) conducted the most comprehensive cross-cultural study of the BFLPE, based on nationally representative samples of approximately 4,000 15-year olds from each of 26 countries (103,558 students, 3,848 schools, 26 countries), who completed the same self-concept instrument and achievement tests. Consistent with the BFLPE, the effects of school-average achievement were negative in all 26 countries and, consistent with previous research, the size of the BFLPE did not vary with the students' initial ability levels.

Diener and Fujita (1997: 350) reviewed BFLPE research in relation to the broader social comparison literature and concluded that Marsh's BFLPE provided the clearest support for predictions based on social comparison theory in an imposed social comparison paradigm. The reason for this, they surmised, was that the frame of reference based on classmates within the same school was more clearly defined in BFLPE research than in most other research settings. Clearly, the importance of the school setting is that the relevance of the social comparisons in school settings is much more ecologically valid than manipulations in typical social

psychology experiments involving introductory psychology students in contrived settings. Indeed, except for opting out altogether, it is difficult for students to avoid the relevance of achievement as a reference point within a school setting or the social comparisons provided by the academic accomplishments of their classmates. Taken together, the research evidence suggests that the BFLPE is very robust, with broad generalizability across educational settings. The results also support the multidimensional perspective, in that self-esteem was nearly unrelated to both individual and school-average levels of achievement.

Internal/external frame of reference (I/E) model

Research in support of the domain specificity of academic self-concept identified a potential problem with the original Shavelson et al. (1976) model. According to this model, verbal, math, and other components of academic self-concept should be substantially correlated with each other and well explained by a higher-order, global component of academic self-concept. The rationale for this hypothesized structure was based on the well-established support for a single higher-order global ability factor (the so-called 'big g' factor) and the typically large correlation between math and verbal academic achievements (typically 0.5 to 0.8). Early self-concept research, however, demonstrated that math and verbal self-concepts were nearly uncorrelated and much more differentiated than the corresponding achievement scores (Marsh, 1986). Furthermore, this near-zero correlation was consistent across different measures of the math and verbal self-concepts and a diversity of settings. In order to explain this surprising lack of correlation between math and verbal self-concepts, Marsh (1986; Marsh and Craven, 1997; Marsh and Yeung, 1998) developed the internal/external frame of reference (I/E) model. According to this model, academic self-concept in a particular school subject is formed in relation to an *external* (social comparison) reference in which students compare their self-perceived performances in a particular school subject with the perceived performances of other students in the same school subject (as in the BFLPE), and an *internal* (ipsative-like) reference in which students compare their performances in the particular school subject with their own performances in other school subjects. The joint operation of these processes, depending on the relative weight given to each, is consistent with the near-zero correlation between math and verbal self-concepts, which led to the revision of the Shavelson et al. model.

Stronger tests of the I/E model are possible when math and verbal achievements are related to math and verbal self-concepts (see Figure 21.2A). The external comparison process predicts that good math skills lead to higher math self-concepts and that good verbal skills lead to higher verbal self-concepts. According to the internal comparison process, however, good math skills should lead to *lower* verbal self-concept (once the positive effects of good verbal skills are controlled). The better I am at mathematics, the poorer I am at verbal subjects (relative to my good math skills). Similarly, better verbal skills should lead to *lower* math self-concept (once the positive effects of good math skills are controlled). In models used to test this prediction (Figure 21.2A), the horizontal paths leading from math achievement to math self-concept and from verbal achievement to verbal self-concept (the grey horizontal lines in Figure 21.2A) are predicted to be substantially positive (indicated by '++' in Figure 21.2A). However, the cross-paths leading from math achievement to verbal self-concept and from verbal achievement to math self-concept (the dark lines in Figure 21.2A) are predicted to be negative. Marsh and Craven (1997) summarized support for these predictions in diverse studies based on SDQ responses. This pattern of results was subsequently

replicated for responses to each of three different self-concept instruments (Marsh et al., 1988), for the nationally representative sample of US high school students in the High School and Beyond Study, and for the nationally representative sample of US high school students in the National Longitudinal Study.

Marsh and Hau (2004) provided particularly persuasive support for the generality of the I/E model based on a cross-cultural study of nationally representative samples of 15-year olds from 26 countries (total $n = 55,577$). As predicted, the two horizontal paths relating math achievement to math self-concept (0.44) and reading achievement to verbal self-concept (0.47) were substantial and positive, whereas the two cross-paths leading from reading achievement to math self-concept (−0.20) and mathematics achievement to verbal self-concept (−0.26) were negative. Also of relevance is the observation that the (zero-order) correlation between math and verbal achievement factors ($r = 0.78$) was very large, whereas the corresponding correlation between math and verbal self-concept factors ($r = 0.10$) was substantially lower. Marsh and Hau then conducted multigroup CFAs and SEMs in which they constrained different parameters to be invariant across the 26 groups. Although the imposition of these added invariance constraints resulted in small decrements in fit, even the highly restrictive model of total invariance (i.e. requiring every parameter to be the same in all 26 groups) provided a good fit to the data that differed only slightly from the baseline model with no invariance constraints. These results support the cross-cultural generalizability of the measures and the relations among them across these 26 countries.

The extreme domain specificity of academic self-concepts, which led to the development of the I/E model, has important implications for any lingering debates about the relative importance of unidimensional and multidimensional perspectives of self-concept. Clearly, the relationship between self-concepts in particular academic areas and corresponding areas of academic achievement cannot be adequately understood if researchers rely solely on global measures of general self-concept or self-esteem. Indeed, the Marsh and Hau results demonstrate that not even global measures of academic self-concept are sufficient to understand the interplay between self-perceptions in different academic domains, which is the basis of the internal comparison process in the I/E model.

PERSONALITY: RELATIONS BETWEEN BIG FIVE PERSONALITY FACTORS, WELL-BEING AND SELF-CONCEPT

In personality research, Marsh et al. (2006c) noted that most researchers still rely primarily on measures of self-esteem rather than on multiple dimensions of self-concept. Personality researchers differentiate between core personality traits such as the Big Five (neuroticism, extraversion, conscientiousness, agreeableness, and openness) and more malleable personality characteristics such as self-concept. Within both the self-concept and personality research literatures, there is strong support for the need to evaluate each of these constructs from a multidimensional perspective, but the research that brings these two multidimensional perspectives together is limited.

In a review of studies relating self-esteem and personality factors, Marsh et al. reported that self-esteem was negatively related to neuroticism and somewhat less positively related to extraversion. Watson et al. (2002) noted that only a few studies have related self-esteem to the complete set of Big Five factors, but that based on this limited research, self-esteem was positively correlated with conscientiousness (*Md r = 0.32*), openness (*Md r = 0.16*), and agreeableness (*Md r = 0.19*). In a large Internet study (Robins et al., 2001), the set of Big Five personality factors accounted for 34% of the variance in self-esteem. Asendorpf and van Aken (2003) related Big Five personality

factors to global self-esteem and to domain-specific social self-concept, measured by Harter's (1985) peer acceptance scale and Marsh's SDQIII. They found that global self-esteem was most closely related to neuroticism, whereas social self-concept was most closely related to extraversion. However, Marsh et al. (2006c) found no previous research in which a well-defined, multidimensional set of personality factors is related to a well-defined, multidimensional set of self-concept factors, leading them to conclude that there was insufficient research to even begin the exciting task of mapping the multivariate pattern of relations between multiple dimensions of personality and multiple dimensions of self-concept.

In order to address this problem, Marsh et al. (2006c) evaluated relations between multiple dimensions of self-concept, personality (Big Five), well-being (positive and negative affect and life satisfaction), and academic outcomes (school grades, test scores, coursework selection) for a large (*n* = 4,475) sample of German adolescents. They found support for the construct validity of a well-defined, multidimensional set of self-concept factors in relation to personality factors, and vice-versa. CFAs of the German adaptation of the SDQIII demonstrated 17 a priori, reasonably independent self-concept factors (*M* correlation = 0.14) which had a highly differentiated pattern of relations with the personality factors and academic outcomes.

In an evaluation of multidimensional and unidimensional perspectives of self-concept, they evaluated how much variance in each of the Big Five and well-being factors could be explained by the specific self-concept factors and by global self-esteem. The percentage of variance that could be uniquely explained by the specific self-concept factors was always substantial, varying between 23 and 60% (*M* = 39%) for the Big Five factors and between 14 and 19% (*M* = 17%) for the well-being factors. In contrast, almost no variance could be uniquely explained by self-esteem in any of the Big Five or the well-being factors. This highly differentiated multivariate pattern of relations between self-concept and personality factors argues against the unidimensional perspective of self-concept still prevalent in personality research.

A detailed evaluation of relations among these constructs provided support for convergent validity (self-concept and personality factors that were logically related were substantially correlated) and divergent validity (self-concept and personality factors that were not logically related were not substantially related). The specificity of this pattern of relations was particularly evident in the seven higher-order factors that incorporated both self-concept and personality factors. Each of the Big Five personality factors loaded primarily on one and only one of these higher-order factors, thus supporting a multidimensional perspective of personality. Furthermore, specific components of self-concept most logically related to each of these Big Five personality factors also loaded on the same higher-order factor as the corresponding personality factor. Two of the higher-order factors (reflecting the quantitative-academic components of self-concept and religious self-concept) were relatively independent of all personality factors. In support of a multidimensional perspective of self-concept, self-esteem loaded substantially on only one of the seven higher-order factors and was not the highest loading self-concept factor on any of the higher-order factors.

Marsh et al. (2006c) also evaluated the patterns of relations among self-concept factors, personality factors, and a diverse set of nine academic indicators that are very important for adolescent students approaching the end of their high school careers and contemplating university. Support for the multidimensional perspective of self-concept was clear and unambiguous; self-esteem was nearly uncorrelated with each of the nine non-academic outcome measures (r's varied from −0.03 to 0.05). In contrast, there was a highly differentiated pattern of substantial relations between these academic outcomes and the academic components of self-concept.

For example, math self-concept was substantially and positively related to math school grades (0.71), math standardized achievement test scores (0.59), and taking advanced math courses (0.51), but was nearly unrelated or even negatively related to English and German outcomes. Math and verbal self-concepts, consistent with the internal/external frame of reference model, were negatively related to each other, and this extreme domain specificity was reflected in the systematic and substantial relations with academic criteria measures. Whereas academic components of self-concept were substantially related to the academic outcomes, the non-academic components of self-concept were almost unrelated to these outcomes. Interestingly, Big Five personality and well-being factors were only moderately related to the academic outcomes and contributed no variance to the prediction of these outcomes that could not also be explained by academic components of self-concept.

By providing a detailed mapping of personality and self-concept factors, Marsh et al. have set the stage for integrating the rich traditions of personality and self-concept research. Although this is beyond the scope of this chapter, it is interesting to speculate on some directions that this research might take – emphasizing the core-surface distinction posited in some personality research (e.g. Asendorpf and van Aken, 2003). In the extreme version of the core-surface distinction, (core) personality factors are expected to cause (surface) self-concept factors, whereas self-concept is expected to have no causal effect on personality traits. In contrast to this extreme position, the pattern of relations is more likely to be reciprocal, such that personality factors and self-concept factors are both causes and effects of each other – although the causal effects of personality are likely to be stronger than those of self-concept on personality. Whereas tests of causal ordering with variables not amenable to experimental manipulation are always a hazardous undertaking, the well-developed REM methodology used to test the causal-ordering of self-concept and achievement (see earlier discussion) is clearly relevant. At least some personality researchers argue that personality should be relatively immune to context, situation, life events, and environmental effects (see McCrae and Costa, 1999). The extreme version of this prediction is unlikely to be supported (cf. Asendorpf and van Aken, 2003; Roberts et al., 2003). Furthermore, to the extent that these external influences do impact personality, the effects are likely to be substantially mediated by changes in multiple dimensions of self-concept. Moreover, it is further suspected that causal effects of personality on behavior are also likely to be mediated at least in part by self-concept. By providing a mapping of core personality and self-concept factors, the Marsh et al. (2006c) study sets the stage for research examining such mediating effects.

REFERENCES

Asendorpf, J.B. and van Aken, M.A.G. (2003) 'Personality-relationship transaction in adolescence: Core versus surface personality characteristics', *Journal of Personality*, 71(4): 629–62.

Baumeister, R.F., Campbell, J.D., Krueger, J.I. and Vohs, K.D. (2003) 'Does high self-esteem cause better performance, interpersonal success, happiness, or healthier lifestyles?', *Psychological Science in the Public Interest*, 4(1): 1–44.

Baumeister, R.F., Campbell, J.D., Krueger, J.I. and Vohs, K.E. (2005) 'Exploding the self-esteem myth', *Scientific American*, 292: 84–92.

Boyle, G.J. (1994) 'Self-Description Questionnaire II', *Test Critiques*, 10(10): 632–43.

Bracken, B.A. (1996) (ed.), *Handbook of Self-concept: Developmental, Social, and Clinical Considerations*. New York: Wiley.

Branden, N. (1994) *Six Pillars of Self-esteem*. New York: Bantam.

Byrne, B.M. (1996a) *Measuring Self-Concept Across the Life Span: Issues and Instrumentation*. Washington, DC: American Psychological Association.

Byrne, B.M. (1996b) 'Academic self-concept: Its structure, measurement, and relation to academic achievement', in B.A. Bracken (ed.), *Handbook of Self-concept: Developmental, Social, and Clinical Considerations*. New York: Wiley, pp. 287–316.

Byrne, B.M. (2002) 'Validating measurement and structure of self-concept: Snapshots of past, present and future research', *American Psychologist*, 57(11): 897–909.

Calsyn, R. and Kenny, D. (1977) 'Self-concept of ability and perceived evaluations by others: Cause or effect of academic achievement?', *Journal of Educational Psychology*, 69(2): 136–45.

Campbell, D.T. and Fiske, D.W. (1959) 'Convergent and discriminant validation by the multitrait-multimethod matrix', *Psychological Bulletin*, 56(2): 81–105.

Coopersmith, S.A. (1967) *The Antecedents of Self-Esteem*. San Francisco: W.H. Freeman.

Diener, E. and Fujita, F. (1997) 'Social comparison and subjective well-being', in B.P. Buunk and F.X. Gibbons (eds), *Health, Coping, and Well-being: Perspectives from Social Comparison Theory*. Mahwah, NJ: Erlbaum, pp. 329–58.

Eccles, J., Wigfield, A., Harold, R.D. and Blumenfeld, P. (1993) 'Age and gender differences in children's self- and task-perceptions during elementary school', *Child Development*, 64(3): 830–47.

Eder, R.A. and Mangelsdorf, S.C. (1997) 'The emotional basis of early personality development: Implications for the emergent self-concept', in R. Hogan, J. Johnson and S. Briggs (eds), *Handbook of Personality Psychology*. San Diego: Academic Press. pp. 209–40.

Fox, K.R. and Corbin, C.B. (1989) 'The physical self-perception profile: Development and preliminary validation', *Journal of Sport and Exercise Psychology*, 11(4): 408–30.

Greenwald, A.G. (1988) 'A social-cognitive account of the self's development', in D.K. Lapsley and F.C. Power (eds), *Self, Ego and Identity: Interpretative Approaches*. New York: Springer-Verlag, pp. 30–42.

Guay, F., Marsh, H.W. and Boivin, M. (2003) 'Academic self-concept and academic achievement: Developmental perspectives on their causal ordering', *Journal of Educational Psychology*, 95(1): 124–36.

Haney, P. and Durlak, J.A. (1998) 'Changing self-esteem in children and adolescents: A meta-analytic review', *Journal of Clinical Child Psychology*, 27(4): 423–33.

Hansford, B.C. and Hattie, J.A. (1982) 'The relationship between self and achievement/performance measures', *Review of Educational Research*, 52(1): 123–42.

Harter, S. (1985) *Manual for the Self-Perception Profile for Children*. Denver, CO: University of Denver.

Harter, S. (1998) 'The development of self-representations', in W. Damon (series ed.) and N. Eisenberg (vol. ed.), *Handbook of Child Psychology: Vol. 3. Social, Emotional and Personality Development* (5th edn). New York: Wiley, pp. 553–617.

Hattie, J. (1992) *Self-Concept*. Hillsdale, NJ: Erlbaum.

James, W. (1890/1963) *The Principles of Psychology*. New York: Holt, Rinehart & Winston (work originally published 1890).

Kagen, S.L., Moore, E. and Bredekamp, S. (1995) 'Considering Children's Early Development and Learning: Toward Common Views and Vocabulary', Report N. 95-03. Washington, DC: National Education Goals Pane.

Kling, K.C., Hyde, J.S., Showers, C.J. and Buswell, B.N. (1999) 'Gender differences in self-esteem: A meta-analysis', *Psychological Bulletin*, 125(4): 470–500.

Marsh, H.W. (1984) 'Self-concept: The application of a frame of reference model to explain paradoxical results', *Australian Journal of Education*, 28(2): 165–81.

Marsh, H.W. (1986) 'Verbal and math self-concepts: An internal/external frame of reference model', *American Educational Research Journal*, 23(4): 129–49.

Marsh, H.W. (1987) 'The big-fish-little-pond effect on academic self-concept', *Journal of Educational Psychology*, 79(3): 280–95.

Marsh, H.W. (1989) 'Age and sex effects in multiple dimensions of self-concept: Preadolescence to early-adulthood', *Journal of Educational Psychology*, 81(3): 417–30.

Marsh, H.W. (1990a) 'The causal ordering of academic self-concept and academic achievement: A multiwave, longitudinal panel analysis', *Journal of Educational Psychology*, 82(4): 646–56.

Marsh, H.W. (1990b) 'A multidimensional, hierarchical self-concept: Theoretical and empirical justification', *Educational Psychology Review*, 2(2): 77–172.

Marsh, H.W. (1991) 'The failure of high ability high schools to deliver academic benefits: The importance of academic self-concept and educational aspirations', *American Educational Research Journal*, 28(2): 445–80.

Marsh, H.W. (1992) 'The content specificity of relations between academic achievement and academic self-concept', *Journal of Educational Psychology*, 84(1): 35–42.

Marsh, H.W. (1993) 'Academic self-concept: Theory measurement and research', in J. Suls (ed.), *Psychological Perspectives on the Self* (Vol. 4). Hillsdale, NJ: Erlbaum, pp. 59–98.

Marsh, H.W. (1994) 'Using the National Educational Longitudinal Study of 1988 to evaluate theoretical models of self-concept: The Self-Description Questionnaire', *Journal of Educational Psychology*, 86(3): 439–56.

Marsh, H.W. (1996) 'Physical Self Description Questionnaire: Stability and discriminant validity', *Research Quarterly for Exercise and Sport*, 67(3): 249–64.

Marsh, H.W. (1997) 'The measurement of physical self-concept: A construct validation approach', in K. Fox (ed.), *The Physical Self: From Motivation to Well-Being*. Champaign, IL: Human Kinetics, pp. 27–58.

Marsh, H.W. (2002) 'A multidimensional physical self-concept: A construct validity approach to theory, measurement, and research', *Psychology: The Journal of the Hellenic Psychological Society*, 9(4): 459–93.

Marsh, H.W. (2005) 'Big fish little pond effect on academic self-concept', *German Journal of Educational Psychology*, 19(3): 119–28.

Marsh, H.W. (2007) *Self-concept Theory, Measurement and Research into Practice: The role of Self-concept in Educational Psychology*. Leicester, UK: British Psychological Society.

Marsh, H.W. and Byrne, B.M. (1991) 'The differentiated additive androgyny model: Relations between masculinity, femininity, and multiple dimensions of self-concept', *Journal of Personality and Social Psychology*, 61(5): 811–28.

Marsh, H.W. and Byrne, B.M. (1993) 'Do we see ourselves as others infer: A comparison of self–other agreement on multiple dimensions of self-concept from two continents',

Australian Journal of Psychology, 45(1): 49–58.

Marsh, H.W., Byrne, B.M. and Shavelson, R. (1988) 'A multifaceted academic self-concept: Its hierarchical structure and its relation to academic achievement', *Journal of Educational Psychology*, 80(3): 366–80.

Marsh, H.W., Byrne, B.M. and Yeung, A.S. (1999) 'Causal ordering of academic self-concept and achievement: Reanalysis of a pioneering study and revised recommendations', *Educational Psychologist*, 34(3): 154–7.

Marsh, H.W., Chanal, J.P., Sarrazin, P.G. and Bois, J.E. (2006a) 'Self-belief does make a difference: A reciprocal effects model of the causal ordering of physical self-concept and gymnastics performance', *Journal of Sport Sciences*, 24(1): 101–11.

Marsh, H.W., Chessor, D., Craven, R.G. and Roche, L. (1995) 'The effects of gifted and talented programs on academic self-concept: The big fish strikes again', *American Educational Research Journal*, 32(2): 285–319.

Marsh, H.W. and Craven, R.G. (1997) 'Academic self-concept: Beyond the dust-bowl', in G. Phye (ed.), *Handbook of Classroom Assessment: Learning, Achievement and Adjustment*. Orlando, FL: Academic Press.

Marsh, H.W. and Craven, R. (2002) 'The pivotal role of frames of reference in academic self-concept formation: The big fish little pond effect', in F. Pajares and T. Urdan (eds), *Adolescence and Education* (Vol. II). Greenwich, CT: Information Age, pp. 83–123.

Marsh, H.W. and Craven, R.G. (2006) 'Reciprocal effects of self-concept and performance from a multidimensional perspective: Beyond seductive pleasure and unidimensional perspectives', *Perspectives on Psychological Science*, 1(2): 133–63.

Marsh, H.W., Craven, R.G. and Debus, R. (1991) 'Self-concepts of young children aged 5 to 8: Their measurement and multidimensional structure', *Journal of Educational Psychology*, 83(3): 377–92.

Marsh, H.W., Craven, R.G. and Debus, R. (1998) 'Structure, stability, and development of young children's self-concepts: A multicohort-multioccasion study', *Child Development*, 69(4): 1030–53.

Marsh, H.W., Debus, R. and Bornholt, L. (2005a) 'Validating young children's self-concept responses: Methodological ways and means to understand their responses', in D.M. Teti (ed.), *Handbook of Research Methods in Developmental Science*. Oxford: Blackwell Publishers, pp. 138–60.

Marsh, H.W. and Hattie, J. (1996) 'Theoretical perspectives on the structure of self-concept', in B.A. Bracken (ed.), *Handbook of Self-concept*. New York: Wiley, pp. 38–90.

Marsh, H.W. and Hau, K.T. (2003) 'Big fish little pond effect on academic self-concept: A crosscultural (26 country) test of the negative effects of academically selective schools', *American Psychologist*, 58(5): 364–76.

Marsh, H.W. and Hau, K.T. (2004) 'Explaining paradoxical relations between academic self-concepts and achievements: Cross-cultural generalizability of the internal-external frame of reference predictions across 26 countries', *Journal of Educational Psychology*, 96(1): 56–67.

Marsh, H.W., Köller, O. and Baumert, J. (2001) 'Reunification of East and West German school systems: Longitudinal multilevel modeling study of the big fish little pond effect on academic self-concept', *American Educational Research Journal*, 38(2): 321–50.

Marsh, H.W., Kong, C-K., Hau, K-T. (2000) 'Longitudinal multilevel modeling of the big fish little pond effect on academic self-concept: Counterbalancing social comparison and reflected glory effects in Hong Kong high schools', *Journal of Personality and Social Psychology*, 78(2): 337–49.

Marsh, H.W. and Myers, M.R. (1986) 'Masculinity, femininity, and androgyny: A methodological and theoretical critique', *Sex Roles*, 14(7–8): 397–430.

Marsh, H.W. and O'Neill, R. (1984) 'Self Description Questionnaire III: The construct validity of multidimensional self-concept ratings by late adolescents', *Journal of Educational Measurement*, 21(2): 153–74.

Marsh, H.W., Papaioannou, A. and Theodorakis, Y. (2006b) 'Causal ordering of physical self-concept and exercise behavior: Reciprocal effects model and the influence of physical education teachers', *Health Psychology*, 25(3): 316–28.

Marsh, H.W., Parada, R.H. and Ayotte, V. (2004a) 'A multidimensional perspective of relations between self-concept (Self Description Questionnaire II) and adolescent mental health (Youth Self-Report)', *Psychological Assessment*, 16(1): 27–41.

Marsh, H.W., Parada, R.H., Craven, R.G. and Finger, L. (2004b) 'In the looking glass: A reciprocal effects model elucidating the complex nature of bullying, psychological determinants and the central role of self-concept', in C.S. Sanders and G.D. Phye (eds), *Bullying: Implications for the Classroom.* Orlando, FL: Elsevier Academic Press, pp. 63–106.

Marsh, H.W. and Parker, J.W. (1984) 'Determinants of student self-concept: Is it better to be a relatively large fish in a small pond even if you don't learn to swim as well?', *Journal of Personality and Social Psychology*, 47(1): 213–31.

Marsh, H.W. and Peart, N. (1988) 'Competitive and cooperative physical fitness training programs for girls: Effects on physical fitness and on multidimensional self-concepts', *Journal of Sport and Exercise Psychology*, 10(4): 390–407.

Marsh, H.W. and Perry, C. (2005) 'Does a positive self-concept contribute to winning gold medals in elite swimming? The causal ordering of elite athlete self-concept and championship performances', *Journal of Sport and Exercise Psychology*, 27(1): 71–91.

Marsh, H.W. and Richards, G. (1988) The Outward Bound Bridging Course for low achieving high-school males: Effect on academic achievement and multidimensional self-concepts', *Australian Journal of Psychology*, 40(3): 281–98.

Marsh, H.W., Richards, G.E., Johnson, S., Roche, L. and Tremayne, P. (1994) 'Physical Self Description Questionnaire: Psychometric properties and a multitrait-multimethod analysis of relations to existing instruments', *Sport and Exercise Psychology*, 16(3): 270–305.

Marsh, H.W., Richards, G. and Barnes, J. (1986a) 'Multidimensional self-concepts: A long term follow-up of the effect of participation in an Outward Bound program', *Personality and Social Psychology Bulletin*, 12(4): 475–92.

Marsh, H.W., Richards, G. and Barnes, J. (1986b) 'Multidimensional self-concepts: The effect of participation in an Outward Bound program', *Journal of Personality and Social Psychology*, 45(6): 173–87.

Marsh, H.W. and Shavelson, R. (1985) 'Self-concept: Its multifaceted, hierarchical structure', *Educational Psychologist*, 20(3): 107–25.

Marsh, H.W., Trautwein, U., Lüdtke, O., Köller, O. and Baumert, J. (2005b) 'Academic self-concept, interest, grades and standardized test scores: Reciprocal effects models of causal ordering', *Child Development*, 76(2): 297–416.

Marsh, H.W., Trautwein, U., Lüdtke, O., Köller, O. and Baumert, J. (2006c) Integration of multidimensional self-concept and core personality constructs: Construct validation and relations to well-being and achievement', *Journal of Personality*, 74(2): 403–55.

Marsh, H.W. and Yeung, A.S. (1998) 'Longitudinal structural equation models of academic self-concept and achievement: Gender differences in the development of math and English constructs', *American Educational Research Journal*, 35(4): 705–38.

Marsh, H.W. and Yeung, A.S. (1999) 'The lability of psychological ratings: The chameleon effect in global self-esteem', *Personality and Social Psychology Bulletin*, 25(1): 49–64.

McCrae, R.R. and Costa, P.T. Jr. (1987) 'Validation of the five-factor model of personality across instruments and observers', *Journal of Personality and Social Psychology*, 52(1): 81–90.

McCrae, R.R. and Costa, P.T. Jr. (1988) 'Different points of view: Self-reports and ratings in the assessment of personality', Paper presented at the XXIV International Congress of Psychology, Sydney, Australia.

McCrae, R.R. and Costa, P.T. Jr. (1999) 'A five-factor theory of personality', in L. Pervin and O.P. John (eds), *Handbook of Personality: Theory and Research* (2nd edn). New York: Guilford, pp. 139–53.

O'Mara, A.J., Marsh H.W., Craven, R.G. and Debus, R. (2006) 'Do self-concept interventions make a difference? A synergistic blend of construct validation and meta-analysis', *Educational Psychologist*, 41(3): 181–206.

Roberts, B.W., Caspi, A. and Moffitt, T. (2003) 'Work experiences and personality development in young adulthood', *Journal of Personality and Social Psychology*, 84(3): 582–93.

Robins, R.W., Tracy, J.L., Trzesniewski, K., Potter, J. and Gosling, S.D. (2001) 'Personality correlates of self-esteem', *Journal of Research in Personality*, 35(4): 463–82.

Rosenberg, M. (1979) *Conceiving the Self*. New York: Basic Books.

Rosenberg, M., Schooler, C., Schoenbach, C. and Rosenberg, F. (1995) 'Global self-esteem and specific self-esteem: Different concepts, different outcomes', *American Sociological Review*, 60: 141–56.

Shavelson, R.J. and Bolus, R. (1982) 'Self-concept: The interplay of theory and methods', *Journal of Educational Psychology*, 74(1): 3–17.

Shavelson, R.J., Hubner, J.J. and Stanton, G.C. (1976) 'Validation of construct interpretations', *Review of Educational Research*, 46(3): 407–41.

Shrauger, J.S. and Schoeneman, T.J. (1979) 'Symbolic interactionist view of self-concept: Through the glass darkly', *Psychological Bulletin*, 86: 549–73.

Valentine, J.C., DuBois, D.L. and Cooper, H. (2004) 'The relation between self-beliefs and academic achievement: A meta-analytic review', *Educational Psychologist*, 39: 111–33.

Watson, D., Suls, J. and Haig, J. (2002) 'Global self-esteem in relation to structural models of personality and affectivity', *Journal of Personality and Social Psychology*, 83(1): 185–97.

Wells, L.E. and Marwell, G. (1976) *Self-esteem: Its Conceptualization and Measurement*. Beverly Hills, CA: Sage Publications.

Wylie, R.C. (1979) *The Self-concept* (Vol. 2). Lincoln: University of Nebraska Press.

Wylie, R.C. (1989) *Measures of Self-concept*. Lincoln: University of Nebraska Press.

22

Optimism and Pessimism as Personality Variables Linked to Adjustment

Rita Chang, Edward C. Chang, Lawrence J. Sanna and Robert L. Hatcher

It is a frigid winter day and the ground is covered with eight inches of snow. You are searching for a parking spot in a crowded lot when a car nearby pulls out. The spot is relatively close to the entrance of the store but would still require a short walk. Do you take it and brave the walk or try to find a closer spot, risking losing the current opening? It depends on who you ask.

HISTORICAL CONCEPTIONS AND CURRENT MODELS OF OPTIMISM AND PESSIMISM

Philosophers and scholars have long been interested in the different ways that optimistic and pessimistic people experience the world (Sicinski, 1972; Tiger, 1979). According to philosophers like Heidegger (1927/1962), it is the power of possibility that represents an important determination of who and what we are, and how we exist in the world. And among the range of possibilities that

influence our existence, two stand out, namely expectations that good things will happen (*bonum futurum*) and expectations that bad things will happen (*malum futurum*), or in more lay terms, optimism and pessimism. While the ultimate question of the meaning of existence has continued to remain a central point of inquiry for philosophers and theologians alike, psychologists have been actively examining the power of optimism and pessimism in our lives.

Psychologists have also known for years that optimism and pessimism exert a great deal of influence on decision-making, risk-taking, and physical and mental health (see Chang, 2001, for a review), but that is where the consensus ends. Existing research on optimism and pessimism is fraught with disagreements about the definitions of optimism–pessimism as well as the relation of optimism to pessimism (Peterson and Chang, 2003). The most accepted description of the constructs at the present is arguably Scheier and Carver's (1985) view of optimism and pessimism as generalized positive and negative outcome expectancies. Other investigators (Dember et al., 1989) have defined those constructs more broadly as a positive and negative outlook on life. Whereas Scheier and Carver conceptualize optimism–pessimism as relating to future expectations only, Dember et al. include present perceptions as well as future expectations in their model. To make matters more complicated, researchers have written about optimistic and pessimistic explanatory styles (Peterson and Seligman, 1987), optimistic biases or illusions (Taylor and Brown, 1988), unrealistic optimism (Weinstein and Klein, 1996), unrealistic pessimism (Dolinksi et al., 1987), and defensive pessimism (Norem and Cantor, 1986), just to name a few. All those models may tap into interrelated but distinct cognitive processes.

MEASURES RELATED TO OPTIMISM AND PESSIMISM

There are as many different measures of optimism–pessimism as there are definitions, and the variety has raised questions about the dimensional structure of optimism and pessimism. It is unclear whether optimism and pessimism are unidimensional, such that high scores on the former preclude high scores on the latter (and vice versa), or whether they represent partially independent dimensions. Scheier and Carver's (1985) life orientation test (LOT) was designed to measure generalized outcome expectancies and consists of eight five-point Likert-type items (plus four filler items), four positively worded and four negatively worded. The test provides a single summary score, with high scores indicating more pessimism. The single score assumes that optimism and pessimism are unidimensional, though Chang et al. (1994) have argued that the original factor analysis of the LOT produced equivocal results. Chang et al. addressed that issue by running exploratory and confirmatory factor analyses on the LOT and found that a two-factor model was more appropriate

than a one-factor model. The correlation between the factors was −0.54. Chang et al. (1997) replicated their previous findings and also found that the separate use of the optimism and pessimism subscales lead to better prediction of variables like life satisfaction and depressive symptoms. Other researchers have obtained similar results (Kubzansky et al., 2004; Marshall et al., 1992; Robinson-Whelen et al., 1997), though Roysamb and Strype (2002) have argued that the bidimensionality of the LOT found in several studies might be partly due to a method artifact. Scheier et al. (1994) later revised the LOT to create the LOT-R by removing a few items that didn't directly relate to the expectation of positive outcomes and replacing one of the removed items while maintaining the unidimensional structure of the test. Interestingly, a recent large-scale study involving over 46,000 adults showed that the LOT-R may actually be better viewed as a measure tapping for bidimensional optimism and pessimism (Herzberg et al., 2006). A bidimensional view of these constructs has also been important in distinguishing optimism from neuroticism (Smith et al., 1989). Indeed, Chang (1998b; 2002b; Chang and D'Zurilla, 1996) has shown that when optimism and pessimism are examined separately, it is largely pessimism, not lack of optimism, that is most strongly associated with measures of neuroticism and negative affective conditions.

Aaron Beck developed the hopelessness scale (HS) (Beck et al., 1974) to reflect the negative expectancies that individuals may have about themselves and their future lives. A measure of pessimism, the HS consists of 20 true-false items, 11 of which are worded negatively (negative expectancies) and nine of which are worded positively (positive expectancies). Higher scores indicate greater pessimism or 'hopelessness'. Beck et al. (1974) performed a principal components analysis on the HS and extracted three factors labeled 'feelings about the future', 'loss of motivation', and 'future expectations'. Since the development of the HS, several researchers have attempted to verify the factor structure of the scale with mixed results. Factor analyses have pointed to a bidimensional structure relating to optimism and pessimism (Marshall et al., 1992), a bidimensional structure relating to pessimism about the future and resignation to the futility of changing the future (Steer et al., 1997), and a unidimensional structure (Aish and Wasserman, 2001).

Andersen's (1990) future events scale (FES) was developed to measure hopelessness as well as pessimism, and the use of the FES as a measure of hopelessness is distinct from its use as a measure of optimism–pessimism (e.g. Andersen and Schwartz, 1992). The FES relies on participants' judgment of the likelihood of specific positive and negative future events as opposed to their self-assessment. The measure is composed of 26 items and participants indicate on a Likert-type scale the likelihood of each event happening to them. The aggregate score for the positive items is typically subtracted from the aggregate score for the negative items; higher scores indicate greater pessimism. But a recent factor analysis of the FES supported a two-factor structure (Wichman et al., 2006). The authors also compared the LOT to the FES and found that the two scale share only 15–24% of the variance, which suggests that the scales measure different constructs.

Finally, Dember et al. (1989) developed the optimism and pessimism scale (OPS) to measure optimism and pessimism in a broad sense. In their model, optimism refers to a perceptual bias and expectancies in favor of the positive features of life and pessimism refers to a bias and expectancies in favor of the negative features of life. The OPS consists of 56 Likert-type items, 18 to assess optimism and 18 to assess pessimism. The remaining 20 items are filler items. Initially, the OPS provided a single summary score, but when the authors obtained separate optimism and pessimism scores and correlated them, they found only a moderate correlation between optimism and pessimism. Given the high internal consistency of the individual items subsets, the authors began to question the assumption that optimism and pessimism represent a single dimension. Interestingly, Chang et al. (1994) found a multidimensional structure for the OPS, and they suggested that the broad definition of optimism–pessimism from which the instrument was created might be tapping into other constructs like life satisfaction, mood, and self-esteem. After analyzing an abbreviated version of the OPS consisting only of items that best fit the definition of optimism and pessimism as positive and negative outcome expectancies, Chang et al. found that a two-factor model fit the data satisfactorily. Comparing the OPS to the LOT-R, Burke et al. (2000) found that the scales may not be measuring similar constructs. According to the authors, the LOT-R may be measuring 'trait' optimism and pessimism, whereas the OPS may be measuring 'state' optimism and pessimism.

A bidimensional model of optimism–pessimism is defensible from a theoretical perspective. In transactional stress theory (Lazarus and Folkman, 1984) and social-learning theory (Bandura, 1986), cognitive appraisals and outcome expectancies are conceived as situation-specific responses rather than trait-like characteristics. So even though there may be some generalization across situations, an individual may have unequal levels of optimism and pessimism across different domains in his or her life. For example, one may be optimistic about receiving a promotion but pessimistic about finding a romantic partner. In a study of older adults suffering from arthritis, Benyamini (2005) showed that high optimism and high pessimism could co-exist and interacted with each other to affect coping strategies. Benyamini suggested that optimism and pessimism may become more independent as one ages because increased problems with health may force even normally optimistic individuals to expect the negative. The author also suggested that optimism–pessimism may appear more unidimensional or bidimensional depending on the particular events or domains of life that came to mind when the participants filled out the measures, citing Robinson-Whelen et al.'s (1997) finding that the optimism–pessimism correlation was significantly higher among caregivers of family members with progressive, dementing illnesses than it was for non-caregivers. Individuals experiencing an extreme life stressor may be less able to perceive the possibility of both good and bad for the future, and they may be more likely to respond to optimism–pessimism measures with their specific stressor in mind. Future studies can shed light on the dimensional nature of optimism–pessimism by designating specific domains of life on which participants should focus or taking into account age or levels of life stress.

ADAPTIVE AND MALADAPTIVE FUNCTIONS OF OPTIMISM AND PESSIMISM

Most models of optimism and pessimism have underscored the inherently adaptive nature of optimism and the maladaptive nature of pessimism, and a large body of research does demonstrate the link between optimism–pessimism and various psychological and physiological outcomes. Overall, optimism seems to be related to psychological benefits such as greater life satisfaction, more positive affect, and fewer depressive symptoms (Chang, 1998c; Chang and Sanna, 2001; Marshall et al., 1992; Scheier et al., 2001) while pessimism seems to be related to detriments such as more depressive symptoms, negative affect, and psychological stress (Chang, 1998c; Chang, 2002a; Strunk et al., 2006). Optimism and pessimism also interact with factors like life stress to affect outcome. Chang and Sanna (2003a) found that when faced with life hassles, adolescents who were pessimistic developed significantly more depressive symptoms and hopelessness than those who were optimistic. Similarly, pessimistic older adults are more likely to develop psychological symptoms when they

are experiencing high levels of self-appraised life stress (Chang, 2002a) than optimistic older adults.

In addition, optimists tend to use more active or problem-focused methods to cope with stressors (see Nes and Segerstrom, 2006, for a review) and exhibit more persistence in mastering difficult tasks (Nes et al., 2005; Segerstrom, 2001a) compared with pessimists, and those tendencies might lead to positive effects in the long run such as greater success and accomplishments. In a study of men who had undergone HIV testing, Taylor et al. (1992) found that individuals with more dispositional optimism engaged in less avoidant coping. Participants who scored high on AIDS-specific optimism (optimism about the likelihood of developing AIDS) were also more likely to adopt health-promoting behaviors like proper diet, rest, and exercise than individuals who were pessimistic, regardless of their HIV status. Of course, such instances of active coping may lead to better psychological adjustment as well, further reinforcing the relation of optimism to variables-like life satisfaction.

Aside from psychological adjustment, there is some evidence that optimism and pessimism have an effect on one's physical health. Studies of cancer patients have showed that pessimism may increase risk of mortality (Allison et al., 2003; Schulz et al., 1996). Compared to pessimists, optimists appear to have better pulmonary function (Kubzansky et al., 2002), lower blood pressure (Räikkönen et al., 1999), better immune function against chronic infections like HPV and HIV, lower risk of health problems after stressful life events (Byrnes et al., 1998; Kivimaki et al., 2005; Milam et al., 2004), and faster recovery rates from surgeries like cardio bypasses (Fitzgerald et al., 1993; Leedham et al., 1995; Scheier et al., 1989). Optimists also appear to be more resistant to post-surgical infections (Leedham et al., 1995). In a prospective study of older adults, Giltay et al. (2004) found that optimism protected against all-cause and cardiovascular mortality a decade later. And in another longitudinal study of patients recruited from the 1960s, pessimism was associated with greater mortality 30 years later, with a 19% increase in risk of mortality for every 10-point increase in the T-score (Maruta et al., 2000). Although not all studies have demonstrated the same relationship between optimism–pessimism and physical health, the above findings at least point to the potential role one's outcome expectations play in shaping one's physical outcome.

COSTS AND BENEFITS OF OPTIMISM AND PESSIMISM

For all the evidence indicating the adaptiveness of optimism and maladaptiveness of pessimism, there is a body of literature indicating the opposite: Optimism comes with its costs while pessimism comes with its rewards. Although some studies have suggested that optimism confers physical health benefits, other studies have failed to replicate those findings or have produced mixed results (e.g. Contrada et al., 2004; Tomakowsky et al., 2001). Additionally, studies have linked optimism with poorer health behaviors because optimists underestimate their risk of developing physical problems. Davidson and Prkachin (1997) found that individuals high in both unrealistic and dispositional optimism showed the largest decrease in exercise frequency and the smallest increase in heart disease prevention knowledge after attending a prevention seminar. Similarly, smokers who had high levels of unrealistic optimism were more likely to endorse smoking myths (e.g. the cause of lung cancer is largely genetic, many lung cancer patients are cured) and were less inclined to quit smoking.

Optimism and pessimism may affect health behavior by biasing the way one attends to and processes information. In a study of eye gaze in optimists and pessimists, optimists spent less time fixating on skin cancer images compared with pessimists, and that finding persisted even after a manipulation

to make the cancer images more relevant to the participants (Isaacowitz, 2005). Segerstrom (2001b) found a similar effect when she administered the emotional Stroop test to optimists, who exhibited greater bias for positive-valence words than for negative-valence words. It is important to note that some studies have obtained the reverse trend, in which participants who were optimistic about their health paid more attention to health information and recalled more details when the information was personally relevant (Aspinwall and Brunhart, 1996). Taken together, the findings suggest there may be differences between dispositional optimists and situation-specific optimists in cognitive processes.

In terms of psychological costs, Tennen and Affleck (1987) have proposed that optimism may backfire because optimists always expect the best and therefore are especially vulnerable when things go very wrong. In line with that theory, Chang and Sanna (2003b) found that optimism exacerbates the impact of accumulated life stress (over the course of one year) in the form of physical and psychological symptoms. Specifically, even though pessimists have higher levels of symptomatology under low levels of life stress, optimists have higher levels of symptomatology under high levels of life stress. Finally, optimists may also be worse at learning from contingent feedback when risks are unlikely to pan out, as in gambling, when optimists tend to maintain positive expectations even after losses (Gibson and Sanbonmatsu, 2004). Conversely, pessimists tend to reduce their bets after poor gambling performance.

STRATEGIES OF OPTIMISTS AND PESSIMISTS

The fact that optimism and pessimism may each have their benefits and costs is perhaps most vividly illustrated when comparing the strategies of optimists with the strategies of a particular type of pessimist, the defensive pessimist (for a review see Norem, 2001). Defensive pessimists are those people who benefit from adopting a negative future outlook (Norem and Cantor, 1986; Norem and Illingworth, 1993; Sanna, 1996; Showers, 1992). They have an objectively high history of success in various situations, such as academic or social settings, but defensive pessimists nonetheless enter those situations 'expecting the worst' (Showers, 1992: 474). Their pessimism is strategic because it serves at least two major goals: (1) a self-protective goal of bracing in case of eventual failure (i.e. having already thought about the possibility of failure makes any actual failure no longer feel so bad or unexpected should it happen) and (2) a motivational goal of increasing preparation to enhance the possibility of doing well (i.e. thinking about the possibility of bad outcomes causes defensive pessimists to redouble their efforts making bad outcomes actually less likely) (Norem and Cantor, 1986; Sanna, 2000; Showers and Rubin, 1990).

In other words, even though they have done well in the past, defensive pessimists experience high anxiety and negative affect as they anticipate the future (Norem and Illingworth, 1993; Sanna, 1998). By focusing on and thinking about worst-case scenarios of all that might go wrong, defensive pessimists attempt to manage their emotions; somewhat ironically, thinking about the prospect of bad outcomes helps defensive pessimists prepare to prevent those outcomes from actually materializing (Norem and Cantor, 1986; Sanna, 1996; Showers, 1992). Their negative expectations thus make bad outcomes less likely. It is noteworthy that the broader idea of pessimism being beneficial is also echoed by other research that has similarly shown the potential benefits of adopting a pessimistic outlook (for a review see Carroll et al., 2006).

Optimists (Norem and Illingworth, 2004) differ in their strategies from defensive pessimists. In particular, whereas defensive pessimists are most likely to employ prospective (before-the-fact) coping strategies, optimists do not use many prospective

strategies and, in fact, may tend to use more retrospective (after-the-fact) coping strategies (Norem and Cantor, 1986; Sanna, 2000). As a contrast to defensive pessimists, optimists set high expectations, do not experience high anxiety, and do not seem to think much about the possibility of negative future outcomes (Norem and Cantor, 1986; Sanna, 1996; Showers, 1992). The key here is that defensive pessimists and optimists function equally well when they are able to use their preferred strategies (for a review see Norem, 2001). However, when strategies are unavailable, or are not possible, they suffer. For example, research has shown that defensive pessimists can be disputed when they are distracted from thinking about the future, when thinking about positive futures, or when put into good moods; because optimists prefer not to think about the future they can be disrupted when asked to do so, whereas distracting them from thinking about the future can sometimes facilitate their performances (Sanna, 1998; Spencer and Norem, 1996).

The specific strategies that defensive pessimists and optimists use in order to attempt to cope with their world illustrate further how they can be either potentially adaptive or maladaptive. Although as described there may be a number of specific strategies that may be used, research has indicated that the strategies of defensive pessimists and optimists differ mainly on the dimension of whether they are prospective or retrospective (for a review see Sanna, 2000). An example is that defensive pessimists and optimists differ in the types of mental simulations, thoughts about alternative possible outcomes, which they use. Defensive pessimists have more prospective upward prefactual thoughts, alternative pre-outcome thoughts that are better than expectations, whereas optimists have more retrospective downward counterfactual thoughts, alternative post-outcome 'what-might-have-beens' that are worse than actuality (Sanna, 1996, 1998). Thinking about upward prefactuals allows defensive pessimists to maintain low expectations, manage anxiety by bracing them in case of failure, and prepare them for the future; thinking about downward counterfactuals allows optimists to maintain a positive outlook by considering how things might have even been worse if they did in fact do poorly (after-the-fact) in a self-serving way, since by contrast to the worst outcome the actual outcome now looks good by comparison (Sanna, 1996, 1998).

Defensive pessimists and optimists also differ in their subjective temporal self-appraisals (Sanna et al., 2006). That is, research on temporal self-appraisals (Ross and Wilson, 2002; Wilson and Ross, 2001; see also Sanna et al., 2004) had proposed that past events with negative implications for self-views feel subjectively farther away (irrespective of identical calendar or clock time) than equally distant past events with positive implications. By appraising the past so that bad events seem far away and good events seem close people can feel positively about themselves in the present. But based on findings that defensive pessimists think the worst will transpire in the future and that they differ from optimists in using other prospective strategies, Sanna et al. (2006) tested another unique twist and reasoned that certain people – defensive pessimists – may actually feel subjectively closer to negative than positive future outcomes. Across several studies (Sanna et al., 2006), defensive pessimists felt closer to possible future failures, performed well when told that manipulated negative futures were close, and close negative futures were related to high anxiety and increased preparation and performance. Optimists did not use prospective self-appraisals as a strategy, but instead they may use other retrospective strategies, such as coping with the past by thinking outcomes were inevitable anyway (e.g. Sanna and Chang, 2003). By coming to believe at least some past outcomes are 'meant to be', optimists may cope by considering these events over and done with, focusing them on more positive futures.

What is clear from this research is that it is overly simplistic to equate optimism with good and pessimism with bad. Setting low expectations, producing bad mood or high anxiety, thinking about futures that are better

(upward) than expectations, and viewing bad futures as subjectively closer may be great for defensive pessimists, although they may be maladaptive for optimists. Likewise, setting high expectations, maintaining good moods and low anxiety, thinking about possible pasts that are worse (downward) than actuality, and seeing at least some past events as inevitable may be great for optimists, although they may be maladaptive for defensive pessimists. Both optimism and defensive pessimism can have adaptive functions.

INHERENT ADAPTIVENESS OR MALADAPTIVENESS

With the array of sometimes seemingly conflicting research, it is difficult to draw any conclusions about the inherent adaptiveness and/or maladaptiveness of optimism and pessimism (for a broader discussion on the multifunctional nature of individual differences variables, see Chang and Sanna, 2003c). Several researchers have proposed theories for the disparity. One possibility with regards to optimism–pessimism and health is that optimism is associated with stronger immunity in reaction to straightforward stressors but with weaker immunity to complicated stressors (Segerstrom and Roach, 2007). For example, in a study of healthy women, optimists had better immune parameters when faced with acute stressors but worse immune parameters when faced with persistent stressors compared with pessimists (Cohen et al., 1999). The finding is consistent with Tennen and Affleck's (1987) theory of vulnerability, and it raises important questions about the adaptiveness of optimism in the real world, where many stressors are likely to be persistent and complicated.

Peterson (2000) has distinguished between 'big' and 'little' optimism in his work and emphasized that the two may be independent. 'Big' optimism refers to larger, less specific expectations, whereas 'little' optimism refers to more limited positive expectations.

Research has shown that 'little' optimism may be a better predictor of mood and immune changes than 'big' optimism (Segerstrom et al., 1998). It may be that the two types of optimism can be adaptive or maladaptive depending on the duration or complexity of the situation.

Finally, researchers might benefit from more consistently distinguishing between realistic (adaptive) and unrealistic (maladaptive) forms of optimism. As Davidson and Prkachin (1997) pointed out, a combination of unrealistic and dispositional optimism might be especially detrimental to health behaviors. Perhaps dispositional optimism, on its own, is a desirable trait, and problems only arise when a rigid refusal to acknowledge risk (unrealistic optimism) is prominent.

CULTURAL AND ETHNIC VARIATIONS IN OPTIMISM AND PESSIMISM

In recent years, a small body of research has emerged that looks at the expression and function of optimism–pessimism in non-European American individuals. What is adaptive among one group of people may not be adaptive among other groups, and cultures may even differ in the extent to which they enable or foster positive expectancies. To date, most cross-cultural and racial/ethnic studies on optimism and pessimism have focused on two groups: African Americans and Asians/Asian Americans. Research on other groups may proliferate as the field of psychology increasingly acknowledges the importance of culture and ethnic membership in personality factors.

The existing literature on African Americans has highlighted the importance of spirituality and religion in the group (e.g. Abernethy et al., 2006; Boyd-Franklin, 2003), a feature that some researchers have speculated derive from African Americans' long history of oppression (Nye, 1992). Overall, African Americans participate more often in organizational and non-organizational religious activities than European Americans (Taylor

and Chatters, 1991; Taylor et al., 1996), and their spiritual/religious convictions play a considerable role in everything from mental health functioning to medical decisions (Constantine et al., 2000; Johnson et al., 2005). Some studies on African Americans have examined the relation of optimism–pessimism to religiosity. Mattis et al. (2003) found that the perception of a good relationship with God positively predicted optimism, and the experience of everyday racism negatively predicted optimism. Social support also marginally predicted optimism in the positive direction. A later study produced similar findings, with age, subjective spirituality and the perception of a good relationship with God positively predicting optimism; education, household income, and subjective spirituality negatively predicting pessimism; and the perception of a negative relationship with God positively predicting pessimism (Mattis et al., 2004).

Researchers have explored the possibility of modifying levels of optimism and pessimism for applied purposes. Jones et al. (2002) looked at the link between parenting style and optimism in a group of African American single mothers and found that maternal optimism was related to positive parenting, a relationship that was partially mediated by maternal depressive symptoms. Positive parenting, in turn, was associated with lower levels of both externalizing and internalizing problems in the children. The authors suggest that future intervention and prevention programs should focus on cultivating optimism in single mothers as well as ameliorating depressive symptoms and teaching parenting skills. Finally, a study by Taylor et al. (2004) exploring health behaviors in African American girls showed that pessimism was positively related to increased sedentary behaviors, suggesting that programs aimed at promoting health may have to target pessimistic tendencies first before they can be successful.

Clearly, the above suggestions for improving parenting style and health behaviors are problematic if one were to accept them in their simplified form. African Americans encounter large amounts of racism and other societal stressors in their daily lives, and to imply that such chronic, institutional problems would resolve themselves with just a bit of positive thinking is unrealistic or even ignorant. But the limited body of available research does evidence the influence optimism and pessimism have on psychological and physical health outcomes in African Americans, and implementing techniques to alter optimism–pessimism levels in intervention programs may not be a bad idea. Developers of such programs are in charge of the difficult task of balancing efforts at individual change with efforts at global change, of providing program participants with a sense of personal control and hope without exonerating governments and institutions of their responsibilities.

Significant differences in the cognitive and emotional styles of people from predominantly Eastern cultures and people from predominantly Western cultures have become apparent in the past few years. One of the most common findings is that Easterners tend to be more collectivistic, with a view of the self that encompasses the important groups (the in-groups) to which they belong, and Westerners tend to be more individualistic, with a view of the self as an autonomous entity (Markus and Kitayama, 1991; Oyserman et al., 2002). Attending to others, harmonious interdependence and fitting in are not only valued but sometimes expected in Asian communities (Weisz et al., 1984; Yee, 1992). In contrast, such relatedness among individuals is neither assumed nor valued in most Western cultures (Doi, 1971/1973; Markus and Kitayama, 1991; Triandis et al., 1988).

Studies have consistently found that compared with European Americans, Asian Americans have higher levels of pessimism but similar levels of optimism (e.g. Chang, 1996a, 1996b, 2002b; Hardin and Leong, 2005). Chang et al. (2001) asked European American and Japanese participants to predict whether certain positive and negative events were more likely to happen to themselves or others. European Americans were more likely than Japanese to predict positive events happening to themselves, and Japanese were more likely than European Americans to predict negative events happening to themselves. Within groups, European American participants demonstrated an optimistic bias only for negative events (i.e. expecting bad things to happen to others), but Japanese participants exhibited both an optimistic bias for negative events and a pessimistic bias for positive events (i.e. expecting good things to happen to others). A related study replicated the between-group differences and found that whereas European American participants showed an optimistic bias for both positive and negative events, Japanese participants showed a pessimistic bias for negative events only (Chang and Asakawa, 2003). Taken together, the two studies suggest that Japanese individuals may not be more pessimistic overall but simply more balanced in their levels of optimism and pessimism, emphasizing either the former or the latter depending on the situation. That would be in line with the findings of several studies indicating a tendency for Asians to be more context-sensitive than European Americans, perhaps because of the importance of attending to others and maintaining group harmony in Asian culture (e.g. Masuda and Nisbett, 2001; Miyamoto et al., 2006).

Other studies have examined the relationship between optimism–pessimism and psychological outcome in Asians/Asian Americans. As one might expect, high pessimism and low optimism appear to be directly or indirectly linked to feelings of hopelessness and other psychological symptoms (Chang, 2002b). Hardin and Leong (2005) found that optimism and pessimism mediated the relations between ideal, ought and undesired self-discrepancies and emotional distress. In both Asian and European Americans, pessimism predicted higher levels of both depression and social anxiety, and lack of optimism predicted higher levels of social anxiety. Pessimism also fully mediated the relationship between undesired self-discrepancies and depressive symptoms. Still, some surprises have emerged in research. In the Hardin and Leong study, despite the finding that Asians/Asian Americans had higher self-discrepancies than European Americans and that undesired self-discrepancies were stronger predictors of pessimism for Asians/Asian Americans, Asians/Asian Americans were no less optimistic and exhibited no more depressive symptoms than European Americans. Chang (1996a) found that although pessimism was a better predictor of maladjustment in European Americans, optimism was a better predictor in Asian Americans. And whereas highly pessimistic European Americans used less problem solving as a coping behavior, highly pessimistic Asian Americans actually used more problem-solving, a finding that has led the author to suggest that pessimism may not be as detrimental for Asian Americans as it may be for European Americans. In the presence of sufficient levels of optimism, pessimism may even be adaptive for Asian Americans.

It is possible that pessimism serves an adaptive function by indirectly reinforcing group harmony in collectivist societies. By focusing on negative outcome expectancies, Asians may work to avoid failures or mistakes that may displease others and upset group harmony, through a process similar to defensive pessimism. As a result, clinicians working with Asian/Asian American clients may actually be doing them a disservice by trying to eliminate pessimism in therapy because pessimism may have an important cultural role. Instead, the emphasis should be on increasing levels of optimism, which appears to be more closely related to adjustment in Asians/Asian Americans. It is clear that more studies on the function of optimism and pessimism in Asian Americans are needed (Chang et al., 2006).

FUTURE DIRECTIONS

It is clear that however one chooses to define and measure optimism and pessimism, there is no doubt these constructs strongly influence everything from basic decision-making to mortality. To solidify and expand on our knowledge base about optimism–pessimism, researchers first need to arrive at an agreement of what the constructs are and how they can be assessed. Should optimism–pessimism denote only expectations about the future, or should they refer to broader self-enhancing and self-critical biases (Chang, in press), which seem to more closely relate to lay terms (e.g. 'rose-colored glasses', 'the glass is half empty')? Is optimism only possible in the absence of pessimism, or can the two co-exist? Furthermore, are the constructs best viewed as dispositional (e.g. genetically determined) (Plomin et al., 1992), situationally determined, or a combination of the two? For example, although studies have shown that optimism is relatively stable across time (e.g. Scheier et al., 1994), findings from other studies have shown that optimism may be strongly determined by a number of contextual factors, including performance feedback (Sheppard et al., 2007). In addition, what are the mechanisms that account for the adaptive and maladaptive functions of optimism and pessimism? Findings from a variety of studies have pointed to the importance of considering coping (Chang et al., 2004; D'Zurilla and Chang, 1995; Lazuras and Folkman, 1984) as a key mechanism linking optimism and pessimism with adjustment. Indeed, studies have shown that optimism and pessimism are not only associated with a host of coping behaviors, including problem solving, positive reframing, and social support seeking, but they are also associated with appraisal processes (Chang, 1998a). Finally, it would be critically important to better understand how constructs like optimism and pessimism relate to, or are distinct from, other conceptually similar variables like hope (Chang, 1998d; Snyder et al., 1991), problem orientation (Chang and D'Zurilla, 1996), and possible varieties of optimism and pessimism (e.g. optimistic biases or illusions, Taylor and Brown, 1988; unrealistic optimism, Weinstein and Klein, 1996; or defensive pessimism, Norem and Cantor, 1986). Until there is more consensus on definition, research on optimism–pessimism will continue to appear to have inconsistencies.

At the moment, it appears that optimism carries with it both mental and physical health benefits and detriments. Although some studies have found a positive relationship between optimism and factors like immune function, active coping and life satisfaction, other studies have linked optimism to poorer health behaviors and more psychological symptoms under accumulated stress. Researchers have proposed several different theories about the situations in which optimism may prove beneficial. For example, Sheppard et al. (2007; see also Carroll et al., 2006) have argued that the need for preparedness determines whether one is optimistic or pessimistic at any given time. Specifically, when a threatening situation or event looms, individuals become more pessimistic to brace for disappointment. At those times, pessimism serves an adaptive function. But when the threat passes, people grow more optimistic because a positive outlook prepares them to capitalize on future opportunities, and then optimism becomes adaptive. Still, Sheppard et al.'s model presupposes a unidimensional view of optimism–pessimism, and in the future, researchers may try to develop a similar model in which levels of optimism and pessimism both fluctuate depending on temporal proximity to a target event.

The study of non-European American cultural and ethnic groups remains a burgeoning field, and in coming years researchers will likely expand on current knowledge about optimism and pessimism in understudied populations. This may be critically important. Ideally, future studies will take into account finer, qualitative differences in the function of optimism–pessimism, rather than assuming that whatever is adaptive in European American culture is adaptive worldwide. In addition, researchers might attempt to develop prevention and intervention programs for at-risk populations that foster adaptive forms of optimism and diminish maladaptive forms of pessimism.

To an optimist, the field of psychology has come a long way in understanding the constructs of optimism and pessimism and their physical and psychological correlates. To a pessimist, there is still a long way to go. In either case, if the current and bourgeoning body of literature gives any indication of what is to come, the future of optimism–pessimism research does look bright.

REFERENCES

Abernethy, A.D., Houston, T.R., Mimms, T. and Boyd-Franklin, N. (2006) 'Using prayer in psychotherapy: Applying Sue's differential to enhance culturally competent care', *Cultural Diversity and Ethnic Minority Psychology*, 12(1): 101–14.

Aish, A.M. and Wasserman, D. (2001) 'Does Beck's Hopelessness Scale really measure several components?', *Psychological Medicine*, 31(2): 367–72.

Allison, P.J., Guichard, C., Fung, K. and Gilain, L. (2003) 'Dispositional optimism predicts survival status 1 year after diagnosis in head and neck cancer patients', *Journal of Clinical Oncology*, 21(3): 543–8.

Andersen, S.M. (1990) 'The inevitability of future suffering: The role of depressive predictive certainty in depression', *Social Cognition*, 8(2): 203–28.

Andersen, S.M. and Schwartz, A.H. (1992) 'Intolerance of ambiguity and depression: A cognitive vulnerability factor linked to hopelessness', *Social Cognition*, 10(3): 271–98.

Aspinwall, L.G. and Brunhart, S.M. (1996) 'Distinguishing optimism from denial: Optimistic beliefs predict attention to health threats', *Personality and Social Psychology Bulletin*, 22(16): 993–1003.

Bandura, A. (1986) *Social Foundations of Thought and Action: A Social Cognitive Theory*. Englewood Cliffs, NJ: Prentice-Hall.

Benyamini, Y. (2005) 'Can high optimism and high pessimism co-exist? Findings from arthritis patients coping with pain', *Personality and Individual Differences*, 38(6): 1463–73.

Beck, A.T., Weissman, A., Lester, D. and Trexler, L. (1974) 'The measurement of pessimism: The Hopelessness Scale', *Journal of Consulting and Clinical Psychology*, 42(6): 861–5.

Boyd-Franklin, N. (2003) *Black Families in Therapy: Understanding the African American Experience* (2nd edn). New York: Guilford.

Burke, K.L., Joyner, A.B., Czech, D.R. and Wilson, M.J. (2000) 'An investigation of concurrent validity between two optimism/pessimism questionnaires: The Life Orientation Test-Revised and the Optimism/Pessimism Scale', *Current Psychology: Developmental, Learning, Personality, Social*, 19(2): 129–36.

Byrnes, D.M., Antoni, M.H., Goodkin, K., Efantis-Potter, J., Asthana, D., Simon, T. et al. (1998) 'Stressful events, pessimism, natural killer cell cytotoxicity, and cytotoxic/suppressor T cells in HIV+ black women at risk for cervical cancer', *Psychosomatic Medicine*, 60(6): 714–22.

Carroll, P., Sweeny, K., Shepperd, J.A. (2006) 'Forsaking optimism', *Review of General Psychology*, 10(1): 56–73.

Chang, E.C. (1996a) 'Cultural differences in optimism, pessimism, and coping: Predictors of subsequent adjustment in Asian American and Caucasian American college students', *Journal of Counseling Psychology*, 43(1): 113–23.

Chang, E.C. (1996b) 'Evidence for the cultural specificity of pessimism in Asians vs Caucasians: A test of a general negativity hypothesis', *Personality and Individual Difference*, 21(5): 819–22.

Chang, E.C. (1998a) 'Dispositional optimism and primary and secondary appraisal of a stressor: Controlling for confounding influences and relations to coping and psychological and physical adjustment', *Journal of Personality and Social Psychology*, 74(4): 1109–20.

Chang, E.C. (1998b) 'Distinguishing between optimism and pessimism: A second look at the "optimism-neuroticism hypothesis"', in R.R. Hoffman, M.F. Sherrik and J.S. Warm (eds), *Viewing Psychology as a Whole: The Integrative Science of William N. Dember*. Washington, DC: American Psychological Association, pp. 415–32.

Chang, E.C. (1998c) 'Does dispositional optimism moderate the relation between perceived stress and psychological well-being?: A preliminary investigation', *Personality and Individual Differences*, 25(2): 233–40.

Chang, E.C. (1998d) 'Hope, problem-solving ability, and coping in a college student population: Some implications for theory and practice', *Journal of Clinical Psychology*, 54(7): 953–62.

Chang, E.C. (2001) (ed.), *Optimism and Pessimism: Implications for Theory, Research, and Practice*. Washington, DC: American Psychological Association.

Chang, E.C. (2002a) 'Optimism–pessimism and stress appraisal: Testing a cognitive interactive model of psychological adjustment in adults', *Cognitive Therapy and Research*, 26(5): 675–90.

Chang, E.C. (2002b) 'Cultural differences in psychological distress in Asian and Caucasian American college students: Examining the role of cognitive and affective concomitants', *Journal of Counseling Psychology*, 49(1): 47–59.

Chang, E.C. and Asakawa, K. (2003) 'Cultural variations on optimistic and pessimistic bias for self versus a sibling: Is there evidence for self-enhancement in the West and self-criticism in the East when the referent group is specified?', *Journal of Personality and Social Psychology*, 84(3): 569–81.

Chang, E.C., Asakawa, K. and Sanna, L.J. (2001) 'Cultural variations in optimistic and pessimistic bias: Do Easterners really expect the worst and Westerners really expect the best when predicting future life events?', *Journal of Personality and Social Psychology*, 81(3): 476–91.

Chang, E.C., Chang, R. and Chu, J.P. (2006) 'In search of personality in Asian Americans: What we know or what we don't know?', in F. Leong, A. Inman, A. Ebreo, L. Yang, L. Kinoshita and M. Fu (eds), *Handbook of Asian-American Psychology* (2nd edn). New York: Sage Publications, pp. 265–301.

Chang, E.C. and D'Zurilla, T.J. (1996) 'Relations between problem orientation and optimism, pessimism, and trait affectivity: A construct validation study', *Behaviour Research and Therapy*, 34(2): 185–94.

Chang, E.C., D'Zurilla, T.J. and Maydeu-Olivares, A. (1994) 'Assessing the dimensionality of optimism and pessimism using a multimeasure approach', *Cognitive Therapy and Research*, 18(2): 143–60.

Chang, E.C., D'Zurilla, T.J. and Sanna, L.J. (2004) (eds), *Social Problem Solving: Theory, Research, and Training*. Washington, DC: American Psychological Association.

Chang, E.C., Maydeu-Olivares, A. and D'Zurilla, T.J. (1997) 'Optimism and pessimism as partially independent constructs: Relationship to positive and negative affectivity and psychological well-being', *Personality and Individual Differences*, 23(3): 433–40.

Chang, E.C. and Sanna, L.J. (2001) 'Optimism, pessimism, and positive and negative affectivity in middle-aged adults: A test of a cognitive-affective model of psychological adjustment', *Psychology and Aging*, 16(3): 524–31.

Chang, E.C. and Sanna, L.J. (2003a) 'Experience of life hassles and psychological adjustment among adolescents: Does it make a difference if one is optimistic or pessimistic?', *Personality and Individual Differences*, 34(5): 867–79.

Chang, E.C. and Sanna, L.J. (2003b) 'Optimism, accumulated life stress, and psychological and physical adjustment: Is it always adaptive to expect the best?', *Journal of Social and Clinical Psychology*, 22(1): 97–115.

Chang, E.C. and Sanna, L.J. (2003c) (eds), *Virtue, Vice, and Personality: The Complexity of Behavior*. Washington, DC: American Psychological Association.

Cohen, F., Kearney, K.A., Zegans, L.S., Kemeny, M.E., Neuhaus, J.M. and Stites, D.P. (1999) 'Differential immune system changes with acute and persistent stress for optimists vs pessimists', *Brain, Behavior and Immunity*, 13(2): 155–74.

Constantine, M.G., Lewis, E.L., Connor, L.C. and Sanchez, D. (2000) 'Addressing spiritual and religious issues in counseling African Americans: Implications for counselor training and practice', *Counseling and Values*, 45(1): 28–38.

Contrada, R.J., Goyal, T.M., Cather, C., Rafalson, L., Idler, E.L. and Krause, T.J. (2004) 'Psychosocial factors in outcomes of heart surgery: The impact of religious involvement and depressive symptoms', *Health Psychology*, 23(3): 227–38.

Davidson, K. and Prkachin, K. (1997) 'Optimism and unrealistic optimism have an interacting impact on health-promoting behavior and knowledge changes', *Personality and Social Psychology Bulletin*, 23(6): 617–25.

Dember, W.N., Martin, S., Hummer, M.K., Howe, S. and Melton, R. (1989) 'The measurement of optimism and pessimism', *Current Psychology: Research and Reviews*, 8(2): 102–19.

Doi, T. (1973) *The Anatomy of Dependence*. (J. Bester, trans.). Tokyo: Kodansha. (Original work published in 1971.)

Dolinski, D., Gromski, W. and Zawisza, E. (1987) 'Unrealistic pessimism', *Journal of Social Psychology*, 127(5): 511–16.

D'Zurilla, T.J. and Chang, E.C. (1995) 'The relations between social problem solving and coping', *Cognitive Therapy and Research*, 19(5): 547–62.

Fitzgerald, T.E., Tennen, H., Affleck, G. and Pransky, G.S. (1993) 'The relative importance of dispositional optimism and control appraisals in quality of life after coronary artery bypass surgery', *Journal of Behavioral Medicine*, 16(1): 25–43.

Gibson, B. and Sanbonmatsu, D.M. (2004) 'Optimism, pessimism, and gambling: The downside of optimism', *Personality and Social Psychology Bulletin*, 30(2): 149–60.

Giltay, E.J., Geleijnse, J.M., Zitman, F.G., Hoekstra, T. and Schouten, E.G. (2004) 'Dispositional optimism and all-cause and cardiovascular mortality in a prospective cohort of elderly Dutch men and women', *Archives of General Psychiatry*, 61(11): 1126–35.

Hardin, E.E. and Leong, F.T.L. (2005) 'Optimism and pessimism as mediators of the relations between self-discrepancies and distress among Asian and European Americans', *Journal of Counseling Psychology*, 52(1): 25–35.

Heidegger, M. (1962) *Being and Time*. (J. Macquarrie and E. Robinson, Trans.). New York: Harper & Row. (Original work published 1927.)

Herzberg, P.Y., Glaesmer, H. and Hoyer, J. (2006) 'Separating optimism and pessimism: A robust psychometric analysis of the Revised Life Orientation Test (LOT-R)', *Psychological Assessment*, 18(4): 433–8.

Isaacowitz, D.M. (2005) 'The gaze of the optimist', *Personality and Social Psychology Bulletin*, 31(3): 407–15.

Johnson, K.S., Elbert-Avila, K.I. and Tulsky, J.A. (2005) 'The influence of spiritual beliefs and practices on the treatment preferences of African Americans: A review of the literature', *Journal of the American Geriatrics Society*, 53(4): 711–19.

Jones, D.J., Forehand, R., Brody, G.H. and Armistead, L. (2002) 'Positive parenting and child psychosocial adjustment in inner-city single-parent African American families: The role of maternal optimism', *Behavior Modification*, 26(4): 464–81.

Kivimaki, M., Vahtera, J., Elovainio, M., Helenius, H., Singh-Manoux, A. and Pentti, J. (2005) 'Optimism and pessimism as predictors of change in health after death or onset of severe illness in family', *Health Psychology*, 24(4): 413–21.

Kubzansky, L.D., Kubzansky, P.E. and Maselko, J. (2006) 'Optimism and pessimism in the context of health: Bipolar opposites or separate constructs?', *Personality and Social Psychology Bulletin*, 30(8): 943–56.

Kubzansky, L.D., Wright, R.J., Cohen, S., Weiss, S., Rosner, B. and Sparrow, D. (2002) 'Breathing easy: A prospective study of optimism and pulmonary function in the normative aging study', *Annals of Behavioral Medicine*, 24(4): 345–53.

Lazarus, R.S. and Folkman, S. (1984) *Stress, Appraisal, and Coping.* New York: Springer.

Leedham, B., Meyerowitz, B.E., Muirhead, J. and Frist, W.H. (1995) 'Positive expectations predict health after heart transplantation', *Health Psychology*, 14(1): 74–9.

Markus, H.R. and Kitayama, S. (1991) 'Culture and the self: Implications for cognition, emotion, and motivation', *Psychological Review*, 98(2): 224–53.

Marshall, G.N., Wortman, C.B., Kusulas, J.W., Hervig, L.K. and Vickers, R.R. (1992) 'Distinguishing optimism from pessimism: Relations to fundamental dimensions of mood and personality', *Journal of Personality and Social Psychology*, 62(6): 1067–74.

Maruta, T., Colligan, R.C., Malinchoc, M. and Offord, K.P. (2000) 'Optimists vs. pessimists: Survival rate among medical patients over a 30-year period', *Mayo Clinic Proceedings*, 75(2): 140–3.

Masuda, T. and Nisbett, R.E. (2001) 'Attending holistically versus analytically: Comparing the context sensitivity of Japanese and Americans', *Journal of Personality and Social Psychology*, 81(5): 922–34.

Mattis, J.S., Fontenot, D.L. and Hatcher-Kay, C.A. (2003) 'Religiosity, racism, and dispositional optimism among African Americans', *Personality and Individual Differences*, 34(6): 1025–38.

Mattis, J.S., Fontenot, D.L., Hatcher-Kay, C.A., Grayman, N.A. and Beale, R.L. (2004) 'Religiosity, optimism, and pessimism among African Americans', *Journal of Black Psychology*, 30(2): 187–207.

Milam, J.E., Richardson, J.L., Marks, G., Kemper, G.A. and McCutchan, A.J. (2004) 'The roles of dispositional optimism and pessimism in HIV disease progression', *Psychology and Health*, 19(2): 167–81.

Miyamoto, Y., Nisbett, R.E. and Masuda, T. (2006) 'Culture and the physical environment: Holistic versus analytic perceptual affordances', *Psychological Science*, 17(2): 113–9.

Nes, L.S. and Segerstrom, S.C. (2006) 'Dispositional optimism and coping: A meta-analytic review', *Personality and Social Psychology Review*, 10(3): 235–51.

Nes, L.S., Segerstrom, S.C. and Sephton, S.E. (2005) 'Engagement and arousal: Optimism's effects during a brief stressor', *Personality and Social Psychology Bulletin*, 31(1): 111–20.

Norem, J.K. (2001) *The Positive Power of Negative Thinking: Using Defensive Pessimism to Harness Anxiety and Perform at your Peak.* New York: Basic Books.

Norem, J.K. and Cantor, N. (1986) 'Defensive pessimism: Harnessing anxiety as motivation', *Journal of Personality and Social Psychology*, 51(6): 1208–17.

Norem, J.K. and Illingworth, K.S.S. (1993) 'Strategy-dependent effects of reflecting on self and tasks: Some implications of optimism and defensive pessimism', *Journal of Personality and Social Psychology*, 65(4): 822–35.

Nye, W.P. (1992) 'Amazing grace: Religion and identity among elderly Black individuals', *International Journal of Aging and Human Development*, 36(2): 103–14.

Oyserman, D. and Coon, H.M. and Kemmelmeier, M. (2002) 'Rethinking individualism and collectivism: Evaluation of theoretical assumptions and meta-analyses', *Psychological Bulletin*, 128(1): 3–72.

Peterson, C. (2000) 'The future of optimism', *American Psychologist*, 55(1): 44–55.

Peterson, C. and Chang, E.C. (2003) 'Optimism and flourishing', in C.L.M. Keyes and J. Haidt (eds), *Flourishing: Positive Psychology and the Life Well-lived.* Washington, DC: American Psychological Association, pp. 55–79.

Peterson, C. and Seligman, M.E. (1987) 'Explanatory style and illness', *Journal of Personality*, 55(2): 237–65.

Plomin, R., Scheier, M.F., Bergeman, C.S., Pedersen, N.L., Nesselroade, J.R. and McClearn, G.E. (1992) 'Optimism, pessimism and mental health: A twin/adoption analysis', *Personality and Individual Differences*, 13(8): 921–30.

Räikkönen, K., Matthews, K.A., Flory, J.D., Owens, J.F. and Gump, B.B. (1999) 'Effects of optimism, pessimism, and trait anxiety on ambulatory blood pressure and mood during everyday life', *Journal of Personality and Social Psychology*, 76(1): 104–13.

Robinson-Whelen, S., Kim, C., MacCallum, R.C. and Kiecolt-Glaser, J.K. (1997) 'Distinguishing optimism from pessimism in older adults: Is it more important to be optimistic or not to be pessimistic?', *Journal of Personality and Social Psychology*, 73(6): 1345–53.

Ross, M. and Wilson, A.E. (2002) 'It feels like yesterday: Self-esteem, valence of personal past experiences, and judgments of subjective distance', *Journal of Personality and Social Psychology*, 82(5): 792–803.

Roysamb, E. and Strype, J. (2002) 'Optimism and pessimism: Underlying structure and dimensionality', *Journal of Social and Clinical Psychology*, 21(1): 1–19.

Sanna, L.J. (1996) 'Defensive pessimism, optimism, and simulating alternatives: Some ups and downs of prefactual and counterfactual thinking', *Journal of Personality and Social Psychology*, 71(5): 1020–36.

Sanna, L.J. (1998) 'Defensive pessimism and optimism: The bitter-sweet influence of mood on performance and prefactual and counterfactual thinking', *Cognition and Emotion*, 12(5): 635–65.

Sanna, L.J. (2000) 'Mental simulation, affect, and personality: A conceptual framework', *Current Directions in Psychological Science*, 9(5): 168–73.

Sanna, L.J. and Chang, E.C. (2003) 'The past is not what it used to be: Optimists' use of retroactive pessimism to diminish the sting of failure', *Journal of Research in Personality*, 37(5): 388–404.

Sanna, L.J., Chang, E.C. and Carter, S.E. (2004) 'All our troubles seem so far away: Temporal pattern to accessible alternatives and retrospective team appraisals', *Personality and Social Psychology Bulletin*, 30(10): 1359–71.

Sanna, L.J., Chang, E.C., Carter, S.E. and Small, E.M. (2006) 'The future is now: Temporal self-appraisals among defensive pessimists and optimists', *Personality and Social Psychology Bulletin*, 32(6): 727–39.

Scheier, M.F. and Carver, C.S. (1985) 'Optimism, coping, and health: Assessment and implications of generalized outcome expectancies', *Health Psychology*, 4(3): 219–47.

Scheier, M.F., Carver, C.S. and Bridges, M.W. (1994) 'Distinguishing optimism from neuroticism (and trait anxiety, self-mastery, and self-esteem): A reevaluation of the Life Orientation Test', *Journal of Personality and Social Psychology*, 67(6): 1063–78.

Scheier, M.F., Carver, C.S. and Bridges, M.W. (2001) 'Optimism, pessimism, and psychological well-being', in E.C. Chang (ed.), *Optimism & Pessimism: Implications for Theory, Research, and Practice.* Washington, DC: American Psychological Association, pp. 189–216.

Scheier, M.F., Matthews, K.A., Owens, J.F., Magovern, G.J., Lefebvre, R.C., Abbott, R.A., et al. (1989) 'Dispositional optimism and recovery from coronary artery bypass surgery: The beneficial effects on physical and psychological well-being', *Journal of Personality and Social Psychology*, 57(6): 1024–40.

Schulz, R., Bookwala, J., Knapp, J.E., Scheier, M., Williamson, G.M. (1996) 'Pessimism, age, and cancer mortality', *Psychology and Aging*, 11(2): 304–9.

Segerstrom, S.C. (2001a) 'Optimism, goal conflict, and stressor-related immune change', *Journal of Behavioral Medicine*, 24(5): 441–67.

Segerstrom, S.C. (2001b) 'Optimism and attentional bias for negative and positive stimuli', *Personality and Social Psychology Bulletin*, 27(10): 1334–43.

Segerstrom, S.C. and Roach, A. (2007) 'On the physical health benefits of self-enhancement', in E.C. Chang (ed.), *Self-criticism and Self-Enhancement: Theory, Research, and Clinical Implications.* Washington, DC: American Psychological Association, pp. 37–54.

Segerstrom, S.C., Taylor, S.E., Kemeny, M.E., Fahey, J.L. (1998) 'Optimism is associated with mood, coping and immune change in response to stress', *Journal of Personality and Social Psychology*, 74(6): 1646–55.

Sheppard, J.A., Carroll, P.J. and Sweeny, K. (2007) 'A functional approach to explaining fluctuations in future outlooks: From self-enhancement to self-criticism', in E.C. Chang (ed.), *Self-criticism and Self-Enhancement: Theory, Research, and Clinical*

Implications. Washington, DC: American Psychological Association, pp. 161–80.

Showers, C. (1992) 'The motivational and emotional consequences of considering positive or negative possibilities for an upcoming event', *Journal of Personality and Social Psychology*, 63(3): 474–84.

Showers, C. and Ruben, C. (1990) 'Distinguishing defensive pessimism from depression: Negative expectations and positive coping mechanisms', *Cognitive Therapy and Research*, 14(4): 385–99.

Sicinski, A. (1972) 'Optimism versus pessimism (Tentative concepts and their consequences for future research)', *The Polish Sociological Bulletin*, 25–26: 47–62.

Smith, T.W., Pope, M.K., Rhodewalt, F. and Poulton, J.L. (1989) 'Optimism, neuroticism, coping, and symptom reports: An alternative interpretation of the Life Orientation Test', *Journal of Personality and Social Psychology*, 56(4): 640–8.

Snyder, C.R., Harris, C., Anderson, J.R., Holleran, S.A., Irving, L.M., Sigmon, S.T., Yoshinobu, L., Gibb, J., Langelle, C. and Harney, P. (1991) 'The will and the ways: Development and validation of an individual-differences measure of hope', *Journal of Personality and Social Psychology*, 60(4): 570–85.

Spencer, S.M. and Norem, J.K. (1996) 'Reflection and distraction: Defensive pessimism, strategic optimism, and performance', *Personality and Social Psychology Bulletin*, 22(4): 354–65.

Steer, R.A., Beck, A.T. and Brown, G.K. (1997) 'Factors of the Beck Hopelessness Scale: Fact or artifact?', *Multivariate Experimental Clinical Research*, 11(3): 131–44.

Strunk, D.R., Lopez, H. and DeRubeis, R.J. (2006) 'Depressive symptoms are associated with unrealistic negative predictions of future life events', *Behaviour Research and Therapy*, 44(6): 861–82.

Taylor, R.J. and Chatters, L.M. (1991) 'Nonorganizational religious participation among elderly Black adults', *Journals of Gerontology*, 46(2): S103–11.

Taylor, R.J., Chatters, L.M., Jayakody, R. and Levin, J.S. (1996) 'Black and White differences in religious participation: A multisample comparison', *Journal for the Scientific Study of Religion*, 35(4): 403–10.

Taylor, S.E. and Brown, J.D. (1988) 'Illusion and well-being: A social psychological perspective on mental health', *Psychological Bulletin*, 103(2): 193–210.

Taylor, S.E., Kemeny, M.E., Aspinwall, L.G. and Schneider, S.G., Rodriguez, R. and Herbert, M. (1992) 'Optimism, coping, psychological distress, and high-risk sexual behavior among men at risk for acquired immunodeficiency syndrome (AIDS)', *Journal of Personality and Social Psychology*, 63(3): 460–73.

Taylor, W.C., Baranowksi, T., Klesges, L.M., Ey, S., Pratt, C., Rochon, J. et al. (2004) 'Psychometric properties of optimism and pessimism: Results from the Girls' health Enrichment Multisite Studies', *Preventive Medicine: An International Journal Devoted to Practice and Theory*, 38(supp): S69–77.

Tennen, H. and Affleck, G. (1987) 'The costs and benefits of optimistic explanations and dispositional optimism', *Journal of Personality*, 55(2): 377–93.

Tiger, L. (1979) *Optimism: The Biology of Hope*. New York: Simon & Schuster.

Tomakowsky, J., Lumley, M.A., Markowitz, N. and Frank, C. (2001) 'Optimistic explanatory style and dispositional optimism in HIV-infected men', *Journal of Psychosomatic Research*, 51(4): 577–87.

Triandis, H.C., Bontempo, R., Villareal, M.J., Asai, M. and Lucca, N. (1988) 'Individualism and collectivism: Cross-cultural perspectives on self-ingroup relationships', *Journal of Personality and Social Psychology*, 54(2): 323–38.

Weinstein, N.D. and Klein, W.M. (1996) 'Unrealistic optimism: Present and future', *Journal of Social and Clinical Psychology*, 15(1): 1–8.

Weisz, J.R., Rothbaum, F.M. and Blackburn, T.C. (1984) 'Standing out and standing in: The psychology of control in America and Japan', *American Psychologist*, 39(9): 955–9.

Wichman, A.L., Reich, D.A. and Weary, G. (2006) 'Perceived likelihood as a measure of optimism and pessimism: Support for the Future Events Scale', *Psychological Assessment*, 18(2): 215–19.

Wilson, A.E. and Ross, M. (2001) 'From chump to champ: People's appraisals of their earlier and present selves', *Journal of Personality and Social Psychology*, 80(4): 572–84.

Yee, A.H. (1992) 'Asians as stereotypes and students: Misperceptions that persist', *Educational Psychology Review*, 4(1): 95–132.

23

Self-Consciousness and Similar Personality Constructs

Jakob Smári, Daníel þór Ólason and Ragnar P. Ólafsson

> To know how to enjoy the present ... is a mental operation that seems to be very difficult and comparable in that way to action and attention to reality (Janet, 1903: 481)

The French psychologist/psychiatrist Pierre Janet emphasized what he called presentification in mental health. By this he meant the absence of ruminations and reveries of the past and the future, and a focus on perception and the actions the person is undertaking. In a similar vein, Ingram (1990) advanced the idea that self-focused attention is largely co-extensive with mental disorder and Nolen-Hoeksema (2004) made the concept of rumination the cornerstone of her theory of depression. All these different conceptualizations distinguish between attention to the self as an object and to the implications of experiences for the self, and attention to what the self is experiencing. But there is much more to self-consciousness and self-awareness than psychopathology. The originators of self-focused attention theory, Shelley Duval and Robert Wicklund (Duval and Wicklund, 1972; Wicklund, 1975) conceived of self-focused attention or objective self-awareness primarily as a self-evaluating mode, leading to a motivation to reduce discrepancies between self and standards. Later,

Fenigstein et al. (1975) operationalized self-focused attention as a bifurcated individual difference variable with the self-consciousness scale (SCS). In the present chapter we will first briefly address the notion of self-awareness as an attentional state, then continue to treat self-consciousness as a personality trait and discuss its main operationalization, the SCS. Finally, we will try to delimit the notion of self-consciousness and its measurement from apparently related concepts.

THE ORIGINAL SELF-AWARENESS THEORY AND ITS DERIVATIVES

Duval and Wicklund (1972) assumed that attention is of a limited capacity. Thus, attention to the self detracts from attentional resources available for other tasks. A fundamental distinction according to Duval and Wicklund is between attention devoted to the self and attention devoted to the environment. They defined what they called a state of objective self-awareness as 'when attention is directed inward and the individual's consciousness is focused on himself, he is the object of his own consciousness' (in Silvia and Duval, 2001: 230). In a state of objective self-awareness according to Duval and Wicklund (1972) the individual's standards and goals become salient. The individual is at the same time motivated to reduce the discrepancy between the self and a standard. While the standard is salient the person tends to see his present state as deficient and dysphoria is likely to ensue. The discrepancy has motivational properties, inasmuch as the person will try to reduce the discrepancy or alternatively avoid self-focus. In more recent versions of the theory an explicit allowance for perceived self-standard consistency during states of objective self-awareness with concomitant positive affect has been made (Silvia and Duval, 2001). It is important to note that according to Duval and Wicklund internal versus external attention is a dichotomous variable, with attention fluctuating from one to the other. Increased self-focus thus implies increased time allocated to the self. This is a central limited capacity model of attention that may be contrasted with a flexible, limited capacity model such as the one presented by Kahneman (1973) (see a discussion in Wells and Matthews, 1994).

In research related to self-focused attention, objective self-awareness has been manipulated in several ways, for example, by putting people in front of a mirror, having them listen to their own voices, distinctive clothing, being observed by other people, telling people that they are different, and so on. In the words of Gibbons, 'Theoretically, any stimulus that directs attention back on the self is capable of inducing a state of self-awareness' (1990: 251). Several alternatives have been proposed to the Duval–Wicklund theory. Buss (1980) is a protagonist of a trait version of self-awareness. He describes the difference between his variety of self-awareness theory and Duval and Wicklund's in four respects: (1) distinction is made between private and public self-awareness, (2) negative discrepancies are not *a priori* assumed as a result of a

state of self-awareness, (3) it is not assumed that people strive for self-consistency, and (4) an assumption of dispositions corresponding to the transient states of self-awareness.

A further relative of Duval and Wicklund's theory is Carver and Scheier's (1981) cybernetic model of self-regulation. There are some differences between these two theories. Carver and Scheier refer, as does Buss (1980), to both private and public self-awareness as a state and public/private self-consciousness as a trait. Moreover, Carver and Scheier emphasize more the informational than the motivational aspects of affect in comparison with Duval and Wicklund.

Objective self-awareness theory has been revised in several ways (Silvia and Duval, 2001). In the revised theory standards are seen as quite malleable rather than relatively immutable as in the original theory. Among the general implications of self-awareness theories is that the state of self-awareness helps the individual to assess and consequently to report more valid and reliable information concerning, for example, his goals, attitudes, personality characteristics, and so on. Similarly these theories generally imply increased attitude-behavior consistency, increased cognizance of own affect and increased effects of affective states on behavior. Subsequent research has supported numerous predictions of these theories (see, for example, Gibbons, 1990; Silvia and Duval, 2001, for reviews).

SELF-AWARENESS/SELF-FOCUSED ATTENTION AS A PERSONALITY TRAIT: SELF-CONSCIOUSNESS

We have already mentioned that Carver and Scheier's (1981) as well as Buss' (1980) contribution to self-awareness theory consisted partly in (a) defining self-consciousness as a trait as well as a state variable, and (b) distinguishing between public and private self-consciousness (awareness). These revisions of self-awareness theory are related to work on the SCS. Fenigstein et al. (1975) constructed the SCS to operationalize self-focused attention as a personality trait (see items in Table 23.1.). It is supposed to reflect individual differences in the frequency and intensity of self-focused attention. The first step in the construction of the scale was the identification of behavioral descriptions that represented the domain of self-consciousness. The items thus generated were then classified into seven categories: (a) preoccupation with past, present, and future behavior; (b) sensitivity to inner feelings; (c) recognition of one's positive and negative attributes; (d) introspective behavior; (e) tendency to picture or imagine oneself; (f) awareness of one's physical appearance and presentation; and (g) concern over the appraisal of others. On the basis of factor analyses of items they distinguished between two main aspects of self-consciousness: private self-consciousness (PrSC); that is, a tendency to attend to the inner self or one's

feelings, motives or attitudes; and public self-consciousness (PuSC) or the tendency to attend to how one might appear in the eyes of other people. They noted a similarity between Jung's notion of introversion and private self-consciousness, and conversely a similarity of public self-consciousness and Mead's conception of the importance of the awareness of another's perspective on the self. The third factor was interpreted as social anxiety that according to Fenigstein et al. (1975) may result from public self-consciousness. These factor analyses were then the rationale for the construction of the three subscales of the SCS. Scheier and Carver (1985) later proposed a slightly revised version of the SCS. The revision consisted mainly in minor changes in wording and deletion of one item (item 3 in the original scale). The SCS has been used in hundreds of studies and several of these

Table 23.1 Items of the Self-Consciousness Scale

Private Self-Consciousness

1. I'm always trying to figure myself out
3. Generally I am not very aware of myself (r)
5. I reflect about myself a lot
7. I am often the subject of my own fantasies
9. I never scrutinize myself (r)
13. I'm generally attentive to my inner feelings
15. I'm constantly examining my motives
18. I sometimes have the feeling that I'm off somewhere watching myself
20. I'm alert to changes in my mood
22. I'm aware of the way my mind works when I work through a problem

Public Self-Consciousness

2. I'm concerned about my style of doing things
6. I'm concerned about the way I present myself
11. I'm self-conscious about the way I look
14. I usually worry about making a good impression
17. One of the last things I do before leaving my house is look in the mirror
19. I'm concerned about what other people think of me
21. I'm usually aware of my appearance

Social Anxiety

4. It takes me time to overcome my shyness in new situations
8. I have trouble working when someone is watching me
10. I get embarrassed very easily
12. I don't find it hard to talk to strangers (r)
16. I feel anxious when I speak in front of a group
23. Large groups make me nervous

r = reversed scoring. Items of the self-consciousness scale reproduced from Fenigstein et al. (1975: 524) studies have found support for the validity of all three scales, although other studies question the proposed unidimensionality of private and public self-consciousness.

VALIDITY OF THE SELF-CONSCIOUSNESS SCALE

The attempts to validate the SCS include studies that aim at testing whether correlates of high self-consciousness (especially private self-consciousness) correspond to the effects of self-awareness as a state, and also studies that focus on testing different outcomes and correlates that theoretically should distinguish between private and public self-consciousness. We will focus here mainly on validity of the PrSC and PuSC scales and not that of private and public awareness states as defined, for example, by Buss (1980). Only a very small portion of the voluminous literature can be addressed because of space limitations.

In a study by Turner et al. (1978) it was found in a sample of 1,400 college students that neither self-consciousness scale correlated with social desirability and that PrSC correlated moderately (0.30 and 0.48) with imagery and thoughtfulness, whereas PuSC had much lower correlations with these variables. Sociability had a low positive correlation with PuSC and a low negative correlation with PrSC. These correlations obtained in a large sample seem to support the validity of both scales.

Private self-consciousness is expected to relate to intensity of affective reactions irrespective of valence. Support for this was obtained by Scheier and Carver (1978) who found that male college students high in private self-consciousness rated their emotions with regard to beautiful nude women as well as to atrocities as stronger than did men low in private self-consciousness. The same authors found stronger reported moods (positive and negative) by people high in private self-consciousness in response to an experimental mood induction.

Similarly, private self-consciousness has been found to be related to resistance to false information about oneself or about one's experiences. Gibbons et al. (1979) found that when people high and low in private self-consciousness were given two identical peppermint drinks one after the other and they were either told that the second was stronger or weaker than the first, the subjects high on PrSC rated the second drink as identical to the first, while the subjects low in private self-consciousness were more likely to rate it as either much weaker or much stronger than the first. There is fair support for the validity of PuSC as well. For example, Scheier (1980) in an intriguing study found support for the validity of both public and private self-consciousness. He divided subjects in highs and lows on both PrSC and PuSC resulting in four groups. The subjects were asked to give their opinion on punishment privately (a questionnaire) and then publicly in an essay on punishment, but after the essay they were to discuss their views on punishment with other participants. The essays were then scored for attitude and the correlation calculated between the essay scores and the questionnaire scores. According to Scheier, subjects that were high on PrSC and at the same time low on PuSC were to be expected to show most consistency between the two sets of scores. This was expected as subjects low in public self-consciousness should be the ones to express their attitudes without regard for others, and subjects high in private self-consciousness the ones to know their own attitudes well. The prediction was borne out. Public self-consciousness is also related to perception of self as a target in social situation. Evidence for this is provided in a study by Fenigstein (1984).

Perhaps the most interesting aspects of private self-consciousness concern its potential relevance with regard to reliability and validity of self-descriptions. There has in general been support for the notion that private self-consciousness is related to the stability and consistency of self-descriptions (Hjelle and

Bernard, 1994; Nasby, 1989a) and a greater consistency between self-report and behavior (Scheier et al., 1978). Scheier et al. (1978) found that private self-consciousness was related to consistency between self-report and objective measures of aggression. Cheek (1982) also found a stronger agreement between self-and peer ratings for people high than low in private self-consciousness. This body of research parallels ample evidence that the state of self-awareness enhances validity of self-report (see Gibbons, 1990, for a review). In a similar vein, Davies (1994) found that subjects high in private self-consciousness judged true feedback based on their responses to the 16PF as more accurate and false feedback as more inaccurate than subjects low in private self-consciousness. There is some support for the contention that self-consciousness is related to accessibility of self-schemata. Thus, Nasby (1985) tested recognition of adjectives previously rated for self-descriptiveness. He found increased false alarms in subjects high compared to subjects low in private self-consciousness for adjectives high in self-descriptiveness, but not for non-descriptive distractor adjectives. Nasby (1989a) argued that if the effects of private self-consciousness on consistency in self-report (test–retest consistency) were due to attention to self-related information at the time of report, similar effects should be obtained for manipulated self-awareness. This was however not the case. Nasby thus concluded that consistency in self-report was due to better articulated self-schemas in people characterized by high private self-consciousness. It has been argued, however, that the 'veridicality effect' results both from better access to self-information and from an increased motivation to report accurately, accuracy being a behavioral standard (Gibbons, 1990). Siegrist (1996) found mixed support for consistency comparing individuals high and low in private self-consciousness. Thus, higher internal consistency was found with regard to self-report of satisfaction and self-representation, but not in self-report of public self-consciousness and ill-being. Some studies have not found

support for the prediction that private self-consciousness moderates the stability of self-report. Thus, Schomburg and Tokar (2003) did not find that private self-consciousness was related to the stability of vocational interest inventory scores. Nasby (1989b) found support for specific articulation of self-schematic information in relation to public and private self-consciousness. This was revealed by a false alarm effect with regard to private components moderated by private (but not public) self-consciousness, and a false alarm effect with regard to public components moderated by public (but not private) self-consciousness. This was interpreted by Nasby as support for the validity of private and public self-consciousness as both were specifically related to processing information with regard to congruent aspects of the self. Finally, an interesting attempt to validate the SCS was reported by De Souza et al. (2005) who compared scores on the private and public self-consciousness scales with classifications of narrative accounts of significant life-events in terms of similar constructs. A reasonable correspondence was found that the authors interpret as support for the non-spurious nature of the notions of public and private self-consciousness as operationalized with the SCS.

FACTORIAL STUDIES OF THE SELF-CONSCIOUSNESS SCALE

The SCS is the primary if not the only operationalization of self-consciousness as a trait. On both *a priori* theoretical grounds and in the light of results of factorial analyses of the SCS, the notion and measure of public, and private self-consciousness have been criticized. The factor analytic studies, especially, have fuelled controversies with regard to the understanding of the notion. This concerns both the distinction of public and private self-consciousness, and possible multidimensionality of both types of self-consciousness. It should be kept in mind however that factor analytic studies of this particular instrument can only to a limited degree inform theoretical discussion of the nature of self-consciousness.

Several factorial studies of the SCS have been conducted, using both confirmatory (CFA) and exploratory factor analysis (EFA). These studies have tended to find support for a unidimensional social anxiety factor, while the public and especially the private self-consciousness factor seem to be more complex. We will now review some of these studies, although an exhaustive review exceeds the space of this chapter. A search on the Web of Science in the 1,340 citations of the Fenigstein et al. (1975) paper yielded more than 30 papers, reporting factorial analyses of the SCS in at least 16 different languages (Arabic, Chinese, Dutch, English, Estonian, French, German, Greek, Italian, Japanese, Persian, Polish, Portuguese, Spanish, Swedish, Turkish). However, in Table 23.2 we have summarized the main findings of some of the factorial studies of the SCS. Also included are studies focusing specifically on the PrSC as well as the few studies addressing the revised SCS. Studies were included in the table if they cited the original Fenigstein et al. (1975) paper and if it could be concluded from the title of the article that it contained results regarding the factor structure of the SCS. In some of the literature on the potential plurifactorial nature of the public and especially private self-consciousness scale a strong emphasis has been on results indicating very different correlations between supposedly distinct subfactors of public and private self-consciousness and outcomes. Whatever weight such considerations should have for the notion of self-consciousness, there is little doubt that such relations are in many cases very different.

Support has been found for the original three-factor structure of the SCS although results are generally in favour of a model with correlated rather then orthogonal factors (Bernstein et al., 1986; Scheier and Carver, 1985). The three-factor structure has also been supported in different language versions of the scale, such as German (Heinemann, 1979; but see also Merz, 1984),

Dutch (Vleeming and Engelse, 1981), French (Rimé and LeBon, 1984), Swedish (Nystedt and Smàri, 1989), Spanish (Baños et al., 1990), Portuguese (Teixeira and Gomes, 1995), Arabic (Alanazi, 2001), and Italian (Comunian, 1994). However, in almost all studies, problems have been encountered with individual items that either fail to load on their hypothesized factor or load on more than one factor. Of the items of the PrSC, problems have commonly been encountered with the reverse scored items number 3 and 9 that often fail to load significantly on any factor. Items number 7, 13, and 22 of the PrSC have also failed to load on their hypothesized factor with item 7 sometimes loading on PuSC and item 22 on SA. Of the PuSC items, problems have commonly been found with item 2 because of weak loadings and often equal or higher loadings on PrSC. Results have generally been more favourable regarding the SA factor but problems have sometimes been encountered with insignificant loading of the reverse scored item 12 of this factor. Internal consistency of the PrSC is often unacceptable (< 0.70), but is generally acceptable for the PuSC and SA scales (0.70 to 0.80.). Internal consistency of all the items (total scale) is less often reported, but tends to be acceptable (around 0.80). Weak to moderate correlations are observed between PrSC and PuSC. Correlations between PuSC and SA tend to be weak, but correlations between PrSC and SA are non-significant in most cases.

Burnkrant and Page (1984) found support for a structure of four instead of three factors of the SCS. The private self-consciousness scale according to these authors should be divided into an internal state awareness (ISA) (items 13, 20, and 22) and a self-reflective-ness (SR) factor (items 1, 5, 7, 15, 18). The results were complicated by the fact that two private self-consciousness items (the reversed items: 3 and 9) actually reduced internal consistency of that scale, as was the case for two items of the public scale (17 and 20) and one item of the social anxiety scale (the reverse item 12). These items were thus dropped in Burnkrant and Page's proposal.

Table 23.2 Studies exploring the factor structure of the self-consciousness scales (SCS and SCS-R)

Study	Sample	Main results
Heinemann (1979)	German university students ($n = 317$)	PCA with oblique rotation shows three factors corresponding with the original structure. Problems with Pr items 3 (loads < 0.20), 7 (loads also on Pu) and 22 (loads also on SA) and with Pu item 2 (loads on Pr).
Vleeming and Engelse (1981)	Older Dutch part-time students ($n = 112$)	PCA with varimax rotation shows three factors corresponding with the original structure. Problems with Pr items 3 and 9 (load < 0.20), 7 (loads on Pu) and 22 (loads also on SA) and with Pu items 2 (loads on Pr) and 6 (loads on Pr).
Burnkrant and Page (1984)	Sample 1: adult women ($n = 360$) Sample 2: college students ($n = 198$)	Fit of the original three-factor model is unacceptable in CFA although a model with correlated factors fits better than with orthogonal factors (both samples). CFA results (both samples) favour a four-factor model compared to the original model. The Pr should be divided into ISA (items 13, 20, 22) and SR (items 1, 5, 7, 15, 18) but items 3 and 9 should be excluded because they reduce reliability estimates. Pu items 17 and 21 and SA item 12 should also be excluded for the same reason. However, fit of the four-factor model does not meet criteria for acceptable fit.
Merz (1984)	German university students ($n = 187$)	PCA with varimax rotation (sample 1) constrained to three factors shows problems with Pr items 3, 20, and 22, with Pu items 2, 6, 11, 14, 17, and 19 and with SA item 12.
Rimé and LeBon (1984)	French speaking Belgian university students ($n = 148$)	PCA with varimax rotation supports the original structure. Problems with Pr items 3 (loads on Pu) and 7 (loads on SA), Pu item 11 (loads on Pr) and SA item 12 (does not load on any of the factors).
Scheier and Carver (1985)	University students ($n = 298$)	PFA with varimax rotation of the SCS supports the original structure. Problems with Pr item 7 (loads weakly on Pu), and Pu item 2 (loads both on Pr and Pu). Results from the revised version, SCS-R, reveal the hypothesized three-factor structure although Pu item 2 loads equally on Pr and Pu.
Bernstein, Teng and Garbin (1986)	University students ($n = 296$)	CFA (oblique multiple groups approach was used) shows support for the original structure but a model with assignment of items based on variances fits almost as well indicating that content and statistical characteristics of the items are highly related.
Gould (1986)	Adult community sample ($n = 169$)	CFA indicates that the original three-factor model is inferior to the model of Burnkrant and Page (1984). Best fit for revised model with four-item Pr scale (items 1, 5, 7, 15) labelled private reflective self-consciousness and modified Pu (items 2, 6, 11, 14, 19) and SA (items 4, 8, 10, 23) scales.
Cyr, Bouchard, Valiquette, Lecomte and Lalonde (1987)	Canadian-French university students ($n = 196$, $n = 217$) and psychologist ($n = 411$)	PCA performed separately in the three samples support the original structure although problems were encountered with some of the Pr (items 3, 7, 18, 20) and Pu (item 2) items
Mittal and Balasubramanian (1987)	College students ($n = 228$)	Results based on internal and external consistency tests of unidimensionality based on classical test theory support the separation of Pr into ISA (items 3, 13, 20, 22) and SR (items 1, 5, 15, 18). Pr items 7 and 9 were excluded. Support was found for the separation of Pu into AC (items 11, 17, 21) and SC (items 2, 6, 14, 19). SA items 12 and 23 were excluded.
Abrams (1988)	University students ($n = 478$) and 16 to 17, 13, and 11 year old adolescents ($n = 176$, $n = 183$ and $n = 63$)	EFA with oblique rotation in different samples give some support for the original structure but indicate that items 3, 7 and 13 may not be stable components of the Pr factor.
Piliavin and Charng (1988)	American ($n = 658$) and Polish ($n = 149$) blood donors	PAF of the Pr and Pu items show that a constrained three-factor solution in the American sample supports the division of Pr into ISA and SR but Pr items 3 (loads on ISA) and 9 (loads on SR) were not excluded. For the Pu items, all items load

	> 0.20 on their factor. Problem with Pu item 2 (higher loading on SR). In the Polish sample, results are similar for the Pr items except that item 3 loads neither on the ISA or the SR. However, only items 6 and 19 load on the Pu factor in this sample.
Nystedt and Smári (1989)	PFA with oblique rotation performed by groups support the original structure for university and female high-school students, although some problems with items 13 and 22 were observed in the former group and with items 2, 3, and 9 in the latter group. For male high-school students only two factors emerged (most Pr and Pu items loading on the same factor).
Baños, Belloch and Perpiña (1990)	PFA of the SCS-R with constrained three factors supports the original structure (total sample, n = 93). Problem with Pu item 18 (equal loadings on Pu and SA).
Pelletier and Vallerand (1990)	CFA of the SCS-R supports the original structure although Pr items 6, 19, and 21 and Pu item 2 have low loadings. CFA performed on the data from Scheier and Carver (1985) shows that all items except item 21 have acceptable loadings on their factors. Multigroup analysis supports the equivalence of the three-factor structure across the English and French versions.
Britt (1992)	PAF with varimax rotation shows that a three-factor solution results in greater approximation to simple structure than a four-factor solution with Pr divided into ISA and SR. The three-factor solution is also relatively invariant across different communality estimates and rotations. Results from a CFA with orthogonal factors do not indicate a better fit of the four-factor model compared with the original three-factor model.
Comunian (1994)	PCA with varimax rotation performed by gender generally supports the original structure. Problems in both groups with Pr items 3 and 20 and Pu items 2 and 17 that do not load on any factor.
Shek (1994)	PCA of the SCS-R with varimax rotation supports the original structure. Problems with Pr item 6 (loads on Pu) and 19 (equal loadings on Pr and Pu) and Pu item 2 (loads on Pr). CFA shows better fit of a three-factor model with these adjustments compared with the original model.
Ruganci (1995)	EFA of an abbreviated version of the Pr and Pu scales (items 3, 7, 9, 18, and 21 dropped because they were identified as weak items in a pilot study) revealed three factors with the six items from the Pu scale loading on one factor and six items from the Pr scale loading on two factors that are comparable to ISA and SR factors. However, in this study item 22 loaded on SR but not ISA.
Teixeira and Gomes (1995)	PCA with a constrained three-factor solution (varimax rotation) supports in general the original structure. Problems with Pr items 3 and 13 (load higher on Pu) and Pu item 2 (equal loadings on Pr and Pu), 17 (loads on Pr), 19 (loads on SA), and 22 (loads on SA). All of the SA items load on the same factor.
Anderson, Bohon and Berrigan (1996)	PAF with oblique rotation (several other analytic procedures revealed similar results) of the Pr items after dropping items 9 and 22 (formed trivial single-item factors), shows two factors similar to SR and ISA. Item 5 loaded on ISA in this study.
Kingree and Ruback (1996)	EFA with varimax rotation of the Pr items generally supports a two-factor model of the scale. However, the authors suggest that rumination and self-awareness are more appropriate labels than SR and ISA for these factors. Items 3 and 9 were problematic and were not retained in the final solution.
Bendania and Abed (1997)	PCA with varimax rotation shows that in a constrained three-factor solution problems were encountered with a number of items from the Pr (items 3, 13, 15, 20, 22) and Pu (items 2, 6, 14, 19) scales but items from the SA scale loaded together on one factor. Two- and four-factor solutions were explored but did not give more simpler structure.

Table 23.2 Studies exploring the factor structure of the self-consciousness scales (SCS and SCS-R)—cont'd

Study	Sample	Main results
Creed and Funder (1998)	University students (n = 149)	PCA supports a four-factor model with Pr divided into SR and ISA and the original Pu and SA factors. Problems with Pu item 2 (loaded on the SR) and Pr item 9 (dropped because it did not load on any factor).
Realo and Allik (1998)	Estonian university students (n = 246)	PCA with varimax rotation was performed on the SCS but detailed results are not reported. None of the factor solutions analyzed yielded a simple factor structure. Factor analysis of a new 26-item version of the (Estonian) SCS supported a three-factor structure (Pr, Pu, SA). This version contains 16 of the original items.
Martin and Debus (1999)	High-school students (n = 468)	The original Pr and Pu two-factor structure of the SCS-R was not supported in a CFA. After removing item 10 (cross loading) an adequate and equally good fit was found for the three-factor model of Anderson et al. (1996) and a three factor model with Pr divided into RGS (items 1, 2, and 3) and MSS (items 5, 6, 7, 8, 9) and Pu (items 11 through 16). This latter model was found to be relatively invariant across gender and two age groups.
Cramer (2000)	University students (n = 350) and data from Bernstein et al. (1986) study	None of the five full models (no items dropped) analyzed showed adequate fit in CFA. The reduced four-oblique-factor model of Burnkrant and Page (1984) had the best fit in both samples. However, internal consistency was unacceptable for three of the factors. Deleting Pu item 21 might not be warranted based on item-total correlation and negative alpha change.
Alanazi (2001)	Arabic university (n = 586) and high-school (n = 599) students	PCA with oblique rotation of the SCS-R performed on the total sample and the two samples separately revealed the original structure in all analysis. Some items of the Pr scale loaded also on the SA factor (item 21 in all analyses).
Nystedt and Ljungberg (2002)	High-school students (n = 367) and university students (n = 200)	PCA with oblique rotation performed separately for the Pr and Pu scales revealed two Pr factors, SR (items 1, 5, 7, and 18) and ISA (items 13, 15, 20, and 22). Problems with Pr items 3 and 9 that were dropped. Two Pu factors emerged, AC (items 11, 17, and 21) and SC (items 2, 6, 14, and 19). Roughly the same factors emerged in joint analysis of all items. In a CFA two-dimensional models of the Pr and Pu scales showed improvement in fit compared to unidimensional models. A four-factor model of the Pr and Pu scales when analyzed together had a better fit than a two-factor model. However, the fit indices failed to reach the required minimum for adequate fit.
Ben-Artzi (2003)	Israeli university students (n = 182, n = 183 and n = 182)	PCA of the Pr items revealed two factors, ISA (items 1, 3, 13, 15, 20, 22) and SR (items 5, 7, 9, 18). CFA showed the superiority of the two-factor model compared with the single-factor model. Fit indices for the two-factor model indicated acceptable fit to the data. However, EFA and CFA results indicated that when all items contained words reflecting extreme rate of occurrence only one factor emerged but when none of the items contained such words, two factors emerged but very different in item composition from the SR/ISA division.
Lindwall (2004)	University students (n = 510)	Fit indices in a CFA for different models supported a four-factor model with ISA, SR (excluding items 3, 8 and 9), Pu (excluding items 17 and 21), and SA (excluding items 8 and 12) for both males and females. Assigning item 15 to ISA rather than SR resulted in improved fit. This is a modified version of the model from Burnkrant and Page (1984). Multigroup comparisons across gender indicated that this model was invariant.
Panayiotou and Kokkinos (2006)	Mixed sample of Cypriots (n = 519)	EFA partially supported the two-factor structure of the Pr with some divergences. However, fit of three-, four- and five-factor models using CFA was unacceptable. Unidimensionality of the Pu and SA scales was supported in CFA but not that of the Pr scale. The two-factor structure of the Pr was not tested using CFA.

Note: SCS = self-consciousness scale; SCS-R = self-consciousness scale-revised; Pr = private self-consciousness; Pu = public self-consciousness; SA = social anxiety; ISA = internal state awareness; SR = self reflectiveness; AC = appearance consciousness; SC = style consciousness; RGS = rumination on the general self; MSS = monitoring of specific aspects of self; PCA = principal components factor analysis; PAF = principal axis factor analysis; PFA = principal factor analysis; EFA = explorative factor analysis; CFA = confirmatory factor analysis.

However, their results using CFA show that the fit of this abbreviated four-factor model did not meet criteria for acceptable fit although the fit was superior to the original three-factor model. The four-factor model of Burnkrant and Page (1984) has been evaluated in a number of studies since then with results generally in favour of the division of PrSC into two factors although some divergences are observed. Mittal and Balasubramanian (1987) investigated the factor structure of the SCS using internal and external consistency tests of unidimensionality based on classical test theory. Their results support the separation of PrSC into ISA and SR with item 3 included in the ISA factor but item 7 omitted from the SR factor. Item 9 was excluded in this analysis. However, Mittal and Balasubramanian's results also support a two-dimensional PuSC scale labelled 'style consciousness' (items 2, 6, 14, 19) and 'appearance consciousness' (items 11, 17, 21) thus introducing a five-factor model of the SCS. Nystedt and Ljungberg (2002) report similar results in Sweden although their CFA results show that fit indexes for this two-dimensional structure of both PrSC and PuSC scales do not meet required minimum values. Piliavin and Charng (1988) used EFA to analyze the PrSC and PuSC items in samples of American and Polish blood donors and found support in the American sample for the separation of the PrSC into ISA and SR. In their analyses items 3 and 9 were not excluded and loaded on the ISA and SR factors respectively. All the PuSC items loaded on their hypothesized factor although item 2 had a higher loading on the SR factor. This problem with item 2 also emerged in a study by Creed and Funder (1998) where support was found for the two-factor structure of the PrSC. Finally, fit of the three-, four- and five-factor models has been compared with CFA in two studies. Cramer (2000) tested these structures using both full (all items included) and reduced (items dropped according to the original studies) models in a sample of 350 university students and data from the Bernstein et al.'s (1986) study. Results show

that all of the full models were rejected in both samples based on the fit indexes used in the analysis. The four-factor model of Burnkrant and Page (1984) had the best fit in both samples when reduced models were tested and met minimum requirements for an adequate fit. Lindwall (2004) evaluated the reduced versions of the aforementioned models in a sample of 510 Swedish university students with results also favouring the Burnkrant and Page model. Thus, the general conclusion can be drawn that a three correlated factor model of the SCS is not an adequate representation of its factor structure and that a more complex model is needed. It however is unclear to what extent a more complex structure (for example with PrSC divided into ISA and SR) is in agreement with the theory of self-consciousness. Bernstein et al. (1986) pointed out that item statistics vary systematically between the different subscales of the SCS. The same is observed for the PrSC subscales proposed by Burnkrant and Page. Moreover, it was found that an assignment of items based on variance led to a fit similar to that based on Fenigstein et al.'s (1975) three factors. They found however little evidence for erroneous assignment of items to factors, as had Burnkrant and Page, and argue that there is little evidence to reject an interpretation of the SCS in the light of substance. Bernstein et al., (1986) reject Burnkrant and Page's proposal of purified four factors on the grounds of parsimony. They maintain that there is no solid evidence that interesting criteria are differentially predicted by the two PrSC subscales (this picture may have changed subsequently). The original scales should in their view thus be retained but expanded. Ben-Artzi (2003) using a Hebrew version of the SCS with an Israeli student population advanced the hypothesis that what lies behind the putative factors of the private self-consciousness scale is the wording of items rather than different content. He points out that some of the items of the PrSC include words referring to extreme rates of occurrence ('always', 'a lot', 'often') and others do not. Conducting factor analyses on the original scale items, items where words noting extremity of occurrence were introduced /or deleted from all items yielded quite different structures. Furthermore SR and ISA scales showed different correlations with a depression measure (Beck Depression Inventory) dependent on presence/absence of terms denoting extremity of occurrence. Ben-Artzi thus concurs with Bernstein et al. (1986) that the results cast some doubt on content interpretations of the PrSC subscales. It seems possible in the light of this study that words related to extreme rates of occurrence might, for example tip items in the direction of measuring neurotic tendencies.

Silvia (1999) criticizes the inferences that have been drawn from studies showing multidimensionality of the private self-consciousness scale, making an example of the study of Creed and Funder (1998). According to Silvia the multidimensionality of the scale tells us practically nothing of the underlying construct. Creed and Funder (1999) in response to Silvia cite J.P. Sartre as support that the distinction between the two aspects of private self-consciousness has not fallen from the sky of factor analysis alone. They emphasize the different correlates of these two aspects of private self-consciousness that to them make theoretical sense. The arguments of Silvia are important, however, as they point to the requirement that personality research should be guided by theory, rather than (or in addition to) blind exploration of contingent and debatable operationalizations of constructs.

The studies concerning the factor structure of the SCS are quite numerous and have been conducted in different countries and in different languages. There is thus a substantial heterogeneity in the populations addressed, even though most studies have addressed college students. There is further a great heterogeneity in the methods used and criteria applied. However, many of the studies are unfortunately methodologically suboptimal in several respects (e.g. factor method, sample size, rotations etc.; see Boyle et al.,

1995, for a discussion of methodological guidelines in research on personality and intelligence). These studies as a whole seem in spite of this to permit some quite definite conclusions. Primarily, the internal consistency of the private self-consciousness scale is generally lower than that of the other two scales, if not precisely low. This points to some heterogeneity of that scale. There seem to be problems with some items, especially on the PrSC, that may perhaps to some extent be attributed to method (reverse scoring or wording). There is overall some support for two subfactors of PrSC, even though composition of items loading on each subfactor is somewhat variable across studies. The support for PuSC subfactors is much weaker. Apart from results of factor analyses the question arises as to whether the SR and ISA factors of the PrSC have different substantive meanings. Results from a number of studies, some of them mentioned in this chapter, seem to indicate that they may (for example, Creed and Funder, 1998; Nystedt and Ljungberg, 2002). Thus, ISA seems to be related to positive and SR to negative outcomes. This might be construed as the strongest evidence for a double-headed notion and measure of private self-consciousness. However, it is not clear what the meaning of the new constructs is or whether a purification of the measure or a revision of the notion of private self-consciousness is in order. Perhaps future studies should focus more on this aspect of the construct validity of measures of self-consciousness rather than limiting their scope to the factor validity of the measures.

WICKLUND AND GOLLWITZER'S CRITICISM OF THE PRIVATE–PUBLIC DISTINCTION

Wicklund and Gollwitzer (1987) criticized the private–public distinction of self-consciousness generally, and the notion and measure of public self-consciousness in particular. Fenigstein (1987) and Carver and Scheier (1987) replied to the criticism.

This debate touches on fundamental issues in self-consciousness research that have not yet been resolved in a satisfactory manner. The main thrust of the argument of Wicklund and Gollwitzer (1987) is that work on private–public self-consciousness distinction reflects an Aristotelian as contrasted with a Galilean approach to science. By this they mean that the person is reduced to a status of category membership instead of a dynamic interplay of forces. They are however adamant in emphasizing that this does not mean that they are opposed to individual difference approaches to self-awareness in general. Their analysis leads to the conclusion that the SCS rests on too feeble theoretical grounds. They point out that the three scales of the SCS are the results of factor analysis rather than based on theoretical argument. Instead of positing new self-consciousness dimensions on such grounds a revision of the item pool would have been a sounder approach. Wicklund and Gollwitzer have serious doubts concerning dividing self-directed attention according to the aspects of the self. While different aspects of the self may be the object of such attention this would not affect its quality. With regard to public self-consciousness Wicklund and Gollwitzer maintain it is not consciousness at all but rather reflects concepts like conformity. In support for this statement they advance the following arguments: (1) data (e.g. Cheek, 1982; Tunnell, 1984) indicating that public self-consciousness is related to measures of social dependency; (2) more importantly, perhaps, studies (e.g. Carver and Scheier, 1978) that show no correlation or negative correlations of PuSC with measures of a tendency to think in the first person or responding to incomplete sentences with 'I' or 'me'.

Carver and Scheier (1987) and Fenigstein (1987) retorted to Wicklund and Gollwitzer. The most important points in Carver and Scheier's and Fenigstein's defence run as follows:

1 Wicklund and Gollwitzer are wrong when they identify research on self-consciousness as personality traits as Aristotelian. In fact even a superficial glance at the literature shows an emphasis on process in research on self-consciousness.

2 Wicklund and Gollwitzer seem to equate public self-consciousness with social dependency. This is however done without much justification, and in fact public self-consciousness has in some studies been found to be unrelated to social desirability (e.g. Turner et al., 1978).

3 While the failure to find public self-consciousness to be related to a projective measure of self-focus was disturbing, other evidence for the construct validity of public self-consciousness has reduced these concerns. Carver and Scheier (1987) take as an example Franzoi and Brewer's (1984) study showing a positive correlation between public self-consciousness and online estimates of subjects' thoughts about themselves as social objects during two consecutive days.

4 There is a strong correspondence between effects obtained through manipulation of self-awareness with stimuli related to public aspects of the self and correlates of public self-consciousness as a trait

5 Wicklund and Gollwitzer (1987) seem to assume that public and private self-consciousness are supposed to be two different types of consciousness, and that one precludes the other. This is however not the case: To the same extent that attention can be divided between the external environment and the self, it can be divided between different aspects of the self.

6 Wicklund and Gollwitzer seem to put up their own theory as a standard in comparison to which other theoretical approaches are found lacking. Thus, they emphasize the pivotal role of discrepancy reduction in relation to self-awareness, forgetting that several effects of self-awareness (for example on heightened self-attribution or intensification of affect) cannot be explained by this construct. Also, Fenigstein maintains that the notion of self-focus avoidance emphasized by Wicklund obfuscates the theory and leaves it non-falsifiable.

8 Fenigstein (1987) admits that the distinction between public and private self-consciousness in the SCS was based on empirical results rather than a priori theoretical analysis, but maintains at the same time that once observed it was found to reflect time-honoured conceptualizations.

It is difficult in the light of Wicklund and Gollwitzer's arguments and with hindsight on subsequent research on public self-consciousness not to entertain some doubts concerning its status as a measure of attention. Apart from highlighting the importance of showing that self-consciousness reflects in fact direction of attention, this debate concerns the role of theory in personality research. But while the present authors concur with an emphasis on the need for theory in the construction of psychological measures, it is important not to overstate the case in a dogmatic manner. A measure like the SCS reflects (hopefully) a construct, but no doubt the construct is to some extent changed/refined through the use of the measurement in research.

SELF-CONSCIOUSNESS AND PSYCHOPATHOLOGY

Inherent in Fenigstein et al.'s (1975) conceptualization is that public self-consciousness plays a role in social anxiety, and self-focused attention has been given a crucial role in some theories of depression. For example, Pyszczynski and Greenberg (1987) proposed a theory of depression where a self-focusing style plays a central role. More generally Ingram (1990) hypothesized that self-awareness is a common denominator of various, if not all, psychopathological conditions. The support for the role of self-consciousness in depression is more extensive than for symptoms of other psychological disorders. Gibbons (1990), referring to his own results based on more than 6,000 college students where the correlation between depression and private self-consciousness was 0.16, suggests that the relationship is weak but consistent. Mor and Winquist (2002) presented a meta-analysis of the relationship between self-focused attention and negative affect. They attended to self-focused attention both as a state and as a trait, to different foci of self-attention, as public and private, ruminative, and non-ruminative. Private self-focus was found to be more related to depression and general anxiety,

whereas public self-focus was more related to social anxiety.

Several cognitive models have been advanced that give a prominent role to self-focused attention in social anxiety (Clark and McManus, 2002). Numerous studies have also found correlations between public self-consciousness and social anxiety, both as measured with the SCS and other measures of social anxiety. Socially anxious people tend to perceive the self as they expect themselves to be perceived by others and it has been demonstrated that enhancing attention to the environment (instead of the self) decreases social anxiety. Bögels and Mansell (2004) offer a review of this literature. Hull studied the role of private self-consciousness in alcohol abuse (Hull, 1981). In a series of interesting studies Hull found that alcohol decreased self-relevant recall of subjects high in private self-consciousness and that failure in comparison with success increased alcohol consumption of subjects high (but not low) in private self-consciousness (Hull and Young, 1983). Fenigstein and Vanable (1992) found that public self-consciousness was related to a measure of paranoia in a college population. Subsequently Smári et al. (1994) investigated the relationship between the same measure of paranoia and self-consciousness among hospitalized schizophrenics. They found that private rather than public self-consciousness was related to paranoia. Several recent studies have, however, found a relationship between subclinical paranoia and public self-consciousness (see Combs and Penn, 2004, for example). In several studies researchers have addressed the differential relationships of internal state awareness and self-reflectiveness with measures of mental health and mental disorder. Ruiperez and Belloch (2003) conclude that whereas the use of the original SCS components might seem to support a non-specificity position with regard to self-consciousness and psychopathology, the use of subcomponents, at least partially, would support specificity across psychopathological groups.

When taken together the picture, albeit somewhat complex, or even confusing, seems to indicate that private self-consciousness is related to various aspects of psychopathology, but that it is probably the self-reflectiveness core that explains this relationship. On the other hand public self-consciousness, even though in some studies found to be related to paranoia or eating disorders, seems most consistently related to social anxiety and social phobia. It seems doubtful (in spite of some studies indicating the contrary) that taking subcomponents of PuSC into account adds anything to the picture.

ALTERNATIVE MEASURES AND ALTERNATIVE CONCEPTUALIZATIONS OF SELF-CONSCIOUSNESS

As already mentioned, there exist variations of the SCS, of which the Scheier and Carver (1985) scale is the best known. In most cases the divergences from the original are probably inconsequential. There are however also more radical departures from the original measure. A major criticism of the Fenigstein et al. (1975) conception is that the SCS may confound frequency of attention to the self with motives for such an attention (Franzoi et al., 1990; Trapnell and Campbell, 1999). Franzoi et al. (1990) found in accordance with a motivational view of PrSC that high PrSC individuals placed higher value on accurate self-knowledge than low PrSC individuals, and that low PrSC individuals may desire to avoid unpleasant self-knowledge in comparison with high PrSC individuals. Trapnell and Campbell (1999) take as a point of departure the apparently contradictory relationships of private self-consciousness with outcomes that are reflective of clarity of self and self-integration, reduced compliance and suggestibility, but at the same time outcomes such as depression and anxiety. Trapnell and Campbell argue that the complex pattern of relationships is explained by the fact that PrSC does not differentiate between motives for self-attention. Thus, the neurotic's rumination is equated with the

philosopher's epistemologically motivated reflection on the self. Trapnell and Campbell further show that the subfactors of the PrSC obtained by previous authors, internal state awareness, and self-reflectiveness show quite different relationships with the five-factor dimensions of openness-to-experience and neuroticism that underline in their view this duality of the private self-consciousness scale. They conclude that: (1) even though there may be after all sufficient common variance in the PrSC scale to justify its continued use as a whole, the precaution should be heeded that attention to subfactors may be necessary in some situations and (2) the SR and ISA subfactors do not sufficiently well correspond to the important reflection and rumination distinction, as the SR does not differentiate intellective from neurotic self-consciousness and ISA items intellective from conscientious self-consciousness. Thus, Trapnell and Campbell (1999) proposed a new measure explicitly intended to capture on the one hand *reflection* or intellective self-consciousness, and *rumination* or rehearsing the past or painful life experiences. They argue on the basis of research with these scales that reflection seems to measure the common core of the two subfactors of private self-consciousness. It has however to be noted that while the relationships between self-consciousness measures and openness, neuroticism and conscientiousness are instructive, too much weight should not be put on these. While the five-factor model of personality and its various operationalizations are widespread it does not go without saying as Trapnell and Campbell seem to assume that it is a procrustean bed every psychological measure has to be tailored to fit. The Big Five dimensions are notoriously devoid of any sophisticated psychological theory (Block, 1995; see also Boyle and Smári, 1997, 2002). There has been some research on the rumination and reflection scales by other authors that throws some doubt on whether these measures reflect the constructs intended by Trapnell and Campbell. Thus, in a recent study Silvia et al. (2005) investigated the construct validity of rumination and reflection as measured by Trapnell and Campbell's (1999) Rumination and Reflection Questionnaire (RRQ). As Silvia et al. (2005) mention, a basic test is whether these measures are related to self-focused attention. They conducted two studies where self-focus was measured by recognition latencies for self-relevant words and completion of ambiguous sentences with first person pronouns. In neither study did rumination nor reflection predict self-focus. Silvia et al. (2005) conclude that in their emphasis on motivational aspects Trapnell and Campbell may have eliminated the attentional aspects of the original private self-consciousness scale. Trapnell and Campbell's study, however, adds to the evidence that different aspects of private self-consciousness should probably be distinguished.

CONSTRUCTS RELATED TO SELF-CONSCIOUSNESS AND SELF-AWARENESS

Several constructs used in social psychology, clinical psychology, and personality seem to overlap to different degrees with the concepts of self-consciousness and self-awareness. Buss (1980) compares his notion of private self-consciousness with Jung's notion of introversion. While there are some similarities according to Buss, Jung's concept is a 'general tendency to focus attention inward and engage in mental activities', whereas 'private self-consciousness is a specific tendency to reflect ... not about all thoughts, ideas and feelings, but only those that center on oneself' (1980: 80–81). Other notions that seem close to that of (especially private) self-consciousness are, for example, rumination and mindfulness.

Rumination

We have already touched upon Trapnell and Campbell's (1999) notion of rumination in contrast with reflection. Nolen-Hoeksema's (2004) version of rumination is however

perhaps currently the most influential. In the response styles theory of Nolen-Hoeksema (Nolen-Hoeksema, 2004), rumination is (in opposition to distraction) a vulnerability factor to depression. It is conceived of both as a trait and a state variable. Nolen-Hoeksema defines rumination as 'repetitive and passive thinking about one's symptoms of depression and the possible causes and consequences of these symptoms' (2004: 107). There exist, however, different approaches to the notion of rumination (see Martin and Tesser, 1996; Papageorgiou and Wells, 2004). In that context Nolen-Hoeksema's notion is relatively narrow as rumination is often taken to mean 'generic term that refers to the entire class of thought that has a tendency to recur' (Papageorgiou and Wells, 2004: 4, refering to Martin and Tesser). In comparison with private self-consciousness, Papageorgiou and Wells (2004: 6) state: 'Rumination may also be differentiated from private self-consciousness, a disposition to chronically self-focus and self-analyse regardless of mood.' Papageorgiou and Wells (2004: 7) further note that 'not all forms of ruminative thinking are necessarily self-relevant'. It seems clear that the notions of rumination and private self-consciousness are conceptually quite distinct even though there may be in some contexts important empirical overlaps.

Mindfulness

The construct of mindfulness has recently come to the fore as a central idea in clinical psychology. Mindfulness as described by Brown and Ryan (2003) is attentiveness and acceptance with regard to the present. Attention is here understood without reference to its object otherwise than that the object or sensation is present- rather than past- or future-oriented. Mindfulness is conceptualized both as a state and as a trait variable. While noting a certain overlap with the aspect of private-self-consciousness and internal self-awareness, Brown and Ryan (2003) distinguish the notion of mindfulness from notions of self-awareness and self-consciousness as differing 'from these approaches in that its mode of functioning is perceptual or "prereflexive" operating on, rather than within, thought, feeling, and other contents of consciousness' (2003: 823). Citing Shear and Jevning (1999) they maintain that 'rather than generating mental accounts about the self, mindfulness offer(s) a bare display of what is taking place' (2003: 823). Without putting the burden of the argument to heavily on the shoulder of the philosopher Jean-Paul Sartre, a text he dedicated to the poet Baudelaire exemplifies very well the notion of a reflexive consciousness as an opposite to mindfulness: 'Baudelaire is a man who never forgets himself. He watches himself watching, he watches to see himself watch, it is his awareness of the tree, of the house he contemplates' (1963: 26).

Mindfulness has generally been found to be related to positive mental health. Among various measures of mindfulness as a trait variable are for example KIMS and MAAS. Brown and Ryan (2003) found that the MAAS was as expected uncorrelated with PrSC, but negatively related to SR and positively related to ISA. Similarly it had low positive correlations with reflection and higher negative correlations with rumination. Correlations with public self-consciousness were, as expected, negative, but low. All these correlations were low or moderate at best. Whatever stance we take towards mindfulness it seems, in spite of superficial similarity, quite distantly related to self-consciousness. The key differences conceptually are on the one hand the non-judgmental aspect of mindfulness, whereas at least Wicklund's notion of self-awareness implies a comparison to standards, and on the other hand that mindfulness is not restricted to the self or self-relevant stimuli.

CONCLUSION

The self-consciousness scales of Fenigstein et al. (1975) combine an unusual empirical

fertility with some ambiguity in the meaning of these scales. In spite of criticism, research on self-consciousness as a trait seems to rejoin in interesting ways research on self-awareness as a state. This research has however run into both theoretical and empirical problems. The problems touch basic issues in how to conduct research in the domain of personality. Originally proposed as trait-like measures of the state-awareness discussed by Duval and Wicklund (1972), there is some doubt as to what the two scales really measure. Do they reflect individual differences in the frequency or the intensity of attention directed to the different aspects of the self, or additionally or even mainly individual differences in psychological turmoil (private self-consciousness) or even conformity (public self-consciousness)? Do these scales moreover confound attention with motives for paying attention as suggested by Trapnell and Campbell (1999)? The factorial structure is also somewhat in doubt for both the public and (especially) the private scale of the SCS. Both scales may be multifactorial. There seems however to be a consensus that there is an important core (be it one or two-headed) reflected by the private self-consciousness scale in particular. The notion does not seem to be redundant, but relatively different from and independent of notions like rumination. It seems thus important to titrate this core and try to distill an alternative and more satisfactory measure of the construct. While we tend to concur with the argument advanced by Silvia that researchers should be careful not to limit their thinking to results of factorial analyses, the results of such analyses may be useful supplementary information to conceptual analysis. New proposals should optimally be grounded in theory as well as factor structures.

REFERENCES

Abrams, D. (1988) 'Self-consciousness scales for adults and children: Reliability, validity and theoretical significance', *European Journal of Personality*, 2(1): 11–37.

Alanazi, F.M. (2001) 'The Revised Self-Consciousness Scale: An assessment of factor structure, reliability, and gender differences in Saudi Arabia', *Social Behavior and Personality*, 29(8): 763–76.

Anderson, E.M., Bohon, L.M. and Berrigan, L.P. (1996) 'Factor structure of the Private Self-Consciousness Scale', *Journal of Personality Assessment*, 66(1): 144–52.

Baños, R.M., Belloch, A. and Perpiña, C. (1990) 'Self-consciousness scale: A study of Spanish housewives', *Psychological Reports*, 66(3): 771–4.

Bendania, A. and Abed, A.S. (1997) 'Reliability and factorial structure of an Arabic translation of the self-consciousness scale', *Psychological Reports*, 81(3): 1091–101.

Ben-Artzi, E. (2003) 'Factor structure of the Private Self-Consciousness Scale: Role of item wording', *Journal of Personality Assessment*, 81(3): 256–64.

Bernstein, I.H., Teng, G. and Garbin, C.P. (1986) 'A confirmatory factoring of the self-consciousness scale', *Multivariate Behavioral Research*, 21(4): 459–75.

Block, J. (1995) 'A contrarian view of the 5 factor approach to personality description', *Psychological Bulletin*, 117(2): 187–215.

Bögels, S.M. and Mansell, W. (2004) 'Attention processes in the maintenance and treatment of social phobia: Hypervigilance, avoidance and self-focused attention', *Clinical Psychology Review*, 24(7): 827–56.

Boyle, G.J., Stankov, L. and Cattell, R.B. (1995) 'Measurement and statistical models in the study of personality and intelligence', in D.H. Saklofske and M. Zeidner (eds), *International Handbook of Personality and Intelligence*. New York: Plenum, pp. 417–46.

Boyle, G.J. and Smári, J. (1997) 'De fem stora och personlighetspsykologins mätningsproblem [The big five and measurement problems in personality psychology]. *Nordisk Psykologi (Nordic Psychology)*, 49(1): 12–21.

Boyle, G.J. and Smári, J. (2002) 'Vers une simplification du modèle cattellien de la personnalité [Towards a simplification of the Cattellian model of personality]. *Bulletin de Psychologie*, 55(6): 635–43.

Britt, T.W. (1992) 'The Self-Consciousness Scale: On the stability of the three-factor structure', *Personality and Social Psychology Bulletin*, 18(6): 748–55.

Brown, K.W. and Ryan, R.M. (2003) 'The benefits of being present: mindfulness and its role in psychological well-being', *Journal of Personality and Social Psychology*, 84(4): 822–48.

Burnkrant, R.E. and Page, T.J. (1984) 'A modification of the Fenigstein, Scheier and Buss Self-Consciousness Scales', *Journal of Personality Assessment*, 48(6): 629–37.

Buss, A.H. (1980) *Self-consciousness and Social Anxiety*. San Francisco: W.H. Freeman.

Carver, C.S. and Scheier, M.F. (1981) *Attention and Self-regulation: A Control Theory Approach to Human Behavior*. New York: Springer Verlag.

Carver, C.S. and Scheier, M.F. (1978). Self-focusing effects of dispositional self-consciousness, mirror presence and audience presence. *Journal of Personality and Social Psychology*, 36(3): 324–32.

Carver, C.S. and Scheier, M.F. (1987) 'The blind men and the elephant: selective examination of the public-private literature gives rise to a faulty perception', *Journal of Personality*, 55(3): 525–41.

Chang, L. (1998) 'Factor interpretations of the Self-Consciousness Scale', *Personality and Individual Differences*, 24(5): 635–40.

Cheek, J.M. (1982) 'Aggregation, moderator variables, and the validity of personality tests-a peer-rating study', *Journal of Personality and Social Psychology*, 43(6): 1254–69.

Clark, D.M. and McManus, F. (2002) 'Information processing in social phobia', *Biological Psychiatry*, 51(1): 92–100.

Combs, D.R. and Penn, D.L. (2004) 'The role of subclinical paranoia on social perception and behavior', *Schizophrenia Research*, 69(1): 93–104.

Comunian, A.L. (1994) 'Self-consciousness scale dimensions: An Italian adaptation', *Psychological Reports*, 74(2): 483–9.

Cramer, K.M. (2000) 'Comparing the relative fit of various models of the self-consciousness scale in two independent samples', *Journal of Personality Assessment*, 75(2): 295–307.

Creed, A.T. and Funder, D.C. (1998) 'The two faces of private self-consciouness: Self-report, peer-report, and behavioral correlates', *European Journal of Personality*, 12(6): 411–31.

Creed, A.T. and Funder, D.C. (1999) 'Shining the light on private self-consciousness: A response to Silvia (1999)', *European Journal of Personality*, 13(6): 539–42.

Cyr, M., Bouchard, M-A., Valiquette, C., Lecomte, C. and Lalonde, F. (1987) 'Analyse psychométrique d'une adaptation en langue française de l'échelle de conscience de soi', *Revue Canadienne des Sciences du Comportement*, 19(3): 287–97.

Davies, M.F. (1994) 'Private self-consciousness and the perceived accuracy of true and false personality feedback', *Personality and Individual Differences*, 17(5): 697–701.

De Souza, M.L., Gomes, W.B. and McCarthy, S. (2005) 'Reversible relationship between quantitative and qualitative data in self-consciousness research: A normative semiotic model for the phenomenological dialogue between data and capta', *Quality and Quantity*, 39(2): 199–215.

Duval, S. and Wicklund, R.A. (1975) *A Theory of Objective Self-awareness*. New York: Academic Press.

Eichstaedt, J. and Silvia, P.J. (2003) 'Noticing the self: Implicit assessment of self-focused attention using word recognition latencies', *Social Cognition*, 21(5): 349–61.

Fenigstein, A. (1984) 'Self-consciousness and the overperception of self as target', *Journal of Personality and Social Psychology*, 47(4): 406–24.

Fenigstein, A. (1987) 'On the nature of public and private self-consciousness', *Journal of Personality*, 55(3): 75–86.

Fenigstein, A., Scheier, M.F. and Buss, A.H. (1975) 'Public and private self-consciousness: assessment and theory', *Journal of Consulting and Clinical Psychology*, 43(4): 522–7.

Fenigstein, A. and Vanable, P.A. (1992) 'Paranoia and self-consciousness', *Journal of Personality and Social Psychology*, 62(1): 129–38.

Franzoi, S.L. and Brewer, L.C. (1984) 'The experience of self-awareness and its relation to level of self-consciousness: An experiential sampling study', *Journal of Research in Personality*, 18(4): 522–40.

Franzoi, S.L., Davis, M.H. and Markwisse, B. (1990) 'A motivational explanation for the existence of private self-consciousness differences', *Journal of Personality*, 58(4): 641–59.

Gibbons, F.X. (1990) 'Self-attention and behavior: A review and theoretical update', in M.P. Zanna (ed.), *Advances in Experimental Social Psychology* (Vol. 23). Academic Press, pp. 249–303.

Gibbons, F.X., Scheier, M.F., Carver, C.S. and Hormuth, S.E. (1979) 'Self-focused attention and the placebo effect-fooling some people some of the time', *Journal of Experimental Social Psychology*, 15(3): 263–74.

Gould, S.J. (1986) 'The self-consciousness scale: A confirmatory factor analysis', *Psychological Reports*, 59(2): 809–10.

Heinemann, W. (1979) 'The assessment of private and public self-consciousness: A German replication', *European Journal of Personality*, 9(3): 331–7.

Hjelle, L.A. and Bernard, M. (1994) 'Private self-consciousness and the retest reliability of self-reports', *Journal of Research in Personality*, 28(1): 52–67.

Hull, J.G. (1981) 'A self-awareness model of the causes and effects of alcohol consumption', *Journal of Abnormal Psychology*, 90(6): 586–600.

Hull, J.G. and Young, R.D. (1983) 'Self-consciousness, self-esteem, and success failure as determinants of alcohol-consumption in male social drinkers', *Journal of Personality and Social Psychology*, 44(6): 1097–109.

Ingram, R.E. (1990) 'Self-focused attention in clinical disorders: Review and a conceptual model', *Psychological Bulletin*, 107(2): 156–76.

Janet, P. (1903) *Les Obsessions et al Psychasthénie. Volume 1, Études Générales*. Paris: Félix Alcan.

Kahneman, D. (1973) *Attention and Effort*. Englewood Cliffs, NJ: Prentice Hall.

Kingree, J.B. and Ruback, R.B. (1996) 'Reconceptualizing the private self-consciousness subscale', *Social Behavior and Personality*, 24(1): 1–8.

Lindwall, M. (2004) 'Factorial structure and invariance across gender of the Swedish Self-Consciousness Scale', *Journal of Personality Assessment*, 82(2): 233–40.

Martin, A.J. and Debus, R.L. (1999) 'Alternative factor structure of the Revised Self-Consciousness Scale', *Journal of Personality Assessment*, 72(2): 266–81.

Martin, L.L. and Tesser, A. (1996) 'Some ruminative thoughts', in R.S. Wyer (ed.), *Advances in Social Cognition* (Vol. IX). New Jersey: Lawrence Erlbaum, pp. 1–47.

Merz, J. (1984) 'Erfahrungen mit der Selbsaufmerksamkeitsskala von Fenigstein, Scheier und Buss (1975)', *Psychologische Beiträge*, 26(2): 239–49.

Mittal, B. and Balasubramanian, S.K. (1987) 'Testing the dimensionality of the Self-Consciousness Scales', *Journal of Personality Assessment*, 51(1): 53–68.

Mor, N. and Winquist, J. (2002) 'Self-focused attention and negative affect: A meta-analysis', *Psychological Bulletin,* 128(4): 638–62.

Nasby, W. (1985) 'Private self-consciousness, articulation of the self-schema, and recognition memory of trait adjectives', *Journal of Personality and Social Psychology,* 49(3): 704–9.

Nasby, W. (1989a) 'Private self-consciousness, self-awareness and the reliability of self-reports', *Journal of Personality and Social Psychology,* 56(6): 950–7.

Nasby, W. (1989b) 'Private and public self-consciousness and articulation of the self-schema', *Journal of Personality and Social Psychology,* 56(1): 117–23.

Nasby, W. (1997) 'Self-consciousness and cognitive prototypes of the ideal self', *Journal of Research in Personality,* 31(4): 543–63.

Nolen-Hoeksema, S. (2004) 'Response styles theory', in C. Papageorgiou and A. Wells (eds), *Depressive Rumination: Nature, Theory and Treatment.* Chichester, UK: John Wiley & Sons, pp. 117–124.

Nystedt L. and Ljungberg, A. (2002) 'Facets of private and public self-consciousness: Construct and discriminant validity', *European Journal of Personality,* 16(2): 143–59.

Nystedt, L. and Smári, J. (1989) 'Assessment of the Fenigstein, Scheier and Buss self-Consciousness Scale: A Swedish translation', *Journal of Personality Assessment,* 53(3): 342–52.

Panayiotou, G. and Kokkinos, C.M. (2006) 'Self-consciousness and psychological distress: A study using the Greek SCS', *Personality and Individual Differences,* 41(1): 83–93.

Papageorgiou, C. and Wells, A. (2004). 'Nature, functions and beliefs about depressive rumination, in C. Papageorgiou and A. Wells (eds), *Depressive Rumination: Nature, Theory and Treatment.* Chichester, UK: John Wiley & Sons, pp. 3–20.

Pelletier, L.G. and Vallerand, R.J. (1990) 'L'échelle révisée de conscience de soi: Une traduction et une validation canadienne-franÁaise du Revised self-consciousness scale', *Revue Canadienne des Sciences du Comportement,* 22(2): 191–206.

Piliavin, J.A. and Charng, H. (1988) 'What is the factorial structure of the private and public self-consciousness scales', *Personality and Social Psychology Bulletin,* 14(3): 587–95.

Pyszczynski, T. and Greenberg, J. (1987) 'Self-regulatory perseveration and the depressive self-focusing style: A self-awareness theory of reactive depression', *Psychological Bulletin,* 102(1): 122–38.

Realo, A. and Allik, J. (1998) 'The Estonian Self-Consciousness Scale and its relation to the five factor model of personality', *Journal of Personality Assessment,* 70(1): 109–24.

Rimé, B. and LeBon, C. (1984) 'Le concept de conscience de soi et ses opérationnalisations', *L'Année Psychologique,* 84(4): 535–53.

Ruganci, R.N. (1995) 'Private and public self-consciousness subscales of the Fenigstein, Scheier and Buss self-consciousness scale: A Turkish translation', *Personality and Individual Differences,* 18(2): 279–82.

Ruiperez, M.A. and Belloch, A. (2003) 'Dimensions of the self-consciousness scale and their relationship with psychopathological indicators', *Personality and Individual Differences,* 35(4): 829–41.

Sartre, J.-P. (1963) *Baudelaire.* Gallimard, Paris.

Scheier, M.F. (1980) 'Effects of public and private self-consciousness on the public expression of personal beliefs', *Journal of Personality and Social Psychology,* 39(3): 514–21.

Scheier, M.F., Buss, A.H. and Buss, D.M. (1978) 'Self-consciousness, self-report of aggressiveness and aggression', *Journal of Research in Personality,* 12(2): 133–40.

Scheier, M.F. and Carver, C.S. (1978) 'Self-focused attention and the experience of emotion: Attraction, repulsion, elation and depression', *Journal of Personality and Social Psychology,* 35(9): 624–36.

Scheier, M.F. and Carver, C.S. (1985) 'The Self-Consciousness Scale: A revised version for use with general population', *Journal of Applied Social Psychology,* 15(8): 687–99.

Schomburg, A.M. and Tokar, D.M. (2003) 'The moderating effect of private self-consciousness on the stability of vocational interests', *Journal of Vocational Behavior,* 63(3): 368–78.

Shek, D.T.L. (1994) 'Assessment of private and public self-consciousness: A Chinese replication', *Journal of Clinical Psychology,* 50(3): 341–8.

Siegrist, M. (1996) 'The influence of self-consciousness on the internal consistency of different scales', *Personality and Individual Differences*, 20(1): 115–7.

Silvia, P.J. (1999) 'Explaining personality or explaining variance? A comment on Creed and Funder (1998)', *European Journal of Personality*, 13(6): 533–8.

Silvia, P.J. and Duval, T.S. (2001) 'Objective self-awareness theory: Recent progress and enduring problems', *Personality and Social Psychology Review*, 5(3): 230–41.

Silvia, P.J., Eichstaedt, J. and Phillips, A.G. (2005) 'Are rumination and reflection types of self-focused attention?', *Personality and Individual Differences*, 38(4): 871–81.

Smari, J., Stefansson, S.B. and Thorgilsson, H. (1994) 'Paranoia, self-consciousness and social cognition in schizophrenics', *Cognitive Therapy and Research*, 18(4): 387–99.

Teixeira, M.A.P. and Gomes, W.B. (1995) 'Self-consciousness scale: A Brazilian version', *Psychological Reports*, 77(2): 423–7.

Trapnell, P.D. and Campbell, J.D. (1999) 'Private-self consciousness and the five factor model of personality: Distinguishing rumination from reflection', *Journal of Personality and Social Psychology*, 76(2): 284–304.

Tunnell, G. (1984) 'The discrepancy between private and public selves: Public self-consciousness and its correlates', *Journal of Personality Assessment*, 48(5): 549–55.

Turner, R.G., Scheier, M.F., Carver, C.S. and Ickes, W. (1978) Correlates of self-consciousness', *Journal of Personality Assessment*, 42(3): 285–9.

Vleeming, R.G. and Engelse, J.A. (1981) 'Assessment of private and public self-consciousness – A Dutch replication', *Journal of Personality Assessment*, 45(4): 385–9.

Wells, A. and Matthews, G. (1994) *Attention and Emotion: A Clinical Perspective*. Hove: Lawrence Erlbaum.

Wicklund, R.A. (1975) 'Objective self-awareness', in L. Berkowitz (ed.), *Advances in Experimental Social Psychology* (Vol. 8). New York: Academic Press, pp. 223–75.

Wicklund, R.A. and Gollwitzer, P.M. (1987) 'The fallacy of the private–public self-focus distinction', *Journal of Personality*, 55(3): 491–523.

24

Personality and the Coping Process

James D.A. Parker and Laura M. Wood

The study of individuals' responses to stressful and upsetting situations has a long research history. Work on the concept of defense, for example, extends back to the nineteenth century and events surrounding the origins of psychoanalysis. On the other hand, some of the work that has examined the way people cope with stressful situations has a history spanning only a few decades. In fact, the category for 'coping' was not included in *Psychological Abstracts* until 1967 (Popplestone and McPherson, 1988), although since this time related categories like 'coping styles' and 'coping resources' have been added – an obvious response to the voluminous amount of research that is now produced on coping-related topics. This chapter presents an overview of research related to the study of people's reactions and responses to stressful situations and individual differences in the use of such reactions and responses.

DEFENSE

One of Freud's earliest contributions was the observation that unpleasant or disturbing thoughts are sometimes kept away from consciousness (Breuer and Freud, 1893/1955). Freud's early writings outlined a variety of psychological maneuvers that individuals use to deflect, distort, or disguise undesirable thoughts and feelings. As Freud's theories evolved, the concepts of 'defence' and 'repression' came to play an increasingly important role (for more discussion on this point, see Brenner, 1957; Hentschel et al., 2004; Madison, 1956; Van der Leeuw, 1971). In his influential history on the psychoanalytic movement, for example, Freud declared that the 'theory of repression is the foundation stone on which the structure of psychoanalysis rests' (1914/1955: 16). Although Freud used the concepts of repression and defense interchangeably in his early psychoanalytic writings (see, for example, Freud, 1896/1955), an important modification was introduced in 1926, when Freud designated the word 'defence' to represent the ego's struggle with unpleasant ideas and feelings (Freud, 1926/1959). At the same time, Freud modified the concept of 'repression', noting from that point on in his work that it should be treated as but one type of defense mechanism.

Perhaps the next most significant event in the evolution and popularization of ideas about defense was the publication of Anna Freud's *Ego and the Mechanisms of Defense* (A. Freud, 1936/1946). A number of important theoretical developments can be found in this work that has attracted the attention of ensuing generations of researchers. Along with cataloguing various defense mechanisms described by her father (e.g. 'regression', 'repression', 'projection', and 'sublimation'), Anna Freud introduced several new mechanisms (e.g. 'identification with the aggressor', 'ego restriction', and 'intellectualization'). Of lasting influence was her observation that despite the existence of a variety of defense mechanisms, individuals tend to use only a narrow few. She argued, in short, that each person has preferred techniques for dealing with stressful or traumatic experiences. The idea that individuals have habitual strategies for dealing with stressful situations has not only interested researchers working with the defense mechanism construct, but many coping researchers as well (Carver et al., 1989; Endler and Parker, 1990a, 1990b; Skinner et al., 2003).

Another influential idea that came from Anna Freud's (1936/1946) work was that some defense mechanisms should be viewed as potentially more pathological than others. This idea was quickly embraced by a number of post-Freudian theorists who began to emphasize the adaptive (non-pathological) features of some defensive responses (e.g. Groot, 1957; Hartmann, 1939). A rather extensive literature has evolved on the classification of defense mechanisms based on potential for pathology. Several theorists have proposed models that distinguish between adaptive and non-adaptive defenses (cf. Haan, 1963, 1977; Kroeber, 1963; Steiner et al., 2001), while others have proposed models that organize defenses along a hierarchy of psychopathology (cf. Bond, 2004; Bond et al., 1983; Perry and Cooper, 1989; Semrad et al., 1973).

Although several different theorists have taken a hierarchical approach to the concept of defense, the model originally developed

by Vaillant (1971) has probably had the most extensive impact on the recent defense literature. Vaillant proposed a hierarchical model that extends from 'immature' to 'mature defenses'. Immature defenses include activities such as projection, hypochondriasis, and passive aggression, while mature defenses include activities like sublimation, humor, and suppression. An intermediate class of defense, neurotic defenses, has also been proposed and includes activities like intellectualization, repression, and reaction formation. This model suggests that individuals who utilize mature defenses have better mental health and more gratifying relationships than individuals who employ immature defenses. A large literature has materialized over the past few decades to empirically test this defense/pathology model (Vaillant, 1986, 1994).

Assessing defenses

Following the publication of Freud's theoretical modifications to the concepts of defense and repression (Freud, 1926/1959), a literature quickly developed that sought to improve the ability to identify various defenses. The three basic traditions that emerged in the assessment of defense mechanisms were observer-rated approaches, self-report approaches, and projective approaches. Only observer-rated and self-report approaches will be discussed in this chapter, since there is a large pre-existing literature on projective measures (Cramer, 1990, 2006; Hilsenroth, 2004; Lerner, 1991).

Development of observer-rated approaches for measuring defenses began in the 1960s (Perry and Ianni, 1998). One of the first systems for identifying a variety of defense mechanisms was developed by Haan (1963), who defined 10 defense mechanisms (e.g. denial, projection) and 10 coping mechanisms (e.g. sublimation, suppression). These definitions were developed so that a summary of individual interviews could be rated for the presence of each defense. Haan's work led to the development of several similar observer-rating systems (e.g. Beardslee et al., 1985; Perry and Cooper, 1989; Semrad et al., 1973).

In the 1970s, Vaillant (1971, 1977) developed a glossary of 18 defense mechanisms that can be used to rate various types of clinical information (e.g. open-ended interviews, interview transcripts). Vaillant's rating system was initially validated using autobiographical data from 95 men that described how they had reacted to a variety of stressful situations over their lifetime (Vaillant, 1971, 1977). Vaillant and colleagues have since contributed the largest literature on defense to date (Steiner et al., 2001).

Because observer-based methods for measuring defenses require much effort to rate and achieve consistent reliability (see Cramer, 2006), it is not surprising that a large body of work has also focused on creating appropriate self-report measures. One of the first of these types of measures was developed by Hann (1965). Using items from the Minnesota Multiphasic Personality Inventory (MMPI) and the California Personality Inventory, and groups of individuals rated high (top 25%) and low (bottom 25%) on Haan's (1963) observer-rated defense scales, nine 'coping mechanism' scales (e.g. objectivity and suppression) and seven 'defense mechanism' scales (e.g. projection and regression) were developed. Using more rigorous procedures, Joffe and Naditch (1977) extended Haan's work, developing 20 self-report defense scales (10 coping mechanism scales and 10 defense mechanism scales).

The most widely used self-report measure of defense is the Defense Mechanism Inventory (DMI) (Gleser and Ihilevich, 1969). The DMI was developed to assess five defense styles: turning against the self, turning against the object, projection, reversal, and principalization. In order to assess these five defense styles, individuals are asked to respond to 10 conflict stories. Although developed to measure five distinct defense styles, high intercorrelations among some of the scales have been reported (see Cramer, 1990). Due to this finding, some researchers have suggested that the DMI may assess a single defense dimension (aggression/inhibition) rather than 5 separate dimensions (Juni and Masling, 1980).

In 1983, Bond et al. developed the Defense Style Questionnaire (DSQ) in an attempt to assess 24 defense mechanisms. The original scale consisted of 97 items, which was later reduced to 81. A second-order factor analysis of the 24 DSQ subscales produced a four-factor defense model: immature defenses, image-distorting defenses, self-sacrificing defenses, and adaptive defenses. Several revisions have been made to the DSQ including a modified scoring system that reflects a more parsimonious three-factor model of defense and includes 20 defense subscales (Andrews et al., 1989). The revised scoring system also allows for the assessment of a mature defense dimension (e.g. sublimation, humor), a neurotic defense dimension (e.g. reaction formation, undoing), and an immature defense dimension (e.g. projection, somatization).

In more recent work, conceptually related to research on the DSQ, Steiner and colleagues developed the 71-item Response Evaluation Measure (REM-71) (Steiner et al., 2001). This self-report measure was developed to include subscales assessing 21 different defenses. Factor analyses with these subscales have consistently produced a two-factor higher-order structure: one dimension related to 'less adaptive' defensive strategies and the other related to 'adaptive' strategies. Although developed for adult populations, the REM has also been developed for use with younger populations (Araujo et al., 2006).

COPING

Despite being used informally in the medical and social science literature for some time, it was not until the 1960s that the word 'coping' began to acquire a technical meaning (Folkman and Moskowitz, 2004).

Initially, some researchers began to label certain 'adaptive' defense mechanisms like 'sublimation' or 'humor' as coping strategies (e.g. Hunter and Goodstein, 1967; Speisman et al., 1964; Weinstock, 1967). According to Haan, for example, 'coping behaviour is distinguished from defensive behaviour, since the latter by definition is rigid, compelled, reality distorting, and undifferentiated, whereas, the former is flexible, purposive, reality oriented, and differentiated' (1965: 374).

The initial work on adaptive defenses led to an independent interest in the 1960s and early 1970s in the study of the conscious strategies used by individuals in stressful situations (e.g. Sidle et al., 1969). Conscious strategies for reacting to stressful or upsetting situations were conceptualized, in this new research tradition, as 'coping responses'. Within a few short years this type of coping research had become a large and self-contained research area quite distinct from the older literature on defense mechanisms (see Lazarus et al., 1974). This first generation of coping researchers shared a number of common concerns that have had a lasting impact in the literature. Although there is a vast number of coping strategies available to individuals in stressful situations, the first generation of coping researchers identified and studied a fairly limited range of basic coping strategies.

Two coping dimensions that were identified by coping researchers early on were emotion-focused and problem-focused coping strategies (see, for example, Averill and Rosenn, 1972; Cohen and Lazarus, 1973; Pearlin and Schooler, 1978). To summarize a large but not always consistent literature (for reviews, see Folkman and Moskowitz, 2004; Parker and Endler, 1992; Skinner et al., 2003; Zeidner and Saklofske, 1996), problem-focused coping involves attempts to solve, reconceptualize, or minimize the effects of a stressful situation, while emotion-focused coping involves self-preoccupation, fantasy, or other conscious activities related to affect regulation. One sign of the importance of these dimensions to researchers in the coping area is that the majority of coping measures developed assess these two coping dimensions (e.g. Billings and Moos, 1981; Carver et al., 1989; Endler and Parker, 1990a, 1990b; Epstein and Meier, 1989; Folkman and Lazarus, 1980, 1985; Nowack, 1989; Patterson and McCubbin, 1987; Tobin et al., 1989).

Another basic dimension, identified early in the coping literature, is avoidance-oriented coping (Roth and Cohen, 1986; Suls and Fletcher, 1985). Avoidance-oriented coping may involve person-oriented and/or task-oriented responses. An individual may react to a stressful or upsetting situation by seeking out other people (social diversion), but they may also respond by engaging in a substitute task (distraction). Along with assessing problem-focused and emotion-focused dimensions, most of the coping measures that have appeared include scales that assess avoidance-like coping responses (e.g. Amirkhan, 1990; Billings and Moos, 1981; Endler and Parker, 1990a, 1990b; Feifel and Strack, 1989; Krohne et al., 2000; Nowack, 1989).

The type of stressful situations examined by early coping researchers has been influential in shaping most of the conceptual models used in research. Early in the coping literature researchers focused almost exclusively on the study of coping reactions to life-threatening or traumatic events (see, for example, the early coping research by Bazeley and Viney, 1974; Dimsdale, 1974; McCubbin et al., 1975; Viney and Clarke, 1974). Interest in the study of responses to life-threatening or traumatic situations became so commonplace that some writers began to define the coping area as the study of responses and reactions to extreme situations (e.g. Hamburg, 1974; White, 1974). Although later generations of coping researchers would turn their attention to studying a broader range of stressful situations, Parker and Endler (1992) have suggested that the initial preoccupation with studying extreme situations had the unanticipated effect of limiting interest in predispositional or stable trait-like coping constructs.

By focusing their attention on coping strategies in highly stressful situations the early coping researchers increased the likelihood that personality variables would be poor predictors of specific coping responses. Although individuals may have habitual coping preferences, life-threatening or extreme situations often permit a relatively narrow range of possible coping responses (Cheng and Cheung, 2005).

Given these trends in the discipline, it is not surprising to see that during the 1970s and early 1980s more coping researchers came to believe that 'coping patterns were not greatly determined by person factors' (Folkman and Lazarus, 1980: 229). Researchers began to stress the importance of studying the situational context in which coping took place (Billings and Moos, 1981; Felton and Revenson, 1984; Folkman and Lazarus, 1985; Pearlin and Schooler, 1978; Stone and Neale, 1984). Consistent with the orientation that situational factors determine specific coping responses, researchers began studying variables like the cognitive appraisals of stressful situations (e.g. Lazarus and Folkman, 1984) and coping resources (e.g. Antonovsky, 1979).

Despite some researchers continuing to downplay the importance of person variables (see Folkman, 1992; Lazarus, 1993), the late 1980s and early 1990s saw renewed interest in person variables in coping research. In fact, subsequent work has demonstrated that both situation and person variables explain significant amounts of variation in coping responses (Suls et al., 1996). An important distinction emerged in the coping literature between those researchers who emphasize the importance of predisposition variables (traits) and those researchers who emphasize situational factors (coping as a process) in the coping literature. This distinction has been referred to in the coping literature as the difference between an *interindividual* and an *intraindividual* approach (Endler and Parker, 1990b; Endler et al., 1998; Folkman et al., 1986; Lazarus, 1993; Parker and Endler, 1992). The *interindividual* approach to

coping attempts to identify habitual coping strategies used by particular individuals across different types of stressful situations, while the *intraindividual* approach to coping attempts to identify basic coping behaviors or strategies used by individuals in specific stressful or upsetting situations. The latter approach assumes that people have a 'repertoire of coping options available to them from which they can build what they believe to be the most effective strategy, depending on the nature of the situation' (Cox and Ferguson, 1991: 20).

Coping assessment

A vast literature has developed on the assessment of coping responses. Unlike the assessment of defense mechanisms, where a variety of methods have been utilized (projective, observer-rated, self-report), most researchers studying coping (whether they advocate an interindividual or intraindividual approach) have used self-report measures to assess coping strategies.

One popular type of intraindividual coping measure takes a situation-specific approach. This type of measure assesses basic coping strategies or responses for responding to a specific stressful situation (e.g. pain symptoms, job loss, cancer, etc.). A variety of situation-specific measures have been developed to assess coping responses to various types of health problems (see, for example, Butler et al., 1989; Sinclair and Wallston, 2004; Willebrand et al., 2001). Job loss and unemployment is another stressor that has generated a large number of situation-specific coping measures (for a detailed review of this literature, see Armstrong-Stassen, 2005; Latack and Havlovic, 1992).

The relationship between coping and health has evolved into one of the most popular topics in the coping literature (Austenfeld and Stanton, 2004; Endler et al., 1998; Somerfield and McCrae, 2000; Worthington and Scherer, 2004). A variety of models have appeared that conceptualize coping as an integral part of well-being (see Endler et al., 1998; Lazarus and Folkman, 1984; Thomae, 1987). In reviewing this literature, Aldwin (1994) and Aldwin and Park (2004) have noted that three general coping and health models have tended to be utilized. The model most often used in the coping and health literature assumes that coping strategies have a direct effect on specific health variables (e.g. blood pressure, rate of recovery, etc.). Another model, used less frequently in the coping literature, views coping as having an indirect effect on health by creating change in some health-related behavior (e.g. maintaining regular contact with health professionals). The last model, also used less frequently in the literature, takes the view that coping strategies moderate the stress generated by a specific health problem.

A second popular type of intraindividual coping measure takes a cross-situational approach. This type of measure assesses a number of basic coping strategies or responses that could be used in a variety of different situations. The items used with these measures assess a broad range of potential coping strategies so that these instruments can be used with individuals experiencing an array of stressors. Respondents identify a recent stressful event and respond to the coping items in relation to that specific situation. Both cross-situation and situation-specific measures can be used on multiple occasions with the same respondent to study coping responses over the course of a specific stressful situation or across similar stressful situations (for examples, see Endler et al., 1998; Sinclair and Wallston, 2004).

The intraindividual coping measure that has had the greatest impact on the coping area is the Ways of Coping Checklist (WCC) (Folkman and Lazarus, 1980), later revised and renamed as the Ways of Coping Questionnaire (WCQ) (Folkman and Lazarus, 1988; for reviews of these scales see Ben-Porath et al., 1991; Ising et al., 2006; Parker et al., 1993; Stone et al., 1991). The WCC or WCQ have been used to study coping in hundreds of published studies, as well as been used as starting points in the development of other coping measures (see, for example, Amirkhan, 1990; Billings and Moos, 1981). The WCC (Folkman and Lazarus, 1980) was developed to assess two basic coping strategies: problem-focused coping and emotion-focused coping. Respondents were asked to respond to the coping items with respect to how they have reacted to a specific stressful situation. Due to issues that arose when attempting to cross-validate the factor structure of the WCC, Folkman and Lazarus (1985) modified the measure and renamed it the Ways of Coping Questionnaire (WCQ). The revised measure consists of eight coping scales (confrontive coping, distancing, self-controlling, seeking social support, accepting responsibility, escape-avoidance, planful problem solving, and positive reappraisal) included in the test-manual for the WCQ (Folkman and Lazarus, 1988). However, some researchers have had problems replicating the factor structure of the WCQ as well (see Edwards and O'Neill, 1998; Parker et al., 1993).

Person variables and coping research continues to be a controversial topic within the literature. Folkman, for example, stated that 'measures of coping traits and dispositions are generally not predictive of how a person copes in an actual, naturally occurring, stressful event' (1992: 33; see also the recent comments by Carpenter, 1992; Lazarus, 1993). During the 1980s and early 1990s the topic of coping styles again attracted the attention of some coping researchers (for some interesting comments on this literature, see McCrae, 1992; Miller, 1992). Much of this research has focused on developing reliable and valid interindividual coping measures.

For example, the Coping Inventory for Stressful Situations (CISS) was developed by Endler and Parker (1990a, 1990b, 1993, 1994, 1999) to reliably assess three basic coping styles: task-oriented coping, emotion-oriented coping, and avoidance-oriented coping. The factor structure of the CISS has been cross-validated in a series of factor-analytic studies with samples of undergraduate students, normal adults, and psychiatric inpatients (Endler and Parker, 1990a, 1994, 1999). The factor structure of the measure was also found to be virtually identical for men and women in the various samples (Cosway et al., 2000; Endler and Parker, 1990a, 1999; Rafnsson et al., 2006).

The most widely used cross-situational coping measure, however, continues to be the Coping Orientation to Problems Experienced scale (COPE) (Carver et al., 1989). The 60-item instrument was developed to assess 15 subscales that assess distinct, but theoretically derived dimensions of coping. Five subscales are associated with various problem-focused strategies (active-coping, planning, suppression of competing activities, restraint-coping, and instrumental social support) and another five subscales are linked with emotion-focused strategies (positive reinterpretation, acceptance, denial, turning to religion, emotional social support). The other five subscales assess a broad heterogeneous set of other coping strategies (wanting to express feelings, behavioral disengagement, mental disengagement, substance use, and humor). A recent review of nine published studies, in which the COPE scales were factor analyzed, reported that highly similar factor structures had emerged (Litman, 2006). The COPE has now been used to study coping in hundreds of published studies and has been the starting point for the development of other coping measures (see, for example, Stanton et al., 2000; Zuckerman and Gagne, 2003).

COPING AND BASIC PERSONALITY

In the late 1980s personality trait research began to flourish again in the study of personality psychology (Angleitner, 1991; Digman, 1990; Endler and Parker, 1992; Wiggins and Pincus, 1992). Not surprisingly there was a renewed interest in person variables in the study of coping processes. This renewed

interest was likely encouraged because of the limited explanatory power of situational models of coping behavior. There is increasing evidence that situation variables account for only modest amounts of coping behaviors (Kozak et al., 2005; Suls et al., 1996). An increasing amount of research suggests that there is considerable consistency in an individual's coping responses (Costa et al., 1996; Moorey et al., 2003; Oxlad et al., 2004; Romano et al., 2003). Terry (1994), for example, collected retrospective reports of how respondents had coped with two different stressful events (6 weeks apart). The way respondents had coped with the first stressful event was one of the best predictors in how they had coped with the second event. Given this type of cross-situational stability, it seems reasonable, therefore, to assume that individual differences in coping styles are related to basic personality (Kato and Pedersen, 2005). For example, in a recent study of occupational stress, Grant and Langan-Fox (2006) found personality (as measured by the NEO-Five Factor Inventory; Costa and McCrae, 1992) accounted for 11% of the variability in coping behaviors (measured using the COPE).

Although many researchers had started investigating the link between personality and coping in the early 1980s, much of the focus of this work was on a disparate set of specific traits like hardiness (Nowack, 1989), Type A behavior (Pittner and Houston, 1980; Vickers et al., 1981), locus of control (Holahan and Moos, 1985; Suls et al., 1996), and self-esteem (Fleishman, 1984). There is a piecemeal quality to this early work that is not surprising, since a comprehensive taxonomy of basic personality dimensions had not yet been widely embraced by the research community. The development of the 'Big Five' personality model certainly contributed to the renewed interest, over the past two decades, in the link between basic personality and coping behaviors (Suls et al., 1996).

Much of the research examining the role of personality in coping has focused on neuroticism and extraversion (Hewitt and Flett, 1996; Lee-Baggley et al., 2005). These Big Five personality dimensions have consistently predicted differential use of emotion-focused and problem-focused coping strategies. For example, neuroticism, has positively predicted emotion-focused strategies such as emotional venting, hostile reactions, and avoidance; it has also negatively predicted problem-focused strategies like planning (Endler and Parker, 1999; Hooker et al., 1994; McCrae and Costa, 1986; O'Brien and DeLongis, 1996; Watson and Hubbard, 1996). Extraversion has negatively predicted emotion-focused strategies such as accepting responsibility (O'Brien and DeLongis, 1996); it positively predicted problem-focused coping strategies like rational action (Watson and Hubbard, 1996).

Less systematic work exists on the role of openness, conscientiousness, and agreeableness (Hewitt and Flett, 1996; Penley and Tomaka, 2002). There is some evidence to suggest a positive relationship exists between openness and the use of humor (McCrae and Costa, 1986) and positive reappraisal (O'Brian and Delongis, 1996) as coping strategies. Other studies, however, have found low or non-significant relationships between Openness and diverse types of coping strategies (Hooker et al., 1994). Although there is some empirical evidence that individuals high on agreeableness are more likely to seek social support (O'Brian and Delongis, 1996), other work has found no relationship between this personality dimension and various types of coping strategies used in stressful situations (David and Suls, 1999). A recent review of the coping literature found a similar pattern of contradictory or non-significant findings for the relationship between conscientiousness and coping behaviors (Lee-Baggley et al., 2005). The use of different types of coping assessment strategies (e.g. interindividual versus intraindividual measures) has undoubtedly contributed to some of the contradictory research on the relationships between basic personality and coping.

FUTURE DIRECTIONS

A distinctive feature of contemporary coping research is the lack of interest in integrating the interindividual (person) and intraindividual (situational) measurement approaches. Reminiscent of the 'person–situation' debate in the personality area several decades ago (for a review, see Endler and Parker, 1992; Kenrick and Funder, 1988), coping researchers rarely assess both situational and person coping variables in the same research study. When both types of variables are used in a particular study, it is usually due to the desire on the part of the researcher to demonstrate the importance of one type of variable over the other (e.g. Ptacek et al., 1994; Schwartz et al., 1999). Individuals working in the coping area would benefit from an examination of some of the lessons that personality researchers learned from the person–situation debate (Kenrick and Funder, 1988). Rather than focusing exclusively on either person or situational variables, many personality researchers began to emphasize the need to study both types of variables simultaneously. Interactional models of personality, like the one proposed by Endler and Magnusson (1976), were viewed at the time as important advancements in the study of personality. Work related to these types of models certainly contributed to the re-emergence, in the mid-1980s, of personality psychology's enhanced role in the discipline. They helped the personality area overcome the doldrums that had set in, earlier in the century, from internal debates about the legitimacy of studying trait constructs (e.g. Mischel, 1973). The coping area will have taken an important step forward when researchers routinely assess both person and situational coping variables in their work.

REFERENCES

Aldwin, C.M. (1994) *Stress, Coping, and Development: An Integrative Perspective.* New York: Guilford.

Aldwin, C.M. and Park, C.L. (2004) 'Coping and physical health outcomes: An overview', *Psychology and Health*, 19(3): 277–81.

Amirkhan, J.H. (1990) 'A factor analytically derived measure of coping: The Coping Strategy Indicator', *Journal of Personality and Social Psychology*, 59(5): 1066–74.

Andrews, G., Pollock, C. and Stewart, G. (1989) 'The determination of defense style by questionnaire', *Archives of General Psychiatry*, 46(5): 455–60.

Angleitner, A. (1991) 'Personality psychology: Trends and developments', *European Journal of Personality*, 5(3): 185–97.

Antonovsky, A. (1979) *Health, Stress, and Coping*. San Francisco: Jossey-Bass.

Araujo, K.B., Medic, S., Yasnovsky, J. and Steiner, H. (2006) 'Assessing defense structure in school-age children using the Response Evaluation Measure-71-Youth Version (REM-Y-71)', *Child Psychiatry and Human Development*, 36(4): 427–36.

Armstrong-Stassen, M. (2005) 'Coping with downsizing: A comparison of executive-level and middle managers', *International Journal of Stress Management*, 12(2): 117–41.

Austenfeld, J.L. and Stanton, A.L. (2004) 'Coping through emotional approach: A new look at emotion, coping, and health-related outcomes', *Journal of Personality*, 72(6): 1335–63.

Averill, J.R. and Rosenn, M. (1972) 'Vigilant and nonvigilant coping strategies and psychophysical stress reactions during anticipation of electric shock', *Journal of Personality and Social Psychology*, 23(1): 128–41.

Bazeley, P. and Viney, L.L. (1974) 'Women coping with crisis: A preliminary community study', *Journal of Community Psychology*, 2(4): 321–9.

Beardslee, W., Jacobson, A., Hauser, S., Noam, G. and Powers, S. (1985) 'An approach to evaluating adolescent adaptive processes: Scale development and reliability', *Journal of American Child Psychiatry*, 24(5): 637–42.

Ben-Porath, Y.S., Waller, N.G. and Butcher, J.W. (1991) 'Assessment of coping: An empirical illustration of the problem of inapplicable items', *Journal of Personality Assessment*, 57(1): 162–76.

Billings, A.G. and Moos, R.H. (1981) 'The role of coping responses and social resources in attenuating the impact of stressful life events', *Journal of Behavioral Medicine*, 4(2): 139–57.

Bond, M. (2004) 'Empirical studies of defense style: Relationships with psychopathology and change', *Harvard Review of Psychiatry*, 12(5): 263–78.

Bond, M., Gardiner, S.T., Christian, J. and Sigel, J.J. (1983) 'An empirical examination of defense mechanisms', *Archives of General Psychiatry*, 40: 333–8.

Brenner, C. (1957) 'The nature and development of the concept of repression in Freud's writings', *Psychoanalytic Study of the Child*, 12: 19–46.

Breuer, J. and Freud, S. (1955) *On the Psychical Mechanisms of Hysterical Phenomena: Preliminary Communication. Standard Edition* (Vol. 2). London: Hogarth. (Original work published 1893.)

Butler, R.W., Damarin, F.L., Beaulieu, C., Schwebel, A.I. and Thorn, B.E. (1989) 'Assessing cognitive coping strategies for acute postsurgical pain', *Psychological Assessment*, 1(1): 41–5.

Carpenter, B.N. (1992) 'Issues and advances in coping research', in B.N. Carpenter (ed.), *Personal Coping: Theory, Research, and Application*. Westport, CT: Praeger, pp. 1–13.

Carver, C.S., Scheier, M.F. and Weintraub, J.K. (1989) 'Assessing coping strategies: A theoretically based approach', *Journal of Personality and Social Psychology*, 56(2): 267–83.

Cheng, C. and Cheung, M.W.L. (2005) 'Cognitive processes underlying coping flexibility: Differentiation and integration', *Journal of Personality*, 73(4): 859–86.

Cohen, F. and Lazarus, R.S. (1973) 'Active coping processes, coping dispositions, and recovery from surgery', *Psychosomatic Medicine*, 35(5): 375–89.

Costa, P.T. and McCrae, R.R. (1992) *Revised NEO Personality Inventory (NEO-PI-R) and NEO Five-Factor Inventory (NEO-FFI) Professional Manual*. Odessa, FL: Psychological Assessment Resources.

Costa, P.T., Sommerfield, M.R. and McCrae, R.R. (1996) 'Personality and coping: A reconceptualization', in M. Zeidner and N.S. Endler (eds), *Handbook of Coping: Theory, Research, Applications*. New York: John Wiley & Sons, pp. 44–61.

Cosway, R., Endler, N.S., Sadler, A.J. and Deary, I.J. (2000) 'The Coping Inventory for Stressful Situations: Factorial structure and associations with personality traits and psychological health', *Journal of Applied Biobehavioral Research*, 5(2): 121–43.

Cox, T. and Ferguson, E. (1991) 'Individual differences, stress and coping', in C.L. Cooper and R. Payne (eds), *Personality and Stress: Individual Differences in the Stress Process*. Chichester: Wiley, pp. 7–30.

Cramer, P. (1990) *The Development of Defense Mechanisms: Theory, Research, and Assessment*. New York: Springer-Verlag.

Cramer, P. (2006) *Protecting the Self: Defense Mechanisms in Action*. New York: Guilford Press.

David, J.P. and Suls, J. (1999) 'Coping efforts in daily life: Role of Big Five traits and problems appraisals', *Journal of Personality*, 67(2): 265–94.

Digman, J.M. (1990) 'Personality structure: Emergence of the five-factor model', *Annual Review of Psychology*, 41: 417–40.

Dimsdale, J.E. (1974) 'The coping behavior of Nazi concentration camp survivors', *American Journal of Psychiatry*, 131(7): 792–7.

Edwards, J.R. and O'Neill, R.M. (1998) 'The construct validity of scores on the Ways of Coping Questionnaire: Confirmatory analysis of alternative factor structures', *Educational and Psychological Measurement*, 58(6): 955–83.

Endler, N.S. and Magnusson, D. (1976) 'Toward an interactional psychology of personality', *Psychological Bulletin*, 83: 956–74.

Endler, N.S. and Parker, J.D.A. (1990a) *Coping Inventory for Stressful Situations (CISS): Manual*. Toronto: Multi-Health Systems.

Endler, N.S. and Parker, J.D.A. (1990b) 'Multidimensional assessment of coping: A critical evaluation', *Journal of Personality and Social Psychology*, 58(5): 844–54.

Endler, N.S. and Parker, J.D.A. (1992) 'Interactionism revisited: The continuing crisis in the personality area', *European Journal of Personality*, 6(3): 177–98.

Endler, N.S. and Parker, J.D.A. (1993) 'The multidimensional assessment of coping: Concepts, issues and measurement', in G.L. VanHeck, P. Bonaiuto, I. Deary and W. Nowack (eds), *Personality Psychology in Europe*. Tilburg,

Netherlands: Tilburg University Press, pp. 309–19.

Endler, N.S. and Parker, J.D.A. (1994) 'Assessment of multidimensional coping: Task, emotion, and avoidance strategies', *Psychological Assessment*, 6(5): 50–60.

Endler, N.S. and Parker, J.D.A. (1999) *Coping Inventory for Stressful Situations (CISS): Manual* (second edition). Toronto: Multi-Health Systems.

Endler, N.S., Parker, J.D.A. and Summerfeldt, L.J. (1998) 'Coping with health problems: Developing a reliable and valid multidimensional measure', *Psychological Assessment*, 10(3): 195–205.

Epstein, S. and Meier, P. (1989) 'Constructive thinking: A broad coping variable with specific components', *Journal of Personality and Social Psychology*, 57(2): 332–50.

Feifel, H. and Strack, S. (1989) 'Coping with conflict situations: Middle-aged and elderly men', *Psychology and Aging*, 4(1): 26–33.

Felton, B.J. and Revenson, T.A. (1984) 'Coping with chronic illness: A study of illness controllability and the influence of coping strategies on psychological adjustment', *Journal of Consulting and Clinical Psychology*, 52(3): 343–53.

Fleishman, J.A. (1984) 'Personality characteristics and coping patterns', *Journal of Health and Social Behavior*, 25(2): 229–44.

Folkman, S. (1992) 'Making the case for coping', in B.N. Carpenter (ed.), *Personal Coping: Theory, Research, and Application*. Westport, CT: Praeger, pp. 31–46.

Folkman, S. and Lazarus, R.S. (1980) 'An analysis of coping in a middle-aged community sample', *Journal of Health and Social Behavior*, 21(3): 219–239.

Folkman, S. and Lazarus, R.S. (1985) 'If it changes it must be a process: A study of emotion and coping during three stages of a college examination', *Journal of Personality and Social Psychology*, 48(1): 150–70.

Folkman, S. and Lazarus, R.S. (1988) *Manual for the Ways of Coping Questionnaire*. Palo Alto, CA: Consulting Psychologists Press.

Folkman, S., Lazarus, R.S., Dunkel-Schetter, C., DeLongis, A. and Gruen, R. (1986) 'The dynamics of a stressful encounter', *Journal of Personality and Social Psychology*, 50(5): 992–1003.

Folkman, S. and Moskowitz, J.T. (2004) 'Coping: Pitfalls and promise', *Annual Review of Psychology*, 55: 745–74.

Freud, A. (1946) *The Ego and the Mechanisms of Defense*. New York: International Universities Press. (Original work published 1936.)

Freud, S. (1955) *Further Remarks on the Neuro-Psychoses of Defence. Standard edition* (Vol. 3). London: Hogarth. (Original work published 1896.)

Freud, S. (1955) *History of the Psychoanalytic Movement. Standard edition* (Vol. 14). London: Hogarth. (Original work published 1914.)

Freud, S. (1959) *Inhibitions, Symptoms, and Anxiety. Standard edition* (Vol. XX). London: Hogarth. (Original work published 1926.)

Gleser, G.C. and Ihilevich, D. (1969) 'An objective instrument for measuring defense mechanisms', *Journal of Consulting and Clinical Psychology*, 33(1): 51–60.

Grant, S. and Langan-Fox, J. (2006) 'Occupational stress, coping and strain: The combined/interactive effect of the Big Five traits', *Personality and Individual Differences*, 41(4): 719–32.

Groot, J.L. (1957) 'On defense and development: Normal and pathological', *Psychoanalytic Study of the Child*, 12: 114–26.

Haan, N. (1963) 'Proposed model of ego functioning: Coping and defense mechanisms in relationship to IQ change', *Psychological Monograph*, 77(8): 1–27.

Haan, N. (1965) 'Coping and defense mechanisms related to personality inventories', *Journal of Consulting Psychology*, 29(4): 373–8.

Haan, N. (1977) *Coping and Defending: Processes of Self-environment Organization*. New York: Academic Press.

Hamburg, D.A. (1974) 'Coping behavior in life-threatening circumstances', *Psychotherapy and Psychosomatics*, 23(1–6): 13–25.

Hartmann, H. (1939) 'Psycho-analysis and the concept of health', *International Journal of Psychoanalysis*, 20: 308–21.

Hentschel, U., Draguns, J.G., Ehlers, W. and Smith, G. (2004) 'Defense mechanisms: Current approaches to research and measurement', in U. Hentschel, G. Smith, J.G. Draguns and W. Ehlers (eds), *Defense Mechanisms: Theoretical, Research and Clinical Perspectives*. Oxford: Elsevier Science, pp. 3–41.

Hewitt, P.L. and Flett, G.L. (1996) 'Personality traits and the coping process', in M. Zeidner and N.S. Endler (eds), *Handbook of Coping: Theory, Research, Applications*. New York: John Wiley & Sons, pp. 410–33.

Hilsenroth, M.J. (2004) 'Projective assessment of personality and psychopathology: An overview', in M.J. Hilsenroth and D.L. Segal (eds), *Comprehensive Handbook of Psychological Assessment, Vol. 2: Personality Assessment*. Hoboken, NJ: John Wiley & Sons, pp. 283–96.

Holahan, C.J. and Moos, R.H. (1985) 'Life stress and health: Personality, coping, and family support in stress resistance', *Journal of Personality and Social Psychology*, 49(3): 739–47.

Hooker, K., Frazier, L.D. and Monahan, D.J. (1994) 'Personality and coping among caregivers of spouses with dementia', *Gerontologist*, 34(3): 386–92.

Hunter, C.G. and Goodstein, L.D. (1967) 'Ego strength and types of defensive and coping behavior', *Journal of Consulting Psychology*, 31(4): 432.

Ising, M., Weyers, P., Reuter, M. and Janke, W. (2006) 'Comparing two approaches for the assessment of coping: Part II. Differences in stability in time', *Journal of Individual Differences*, 27(1): 15–19.

Joffe, P.E. and Naditch, M. (1977) 'Paper and pencil measures of coping and defense processes', in N. Haan (ed.), *Coping and Defending: Processes of Self-environment Organization*. New York: Academic Press, pp. 280–97.

Juni, S. and Masling, J. (1980) 'Reaction to aggression and the Defense Mechanism Inventory', *Journal of Personality Assessment*, 44(5): 484–6.

Kato, K. and Pedersen, N.L. (2005) 'Personality and coping: A study of twins reared apart and twins reared together', *Behavior Genetics*, 35(2): 147–58.

Kenrick, D.T. and Funder, D.C. (1988) 'Profiting from controversy: Lessons from the person-situation debate', *American Psychologist*, 43(1): 23–34.

Kozak, B., Strelau, J. and Miles, J.N.V. (2005) 'Genetic determinants of individual differences in coping styles', *Anxiety, Stress and Coping: An International Journal*, 18(1): 1–15.

Kroeber, T.C. (1963) 'The coping functions of the ego mechanisms', in R.W. White (ed.), *The Study of Lives: Essays on Personality in Honor of Henry A. Murray*. New York: Atherton Press, pp. 178–89.

Krohne, H.W., Egloff, B., Varner, L.J., Burns, L.R., Weidner, G. and Ellis, H.C. (2000) 'The assessment of dispositional vigilance and cognitive avoidance: Factorial structure, psychometric properties, and validity of the Mainz Coping Inventory', *Cognitive Therapy and Research*, 24(3): 297–311.

Latack, J.C. and Havlovic, S.J. (1992) 'Coping with job stress: A conceptual evaluation framework for coping measures', *Journal of Organizational Behavior*, 13(5): 479–508.

Lazarus, R.S. (1993) 'Coping theory and research: Past, present, and future', *Psychosomatic Medicine*, 55(3): 234–47.

Lazarus, R.S., Averill, J.R. and Opton, E.M. (1974) 'The psychology of coping: Issues of research and assessment', in G.V. Coelho, D.A. Hamburg and J.E. Adams (eds), *Coping and Adaptation*. New York: Basic Books, pp. 47–68.

Lazarus, R.S. and Folkman, S. (1984) *Stress, Appraisal, and Coping*. New York: Springer.

Lee-Baggley, D., Preece, M. and DeLongis, A. (2005) 'Coping With Interpersonal Stress: Role of Big Five Traits', *Journal of Personality*, 73(5): 1141–80.

Lerner, P.M. (1991) *Psychoanalytic Theory and the Rorschach*. Hillsdale, NJ: The Analytic Press.

Litman, J.A. (2006) 'The COPE inventory: Dimensionality and relationships with approach- and avoidance-motives and positive and negative traits', *Personality and Individual Differences*, 41(2): 273–84.

Madison, P. (1956) 'Freud's repression concept: A survey and attempted clarification', *International Journal of Psychoanalysis*, 37: 75–81.

McCrae, R.R. (1992) 'Situational determinants of coping', in B.N. Carpenter (ed.), *Personal Coping: Theory, Research, and Application*. Westport, CT: Praeger, pp. 65–76.

McCrae, R.R. and Costa, P.T. (1986) 'Personality, coping, and coping effectiveness in an adult sample', *Journal of Personality*, 54(2): 385–405.

McCubbin, H.I., Hunter, E.J. and Dahl, B.B. (1975) 'Residuals of war: Families of prisoners of war and servicemen missing in action', *Journal of Social Issues*, 31(4): 95–109.

Miller, S.M. (1992) 'Individual differences in the coping process: What to know and when to know it', in B.N. Carpenter (ed.), *Personal Coping: Theory, Research, and Application*. Westport, CT: Praeger, pp. 65–76.

Mischel, W. (1973) 'Toward a cognitive, social learning reconceptualization of personality', *Psychological Review*, 80(4): 252–83.

Moorey, S., Frampton, M. and Greer, S. (2003) 'The Cancer Coping Questionnaire: A self-rating scale for measuring the impact of adjuvant psychological therapy on coping behaviour', *Psycho-Oncology*, 12(4): 331–44.

Nowack, K.M. (1989) 'Coping style, cognitive hardiness, and health status', *Journal of Behavioral Medicine*, 12(2): 145–58.

O'Brien, T.B. and DeLongis, A. (1996) 'The interactional context of problem-, emotion-, and association-focused coping: the role of the big five personality factors', *Journal of Personality*, 64(4): 775–813.

Oxlad, M., Miller-Lewis, L. and Wade, T.D. (2004) 'The measurement of coping responses: Validity of the Billings and Moos Coping Checklist', *Journal of Psychosomatic Research*, 57(5): 477–84.

Parker, J.D.A. and Endler, N.S. (1992) 'Coping with coping assessment: A critical review', *European Journal of Personality*, 6(5): 321–44.

Parker, J.D.A., Endler, N.S. and Bagby, R.M. (1993) 'If it changes, it might be unstable: Examining the factor structure of the Ways of Coping Questionnaire', *Psychological Assessment*, 5(3): 361–8.

Patterson, J.M. and McCubbin, H.I. (1987) 'Adolescent coping style and behaviors: Conceptualization and measurement', *Journal of Adolescence*, 10(2): 163–86.

Penley, J.A. and Tomaka, J. (2002) 'Associations among the Big Five, emotional responses and coping with acute stress', *Personality and Individual Differences*, 32(7): 1215–28.

Perry, J.C. and Cooper, S.H. (1989) 'What do cross-sectional measures of defense mechanisms predict', in G.E. Vaillant (ed.), *Empirical Studies of Ego Mechanisms of Defense*. Washington, DC: American Psychiatric Press, pp. 47–59.

Perry. J.C. and Ianni, F.F. (1998) 'Observer-rated measures of defense mechanisms', *Journal of Personality*, 66(6): 993–1024.

Pearlin, L.I. and Schooler, C. (1978) 'The structure of coping', *Journal of Health and Social Behavior*, 19(1): 2–21.

Pittner, M.S. and Houston, B.K. (1980) 'Response to stress, cognitive coping strategies, and the Type A behavior pattern', *Journal of Personality and Social Psychology*, 39(1): 147–57.

Popplestone, J.A. and McPherson, M.W. (1988) *Dictionary of Concepts in General Psychology*. New York: Greenwood Press.

Ptacek, J.T., Smith, R.E., Espe, K. and Raffety, B. (1994) 'Limited correspondence between daily coping reports and retrospective coping recall', *Psychological Assessment*, 6(1): 41–49.

Rafnsson, F.D., Smari, J., Windle, M., Mears, S.A. and Endler, N.S. (2006) 'Factor structure and psychometric characteristics of the Icelandic version of the Coping Inventory for Stressful Situations (CISS)', *Personality and Individual Differences*, 40(3): 1247–58.

Romano, J.M., Jensen, M.P. and Turner, J.A. (2003) 'The chronic pain coping inventory-42: Reliability and validity', *Pain*, 104(1–2): 65–73.

Roth, S. and Cohen, L.J. (1986) 'Approach, avoidance, and coping with stress', *American Psychologist*, 41(7): 813–19.

Schwartz, J.E., Neale, J., Marco, C., Shiffman, S.S. and Stone, A.A. (1999) 'Does trait coping exist? A momentary assessment approach to the evaluation of traits', *Journal of Personality and Social Psychology*, 77(2): 360–9.

Semrad, E., Grinspoon, L. and Fienberg, S.E. (1973) 'Development of an Ego Profile Scale', *Archives of General Psychiatry*, 28(1): 70–77.

Sidle, A., Moos, R.H., Adams, J. and Cady, P. (1969) 'Development of a coping scale', *Archives of General Psychiatry*, 20(2): 225–32.

Sinclair, V.G. and Wallston, K.A. (2004) 'The Development and Psychometric Evaluation of the Brief Resilient Coping Scale', *Assessment*, 11(1): 94–101.

Skinner, E.A., Edge, K., Altman, J. and Sherwood, H. (2003) 'Searching for the structure of coping: A review and critique of category systems for classifying ways of coping', *Psychological Bulletin*, 129(2): 216–69.

Somerfield, M.R. and McCrae, R.R. (2000) 'Stress and coping research: Methodological challenges, theoretical advances, and clinical applications', *American Psychologist*, 55(6): 620–5.

Speisman, J., Lazarus, R., Mordkoff, A. and Davison, L. (1964) 'Experimental reduction of stress based on ego-defense theory', *Journal of Abnormal and Social Psychology*, 68(4): 367–80.

Stanton, A.L., Kirk, S.B., Cameron, C.L. and Danoff-Burg, S. (2000) Coping through emotional approach: Scale construction and validation', *Journal of Personality and Social Psychology*, 78(6): 1150–69.

Steiner, H., Araujo, K. and Koopman, C. (2001) 'The response evaluation measure (REM-71): A new instrument for the measurement of defenses in adults and adolescents', *American Journal of Psychiatry*, 158(3): 467–73.

Stone, A.A., Greenberg, M.A., Kennedy-Moore, E. and Newman, M.G. (1991) 'Self-report, situation-specific coping questionnaires: What are they measuring?', *Journal of Personality and Social Psychology*, 61(4): 648–58.

Stone, A.A. and Neale, J.M. (1984) 'New measure of daily coping: Development and preliminary results', *Journal of Personality and Social Psychology*, 46(4): 892–906.

Suls, J., David, J.P. and Harvey, J.H. (1996) 'Personality and coping: Three generations of research', *Journal of Personality*, 64(4): 711–35.

Suls, J. and Fletcher, B. (1985) 'The relative efficacy of avoidant and nonavoidant coping strategies: A meta-analysis', *Health Psychology*, 4(3): 249–88.

Terry, D.J. (1994) 'Determinants of coping: The role of stable and situational factors', *Journal of Personality and Social Psychology*, 66(5): 895–910.

Thomae, H. (1987) 'Conceptualizations of responses to stress', *European Journal of Personality*, 1(3): 171–92.

Tobin, D.L., Holroyd, K.A., Reynolds, R.V. and Wigal, J.K. (1989) 'The hierarchical factor structure of the Coping Strategies Inventory', *Cognitive Therapy and Research*, 13(4): 343–61.

Vaillant, G.E. (1971) 'Theoretical hierarchy of adaptive ego mechanisms', *Archives of General Psychiatry*, 24(2): 107–18.

Vaillant, G.E. (1977) *Adaptation to Life*. Boston: Little, Brown.

Vaillant, G.E. (1986) *Empirical Studies of Ego Mechanisms of Defense*. Washington, DC: American Psychiatric Press.

Vaillant, G.E. (1994) 'Ego mechanisms of defense and personality psychopathology', *Journal of Abnormal Psychology*, 103(1): 44–50.

Van der Leeuw, P.J. (1971) 'On the development of the concept of defense', *International Journal of Psychoanalysis*, 52(1): 51–8.

Vickers, R.R., Hervig, L.K., Rahe, R.H. and Rosenman, R.H. (1981) 'Type A behavior pattern and coping and defense', *Psychosomatic Medicine*, 43(5): 381–96.

Viney, L.L. and Clarke, A.M. (1974) 'Children coping with crisis: An analogue study', *British Journal of Social and Clinical Psychology*, 13(3): 305–13.

Watson, D. and Hubbard B., (1996) 'Adaptational style and dispositional structure: Coping in the context of the Five-factor model', *Journal of Personality*, 64(4): 735–74.

Weinstock, A.R. (1967) 'Family environment and the development of defense and coping mechanisms', *Journal of Personality and Social Psychology*, 5(1): 67–75.

White, R.W. (1974) 'Strategies of adaptation: An attempt at systematic description', in G.V. Coelho, D.A. Hamburg and J.E. Adams (eds), *Coping and Adaptation*. New York: Basic Books, pp. 47–68.

Wiggins, J.S. and Pincus, A.L. (1992) 'Personality: Structure and assessment', *Annual Review of Psychology*, 43: 473–504.

Willebrand, M., Kildal, M., Ekselius, L., Gerdin, B. and Andersson, G. (2001) 'Development of the Coping with Burns Questionnaire', *Personality and Individual Differences*, 30(6): 1059–72.

Worthington, E.L. and Scherer, M. (2004) 'Forgiveness is an emotion-focused coping strategy that can reduce health risks and promote health resilience: Theory, review, and hypotheses', *Psychology and Health*, 19(3): 385–405.

Zeidner, M. and Saklofske, D. (1996) 'Adaptive and maladaptive coping', in M. Zeidner and N.S. Endler (eds), *Handbook of Coping: Theory, Research, Applications*. Oxford: John Wiley & Sons, pp. 505–31.

Zuckerman, M. and Gagne, M. (2003) 'The COPE revised: Proposing a 5-factor model of coping strategies', *Journal of Research in Personality*, 37(3): 169–204.

PART V

New Trait and Dynamic Trait Constructs

25

Motivational Traits: New Directions and Measuring Motives with the Multi-Motive Grid (MMG)

Thomas A. Langens and Heinz-Dieter Schmalt

Traits have been conceptualized as stable habits or styles that consistently characterize a person's behavior (Maddi, 1980), as enduring dispositions that have affective, behavioral, or attitudinal aspects (Costa and McCrae, 1980), and as 'stylistic and habitual patterns of cognition, affect, and behavior' (Emmons, 1989: 32). To describe stylistic patterns of behavior, most trait theorists recommend the five-factor model (FFM) of personality (Tupes and Christal, 1992), which identifies the traits of neuroticism, extraversion, openness to experience, agreeableness, and conscientiousness as the general building blocks of personality (Costa and McCrae, 1992). Such traditional conceptions of traits are primarily concerned with the 'how' of behavior, or how people typically behave in a given situation: Do they appear anxious or rather relaxed? Do they readily interact with strangers or do they prefer to be by themselves? Do they behave in a friendly or in a domineering way toward other persons?

Motivational psychologists (e.g. McClelland, 1985; Heckhausen, 1992; Heckhausen and Heckhausen, in press; Schneider and Schmalt, 2000), on the other hand, are primarily concerned with the 'why' of behavior: why do people act the way they do? What goal are they trying to accomplish or which end-state are they trying to attain, in a situation? It is important to note that 'how' and 'why' approaches may result in completely different explanations for any given behavior. Imagine a student who works hard and spends long hours each night reading her books and preparing papers for school. Based on this short description, trait theorists may likely characterize this student as highly conscientious. From a motivational perspective, there are several ways to approach an explanation for this behavior. First, it is possible that the student is driven by a strong *achievement motive*. She may work hard because gaining skills and exceeding standards of excellence gives her a sense of pride and accomplishment. Second, the student may be motivated by a strong *affiliation motive*. She may have learned that good grades are a means to secure her parents' affection and thus help to maintain or restore an important interpersonal relationship. Third, the student may have a strong *power motive*. Students who achieve good grades stand out, receiving attention from their classmates as well as from their teachers; this prospect is highly affectively charged for individuals high in power motivation. Thus, a single specific behavior may serve to attain completely different goal states. Simply knowing that a student works hard to attain good grades in school may not be sufficient to identify the motivational basis of behavior; that is, to explain why this behavior is exhibited. In order to do this, motivational psychologists turn to motivational traits as a basic explanatory construct. These different forms of theorizing were already emphasized by Henry Murray, who stated that 'the psychologists who think of personality as ... traits and those who think of it as ... motives focus attention on different phenomena, use different methods and end up with different accounts' (1938: 714).

In personality psychology, the concept of dynamic motivational traits was first introduced by Cattell (1957) to characterize increases and decreases of motivational tendencies which occur in response to the incentives present in different situations. We agree with Cattell (1965) that motivational processes are at the heart of personality theorizing, and that dynamic motivational traits constitute the main window to personality. As understood in this chapter, motives are decidedly similar to ergs, one of three types of dynamic traits identified by Cattell (1957). Cattell considered ergs to be innate motivators characterized by the emotions attached to them and by the biological goals they serve. Influenced by McDougall's (1932) conception of instinct, Cattell (1957) asserted that ergs direct attention to classes of objects related to the consummation of a specific incentive in the past, which then leads the person to experience a certain anticipatory

emotion and to initiate a course of action which leads to full consummatory activity. The pursuit of conscious goals – called sentiments in Cattell's system – has its roots in one or more ergs, and the main reason for goal pursuit is that it satisfies the erg or ergs which fuel goal pursuit. Thus, ergs are the motivational basis for goal pursuit; without ergs, behavior would simply be cut off from its energizing basis.

In the following, we will sketch out the main properties of motivational traits as described in present-day motivational psychology. While motivational traits have a number of unique properties which distinguish motives from traditional trait conceptions, the reader will recognize parallels to Cattell's theorizing. We will then introduce a recently developed measure which assesses motives using a semiprojective technique which does not rely on potentially biased self-descriptions. We will proceed by presenting some key empirical findings which illustrate the application and scope of motivational traits. Finally, we will point to directions for future research on dynamic motivational traits.

PROPERTIES OF MOTIVATIONAL TRAITS

In what follows, we will argue that motives can regulate behavior without necessarily resorting to conscious goals as a mediating process. Instead, motivational processes instigate behavior by means of affective processes which largely operate outside of conscious awareness. As a result, motives can only be assessed by indirect methods which do not rely on self-reports of goals or conscious aspirations. Most researchers agree that motives share the following qualities.

Motives have an affective core

The single most important assumption shared by most researchers of human motivation is that people pursue certain end-states – like surpassing standards of excellence, establishing and maintaining close relationships with other people, or trying to impress or dominate others – because of the affective consequences of attaining these end-states. Accordingly, motives are conceptualized as being based on affective preferences; that is, on the capacity to experience the consummation of motive-specific incentives as rewarding and pleasurable (McClelland, 1985; Schneider and Schmalt, 2000; Schultheiss and Brunstein, 2005). Alternatively, motives represent the 'disposition to be concerned with and to strive for a certain class of incentives or goals' (Emmons, 1989: 32). For example, people who are high in achievement motivation have 'the *capacity* to take pride in accomplishments' (Atkinson, 1964: 241) which are due to their own effort and persistence. Those low in achievement motivation, in contrast, may have the ability to perform as well or even better on the same tasks, but may lack the capacity to reap the emotional rewards of surpassing a standard of excellence. Similarly, those with a strong affiliation motive are able to enjoy a close and secure relationship more than individuals low in affiliation motivation. Finally, people who have a strong need for power are emotionally simulated by the experience of 'feeling strong' (McClelland, 1975: 77) – by dominating, impressing, or having an impact on other people – in a way those low in power motivation are not. Hence, people differ in the persistence and effort they invest in pursuing certain end-states because they differ in the capacity to experience positive emotions which result from attaining these end-states.

Motives regulate behavior by assigning emotional significance to stimuli

Through a life-long history of experience, people learn not only which stimuli or situations satisfy a particular motive, but also which cues predict the availability of a motive-specific incentive. By associative learning, these stimuli acquire the capacity to trigger an anticipatory emotional response which attracts people to certain situations while making them avoid others (Weinberger and McClelland, 1990). For example, if a child has learned that confronting a challenging task introduced by a parent eventually leads to solving the challenge and, in turn, to positive emotions like joy or pride, then the presentation of similar tasks will trigger anticipatory positive emotions which draw the child to these tasks in the future. If, on the other hand, parents consistently set tasks which are too difficult for the child and lead to frustration, then similar tasks will trigger negative emotional responses which direct the child away from them (Heckhausen and Heckhausen in press; Schultheiss and Brunstein, 2005). It follows from this description that the primary manifestation of motivational processes may be conceived of as a set of *forces* acting upon and directing a person either toward a desired object or away from a dreaded or potentially harmful situation. Indeed, this idea has a long history in motivational theory, beginning with Lewin's (1935) field theory which introduced a *dynamic* interpretation of behavior.

Approach and avoidance tendencies can be distinguished for each of the three basic motives. In the domain of achievement motivation, persons may be motivated either by hope of success or by fear of failure, such that any situation in which performance can be compared to a standard of excellence will acquire a positive emotional significance for individuals with a strong hope of success and a negative emotional significance for individuals with a high fear of failure. Similarly, power-motivated individuals may be characterized by hope of power or by fear of loss of power, while affiliation motivation can take the form of hope of affiliation or fear of rejection. It is important to note that the strength of hope and fear components of a motive are generally independent of each other. Thus, a person may be high in both hope of affiliation and fear of rejection, being attracted to social encounters as well as being driven away from them.

Motives have to be aroused in order to regulate behavior

A motive does not instigate behavioral tendencies on its own. Thus, a person with a strong achievement motive is not expected to strive for excellence in each and every situation, but only if a situation offers an incentive which signals that achievement needs may be satisfied (Heckhausen, 1992; Schneider and Schmalt, 2000). In order to influence thought and behavior, motives have to be aroused by an incentive which is tailored to the specific demands of the motive. In the case of the achievement motive, a strong incentive is a task of medium difficulty which offers immediate and contingent performance feedback (Heckhausen et al., 1985). Thus, a strong hope of success will lead to high effort and persistence only if the present task offers these characteristics. The general principle that motives have to be aroused by a specific incentive in order to influence behavior can explain the lack of empirical findings sometimes reported. For example, there is no evidence that students high in achievement motivation generally attain better grades than students low in achievement motivation (Entwisle, 1972). However, such a finding may be expected, given that students differ greatly in ability and knowledge, so that each task set by a teacher is of medium difficulty only for a small fraction of students. In addition, explicit social demands to do well, so often encountered in educational settings, may undermine spontaneous or self-determined behavior regulated by implicit achievement motivation (Deci and Ryan, 1991; Spangler, 1992). Hence, achievement motivation is most closely related to performance if an individual encounters a challenging task but is free to choose task difficulty. It may be for this reason that achievement motivation is strongly related to entrepreneurial success (Collins et al., 2004).

In summary, individual differences in motive strength will only translate into behavioral differences if a motive is aroused by an appropriate incentive, with the effect that 'motivated goal-directed behavior shows intelligent variation in relation to the situation' (Winter et al., 1998). This position was already a basic element of interactionism, which stressed the need to study personality relative to the subjective significance of situations (Endler and Magnusson, 1974; Mischel and Shoda, 1995). Likewise, Funder (2006) reiterated this claim for developing a way to conceptualize and measure aspects of situations that are psychologically relevant.

Motivational states are dynamic

While traits are conceptualized to vary between persons, they are assumed to remain rather stable within a person. Although an extraverted person is not expected to behave in an extraverted manner in each and every situation, a central proposition of traditional trait theory assumes that people occupy the same rank with respect to the criterion behavior in a variety of situations. In contrast, it is assumed not only that motives differ between persons, but also that motivational states fluctuate within a person over time. As outlined above, a motive may remain in a dormant state as long as it is not aroused by an incentive. Once triggered by an appropriate incentive, however, motivational states tend to persist or even increase over time (Bargh et al., 2001). A state of an aroused motivation diminishes only if the person comes into contact with the desired incentive and consummates the rewards associated with it, or if he or she disengages from goal pursuit. After attaining a motivational incentive, there might even be a 'refractory phase', which may prevent a successive arousal of the same motivational state over extended periods of time (Atkinson and Birch, 1970). Such dynamic fluctuations of motivational states may sometimes give the impression of erratic behavior. From a broader perspective, however, motivated behavior is coherent when taking into account the motivational incentives present in a given situation and the person's history of motivated goal pursuit.

Since motives operate outside of conscious awareness, they have to be assessed by indirect methods

Traditional trait theory assumes that people have the capacity to validly reflect on their traits and the behavior which corresponds to a certain trait. As a telling example, consider the ten-item measure of the Big Five personality traits, which, although only providing brief verbal descriptions of each trait, correlates strongly with extended measures of the FFM (Gosling et al., 2003). In contrast, asking individuals to report on their personal dispositions, preferences, or behavioral inclinations does not work when attempting to assess motivational traits because, unlike traditional traits, motives operate outside of conscious awareness and therefore cannot be measured in self-report. As outlined above, motives shape behavior indirectly by assigning emotional significance to environmental stimuli and not by initiating a declarative process which is available to conscious processing. People are typically unaware that their behavior has been influenced by their motives and, consequently, cannot validly reflect on their motives. In support of this claim, a wealth of studies show that self-report measures of motives (which are also called self-attributed motives or explicit motives) are unrelated to affect-based motives (which are also called implicit motives), which we focus on in this chapter (McClelland et al., 1989; Spangler, 1992). Since motives cannot be assessed using self-report measures, they have to be assessed using indirect measures, a problem we will turn to shortly.

Because motives are not represented in conscious awareness, motivational psychology distinguishes between end-states (which

a person may not be aware of pursuing) and goals (conscious conceptions of things a person strives to attain). Motives are generally unrelated to the conscious goals a person is pursuing at any time (Woike, 1995; Emmons and McAdams, 1991). Even more to the point, conscious goals may often be little more than rationalizations people construe to explain to themselves and others their efforts to attain a certain end-state (Nisbett and Wilson, 1977; Wilson and Dunn, 2004). Thus, a person high in power motivation is unlikely to explain his behavior by saying 'I wanted to tell him off and make him look like a fool because doing so makes me feel good', but rather by formulating a sensible and rational explanation like 'My belief in the importance of egalitarian values urged me to demonstrate my point of view', because the latter is socially accepted. Similarly, in an argument, a person high in the need for power may raise his voice without even realizing it, simply because this behavior has previously had positive consequences (the opponent backed off) which led to a feeling of elation, strength, and dominance.

So, while self-report is not a valid indicator of implicit motives, motives can be assessed by indirect methods which assess spontaneous associations, thoughts and fantasies elicited by an aroused state of motivation. In the following, we will present a newly developed method to assess implicit motives which operates on the premise that motives assign emotional significance to stimuli, which then lead a person either to confront or to avoid a particular situation.

MEASURING MOTIVATIONAL TRAITS WITH THE MULTI-MOTIVE GRID (MMG)

General principles of motive assessment

The measurement of implicit motivational traits has a long and venerable tradition in psychology, which can be traced back to Freud's (1900) claim that motives manifest themselves indirectly, for example in fantasies and dreams. Some of the major issues of the psychoanalytic theory of motivation were incorporated into a dynamic theory of personality by Murray (1938), who also developed a seminal technique to measure implicit motives, the Thematic Apperception Test (TAT). McClelland and his associates (McClelland et al., 1953; Atkinson, 1958) refined Murray's technique by confronting individuals with a set of somewhat ambiguous pictures which yield the appropriate incentives for arousing a targeted motive (achievement, affiliation, or power) and asking them to make up a fanciful story about the situation portrayed in the picture. Stories written in response to the pictures were scored for a variety of subcategories, such as a stated need, anticipatory positive or negative goal states associated with the aroused motivational tendency, and instrumental activities (Atkinson, 1958; Smith, 1992).

Researchers who relied on the TAT for measuring motives always emphasized the unique feature of this measure, which is that motives are aroused by picture cues. It was argued that a TAT picture operates like a *real-life situation* (Heckhausen, 1967) and gives rise to motivational processes (e.g. goal anticipation, expectancies) corresponding to those processes elicited in a real-life situation (Atkinson, 1958). Whereas words primarily activate declarative knowledge about the self, pictures automatically and efficiently activate the affective networks resulting from one's life-long experience with incentives, which are the building blocks of implicit motives (Kuhl et al., 2003). Hence, it is contended that motive arousal by picture cues represents the *via regia* to assess implicit motivational traits. Triggering motives with pictured situations allows a quick, unobtrusive, and undisturbed activation of memory structures which correspond to processes observed in real-life situations.

Cognitive psychology has elaborated this position, giving special attention to the analysis of visual images (mental imagery; e.g. Anderson, 1983). Most of this research used an experimental paradigm which analyzed the retrieval processes of encoding pictures versus words, using the process dissociation procedure developed by Jacoby and Kelley (1990). One of the basic tenets of this research states that the mental processes operating upon a visual image are similar to those underlying the perception of a real object (Azizian et al., 2006; Johnson-Laird, 1989: 147). Jacoby and Kelley (1990) elaborated this theoretical position in regard to episodic memory. They argue that highly motivated individuals have repeatedly acted in ways consistent with their motivational predisposition. When motivated to attain a certain end-state, memories of these prior episodes are used unconsciously to guide the perception and interpretation of a situation. However, individuals may later be unable to consciously report their motives, because these motives were not part of their conscious experience in the original situation. Indeed, experiments designed to manipulate motivational orientations often produce behavioral changes without corresponding changes in the self-reports of the underlying motives (Nisbett and Wilson, 1977; Wilson and Dunn, 2004). It is argued that mental processing of these motivational states is simply inaccessible to conscious scrutiny. Schacter and colleagues directly examined the memory processes involved in encoding pictures versus those involved in encoding words (Dodson and Schacter, 2002; Budson et al., 2005). They found that memorizing pictures (as opposed to words) was related to lower rates of false recognition in a subsequent memory task. These authors suggest that picture cues generate a particular 'retrieval orientation' based on individuals' meta-memorial assessments of the kinds of information they 'feel they should remember' (Strack and Bless, 1994). Additional analyses based on event-related potentials examined the neural correlates of this retrieval orientation. Schacter and his associates report that individuals memorizing pictures adopted a meta-cognitive strategy leading to a retrieval orientation relying upon recollection. Individuals studying words, on the other hand, did not rely upon recollection and needed to engage in additional post retrieval processing in order to consciously evaluate contents of memory. Such judgmental inferences are reminiscent of a deliberative mindset described by Gollwitzer and his co-workers (Gollwitzer et al., 2004), whereas the former is reminiscent of the automatic activation of motivational tendencies created by priming procedures (Bargh and Chartrand, 1999).

To summarize, research on the processing of pictures versus words has documented a differential impact on memory. First, it has been shown that pictures (as compared to words) are processed with higher priority (the 'picture superiority effect') and, second, that the right medial temporal lobe is involved in picture recognition, testifying to the affective nature of the information being processed. It is contended that the superior processing of pictorial information in memory is due to humans' long-lasting interaction with the world, which is largely visual and based on pictorial information and not some abstract, amodal representation, like propositional networks.

The development of the multi-motive grid as a measure of implicit motives

Taken together, the merits of the TAT seem to hinge on the assumption that motives are aroused unconsciously by picture cues, providing a direct representation of basic motivational processes. The grid technique, developed by Schmalt and colleagues (Schmalt, 1976, 1999, 2005; Sokolowski et al., 2000), combines features of the TAT and traditional questionnaire measures. Analogous to the TAT, a series of ambiguous pictures is presented to arouse motive dispositions,

but instead of requiring participants to write stories in response to the pictures, a set of statements representing motivational tendencies in terms of needs, emotional responses, goal anticipations, and instrumental acts is appended to each picture. Typically, these statements cover those areas of content that were originally measured by the TAT scoring categories. Thus the grid technique resembles the TAT in that motives are aroused by pictorial stimuli, but resembles traditional questionnaires in the test responses. This combination has two advantages: it allows for an arousal of motives by unconsciously tapping into the subjective 'incentive landscapes' of an individual while at the same time yielding standardized test responses which are amenable to classical test theory. Additionally, having participants write fanciful stories which have to be analyzed using elaborate coding systems (which is a time-consuming procedure requiring a high level of expertise) is avoided and replaced by a more advantageous traditional item format.

Our considerations concerning the theoretical background of measuring motivational traits with the help of picture interpretations have highlighted the crucial role of the picture cues themselves. In contrast to the rather intuitive selection of pictures to assess motives using the TAT (Smith, 1992; for an exception see Schultheiss and Brunstein, 2001), the development of the MMG and the selection of pictures was based on an empirical strategy. Two stimulus dimensions of the pictured situations seem to be important in this respect: *ambiguity* and *stimulus pull* (Epstein, 1962; Murstein, 1963). Stimulus pull refers to the strength of the incentive for a certain motive. Ambiguity refers to the diversity of motivational themes (power, affiliation, achievement) a picture can arouse. A picture is identified as ambiguous if it arouses more than one motive with a substantial level of pull.

When we developed the MMG (Sokolowski et al., 2000), we first drew on a screening procedure in which we collected TAT pictures, verbal descriptions, newspaper ads, and photographs which seemed to be appropriate for measuring the three motives. Next, an artist was commissioned to draw approximately 60 pictures. In order to give enough latitude in interpreting the pictures, it was decided to use line drawings which do not depict the facial expression of the pictured persons. In an initial study, experts were asked to rate how strongly each picture exerted a pull for the achievement, power, and affiliation motives. The obtained means indicate the stimulus pull of each picture in relation the three motives under consideration (see Sokolowski, et al., 2000: table 2). There are pictures that arouse only one motive and hence possess low ambiguity, like 'Taking a test' (see Picture 9 in Figure 25.1) which arouses only the achievement motive. The picture portraying a group at work (Picture 14, Figure 25.1), on the other hand, arouses all three motives simultaneously and thus possesses high ambiguity. Our selection strategy was to provide a set of pictures covering all three thematic domains with different levels of ambiguity.

In the next step, we generated statements which reflect the motivational orientation aroused by the pictures for each of the three motivational domains. Again the principles of selecting the concrete thematic content

were tailored according to the relevant TAT conventions. The statements employed in the MMG represent motivational tendencies in terms of positive and negative goal anticipations, positive and negative affective states while pursuing a goal, and instrumental activities.

Right from the beginning of motive assessment using the TAT, it was clear that approach and avoidance tendencies had to be discerned, but adequate measurement of these tendencies proved to be difficult. The only measure that worked satisfactorily, judged on theoretical as well as empirical grounds, was Heckhausen's TAT measure (Heckhausen, 1963) which contains different scoring categories for approach and avoidance tendencies (Heckhausen et al., 1985). The statements of the MMG were developed according to these standards. The statements retained for the final version of MMG had the highest factor loadings in different factor analyses computed on earlier versions. In this version, the MMG comprises 12 statements measuring hopes and fears for the three motives (see Table 25.1). Each statement appears in only 6 situations, resulting in a 6 (motives) × 2 (statements) × 6 (situations) = 72 items test format. This version of the MMG (which we call MMG-S) outperforms earlier versions with respect to psychometric

Table 25.1   Statements of the MMG which are used to assess the approach and avoidance tendencies of the achievement, power, and affiliation motive

Domain	Approach	Avoidance
Achievement	Hope of success (HS)	Fear of failure (FF)
	Feeling confident to succeed at this task	Thinking about lacking abilities at this task
	Feeling good about one's competency	Wanting to postpone a difficult task for a while
Power	Hope of power (HP)	Fear of loss of power (FP)
	Trying to influence other people	Anticipating to lose standing
	Hoping to acquire a good standing	Being afraid of being overpowered by other people.
Affiliation	Hope of affiliation (HA)	Fear of rejection (FR)
	Feeling good about meeting other people	Being afraid of being rejected by others
	Hoping to get in touch with other people	Being afraid of being boring to others

Picture 9: Taking a test

Picture 11: Badminton

Picture 14: Work group

Figure 25.1   Three pictures of the Multi-Motive Grid characterized by low ambiguity (Picture 9, 'Taking a Test'), moderate ambiguity (Picture 11, 'Badminton'), and high ambiguity (Picture 14, 'Work Group')

properties and construct validity. It takes about 15 minutes to complete the test.

Applying the instructions typically used for the TAT measurement of motives, participants are asked to 'put yourself in the position of one of the persons shown in these pictures' and to imagine what is going on in the picture, and what the people shown are thinking and feeling. Next, participants are asked to decide for each statement whether it fits this situation by checking either 'YES' or 'NO'. The score of individual motive strength is calculated by adding up all the motive-relevant statements answered with a 'YES' for all the 14 situations.

Internal consistencies of the resulting scales are medium to high, ranging from 0.65 to 0.80. To explore the underlying structure of the MMG, we employed both exploratory and confirmatory factor analyses (see Sokolowski et al., 2000) which yielded two main results. First, we found that the approach tendencies cluster together to form a generalized approach factor, whereas the avoidance tendencies make up a generalized avoidance factor. This result is in accord with recent research suggesting that approach and avoidance are the general building blocks of personality which determine whether people are generally responsive to incentives or threats (Elliot and Thrash, 2002). Likewise, Gable et al. (2003) found that the hope and the fear scales of the MMG loaded significantly on the appropriate latent variables in a two-factor model with one approach and one avoidance factor. Second, evidence from confirmatory factor analysis suggested that the three motivational domains of achievement, power, and affiliation can still be distinguished. The model that fitted the data best was a six-factor model which allowed for hopes and fears to be correlated (see Sokolowski et al., 2000: 133).

Earlier, we claimed that implicit motives are unrelated to self-reports of needs and goals. To test this claim, we (Schmalt and Langens, 1996) correlated the MMG scales with the corresponding scales of the personality research form (PRF), a well-established self-report measure of motivational needs, and the thematic content of personal strivings which are conceptualized as the goals a person is typically pursuing in his daily life (Emmons, 1989). As expected, there were no significant relationships between the MMG on the one hand, and the PRF and goals on the other (all r's < 0.13), which clearly demonstrates that MMG scores are independent of conscious conceptions of one's needs and desires. The next section complements these results by showing that the MMG predicts a variety of key indicators of motivational processes.

EMPIRICAL STUDIES RELATING MOTIVATIONAL TRAITS TO THOUGHT AND BEHAVIOR

In this section, we will summarize empirical studies which demonstrate that motivational traits shape thought, emotional processes, and behavior in an indirect yet meaningful way. We will first focus on how motives sensitize individuals to emotional stimuli and induce a readiness to respond by moving towards or away from stimuli. Then, focusing on achievement motivation, we will illustrate how motives indirectly lead individuals to approach or avoid standards of excellence. The next section illustrates how distinguishing between approach and avoidance motivation

helps to integrate diverse findings on power motivation. Finally, focusing on affiliation motivation, we will give an overview of studies which show how motives influence long-term emotional well-being.

Sensitivity to emotional stimuli and motor behavior

As alluded to before, motives exert their influence on basic perceptual and motor processes, sensitizing individuals for certain classes of stimuli and acting like forces drawing them toward desired stimuli or away from harmful situations. In the following, we will discuss empirical studies which employed the MMG to illustrate these propositions. A study by Langens and Dorr (2006) demonstrated that motives are sensitive to relevant stimuli even if these stimuli are not accessible to conscious awareness. Participants worked on a computerized version of the emotional Stroop task in which they had to name the color of a circle presented on a computer screen as quickly as possible. In some trials, schematic faces with neutral, angry, or friendly expressions were presented before the colored circle appeared. In one condition, the faces were presented subliminally (for about 16 ms), so that in effect participants were unable to consciously recognize the faces. In another condition, the faces were presented supraliminally (for 250 ms). We reasoned that the performance of participants predominantly high in fear of failure (as opposed to participants who were predominantly high in hope of success) would be disrupted by faces which could be interpreted as evaluating their performance on this task (i.e. friendly and angry faces). The results showed that resultant achievement motivation (a measure calculated by subtracting fear of failure from hope of success, see Heckhausen et al., 1985) as measured by the MMG was significantly correlated with response latencies on the Stroop task when emotional faces were presented subliminally, but not when emotional faces were presented supraliminally (see Figure 25.2). The longest response latencies were evident when emotional faces were presented subliminally to participants who were predominantly high in fear of failure, suggesting that failure-oriented individuals (FF > HS) were distracted by emotional faces without being able to consciously perceive them. Additionally, individuals who were predominantly motivated by hope of success (HS > FF) tended to respond faster on the Stroop task when emotional faces were presented subliminally. Thus, the achievement motives seem to be susceptible to relevant cues (i.e. cues signaling approval or disapproval) even if these cues are not represented in conscious awareness. In fact, the distracting effect of emotional faces was absent when faces could be consciously perceived. We suspect that presenting emotional faces supraliminally may have triggered additional strategic processes (e.g. conscious intentions to do well) which may have overridden the

effects of emotional faces on automatic evaluative processes (mediated by motives) which were evident when the faces were presented subliminally (for a similar argument, see Lundh et al., 2001).

Whereas the study by Langens and Dorr (2006) suggests that motives sensitize individuals to relevant emotional stimuli, a recent study by Puca et al. (2006) investigated whether motives preactivate approach or avoidance motor responses in response to environmental stimuli. The main dependent variable in these studies was response force. Since response force is essential for regulating the distance between an individual and a desired or feared object, it is a more direct indicator of motor processes than response time. The main hypothesis of this research was that basic motivational systems like approach and avoidance preactivate the motor system, such that a strong (relative to weak) avoidance motivation prepares an individual to perform avoidance movements more forcefully, whereas a strong (relative to

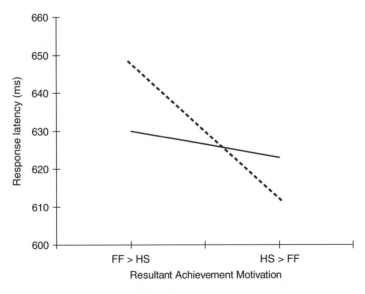

Figure 25.2   Response latencies on the emotional Stroop task for trials in which emotional faces (friendly or angry) were presented just before the target stimulus as a function of resultant achievement motivation (FF: fear of failure; HS: hope of success). Faces were either presented subliminally (dashed line) or supraliminally (solid line)

weak) approach motivation prepares an individual to perform approach movements more forcefully. In the first experiment, participants worked on a lexical decision task in which they had to respond to words presented on a computer screen by either moving their forearm towards the screen (approach movement) or away from the screen (avoidance movement). Using MMG scores as predictors, the results showed that participants with strong avoidance motives performed avoidance movements more forcefully than participants with weak avoidance motives. A second study replicated and extended this finding. Participants were asked to respond to an acoustic signal which came from behind or in front of them by moving their arm either forward or backward. The results showed that highly avoidance motivated individuals exerted more powerful movements aimed at increasing the distance to external stimuli than low avoidance motivated individuals (see Figure 25.3). These studies thus conclusively show that

avoidance motivation induces a readiness to increase one's distance from environmental stimuli, which directly translates into more forceful and vigorous motor responses away from them.

Indirect influences on behavior: The case of achievement motivation

Earlier, we contended that motives shape behavior not by running of declarative processes which result in conscious goals, but rather indirectly by assigning emotional significance to stimuli, attracting a person towards desired objects and tasks and repelling them from dreaded situations. We will now look at empirical studies which illustrate how the achievement motives – hope of success and fear of failure – exert their influence on behavior and performance.

As noted before, the optimal incentive for hope of success (HS) is a task of medium difficulty which provides immediate and

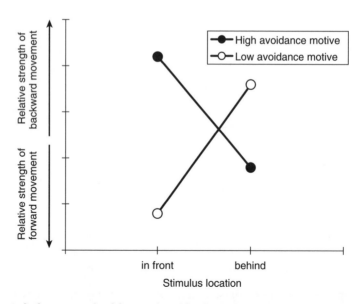

Figure 25.3   Relative strength of forward and backward movements in response to acoustic signals coming from behind or in front of participants as a function of avoidance motivation (adapted from Puca et al., 2006)

accurate performance feedback. Tasks which meet these criteria are especially likely to arouse positive emotions such as enjoyment and elation in individuals high in HS. Hence, a person high in HS may persist in struggling to complete a task not because she tries to reach a pre-set goal, but because of the positive emotions aroused by competing with a standard of excellence. Testing this assumption, Puca and Schmalt (1999) had participants work on a challenging reaction time task, telling them either that they would receive feedback for their performance or that they would not. Participants predominantly high in HS reported having enjoyed the task more and demonstrated better performance than participants predominantly high in fear of failure (FF). In addition, the connection between the achievement motives and performance was mediated by task enjoyment, but only when participants were anticipating performance feedback. In summary, arousal of positive emotions (task enjoyment) mediated the relationship between achievement motivation and performance only if the task provided all the elements constituting an optimal incentive for achievement motivation (i.e. challenge and feedback). In this way, enjoyment indirectly led participants high in HS to excel at this task without necessarily inducing a conscious goal to do so.

Recently, the results of Puca and Schmalt (1999) were nicely complemented by a study by Schüler (submitted), who investigated the antecedents of flow-experience in academic settings. Csikszentmihalyi (1975) proposed that flow experience – a subjective state characterized by complete task-involvement and, typically, high performance – results from a balance of personal skills and the challenge presented by a task. Atkinson's (1964) theory of achievement motivation, on the other hand, posits that a challenge–skill balance presents an optimal incentive only for individuals who are predominantly high in hope of success. Integrating these two lines of research, Schüler argues that a challenge–skill balance should be related to

flow experience only among individuals who are characterized by high hope of success, and should be absent for failure-motivated individuals. This hypothesis was supported by two studies which assessed motives (MMG), challenge–skill balance, flow, and performance (exam grades) among university students: The highest level of flow-experience was evident among participants high in hope of success who reported that the challenge posed by the academic environment matched their skills; flow, in turn, predicted exam grades. Again, these studies demonstrate how motives indirectly exert their influence on behavior, in this case by promoting a complete task-involvement which fosters optimal performance. In the next paragraph, we will illustrate how fear of failure indirectly shapes behavior by generating fantasies and daydreams.

As already alluded to, we subscribe to Freud's (1900) view that motives primarily manifest themselves in conscious awareness in the form of spontaneous fantasies like dreams and daydreams. Klinger (1990) posits that daydreaming occurs when a motivational impulse cannot be translated into behavior due to a lack of an opportunity to act or a strong avoidance motivation. For example, a person high in power motivation who has just been provoked by someone else may not act upon this provocation, but rather daydream of getting back to the person because retaliation is impossible in the current situation (e.g. a classroom setting) and/or because he or she is high in fear of loss of power. Similarly, a person high in fear of failure may often daydream about succeeding in school or business while at the same time avoiding real-life opportunities to get ahead. Hence, we expected a substantial relationship between avoidance motives and the content of spontaneous daydreaming. A study by Schmalt and Langens (1996) investigated this issue. Participants monitored their daydreaming over a one-week period and subsequently reported the most frequent and most meaningful daydreams they had. Daydreams were then coded for thematic content; that is, whether they revolved around the themes of achievement, power, or affiliation. Table 25.2 shows that the MMG motive scores predict daydreaming activity in the domains of achievement and power. Note also that daydreaming is unrelated to the PRF measure of self-reported motivation. This finding is in accord with the more general assumption that individuals with strong avoidance motives are inclined to seek vicarious satisfaction of their motives. For example, studies which employed the MMG found that video games are especially attractive for adolescents high in fear of failure (Wegge et al., 1994).

Having collected evidence that failure-motivated individuals tend to daydream about attaining achievement-related goals, we (Langens and Schmalt, 2002) next investigated how such daydreams further shape goal pursuit of real-life goals. We first found that individuals high in fear of failure who heavily daydream about attaining achievement-related goals reported lower levels of emotional well-being compared to (1) individuals high in fear of failure who did not have such daydreams and (2) individuals low in fear of failure who did have many achievement-related daydreams. These results seemed to suggest that positive day dreaming somehow reduced emotional well-being among individuals high in fear of failure. In a second study, we had participants

either imagine the successful attainment of an achievement-related goal or failure to attain such a goal. This study showed that individuals high in fear of failure reduced their commitment to pursue the imagined goal in real life when they imagined a successful goal pursuit (but not when they imagined failing at goal pursuit). Employing a behavioral indicator of motivation, Langens (2003) found that individuals high in fear of failure showed the lowest levels of motivation to prepare for an upcoming exam if they imagined successfully taking the exam. These studies suggest that positive daydreaming seems to have an array of detrimental emotional and motivational effects on individuals high in fear of failure; for them, imagining the successful attainment of an important personal goal seems to induce negative mood, provokes disengagement from goal pursuit, and is followed by lower levels of motivation to pursue this goal. Langens and Schmalt (2002) argue that such a pattern of responses can best be explained by assuming that individuals high in fear of failure are especially sensitive to having their hopes confounded. Daydreaming about successes in school or sports may give failure-motivated individuals a vivid idea how beautiful it would be to attain their goals. However, because they are high in fear of failure, they typically doubt that they will be able to do so in reality. This contrast of imagining success and then realizing that it will be out of reach is likely to lead to anticipatory disengagement from goal pursuit and low levels of motivation.

In summary, the studies presented in this section suggest that enjoyment and flow mediates the relationship between hope of success and high performance on challenging tasks, whereas spontaneous fantasies such as daydreams mediate the relationship between fear of failure and disengagement from goal pursuit. In either case, these studies show how motives as assessed by the MMG indirectly shape behavior and performance.

Table 25.2 Relationships between motives as measured by the MMG and the PRF and the content of spontaneous daydreaming

	Content of daydreaming	
	Achievement	Power
Achievement		
MMG-hope of success	0.13	0.15
MMG-fear of failure	0.31**	0.23+
PRF-achievement	−0.05	−0.06
Power		
MMG-hope of power	0.17	0.25*
MMG-fear of loss of power	0.32**	0.28*
PRF-power	0.16	0.17

Note: **p< .01.*p<.05. + p<.10.

Differentiating approach and avoidance motivation: The case of power motivation

A central feature which distinguishes the MMG from the Thematic Apperception Test is its ability to measure both the approach and avoidance components of motivation. Because TAT measures of motives do not distinguish between approach and avoidance, the features and functional properties of avoidance motivation have received only cursory attention in the past decades (McGregor and Elliot, 2005). Using the power motive as an example, we will next outline how differentiating between approach and avoidance motivation can help to integrate an array of seemingly contradictory findings reported in the empirical literature.

The power motive has been related to a wide variety of socially accepted behaviors such as managerial success, office holding, and persuasiveness, as well as a cluster of 'profligate' behaviors such as exploitative sexual behavior, vicarious sexual behavior (e.g. reading 'Playboy'), drinking and drug use (Winter, 1988). There have been quite a few attempts to identify moderators which explain whether the power motive is expressed by socially acceptable means or by profligate behavior. These attempts include the formulation of such concepts as socialized and personalized power (McClelland et al., 1972), activity inhibition (McClelland, 1975), and responsibility (Winter and Barenbaum, 1985). Schmalt (submitted) has recently suggested that the motivational orientation of power motivation may be the most valid way to conceptualize how power motivation is expressed in behavior. Office holding as well as managerial success and persuasiveness require confidence, skill, and expertise as well as a willingness to directly interact with others in order to gain or maintain a position of high status. Behaviors which meet these criteria may therefore be related to approach motivation characterized by *hope of power*. On the other hand, alcohol, exploitative sex, and drug abuse may

function as substitutes which give satisfaction to those individuals who avoid direct, socially approved attempts to assert themselves against the opposition of another person, because they are fearful that their attempts to dominate and feel strong will not meet with success. Thus, profligate behavior may be an outlet for avoidance motivation characterized by a *fear of loss of power*. A joint factor analysis of various behavioral indicators of power motivation, as well as the MMG scores of hope of power and fear of loss of power clearly demonstrated that approach and avoidance are central dimensions of power-related behaviors (see Figure 25.4). The approach factor was characterized by office holding, an interest in prestige possessions and hope of power as measured by the MMG. Conversely, drinking alcohol as a means to regulate negative mood, exploitative sexual behavior and drug abuse, and fear of loss of power all loaded high on the avoidance factor. Thus, there is some evidence that socially acceptable means to gain or maintain power are primarily utilized by individuals high in hope of power, whereas people high in fear of loss of power resort to vicarious experiences which may give them the experience of 'feeling strong' without having to risk social defeat.

To further investigate the effects of approach and avoidance power motivation on social behavior, we will next consider a set of studies which focused on dating behavior. Generally speaking, approach motivation should induce a motivational focus which is sensitive to potential gains, whereas avoidance motivation should sensitize an individual to potential losses (Higgins, 1997). Applied to the context of dating behavior, hope of power should increase the salience of characteristics which indicate an individual's attractiveness, whereas fear of loss of power may sensitize an individual to potential threats to a relationship. These assumptions were investigated by two recent studies.

Focusing on approach motivation, Schmalt (2006) investigated whether the attractiveness ratings of females who differed in their

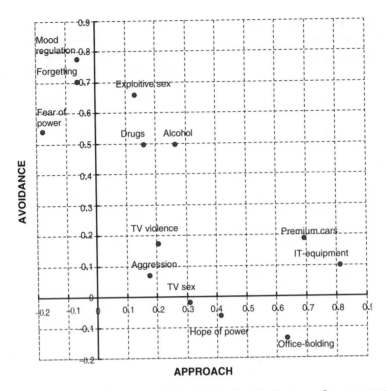

Figure 25.4 Result of a joint factor analysis of behavioral indicators of power motivation and MMG-hope of power and MMG-fear of loss of power (cf. Schmalt, 2006)

waist-to-hip ratio (WHR) are moderated by the power motive. Singh (1993) has argued that female body shape, and particularly WHR, is a reliable indicator of a female's reproductive status, reproductive capability, and health, such that a WHR of 0.7 signals optimal reproductive capability and health and is consequently appraised as highly attractive. There are several lines of argumentation which suggest that men high in hope of power may differentially prefer women with a WHR of 0.7. First, power-motivated men may conceive of women as 'prestige possessions' and may therefore prefer highly attractive women who stand out and draw the attention of other men. From the perspective of evolutionary psychology, a strong power motivation may have proved adaptive because high status seems to be related to reproductive success in human as well as non-human primates (Harcourt, 1989), suggesting that power motivation is related to a capacity to identify cues which are related to reproductive success. Both arguments suggest that high (relative to low) power-motivated individuals are more discriminative concerning WHR information and that, accordingly, attractiveness ratings of females should co-vary more strongly with WHR. Supporting this assumption, Schmalt (2006) found that the variance of attractiveness ratings of females with WHRs ranging from 0.7 to 1.0 was related to power motivation, such that high (relative to low) resultant power motivation (HP > FP) was associated with a stronger preference for a WHR of 0.7 (as compared to larger WHRs). In other words, individuals low in power motivation did not base their attractiveness ratings as much on WHR as individuals high in resultant power motivation. These results thus show that hope of power seems to sensitize individuals to information concerning possible gains, such as a female's attractiveness as indicated by WHR.

A study by Esters (2006) scrutinized the relationship between fear of loss of power and potential losses by investigating emotional responses to sexual infidelity. Participants were shown a series of six pictures of a man and a woman in situations which depicted possible situations of sexual infidelity with varying degrees of explicitness and ambiguity. For example, while the first picture showed a man applying sun tan lotion to the back of a female lying on a beach, the last picture of the series showed a couple having an overt sexual relationship. Participants were asked to imagine that they happen to observe their romantic partner in the situation depicted in the pictures and to rate the emotions they would experience. Not surprisingly, jealousy (which was operationalized as the sum of negative emotional responses to the picture) was directly related to explicitness of sexual infidelity. In addition, there was a significant interaction between explicitness and fear of loss of power (FP) among male participants: whereas men both high and low in FP responded similarly to ambiguous pictures,

the difference between the two groups grew larger as the pictures became more explicit. The highest level of jealousy was reported by men high in FP who rated the most explicit picture (see Figure 25.5).

Taken together, the results of Schmalt (2006) and Esters (2006) clearly demonstrate a differential sensitivity for potential gains and losses in individuals high in HP and FP. Whereas individuals high in hope of power are especially sensitive to information regarding potential gains (attractiveness of a potential female dating partner), individuals high in fear of loss of power are especially sensitive to information regarding a potential loss (a partner's infidelity). This research again underlines the importance to distinguish between approach and avoidance motivation and the need for diagnostic instruments which allow the assessment of both.

Affiliation motivation and emotional wellbeing

An increasingly large body of research suggests that motivational processes are closely intertwined with emotional well-being and physical health (e.g. McClelland, 1989). Recent research employing the MMG has

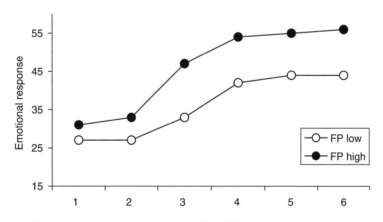

Figure 25.5   Emotional responses to situations which differ in explicitness of sexual infidelity (1 = low explicitness, high ambiguity; 6 = high explicitness, low ambiguity) by men high vs. low in fear of loss of power (FP)(Esters,2006)

focused on the affiliation motives as key pre-dictors of subjective well-being. For exam-ple, Gable (2006) found that whereas hope of affiliation was related to less loneliness and more positive attitudes towards social bonds, fear of rejection was associated with more loneliness, less satisfaction with, and more anxiety about social bonds, and lower levels of emotional wellbeing. A study by Strachman and Gable (2006) investigated the effect of fear of rejection (MMG) on memory. Participants received an adjective-checklist ostensibly filled in by a person they were to meet at some later point in the study. On an unannounced test assessing their recall of this list, participants high (relative to low) in fear of rejection remembered more negative words, but only if avoidance social goals were made salient. These results are in accord with research showing that individ-uals high in fear of rejection feel more insecure in social situations and typically transmit feelings of insecurity to the people around them; they feel more uncom-fortable and anxious in social groups, believe they are less liked by peers and friends, and frequently anticipate being rejected by other people (Sokolowski and Schmalt, 1996).

A study by Langens and Schüler (2005) further investigated how fear of rejection as measured by the MMG plays an important role in how people deal with and adapt to stressful events. A starting point for this research was the assumption that the percep-tion of high social support predicts speedier and better adjustment to stressful events (e.g. Cohen, 1992; Stroebe and Stroebe, 1996). Yet this resource may be unavailable to people who are high in fear of rejection, since – as the aforementioned results have shown – individuals high in fear of rejection tend to doubt that they are liked, cared for, and valued. Therefore, individuals high (rel-ative to low) in fear of rejection may benefit from strategic interventions which aim to help people adapt to stressful events. To test this assumption, Langens and Schüler (2005) employed an intervention originally designed

by Pennebaker (1997) in which participants write about highly emotional experiences over several sessions. This experimental con-dition was compared to a control condition in which participants did not write about emo-tional experiences. In two longitudinal stud-ies, they found that individuals high in fear of rejection typically report higher levels of negative mood, which is consistent with the notion that fear of rejection undermines the stress-buffering effects of perceived social support. However, if instructed to write about emotional experiences, individuals high in fear of rejection not longer showed mood impairments over the course of two months. Most likely, writing about emotional experi-ences compensated for their vulnerability to stressful events induced by a high fear of rejection. This study suggests that knowledge of motivational traits may help to identify people who are at risk of developing impair-ments of emotional wellbeing. It also illus-trates how a vulnerability associated with a particular motive (i.e. fear of rejection) may be compensated by effective emotion regulation strategies.

CONCLUSIONS AND FUTURE DIRECTIONS

In the present chapter, we aimed to present an up-to-date picture of the concept and measurement of motivational traits in per-sonality. Although Cattell (1957) underlined the importance of motivational processes in understanding the structure of personality many years ago, his ideas have rarely been followed up by researchers in personality. We believe that conceptual advancements in the field of motivational psychology as well as the availability of new methods to assess motives and to study motivational processes offer a variety of incentives to further inte-grate the concept of motivational traits in the larger field of personality. Doing so will enable us to more clearly understand the hidden forces which so efficiently direct our behavior and characterize our personality.

REFERENCES

Anderson, J.R. (1983) *The Architecture of Cognition*. Cambridge: Harvard University Press.

Atkinson, J.W. (1958) *Motives in Fantasy, Action, and Society*. Princeton, NJ: Van Nostrand.

Atkinson, J.W. (1964) *An Introduction to Motivation*. Princeton, NJ: Van Nostrand.

Atkinson, J.W. and Birch, D. (1970) *The Dynamics of Action*. New York: Wiley.

Azizian, A., Watson, T.D., Parvaz, M.A. and Squires, N.K. (2006) 'Time course of processes underlying picture and word evaluation: An event-related potential approach', *Brain Topography*, 18(3): 213–22.

Bargh, J.A. and Chartrand, T.L. (1999) 'The unbearable automaticity of being', *American Psychologist*, 54(7): 462–79.

Bargh, J.A., Gollwitzer, P.M., Lee-Chai, A., Barndollar, K. and Trötschel, R. (2001) 'The automated will: Nonconscious activation and pursuit of behavioural goals', *Journal of Personality and Social Psychology*, 81(6): 1014–27.

Budson, A.E., Droller, D.B., Dodson, C.S., Schacter, D.L., Rugg, M.D., Holcomb, P.J. and Daffner, K.R. (2005) 'Electrophysiological dissociation of picture versus word encoding: The distinctiveness heuristic as a retrieval orientation', *Journal of Cognitive Neuroscience*, 17(8): 1181–93.

Cattell, R.B. (1957) *Personality and Motivation: Structure and Measurement*. New York: World Book.

Cattell, R.B. (1965) *The Scientific Analysis of Personality*. Harmondsworth: Penguin.

Cohen, S. (1992) 'Stress, social support, and disorder', in H.O.F. Veiel and U. Baumann (eds), *The Meaning and Measurement of Social Support*. New York: Hemisphere, pp. 109–24.

Csikszentmihalyi, M. (1975). *Beyond Boredom and Anxiety*. San Francisco: Jossey-Bass.

Collins, C.J., Hanges, P.J. and Locke, E.A. (2004) 'The relationship of achievement motivation to entrepreneurial success: A meta Analysis', *Human Performance*, 17(1): 95–117.

Costa, P.T. Jr. and McCrae, R.R. (1980) 'Still stable after all these years: Personality as a key to some issues in adulthood and old age', in P.B. Baltes and O.G. Brim (eds), *Life Span Development and Behavior*. New York: Academic Press, pp. 65–102.

Costa, P.T. Jr. and McCrae, R.R. (1992) *Revised NEO Personality Inventory (NEO PI-R) and NEO Five Factor Inventory. Professional Manual*. Odessa: Psychological Assessment Resources.

Deci, E.L. and Ryan, R.M. (1991) 'A motivational approach to self: Integration in personality', in R. Dienstbier (ed.), *Nebraska Symposium on Motivation: Perspectives on Motivation* (Vol. 38). Lincoln: University of Nebraska Press, pp. 237–88.

Dodson, C.S. and Schacter, D.L. (2002) 'When false recognition meets metacognition: The distinctiveness heuristic', *Journal of Memory and Language*, 46(4): 782–803.

Elliot, A.J. and Thrash, T.M. (2002) 'Approach-avoidance motivation in personality: Approach and avoidance temperaments and goals', *Journal of Personality and Social Psychology*, 82(5): 804–18.

Emmons, R.A. (1989) 'The personal striving approach to personality', in L.A. Pervin (ed.), *Goal Concepts in Personality and Social Psychology*. Hillsdale, NJ: Erlbaum, pp. 87–126.

Emmons, R.A. and McAdams, D.P. (1991) 'Personal strivings and motive dispositions: Exploring the links', *Personality and Social Psychology Bulletin*, 17(6): 648–54.

Endler, N.S. and Magnusson, D. (1974) 'Interactionism, trait psychology, psychodynamics, and siutationism', Reports from the Psychological Laboratories (Number 418), University of Stockholm.

Entwisle, D.R. (1972) 'To dispel fantasies about fantasy-based measures of achievement motivation', *Psychological Bulletin*, 77(6): 377–91.

Epstein, S. (1962) 'The measurement of drive and conflict in humans: Theory and experiment', in M.R. Jones (ed.), *Nebraska Symposium on Motivation*. Lincoln: University of Nebraska Press, pp. 127–209.

Esters, F. (2006) 'Eifersucht bei bildlich dargestellter sexueller und emotionaler Untreue [Jealousy in response to pictures arousing sexual and emotional infidelity]', unpublished thesis, University of Wuppertal.

Freud, S. (1900) *Die Traumdeutung [The Interpretation of Dreams]*. Gesammelte Werke, Bd. X. Frankfurt: Fischer.

Funder, D.C. (2006) 'Towards a resolution of the personality triad: Persons, situations, and behaviors', *Journal of Research in Personality*, 40(1): 21–34.

Gable, S.L. (2006) 'Approach and avoidance social motives and goals', *Journal of Personality*, 74(1): 175–222.

Gable, S.L., Reis, H.T. and Elliot, A.J. (2003) 'Evidence for bivariate systems: An empirical test of appetition and aversion across domains', *Journal of Research in Personality*, 37(5): 349–72.

Gollwitzer, P.M., Fujita, K. and Oettingen, G. (2004) 'Planning and the implementation of goals', in R. Baumeister and K. Vohs (eds), *Handbook of Self-regulation*. New York: Guilford, pp. 211–28.

Gosling, S.D., Rentfrow, P.F. and Swann, W.B. (2003) 'A very brief measure of the Big-Five personality domains', *Journal of Research in Personality*, 37(6): 504–28.

Harcourt, A.H. (1989) 'Social influences on competitive ability: alliances and their consequences', in V. Standen, R.A. Foley (eds), *Comparative Socioecology–The Behavioural Ecology of Humans and Other Mammals*. Oxford: Blackwell, pp. 223–42.

Heckhausen, H. (1963) *Hoffnung und Furcht in der Leistungsmotivation [Hope and Fear in Achievement Motivation]*. Meisenheim\ Glan: Hain.

Heckhausen, H. (1967) *The Anatomy of Achievement Motivation*. New York: Academic Press.

Heckhausen, H. (1992) *Motivation and Action*. New York: Springer.

Heckhausen, J. and Heckhausen, H. (in press) *Motivation and Action*. Berlin: Springer.

Heckhausen, H., Schmalt, H.-D. and Schneider, K. (1985) *Achievement Motivation in Perspective*. New York: Academic Press.

Higgins, E.T. (1997) 'Beyond pleasure and pain', *American Psychologist*, 52(12): 1280–1300.

Jacoby, L.L. and Kelley, C.M. (1990) 'An episodic view of motivation: Unconscious influences of memory', in E.T. Higgins and R.M. Sorrentino (eds), *Handbook of Motivation and Cognition: Foundations of Social Behavior*. New York: Guilford, pp. 451–81.

Johnson-Laird, P.N. (1989) 'Mental models', in M.I. Posner (ed.), *Foundations of Cognitive Science*. Cambridge: MIT Press, pp. 469–99.

Klinger, E. (1990) *Daydreaming. Using Waking Fantasy and Imagery for Self-knowledge and Creativity*. Los Angeles: Jeremy P. Tarcher.

Kuhl, J., Scheffer, D. and Eichstaedt, J. (2003) 'Der Operante Motiv-Test (OMT): Ein neuer Ansatz zur Messung impliziter Motive', in J. Stiensmeier-Pelster und F. Rheinberg (eds.), *Diagnostik von Motivation und Selbstkonzept*. Göttingen: Hogrefe, pp. 129–50.

Langens, T.A. (2003) 'Potential costs of goal imagery: The moderating role of fear of failure. *Imagination, Cognition and Personality*, 23(1): 27–44.

Langens, T.A. and Dorr, S. (2006) 'Fear of failure and sensitivity to emotional faces', Unpublished data, University of Wuppertal.

Langens, T.A. and Schmalt, H.D. (2002) 'Emotional consequences of positive daydreaming: The moderating role of fear of failure', *Personality and Social Psychology Bulletin*, 28(12): 1725–35.

Langens, T.A. and Schüler, J. (2005) 'Written emotional expression and emotional well-being: The moderating role of fear of rejection', *Personality and Social Psychology Bulletin*, 31(6): 818–30.

Lewin, K. (1935) *A Dynamic Theory of Personality: Selected Papers*. New York: McGraw-Hill.

Lundh, L.G., Wikström, J. and Westerlund, J. (2001) 'Cognitive bias, emotion and somatic complaints in a normal sample', *Cognition and Emotion*, 15(3): 249–77.

Maddi, S.R. (1980) *Personality Theories: A Comparative Analysis* (4th edn). Homewood, IL: Dorsey Press.

McClelland, D.C. (1975) *Power: The Inner Experience*. New York: Irvington.

McClelland, D.C. (1985) *Human Motivation*. Glenview: Scott, Foresman and Co.

McClelland, D.C. (1989) 'Motivational factors in health and disease', *American Psychologist*, 44(4): 675–83.

McClelland, D.C., Atkinson, J.W., Clark, R.A. and Lowell, E.L. (1953) *The Achievement Motive*. New York: Appleton-Century-Crofts.

McClelland, D.C., Davis, W.N., Kalin, R. and Wanner, E. (1972) *The Drinking Man*. New York: Free Press.

McClelland, D. C., Koestner, R. and Weinberger, J. (1989) 'How do self-attributed and implicit motives differ?', *Psychological Review*, 96(4): 690–702.

McDougall, W. (1932) *The Energies of Men*. London: Methuen.

McGregor, H.A. and Elliot, A.J. (2005) 'The shame of failure: Examining the link between fear of failure and shame', *Personality and Social Psychology Bulletin*, 31(2): 218–31.

Mischel, W. and Shoda, Y. (1995) 'A cognitive-affective system theory of personality: Reconceptualizing situations, dispositions, dynamics, and invariance in personality structure', *Psychological Review*, 102(2): 246–68.

Murray, H.A. (1938) *Explorations in Personality.* New York: Oxford University Press.

Murstein, B.I. (1963) *Theory and Research in Projective Techniques (Emphasizing the TAT).* New York: Wiley.

Nisbett, R.E. and Wilson, T.D. (1977) 'Telling more than we can know: Verbal reports on mental processes', *Psychological Review*, 84(3): 231–59.

Pennebaker, J.W. (1997) *Opening Up: The Healing Power of Expressing Emotions* (2nd edn). New York: Guilford.

Puca, R.M., Rinkenauer, G. and Breidenstein, C. (2006) 'Individual differences in approach and avoidance motivation: How the avoidance motive influences response force', *Journal of Personality*, 74(4): 979–1014.

Puca, R.M. and Schmalt, H.-D. (1999) 'Task enjoyment: A mediator between achievement motives and performance', *Motivation and Emotion*, 23(1): 15–29.

Schmalt, H.-D. (1976) *Die Messung des Leistungsmotivs [The Assessment of Achievement Motivation].* Göttingen: Hogrefe.

Schmalt, H.-D. (1999) 'Assessing the achievement motive using the grid technique', *Journal of Research in Personality*, 33(2): 109–30.

Schmalt, H.-D. (2005) 'Validity of a short form of the Achievement-Motive Grid (AMG-S): Evidence for the three-factor structure emphasizing active and passive forms of fear of failure', *Journal of Personality Assessment,* 84(2): 172–84.

Schmalt, H.-D. (2006) 'Waist-to-hip ratio and female physical attractiveness: The moderating role of power motivation and the mating context', *Personality and Individual Differences*, 41(3): 455–65.

Schmalt, H.-D. (submitted) 'Fear of power motivates alcohol, sex, and drugs', *Journal of Research of Personality*.

Schmalt, H.-D. and Langens, T. (1996) 'Projective, semiprojective, and self-report measures of human motivation predict private cognitive events: strivings, memories, and daydreams', Unpublished manuscript, University of Wuppertal.

Schneider, K. and Schmalt, H.-D. (2000) *Motivation.* Stuttgart: Kohlhammer.

Schüler, J. (submitted) 'Arousal of flow-experience in a learning setting and its effects on exam performance'.

Schultheiss, O.C. and Brunstein, J.C. (2001) 'Assessment of implicit motives with a research version of the TAT: Picture profiles, gender differences, and relations to other personality measures', *Journal of Personality Assessment*, 77(1): 71–86.

Schultheiss, O.C. and Brunstein, J.C. (2005) 'An implicit motive approach to competence', in A.J. Elliot and C.S. Dweck (eds), *Handbook of Competence and Motivation.* New York: Guilford, pp. 31–51.

Singh, D. (1993) 'Adaptive significance of female physical attractiveness: Role of waist-to-hip ratio', *Journal of Personality and Social Psychology*, 65(2): 293–307.

Smith, C.P. (1992) *Motivation and Personality: Handbook of Thematic Content Analysis.* Cambridge: Cambridge University Press.

Sokolowski, K. and Schmalt, H.-D. (1996) 'Emotionale und motivationale Einflußfaktoren in einer anschlußthematischen Konfliktsituation [Effects of emotion and motivation in an affiliation conflict]', *Zeitschrift für Experimentelle Psychologie*, 3(3): 461–82.

Sokolowski, K., Schmalt, H.-D., Langens, Th. and Puca, R.M. (2000) 'Assessing achievement, affiliation, and power motives all at once – the Multi-Motive Grid (MMG)', *Journal of Personality Assessment*, 74(1): 126–45.

Spangler, W.D. (1992) 'Validity of questionnaire and TAT measures of need for achievement', *Psychological Bulletin*, 112(1): 140–54.

Strack, F. and Bless, H. (1994) 'Memory for nonoccurrences: Metacognitive and presuppositional strategies', *Journal of Memory and Language*, 33(2): 203–17.

Stroebe, W. and Stroebe, M. (1996) 'The social psychology of social support', in E.T. Higgins and A.M. Kruglanski (eds), *Social Psychology: Handbook of Basic Principles.* New York: Guilford, pp. 597–621.

Tupes, E.C. and Christal, R.E. (1992) 'Recurrent personality factors based on trait ratings', *Journal of Personality*, 60(2): 225–51.

Wegge, J., Quäck, A. and Kleinbeck, U. (1994) 'Zur Faszination von Video- und Computer-spielen bei Studenten: Welche Motive befriedigt die "bunte Welt am Draht"?', in K. Bräuer, U. Kittler and H. Metz-Göckel (ed.), *Pädagogische Psychologie und ihre Anwendungen (Bd. 2)*. Essen: Verlag "Die blaue Ente".

Weinberger, J. and McClelland, D.C. (1990) 'Cognitive versus traditional motivational models: Irreconcilable or complementary?', in E.T. Higgins and R.M. Sorrentino (eds), *Handbook of Motivation and Cognition. Foundations of Social Behavior* (Vol. 2). New York: Guilford, pp. 562–97.

Wilson, T.D. and Dunn, E.W. (2004) 'Self-knowledge: Its limits, value and potential for improvement', *Annual Review of Psychology*, 55(1): 493–518.

Winter, D.G. (1988) 'The power motive in women-and men', *Journal of Personality and Social Psychology*, 54(3): 510–19.

Winter, D.G. and Barenbaum, N.B. (1985) 'Responsibility and the power motive in women and men', *Journal of Personality*, 53(2): 335–55.

Winter, D.G., John, O.P., Stewart, A.J., Klohnen, E.C. and Duncan, L.E. (1998) 'Traits and motives: Toward an integration of two traditions in personality research', *Psychological Review*, 105(2): 230–50.

Woike, B.A. (1995) 'Most-memorable experi-ences: Evidence for a link between implicit and explicit motives and social cognitive processes in everyday life', *Journal of Personality and Social Psychology*, 68(6): 1081–91.

AUTHORS NOTE AND ACKNOWLEDGEMENTS

Thomas A. Langens and Heinz-Dieter Schmalt, University of Wuppertal, Wuppertal, Germany. Part of the research reported in this chapter was supported by German Science Foundation Grant LA 1155/3-1. Correspondence concern-ing this article should be addressed to Heinz-Dieter Schmalt, Department of Psychology, University of Wuppertal, Gauss-Strasse 20, 42097 Wuppertal, Germany. Email: schmalt@uni-wuppertal.de

26

Processes on the Borderline Between Cognitive Abilities and Personality: Confidence and its Realism

Lazar Stankov and Sabina Kleitman

Some psychological processes, typically captured by individual differences methodology, are related to but conceptually different from both cognitive ability and personality traits (Messick, 1996; Stankov, 1999). Cognitive traits refer to consistent variations in behavior that accompany variations in complexity of stimulus patterns. Personality is usually defined as a collection of a person's unique emotional thought, and behavioral patterns that are captured by statements that describe the way we 'think, feel, or act'. For Messick (1996), cognitive styles are the most important processes that lie in-between abilities and personality traits. His emphasis was on field independence versus field sensitivity and stylistic dimensions of attentional scanning. For Stankov (1999), these include different self-related constructs (e.g. self-concept as described by Marsh, 1986), aspects of trait complexes (see Ackerman, 2003) and outlooks, and perhaps what we have become accustomed to calling emotional intelligence.

In this chapter, we shall focus on recent work on confidence and its relationship to accuracy. The discrepancy between confidence and accuracy of performance will be referred to as realism of confidence – the area that captures the essence of processes that are related to ability and personality and yet differ from both. What we have found is that confidence is a useful construct that can be profitably employed in research and practice.

THEORETICAL AND HISTORICAL BACKGROUND OF RESEARCH ON CONFIDENCE

There are two traditions in psychological studies of confidence. One tradition treats confidence as a personality trait and employs a typical format for the self-assessment of such traits. For example, 'assertiveness' and 'bold and bashful' aspects of the extroversion dimension include features of self-confidence (e.g. McCrae and Costa, 1990). Although we have used these and other related scales in our work, confidence-as-personality trait will be treated as a marginal topic in this chapter. This is because empirical evidence suggests that such personality measures do not correlate to any substantial degree with our own procedures for assessing confidence (Kleitman et al., 2003; Pallier et al., 2002).

The second tradition of research on confidence has a long history in psychology that is inextricably linked to well-defined cognitive activities, typically in providing an answer to a test item. There are three distinct streams in this tradition. *Psychophysical* studies of confidence started with the work of Fullerton and J.M. Cattell (1892). Classical psychophysicists routinely collected three bits of information in their studies of threshold performance: accuracy, speed, and confidence. These three dependent measures provided relevant information for the interpretation of psychophysical functions. More recent research following this stream of work was reviewed by Vickers (1979) and Baranski and Petrusic (1999).

The second stream comes from psychologists in the area of *decision-making*. Their typical question is whether those who know more also know more about how much they know. 'Know' refers to accuracy, and 'knowing how much they know' relates to confidence (Lichtenstein and Fischoff, 1977). Two important theoretical approaches have been dominant in the study of confidence: the heuristics and biases approach (Kahneman et al., 1982) and the ecological approach (Gigerenzer et al., 1991). As we shall elaborate later, the heuristics and biases approach attributes the discrepancy between 'knowing how much they know' and 'know' to systematic personal tendencies. The ecological approach attributes this discrepancy to the characteristics of tasks that may attract the use of wrong cues in choosing the answer to a test question and adapting a wrong normative model.

The third stream is found within the area of *educational and psychological assessment* where confidence is treated within the rubric of metacognition (Paulhus and Harms, 2004; Schraw and Dennison, 1994; Tobias and Everson, 2000). In general, the central issue

is the same as that of the decision-making literature. In the late 1960s and 1970s, attempts were made to incorporate confidence ratings in the scoring practice for cognitive tests, and much of the psychometric work that employed subjective probability (i.e. confidence) measures was carried out. This method of measuring confidence became known as 'confidence scoring'. In this procedure, the examinee indicated the degree of confidence, namely subjective probability, that the option he or she had chosen was correct. One of the scoring procedures employed by Hakstian and Kansup (1975) involved expressing a confidence in a given answer on a ten-point scale and taking as an item score the level of confidence assigned to the keyed alternative. All other scoring schemes employed during that period of research used a single score of that nature – that is, a score that was a combination of information from accuracy and confidence.

Studies have shown higher reliabilities of such confidence-corrected accuracy scores than reliabilities of accuracy scores alone. The findings regarding their validity were mixed but generally unsatisfactory. One early finding was that personality traits do not correlate with confidence (Echternacht et al., 1972). Not much work on confidence scoring was carried out after the Hakstian and Kansup (1975) study that concluded with the statement, 'In terms of current methods of implementing it and common scholastic criteria, confidence testing appears to have little to recommend it over conventional testing' (1975: 238). Following this conclusion, the interest in confidence scoring ceased. However, one area that seems to be benefiting from confidence scoring nowadays is speech recognition (see Sankar and Kannan, 2004).

Important to the main theme of this chapter is the following claim by Hakstian and Kansup (1975) who put the nail in the coffin of confidence scoring: 'It appears from the validity data, that by measuring subjects' confidence in their responses in addition to their grasp of item content, we measure an additional trait largely unrelated to several criteria of interest' (1975: 238). In other words, they implied that we might be able to measure subjective (confidence) and objective (accuracy) probabilities as two different constructs and to predict different criteria with each of the two constructs. Thus, although in combination no incremental validity can be claimed, separate accuracy and confidence scores could be used. As it turned out, the impetus for formal research did not come until the mid-1990s from the decision-making literature. We will return to this link in a later section that deals with realism scores.

THE MEASUREMENT OF CONFIDENCE

Our preference for examining the role of confidence within the overall structure of individual differences derives from a realization that measurement properties of the assessment procedures for this construct are psychometrically sound, probably sounder than most other constructs on 'the no-man's-land' between personality and abilities, and at least comparable to the well-established measures from each domain. This conclusion was arrived at on the basis of empirical evidence accumulated over the past ten years.

To illustrate the point, consider the findings from a recently completed study that collected accuracy and confidence measures from the Internet-administered Test of English as a Foreign Language, better known as TOEFL iBT. The data presented here are based on the validation sample of 824 *native English speakers* (see Stankov and Lee, 2007). This version of TOEFL iBT consists of four subtests: reading, listening, writing, and speaking. Confidence ratings were collected for the first two subtests. Figure 26.1 provides an example of the reading subtest of

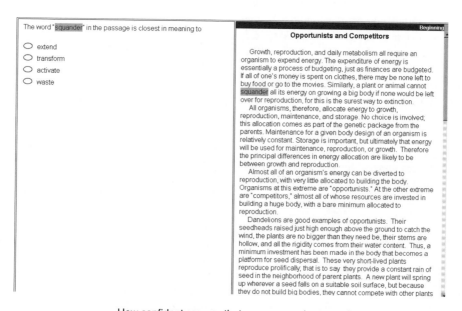

Note: After providing the answer to an item, participants are asked to answer confidence question

Figure 26.1   Screen capture of an item from the TOEFL iBT, form B

TOEFL iBT. In this subtest, participants are asked to read some material and answer questions regarding the meaning of a particular word in the text. From each text, several questions are asked; therefore one can treat each text as a testlet. The testlets can be treated as parallel forms of the reading subtest of TOEFL iBT. Two reading and two listening testlets were given in this study.

As illustrated in Figure 26.1, after each question (left side of the panel), participants are asked to indicate on a percentage scale how confident they are in the answer they have provided. Confidence ratings are illustrated at the bottom of the panel. Two total scores are calculated: (a) percentage of items correct; that is, typical total score divided by the total number of items in the test; and (b) confidence expressed as the mean of confidence scores over all items in the test.

Table 26.1 serves a dual purpose showing first that reliabilities of the confidence scores are higher than reliabilities of accuracy scores and second that two factors that correspond to accuracy (labeled as the primary factor of verbal comprehension that is the source for listening and reading items) scores and confidence can be extracted from the 8-by-8 correlation matrix. To fully evaluate these findings, one needs to know the correlation between raw accuracy and confidence scores from the same test. In general, average

Table 26.1 Reliability coefficients and factor pattern matrix* for two testlets from reading and listening subtests of TOEFL iBT ($n = 824$)

Variables	Cronbach alpha	Verbal comprehension factor	Confidence factor
Accuracy scores			
1. Reading 1	0.82	0.92	
2. Reading 2	0.79	0.97	
3. Listening 1	0.78	0.60	
4. Listening 2	0.72	0.57	0.21
Confidence scores			
5. Reading 1	0.91	0.36	0.59
6. Reading 2	0.94		0.75
7. Listening 1	0.94		0.96
8. Listening 2	0.90		0.96

* PROMAX-rotated maximum likelihood solution

correlations between raw accuracy and confidence scores range between 0.40 and 0.60. The correlation between the two factors in Table 26.1 is 0.578. Thus, even though the correlations between accuracy and confidence scores tend to be moderate to high, correlations between confidence scores from different tests are sufficiently high to pull out a separate confidence factor.

The same findings – high reliabilities and separation of measures of confidence from measures of accuracy – have been reported in several studies (Kleitman and Stankov, 2001; Pallier et al., 2002; Stankov, 1998, 2000; Stankov and Crawford, 1996, 1997). Replicable patterns of satisfactory psychometric properties, identification of a confidence factor, and evidence for factorial separation of confidence and accuracy (or ability) factors that are derived from the same battery of tests are only a part of the validity argument for a construct. This argument also calls for a proof of discriminant validity, addressed in the next section.

CONFIDENCE TRAIT VIS-À-VIS PERSONALITY TRAITS

Given that the first tradition of confidence research points to its link to personality, what is the relationship between confidence scores and established personality traits? To determine this, we correlated scores from the International Personality Item Pool (IPIP) (Goldberg et al., 2006) with factor scores for the confidence factor reported in Table 26.1. These are presented in Table 26.2. For comparison purposes, Table 26.2 also displays correlations between accuracy scores (total TOEFL iBT scores) and the Big Five IPIP personality factors. Again, these accuracy scores can be interpreted as measures of verbal comprehension. Our purpose is to compare the patterns of correlation of cognitive ability and confidence. Table 26.2 shows that correlations with the personality measures of agreeableness and openness are

Table 26.2   Correlations between Big Five personality factors and reading and listening confidence scores and TOEFL iBT total score

	Accuracy scores TOEFL total score	Confidence scores reading and listening
1. Extraversion	0.04	0.04
2. Agreeableness	0.34	0.23
3. Conscientiousness	0.14	0.16
4. Emotional Stability	0.05	0.12
5. Openness	0.39	0.33

slightly higher for the TOEFL iBT total (accuracy) score than for confidence scores. The pattern of correlations, however, is very similar. We can therefore conclude that these confidence and accuracy measures are about equally correlated with these personality measures. Thus, if ability is conceptually different from personality, so must be confidence.

CONFIDENCE AND QUESTIONNAIRE MEASURES OF METACOGNITION

Conceptually, confidence and its realism are related to several other constructs that may be seen as residing on the borderline between personality and abilities. Of particular interest are measures of metacognitive processes. These are usually assessed with questionnaires. One of the better known instruments is Schraw and Denison's (1994) Metacognitive Awareness Inventory (MAI), a 52-item questionnaire specifically developed to assess: (1) knowledge about cognition; and (2) regulation of cognition. The other inventory that has been used extensively in our work is the Memory and Reasoning Competence Inventory (MARCI), which was analogously designed to measure self-concept – a generic term that refers to subjective perceptions of one's own relative strengths and weaknesses in relation to some general or specific activities (Kleitman and Stankov, 2007). As the title indicates, the focus in MARCI is on self-assessment of

memory and reasoning processes that are deemed to be crucial for the majority of tests of intelligence.

Kleitman and Stankov (2007) report on the outcomes of factor analysis of an extensive battery of tests that contained measures of cognitive abilities (fluid and crystallized intelligence), speed, confidence, and three measures of metacognition (MAI total score and memory and reasoning scores from MARCI). This study was specifically designed to answer the question about the relationship between confidence and metacognition. Their finding was that confidence defines a separate factor from metacognition using a sample of college students ($n = 296$). The correlation between the two factors ($r = 0.41$) is moderate. On the basis of these findings, it appears that confidence and metacognition are separate but correlated processes.

Essentially the same outcome was obtained in the study with TOEFL iBT, which contained the same metacognitive measures. Table 26.3 shows that three factors emerged in this study – crystallized intelligence, confidence, and metacognition. The correlation between metacognition and confidence in Table 26.3 is 0.32, similar to

Table 26.3   Exploratory factor analysis of the correlations among accuracy and confidence scores and metacognitive inventories

Variable*	Factor		
	Crystallized intelligence	Confidence	Metacognition
Accuracy scores			
Reading	0.96		
Listening	0.64		
Numeracy	0.63		
Overclaiming *d'*	0.41		
Confidence scores			
Reading	0.31	0.62	
Listening		0.99	
Inventories			
Memory			0.63
Reasoning			0.72
Metacognitive Awareness			0.45

* Overclaiming *d'* refers to the accuracy measure based on signal detection theory (see Paulhus and Harms, 2004)

what was found by Kleitman and Stankov (2007). Again, confidence and metacognition as assessed by the questionnaire measures are separate but related psychological constructs.

INCREMENTAL VALIDITY OF CONFIDENCE RATINGS

The incremental validity of confidence ratings has not been explored extensively. However, the little evidence for incremental validity using performance criteria such as grade point average (GPA) that has been accumulated is somewhat encouraging. In Table 26.4, we present R-square values for two regression models. The criteria are writing and speaking scores, a numeracy test (ETS-developed subtest of adult literacy with quantitative material which for our purposes is just another cognitive measure), and self-reported SAT and GPA scores. In the first model based on $n = 824$, these measures were regressed on reading and listening accuracy scores of the TOEFL iBT. In the second model, the criteria measured were regressed on both accuracy and confidence scores from the reading and listening scores of the TOEFL iBT. The difference in R-squares between the

two models represents the incremental validity of confidence ratings over accuracy scores; statistical significance is indicated by asterisks.

In Table 26.4, incremental validity is present for the writing, speaking, and numeracy criterion test scores and is not present for the two self-reported SAT and GPA scores. Note that from a practical point of view, even significant R-square changes presented in Table 26.4 are small – 1% or less. On the other hand, given that accuracy scores from all four TOEFL iBT subtests are highly correlated (0.65 and above), it is surprising that any incremental validity for confidence can be detected at all.

There may be many reasons for the lack of incremental validity for GPA and SAT scores, and there is probably no need to speculate at this stage. We may note, however, that although performance on measures of achievement has traditionally been the most important criterion variable in working with college students, there may be other important criteria for success at college that are likely to have a close relationship to confidence. For example, confidence may be related to dropout rates at college or, perhaps, to the publication rate (including conference presentations) in graduate school. Needless to say, measures of GPA and SAT that

Table 26.4 Summary of regression analysis results: *R*-square coefficients showing incremental validity of reading and listening confidence scores in predicting various accuracy score criteria above and beyond reading and listening accuracy scores

	R-squares from regression analysis	
Criteria	Regression model predictors: accuracy scores only	Regression model predictors: accuracy and confidence scores
	1. Reading accuracy 2. Listening accuracy	1. Reading accuracy 2. Listening accuracy 3. Reading confidence 4. Listening confidence
TOEFL		
Writing	0.385	0.395**
Speaking	0.269	0.273*
Numeracy	0.401	0.404*
SAT (subsample of $n = 384$)	0.307	0.307
High-school GPA	0.079	0.079

* Indicates statistically significant incremental validity change from the first model to the second model are real, not self-reported, and different tests for the calculation of accuracy and confidence scores may also lead to an improved predictive validity.

There is already some evidence that confidence scores may be effective in predicting criteria other than academic success. In our work with TOEFL iBT, there were two administrations of the reading and listening items: one under normal conditions and (usually later in the same day) one with confidence ratings attached. Therefore it was possible to calculate an index of change – a measure of the degree to which a person chose to change his or her answer to an item between two presentations of the same item. We found that such change-scores correlate negatively with confidence. In other words, less confident people tended to change their answers more frequently than more confident people in the repeated testing. One conclusion is that test–retest reliability estimates for accuracy may contain a systematic variance due to a person's lack of confidence. An extrapolation from this finding may be the possibility that less confident people may be prone to take the same test repeatedly.

CONFIDENCE AND MALADAPTIVE BEHAVIOR

Evidence also suggests that confidence scores are valuable in predicting some maladaptive personality styles, such as the feeling of being an impostor, also known as an 'impostor phenomenon' (Clance and Imes, 1978), which is characterized by a sense of inferiority, self-criticism, and a pervasive fear of the inability to replicate one's own success despite previous evidence of the contrary (see also Ross and Krukowski, 2003). Supporting the nature of the impostor phenomenon, impostors showed a 'gap' between assessment of their performance via the confidence and *actual* task-related achievements. That is, people higher on impostor tendencies tended to have lower

confidence, but not the accuracy scores (Want and Kleitman, 2006).

REALISM OF CONFIDENCE RATINGS: THE DIFFERENCE BETWEEN CONFIDENCE AND ACCURACY SCORES

The continual attractiveness of confidence measures is due to their link to other types of scores – for example, accuracy and speed measures – that are more commonly used in psychological assessment. Although the link between speed and confidence has been of particular interest to psychophysicists, relatively little effort was invested in looking at their relationship in complex cognitive tasks (however, see Stankov, 2000). The decision-making and educational assessment tradition, however, was mostly interested in the confidence–accuracy relationship. For example, early attempts to link these measures have their origins in the forecasting (weather and economic) and medical diagnoses, among others. The question was whether high confidence leads to a better forecasting performance.

In the decision-making tradition, the most commonly cited first attempt to link confidence and accuracy was through what became known as the Brier score (see Brier, 1950). In the 1970s, several authors showed that the Brier score may be conveniently decomposed into two components – calibration and resolution. Stankov and Crawford (1996) examined the psychometric properties of several scores, including calibration and resolution, and found out that reliability of these scores was generally low. The only measure of calibration employed in Stankov–Crawford study that held promise was given different labels but has been commonly referred to as 'overconfidence bias' (or simply 'bias'), 'accuracy of self-assessment,' or 'realism of confidence ratings.' In this paper, we shall use the term 'realism' as a short-hand label for the accuracy of self-assessment of cognitive test performance. The score is easy to calculate:

Realism = (Average confidence score) − (percentage correct over all items in the test).

For each participant, this is the difference between subjective and objective probabilities. Note that high (overconfidence) or low (underconfidence) values of the realism score indicate the presence of poor realism of confidence ratings. A score close to zero indicates good calibration or good realism of confidence. Also, since the realism score can be both positive and negative, sometimes researchers calculate the absolute value of the realism scores.

For large-scale testing programs, realism scores are interesting for two reasons. First, they may correlate with some yet-to-be-identified criterion measures. They can be interpreted as indices of the metacognitive process of self-monitoring. Zero realism scores are an index of perfect calibration and therefore suggest that, over all items, the person is reasonably aware of the quality of answers provided – he or she is a good self-monitor. This, in turn, implies good metacognition; that is, those who know more also know more about how much they know. Second, although confidence can be coached and therefore faked, due to the yoked nature between confidence and accuracy, realism scores cannot be faked. High under- or overconfidence score implies either non-compliance or severe metacognitive deficit. These realism scores are therefore candidates for use in high-stakes testing. Most existing non-cognitive measures can be coached and, mainly for that reason, have not been used for college admission purposes and have been used cautiously for job selection.

The main drawback in the use of realism scores is their theoretically grounded lower reliability. They belong to a class of difference scores whose reliability depends not only on the reliability of component scores but also on the correlation between the components (i.e. high correlation implies low reliability of the difference scores). Empirical evidence for reliability of realism scores varies and can reach satisfactory level (Stankov and Crawford, 1997). For the listening and reading realism scores that are the focus of our paper, reliabilities are 0.71 and 0.69 respectively.

OVERCONFIDENCE AT INDIVIDUAL AND GROUP LEVELS

Realism rather than confidence per se is often of interest to investigators. The typical finding in studies that compared confidence and accuracy on cognitive tests has been a pronounced overconfidence. In short, on typical verbal tests of intelligence, people tend to think that they know more then they, in fact, do know. With visual perceptual tasks, however, Juslin and Olsson (1997) report the presence of underconfidence.

While reduced reliability of realism scores may lead to lower correlations with other variables of interest and therefore question the utility of these scores at the individual level, group comparisons that rely on mean differences may still be useful and informative. In other words, low reliability is less of a threat to comparisons between groups of participants, the mean of the observed scores is the same as the mean of the true scores (i.e. the mean of the error scores is assumed to be equal to zero).

Early work by Stankov and Crawford (1997) examined age differences under the assumption that realism scores measure metacognitive processes which, in turn, represent an aspect of wisdom. They hypothesized that older participants will be better calibrated than younger participants. Their data showed the opposite – older participants tended to have higher overconfidence bias scores than younger participants. This finding was attributed to a tendency in our society to avoid questioning older people's beliefs and judgment and therefore leaving them with a false impression of their competence.

GENDER AND ETHNIC DIFFERENCES IN THE REALISM OF CONFIDENCE RATINGS

Some earlier studies (see especially Crawford and Stankov, 1996; Stankov, 1998; Stankov and Crawford, 1997) have reported that there are no meaningful gender differences in realism score. Pallier (2003) studied gender differences on a variety of cognitive tasks ranging from measures of visual perception to general knowledge. His findings clearly point out that: (a) there are significant gender differences in confidence, with males showing higher confidence ratings; (b) there are no pronounced differences in accuracy; and (c) hence, there are significant differences in realism scores with males, again, showing higher overconfidence.

The results with TOEFL iBT subtests of reading and listening presented in Table 26.5 show a different pattern: (a) no gender differences in confidence; (b) significant gender differences in accuracy, with females performing better on both TOEFL iBT subtests; and (c) hence, significant gender differences in realism scores. The different patterns of gender differences in confidence and accuracy in the two studies may be due to the nature of the tasks employed in Pallier (2003) and in TOEFL iBT, and the differences in the samples of participants. Pallier employed Australian University students, and TOEFL iBT scores were obtained in the US from community college students. Importantly, gender differences in overconfidence that are reflected in realism scores remain – males are

more unrealistic (overconfident) in their self-assessments of performance.

Table 26.6 compares three ethnic groups – Whites, Hispanics, and Blacks – in terms of their accuracy, confidence, and realism scores. The order of the three groups on measures of accuracy and confidence is the same. The ordering on realism is reversed, with Whites showing the lowest overconfidence and Blacks the highest. Hispanics are in the middle.

IS OVERCONFIDENCE AN INSTANCE OF A SYSTEMATIC BIAS IN HUMAN REASONING?

The explanation of miscalibration as reflected in realism scores has been debated extensively in the knowledge calibration literature. The adherents of the 'heuristics and biases' approach maintain that miscalibration is an example of systematic personal tendencies which may take place at the rational/metacognitive level (e.g. Kahneman et al., 1982; Klayman et al., 1999; Koehler et al., 1996; Koriat et al., 1980). Within this approach, again, confidence judgments are seen as subjective probability judgments that reflect one's belief in the accuracy of a decision. Thus, their importance in effective decision-making is often emphasized. Miscalibration is seen as a bias that marks yet another instance of human irrationality. Thus, Kleitman (2003) applied an individual differences approach in her work with realism scores and showed that miscalibration is related to another type of

Table 26.5   Means for accuracy, confidence, and realism scores on TOEFL iBT reading and listening tests

	Reading accuracy	Confidence	Realism	Listening accuracy	Confidence	Realism
Males[a]	74.57	87.58	13.01	79.88	88.27	8.39
Females[b]	77.23	88.16	10.93	84.19	89.20	5.01
t-test[c]	2.04*	0.748	2.11*	4.20**	1.482	3.93**

*$p < 0.05$; **$p < 0.01$
[a] $n = 304$; [b] $n = 518$; [c] df = 821

Table 26.6   Means for accuracy, confidence, and realism scores on TOEFL iBT reading and listening by ethnicity

	Reading accuracy	Confidence	Realism	Listening accuracy	Confidence	Realism
White [a]	79.32	89.02	9.69	85.27	89.52	3.92
Hispanic [b]	70.41	86.51	16.10	79.19	89.31	10.12
African-American [c]	61.75	83.02	21.27	68.87	84.98	16.11
F-test [d]	59.41**	17.28**	21.673**	51.24**	9.30**	19.41**

$*p < 0.05; **p < 0.01$
[a] $n = 605;$ [b] $n = 60;$ [c] $n = 113;$ [d] $df = 2,769$

systematic personal tendency – a lack of awareness of additivity in the assignment of subjective probabilities.

In a series of studies, Kleitman (2003) employed a multiple-choice verbal reasoning test. The procedure was inspired by the work of Brenner and Koehler (1999) and involved assessment of the strength of each alternative in a multiple-choice item. Used to identify partial uncertainty and an alternative scoring rule, this procedure is sometimes referred to as probability scoring. The typical requirement for the application of this method is partitioning 100 points among the k options. In contrast to the typical procedure, participants ($n = 769$) in Kleitman's (2003) studies were not instructed to partition a 100% scale among alternatives. They were asked to indicate for each alternative how confident they were that the alternative was the correct answer. To do so, participants had to write down a number between 0 and 100 (conf(a)-conf(e), see Figure 26.2), with no additional restrictions (i.e. no enforcement of the additivity rule of probabilities). Participants were told, however, that only one answer was correct, and they were also asked to answer each question and indicate how confident they were that their answer was correct. A final, or global, confidence judgment labeled as Conf (ψ) was provided at the bottom of the page (see Figure 26.2).

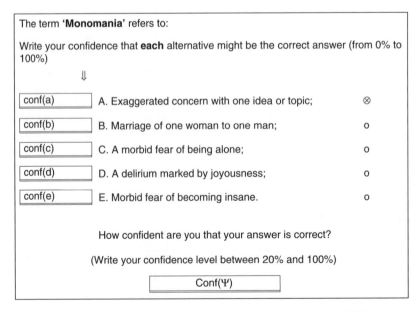

Figure 26.2   An item used for testing the assumption of additivity

Kleitman (2003) was particularly interested in finding out the percentage of people who were behaving according to the additivity rule (the probabilities add up to approximately 100) and those who are sub- (below 100) and super-additive (above 100). She found that the total sample was divided fairly evenly across the three groups, with about 60% of participants *not* behaving in the additive fashion. She also found that those who were super-additive tended to show overconfidence bias, while those who were sub-additive tended to show underconfidence bias. The correlation between realism scores and additivity indices is not very high (about 0.30). Nevertheless, it is sufficiently high to conclude that a non-trivial part of the realism scores' variance can be accounted for by the lack of appreciation of the additivity property of probability theory. This supports the claim that personal tendencies towards non-additivity and overconfidence share something in common. This, in turn, supports the view that both overconfidence and non-additivity are a part of a conglomerate of systematic personal tendencies postulated by the heuristics and biases approach.

OVERCONFIDENCE: IGNORANCE OF INCOMPETENCE OR 'APPLES AND ORANGES'?

Kruger and Dunning (1999) published a paper claiming that people tend to hold unreasonably favorable views about their own abilities. They claim this because people who have low abilities tend to make more errors on cognitive tests, and their incompetence robs them of the metacognitive ability to realize that. They reported the results of four experiments that asked the participants to do a cognitive test and to indicate at what percentile, for the population in which they belong, their own scores will lie. Kruger and Dunning (1999) found that people at the twelfth percentile in their cognitive performance rated themselves as

falling at the sixty-second percentile. The interpretation in terms of the alleged ignorance of their own incompetence may be seen as a 'tweak-your-nose' attitude toward low achievers. Although questions about percentile ranks in the Kruger and Dunning (1999) paper may appear different from the calculation of realism scores, their 'tweak-your-nose' interpretation can be tested by closer examination of the relationship between accuracy and confidence measures. Already considered, Tables 26.5 and 26.6 contain some clues about the relationship between realism scores and the constituent components. In particular, for both gender and ethnicity, the size of the differences between arithmetic means is smaller for confidence than it is for the accuracy scores. This is confirmed by the t- and F-tests in the last row in each table.

To gain more clarity, consider the data presented in Figure 26.3. This figure displays the application of the item response theory (IRT), Rasch model, for the accuracy data. The vertical axis in this figure represents the total raw score on the reading test. The horizontal axis represents a person's ability. Zero on the horizontal axis indicates average ability, and negative signs indicate a lower-than-average ability level. Triangles define the IRT curve, calculated in the traditional way with the 0, 1 scoring. Thus, a person of average ability (theta = 0) is expected to obtain a score of 18 on the reading test. This is the approximate value one obtains by drawing a vertical line above zero until it reaches the triangle-labeled curve and then moving horizontally to the y-axis. Circles are means of the confidence scores for people who have a particular ability score. (The listening test shows an identical trend but we do not present these findings here in order to save space.)

For our purposes, the main message is contained in a clear separation between the two lines – triangles and circles in Figure 26.3 – as the ability level decreases. The interpretation is that people with low ability tend to be more overconfident (reflected in

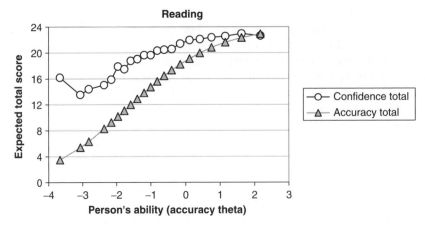

Figure 26.3 Overconfidence: the difference between confidence (circles) and IRT accuracy curves (triangles) for the reading subtest of TOEFL iBT

higher realism scores). Thus, on face value, the data are in agreement with the Kruger and Dunning (1999) findings. Thinking in terms of evolutionary theory, realization that one is performing badly on a test may conceivably lead to depression and giving up on life activities. Consequently, high confidence can be seen as serving a protective purpose in life.

Another interpretation of the trends presented in Figure 26.3 has to do with the observation that the two curves follow different trajectories. This could mean that subjective (confidence) and objective (accuracy) probabilities not only measure different constructs as evidenced by factor analysis but, like height and weight, are also measured on different scales. The problem, we believe, is mostly in the measurement of confidence. First, there is a ceiling effect at the top level of the confidence curve which may be taken as the main cause of the rapprochement between accuracy and confidence at the high ability levels. Second, as pointed out in the previous section, there is evidence that people have unclear ideas about the concept and axioms of probability. Third, for the items of the reading test we have been considering in this chapter, confidence ratings below 50% are extremely rare (8% or less). Perhaps many people interpret 50% confidence to mean a 50–50 chance of

being correct, again related to the problems in understanding probability theory.

Together, these three observations about the measurement of confidence point to the possibility that a different measurement scale underlies confidence ratings. Maybe a common scale can be developed in the future along the lines of the Body Mass Index that combines height and weight. For the time being, however, it is probably best to ignore the 'tweak-your-nose' interpretation of Kruger and Dunning (1999; see also Dunning, 2005) – it is disrespectful and may be wrong. After all, if there are difficulties in working with probabilities, why should we assume that estimating one's position on a percentile scale is different or problem-free?

OVERCONFIDENCE AND CHARACTERISTICS OF THE TASKS

In addition to the possible scaling issues that question the interpretation of the 'tweak-your-nose' interpretation of realism scores, there are questions related to the generality of the reported overconfidence phenomenon. The claim is that overconfidence depends on the nature of the task. First, in the studies of others and in our own work, overconfidence is not a general finding. As mentioned above, Juslin and Olsson (1997) report under confidence with the perceptual tasks. In our own work (see Stankov, 1998, 2000), fluid intelligence tasks often tend to display relatively good calibration, usually better than crystallized intelligence tasks. Thus, at the very least, ignorance of incompetence may be restricted to a class of cognitive tasks that calls for the use of acculturated knowledge. Second, a recent paper by Burson et al. (2006) addresses the claim of Kruger and Dunning (1999) directly. Their main focus is on task difficulty. Burson et al. report the findings from three studies and 12 tasks that show that judges at all skill levels (i.e. not just those that show poor ability/ performance) are subject to a similar degree of error in predicting their relative standing on a percentile scale.

Since we do not want to end this section with a damning conclusion about realism scores, we add the following caveat. While realism scores may be problematic as a way to assess individuals' metacognitive (in)competence, they may be informative if one is interested in group effects. Furthermore, these scores may be the only available non-cognitive measure that is resistant to coaching and faking, and therefore may be useful in high-stake testing programs.

CONCLUSIONS

The evidence reviewed in this chapter is focused on our work with confidence ratings and on realism of confidence ratings. With respect to confidence, there can be little doubt that it is a trait that can be reliably measured. This trait is distinct from ability traits (accuracy), personality measures, and questionnaire measures of metacognition. Some limited evidence for its incremental validity with cognitive performance measures and some personality 'miscalibration' is becoming available. Our suggestion would be to explore its incremental validity with other criterion measures, such as attrition rates and scholarly productions in graduate school.

The evidence related to measures of realism of confidence ratings is mixed. The ratings may be useful in group comparisons. For example, there are meaningful gender and ethnic differences, with males being more overconfident than females and Blacks being more overconfident than Whites. Although we did not review this literature in the present chapter, there is also evidence from cross-cultural comparisons that Confucians (i.e. East Asians) tend to show less overconfidence than Americans (see Stankov, submitted). Also, older people tend to be a bit more overconfident than young people (Stankov and Crawford, 1997). All these comparisons need to be evaluated with caution because of the problems listed below.

The problems with the use of realism scores are at the individual level. As difference scores, they tend to be less reliable than their constituent accuracy and confidence scores. Therefore, their correlation with other variables is expected to be lower. For the two tests that are the focus of this chapter, reliabilities of the realism scores are not of concern; they are reasonable.

Although these scores increase with the decrease in a person's ability, the 'twist-your-nose' interpretation in terms of ignorance of incompetence is not warranted. We believe that there is evidence that objective and subjective probabilities are measured on different scales, and simple comparisons between them make no sense. This is due to a ceiling on confidence ratings, the possibility that people do not understand the meaning of probability, and the tendency to avoid the use of probabilities lower than 0.50. These problems do not exist for objective probabilities. In addition, the size and direction of realism scores depend on the nature of the tasks under consideration – perceptual and fluid intelligence tasks are less prone to overconfidence than crystallized intelligence tasks.

Anything of substance to realism scores may reside in the finding of a moderate correlation between realism and additivity – that is, a tendency to over- or underestimate probabilities of mutually exclusive and exhaustive events like the alternatives in multiple-choice items. This places realism of confidence ratings and commonly observed overconfidence on acculturated knowledge tasks within the category of systematic personal tendencies that have been identified within the 'heuristics and biases' approach to human decision-making.

REFERENCES

Ackerman, P.L. (2003) 'Aptitude complexes and trait complexes', *Educational Psychologist*, 38(2): 85–93.

Baranski, J.V. and Petrusic, W.M. (1999) 'Realism of confidence in sensory discrimination', *Perception and Psychophysics*, 61(7): 1369–83.

Brenner, L.A. and Koehler, D.J. (1999) 'Subjective probability of disjunctive hypotheses: Local-weight models for decomposition of evidential support', *Cognitive Psychology*, 38(1): 16–47.

Brier, G.W. (1950) 'Verification of forecasts expressed in terms of probability', *Monthly Weather Review*, 78: 1–3.

Burson, K.A., Larrick, R.P. and Klayman, J. (2006) 'Skilled or unskilled, but still unaware of it: How perceptions of difficulty drive miscalibration in relative comparisons', *Journal of Personality and Social Psychology*, 90(1): 60–77.

Clance, P.R. and Imes, S.A. (1978) 'The impostor phenomenon in high achieving women: Dynamics and therapeutic intervention', *Psychotherapy: Theory, Research, and Practice*, 15(3): 241–7.

Crawford, J.D. and Stankov, L. (1996) 'Age differences in the realism of confidence judgments: A calibration study using tests of fluid and crystallized intelligence', *Learning and Individual Differences*, 8(2): 83–103.

Dunning, D. (2005) *Self-insight: Roadblock and Detours on the Path of Knowing Thyself*. New York: Psychology Press.

Echternacht, G.J., Boldt, R.F. and Sellman, W.S. (1972) 'Personality influences on confidence test scores', *Journal of Educational Measurement*, 9(3): 235–41.

Fullerton, G.S. and Cattell, J.M. (1892) 'On the perception of small differences', University of Pennsylvania Philosophy Series No. 2. Philadelphia: University of Pennsylvania Press.

Gigerenzer, G., Hoffrage, U. and Kleinbolting, H. (1991) 'Probabilistic mental models – a Brunswikian theory of confidence', *Psychological Review*, 98(4): 506–28.

Goldberg, L.R., Johnson, J.A., Eber, H.W., Hogan, R., Ashton, M.C., Cloninger, C.R. and Gough, H.C. (2006) 'The International Personality Item Pool and the future of public-domain personality measures', *Journal of Research in Personality*, 40(1): 84–96.

Hakstian, A.R. and Kansup, W. (1975) 'A comparison of several methods of assessing partial knowledge in multiple-choice tests: II. Testing procedures', *Journal of Educational Measurement*, 12(4): 231–9.

Juslin, P. and Olsson, H. (1997) 'Thurstonian and Brunswikian origins of uncertainty in judgment: A sampling model of confidence in sensory discrimination', *Psychological Review*, 104(2): 344–636.

Kahneman, D., Slovic, P. and Tversky, A. (1982) *Judgments Under Uncertainty: Heuristics and Biases*. Cambridge, UK: Cambridge University Press.

Klayman, J., Soll, J.B., Gonzalez-Vallejo, C. and Barlas, S. (1999) 'Overconfidence: It depends on how, what, and whom you ask', *Organizational Behavior and Human Decision Processes*, 79(3): 216–47.

Koehler, D.J., Brenner, L.A., Liberman, V. and Tversky, A. (1996) 'Confidence and accuracy in trait inference: Judgment by similarity', *Acta Psychologica*, 92(1): 33–57.

Kleitman, S. (2003) 'Bias score – an instance of systematic irrationality?' in P. Slezak (ed.), *Proceedings of Joint International Conference on Cognitive Science*, Vol. 1. Sydney: University of New South Wales, pp. 311–17.

Kleitman, S. and Stankov, L. (2001) 'Ecological and person-oriented aspects of metacognitive processes in test-taking', *Applied Cognitive Psychology*, 15(3): 321–41.

Kleitman, S. and Stankov, L. (2007) 'Self-confidence and metacognitive processes', *Learning and Individual Differences*, 17(2): 167–73.

Kleitman, S., Stankov, L. and Marsh, H. (2003) 'Metacognition: Self-Concept, personality and cognitive correlates',

Proceedings of the AARE/NZARE Conference SELF Research Centre Symposium, Auckland, New Zealand.

Koriat, A., Lichenstein, S. and Fischhoff, B. (1980) 'Reasons for confidence', *Journal of Experimental Psychology: Human Learning and Memory*, 6(2): 107–18.

Kruger, J. and Dunning, D. (1999) 'Unskilled and unaware of it: how difficulties in recognizing one's own incompetence lead to inflated self-assessments', *Journal of Personality and Social Psychology*, 77(6): 1121–34.

Lichtenstein, S. and Fischhoff, B. (1977) 'Do those who know more also know more about how much they know?', *Organizational Behavior and Human Decision Processes*, 20(2): 159–83.

Marsh, H.W. (1986) 'Verbal and math self-concepts: An internal/external frame of reference model', *American Educational Research Journal*, 23(1): 129–49.

McCrae, R.R. and Costa, P.T. (1990) *Personality in Adulthood*. New York: Guilford.

Messick, S. (1996) 'Bridging cognition and personality in education: The role of style in performance and development', *European Journal of Personality*, 10(5): 353–76.

Pallier, G. (2003) 'Gender differences in the accuracy of self-assessment on cognitive tasks', *Sex Roles: A Journal of Research*, 48(5–6): 265–76.

Pallier, G., Wilkinson, R., Danthiir, V., Kleitman, S., Knezevic, G., Stankov, L. and Roberts, R. (2002) 'The role of question format and individual differences in the realism of confidence judgments', *Journal of General Psychology*, 129(3): 257–300.

Paulhus, D.L. and Harms, P.D. (2004) 'Measuring cognitive ability with the over-claiming technique', *Intelligence*, 32(3): 297–314.

Ross, S.R. and Krukowski, R.A. (2003) 'The imposter phenomenon and maladaptive personality: Type and trait characteristics', *Personality and Individual Differences*, 34(3): 477–84.

Sankar, A. and Kannan, A. (2004) 'A comprehensive study of task-specific adaptation of speech recognition models', *Speech Communication*, 42(1): 125–139.

Schraw, G. and Dennison, R.S. (1994) 'Assessing metacognitive awareness', *Contemporary Educational Psychology*, 19(4): 460–75.

Stankov, L. (1998) 'Calibration curves, scatterplots and the distinction between general knowledge and perceptual tasks', *Learning and Individual Differences*, 10(1): 29–50.

Stankov, L. (1999) 'Mining on the "no man's land" between intelligence and personality', in P.L. Ackerman, P.C. Kyllonen and R.D. Roberts (eds), *Learning and Individual Differences: Process, Trait, and Content Determinants*. Washington, DC: American Psychological Association, pp. 315–37.

Stankov, L. (2000) 'Complexity, metacognition, and fluid intelligence', *Intelligence*, 28(2): 121–43.

Stankov, L. (submitted) 'Psychological aspects of culture'.

Stankov, L. and Crawford, J.D. (1996) 'Confidence judgments in studies of individual differences', *Personality and Individual Differences*, 21(6): 971–86.

Stankov, L. and Crawford, J.D. (1997) 'Self-confidence and performance on tests of cognitive abilities', *Intelligence*, 25(2): 93–109.

Stankov, L. and Lee, J. (2006) 'Confidence and cognitive test performance', Research Report #(3). Educational Testing Service, Princeton, NJ.

Tobias, S. and Everson, H.T. (2000) 'Assessing metacognitive knowledge monitoring', in G. Schraw and J.C. Impara (eds), *Issues in the Measurement of Metacognition*. Lincoln, NE: Buros Institute of Mental Measurements, pp. 147–222.

Vickers, D. (1979) *Decision Processes in Visual Perception*. New York: Academic Press.

Want, J. and Kleitman, S. (2006) 'Feeling "phony": adult achievement behaviour, parental rearing style and self-confidence', *Journal of Personality and Individual Differences*, 40(5): 961–71.

27

Culture: Ways of Thinking and Believing

Lazar Stankov and Jihyun Lee

Numerous definitions of culture exist in the literature today, but there is a common thread on its definition that researchers across disciplines tend to agree upon. Culture has been defined as:

> The collective programming of the mind that distinguishes the members of one group or category of people from another. (Hofstede, 2002: 9)

> [S]hared meaning systems that provide the standards for perceiving, believing, evaluating, communicating, and acting among those who share a language, a historic period, and a geographic location. (Triandis, 1996: 207)

> [A] meaning and information system shared by a group and transmitted across generations. (Matsumoto and Yoo, 2006: 234)

The above definitions by psychologists emphasize a set of shared beliefs, values, and social norms which can influence the behavior of a certain group of people in similar ways (cf. Lustig and Koester, 1996). This echoes the view of Adda B. Bozeman (1975), a political scientist, who referred to culture (and civilization) as 'values, norms, institutions, and modes of thinking to which successive generations in a given society have attached primary importance' (see also Huntington, 1997: 41). The culture, then, can

be conveniently described as patterns of human thought. We can divide these patterns of thought into two main streams of human functions – cognitive and non-cognitive. Cognitive patterns of thought are captured by tests of achievement and ability.

Contemporary cross-cultural researchers have shown an increased interest in non-cognitive, as opposed to different cognitive aspects of culture. At least two reasons seem to exist for this trend. One is the need for co-operation on an international scale in business. Rarely do we need to know an average IQ of our contacts from the other parts of the world. It is more important to be able to understand subtle meanings in the course of verbal and non-verbal communication and to predict how they would react to our demands and needs during business interactions. The other reason comes from recent clashes between countries and civilizations. Humans have always fought for the causes related to their beliefs and values. In this chapter, we will focus on non-cognitive aspects of culture, which seem more related to the need of the modern world, although we recognize that cognitive abilities also vary across cultures (see Sternberg and Grigorenko,

2004; Nisbett, 2003). Indeed, non-cognitive patterns of thought are the essence of psychological definitions of culture.

The aim in this chapter is to present the results of our recent studies (Stankov, 2007; Stankov and Lee, in press). Some aspects of these reports are more technical than others, but we summarize the main findings in a non-technical fashion here. This chapter first deals with psychometric properties of measures of culture based on data from different countries and groups of countries. In the second part, we show patterns of arithmetic mean differences for different groups of participants. We start by considering the theoretical background for the design of our studies.

ASSESSMENT OF NON-COGNITIVE ASPECTS OF CULTURE

Questionnaire measures of four psychological domains were given following the administration of Test of English as a Foreign Language (TOEFL iBT) to 1,252 US students and 1,600 foreign students. The battery was delivered via the Internet. The Stankov (in press) and Stankov and Lee (in press) studies are based on 1,600 foreign students and 431 US students. Stankov (2007) is based on 1,252 US students (i.e. native speakers of English) only. It is assumed in our work that ethnic background of participants captures salient features of the culture they identify with.

Two main criteria guided the selection of variables in these three studies: they had to be non-cognitive and their relevance for cross-cultural comparisons had to be well documented in the literature. Broad framework for the selection of measures was provided by the definitions of culture as a shared system of beliefs, values, and social norms and includes measures of personality traits.

All selected measures that were used in our work have a long history in cross-cultural studies. An advantage of our recent work (Stankov, in press; Stankov and Lee, in press) over much of the previous work in this area was in bringing together in a single battery a large number of scales (43 scales, see Table 27.1) from four distinct domains that had never been studied together. The domains are:

1 *Personality.* A collection of emotion, thought, and behavior patterns unique to a person. These patterns are captured by statements that describe the way we 'think, feel, or act'.
2 *Social attitudes.* States of mind and feelings toward a specific object or social interaction. They are captured by statements that can elicit the expression of beliefs about what is true, real, or good in social situations (cf. Saucier, 2004).
3 *Values.* Guiding principles, standards, about some desirable end-state of existence (Rokeach, 1973; see also Schwartz, 2003). They are criteria people use to evaluate others, themselves, actions, and events.
4 *Social norms.* A set of beliefs (or perceptions) about the expected standards of behavior that is sanctioned and enforced, sometimes implicitly, by the society.

It is apparent that cross-cultural psychology has focused on domains that are important for social interactions. It is also noticeable that these four distinct domains can be ordered in such a way that suggests a particular psychological–social progression in human interactions. As we move from personality to social norms, there is change in focus from self (inside oriented) to the perceived regulations imposed by a society.

FACTORIAL STRUCTURE OF THE FOUR DOMAINS

Table 27.2 presents the results of factor analysis (Stankov, in press a; Stankov and Lee, in press) based on 'pancultural' design – no distinction is made between the countries. All participants are treated as if they come from the same population. The obtained factors can be interpreted as:

1 *Personality/social attitudes.* Clearly, this is a bipolar factor contrasting 'good' self-evaluative aspects of personality and negative or nasty-toward-others social attitudes and personality dimensions. Negative loadings are higher

Table 27.1 Constructs within the domains of personality, social attitudes, values, and social norms

I. Big Five personality traits (IPIP):	
1. Extraversion	Outgoing and physical-stimulation-oriented vs. introversion, quiet, and physical-stimulation-averse
2. Agreeableness	Affable, friendly, conciliatory vs. aggressive, dominant, disagreeable
3. Conscientiousness	Dutiful, planful, and orderly vs. spontaneous, flexible, and unreliable
4. Neuroticism	Emotionally reactive, prone to negative emotions vs. calm, unperturbable, optimistic, emotional stability
5. Openness	Open to new ideas and change vs. traditional and staid. See Saucier and Goldberg (2002). The scales were downloaded from the following web site: <ipip.ori.org/ipip/>
II. Social attitudes	
1. Toughness	Machoism, hard realism, street wiseness, Machiavellianism
2. Maliciousness	Poor impulse control, sadism, resentment, brutality
	Source: Stankov and Knezevic (2005)
III. Social attitudes	
1. Alphaisms	Religious sources of authority, legalism, institutionalism, secularism, evolutionism
2. Betaisms	Non-PC motives for behavior, materialism, sensualism, fascism
3. Gammaisms	Western democracy beliefs, constitutionalism, humanism, existentialism, neoliberalism
4. Deltaisms	Personal mysticism, Hinduism, transcendentalism, Zen Buddhism, animism
5. Government interventionism	See Method Section
6. Harshness to outsiders	See Method Section
	Source: Saucier (2000)
IV. Values	
1. Power	Authority, wealth, social power, public image, social recognition
2. Achievement	Ambition, success, capability, influence, intelligence
3. Hedonism	Pleasure, enjoyment of life
4. Stimulation	Variety, excitement
5. Self-direction	Creativity, freedom, independence, curiosity, choosing own goals
6. Universalism	Broadmindedness, social justice, equality, world at peace, unity with nature, wisdom, protection of the environment
7. Benevolence	Helpfulness, loyalty, forgiveness, honesty, responsibility, truth, friendship, mature love
8. Tradition	Respect for the tradition, humility, devoutness, acceptance of one's portion in life, moderation
9. Conformity	Obedience, self-discipline, politeness, honoring parents and elders
10. Security	Social order, family security, national security, reciprocation of favors, cleanliness, sense of belonging, health
11. Spirituality	Spirituality, meaning of life, sense of inner harmony, sense of detachment
	Source: Schwartz and Bardi (2001)
V. Social norms	
1. Uncertainty avoidance	The extent to which members of an organization or society strive to avoid uncertainty by relying on established social norms, rituals, and bureaucratic practices
2. Future orientation	The degree to which individuals in organizations or societies engage in future-oriented behaviors such as planning, investing in the future, and delaying individual or collective gratification
3. Power distance	The degree to which members of an organization or society expect and agree that power should be stratified and concentrated at higher levels of an organization or government
4. Institutional collectivism	The degree to which organizational and societal institutional practices encourage and reward collective distribution of resources and collective action
5. Humane orientation	The degree to which individuals in organizations or societies encourage and reward individuals for being fair, altruistic, friendly, generous, caring, and kind to each other
6. Performance orientation	The degree to which an organization or society encourages and rewards group members for performance improvement and excellence
7. In-group collectivism	The degree to which individuals express pride, loyalty, and cohesiveness in their organizations or families
8. Gender egalitarianism	The degree to which an organization or society minimizes gender role differences while promoting gender equality
9. Assertiveness	The degree to which individuals in organizations or societies are assertive, confrontational, and aggressive in social relationships
	Source: House et al. (2004)

Table 27.2   Factor pattern matrix (maximum likelihood followed by PROMAX). Note that loadings lower than 0.30 are omitted

Measures	Factors			
	Personality/social attitudes	Values	Social norms	Conservatism
Big Five personality traits (IPIP):				
1. Extraversion				
2. Agreeableness	0.56			
3. Conscientiousness	0.45			
4. Neuroticism*	0.46			
5. Openness	0.38	0.30		
Additional personality traits (IPIP)				
6. Belligerence	−0.66			
7. Conservatism				0.74
8. Distrust	−0.62			
9. Achievement seeking	0.48			
10. Risk avoidance	0.35			0.31
Dimensions of social attitudes (Stankov/Knezevic):				
11. Toughness	−0.82			
12. Maliciousness	−0.78			
Dimensions of social attitudes (Saucier):				
13. Alphaism				0.51
14. Betaism	−0.38			
15. Gammaism				0.45
16. Deltaism				0.48
17. Gov't. intervention				0.40
18. Harsh to outsiders				0.35
Values (Schwartz):				
19. Power	−0.39	0.57		
20. Achievement		0.85		
21. Hedonism		0.73		
22. Stimulation		0.76		
23. Self-direction		0.92		
24. Universalism		0.82		
25. Benevolence		0.78		
26. Tradition		0.54		0.46
27. Conformity		0.63		0.39
28. Security		0.77		
29. Spirituality		0.61		
Dimensions of social norms (GLOBE):				
30. Uncertainty avoidance			0.36	
31. Future orientation			0.45	
32. Power distance			−0.61	
33. Institutional collectivism				
34. Humane orientation				
35. Performance orientation			0.54	
36. In-group collectivism				0.37
37. Gender egalitarianism			0.31	
38. Assertiveness				
Dimensions of social norms (Hofstede/Stankov):				
39. Power distance			0.37	
40. Uncertainty avoidance	−0.32		−0.46	
41. Individualism/collectivism				
42. Masculinity/femininity				
43. Long-/short-term orientation				

*Neuroticism is scored in the opposite direction, indicating emotional stability implying that this is predominantly (anti-) social attitudes factor, and to a smaller degree a personality factor.

2 *Values.* This factor has high loadings from all eleven Schwartz Value Survey (SVS) scales.

3 *Social norms.* This factor differs from the other factors in the sense that it does not refer to one's own feelings (personality and social attitudes) but rather an 'objective' view of societal norms.

4 *Conservatism.* People scoring high on this factor hold conservative values; they are hard-working, religious, with strong Western democracy beliefs and are proud of their family. This factor cuts across the four domains. It is defined by Schwartz's scales of tradition and conformity, virtually all Saucier's scales but beta, the personality trait of conscientiousness, and GLOBE's in-group collectivism. This factor also has loadings from the conservatism and risk-avoidance scales as well as from the harshness toward outsiders and government interventionism scales.

This four-factor structure has important implications for our understanding of social interactions. First, the factor structure described above was obtained from both samples – the US sample and the non-US sample. This overrides the claim that insufficient command of English might have affected the factorial structure. Such an objection cannot possibly hold with the native English speakers of the US sample. Second, the emergence of a conservatism factor indicates that this dimension can operate, and therefore can be assessed, at the individual level. We may note that one of the most commonly discussed dimensions in cross-cultural work, collectivism versus individualism, did not emerge as a factor in our data even though there was a sufficient number of variables that may be indicative of this factor. Third, although not shown here, the correlations among these four factors are low, suggesting a structure that can, perhaps, be best described as a truncated hierarchy with no evidence for the general factor of culture. Fourth, we wish to point out that Stankov (in press) reports a slightly different factor structure with these variables. With only

two out of five personality variables having loadings on this factor, it clearly shows that this first factor is predominantly a social attitudes factor. Thus, we acknowledge that the domain of personality may be separate from the domain of social attitudes (see Saucier, 2000). Fifth, three out of four factors conform to what we refer to as the domains of cross-cultural differences. This came as a surprise to us. It seems that people see social interactions in terms of the four major domains. Constructs that appear to be quite distinct are included within each domain. However, when constructs from within each domain were put together with constructs from other domains, the distinctiveness of each construct within the domain seems to lose its existence as a separate factor. For example, Schwartz' dimensions of hedonism and benevolence are at the opposite sides of his circumplex model but they merge into the same factor in our analyses.

Before proceeding to the next topic, we wish to point out that possible threats to the validity of our studies have been checked. No effects were found for the order of instrument presentation, the number of alternatives of Likert scales, the differences in the number of items for each scale, and several other methodological issues (see Stankov, in press, for further details).

WHAT ABOUT PERSONALITY ACROSS CULTURES?

An important recent work on cross-cultural differences in personality traits was reported by Terraciano et al. (2005). Their emphasis has been on comparison between stereotypes held about a particular nation and the actual personality traits characteristic of that nation. The conclusion was that there is no correspondence between the two. More important for our purposes here is their finding that personality structure (i.e. the Big Five) is rather similar across the cultures (see also McCrae, 2002).

A reasonable question is why four of the Big Five personality factors load on the same personality/social attitudes factor. The answer to this question is in two parts. First, even though the construction of the Big Five scales was based on the assumption of orthogonality (varimax was often the preferred method of factor rotation), personality traits measured by these scales are still moderately correlated. Stankov (2004) points out that the first principal component from the personality measures is only slightly lower than the first principal component from the ability domain based on a wide sample of cognitive tasks. And yet cognitive abilities are often interpreted in terms of a single 'g' factor while in the domain of personality separate Big Five factors have received wide popularity. In fact, in the review by Saucier and Goldberg (2003), it was shown that studies of personality structure sometimes report a single evaluation factor. DeYoung (2006) also shows that there exist higher order factors among the Big Five. Second, when studied within a broad range of non-cognitive measures like the domains in our studies, factors of the Big Five personality traits coalesce into a single factor.

CULTURE IS MOSTLY ETIC, NOT EMIC

Pancultural analyses – analyses based on a whole group of participants regardless of their group memberships – are useful, but often raise questions about the possibility that a different factorial structure may emerge in a particular country or region. Cross-cultural psychologists use the term *etic* to refer to comparative analyses which focus on the universality of the constructs across cultures. On the other hand, *emic* refers to internal explorations of psychological phenomena in local constructs that informs about culture-specific features (Segall et al., 1998).

We employed multi-group factor analysis to examine the components of etic and emic

variance in the solution presented in Table 27.2 (Stankov and Lee, in press). To accomplish this, we first grouped countries into world regions. Although our sample of TOEFL iBT test takers came from 73 different countries, the number of participants for some countries was small (less than five) and thus the decision was made to combine countries into cultural groups based on GLOBE classification (see House et al., 2004). The nine GLOBE societal clusters are 1. Latin Europe, 2. Germanic Europe, 3. Eastern Europe, 4. Latin America, 5. Sub-Saharan Africa, 6. Middle East, 7. Southern Asia, 8. Confucian Asia, and 9. Anglo (largely US sample). Second, among different ways of examining factorial invariance, we decided to focus on configural invariance. In this solution, only the same pattern of factor loadings exists across the societal clusters but actual sizes of these loadings can vary from one cluster to another. We also examined modification indices for each of the nine societal clusters. If modification indices suggested that freeing a particular loading within a given societal cluster was likely to improve model fit indices, these loadings were released and left 'free'. By doing so, we obtain information about etic features of the data from the configural invariance model and, at the same time, we also obtain the emic information from factor loadings that are unique to a societal cluster.

The results of these multi-group factor analyses show that etic component is much stronger than the emic component in our data. The factor structure presented in Table 27.2 holds well across the societal clusters – loadings that are unique to a particular cluster are minuscule in comparison to the overall similarity between the societal clusters. We humans are very much alike in terms of the main dimensions of personality, social attitudes, values, and social norms. This provides good justification for comparing different clusters in terms of arithmetic means – factorial invariance implies that these comparisons are valid. We turn to this topic in the following sections.

RELATIVE CONTRIBUTIONS OF VARIANCE DUE TO INDIVIDUALS, COUNTRIES, AND SOCIETAL CLUSTERS TO THE TOTAL VARIANCE OF FACTOR SCORES

We report in this section the outcomes of a three-level hierarchical linear modeling (HLM) analysis. The HLM analyses address two issues: the relative contribution of individuals versus countries/societal clusters in explaining the variance in factor scores and which of the four factors are more prone to individual versus cultural (i.e. countries and societal clusters) influences.

Table 27.3 shows the result of HLM analyses. To address the first issue, we compared the three level in Table 27.3. It is apparent that the variances due to individual differences are larger than any other source of variability. These range from 92.89 for 'values' to 74.95 for 'social norms'. Individual variability (which is the main focus in psychology) is so much more powerful than the variability among countries or societal clusters. It is also apparent that, except for the 'values' factor, the variances explained by societal clusters (Level 3) are larger than the variances explained by countries (Level 2). This can be seen as supportive evidence for the GLOBE classification of world regions.

The finding of preponderance of variance due to individuals in the HLM analysis is not surprising. Sometimes the kind of analysis reported in Table 27.3 is referred to as 'value added' (i.e. the interest is in the effects of country and culture over the effects due to individual differences). Its application has become common in education due to the implementation of the No Child Left Behind Act. In education, it is the effect of schools that is being evaluated. In educational studies when comparing school and individual effects, the ratio of variance explained by individuals versus the school variances is approximately in the same range as that reported in Table 27.3. The general pattern seems to be the same for the group/country effects in our study and for the group/school effects in educational studies.

Looking down the columns in Table 27.3 we can address the second issue. The smallest effect of countries and societal clusters is found on the 'values' factor. It seems that a popular notion that people value similar things regardless where they live seems to be supported by our data. People in all cultures seem to appreciate in their lives achievement, power, self-direction, security, and so on. The other three factors do show stronger influence of countries and societal clusters. The strongest influence, as one would expect, is on the 'social norms' factor – 25.05% of the total variance is due to

Table 27.3   Breakdown of the total variance into the components due to individual, country, and societal clusters (hierarchical linear modeling (HLM) results)

	Personality/social attitudes	Value systems	Social norms	Conservatism
Total variance	8.20	12.47	11.01	14.21
Level-1				
Variance due to individuals within countries	7.11	11.58	8.25	10.83
% of total variance	86.75	92.89	74.95	76.16
Level-2				
Variance due to countries within clusters	0.33	0.78	1.23	0.96
% of total variance	4.05	6.19	11.19	6.76
Level-3				
Variance between clusters	0.75	0.11	1.53	2.43
% of total variance	9.19	0.92	13.86	17.08
ANOVA *F*-tests for nine	29.828	11.348	40.071	51.302
Societal clusters *df* = 8,1970				

countries (11.19%) and societal clusters (13.86%). This is closely followed by the conservatism factor – 23.75% of the total variance is due to countries (6.67%) and societal clusters (17.08%). Clearly, cultures differ a lot on conservatism/liberalism dimension. Finally, for the 'personality/social attitudes' factor, the amount of variance due to the combined effects of countries and societal clusters is 13.24%. Although this is not apparent in the analyses presented in Table 27.3, there is indication in our data that if we split this factor into its two constituents – that is, personality variables and social attitudes variables – personality is less affected by culture than social attitudes. This is in accordance with the expectations. Thus, the ordering of factors from the most to the least influenced by group/cultures is as follows:

Social norms – conservatism – social attitudes/personality – values

The last row of Table 27.3 shows the *F*-tests for the differences between the nine societal clusters. As can be seen, the ordering of the magnitude of *F*-tests parallels the ordering of the percentage of total variance that is due to societal clusters. The only difference is the swap of 'conservatism' and 'social norms' factors.

Apart from the surprising position of the 'values' factor, it is interesting that 'conservatism' factor shows such large cultural differences. We shall have a closer look at the pattern of means of societal clusters below.

BETWEEN-COUNTRIES VERSUS WITHIN-STRUCTURE

There is a methodology-related issue in contemporary cross-cultural psychology that, despite our efforts, we were unable to resolve. This has to do with the differences between individual-level analysis and country-level analysis. Individual-level analysis is pretty much what we have been dealing with up until now in this chapter.

In the early 1980s, country-level analysis was championed by Hofstede (see Hofstede, 2002). In this type of analysis, a sample of people from the same country is assessed and arithmetic means for the sample are calculated. The analyses then proceed at the country level in which countries are being treated as units of analysis. Country scores (i.e. mean of people from the same country) can then be correlated among themselves or with measures of economic development or climatic features, and the like. The argument is that these between-countries analyses, in contrast to individual-level analyses, tell us about 'true' cultural differences. A question, then, can be raised whether individual and country level analyses produce the same factors. If they don't, the situation is considerably complicated since we would need separate explanations for cross-cultural differences at the individual and country levels.

A method known as multi-level structural equation modeling has been increasingly employed in contemporary cross-cultural studies. In this approach, one obtains separate factor analytic solutions from the 'within' and 'between countries' covariance matrices. In our work, we chose 33 countries with more than five participants and carried out multi-level analyses using Mplus (Muthen and Muthen, 2004) program. In the outcome, the 'within' factors turned out to be identical to the pancultural factors reported in Table 27.2. The 'between' countries factors, at first, were hard to fit due to a problem of convergence and, when we finally arrived at the solution, only two rather than four factors emerged. These obtained 'between' factors can be interpreted as 'style' factors. The first factor seems to contrast Latin Americans' tendency to assign extreme values to the attitude statement and Confucians' preference for middle values on the scale. The second factor correlates with economic development and may be, tentatively at this stage, interpreted as an acquiescence response style.

However, we retain our skepticism about the outcomes on the 'between' factors of the multi-level analysis. This is partly due to the difficulties in arriving at an acceptable solution and partly to our additional analysis using an exploratory factor analytic approach along the lines of Hofstede (2002). Using the country-means, four (rather than two) between-countries factors appeared. They are similar to the solution presented in Table 27.2.

MEAN DIFFERENCES BETWEEN THE WORLD REGIONS

Figures 27.1–27.4 show the arithmetic means for each of the nine societal clusters on four factor scores: personality/social attitudes,

values, social norms, and conservatism. Factor scores are standardized to have the mean of zero and unit standard deviation. Although the F-tests in Table 27.3 show that the variances explained by the societal clusters on all four factors were significantly different, the 'values' factor has relatively less variance explained by the societal clusters than any of the other factors. This is reflected in the range of the factor scores means; the 'values' factor shows a smaller range than the other three factors do. We can also read out in Figure 27.2 that the smallest effect of the societal clusters expressed as the Cohen's d' is on Values (approx. $d' = 0.70$) and the largest effect is on conservatism in Figure 27.4 (approx. $d' = 1.80$).

Figure 27.1 shows the factor score means for personality/social attitudes. In interpreting

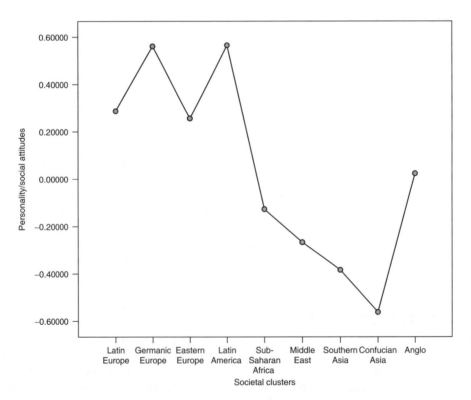

Figure 27.1   Mean personality/social attitudes scores by societal cluster. Note that low scoring societal clusters have high endorsement of negative pole (e.g. toughness and maliciousness) and lower endorsement of positive pole ('evaluative' personality traits) on factor 1

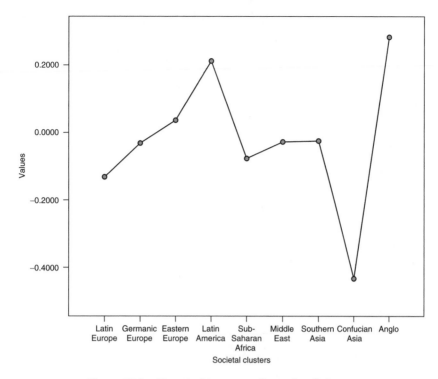

Figure 27.2 Mean values scores by societal cluster

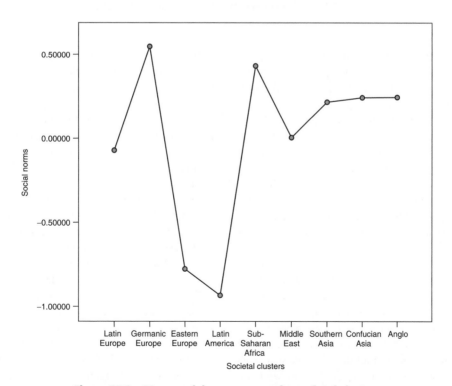

Figure 27.3 Mean social norms scores by societal clusters

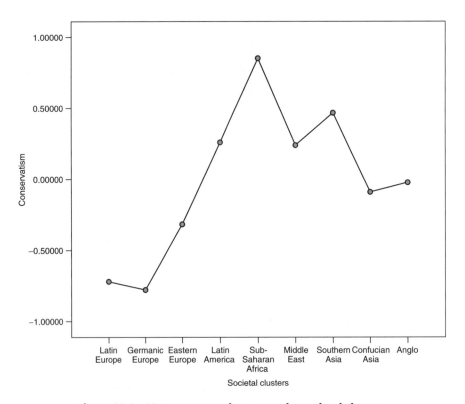

Figure 27.4   Mean conservatism scores by societal clusters

the pattern of means in Figure 27.1, it is important to recall that 'personality/social attitudes' factor is made up of positive personality traits and negative social attitudes but is predominantly defined by the latter. Thus, high scores on this factor can be interpreted as 'anti' or 'amoral' social attitudes. We use the term 'toughness' as shorthand to describe this factor. Societal clusters showing high mean scores in Figure 27.1 – three European clusters (Germanic, Eastern, and Latin) and Latin America – represent groups that are low on toughness – they seem to hold 'soft' views relative to other clusters.

Figure 27.2 presents factor score means of the 'values' factor. As can be seen, the mean values among most societal clusters are very close to each other. The largest mean difference appears between Confucian and Anglo clusters; the importance of values was endorsed the least by Confucians and the most by Anglo people.

Figure 27.3 shows the pattern of factor score means for the 'social norms' factor. Social norms may impose subtle or overt influences on individuals' behaviors or decision-making. Societal clusters that are low on this factor in Figure 27.3 are Eastern Europe and Latin America. These are the world regions that are experiencing significant political and social changes and are, perhaps, cynical in their view of social norms. Alternatively, the construct of social norms in those regions is not clearly defined.

High scores on the 'conservatism' factor in Figure 27.4 mean that the region is high on conservatism. Low scores, on the other hand, indicate liberalism. As can be seen in Figure 27.4, societal clusters that show low conservatism are those three European clusters that showed low 'toughness' in Figure 27.1. On the other hand, Latin Americans with a low score on 'toughness' scored high on conservatism.

Table 27.4 Correlations between four-factor scores and cognitive measures

Variable	Personality/amoral social attitudes	Values	Social norms	Conservatism
High-school GPA	0.22**	−0.01	−0.01	−0.08
SAT (self-report) n = 732	0.28**	−0.10	−0.09	−0.35**

In summary, the most salient feature seems to appear in the comparisons of Figures 27.1 and 27.4. Europeans tend to be more liberal and lower on '(anti-)social attitudes' than people from other parts of the world. Anglo participants, including the US, lay themselves about in the middle of both 'conservatism' and '(anti)-social attitudes'. In addition, East Europeans and Latin Americans tend to score low on 'Social norms' factors indicating that, perhaps, these societies are more cynical in their perceptions of the role of society's implicit and explicit norms in their personal lives.

CULTURAL DIMENSIONS AND COGNITIVE, GENDER, AND ETHNIC DIFFERENCES

In this section we present our findings on correlations with cognitive performance and differences with respect to gender and race/ethnicity. The results are based on the US sample only.

Cognitive correlates of cultural dimensions

Table 27.4 presents correlations of the four sets of factor scores with SAT and high-school grade point average scores (GPA). As can be seen in this table, the significant

correlations of SAT and GPA are with 'personality/social attitudes' factors and with the 'conservatism' factors. The positive correlation with 'anti-social attitudes' factor and the negative correlation with the 'conservatism' factor indicate that those who are conservative and hold 'tough' social attitudes tend to have low SAT or GPA scores. Similar patterns of correlations with 'anti-social attitudes' and 'conservatism' were obtained with a sample of native TOEFL iBT test-takers (Stankov, 2007). For our purposes here, TOEFL iBT is just another cognitive test. Together, our findings suggest that conservative and 'tough' people tend to have lower cognitive ability.

Gender differences

Table 27.5 presents the means for males and females on all four set of factor scores. The main gender difference appears on the 'personality/social attitudes' factor – males subscribe more strongly to 'tough' attitude statements. Although statistically significant, gender differences on the other three factors are small from the practical point of view.

Ethnic differences

Table 27.6 presents arithmetic means by race/ethnicity on all four factors. Three observations from this table are noteworthy. First, no statistically significant differences

Table 27.5 Gender differences

Variable	Personality/amoral social attitudes	Values	Social norms	Conservatism
Male (n = 436)	−0.325	−0.143	0.117	−0.144
Female (n = 738)	0.193	0.085	−0.070	0.084
Cohen's d′	0.518	0.215	0.187	0.228
t-test (df = 1,1172)	8.33**	3.75**	2.62**	3.40**

Note: Factor scores are in standard score units (i.e. mean = 0; sd = 1)

Table 27.6   Ethnic differences

Variable	Factor 1: Personality/ amoral social attitudes	Factor 2: Values	Factor 3: Social norms	Factor 4: Conservatism
White ($n = 727$)	0.092	−0.117	−0.060	−0.107
Black ($n = 239$)	−0.276	0.249	0.087	0.324
Hispanic ($n = 91$)	0.039	0.213	0.214	0.151
Asian ($n = 91$)	−0.068	0.265	0.076	−0.148
Other ($n = 49$)	0.078	−0.070	−0.084	−0.054
F-test ($df = 41,165$)	5.70**	8.39**	1.687(ns)	7.50**

Note: Factor scores are in standard score units (i.e. mean = 0; sd = 1)

were found between racial/ethnic groups on the 'social norms' factor. The racial/ethnic group differences on the other three factors were statistically significant at the 0.05 level. Second, although the difference is small (less than one-half of the standard deviation), it appears that Blacks, in comparison to their White counterparts, score lower on the 'personality/social attitudes' factor and on the 'conservatism' factor. In other words, Blacks show tougher and more conservative attitudes than Whites do. Third, Whites seem to attach lower importance to values than Blacks, Hispanics, or Asians.

HOW DO WE SEE OUR WORLD? INSIDE-OUT LAYERS OF SOCIAL INTERACTIONS

What we have shown in this chapter is that there are four major dimensions of culture: personality/social attitudes, values, social norms, and conservatism. With the exception of the 'conservatism' factor, what we had conceptualized initially as 'domains' – a loose collection of constructs – has appeared as 'the' dimensions of culture. Our data show that we tend to make clear distinctions among our activities of thinking about ourselves (personality), dealing with others (social attitudes), attaching meanings to long-term goals (values), and considering societal milieu (social norms).

As we move from personality to social norms, there is a decreasing amount of person-to-person contact. In addition, the focal points move from self to others. Personality is a private entity that can be revealed to others who are within a close proximity in terms of physical distance or social relations. Social attitudes can be expressed when we deal with people that are both close and somewhat removed from us in terms of physical and social interactions. Value systems are less directly and only occasionally involved in immediate social interchanges. Values take place typically in planning or decision-making of a person's long-term activities, and involve organizations or institutions in addition to social interactions. Finally, social norms act as conscious and unconscious controls over our behaviors. Social norms can only be reflected in our perceptions of institutionalized behaviors of people in a given society, and thus there are no immediate person-to-person interactions. The cascade of domains/dimensions in Figure 27.5 depicts this diminishing role of direct social interactions in the four domains from the highest on personality traits to the lowest on social norms.

We can also speculate that there may be a developmental trend that is reflected in the cascade in Figure 27.5. We usually see that child's personality traits emerge early, within the first two or three years of life. Attitudes toward others such as parents, siblings, and friends seem to develop next, possibly prior to the beginning of schooling. Values are likely to develop prominently during adolescence. Finally, the awareness of social norms emerges when a person makes choices in

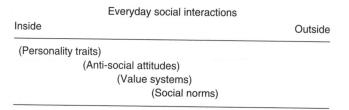

Figure 27.5   Inside-out and developmental stages of social interactions

other settings than in school-related activities. For an adult, all four domains can be identified and stand as separate dimensions. However, empirical evidence for such a developmental trend may be difficult to gather.

We would like to point out that ecological factors such as political traditions and institutions, economic forces, geographical factors, family structure, socialization practices, educational institutions, social stratification, and mobility are not included in this model. Only subjective experiences – the way people see themselves and their immediate and distant social worlds and express their beliefs and values – are the focal points for the studies reviewed in this chapter.

CONCLUSIONS

In this chapter, we have presented our work on dimensions of cultural differences captured by a battery of 43 scales. Our focus was on studying how people from 73 countries answer questions that measure five personality traits, eight different ways to express social attitudes, eleven distinctive values, and nine aspects of looking at their own culture. Much to our surprise, the distinctions within each domain did not show up in the factor analyses – using three different approaches: pancultural, multi-group, and multi-level. On the other hand, people across all cultures see the distinction among the four main domains providing the evidence that psychological aspects of culture are made up of personality/social attitudes, values, social norms, and conservatism.

Our multi-group factor analyses based on the nine GLOBE societal clusters show that etic component is much stronger than the emic component among the psychological dimensions culture. The factor loadings that are unique to a particular cluster (emic) are minimal in comparison to the overall similarity between the societal clusters (etic). Our three-level HLM analyses, with individual, countries, and societal clusters as the three levels of analyses, show that individual variability (which is often the focus in psychology) is much more pronounced than the variability between countries or between the societal clusters. It is interesting that, with the exception of the 'values' factor, the variances of the other three factors explained by societal clusters are larger than the variances explained by countries. As one would expect, the 'social norms' factor was more influenced by countries and societal clusters than the other factors, followed by 'conservatism', and then by 'personality/social attitudes' factors. The 'values' factor was the least influenced by countries and societal clusters, supporting the evidence that individuals rather than culture play a strong role in deciding what they value in life.

We also present evidence for different patterns of factor score means for each of the nine societal clusters on the four dimensions of cultural differences. Our data show that three European clusters (Germanic, Eastern, and Latin) and Latin America represent groups that possess 'soft' views of others. Confucians and Anglo people show the largest difference in their value systems. People from Eastern Europe and Latin America show low endorsements of social norms. Three European clusters – Germanic,

Eastern, and Latin – seem to be the least conservative attitudes among all the clusters.

The relationship of four dimensions of culture to cognitive performance, gender, and race/ethnicity was also described in this chapter. In summary, those who are conservative and hold 'tough' social attitudes toward others tend to have low scores on measures of cognitive performance such as SAT, TOEFL iBT, and GPA. Although gender differences were apparent on all four dimensions, the most prominent gender differences were on the '(anti-) social attitudes' factor – males showed more strong and tough attitudes toward others than females did. The racial/ethnic group differences were also found in three out of four factors with the 'values' factor being the exception. It appears that Blacks, in comparison to their White counterparts, show tougher and more conservative attitudes toward others and the world. On the other hand, Whites seem to endorse lower importance to 'values' than Blacks, Hispanics, or Asians.

There are many ways to proceed with this type of work. Our own focus will be on the expansion of the domains to be covered. Thus, we think that measures of religiosity, psychoticism, and social axioms – defined as generalized sets of beliefs that are central to a person's belief system (see Leung and Bond, 2004) – should be added to the battery. In addition, we believe that studying dimensions of cultural differences may be useful in studying fanaticism and extremism which underlie anti-social terrorist activities. An important question today is whether extremist views can be reduced to the four dimension of culture or whether we need another scale for its assessment.

REFERENCES

Bozeman, A.B. (1975) 'Civilizations under stress', *Virginia Quarterly Review*, 51(4): 1–18.

DeYoung, C.G. (2006) 'Higher-order factors of the Big Five in a multi-informant sample', *Journal of Personality and Social Psychology*, 91(6): 1138–51.

Hofstede, G. (2002) 'The pitfalls of crossnational survey research: A reply to the article by Spector et al. on the psychometric properties of the Hofstede Values Survey Module 1994', *Applied Psychology: An International Review*, 51(1): 170–18.

House, R.J., Hanges, P.J., Javidan, M., Dorfman, P.W. and Gupta, V. (2004) *Culture, Leadership, and Organizations: The GLOBE Study of 62 Societies*. Thousand Oaks, CA: Sage Publications.

Huntington, S. (1997) *The Clash of Civilizations and the Remaking of World Order*. New York: Touchstone.

Leung, K. and Bond, M.H. (2004) 'Social axioms: A model for social beliefs in multicultural perspective', *Advances in Experimental Social Psychology*, 36(5): 119–97.

Lustig, M. and Koester, J. (1996) *Intercultural Competence: Interpersonal Communication Across Cultures*. New York: Harper Collins.

Matsumoto, D. and Yoo, S.H. (2006) 'Toward a new generation of cross-cultural research', *Perspectives on Psychological Science*, 1(3): 234–47.

McCrae, R.R. (2002) 'The five-factor model of personality across cultures', in R.R. McCrae, J. Allik (eds), *The Five 'Factor Model of Personality Across Cultures'*, New York: Kluwer Academic/Plenum, pp. 105–25.

Muthen, L.K. and Muthen, B.O. (2004) *Mplus: The Comprehensive Modeling Program for Applied Researchers. User's Guide* (3rd edn). Los Angeles: Muthen & Muthen.

Nisbett, R. (2003) *The Geography of Thought*. New York: Free Press.

Rokeach, M. (1973) *The Nature of Human Values*. New York: Free Press.

Saucier, G. (2000) 'Isms and the structure of social attitudes', *Journal of Personality and Social Psychology*, 78(2): 366–85.

Saucier, G. and Goldberg, L.R. (2002) 'Assessing the Big Five: Applications of 10 psychometric criteria to the development of marker scales', in B. de Raad and M. Perugini (eds), *Big Five Assessment*. Goettingen: Hogrefe & Huber, pp. 29–58.

Saucier, G. (2004) 'Personality and ideology: one thing or two?', Unpublished manuscript, University of Oregon.

Saucier, G. and Goldberg, L.R. (2003) 'The structure of personality attributes', in M.B. Barrick and A.M. Ryan (eds), *Personality and Work: Reconsidering the Role of Personality in Organizations*. San Francisco: Jossey-Bass.

Schwartz, S.H. (2003) 'Basic human values: Their content and structure across countries', in A. Tamayo and J. Porto (eds), *Values and Work*. Brasilia: Editora Universidade de Brasilia.

Schwartz, S.H. and Bardi, A. (2001) 'Value hierarchies across cultures: Taking a similarities perspective', *Journal of Cross Cultural Psychology*, 32(3): 268–90.

Segall, M.H., Lonner, W.J. and Berry, J.W. (1998) 'Cross-cultural psychology as a scholarly discipline: On the flowering of culture in behavioural research', *American Psychologist*, 53(5): 1101–10.

Stankov, L. (2004) "g" factor: Issues of design and interpretation', in O. Wilhelm and R. Engle (eds), *Understanding and Measuring Intelligence*. Sage Publications.

Stankov, L. (in press) 'Psychological aspects of culture', *European Journal of Social Psychology.*

Stankov, L. (2007) 'The structure among measures of personality, social attitudes, values, and social norms', *Journal of Individual Differences,* 28: 240–51.

Stankov, L. and Knezevic, G. (2005) 'Amoral social attitudes and value orientations among Serbs and Australians', *Australian Journal of Psychology*, 57: 115–29.

Stankov, L. and Lee, J. (in press) 'Dimensions of cultural differences: pancultural, etic/emic, and ecological approaches', *Learning and Individual Differences.*

Sternberg, R.J. and Grigorenko, E.L. (2004) *Culture and Competence: Context of Life Success*. Washington, DC: American Psychological Association.

Terraciano et al. (2005) 'National character does not reflect mean personality trait levels in 49 cultures', *Science*, 310(5745): 96–100.

Triandis, H.C. (1996) 'The psychological measurement of cultural syndromes', *American Psychologist*, 51(4): 407–15.

28

Emotional Intelligence

Elizabeth J. Austin, James D.A. Parker, K.V. Petrides and
Donald H. Saklofske

INTRODUCTION

Emotional intelligence (EI) is a relatively new arrival in the field of individual differences. The term first appeared in Leuner (1966), Greenspan (1989), and in a dissertation by Payne (1986). The field was launched by Goleman's (1995) book, which was influenced by an earlier theoretical article by Salovey and Mayer (1990). This work also drew on earlier literature, in particular that on social intelligence (e.g. Marlowe, 1986; Thorndike, 1920) and Gardner's (1983) multiple intelligence theory. The intense interest in EI outside academic psychology, sparked by Goleman (1995), together with the relatively sparse empirical research findings then available, led to claims in the popular media for outcomes of EI not substantiated by research findings. More recently, empirical EI research has expanded, allowing popular beliefs about how EI relates to outcomes such as academic and career success to be scientifically tested. This rapid growth in EI research has led to the publication of a number of books which both summarise the current state of the field and discuss problematic issues in more detail than is possible here (e.g. Bar-On and Parker, 2000b; Ciarrochi

et al., 2006; Matthews et al., 2002; Murphy, 2006; Schulze and Roberts, 2005). The text by Murphy provides a critical review of EI research and applications, including an analysis of why the adoption of EI tests in the business world has tended to precede or ignore empirical findings.

Two problematic issues in EI research relate to disagreements on both the definition of EI and on how it should be measured. Examples of EI definitions are: 'an array of non-cognitive capabilities, competencies, and skills, that influence one's ability to succeed in coping with environmental demands and pressures' (Bar-On, 1997: 14) and 'an ability to recognise the meanings of emotion and their relationships, and to reason and problem-solve on the basis of them' (Mayer et al., 1999: 267). The models proposed by different researchers vary, although most include core features of perceiving, understanding and managing emotions, and also that these abilities can be exercised both intrapersonally and interpersonally. Further work may lead to an agreed EI model, but the measurement issue appears more intractable. Although there are a number of EI measures for which evidence of reliability and validity has been obtained, two different measurement methods are currently in use.

Some tests are problem-based, resembling intelligence tests, while others are self-report questionnaires, resembling personality tests.

In this chapter we first address the current status of EI measurement, including the issue of whether EI meets the agreed definition of an intelligence. Research findings on real-life correlates of EI in the areas of health, academic success and occupational success are then summarised. We conclude with suggestions for future work on EI.

EI MEASUREMENT

Introduction

One approach to measuring EI involves solving problems with emotion-related content, while the other involves the use of self-report questionnaires. Petrides and Furnham (2001) proposed the use of the respective terms ability and trait EI; these labels relate to the well-known distinction between maximal and typical performance. There are a number of problems associated with extending maximum performance measurement from the cognitive to the emotional domain but trait EI measurement appears reasonably unproblematic. Using these labels does not address the issue of whether trait and ability EI are the same. Correlations between trait and ability measures have been found to be modest (e.g. Zeidner et al., 2005) and similar to those between tested and self-reported intelligence (e.g. Furnham and Rawles, 1999). This suggests a (limited) capability for self-assessment of EI but does not imply that questionnaire EI measures an intelligence.

Ability EI

General issues

Advocates of ability EI argue that it is a subcomponent of cognitive ability and can be measured with tests which resemble intelligence tests. Ability EI tests assess emotion-related capabilities using problems

(e.g. how to resolve a conflict with a work colleague) requiring understanding and/or use of emotions. Scoring such items is non-obvious; the two most-used scoring systems are expert and consensus scoring. Expert scoring utilises individuals with specialist knowledge (emotion researchers) to determine the correct answers. It is not clear that such individuals actually qualify as experts (knowledge of emotion theory is not the same as high EI). Consensus scoring defines the right answer as that most frequently endorsed by a normative group. In either case responses to test items are awarded a score which is equal to the proportion of the relevant group endorsing them. Consensus scoring is problematic because the option chosen by the majority may not reflect the solution favoured by a high-EI minority, and is also discordant with the veridical scoring used in intelligence testing (Matthews et al., 2002). Another method, target scoring, can be applied where the person generating the item was seeking to convey a particular emotion. This represents an alternative approach to the issue of 'right' answers, but is not widely used.

Instruments and psychometrics

The main proponents of ability EI are Salovey, Mayer and co-workers. In the interests of brevity we will only discuss this group's most recent ability EI measure, the Mayer–Salovey–Caruso emotional intelligence test (MSCEIT; Mayer et al., 2003). For a description of the MSCEIT's predecessor, the MEIS, see Mayer et al. (1999). The MSCEIT is constructed in accordance with a hierarchical model of EI mimicking that for psychometric intelligence (Carroll, 1993). The eight MSCEIT subscales (two per branch) give scores on the EI branches of perceiving emotions, using emotions to facilitate thought, understanding emotions and managing emotions. Branch scores are combined to give experiential (perceiving, facilitating) and strategic (understanding, managing) area scores and the area scores are combined to give a total score.

The MSCEIT has been reported to have good internal reliability and high correlations are also found between consensus and expert scores. Findings on the fit of MSCEIT data to its theoretical factor structure have however been mixed (Mayer et al., 2003; Palmer et al., 2005). Other ability EI measures are available, for example the EARS (Mayer and Geher, 1996), TEMINT (Amelang and Steinmayr, 2006). Two recent tests, the STEU and STEM (MacCann, 2006), seek to avoid the problems of consensus scoring by allowing standards-based scoring linked to theoretical models of emotion and coping. Although not developed as an EI measure, the levels of emotional awareness scale (LEAS; Lane et al., 1990) has been found to be significantly correlated with MEIS and MSCEIT scores (Barchard and Hakstian, 2004; Ciarrochi et al., 2003). Further work is needed to clarify the associations amongst current ability EI tests.

Ability EI as an intelligence?

The accepted structure of psychometric intelligence is hierarchical, with general ability (g) at the apex and more specific abilities at lower levels (Carroll, 1993). This structure is underpinned by the well-known 'positive manifold' of positively intercorrelated ability tests. Any new intelligence should fit this structure; that is, it should show positive associations with existing intelligence measures, whilst also being non-redundant with them. Evidence that ability EI fits the positive manifold comes from findings that MEIS and MSCEIT scores have moderate positive correlations with conventional intelligence measures (e.g. MacCann et al., 2004; Roberts et al., 2001). However, the construct validity value of these correlations has been called into question (Brody, 2004). Both MEIS and MSCEIT scores are more strongly correlated with crystallised than with fluid ability (e.g. McCann et al., 2004; Roberts et al., 2001).

An alternative perspective on EI as an intelligence is to establish links with the information-processing approach to intelligence. Higher (particularly fluid) intelligence is well known to be associated with superior performance on information-processing tasks (Deary, 2000), in particular inspection time (IT). If ability EI is an intelligence then it would be expected to show similar associations. Emotional IT task performance has been found to correlate with fluid ability (Austin, 2005), while MSCEIT scores have been found to correlate with emotional but not with non-emotional IT performance (Farrelly and Austin, 2007). It has also been found that high scorers on emotional management ability show EEG evidence of more efficient cortical information processing (Freudenthaler et al., 2006).

Although there is some evidence that ability EI has intelligence properties, the only broad-bandwidth measure currently available (MSCEIT) does not appear to measure fluid EI, so the development of alternative ability tests targeted at this is important. It would also be helpful to researchers to have access to a more diverse set of ability EI tests, in particular tests which can be veridically scored. This would allow the construct of ability EI, as opposed to its particular realisation in one test, to be examined more generally.

Trait EI

General issues

The construct of trait EI has its roots in the distinction between trait and ability EI (Petrides and Furnham, 2001), which mirrors the deep distinction in differential psychology between typical behaviour and maximal performance (Cronbach, 1949). A true intelligence should be assessed through items that can be veridically scored according to objective criteria. The explosion of interest in EI following the publication of Goleman (1995) led to the development of dozens of 'EQ tests' with little theoretical or psychometric rationale. There was also an erroneous insistence that these measures assessed abilities. The trait/ability dichotomy was introduced to address these issues and is based on the method used to operationalise the construct. As such, it is unrelated to the distinction between mixed and ability models of EI (Mayer et al., 2000b), with which it is sometimes confused and which concerns whether or not a theoretical model 'mixes' cognitive abilities with other characteristics.

The introduction of trait EI spurred several similar labels (e.g. self-reported EI). This proliferation of labels is a classic manifestation of the jangle fallacy, whereby the same variance is repeatedly rechristened (Kelley, 1927). All of these labels refer to the same underlying construct, for which trait EI theory provides a psychological foundation. Trait EI goes beyond a mere offer of an accurate label for EI measured through self-report. The crux of the matter is the nature and scientific plausibility of the underlying construct and it is here that trait EI has the compelling advantage of being compatible with mainstream models of individual differences (Petrides et al., 2007a).

Models of EI that do not view it as a personality trait are problematic for two reasons. First, models operationalised via self-report are entirely incongruent with what we know about cognitive ability (e.g. Deary, 2000). Correlations between measured and self-estimated IQ are, at best, about 0.3 (Furnham and Rawles, 1999). Consequently, any EI model that theorises about ability-related concepts and then uses questionnaires in its operationalisation is a scientific non-starter. Research conducted with EI questionnaires based on unsound models is not however futile. The results can be linked to mainstream psychology if interpreted through the perspective of trait EI theory (Petrides et al., 2007a). Trait EI theory is general and can provide a platform for the correct interpretation of data from any emotion-related questionnaire. Secondly, ability EI models are problematic because the subjectivity of emotional experience (Watson, 2000) prevents the development of items that can be veridically scored and that cover the entire sampling domain of the construct. The one test that claims to offer a valid operationalisa-

tion of ability EI has been dismissed by cognitive ability experts on the grounds that it relies on scoring procedures that are fundamentally different from those of standard IQ tests (Brody, 2004). The trait/ability EI distinction views the two constructs as essentially different. Therefore, the operationalisation of one has no bearing on the operationalisation of the other and the two could theoretically co-exist (Tett et al., 2005).

So what is trait EI? It is superficial and incorrect to view trait EI as a mere label that denotes emotional intelligence measured by questionnaire. Trait EI is a constellation of emotion-related self-perceptions and dispositions located at the lower levels of personality hierarchies. This definition has significant implications for the construct and leads to a coherent psychological theory (as distinct from 'models', 'tests', etc.) that is testable, falsifiable and general. Trait EI as a construct seeks to provide a comprehensive operationalisation of affective aspects of personality. Leaving aside claims about the discovery of an escalating number of new 'intelligences', Thorndike (1920), Gardner (1983), Salovey and Mayer (1990), Goleman (1995) and others simply discuss the possibility of unexplored emotion-related variance. Trait EI research has sought to establish empirically the extent to which these ideas have already been incorporated in mainstream differential psychology taxonomies and to find ways to operationalise the remainder. The conversion, extension and incorporation of these ideas in personality taxonomies has led to the detection of some new variance (trait EI consistently shows incremental validity over the Giant Three and the Big Five) and, more importantly, has created exciting theoretical advances.

Sampling domain

The current sampling domain of trait EI (see Table 28.1) was derived from a content analysis of early models of 'emotional intelligence'. The rationale was to include core elements common to more than a single model, but exclude peripheral elements appearing in

Table 28.1   The adult sampling domain of trait emotional intelligence

Facets	High scorers perceive themselves as ...
Adaptability	... flexible and willing to adapt to new conditions
Assertiveness	... forthright, frank and willing to stand up for their rights
Emotion perception (self and others)	... clear about their own and other people's feelings
Emotion expression	... capable of communicating their feelings to others
Emotion management (others)	... capable of influencing other people's feelings
Emotion regulation	... capable of controlling their emotions
Impulsiveness (low)	... reflective and less likely to give in to their urges
Relationships	... capable of maintaining fulfilling personal relationships
Self-esteem	... successful and self-confident
Self-motivation	... driven and unlikely to give up in the face of adversity
Social awareness	... accomplished networkers with superior social skills
Stress management	... capable of withstanding pressure and regulating stress
Trait empathy	... capable of taking someone else's perspective
Trait happiness	... cheerful and satisfied with their lives
Trait optimism	... confident and likely to 'look on the bright side' of life

only one conceptualisation. This is analogous to procedures used in classical scale development, whereby the commonalities (shared core) of the various items comprising a scale are carried over into a total (internally consistent) score, while their random or unique components (noise) are cancelled out in the process. The systematic nature of this method is to be contrasted with the haphazard procedures through which other sampling domains have been established wherein the inclusion or exclusion of facets is typically the outcome of unstated or arbitrary decisions. Nonetheless, as the theory develops and the empirical base expands, this sampling domain will have to be adjusted to reflect theoretical and empirical developments.

Trait EI and personality

Since trait EI is a personality trait, a crucial question concerns its location within the major trait taxonomies. This question is of vital theoretical importance and has implications for both discriminant and incremental validity. A series of joint factor analyses with various measures of the Giant Three and Big Five have revealed that trait EI is located at the lower levels of the trait hierarchies. Thus, trait EI is a distinct (because it can be isolated in personality space) and compound (because it is partially determined by several personality dimensions) construct that lies at the lower levels of personality hierarchies (because the trait EI factor is oblique, rather than orthogonal to the Giant Three and the Big Five) (Petrides et al., 2007c). This conclusion allows us to connect the construct to established theories of differential psychology – a critical advantage of trait EI theory.

Incremental validity

An increasing number of studies have supported the incremental validity of trait EI. Possibly the largest is by Petrides et al. (2007b), who examined incremental validity vis-à-vis the Big Five and mood in relation to over 20 distinct criteria and found statistically significant effects in the vast majority of cases. Other studies with positive results include Mikolajczak et al. (2006; alexithymia and optimism), Petrides et al. (2004; Giant Three), Saklofske et al., (2003; Big Five) and Van der Zee and Wabeke (2004; Big Five).

While the above-mentioned findings clearly show that trait EI can account for variance over and above the basic personality dimensions, the single important message we would like to highlight is that incremental validity is of limited theoretical importance. Even if there were complete overlap between trait EI and the main personality dimensions, the explanatory power of the former would not be compromised. Describing personality constructs in terms of broad personality dimensions, although frequently possible, fails to capture their nature (Funder, 2001). The main advantages of trait EI are to be found in conceptual content and explanatory power, rather than in predictive and incremental utility.

RESEARCH ON CORRELATES OF EI

Introduction

The idea that EI can explain variance in life outcomes not accounted for by intelligence and personality is interesting and important. There is considerable interest in the associations of EI with health and also in whether EI is a predictor of career and academic success. If it is then EI is potentially a useful selection tool, and training people to enhance their EI levels might also be appropriate.

EI and health

There are theoretical reasons to anticipate associations between EI and psychological health. Intrapersonal EI should associate with mood regulation and stress management, and with happiness and positive emotions, associations which should protect against depression and anxiety. Interpersonal EI should be related to social network size and quality of relationships, which are associated with mental health (e.g. Fuhrer et al., 1998). Several studies have confirmed these associations, with EI being found to be positively related to health-related quality of life, life satisfaction, and social network quality and size (Austin et al., 2005; Ciarrochi et al., 2001; Extremera and Fernández-Berrocal, 2002), and negatively related to psychological distress, loneliness and depression (e.g. Saklofske et al., 2003). The association of EI with mental health has been verified in a recent meta-analysis (Schutte et al., 2007).

It has also been found that high EI is associated with increased capability for maintenance and repair of positive mood (Ciarrochi et al., 2000; Schutte et al., 2002).

The associations of EI with health behaviours and physical health have been less extensively studied. High EI would be expected to lead to positive interactions with health professionals and ability to resist peer pressure towards risky behaviours. High EI has been found to be related to willingness to seek help for personal-emotional problems, depression and suicidal ideation (Ciarrochi and Deane, 2001). Resistance of peer pressure may explain the negative associations found between EI and cigarette, drug and alcohol use (e.g. Austin et al., 2005; Riley and Schutte, 2003; Trinidad and Johnson, 2002), although the superior ability of high-EI individuals to regulate their mood without these agents could also be relevant. EI has been found to be positively associated with self-rated health and negatively with number of recent illnesses reported, symptom reporting and subjective fatigue (Brown and Schutte, 2006; Extremera and Fernández-Berrocal, 2002; Salovey et al., 2002; Tsaousis and Nikolaou, 2005). As for psychological health, lower levels of symptom/illness reporting are likely to be related to subcomponents and correlates of EI such as better mood management, lower stress and positive mood. The findings on associations between alexithymia and somatic symptoms (which relates to confusion between experienced emotions and physical symptoms) discussed below are also relevant.

Taking exercise provides an example of a health behaviour for which theoretical links to EI can be proposed. Since exercise is known to be associated with mood enhancement (e.g. Penedo and Dahn, 2005), the mood regulation skills of high EI scorers might facilitate the use of exercise as a mood management mechanism, whilst the positivity and optimism associated with high EI may assist in overcoming barriers to taking exercise. The social opportunities afforded by some forms of exercise could also motivate high-EI individuals. EI has been found to be positively related to frequency of planned exercise (Tsaousis and Nikolaou, 2005), and with reports of taking regular exercise (Saklofske et al., 2007b). In addition to these associations for overall EI, the intrapersonal, interpersonal and general mood subscales of the EQ-i:S (Bar-On, 2002), corresponding to EI components expected to be linked to taking exercise, have been found to be significantly correlated with taking regular exercise, although only the intrapersonal scale was correlated with amount of exercise taken (Saklofske et al., 2007b).

An interesting perspective on EI/health associations can be obtained by considering possible links between EI and coping. If EI acts as a coping resource, it could potentially mediate the effect of personality on health-related outcomes. EI has been found to be positively associated with rational coping and negatively associated with emotion-focused coping. In addition a positive association with internal health locus of control and a negative association with chance health locus of control was found (Saklofske et al., 2007a). Thus high-EI individuals may have resources allowing them to deal constructively with health problems.

Clinical implications of EI

Although various EI models have been proposed (e.g. Bar-On, 1997; Mayer et al., 1999), all identify dimensions with important implications for clinical psychology. The ability to identify and communicate internal mental states, the ability to link particular mental events with specific situations and personal behaviours, the ability to guide future behaviour from information about feelings and emotions, as well as the ability to mentally regulate negative or extreme emotional states, comprise core abilities in virtually all models for EI. This broad range of abilities has obvious clinical implications, given that they have long been associated with numerous disorders such as substance use disorders, somatoform disorders, eating disorders and anxiety disorders; and with a

variety of physical, lifestyle and interpersonal problems (Taylor et al., 1997). Successful outcomes from various types of clinical intervention have also been found to be linked with many of these basic types of ability (Ackerman and Hilsenroth, 2003; Krystal, 1988; Taylor, 1987). For example, successful insight-oriented psychotherapy often depends on a client's 'ability to see relationships among thoughts, feelings, and actions, with the goal of learning the meanings and causes of his experiences and behaviour' (Applebaum, 1973: 36).

While theoretical models of EI have obvious clinical implications, little direct empirical evidence exists. However, a fairly substantial amount of literature can be found if the search is broadened to include research on related constructs. One of these comes from research that attempts to predict the successful outcomes of psychotherapy. Many individuals respond quite poorly to insight-oriented psychotherapy (Silver, 1983; Taylor, 1977). Often, this lack of 'client fit' is apparent from the very start of treatment, where some individuals seem to be more difficult to help than others. These are often the same clients who stop treatment after only a few sessions, report being discouraged by the slow pace of the therapy, and habitually complain that the topics raised by the therapist have little relevance to their 'problems' (Beckham, 1992; Saltzman et al., 1976). Not only do these clients often feel frustration in the therapeutic situation but, as noted by Taylor (1977), they create frustrations for the psychotherapist as well. The results, as noted by Silver (1983) and Taylor (1977), are counter transference problems. One of the most drastic of these problems is termination of therapy by the client. Dropout rates from psychotherapy can run as high as 80% to 90% (Owen and Kohutek, 1981), with almost half of these terminations occurring after the first few sessions (Pekarik, 1983; Reder and Tyson, 1980).

Not surprisingly, given the high dropout rates, there has been a long history of research dedicated to discovering the variables that might identify individuals not likely to benefit from psychotherapy (e.g. Bachrach and Leaff, 1978; Tolor and Reznikoff, 1960). Although individuals terminate psychotherapy for many reasons, (Luborsky et al., 1985), numerous emotional and social competencies appear to play a role (Krystal, 1988; Mallinckrodt et al., 1998; McCallum et al., 1992; Pierloot and Vinck, 1977; Piper et al., 1998). A sizeable research literature has developed on the personality variables that predict successful outcomes in psychotherapy (Bachrach and Leaff, 1978). Parker (2005) has noted that there is considerable overlap between these constructs and EI, particularly psychological mindedness. In an early definition of psychological mindedness, Conte et al. (1990) have suggested that it involves several related abilities: having access to one's feelings, a willingness to talk about one's feelings and interpersonal problems to others, an active interest in the behaviours of others, and a capacity for behavioural change. Given the nature of this broad set of abilities, it is not surprising that individuals with limited levels of psychological mindedness often find psychotherapy to be a frustrating experience with limited benefits (McCallum et al., 1992; Piper et al., 1998, 2001).

Alexithymia is another construct that has considerable overlap with EI (Parker et al., 2001), but has also generated a sizeable empirical literature (Parker, 2005). Sifneos (1973) coined the term 'alexithymia' (from the Greek: a = lack, lexis = word, thymos = emotion) to identify individuals with a similar set of cognitive and affective characteristics. Research on alexithymia has led to a definition with the following core features: difficulty identifying feelings and distinguishing between feelings and the bodily sensations of emotional arousal; difficulty describing feelings; constricted imaginal processes; and a stimulus-bound, externally orientated, cognitive style (see Taylor, 2000; Taylor et al., 1997). A number of researchers have found evidence of an important empirical relationship between alexithymia and EI. These studies have used a number of different EI measures and also different versions of the Toronto alexithymia scale (TAS) (Bagby et al., 1994; Taylor et al., 1986), but give consistent findings of a moderate to high (negative) EI/alexithymia association (e.g. Parker et al., 2001; Saklofske et al., 2003).

Along with the core characteristics of alexithymia described above, several other common features have been observed in alexithymic individuals that have important clinical implications. Several different researchers have found alexithymia to be linked with a limited capacity for empathy (Guttman and Laporte, 2002; McDougall, 1989; Taylor, 1987), problems processing emotionally toned or charged information (Stone and Nielson, 2001; Suslow and Junghanns, 2002), as well as difficulties in identifying facial expressions of emotion (Lane et al., 1996; Parker et al., 1993). Alexithymic individuals also appear to be less likely to turn to others for emotional support, in part because of their problems communicating emotional experiences to others and are less likely to regulate emotional distress via daydreams or other imaginative mental activities due to their limited range of 'healthy' affect regulating abilities (Mayes and Cohen, 1992; Taylor et al., 1997). Alexithymia has been identified as a vulnerability factor for individuals experiencing a number of psychiatric disorders, such as post-traumatic stress disorder (Badura, 2003), substance use disorders (Cecero and Holmstrom, 1997), eating disorders (Zonnevijlle-Bender et al., 2002), attention-deficit/hyperactivity disorder (Friedman et al., 2003), and problem gambling (Parker et al., 2005d). It is also worth noting that alexithymia was initially linked to individuals experiencing a broad range of psychosomatic problems (for a review of this literature see De Gucht and Heiser, 2003).

EI and educational performance

Introduction

While the EI construct is in many ways not new to psychology, its acceptance into mainstream research and practice has met with some controversy (Matthews et al., 2002).

However, EI appears to have been embraced somewhat more quickly in education than in other fields, and by school psychologists (Ross and Powell, 2002) more than by other areas of psychological practice and specialisation. Examination of published papers on EI shows a large increase after 2000 in contrast to the previous decade and these publications have been most frequently focused on assessment and education. Further, there are numerous school-based programmes that are grounded in EI themes and that have a specific focus on enhancing social and emotional learning (e.g. Axelrod et al., 2004; Collaborative for Academic, Social, and Emotional Learning, 2005). This increase in interest appears to be related to the recent focus on affective education, the influence of popular psychologists such as Gardner and Sternberg in educational circles, and a growing concern with bullying, aggression and tragic events (e.g. shootings), at least in North American schools. At post-secondary level there is considerable interest in ensuring academic completion and success. Although recent changes in US federal legislation regarding education have placed the greatest emphasis on academic achievement, the question still remains: what are the factors that predict learning and achievement and how can they be included in a prescription for learning and teaching?

There is compelling evidence that intelligence tests are the best predictors of academic success in the elementary school years, and together with previous school achievement, are good predictors of success in high school (Sattler, 2001). At the same time, relying on IQ scores alone limits expectations about a student's capacity to learn. This perspective is challenged by arguing that other factors such as EI are modifiable, can be learned, and influence student learning outcomes. In particular, the predictive power of IQ decreases substantially in post-secondary settings. If students entering university are above average intelligence and have high entry level GPAs, then not only is the range restricted on these predictors,

but other factors are needed to account for failure and dropout. As noted by Bar-On and Parker (2000a), there are key points of life transitions that can impact both the social-emotional well-being and academic accomplishments of students. Taking university students as an example, personal factors that can lead to failure or withdrawal prior to graduation could include the need to develop new study habits, learning to be independent, and the high likelihood that existing relationships may need to be modified. A similar list could be constructed for personal factors that can affect school achievement. In either case, an examination of the EI sampling domain in Table 28.1 shows that there are aspects of EI related to interpersonal and intrapersonal skills and the capacity to manage stress and adapt to changing circumstances that are likely to be of relevance to personal issues that can impact academic success.

While there is surface appeal to the importance of EI as a predictor of various life outcomes, including school achievement, evidence to support claims (e.g. Goleman, 1995; Liff, 2003; Ross and Powell, 2002) that EI accounts for a significant amount of the variance beyond IQ tests and should be part of the school curriculum is lacking. There is some evidence that programmes targeting social and emotional learning have positive results and in turn impact academic success (e.g. Weissberg and O'Brien, 2004) but it is clear that evidence-based support for the relevance of EI to education and student achievement and well-being is much needed (e.g. Matthews et al., 2002; Rossen, 2006).

Post-secondary/university education

Turning first to recent research findings of the relevance of EI to university settings, it is well known that the transition from a high school to university or college is stressful for many individuals (Perry et al., 2001). One of the most frequently cited indicators of this is the fact that 25% or more of North American high-school students who enter university or college will fail or withdraw from that institution before graduation (Pancer et al., 2000).

While these figures vary between region and university, and between countries (with UK dropout rates being around 10% and dropout being rare in countries such as Japan and China), this does not preclude the argument that, even in situations where dropout rates are low, many students face considerable stress as they attempt to adjust to university life.

Studies by Parker et al. (2004b) and Parker et al. (2005a) on US and Canadian first-year students showed that academically successful students scored higher on EI components than their unsuccessful counterparts, controlling for the effects of age, course load, and high-school GPA. Parker et al. (2006b) examined the relationship between academic retention and EI in a large sample of first-year students. Two groups of students were compared, those who withdrew from the university before their second year and a matched (age, gender, ethnicity) sample of students who remained at the university. Results revealed that students who persisted in their studies were significantly higher than those who withdrew on most EI dimensions. These findings contrast with those from earlier studies (e.g. Barchard, 2003) using a mixture of part-time and full-time students, mature students, students recently graduated from high school, and students in different years of study, where weak or non-existent relationships between EI and academic achievement were reported. Possible reasons for this discrepancy are that part-time students often face different challenges from younger students when pursuing post-secondary education, as do students at different stages of their post-secondary programmes of study (Gall et al., 2000). Furthermore, since EI levels are thought to increase across the lifespan (Mayer et al., 2000a), combining young and older adults is an important confound.

The relationship between EI and post-secondary achievement suggests a number of possible interventions with at-risk students. Recently, Wood et al. (2006) reported on a student mentoring project that was conducted with first-year students attending a small Ontario university. The students were full-time at the start of their studies and had graduated from high school within the previous 24 months. Using a cut-off EI score as a criterion, students at risk of dropping out were identified and randomly assigned to a group who received a four-month peer-mentoring programme or to a control group. The peer-mentoring programme was delivered by phone and was customised for each student, since core issues for at-risk students varied considerably. It was found that students identified as at-risk based on low EI scores were less likely to return for their second year of study compared to students not at risk, but that at-risk students in the mentoring programme were significantly more likely to return for than those in the control group. This study is relevant for several reasons. It clearly operationalises both EI and the intervention programme; this is critical in determining the impact of independent on dependent variables. It also demonstrates the efficacy that prevention programmes targeting EI factors might have in post-secondary settings, and suggests that while EI is a somewhat stable characteristic, it is also modifiable (Parker et al., 2005c). At a practical level, the economic loss to the university and potentially to society of students not completing their programmes can be staggering. Society invests huge sums of money in the education of students, and statistics abound showing the increased income of those who have received the greatest amount of education. The loss to universities in relation to student tuition and transfer grants can also be substantial. This is another very good reason to look closely at those factors, including EI components, which impact student success at university.

School-level education

In view of the intense interest in associations between EI and educational success, a considerable amount of work has been done on developing EI scales suitable for use with children and adolescents, with the main current examples being the youth form of the EQ-i (EQ-i:YV; Bar-On and Parker, 2000a) and the adolescent short form of the TEIQue (TEIQue-ASF; Petrides et al., 2006). These scales have been developed from the corresponding adult scales via syntactic and vocabulary simplifications. This approach leaves open the issue of whether the EI sampling domain is developmentally invariant; that is, that the constituent facets (if not necessarily their mean level), remain the same throughout life. Studies of children and adolescents have focused on two issues which are regarded as inter-related. These are associations of EI scores with academic success, and with a range of indicators of social adjustment in the school environment, with the underlying assumption that adjustment may be one of the determinants of academic performance.

High-school/secondary-school education

Parker et al. (2004a) examined the relationship between EI and academic achievement in a sample of American high-school students. Students completed a youth form for the EQ-i:YV (Bar-On and Parker, 2000a) and EI scores were matched with end-of-year GPA. Based on GPA, students were placed into one of three groups: 'successful', 'middle', and 'less successful'. It was found that the successful group scored significantly higher than the other two groups on the EI dimensions of interpersonal, adaptability and stress management. A similar study (Petrides et al., 2004), using British high-school students and the adult TEIQue (Petrides and Furnham, 2003), found that while trait EI had no direct effects on academic performance, it moderated the effects of IQ. For low IQ pupils, high EI was a significant positive predictor of academic performance. As IQ increased the effects of EI diminished, so that high-IQ pupils performed very well academically, irrespective of their EI levels. In the same study, high-EI pupils were found to have significantly fewer unauthorised absences (truancy) and were significantly less likely to have been expelled from school

due to antisocial behaviour, compared to their low-EI peers.

Petrides et al. (2006) investigated whether trait EI is related to how schoolchildren are perceived by their classmates. Pupils completed the TEIQue-ASF and were subsequently asked to nominate classmates on seven distinct behavioural descriptions ('cooperative', 'disruptive', 'shy', 'aggressive', 'dependent', 'a leader', and 'intimidating'). It was found that high-EI pupils received significantly more nominations for being cooperative and for having leadership qualities, and significantly fewer nominations for being disruptive, aggressive and dependent. These results suggest that high-EI children are perceived as more sociable and better adjusted than their low-EI peers, which is consistent with the positive correlation found between trait EI scores and social network size (Austin et al., 2005). Similar results were obtained in a study of Dutch children (Mavroveli et al., 2007) that examined the relationship between trait EI, coping styles and peer-rated social competence. High EI scores were associated with adaptive coping styles, whereas low EI scores were associated with maladaptive coping styles (in boys only). Four behavioural descriptions were employed in this study ('cooperative', 'aggressive', 'disruptive', 'a leader') and it was possible, due to the large sample size, to perform gender-specific analyses. These revealed significant correlations, with nominations on aggression (negative) and cooperation (positive) in boys, and with nominations on aggression (negative – one-tailed test), cooperation (positive), and leadership (positive) in girls.

Taken together, the above results suggest that trait EI has a significant role to playduring late childhood and adolescence, which calls for a much closer look at the conceptual and psychometric foundations of the construct within this age range.

Elementary education

There has been a strong call to develop and include EI programmes in the elementary school curriculum, both to promote psychological well-being and also to serve an early intervention/prevention role (e.g. Goleman, 1995; Liff, 2003; Ross and Powell, 2002). For example, the First Nations or Aboriginal population in Canada comprises one of the least educated and most impoverished groups with many students not completing public schooling or university training. Preliminary findings with First Nations children have shown lower scores on several EI factors that may suggest the need for schools to place a greater emphasis on the social and emotional needs of these children (Parker et al., 2005b). Of interest is that a somewhat similar question has been raised about children who have been identified as academically and intellectually gifted. The question of whether these children require special education programmes or are best served in regular classroom settings is also raised in the context of whether they are more socially and emotionally vulnerable because of their 'giftedness' (Schwean et al., 2006).

It has been argued that EI accounts for a large part of the variance in school and future success beyond that predicted by cognitive tests. In recent years, an increasing number of programmes have been developed that can be employed by teachers and parents to enhance the EI of children (Grewal and Salovey, 2005). Rossen (2006: 79) states, 'As a result, intervention programs aimed at improving students' emotional intelligence have entered the curriculum of thousands of American schools.' However Rossen further contends that many of these programmes are unrelated and inconsistent in their definition of EI and lack clear objectives. Furthermore, until recently there has been little convincing research to support the claims made by Goleman (1995) and others (e.g. Ross and Powell, 2002) relating to EI and school success.

A recent study examining the relationship between emotional intelligence and academic achievement in elementary school children (Parker et al., 2006a) provides a first step in providing the data needed to counteract the 'belief trumps evidence' position that

can arise when public opinion plays a considerable role in education policy and programmes. Parker et al. noted that much of the previous research on academic success in children and adolescents has focused on the impact of cognitive abilities, gender, ethnicity, socioeconomic status and peer relationships (e.g. Bjarnason, 2000; Newcomb et al., 2002). However, the fact that a large part of the variance remains unaccounted for has encouraged research on a broader range of predictors (McLaughlin et al., 1998), including personality factors and conative variables such as self-efficacy. Following from the earlier reported study with high-school students that showed academically successful students scoring significantly higher than lower achieving students on several dimensions of emotional intelligence, Parker et al. (2006) attempted to replicate these results by examining the relationship between emotional intelligence and academic achievement among a group of elementary aged children. A relatively broad range of emotional and social competencies were examined using Bar-On's (1997) model of emotional intelligence. The sample consisted of 72 students (42 males, 30 females) attending an elementary school in central Canada. End-of-year GPA was used to identify academic groups of students who were below average, average and above average. Comparing these groups showed that the top third students scored significantly higher than the middle third and bottom third students on the interpersonal, adaptability, and total EI scales. There were no significant differences between the middle and bottom groups. A discriminant function analysis using the intrapersonal, interpersonal, adaptability and stress management scales showed that the scales could significantly discriminate between the high-achieving group and other students. The overall correct classification rate was 84.21%. At the start of the academic year, the elementary school students were found to score lower than a community-based normative sample of children on several EI dimensions. At the end of the school term, however,

EQ-i:YV scores had improved significantly on several dimensions. There are many untested educational programmes that claim to increase EI scores, and further contend that EI is directly and positively related to school achievement. This study provides strong empirical evidence that EI scores can change (and so may be responsive to training programmes) and further that those with higher EI also show greater levels of school accomplishment. Together with the data from secondary and post-secondary settings, this would appear to be a fairly robust finding.

EI and occupational performance

Introduction

The use of EI to predict workplace success and of EI training to enhance the effectiveness of employees are ideas which have attracted an amount of interest comparable to that in associations of EI with academic success. Claims that EI is an important predictor, or even the most important predictor, of occupational success have been widely disseminated (e.g. Goleman, 1995). Examination of research findings however reveals that there is no support for assertions that EI explains substantial amounts of variance in work performance, but that there is evidence for more modest associations. Before reviewing this evidence, some general comments are in order. Theoretically it appears unlikely that EI could act as a universal predictor of success and effectiveness in the workplace, as seems to be the case for general ability (Schmidt and Hunter, 2004) and conscientiousness (Salgado, 2003). Put simply, the criteria for workplace success are context-dependent, and it is possible to imagine occupations where high EI would not help performance. By contrast, it is difficult to envisage occupations where being unintelligent and/or unconscientious would be an advantage. The social skills associated with high EI are often cited as being relevant to work performance, and it is certainly true that many occupations require employees to interact effectively with one another and/or

with customers, clients, etc. There are however also occupations where interpersonal EI is not highly relevant, where employees either do not interact with others a great deal, or where a high level of specialist or technical ability is the main criterion for effective performance. In addition, high interpersonal EI might actually be detrimental in, for example, management roles where tough firing decisions need to be made and sympathy for others over-ridden. There is perhaps a better case for high intrapersonal EI being generally helpful for employees, since most workplace environments require mood regulation and stress management, but the extent to which these are needed varies widely between occupations. Zeidner et al. (2004) suggest that serious attempts to use EI for selection or prediction of occupational success require occupation-specific 'emotional task analysis' as a prerequisite.

Studies of workplace performance

Individual studies of EI and occupational performance have shown, perhaps unsurprisingly in view of the above comments, mixed results. A recent meta-analysis (Van Rooy and Viswesvaran, 2004) does however report a sample-weighted mean correlation of 0.22 between overall EI and job performance, based on 19 studies, and subsequent studies have found similar results (e.g. Sy et al., 2006). A methodological issue in job performance assessment is that this is often done using ratings by superiors which can be subjective and may indeed be related to subordinate EI. The use of more objective performance indicators (e.g. sales achieved) would be helpful. Less direct evidence for EI/performance associations comes from studies in which EI has been found to be linked to attributes likely to be associated with better job performance such as lower stress levels, better stress management and higher job satisfaction (Petrides and Furnham, 2006; Slaski and Cartwright, 2002; Sy et al., 2006).

There is also a growing literature on EI and leadership with high-EI managers being expected to be more successful in the workplace because they can elicit better performance from their subordinates. Much of the discussion has centred on the transformational leadership style, in which the leader is strongly focused on motivating subordinates, is inspirational, and deals with subordinates as individuals (Bass, 1997). In this context there are clearly several EI subcomponents, for example recognition of and managing others' emotions, which are theoretically linked to effective leadership. These connections are discussed in detail by George (2000). A number of empirical studies on managers have shown EI to be positively associated both with transformational leadership style and with leadership ability and effectiveness (e.g. Butler and Chinowsky, 2006; Downey et al., 2006). More work is needed in this area, since it seems likely that the context in which leadership occurs determines the effectiveness of the trans-formational style, and therefore would be expected to moderate EI/leadership associations.

There has been considerable activity on the development of training programmes to improve EI skills in the workplace, particularly for managers. There is some evidence that intervention programmes can improve EI scores (Dulewicz and Higgs, 2004; Slaski and Cartwright, 2003) but the effectiveness of EI interventions in the workplace requires further study.

In summary, there is a growing body of evidence that EI is positively associated with occupational success, but more work needs to be done on the effects of specific occupational context on the strength of this association, and on the incremental validity of EI over intelligence and personality in predicting occupational outcomes. It is also important that workplace-based EI interventions are appropriately tested and validated.

SUMMARY

In this chapter the current status of EI research both as regards theory and measurement and in relation to key real-life associations of EI

have been discussed. It is clear from this material that there is much work still to be done on EI.

Within EI psychometrics there are particular issues in the measurement of ability EI, relating to problems of reconciling the use of consensus and expert scoring with veridical scoring as used in conventional intelligence tests, and in developing tests which could assess the fluid component of EI (if it exists). Compared to the situation with trait EI, where a diverse range of tests is available, there are relatively few ability EI measures available. The MSCEIT is currently the only available ability EI measure which claims to sample the whole EI domain; the development of additional instruments of this type is desirable in order to obtain a diversity of test batteries comparable to the situation for cognitive ability. What remains unclear, however, is how such tests can square the subjective nature of emotions with the objectivity required in mental ability measurement. Studies of associations of EI with health, well-being, and educational and occupational performance have produced interesting results, but in most of these areas the total number of studies is still small and more work needs to be done in order to obtain a substantial body of knowledge on how EI relates to these factors. Within the occupational and educational area it is also important that studies using treatment and control groups are performed when EI intervention programmes are proposed, and that such programmes are tailored to the needs of the particular target group. Emotion-related capabilities clearly are important in the real world, but the capabilities required are context-dependent, so it is important to both establish what type of emotion skills different groups (schoolchildren, students, employees) need to develop and to verify that training programmes actually do develop these skills and improve outcomes.

REFERENCES

Ackerman, S.J. and Hilsenroth, M.J. (2003) 'A review of therapist characteristics and

techniques positively impacting the therapeutic alliance', *Clinical Psychology Review*,
23(1): 1–33.

Amelang, M. and Steinmayr, R. (2006) 'Is there
a validity increment for tests of emotional
intelligence in explaining the variance of
performance criteria?', *Intelligence*, 34(5):
459–68.

Applebaum, S.A. (1973) 'Psychological-
mindedness: Word, concept, and essence',
International Journal of Psychoanalysis,
54(1): 35–45.

Austin, E.J. (2005) 'Emotional intelligence and
emotional information processing', *Personality
and Individual Differences*, 39(2): 403–14.

Austin, E.J., Saklofske, D.H. and Egan, V.
(2005) 'Personality, well-being and health
correlates of trait emotional intelligence',
Personality and Individual Differences, 38(3):
547–58.

Axelrod, J., O'Brien, M.U. and Weissberg, R.P.
(2004) 'Social and emotional learning as a
framework for school improvement and student success', *The Community Psychologist*,
37(2): 8–10.

Bachrach, H.M. and Leaff, L.A. (1978)
'"Analyzability": A systematic review of the
clinical and quantitative literature', *Journal of
the American Psychoanalytical Association*,
26(4): 881–920.

Badura, A.S. (2003) 'Theoretical and empirical
exploration of the similarities between
emotional numbing in posttraumatic stress
disorder and alexithymia', *Journal of Anxiety
Disorders*, 17(3): 349–60.

Bagby, R.M., Parker, J.D.A. and Taylor, G.J.
(1994) 'The Twenty-Item Toronto Alexithymia
Scale-I. Item selection and cross-validation
of the factor structure', *Journal of
Psychosomatic Research*, 38(1): 23–32.

Barchard, K.A. (2003) 'Does emotional intelligence assist in the prediction of academic
success?', *Educational and Psychological
Measurement*, 63(5): 840–58.

Barchard, K.A. and Hakstian, A.R. (2004) 'The
nature and measurement of emotional intelligence abilities: Basic dimensions and their
relationships with other cognitive ability
and personality variables', *Educational and
Psychological Measurement*, 64(3): 437–62.

Bar-On, R. (1997) *Bar-On Emotional Quotient
Inventory: Technical Manual*. Toronto: Multi-
Health Systems.

Bar-On, R. (2002) *Bar-On Emotional Quotient
Short form (EQ-i:Short): Technical Manual*.
Toronto: Multi-Health Systems.

Bar-On, R. and Parker, J.D.A. (2000a) *Bar-On
EQ-i:YV: Technical Manual*. Toronto: Multi-
Health Systems.

Bar-On, R. and Parker J.D.A. (2000b) (eds),
Handbook of Emotional Intelligence. San
Francisco: Jossey-Bass.

Bass, B.M. (1997) 'Does the transactional-
transformational paradigm transcend organizational and national boundaries?',
American Psychologist, 52(2): 130–9.

Beckham, E. (1992) 'Predicting patient dropout
in psychotherapy', *Psychotherapy*, 29(2):
177–82.

Bjarnason, T. (2000) 'Grooming for success?
The impact of adolescent society on early
intergenerational social mobility', *Journal of
Family and Economic Issues*, 21(4): 319–42.

Brody, N. (2004) 'What cognitive intelligence is
and what emotional intelligence is not',
Psychological Inquiry, 15(3): 234–8.

Brown, R.F. and Schutte, N.S. (2006) 'Direct
and indirect relationships between emotional
intelligence and subjective fatigue in university students', *Journal of Psychosomatic
Research*, 60(6): 585–93.

Butler, C.J. and Chinowsky, P.S. (2006)
'Emotional intelligence and leadership behav-
ior in construction executives', *Journal of
Management in Engineering*, 22(3): 119–25.

Carroll, J.B. (1993) *Human Cognitive Abilities:
A Survey of Factor Analytic Studies*.
Cambridge, MA: Cambridge University Press.

Cecero, J.J. and Holmstrom, R.W. (1997)
'Alexithymia and affect pathology among
adult male alcoholics', *Journal of Clinical
Psychology*, 53(3): 201–8.

Ciarrochi, J., Caputi, P. and Mayer, J.D. (2003)
'The distinctiveness and utility of a measure
of trait emotional awareness', *Personality
and Individual Differences*, 34(8): 1477–90.

Ciarrochi, J., Chan, A.Y.C. and Bajgar, J. (2001)
'Measuring emotional intelligence in adolescents', *Personality and Individual Differences*,
31(7): 1105–19.

Ciarrochi, J.V., Chan, A.Y.C. and Caputi, P.
(2000) 'A critical evaluation of the emotional
intelligence construct', *Personality and
Individual Differences*, 28(5): 539–61.

Ciarrochi, J.V. and Deane, F.P. (2001)
'Emotional competence and willingness to

seek help from professional and non professional sources', *British Journal of Guidance and Counselling*, 29(2): 233–46.

Ciarrochi, J., Forgas, J.P. and Mayer, J.D. (2006) (eds), *Emotional Intelligence in Everyday Life*. New York: Psychology Press.

Collaborative for Academic, Social, and Emotional Learning (2005) *The Illinois Edition of Safe and Sound: An Educational Leader's Guide to Evidence-based Social and Emotional Learning Programs*. Chicago, IL: Author.

Conte, H.R., Plutchik, R., Jung, B.B., Picard, S., Karasu, T.B. and Lotterman, A. (1990) 'Psychological mindedness as a predictor of psychotherapy outcome: A preliminary report', *Comprehensive Psychiatry*, 31(5): 426–31.

Cronbach, L.J. (1949) *Essentials of Psychological Testing*. New York: Harper & Row.

Deary, I.J. (2000) *Looking Down on Human Intelligence*. Oxford: Oxford University Press.

De Gucht, V. and Heiser, W. (2003) 'Alexithymia and somatisation: A quantitative review of the literature', *Journal of Psychosomatic Research*, 54(5): 425–34.

Downey, L.A., Papageorgiou, V. and Stough, C. (2006) 'Examining the relationship between leadership, emotional intelligence and intuition in senior female managers', *Leadership and Organization Development Journal*, 27(4): 250–64.

Dulewicz, V. and Higgs, M. (2004) 'Can emotional intelligence be developed?', *International Journal of Human Resource Management*, 15(1): 95–111.

Extremera, N. and Fernández-Berrocal, P. (2002) 'Relation of perceived emotional intelligence and health-related quality of life of middle-aged women', *Psychological Reports*, 91(1): 47–59.

Farrelly, D. and Austin, E.J. (2007) 'Ability EI as an intelligence? A preliminary study of associations of the MSCEIT with performance on emotion-processing and social tasks, and with cognitive ability', *Cognition and Emotion,* 21(5):1043–63.

Freudenthaler, H.H., Fink, A. and Neubauer, A. (2006) 'Emotional abilities and cortical activation during emotional information processing', *Personality and Individual Differences*, 41(4): 685–95.

Friedman, S.R., Rapport, L.J., Lumley, M., Tzelepis, A., VanVoorhis, A., Stettner, L.

and Kakaati, L. (2003) 'Aspects of social and emotional competence in adult attention-deficit/hyperactivity disorder', *Neuropsychology*, 17(1): 50–8.

Fuhrer, R., Stansfeld, S.A., Chemali, J. and Shipley, M.J. (1998) 'Gender, social relations and mental health: Prospective findings from an occupational cohort (Whitehall II study)', *Social Science and Medicine*, 48(1): 77–87.

Funder, D.C. (2001) 'Personality', *Annual Review of Psychology*, 52: 197–221.

Furnham, A. and Rawles, R. (1999) 'Correlations between self-estimated and psychometrically measured IQ', *Journal of Social Psychology*, 139(4): 405–10.

Gall, T.L., Evans, D.R. and Bellerose, S. (2000) 'Transition to first year university: Patterns of change in adjustment across life domains and time', *Journal of Social and Clinical Psychology*, 19(4): 544–67.

Gardner, H. (1983) *Frames of Mind: The Theory of Multiple Intelligences*. New York: Basic Books.

George, J.M. (2000) 'Emotions and leadership: the role of emotional intelligence', *Human Relations*, 53(8): 1027–55.

Goleman, D. (1995) *Emotional Intelligence: Why it Can Matter More than IQ*. London: Bloomsbury.

Greenspan, S.I. (1989) 'Emotional intelligence', in K. Field, B.J. Cohler and G. Wool (eds), *Learning and Education: Psychoanalytic Perspectives*. Madison, CT: International Universities Press, pp. 209–43.

Grewal, D. and Salovey, P. (2005) 'Feeling smart: The science of emotional intelligence', *American Scientist*, 93(4): 330–9.

Guttman, H. and Laporte, L. (2002) 'Alexithymia, empathy, and psychological symptoms in a family context', *Comprehensive Psychiatry*, 43(6): 448–55.

Kelley, T.L. (1927) *Interpretation of Educational Measurements*. New York: World Book.

Krystal, H. (1988) *Integration and Self-healing: Affect, Trauma, Alexithymia*. Hillsdale, NJ: Analytic Press.

Lane, R.D., Quinlan, D.M., Schwartz, G.E., Walker, P.A. and Zeitlin, S.B. (1990) 'The Levels of Emotional Awareness Scale – a cognitive-developmental measure of emotion', *Journal of Personality Assessment*, 55(1–2): 124–34.

Lane, R., Sechrest, L., Reidel, R., Weldon, V., Kaszniak, A. and Schwartz, G. (1996)

'Impaired verbal and nonverbal emotion recognition in alexithymia', *Psychosomatic Medicine*, 58(6): 203–10.

Leuner, B. (1966) 'Emotionale intelligenz und emanzipation. [Emotional intelligence and emancipation.] *Praxis der Kinderpsychologie und Kinderpsychiatry*, 15(6): 196–203.

Liff, S.B. (2003) 'Social and emotional intelligence: Applications for developmental education', *Journal of Developmental Education*, 26(3): 28–34.

Luborsky, L., McLellan, A., Woody, G., O'Brien, C. and Auerbach, A. (1985) 'Therapist success and its determinants', *Archives of General Psychiatry*, 42(6): 602–11.

MacCann, C.E. (2006) 'New approaches to measuring emotional intelligence: Exploring methodological issues with two new assessment tasks', PhD thesis, University of Sydney.

MacCann, C., Roberts, R.D., Matthews, G. and Zeidner, M. (2004) 'Consensus scoring and empirical option weighting of performance-based emotional intelligence (EI) tests', *Personality and Individual Differences*, 36(3): 645–62.

Mallinckrodt, B., King, J.L. and Coble, H.M. (1998) 'Family dysfunction, alexithymia, and client attachment to therapist', *Journal of Counselling Psychology*, 45(4): 497–504.

Marlowe, H.A. (1986) 'Social intelligence: Evidence for multidimensionality and construct independence', *Journal of Educational Psychology*, 78(1): 52–8.

Matthews, G.D., Zeidner, M. and Roberts, R.D. (2002) *Emotional Intelligence. Science and Myth*. Cambridge, MA: MIT Press.

Mavroveli, S. Petrides. K.V., Rieffe, C. and Bakker, F. (2007) 'Trait emotional intelligence, psychological well-being, and peer-rated social competence in adolescence', *British Journal of Developmental Psychology*, 25(2): 263–75.

Mayer, J.D., Caruso, D.R. and Salovey, P. (1999) 'Emotional intelligence meets traditional standards for an intelligence', *Intelligence*, 27(4): 267–98.

Mayer, J.D., Caruso, D.R. and Salovey, P. (2000a) 'Selecting a measure of emotional intelligence: The case for ability scales', in R. Bar-On and J.D.A. Parker (eds), *Handbook of Emotional Intelligence*. San Francisco, CA: Jossey-Bass, pp. 320–42.

Mayer, J.D. and Geher, G. (1996) 'Emotional intelligence and the identification of emotion', *Intelligence*, 22(2): 89–113.

Mayer, J.D., Salovey, P. and Caruso, D.R. (2000b) 'Models of emotional intelligence', in R.J. Sternberg (ed.), *Handbook of Human Intelligence*. New York: Cambridge University Press.

Mayer, J.D., Salovey, P., Caruso, D.R. and Sitarenios, G. (2003) 'Measuring emotional intelligence with the MSCEIT V2.0', *Emotion*, 3(1): 97–105.

Mayes, L.C. and Cohen, D.J. (1992) 'The development of a capacity for imagination in early childhood', *Psychoanalytic Study of the Child*, 47(1–2): 23–47.

McCallum, M., Piper, W. and Joyce, A. (1992) 'Dropping out from short-term group therapy', *Psychotherapy*, 29(2): 206–15.

McDougall, J. (1989) *Theatres of the Body: A Psychoanalytic Approach to Psychosomatic Illness*. New York: Norton.

McLaughlin, G.W., Brozovsky, P.V. and McLaughlin, J.S. (1998) 'Changing perspectives on student retention: A role for institutional research', *Research in Higher Education*, 39(1): 1–17.

Mikolajczak, M., Luminet, O. and Menil, C. (2006) 'Predicting resistance to stress: Incremental validity of trait emotional intelligence over alexithymia and optimism', *Psicothema*, 18 (suppl.s): 79–88.

Murphy, K.R. (2006) (ed.), *A Critique of Emotional Intelligence. What are the Problems and How Can They Be Fixed?*. Mahwah: Lawrence Erlbaum.

Newcomb, M.D., Abbott, R.D., Catalano, R.F., Hawkins, J.D., Battin-Pearson, S. and Hill, K. (2002) 'Mediational and deviance theories of late high school failure: Process roles of structural strains, academic competence, and general versus specific problem behavior', *Journal of Counseling Psychology*, 49(2): 172–86.

Owen, P. and Kohutek, K. (1981) 'The rural mental health dropout', *Journal of Rural Community Psychology*, 2(2): 38–41.

Palmer, B.R., Gignac, G., Manocha, R. and Stough, C. (2005) 'A psychometric evaluation of the Mayer-Salovey-Caruso Emotional Intelligence Test Version 2.0', *Intelligence*, 33(3): 285–305.

Pancer, S.M., Hunsberger, B., Pratt, M.W. and Alisat, S. (2000) 'Cognitive complexity of expectations and adjustment to university in the first year', *Journal of Adolescent Research*, 15(1): 38–57.

Parker, J.D.A. (2005) 'Relevance of emotional intelligence for clinical psychology', in R. Schulze and R.D. Roberts (eds), *International Handbook of Emotional Intelligence*. Berlin: Hogrefe & Huber, pp. 271–87.

Parker, J.D.A., Creque, R.E., Barnhart, D.L., Harris, J., Majeski, S.A., Wood, L.M., Bond, B.J. and Hogan, M.J. (2004a) 'Academic achievement in high school: Does emotional intelligence matter?', *Personality and Individual Differences*, 37(7): 1321–30.

Parker, J.D.A., Duffy, J., Wood, L.M., Bond, B.J. and Hogan, M.J. (2005a) 'Academic achievement and emotional intelligence: Predicting the successful transition from high school to university', *Journal of First-Year Experience and Students in Transition*, 17(1): 67–78.

Parker, J.D.A., Duncan, A., Woon, S., Eldridge, B., Wood, L.M. and Eastabrook, J.M. (2006a) 'Emotional intelligence and academic achievement in elementary school children', Emotion and Health Research Laboratory, Research Report Series, Report Number 17.

Parker, J.D.A., Hogan, M.J., Eastabrook, J.M., Oke, A. and Wood, L.M. (2006b) 'Emotional intelligence and student retention: Predicting the successful transition from high school to university', *Personality and Individual Differences*, 41(7): 1329–36.

Parker, J.D.A., Saklofske, D.H., Shaughnessy, P.A., Huang, S.H.S., Wood, L.M. and Eastabrook, J.M. (2005b) 'Generalizability of the emotional intelligence construct: A cross-cultural study of North American aboriginal youth', *Personality and Individual Differences*, 39(1): 215–27.

Parker, J.D.A., Saklofske, D.H., Wood, L.M., Eastabrook, J.M. and Taylor, R.N. (2005c) 'Stability and change in emotional intelligence: Exploring the transition to young adulthood', *Journal of Individual Differences*, 26(2): 100–6.

Parker, J.D.A., Summerfeldt, L.J., Hogan, M.J. and Majeski, S. (2004b) 'Emotional intelligence and academic success: Examining the transition from high school to university', *Personality and Individual Differences*, 36(1): 163–72.

Parker, J.D.A., Taylor, G.J. and Bagby, R.M. (1993) 'Alexithymia and the recognition of facial expressions of emotion', *Psychotherapy and Psychosomatics*, 59(3–4): 197–202.

Parker, J.D.A., Taylor, G.J. and Bagby, R.M. (2001) 'The relationship between emotional intelligence and alexithymia', *Personality and Individual Differences*, 30(1): 107–15.

Parker, J.D.A., Wood, L.M., Bond, B.J. and Shaughnessy, P. (2005d) 'Alexithymia in young adulthood: A risk-factor for pathological gambling', *Psychotherapy and Psychosomatics*, 74(1): 55.

Payne, W.L. (1986) 'A study of emotion: Developing emotional intelligence; Self-integration, relating to fear, pain and desire', *Dissertation Abstracts International*, 47(01), 203A.

Pekarik, G. (1983) 'Follow-up adjustment of outpatient dropouts', *American Journal of Orthopsychiatry*, 53(3): 501–11.

Penedo, F.J. and Dahn, J.R. (2005) 'Exercise and well-being: A review of mental and physical health benefits associated with physical activity', *Current Opinion in Psychiatry*, 18(2): 189–93.

Perry, R.P., Hladkyj, S., Pekrun, R.H. and Pelletier, S.T. (2001) 'Academic control and action control in the achievement of college students: A longitudinal field study', *Journal of Educational Psychology*, 93(4): 776–89.

Petrides, K.V., Frederickson, N. and Furnham, A. (2004) 'The role of trait emotional intelligence in academic performance and deviant behavior at school', *Personality and Individual Differences*, 36(2): 277–93.

Petrides, K.V. and Furnham, A. (2001) 'Trait emotional intelligence: psychometric investigation with reference to established trait taxonomies', *European Journal of Personality*, 15(6): 425–48.

Petrides, K.V. and Furnham, A. (2003) 'Trait emotional intelligence: Behavioural validation in two studies of emotion recognition and reactivity to mood induction', *European Journal of Personality*, 17(1): 39–57.

Petrides, K.V. and Furnham, A. (2006) 'The role of trait emotional intelligence in a gender-specific model of organizational variables', *Journal of Applied Social Psychology*, 36(2): 552–69.

Petrides, K.V., Furnham, A. and Mavroveli, S. (2007a) 'Trait emotional intelligence: Moving forward in the field of EI', in G. Matthews, M. Zeidner and R. Roberts, R. (eds), *Emotional Intelligence: Knowns and Unknowns* (Series in Affective Science). Oxford: Oxford University Press.

Petrides, K.V., Pérez-González, J.C. and Furnham, A. (2007b) 'On the criterion and incremental validity of trait emotional intelligence', *Cognition and Emotion*, 21(1): 26–55.

Petrides, K.V., Pita, R. and Kokkinaki, F. (2007c) 'The location of trait emotional intelligence in personality factor space', *British Journal of Psychology*, 98(2): 273–89.

Petrides, K.V., Sangareau, Y., Furnham, A. and Frederickson, N. (2006) 'Trait emotional intelligence and children's peer relations at school', *Social Development*, 15(3): 537–47.

Pierloot, R. and Vinck, J. (1977) 'A pragmatic approach to the concept of alexithymia', *Psychotherapy and Psychosomatics*, 28(1–4): 156–66.

Piper, W.E., Joyce, A.S., McCallum, M. and Azim, H.F. (1998) 'Interpretive and supportive forms of psychotherapy and patient personality variables', *Journal of Consulting and Clinical Psychology*, 66(3): 558–67.

Piper, W.E., McCallum, M., Joyce, A.S., Rosie, J.S. and Ogrodniczuk, J.S. (2001) 'Patient personality and time-limited group psychotherapy for complicated grief', *International Journal of Group Psychotherapy*, 51(4): 525–52.

Reder, P. and Tyson, R. (1980) 'Patient dropout from individual psychotherapy', *Bulletin of the Menninger Clinic*, 44(3): 229–52.

Riley, H. and Schutte, N.S. (2003) 'Low emotional intelligence as a predictor of substance-use problems', *Journal of Drug Education*, 33(4): 391–8.

Roberts, R.D., Zeidner, M. and Matthews, G. (2001) 'Does emotional intelligence meet traditional standards for an intelligence? Some data and conclusions', *Emotion*, 1(3): 196–231.

Ross, M.R. and Powell, S.R. (2002) 'New roles for school psychologist: Addressing the social and emotional learning needs of students', *School Psychology Review*, 31(1): 45–52.

Rossen, E. (2006) 'Emotional intelligence in our schools: Are we jumping the gun?', *The School Psychologist*, 60(2): 79–81.

Saklofske, D.H., Austin, E.J., Galloway, J. and Davidson, K. (2007a) 'Individual difference correlates of health-related behaviours: preliminary evidence for links between emotional intelligence and coping', *Personality and Individual Differences*, 42(3): 491–502.

Saklofske, D.H., Austin, E.J. and Minski, P.S. (2003) 'Factor structure and validity of a trait emotional intelligence measure', *Personality and Individual Differences*, 34(4): 1091–100.

Saklofske, D.H., Austin, E.J., Rohr, B.A. and Andrews, J.J.W. (2007b) 'Personality, emotional intelligence and exercise', *Journal of Health Psychology*, 12(6): 937–48.

Salgado, J.F. (2003) 'Predicting job performance using FFM and non-FFM personality measures', *Journal of Occupational and Organizational Psychology*, 76(3): 323–46.

Salovey, P. and Mayer, J.D. (1990) 'Emotional intelligence', *Imagination, Cognition, and Personality*, 9(3): 185–211.

Salovey, P., Stroud, L.R., Woolery, A. and Epel, E.S. (2002) 'Perceived emotional intelligence, stress reactivity, and symptom reports: further explorations using the trait meta-mood scale', *Psychology and Health*, 17(5): 611–27.

Saltzman, C., Luetgert, M.J., Roth, C.H., Creaser, J. and Howard, L. (1976) 'Formation of a therapeutic relationship: Experiences during the initial phase of psychotherapy as predictors of treatment duration and outcome', *Journal of Consulting and Clinical Psychology*, 44(4): 546–55.

Sattler, J.M. (2001) *Assessment of Children: Cognitive Applications* (4th edn). San Diego: Author.

Schmidt, F.L. and Hunter, J. (2004) 'General mental ability in the world of work: occupational attainment and job performance', *Journal of Personality and Social Psychology*, 86(1): 162–73.

Schulze, R. and Roberts, R.D. (2005) (eds), *Emotional Intelligence. An International Handbook*. Cambridge, MA: Hogrefe

Schutte, N.S., Malouff, J.M., Simunek, M., McKenley, J. and Hollander, S. (2002) 'Characteristic emotional intelligence and emotional well-being', *Cognition and Emotion*, 16(6): 769–85.

Schutte, N., Malouff, J.M., Thorsteinsson, E.B., Bhullar, N. and Rooke, S.E. (2007) 'A meta-analytic investigation of the relationship between emotional intelligence and health', *Personality and Individual Differences*, 42(6): 921–33.

Schwean, V.L., Saklofske, D.H., Widdifield-Konkin, L., Parker, J.D.A. and Kloosterman, P. (2006) 'Emotional intelligence and gifted children', *E-Journal of Applied Psychology*, 2(2): retrieved January 23, 2007, from http://ojs.lib.swin.edu.au/index.php/ejap/article/view/70/99

Sifneos, P.E. (1973) 'The prevalence of "alexithymic" characteristics in psychosomatic patients', *Psychotherapy and Psychosomatics*, 22(2–6): 255–62.

Silver, D. (1983) 'Psychotherapy of the characterologically difficult patient', *Canadian Journal of Psychiatry*, 28(7): 513–21.

Slaski, M. and Cartwright, S. (2002) 'Health, performance and emotional intelligence in retail managers: an exploratory study', *Stress and Health*, 18(2): 63–8.

Slaski, M. and Cartwright, S. (2003) 'Emotional intelligence training and its implications for stress, health and performance', *Stress and Health*, 19(2): 233–9.

Stone, L. and Nielson, K.A. (2001) 'Intact physiological responses to arousal with impaired emotional recognition in alexithymia', *Psychotherapy and Psychosomatics*, 70(2): 92–102.

Suslow, T. and Junghanns, K. (2002) 'Impairments of emotion situation priming in alexithymia', *Personality and Individual Differences*, 32(3): 541–50.

Sy, T., Tram, S. and O'Hara, L.A. (2006) 'Relation of employee and manager emotional intelligence to job satisfaction and performance', *Journal of Vocational Behavior*, 68(3): 461–73.

Taylor, G.J. (1977) 'Alexithymia and the counter-transference', *Psychotherapy and Psychosomatics*, 28(1–4): 141–7.

Taylor, G.J. (1987) *Psychosomatic Medicine and Contemporary Psychoanalysis*. Madison, CT: International Universities Press.

Taylor, G.J. (2000) 'Recent developments in alexithymia theory and research', *Canadian Journal of Psychiatry*, 45(2): 134–42.

Taylor, G.J., Bagby, R.M. and Parker, J.D.A. (1997) *Disorders of Affect Regulation*. Cambridge: Cambridge University Press.

Taylor, G.J., Ryan, D. and Bagby, R.M. (1986) 'Toward the development of a new self-report alexithymia scale', *Psychotherapy and Psychosomatics*, 44(4): 191–9.

Tett, R.P., Fox, K.E. and Wang, A. (2005) 'Development and validation of a self-report measure of emotional intelligence as a multidimensional trait domain', *Personality and Social Psychology Bulletin*, 31(7): 859–88.

Thorndike, E.L. (1920) 'Intelligence and its uses', *Harper's Magazine*, 140(1): 227–35.

Tolor, A. and Reznikoff, M. (1960) 'A new approach to insight: A preliminary report', *Journal of Nervous and Mental Disease*, 130(4): 286–96.

Trinidad, D.R. and Johnson, C.A. (2002) 'The association between emotional intelligence and early adolescent tobacco and alcohol use', *Personality and Individual Differences*, 32(1): 95–105.

Tsaousis, I. and Nikolaou, I. (2005) 'Exploring the relationship of emotional intelligence with physical and psychological health functioning', *Stress and Health*, 21(2): 77–86.

Van der Zee, K. and Wabeke, R. (2004) 'Is trait emotional intelligence simply or more than just a trait?', *European Journal of Personality*, 18(4): 243–63.

Van Rooy, D.L. and Viswesvaran, C. (2004) 'Emotional intelligence: A meta-analytic investigation of predictive validity and nomological net', *Journal of Vocational Behavior*, 65(1): 71–95.

Watson, D. (2000) *Mood and Temperament*. New York: Guilford.

Weissberg, R.P. and O'Brien, M.U. (2004) 'What works in school-based social and emotional learning programs for positive youth development', *The Annals of the American Academy of Political and Social Science*, 591(1): 86–97.

Wood, L.M., Parker, J.D.A., Rowbotham, A., Taylor, R.N. and Eastabrook, J.M. (2006) 'Teaching emotional intelligence: A mentoring program for students at-risk of academic failure', Paper presented at the Annual Meeting of the Canadian Psychological Association, Calgary.

Zeidner, M., Matthews, G. and Roberts, R.D. (2004) 'Emotional intelligence in the workplace: A critical review', *Applied Psychology: An International Review*, 53(3): 371–99.

Zeidner, M., Shani-Zinovich, I., Matthews, G. and Roberts, R.D. (2005) 'Assessing emotional intelligence in gifted and non-gifted high school students: Outcomes depend on the measure', *Intelligence*, 33(4): 369–91.

Zonnevijlle-Bender, M.J.S., van Goozen, S.H.M., Cohen-Kettenis, P.T., van Elburg, A. and van Engeland, H. (2002) 'Do adolescent anorexia nervosa patients have deficits in emotional functioning?', *European Child and Adolescent Psychiatry*, 11(2): 38–42.

PART VI

Applications

29

Personality Disorders and the DSM: A Critical Review

Mary L. Malik, Brynne E. Johannsen and Larry E. Beutler

Human beings long have been fascinated by individual difference, and efforts to understand the cause and nature of these differences have spanned many disciplines and cultures, perhaps dating back as far as our origins as humans. Within Western European culture, the study of individual difference at times has been linked with the study of psychopathology, with some models historically proposing links between personality and psychopathology while others have viewed 'mental illness' as involving qualitatively different processes than those of 'normal' functioning (Maher and Maher, 1994). These tensions are summarized by Clark (2005b), who notes both the long history of studying connections between personality and psychopathology as well as the opposing tendency to split these studies across (and even within) fields, with psychiatry traditionally focusing on 'abnormal' functioning (i.e. psychopathology), while psychology historically has focused on 'normal' functioning/personality.

These long-standing questions about the nature of the relationship among normal versus abnormal functioning, personality, and psychopathology can be seen in the evolution of the classification system used by clinicians in the United States to organize and to define mental illness: the *Diagnostic and Statistical Manual for Mental Disorders* (DSM). In terms of normal versus abnormal functioning, the focus of the DSM from the start (DSM-I; American Psychiatric Association, 1952) has been on the categorical classification of 'disorders', with each individual in question being determined either to have or not to have a given disorder, based on the qualifying criteria. This 'disease' based, categorical approach to diagnosis reflects the development of the manual within the field of psychiatry, and the desires of this field to ground itself within the traditional medical model that distinguishes between disease and health and places importance on precisely defining disease. In this sense, the DSM is intended to advance a political as well as a scientific and practical purpose.

It is notable that the proposed relationship between problems of personality and other types of psychopathology has changed markedly during the development of the

DSM. In both DSM-I and in its first revision (DSM-II; American Psychiatric Association, 1968), problems of personality were not distinguished from other disorders, and all diagnoses were presented in a glossary format in which lists of disorders were associated with descriptions to aid in diagnosis. With the introduction of the third edition of the *Diagnostic and Statistical Manual for Mental Disorders* (DSM-III; American Psychiatric Association, 1980), the conceptualization of personality disorders changed through a move to a multiaxial system, with clinical syndromes such as schizophrenia and depression placed on Axis I, while personality disorders were placed on Axis II. This was done explicitly to call more attention to the personality disorders, which had previously been overlooked (Krueger and Tackett, 2003). However, the placement of personality disorders on a separate Axis also presented an implicit assumption that personality disorders represent a distinct type of psychopathology – a qualitative distinction – rather than simply a difference in severity, as compared to other types of mental illness (Clark, 2005b).

This separation of the personality disorders from other mental health issues has been sustained during subsequent editions of the DSM, including the DSM-IV (American Psychiatric Association, 1994) and the text revision of DSM-IV, the DSM-IV-TR (American Psychiatric Association, 2000). The multiaxial approach to diagnosis has also been preserved, and currently (DSM-IV, DSM-IV-TR), each individual is evaluated along five separate dimensions. The first Axis, Axis I, is used to code 'all the various disorders or conditions in the classification except for the personality disorders and mental retardation', which are listed on Axis II. General medical conditions are noted on Axis III, with psychosocial or environmental problems (such as financial or marital stress) noted on Axis IV. Finally, Axis V consists of a number that represents the individual's overall level of functioning. The implication of this system is that these are independent

dimensions from one another and that there is a discontinuity or class distinction among them.

In the 50-odd years since its introduction, the DSM has received many criticisms (cf. critical reviews by Blashfield, 1984; Kirk and Kutchins, 1992; Malik and Beutler, 2002), and subsequent revisions increasingly have made efforts to address the problems raised by these critics. The descriptive approach to diagnosis initially used in the DSM (DSM-I, DSM-II) was associated with problems of reliability (e.g. Blashfield, 1984; Klonsky, 2000). In addition, the DSM-I and II were criticized as 'diagnosis by committee', because the diagnoses themselves (as well as their definitions) were obtained through consensus by a small number of predominantly psychoanalytically grounded 'experts', who drew on their experience and opinions to develop the diagnoses (e.g. Kirk and Kutchins, 1992; Pincus and McQueen, 2002). Thus, the diagnoses described in the first two editions of the DSM were not only unreliable, but also of questionable validity due to the implicit grounding of these diagnoses in theory rather than empirical findings.

In response to these critiques, efforts were made in subsequent editions to increase the reliability of DSM diagnoses by moving from the narrative descriptions of diagnoses used in the DSM-I and DSM-II to lists of specific criteria, with patients said to meet a given diagnosis if they were deemed to be positive for a certain number of criteria. In addition, attempts to enhance reliability were made by developing standard ways of obtaining diagnostic information via structured clinical interviews such as the Schedule for Affective Disorders and Schizophrenia (SADS; Endicott and Spitzer, 1978) and the Structured Clinical Interview for DSM-III (SCID; Spitzer, 1983). Finally, those who have been called upon to revise the DSM have attempted to address questions regarding the validity of DSM diagnoses through an increasing reliance on research findings rather than a consensus of experts. For example, the DSM-IV was developed via a three-stage process during which more than a dozen work groups reviewed the available literature to locate gaps of information in diagnostic areas of interest, determined whether or not these gaps could be filled with existing data, and carried out field trials to fill the gaps for which data were lacking (Nathan, 1998). Efforts were also made to include women, racial and ethnic minorities, and non-psychiatrists in the development of the DSM-IV, to counter the criticism that the DSM represented the views of a relatively small group of predominantly male Caucasian psychiatrists.

Despite these efforts, the general consensus by even its supporters is that the DSM-IV (and its recent text revision, the DSM-IV -TR, American Psychiatric Association, 2000) remains an imperfect classification system. Some critiques of the DSM have focused on general shortcomings, such as the use of a disease-based medical model (e.g. Gonçalves et al., 2002), the constraints of a categorical classification system (e.g. Widiger, 1992; Widiger and Samuel, 2005), ongoing problems with reliability (Kirk and Kutchins, 1992), problems with co-morbidity (Clark et al., 1995), and the rapid proliferation of disorders with each edition that arguably has outstripped the research (e.g. Houts, 2002).

Personality researchers have been especially critical of the DSM, and as the mental health field looks toward the development of the DSM-V, these researchers have been putting forward a strong case that significant modifications are needed in the established approach in order to improve the classification of personality disorders. This critique has been convincing to the point of near unanimous agreement by those involved in developing the DSM-V that the current Axis II is sufficiently flawed to warrant significant reworking. Significantly, a Gaps Work Group sponsored by the American Psychiatric Association (APA) and the National Institute of Mental Health (NIMH) cited 'notable dissatisfaction' with the current

DSM-IV-TR conceptualization and classification of personality disorders, and argued for an empirically supported alternative dimensional model of classification (First et al., 2002: 124). This recommendation was echoed by the steering committee of a conference sponsored for the sole purpose of reviewing existing research on personality disorder and of setting a research agenda to move the field toward a dimensional personality disorder classification system (Widiger et al., 2005). In fact, some of the research spearheaded by personality disorder researchers to illustrate the conceptual weaknesses of the current Axis II classification system has led to an increasing acknowledgment that the entire classification system ultimately may need to be revised. Notably, the nomenclature work group appointed by the APA and NIMH to examine the basic assumptions of the current diagnostic system concluded that it is 'important that consideration be given to advantages and disadvantages of basing part or all of DSM-V on dimensions rather than categories' (Rounsaville et al., 2002: 12). The work group additionally recommended that a dimensional approach to classification might initially be implemented for the personality disorders and later expanded to other areas should it perform adequately and be acceptable to clinicians.

Although a complete abandonment of all categorical diagnoses remains controversial at this point (cf. Brown and Barlow, 2005), it does appear quite likely that the DSM-V will include at least some dimensional elements in the diagnosis of personality disorders, and ultimately this growing body of research shows promise of leading us toward more useful and empirically grounded approaches to diagnosis. In the remainder of this chapter, we will summarize the research to date involving the ability of the current DSM to meet the needs of a classification system, with a focus on two functions of classification that are frequently discussed in the debate over the effectiveness of the DSM: (1) the degree to which the DSM (and especially the DSM-defined Axis II personality disorders) are empirically grounded; and (2) the degree to which the current DSM Axis II provides insight into etiology and guidance for treatment. Next, we will critically review the growing body of research supportive of alternative, dimensional models. Finally, we will draw on what is known to date about empirically validated principles of therapeutic change to suggest ways in which fruitful connections might be made between the personality assessment and clinical outcome literatures. Although some have expressed concerns that the shift toward dimensional models of diagnosis may create a rift between researchers and clinicians (Watson and Clark, 2006), we will argue here that an empirically based, dimensional model of personality assessment provides us with the structure needed to build required connections between diagnosis, treatment, and prognosis in ways likely to be useful to researchers and clinicians alike.

THE EMPIRICAL GROUNDING OF THE DSM

Although early versions of the DSM were arguably at least implicitly theoretical, the pendulum has swung in the opposite direction, and there is little argument at present against the idea that a 'good' classification system should be one that reflects nature. Consequently, the DSM has increasingly made efforts to ground diagnoses empirically by relying on research rather than clinical judgment. The degree to which it is effective in doing so is an area of active debate, and, as we will discuss, the bulk of the evidence to date suggests that the DSM does an especially poor job of presenting an empirically accurate representation of the personality disorders.

The current structure of the DSM

As it currently stands, the DSM-IV assigns diagnoses using a *categorical* system, with each diagnosis determined to be present if sufficient criteria are met, and absent otherwise. The current system is also described as *polythetic*, meaning that a diagnosis is assigned if an individual meets a certain number of criteria but with no obligate criterion (Johansen et al., 2004). Thus, one question to be addressed is the degree to which a polythetic, categorical classification system represents the range and scope of mental health problems and symptoms.

Next, within this multiaxial system, a distinct division is drawn between the Axis I and Axis II disorders, although the Axis I disorders explicitly include some pervasive problems with very early onset (such as autism) that parallel what we usually think of as the providence of Axis II. The 'dis-orders' included in Axis I implicitly tend to be conceptualized as 'disease' states that may be imposed on an otherwise healthy individual, and are thus identified with an onset and end point. In contrast, the Axis II personality disorders are defined as 'an enduring pattern of inner experience and behavior' that 'is pervasive and inflexible', 'has an early, developmental onset in adolescence or early adulthood', and once developed 'is stable over time'. Thus, Axis II personality disorders are explicitly conceived of as maladaptive *traits* that are relatively unchanging, whereas Axis I disorders are implicitly conceptualized as *states*, which may or may not intensify (or remit) over time. Because the first two axes are conceived of as independent, an individual may have diagnoses on Axis I alone, on Axis II alone, on both axes, or on neither. However, the Axis I disorder (if any) is assumed to be the primary focus unless otherwise stated, and Axis I disorders have hierarchical precedence, as a personality disorder may not be diagnosed if the symptoms of the disorder are present exclusively during the course of an Axis I disorder (e.g. paranoid personality disorder may not be diagnosed if the symptoms of this disorder occur only during the course of a psychotic disorder). Thus, another question of concern is the degree to which Axis I and Axis II truly represent separate (and implicitly independent) types of disorders.

Finally, the DSM-IV further divides Axis II into ten distinct personality disorders that are grouped into three relatively independent (it is assumed) clusters based on descriptive similarities (see Table 29.1): Cluster A (paranoid, schizoid, and schizotypal personality disorder); Cluster B (antisocial, borderline, histrionic, and narcissistic personality disorder); and Cluster C (avoidant, dependent, and obsessive-compulsive personality disorder). Individuals may be assigned multiple personality disorders if they meet the criteria for more than one disorder, and an individual whose personality pattern meets the general criteria for a personality disorder but who does not meet the specific criteria for any given disorder may be assigned a diagnosis of 'personality disorder NOS' (not otherwise specified). Therefore, a question to be addressed is the degree to which this arrangement of ten discrete disorders falling into three separate and distinct clusters is supported by current understanding and research.

Empirical support for the DSM's current structure

A desired characteristic of an empirically sound, categorical classification system is that it 'carves Nature at her joints'. That is, such a system should assist us in deciding whether or not an individual has or does not have a given disorder, and ultimately this decision should be consistent with a reality where disorders can be said to be either present or absent, but not both. And, if present, they are not simply a different degree of severity than a usual or normal presentation. This is a strong demand of a classification system, and in fact is stronger than that made by the authors of the DSM-IV, who admit of the DSM that 'there is no assumption that each category of mental disorder is a completely discrete entity with absolute boundaries dividing it from other mental disorders or from no mental disorder' (American Psychiatric Association, 2000: xxxi). Given the complex nature of human thought, emotion, and behavior, we would agree that some flexibility is required in a classification

Table 29.1   DSM-IV Axis II personality disorders and characteristics

Disorder[1]	Cluster	Essential characteristic(s)	Minimum no symptoms required
Paranoid	A	Pervasive distrust and suspiciousness of others	4 of 7
Schizoid	A	Social detachment/restricted interpersonal emotional expression	4 of 7
Schizotypal	A	Social and interpersonal deficits/eccentricity/cognitive or perceptual distortion	5 of 9
Antisocial[2]	B	Pervasive disregard for others' rights since age 15	3 of 7
Borderline	B	Instability of relationships, self-image and affect/marked impulsivity	5 of 9
Histrionic	B	Excessive emotionality and attention-seeking	5 of 8
Narcissistic	B	Grandiosity/need for admiration/lack of empathy	5 of 9
Avoidant	C	Social inhibition/feelings of inadequacy/hypersensitivity	4 of 7
Dependent	C	Excessive need for care/submissive and clinging behavior/fear of separation	5 of 8
Obsessive-compulsive	C	Preoccupation with orderliness, perfectionism,and mental/ interpersonal control	4 of 8

[1] All personality disorder diagnoses require that the personality patterns in question have begun 'by early adulthood' and are present 'in a variety of contexts'

[2] A diagnosis of antisocial personality disorder requires evidence of conduct disorder prior to age 15

Source: American Psychiatric Association, 1994

system purporting to organize the wide range of problems described by the DSM. Yet should we retain a categorical approach to classification despite evidence to the contrary, we risk 'the misleading, unstable, and illusory efforts to carve psychological functioning at nonexistent discrete joints' (Widiger and Samuel, 2005: 500).

The most troublesome problems overall with the current approach to diagnosis have been the high levels of within-category heterogeneity and the large degree of diagnostic co-occurrence (cf. Krueger et al., 2005b). This within-category heterogeneity is due to the polythetic approach to classification, whereby individuals are said to meet criteria for a given disorder if they meet a certain number out of a list of symptoms for the disorder, with no obligate criterion. This results in any myriad of symptom presentations among patients diagnosed with a given disorder. There is no particular reason why a polythetic system could not be consistent with an underlying diagnostic reality, and there are many medical syndromes that can be challenging to diagnose because of individual variation in symptom presentation. For example, the autoimmune disease rheumatoid arthritis (RA) can be challenging to diagnose due to the variable nature of its symptoms and a wide array of related autoimmune and arthritic conditions. To assist in the diagnosis, the American Rheumatism Association recommends that clinicians evaluate patients with respect to seven criteria, with a diagnosis of RA assigned if a patient meets at least five of these criteria for six or more weeks (Duke Orthopedics Department, 2007). An RA diagnosis also includes multiple exclusion criteria; for example, RA should not be diagnosed if the patient is also displaying a rash consistent with systemic lupus erythematosus, another autoimmune disease. Of course, in the case of most medical issues of this sort, we have at least some degree of understanding of the etiology of the disorder, as well as an idea of how the disease impacts the body (RA, for example, is an autoimmune-mediated disease whereby sufferers' immune systems attack the joints as well as other organs).

These things are more poorly understood in the case of psychiatric diagnoses (and almost by definition, since conditions such as porphyria for which we uncover clear-cut etiologies and physical manifestations are generally removed from psychiatry and reclassified in another area of medicine). Thus, the current categorical polythetic approach was developed less because it allows us to define a complex reality than because we have had little information as to the nature of that reality, and such an approach allows us flexibility in our attempts to classify and categorize. This general lack of data to support our current system is openly acknowledged in the DSM-IV, which states that a polythetic approach is used because, 'There is no assumption that all individuals described as having the same mental disorder are alike in all important ways' (American Psychiatric Association, 2000: xxxi). However, this flexibility comes at a cost of potentially great variation between individuals diagnosed with the same condition. An extreme example is the case of obsessive-compulsive personality disorder, which is defined in such a way that two individuals could be diagnosed with this disorder while sharing no symptoms in common.

High levels of diagnostic co-occurrence (or 'co-morbidity') have also been cited to challenge the empirical groundings of the DSM. Again, co-morbidity (i.e. patients having clinical presentations that meet criteria for two or more DSM diagnoses) is not necessarily problematic, and people often do present with symptoms of more than one disease in other areas of medicine (e.g. a patient with rheumatoid arthritis could also come down with the flu). However, as described by First (2005b), much of the co-morbidity in the DSM is either artifactual, due to the tendency of the DSM to 'split' rather than lump diagnoses (e.g. the ten diagnoses associated with the particular substance abused in the case of substance abuse), or spurious, due to the tendency of the DSM to define some disorders in such a way that more narrowly defined disorders are contained within them (e.g. by definition, all individuals who meet criteria for dementia will also meet criteria for amnestic disorder). The personality disorders have been seen as especially problematic from a co-morbidity standpoint, as two-thirds of patients with one personality disorder also meet criteria for another, and many in fact have several (Harvard Mental Health Letter, 2000). There is little evidence for boundaries among the personality disorders (Grant et al., 2005), and certain pairs of disorders (avoidant and dependent, schizoid and schizotypal, borderline and histrionic) are often indistinguishable when rated by clinicians (Clark et al., 2005). Although some of these problems with co-morbidity are likely due to methodological factors (e.g. similarity in diagnostic method used, such as self-report), co-morbidity remains notably higher than would be expected if each DSM personality disorder represented an independent diagnostic entity (Clark, 2005b). Moreover, this co-morbidity is not due to some underlying commonality within each of the three higher order clusters (A, B, and C), as there are correlations between disorders in different clusters. For example, avoidant personality disorder (from Cluster C) has been found to be significantly correlated with paranoid and schizoid personality disorders (placed in Cluster A). Observations such as these fail to support the idea of relatedness of disorders within clusters and independence among clusters (Clark et al., 2005).

As can be seen, the DSM's polythetic categorical approach is not well supported by data, and performs especially poorly with respect to the personality disorders. In fact, there is a growing body of research that challenges another structural aspect of the DSM, namely the separation between Axis I and Axis II. This research is emerging both from the fields of personality disorder and from the Axis I mood and anxiety disorders, and suggests that our approach to the classification of disorders on both axes ultimately may require significant revision (Krueger et al., 2005b).

As previously discussed, the personality disorders have been conceptualized as representing deep seated and pervasive problems that remain unchanging over time, in contrast to the Axis I disorders, which are seen as having a fairly distinct onset, as well as having the possibility of remitting. In the language of the DSM-IV,

> A Personality Disorder is an enduring pattern of inner experience and behavior that deviates markedly from expectations of the individual's culture, is pervasive and inflexible, has an onset in adolescence or early adulthood, is stable over time, and leads to distress or impairment. (American Psychiatric Association, 2000: 685)

This idea of the temporal stability of the personality disorders has been challenged by three recent major longitudinal studies of personality disorder, the results of which were reviewed by Clark (2005a). Clark noted that all three studies observed surprisingly high rates of remission of personality disorder, with two of the studies reporting remission rates estimated at 35–50% over the course of several years, whereas the third study noted a pattern of 'linear decline' in personality pathology of approximately 1% a year from adolescence up to age 27. Furthermore, the studies suggested that the presence of an Axis I disorder may 'enhance' the stability of personality disorder, effectively increasing the likelihood that an Axis II disorder will persist rather than remit. This challenges the generally accepted notion in clinical practice that the presence of an Axis II disorder will enhance the likelihood that an Axis I disorder will persist (rather than vice versa), and suggests a dynamic, two-way relationship between these two types of psychopathology. Finally, two of the studies (Skodol et al., 2005; Zanarini et al., 2005) suggest that the affective components of personality disorder are more stable than the behavioral components. Drawing on these results, Clark (2005a) argues that DSM personality disorders are best conceived of as 'hybrid' disorders, consisting of acute,

'Axis I-like' symptoms that resolve relatively quickly, combined with more persistent cognitive, behavioral, and especially affective components that represent longer lasting, temperamentally based personality dysfunction.

This conceptualization of 'hybrid' disorders does not appear to be limited to the personality literature, and there is growing evidence from researchers who focus on Axis I disorders (and especially from the mood and anxiety literature) to suggest that our current categorical models of these disorders fail to include information important to diagnosis and treatment. In a recent special section in the *Journal of Abnormal Psychology*, Brown and Barlow (2005) summarize a growing body of literature that supports the idea that broad, biological-genetic and psychosocial vulnerabilities appear to underlie many of the DSM disorders. Within this framework, the high levels of co-morbidity and symptom overlap within and between many Axis I and Axis II disorders can be explained by variation along these common core vulnerabilities, with variation in clinical presentation due to the influence of other, more specific biological, genetic, or psychosocial influences. Citing work from the anxiety and mood disorder literature, Brown and Barlow emphasize the importance of attending to these underlying dimensions in the treatment of psychiatric problems. They describe results from one of their own studies on panic disorder in which the level of co-morbid disorders had returned to its prior level at a two-year follow-up, despite the fact that the study patients had maintained (or even improved) their panic disorder gains (Brown et al., 1995). They argue that these results may indicate that their treatment (cognitive-behavioral therapy focused on reducing the symptoms of panic disorder) was effective in treating the panic disorder but ineffective in addressing an underlying predispositional dimensional factor (such as neuroticism), leaving the study participants vulnerable to developing additional disorders. Arguments such as these have led to a

growing conviction that the Axis I and Axis II disorders are not well distinguished empirically, and that modifications or rearrangements to the current DSM's Axis II may ultimately lead to a significant reworking of the DSM Axis I disorders (Krueger et al., 2005a, 2005b; Widiger et al., 2005).

In summary, a review of the literature indicates that the empirical grounding of the current DSM is rather weak. These problems associated with a categorical, polythetic approach to classification have been most obvious for the personality disorders, for which the current arrangement of three clusters of ten disorders on a separate Axis from other psychiatric problems has little support. Moreover, there is increasing evidence to suggest that the problem is more pervasive than this, and that ultimately, the entire DSM may well warrant significant reworking to be considered a good fit for our current understandings of the nature of psychopathology.

THE DSM AS A GUIDE TO ETIOLOGY AND TREATMENT

In addition to being empirically grounded, a good classification system arguably should provide us with some information on the etiology and course of psychiatric disorders; this information not only can allow us to form more accurate ideas about the relationships between different types of problems, but also may assist us in developing prophylactic measures to prevent or minimize the emergence of problems. Furthermore, a good classification system should also provide us with guidance in selecting and administering treatments.

Despite years of research and effort, few would challenge the notion that the current DSM falls short of these goals. With respect to etiology, even those who advise a conservative approach to implementing changes admit that the DSM provides us with little guidance as to the pathophysiology underlying most DSM disorders (First, 2005b).

With respect to treatment, the DSM's approach to defining disorders provides no direct information in these definitions that would assist in developing treatments for any particular disorder. This does not mean that we entirely lack such information, however, as the growing emphasis on empirically supported treatment (and especially the American Psychological Association's Division 12 Task Force on the Promotion and Dissemination of Psychological Procedures (1995), Chambless et al., 1996; Chambless, et al., 1998) has resulted in a large body of literature providing guidance as to the empirical support of various psychosocial and medication-based therapies for a wide array of psychiatric disorders. Nonetheless, even this large body of empirically based research is subject to serious caveat. First, the empirically supported treatment movement has focused almost entirely on Axis I disorders, and, with the exception of borderline and avoidant personality disorders, little is known about effective treatments for specific personality disorders (Critchfield and Benjamin, 2006). Second, the DSM's categorical approach to diagnosis has led some to express concerns about the feasibility of conducting a sufficient number of diagnosis-based studies to evaluate an ever-proliferating array of psychosocial and psychopharmaceutical treatment options (e.g. Beutler and Clarkin, 1990; Malik et al., 2003). Furthermore, there is little evidence that the effects of different psychotherapies are specific to the particular symptoms used to define DSM diagnoses (e.g. Kirsch and Sapirstein, 1998; Beutler et al., 2000; Beutler, 2002). Conversely, as previously discussed, there is a growing body of research to suggest that our current diagnostic system fails to include broad dimensional elements that cut across current diagnostic categories (e.g. Brown and Barlow, 2005; Clark, 2005a), raising the concern that 'current psychosocial treatments have become overspecialized because they focus on disorder-specific features (e.g. fear of pain in PDA), neglecting broader dimensions

that are more germane to favorable long-term outcomes' (Brown and Barlow, 2005: 553).

With regard to the personality disorders, there is nothing to indicate that the DSM classification system adds much to our understanding of the etiology of personality disorders (Harvard Mental Health Letter, 2000), and for the most part, treatments specific for most of the ten DSM-defined disorders have been lacking. All in all, the challenges associated with developing treatment for the Axis II disorders are similar to those associated with the Axis I disorders, albeit arguably even more profound. First, many of the current symptoms used to diagnose personality disorders are behavioral, with little emphasis on other areas of clinical interest, such as inner experiences (Shedler and Weston, 2004a). Although this behavioral focus was developed in an effort to increase diagnostic reliability, there is little evidence that it actually does so (Clark et al., 2005). Furthermore, as will be discussed, this focus on behavioral criteria neglects broad, temperament-based dimensions that increasingly are seen as important in the etiology, diagnosis, and treatment of personality disorders (Clark, 2005b). Next, the large number of distinct personality disorders, in combination with the polythetic approach to classification and the very high levels of co-morbidity, makes the development of treatments for individual disorders a daunting task. For example, given that two individuals with antisocial personality disorder may have no symptoms in common, will the same treatment be effective for each? How should treatment differ for an individual with borderline personality disorder alone as compared to treatment for an individual who also meets criteria for dependent personality disorder? In the case of multiple personality disorders, do we need separate treatments for each? And how do we develop treatments for the large percentage of individuals diagnosed with personality disorder not otherwise specified? The DSM provides us with little guidance.

The question of how to treat personality disorders most effectively was recently addressed by the Task Force on Empirically Based Principles of Therapeutic Change, chaired by Castonguay and Beutler (2006). This task force was inspired by the work of two previous task forces: the Task Force on the Promotion and Dissemination of Psychological Procedures sponsored by Division 12 (Society of Clinical Psychology) of the American Psychological Association (Chambless et al. 1996; Chambless et al., 1998; American Psychological Association Task Force, 1995) and a task force sponsored by Division 29 (Psychotherapy) of the American Psychological Association (Norcross, 2002). While both of these latter task forces sought to provide guidance about the empirical support for various psychotherapeutic interventions, the Division 12 task force focused on elucidating empirically supported treatments for specific diagnostic disorders (i.e. defining specific psychotherapeutic treatment models that performed better than controls in controlled trials) whereas the Division 29 task force emphasized the role of patient and relationship factors that cut across disorders and interventions to moderate treatment outcomes. Noting the perception that the results of these two task forces were often seen as contrasting and contradictory, Castonguay and Beutler formed their task force with the aim of integrating the results of the two groups.

Focusing on four main symptom groups (dysphoric disorders, anxiety disorders, personality disorders, and substance use disorders), the task force members undertook an exhaustive critical review of existing outcome research to identify the roles of participant, relationship, and technique factors in the effective treatment of each of these problem clusters. These relationships were then formulated as 'empirically informed principles' that could be used as strategies to guide clinicians' treatment efforts. Unsurprisingly, the task force work group that focused on the personality disorders noted difficulty in finding sufficient research of a high enough

quality to clearly delineate well-supported participant and relationship factors connected to treatment outcome (Fernández-Alvarez et al., 2006; Smith et al., 2006). Furthermore, the empirically supported technique factors for personality disorder uncovered by the task force (Linehan et al., 2006) were noted to be derived primarily from the avoidant and borderline personality disorder literature, since little research to date has focused on other personality disorders. The reasons cited for this lack of suitable research were very similar to those given earlier in this chapter to illustrate the problems with the DSM approach to personality disorder diagnosis (e.g. the high degree of intra-diagnostic heterogeneity and high levels of co-morbidity). Thus, not only does the DSM-IV categorical approach to personality disorder diagnosis provide little guidance regarding etiology or treatment, but arguably can be said to complicate the task of uncovering information that would allow us to progress in these areas.

ALTERNATIVE MODELS

Many researchers and clinicians (e.g. Clark, 2005b; Verheul, 2005) have proposed a move toward incorporating dimensional elements into the classification for personality disorders, including those involved in setting the personality disorder research agenda for the DSM-V (Widiger et al., 2005). From the perspective of many of these scholars, personality is seen to exist on a continuum between normal personality and maladaptive or abnormal variants of normal personality traits. This view of personality disorders is therefore quite different than the categorical perspective that underlines the DSM. The majority of the research performed on personality disorders to date supports the idea that these disorders are most accurately conceptualized as continuous variables, with quantitative but not qualitative differences between normal and abnormal functioning

(Schroeder et al., 1992). Schizotypal personality disorder, which appears to be discontinuous, appears to be an exception to this general rule (Endler and Kocovski, 2002). Thus, dimensional models of personality functioning not only provide a bridge between abnormal and normal functioning, but also allow for patients readily to be compared to other persons in the population, making the scores portable (Krueger and Piasecki, 2002).

Because much of the research on personality functioning has been conducted by researchers interested in 'normal' functioning, many of the proposed dimensional models of abnormal personality originate from models used to describe normal personality. However, some models were constructed by adding dimensional elements to symptoms drawn from Axis II of the DSM. Typically, these models are tested to determine whether they can adequately represent personality disorder in two ways: (1) by examining whether DSM personality diagnoses can be appropriately described with models of normal personality, and (2) by examining the relationship between personality disorder traits and models of normal personality (Livesley and Jang, 2005).

A large number of these dimensional models exist, including models by Eysenck (1987), Costa and McCrae (1992), Harkness and McNulty (1994), Millon et al. (1996), Tellegen (Watson et al., 1999), Cloninger (2000), Tyrer (2000), Zuckerman (2002), Livesley (2003), Wiggins (2003), Shedler and Westen (2004b), and Skodol et al. (2005). The sheer magnitude of these alterative models has led many to question which of these models (if any) provides us with the best fit. Thus, despite a general agreement that dimensional models appear an appropriate approach in the classification of personality disorder, many have agreed with Frances that 'the time is not ripe, and it is not yet clear which dimensional system will be optimal' (1993: 110). Recently, however, there appears to be a convergence of findings from several fields of research that would appear

to provide us with the guidance we need in laying the foundation for an empirically grounded and clinically useful dimensional approach to personality assessment. As we will discuss, many of the models developed and tested by personality researchers (including the well-studied five-factor model described below) correspond quite well to broad factors of temperament uncovered in multivariate genetic research. These factors, in turn, are quite similar to some of the participant and treatment factors that have emerged from the outcome literature.

With respect to contributions from the area of personality assessment, the five-factor model of personality (FFM; Costa and McCrae, 1992) is one of the oldest and most widely used models of personality functioning. The FFM was derived based on the lexical-semantic hypothesis which asserts that language evolves over time to reveal what is important, and that the most relevant personality characteristics have been encoded in the natural language (John and Srivastava, 1999). Lay adjectives that describe personality were extracted from the dictionary, and then factor analysis was performed on non-pathological samples. The traits that were found consisted of five broad trait domains: neuroticism, conscientiousness, agreeableness/antagonism, extraversion/introversion, and openness. These traits have been found to exist in every culture studied, and are thus proposed as sufficient to describe diagnostic personality criteria worldwide (McCrae et al., 2005).

Studies have examined the extent to which the FFM can adequately describe personality disorder. Bagby and colleagues (2005a) found that the FFM was able to adequately conceptualize the DSM-IV personality disorders. Descriptions of antisocial personality disorder, for example, revealed that prototypic patients are low in conscientiousness and agreeableness at the trait level, low in anxiousness, self-consciousness and modesty, and high in assertiveness. General support was found for paranoid, schizoid, schizotypal, borderline, narcissistic, dependent and avoidant personality disorders, with weaker support for antisocial, histrionic, and obsessive-compulsive personality disorders. Bagby and colleagues (2005b) found that neuroticism and extraversion were significantly associated with symptom counts for nearly all disorders, and that the openness domain was associated with symptom counts for only two disorders. They also found that the agreeableness and conscientiousness domains were significantly associated with specific disorders. They concluded that the neuroticism and extraversion domains are associated with all forms of DSM-IV personality disorders on a general level, while the co-variation of the remaining domains define the specific features of the individual personality disorders.

The results from the FFM are quite remarkably consistent with existing multivariate genetic research, which suggests that four broad secondary traits (emotional dysregulation, constraint/conscientiousness, antagonism/dissocial, and inhibition/introversion) are sufficient to represent the range of normal and abnormal personality functions (Livesley et al., 1998). Such models provide good correspondence between genotype and the observable aspects of personality (phenotype), which contrasts with the relatively poor correspondence between genotype and phenotype observed for many categorical diagnoses (Merikangas, 2002). As noted by Widiger and Samuel (2005), these four dimensions correspond well to four of the five domains developed by McCrae and Costa, with emotional dysregulation corresponding to the FFM neuroticism factor, the constraint domain corresponding with FFM's conscientiousness, the dissocial domain corresponding with FFM's agreeableness/ antagonism, and inhibition/ introversion corresponding with FFM's introversion/ extroversion. Thus, only the 'openness to experience' factor from the FFM lacks a clear match in the multivariate genetic results.

In their review of these and other personality data, Widiger and Simonsen (2005) argue convincingly that most existing models of personality structure could be well represented by a single hierarchical model. They suggest that the highest level of this model should be the two broad clinical dimensions of internalization and externalization. Nested just beneath this level would be the four to five broad domains of personality functioning, as suggested by the personality assessment and genetic data. They visualize personality trait scales nested at the next level of the hierarchy, with behaviorally specific diagnostic criteria at the lowest level.

Although there are many details yet to be resolved, this proposal by Widiger and Simonsen does demonstrate that we are coming very close to the development of a workable dimensional model of personality functioning. Such a model also one day might be expanded to include some of the disorders currently placed on Axis I. For example, Krueger and colleagues (2005a) have suggested that externalizing disorders such as substance abuse and antisocial behavior would be better understood as problems existing on a continuum rather than as categorical problems. At present, such a model holds the promise not only of providing a better fit to the personality data, but also of allowing the establishment of links between assessment, etiology, and treatment.

In terms of etiology, the link between dimensional models of personality dysfunction and etiology is easily made by grounding these models in genetic propensities, as described by Livesley and colleagues (1998). Consistent with this approach, Clark (2005b) has provided an interesting discussion of the ability of three broad dimensions of temperament to provide a link between normal personality functioning and psychopathology. Clark suggests that three broad, innate dimensions of temperament (negative affectivity, positive affectivity, and disinhibition) might serve as risk factors for the development of psychopathology in the face of relevant stressors. Thus, a shift to a dimensional system of personality diagnosis would provide us with considerably more guidance as to etiological links than the existing categorical approach.

With respect to treatment, these dimensional approaches to personality assessment suggested by Widiger and others would appear to correspond quite nicely with the treatment guidelines developed independently by researchers with an interest in psychotherapy outcome. Specifically, Beutler and colleagues (e.g. Beutler and Clarkin, 1990; Beutler et al., 2000) have long been interested in uncovering cross-cutting principles of therapeutic change to provide guidance to therapists in optimizing treatment outcomes for their clients. Their work was inspired by the observation that a wide range of treatments are effective for depression, with very different treatments producing quite similar results (e.g. Smith et al., 1980). Despite this average effectiveness, however, in any group of depressed patients, some will benefit much from treatment while others benefit less and some may even become worse (Beutler et al., 2000). This suggested that moderating variables might be important in impacting treatment outcome, and, after extensively reviewing the outcome literature, Beutler and colleagues indeed uncovered several participant and treatment variables that appear to interact in ways affecting therapeutic results (e.g. Beutler et al., 2000).

Initially limited to the depression literature, this effort to uncover moderating factors has recently been expanded into other diagnostic areas by the Task Force on Empirically Based Principles of Therapeutic Change (Castonguay and Beutler, 2006). As previously described, the task force members charged with uncovering empirically supported participant, therapist, and technique factors related to outcome for individuals with personality disorder (Critchfield and Benjamin, 2006; Fernandez-Alvarez et al., 2006; Linehan et al., 2006; Smith et al., 2006) found some suggestive factors, but were able to uncover relatively few that could be considered truly empirically supported, largely due to a relative lack of suitable research studies to review. However, the research used by the task force in their reviews was, out of necessity, conducted on studies using the current categorical classification system. In contrast, if we follow the lead of Widiger and Simonsen (2005) in defining personality functioning in terms of the four broad dimensions common to multiple models, it is possible to suggest some plausible hypotheses as to the likely interactions between these broad personality dimensions and some of the variables important in therapeutic change described by the recent task force (Beutler et al., 2006).

By accepting the idea of four broad dimensions of personality, two of these dimensions (introversion/extroversion and agreeableness/antagonism) can readily be matched with several of the task force's change principles. With respect to introversion/extroversion, the task force recommended that externalizing patients will benefit most from treatments focused on behavioral change and symptom reduction (such as skills building and impulse management), whereas internalizing patients will benefit most from treatments that foster insight, self-understanding, interpersonal attachments, and self-esteem (Beutler et al., 2006). If we consider agreeableness/antagonism to be related to the therapeutic concept of 'resistance', the task force notes that interventions that increase patient resistance (such as therapist control and confrontation) are associated with poorer outcomes than interventions that allow the patient more freedom and do not confront the patient's resistance directly. Given this observation, the task force recommended that therapists adjust their use of directive therapeutic techniques based on the patient's level of resistance (Beutler et al., 2006). This could be translated into language consistent with that of the evolving dimensional models of assessment by noting that patients with lower levels of agreeableness will have better outcomes when therapists use a relatively less directive approach and avoid taking control and initiating confrontation. In contrast, patients with higher levels of agreeableness should be able to tolerate a greater degree of therapist directiveness, control, and confrontation.

The other two personality dimensions (emotional dysregulation/neuroticism and constraint/impulsivity) might also fit into the task force recommendations. The task force notes that a patient's overall functional impairment is an indicator for the length and intensity of treatment needed, with highly impaired patients tending to get little benefit from short-term interventions (Beutler et al., 2006). To the extent that emotional dysregulation and neuroticism are associated with impairment in functioning, the task force recommendations may well be applicable to this dimension. Interestingly, the task force does note constraint/impulsivity to be an important participant factor impacting outcome, but associates 'constraint' with 'introversion' and 'impulsivity' with 'extroversion.' Thus, the task force recommendations for participants who are high versus low in impulsivity is identical to the recommendations for those who are high versus low in extroversion, and there are no unique treatment recommendations associated with the constraint/impulsivity dimension (Beutler et al., 2006). Given the solid research support from the personality literature for introversion/extroversion and constraint/impulsivity as separate factors, the task force's failure to differentiate these variables may reflect a failure in the psychotherapy literature to sufficiently attend to literature on personality. Such a failure in the treatment outcome literature may have not allowed these factors to be explored separately. This observation underlines the importance of communion among lines of research in personality and psychotherapy. Until specific differentiation is explored in a psychotherapy context, it will not be known if impulsivity and extroversion respond best to similar treatment approaches, whereas constraint and introversion are best treated with a different approach. If current trends continue and we begin to shift toward dimensional models of personality assessment, we should at some point have sufficient information to address this question.

One final issue that a shift to a dimensional model of personality might allow us to address is prevention. In medicine, the Western model of focus on disease and dysfunction is gradually shifting to one of prevention and whole body health. For example, early attempts to identify predictors of later problems such as high blood pressure or high blood sugar levels have led to early interventions (diet, exercise, sometimes medications) that minimize the long-term health impact of these conditions. Similarly, dimensional models of personality functioning (and quite possibly other types of mental health issues), if assessed along a continuum, might provide us with early warning signs of developing problems, as well as the potential to intervene prior to the development of a fully fledged disorder. As prevention of problems is always desirable when possible, the better our field is grounded in good explanations for etiology, the better our chances of preventing or minimizing suffering through early intervention.

OTHER ISSUES

There seems to be little doubt that a dimensional approach to personality assessment would be a clear improvement over the current categorical diagnostic system with respect to empirical grounding, etiology, and treatment. However, the idea of abandoning the current DSM Axis II typology has raised several concerns. The most serious of these concerns have focused on the potential difficulties that a move to a dimensional system might cause for clinicians (e.g. Sprock, 2003; First, 2005a; Watson and Clark, 2006), as well as the potential problems caused by a lack of clear cutoffs or thresholds between normal personality and problematic personality functioning (e.g. Kupfer, 2005).

It is true that changing to a dimensional approach would require new learning for clinicians. However, there are indications that such a transition might not be as difficult as some fear. Proponents of dimensional models argue that dimensional models would improve professional communication because they allow for the provision of more information than is currently allowed with categorical models (Widiger et al., 2005). Dimensional models also allow for the description of borderline or doubtful cases, in contrast to categorical models where a patient either meets criteria or not (Harvard Mental Health Letter, 2000). Furthermore, dimensional models allow for the diagnosis of subthreshold conditions such as minor degrees of mood disorders and non-specific complaints, which comprise the bulk of mental health needs in primary care settings (Jablensky, 2005). In addition, the current conceptualization of personality disorders excludes personality strengths, which might rule out a personality disorder diagnosis for some clients (Westen and Shedler, 1999). Finally, dimensional models might provide better coverage for idiosyncratic traits and may eliminate the need for the most commonly used personality disorder diagnosis: 'personality disorder not otherwise specified' (Widiger et al., 2005).

Several studies conducted on dimensional models of personality also indicate that they should perform quite well in clinical settings. For example, Skodol and colleagues (2005) studied a model that translated DSM-IV personality disorder categories into dimensional information by allowing for clinically significant traits and subthreshold disorders, as well as for different degrees of severity. They then assessed the model to determine whether this adaptation was clinically useful. They found that the dimensional representations provided more clinically relevant descriptive information than the categories currently used, as it allowed for subthreshold information to be included. They also found that the dimensional representations of personality disorder bore a stronger relationship to measures of functional impairment, one of the hallmarks of personality pathology, than did the categorical representations. In another recent study, Samuel and Widiger (2004) asked practicing clinicians to rate prototypic cases of each DSM-IV personality disorder in terms of the FFM. They found that clinicians were able to conceptualize the DSM-IV

personality disorders with 'good to excellent reliability' (2004: 296). Further, they assert that the FFM allows for a richer and more comprehensive description of DSM-IV personality disorders than the current categorical system.

With respect to the absence of thresholds in a dimensional classification system, it is important to note that this problem is not limited to a dimensional approach to classification, but can be problematic for a categorical classification system as well. For example, clinicians working with Axis I depressive and anxiety disorders have noted significant problems with inter-rater reliability due to disagreements as to the severity or duration of relevant symptoms (Brown and Barlow, 2005), and the process of generating cut-points to define categories arguably involves working with dimensional data (Kupfer, 2005). In terms of revisions to the DSM Axis II, Widiger and colleagues (2005) agree that cutoff points would be required to make clinical decisions, such as whether to provide treatment, medication, or insurance coverage. Widiger and Samuel (2005) elaborate on this point using the case of mental retardation. They point out that using an IQ of 70 as a demarcation point to define mental retardation is an arbitrary decision (in that we could just as easily use an IQ of 69 or of 71), but one that is clinically relevant and useful. Thus, they argue that the use of a dimensional approach is not mutually exclusive to the development of categories or decision points needed for treatment decisions. Livesley and Jang (2005) agree, pointing out that when providing cutoff points for continuous variables, the thresholds may end up being artifactual, but they need not be arbitrary, and that empirically derived cutoff points could be determined based on risk associated with certain levels of trait expression.

In summary, although no classification system will be perfect, there appears to be little doubt at this stage that a dimensional approach to personality assessment is a better fit to the data than the current categorical system, and that we have sufficient information about the nature of personality functioning (both normal and abnormal) to begin working to develop such a system. Dimensional models also seem more promising than categorical approaches in providing us with guidance as to the etiology and treatment of personality disorders, with the primary drawback being that such an approach would be novel, and, as such, would require new learning from clinicians. While ease of use is very important and should be taken into account in the development of any new model, we agree with Clark (1993), who argued that retaining an existing diagnostic system primarily because it is familiar, bears 'a disturbing resemblance to the old story of searching for a lost key under the lamppost because the light is better there . . . a traditional, familiar, and conceptually simple system is of little scientific or clinical value if it has low validity' (1993: 100; cited in Verheul, 2005).

CONCLUSIONS

There is no doubt that we are living in a very exciting time in the history of psychiatric classification, and an explosion of research in the past several years is beginning to have a significant impact on the way we understand and conceptualize mental health issues and diagnoses. To place this in a historical perspective, when two of the authors of this chapter edited a book critical of the DSM (Beutler and Malik, 2002), we began work on this book at a time when such a project was still considered by many to reflect a fringe movement in the field of psychiatric diagnoses. We felt at the time that the criticisms of the DSM approach to classification were significant enough to warrant attempts to present alternatives. In the process of developing the book, however, we came to realize that although there was a growing dissatisfaction with the DSM approach to diagnoses, we were not yet at the point to provide a single effective alternative (but see some interesting proposals

by Beutler and Malik, 2002; Doucette, 2002; Gonçalves et al., 2002; Kihlstrom, 2002; Schneider et al., 2002; Westen et al., 2002). As such, we were very gratified when reviewing the literature for this current chapter to see how far the field has come in just a few short years.

At this point in time (early 2008), the idea that we should be developing an alternative approach to the classification of personality disorders has gained widespread acceptance (e.g. Widiger et al., 2005) and the idea that the DSM approach itself is in need of significant reworking is gaining ground (e.g. Rounsaville et al., 2002). We have also made marked progress in empirically grounded approaches to the development of cross-cutting, dimensionally based models, to the point where the exploration of alternatives can no longer be dismissed due to lack of data. Furthermore, these models provide connections both to the etiology of personality dysfunction and to the clinical outcome literature in ways that should prove very useful in the design and implementation of an empirically based diagnostic system that also provides suggestions for treatment. These advances can be credited to the hard work and dedication of many researchers and clinicians in the field, including individuals involved in assessment (and especially personality researchers) as well as those with a commitment to an improved understanding in treatment outcome. It is encouraging to see the rapid progress of the past several years, and we (the authors) are hopeful that we are truly on the verge of a marked improvement in our ability to understand and help the people with whom we work, whether in the laboratory, the classroom, or the community.

REFERENCES

American Psychiatric Association (1952) *Diagnostic and Statistical Manual of Mental Disorders* (1st edn). Washington, DC: APA.
American Psychiatric Association (1968) *Diagnostic and Statistical Manual of Mental Disorders* (2nd edn). Washington, DC: APA.

American Psychiatric Association (1980) *Diagnostic and Statistical Manual of Mental Disorders* (3rd edn). Washington, DC: APA.

American Psychiatric Association (1994) *Diagnostic and Statistical Manual of Mental Disorders* (4th edn). Washington, DC: APA.

American Psychiatric Association (2000) *Diagnostic and Statistical Manual of Mental Disorders* (4th edn, revised). Washington, DC: APA.

American Psychological Association Task Force on Promotion and Dissemination of Psychological Procedures (1995) 'Training in and dissemination of empirically validated psychological treatments: Report and recommendations', *The Clinical Psychologist*, 48(1): 3–23.

Bagby, R.M., Costa, P.T., Widiger, T.A., Ryder, A.G. and Marshall, M. (2005a) 'DSM-IV personality disorders and the Five-Factor Model of personality: A multi-method examination of domain- and facet-level predictions', *European Journal of Personality*, 19(4): 307–24.

Bagby, R.M., Marshall, M.B. and Georgiades, S. (2005b) 'Dimensional personality traits and the prediction of DSM-IV personality disorder symptom counts in a nonclinical sample', *Journal of Personality Disorders*, 19(1): 53–67.

Beutler, L.E. (2002) 'The dodo bird really is extinct', *Clinical Psychology: Science and Practice*, 9(1): 30–4.

Beutler, L.E., Castonguay, L.G. and Follette, W.C. (2006) 'Integration of therapeutic factors in dysphoric disorders', in L.G. Castonguay and L.E. Beutler (eds), *Principles of Therapeutic Change that Work*. New York: Oxford University Press, pp. 111–17.

Beutler, L.E. and Clarkin, J. (1990) *Systematic Treatment Selection: Toward Targeted Therapeutic Interventions*. New York: Brunner/Mazel.

Beutler, L.E., Clarkin, J. and Bongar, B. (2000) *Guidelines for the Systematic Treatment of the Depressed Patient*. New York: Oxford University Press.

Beutler, L.E. and Malik, M.L. (2002) 'Diagnosis and treatment guidelines: The example of depression', in M. L. Malik and L.E. Beutler (eds), *Rethinking the DSM: A Psychological Perspective*. Washington, DC: American Psychological Association, pp. 251–78.

Blashfield, R.K. (1984) *The Classification of Psychopathology: Neo-Kraepelian and Quantitative Approaches*. New York: Plenum.

Brown, T.A., Anthony, M.M. and Barlow, D.H. (1995) 'Diagnostic comorbidity in panic disorder: Effect on treatment outcome and course of comorbid diagnoses following treatment', *Journal of Consulting and Clinical Psychology*, 63(3): 408–18.

Brown, T.A. and Barlow, D.H. (2005). 'Dimensional versus categorical classification of mental disorders in the fifth edition of the *Diagnostic and Statistical Manual of Mental Disorders* and beyond: Comment on the Special Section', *Journal of Abnormal Psychology*, 114(4): 551–6.

Castonguay, L.G. and Beutler, L.E. (2006) (eds), *Principles of Therapeutic Change that Work*. New York: Oxford University Press.

Chambless, D.L., Baker, M.J., Baucom, D.H., Beutler, L.E., Calhoun, K.S., Crits-Christoph, P., Daiuto, A., DeRubeis, R., Detweiler, J., Haaga, D.A.F., Johnson, S.B., McCurry, S., Mueser, K.T., Pope, K.S., Sanderson, W.C., Shoham, V., Stickle, T., Williams, D.A. and Woody, S.R. (1998) 'Update on empirically validated therapies, II', *Clinical Psychologist*, 51(1): 3–16.

Chambless, D.L., Sanderson, W.C., Shoham, V., Johnson, S.B., Pope, K.S., Crits-Christoph, P., Baker, M., Johnson, B., Woody, S.R., Sue, S., Beutler, L.E., Williams, D.A. and McCurry, S. (1996) 'An update on empirically validated therapies', *Clinical Psychologist*, 49(2): 5–14.

Clark, L.A. (1993). 'Personality disorder diagnosis: Limitations of the Five-Factor Model', *Psychological Inquiry*, 4(2): 100–4.

Clark, L.A. (2005a) 'Stability and change in personality pathology: Revelations of three longitudinal studies', *Journal of Personality Disorders*, 19(5): 524–32.

Clark, L.A. (2005b) 'Temperament as a unifying basis for personality and psychopathology', *Journal of Abnormal Psychology*, 114(4): 505–21.

Clark, L.A., Livesley, W.J., Shedler, J. and Westen, D. (2005) 'Revamping DSM-IV personality disorder diagnoses', *Clinician's Research Digest*, 23(1): 5.

Clark, L.A., Watson, D. and Reynolds, A. (1995) 'Diagnosis and classification in psychopathology: Challenges to the current system and future directions', *Annual Review of Psychology*, 46: 121–53.

Cloninger, C.R. (2000) 'A practical way to diagnose personality disorders: A proposal', *Journal of Personality Disorders*, 14(2): 99–108.

Costa, P.T. Jr. and McCrae, R.R. (1992) *Revised NEO Personality Inventory (NEO-PI-R) and NEO Five-factor Inventory (NEO-FFI) Professional Manual*. Odessa: FL: Psychological Assessment Resources.

Critchfield, K.L. and Benjamin, L.S. (2006) 'Integration of therapeutic factors in treating personality disorders', in L.G. Castonguay and L.E. Beutler (eds), *Principles of Therapeutic Change that Work*. New York: Oxford University Press, pp. 253–71.

Doucette, A. (2002) 'Child and adolescent diagnosis: The need for a model-based approach', in M.L. Malik and L.E. Beutler (eds), *Rethinking the DSM: A Psychological Perspective*. Washington, DC: American Psychological Association, pp. 201–220.

Duke Orthopedics Department (2007) 'American Rheumatology Association diagnostic criteria for R.A.', in: *Wheeless Textbook of Orthopedics*. <http:// www.wheelesson-line.com/ortho/american_rheumatism _association_diagnostic_criteria_for_ra>

Endicott, J. and Spitzer, R.L. (1978) 'A diagnostic interview', *Archives of General Psychiatry*, 35(7): 837–44.

Endler, N.S. and Kocovski, N.L. (2002) 'Personality disorders at the crossroads', *Journal of Personality Disorders*, 16(6): 487–502.

Eysenck, H.J. (1987) 'The definition of personality disorders and the criteria appropriate for their description', *Journal of Personality Disorders*, 1(2): 211–19.

Fernández-Alvarez, H., Clarkin, J.F., Salgueiro, M. del C. and Critchfield, K.L. (2006) 'Participant factors in treating personality disorders', in L.G. Castonguay and L.E. Beutler (eds), *Principles of Therapeutic Change that Work*. New York: Oxford University Press, pp. 203–18.

First, M.B. (2005a) 'Clinical utility: A prerequisite for the adoption of a dimensional approach in DSM', *Journal of Abnormal Psychology*, 114(4): 560–4.

First, M.B. (2005b) 'Mutually exclusive versus co-occurring diagnostic categories: The challenge of diagnostic comorbidity', *Psychopathology*, 38(4): 206–10.

First, M.B., Bell, C.B., Cuthbert, B., Krystal, J.H., Malison, R., Offord, D.R., Reiss, D., Shea, M.T., Widiger, T.A. and Wisner, K.L. (2002) 'Personality disorders and relational disorders: A research agenda for addressing crucial gaps in DSM', in D.J. Kupfer, M.B. First and D.A. Reigier (eds), *A Research Agenda for DSM-V*. Washington, DC: American Psychiatric Association, pp. 123–99.

Frances, A. (1993) 'Dimensional diagnosis of personality: Not whether, but when and which', *Psychological Inquiry*, 4(2): 110–11.

Gonçalves, O.F., Machado, P.P., Korman, Y. and Angus, L. (2002) 'Assessing psychopathology: A narrative approach', in M.L. Malik and L.E. Beutler (eds), *Rethinking the DSM: A Psychological Perspective*. Washington, DC: American Psychological Association, pp. 149–76.

Grant, B.F., Stinson, F.S., Dawson, D.A., Chou, S.P. and Ruan, W.J. (2005) 'Co-occurrence of *DSM-IV* personality disorders in the United States: Results from the National Epidemiologic Survey on Alcohol and Related Conditions', *Comprehensive Psychiatry*, 46(1): 1–5.

Harkness, A.R. and McNulty, J.L. (1994) 'The Personality Psychopathology Five (PSY-5): Issue from the pages of a diagnostic manual instead of a dictionary', in S. Strack and M. Lorr (eds), *Differentiating Normal and Abnormal Personality*. New York: Springer, pp. 291–315.

Harvard Mental Health Letter (2000) 'Personality disorders – part I', *Harvard Mental Health Letter*, 16(9): 1–5.

Houts, A.C. (2002) 'Discovery, invention, and the expansion of the modern *Diagnostic and Statistical Manuals of Mental Disorders*', in M.L. Malik and L.E. Beutler (eds), *Rethinking the DSM: A Psychological Perspective*. Washington, DC: American Psychological Association, pp. 17–65.

Jablensky, A. (2005) 'Categories, dimensions and prototypes: Critical issues for psychiatric classification', *Psychopathology*, 38(4): 201–5.

Johansen, M., Karterud, S., Pedersen, G., Gude, T. and Falkum, E. (2004) 'An investigation of the prototype validity of the borderline DSM-IV construct', *Acta Psychiatrica Scandinavica*, 109(4): 289–98.

John, O.P. and Srivastava, S. (1999) 'The big five trait taxonomy: History, measurement, and theoretical perspectives', in L.A. Pervin and O.P. John (eds), *Handbook of*

Personality: Theory and Research (2nd edn). New York: Guilford, pp. 102–38.

Kihlstrom, J.F. (2002) 'To honor Kraepelin: From symptoms to pathology in the diagnosis of mental illness', in M.L. Malik and L.E. Beutler (eds), *Rethinking the DSM: A Psychological Perspective*. Washington, DC: American Psychological Association, pp. 279–303.

Kirk, S.A. and Kutchins, H. (1992) *The Selling of the DSM: The Rhetoric of Science in Psychiatry*. New York: Aldine de Gruyter.

Kirsch, I. and Saparstein, G. (1998) 'Listening to Prozac by hearing placebo: A meta-analysis of antidepressant medications', *Treatment and Prevention*, 1(1): Article 0001c. Available at: <http://journals.apa.org/prevention/volume1/pre 0010001c.html>

Klonsky, E.D. (2000) 'The DSM classification of personality disorder: Clinical wisdom or empirical truth? A response to Alvin R. Mahrer's problem 11', *Journal of Clinical Psychology*, 56(12): 1615–21.

Krueger, R.F., Markon, K.E., Patrick, C.J. and Iacono, W. (2005a) 'Externalizing Psychopathology in adulthood: A dimensional-spectrum conceptualization and its implications for DSM-V', *Journal of Abnormal Psychology*, 114(4): 537–50.

Krueger, R.F. and Piasecki, T.M. (2002) 'Toward a dimensional and psychometrically informed approach to conceptualizing psychopathology', *Behavior Research and Therapy*, 40(5): 485–99.

Krueger, R.F. and Tackett, J.L. (2003) 'Personality and psychopathology: Working toward the bigger picture', *Journal of Personality Disorders*, 17(2): 109–28.

Krueger, R.F., Watson, D. and Barlow, D.H. (2005b) 'Introduction to the Special Section: Toward a dimensionally based taxonomy of psychopathology', *Journal of Abnormal Psychology*, 114(4): 491–3.

Kupfer, D.J. (2005) 'Dimensional models for research and diagnosis: A current dilemma', *Journal of Abnormal Psychology*, 114(4): 557–9.

Linehan, M.M., Davison, G.C., Lynch, T.R. and Sanderson, C. (2006) 'Technique factors in treating personality disorders', in L.G. Castonguay and L.E. Beutler (eds), *Principles of Therapeutic Change that Work*.

New York: Oxford University Press, pp. 239–52.

Livesley, W.J. (2003) 'Diagnostic dilemmas in classifying personality disorder', in K.A. Phillips, M.B. First and H.A. Pincus (eds), *Advancing DSM: Dilemmas in Psychiatric Diagnosis*. Washington, DC: American Psychiatric Association, pp. 153–90.

Livesley, W.J. and Jang, K.L. (2005) 'Differentiating normal, abnormal, and disordered personality', *European Journal of Personality*, 19(4): 257–68.

Livesley, W.J., Jang, K.L. and Vernon, P.A. (1998) 'Phenotypic and genetic structure of traits delineating personality disorder', *Archives of General Psychiatry*, 55(10): 941–8.

Maher, B.A. and Maher, W.B. (1994) 'Personality and psychopathology: A historical perspective', *Journal of Abnormal Psychology*, 103(1): 72–7.

Malik, M.L. and Beutler, L.E. (2002) 'The emergence of dissatisfaction with the DSM', in M.L. Malik and L.E. Beutler (eds), *Rethinking the DSM: A Psychological Perspective*. Washington, DC: American Psychological Association, pp. 3–15.

Malik, M.L., Beutler, L.E., Gallagher-Thompson, D., Thompson, L. and Alimohamed, S. (2003) 'Are all cognitive therapies alike? A comparison of cognitive and non-cognitive therapy process and implications for the application of empirically supported treatments (ESTs)', *Journal of Consulting and Clinical Psychology*, 71(1): 150–8.

McCrae, R.R., Löckenhoff, C.E. and Costa, P.T. (2005) 'A step toward DSM-V: Cataloguing personality-related problems in living', *European Journal of Personality*, 19(4): 269–86.

Merikangas, K.R. (2002) 'Implications of genetic epidemiology for classification', in J.E. Helzer and J.J. Hudziak (eds), *Defining Psychopathology in the 21st Century: DSM-V and Beyond*. Washington, DC: American Psychiatric Publishing, pp. 195–209.

Millon, T.R., Davis, R.D., Millon, C.M., Wenger, A.W., Van Zuilen, M.H., Fuchs, M. and Millon, R.B. (1996) *Disorders of Personality. DSM and Beyond*. New York: John Wiley & Sons.

Nathan, P.E. (1998) 'The DSM-IV and its antecedents: Enhancing syndromal diagnosis', in J.W. Barron (eds), *Making Diagnosis Meaningful: Enhancing Evaluation and Treatment of Psychological Disorders*. Washington, DC: American Psychological Association, pp. 3–27.

Norcross, J.C. (2002) (ed), *Psychotherapy Relationships that Work*. New York: Oxford University Press.

Pincus, H.A. and McQueen, L. (2002) 'The limits of an evidence-based classification of mental disorders', in M.D. Sadler and Z. John (eds), *Descriptions and Prescriptions: Values, Mental Disorders, and the DSMs*. Baltimore, MD: Johns Hopkins University Press, pp. 9–24.

Rounsaville, B.J., Alarcon, R.D., Andrews, G., Jackson, J.S., Kendell, R.E. and Kendler, K. (2002) 'Basic nomenclature issues for DSM-V', in D.J. Kupfer, M.B. First and D.E. Regier (eds), *A Research Agenda for DSM-V*. Washington, DC: American Psychiatric Association, pp. 2–29.

Samuel, D.B. and Widiger, T.A. (2004) 'Clinicians' personality descriptions of prototypic personality disorders', *Journal of Personality Disorders*, 18(3): 286–308.

Schneider, W., Buchheim, P., Cierpka, M., Dahlbender, R.W., Freyberger, H.J., Grande, T., Hoffmann, S.O., Jannssen, P.L., Küchenhoff, J., Muhs, A., Rudolf, G., Rüger, U. and Schüssler, G. (2002) 'Operationalized psychodynamic diagnostics: A new diagnostic approach in psychodynamic psychotherapy', in M.L. Malik and L.E. Beutler (eds), *Rethinking the DSM: A Psychological Perspective*. Washington, DC: American Psychological Association, pp. 177–200.

Schroeder, M.L., Wormworth, J.A. and Livesley, W.J. (1992) 'Dimensions of personality disorder and their relationship to the Big Five Dimensions of personality', *Psychological Assessment*, 4(1): 47–53.

Shedler, J. and Westen, D. (2004a) 'Refining personality disorder diagnosis: Integrating science and practice', *The American Journal of Psychiatry*, 161(8): 1350–65.

Shedler, J. and Westen, D. (2004b) 'Dimensions of personality pathology: An alternative to the Five-Factor Model', *The American Journal of Psychiatry*, 161(10): 1743–54.

Skodol, A.E., Gunderson, J.G., Shea, M.T., McGlashan, T.H., Morey, L.C., Sanislow, C.A., Bender, D.S., Grilo, C.M., Zanarini, M.C., Yen, S., Pagano, M.E. and Stout, R.L. (2005) 'The Collaborative Longitudinal Personality Disorders Study (CLPS): Overview and implications', *Journal of Personality Disorders*, 19(5): 487–504.

Skodol, Oldham, Shea, M.T., Zanarini, M.C., Sanislow, C.A., Grilo, C.M., McGlashan, T.H. and Gunderson, J.G. (2005) 'Dimensional representations of DSM-IV personality disorders: Relationships to functional impairment', *The American Journal of Psychiatry*, 162(10): 1919–25.

Smith, T.L., Barrett, M.S., Benjamin, L.S. and Barber, J.P. (2006) 'Relationship factors in treating personality disorders', in L.G. Castonguay and L.E. Beutler (eds), *Principles of Therapeutic Change that Work*. New York: Oxford University Press, pp. 219–38.

Smith, M.L., Glass, G.V. and Miller, T.I. (1980) *The Benefits of Psychotherapy*. Baltimore: John Hopkins University Press.

Spitzer, R.L. (1983) 'Psychiatric diagnosis: Are clinicians still necessary?', *Comprehensive Psychiatry*, 24(5): 399–411.

Sprock, J. (2003) 'Dimensional versus categorical classification of prototypic and nonprototypic cases of personality disorder', *Journal of Clinical Psychology* 59(9): 991–1014.

Tyrer, P. (2000) (ed), *Personality Disorders: Diagnosis, Management, and Course* (2nd edn). London: Arnold.

Verheul, R. (2005) 'Clinical utility of dimensional models for personality pathology', *Journal of Personality Disorders*, 19(3): 283–302.

Watson, D. and Clark, L.A. (2006) 'Clinical diagnosis at the crossroads', *Clinical Psychology: Science and Practice* 13(3): 210–15.

Watson, D., Wiese, D., Vaidya, J. and Tellegen, A. (1999) 'The two general activation systems of affect: Structural findings, evolutionary considerations, and psychobiological evidence', *Journal of Personality and Social Psychology*, 76(5): 820–38.

Westen, D.W., Heim, A.K., Morrison, K., Patterson, M. and Campbell, L. (2002) 'Simplifying diagnosis using a prototype-matching approach: Implications for the next edition of the DSM', in M.L. Malik and L.E. Beutler (eds), *Rethinking the DSM: A Psychological Perspective*. Washington,

DC: American Psychological Association, pp. 221–50.

Westen, D. and Shedler, J. (1999) 'Revising and assessing Axis II, part I: Developing a clinically and empirically valid assessment method', *The American Journal of Psychiatry*, 156(2): 258–72.

Widiger, T.A. (1992) 'Categorical versus dimensional classification: Implications from and for research', *Journal of Personality Disorders*, 6(4): 287–300.

Widiger, T.A. and Samuel, D.B. (2005) 'Diagnostic categories or dimensions? A question for the *Diagnostic and Statistica Manual of Mental Disorders – Fifth Edition*', *Journal of Abnormal Psychology*, 114(4): 494–504.

Widiger, T.A. and Simonsen, K. (2005) 'Alternative dimensional models of personality disorder: Finding a common ground',

Journal of Personality Disorders, 19(2): 110–30.

Widiger, T.A., Simonsen, E., Krueger, R., Livesley, W.J. and Verheul, R. (2005) 'Personality disorder research agenda for the DSM-V', *Journal of Personality Disorders*, 19(3): 315–38.

Wiggins, J.S. (2003) *Paradigms of Personality Assessment*. New York: Guilford.

Zanarini, M.,C., Frankenburg, F.R., Hennen, J., Reich, D.B. and Silk, K.R. (2005) 'The McLean Study of Adult Development (MSAD): Overview and implications of the first six years of prospective follow-up', *Journal of Personality Disorders*, 19(5): 505–23.

Zuckerman, M. (2002) 'Zuckerman-Kuhlman Personality Questionnaire (ZKPQ): An alternative five-factorial model', in B. de Raad and M. Perugini (eds), *Big Five Assessment*. Kirkland, WA: Hogrefe and Huber, pp. 377–97.

30

Personality and Treatment Planning for Psychotherapy: The Systematic Treatment Selection Model

Gary Groth-Marnat, Elisa Gottheil, Weiling Liu,
David A. Clinton and Larry E. Beutler

INTRODUCTION

A crucial question facing professional psychologists is understanding why people change and what can be done to enhance it. One approach has been to research common factors such as the quality of the therapeutic alliance, as for example the work of Lambert (1992). Another has been to understand specific treatments tailored toward a specific diagnosis, as for example the descriptions of research-supported treatments for different diagnostic groups by Nathan and Gorman (2002). In contrast, the focus of this chapter will be to review various client factors that have been found to be relevant in both understanding change as well as tailoring psychotherapeutic interventions.

In the early years of psychotherapy, folklore emerged related to which types of clients would and would not benefit from psychotherapy. Such factors included the importance of the client being 'psychologically minded', having a 'high level of motivation', or not being 'resistant'. It was believed that if these qualities were absent, the client would not be a good candidate for therapy. Over 200 possible client characteristics have been identified of which approximately 100 have been researched. This research has identified that the most relevant characteristics include coping style, reactance, problem complexity, functional impairment, social support, and subjective distress (Beutler and Clarkin, 1990; Beutler et al., 2000a).

A further line of research has been to investigate the extent to which psychotherapy in general is effective. The classic meta-analysis by Smith et al. (1980) found that indeed persons receiving psychotherapy were more improved than those who did not. This finding has been replicated in numerous meta-analytic and single studies. However, this early data reported summarized or averaged results and did little to investigate the mechanisms, including personality factors, underlying change. It later became clear that some types of clients would improve with certain interventions and yet others, with different characteristics, would not improve using these same interventions. As a result of identifying the relevant characteristics, it could be determined who would and who would not benefit from certain types of treatment. This sort of analysis goes above and beyond summarized data to provide a more nuanced understanding of principles of change.

An important rationale for the above client matching approach was to determine its relative importance in understanding and predicting client outcome from psychotherapy. Research indicates that, when matching interventions with client characteristics is combined with the quality of the therapeutic relationship, up to 90% of the variance can be accounted for (Beutler et al., 1999; Beutler et al. 2000b). When the quality of the therapeutic relationship is evaluated in isolation, it only accounts for between 7% and 30% of the variance (Horvath and Symonds, 1991; Lambert, 1992). A contrasting approach is to consider the variance accounted for by matching client diagnosis with type of treatment. Since this follows the medical model typified by medicine, it is often believed that this is a highly effective means of treatment planning. However, research indicates that it only accounts for 10% of the variance in treatment outcome (Lambert, 1992; Wampold et al., 1997). Thus, tailoring treatment according to diagnosis seems to be far less useful than tailoring treatment according to client characteristics.

The underlying theme is that psychotherapy outcome can be increased when there is an optimal *fit* between the client's personality and various strategies of psychotherapy. For example, a therapist might adjust what they do based on the extent the client can tolerate external control, whether they are likely to benefit from symptom removal as opposed to insight-oriented approaches, or whether they

need to increase versus decrease their level of arousal as a means of optimizing motivation. Each of these choices can be guided by relevant personality variables the most important ones being functional impairment, social support, problem complexity/chronicity, coping style, and traits related to resistance.

A crucial feature of the STS model is accurate assessment of clients prior to commencing therapy. A variety of instruments can be useful including the Minnesota Multiphasic Personality Inventory-2, Personality Assessment Inventory, the DSM-IV-TR Global Assessment of Functioning, Beck Depression Inventory-II, Millon Clinical Multiaxial Inventory-III, Sarason Social Support Scale, and the Dowd Therapeutic Reactance Scale (see Groth-Marnat, 2003). Despite their potential value, the expectations of both clients and the healthcare system typically require more rapid assessment. One option is the paper–pencil rating scale which allows clinicians to rate relevant client characteristics (Systematic Treatment Selection-Clinician Rating Form; Beutler, 2001; Beutler et al., 2000a; Fisher et al., 1999). Ratings can be made on all available data regardless of whether this is based on interview, client records, formal tests, or information provided by informants. The psychometric properties of the STS-Clinician Rating Form have been found to be moderate to good (Beutler, 2001; Beutler et al., 2000; Fisher et al., 1999). For example inter-rater agreement on the STS-Clinician Rating Form was good ($\kappa = 0.89–0.90$) and correlations between clinicians rating clients independently and STS-based ratings were also good ($\kappa = 0.83–0.85$). Convergent validity based on correlations with formal tests was moderate (i.e. MMPI-2 scores for internalization were 0.42; Millon Clinical Multiaxial Inventory-III ratings for internalization were 0.75). Thus the STS-Clinician Rating Form shows promise for being a brief, accurate assessment tool for evaluating clients based on STS dimensions.

A computer program is available for each of the domains described below (see Beutler and

Williams, 1999; Harwood and Williams, 2003) that can evaluate relevant client characteristics, provide treatment recommendations, develop a narrative report (clinician as well as client oriented), and track client outcomes (see www.systematictreatmentselection.com). Incorporated into this program is the STS-Clinician Rating Form.

Above and beyond formal assessment, the STS model represents a way of prioritizing and thinking through the entire process of client care extending from initial contact to termination and follow-up. In particular, assessment can be refined to focus primarily on STS dimensions since these have been demonstrated to have the highest benefit for optimizing outcome. An interviewer might structure the intake interview in order to obtain relevant STS information. A therapist might also benefit from monitoring the progress of psychotherapy based on relevant STS domains. For example, if a client is not progressing in psychotherapy, the therapist might think through the therapist/client relationship dynamics by considering the client level of resistance (or complexity, coping style, etc.). This might lead to the realization that they have not been adapting their style to relevant personality characteristics (i.e. they might have been too directive and need to be more collaborative and egalitarian). It would also be important to insure that professional training focus on relevant STS dimensions along with the skills to competently work within this model (see Groth-Marnat et al., 2001). Since STS focuses on strategies of intervention and is eclectic, it might easily be adapted by most 'models' of psychotherapy (i.e. cognitive behavioral, humanistic, psychodynamic).

Whereas the above conceptualization has focused primarily on professional psychologists, the STS might also be expanded to include client/consumer awareness. In this case the responsibility might be on the client to develop self-assessment with a resulting self-awareness that can then be used to provide them with better tools on how they could most benefit from psychotherapy.

STS DIMENSIONS: DESCRIPTION, ASSESSMENT, AND TREATMENT IMPLICATIONS

The following information provides the core of the STS model by describing each dimension, summarizing assessment strategies, and discussing treatment implications. A summary of the various types of decisions based on these dimensions is included in Table 30.1.

Functional impairment

One of the most crucial levels of client evaluation relates to the extent they are impaired. Such an assessment should focus on objective indicators of difficulties related to family problems, social support, occupation, and social isolation/withdrawal (Beutler et al., 2000a). It should be stressed that *functional* impairment is not necessarily the same as *subjective* distress. For example, some clients do not feel particularly anxious or

Table 30.1 Summary of treatment implications for ratings on STS dimensions

Dimension	Treatment consideration
Functional impairment	Restrictiveness (inpatient/outpatient)
	Intensity (duration/frequency)
	Medical vs. psychosocial interventions
	Prognosis
	Urgency of providing symptom relief
Social support	Duration of treatment
	Psychosocial interventions vs. medication
	Cognitive behavioral vs. relationship enhancement
	Possible group interventions
Problem complexity/ chronicity	Resolution of thematic, unresolved conflicts vs. narrow symptom focus
Coping style	Internal, insight oriented vs. behavioral symptom oriented interventions
Resistance traits	Structured, directive vs. supportive, nondirective or paradoxical interventions
Distress level	Decrease/increase arousal

disturbed regarding their impairments (low subjective distress) and yet they are highly dysfunctional. This may include an antisocial personality who, as a result of their personality, experiences considerable difficulty working and sustaining relationships but feels little anxiety over these impairments. Additional examples might be persons with schizoid or autistic characteristics. For these reasons, the focus is on more objective indicators that the client is functioning poorly rather than subjective reports.

The determination of the extent of functional impairment will decide the frequency and intensity of treatment provided (Beutler et al., 2000a; Beutler and Harwood, 2000). Generally, mild and moderate impairment suggest limited treatment needs; whereas mild impairment questions whether or not treatment is warranted, moderate impairment might suggest time-limited interventions (Beutler and Harwood, 2000). These will most likely be psychosocial in nature and there will be less urgency to rapidly define and achieve specific, symptom-oriented goals. When levels of functional impairment are high, however, the following five areas of treatment need to be considered interdependently: (1) restrictiveness of treatment (inpatient versus different levels of treatment in outpatient care); (2) intensity of interventions (duration and frequency); (3) use of medical/somatic versus psychosocial interventions; (4) prognosis; and (5) the urgency of achieving initial goals (Beutler et al., 2003a).

Beutler and his colleagues (Beutler and Harwood, 2000; Gaw and Beutler, 1995) have summarized the relevant assessment dimensions of functional impairment to include the following: multiple impaired areas of performance in the client's daily life, general incapacity to function, difficulty interacting with the clinician, a problem that interferes with the client's ability to function during the interview, poor concentration during assessment tasks, and level of distraction by minor events. There are also several structured means of obtaining useful information related to functional impairment

(Gaw and Beutler, 1995; Groth-Marnat, 2003) in particular the computerized program mentioned above (www.systematic treatmentselection.com). These are:

- A mental status examination.
- *Diagnostic and Statistical Manual-IV-TR* (APA, 2000) specific type of diagnoses. Functional impairment is likely to be more severe if there are diagnoses on both Axis I and II, and if there is the presence of severe disorders in the psychotic domain (schizophrenia, bipolar).
- Global Assessment of Functioning (GAF) scale of the *Diagnostic Statistical Manual-IV-TR* (APA, 2000).
- The presence of elevated scales on the Minnesota Multiphasic Personality Inventory-2/Minnesota Multiphasic Personality Inventory-A, especially on the right side of the profile (paranoia, schizophrenia, hypomania).
- The Beck Depression Inventory-II when scores are 30 or above.
- General elevations on the Millon Clinical Multiaxial Inventory-III scales, particularly on the severe personality pathology or severe syndrome scales.
- A high number of reported problems (T above 63) on the Brief Symptom Inventory (Derogatis, 1992).
- High scores on the trait anxiety scale of the State-Trait Anxiety Inventory (Spielberger et al., 1983).

Social support

Level of environmental support refers to the presence and quality of the relationships available to the person in terms of family and friends. On one end of the spectrum, the person feels respected by family and friends and can also trust and confide in them. In particular, she/he feels an integral part of his or her family network and has a number of friends with common interests. On the other end, the person is experiencing differing degrees of loneliness and abandonment from family and friends. The importance of these external means of support is that they can often modify the impact of other forms of stressors. High social support has been associated with a shorter duration of therapy. Indeed, long-term intervention may even be contraindicated. High social support has also been associated with a favorable response to treatment (Mallinckrodt, 1996), the ability to maintain the gains made through treatment (Zlotnick et al., 1996), and with gains that are achieved in a shorter period of time (Moos, 1990). In addition, high social support is a good predictor of positive treatment outcome for substance abuse disorders (where secure forms of employment represent the high social support variable; Beutler and Harwood, 2000). Clients with high social support have also been found to respond better to therapies that enhance and rely on their existing social support rather than utilize more individually oriented interventions such as cognitive and behavioral therapies (Beutler et al., 2000b). In contrast, low social support has been associated with requiring more time to benefit from treatment and with pharmacological interventions (Beutler et al., 2000b). In these cases, cognitive behavioral therapy is more effective than therapies that enhance relationships. However, it is also possible that a supportive group intervention should be used to provide enough support to activate interpersonal types of therapies.

The following are formal strategies for assessing social support:

- The Social Support Questionnaire (Sarason et al., 1983).
- Minnesota Multiphasic Personality Inventory-2/Minnesota Multiphasic Personality Inventory -2) scales provide valuable information regarding social supports:
  - Social introversion (0). High scores suggest a person who may find it difficult to have a large network of friends.
  - Paranoia (6) and schizophrenia (8). Elevations in these scales suggest that the number and quality of social supports may be low.
  - Hypochondriasis (1) and hysteria (3). High scores in these scales may indicate that even though the number of supports may be high, the quality is poor.
- Millon Clinical Multiaxial Inventory-III elevations may also provide useful information regarding social supports:
  - High scores on schizoid, avoidant, schizotypal, paranoid, and thought disorder scales indicate

low number as well as poor quality of social support.
- Dependent, histrionic, narcissistic, passive-aggressive (negativistic), self-defeating, and borderline scales may have moderate to high social supports but these supports are likely to be conflicted, through such issues as tension between autonomy and dependency, fear, anxiety, need for admiration, or covert hostility.

Problem complexity/chronicity

It is common sense to assume that the more complex an individual's symptoms, the more complicated and time consuming their treatment would become. This dimension, however, is not as simple as it initially seems. Complexity itself can be related to issues of co-morbidity, enduring personality disturbances, and recurrence of their symptoms (Beutler et al. 2000b). It reflects the multiplicity and recurrence of problems and their pattern of change over time (Beutler and Groth-Marnat, 2003). Problem complexity can be determined through an evaluation of the individual's symptoms, with the simple understanding that the more numerous the symptoms and the more pervasive their developmental pattern, the more complex the treatment. However, the chronicity of their symptoms must also be taken into the evaluation; the complexity of an individual's symptoms is highly correlated with the chronicity of their distress (Beutler and Groth-Marnat, 2003).

Issues of chronicity can raise an individual's level of distress, enforce an acceptance of their symptoms, impede their motivational efforts and reduce their belief in their ability to change. In a review of the literature on anxiety symptoms, Newman et al. (2006) found that the duration of the illness, history of psychiatric services, and age of symptom onset all were predictors of therapeutic outcome. Specifically, the longer the duration of the illness, the greater history of psychiatric services, and the younger the onset of symptoms, all indicate negative prognostic factors (Newman et al., 2006). In an earlier review by

Beutler et al. (2000b), 23 studies were evaluated using depression relevant factors. The results of this review lead to the development of two principles relating to the complexity and chronicity of an individual's symptoms: (1) high problem complexity should favor the effects of a broad-band treatment, both of a psychosocial and a medical type; and (2) pharmacotherapy, though not necessarily psychotherapy, achieves its greatest efficacy among patients with complex and chronic depressive symptoms. Both such principles argue for the need for multi-modal treatments for individuals with complex and/or chronic problems. Such evidence suggests that both chronicity and complexity of psychological distress is related to the severity and the extent of required treatments.

There are a number of informal and formal means of assessing complexity/chronicity, outlined as follows.

- *Diagnostic interview.* The most efficient method of determining an individual's level of complexity and chronicity, this includes information on the circumstances under which the symptoms were first noticed, how those symptoms were initially explained, the frequency and nature of the circumstances that evoked the problem, any changes over time that have occurred in the behaviors, family history, history of problem development, remission and recurrence, and resolution can indicate different prognostic outcomes (see Beutler and Groth-Marnat, 2003). Note that recently developed and single-episode problems have a better prognosis while longer periods of reduced functioning indicates a poorer outcome (Beutler and Groth-Marnat, 2003).
- *Millon Clinical Multiaxial Inventory-III.* The presence of clear personality disorders, co-morbid Axis I and Axis II conditions.

Coping style

Coping style can be defined as a personal quality that comprises the typical and usual way an individual interacts with others and responds to a threatened loss of safety and well-being (Beutler and Harwood, 2000). These patterns of responding are stable over time and occur upon a continuum, rather than distinct states of existence. Systematic treatment selection adopts the principle that an individual's coping style is an enduring propensity or disposition that characterizes their interpersonal interactions (Beutler and Harwood, 2000). Coping styles are invoked during experiences in which the individual is attempting to achieve a desired goal or attempting to avoid an unwanted, negative experience (Beutler and Harwood, 2000).

According to the systematic treatment selection model, coping styles range from an internalizing personal style to an externalizing one. An internalizing coping style incorporates concepts such as introversion, obsessiveness, inhibition, inner directedness, and restraint or control (Beutler et al., 2000a). In contrast, an externalizing coping style includes characteristics such as extroversion, impulsivity, sociopathy, and projection (Beutler et al., 2000). In summary, individuals who tend to view the cause of their problems or distress as being internal to themselves can be classified as possessing an internalizing coping style, whereas individuals who project the causes of their problems as being external to themselves have a decidedly externalizing coping style.

Beutler et al. (2000) reviewed a number of studies in the depression literature and determined two overall guiding principles in regards to incorporating coping style into treatment planning: (1) externalizing coping styles indicate the use of interventions designed to directly affect symptoms or build skills; and (2) internalizing coping styles indicate the use of interventions designed to enhance insight and awareness. The basis of these principles should be plainly obvious: interventions asking an externalizing individual to make changes inside themselves and the ways in which they interact with the world would not be effective considering that they do not see themselves as being a casual factor in their distress. Similarly, internalizing individuals already see their own internal states and interactions as playing a casual role thus enacting change and promoting insight would be more effective than teaching such an individual external behavioral coping strategies. In some cases, however, the preferred style is not clearly defined since the client uses both external and internal coping styles. For example, a client with overcontrolled hostility might intermittently externalize their anger but, for the most part, works to control and internalize it.

Both clinical interviews and formal assessment procedures can assist in evaluating a client's preferred coping style.

- *Clinical interview.* Self-reported and observed interpersonal and intrapersonal information, inquire how the individual conceptualizes their problems and to whom they attribute responsibility, determine how the individual reacts around others (Beutler and Groth-Marnat, 2003).
- *Minnesota Multiphasic Personality Inventory-2.* An externalizing style is suggested by elevations on psychopathic deviance (4), paranoia (6), and mania (9). In contrast, an internalizing style is indicated by high scores on depression (2), psychasthenia (7), and social introversion (0).
- *Millon Clinical Multiaxial Inventory-III.* Externalizing styles are indicated by elevations on histrionic, antisocial, aggressive/sadistic, and paranoid; internalizing styles are suggested by high scores on avoidant, depressive, dependent, and compulsive.

Resistance traits

Interpersonal reactance, and its more general but less extreme form 'resistance', are concepts that are used to describe an interpersonal reaction by an individual to the perceived loss of a freedom or right (i.e. some form of interpersonal control). Each individual has developed through his or her life a sense of freedom, a sense of control, over an inherently uncontrollable world. Resistance is thus a defensive formation that people create in order to cope with external events, regardless of the fact that this sense of freedom is an inherently false or tenuous state (Beutler and Clarkin, 1990). As such, when this self-perceived state of control or freedom

is threatened, the individual forms a resistant reaction toward that threat in order to maintain their sense of control. Thus, resistance occurs when an individual's sense of freedom, image of self, safety, psychological integrity, or power is threatened (Beutler and Hardwood, 2000a).

When forming a conceptualization of an individual's level of resistance, it is important to note that reactant behaviors are a result of enduring traits and situation induced reactions; it has both state and trait characteristics and needs to be evaluated and treated based upon the type of resistance incurred (Beutler and Harwood, 2000). Resistant *traits* are ones that are stable, cross-situational dispositions, or reactions to vulnerabilities and threats whereas resistant *states* are a function of the particular constraints of the individual's immediate environment and interpersonal interactions (Beutler and Harwood, 2000).

Reviews of the literature have consistently supported the use of tailoring interventions according to a client's level of trait-like resistance. Beutler et al. (2000) performed an extensive search of the available literature on the subject of resistance. The assumption behind their review, based upon the empirical evidence for using patient resistance in treatment planning and implementation, was that similar guidelines regarding reactance could be used throughout a wide variety of diagnostic groups (Beutler et al., 2000). This review comprised 31 studies of samples related to, or involving, depressed individuals. Through this review they were able to draw two conclusions: (1) minimally structured, self-directed interventions, non-directive procedures, or paradoxical directives are effective among patients who are highly prone to interpersonal resistance; and (2) directive treatment interventions and clinician guidance are advantageous to patients who have low resistance tendencies (Beutler et al., 2000; see also Horvath and Goheen, 1990).

A firm understanding of the concept of resistance is doubly important when treating an individual in a therapeutic setting.

The process of psychotherapy inherently clashes with an individual's perceived sense of freedom either intentionally or simply by accident. Due to the inevitability of reactance formation, adequate assessment of the level of individual reactance is essential for psychotherapy to be effective. Resistance levels can be assessed using the following measures:

- *Clinical interview.* High levels of resistance can be inferred through behaviors and cues that include frequent resentment of others, enjoyment of competition, attempts to 'get even' with others when provoked (Beutler and Groth-Marnat, 2003).
- *Dowd Therapeutic Reactance Scale (DOWD-TRS)* (Dowd et al., 1991). Scores above 68.
- *Minnesota Multiphasic Personality Inventory-2.* Elevations on negative treatment indicators (difficulty trusting and disclosing to health professionals), psychopathic deviance-2 subscale (authority problems), type A-2 subscale (competitive drive), or dominance (need to be in control)
- *Systematic Treatment Selection-Clinician's Rating Form.* Rating for resistance (Fisher et al., 1999) and www.systematictreatmentselection.com.

Distress level

While subjective distress and level of impairment have frequently been confounded, a patient's distress represents an internal state rather than objective performance. At times, level of functional impairment can be the same as subjective distress but at other times they can be quite different. The practical importance of this is that the relative elevation of these two variables can have different implications for treatment (Beutler and Clarkin, 1990). Subjective distress is manifested primarily in heightened anxiety, confusion, or depression (Beutler and Harwood, 2000). Subjective distress is relatively independent of specific diagnoses and represents transient states of well-being.

The variations of levels of distress and their manifestations vary in their utility for treatment, so there is an optimum window of distress clinicians should try to achieve. If a client's distress becomes too high, the person has difficulty appropriately processing information and concentrating. Not only will it be disruptive and result in a deteriorated ability to function, but it will also interfere with the problem solving and behavioral experimentation required in therapy. A client whose level of subjective distress is too low will have difficulty becoming engaged in actively working to change behavior. A moderate level of subjective distress can lead to cognitive improvements including enhanced memory, faster performance, and higher intellectual efficiency. This is useful because it motivates a client to become involved with change.

The correlation of subjective distress to such variables as type or style of treatment, commitment, and participation in treatment suggest that moderate distress may be necessary to sustain commitment and participation in treatment. The presence of high initial distress may be an indicator for the use of supportive and self-directed therapy but bears no relationship to the effectiveness of active and therapist-guided interventions. High distress may also be an indicator for interpersonally focused interventions, perhaps including group or family formats.

Assessment of subjective distress can be based on the following:

- Clinical interview. Behavioral observations and examining relevant history are two of the best methods of monitoring a client's distress levels. High distress is expressed by motor agitation, high emotional arousal, poor concentration, unsteady voice, autonomic symptoms, hyperventilation, excited affect, and intense feelings (Beutler and Harwood, 2000; Gaw and Beutler, 1995); low levels of distress are indicated by reduced motor activity, poor emotional investment in treatment, low energy level, blunted or constricted affect, slow speech, unmodulated verbalizations, and the absence of symptoms. Patient distress is also ordinarily assessed through patient self-reports.
- *Beck Depression Inventory-II* (BDI; Beck et al., 1996). Scores above 29 suggest high levels of subjective distress.

- *Symptom Checklist-90R* (Derogatis, 1994). Scores above 75
- *State Trait Anxiety Inventory (STAI)* (Spielberger et al., 1983).

PRINCIPLES OF THERAPEUTIC CHANGE THAT WORK

Born from the desire to establish broad principles of change derived from empirical research, the Task Force on Therapeutic Principles that Work sought the answers to several questions, primary among them: What is known about the nature of the participants, relationships, *and* procedures within treatment that induces positive effects across theoretical models? And how do factors related to these domains work together to enhance change? (Castonguay and Beutler, 2006). The specific goals of the task force comprised an attempt to integrate participant, relationship, and treatment factors while at the same time creating working principles that were supported by empirical research. These principles were to provide effective guidelines for planning and implementing treatment, while not being tied to any one particular therapeutic model. A wide number of principles were extracted and summarized. These related to participant (client) characteristics, the therapeutic relationship, and technique factors. The principles that are most relevant to participant characteristics are summarized:

1. Clients with high levels of impairment are associated with less benefit from treatment when compared with clients who begin treatment with better levels of functioning.
2. Clients who begin therapy with high levels of impairment do better when offered intensive, long-term treatment than when they are given brief, non-intensive treatment (regardless of the type/model of treatment). Patients with low impairment do equally well with either low or high intensive treatment.
3. Perceived levels of social support are positive predictors of treatment benefit. Absence of either actual or perceived social support may be indicative of the severity of the problem and the degree of experienced impairment (e.g. co-morbidity and personality disorders). Evidence is inconsistent as to whether efforts to improve social support add benefit to the effects of treatment across problem areas. In depression, improving social support adds some benefit, suggesting that it may be a specific treatment factor.

4. Patients who conceptualize their problems as being due to an outside source (external blame) and are gregarious and impulsive are more likely to benefit from direct behavioral change and symptom reduction (i.e. building new skills, managing impulses) rather than interventions that emphasize self-awareness and insight.
5. Patients who are reflective (non-impulsive) use self-inspection, and are overcontrolled and indecisive improve the most with interventions that focus on insight, self-understanding, improving interpersonal attachments, and building self-esteem than interventions that emphasize building new social skills and focus on directly reducing symptoms.
6. Treatments are most effective when they avoid activating client resistance.
7. Directive treatments should be used for clients with low resistance and non-directive or paradoxical interventions should be used with clients who have a high level of resistance.
8. Anxious clients who also attribute their anxiety to external (rather than internal) factors (low internal locus of control) and who have negative self-attributions are likely to have less improvement than those who perceive their anxiety as due to internal factors and have more positive attributions.
9. Patients who have had early significant interpersonal problems are likely to have difficulties responding to and benefiting from psychotherapy
10. Positive client expectations are likely to enhance the likelihood of benefiting from psychotherapy for clients with substance abuse. Information is lacking on the effects of patient expectations in the treatment of personality disorder. Interestingly, however, expectations do not appear to be associated with outcome in the treatment of depression.
11. Patients who have been diagnosed with a personality disorder are less likely to benefit from therapy than those who have not been diagnosed with a personality disorder.
12. Among patients with a personality disorder or who experience depression, therapist flexibility in changing strategies, adapting to patient

presentations, tolerance, and creativity are related to improvement. In the treatment of depression, for example, this refers to the importance for the therapist to be open, informed, and tolerant of religious views. There is little data on this cluster of variables among other disorders, but it is logical to suggest that it represents a general phenomenon.

13 The effectiveness of therapy is not substantially benefited by a therapist who has had a personal experience with the same type of problem as the patient. Openness and tolerance on the part of the therapist are more important than shared experience. This has been documented in the treatment of substance use but it is likely that this is a general phenomenon.

14 Therapists who have secure attachment patterns have better success than those who do not. Success is also optimal with therapists who are comfortable with long-term emotionally intense relationships.

15 Therapists who have the following characteristics tend to have the best outcomes: tolerance to his/her own negative feelings regarding the treatment process and the client, openmindedness, flexibility, and creativity.

16 Patient pretreatment readiness for change is a reliable predictor of benefit in substance abuse disorders and likely to be involved in other problem areas, but research is largely absent. However, there is little evidence to suggest that efforts to alter one's readiness contribute substantially to benefit.

17 Among most problems, especially among patients with depression, anxiety, or personality disorders, the patient's attachment/interpersonal style interferes with the process of change and/or outcome. Prognosis is best among those with social approach or non-avoidant styles.

The incorporation of these principles into a systematic treatment model would allow for a further elaboration of our understanding in regards to the factors that a client brings with them to the therapeutic process. When used in conjunction with the STS, both sets of principles provide a large base of knowledge with which to plan, implement, and manage a variety of potential factors into the therapeutic process. All of which promote progress toward the goal of integrating treatment variables regardless of therapeutic orientation and allowing for the maximization of positive outcomes in therapy.

CASE EXAMPLE

M is a 27-year-old Italian-American married female. She is currently a graduate student working toward her MSc in counseling psychology and working as a clinical manager in a transitional home for disabled individuals. M is also 6 months pregnant. She reports having 'a lot of anxiety'. Given the information provided, she was given a provisional diagnosis of generalized anxiety *disorder* (300.02, DSM-IV).

M grew up in the United States. Her mother and father are of Italian descent. She has three siblings, two older sisters and a younger brother. Her father was a laborer and her mother had multiple jobs. M's mother was rarely home because she worked during the day and night. Thus, M reports not having a strong relationship with her mother. M stated that her father's work ethic was strong and she takes after him. M reported having worked since she was 16 years old as it was expected of her. M reported that she was brought up in a traditional Italian home where 'men go out and work, come home, and do nothing while women do everything.' M stated that this cultural belief, which is held by both her and her husband, has been highly anxiety provoking. M also believes that since she is a woman, she should be able to do everything without praise or acknowledgment. At the same time she stated that she would appreciate it if she were acknowledged for her accomplishments. M stated she is under considerable pressure from school, work, and tries to control everything around the house. She stated she needs help from her husband but he 'shuts down when he comes home from work'.

M has a history of anxiety and panic attacks. M's range of physical symptoms include shakiness, dizziness, shortness of breath, sweating, and then passing out. She reported having panic attacks since she was 15 or 16. These have occurred on an average of once or twice a month. M stated the pregnancy has helped her control her stress better since she allows herself to relax since she does not want her level of stress to affect the baby. As a result, she currently is experiencing less anxiety than prior to her pregnancy. She sought treatment to find techniques and tools to help with her anxiety because she 'suffers from a lot of anxiety'. M stated that even though she has anxiety-related symptoms, she still perseveres with tasks until she has to stop because she 'keels over and needs to stop physically'. M stated she is often overwhelmed when thinking about how she can actually get everything done. Sometimes, she has difficulty speaking because she feels unable to keep up with what she is thinking about. M reported not being concerned about death because she is too young to die of a heart attack. However, she is 'worried about passing out and hitting my head on something'. M identifies work, school, and home as triggers to her anxiety. M believes that she

needs to complete everything on her own without help because 'that is what an Italian woman should be able to do'. When asked to give up some of the load of her work, she saw it as weakness. She was unable to identify any responsibilities that she can designate to others. She states, 'I don't see how change can help.' M asserted that 'I am stuck. I am a person that wants things to change but am not willing to change. I just don't see how to do any of that.'

A clinical interview was conducted to gain further insight into the exact nature of M's distress. Formal assessment tools were also administered to provide more information about the patient's patterns of behaving, feeling, and thinking associated with the maintenance of problems. In order to develop an optimal treatment program, the assessment results were organized on dimensions of the STS (demographic information, coping style, functional impairment, resistance, level of distress, and complexity/chronicity). As suggested in Figure 30.1, M's coping style is characterized by lower than average

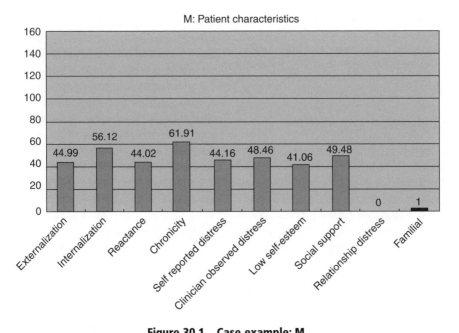

Figure 30.1   Case example: M

(for psychiatric outpatients) levels of both externalizing and internalizing patterns. This suggests that her defenses are well modulated, a perspective that is confirmed by the low levels of self-reported and clinician observed distress, both of which are below the outpatient mean by almost one standard deviation. Problems with self-esteem are also low, further confirming the mild nature of her current difficulties. It should be noted that, given that her problems are relatively mild, her defenses are moderate. Finally, M's social support levels are relatively high and her level of resistance (reactance) is relatively low (below the outpatient mean of $T = 50$), both of which further confirm her good prognosis and overall strengths. Thus, her assessment suggests a person with mild difficulties, stable defenses, and good social support. Her prognosis is good and her defenses are quite stable.

Following a thorough assessment, formulating a specific treatment plan that utilizes the principles of change outlined earlier in the chapter would be the next step. Given M's initial report of anxiety, a diagnosis of transitory adjustment disorder is suggested. Her expectations will likely play an important role in the change process. Therefore, an individually tailored treatment plan should incorporate strategies for raising her expectations for therapeutic change. In the absence of major difficulties with adjustment, it would seem that a treatment that emphasizes the healing power of the therapeutic relationship may be sufficient. Therapeutic change is likely to be greatest when the therapist is skillful and provides trust, acceptance, acknowledgement, collaboration, and respect for the patient within an environment that both supports and provides maximal safety. Moreover to fully optimize treatment, clear and explicit goals should be collaboratively made in order to allow M to understand and actively participate in her treatment.

If the foregoing proves to be insufficient, then an intervention that focuses on insight and self-awareness would be a good option, based on the nature of her internalizing defenses. Possible technical interventions in

the case of M would be: (1) identify some basic themes that characterize her relationship with family, friends, husband, and other significant people in her life; (2) associate these themes with the nature and specificity of core beliefs which may be dysfunctional or at the very least less than optimal; and (3) challenge her to explore new patterns that may break the rigidity of established themes. M's low resistance levels are likely to bode well for an active intervention in which the therapist can be challenging as well as supportive.

Improving M's ability to manage her emotional and cognitive processes may alleviate some of her anxiety symptoms. Finally, by helping M accept, tolerate, and fully experience her emotions in a safe environment may allow problematic responses to diminish or extinguish entirely. Throughout this process, working to facilitate incremental change and keeping M in a moderate level of arousal would best promote therapeutic outcomes.

DISCUSSION

The validity of STS is inherently tied to the validity of the various principles on which it is based. The principles themselves derive from a close inspection of the generality of research findings. There is no rigid adherence to any one or any collection of these principles and indeed they are constantly in the process of being revised and updated as data accumulates. For example, the original collection of principles by Beutler (1979) continue to form a base for the STS system, but they were expanded and updated in subsequent reviews by Beutler (1983), Beutler and Clarkin (1990), and Beutler et al. (2000). Each revision has both narrowed or deleted some principles and expanded the application of others. Most recently, the Task Force on Therapeutic Principles that work (Castonguay and Beutler, 2006) expanded the list of research-informed principles and separated them into categories based upon their relative value for different diagnostic groups of patients.

Independent validation of the principles was first undertaken by Beutler et al. (2000b) via an independent analysis of a combined sample of patients from five data sets, four of which were done as randomized clinical trial studies of psychotherapy outcome. Nine different models of intervention, including a drug treatment condition, were represented as well as a very wide range of patients and problems. This archival study was conducted as a prospective validation of the STS system. It gathered all intake interviews on nearly 300 patients in the original study, along with available intake data. Using the STS Clinician Rating Form, trained clinicians then identified the STS patient variables on all patients, remaining blind to their psychotherapy assignment, process, or outcome. The psychotherapy of these patients was then reviewed via audio and videotapes by trained psychotherapy raters who assigned the psychotherapy process dimensions that were identified as important in the STS system. Early and late sessions were reviewed on all patients. Outcomes were all based on the Beck Depression Scale and the Hamilton Depression Rating Scale administered by all of the original investigators using trained and independent clinicians. The outcomes supported the validity of both patient prognostic dimensions, therapeutic relationship factors, and treatment matching variables that had been independently identified in a comprehensive review of the research literature to that point.

A second prospective evaluation of the STS system was undertaken by Beutler et al. (2003a) on a sample of co-morbid stimulant abusing and depressed patients. Patients were randomly assigned to therapies and to therapists within therapies. Thus, they were also randomly assigned to different levels of 'fit' between patient and treatment offered. Analysis indicated that patient prognostic variables from the STS model predicted both end of treatment and follow up change, as did the STS treatment variables, relationship factors, and the dimensions of fit or match between patient and treatment factors. Each

domain, patient, treatment, relationship, and goodness of treatment fit, each added variance to the overall prediction of change at end of treatment and at follow-up. The STS variables, however, appeared to extract much of the power that is usually assigned or represented in the therapeutic relationship in accounting for change.

While, as these findings suggest, there are some conceptual and real-event benefits to constructing treatments around principles of change and common patient, treatment, relationship, and treatment fit qualities, the major advantages of this approach are yet to be realized. We are only beginning the process of integrating among the different principles that are embodied in these separate domains of predictors in order to construct a coherent treatment. Housley and Beutler (2007), for example, have recently proposed a treatment for the victims of mass trauma by applying the expanded list of STS principles drawn from the Task Force on Principles of Therapeutic Change that Work. This treatment is embodied within a treatment manual that integrates the use of cognitive therapy, behavior therapy, and relationship therapy techniques in working with patients who have been exposed to mass trauma.

The Housley and Beutler manual contrasts with the usual manual for working with targeted populations in several respects. For example, it is not focused on specific diagnoses like post-traumatic stress disorder (PTSD). It is focused on a range of effects that tend to follow disaster. That is, it follows the observation of research that the effects of mass trauma are very broad, rather than focusing solely on the narrow definition of PTSD that would follow from a diagnostic or theoretical view alone. Diagnostic logic, in other words, would (and does) result in a focus on PTSD, but epidemiological studies confirm that PTSD is only one of many results that occur following mass trauma (Gelea et al., 2005). Response to trauma comprises a large number of symptoms and problems, including anxiety, depression, PTSD symptoms, chemical abuse, and family distress, a point that is central to an integrative, principle-based approach to treatment. In this context, therefore, an approach based on research-informed principles rather than theoretically derived concepts of diagnosis and treatment is more targeted and truer to the form of the reactions that follow from an evoking event.

Following the STS logic, the principle-driven manual by Housley and Beutler (2007) incorporates a broad range of techniques drawn from several different models. The particular techniques are included because they have been demonstrated to be efficacious for different symptoms and problems, but they are only representative of those that can be incorporated by the principles employed. This ensures that the principle-driven approach will be more flexible than the usual diagnostically or theory-driven approach.

By combining principles with representative treatments, moreover, the Housley and Beutler manual incorporates a developmental perspective into treatment and identifies clusters of interventions that are likely to work at a given time and those that are not. These decisions follow the principles defined by the task force. Thus, principles that draw attention to the progressive nature of treatment emphasize the role of patient factors in determining prognosis and the early formation of relationship as an important factor. Following this logic, the three stages of intervention outlined by Housley and Beutler (2007) emphasizes principles that address patient factors in the first phase of treatment, those that optimize the therapeutic relationship in the second phase, and those that contribute to a fit of patient to treatment in the more advanced, third phase of treatment.

Such research as the foregoing provides a broad base of application for the STS model and opens doors for research and practice that cut across disorder, problem, theoretical model, and clinician. Many avenues for research and for modifying the applications and efficacy of the STS approach are just opening.

REFERENCES

American Psychiatric Association (2000) *Diagnostic and Statistical Manual of Mental Disorders-Text Revision* (4th edn). Washington, DC: APA.

Beck, A.T., Steer, R.A. and Brown, G.E. (1996) *BDI-II Manual*. San Antonio, CT: Psychological Corporation.

Beutler, L.E. (1979) 'Toward specific psychological therapies for specific conditions', *Journal of Consulting and Clinical Psychology*, 47(5): 882–97.

Beutler, L.E. (1983) *Eclectic Psychotherapy: A Systematic Approach*. New York: Pergamon.

Beutler, L.E. (2001) 'Comparisons among quality assurance systems: From outcome assessment to clinical utility', *Journal of Consulting and Clinical Psychology*, 69(2): 197–204.

Beutler, L.E. and Clarkin, J.F. (1990) *Systematic Treatment Selection: Towards Targeted Therapeutic Interventions*. New York: Bruner/Mazel.

Beutler, L.E., Albanese, A.L., Fisher, D., Karno, M., Sandowicz, M., Williams, O.B., Gallagher-Thompson, D. and Thompson, L. (1999 June) *'Selecting and Matching to Patient Variables'*, Paper presented at the annual meeting of the Society for Psychotherapy Research, Braga, Portugal.

Beutler, L.E., Clarkin, J.F. and Bongar, B. (2000a) *Guidelines for the Systematic Treatment of the Depressed Patient*. New York: Oxford.

Beutler, L.E. and Groth-Marnat, G. (2003) *Integrative Assessment of Adult Personality* (2nd edn). New York: Guilford.

Beutler, L.E. and Harwood, T.M. (2000) *Prescriptive Psychotherapy: A Practical Guide to Systematic Treatment Selection*. New York: Oxford.

Beutler, L.E., Harwood, T.M., Alimohamed, S. and Malik, M. (2003a) 'Functional impairment and coping style', in J.C. Norcross (ed.) *Psychotherapy Relationships that Work: Therapist Contributions and Responsiveness to Patient's Needs*. New York: Oxford University Press.

Beutler, L.E., Moleiro, C., Malik, M. and Harwood, M.T. (2000b) 'University of California Matching Study: First Findings', Paper presented at the Annual Meeting of the Society for Psychotherapy Research, Chicago.

Beutler, L.E., Moleiro, C., Malik, M., Harwood, T.M., Romanelli, R., Gallagher-Thompson, D. and Thompson, L. (2003a) 'A comparison of the Dodo, EST, and ATI indicators among co-morbid stimulant dependent, depressed patients', *Clinical Psychology and Psychotherapy*, 10(2): 69–85.

Beutler, L.E. and Williams, O. (1999) *Systematic Treatment Selection (STS). A Software Package for Treatment Planning*. Ventura, CA: Center for Behavioral Health Technology.

Castonguay, L.G. and Beutler, L.E. (2006) (eds), *Principles of Therapeutic Change that Work*. New York: Oxford.

Derogatis, L.R. (1992) *BSI: Administration, Scoring, and Procedures Manual-II* (2nd edn). Baltimore: Clinical Psychometric Research.

Derogatis, L.R. (1994) *SCL-90-R: Administration, Scoring, and Procedures Manual*. Minneapolis: National Computer Systems.

Dowd, E.T., Milne, C.R. and Wise, S.L. (1991) 'The Therapeutic Reactance Scale: A measure of therapeutic reactance', *Journal of Counseling and Development*, 69(6): 541–5.

Fisher, D., Beutler, L.E. and Williams, O.B. (1999) 'Making assessment relevant to treatment planning: The STS clinician rating form', *Journal of Clinical Psychology*, 55(7): 825–42.

Galea, S., Nandi, A. and Vlahov, D. (2005) 'The epidemiology of post-traumatic stress disorder after disasters', *Epidemiological Review*, 27(1): 78–91.

Gaw, K.F. and Beutler, L.E. (1995) 'Integrating treatment recommendations', in L.E. Beutler and M.R. Berren (eds), *Integrative Assessment of Adult Personality*. New York: Guilford, pp. 280–319.

Groth-Marnat, G. (2003) *Handbook of Psychological Assessment*. New Jersey: John Wiley & Sons.

Groth-Marnat, G., Roberts, R. and Beutler, L.E. (2001) 'Client characteristics and psychotherapy: Perspectives, support, interactions, and implications for training', *Australian Psychologist*, 36: 115–21.

Housley, J. and Beutler, L.E. (2007) *Treating Victims of Mass Trauma and Terrorism*. Gottengen: Hogrefe & Huber.

Horvath, A.O. and Goheen, M.D. (1990) 'Factors mediating the success of defiance- and compliance-based interventions', *Journal of Consulting and Clinical Psychology*, 37(4): 363–71.

Horvath, A.O. and Symonds, B.D. (1991) 'Relation between working alliance and outcome in psychotherapy: A meta-analysis', *Journal of Counseling Psychology*, 38(2): 139–49.

Harwood, M., and Williams, O.B. (2003) 'Identifying treatment-relevant assessment: Systematic Treatment Selection', in L.E. Beutler and Groth-Marnat, G. (eds), *Integrative Assessment of Adult Personality* (2nd edn). New York: Guilford.

Lambert, M.J. (1992) 'Psychotherapy outcome research: Implications for integrative and eclectic therapies', in J.C. Norcross and M.R. Goldfried (eds), *Handbook of Psychotherapy Integration*. New York: Basic Books, pp. 94–129.

Mallinckrodt, B. (1996) 'Change in working alliance, social support, and psychological symptoms in brief therapy', *Journal of Counseling Psychology*, 43(4): 448–55.

Moos, R.H. (1990) 'Depressed patients' life context, amount of treatment, and treatment outcome', *Journal of Nervous and Mental Diseases*, 178(4): 105–12.

Nathan, P.E. and Gorman, J.M. (2002) (eds), *A Guide to Treatments that Work* (2nd edn). New York: Oxford University Press.

Newman, M.G., Crits-Christoph, P., Gibbons, M.B. and Erickson, T.M. (2006) 'Participant factors in treating anxiety disorders', in L. Castonguay and L.E. Beutler (eds), *Empirically Supported Principles of Change*. New York: Oxford University Press, pp. 187–200.

Sarason, I.G., Levine, H.M., Basham, R.B. and Sarason, B.R. (1983) 'Assessing social support: The Social Support Questionnaire', *Journal of Personality and Social Psychology*, 44(4): 127–39.

Smith, M.L., Glass, G.V. and Miller, T.L. (1980) *The Benefits of Psychotherapy*. Baltimore: Johns Hopkins University Press.

Spielberger, C.D., Gorsuch R.L., Lushene, R., Vagg, P.R. and Jacobs, G.A. (1983) *Manual for the State-Trait Anxiety Inventory*. Palo Alto, CA: Consulting Psychologists Press.

Wampold, B.E., Mondin, G.W., Moody, M., Stitch, F., Benson, K. and Ahn, H. (1997) 'A meta-analysis of outcome studies comparing "bona fide" psychotherapies: Empirically, "All must have prizes"' *Psycholological Bulletin*, 122(3): 203–315.

Zlotnick, C., Shea, M.T., Pilkonis, P., Elkin, I. and Ryan, C. (1996) 'Gender of dysfunctional attitudes, social support, life events, and depressive symptoms over naturalistic follow-up', *American Journal of Psychiatry*, 153: 1021–7.

31

Personality and Health: Current Evidence, Potential Mechanisms, and Future Directions

Paula G. Williams, Timothy W. Smith and Matthew R. Cribbet

Research on the relationship between personality and physical health has a long and lively history characterized by growing support, healthy skepticism, and recurring methodological and conceptual challenges. Personality characteristics can confer either protection or vulnerability for illness, including life-threatening conditions. Indeed, the risk associated with some personality factors is equal to several well-established medical risk factors (Hampson et al., 2006). This research is a cornerstone of health psychology and behavioral medicine, and evidence that personality predicts health and longevity has helped revitalize personality research by challenging the critique of personality traits and measures as having limited predictive utility.

That stable individual differences in cognition, emotion, and behavior influence health is not surprising. Leading causes of morbidity and mortality (e.g. heart disease, cancer) involve repeated behaviors and prolonged exposure to particular environments, and personality clearly involves enduring processes. In this chapter, we provide an overview of the major associations between personality and health, framed within current thinking about the nature of personality and methodological issues inherent in examining associations with health. Additionally, potential mechanisms for personality–health relations are examined. Finally, we discuss how new frontiers in personality research, such as behavioral genetics and neuroscience, may play a role in our evolving understanding of how personality influences health.

CONCEPTUAL AND METHODOLOGICAL ISSUES

Research on personality and health requires sound conceptualization and measurement of the two components of the general hypothesis, and care in testing their association. These seemingly simple considerations have proven to be challenging throughout the history of the topic.

Conceptualization and measurement of personality

Many challenges in the study of personality and health would become more tractable through consistent incorporation of concepts and methods of current personality research. For example, many different personality characteristics have been studied, often with minimal attention to their overlap with previously studied traits. Basic measurement issues such as convergent and divergent validity are often given fleeting attention beyond an implicit assertion that scale labels accurately and specifically identify the constructs assessed. As a result, prior warnings that the field often reinvents previously identified risk factors under new labels (Holroyd and Coyne, 1987) or fails to identify basic dimensions of risk within an illusory diversity of personality constructs (Smith and Williams, 1992) remain relevant.

Three perspectives in personality science are valuable in addressing problems in conceptualization and measurement of personality in studies of health. Perhaps the most obvious, the five-factor model (FFM) is a generally accepted taxonomy (Digman, 1990) with well-validated measures (e.g. Costa and McCrae, 1992), providing a nomological net (Cronbach and Meehl, 1955) for comparing, contrasting, validating, and integrating the array of personality concepts and scales used to study physical health (Smith and Williams, 1992). The FFM is embedded in a psychometric tradition which includes well-established procedures for development and evaluation of measures (Ozer, 1999; West and Finch, 1997), an essential aspect of personality science that is inconsistently used in this research area. Examination of the associations of specific scales with the broad domains of the FFM, as well as the more

specific facets they comprise, would facilitate the identification of common dimensions of risk and resilience, and more specific differences in this regard, fostering a more systematic, integrated, and cumulative science of personality and health.

The FFM is maximally useful in clarifying *which* aspects of personality confer risk or resilience; it is less useful in describing *how* personality influences health. That is, trait taxonomies focus on characteristics that people *have* rather than things they *do* (Cantor, 1990), and the latter type of analysis is more useful in understanding the processes that might link personality with health-relevant changes in physiology. Although there have been important efforts to tie FFM traits to personality processes (e.g. McCrae and Costa, 1996), a second major aspect of personality science – the social-cognitive perspective (Mischel and Shoda, 1998) – is more useful in describing the processes through which enduring characteristics of individuals influence day-to-day adaptation in ways that could alter risk of disease.

The social-cognitive perspective has not achieved the same level of consensus as the FFM in terms of a taxonomy of these 'middle-units' of personality that lie between broad traits and specific behavior, though valuable descriptions of this domain have been offered (Mischel and Shoda, 1998). Examples of these active personality characteristics and processes include: mental representations of self, others, and relationships (i.e. schemas) or interaction sequences (i.e. scripts); motivational constructs such as expectancies, goals, and life tasks; appraisals, encodings, or attributions regarding people and situations; self-regulation and coping; and strategies, competencies and tactics in goal-directed action. In the social-cognitive perspective, personality is described through the content of such characteristics (e.g. positive vs. negative representations of others) and the connections or associations among them (i.e. easily activated negative schemas following appraisals of threat). A major tenet of the social-cognitive view is that the consistency of personality is best captured as patterns of behavioral response to variations in psychologically distinct situations (Mischel, 2004), rather than the pan-situational differences in behavior implied by broad trait models. In this view, 'if–then' patterns of specific situation-response profiles or 'behavioral signatures' (Mischel, 2004) are more accurate descriptions of individual differences. Whereas FFM traits describe broad regularities in behavior, elements of the social-cognitive approach provide a more specific and dynamic account of individual differences. These two approaches are complementary, and there are a growing number of integrative efforts examining social-cognitive correlates of FFM traits (e.g. Graziano et al., 1996). By articulating psychological mechanisms linking personality traits to health-relevant processes, the social-cognitive perspective might be particularly useful in the development of related interventions.

Studies of personality and health are a major component of the broader study of psychosocial influences on health. Psychosocial influences on health are typically separated into characteristics of people (i.e. personality traits) and characteristics of the social contexts they inhabit (e.g. chronic job stress, social isolation, conflict in close relationships). Yet, personality characteristics and health-relevant aspects of the social environment are reciprocally related; personality traits both predict and are predicted by experiences in personal relationships and at work (Roberts et al., 2003; Robins et al., 2002). Further, some social-environmental risk factors, such as social support, demonstrate stability over time and across situations, significant correlations with personality traits, and evidence of heritability in behavioral genetics research. That is, social-environmental risk factors often 'behave' like personality traits. Traditionally, personality research conceptualizes personality and social circumstances as separate sources of influence on behavior, emotion, and stress, which interact only statistically in

influencing these health-relevant responses (Endler and Magnusson, 1976). Yet personality characteristics influence exposure to health-relevant features of social environments at home and work, rather than only moderating responses to this hypothetically separate type of influence on physical health. The field's implicit separation of social-environmental and personality risk factors could impede the development of integrative models of risk and resilience.

In this regard, a third major perspective in current personality science – the interpersonal view (Kiesler, 1996; Pincus and Ansell, 2003) – can be valuable. In a foundational description of this approach, Sullivan defined personality as 'the relatively enduring pattern of interpersonal situations which characterize a human life' (1953: 111). In this approach, personality and social situations are reciprocally related, as they are in the social-cognitive perspective (Bandura, 1978; Mischel and Shoda, 1998). The particular concept that describes this reciprocal influence is the transactional cycle (Carson, 1969; Pincus and Ansell, 2003), in which intra-individual elements of personality (e.g. schemas, affect, expectancies, goals, appraisals) guide overt interpersonal behavior, as in the social-cognitive approach. The initial actor's overt behavior tends to influence the covert experience (e.g. affect, appraisals) of interaction partners so as to increase the likelihood that the partner will behave overtly in such a way as to complement or confirm the initial actor's expectations or beliefs. For example, given their negative expectations, characteristically suspicious persons are likely to behave in a cold or quarrelsome manner, increasing the likelihood that interaction partners will respond in kind rather than with expectancy-disconfirming warmth (Wagner et al., 1995). The resulting consistency in social interactions promotes stability in personality (Caspi et al., 1989; Smith and Spiro, 2002).

For individual differences in social behavior (i.e. personality traits) and aspects of the social situations, the interpersonal approach identifies two basic dimensions of social behavior. Friendliness or warmth versus hostility, quarrelsomeness, or coldness defines the affiliation axis of the interpersonal circumplex (IPC) (Kiesler, 1983; Wiggins, 1979), whereas dominance versus submissiveness defines the control axis. The IPC can be used (Gurtman and Pincus, 2003) to compare, contrast, and integrate personality traits studied as risk factors (Gallo and Smith, 1998), as well as social-environmental risk or resilience factors such as social support (Trobst, 2000), marital discord (Traupman et al., submitted), and interpersonal correlates of SES (Gallo et al., 2006). This function of the interpersonal approach can be enhanced with the version of the IPC that incorporates the FFM (Trapnell and Wiggins, 1990). The FFM traits of agreeableness versus antagonism and extraversion versus introversion are rotational equivalents of the IPC affiliation and dominance axes (McCrae and Costa, 1989). Hence, the interpersonal approach combines assets of the FFM and social-cognitive approaches in facilitating conceptually integrative and methodologically rigorous research on health, including both structural and dynamic issues.

In addition to methodological issues involving convergent and discriminant validity of personality measures, it is important to note that most studies rely on self-report measures of personality. In some instances, interview-based behavioral ratings or ratings provided by significant others are used, but this is an exception to the general rule of self-reports. Importantly, interview-based behavioral ratings and ratings by significant others are often stronger predictors of health endpoints and outcomes than self-report measures of personality are (Miller et al., 1996; Smith et al., 2007). Self-reports of personality and ratings by others converge significantly but modestly, and often are differentially related to important outcomes (e.g. Oltmanns and Turkhiemer, 2006). Hence, over-reliance on self-report assessments could be producing an inaccurate or at least incomplete account of personality traits as health risk factors, one that may in fact underestimate their importance.

Conceptualization and measurement of health outcomes

Studies of personality and health have examined many different health outcomes. Some are straightforward and obviously important, such as longevity among initially healthy persons or survival among those with established illness. The development and course of specific illness (e.g. coronary heart disease) are increasingly studied with well-grounded diagnostic methods. In particular, when used in prospective designs, these unambiguous health outcomes provide strong and clear tests of psychosomatic hypotheses. However, the study of personality and health has also included more ambiguous outcomes, such as self-rated health, symptom reports, and utilization of medical services. These outcomes are important; self-rated health predicts longevity (Idler and Benyamini, 1997) and both physical symptom reports and general perceptions of health are key components of quality of life (Ryff and Singer, 1998). Given daunting healthcare expenditures, personality predictors of utilization have obvious practical importance. Yet, each of these outcomes involves illness behavior (i.e. actions of people when they might be physically ill) rather than a direct measure of the underlying medical condition. There is a clear correspondence between disease and illness behavior, but they are not synonymous. Individuals sometimes engage in less illness behavior than expected on the basis of their underlying physical condition, as when a stoic denies symptoms. Others display excessive illness behavior, as in somatoform disorders. Hence, when outcomes mix actual health and illness behavior, it is unclear if personality is associated with the actual illness or only the illness behavior.

Testing associations between personality and health

Some studies of personality and health compare individuals with existing disease with healthy controls. These concurrent associations between personality and disease could reflect psychological responses to illness rather than potential causes (Cohen and Rodriguez, 1995), as when patients with cancer report more anxiety or depressive symptoms than healthy controls. Non-invasive imaging technologies (e.g. ultrasound measures of carotid artery atherosclerosis, CT scans of aortic or coronary artery calcification) can provide more informative cross-sectional tests, since health endpoints can be measured in persons who have no subjective or outward indication of disease. However, prospective studies with careful assessments of initial health status are the current 'gold standard' design.

By necessity, even well-designed prospective studies are correlational; experimental manipulation of personality is neither feasible nor ethical in human studies. Further, personality is often confounded with other health-relevant factors, such as socioeconomic status, age, gender, and health behavior (e.g. smoking, diet, alcohol use, exercise, etc.). Even when such 'third variables' are statistically controlled, limitations in their measurement can result in their 'under-correction' and hence unrecognized continuation as confounds (Phillips et al., 1991).

Yet even if it could be accomplished with precision, statistical control of potential confounds should be driven by clear theory and full awareness of the limitations of a tool that appears to provide more control than it in fact can. A correlation between smoking and personality could be seen as a confound to be eliminated through statistical control, or it

could be seen as a potential mediating explanation for the effects of personality on health. In the latter case, this hypothesis should be articulated and tested through theory-driven analyses (Baron and Kenny, 1986), rather than discarded through an atheoretical compulsion to discern statistically independent predictors. Efforts to identify independent predictors of disease and longevity are, of course, worthwhile, but they should be guided by clear thinking.

In addition, forcing statistical independence on correlated risk factors must be pursued cautiously. For example, negative affective traits such as anxiety, depressive symptoms, and anger are each associated with increased risk of CHD (Suls and Bunde, 2005), as we discuss in more detail later. These traits are typically closely correlated. It seems obviously important to determine if anxiety and depressive symptoms are independent predictors of CHD, but the variance in anxiety that is statistically independent of depression does not unambiguously reflect the original conceptualization of this trait. Forced statistical separation of naturally confounded constructs creates 'counterfactuals' (Meehl, 1970) in which measured constructs shorn of their natural associations do not fully resemble the original constructs of interest. Statistical control in the analysis of non-experimental studies of personality and health is not inherently unwise. Rather, it should be guided and interpreted with full appreciation of the imprecise, likely incomplete and somewhat illusory nature of the 'control' that has been achieved.

REPLICATED ASSOCIATIONS BETWEEN PERSONALITY AND HEALTH

A wide variety of traits have been studied as risk factors, many of which have been examined in single studies or with limited measures of personality or health outcomes.

Rather than attempt a comprehensive review, we present specific traits – or related sets of traits – found to have replicated prospective associations with health in well-designed studies of longevity or specific outcomes such as coronary heart disease (CHD).

The type A behavior pattern legacy: hostility and dominance

Following Friedman and Rosenman's (1959) seminal description of this composite of achievement striving, competitiveness, impatience, easily provoked hostility, excessive job involvement, and a vigorous speech style, 20 years of generally supportive research led an expert panel to conclude that the type A pattern was a reliable CHD risk factor (Cooper et al., 1981). However, several failures to replicate this association (e.g. Shekelle et al., 1985) gave cause for concern. A quantitative review indicated that the association with CHD was reliable and inconsistencies could be attributed to methodological issues; the association was more evident in initially healthy than high-risk samples, and when type A behavior was assessed through behavioral ratings rather than self-reports (Miller et al., 1991).

Subsequent examination of individual elements within this multi-component pattern quickly identified hostility as the primary unhealthy type A trait (Hecker et al., 1988; Matthews et al., 1977). Initially, these studies were based on behavioral ratings derived from the type A structured interview (Rosenman, 1978), but were soon followed by studies using self-report measures that also found prospective associations between hostility and CHD morbidity and mortality, as well as reduced longevity (Barefoot et al., 1983; Shekelle et al., 1983). Although some failures to replicate appeared, a quantitative review of studies indicated that hostility was associated with reduced longevity and greater risk of CHD (Miller et al., 1996), and these effects were stronger for behavioral ratings of hostility than for self-reports.

Recent research has used a variety of self-report and behavioral measures of individual differences in anger, hostile beliefs and attitudes, and aggressive social behavior (Smith et al., 2004a). Some subsequent studies of initially healthy individuals have failed to replicate the association between hostility and subsequent health (e.g. Surtees et al., 2005), but the majority support the prior conclusion (e.g. Everson et al., 1997; Matthews et al., 2004a). Several – but not all – studies have indicated that these traits influence the initial development and progression of asymptomatic atherosclerosis (e.g. Smith et al., 2007), and the emergence and course of clinically apparent cardiovascular disease (e.g. Boyle et al., 2004; Olson et al., 2005) (for reviews, see Smith et al., 2004b; Smith and MacKenzie, 2006)

Although the legacy of the type A pattern has primarily focused on anger, hostility, and aggressiveness, research indicates that descriptions of this construct contained a second unhealthy trait – social dominance. Based on behavioral ratings from the structured interview, hostility and a socially dominant verbal style comprising loud, rapid, and vigorous speech and the tendency to 'talk over' others have been found to be independent predictors of CHD and reduced longevity (Houston et al., 1992, 1997). Subsequent studies using self-reports of dominance replicated this association with CHD (e.g. Siegman et al., 2000).

Negative affectivity and neuroticism

Individual differences in the experience of anxiety, sadness, irritability, and related negative affects define a broad dimension labeled 'neuroticism' or 'negative affectivity' (Costa and McCrae, 1992; Watson and Clark, 1984), contrasting susceptibility to emotional distress with stability and adjustment. An early and influential review concluded that this trait was a risk factor for subsequent illness (Friedman and Booth-Kewley, 1987), but it was criticized for being based in part on studies in which health outcomes reflected illness behavior (Matthews, 1988; Stone and Costa, 1990), as neuroticism and negative affectivity are associated with somatic complaints and other illness behaviors in excess of actual levels of disease (Costa and McCrae, 1987; Watson and Pennebaker, 1989). However, subsequent, more methodologically sound studies demonstrated that a variety of specific negative affective traits, as well as the broader trait of N/NA, confer increased risk of reduced longevity and specific diseases such as CHD (Suls and Bunde, 2005).

Neuroticism includes a variety of specific characteristics that have been studied as health risk factors, such as anxiety, depressive symptoms, worry, and low self-esteem. Because this domain includes anger, it overlaps with the literature on hostility discussed previously. N/NA is associated with anxiety and mood disorders (Clark et al., 1994; Zonderman et al., 1993). Hence, studies of the health consequences of these disorders are also relevant to this risk trait.

Anxiety and depressive symptoms have been found to predict increases in blood pressure and the incidence of hypertension (Rutledge and Hogan, 2002), although not all studies support this conclusion. Among initially healthy persons, anxiety, depressive symptoms, general emotional distress, and related characteristics (e.g. worry, poor self-esteem) have been found to predict CHD (Albert et al., 2005; Barefoot and Schroll, 1996; Kubzansky et al., 1997; Rowan et al., 2005), atherosclerosis (Haas et al., 2005), stroke (May et al., 2002), diabetes (Golden et al., 2004), and reduced longevity or earlier all-cause mortality (Gump et al., 2005; Hermann et al., 1998; Stamatakis et al., 2004). Among persons with existing disease such as CHD, stoke, or renal failure, measures of emotional distress have been associated with recurrent cardiovascular events (e.g. reinfarction) and reduced survival (e.g. Blumenthal et al., 2003; Christensen et al., 2002; Frasure-Smith et al., 1995; Strik et al., 2003). It is

important to note that several studies have failed to replicate these effects (e.g. Lane et al., 2001). However, the balance of evidence from well-designed studies supports the conclusion that individual differences in negative affect are associated with risk of serious illness and reduced longevity.

Optimism/pessimism

Individual differences in the tendency to hold optimistic expectations about future events have been identified as a protective factor in studies of health outcomes. Pessimistic expectations and beliefs appear to confer increased risk, as do related traits such as hopelessness. Several different conceptualizations of this domain have been offered, along with related measures (Everson et al., 1996; Gillham et al., 2001; Scheier and Carver, 1985). These measures are often only modestly correlated, raising concerns about whether they reflect the same construct (Norem and Chang, 2001). Recent evidence also suggests that optimism and pessimism are separable dimensions, rather than opposite ends of a single continuum (Herzberg et al., 2006; Kubzansky et al., 2004). Hence, associations with subsequent health could reflect benefits of optimism, the risks of pessimism, or both.

Prospective studies indicate that various measures of this domain are associated with onset of cardiovascular and other serious diseases and reduced longevity among initially healthy persons (Anda et al., 1993; Brummett et al., 2006; Everson et al., 1996; Giltay et al., 2004; Kubzansky et al., 2001; Maruta et al., 2000; Peterson et al., 1998; Stern et al., 2001), and with development of hypertension and progression of atherosclerosis (Everson et al., 1997; Everson et al., 2000; Matthews et al., 2004b). Among individuals with established disease (e.g. CHD, stroke, cancer), optimism and/or pessimism has been associated with recurring disease, complications, and reduced survival (Helgeson and Fitz, 1999; Lewis et al., 2001;

Scheier et al., 1989, 1999; Schultz et al., 1996). Yet some studies failed to support this association with subsequent health (Cassileth et al., 1985). Further, measures of optimism/pessimism are often closely correlated with the N/NA domain, and as a result it is sometimes unclear whether the health consequences of optimism/pessimism are due to this broader personality domain (Smith et al., 1989).

Conscientiousness

Individual differences in organization and orderliness, persistence, dutifulness, self-discipline, deliberateness, and perceived competence are all aspects of the FFM domain of conscientiousness (sometimes termed 'constraint'). Although less frequently studied as a predictor of health, measures of conscientiousness have been found to predict longevity in initially healthy samples and survival among persons with established disease (Christensen et al., 2002; Friedman et al., 1993; Martin and Friedman, 2000; Weiss and Costa, 2005; Wilson et al., 2004). These effects are similar when conscientiousness is assessed from childhood (Friedman et al., 1993) to later adulthood (Weiss and Costa, 2005; Wilson et al., 2004), suggesting that conscientiousness influences health across the lifespan. However, compared to some other personality domains, the effects of conscientiousness on health are not as extensively documented. Further, it is not yet clear which aspects of this multi-faceted domain are most closely and consistently related to later health.

MECHANISMS IN THE ASSOCIATION BETWEEN PERSONALITY AND HEALTH

A variety of models have been proposed to describe processes that underlie associations between personality and health. Some models highlight health behavior (e.g. smoking) or illness behavior (e.g. adopting the sick role). Others consider physiological mechanisms, especially in response to life stress, to be the critical link. For the sake of presentation, these models will be considered separately; however, the proposed mechanisms are clearly interrelated.

Illness behavior

The multi-faceted construct involving perception and reporting of physical sensations, and responses to perceived illness (e.g. taking medications, staying home from work, seeking medical attention, and discussing physical problems with others) has been termed *illness behavior* (Mechanic, 1972). Positing illness behavior as a potential mechanism can suggest that personality may not be related to objective illness, only to subjective perceptions (i.e. self-assessed health) or behavior. Yet, illness behavior can influence health directly. For example, an undetected (or ignored) sign of illness may lead to a decline in health that might have been avoided, or failure to follow a prescribed medical regimen may undermine health. These latter aspects of illness behavior are self-regulatory processes, and represent a potential pathway between personality and actual illness (Wiebe and Fortenberry, 2006).

Judgments about the status of health and illness (i.e. self-assessed health) influence self-care decision-making, healthcare utilization, and communication with healthcare providers. Importantly, self-assessed health, especially global health assessments (i.e. ratings from 'poor' to 'excellent'), predict mortality over and above biomedical markers (Idler and Benyamini, 1997). Thus, to the extent that personality factors are related to self-assessed health, this represents a pathway to important health outcomes. A large body of research has demonstrated significant relations between neuroticism and poorer self-assessed health (e.g. Brown and Moskowitz, 1997; Costa and McCrae, 1987; Watson and Pennebaker, 1989; Williams et al., 2004; Williams and Wiebe, 2000).

Dispositional optimism has also been associated with better general perceptions of health (Achat et al., 2000) and fewer physical symptoms (Scheier and Carver, 1985).

An important aspect of illness behavior involves self-care activities, including treatment adherence. In the case of chronic illness, self-care and treatment adherence may require long-term persistence in disease management activities. There are substantial individual differences in illness self-management, suggesting that personality may influence these activities, which may have implications for disease progression. For example, both neuroticism and conscientiousness have been linked to renal deterioration in patients with type 1 diabetes (Brickman et al., 1996) and mortality among renal dialysis patients (Christensen et al., 2002).

Whereas functional disability constitutes tendencies to reduce activities in the face of illness, the other end of the illness behavior continuum – neglecting to take time from work to recover, and so on – is an often overlooked area of research on illness behavior. One exception has been the examination of the type A behavior pattern and sick role behavior; individuals exhibiting aspects of the type A behavior pattern have been found to be more likely to reject the sick role and return to work before full recovery (Alemagno et al., 1991).

Appropriate use of health services is also an avenue by which personality may affect health. There are large individual differences in the use of health services, including delay behavior – the lag time between detecting a symptom and seeking healthcare. For some conditions, such as myocardial infarction or stroke, delay has life-threatening implications. In a study of seeking medical care after myocardial infarction, O'Carroll and colleagues (2001) found that low scores on neuroticism differentiated those that delayed (waited over 4 hours) from those that did not. Similarly, Kenyon and colleagues (1991) found that 'somatic and emotional awareness' was related to earlier treatment seeking for acute myocardial infarction, suggesting

that a relative lack of such awareness among low-neurotic individuals may promote delay. Neither of these studies, however, distinguished among delay in initially detecting the physical sensations, deciding symptoms warrant medical attention, and delay between deciding they were ill and seeking treatment. Some research has suggested that whereas type A characteristics predict delay in deciding that symptoms constitute illness, individuals who are more relaxed and easygoing are more likely to delay in the later phase of treatment seeking (Matthews et al., 1983).

Constitutional predisposition

It is possible that prospective associations between personality traits and subsequent disease do not reflect a causal effect, but instead a non-causal association between co-effects of an underlying third variable. That is, it is possible that an underlying genetic/constitutional individual difference may produce a stable individual difference in affect, behavior, and/or cognition (i.e. personality), and also confer risk or resilience for a specific disease or for general health. In this way, personality traits would predict subsequent health, without actually playing a causal role in disease development. Virtually all of the personality traits identified as risk factors also demonstrate moderate levels of heritability in behavioral genetics studies, attesting to the plausibility of the constitutional predisposition model. Further, in recent years molecular genetic studies of personality have identified candidate genes in the case of individual differences in anger, aggressiveness, and negative affectivity or neuroticism. However, no studies to date have tested the constitutional model directly, as when the association of personality and subsequent health is tested with and without controlling genetic variance or a specific genotype.

These advances in quantitative and molecular genetics also provide opportunities to test other potentially important models of risk not yet addressed in the study of personality and health. For example, personality traits might influence health differentially among genetically vulnerable or resilient individuals (e.g. genetic diathesis by stress interactions), or genetic factors might predispose individuals to greater exposure to high or low risk environments over time (i.e. gene–environment correlations). These more complex models of the relative effects of personality and genetic factors go well beyond older 'nature versus nurture' debates, and have been fruitfully applied to research in other psychological fields (e.g. Moffitt et al., 2005).

Health behavior

Another potential mechanism is health-damaging and health-enhancing behavior. Considerable evidence supports this possibility. For example, neuroticism is related to some health behaviors that are potentially detrimental to health (e.g. substance use, Booth-Kewley and Vickers, 1994; Cooper et al., 2000), whereas conscientiousness is related to positive health behavior (Bogg and Roberts, 2004). Additionally, the combination of low conscientiousness and either high neuroticism or high extraversion is associated with engaging in riskier health behaviors (Vollrath and Torgersen, 2002). Personality factors, such as excitement seeking, have also been related to risky behaviors (e.g. unsafe driving, exposure to violent situations) that may lead to injury or death (Zuckerman and Kuhlman, 2000).

Although such associations between personality factors and health behavior suggest this model is plausible, actual tests of mediation have rarely been conducted. Indeed, when health behaviors and personality are both examined, studies often treat health behaviors as covariates, missing the opportunity to test mediation (Friedman, 2006). When mediation has been tested, it has not been the case that health behaviors fully account for known associations between personality factors and health. For example, relations between conscientiousness and

prudent health behavior do not fully explain the association with mortality (Friedman et al., 1995). Hostility is also associated with a variety of negative health behaviors, and some mediational studies indicate that this mechanism explains associations of this trait with subsequent health (Everson et al., 1996). However, the association of hostility with subsequent morbidity and mortality generally remains significant when measures of health behavior are controlled (Smith et al., 2004a). Much of the prior research is limited by examining personality relations to single health behaviors, such as smoking, independently. Negative health behaviors tend to co-occur, especially those related to substance use, as do positive health behaviors (Friedman, 2006).

Stress moderation

Perhaps the most frequently studied mechanism for personality–health relations centers on the interaction between personality and life stressors. From this perspective, personality is thought to make individuals more or less vulnerable to the deleterious effects of stress. Although this proposition appears simple at first blush, the inter-relations among personality, stress, and illness are quite complex. One must consider the many ways that personality might influence the experience of stress and the pathways by which stress influences health. For example, personality style might be related to stress by increasing the tendency to be exposed to stressors, by influencing an individual's reaction to stress, by shortening or extending the length of time it takes an individual to 'recover' from the effects of stress, or by affecting the restoration processes that are crucial to the body's ability to repair itself in response to stress (Uchino et al., in press). To this end, we consider the associations between personality and stress exposure, reactivity, recovery, and restoration.

Stress exposure

A transactional stress moderation perspective on relations between personality and health suggests a reciprocal relationship between individuals and their environments, consistent with the social-cognitive and interpersonal perspectives in personality discussed above. In this view, personality traits and stressful events are not independent influences on health; life stress is not randomly distributed across levels of various personality traits. Rather, by the nature of personality style, individuals may be more or less likely to find themselves in, or create for themselves, stressful circumstances.

Indeed, there is considerable evidence that personality factors are related to differential stress exposure. For example, hostile individuals may interact with others in a manner that creates conflict and thwarts the probability of receiving social support from others. Thus, a hostile individual's style may both increase the probability of stressful circumstances and reduce the likelihood of having access to stress-buffering resources (Smith et al, 2004a). Individuals high in neuroticism are more frequently exposed to major life events (Magnus et al., 1993), daily hassles, and chronic stressors such as conflict in close relationships (Affleck et al., 1994; Bolger and Zuckerman, 1995; David et al., 1997; Gunthert et al., 1999; Suls et al., 1998). Current thinking on the behavioral motivation systems that underlie trait-negative affectivity can inform our understanding of why this might be. N/NA is thought to derive from a highly active behavioral inhibition system (BIS) (Gray, 1987), increasing sensitivity to signs of threat or punishment. This sensitivity can, in turn, lead to defensive behavior that may create stressful situations.

Stress reactivity

This term describes the immediate response to a potentially stressful event and involves one's perception of the event (i.e. appraisal) (Lazarus and Folkman, 1984), subjective distress, and physiological arousal (e.g. increased heart rate, release of stress hormones such as cortisol). The onset or progression of disease may be influenced via repeated activation of the sympathetic adrenomedullary (SAM) system and the hypothalamic–pituitary–adrenocortical (HPA) axis, which are central to the body's

characteristic responses to stress. Additionally, there are a variety of anatomical links between the nervous and immune systems, including immune cell receptors for neurotransmitters and hormones that are either produced or regulated by the nervous system (Ader et al., 2001), indicating that physiological responses to stress also includes immune system responses (Segerstom and Miller, 2004).

Physiological reactivity to stress is associated with traits reflecting propensity to negative affect. Anger, hostility, and depression have been associated with elevations of both SAM and HPA system activation in response to stress (Smith and Ruiz, 2002). Findings regarding relations between individual differences in hostility and cardiovascular reactivity to laboratory stressors are particularly robust (Smith et al., 2004a). Additionally, chronic anxiety and depressive symptoms are associated with altered autonomic regulation of the cardiovascular system (Berntson et al., 1998, Carney et al., 1995; Watkins et al., 1998). Each of these traits, in turn, has been found to be associated with various aspects of immune functioning, both in terms of response to stressors and more enduring levels of immune activity (Segerstrom and Smith, 2006).

One concern about associations between personality traits and physiological responses to controlled presentations of laboratory stressors involves the extent to which they occur in 'real life'. Ambulatory studies are particularly valuable in this regard. For example, optimism has been associated with lower ambulatory blood pressure during daily activities (Raikkonen et al., 1999), whereas hostility has been associated with higher levels (Benotsch et al., 1997; Brondolo et al., 2003). However, it is difficult to determine if these findings reflect greater reactivity to or greater exposure to daily stress. As noted above, individuals high in negative affectivity demonstrate both greater exposure and greater affective reactivity to daily events (Bolger and Zuckerman, 1995; Suls and Martin, 2006).

Despite the evidence for associations between personality and physiological reactivity to stress, there have been few tests of mediation in which personality, physiological stress responses, and subsequent health are assessed and the mediational hypotheses tested directly (Segerstrom and Smith, 2006). Moreover, cardiovascular and psychoneuroimmunological mechanisms are often explored independently and focus on different disease outcomes (e.g. CHD vs. HIV/AIDS, cancer) making it less likely that common pathways, such as inflammation, will be implicated as a mechanism for personality–health relations (Friedman, 2006). Studies that have examined both cardiovascular and immunologic reactivity to stress have found reliable correspondence between the two systems (e.g. Bosch et al., 2003; for a review, see Uchino et al., in press).

Recovery

In the context of the stress response, recovery typically refers to levels of emotional or physiological arousal after termination of the stressor or the time required for the individual to return to baseline levels after termination of the stressor. In the case of cardiovascular recovery, it has been hypothesized that the duration of stress-related cardiovascular responses may be as important as the magnitude of initial reactivity in the development of cardiovascular diseases (Brosschot et al., 2006; Schwartz et al., 2003). Indeed, poor cardiovascular recovery has been associated with increases in blood pressure over several years (Mosely and Linden, 2006; Stewart et al., 2006). Further, individual differences in hostility and other personality risk factors have been associated with delayed recovery of cardiovascular responses to stress (e.g. Anderson et al., 2005). Individuals high in neuroticism tend to experience 'negative emotional spillover' after the experience of a negative event and concomitant negative mood, meaning that negative mood states tend to persist over time (Suls and Martin, 2005). Thus, it takes longer for these individuals to recover from negative daily events.

Related to physiological recovery are the characteristic coping styles that accompany personality traits. Some coping strategies, such as rumination (Brosschot et al., 2006),

may impede recovery following stressful events. To the extent that personality is reliably associated with stress-coping patterns, this may be an additional mechanism for relations to poor health. Indeed, prior research suggests that each trait of the FFM is significantly and independently related to different coping strategies and that personality interacts with type of stressor to predict coping responses (Lee-Baggley et al., 2005). Again, however, direct tests of coping style as a mediator of personality–health relations have not been conducted.

Peri- and post-stress restoration

During and after the experience of stress, restorative processes operate to 'refresh, buttress, and repair various forms of cellular damage' and to return an individual to baseline levels (Cacioppo and Berntson, 2007). A related concept is allostatic load – the disruption of homeostatic mechanisms related to either repeated stress and/or poor management of systems that promote allostasis (McEwen, 1998). Sleep, wound healing, and humoral immunity are examples of restorative processes. Additionally, one aspect of restoration corresponds closely to illness behavior – the capacity for some individuals to retreat from daily stress to recuperate following a time of increased stress and/or illness. A weakened immunologic state may increase stress resulting in a positive feedback loop that may foster the development of more frequent or chronic illness (Cacioppo and Berntson, 2006). Although it has been less the focus of research compared to other aspects of the stress response, personality is associated with restoration, making this another potential pathway by which personality may influence health.

Sleep quality has emerged as a potent predictor of poor health. Poor sleep, especially sleep deprivation, is related to impaired immune functioning (Lange et al., 2003) and predicts all-cause mortality (Dew et al., 2003). Relations between personality and sleep quality suggest this may be an important mechanism for personality–health relations. Of the traditional personality factors, neuroticism and other anxiety-related constructs have been most implicated in the incidence of poor sleep (Gray and Watson, 2002). Moreover, high trait-anxious individuals have been found to take longer to fall sleep, have greater percentage of and more frequent transitions to light sleep, and lower REM density compared to low trait-anxious individuals (Fuller et al., 1997).

Multiple mechanisms underlying personality–health relations

There is evidence that personality factors are related to each of the potential mechanisms outlined above, although specific tests of mediation and longitudinal relations among predictors and proposed mediators have rarely been tested. Moreover, it is clear that the various models are not independent from one another, as when health behavior declines under conditions of stress. Even individuals who maintain reasonable health habits under most circumstances find it difficult to sustain health behavior when under stress. Moreover, negative health habits, particularly substance use and overeating, may be maladaptive attempts to cope with stress. It is also clear that the components of stress – exposure, reactivity, recovery, and restoration – are not independent. For example, difficulties recovering from a stressful event (i.e. prolonged distress, rumination) will likely influence sleep quality. Poor sleep quality, in turn, may affect emotion regulation abilities and daily functioning, thereby creating the fertile ground for further stress and illness. Personality may be related to the propensity for escalating difficulties under stressful circumstances. Consistent with this notion, neuroticism is associated with stronger negative reactions to recurring problems over time, a process Suls and Martin (2005) term the 'neurotic cascade'. Hence, it is unlikely that any single, specific mechanism would ever fully account for the association between a given personality characteristic and a health outcome. The predictive utility of personality

constructs in studies of health outcomes may instead reflect that most personality characteristics influence a variety of these pathways that combine over time in potentially synergistic ways to influence subsequent health.

CONCLUSIONS AND FUTURE DIRECTIONS

Recent decades of research have produced evidence that personality characteristics are associated with important health outcomes. The quality of this growing body of research could be enhanced further by more consistent and complete incorporation of theoretical frameworks and methods from personality science. Such efforts would be useful in developing a more complete account of which personality traits confer risk and resilience, as well as the likely multiple mechanisms underlying these associations. This more complete account of personality and health will provide a firmer foundation for preventive efforts to enhance health.

There are additional issues that if addressed in future research could also advance this basic and applied agenda. For example, much of the prior personality and health research has focused on single traits, single mechanisms, and single disease outcomes. Future research should, where possible, examine multiple personality dimensions, but not only so as to distinguish their unique and overlapping effects on health. Although the majority of the research on personality and health has focused on direct effects of individual traits (i.e. main effects), personality factors do not exist in isolation and may moderate each other. For example, the combination of low conscientiousness and either high neuroticism or high extraversion is associated with engaging in riskier health behaviors (Vollrath and Torgersen, 2002). This finding is consistent with the hypothesis that conscientiousness reflects underlying individual differences in effortful control abilities and, thus, may moderate the effects of personality factors related to emotional reactivity. To the extent that conscientiousness is related to effortful or attentional control and the ability to overcome emotional reactivity, one can hypothesize that these interactions (i.e. N × C, E × C) may have important implications for relations between personality and physical well-being. In general, moving toward delineating interactive combination of traits or personality *profiles* that confer risk for future poor health would help avoid the pitfalls of examining traits in isolation.

It is also apparent that the effects of personality variables may differ depending on the level of the personality factor (i.e. curvilinear effects). For instance, moderate neuroticism may be related to better health-relevant self-care than either high or low neuroticism. Moreover, low neuroticism may be related to treatment-seeking delay in the face of potentially serious illness. Thus, the assumption that lower neuroticism is uniformly related to better physical and mental well-being may be false. Additionally, better theoretical explication of why varying levels of individual difference factors should be differentially related to health and illness is needed.

Personality–illness relations may also be moderated by other individual differences such as gender and ethnicity, as well as by environmental factors such as socioeconomic status. There are reliable gender differences in personality (e.g. women are higher in neuroticism compared to men) and psychopathology that may influence the development of illness, especially via the stress response (see Williams and Gunn, 2005). Socioeconomic status influences virtually all the proposed mechanisms for personality–illness relations. Testing the appropriate interactions between personality and theoretically determined potential moderators will help elucidate the circumstances under which personality factors are related to illness outcomes. Further, as discussed above, personality traits are consistently related to interpersonal processes and characteristics of the social environment that also confer risk and resilience for physical

health. Hence, concepts and methods that foster the integrative study of personality and social risk factors – such as the interpersonal perspective (Smith et al., 2003, 2004b) – can facilitate the development of a more complete understanding of psychosocial risk, rather than one based on an artificial separation of characteristics of persons and the social circumstances they inhabit.

Most of the health outcomes of interest in personality and health research (e.g. coronary heart disease, cancer, etc.) involve long etiologies, often beginning many years before the occurrence of outward signs of disease. Further, most of the personality characteristics identified as risk factors have been identified in childhood and adolescence (Shiner and Caspi, 2003). Hence, developmental approaches to understanding the emergence and continuity of personality may be particularly important in understanding the influence of personality on physical health across the life course (Smith and Spiro, 2002). Increasingly, epidemiological studies are examining the association of life course exposures (e.g. childhood and adult SES) and risk factory trajectories over time as influences on later health, based on the assumption that patterns of risk and resilience over long periods of time might better capture the impact of such characteristics on disease compared to these factors at a single point in time. A small but growing body of research suggests that personality traits measured in childhood are associated with levels of health risk factors in adulthood (Caspi et al., 2006), and that patterns of change over time in such characteristics are related to adult health status. Further, a growing body of evidence indicates that early life experiences shape the physiological mechanisms identified as potentially linking personality and health outcomes (Danese et al., 2007; Gutman and Nemeroff, 2003; Luecken and Lemery, 2004; Taylor et al., 2004). Hence, research on personality and health could also benefit from incorporation of recent developmental approaches to the emergence, continuity, and change of personality characteristics (Caspi et al., 2006).

The study of personality and health will also likely benefit from the incorporation of evolving developments in the biological bases of personality and individual differences, such as those made available through advances in molecular genetics and functional neuroimaging techniques (Canli, 2006). For example, in the modern era of behavioral genomics, research has increasingly focused on identifying specific biological pathways that contribute to complex cognitive and emotional behaviors. Research of this form will contribute to our understanding of how individual differences in temperament and personality emerge and how such differences may confer vulnerability to both mental and physical health outcomes. The 'candidate gene association approach' involves testing the relationship between a particular phenotype (e.g. personality traits) and a specific allele of a gene. Relevant to personality effects on health, genes controlling serotonin (e.g. 5-HT) are strong candidates for individual differences in neuroticism–anxiety–depression. Importantly, variation in the serotonin transporter gene (5-HTTLPR) has been found to moderate the influence of stressful life events on major depression (Caspi et al., 2003), suggesting that variation in this gene may underlie individual differences in physiological stress responses that may also be relevant to health outcomes.

Research utilizing neuroimaging techniques to examine brain activity among individuals with particular genetic variations also hold promise for understanding personality effects on health. For example, individuals with 5-HTTLPR S allele exhibit increased amygdala activity while processing emotional information (Hariri et al., 2002), suggesting that anxiety and fearfulness associated with the short allele may reflect hyperresponsiveness of the amygdala to relevant environmental stimuli. Recent research has examined the effects of environmental stress on brain regions, most notably the prefrontal cortex, that are critical in the regulation of amygdala activity, suggesting the need to examine interactive effects of the amygdala and prefrontal cortex during affect processing. To the extent that the genetics and brain circuitry underlying personality constructs can be identified, along with cognitive tasks (i.e. endophenotypes) that reliably activate particular brain circuits, mechanisms for the effects of personality on health via stress responses over time can be articulated. Despite the promise of behavioral genetics and neuroscience in advancing our understanding of personality effects on health, it is unlikely that single-gene variations will have much explanatory value. Examining the contributions of multiple genes acting in response to environmental pressures is necessary for the development of truly predictive markers that account for the majority of variance in any given phenotype, including personality factors related to stress resiliency.

The centuries-old hypothesis that individual differences in thought, emotion, and behavior can influence physical health has received considerable support from methodologically sound studies in recent decades. Further application of the concepts and methods of current personality science, as well as incorporation of emerging advances in the molecular genetics and neuroscience of personality, may help to further refine our understanding of the link between psyche and soma. Such advances represent historic progress on age-old questions regarding mind and body, and important elements in efforts to prevent disease and promote health.

REFERENCES

Achat, H., Kawachi, I., Spiro, A., DeMolles, D.A. and Sparrow, D. (2000) 'Optimism and depression as predictors of physical and mental health functioning: The Normative Aging Study', *Annals of Behavioral Medicine*, 22(2): 127–30.

Ader, R., Felten, D.L. and Cohen, N. (2001) (eds), *Psychoneuroimmunology* (3rd edn). New York: Academic Press.

Affleck, G., Tennen, H., Urrows, S. and Higgins, P. (1994) 'Person and contextual features of daily stress reactivity: Individual differences in relations of undesirable daily events with mood disturbances and chronic pain intensity', *Journal of Consulting and Clinical Psychology*, 67(2): 746–54.

Albert, C.M., Chae C.U., Rexrode, K.M., Manson, J.E. and Kawachi, I. (2005) 'Phobic anxiety and risk of coronary heart disease and sudden cardiac death among women', *Circulation*, 111(4): 480–87.

Alemagno, S.A., Zyzanski, S.J., Stange, K.C., Kercher, K., Medalie, J.H. and Kahana, E. (1991) 'Health and illness behavior of Type A persons', *Journal of Occupational Health*, 33(8): 891–5.

Anda, R., Williamson, D., Jones, D., Macera, C., Eaker, E., Glassman, A., Marks, J. (1993) 'Depressed affect, hopelessness, and the risk of ischemic heart disease in a cohort of U.S. adults', *Epidemiology*, 4(4): 285–94.

Anderson, J.C., Linden, W. and Habia, M.E. (2005) 'The importance of examining blood pressure reactivity and recovery in anger provocation research', *International Journal of Psychophysiology*, 57(3): 159–63.

Bandura, A. (1978) 'The self-system in reciprocal determinism', *American Psychologist*, 33(4): 1175–84.

Barefoot, J.C., Dahlstrom, W.G. and Williams, R.B. (1983) 'Hostility, CHD incidence, and total mortality: A 25-year follow-up study of 255 physicians', *Psychosomatic Medicine*, 45(1): 59–63.

Barefoot, J.C. and Schroll, M. (1996) 'Symptoms of depression, acute myocardial infarction, and total mortality in a community sample', *Circulation*, 93(11): 1976–80.

Baron, R.M. and Kenney, D.A. (1986) 'The moderator-mediator variable distinction in social psychological research: Conceptual, strategic, and statistical considerations', *Journal of Personality and Social Psychology*, 51(6): 1173–82.

Benotsch, E.G. Christensen, A.J. and McKelvey, L. (1997) 'Hostility, social support and ambulatory cardiovascular activity', *Journal of Behavioral Medicine*, 20(2): 163–76.

Berntson, G.G., Sarter, M. and Cacioppo, J.T. (1998) 'Anxiety and cardiovascular reactivity: The basal forebrain cholinergic link', *Behavioural Brain Research*, 94(2): 225–48.

Blumenthal, J.A., Lett, H.S., Babyak, M.A., White, W., Smith, P.K., Mark, D.B., Jones, R., Matthew, J.P. and Newman, M.F. (2003) 'Depression as a risk factor for mortality after coronary artery bypass surgery', *Lancet*, 362(9384): 604–9.

Bogg, T. and Roberts, B.W. (2004) 'Conscientiousness and health-related behaviors: A meta-analysis of the leading behavioral contributors to mortality', *Psychological Bulletin*, 130(6): 887–919.

Bolger, N. and Zuckerman, A. (1995) 'A framework for studying personality in the stress process', *Journal of Personality and Social Psychology*, 69(5): 890–902.

Booth-Kewley, S. and Vickers, R.R. (1994) 'Associations between major domains of personality and health behavior', *Journal of Personality*, 62(3): 281–98.

Bosch, J.A., Berntson, G.G., Cacioppo, J.T., Dhabhar, F.S. and Marucha, P.T. (2003) 'Acute stress evokes selective mobilization of T cells that differ in chemokine receptor expression: A potential pathway linking immunologic reactivity to cardiovascular disease', *Brain, Behavior, and Immunity*, 17(4): 251–9.

Boyle, S.H., Williams, R.B., Mark, D.B., Brummett, B.H., Siegler, J.C., Helms, M.J. et al. (2004) 'Hostility as a predictor of survival in patients with coronary artery disease', *Psychosomatic Medicine*, 66(5): 629–32.

Brickman, A.L., Yount, S.E., Blaney, N.T., Rothberg, S.T. and Kaplan De-Nour, A. (1996) 'Personality traits and long-term health status: The influence of neuroticism and conscientiousness on renal deterioration in Type-1 diabetes', *Psychosomatics*, 37(5): 459–68.

Brondolo, E., Rieppi, R., Erickson, S.A., Bagiella, E., Shapiro, P.A., McKinley, P. et al. (2003) 'Hostility, interpersonal interactions, and ambulatory blood pressure', *Psychosomatic Medicine*, 65(6): 1003–111.

Brosschot, J.F., Gerin, W. and Thayer, J.F. (2006) 'The perseverative cognition hypothesis: A review of worry, prolonged stress-related physiological activation, and health', *Journal of Psychosomatic Research*, 60: 113–24.

Brown, K.W. and Moskowitz, D.S. (1997) 'Does unhappiness make you sick? The role of affect and neuroticism in the experience of common physical symptoms', *Journal of Personality and Social Psychology*, 72(4): 907–17.

Brummett, B.H., Helms, M.J., Dahlstrom, W.G. and Siegler, I.C. (2006) 'Prediction of all-cause mortality by the Minnesota Multiphasic Personality Inventory Optimism-Pessimism scale scores: Study of a college sample during a 40-year follow-up period', *Mayo Clinic Proceedings*, 81(12): 1541–4.

Cacioppo, J.T. and Berntson, G.G. (2007) 'The brain, homeostasis, and health: Balancing demands of the internal and external milieu', in H.S. Friedman and R. Cohen Silver (eds), *Foundations of Health Psychology*. New York: Oxford University Press, pp. 73–91.

Canli, T. (2006) (ed.), *Biology of Personality and Individual Differences*. New York: Guilford.

Cantor, N. (1990) 'From thought to behavior: "having" and "doing" in the study of personality and cognition', *American Psychologist*, 45(2): 735–50.

Carney, R.M., Freedland, K., Rich, M. and Jaffe, A.S. (1995) 'Depression as a risk factor for cardiac events in established coronary heart disease: A review of possible mechanisms', *Annals of Behavioral Medicine*, 17(2): 142–9.

Carson, R.C. (1969) *Interaction Concepts in Personality*. Chicago: Aldine.

Caspi, A., Bem, D.J. and Elder, G.H. (1989) 'Continuities and consequences of interactional styles across the life course', *Journal of Personality*, 57(2): 375–406.

Caspi, A., Harrington, H., Moffitt, T.E., Milne, B.J. and Poulton, R. (2006) 'Socially isolated children 20 years later: Risk of cardiovascular disease', *Archives of Pediatric and Adolescent Medicine*, 160(8): 805–11.

Caspi, A., Sugden, K., Moffitt, T.E., Taylor, A., Craig, I.W., Harrington, H. et al. (2003) 'Influence of life stress on depression: Moderation by a polymorphism in the 5-HTT gene', *Science*, 301(5631): 386–9.

Cassileth, B.R., Lusk, E.J. and Miller, D.S. (1985) 'Psychosocial correlates of survival in advanced malignant disease', *New England Journal of Medicine*, 312(24): 1551–5.

Christensen, A.J., Ehlers, S.L., Wiebe, J.S., Moran, P.J., Raichle, K., Ferneyhough, K. et al. (2002) 'Patient personality and mortality: A 4-year prospective examination of chronic renal insufficiency', *Health Psychology*, 21(4): 315–20.

Clark, L.A., Watson, D. and Mineka, S. (1994) 'Temperament, personality, and the mood and anxiety disorders', *Journal of Abnormal Psychology*, 103(1): 103–16.

Cohen, S. and Rodriguez, M. (1995) 'Pathways linking affective disturbances and physical disorders', *Health Psychology*, 14(5): 374–80.

Cooper, M.L., Agocha, V.B. and Sheldon, M.S. (2000) 'A motivational perspective on risky behaviors: The role of personality and affect regulatory processes', *Journal of Personality*, 68(6): 1069–88.

Cooper, T., Detre, T. and Weiss, S.M. (1981) 'Coronary-prone behavior and coronary heart disease: A critical review', *Circulation*, 63(6): 1199–215.

Costa, P.T. Jr. and McCrae, R.R. (1987) 'Neuroticism, somatic complaints, and disease: Is the bark worse than the bite?', *Journal of Personality*, 55(2): 299–316.

Costa, P.T. Jr. and McCrae, R.R. (1992) *Professional Manual: Revised NEO Personality Inventory (NEO-PI-R) and the NEO Five-Factor Inventory (NEO-FFI)*. Odessa, FL: Psychological Assessment Resources.

Cronbach, L.J. and Meehl, P.E. (1955) 'Construct validity in psychological tests', *Psychology Bulletin*, 52(4): 281–302.

Danese, A., Pariente, C.M., Caspi, A., Taylor, A. and Poulton, R. (2007) 'Childhood maltreatment predicts adult inflammation in a life-course study', *Proceedings of the National Academy of Sciences*, 104(4): 1319–24.

David, J., Green, P., Martin, R. and Suls, J. (1997) 'Differential roles of neuroticism and extraversion and event desirability for mood in daily life: An integrative model of top-down and bottom-up influences', *Journal of Personality and Social Psychology*, 73(1): 149–59.

Dew, M.A., Hoch, C.C., Buysse, D.J., Monk, T.H., Begley, A.E., Houck, P.R. et al. (2003) 'Healthy older adults sleep predicts all-cause mortality at 4 to 19 years of follow-up', *Psychosomatic Medicine*, 65(1): 63–73.

Digman, J.M. (1990) 'Personality structure: Emergence of the Five-Factor Model', *Annual Review of Psychology*, 41: 417–40.

Endler, N.S. and Magnusson, D. (1976) 'Toward an interactional psychology of personality', *Psychology Bulletin*, 83(5): 956–79.

Everson, S.A., Goldberg, D.E., Kaplan, G.A., Cohen, R.D., Pukkala, E., Tuomilehto, J. et al. (1996) 'Hopelessness and risk of mortality and incidence of myocardial infarction and cancer', *Psychosomatic Medicine*, 58(1): 113–21.

Everson, S.A., Kaplan, G.A., Goldberg, D.E. and Salonen, J.T. (2000) 'Hypertension incidence is predicted by high levels of hopelessness in Finnish men', *Hypertension*, 35(9): 561–7.

Everson, S.A., Kaplan, G.A., Goldberg, D.E., Salonen, R. and Salonen, J.T. (1997) 'Hopelessness and 4-year progression of carotid atherosclerosis', *Arteriosclerosis Thrombosis and Vascular Biology*, 17(8): 1490–5.

Everson, S.A., Kauhanen, J., Kaplan, G., Goldberg, D., Julkunen, J., Tuomilehto, J. et al. (1997) 'Hostility and increased risk of mortality and myocardial infarction: The mediating role of behavioral risk factors', *American Journal of Epidemiology*, 146(2): 142–52.

Frasure-Smith, N., Lesperance, F. and Taljic, M. (1995) 'Depression and 18-month prognosis after myocardial infarction', *Circulation*, 91(4): 999–1005.

Friedman, H.S. (2006) 'Personality, disease, and self-healing', in H.S. Friedman and R. Cohen Silver (eds), *Foundations of Health Psychology*. New York: Oxford University Press, pp. 172–99.

Friedman, H.S. and Booth-Kewley, S. (1987) 'The disease-prone personality: A meta-analytic view of the construct', *American Psychologist*, 42(6): 539–55.

Friedman, H.S., Tucker, J.S., Tomlinson-Keasey, C., Schwartz, J.E., Wingard, D.L. and Criqui, M.H. (1993) 'Does childhood personality predict longevity?', *Journal of Personality and Social Psychology*, 65(1): 176–85.

Friedman, M. and Rosenman, R.H. (1959) 'Association of a specific overt behavior pattern with increases in blood cholesterol, blood clotting time, incidence of arcus senilis and clinical coronary artery disease', *Journal of the American Medical Association*, 169: 1286–96.

Fuller, K.H., Waters, W.F., Binks, P.G. and Anderson, T. (1997) 'Generalized anxiety and sleep architecture: A polysomnographic investigation', *Sleep: Journal of Sleep Research and Sleep Medicine*, 20(5): 370–6.

Gallo, L.C. and Smith, T.W. (1998) 'Construct validation of health-relevant personality traits: Interpersonal circumplex and five-factor model analyses of the Aggression Questionnaire', *International Journal of Behavioral Medicine*, 5(2): 129–47.

Gallo, L.C., Smith, T.W. and Cox, C.M. (2006) 'Socioeconomic status, psychosocial processes, and perceived health: An interpersonal perspective', *Annals of Behavioral Medicine*, 31(2): 109–19.

Gillham, J.E., Shatte, A.J. Reivich, K.J. and Seligman, M.E.P. (2001) 'Optimism, pessimism, and explanatory style', in E.C. Chang (ed.), *Optimism and Pessimism: Implications for Theory, Research, and Practice*. Washington, DC: American Psychological Association, pp. 53–76.

Giltay, E.J., Geleijnse, J.M., Zitman, F.G., Hoekstra, T. and Schouten, E.G. (2004) 'Dispositional optimism and all-cause and cardiovascular mortality in a prospective cohort of elderly Dutch men and women', *Archives of General Psychiatry*, 61(11): 1126–35.

Golden, S.H., Williams, J.E., Ford, D.E., Yeh, H.C., Paton Sanford, C., Nieto, F.J. et al. (2004) 'Depressive symptoms and the risk of type 2 diabetes: The Atherosclerosis Risk in Communities study', *Diabetes Care*, 27(2): 429.

Gray, E.K. and Watson, D. (2002) 'General and specific traits of personality and their relation to sleep and academic performance', *Journal of Personality*, 70(2): 177–206.

Gray, J.A. (1987) *The Psychology of Fear and Stress*. New York: Cambridge University Press.

Graziano, W.G., Jensen-Campbell, L.A. and Hair, E.C. (1996) 'Perceiving interpersonal conflict and reacting to it: The case for agreeableness', *Journal of Personality and Social Psychology*, 70(5): 820–35.

Gump, B.B., Matthews, K.A., Eberly, L.E., Change, Y.F., MRFIT Research Group (2005) 'Depressive symptoms and mortality in men: Results from the Multiple Risk Factor Intervention Trial', *Stroke*, 36(1): 98–102.

Gunthert, K.C., Cohen, L. and Armelli, S. (1999) 'The role of neuroticism in daily stress and coping', *Journal of Personality and Social Psychology*, 77(5): 1087–100.

Gurtman, M.B. and Pincus, A.L. (2003) 'The circumplex model: Methods and research applications', in J.A. Schinka and W.F. Velicer (eds), *Handbook of Psychology: Research Methods in Psychology* (Vol. 2). New York: Wiley, pp. 407–28.

Gutman, D.A. and Nemeroff, C.B. (2003) 'Persistent central nervous system effects of an adverse early environment: Clinical and preclinical studies', *Physiology and Behavior*, 79(3): 471–8.

Haas, D.C., Davidson, K.W., Schwartz, D.J., Rieckmann, N., Roman, M.J., Pickering, T.J. et al. (2005) 'Depressive symptoms are independently predictive of carotid atherosclerosis', *American Journal of Cardiology*, 95(5): 547–50.

Hampson, S., Goldberg, L.R., Vogt, T.M. and Dubanoski, J.P. (2006) 'Forty years on: Teachers assessment of childrens personality traits predict self-reported health behaviors and outcomes at midlife', *Health Psychology*, 25(1): 57–64.

Hariri, A.R., Mattay, V.S., Tessigore, A., Kolachana, B., Fera, F., Goldman, D. et al. (2002) 'Serotonin transporter genetic variation and the response of the human amygdala', *Science*, 297(5580): 400–3.

Hecker, M.H.L., Chesney, M.A., Black, G.W. and Frautchi, N. (1988) 'Coronary-prone behaviors in the Western Collaborative Group Study', *Psychosomatic Medicine*, 50(2): 153–64.

Helgeson, V.S. and Fritz, H.L. (1999) 'Cognitive adaptation as a predictor of new coronary events after percutaneous transluminal coronary angioplasty', *Psychosomatic Medicine*, 61(4): 488–95.

Hermann, C., Brano-Driehorst, S., Kaminsky, B., Leibring, E., Staats, H. and Ruger, U. (1998) 'Diagnostic groups and depressed mood as predictors of 22-month mortality in medical inpatients', *Archives of General Psychiatry*, 46(4): 345–50.

Herzberg, P.Y., Glaesmer, H. and Hoyer, J. (2006) 'Separating optimism and pessimism: A robust psychometric analysis of the revised Life Orientation Test (LOT-R)', *Psychological Assessment*, 18(4): 433–8.

Holroyd, K.A. and Coyne, J. (1987) 'Personality and health in the 1980s: Psychosomatic medicine revisited?', *Journal of Personality*, 55(2): 360–75.

Houston, B.K., Babyak, M.A., Chesney, M., Black, G. and Ragland, D. (1997) 'Social dominance and 22-year all-cause mortality in men', *Psychosomatic Medicine*, 59(1): 5–12.

Houston, B.K., Chesney, M.A., Black, G.W., Cates, D.S. and Hecker, M.L. (1992) 'Behavioral clusters and coronary heart disease risk', *Psychosomatic Medicine*, 54(4): 447–61.

Idler, E.L. and Benyamini, Y. (1997) 'Self-rated health and mortality. A review of twenty-seven community studies', *Journal of Health and Social Behavior*, 38(1): 21–37.

Kenyon, L.W., Ketterer, M.W., Gheorghiade, M. and Goldstein, S. (1991) 'Psychological factors related to prehospital delay during acute myocardial infarction', *Circulation*, 84(5): 1969–76.

Kiesler, D.J. (1983) 'The 1982 interpersonal circle: A taxonomy for complementarity in human transactions', *Psychology Review*, 90: 185–214.

Kiesler, D.J. (1996) (ed.), *Contemporary Interpersonal Theory and Research: Personality, Psychopathology, and Psychotherapy*. New York: Wiley.

Kubzansky, L.D., Kawachi, I., Spiro, A., Weiss, S.T., Vokonas, P.S. and Sparrow, D. (1997) 'Is worrying bad for your heart? A prospective study of worry and coronary heart disease in the Normative Aging Study', *Circulation*, 95(4): 818–24.

Kubzansky, L.D., Kubzansky, P.E. and Maselko, J. (2004) 'Optimism and pessimism in the context of health: Bipolar opposites or separate constructs?', *Personality and Social Psychology Bulletin*, 30(8): 943–56.

Kubzansky, L.D., Sparrow, D., Vokonas, P. and Kawachi, I. (2001) 'Is the glass half empty or half full? A prospective study of optimism and coronary heart disease in the normative aging study', *Psychosomatic Medicine*, 63(6): 910–16.

Lane, D., Carroll, D., Ring, C., Beevers, D.G. and Lip, G.Y.H. (2001) 'Mortality and quality of life 12 months after myocardial infarction: Effects of depression and anxiety', *Psychosomatic Medicine*, 63(2): 221–30.

Lange, T., Perras, B., Fehm, H.L. and Born, J. (2003) 'Sleep enhances the human antibody response to hepatitis A vaccination', *Psychosomatic Medicine*, 65(5): 831–5.

Lazarus, R.S. and Folkman, S. (1984) *Stress, Appraisal, and Coping*. New York: Springer.

Lee-Baggley, D., Preece, M. and DeLongis, A. (2005) 'Coping with interpersonal stress: Role of Big Five traits', *Journal of Personality*, 73(5): 1141–80.

Luecken, L.J. and Lemery, K.S. (2004) 'Early caregiving and physiological stress responses', *Clinical Psychology Review*, 24(2): 171–91.

Lewis, S.C., Dennis, M.S., O'Rourke, S.J. and Sharpe, M. (2001) 'Negative attitudes among short-term stroke survivors predict worse long-term survival', *Stroke*, 32(7): 1640–5.

Magnus, K., Diener, E., Fugita, F. and Pavot, W. (1993) 'Extraversion and neuroticism as predictors of objective life events: A longitudinal analysis', *Journal of Personality and Social Psychology*, 65(6): 1046–53.

Martin, L.R. and Friedman, H.S. (2000) 'Comparing personality scales across time: An illustrative study of validity and consistency in life-span archival data', *Journal of Personality*, 68(1): 85–110.

Maruta, T., Colligan, R.C., Malinchoc, M. and Offord, K.P. (2000) 'Optimists vs. pessimists: survival rate among medical patients over a 30-year period', *Mayo Clinic Proceedings*, 75: 140–3.

Matthews, K.A. (1988) 'CHD and Type A behaviors: update on an alternative to the Booth-Kewley and Friedman quantitative review', *Psychological Bulletin*, 104(3): 373–80.

Matthews, K.A., Glass, D.C., Rosenman, R.H. and Bortner, R.W. (1977) 'Competitive drive, pattern A, and coronary heart disease: A further analysis of some data from the Western Collaborative Group Study', *Journal of Chronic Disease*, 30(8): 489–98.

Matthews, K.A., Gump, B.B., Harris, K.F., Haney, T.L. and Barefoot, J.C. (2004a) 'Hostile behaviors predict cardiovascular mortality among men enrolled in the Multiple Risk Factor Intervention Trial', *Circulation*, 109(1): 66–70.

Matthews, K.A., Raikkonen, K., Sutton-Tyrrell, K. and Kuller, L.H. (2004b) 'Optimistic attitudes protect against progression of carotid atherosclerosis in health middle-aged women', *Psychosomatic Medicine*, 66(5): 640–4.

Matthews, K.A., Siegel, J.M., Kuller, L.H., Thompson, M. and Varat, M. (1983) 'Determinants of decisions to seek medical treatment by patients with acute myocardial infarction symptoms', *Journal of Personality and Social Psychology*, 44(6): 1144–56.

May, M., McCarron, P., Stansfeld, S., Ben-Shlomo, Y., Gallacher, J., Yarnell, J. et al. (2002) 'Does psychological distress predict the risk of ischemic stroke and transient ischemic attack? The Caerphilly Study', *Stroke*, 33(1): 7–12.

McCrae R.R. and Costa P.T. Jr. (1989) 'The structure of interpersonal traits: Wiggins circumplex and the five-factor model', *Journal of Personality and Social Psychology*, 56(4): 586–95.

McCrae, R.R and Costa, P.T. Jr. (1996) 'Toward a new generation of personality theories: theoretical contexts for the five-factor model', in J.S. Wiggins (ed.), *The Five-Factor Model of Personality*. New York: Guilford, pp. 51–87.

McEwen, B.S. (1998) 'Stress, adaptation, and disease – allostasis and allostatic load', *Annals of the New York Academy of Sciences,* 840: 33–44.

Mechanic, D. (1972) 'Social psychological factors affecting the presentation of bodily complaints', *New England Journal of Medicine*, 286(21): 1132–9.

Meehl, P.E. (1970) 'Nuisance variables and the ex post facto design', in M. Radner and S. Winokur (eds), *Minnesota Studies in the Philosophy of Science: Vol. IV Analyses of Theories and Methods of Physics and Psychology*. Minneapolis: University of Minnesota Press, pp. 373–402.

Miller, T.Q., Smith, T.W., Turner, C.W., Guijarro, M.L. and Hallet, A.J. (1996) 'A meta-analytic review of research on hostility and physical health', *Psychology Bulletin*, 119(2): 322–48.

Miller, T.Q., Turner, C.W., Tindale, R.S., Posavac, E.J. and Dugoni, B.L. (1991) 'Reasons for the trend toward null findings in research on Type A behavior', *Psychology Bulletin*, 110(3): 469–85.

Mischel, W. (2004) 'Toward an integrative science of the person', *Annual Review of Psychology*, 55: 1–22.

Mischel, W. and Shoda, Y. (1998) 'Reconciling processing dynamics and personality dispositions', *Annual Review of Psychology*, 49: 229–58.

Moffitt, T.E., Caspi, A. and Rutter, M. (2005) 'Strategy for investigating interactions between measured genes and measured environments', *Archives of General Psychiatry*, 62(5): 473–81.

Mosely, J.V. and Linden, W. (2006) 'Predicting blood pressure and heart rate change with cardiovascular reactivity and recovery: Results from a 3-year and 10-year follow-up', *Psychosomatic Medicine*, 68(6): 833–43.

Norem, J.K. and Chang, E.C. (2001) 'A very full glass: adding complexity to our applications of optimism and pessimism research', in E.C. Chang (ed.), *Optimism and Pessimism: Implications for Theory, Research and Practice.* Washington, DC: American Psychological Association, pp. 347–67.

O'Carroll, R.E., Smith, K.B., Grubb, N.R., Fox, K.A. and Masterton, G. (2001) 'Psychological factors associated with delay in attending hospital following a myocardial infarction', *Journal of Psychosomatic Medicine*, 51(4): 611–4.

Olson, M.B., Krantz, D.S., Kelsey, S.F., Pepine, C.J., Sopko, G., Handberg, E. et al. (2005) 'Hostility scores are associated with increased risk of cardiovascular events in women undergoing coronary angiography: a report from the NHLBI-Sponsored WISE study', *Psychosomatic Medicine*, 67(4): 546–52.

Oltmanns, T.E. and Turkheimer, E. (2006) 'Perceptions of self and others regarding pathological personality traits', in R.F. Krueger and J.L. Tackett (eds), *Personality and Psychopathology.* New York: Guilford, pp. 71–111.

Ozer, D.J. (1999) 'Four principles for personality assessment', in L.A. Pervin and O.P. John (eds), *Handbook of Personality: Theory and Research.* New York: Oxford, pp. 671–86.

Peterson, C., Seligman, M., Yurko, K., Martin, L.R. and Friedman, H. (1998) 'Catastrophizing and untimely death', *Psychological Science*, 9(2): 127–30.

Phillips, A.N. and Davey Smith, G. (1991) 'How independent are "independent" effects? Relative risk estimation when correlated exposures are measured imprecisely', *Journal of Clinical Epidemiology*, 44(11): 1223–31.

Pincus, A.L. and Ansell, E.B. (2003) 'Interpersonal theory of personality', in T. Millon and M.J. Lerner (eds), *Handbook of Psychology: Personality and Social Psychology* (Vol. 5). New York: Wiley, pp. 209–29.

Raikkonen, K., Matthews, K.A., Flory, J.D., Owens, J.F. and Gump, B. (1999) 'Effects of optimism, pessimism, and trait anxiety on ambulatory blood pressure and mood during everyday life', *Journal of Personality and Social Psychology*, 76(1): 104–13.

Roberts, B.W., Caspi, A. and Moffitt, T.E. (2003) 'Work experiences and personality development in young adulthood', *Journal of Personality and Social Psychology*, 84(3): 582–93.

Robins, R.W., Caspi, A. and Moffitt, T.E. (2002) 'It's not just who you're with, it's who you are: Personality and relationship experiences across multiple relationships', *Journal of Personality*, 70(6): 925–64.

Rosenman, R.H. (1978) 'The interview method of assessment of the coronary-prone behavior behavior pattern', in T.M. Dembroski, S.M. Weiss, J.L. Shields, S.G. Haynes and M. Feinleig (eds), *Coronary-prone Behavior.* New York: Springer-Verlag, pp. 55–70.

Rowan, P.J., Haas, D., Campbell, J.A., Maclean, D.R. and Davidson, K.W. (2005) 'Depressive symptoms have an independent gradient risk for coronary heart disease incidence in a random, population-based sample', *Annals of Epidemiology*, 15(4): 316–20.

Rutledge, T. and Hogan, B.E. (2002) 'A quantitative review of prospective evidence linking psychological factors with hypertension development', *Psychosomatic Medicine*, 64(5): 758–66.

Ryff, C.D. and Singer, B. (1998) 'The contours of positive human health', *Psychological Inquiry*, 9(1):1–28.

Scheier, M.F. and Carver, C.S. (1985) 'Optimism, coping, and health: Assessment and implications of generalized outcome expectancies', *Health Psychology*, 4(3): 219–47.

Scheier, M.F., Matthews, K.A., Owens, J., Magovern, G., Lefebure, R., Abbott, R. and Carver, C. (1989) 'Dispositional optimism and recovery from coronary artery bypass surgery: the beneficial effects of physical and psychological well-being', *Journal of Personality and Social Psychology*, 57(6): 1024–40.

Scheier, M.F., Matthews, K.A., Owens, J.F., Schulz, R., Bridges, M.W., Magovern, G.J. and Carver, C.S. (1999) 'Optimism and rehospitalization after coronary artery bypass graft surgery', *Archives of Internal Medicine*, 159(8): 829–35.

Schwartz, A.R., Gerin W., Davidson, K.W., Pickering, T.G., Brosschot, J.F., Thayer, J.F.,

Christenfeld, N. and Linden, W. (2003) 'Toward a causal model of cardiovascular responses to stress and the development of cardiovascular disease', *Psychosomatic Medicine*, 65(1): 22–35.

Schultz, R., Bookwala, J., Knapp, J.E., Scheier, M. and Williamson, G.M. (1996) 'Pessimism, age, and cancer mortality', *Psychology and Aging*, 11(2): 304–9.

Segerstrom, S.C. and Miller, G.E. (2004) 'Psychological stress and the human immune system: A meta-analytic study of 30 years of inquiry', *Psychological Bulletin*, 130(4): 601–30.

Segerstrom, S.C. and Smith, T.W. (2006) 'Physiological pathways from personality to health: The cardiovascular and immune systems', in M. Vollrath (ed.), *Handbook of Personality and Health*. New York: Wiley, pp. 175–94.

Shekelle, R.B., Gale, M., Ostfeld, A.M. and Paul, O. (1983) 'Hostility, risk of coronary heart disease, and mortality', *Psychosomatic Medicine*, 45(2): 109–14.

Shekelle, R.B., Gale, M. and Norusis, M. (1985) 'Type A score (Jenkins Activity Survey) and risk of recurrent coronary heart disease in the Aspirin Myocardial Infarction Study', *American Journal of Cardiology*, 56(4): 221–5.

Shiner, R. and Caspi, A. (2003) 'Personality differences in childhood and adolescence: Measurement, development, and consequences', *Journal of Child Psychology and Psychiatry*, 44(1): 2–32.

Siegman, A.W., Kubzansky, L.D., Kawachi, I., Boyle, S., Vokonas, P.S. and Sparrow, D. (2000) 'A prospective study of dominance and coronary heart disease in the normative aging study', *American Journal of Cardiology*, 86(2): 145–9.

Smith, T.W., Gallo, L.C. and Ruiz, J.M. (2003) 'Toward a social psychophysiology of cardiovascular reactivity: interpersonal concepts and methods in the study of stress and coronary disease', in J. Suls and K. Wallston (eds), *Social Psychological Foundations of Health and Illness*. Oxford: Blackwell, pp. 335–66.

Smith, T.W., Glazer, K., Ruiz, J.M. and Gallo, L.C. (2004a) 'Hostility, anger, aggressiveness and coronary heart disease: An interpersonal perspective on personality, emotion and health', *Journal of Personality*, 72(6): 1217–70.

Smith, T.W. and MacKenzie, J. (2006) 'Personality and risk of physical illness', *Annual Review of Clinical Psychology*, 2: 435–67.

Smith, T.W., Orleans, C.T. and Jenkins, C.D. (2004b) 'Prevention and health promotion: decades of progress, new challenges, and an emerging agenda', *Health Psychology*, 23(2): 126–31.

Smith, T.W., Pope, M.K., Rhodewalt, F. and Poulton, J.L. (1989) 'Optimism, neuroticism, coping, and symptom reports: an alternative interpretation of the Life Orientation Test', *Journal of Personality and Social Psychology*, 56(4): 640–8.

Smith, T.W. and Ruiz, J.M. (2002) 'Psychosocial influences on the development and course of coronary heart disease: Current status and implications for research and practice', *Journal of Consulting and Clinical Psychology*, 70(3): 548–68.

Smith, T.W. and Spiro, A. (2002) 'Personality, health, and aging: Prolegomenon for the next generation', *Journal of Research in Personality*, 36(4): 363–94.

Smith, T.W., Uchino, B.N., Berg, C.A., Florsheim, P., Pearce, G., Hawkins, M., Hopkins, P.N. and Yoon, H.C. (2007) 'Hostile personality traits and coronary artery calcification in middle-aged and older married couples: Different effects for self-reports versus spouse ratings', *Psychosomatic Medicine*, 69(5): 441–8.

Smith, T.W. and Williams, P.G. (1992) 'Personality and health: Advantages and limitations of the five factor model', *Journal of Personality*, 60(2): 395–423.

Stamatakis, K.A., Lynch, J., Everson, S.A., Raghunathan, T., Salonen, J.T. and Kaplan, G.A. (2004) 'Self-esteem and mortality: prospective evidence from a population-based study', *American Journal of Epidemiology*, 14(1): 58–65.

Stern, S.L., Dhanda, R. and Hazuda, H.P. (2001) 'Hopelessness predicts mortality in older Mexican and European Americans', *Psychosomatic Medicine*, 63(3): 344–51.

Stewart, J.C., Janicki, D.L. and Kamarck, T.W. (2006) 'Cardiovascular reactivity and recovery from psychological challenge as predictors of 3-year change in blood pressure', *Health Psychology*, 25(1): 111–18.

Stone, S.V. and Costa, P.T. Jr. (1990) 'Disease-prone personality or distress-prone personality?

The role of neuroticism in coronary heart disease', in H.S. Friedman (ed.), *Personality and Disease*. New York: Wiley, pp. 178–200.

Strik, J.J., Denollet, J., Lausberg, R. and Honig, A. (2003) 'Comparing symptoms of depression and anxiety as predictors of cardiac events and increased health care consumption after myocardial infarction', *Journal of the American College of Cardiology*, 42(10): 1801–7.

Suls, J. and Bunde, J. (2005) 'Anger, anxiety, and depression as risk factors for cardiovascular disease: The problems and implications of overlapping affective dispositions', *Psychological Bulletin*, 131(2): 260–300.

Suls, J. and Martin, R. (2005) 'The daily life of the garden-variety neurotic: Reactivity, stressor exposure, mood spillover, and maladaptive coping', *Journal of Personality*, 73(1): 1–25.

Suls, J., Martin, R. and David, J. (1998) 'Person–environment fit and its limits: Agreeableness, neuroticism and emotional reactivity to interpersonal conflict', *Personality and Social Psychology Bulletin*, 24(1): 88–98.

Surtees, P.G., Wainwright, N.W., Luben, R., Day, N.E. and Khaw, K-T. (2005) 'Prospective cohort study of hostility and the risk of cardiovascular disease mortality', *International Journal of Cardiology*, 100(1): 155–61.

Taylor, S.E., Lerner, J.S., Sage, R.M., Lehman, B.J. and Seeman, T.E. (2004) 'Early environment, emotions, responses to stress, and health', *Journal of Personality*, 72(6): 1365–93.

Trapnell, P.D. and Wiggins, J.S. (1990) 'Extension of the Interpersonal Adjective Scales to include the big five dimensions of personality', *Journal of Personality and Social Psychology*, 59(4): 781–90.

Trobst, K. (2000) 'An interpersonal conceptualization and quantification of social support transactions', *Personality and Social Psychology Bulletin*, 26(9): 971–86.

Traupman, E., Smith, T.W., Uchino, B.N., Berg, C.A., Trobst, K.K. and Costa, P.T. Jr. (submitted) 'Interpersonal circumplex descriptions of psychosocial risk factors for physical disease: Application to the domains of hostility, neuroticism, and marital adjustment.

Uchino, B.N., Vaughn, A.A., Matwin, S. (in press) 'Social processes linking personality to physical health: A multilevel analysis with emphasis on hostility and optimism', in F. Rhodewalt (ed.), *Personality and Social Behavior*. New York: Psychology Press.

Vollrath, M. and Torgersen, S. (2002) 'Who takes health risks? A probe into eight personality types', *Personality and Individual Differences*, 32(7): 1185–97.

Wagner, C.C., Kiesler, D.J. and Schmidt, J.A. (1995) 'Assessing the interpersonal transaction cycle: convergence of action and reaction interpersonal circumplex measures', *Journal of Personality and Social Psychology*, 69(5): 938–49.

Watkins, L.L., Grossman, P., Krishnan, R. and Sherwood, A. (1998) 'Anxiety and vagal control of heart rate', *Psychosomatic Medicine*, 60(4): 498–502.

Watson, D. and Clark, L.A. (1984) 'Negative affectivity: The disposition to experience aversive emotional states', *Psychology Bulletin*, 96(3): 465–90.

Watson, D. and Pennebaker, J.W. (1989) 'Health complaints, stress, and distress: Exploring the central role of negative affectivity', *Psychology Review*, 96(2): 234–54.

Weiss, A. and Costa, P.T. Jr. (2005) 'Domain and facet predictors of all-cause mortality among Medicare patients aged 65–100', *Psychosomatic Medicine*, 67(5): 724–33.

West, S.G. and Finch, J.F. (1997) 'Personality measurement: Reliability and validity issues', in Hogan et al. (eds), *Handbook of Personality Psychology*. Academic Press: New York, pp. 143–64.

Wiebe, D.J. and Fortenberry, K.T. (2006) 'Mechanisms linking personality and health', in M.E. Vollrath (ed.), *Handbook of Personality and Health*. West Sussex: Wiley, pp. 137–56.

Wiggins, J.S. (1979) 'A psychological taxonomy of trait-descriptive terms: The interpersonal domain', *Journal of Personality and Social Psychology*, 37(3): 395–412.

Williams, P.G. and Gunn, H.E. (2005) 'Gender, personality, and psychopathology', in J.C. Thomas and D.L. Segal (eds), *Comprehensive Handbook of Personality and Psychopathology: Vol. 1 Personality and Everyday Functioning*. Hoboken, NJ: Wiley, pp. 432–42.

Williams, P.G., O'Brien, C.D. and Colder, C.R. (2004) 'The effects of neuroticism and extraversion of self-assessed health and health-relevant cognition', *Personality and Individual Differences,* 37(1): 83–94.

Williams, P.G. and Wiebe, D.J. (2000) 'Individual differences in self-assessed health: Gender, neuroticism, and physical symptom reports', *Personality and Individual Differences,* 28(5): 823–35.

Wilson, R.S., Mendes de Leon, C.F., Bienias, J.L., Evans, D.A. and Bennett, D.A. (2004) 'Personality and mortality in old age', *The Journals of Gerontology, Series B, Psychological Sciences and Social Sciences,* 59(3): 110–16.

Zonderman, A.B., Herbst, J., Schmidt, C., Costa, P.T. and McCrae, R.R. (1993) 'Depressive symptoms as a non-specific graded risk for psychiatric diagnoses', *Journal of Abnormal Psychology,* 102(1): 544–52.

Zuckerman, M. and Kuhlman, D.M. (2000) 'Personality and risk-taking: Common biosocial factors', *Journal of Personality,* 68(6): 999–1029.

32

Anxiety, Depression, and Anger: Core Components of Negative Affect in Medical Populations

Ephrem Fernandez and Robert D. Kerns

NEGATIVE AFFECT

Within psychology, the term 'affect' has evolved out of restricted usages within psychoanalysis and clinical psychiatry into a general term that refers to any kind of subjective feeling (Tomkins, 1962). Imposed with a metaphor from chemistry, affect is now regarded as either positive or negative in valence, the former implying pleasant feelings and the latter implying unpleasant feelings. Other terms used interchangeably with negative affect are 'dysphoria' and 'distress', though sometimes the words 'stress' and 'suffering' are also used to loosely suggest negative affect. The main point of consensus is that negative affect refers to any form of subjective feeling that is experienced as unpleasant in quality. Such unpleasantness can also vary quantitatively, that is, on a dimension of intensity. This common property of affect (be it positive or negative) is also labeled as activation or arousal.

Various types of negative affect have appeared in the diagnostic criteria for psychiatric disorders (e.g. schizophrenia, post-traumatic disorder, borderline personality disorder, obsessive-compulsive disorder) partly because 'distress' is regarded as one of the associated features of all mental disorders (American Psychiatric Association, 2000). Yet people with somatic complaints of medical disease have rarely been examined for clinically significant levels of negative affect. This is probably an outcome of the mind–body dualism that has infused the health sciences for centuries. In this chapter, we report on some of the recent findings that do point to a spectrum of negative affect in medical populations. Supported by theoretical foundations and empirical data, we direct our attention to three specific types of negative affect: anger, fear, and sadness, or their clinical equivalents of anger, anxiety, and depression, respectively. This, we call the core of negative affect (CONA). With reference to medical populations, we focus on the three highly prevalent ailments in developed as well as developing countries of the world: cardiovascular disease (CVD), cancer, and HIV/AIDS. Furthermore, we draw parallels between the CONA as manifested in these populations and CONA as already researched in one population: patients who suffer from pain.

ANXIETY, DEPRESSION, AND ANGER

Anxiety and depression have often been studied as twin features of negative affect, but more recently, anger has been introduced as a close relative to form a new triad of negative affect. Barlow (1991) made a bridge between the experimental psychology of emotions and the clinical psychology of emotional disorders, by postulating how fear, sadness, and anger lie at the root of anxiety, depression, and anger disorders. Spielberger et al. (1995) grouped depression, anxiety, and anger under the label of 'emotional vital signs', a construct later echoed by Ghosh and Puja (2004). Examining pain patients as a 'test population', Fernandez et al. (1999) and Fernandez (2002) showed that there is ample empirical evidence to position anxiety, depression, and anger within the core of negative affect.

Vital signs

The idea of emotional vital signs was originally spun out of Spielberger's view that anxiety was analogous with heart rate, anger with blood pressure, and depression with fever. The analogy may not be perfect since the term 'vital signs' as used in medicine refers to objective signs that the systems of the body (required to keep a person alive) are in working order or normal. When measured values for respiration, heart rate, blood pressure, and temperature are zero, the person is evidently dead; when they reach a certain norm for the species, the organism is essentially

alive and well. In the case of anxiety, depression, and anger, zero values would point to healthy emotional functioning, while high values, though not necessarily a sign that life is threatened, do raise concerns for the well-being of oneself or others. Profound depression could forebode suicidality, extreme anger could potentiate acts of destruction, and high-grade fear could be crippling or disabling. In that sense, if one were to select three affective types as indices of a person's emotional health, anxiety, depression, and anger would probably be the most appropriate choices.

The core

In using the word 'core' to refer to the group of three negative affects, we do not imply anything that resides deep within the individual. These subjective feelings are not necessarily hidden as part of an individual's inner life. In fact, they are quite open to observation and measurement. It is their ubiquity and functional significance that earns them membership within the core of negative affect. This kind of pervasiveness and importance is also captured in the common adage that depression is the common cold of psychiatry, the notion in much of psychology that anxiety is inherent in neuroses if not in our very existence as humans, and the vast and recurrent media coverage of acts of anger and rage.

Evolutionary roots

The clinical syndromes of anxiety, depression, and anger are rooted in fear, sadness, and anger, respectively. These three discrete emotions play a primordial and universal role in the defense against aversive stimuli. Fear, for instance, is regarded as the most basic of all emotions because it motivates escape or avoidance from predators or other insurmountable threats, thereby being crucial for survival. As Marks puts it 'Fear is a vital evolutionary legacy ... Without fear, few would survive long under natural conditions' (1987: 3). Anger is a twin emotion of fear in the defense against aversive stimuli. Thus Walter Cannon (1929) coined the term 'fight or flight' to refer to the twin options of fleeing out of fear or fighting out of anger during an emergency. Inasmuch as anger mobilizes the organism to retaliate in the face of provocation or assault, it promotes survival.

Surprisingly omitted from evolutionary accounts of basic emotion is sadness. This emotion may be viewed as a third option in the repertoire of responses toward threat or attack. When escape is not possible, when retaliation is not feasible, and the prospect of defeat is looming, then sadness is the emotion that arises in the service of the next most appropriate response of yielding or submission. A variant of it is what Seligman and colleagues term 'learned helplessness' (Peterson et al., 1993; Seligman, 1972). Buerki and Adler simply call it 'giving up' in order to conserve resources:

> If a person has experienced certain situations, in which fight or flight was impossible or of no avail, he or she might react with conservation–withdrawal when exposed anew … Conservation–withdrawal is primarily a biological reaction pattern, the counterpart of Cannon's fight–flight reaction. Both reaction patterns are directed toward adaptation to stressful situations. They are aimed at self-protection and self-preservation. Fight–flight attempts to reach its goal by engaging, conservation–withdrawal by disengaging and saving of energy. (2005: 5–6)

In the face of an overwhelming offensive, fighting would be a waste of resources if not an acceleration toward death. Similarly, when fighting or fleeing are not viable options in the face of overwhelming adversity, the emotion is likely to be sorrow and dejection which primes the individual to yield or surrender.

Physiological mechanisms

It has been portrayed that certain emotions have biochemical commonalities such as hormones and neurotransmitters (serotonin, dopamine), and involve the same brain structures. The evidence for this has been highly conflicting and no attempt will be made to review these findings here. Besides, it is not necessary to show biochemical specificity to justify the existence of different emotions or to show biochemical commonality to argue for the similarity of emotions.

What is relatively clear is that anger and fear involve the hypothalamic–pituitary axis in order to mobilize the organism toward vigorous action of fight or flight. However, sympathetic reactivity is not only the result of negative affect but can be even greater during positive affect (Heponiemi et al., 2006). Also, depression is the one component of negative affect that is least likely to involve sympathetic activation, and that makes sense because the goal in depression is not one of action as much as inaction.

Recently, Ryff et al. (2006) found that anxiety and anger had more in common with regard to biological correlates. Women with an average age of 74 years old completed psychometric tests of anxiety, depression, and anger in addition to providing urine and blood samples on multiple occasions. It was found that traits of anxiety were negatively associated with systolic blood pressure (SBP) and positively associated with glycosylated hemoglobin. Traits of anger were inversely correlated with SBP and positively associated with glycosylated hemoglobin. Depression did not have any significant associations with the above biological correlates but was positively associated with weight.

AFFECTIVE FORM

As pointed out earlier, research has resoundingly demonstrated that affect can be characterized in terms of valence and intensity. In other words, it can be distinguished qualitatively as well as quantitatively. Being high in affective arousal says nothing about whether the person is elated or upset, just as being low in emotional arousal leaves open the possibility that the person may be gloomy or just glad. In addition to valence and intensity, affect can also be described in terms of form. By this we mean that affect (which we introduced as a general term) can assume different configurations depending on its patterns of occurrence.

State versus trait

One binary distinction, now popular in psychology, is between affect as a momentary state versus affect as an enduring trait. Thus, the anger a person experiences can be qualified in terms of whether it is a passing event or a habitual occurrence. Most of the effort in making this distinction is credited to Spielberger and colleagues who first published the state–trait anxiety scale (STAI; Spielberger et al., 1977), then the state–trait anger expression inventory (STAXI; Spielberger, 1988), and more recently, the state–trait depression scale (STDS; Krohne et al., 2002). In doing so, they have proposed that affective quality be distinguished according to whether it is a state happening 'right now' or a trait that is present 'most of the time'. This mirrors the dichotomy between situational and dispositional aspects of behavior that have been the subject of much discussion by personality theorists and behaviorists.

Emotion, mood, temperament

The state–trait dichotomy was certainly an advancement upon vernacular labels for affect, and it soon caught on as a practice in psychological research to describe both state and trait when assessing anxiety, anger, or depression. However, the state–trait instruments are limited by some ambiguities (Fernandez, 2002). Asking subjects to report how they feel 'right now' still leaves unclear the distinction between emotion and mood, both of which may be present at a point in time and hence get subsumed under 'state'.

Similarly, asking how a person 'feels generally' may elicit answers that could pertain to either mood or trait because both mood and trait share the property of taking up more time. Clearly, the domain that is most obscured by the state–trait distinction of affect is mood.

A further improvement would be to refine the dichotomy into a trichotomy which allows for any affective quality to assume the form of an emotional episode, a mood state, or a temperamental trend (Table 32.1). The first of these three forms represents a relatively sharp and short-lived change in affective intensity, the second represents a medium-term duration of affect, and the third represents the recurrent frequency of a particular affect. These in turn correspond to the phasic, tonic, and cyclic properties of all affect. Emotion occurs as an episode and is therefore phasic, mood persists and is therefore tonic, and temperament is the recurrence of a particular emotion and therefore has a cyclic quality.

These three different forms of any affective quality are sometimes reflected by the semantic variations within many languages. In English for example, when a person becomes angry, that condition may be labeled anger or fury; when the anger persists for an extended time, the person may be said to be in a 'crabby' or irritable' mood, whereas one who is habitually angry may be deemed a hostile or fractious person (Table 32.1). Language, however, turns out to be a crude instrument for labeling affect because of numerous individual differences in word

Table 32.1 Emotion, mood, and temperament forms of affect

Affective quality	Affective form		
	Emotion	*Mood*	*Temperament*
Fear	Afraid	Anxious	Nervous
Anger	Angry	Irritable/ irascible	Hostile
Sadness	Sad	Depressive/ dysthymic	Melancholic

usage and the fact that any single language has its fair share of gaps and redundancies in labeling phenomena.

CORE OF NEGATIVE AFFECT (CONA) IN MEDICAL POPULATIONS

In our present review of the research on anger, fear, and sadness in medical populations, it was not always possible to clearly delineate what was emotion from what was mood-related, or temperament but we do regard this tripartite form of affect as a necessary frame of reference for future research in this field. Another obstacle to firm conclusions in this endeavor was the uncertainty of the exact role or influence played by each affective type within each medical condition. As in the context of pain, affect could be a precipitant, a predisposing factor, an aggravator, a perpetuating factor, a consequence, or just a correlate (Fernandez, 2002). With regard to the last of these, it would also help to know if we are referring to co-occurrence, covariance, or equivalence between two variables. This is another proposed extension of our methodological approach to studying affect in illness, even though past literature may not lend itself to such a level of discrimination.

Surveying the last five years of published research, we set out to find studies of CVD, cancer, and HIV/AIDS in which all three core components of negative affect had been investigated. The product was a handful of studies quite divergent in terms of their design and their hypotheses. Nevertheless, these studies mark the beginnings of a new line of enquiry into the CONA and they are therefore the subject of review in the accompanying section.

Cardiovascular disease (CVD)

In an extensive narrative review of CONA in coronary heart disease (CHD), Suls and Bunde (2005) reported (1) evidence for depression in the development (precipitation) of CHD; (2) some evidence for depression leading to disease progression (exacerbation) in CHD; (3) evidence for anxiety in the development of CHD; (4) meager evidence for anxiety in the progression of CHD; (5) some evidence for hostility in the development of CHD; and (6) minimal evidence of hostility in the progression of CHD. This means that anxiety, depression, and anger are primarily precipitants rather than aggravators of CHD. This is only in partial agreement with the findings on pain, where anxiety is a definitely a precipitator, depression is largely a consequence, and anger is at least a correlate of pain. Suls and Bunde do not comment on the relative or collective effects of the triad of emotions on CHD because of insufficient research on all three affective qualities within the same samples.

Mixed results in the review by Suls and Bunde may be due to methodologically diverse studies – especially the use of different measures of affect across studies. Also, Suls and Bunde relied on significance levels rather than effect sizes to reach their inferences. Their interpretations that anxiety and depression (but not anger) are related to increased CHD risk in healthy samples may be re-evaluated on close inspection of their data as summarized in Table 32.2. As shown in the table, the actual percentage of studies reporting significant relationships between affect and development of CHD never deviated far from chance levels nor did it differ appreciably across the three affective types: 53% for depression, 42% for anxiety, and 48% for anger (Table 32.2). The role of depression as an aggravator of existing CHD is unclear due to what the authors identified as negative significant effects. Unfortunately, the exact number of negative significant effects was not specified. Other than that, the percentage of studies reporting significant aggravation of CHD by affect is remarkably similar: 29% for anxiety, and 27% for anger. Despite these findings, the role of anger (relative to its CONA counterparts) is seemingly understated in the etiology of CHD.

Table 32.2   Number of studies showing affective influences on coronary heart disease (CHD), based on Suls and Bunde (2005)

			Significance of effect			
Direction of effects			Significant	Marginal or select significant	Non-significance	Total
Depression	→	CHD	10	7	2	19
Depression	↑	CHD	24	5	15	44
Anxiety	→	CHD	5	3	3	12 or 11
Anxiety	↑	CHD	4	1	9	14
Anger	→	CHD				
	Cynical hostility		5	2	4	11
	Trait anger		1	1	1	3
	Anger expression		5	2	2	9
	Σ		11	5	7	23
Anger	↑	CHD				
	Cynical hostility		1	0	5	6
	Trait anger		1	1	1	3
	Anger expression		2	0	4	6
	Σ		4	1	10	15

→ Precipitating factor
↑ Exacerbating factor

It must also be pointed out that Suls and Bunde used measures of anger expression as predictors of CHD prognosis, when alternatively anger inhibition has also been implicated in CHD (Brosschot and Thayer, 1998; Magai et al., 2003; Smith and MacKenzie, 2006). The suppression or internalization of anger may demand greater cognitive effort and involve vagal mechanisms that increase the risk of cardiovascular deterioration. Given that many of the studies reported used the STAXI to assess anger, a distinction could have been made between internalized and externalized anger.

A subsequent study by Kubzansky et al. (2006) appeared in response to the limitations of previous research in which anxiety, depression, and anger had been measured either singly or else as parts of a broader construct. The authors proposed a measure of general distress common to anxiety, depression, and anger in addition to orthogonal measures that were termed 'iso-anxiety', 'iso-depression', and 'iso-anger', respectively. They turned to the MMPI-2 which has 72 items that make up three content scales for measuring anxiety, depression, and anger, respectively. Responses to these 72 items were extracted from a sample of 1,306 men who had completed the MMPI-2, and these data were subsequently analyzed using principal factor analysis with orthogonal varimax rotation. Based on this, three near-orthogonal scales were created for measuring the three corresponding affective types. Additionally, a fourth 'general distress' scale was constructed to include items that loaded equally strongly on more than one factor. The same sample of men was followed up for an average of 11 years at which point the MMPI-2 was re-administered. Data were analyzed in terms of multivariate-adjusted relative risks of CHD for those highest versus lowest on each of the scales. Results showed a strong association between general distress and the incidence of CHD. Iso-anxiety was significantly associated with CHD outcomes, especially for myocardial infarction; iso-anger was associated primarily with angina pectoris; and iso-depression was not significantly associated with any CHD outcome. The authors concluded that their results call for an appreciation of the shared as well as unique contributions of negative emotions in the development of CHD.

It should also be noted that independent investigations have shown that acute outbursts of anger, fear, and sadness can trigger heart attacks (Carroll et al., 2002; Kamarck and Jennings, 1991; Lear and Kloner, 1996; Mittleman et al., 1995). However, cardiovascular reactivity is not only the result of negative affect and can be even greater during intensely positive affect (Heponiemi et al. 2006). By implication, it is the sudden intensification of arousal during emotion that seems to be a precipitating factor in cardiac incidents. In the long term, anger, depression, and anxiety may also encourage other unhealthy behaviors (e.g. smoking) that increase the risk of CHD (Smith and Ruiz, 2002).

The role of multiple affective qualities in cardiac incidents is also reflected in the relatively new construct called vital exhaustion (VE). As conceptualized by its originator, this includes irritability, demoralization, and fatigue (Appels, 1990; Appels and Mulder, 1988a, 1988b). Here, elements of anger and sadness are combined with fatigue. The anger seems to be internalized rather than externalized in people with this condition (Bages et al., 1999). VE seems to overlap partially with the type A personality which is characterized as a pattern of hostility, impatience, and competitiveness (Rosenman et al., 1975). It is quite possible that the fatigue and depression of VE may actually be a byproduct of (prolonged) type A-related behavior. In terms of life events, sustained job stress/conflict, unemployment, and bereavement have been known to culminate in VE (Falger and Schouten, 1992).

Whatever its bases, VE was initially regarded as a precipitator of myocardial infarction (Appels, 1990). It has also been shown to be associated with angina pectoris (Appels and Mulder, 1988a) and cardiac events following angioplasty (Kop, 1995). It is not a stretch to find the depressive and anergic elements of VE following serious cardiac incidents.

It bears mentioning that both the type A and VE constructs have had their share of mixed results in their relationship to CVD (e.g. Miller et al., 1991). This is not surprising

given the curious admixture of somatic, affective, and behavioral features within these constructs. Nonetheless, what is common to both constructs is a role of affect, even though VE emphasizes depression and type A emphasizes anger. Yet other psychological investigations have revealed a part played by anxiety in CVD (e.g. Barger and Sydeman, 2005; Herrmann-Lingen and Buss, 2007). In sum, it pays to go in search of all three of these core affective qualities, keeping in mind that each may enter the picture through a different pathway, namely as precipitator, exacerbator, consequence, or perpetuator of CVD.

Cancer

Almost opposite to the anger-prone type A personality that is implicated in CHD, a personality prone to repressing negative emotions was articulated (Temoshok, 1987). Such non-expression of negative affect was suspected as a factor in the etiology of cancer. It came to be known as the type C personality.

Lieberman and Goldstein (2006) therefore investigated whether the ventilation of anxiety, depression, fear, and anger would have an impact on depression and quality of life in patients already diagnosed with breast cancer. The patients engaged in emotional expression through the medium of Internet bulletin boards for a period of about six months. The use of negative emotional words in each of the affective categories was examined in relation to the dependent measures. Regression analyses revealed that anger expression was associated with improved quality of life and reduced depression, thus hinting at the psychodynamic notion of depression as anger turned inward. However, the expression of anxiety or fear was associated with increased depression and reduced quality of life. The expression of sadness was not significantly related to the outcome measures. While these findings by no means show that suppression of negative affect causes cancer, they encourage the view that unexpressed anger is related to psychosocial impairment in breast cancer.

More extensive coverage of the research in this area was achieved in a meta-analysis by McKenna et al. (1999). Aggregating effect sizes across 46 studies, they found only a modest relationship between the presence of anxiety, depression, or anger (or their equivalent temperaments) and the development of breast cancer. The average effect sizes did not exceed 0.38 even when some of the dependent measures were combined into a broader construct of emotional denial/ repression.

A recent prospective study by Tijhuis et al. (2000) attempted to find out cancer incidence and mortality as a function of emotional control of anxiety, depression, and anger. Almost a thousand men born between 1900 and 1920 and living in Zutphen, Netherlands were examined medically for cancer and also interviewed and assessed using the Courtald Emotional Control Scale (CECS) (Watson and Greer, 1983) in 1985, 1990, 1993, and 1995. Focusing on a final sample of 590 men, it was found that from 1985 to 1995, 119 of them were diagnosed with cancer and 71 died of cancer. Descriptive statistics for the sample revealed the highest level of emotional control for anxiety (19.2), a slightly lower level for depression (18.4) and a slightly lower level for anger (16.4) with almost equivalent degrees of variability. When Cox proportional hazards models were used to determine effects of emotional control on cancer incidence and mortality, it was found that men within the highest and intermediate tertiles of controlled depression had a significantly increased risk of cancer mortality even after adjustment for other risk factors such as age, marital status, and SES; this was not the case for men who suppressed anxiety or anger. Control of depression was also significantly related to cancer incidence, but anger control or anxiety control were not. This study is nevertheless informative because it shows that cancer patients are consumed not only by the somatic demands of their disease but also by a struggle to control anxiety, anger, and depression even though

only one of these (when controlled) seems to increase the incidence and mortality associated with cancer.

Also using the CECS, an Australian study on breast cancer failed to find any significant associations between cancer outcome and emotional suppression of any kind, before or after controlling for age effects (O'Donnell et al., 2000). Once again, the more important message for our purposes is that the cancer patients did seem to experience components of the core of negative affect, as implied by their scores on emotional control for each of these.

A qualitative illustration of core components of negative affect in cancer patients is visible in some of the nursing literature. For example, Bowers et al. (2002) mention that even though many women with cervical cancer were depleted of physical energy, they would utter statements such as:

> That was once in my mind I was angry. I wanted to get in and get over with as soon as possible and not wait a month. Then I was too weak and tired to display it very much ... One day I came home and went to bed. The longer I laid in bed the madder I got. I was screaming to myself. I thought I would call a friend, but I did not want to dump on her so I said I can't take it anymore and I came downstairs and banged and slammed and got supper. (2002: 144–145)

A further quote by Bowers et al. captures the almost existential anxiety of the cancer patient: 'There is a reason for everything. I don't know it is. I don't know why. I began to think. Get a grip on yourself and find a purpose' (2002: 139). A final quote by Bowers et al. captures the despair/depression of the cancer patient. 'I guess my life was interesting, with so many things, and now it is not. Life is destroyed. It was so good before' (2002: 145). These anecdotes help remind us of the cognitive appraisals that underlie the statistical data on anxiety, depression, and anger in medical populations.

HIV/AIDS

One of the few recent empirical studies of the CONA in the context of HIV/AIDS was conducted by Atwine et al. (2005). In a rural district of southwestern Uganda, 123 children aged 11–15 years old whose parents had reportedly died from AIDS were compared with a normative sample of 110 children of similar age and gender living in intact households. They were all administered an appropriately translated version of the Beck Youth Inventories (Beck et al., 2001) which had been designed as a diagnostic aid for anxiety, depression, and anger, and for self-concept problems and disruptive behavior in youth. Results revealed significantly higher levels of disruptiveness as well as all three components of CONA in the orphaned group as compared to the non-orphaned group.

Another group of researchers (Teva et al., 2005) studied 100 HIV/AIDS patients between 18 and 70 years old who were recruited from various hospitals in Andalusia, Spain. They were administered a battery of tests suitable for assessing the CONA: the BDI, the STAI, and the STAXI. It was found that most of the 63 men and 37 women in the group reported low levels of state anger, with about one-third not expressing anger. This may be related to the additional finding that most participants were low in trait anger to begin with. Anger was higher during the symptomatic stage as opposed to the pre-symptomatic stage. Similarly, anxiety was greater during lypodystrophy than before it. Anxiety was far more prevalent in men than women. Most men also showed some depression but most women did not. The authors explain these differences with reference to cognitive appraisals that differ according to gender and stage of infection.

To the extent that pain is often a symptom in HIV/AIDS, the kinds of affective distress observed in chronic pain patients are also likely to manifest in HIV/AIDS patients (Marcus et al., 2000). Morever, HIV/AIDS patients, like cancer patients, often go through stages of adjustment to this (presumably) terminal illness. In the traditional model of Elizabeth Kubler-Ross (1974, 1997), this begins with shock and anxiety, proceeds to anger, and ends in depression. The core components of negative affect may thus unfold in sequence rather than appear concurrently.

Pain

Over the last half of the twentieth century, considerable research accumulated on anxiety, depression, and (to a lesser extent) anger in pain patients. This has already been critiqued and synthesized (e.g. Banks and Kerns, 1996; Fernandez, 2002). We now turn to a few recent empirical articles on the core of negative affect in pain, followed by a discussion of how this parallels the experience of negative affect associated with cancer, HIV/AIDS, or CVD.

Feeney (2004) evaluated 100 post-surgical orthopedic patients above the age of 65. These individuals were administered the geriatric depression scale (stripped of its somatic items because these do not discriminate between depressed elderly and non-depressed elderly). Patients were also administered the STAI and the STAXI to generate state and trait measures of anxiety and anger, respectively. The McGill Pain Questionnaire (MPQ) (Melzack, 1975) was used to derive a total pain score by summing the rank values of pain descriptors endorsed by patients. The authors found that pain was significantly correlated with state anxiety and depression but not with any of the measures of anger. Standard multiple linear regression analysis revealed that about 31% of the variance in total pain was explained by the five affective variables but only state anxiety had a significant standardized weight, accounting for about 18% of the variance in pain. The remaining four variables did not contribute significantly to the prediction of pain over and above that accounted for by state anxiety. This is quite likely due to the particular pain measure that was chosen. In using the rank values of pain descriptors from the MPQ, the authors were opting for a crude index of pain in comparison to the scales of the multidimensional pain inventory (Kerns et al., 1985) or even other measures offered by the MPQ itself such as the present pain intensity. The MPQ also allows measurement of affective pain as a separate factor, and examining this variable would probably have led to more significant results beyond those witnessed for anxiety.

Ghosh and Puja (2004) administered the BDI, STAI, and STAXI to 50 female outpatients with migraine headache and an equally sized group of age-matched females with no headaches. T-tests showed significantly higher scores for the patient group on six measures (trait anxiety, trait anger, anger-in, anger-out, anger control, and depression). The significant differences on trait rather than state anger and anxiety raise the likelihood that patients' headaches were not precipitated by affective episodes but were predisposed by affective temperaments. This conclusion is consistent with the findings of several studies cited by the authors.

In a more specific investigation of anger expression styles as they relate to pain, Kerns et al. (1994) found that anger-in and anger expression are correlated with chronic low back pain severity, though the former is associated with poorer adjustment. Similarly, Bruehl et al. (2002) found that both anger-in and anger-out affected pain sensitivity, but only the latter seemed to be mediated by impairment in antinociceptive effects of endogenous opioids.

In a broader investigation of the inhibition and expression of multiple emotions, Burns et al. (2003) randomly assigned students to three conditions: anger, sadness, and joy, respectively. In each condition, subjects recalled and described a recent event that evoked the relevant emotion. This was accompanied by a cold pressor pain test. Pain response was assessed by temporal measures of threshold and tolerance as well as by verbal descriptors on the MPQ. Unlike other findings by the same authors, a significant positive association was found between anger-out and pain threshold (but not pain tolerance or MPQ scores); this effect was paralleled by decreases in systolic blood pressure but not diastolic blood pressure. In contrast, induced sadness led to the largest increases

in MPQ scores of pain severity. It would be interesting to extend this line of enquiry by investigating any changes in pain sensitivity that might occur when fear is evoked using the same recall procedure as used for anger and sadness.

Our understanding of the emotions experienced by those in pain can be further deepened by an exploration of how exactly their pain is interpreted. As pointed out earlier, beneath the statistical data on negative affect are undercurrents of cognitive appraisals about the medical condition. Thus, pain patients are less likely to be angry at the pain itself and more likely to be angry at the ramifications of their painful condition (Fernandez and Turk, 1995). Similarly, anger is to be expected in any disease or disorder that is diagnostically ambiguous, refractory to treatment, (mis)attributed to psychological mechanisms, financially burdensome, and legally fractious. Consider the emotional reactions that arise in cancer patients. As Bowers, Tamlyn, and Butler mention,

> Most women experienced anger not at the cancer itself, but rather in relation to the communication and contact with others as they lived with ovarian cancer. In general, the causes of women's anger were related to misdiagnosis, late diagnosis, multiple testing, physicians discounting their symptoms and/or waiting for treatment, or inaccessibility to prompt treatment. (2002: 144)

Just as chronic pain can generate life interference which culminates in depression (Rudy et al., 1988), so can cancer, CVD or HIV/AIDS become depressing via their limiting effects on day-to-day functioning. The process of functional decline can be met with considerable apprehension, worry, and outright dread, especially if death is imminent. It is therefore not far-fetched to also consider the existential anxieties that are probably added to the other objects of anxiety, depression, and anger in these patients.

CONA COMORBIDITY

The preceding literature review shows that anxiety, depression, and anger do exist (sometimes in isolation, sometimes in combination) to a clinically significant degree in patients with medical ailments. The next issue concerns the extent to which the components of CONA are comorbid with one another, and what corollaries arise thereby. Across studies of medical patients, there have been repeated observations of a close relationship between anxiety and depression. The association between anger and each of its two counterparts in the CONA has been less researched. Given that anger and fear are twin emotions that mobilize the individual to fight or flight, it is likely that in any set of nomothetic data from individuals facing provocation or danger, there would be traces of both anger and fear. Up to this time, however, the emphasis has been on the so-called comorbidity between anxiety and depression.

Comorbidity statistics

Comorbidity, at its simplest, refers to the co-occurrence of two disorders in the same individual. However, it makes a difference whether the individual is evaluated for episode comorbidity or lifetime comorbidity. The former refers to multidiagnostic co-occurrence at one point in time. This is likely to be exceeded by the latter which means multiple diagnoses occurring at any point in the individual's lifetime. Based on an extensive epidemiological study, Robins et al. (1991) reported a 60% lifetime comorbidity of psychiatric disorders. About one-third of patients diagnosed with anxiety disorder were also diagnosed with a depressive disorder (Sanderson et al., 1990).

Going beyond co-occurrence to correlation, the picture remains similar. Anxiety and depression have been repeatedly shown to co-vary in a positive direction. Dobson's (1985) review of the relevant literature showed that the correlation between scores on anxiety and scores on depression ranged from +0.27 to +0.94, with an average correlation of +0.61. This average correlation was

only a little less than the average correlation of +0.66 between anxiety scales.

Principally, there are five main explanations for comorbidity of the core components of negative affect: definitional overlap, instrument overlap, response set, misinterpretation of data, and phenomenological bases. It is necessary to evaluate the tenability of each of these explanations as they have implications for the theoretical and applied potential of CONA as a construct.

Definitional overlap

The definitional overlap pertains to a similarity of conceptualization, in this case, between multiple diagnostic labels. Specifically, if there are similarities in the way anxiety and depression are operationally defined, it would not be surprising that when one is identified, so is the other. For the definition of clinically significant depression and anxiety, we turn to the *Diagnostic and Statistical Manual of Mental Disorders, version IV-Text Revision (DSM-IV-TR)*. In this nosological system, the dysthymic variant of depressive disorder comprises at least two years of at least two of the following symptoms: poor appetite, sleep disturbance, fatigue, low self-esteem, poor concentration, and perceived hopelessness. By comparison, generalized anxiety disorder (GAD) comprises more than six months of worry/anxiety with at least three of the following symptoms: restlessness, fatigue, difficulty concentrating, irritability, muscle tension, and sleep disturbance. As immediately apparent, 50% of the symptoms of dysthymia are found in GAD and vice versa. This degree of overlap may account for the high comorbidty between these two disorders, as reported in the National Comorbidity Survey (NCS) of 8,000 respondents across the US (Kessler et al., 1994). In this study, the six-month comorbidity of GAD and dysthmia was quantified by an odds ratio of 21.5, odds ratio being the ratio of frequency of two disorders being simultaneously present or absent to the frequency of each one being present on its own – in other words, the ratio of a joint occurrence to a singular occurrence. The GAD–dysthymia odds ratio was among the highest for any pair of psychiatric disorders. Similarly high odds ratios have been reported for other pairs of anxiety and depressive disorders, in particular panic disorder and major depression, with an odds ratio of 21.3 in the Epidemiological Catchment Area (ECA) study of 20,000 respondents in five US communities (Robins et al., 1991). In fact, the average pairwise associations between affective disorders (inclusive of mania) and anxiety disorders have been higher than that between anxiety disorders (Kessler, 1995). In short, the overlap of DSM diagnostic criteria may account for some of the comorbidity between clinical anxiety and depression.

Instrument overlap

The idea that high comorbidity between anxiety and depression could be due to instrument overlap occurred to various scholars who noticed that many psychological tests discriminated poorly between the two affective types (Clark et al., 1990). The same applies to the comorbidity of anger, depression, and anxiety. An inspection of the items in the Beck Depression Inventory (BDI) (Beck and Steer, 1993a) and the Beck Anxiety Inventory (BAI) (Beck and Steer, 1993b) reveals similarity of content as does a comparison of the STAI and STAXI. Anxiety and anger are likely to share common physiological reactivity by virtue of their common roots in sympathetic activation. However, if psychological tests rely on the subjective feelings as defining features of these syndromes, then they are less likely to generate overlapping profiles.

Interpretation of data

Suls and Bunde (2005) adopt Watson's view that the frequent correlation in self-report data for anxiety and depression must be partly rooted in a common latent factor or shared underlying dimension called negative affect. Reacting to this multicollinearity, Ketterer (1996) and others have suggested that we replace the measurement of anxiety, depression, and anger as separate entities with a global measure of negative affect.

Certainly, multicollinearity between variables (especially if it exceeds 0.80) suggests redundancy. But just because entities are correlated does not mean that they are connected. It simply means they co-vary. Thus, the strong collinearity between height and weight is not grounds for collapsing the two into one construct. Culture is closely associated with race, but it still makes much sense to tease the two apart. Verbal and quantitative IQ tend to be highly correlated, yet they are often viewed as distinct areas of ability.

A useful lesson in the interpretation of multicollinearity can be found in the context of measuring pain components. Turk et al. (1985) discovered that in a multiple-group confirmatory factor analysis, the sensory, affective, and evaluative subscales of the MPQ turned out to be highly intercorrelated: $r = 0.81$ between sensory and affective, $r = 0.67$ between affective and evaluative, and $r = 0.64$ between evaluative and sensory, thus yielding an average correlation of 0.71 among the three constructs. Moreover, the cross-construct correlations exceeded the within-construct correlations. The authors took this as a sign of lack of distinctiveness of the subscales and therefore recommended using the total factor score rather than individual scores on the three subscales. However, in a rebuttal, Melzack adduced several bits of evidence from perceptual psychophysics to show that a high correlation among variables is not a sign of redundancy and does not necessitate collapsing the variables into one. Specifically, increases in light intensity are associated with enhanced discriminability of color, contours, texture, and distance, yet we do not suggest conflating color and texture into one variable. Similarly, in audition, increased volume enhances discrimination of pitch, timbre, and spatial location, but this is not grounds for abandoning separate measures of timbre and pitch (Melzack and Katz, 1992).

Response set

In an extensive and seminal review paper, Russell and Carroll (1999) strongly disputed the idea proposed by Watson et al. (1988) that positive and negative affect are independent unipolar dimensions. In the process, Russell and Carroll also offered empirical data and reasoned arguments that now allow us to seriously doubt the value of collapsing anxiety and depression (and anger for that matter) into an undifferentiated phenomenon called 'negative affect'. Citing the classic work of Bentler (1969), it was pointed out that spurious correlations can emerge from self-report tests when there is an acquiescent response style in test-taking. Russell and Carroll then went on to cite about a dozen other studies containing empirical evidence of how this acquiescent response set has in fact influenced measures of affect. This may well account for the frequently observed correlations between self-report measures of anxiety and depression as well as of anger.

Phenomenological bases

Of course, anxiety, depression, and anger (or their corresponding emotions of fear, sadness, and anger) often co-occur, but this is not sufficient grounds for resorting or reverting to a general concept of 'negative affect'. Some of the association is phenomenologically based. First, at any point in time, each of the three emotions may be rooted in quite different events: a patient may be angry because of conflict on the job, depressed because of illness, and anxious about the welfare of family members. Second, the same things that make people depressed can also make them anxious and angry. Failure in a task/test often leaves one feeling sorry or

sad for oneself, angry at the person evaluating one's performance, and worried about the consequences for one's goal attainment. Killing of an admired leader often leads to sorrow for the leader's suffering or deprivation of rights, anger toward the killers, and apprehension about how to cope without the leader. Popularly called 'mixed emotions', these co-occur because of different appraisals of the same event. So, co-occurring emotions can be due to (1) different reactions to different event or (2) different reactions to the same event. It would not make sense to combine such multiple emotions into one amorphous 'negative affect' because these emotions originate from quite different circumstances or else are differentiated by separate appraisals of the same event.

MEASURING CORE COMPONENTS OF NEGATIVE AFFECT

The current componential representation of negative affect is consistent with a major perspective in affect science called differential emotions theory or the theory of discrete emotions. Accordingly, the tests used to assess the core components of negative affect should be selected to allow the differentiation of negative affect into its core components of fear, sadness, or anger, or their respective clinical equivalents of anxiety, depression, and anger. The options for assessing these types of affect would therefore exclude the positive and negative affect scales (PANAS) (Watson, et al., 1988) which are predicated on a view of undifferentiated negative affect. Moreover, the single word descriptors that make up the PANAS (distressed, upset, hostile, irritable, scared, afraid, ashamed, guilty, nervous, and jittery) are gross labels that are unsuited for accessing the underlying appraisals of each emotion. If anything, this is what may obscure some of the fine differences among anxiety, depression, and anger or their emotional equivalents of fear, sadness, and anger. It should also be noted that the concept of negative affect as proposed by Watson et al. does not pertain to negative emotions as much as 'subjective distress and unpleasurable engagement that subsumes a variety of aversive mood states, including anger, contempt, disgust, guilt, fear, and nervousness, with low NA being a state of calmness and serenity' (1988: 1063).

The use of single-word adjectives for assessing affect dates back to the multiple affect adjective checklist (MAACL) (Zuckerman and Lubin, 1965) – revised as the MAACL-R (Zuckerman and Lubin, 1985). This instrument does generate scores for anxiety, depression, and hostility but its factor structure is still an unsettled matter (e.g. Gotlib and Meyer, 1986). Another instrument of the same genre is the profile of mood states (POMS) (McNair et al., 1981) which lists 65 adjectives of affect to be rated on a four-point scale of amount/frequency. Subscale scores are generated for all three components of the CONA in addition to three other subscales pertaining to energy levels and cognitive function. Psychometrically, it has received some support though questions remain about how to interpret its results (e.g. Boyle, 1987).

The differential emotions scale (DES-IV; Izard et al., 1974) takes affect assessment a step deeper by replacing single word adjectives with actual statements that better reflect the experience of emotion. Subscale scores are generated for 11 types of affect, among them anger, fear, and sadness. There has been limited psychometric evaluation of the DES-IV although some of the empirical outcomes are encouraging (Boyle, 1986).

Apart from the above instruments directed specifically at affect, there are more general tests such as the SCL-90-R and the MMPI-2. Both of these are commonly used in health psychology to cast a wide net for detecting psychopathology. In the process, they allow the identification of clinically significant levels of the CONA. One special advantage of these tests is that their psychometric validity and reliability have been the subject of extensive research and are now fairly well established. However, they are broad in scope and therefore bring in more data than is needed for our current goals of assessing negative affect.

CONCLUSION

It is the thesis of this chapter that there are three key components to negative affect: fear, sadness, and anger, which can take the form of emotions, moods, or temperaments. Previous research has studied them mainly as discrete emotions or else as the clinical syndromes of anxiety, depression, and anger.

The three core components of negative affect have an evolutionary history that has earned them special roles in survival. In particular, they are part of the individual's repertoire of defenses against threat, attack, or adversity in general. Thus, anxiety, depression, and anger are prevalent in medical populations such as those afflicted with CVD, cancer, or HIV/AIDS. Research has pointed to the comorbidity of these affective types. The frequent co-occurrence or covariation of these affective types does not mean that they should be collapsed into one broad category called negative affect. Close scrutiny has revealed that the comorbidity is in part due to overlap in nosological criteria for anxiety and depression and in part due to overlapping items across psychological tests. The comorbidity may also be an artifact of response sets. Most important, anger, fear, and sadness are linked by unique threads of cognitive appraisals in response to the same situation or else by multiple appraisals in response to multiple stimuli.

Future research may benefit greatly from the assessment of the three core components of negative affect in medical populations. This is not strictly tied to any premise that anxiety, depression, and anger co-occur, co-vary, or are equivalent. Rather, the prime reason is that there is a high probability of one or more of these affective types in anyone who faces adversity. Perhaps, by including three subscales on one and the same test of affect, scores for anxiety, depression, and anger can be output on the same metric, yet on three separate but parallel continua. This would enable the charting of a profile of the individual's core components of negative affect. Protracted over time, such a chart might also reveal patterns that allow us to differentiate the emotional, mood-related, or temperamental aspects of anger, fear, and sadness. In this way, the landscape of a person's affective function can be better mapped to identify, with greater specificity, the areas in need of clinical attention.

REFERENCES

American Psychiatric Association (2000) *Diagnostic and Statistical Manual of Mental Disorders Fourth Edition Text Revision (DSM-IV-TR)*. Washington, DC: American Psychiatric Publishing.

Appels, A. (1990) 'Mental precursors of myocardial infarction', *British Journal of Psychiatry*, 156(2): 465–71.

Appels, A. and Mulder, P. (1988a) 'Excess fatigue as a precursor of myocardial infarction', *European Heart Journal*, 9(7): 758–64.

Appels, A. and Mulder, P. (1988b) 'A questionnaire to assess premonitory symptoms of myocardial infarction', *International Journal of Cardiology*, 17(1): 15–24.

Atwine, B., Cantor-Graae, E. and Bajunirwe, F. (2005) 'Psychological distress among AIDS orphans in rural Uganda', *Social Science and Medicine*, 61(3): 551–64.

Bages, N., Appels, A. and Falger, P.R.J. (1999) 'Vital exhaustion as a risk factor of myocardial infarction: A case control study in Venezuela', *International Journal of Behavioral Medicine*, 6(3): 279–90.

Banks, S.M. and Kerns, R.D. (1996) 'Explaining high rates of depression in chronic pain: A diathesis-stress framework', *Psychological Bulletin*, 119(1): 95–110.

Barger, S.D. and Sydeman, S.J. (2005) 'Does generalized anxiety disorder predict coronary heart disease risk factors independently of major depressive disorder?', *Journal of Affective Disorders*, 88(1): 87–91.

Barlow, D.H. (1991) 'Disorders of emotion', *Psychological Inquiry*, 2(1): 58–71.

Beck, A.T. and Steer, R.A. (1993a) *Manual for the Beck Anxiety Inventory*. San Antonio, TX: Psychological Corporation.

Beck, A.T. and Steer, R.A. (1993b) *Manual for the Beck Depression Inventory*. San Antonio, TX: Psychological Corporation.

Beck, J., Beck, A. and Jolly, J. (2001) *Beck Youth Inventories of Emotional and Social Impairment Manual*. San Antonio, TX: Psychological Corporation.

Bentler, P.M. (1969) 'Semantic space is approximately bipolar', *Journal of Psychology*, 71(1): 33–40.

Bowers, D.E., Tamlyn, D. and Butler, L.J. (2002) 'Women living with ovarian cancer: Dealing with an early death', *Health Care for Women International*, 23(2): 135–48.

Boyle, G.J. (1986) 'Higher-order factors in the Differential Emotions Scale (DES-III)', *Personality and Individual Differences*, 7(3): 305–10.

Boyle, G.J. (1987) 'A cross-validation of the factor structure of the Profile of Mood States: Were the factors correctly identified in the first instance?', *Psychological Reports*, 60(2): 343–54.

Brosschot, J.F. and Thayer, J.F. (1998) 'Anger inhibition, cardiovascular recovery, and vagal function: A model of the link between hostility and cardiovascular disease', *Annals of Behavioral Medicine*, 20(4): 326–32.

Bruehl, S., Burns, J., Chung, O.Y., Ward, P. and Johnson, B. (2002) 'Anger and pain sensitivity in chronic low back pain patients and pain-free controls: The role of endogenous opioids', *Pain*, 99(1–2): 223–33.

Buerki, M.D. and Alder, M.D. (2005) 'Negative affect states and cardiovascular disorders: a review and the proposal of a unifying biopsychosocial concept', *General Hospital Psychiatry*, 27(3): 180–8.

Burns, J.W., Kubilus, A. and Bruehl, S. (2003) 'Emotion induction moderates effects of anger management style on acute pain sensitivity', *Pain*, 106(1–2): 109–18.

Cannon, W.B. (1929) *Bodily Changes in Pain, Hunger, Fear, and Rage* (2nd edn). New York: Appleton.

Carroll, D., Ebrahim, S., Tilling, K., Macleod, J. and Smith, G.D. (2002) 'Admissions for myocardial infarction and World Cup football: database survey', *British Medical Journal*, 325(7378): 1439–42.

Clark, D.A., Beck, A.T. and Stewart, B. (1990) 'Cognitive specificity and positive-negative affectivity: Complementary or contradictory views on anxiety and depression?', *Journal of Abnormal Psychology*, 99(2): 148–55.

Dobson, K.S. (1985) 'The relationship between anxiety and depression', *Clinical Psychology Review*, 5(4): 307–24.

Falger, P.R.J. and Schouten, E.G.W. (1992) 'Exhaustion, psychological stressors in the work environment, and acute myocardial infarction in men', *Journal of Psychosomatic Research*, 36(8): 777–86.

Feeney, S.L. (2004) 'The relationship between pain and negative affect in older adults: anxiety as a predictor of pain', *Journal of Anxiety Disorders*, 18(6): 733–44.

Fernandez, E. (2002) *Anxiety, Depression, and Anger in Pain: Research Findings and Clinical Options*. Dallas, TX: Advanced Psychological Resources.

Fernandez, E., Clark, T.S. and Rudick-Davis, D. (1999) 'A framework for conceptualization and assessment of affective disturbance in pain', in A.R. Block, E.F. Kremer and E. Fernandez (eds), *Handbook of Pain Syndromes: Biopsychosocial Perspectives*. Mahwah, NJ: Erlbaum, pp. 123–47.

Fernandez, E. and Turk, D.C. (1995) 'The scope and significance of anger in the experience of chronic pain', *Pain*, 61(2): 165–75.

Ghosh, S.N. and Puja (2004) 'The emotional vital signs in migraine', *Psychological Studies*, 49(4): 272–7.

Gotlib, I.H. and Meyer, J.P. (1986) 'Factor analysis of the Multiple Affect Adjective Check List: A separation of positive and negative affect', *Journal of Personality and Social Psychology*, 50(6): 1161–5.

Heponiemi, T., Ravaja, N., Elovainio, M., Naatanen, P. and Jarvinen, L.K. (2006) 'Experiencing positive affect and negative affect during stress: Relationships to cardiac reactivity and to facial expressions', *Scandinavian Journal of Psychology*, 47(5): 327–37.

Herrmann-Lingen, C. and Buss, U. (2007) 'Anxiety and depression in patients with coronary heart disease', in J. Jordan, B. Bardé and A.M. Zeiher (eds), *Contributions Toward Evidence-based Psychocardiology: A Systematic Review of the Literature*. Washington, DC: American Psychological Association, pp. 125–57.

Izard, C.E., Dougherty, F.E., Bloxom, B.M. and Kotsch, W.E. (1974) 'The differential emotions scale: A method of measuring the subjective experience of discrete emotions', Unpublished manuscript, Vanderbilt University.

Kamarck, T. and Jennings, J.R. (1991) 'Biobehavioural factors in sudden cardiac death', *Psychological Bulletin*, 109(1): 42–75.

Kerns, R.D., Rosenberg, R. and Jacob, M.C. (1994) 'Anger expression and chronic pain', *Journal of Behavioral Medicine*, 17(1): 57–67.

Kerns, R.D., Turk, D.C. and Rudy, T.E. (1985) 'The West Haven-Yale Multidimensional Pain Inventory (WHYMPI)', *Pain*, 23(4): 345–56.

Kessler, R.C., McGonagle, K.A., Zhao, S., Nelson, C.B., Hughes, M., Eshleman, S., Wittchen, H-U. and Kendler, K.S. (1994) 'Lifetime and 12-month prevalence of DSM-III-R psychiatric disorders among persons aged 15–54 in the United States: Results from the National Comorbidity Survey', *Archives of General Psychiatry*, 51(1): 8–19.

Kessler, R.C. (1995) 'Epidemiology of psychiatric comorbidity', in M.T. Tsuang, M. Tohen and G.E.P. Zahner (eds), *Textbook in Psychiatric Epidemiology*. New York: Wiley, pp. 179–97.

Ketterer, M.W. (1996) 'Anger and myocardial infarction [Letter]', *Circulation*, 94(7): 1788–9.

Kop, W.J. (1995) 'Vital exhaustion, cardiac events and the relationship to depression', *European Psychopharmacology*, 5(3): 220–1.

Krohne, H.W., Schmukle, S.C., Spaderna, H. and Spielberger, C.D. (2002) 'The State-Trait Depression Scales: An international comparison', *Anxiety, Stress and Coping: An International Journal*, 15(2): 105–22.

Kubler-Ross, E. (1974) *Questions and Answers on Death and Dying*. New York: Macmillan.

Kubler-Ross, E. (1997) *AIDS: The Ultimate Challenge*. New York: Touchstone.

Kubzansky, L.D., Cole, S.R., Kawachi, I., Vokonas, P. and Sparrow, D. (2006) 'Shared and unique contributions of anger, anxiety, and depression to coronary heart disease: A prospective study in the normative aging study', *Annals of Behavioral Medicine*, 31(1): 21–9.

Lear, J. and Kloner, R.A. (1996) 'The Northridge earthquake as a trigger for acute myocardial infarction', *American Journal of Cardiology*, 77(14): 1230–2.

Lieberman, M.A. and Goldstein, B.A. (2006) 'Not all negative emotions are equal: The role of emotional expression in online support groups for women with breast cancer', *Psycho-Oncology*, 15(2): 160–8.

Magai, C., Kerns, M.D., Gillespie, M. and Huang, B. (2003) 'Anger experience and anger inhibition in sub-populations of African American and European American older adults and relation to circulatory disease', *Journal of Health Psychology*, 8(4): 413–32.

Marcus, K.S., Kerns, R.D., Rosenfeld, B. and Breitbart, W. (2000) 'HIV/AIDS-related pain as a chronic pain condition: Implications of a biopsychosocial model for comprehensive assessment and effective management', *Pain Medicine*, 1(3): 260–73.

Marks, I. (1987) *Fears, Phobias, and Rituals: Panic, Anxiety, and their Disorders*. New York: Oxford University Press.

McKenna, M.C., Zevon, M.A., Corn, B. and Rounds, J. (1999) 'Psychosocial factors and the development of breast cancer: A meta-analysis', *Health Psychology*, 18(5): 520–31.

McNair, D.M., Lorr, M. and Droppleman, L.F. (1981) *Profile of Mood States*. San Diego: Educational and Industrial Testing Service.

Melzack, R. (1975) 'The McGill Pain Questionnaire: Major properties and scoring methods', *Pain*, 1(3): 277–259.

Melzack, R. and Katz, J. (1992) 'The McGill Pain Questionnaire: Appraisal and current status', in D.C. Turk and R. Melzack (eds), *Handbook of Pain Assessment*. New York: Guilford, pp. 152–68.

Miller, T.Q., Turner, C.W., Tindale, R.S., Posavac, E.J. and Dugoni, B.L. (1991) 'Reasons for the trend toward null findings in research on Type A behavior', *Psychological Bulletin*, 110(3): 469–85.

Mittleman, M.A., Maclure, M., Sherwood, J.B., Mulry, R.P., Tofler, G.H., Jacobs, S.C., Friedman, R., Benson, H. and Muller, J.E. (1995) 'Triggering of acute myocardial infarction onset by episodes of anger', *Circulation*, 92(7): 1720–5.

O'Donnell, M.C., Fisher, R., Irvine, K., Rickard, M. and McConaghy, N. (2000) 'Emotional suppression: Can it predict cancer outcome in women with suspicious screening', *Psychological Medicine*, 30(5): 1079–88.

Peterson, C., Maier, S.F. and Seligman, M.E.P. (1993) *Learned Helplessness: A Theory for the Age of Personal Control*. New York: Oxford University Press.

Robins, L.N., Locke, B.Z. and Reiger, D.A. (1991) 'An overview of psychiatric disorders in America', in L.N. Robins and D.A. Reiger (eds), *Psychiatric Disorders in America: The Epidemiological Catchment Area Study*. New York: The Free Press, pp. 328–66.

Rosenman, R.H., Brand, R.J., Jenkins, C.D., Friedman, M., Straus, R. and Wurm, M. (1975) 'Coronary heart disease in the Western Collaborative Group Study: Final follow-up experience of 8 1/2 years', *Journal of the American Medical Association*, 233(8): 872–7.

Rudy, T.E., Kerns, R.D. and Turk, D.C. (1988) 'Chronic pain and depression: Toward a cognitive-behavioral mediation model', *Pain*, 35(2): 129–40.

Russell, J.A. and Carroll, J.M. (1999) 'On the bipolarity of positive and negative affect', *Psychological Bulletin*, 125(1): 3–30.

Ryff, C.D., Love, G.D., Urry, H.L., Muller, D., Rosenkranz, M.A., Friedman, E.M., Davidson, R.J. and Singer, B. (2006) 'Psychological well-being and ill-being: Do they have distinct or mirrored biological correlates?', *Psychotherapy and Psychosomatics*, 75(2): 85–95.

Sanderson, W.C., DiNardo, Rapee, R.M. and Barlow, D.H. (1990) 'Syndrome comorbidity in patiens diagnosed with a DSM-III-R anxiety disorder', *Journal of Abnormal Psychology*, 99(3): 308–12.

Seligman, M.E. (1972) 'Learned helplessness', *Annual Review of Medicine*, 23(5): 407–12.

Smith, T.W. and MacKenzie, J. (2006) 'Personality and risk of physical illness', *Annual Review of Clinical Psychology*, 2: 435–67.

Smith, T.W. and Ruiz, J. (2002) 'Psychosocial influences on the development and course of coronary heart disease: Current status and implications for research and practice', *Journal of Consulting and Clinical Psychology*, 70(3): 548–68.

Spielberger, C.D. (1988) *State-Trait Anger Expression Inventory Professional Manual*. Odessa, FL: Psychological Assessment Resources.

Spielberger, C.D., Gorsuch, R.L., Lushene, R.E., Vagg, P.R. and Jacobs, G.A. (1977) 'The State–Trait Anxiety Inventory: Test Manual for Form Y', Palo Alto: Consulting Psychologists Press.

Spielberger, C.D., Ritterband, L.M., Sydeman, S.J., Reheiser, E.C. and Unger, K.K. (1995) 'Assessessment of emotional states and personality traits, measuring psychological vital signs', in J.N. Butcher (ed.), *Clinical Personality Assessment: Practical Approaches*. New York: Oxford University Press, pp. 42–58.

Suls, J. and Bunde, J. (2005) 'Anger, anxiety, and depression as risk factors for cardiovascular disease: The problems and implications of overlapping affective dispositions', *Psychological Bulletin*, 131(2): 260–300.

Teva, I., Bermúdez, M., Hernández-Quero, J. and Buela-Casal, G. (2005) 'Evaluación de la depresión, ansiedad e ira en pacientes con VIH/SIDA [Assessment of depression, anxiety, and anger in HIV/AIDS patients]', *Salud Mental*, 28(5): 40–9.

Temoshok, L. (1987) 'Personality coping style, emotion and cancer: Towards an integrative model', *Cancer Surveys*, 6(3): 545–67.

Tijhuis, M.A.R., Elshout, J.R.A.F. Feskens, E.J.M., Janssen, M. and Kromhout, D. (2000) 'Prospective investigation of emotional control and cancer risk in men (the Zutphen Elderly Study) (The Netherlands)', *Cancer Causes and Control*, 11(7): 589–95.

Tomkins, S.S. (1962) *Affect Imagery Consciousness (Vol I). The Positive Affects*. New York: Springer.

Turk, D.C., Rudy, T.E. and Salovey, P. (1985) 'The McGill Pain Questionnaire reconsidered: Confirming the factor structure and examining appropriate uses', *Pain*, 21(4): 386–97.

Watson, D., Clark, L.A. and Tellegen, A. (1988) 'Development and validation of brief measures of positive and negative affect: The PANAS scales', *Journal of Personality and Social Psychology*, 54(6): 1063–70.

Watson, M. and Greer, S. (1983) 'Development of a questionnaire measure of emotional control', *Journal of Psychosomatic Research*, 27(4): 299–305.

Zuckerman, M. and Lubin, B. (1965) *Manual for the Multiple Affect Adjective Check List*. San Diego: Educational and Industrial Testing Service.

Zuckerman, M. and Lubin, B. (1985) *Manual for the MAACL-R: The Multiple Affect Adjective Check List Revised*. San Diego: Educational and Industrial Testing Service.

33

Personality and Alcohol Use

Manuel I. Ibáñez, María A. Ruipérez, Helena Villa,
Jorge Moya and Generós Ortet

INTRODUCTION

Alcohol is one of the world's most commonly used drugs, and its misuse, especially among adolescents and young adults, causes serious health, economic and social problems (Goldman et al., 2005). Low to moderate amounts of alcohol are associated with a reduced risk of coronary heart disease, but high alcohol consumption is related to many diseases, such as hypertension and stroke, liver disease and different types of cancer. The estimated economic cost of alcohol abuse in the US, for example, was $184.6 billion in 1998 (National Institute on Alcohol Abuse and Alcoholism (NIAAA), 2000). Furthermore, early alcohol use in adolescents is often associated with other high-risk behaviours, such as antisocial behaviour, use of other drugs, poor school performance and violence, as well as engaging in unprotected sex and drunk driving (Clark et al., 2002; Zuckerman and Kuhlman, 2000). For example, around half of the drivers aged between 21 and 24 who died in car crashes in 2003 in the US had measurable alcohol in their blood (National Highway Traffic Safety Administration (NHTSA), 2004). In Spain, more than 30% of total deaths from car crashes presented with alcohol in the blood which exceeded the legal limits (Plan Nacional Sobre Drogas (PNSD), 2004).

Although alcohol is available to any adult, and illegally to many minors, its misuse is not evenly distributed throughout the population. Almost everybody has tried alcohol at least once, and a large number of people show low to moderate alcohol consumption. However, a sizable minority of the population abuses alcohol. For instance, the total prevalence of 12-month DSM-IV alcohol abuse and dependence was 8.46% (Grant et al., 2004). In Spain, almost half of the population takes one or more drinks each week, and 5.3% is estimated to present a risky alcohol use (PNSD, 2004). Understanding the causes of these individual differences in alcohol use and misuse will help the development of prevention programmes and more effective interventions to reduce the incidence and prevalence of alcohol-related problems.

PERSONALITY AND ALCOHOL

Personality is one of the most studied psychological factors in the development of alcohol use and abuse. From LeGrain's alcoholic classification in the late nineteenth century (Babor, 1996) to Cloninger's more recent types of alcoholism (1987; Cloninger et al., 1996), several typologies in which personality played a prominent role have been proposed (Babor, 1996; Ball, 1996). Despite some early simplistic proposals of 'alcoholic personality', however, research has consistently failed to find a single addictive or alcoholic personality (Nathan, 1988). Nonetheless, a variety of personality traits have been reliably associated with both the development and manifestation of alcohol use disorders (Ball, 2005; Eysenck, 1997; Rose, 1998; Sher et al., 2005). Indeed, personality traits would be the basis for a broader range of disinhibited or externalising behaviours, such as hyperactivity, conduct problems, deviant and risky behaviours, or other drugs use and abuse (Khan et al., 2005; Krueger et al., 2002; Sher and Trull, 1994; Zuckerman and Kuhlman, 2000).

In order to describe several lines of evidence that support the relationship between personality and alcohol use and abuse, in both man and non-human animals, we will group temperamental and personality traits into three broad clusters (see Figure 33.1).

These three clusters are: neuroticism/negative emotionality (N), which includes anxiety, harm avoidance, negative emotionality and neuroticism; extraversion/sociability (E), including sociability, activity, positive emotionality and extraversion; and impulsivity/disinhibition (IMP), including sensation seeking, aggressivity, novelty seeking, low constraint (impulsiveness), psychoticism, low agreeableness and low conscientiousness (Ortet et al., 2002; Sher and Trull, 1994; Zuckerman, 1999; Zuckerman and Cloninger, 1996; Zuckerman et al., 1993).

Cross-sectional studies

Cross-sectional studies are important in determining the co-occurrence of personality traits and different patterns of alcohol consumption. Studies in adolescent and adult non-clinical samples would be useful in exploring the relationship between personality and the onset and development of moderate non-pathological alcohol use. The association between personality and pathological patterns of alcohol consumption are usually explored in alcohol-related samples, such as patients with alcohol abuse and dependence or in children of alcoholics.

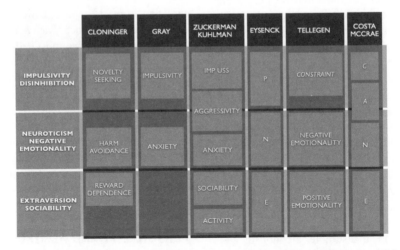

Figure 33.1   Three broad clusters for organizing personality traits. IMP USS: impulsive unsocialised sensation seeking; P: psychoticism; N: neuroticism; E: extraversion; C: conscientiousness; A: agreeableness. Traits in *italics* are related inversely

Studies in adolescents and young adults have described that the IMP cluster is the most prominent in alcohol use development. Sensation seeking, novelty seeking, impulsivity, low conscientiousness or low agreeableness have been related to the onset and use of alcohol and other drugs, especially legal drugs, in different sociocultural contexts (e.g. Cooper et al., 2000; Gerra et al., 2004; Knyazev et al., 2004; Kuo et al., 2002; Villa et al., 2006; Wills et al., 1998, 2000). In relation to the E cluster, these traits have been more related to alcohol use during adolescence than adulthood. Thus, some studies have shown a moderate positive relation to different drinking behaviours (Cooper et al., 2000; Knyazev et al., 2004; Kuo et al., 2002; Villa et al., 2006; Wills et al., 1998). Finally, the N cluster has been inconsistently related to alcohol use during adolescence (Cooper et al., 2000; Knyazev et al., 2004; Kuo et al., 2002; Villa et al., 2006; Wills et al., 1998).

Studies in adults also show that alcohol use is mainly associated with IMP-related traits, like sensation seeking (e.g. Finn et al., 2000; Grau and Ortet, 1999; Zuckerman and Kuhlman, 2000), novelty seeking (e.g. Cloninger et al., 1995; Earlywine et al., 1992), low constraint (Clarck and Watson, 1999; Schuckit, 1998), psychoticism (e.g. Conrod et al., 1997; Grau and Ortet, 1999) or low agreeableness and low conscientiousness (Chassin et al., 2004; Ruiz et al., 2003; Theakston et al., 2004). N-related traits are not usually associated with alcohol use (e.g. Cloninger et al., 1995; Earlywine et al., 1992; Grau and Ortet, 1999; Zuckerman and Kuhlman, 2000), whereas some studies have found a modest association between E-related traits and alcohol use, although not as consistently as IMP (e.g. Grau and Ortet, 1999; Zuckerman and Kuhlman, 2000).

In relation to pathological patterns of alcohol use, numerous cross-sectional researches have studied whether alcoholics and non-alcoholics differ in multiple variables, including personality. Sher and Trull (1994)

concluded that IMP is the cluster most clearly associated with alcoholism. In addition, samples of alcoholics tend to present higher scores in N-cluster traits, although it is not clear whether this cluster is causally implied or is a consequence of the problems associated with alcohol abuse and dependence. Finally, the E-cluster does not seem to be related to alcoholism. Subsequent studies tend to confirm these conclusions (Krueger et al., 2000; McGue et al., 1997). Furthermore, IMP-related traits (i.e. novelty seeking) not only were associated with an increased risk for alcohol dependence, but also accounted for a modest proportion of the comorbidity between alcohol dependence and other externalising disorders, such as drug dependence, antisocial personality disorder and conduct disorder (Khan et al., 2005).

Another cross-sectional line of evidence comes from the study on children of alcoholics (COAs). COAs are of interest in alcoholism because they are at substantially increased risk of developing alcoholism. Thus, the identification of personality traits that differentiate COAs from non-COAs could lead to a discovery in personality factors involved in the alcoholism aetiology. According to Sher's review (Sher, 1997), IMP traits, but not N and E traits, seem to be related to a family history of alcoholism (FHA), although the magnitude of this effect is not large.

These and other findings have led some authors to propose different influential alcoholism typologies based, in part, on personality characteristics. Based on prospective, genetic and psychobiological studies, C.R. Cloninger (1987; Cloninger et al., 1996) has proposed two types of alcoholism – type I and type II. Type I alcoholism is characterised by a later onset of alcohol misuse, feelings of worry and guilt about their alcohol use, and it is more influenced by environmental than genetic factors. Personality traits, such as harm avoidance or anxiety, are core traits of type I alcoholics, and their main motivation is tension reduction. Type II alcoholism is present in a greater proportion of males than in females. It is characterised by an early onset of alcohol misuse, is associated with antisocial behaviour, and is more influenced by genetic than by environmental factors. Novelty seeking and impulsivity are personality traits that characterise type II alcoholics, and the main motivation is related to reinforcement properties of alcohol. Noteworthy, other models of alcoholism present a high degree of convergence with Cloninger's typology. Type I and type II closely resemble Babor's type A and B alcoholism (Ball, 1996; Babor, 1996). Furthermore, type I alcoholism would be similar to Zucker's negative affect alcoholism, whereas type II alcoholism is related to Zucker's antisocial and developmentally limited alcoholism (Zucker, 1994).

Cross-sectional studies have shown a moderate but consistent role of personality in alcohol use and abuse. However, cross-sectional research has limitations in approaching the causal direction of the personality–alcoholism correlation (Sher and Trull, 1994). For example, it could be interpreted that impulsivity/disinhibition traits lead to involvement with alcohol use and abuse (Cloninger, 1987; Eysenck, 1997; Kreek et al., 2005) or, alternatively, that an antisocial and substance-abusing lifestyle leads to impulsivity (Nathan, 1988). In addition, anxiety and depression traits could be related to alcoholism because the anxiolytic properties of ethanol make those individuals with higher negative emotionality traits more vulnerable or because the social and personal problems produced by alcohol abuse and dependence increase the negative affect (Sher and Trull, 1994). Prospective research, genetically informative data or animal studies are required to determine which of these hypotheses is more plausible.

Prospective studies

Prospective studies are of special interest because they allow for the exploration of alcohol use and abuse precursors, and thus clarify the causal role of personality in alcohol consumption. Different studies, carried out in various countries and cultures, suggest that temperament and personality predictors of an increased liability to alcoholism can be seen even in early childhood (Rose, 1998).

Cloninger et al. (1988) assessed temperament traits of Swedish children aged 10 to 11 using interviews with their teachers. The participants' alcohol-related problems were assessed at the age of 27. Boys classified as high novelty seekers and low harm avoidance presented a 20-fold higher risk of alcoholism than boys without those characteristics. Masse and Tremblay (1997) reported similar results in a prospective study in Canada. They found that 6-year-old boys who presented higher novelty-seeking scores and lower harm avoidance levels were more likely to initiate alcohol and other drug use in early adolescence than boys without those traits.

Also in Sweden, Wennberg and Bohman (2002) assessed temperament traits in children and correlated them to different alcohol consumption patterns in adulthood. Aggressive traits at the age of 4 predicted frequency of intoxication at the age of 25, whereas extravert/outgoing traits, such as activity and low orderliness, predicted lifetime alcohol problems at the age of 36. In accordance with these results, Pulkkinen and Pitkänen (1994) found in Finland that aggressiveness at the age of 8 predicted an increased risk for alcoholism 18 to 20 years later for males, but not for females. Conversely, anxiety/shyness was positively related to alcohol and other drug use in females, but negatively associated in men.

In New Zealand, Caspi et al. (1996) assessed temperamental characteristics at the age of 3, such as undercontrol (which included behaviour traits such as irritability, impulsivity and low persistency) and inhibition (referred to behaviour traits of fear, anxiety or reticence). Undercontrolled boys, but not girls, were more than twice as likely to be diagnosed with alcoholism at the age of 21. Furthermore, undercontrolled and inhibited boys had more alcohol-related problems than children without these characteristics. In addition, personality was assessed in this sample at the age of 18. Low constraint (impulsivity) and negative emotionality predicted alcohol abuse 3 years later in both men and women (Krueger et al., 2000).

Kubicka et al. (2001) found in participants from the Czech Republic that low conscientiousness at the age of 9–10 predicted high drinking quantity per occasion, heavy episodic drinking and smoking 24 years later. Furthermore, extraversion predicted average daily alcohol consumption.

In the US, Chassin et al. (2004) found that parents' rates of impulsivity in young adolescents (mean age around 13) predicted heavy drinking/heavy drug use; whereas parents' rates of impulsivity and emotionality predicted drug dependence, and alcohol and drug comorbidity 7 and 12 years later. Furthermore, neuroticism, low conscientiousness and especially openness and low agreeableness in young adulthood predicted heavy drinking/heavy dug use, alcohol dependence, drug dependence, and alcohol and drug comorbidity around 5 years later.

Also in the US, Sher et al. assessed the personality of young adults (mean age of 18). Different substance use disorders were examined 6 (Sher et al., 2000) and 11 (Jackson and Sher, 2003) years later. A broad impulsive sensation-seeking trait was the best predictor of alcohol abuse and dependence, together with other substance use disorders. In addition, negative emotionality-related traits were a modest but significant predictor of alcohol and other substance use disorders, whereas extraversion-related traits were not associated with any substance use disorder. Recently, Elkins et al. (2006) reported similar results. They found that personality at the age of 17 predicted early onset and development of alcohol, nicotine and illicit drug disorders 3 years later. Specifically, low constraint (i.e. impulsivity) and high negative emotionality predicted early alcohol onset and the development of alcohol abuse and dependence.

Overall, prospective studies support the causal role of IMP-related traits on development of alcohol use and abuse in men. Results show a similar tendency in women, although studies in young girls are not as conclusive as in young boys. There is also evidence of a possible role of N-related traits on alcoholism, and a slight influence of E-related traits. Noteworthy, these findings are independent of the sociocultural context.

Genetic studies

A preliminary multivariate genetic analysis from a large twin sample found that the genetic risk for alcoholism might be mediated, in part, through novelty seeking (Heath et al., 1994). This result has been replicated and extended in both adolescent and adult samples. Young et al. (2000), Krueger et al. (2002) and Mustanski et al. (2003) found that IMP-related traits in adolescent twin samples share common genes with alcohol use and abuse, other substance experimentation and abuse, conduct disorders, antisocial behaviour and hyperactivity. Slutske et al. (1998, 2002) found that genetic factors in adult twins contributing to variations in the IMP traits account for around 40% of the genetic diathesis for alcohol dependence, and for approximately 90% of the common genetic diathesis for alcohol dependence and conduct disorders among both men and women. These studies have also shown that E-related traits are not genetically related to alcohol dependence, and that N-related traits present a weak but significant genetic relationship with alcohol dependence.

In this line, a recent result obtained within the COGA project (Collaborative Study on the Genetics of Alcoholism), a multi-centre effort to identify genes involved in alcoholism, found evidence of linkage to several chromosomal loci for a quantitative phenotype related to aspects of alcohol use and anxiety (Dick et al., 2002), a phenotype similar to Cloninger's type I alcoholism (Cloninger, 1987). Furthermore, a reanalysis of the COGA linkage study has reported a genetic association between novelty seeking and alcoholism (Czerwinski et al., 1999).

Association genetic studies could be useful in the search of promising gene candidates at the basis of the genetic covariation of personality traits and alcohol use and abuse. Dopamine receptor genes are potentially candidate genes at the basis of the disinhibition/externalising spectrum that include IMP-related traits and alcohol use and abuse. Although far from conclusive, some studies have found associations between polymorphisms of the dopamine receptor D4DR and alcohol abuse, alcoholism and alcohol craving (Ebstein and Kotler, 2002; Hutchison et al., 2002; Laucht et al., 2007; Muramatsu, et al., 1996). However, the gene that has received most attention in alcoholism is D2DR. Blum et al. (1990) first reported that the *Taq*I-A1 polymorphism in the dopamine receptor gene D2DR was associated with alcoholism. Although posterior studies have provided mixed support to this finding, recent revisions still consider D2DR as a candidate gene for alcoholism liability (Bowirrat and Oscar-Berman, 2005; Noble, 2003).

Since the two independent reports in 1996 (Benjamin et al., 1996; Ebstein et al., 1996), nearly 15 papers have studied the association between several D4DR gene polymorphisms and IMP-related traits, with positive and negative reports (Ebstein and Kotler, 2002; Savitz and Ramesar, 2004; Schinka et al., 2002). To date, no clear conclusion has been reached, although a meta-analysis by Schinka et al. (2002) suggested a slight but real effect of the -521 C/T SNP variant on novelty seeking. In any case, theoretical conceptualisation of personality and convergent results from psychobiological (Burgdorf and Panksepp, 2006; Cloninger et al., 1993; Depue and Collins, 1999; Pickering and Gray, 1999), animal (Cardinal et al., 2001; Dulawa et al., 1999) or neuroimage research (see later section in this chapter) highlight the importance of dopamine on IMP-related traits, and D2DR or D4DR still continue to be promising candidates at the basis of

impulsive personality. Interestingly, both dopamine receptor genes have also been related to other drug disorders, pathological gambling, attention deficit hyperactivity disorder (ADHD), cognitive impulsivity or the normal personality trait of novelty seeking. This led to consider D2DR and D4DR as non-specific genes of vulnerability to a wide range of impulsive and reward-motivated behaviours (Bowirrat and Oscar-Berman, 2005; Ebstein and Kotler, 2002; Noble, 2003).

Overall, multivariate and association genetic studies suggest that IMP-related personality traits share common genes with other disinhibitory behaviours and externalising disorders, such as abuse of alcohol and other substances. Consequently, IMP-related traits could be considered mediator variables between some dopamine genes and certain pathological behaviours. Two recent studies showed evidence of this hypothesis. Laucht et al. found associations between D4DR, and heavy drinking (Laucht et al., 2007) and smoking initiation (Laucht et al., 2005) in adolescent boys. However, these studies suggest that D4DR exerts its influence through being mediated by the 'novelty seeking' personality trait. The authors emphasised the implication of personality traits in mediating between genetic liability and onset of substance use.

In addition, alcohol also presents anxiety-reduction effects that could be mediated by serotonergic and GABAergic systems, among others (Lesch, 2005; Mihic and Harris, 1997; Naranjo et al., 2002). Genetic studies have also pointed out the role that g-aminobutyric acid (GABA) and 5-hydroxytryptamyne (5-HT), or serotonin, play on alcoholism. In relation to GABA, several subunits of the $GABA_A$ receptor gene have been associated with alcoholism, especially the $\alpha 6$ and $\gamma 2$ subunits (Loh and Ball, 2000; Tyndale, 2003), and recent association and linkage studies strongly point to the role of the *GABRA2* gene in alcohol dependence, which codes for the $\alpha 2$ subunit of $GABA_A$ (Goldman et al., 2005).

In reference to serotonin, a meta-analysis of the association of polymorphisms in the promoter region of the gene encoding the serotonin transporter protein (5-HTTLPR) and alcoholism concludes that allelic variations in 5-HTT gene contribute to the risk of alcohol dependence, although the effect is small (Feinn et al., 2005). Moreover, several studies found associations between the 5-HTT gene and N-related traits (Aguilera et al., 2006; Lesch et al., 1996). For example, Sen et al. (2004b) reported an association of the 5-HTT and GABA$_A$ $\alpha 6$ subunit with neuroticism. A recent meta-analysis of the 5-HTT gene and N-related traits has concluded that there is a strong association between the serotonin transporter promoter variant and neuroticism (Sen et al., 2004a).

Taken together, genetic studies suggest that some of the genes contributing to the liability to alcoholism are shared with personality traits, especially those associated with IMP-related traits. Candidate genes could be related to dopamine activity; that is, D4DR and D2DR (Bowirrat and Oscar-Berman, 2005; Ebstein and Kotler, 2002). With regard to N-related traits, their role would be more modest and may likely be genetically related only to some alcoholism phenotypes. Candidate genes could be those related to GABA and serotonin regulation, such as GABA$_A$ and 5-HTT (Lesch, 2005; Sen et al., 2004a, 2004b).

Nevertheless, one caveat of these studies is that they do not account for those processes underlying this genetic association (Slutske et al., 2002). For example, personality traits may indirectly influence alcohol use via the social milieu, leading to an association with deviant heavy-drinking peers (Wills et al., 2000), or because there are underlying common psychobiological processes to both personality and alcohol use and abuse (Bardo et al., 1996; Eysenck, 1997; Kreek et al., 2005; Lesch, 2005). Animal and neuroimage studies can address this question.

Animal studies

Since laboratory conditions allow a strict control of environmental variables, the study in animals (the majority in rodents) of the relationship between temperament traits and alcohol consumption may provide evidence about the biological (or environmental) nature of this relationship. Two main procedures have been used in rodent: (1) the study of a predictive relation of behavioural patterns and voluntary alcohol consumption in genetically heterogeneous outbred rodents and (2) the study of behavioural characteristics in inbred rats that have been selected for their high consumption versus low consumption of alcohol.

Genetically heterogeneous animals show individual differences in their alcohol consumption, and some studies have explored the predictive influence of several behavioural traits. Specifically, trait activity has been found to be unrelated to alcohol consumption (Ibáñez et al., 2003; Johansson and Hansen, 2002; Koros et al., 1998; Nielsen et al., 1999). Results are inconsistent in relation to anxiety; Sandbak and Murison (2001) found no relation between anxiety and alcohol consumption. However, Spanagel et al. (1995) and Ibáñez et al. (2003) showed that anxiety predicted later alcohol consumption. Furthermore, although Johansson and Hansen (2002) did not find a relationship between anxiety and voluntary alcohol consumption, they found that lesions in the amygdala decreased anxiety and alcohol consumption, suggesting a common biological link for both behaviours. Finally, despite some negative findings (Bienkowski et al., 2001; Gingras and Cools, 1995), the majority of studies support the notion that novelty seeking is related to alcohol consumption, at least in the initiation phase of ethanol drinking (Hoshaw et al., 1999; 2000; Johansson and Hansen, 2002; Ibáñez et al., 2003; Nadal et al., 2002). Furthermore, Gingras and Cools (1996) and Hoshaw and Lewis, (2001) found that high novelty-seeking rats presented a greater sensitisation for acute ethanol doses than low novelty seekers.

In addition, Poulos et al. (1995) showed that impulsivity (operationally defined as the choice of a small, sooner reward over a large, delayed reward) predicted alcohol consumption in rats. Furthermore, Poulos et al. (1998) found that impulsivity behaviours following ethanol injections predicted subsequent ethanol consumption. Recently, Mitchell et al. (2006) have described that outbred mice with greater impulsivity showed higher levels of sensitisation to the stimulating effects of ethanol. As mentioned, impulsivity along with novelty seeking are considered central traits of the IMP cluster (Cloninger et al., 1993; Pickering and Gray, 1999).

Genetically homogeneous strains that present extreme differences in alcohol preference have been developed by selective inbreeding of rats that prefer 10% ethanol concentrations, and the inbreeding of rats that avoid it. The most important lines are: P-NP lines (preferent vs. non preferent) and HAD-LAD lines (high alcohol drinking vs. low alcohol drinking; Li et al., 1993), AA-ANA lines (alcohol acceptant vs. alcohol non-acceptant; Kiianmaa et al., 1992), and sP-sNP lines (Sardinian preferent vs. Sardinian non-preferent; Colombo et al., 1995). However, although alcohol preference versus non-preference phenotypes are similar across different strains, it is probable that genotypes of these lines present some differences due to the polygenic nature of this behaviour (Crabbe et al., 1999).

It has been consistently shown that P-NP lines do not present differences in activity trait (Badishtov et al., 1995; Overstreet et al., 1997). Anxiety, however, would be positively related to alcohol consumption in P-NP (Stewart et al., 1993) and sP-sNP strains (Colombo et al., 1995), negatively related in AA-ANA strains (Möller et al., 1997) and not related in HAD-LAD strains (Overstreet et al., 1997). These data suggest that anxiety is relevant to alcoholism only in some phenotypes, and clearly point out that other genetic factors are implied in the development of alcoholism. Finally, and as far we know, novelty seeking has only been explored in the P-NP and HAD-LAD lines. Results suggest a moderate but significant role of this trait in alcohol preference (Nowack et al., 2000).

Overall, animal data seem to parallel human findings. They suggest a moderate but consistent predictive relation of IMP-associated traits (i.e. novelty seeking and impulsivity) with alcohol use and abuse, a less clear relationship of N-associated traits (i.e. anxiety) with ethanol consumption, and no relation of extraversion/sociability-related traits (i.e. activity) with alcohol consumption.

Neuroimage studies

Animal studies suggest that the relationship between some personality traits and alcohol use and abuse may be, in part, explained by shared biological systems. *In vivo* neuroimaging studies of the human brain can contribute significantly to our knowledge of these biological systems.

Although many drugs of abuse, including alcohol, have different primary molecular targets, they all have the common action of increasing dopamine (DA) transmission in the nucleus accumbens (NAcb). This fact has led to the widely held view that the mesolimbic DA system is related to the reinforcing effects of drugs (Everitt and Robbins, 2005), as well as to the appetitive motivation in general (Ikemoto and Panksepp, 1999; Kalivas and Volkow, 2005). Additionally, it has been hypothesised that individual differences in the mesolimbic DA system would be related to personality traits associated with incentive motivation, positive affective states, and goal-directed behaviours, such as positive emotionality (Burgdorf and Panksepp, 2006; Depue and Collins, 1999), novelty and sensation seeking (Cloninger et al., 1993; Zuckerman and Kuhlman, 2000), and impulsivity (Pickering and Gray, 1999). Consequently, DA areas are key targets in human neuroimage studies of alcohol and personality.

Human neuroimaging studies have found some suggestive evidence of the role of mesolimbic pathways and DA activity associated with IMP-related traits, such as novelty seeking, sensation seeking and impulsivity (Barrós-Loscertales et al., 2006a; Boileau et al., 2003; Horn et al., 2003; Laine et al., 2001; Leyton et al., 2002; Suhara et al., 2001; Youn et al., 2002). In a recent paper, Abler et al. (2006) showed that NAcb activity increased linearly with the probability of reward, and was related to the personality traits of sensation and novelty seeking. These studies suggest the implication of the dopaminergic system on IMP-related traits, and its possible role in sensitivity to reward cues.

In relation to alcohol, several neuroimage studies have shown the decreased dopamine D2 receptor in the ventral striatum of alcohol-dependent individuals and detoxified male alcoholics compared to control participants (Heinz et al., 2004; Volkow et al., 2002). Furthermore, alcohol-associated stimuli elicited a greater activation of areas of the prefrontal cortex and limbic systems related to the reward and dopaminergic function in alcoholics (Heinz et al., 2004; Myrick et al., 2004), or adolescents with alcohol use disorder (Tapert et al., 2003). Moreover, alcohol craving has been related to dopaminergic brain regions and DA activity on alcoholics (Heinz et al., 2004; Myrick et al., 2004). Yoder et al. (2005) also found that in healthy non-alcoholic participants, baseline D2 receptor availability in the left NAcb was correlated with peak-perceived 'intoxication' and marginally correlated with a peak-perceived 'high'. These findings suggest that DA activity in the ventral striatum of alcoholics might contribute to an incentive salience to alcohol-associated stimuli.

Overall, psychobiological substrates related to incentive motivation and reward have been found to be associated with both IMP-related traits and alcohol use. Direct evidence of this association has been documented. Boileau et al. (2003) presented the first results in humans that show that alcohol promotes DA release in the brain with a preferential effect in the NAcb. Importantly, this

magnitude of activation also correlated with impulsivity (Boileau et al., 2003). Furthermore, Leyton et al. (2002) have reported that amphetamine-induced DA release targeted the NAcb, and that this release highly correlated with novelty seeking. These studies show a differential response to drugs, including alcohol, in DA brain areas related to appetitive motivation, reward and addiction. This response is also associated with IMP-related traits, suggesting that personality would be the basis of individual differences in sensitivity to rewarding and/or incentive motivational properties of different drugs.

On the other hand, N-related traits like neuroticism, negative emotionality or harm avoidance have been mainly related to amygdala and serotonin activity (Abercrombie et al., 1998; Barrós-Loscertales et al., 2006b; Moresco et al., 2002; Reuter et al., 2004; Tabert et al., 2001; Tauscher et al., 2001; Youn et al., 2002). Hariri et al. (2006) reviewed genetic and neuroimage studies that connect serotonin genes with amygdala activity and trait anxiety. The 5-HTT gene has been demonstrated to bias the reactivity of the amygdala in the face of negative and other salient stimuli. Moreover, cingulate–amygdala functional connectivity predicted almost 30% of variation in trait anxiety (Pezawas et al., 2005).

Neuroimage studies have also related serotonin activity to alcoholism. Szabo et al. (2004) found a lower binding of the serotonin reuptake transporter in the brain of abstinent or recovering alcoholics compared with control participants. In addition, Heinz et al. (1998) found lower 5-HTT density in type I alcoholics, a subtype characterised by high anxiety (Cloninger, 1987). These and other evidence have led to highlight the role of anxiety on alcoholism through common psychobiological factors, especially the amygdala, and to propose serotonin as the possible link between alcohol dependence and negative emotions (Lesch, 2005).

To summarise, human neuroimage studies together with findings in animals indicate the existence of shared biological systems between personality and alcohol use and abuse. These biological systems would regulate positive and negative affective processes, such as incentive motivation and anxiety, suggesting that personality variables could be understood as unspecific traits of sensitivity to the reinforcing and anxiolytic properties of alcohol and other drugs.

PERSONALITY PATHWAYS TO ALCOHOL USE AND ALCOHOLISM

Several theoretical models have been proposed for the aetiology of alcohol use and abuse. These hypothetical models are not mutually exclusive but may represent multiple pathways into alcohol use and abuse. Based in part on Sher et al. (2005) proposal, four main aetiological pathways to alcohol consumption could be considered: (1) specific sensitivity to alcohol; (2) negative affect regulation; (3) positive affect regulation; and (4) deviance proneness. Personality would play a relevant role in most of them (see Figure 33.2).

Specific sensitivity to alcohol

'Alcohol specific effects' models are based on the hypothesis that individuals experience particular effects when they drink alcohol, and that these effects are alcohol-specific. This pathway was strongly supported by genetic studies. It has been found that adolescent alcohol use (Young et al., 2006) and adult alcoholism (Tsuang et al., 1996) show alcohol-specific genetic influences. Accordingly, molecular genetic studies have found that gene polymorphisms related to alcohol metabolism are of importance in alcoholism, particularly in Asians. Specifically, variants of the ALDH2 and ADH1B genes may reduce the risk of developing alcoholism, probably because of its implication on the aversive effects caused by the accumulation of metabolite acetaldehyde in the bloodstream (facial flushing, lightheadedness, palpitations or nausea) (Goldman et al., 2005; Luczak et al., 2006). These and other genes would produce psychobiological effects that *specifically* influence alcohol use and abuse.

However, genetic studies also point to other genetic and environmental pathways. Twin studies have found that alcohol use

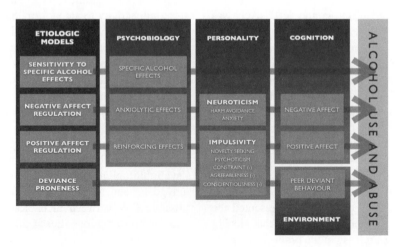

Figure 33.2 The role of personality on main theoretical pathways to alcoholism risk

and abuse also share genes with other drug addictions (Tsuang et al., 1996; Young et al., 2006), externalising disorders (Kendler et al., 2003; Krueger et al., 2002) and impulsive/disinhibited personality (Krueger et al., 2002; Mustanski et al., 2003; Slutske et al., 2002; Young et al., 2000), suggesting unspecific factors as the basis of alcoholism. These unspecific genetic factors may influence liability to alcoholism and other impulsive and reward-motivated behaviours through psychobiological processes of affect regulation, such as animal and neuroimage studies suggest and through environmental variables as most psychosocial studies have found.

Negative affect regulation

Halfway through the last century, Conger proposed a tension-reduction hypothesis of alcohol (see Sayette, 1999). This states that alcohol consumption reduces anxiety, so people will be especially motivated to drink alcohol when faced with stress. Hypothetically, individual differences in anxiety would be related to the anxiolytic effect perception of alcohol, so this effect would be relevant in alcohol use and alcoholism.

Studies in animals have demonstrated that alcohol reduces anxiety, and that alcohol withdrawal, once alcohol consumption is established, produces anxiety (Hölter et al., 1998). In addition, stress facilitates both the initiation and the reinstatement of alcohol and other drugs use after a period of abstinence (Piazza and Le Moal, 1998). However, and as already described, individual differences in the level of anxiety in animals have been only moderately related to alcohol in certain conditions, individuals or strains (Ibáñez et al., 2003).

In humans, the anxiolytic properties of alcohol are important motivational factors in alcohol consumption (Kuntsche et al., 2005), and anxiety-related traits modulate this motivation (Cooper et al., 2000). However, it is not clear that alcohol reduces stress in all individuals or in all situations (Sayette, 1999). In addition, life stressors have not been unequivocally related to alcohol use and alcoholism (Brady and Sonne, 1999; Jackson and Sher, 2003; Schuckit, 1998). Furthermore, individual differences in N-related traits are modestly related only to some alcoholism phenotypes, such as type I (Cloninger, 1987) or negative affect alcoholism (Zucker, 1994).

In other words, complex interactive effects would exist among genetic background, life stressors, personality and alcohol use history. Probably, environmental factors such as problematic family relationships, child abuse and other stressing negative life events would interact with personality variables, such as N-related traits, in order to cope by means of alcohol (Jackson and Sher, 2003). It is probable, however, that this pathway would be important once patterns of alcohol use are well established.

Positive affect regulation

Most people drink alcohol because they expect positive reinforcement effects and, consequently, motivation to 'enhance' (e.g. drinking 'to feel good') is an important factor in alcohol use and abuse (Kuntsche et al., 2005). Importantly, positive expectancies and enhancing motivations are influenced by IMP-related traits (Cooper et al., 2000; Finn et al., 2000). Accordingly, IMP-related traits have a moderate but consistent role in alcohol onset, alcohol use and alcoholism, as we have described.

Motivation for positive reinforcement would be attributed to alcohol psychobiological effects on those brain areas related to appetitive motivation for natural rewards (Everitt and Robins, 2005; Ikemoto and Panksepp, 1999; Kalivas and Volkow, 2005). According to animal and neuroimaging studies reviewed in this chapter, IMP-related traits would influence alcohol use and abuse due in part to its moderating role on the sensitivity to the incentive motivational and rewarding properties of alcohol.

Deviance proneness

One of the most relevant social factors in alcohol use among adolescents is the affiliation with deviant peers who consume alcohol and other drugs (Swadi, 1999). However, the selection of peer groups is not only casual; personality, among other variables, also plays a significant role in choosing friends.

Several studies have found that IMP-related traits facilitate in individuals an affiliation with peers with a high alcohol and other drug consumption. This in turn would increase the probability of their own alcohol (and other drug) use (Finn et al., 2000; Moya et al., 2006; Villa et al., 2006; Wills et al., 1998, 2000). For example, Tarter et al. (1998) found that difficult temperament at ages of 10 to 12, such as high activity and low sociability, was related to deviant peer affiliation, which in turn was associated with tolerance towards deviant behaviour. This last attitudinal factor predicted alcohol and other drug use 2 years later. In other words, personality characteristics, together with other factors, lead to seek deviant peers and situations where alcohol and other drugs are available and their use is promoted.

CONCLUSIONS

Cross-sectional, prospective, genetic, animal and neuroimaging studies have shown that personality constitutes a relevant variable in the development of alcohol use and abuse. However, *different* personality traits could be related to alcohol use and alcoholism through *different* processes. Animal and neuroimaging studies suggest that impulsivity/disinhibition (IMP) would be related to alcohol use

and alcoholism through its mediation on reinforcement alcohol properties, whereas neuroticism/emotionality (N) would be related to alcoholism through its mediation on anxiolytic alcohol effects. Furthermore, the *same* personality traits could be aetiologically connected to alcohol use and abuse through *different* pathways. For example, IMP-related traits may influence alcohol use not only through its mediation on reward sensitivity, but also through its role on deviant peer affiliation. Moreover, even *different* personality traits could influence alcohol consumption through *similar* processes. For example, IMP and E traits would influence the choice of deviant peers that, in turn, facilitates alcohol use and abuse.

In addition, the role of personality is probably different in several stages or patterns of alcohol consumption. IMP-related traits, and E-related traits to a lesser extent, are more relevant at the first stages of alcohol consumption, probably facilitating the affiliation with deviant peers that, in turn, increases the probability of alcohol use. When a stable pattern of alcohol consumption is established, IMP would favour alcohol use probably through the sensitivity to alcohol reinforcing properties. Finally, in the pathological use of alcohol, IMP-related traits, and probably also N-related traits, would be prominent due to sensitivity to both reinforcing and anxiolytic alcohol effects.

However, the influence of personality in alcohol use and alcoholism is limited. For example, in our studies we have found that personality variables account for around 15–20% of the alcohol consumption variance in non-pathological adult samples. Consequently, personality is only one piece in the complex puzzle of multiple biological, psychological and social variables as the basis of the onset, use and abuse of alcohol (Ruipérez et al., 2006; Zucker et al., 1994). A comprehensive view should consider the dynamics and multiple processes of the biopsychosocial factors implied in the development of alcohol use and alcoholism (see Figure 33.3).

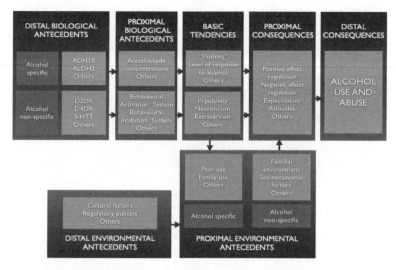

Figure 33.3 A temptative model of biopsychosocial risk and protective factors for alcohol use and alcoholism

ACKNOWLEDGEMENTS

Preparation of this chapter was supported in part by grants from the Spanish Ministry of Education and Science and FEDER founds (BSO2002-03875 and SEJ2005-09307), the Spanish Ministry of Health (PNSD 2005), the Valencian Autonomous Government (GV05/128) and the Bancaixa-Universitat Jaume I foundation (P1·1A2004-19).

REFERENCES

Abercrombie, H.C., Schaefer, S.M., Larson, C.L., Oakes, T.R., Holden, J.E., Perlman, S.B., Krahn, D.D., Benca, R.M. and Davidson, R.J. (1998) 'Metabolic rate in the right amygdala predicts negative affect in depressed patients', *Neuroreport* 9(14): 3301–7.

Abler, B., Walter, H., Erk, S., Kammerer, H. and Spitzer, M. (2006) 'Prediction error as a linear function of reward probability is coded in human nucleus accumbens', *NeuroImage*, 31(2): 790–5.

Aguilera, M., Arias, B., Barrantes-Vidal, N., Villa, H., Moya, J., Ibáñez, M.I., Ruipérez, M.A., Ortet, G. and Fañanás, L. (2006) 'Contributions of SERT and BNDF genes on Neuroticism in healthy general population', *American Journal of Medical Genetics Part B Neuropsychiatric Genetics*, 141B(7): 763.

Babor, T.F. (1996) 'The classification of alcoholism', *Alcohol Health and Research World*, 20(1): 6–14.

Badishtov, B.A., Overstreet, D.H., Kashevskaya, O.P., Viglinskaya, I.V., Kampov-Polevoy, A.B., Seredenin, S.B. and Halikas, J.A. (1995) 'To drink or not to drink: Open field activity in alcohol-preferring and alcohol-nonpreferring rat lines', *Physiology and Behavior*, 57(3): 585–9.

Ball, S.A. (1996) 'Type A and type B alcoholism', *Alcohol Health and Research World*, 20(1): 30–5.

Ball, S.A. (2005) 'Personality traits, problems, and disorders: clinical applications to substance use disorders', *Journal of Research in Personality*, 39(1): 84–102.

Bardo, M.T., Donohew, R.L. and Harrington, N.G. (1996) 'Psychobiology of novelty seeking and drug seeking behavior', *Behavioural Brain Research*, 77(1–2): 23–43.

Barrós-Loscertales, A, Meseguer, V., Sanjuán, A., Belloch, V., Parcet, M.A., Torrubia, R. and ávila, C. (2006a) 'Striatum gray matter reduction in males with an overactive Behavioral Activation System (BAS)', *European Journal of Neuroscience*, 24(7): 2071–4.

Barrós-Loscertales, A, Meseguer, V., Sanjuán, A., Belloch, V., Parcet, M.A., Torrubia, R. and ávila, C. (2006b) 'Behavioral Inhibition System activity is associated with increased amygdala and septo-hippocampal gray matter volume: A voxel-based morphometry study', NeuroImage, 33(3): 1011–15.

Benjamin, J., Li, L., Patterson, C., Greenberg, B.D., Murphy, D.L. and Hamer, D.H. (1996) 'Population and familial association between the D4 dopamine receptor gene and measures of Novelty Seeking', Nature Genetics, 12(1): 81–4.

Bienkowski, P., Koros, E. and Kotowski, W. (2001) 'Novelty seeking behaviour and operant oral ethanol self-administration in wistar rats', Alcohol and Alcoholism, 36(6): 525–8.

Blum, K., Noble, E.P, Sheridan, P.J., Montgomery, A., Ritchie, T., Jagadeeswaran, P., Nogami, H., Briggs, A.H. and Cohn, J.B. (1990) 'Allelic association of human dopamine D2 receptor gene in alcoholism', Journal of the American Medical Association, 263(15): 2055–60.

Boileau, I., Assaad, J.M., Pihl, R.O., Benkelfat, C., Leyton, M., Diksic, M., Tremblay, R.E. and Dagher, A. (2003) 'Alcohol promotes dopamine release in the human nucleus accumbens', Synapse, 49(4): 226–31.

Bowirrat, A. and Oscar-Berman, M. (2005) 'Relationship between dopaminergic neurotransmission, alcoholism, and Reward Deficiency syndrome', American Journal of Medical Genetics Part B Neuropsychiatric Genetics, 132(1): 29–37.

Brady, K.T. and Sonne, S.C. (1999) 'The role of stress in alcohol use, alcoholism, treatment and relapse', Alcohol Research and Health, 23(4): 263–71.

Burgdorf, J. and Panksepp, J. (2006) 'The neurobiology of positive emotions', Neuroscience and Biobehavioral Reviews, 30(2): 173–87.

Cardinal, R.N., Pennicott, D.R., Sugathapala, C.L., Robbins, T.W. and Everitt, B.J. (2001) 'Impulsive choice induced in rats by lesions of the nucleus accumbens core', Science, 292(5526): 2499–501.

Caspi, A., Moffit, T.E., Newman, D.L. and Silva, P.A. (1996) 'Behavioral observations at age 3 years predict adult psychiatric disorders: Longitudinal evidence from a birth cohort', Archives of General Psychiatry, 53(11): 1033–9.

Chassin, L., Flora, D.B. and King, K.M. (2004) 'Trajectories of alcohol and drug use and dependence from adolescence to adulthood: The effects of familial alcoholism and personality', Journal of Abnormal Psychology, 113(4): 483–98.

Clarck, L.A. and Watson, D. (1999) 'Temperament: A new paradigm for trait psychology', in L.A. Pervin and O.P. John (eds), Handbook of Personality. Theory and Research (2nd edn). New York: Guilford, pp. 399–423.

Clark, D.B., Vanyukov, M. and Cornelius, J. (2002) 'Childhood antisocial behavior and adolescent alcohol use disorders', Alcohol Research and Health, 26(2): 109–15.

Cloninger, C.R. (1987) 'Neurogenetic adaptive mechanism in alcoholism', Science, 236(4800): 410–6.

Cloninger, C.R., Sigvardsson, S. and Bohman, M. (1988) 'Childhood personality predicts alcohol abuse in young adults', Alcoholism: Clinical and Experimental Research, 12(4): 494–505.

Cloninger, C.R., Sigvardsson, S. and Bohman, M. (1996) 'Type I and Type II alcoholism: An update', Alcohol Health and Research World, 20(1): 18–23.

Cloninger, C.R., Sigvardsson, S., Przybeck, T.R. and Svrakic, D.M. (1995) 'Personality antecedents of alcoholism in a national area probability sample', European Archives of Clinical Neuroscience, 245(4-5): 239–44.

Cloninger, C.R., Svrakic, D.M. and Przybeck, T.R. (1993) 'A psychobiological model of temperament and character', Archives of General Psychiatry, 50(12): 975–90.

Colombo, G., Agabio, R., Lobina, C., Reali, R., Zocchi, A., Fadda, F. and Gessa, G.L. (1995) 'Sardinian alcohol-preferring rats: A genetic animal model of anxiety', Physiology and Behavior, 57(6): 1181–5.

Conrod, P.J., Petersen, J.B. and Pihl, R.O. (1997) 'Disinhibited personality and sensitivity to alcohol reinforcement: Independent correlates of drinking behavior in sons of alcoholics', Alcoholism: Clinical and Experimental Research, 21(7): 1320–32.

Cooper, M.L., Agocha, V.B. and Sheldon, M.S. (2000) 'A motivational perspective on risky behaviors: the role of personality and affect regulatory processes', Journal of Personality, 68(6): 1059–88.

Crabbe, J.C., Philips, T.J., Buck, K.J., Cunningham, C.L. and Belknap, J.K. (1999) 'Identifying genes for alcohol and drug sensitivity: recent progress and future directions', *Trends in Neuroscience*, 22(4): 173–9.

Czerwinski, S.A., Mahaney, M.C., Williams, J.T., Almasy, L. and Blangero, J. (1999) 'Genetic analysis of personality traits and alcoholism using a mixed discrete continuous trait variance component model', *Genetic Epidemiology*, 17(suppl. 1): 121–6.

Depue, R.A. and Collins, P.F. (1999) 'Neurobiology of the structure of personality: Dopamine, facilitation of incentive motivation, and extraversion', *Behavioral Brain Sciences*, 22(3): 491–569.

Dick, D.M., Nurnberger, J. Jr., Edenberg, H.J., Goate, A., Crowe, R., Rice, J., Bucholz, K.K., Kramer, J., Schuckit, M.A., Smith, T.L., Porjesz, B., Begleiter, H., Hesselbrock, V. and Foroud, T. (2002) 'Suggestive linkage on chromosome 1 for a quantitative alcohol-related phenotype', *Alcoholism: Clinical and Experimental Research*, 26(10): 1453–60.

Dulawa, S.C., Grandy, D.K., Low, M.J., Paulus, M.P. and Geyer, M.A. (1999) 'Dopamine D4 receptor-knock-out mice exhibit reduced exploration of novel stimuli', *Journal of Neuroscience*, 19(21): 9550–6.

Earlywine, M., Finn, P.R., Peterson, J.B. and Pihl, R.O. (1992) 'Factor structure and correlates of the Tridimensional Personality Questionnaire', *Journal of Studies in Alcohol*, 53(3): 233–8.

Ebstein, R.P. and Kotler, M. (2002) 'Personality, substance abuse, and genes', in J. Benjamin, R.P. Ebstein and R.H. Belmaker (eds), *Molecular Genetics and the Human Personality*. Washington DC: American Psychiatric Publishing, pp. 151–63.

Ebstein, R.P., Novick, O., Umansky, R., Priel, B., Osher, Y., Blaine, D., Benett, E.R., Nemanov, L., Katz, M. and Belmaker, R.H. (1996) 'Dopamine D4 receptor (D4DR) exon III polymorphism associated with the human personality trait of Novelty Seeking', *Nature Genetics*, 12(1): 78–80.

Elkins, I.J., King, S.M. McGue, M. and Iacono, W.G. (2006) 'Personality traits and the development of nicotine, alcohol, and illicit drug disorders: Prospective links from adolescence to young adulthood', *Journal of Abnormal Psychology*, 115(1): 26–39.

Everitt, B.J. and Robins, T.W. (2005) 'Neural system of reinforcement for drug addiction: from actions to habits to compulsion', *Nature Neuroscience*, 8(11): 1481–9.

Eysenck, H.J. (1997) 'Addiction, personality and motivation', *Human Psychopharmacology*, 12(S2): 79–87.

Feinn, R., Nellissery, M. and Kranzler, H.R. (2005) 'Meta-analysis of the association of a functional serotonin transporter promoter polymorphism with alcohol dependence', *American Journal of Medical Genetics Part B Neuropsychiatric Genetics*, 133(1): 79–84.

Finn, P.R., Sharkansky, E.J, Brandt, K.M. and Turcotte, N. (2000) 'The effects of familial risk, personality and expectancies on alcohol use and abuse', *Journal of Abnormal Psychology*, 109(1): 122–33.

Gerra, G., Angioni, L., Zaimovic, A., Moi, G., Bussandri, M., Bertacca, S., Santoro, G., Gardini, S., Caccavari, R. and Nicoli, M.A. (2004) 'Substance use among high-school students: Relationships with temperament, personality traits, and parental care perception', *Substance Use and Misuse*, 39(2): 345–67.

Gingras, M.A. and Cools, A.R. (1995) 'Differential ethanol intake in high and low responders to novelty', *Behavioural Pharmacology*, 6(7): 718–23.

Gingras, M.A. and Cools, A.R. (1996) 'Analysis of the biphasic locomotor response to ethanol in high and low responders to novelty: A study in Nijmegen Wistar rats', *Psychopharmacology (Berlin)*, 125(3): 258–64.

Goldman, D., Oroszi, G. and Ducci, F. (2005) 'The genetics of addictions: uncovering the genes', *Nature Reviews – Genetics*, 6(7): 521–32.

Grant, B.F., Dawson, D.A., Stinson, F.S., Chou, S.P., Dufour, M.C., Compton, W., Pickering, R.P. and Kaplan, K. (2004) 'The 12-month prevalence and trends in DSM-IV alcohol abuse and dependence: United States 1991–1992 and 2001–2002. *Drug and Alcohol Dependence*, 74(3): 223–34.

Grau, E. and Ortet, G. (1999) 'Personality traits and alcohol consumption in a sample of non-alcoholic women', *Personality and Individual Differences*, 27(6): 1057–66.

Hariri, A.R., Drabant, E.M. and Weinberger, D.R. (2006) 'Imaging genetics: Perspectives from studies of genetically driven variation in serotonin function and corticolimbic affective processing', *Biological Psychiatry*, 59(10): 888–97.

Heath, A.C., Cloninger, C.R. and Martin, N.G. (1994) 'Testing a model for the genetic structure of personality: A comparison of the personality systems of Cloninger and Eysenck', *Journal of Personality and Social Psychology*, 66(4): 762–75.

Heinz, A., Ragan, P., Jones, D.W., Hommer, D., Williams, W., Knable, M.B., Gorey, J.G., Doty, L., Geyer, C., Lee, K.S., Coppola, R., Weinberger, D.R. and Linnoila, M. (1998) 'Reduced central serotonin transporters in alcoholism', *American Journal of Psychiatry*, 155(11): 1544–9.

Heinz, A., Siessmeier, T., Wrase, J., Hermann, D., Klein, S., Grusser-Sinopoli, S.M., Flor, H., Braus, D.F., Buchholz, H.G., Grunder, G., Schreckenberger, M., Smolka, M.N., Rosch, F., Mann, K. and Bartenstein, P. (2004) 'Correlation between dopamine D(2) receptors in the ventral striatum and central processing of alcohol cues and craving', *American Journal of Psychiatry*, 161(10): 1783–9.

Hölter, S.M., Engelmann, M., Kirschke, C., Liebsch, G., Landgraf, R. and Spanagel, R. (1998) 'Long-term ethanol self-administration with repeated ethanol deprivation episodes changes ethanol drinking pattern and increases anxiety-related behaviour during ethanol deprivation in rats', *Behavioural Pharmacology*, 9(1): 41–8.

Horn, N.R., Dolan, M., Elliott, R., Deakin, J.F.W. and Woodruff, P.W.R. (2003) 'Response inhibition and impulsivity: an fMRI study', *Neuropsychologia*, 41(14): 1959–66.

Hoshaw, B.A. and Lewis, M.J. (2001) 'Behavioral sensitisation to ethanol in rats: Evidence from the Sprague-Dawley strain', *Pharmacology, Biochemistry and Behavior*, 68(4): 685–90.

Hoshaw, B.A., Hua, K. and Lewis, M.J. (1999) 'Response to novelty predicts early ethanol self-administration in Sprague-Dawley rats', *Research Society on Alcohol Abstracts*, 76(1): 18.

Hoshaw, B.A., Sulkoski, J. and Lewis, M.J. (2000) 'The role of responses to novelty in self-administration', *Research Society on Alcohol Abstracts*, 53(1): 15.

Hutchison, K.E., McGeary, J., Smolen, A., Bryan, A. and Swift, R.M. (2002) 'The DRD4 VNTR polymorphism moderates craving after alcohol consumption', *Health Psychology*, 21(2): 139–46.

Ibáñez, M.I., Ávila, C., Moro, M. and Ortet, G. (2003) 'Temperamental traits novelty seeking and anxiety predict voluntary ethanol intake in mice', Poster presented at the 11th Biennial Meeting of the International Society for the Study of Individual Differences, July, Graz, Austria.

Ikemoto, S. and Panksepp, J. (1999) 'The role of the nucleus accumbens dopamine in motivated behavior: A unifying interpretation with special reference to reward-seeking', *Brain Research Reviews*, 31(1): 6–41.

Jackson, K.M. and Sher, K.J. (2003) 'Alcohol use disorders and psychological distress: A prospective state-trait analysis', *Journal of Abnormal Psychology*, 112(4): 599–613.

Johansson, A.K. and Hansen, S. (2002) 'Novelty seeking and harm avoidance in relation to alcohol drinking in intact rats and following axon-sparing lesions to the amygdala and ventral striatum', *Alcohol and Alcoholism*, 37(2): 147–56.

Kalivas, P.W. and Volkow, N.D. (2005) 'The neural basis of addiction: A pathology of motivation and choice', *American Journal of Psychiatry*, 162(8): 1403–13.

Khan, A.A., Jacobson, K.C., Gardner, C.O., Prescott, C.A. and Kendler, K.S. (2005) 'Personality and comorbidity of common psychiatric disorders', *British Journal of Psychiatry*, 186(March): 190–6.

Kendler, K.S., Prescott, C.A., Myers, J. and Neale, M.C. (2003) 'The structure of genetic and environmental risk factors for common psychiatric and substance use disorders in men and women', *Archives of General Psychiatry*, 60(9): 929–37.

Kiianmaa, K., Hyytiä, P. and Siclair, J.D. (1992) 'Development of an animal model of ethanol abuse', in A.A. Boulton, G.B. Baker and P.H. Wu (eds), *Animal Models of Drug Addiction*. New Jersey: Humana Press, pp. 24–63.

Knyazev, G.G., Slobodskaya, H.R., Kharchenko, I.J. and Wilson, G.D. (2004) 'Personality and substance use in Russian youths: The predictive and modearting role of behavioural activation and gender', *Personality and Individual Differences*, 37(4): 827–43.

Koros, E., Piasecki, J., Kostowski, W. and Bienkowski, P. (1998) 'Saccharin drinking rather than open field behaviour predicts initial ethanol acceptance in Wistar rats', *Alcohol and Alcoholism*, 33(2): 131–40.

Kreek, M.J., Nielsen, D.A., Butelman, E.R. and LaForge, S. (2005) 'Genetic influences on impulsivity, risk taking, stress responsivity and vulnerability to drug abuse and addiction', *Nature Neuroscience*, 8(11): 1450–7.

Krueger, R.F., Caspi, A. and Moffit, T.E. (2000) 'Epidemiological personology: The unifying role of personality in population-based research on problem behaviors', *Journal of Personality*, 68(6): 967–98.

Krueger, R.F., Hicks, B.M., Patrick, C.J., Carlson, S.R., Iacono, W.G. and McGue, M. (2002) 'Etiologic connections among substance dependence, antisocial behavior, and personality: Modeling the externalizing spectrum', *Journal of Abnormal Psychology*, 111(3): 411–24.

Kubicka, L., Matejcek, Z., Dytrych, Z. and Roth, Z. (2001) 'IQ and personality traits assessed in childhood as predictors of drinking and smoking behavior in middle-aged adults: A 24-year follow-up study', *Addiction*, 96(11): 1615–28.

Kuntsche, E., Knibbe, R., Gmel, G. and Engels, R. (2005) 'Why do young people drink? A review of drinking motives', *Clinical Psychology Review*, 25(7): 841–61.

Kuo, P.-H., Yang, H.-J., Soong, W.-T. and Chen, W.J. (2002) 'Substance use among adolescents in Taiwan: Associated personality traits, incompetence, and behavioral/ emotional problems', *Drug and Alcohol Dependence*, 67(1): 27–39.

Laine, T.P., Ahonen, A., Rasanen, P. and Tiihonen, J. (2001) 'Dopamine transporter density and novelty seeking among alcoholics', *Journal of Addictive Diseases*, 20(4): 91–96.

Laucht, M., Becker, K., El-Faddagh, M., Hohrn E., and Schmidt, M.H. (2005) 'Association of the D4DR exon III polymorphism with smoking in fifteen-years-old: A mediating role for novelty seeking?', *Journal of the American Academy of Child and Adolescent Psychiatry*, 44(5): 477–84.

Laucht, M., Becker, K., Faddagh, M., Hohm, E. and Schmidt, M.H. (2007) 'Novelty seeking involved in mediating the association between dopamine D4 receptor gene exon III polymorphism and heavy drinking in male adolescent: Results from a high-risk community sample', *Biological Psychiatry*, 61(1): 87–92.

Lesch, K.P. (2005) 'Alcohol dependence and gene x environment interaction in emotion regulation: Is serotonin the link?', *European Journal of Pharmacology*, 526(1–3): 113–24.

Lesch, K.P., Bengel, D., Heils, A., Sabol, S.Z., Greenberg, B.D., Petri, S., Benjamin, J., Müller, C.R., Hamer, D.H. and Murphy, D.L. (1996) 'Association of anxiety-related traits with a polymorphism in the serotonin transporter gene regulatory region', *Science*, 274(5292): 1527–31.

Leyton, M., Boileau, I., Benkelfat, C., Diksic, M., Baker, G. and Dager, A. (2002) 'Amphetamine induced increases in extracellular dopamine, drug wanting, and novelty seeking: a PET/ (11C)raclopride study in healthy men', *Neuropsychopharmacology*, 27(6): 1027–35.

Li, T.K., Lumeng, L. and Doolittle, D.P. (1993) 'Selective breeding for alcohol preference and associated responses', *Behavior Genetics*, 23(2): 163–70.

Loh, E.W. and Ball, D. (2000) 'Role of GABAAbeta2, GABAAalfa6, GABAAalfa1 and GABAAgamma2 receptor subunit genes cluster in drug responses and the development of alcohol dependence', *Neurochemistry International*, 37(5–6): 413–23.

Luczak, S.E., Glatt, S.J. and Wall, T.L. (2006) 'Meta-Analysis of ALDH2 and ADH1B with alcohol dependence in Asians', *Psychological Bulletin*, 132(4): 607–21.

Masse, L.C. and Tremblay, R.E. (1997) 'Behavior of boys in kindergarten and the onset of substance use during adolescence', *Archives of General Psychiatry*, 54(1): 62–8.

McGue, M., Slutske, W., Taylor, J. and Iacono, W.G. (1997) 'Personality and substance use disorders: I. Effects of gender and alcoholism subtype', *Alcoholism: Clinical and Experimental Research*, 21(3): 513–20.

Mihic, S.J. and Harris, R.A. (1997) 'GABA and the GABA$_A$ receptor', *Alcohol Health and Research World*, 21(2): 127–31.

Mitchell, S.H., Reeves, J.M., Li, N. and Phillips, T. (2006) 'Delay discounting predicts behavioural sensitization to ethanol in out-bred WSC mice', *Alcoholism: Clinical and Experimental Research*, 30(3): 429–37.

Möller, C., Wiklund, L., Thorsell, A., Hyytiä, P. and Heilig, M. (1997) 'Decreased measures of experimental anxiety in rats bred for high alcohol preference', *Alcoholism: Clinical and Experimental Research*, 21(4): 656–60.

Moresco, F.M., Dieci, M., Vita, A., Messa, C., Gobbo, C., Galli, L., Rizzo, G., Panzacchi, A., De Peri, L., Invernizzi, G. and Fazio, F. (2002) 'In vivo serotonin 5HT2A receptor binding and personality traits in healthy subjects: A positron emission tomography study', *NeuroImage*, 17(3): 1470–8.

Moya, J., Ibáñez M.I., Ruipérez, M.A., Villa, H., Mestre, H. and Ortet, G. (2006) 'Psychosocial variables related to alcohol use in adolescents', Poster presented at the 13th Biennial Meeting of the International Society for the Study of Individual Differences, July, Athens.

Muramatsu, T., Higuchi, S., Murayama, M., Matsushita, S. and Hayashida, M. (1996) 'Association between alcoholism and the dopamine D4 receptor gene', *Journal of Medical Genetics*, 33(2): 113–5.

Mustanski, B.S., Viken, R.J., Kaprio, J. and Rose, R.J. (2003) 'Genetic influences on the association between personality risk factors and alcohol use and abuse', *Journal of Abnormal Psychology*, 112(2): 282–9.

Myrick, H., Anton, R.F., Li, X., Henderson, S., Drobes, D., Voronin, K. and George, M.S. (2004) 'Differential brain activity in alcoholics and social drinkers to alcohol cues: Relationship to craving', *Neuropsychopharmacology*, 29(2): 393–402.

Nadal, R., Armario, A. and Janak, P.H. (2002) 'Positive relationship between activity in a novel environment and operant self-administration in rats', *Psychopharmacology*, 162(3): 333–8.

Naranjo, C.A., Chu, A.Y. and Tremblay, L.K. (2002) 'Neurodevelopmental liabilities in alcohol dependence: Central serotonin and dopamine dysfunction', *Neurotoxicity Research*, 4(4): 343–61.

Nathan, P.E. (1988) 'The addictive personality is the behavior of the addict', *Journal of Consulting and Clinical Psychology*, 56(5): 183–8.

National Highway Traffic Safety Administration (NHTSA) (2004) *Traffic Safety Facts 2003 Annual Report: Early Edition*. Washington, DC: US Dept. of Transportation.

National Institute on Alcohol Abuse and Alcoholism (NIAAA) (2000) *Tenth Special Report to the U.S. Congress on Alcohol and Health*. Bethesda, MD: National Institute on Alcohol Abuse and Alcoholism.

Nielsen, D.M., Crosley, K.J., Keller, R.W., Glick, S.D. and Carlson, J.N. (1999) 'Rotation, locomotor activity and individual differences in voluntary ethanol consumption', *Brain Research*, 823(1–2): 80–7.

Noble, E.P. (2003) 'D2 dopamine receptor gene in psychiatric and neurologic disorders and its phenotypes', *American Journal of Medical Genetics Part B Neuropsychiatric Genetics*, 116(1): 103–25.

Nowack, K.L., Ingraham, C.M., McKinzie, D.L., McBride, W.J., Lumeng, L., Li, T.K. and Murphy, J.M. (2000) 'An assessment of novelty-seeking behavior in alcohol preferring and nonpreferring rats', *Pharmacology Biochemistry and Behavior*, 66(1): 113–21.

Ortet, G., Ibáñez, M.I., Llerena, A. and Torrubia, R. (2002) 'Underlying traits of the Karolinska Scales of Personality (KSP)', *European Journal of Psychological Assessment*, 18(2): 139–48.

Overstreet, D.H., Halikas, J.A., Seredenin, S.B., Kampov-Polevoy, A.B., Viglinskaya, I.V., Kashevskaya, O., Badishtov, B.A., Knapp, D.K., Mormede, P., Kiianmaa, K., Li, T.K. and Rezvani, A.H. (1997) 'Behavioral similarities and differences among alcohol-preferring and nonpreferring rats: Confirmation by factor analysis and extension to additional groups', *Alcoholism: Clinical and Experimental Research*, 21(5): 840–8.

Pezawas, L., Meyer-Lindenberg, A., Drabant, E.M., Verchinski, B.A., Munoz, K.E., Kolachana, B.S., Egan, M.F., Mattay, V.S., Hariri, A.R. and Weinberger, D.R. (2005) '5-HTTLPR polymorphism impacts human cingulate-amygdala interactions: A genetic susceptibility mechanism for depression', *Nature Neuroscience*, 8(6): 828–34.

Piazza, P.V. and Le Moal, M. (1998) 'The role of stress in drug self-administration', *Trends in Pharmacological Sciences*, 19(2): 67–74.

Pickering, A.D. and Gray, J.A. (1999) 'The neuroscience of personality', in L.A. Pervin and O.P. John (eds), *Handbook of Personality*.

Theory and Research (2nd edn). New York: Guilford Press, pp. 277–99.

Plan Nacional Sobre Drogas (PNSD) (2004) *Observatorio Español sobre drogas – Informe 2004 [Spanish drug observatory – 2004 report]*. Madrid: Ministerio de Sanidad y Consumo.

Poulos, C.X., Le, A.D. and Parker, J.L. (1995) 'Impulsivity predicts individual susceptibility to high levels of alcohol self-administration', *Behavioural Pharmacology*, 6(8): 810–14.

Poulos, C.X., Parker, J.L. and Le, D.A. (1998) 'Increased impulsivity after injected alcohol predicts later alcohol consumptrion in rats: evidence for "loss-of-control drinkings" and marked individual differences', *Behavioral Neuroscience*, 112(5): 1247–57.

Pulkinnen, L. and Pitkänen, T.A. (1994) 'Prospective study of the precursors to problem drinking in young adulthood', *Journal of Studies on Alcohol*, 55(5): 578–87.

Reuter, M., Strak, R. Henning, J. Walter, B., Kirsch, P., Schienle, A. and Vaitl, D. (2004) 'Personality and emotion: Test of Gray's personality theory by means of an fMRI study', *Behavioral Neuroscience*, 118(3): 462–9.

Rose, R.J. (1998) 'A developmental behavior-genetic perspective on alcoholism risk', *Alcohol Health and Research World*, 22(2): 131–43.

Ruipérez, M.A., Ibáñez, M.I., Villa, H., Ortet, G. (2006) 'Factores biopsicosociales en el consumo de alcohol [Biopsychosocial factors on alcohol consumption]', in L.A. Oblitas (ed.), *Atlas de Psicología Clínica y de la Salud*. Bogotá: PSICOM.

Ruiz, M.A., Pincus, A.L. and Dickinson, K.A. (2003) 'NEO PI–R predictors of alcohol use and alcohol-related problems', *Journal of Personality Assessment*, 81(3): 226–36.

Sandbak, T. and Murison, R. (2001) 'Behavioural responses to elevated plus-maze and defensive burying testing: Effects on subsequent ethanol intake and effect of ethanol on retention of the burying response', *Alcohol and Alcoholism*, 36(1): 48–58.

Savitz, J.B. and Ramesar, R.S. (2004) 'Genetic variants implicated in personality: A review of the more promising candidates', *American Journal of Medical Genetics Part B Neuropsychiatric Genetics*, 131(1): 20–32.

Sayette, M.A. (1999) 'Does drinking reduce stress?', *Alcohol Research and Health World*, 23(4): 250–5.

Schinka, J.A., Letsch, E.A. and Crawford, F.C. (2002) 'DRD4 and novelty seeking: Results of meta-analyses', *American Journal of Medical Genetics Part B Neuropsychiatric Genetics*, 114(6): 643–8.

Schuckit, M.A. (1998) 'Biological, psychological and environmental predictors of the alcoholism risk: A longitudinal study', *Journal of Studies on Alcohol*, 59(5): 485–94.

Sen, S., Burmeister, M. and Ghosh, D. (2004a) 'Meta-analysis of the association between a serotonin transporter polymorphism (5-HTTLPR) and anxiety-related personality traits', *American Journal of Medical Genetics Part B Neuropsychiatric Genetics*, 127(1): 85–9.

Sen, S., Villafuerte, S., Nesse, R., Stoltenberg, S.F., Hopcian, J., Gleiberman, L., Weder, A. and Burmeister, M. (2004b) 'Serotonin transporter and GABAA alpha 6 receptor variants are associated with neuroticism', *Biological Psychiatry*, 55(3): 244–9.

Sher, K.J. (1997) 'Psychological characteristics of children of alcoholics', *Alcohol Health and Research World*, 21(3): 247–54.

Sher, K.J. and Trull, T.J. (1994) 'Personality and disinhibitory psychopathology: Alcoholism and antisocial personality disorder', *Journal of Abnormal Psychology*, 103(1): 92–102.

Sher, K.J., Bartholow, B.D. and Wood, M.D. (2000) 'Personality and substance use disorders: a prospective study', *Journal of Consulting and Clinical Psychology*, 68(5): 818–29.

Sher, K.J., Grekin, E.R. and Williams, N.A. (2005) 'The development of alcohol use disorders', *Annual Review of Clinical Psychology*, 1(1): 493–523.

Slutske, W.S., Heath, A.C., Madden, P.A.F., Bucholz, K.K., Dinwiddie, S.H., Dunne, M.P., Statham, D.J. and Martin, N.G. (1998) 'Personality and the common genetic risk for conduct disorder and alcohol dependence', *Behavior Genetics*, 28(6): 481.

Slutske, W.S., Heath, A.C., Madden, P.A.F., Bucholz, K.K., Statham, D.J. and Martin, N.G. (2002) 'Personality and the genetic risk for alcohol dependence', *Journal of Abnormal Psychology*, 111(1): 124–33.

Spanagel, R., Montkowski, A., Allingham, K., Stör, T., Shoaib, M., Holsboer, F. and Landgraf, R. (1995) 'Anxiety: A potential predictor of vulnerability to the initiation of ethanol self-administration in rats', *Psychopharmacology*, 122(4): 369–73.

Stewart, R.B., Gatto, G.J., Lumeng, L., Li, T.K. and Murphy, J.M. (1993) 'Comparison of alcohol-preferring (p) and nonpreferring (NP) rats on tests of anxiety and for the anxiolytic effects of ethanol', *Alcohol*, 10(1): 1–10.

Suhara, T. Yasuno, F., Sudo, Y., Yamamoto, M., Inoue, M., Okubo, Y. and Suzuki, K. (2001) 'Dopamine D2 receptor in the insular cortex and the personality trait of novelty seeking', *NeuroImage*, 13(5): 891–5.

Swadi, H. (1999) 'Individual risk factors for adolescent substance use', *Drug and Alcohol Dependence*, 55(3): 209–24.

Szabo, Z., Owonikoko, T., Peyrot, M., Varga, J., Mathews, W.B., Ravert, H.T., Dannals, R.F. and Wand, G. (2004) 'Positron emission tomography imaging of the serotonin transporter in subjects with a history of alcoholism', *Biological Psychiatry*, 55(7): 766–71.

Tabert, M.H., Borod, J.C., Tang, C.Y., Lange, G., Wei, T.C., Johnson, R., Nusbaum, A.O. and Buchsbaum, M.S. (2001) 'Differential amygdala activation during emotional decision and recognition memory tasks using unpleasant words: an fMRI study', *Neuropsychologia*, 39(6): 556–73.

Tapert, S.F., Cheung, E.H., Brown, G.G., Frank, L.R., Paulus, M.P., Schweinsburg, A.D., Meloy, M.J. and Brown, S.A. (2003) 'Neural response to alcohol stimuli in adolescents with alcohol use disorder', *Archives of General Psychiatry*, 60(7): 727–35.

Tarter, R.E., Moss, H., Blackson, T., Vanykov, M., Brigham, J. and Loeber, R. (1998) 'Desegregating the liability for drug abuse', in C.L. Wetherington and J.L. Falk (eds), *Laboratory Behavioral Studies of Vulnerability to Drug Abuse*, NIDA Research Monograph No. 169. Rockville: NIDA, pp. 227–43.

Tauscher, J., Bagby, R.M., Javanmard, M., Christensen, B.K., Kasper, S. and Kapur, S. (2001) 'Inverse relationship between serotonin 5-HT(1A) receptor binding and anxiety: a [(11)C]WAY-100635 PET investigation in healthy volunteers', *American Journal of Psychiatry*, 158(8): 1326–8.

Theakston, J.A., Stewart, S.H., Dawson, M.Y., Knowlden, S.A.B. and Lehman, D.R. (2004) 'Big-Five personality domains predict drinking motives', *Personality and Individual Differences*, 37(5): 971–84.

Tsuang, M.T., Lyons, M.J., Eisen, S.A., Goldberg, J., True, W., Lin, N., Meyer, J.M., Toomey, R., Faraone, S.V. and Eaves, L. (1996) 'Genetic influences on DSM-III-R drug abuse and dependence: A study of 3,372 twin pairs', *American Journal of Medical Genetics Part B Neuropsychiatric Genetics*, 67(5): 473–7.

Tyndale, R.F. (2003) 'Genetics of alcohol and tobacco in humans', *Trends in Molecular Medicine*, 35(2): 94–121.

Villa, H., Ruipérez, M.A., Ibáñez M.I., Moya, J., Mestre, H. and Ortet, G. (2006) 'A cross-cultural study on personality and alcohol consumption in adolescents: Scotland and Spain', Poster presented at the 13th Biennial Meeting of the International Society for the Study of Individual Differences, July, Athens.

Volkow, N., Wang, G., Maynard, L., Fowler, J.S., Jayne, B., Telang, F., Logan, J., Ding, Y.S., Gatley, S.J., Hitzemann, R., Wong, C. and Pappas, N. (2002) 'Effects of alcohol detoxification on dopamine D2 receptors in alcoholics: A preliminary study', *Psychiatry Research*, 116(3): 163–72.

Wennberg, P. and Bohman, M. (2002) 'Childhood temperament and adult alcohol habits. A prospective longitudinal study from age 4 to age 36', *Addictive Behaviors*, 27(1): 63–74.

Wills, T.A., Sandy, J.M. and Yaeger, A. (2000) 'Temperament and adolescent substance use: an epigenetic approach to risk and protection', *Journal of Personality*, 68(6): 1127–52.

Wills, T.A., Windle, M. and Cleary, S.D. (1998) 'Temperament and novelty seeking in adolescent substance use: Convergence of dimensions of temperament with constructs from Cloninger's theory', *Journal of Personality and Social Psychology*, 74(29): 387–406.

Yoder, K.K., Kareken, D.A., Seyoum, R.A., O'Connor, S.J., Wang, C., Zheng, Q.H., Mock, B. and Morris, E.D. (2005) 'Dopamine D(2) receptor availability is associated with subjective responses to alcohol', *Alcoholism: Clinical and Experimental Research*, 29(6): 965–70.

Youn, T., Lyoo, I.K., Kim, J.J., Park, H.J., Ha, K.S., Lee, D.S., Abrams, K.Y., Lee, M.C. and Kwon, J.S., (2002) 'Relationship between personality trait and regional cerebral glucose metabolism assessed with positron emission tomography', *Biological Psychology*, 60(2-3): 109–20.

Young, S.E., Rhee, S.H., Stallings, M.C., Corley, R.P. and Hewitt, J.K. (2006) 'Genetic and environmental vulnerabilities underlying adolescent substance use and problem use: general or specific?', *Behavior Genetics*, 36(4): 603–15.

Young, S.E., Stallings, M.C., Corley, R.P., Krauter, K.S. and Hewitt, J.K. (2000) 'Genetic and environmental influences on behavioural disinhibition', *American Journal of Medical Genetics Part B Neuropsychiatric Genetics*, 96(5): 684–95.

Zucker, R. (1994) 'Pathways to alcohol problems and alcoholism: A developmental account of the evidence for multiple alcoholism and for contextual contributions to risk', in R. Zucker, G. Boyd and J. Howard (eds), *The Development of Alcohol Problems: Exploring the Biopsychosocial Matrix of Risk*. Rockville: NIAAA, pp. 255–89.

Zucker, R., Boyd, G. and Howard, J. (1994) *The Development of Alcohol Problems: Exploring the Biopsychosocial Matrix of Risk*, Research Monograph-26. Rockville: NIAAA.

Zuckerman, M. (1999) 'Incentive motivation: Just extraversion?', *Behavioral and Brain Sciences*, 22(3): 539–40.

Zuckerman, M. and Cloninger, C.R. (1996) 'Relationships between Cloninger's, Zuckerman's and Eysenck's dimensions of personality', *Personality and Individual Differences*, 21(2): 283–5.

Zuckerman, M. and Kuhlman, D.M. (2000) 'Personality and risk-taking: Common biosocial factors', *Journal of Personality*, 68(6): 999–1030.

Zuckerman, M., Kuhlman, D.M., Joireman, J., Teta, P. and Kraft, M. (1993) 'A comparison of three structural models for personality: The Big Three, the Big Five, and the Alternative Five', *Journal of Personality and Social Psychology*, 65(4): 757–68.

34

Personality, Stress and the Determination of Smoking Behaviour in Adolescents

Donald G. Byrne and Jason Mazanov

SMOKING IN ADOLESCENCE

The negative health consequences of cigarette smoking are now established beyond any reasonable doubt. Smoking has been convincingly and causally related to cardiovascular, peripheral vascular and cerebrovascular diseases, and malignant tumours of the respiratory system and the oral cavity. Smoking has also been consistently associated with a range of other malignant tumours. It causes emphysema and triggers attacks of asthma and bronchitis, and has been linked with a variety of gastrointestinal diseases including those of the pancreas. However while the large majority of these conditions become manifest only in middle or late adulthood cigarette smoking has its origins firmly in early or middle adolescence. To the extent that the prevention of smoking onset at that early age could effectively reduce the incidence of many life threatening and debilitating health conditions half a lifetime later, it is understandable that the causes of adolescent smoking onset have been comprehensively researched.

Despite this effort and the consequent application of a multitude of smoking prevention programmes targeted at early and middle adolescence (Byrne and Mazanov, 2005), rates of smoking behaviour in this age group remain alarmingly high. Large numbers of adolescents in developed countries report themselves to be regular smokers and females do so at rates generally greater than males.[1]

COMMON DETERMINANTS OF ADOLESCENT SMOKING BEHAVIOUR

A comprehensive and contemporary review of causal factors in relation to the onset of adolescent smoking (Tyas and Pederson, 1998) suggested a four-category typology of causal influences: socio-demographic, environmental, behavioural and personal.

Socio-demographic factors are self-evident; smoking onset increases with age in adolescence and females are more likely to smoke than males. Smoking onset is related to lower socio-economic status generally though, as Tyas and Pederson (1998) point out, family structure is an ambiguous correlate. Adolescents with higher disposable incomes are more likely than others to smoke. Ethnicity and race have been related to smoking but not in any consistent manner, and while urban or rural location has been investigated there is little conclusive about the evidence.

In relation to what Tyas and Pederson (1998) termed 'environmental factors', the recent literature suggests that adolescent smoking is linked positively to parental smoking behaviours (Peterson et al., 2006) and is negatively related to parental attitudes to smoking, although not in any simple manner (Huver et al., 2006). Smoking behaviour in younger adolescents has a strong positive relationship with older sibling smoking behaviour (Avenevoli and Merikangas, 2003), and also to peer pressure in the same age group (Unger et al., 2001). A school culture of non-smoking is associated with lower rates of adolescent smoking (Aveyard et al., 2004). Adolescents with poor self-esteem are more likely to smoke than those with good self-esteem (Byrne and Mazanov, 2001) and a propensity to risk taking increases the likelihood of smoking (Lejuez et al., 2005). Finally, attitudes to smoking clearly relate to the behavioural intention to smoke in those who have not yet adopted the behaviour (Kremers et al., 2001; Piko, 2001; Markham et al., 2004).

The determinants of adolescent smoking then are clearly complex and diverse. Longitudinal studies testing multivariate causal models (see, for example, Byrne and Reinhart, 1998) have provided conclusive support neither for specific combinations of causal variables nor for the rank ordered importance of those variables. Variation both in the range and nature of variables and in the measures used to assess those variables have plagued comparative interpretations of the evidence on smoking. Moreover, studies frequently mix and confuse outcome variables. Current smoking behaviour, expressed intention to smoke in the future and smoking onset over time in cohorts of current non-smokers all appear as reported outcomes in the literature. The present lack of clarity is not, therefore, surprising, but the importance of the search ensures that it continues.

While the complex explanations of smoking behaviour are daunting, two avenues of research, those bearing on personality and stress, continually present themselves for attention. The theory and testing of personality and stress in relation to adolescent smoking has a long history.

PERSONALITY AND ADOLESCENT SMOKING

As noted above, the role of personality in adolescent smoking is both broad and complex. The volume of psychosocial variables associated with adolescent smoking behaviour makes it impossible to include a comprehensive account of the entire spectrum (Mazanov and Byrne, 2002). This makes the choice of variables for inclusion a difficult task, with some important variables necessarily omitted. This review examines some personality constructs more consistently related to adolescent smoking over time relative to others.

For this review, adolescence has been extended to include the teenage years and early twenties. Western democratic societies tend to define adulthood as the voting age or age at which one can hold an elected seat in parliament, usually 18 years. Experimentation with health risk behaviours characteristic of adolescence also occurs in the early twenties (when around 5% of lifetime smokers initiate; Choi et al., 2001). For this reason results outside the traditional boundary of adolescence are considered.

Each personality construct is considered two ways. The first is a contrast of factors influencing onset and those that influence maintenance. The second contrast of association versus causality is aimed at exploring how results from cross-sectional and longitudinal research vary, and their implications for primary and secondary prevention.

Models

Personality research into adolescent smoking evolved from unidimensional (e.g. Coan, 1973; Matarazzo and Saslow, 1960) to model-based examinations (e.g. the five-factor model, McCrae and Costa, 1996; and the biological theory of personality, Eysenck 1990). Research using instruments to operationalise these models addresses the relationship of traditional personality constructs to adolescent smoking. This review was confined to the two models noted.

Association versus causality

The only 'model' factor with no demonstrable association with adolescent smoking is openness to experience. Harakeh et al. (2005) demonstrate agreeableness, conscientiousness, extraversion and neuroticism have some correlation with adolescent smoking, with additional cross-sectional support for conscientiousness (negative; Kashdan et al., 2005) and extraversion (positive; Kikuchi et al., 1999). Prospective longitudinal results support the associative relationship of conscientiousness and extraversion (Presson et al., 2002). Psychoticism emerges as positively related to changes in smoking behaviour (Canals et al., 1997). Even this narrow range of results suggests that theoretically or empirically demonstrated models of personality have a role to play in adolescent smoking research.

Onset versus maintenance

The role of 'model' personality variables changes from association to specific forms of causation. Only extraversion and neuroticism appeared to consistently predict onset (Harakeh et al., 2005). However, this relationship is by no means established, with White et al.

(1996) suggesting that personality plays only a minor role in transitions between stages of smoking, at least in terms of effect size; extraversion had only a minor role to play and neuroticism became redundant. However, there is some evidence neuroticism may play more of a role in the maintenance rather than onset of regular adolescent smoking (Vink et al., 2003).

The role of model personality in adolescent smoking

This short review demonstrates the range of possible relationships that can emerge from models of personality and adolescent smoking. Any survey of the 'models' literature is likely to find a mixture of results that declare ascendancy of one variable over another. Importantly, this discussion shows such variables need to be included in any explanation of adolescent smoking as theoretically defined primary predictors, covariates, moderators or mediators.

Risk

As a developmental stage, adolescence is conspicuous as a time for experimenting with 'risky' behaviour (Gonzalez et al., 1994). Many theories of health behaviour incorporate risk as fundamental to describing adolescent commencement or continuation of health risk behaviours (Weinstein, 1993). There are several ways of translating this into the context of personality (Gullone et al., 2000).

The first is to consider risk as an individual difference in terms of predisposition to engage with risky behaviour. Behaviours which come with a certain health risk (e.g. smoking, not using condoms or wearing seatbelts) tend to cluster within individuals (comorbidity; Epstein et al., 2003). While helpful aetiologically and epidemiologically, it gives little insight (beyond correlation) into why clustering occurs. Another way of approaching this issue is how adolescents perceive the 'risk' associated with behaviour. This has led to the investigation of how adolescents perceive and process risk in terms of the probability of events (see below) or fulfilling some psychologically relevant drive or predisposition. In this context, risk has been deconstructed to yield several factors that seem consistently related to adolescent smoking behaviour, broadly grouped into rebellion, antisocial behaviour, delinquency and novelty/sensation seeking (cf. Gullone et al., 2000).

Association versus causality

There is a clear relationship between the way adolescents deal with 'risk' in its many forms and smoking behaviour. At a basic level, a number of studies correlate 'risk' with smoking behaviour (smoking status or number of cigarettes smoked) cross-sectionally (Epstein et al., 2003; Kopstein et al., 2001) and longitudinally (Adalbjarnardottir and Rafnsson, 2002; Brook et al., 2004; Burt et al., 2000). That is, an indication 'risk' and smoking behaviour have some kind of systematic relationship. Confirmation of the systematic relationship has come from studies specifically looking at what causes adolescents to start smoking. Some authors have found compelling statistical evidence of risk as independently influential (Botvin et al., 2001) whereas others have found risk influences smoking behaviour in concert with other psychosocial variables (Koval et al., 2001).

Onset versus maintenance

The relationship between 'risk' and onset of adolescent smoking is variable, with some research focusing on risk as the most central variable for prevention (Burt et al., 2000) and others finding no relationship (Mazanov and Byrne, 2006a). However, risk is related to onset more consistently than otherwise. Audrain-McGovern et al. (2004) show that early onset is characteristic of those with a higher novelty/sensation seeking. White et al.'s (2002) analysis showed disinhibition (part of the novelty/sensation-seeking domain) was key for identifying different trajectories in onset. Flay et al. (1998) report risk differentiated non-smokers from onset (to experimental smoking) and maintenance (regular use). Importantly, these studies indicate that risk is as important for maintenance as for onset.

Additional thoughts on adolescent risk

One important aspect of research into adolescent smoking and risk is the way in which adolescents view the potentially negative impact smoking will have on their life. Arnett (2000) and Borland (1997) report an 'optimistic bias', where adolescents consistently underestimate the consequences smoking may have for them (e.g. breaking addiction). This has a significant impact on their decision-making ability when it comes to making rational cost–benefit trade-offs described by theories of health decision making. Halpern-Felsher et al. (2004) note that adolescents tend to minimise future risk, trading off future cost against immediate benefit. Importantly though, adolescent perceptions of risk tend to evolve very rapidly (Mazanov and Byrne, 2006b) as the adolescent progresses towards adulthood (presumably with age and experience).

Smoking and the 'risky' personality

Based on the reliability of the results over time and across studies, the way adolescents deal with risk clearly influences uptake and maintenance. With the risk relationship reasonably established through replication, the next step may be to develop studies seeking to predict change in smoking using change in 'risk' over time (e.g. more sophisticated longitudinal modelling; Collins, 2006; Mazanov and Byrne, 2006a).

Smoking beliefs/knowledge

Individual variation in personal beliefs or knowledge of the health consequences of smoking represents an important component of the rational health decision-making theory cost–benefit analysis thought to drive adolescent smoking behaviour (Weinstein, 1993). This theoretically central individual difference has justified interventions to alter beliefs or knowledge by exposing adolescents to scientifically demonstrated facts about the consequences of smoking (Glied, 2003) with little success (Evans, 2001). This failure brings into question whether beliefs or knowledge are associated with smoking behaviour in the way theory suggests.

Association versus causality

There is evidence that adolescents (at least in the industrialised West) are very knowledgeable about the health consequences of smoking (Tilleczek and Hine, 2006), smokers more than non-smokers (Mazanov and Byrne, 2007). What is less clear is whether this information influences beliefs or smoking behaviour. There is some evidence that beliefs and knowledge predict smoking behaviour cross-sectionally (Hines et al., 1999; Islam and Johnson, 2005) and cross-culturally (Steptoe et al., 2002). However, the association varies across gender, is sometimes more important for boys than girls (Nebot et al., 2005) and vice versa (Epstein et al., 2003). Some suggest that this variable association may be a function of interactions with other variables (e.g. health locus of control; Bennett et al., 1997) or psychometry (Panter and Reeve, 2002). More importantly, there is evidence that beliefs and knowledge are causally irrelevant (Sperber et al., 2001), suggesting that a more systematic examination of beliefs and knowledge is needed in terms of association and causality.

Onset versus maintenance

There is very little literature in relation to onset or maintenance. Mazanov and Byrne (2007) show that adolescent knowledge of the health consequences of smoking has no relationship with onset, maintenance or cessation. Some evidence shows that beliefs or knowledge relate to cessation, which implies that beliefs and knowledge also influence maintenance (Etter et al., 2000; Rose et al., 1996). The relationship between beliefs, knowledge and maintenance is also reflected in smokers tending to have more positive beliefs about smoking (Amos et al., 1997; Hines et al., 1999). It remains to be established whether this difference exists before onset or a post-decisional justification (e.g. avoiding cognitive dissonance).

The role of smoking beliefs and knowledge in adolescent smoking

Despite theoretical and intuitive importance, there is little evidence to support or refute a role for beliefs and knowledge in adolescent smoking. The role of variables in this domain warrant further attention. The first step is to establish the reliability of the relationship. If a reliable relationship is found, further work on the role beliefs and knowledge play in onset or maintenance is needed, especially for education-based intervention or prevention programmes.

Self-esteem/self-efficacy

The influences of self-esteem and self-efficacy on adolescent smoking have been intensively investigated. There is considerable theoretical support for self-esteem/self-efficacy as a key variable of interest to adolescent smoking, being nominated as one of eight variables declared central to understanding health behaviour (Fishbein et al., 2001). The empirical literature supports the theoretical contention with esteem/efficacy established as both a main and secondary predictor of adolescent smoking.

There is an emerging literature that considers the problem of global versus specific esteem/efficacy (see below). Glendinning and Inglis (1999) suggest the relationship between self-esteem and adolescent smoking can be elaborated on the basis of rather blunt global measures, although contextually specific measures (e.g. peer or academic) are warranted. Glendinning (2004) reaffirms that more effort is needed to understand context specific self-esteem while maintaining global esteem still has an important role to play.

Association versus causality

The association of esteem/efficacy with adolescent smoking forms an established part of the literature (Byrne and Mazanov, 2001, 2003), indicating that low esteem/efficacy is associated with adolescent smoking (e.g. Engels et al., 1999; Mazanov and Byrne,

2002; Soldz and Cui, 2001). In terms of specific efficacy, social self-efficacy (Holm et al., 2003), physical self-concept (Thornton et al., 1999) and academic efficacy (Chung and Elias, 1996) have all demonstrated associations with smoking behaviour. In terms of specific esteem, Kawabata et al. (1999) report smokers that have greater physical self-esteem and lower global, cognitive and family esteem than non-smokers. This result supports Glendinning and Inglis's (1999) assertion that global measures still have a role to play. Notably, some cross-sectional studies report the absence of an esteem/efficacy relationship with adolescent smoking (Moore et al., 1996; White et al., 1996).

While measures of association indicate a fairly reliable relationship, the longitudinal literature suggests the role of esteem/efficacy changes over time. Poikolainen et al. (2001) suggest that the predictive effectiveness of self-esteem wanes over time. Engels et al. (2006) indicate that while low esteem/efficacy predicts cross-sectionally, the predictive effect only occurs for females longitudinally (see below). These results agree with Glendinning's (2004) assertion the longitudinal evidence of a relationship between self-esteem and adolescent smoking is less clear-cut than cross-sectional evidence. Whether this assertion extends to efficacy is yet to be determined.

Onset versus maintenance

Glendinning's (2004) assertion of ambiguity appears to hold in relation to onset (Engels et al.'s (2006) result was that self-esteem has a role in onset for girls only). In terms of maintenance, O'Callaghan and Doyle (2002) show a potentially curvilinear relationship between self-esteem and ordinal smoking status, with occasional smokers demonstrating higher self-esteem than regular or non-smokers. The efficacy literature is more consistent with evidence global self-efficacy influences onset (Engels et al., 1999). Specifically, the protective effect of refusal self-efficacy interventions has been shown in studies of association (Islam and Johnson, 2005; Nebot et al., 2005) and retarding onset

(Bruvold, 1993; Byrne and Mazanov, 2005). Self-efficacy also seems to influence the readiness to change smoking status (Stephens et al., 2004) perhaps as a function of cessation (increased self-efficacy and quitting; Etter et al., 2000).

The role of self-esteem/efficacy

The role of self-esteem/efficacy is tied to a broader philosophical debate about how much contextual detail is needed for a psychosocial construct to be useful. The answer is likely to be tied back to the utility of the results. For example, an excruciating level of detail on specific self-esteem/efficacy may be statistically or academically useful, and meaningless for intervention. This is comparable to the debate on the inclusion of past behaviour in models of health behaviour (Conner and Armitage, 1998), where the result provides no assistance for designing intervention programmes.

Outside this debate, more work is needed on the role of esteem/efficacy in terms of how it changes over time. One line of work needs to establish a compelling case for the role of esteem/efficacy longitudinally, especially in relation change. For example, this might include whether esteem/efficacy influences onset or maintenance by provoking stability or instability in smoking behaviour (Mazanov and Byrne, 2006b).

Locus of control

The belief that one has control over one's behaviour is seen as central to health behaviour (Steptoe and Wardle, 2001), especially in the context of self-efficacy (refusal skills; Stuart et al., 1994). There has been a generally replicated result that adolescent smokers have an external locus of control (e.g. Ludtke and Schneider, 1996; Schneider and Busch, 1998). One significant study by Steptoe and Wardle (2001), involving 7,115 university students across 18 European countries, showed external locus of control was unrelated to smoking. With a respondent age range of 18–30, it is difficult to ascertain whether this result is reliable for the adolescent context.

An important change in locus of control research has been the shift from Rotter's (1966) single internal–external continuum to facet locus of control (internality, chance and powerful others). Some studies show that all three influence smoking behaviour (Bennett et al., 1997) and others only for specific facets (e.g. extremely high chance orientation only; Steptoe and Wardle, 2001). There has been little work on the role of locus of control in how smoking behaviour changes. Stephens et al. (2004) suggest that readiness to change smoking behaviour is unrelated to locus of control. Presson et al. (2002) indicate that an internal locus of control has some protective effect against uptake.

In terms of association, locus of control seems to have a relatively strong relationship with smoking behaviour. Whether locus of control remains as a viable predictor in the context of onset or maintenance is something future research needs to address.

Religiosity/morality

Religion or personal morality has been used as the conduit for a range of substance use interventions, notably in relation to alcohol (e.g. Alcoholics Anonymous and evangelical Protestantism; Sarafino, 2006). This has seen research into the role religion or personal morality might play in protecting adolescents from smoking. Most research on the role of religion or personal morality in this review is based on industrialised West English language sources, and may only represent Judeo-Christian faiths.

Association versus causality
The established negative correlation between 'religiosity' (church attendance, claimed faith or self-report) and smoking has been replicated across cohorts (Merrill et al., 2005; Soldz and Cui, 2001; Wallace et al., 2003). Closer examination reveals that the psychology of religiosity or morality may have less effect than the culture minimising exposure (Chen et al., 2004). That is, being part of a religious group provides the protection rather than the psychological character

of the individual (Wallace et al., 2003). Piko and Fitzpatrick (2004) suggest that the correlation may be more important for boys than girls. This review found no concrete evidence of causality in terms of changes in smoking behaviour being demonstrated by those 'finding' or 'losing' religion.

Onset versus maintenance
There was some evidence religion or personal morality was protective against onset (Amey et al., 1996). Timberlake et al. (2006) report religiosity was the only protective factor that overcame genetic effects. An interesting take on this relationship was that a strong 'private' sense of religion protected adolescents from experimenting with cigarettes, and the public demonstration of their religion protected them from regular smoking (Nonnemaker et al., 2003). That is, if religious adolescents take up smoking their religion may retard progression to regular smoking. This contention is supported by religiosity mitigating the rate of growth in smoking over time (Wills et al., 2003) (possibly more so for boys; Van den Bree et al., 2004). This suggests that differential processes are at work.

The role of religiosity/morality
Religiosity or personal morality has some role to play in adolescent smoking; exactly what that role is is open to debate. More research is needed in a wider range of religious contexts. Such research needs designs that establish whether the correlation is psychological in nature or a spurious relationship. Establishing this result provides guidance on whether religion may be viable as a basis for prevention or intervention programmes.

Conclusions

Reviewing the role of personality in adolescent smoking makes it clear that there is significant scope to explore causality more thoroughly. Exploring causality more thoroughly leads to questions looking to differentiate changes in adolescent smoking behaviour, including changes between non-smoking and some form of smoking. The time has come to move research designs aimed at association towards research designs aimed at explaining changes in behaviour over time (see Collins, 2006, for an informative overview).

STRESS AND SMOKING

While links between personality and smoking have been investigated within the clear theoretical framework(s) of trait personality theory, and the scientific acceptance of those postulated links has benefited from this under-pinning, associations between stress and smoking have a more tenuous history. This arises from three important factors. First, research into stress and smoking has largely been empirically driven and is often lacking in a clear theoretical foundation. Second, definitions and conceptualisations of stress have historically been challenged. And third, Nesbitt's paradox (Nesbitt, 1973), in which 'smoking generates physiological and psychological changes which are normally incompatible' (as stated by Parrott, 1998), poses a discord between anecdotal and clinical reports of smoking and stress reduction, and relevant theory and empirical evidence.

Nonetheless, the popular view that smoking reduces stress, and that smoking behaviour is reinforced through its stress reducing properties, prevails. An Internet search using the term 'stress and smoking' yields an abundance of sites, the large majority offering either folk wisdom (stress promotes smoking behaviour), or various intervention packages to assist with stress management during smoking cessation. There is a relatively small scientific literature, and even then often indirect, documenting clear associations between stress and smoking. The hypothesised relationship was first canvassed three decades ago (Schachter et al., 1977) but few studies since have directly addressed the fundamental issues either of whether stress causes (or contributes to) the onset of smoking behaviour or whether among those who have already commenced smoking, stress increases the frequency of cigarette consumption.

Much of the evidence addressing the latter issue is largely indirect; it is also mostly focused on the adult population of smokers (Thommson, 1997; Spigner et al., 2005). Given that the bulk of evidence comes from the adult population, however, it is important to critically discuss this prior to examining the causal influence of stress on adolescent smoking onset.[2] The evidence can best be captured under the three groupings of (a) stress-related psychiatric disorders and smoking (b) stress and smoking in high occupational risk populations and (c) stress and smoking cessation.

Traumatic stress, stress-related mood disorders and smoking

Many psychiatric disorders either claim stress as a causal contributor or manifest stress-like symptoms as part of their clinical presentation (American Psychiatric Association, 2000). It is then reasonable to expect that if stress and smoking are related, smoking rates should be elevated among those suffering such disorders.

Morissette et al. (2006) examined smoking behaviour among individuals with anxiety disorders, and reported smoking to be higher in those with anxiety sensitivity, higher levels of anxiety symptoms, agoraphobic avoidance, negative affect and life interference of anxiety. Smokers were not different from non-smokers, however, on measures of social anxiety, worry or obsessive-compulsive symptoms. A broad influence of anxiety on smoking behaviour could therefore be claimed.

But of the anxiety based psychiatric disorders, post-traumatic stress disorder (PTSD) shows the most consistent association with smoking behaviour. PTSD identified by structured interview in the general population was related to the probability of smoking and of nicotine dependence, and also to a (low) probability of remission from nicotine dependence (Hapke et al., 2005) leading to the conclusion that smokers with PTSD may need particular help with cessation. Thorndike et al. (2006) looked for PTSD in current regular smokers (rather than assessing smoking in those with PTSD) and found PTSD to be related to nicotine dependence but not to numbers of cigarettes consumed daily. Smoking behaviour assessed in various ways has now also been clearly, consistently, and causally linked to the experience of major traumatic events, both civilian (Olff et al., 2006) and war related (Koenen et al., 2006).

Survivors of the attack on the World Trade Centre on 11 September 2001 have recently provided a large group for study in relation to PTSD and smoking. Assessment of a random sample of New York residents five to eight weeks after the attack showed that rates of smoking increased noticeably following the event (Vlahov et al., 2002), and symptoms of PTSD were associated with this increase (Arijit et al., 2005). Even US populations geographically distant from New York at the time of the attack showed traumatic-event-related increases in smoking behaviour in the following week (Formann-Hoffman et al., 2005). Interestingly, re-examination of these data controlling for depression eliminated associations between PTSD and smoking, raising the possibility that mood disorders other than those based on anxiety are associated with smoking behaviour. Depression has been prominent in this regard (Knox et al., 2006; Dierker et al., 2005; Campo-Arias et al., 2006), though associations have not been universally strong (Johnson and Breslau, 2006).

The use of mood disorders as a proxy index of stress has not then provided unambiguous support for the view that stress and smoking are linked in anything but a coincidental manner. While the evidence is strongest for PTSD and smoking, it is confounded in at least one study by the co-existence of depression.

Smoking in stress-prone occupational populations

Some populations of individuals through occupational choice are subjected to greater exposure to stress during periods of their lives than are other populations. If smoking were linked to stress then more individuals in these populations would be expected to be smokers, and among those smokers, the behaviour would be expected to co-vary with fluctuations in stressor load.

Rates of smoking among nurses is high relative to the population at large, and the stress of the nursing workplace has been implicated in this finding (McKenna et al., 2003); while there was no evidence to indicate a causal influence, the maintenance effects of stress on smoking behaviour in nurses was clearly apparent.

Armed service personnel, whether current or retired, constitute another population at apparent risk. Rates of smoking in military populations are recognized to be high (Feigelman, 1994) and speculation has linked this phenomenon to the stress of a potentially hazardous occupation (Prendergast et al., 1973). Smoking rates rise generally when young recruits enter military service (Chisick et al., 1998) and the experience of combat conditions (Wynd and Ryan-Wenger, 1998; Ismali et al., 2000) strengthens links. This has also been evident among those engaged in the provision of medical care during wartime (Creson et al., 1996; Britt and Adler, 1999; Boos and Croft, 2004). And high rates of smoking in military personnel continue into civilian life after discharge (Klevens et al., 1995; Whitlock et al., 1995; Op den Velde et al., 2002). There is evidence to suggest however that continuation is mediated in part by the development of PTSD (Op den Velde et al., 2002) or depression (Whitlock et al., 1995). There is therefore consistent evidence linking smoking with military service, and by inference with the stress of military life, but much of this is indirect and does not inform the debate on stress and smoking in any specific way. Much the same may be said for stress and smoking among police officers (Smith et al., 2005). Empirical evidence for this has been reported in a number of countries including the US (Franke et al., 1998), Australia (Richmond et al., 1998) and France (Bonnet et al., 2005). Importantly, however, this empirical finding has been specifically linked to the occupational stress arising from police work (Bonnet et al., 2005; Smith et al., 2005).

Most directly, however, occupational stress has been related to cigarette smoking in studies extending beyond specific occupational groups with putative high stress levels. Kouvonen et al. (2005) found that high effort–reward imbalance in the workplace was a predictor of smoking behaviour. High levels of job strain and job demand were also related to cigarette smoking, and low job effort was associated with ex-smoker status. The stress of job loss too has been related to increases in cigarette consumption and to relapse into smoking among those who had previously quit (Falba et al., 2005). Occupational stress is therefore clearly associated with smoking behaviour but whether this extends to a causal influence on smoking onset or is limited to some co-variation between stress and smoking behaviour among already established smokers remains to be confirmed by prospective investigation.

Stress and smoking cessation

Clinical observations have consistently indicated that stress impacts adversely on smoking cessation. Recent studies report that perceived stress is associated with lower quit rates in those undergoing a smoking cessation intervention (Norman et al., 2006), and with a failure to maintain abstinence following intervention (Manning et al., 2005). Autonomic arousal during the early stages of smoking abstinence following intervention exacerbates withdrawal symptoms and contributes to rapid relapse for most smokers (al'Absi, 2006). Clinical anecdote is therefore borne out by systematic investigation. Depression, however, has not been shown to predict failure in smoking cessation (Hall, 2004; Lerman et al., 2004). Since the experience of stress most probably interferes with smoking cessation, some practitioners now advocate the inclusion of a stress management component into smoking cessation interventions.

Conclusions

The evidence is sufficiently consistent that in line with anecdote and observation, stress is generally linked with smoking in adult smokers. The bulk of this evidence, however, comes from studies inferring stress either from the presence of diagnosed psychological dysfunction or membership of an occupational group assumed to be stressful. Few studies have reported co-variations of smoking behaviour with naturalistic assessments of stressor exposure and impact. Nonetheless, the broad co-existence of stress and smoking appears to be established. But the target populations for these studies have been regular smokers typically in adulthood, and as we stated earlier, smoking onset is overwhelmingly to be found in adolescents. The evidence on stress and adolescent smoking, both as a causal influence on smoking onset and as a maintaining influence once smoking has been established, must now be examined.

STRESS AND ADOLESCENT SMOKING

The primary theoretical objection to a causal link between stress and smoking onset in adolescence lies with Nesbitt's paradox (Nesbitt, 1973). This aside, however, the past decade has seen a great deal of evidence linking stress with smoking behaviour in adolescence. Most of this evidence falls within the three broad categories of: (a) stress and either current smoking behaviour or smoking onset (b) smoking in adolescents suffering from a psychological disorder linked with stress or (c) stress as an impediment to smoking prevention strategies in adolescents. These are now considered in turn.

Stress and adolescent smoking (onset or current behaviour)

The experience of high levels of stress, often in association with poor mobilization of effective coping skills, has consistently been associated with current smoking behaviour in adolescents. Siqueira et al. (2000) examined 954 patients aged between 12 and 21 attending an urban multidisciplinary clinic; 25% were current smokers and this was clearly related to both high levels of experienced stress and the use of negative coping strategies. The nature of the reported stressors was broadly based but those involving the family were prominent. Family stress was also found to be a correlate of both adolescent smoking behaviour and daily smoking levels in a large population sample (Miller and Volk, 2002).

A study of normal secondary school adolescents (Karatzias et al., 2001) looked both at experimental smoking (having tried smoking) and the maintenance of established smoking behaviour. School stress was the best predictor of experimental smoking but the maintenance of the behaviour, once established, was better predicted by poor quality of school life. While this study was essentially retrospective, the finding that (school) stress predicted experimental smoking but not smoking maintenance hints at the possible link between stress and smoking onset. A large population study (Van den Bree et al., 2004) further reinforced the importance of school stress, reporting associations between stress in the school context and both initiation and progression of smoking among adolescents. High levels of stress predicted progression along a trajectory of smoking in school-aged adolescents (Hunt, 2005). And findings such as these have gone beyond Western samples of adolescents, with similar results recently reported from samples of adolescents in China (Unger et al., 2001; Li et al., 2003; Liu, 2003).

While much of this evidence rests on cross-sectional examination of adolescent smoking behaviour, a number of studies have attempted to move to a more predictive assessment of stress and smoking. In a large sample of sixth and seventh graders, Jones (2004) showed not only that perceived stress related to current smoking behaviour, but that measures of perceived stress in sixth graders predicted smoking when these adolescents were prospectively examined as seventh graders. And reported adolescent intention to smoke is clearly predicted by prior stress (Straub et al., 2003; Booker et al., 2004). In a

truly prospective study (relatively rare in this area) Wills et al. (2002) examined directional hypotheses in regard to stress and smoking in a large sample of adolescents initially assessed at intake (with a mean age of 12.4 years) and followed up at three yearly intervals. The experience of negative life events significantly predicted smoking onset over the follow-up period, and because of the prospective design, the evidence supported the view that stress is associated with smoking onset.

The paucity of prospective evidence on stress and adolescent smoking onset – in contrast to the more abundant associations between stress and current smoking behaviour – has limited conclusions that might be drawn in this area. A quasi-prospective study of more than 6,500 Australian adolescents (Byrne et al., 1995) reported significant associations between stress and smoking onset in previously non-smoking adolescents followed up over a year, with associations represented across a broad range of stressors. Unfortunately, while smoking onset was assessed over the follow-up year, stress was retrospectively measured only at follow-up, and so predictive relationships based on levels of stress at intake could not be claimed.

This issue was addressed in a further study (Byrne and Mazanov, 1999) in which both stress and current smoking were assessed in a large sample of Australian adolescents. Stressor experience was clearly related to current smoking, and while associations were stronger for girls than for boys, most domains of adolescent stressors were correlated with smoking behaviour. The sample was followed up a year after intake; scores on scales of adolescent stress were only weakly predictive of smoking onset in boys. For girls, however, prospective associations were far stronger, and more broadly represented across the domains of adolescent stress, indicating that stress may exert a causal influence on the onset of smoking at least for adolescent girls (Byrne and Mazanov, 2003). Results indicated a broad range of stressor categories (Byrne et al., 2007) as precursors to adolescent smoking, particularly among girls. The breadth of stressors associated with smoking attests to the complex nature of adolescent stress. Examination of intention to smoke in this same cohort revealed that dimensions of stress usefully predicted adolescents' indications intention to be smokers (or non-smokers) at some time into the future (Mazanov and Byrne, 2002). Intention to smoke is a contentious outcome variable, however, since it is not perfectly correlated with the actual behavioural outcome, though it is often used as a variable of convenience where a true prospective methodology is not feasible. Droomers et al. (2005) extended the reasoning to the broader psychosocial contexts in which adolescents live, linking smoking to the stress of low socio-economic class, though findings such as these are prone to a range of interpretations.

Two particular sources of adolescent stress have emerged from the recent literature as worthy of further attention. First, gender differences in relation to stress and smoking are clearly evident (Koval et al., 2000). Female gender has also been associated with smoking rates, with girls tending to have higher rates of smoking than boys, at least in Western samples (Byrne and Reinhart, 1998). Adolescent girls also appear to experience higher levels of stress than boys (Byrne et al., 2006). The possibility that these issues may be linked (Croghan et al., 2006) cannot be overlooked. One pathway which may explain the link is that of pubertal timing. Early puberty in girls has been associated with the experience of stress (Simon et al., 2003), and with both having tried smoking (Simon et al., 2003) and early initiation and greater frequency of smoking (Dick et al., 2000). The potential to understand high smoking rates in adolescent girls through the mechanism of stress associated with early puberty deserves further exploration.

Second, as societies around the World become more multi-ethnic, adolescents in minority groups are experiencing racial discrimination and stress arising from that (Fisher et al., 2000). Early evidence is emerging that stress from this source is associated with adolescent smoking. Guthrie et al. (2002) looked at racial discrimination among African-American adolescent girls and reported a clear association between the experience of discrimination and smoking. Controlling for levels of stress arising from discrimination significantly reduced the size of the relationship between discrimination and smoking, underscoring the importance of stress in understanding the link. Udry et al. (2003) extended this reasoning to adolescents of mixed race origins, associating elevated risk of smoking in mixed race adolescents to stress arising from this situation. This potential link between stress and adolescent smoking also requires vigorous examination.

Anxiety, depression and adolescent smoking

In a manner identical to evidence relating stress to established smoking in adults, it would be expected that where adolescents suffer a psychological disorder involving affective distress, smoking behaviour should vary in some way in relation to the onset or course of that psychological disorder.

Investigation of a population sample of adolescents (Acierno et al., 2000) assessed traumatic stress in relation to cigarette use. Depression was associated with smoking only in girls, and in contrast to the adult literature reviewed earlier; PTSD was not independently related to an increased risk of smoking. Gender differences in relation to depression and smoking were also evident in a study of early adolescents using electronic diary data collection (Whalen et al., 2001; Henker et al., 2002). While 'depressive dispositions' were related both to smoking urges and risk of smoking in this sample, depression was related to a reduction in smoking risks in boys, but only where smoking risks were associated with externalising (aggressive and delinquent) behaviours. By contrast, a telephone survey of girls and young women drawn from a representative population sample revealed that smoking was related to the report of depressive symptoms (Pirkle and Richter, 2006).

Botello-Cabrera (2005) reported broader links between mood disorders and smoking in adolescents, where smoking related to having any psychiatric disorder. A study of current adolescent smoking behaviour (Koval et al., 2004) indicated that while psychosocial variables relate to current smoking, effects are more evident for boys than for girls, leading to the conclusion that for older boys at least, smoking may be used as a coping strategy against depression. Broadening the field further, an extensive study of young people aged 7 to 18 with symptoms of hyperactivity-inattention (Galera et al., 2005) suggested that while these symptoms did not independently predict risk of smoking, symptoms of conduct disorder were significantly related to smoking in both genders. High activity levels were associated with smoking only in boys, but shy girls showed a lower risk of smoking.

Some studies have questioned the direction of causality of the link between psychological disorder and smoking in adolescents. Goodwin et al. (2005) followed a large group of adolescents over three time points from adolescence to young adulthood and found that daily smoking at intake was related to the experience of panic attacks at the first follow-up and to conspicuous panic disorder at the final data collection. While these results were attenuated when the presence of parental anxiety was taken into account they suggest that smoking may lead to anxiety rather than the reverse. Data from a further population sample (Steuber and Banner, 2006) indicated that adolescent smoking status at intake was associated with the report of depression at follow up, and that this finding was most prominent for girls. McGee et al. (2005) reported that early smoking in adolescents predicted suicidal ideation sometime later, though this relationship disappeared when co-existing depression was controlled for.

The evidence linking affective distress with adolescent smoking is therefore tantalizing but not conclusive in regard to adolescent smoking. While firmer conclusions are attractive the complexity of adolescent mental health issues potentially confounds the data.

Stress and adolescent smoking prevention and cessation

The health consequences of adolescent smoking are sufficiently important that a good deal of research is now devoted either to prevention of smoking in younger adolescents or cessation of smoking among those who have already acquired the behaviour. As with the adult literature there is emerging evidence that stress exerts an influence on the ease with which adolescents are either able to resist the behaviour or give it up once acquired.

Common practice in the field of adolescent smoking cessation consistently involves the teaching of stress management as an integral component of intervention (Singleton and Pope, 2000; O'Connell et al., 2004). Indeed, a study of smoking cessation interventions (Turner et al., 2004) actually found that stress predicted attendance at cessation sessions; those with high reported stress were less likely to attend than those with low stress. And stress posed a significant barrier to smoking cessation in another sample interviewed on their likelihood of quitting smoking (Amos et al., 2006). A small qualitative study of young female smokers (Gilbert, 2005) advocated that smoking cessation programmes should be targeted to the needs of young people and that the common belief that smoking leads to stress relief should for a focus for such programmes.

Unlike the adult literature however, few studies have examined stress (or mental health status) in relation to actual outcomes in smoking cessation programmes. Horn et al. (2004) studied a relatively small sample of rural adolescents either undergoing a purpose-designed programme to quit smoking or offered a brief, single intervention. The cessation programme was modestly successful but the co-existence of depression or anxiety reduced the effectiveness of cessation outcomes. On that basis these authors recommended the inclusion of coping and stress management skills into smoking cessation programmes for adolescents.

The literature on smoking prevention in adolescents is, unfortunately, not encouraging (Bruvold, 1993) and there has been little to systematically link stress with the achievement of prevention. Byrne and Mazanov (2005) did present data evaluating an extensive smoking prevention programme in a large sample of Australian adolescents which does bear on the role of stress. Three approaches to smoking prevention based respectively on the health consequences of smoking, the fitness consequences of smoking and resistance to peer pressure were trialled in a one-year prospective study. While the intervention programme focusing on the health consequences of smoking was most effective in reducing smoking onset immediately following intervention, one-year follow-up demonstrated that resistance to peer pressure based on stress management was a more effective long-term prevention strategy.

CONCLUSIONS

The evidence relating adolescent smoking to personality and stress is persuasive but not conclusive. The diversity of theoretical approaches to personality precludes a clear picture either of whether personality is a reliable predictor of adolescent smoking or, where the evidence is positive, what attributes of personality are strongest in this regard. Moreover, much of the work has been retrospective, and while this contributes to indicative conclusions it cannot give truly causal ones.

Work on stress and adolescent smoking is perhaps even less clear-cut. Much of the support has been implied from studies of established adult smokers and focused on the apparent stress-reducing properties of smoking behaviour. One difficulty here continues to lie with Nesbitt's (1973) paradox, and it remains theoretically implausible that an arousing behaviour such as smoking would be acquired in order to combat the effects of stress (also arousing), by previously non-smoking adolescents. Yet the empirical evidence continues to support a link between stress and adolescent smoking, and some evidence (Byrne and Mazanov, 1999, 2003, 2005) suggests that this link may be causal. Prospective evidence restricts the link largely to girls but associations remain evident in boys. And interestingly, there is little evidence that stress influences smoking behaviour over time in adolescents once the behaviour has been established (Mazanov and Byrne, 2006b). But the best evidence on whether stress relates causally to the onset of adolescent smoking will finally rest with intervention studies, and there are now sufficient numbers of these studies to indicate that stress management should be a prominent component of all new programmes focusing on the prevention of smoking behaviour among school-aged adolescents.

ACKNOWLEDGEMENTS

The authors gratefully acknowledge the editorial assistance of Mrs Kerry Thomas in the preparation of this chapter.

NOTES

1 Sources: <http://www.quit.org.au/browse.asp?ContainerID=1727> and <http://www.education.ed.ac.uk/cahru/publications/BriefingPaper6.pdf>

2 Since this work deals mostly with regular adult smokers, and not with smoking onset among adolescents, only recent evidence (post-2000) has been considered.

REFERENCES

Acierno, R., Kilpatrick, D.G., Resnick, H., Saunders, B., De Arellano, M. and Best, C. (2000) 'Assault, PTSD, family substance use, and depression as risk factors for cigarette use in youth: Findings from the National Survey of Adolescents', *Journal of Traumatic Stress*, 13(3): 381–96.

Adalbjarnardottir, S. and Rafnsson, F.D. (2002) 'Adolescent anti-social behaviour and substance use: Longitudinal analyses', *Addictive Behaviours*, 27(2): 227–40.

Ajzen, I. (1991) The Theory of Planned Behaviour. *Organisational Behaviour and Human Decision Processes*, 50(2): 179–211.

al'Absi, M. (2006) 'Hypothalamic–pituitary–adrenocortical responses to psychological stress and risk for smoking relapse', *International Journal of Psychophysiology*, 59(3): 218–27.

Alexander, L., Currie, C., Todd, J. and Smith, R. (2004) How are Scotland's young people doing? *A cross-national perspective on health-related risk*. HBSB Briefing Paper, 6.

American Psychiatric Association (2000) *Diagnostic and Statistical Manual of Mental Disorders* (4th edn Text Revision). Washington DC: APA.

Amey, C.H., Albrecht, S.L. and Miller, M.K. (1996) 'Racial differences in adolescent drug use: The impact of religion', *Substance Use and Misuse*, 31(10): 1311–32.

Amos, A., Elton, R., Gray, D. and Currie, C. (1997) 'Healthy or druggy? Self-image, ideal image and smoking behaviour among young people', *Social Science and Medicine*, 45(6): 847–58.

Amos, A., Wiltshire, S., Haw, S. and McNeill, A. (2006) 'Ambivalence and uncertainty: Experiences of and attitudes towards addiction and smoking cessation in the mid-to-late teens', *Health Education Research*, 21(2): 181–91.

Arijit, N., Galea, S., Ahern, J. and Vlahov, D. (2005) 'Probable cigarette dependence, PTSD, and depression after an urban disaster: Results from New York City residents 4 months after September 11, 2001', *Psychiatry: Interpersonal and Biological Processes*, 68(4): 299–310.

Arnett, J.J. (2000) 'Optimistic bias in adolescent and adult smokers and non-smokers. *Addictive Behaviours*, 25(2): 625–32.

Audrain-McGovern, J., Cuevas, J., Rodgers, K., Rodriguez, D., Tercyak, K.P. and Patterson, F. (2004) 'Identifying and characterising adolescent smoking trajectories', *Cancer Epidemiology Biomarkers and Prevention*, 13(12): 2023–34.

Audrain McGovern, J., Rodriguez, D., Tercyak, K. P., Neuner, G. and Moss, H. B. (2006) The impact of self-control indices on peer smoking and adolescent smoking progression. *Journal of Paediatric Psychology*, 31(2): 139–51.

Avenevoli, S. and Merikangas, K.R. (2003) 'Familial influences on adolescent smoking', *Addiction*, 98(suppl. 1), 1–20.

Aveyard, P., Markham, W.A., Lancashire, E., Bullock, A., Maca, C., Cheng, K.K. and Daniels, H. (2004) 'The influence of school culture on smoking among pupils', *Social Science and Medicine*, 58(9): 1767–80.

Bennett, P., Norman, P., Moore, L., Murphy, S. and Tudor-Smith, C. (1997) 'Health locus of control and value for health in smokers and non-smokers', *Health Psychology*, 16(2): 179–82.

Bina, M., Graziano, F. and Bonino, S. (2006) Risky driving and lifestyles in adolescence. *Accident Analysis and Prevention*, 38(3): 472–81.

Bobak, M., Rose, R., Marmot, M., Pikhart, H. and Hertzman, C. (1998) 'Socioeconomic factors, perceived control and self-reported health in Russia: A cross-sectional survey', *Social Science and Medicine*, 47(2): 269–79.

Bonnet, A., Fernandez, L., Marpeaux, V., Graziani, P., Pedinielli, J.-L. and Rouan, G. (2005) 'Stress, tobacco smoking and other addictive behaviours in the police force', *Alcoologie et Addictologie*, 27(2(suppl.)), 26S–36S.

Booker, C.L., Gallaher, P., Unger, J.B., Ritt-Olson, A. and Johnson, C.A. (2004) 'Stressful life events, smoking behavior, and intentions to smoke among a multiethnic sample of sixth graders', *Ethnicity and Health*, 9(4): 369–97.

Boos, D.J. and Croft, A.M. (2004) 'Smoking rates in the staff of a military field hospital before and after wartime deployment', *Journal of the Royal Society of Medicine*, 97(1): 20–2.

Borland, R. (1997) 'What do people's estimates of smoking related risk mean?', *Psychology and Health*, 12(4): 513–21.

Botello Cabrera, M.T. (2005) 'DSM-IV psychiatric disorders and cigarette smoking among adolescents living in Puerto Rico', *Dissertation Abstracts International: Section B: The Sciences and Engineering*, 66(5-B): 2538.

Botvin, G.J., Griffin, J.W., Diaz, T. and Ifill-Williams, M. (2001) 'Drug abuse prevention among minority adolescents: Post-test and one-year follow-up of a school-based preventive intervention', *Prevention Science*, 2(1): 1–13.

Britt, T.W. and Adler, A.B. (1999) 'Stress and health during medical humanitarian assistance missions', *Military Medicine*, 164(4): 275–9.

Brook, J.S., Pahl, T., Balka, E.B. and Fei, K. (2004) 'Smoking among New Yorican adolescents: Time 1 predictors of time 2 tobacco use', *Journal of Genetic Psychology*, 165(3): 324–40.

Bruvold, W.H. (1993) 'A meta-analysis of adolescent smoking prevention programs', *American Journal of Public Health*, 83(6): 872–80.

Burt, R.D., Dinh, K.T., Peterson, A.V. and Sarason, I.G. (2000) 'Predicting adolescent smoking: A prospective study of personality smoking', *Preventive Medicine*, 30(2): 115–25.

Byrne, D.G., Byrne, A.E. and Reinhart, M.I. (1995) 'Personality, stress and the decision to commence smoking in adolescence', *Journal of Psychosomatic Research*, 39(1): 53–62.

Byrne, D.G., Davenport, S.C. and Mazanov, J. (2007) 'Profiles of adolescent stress: The development of the Adolescent Stress Questionnaire', *Journal of Adolescence*, 30(3): 393–416.

Byrne, D.G. and Mazanov, J. (1999) 'Sources of adolescent stress, smoking and the use of other drugs', *Stress Medicine*, 15(4): 215–27.

Byrne, D.G. and Mazanov, J. (2001) 'Self-esteem, stress and cigarette smoking in adolescents', *Stress and Health*, 17(2): 105–10.

Byrne, D.G. and Mazanov, J. (2003) 'Adolescent stress and future smoking behaviour: A prospective investigation', *Journal of Psychosomatic Research*, 54(4): 313–21.

Byrne, D.G. and Mazanov, J. (2005) 'Prevention of adolescent smoking: A prospective test of three models of intervention', *Journal of Substance Use*, 10(6): 363–74.

Byrne, D.G. and Reinhart, M.I. (1998) Psychological determinants of adolescent smoking behaviour: A prospective study', *Australian Journal of Psychology*, 50(1): 29–34.

Campo-Arias, A., Diaz-Martinez, L.A., Rueda-Jaimes, G.E., Rueda-Sanchez, M., Farelo-Palacin, D., Diaz, F.J. et al. (2006) 'Smoking is associated with schizophrenia, but not with mood disorders, within a population with low smoking rates: A matched case-control study in Bucaramanga, Colombia', *Schizophrenia Research*, 83(2–3): 269–76.

Canals, J., Blade, J. and Domenech, E. (1997) 'Smoking and personality predictors among young Spanish people', *Personality and Individual Differences*, 23(5): 905–8.

Chen, C.Y., Dormitzer, C.M., Bejarano, J. and Anthony, J.C. (2004) 'Religiosity and the earliest stages of adolescent drug involvement in seven countries of Latin America', *American Journal of Epidemiology*, 159(12): 1180–8.

Chisick, M.C., Poindexter, F.R. and York, A.K. (1998) 'Comparing tobacco use among incoming recruits and military personnel on active duty in the United States', *Tobacco Control*, 7(3): 236–40.

Choi, W.S., Gilpin, E.A., Farkas, A.J. and Pierce, J.P. (2001) 'Determining the probability of future smoking among adolescents', *Addiction*, 96(2): 313–23.

Chung, H. and Elias, M. (1996) 'Patterns of adolescent involvement in problem behaviours: Relationship to self-efficacy, social competence and life events', *American Journal of Community Psychology*, 24(6): 771–84.

Coan, R.W. (1973) 'Personality variables associated with cigarette smoking', *Journal of Personality and Social Psychology*, 26(1): 86–104.

Collins, L.M. (2006) 'Analysis of longitudinal data: The integration of theoretical model, temporal design, and statistical model', *Annual Review of Psychology*, 57: 505–28.

Conner, M. and Armitage, C.J. (1998) 'Extending the theory of planned behaviour: A review and avenues for further research', *Journal of Applied Social Psychology*, 28(15): 1429–64.

Creson, D., Schmitz, J.M. and Arnoutovic, A. (1996) 'War-related changes in cigarette smoking: A survey study of health professionals in Sarajevo', *Substance Use and Misuse*, 31(5): 639–46.

Croghan, I.T., Bronars, C., Patten, C.A., Schroeder, D.R., Nirelli, L.M., Thomas, J.L. et al. (2006) 'Is smoking related to body image satisfaction, stress, and self-esteem in young adults?', *American Journal of Health Behavior*, 30(3): 322–33.

Dick, D.M., Rose, R.J., Viken, R.J. and Kaprio, J. (2000) 'Pubertal timing and substance use: Associations between and within families across late adolescence', *Developmental Psychology*, 36(2): 180–9.

Dierker, L.C., Ramirez, R.R., Chavez, L.M. and Canino, G. (2005) 'Association between psychiatric disorders and smoking stages among Latino adolescents', *Drug and Alcohol Dependence*, 80(3): 361–8.

Droomers, M., Schrijvers, C.T.M., Casswell, S. and Mackenbach, J.P. (2005) 'Father's occupational group and daily smoking during adolescence: Patterns and predictors', *American Journal of Public Health*, 95(4): 681–9.

Engels, R.C.M.E., de Vries, J., Hale, W.W. and Noom, M. (2006) 'Self-efficacy and emotional adjustment as precursors of smoking in early adolescence', *Substance Use and Misuse*, 40(12): 1883–93.

Engels, R.C.M.E., Knibbe, R.A. and Drop, M.J. (1999) 'Predictability of smoking in adolescence: Between optimism and pessimism', *Addiction*, 94(1): 115–24.

Epstein, J.A., Botvin, G.J. and Spoth, R. (2003) 'Predicting smoking among rural adolescents: Social and cognitive processes', *Nicotine and Tobacco Research*, 5(4): 485–91.

Etter, J.F., Perneger, T.V., Bergman, M.M. and Humair, J.P. (2000) 'Development and validation of a scale measuring self-efficacy of current and former smokers', *Addiction*, 95(6): 901–13.

Etter, J.F., Perneger, T.V., Humair, J.P. and Bergman, M.M. (2000) 'Development and validation of the Attitudes Towards Smoking Scale (ATS-18)', *Addiction*, 95(4): 613–25.

Evans, R.I. (2001) 'Social influences in etiology and prevention of smoking and other health threatening behaviours in children and adolescents', in A. Baum, T.A. Revenson and J.E. Singer (eds), *Handbook of Health Psychology*. London: Lawrence Earlbaum Associates, pp. 459–68.

Eysenck, H.J. (1990) 'Biological dimensions of personality', in L.A. Pervin (ed.), *Handbook of Personality: Theory and Research*. New York: Guilford, pp. 244–76.

Falba, T., Teng, H.-M., Sindelar, J.L. and Gallo, W.T. (2005) 'The effect of involuntary job loss on smoking intensity and relapse', *Addiction*, 100(9): 1330–9.

Feigelman, W. (1994) 'Cigarette smoking among former military service personnel: A neglected social issue', *Preventive Medicine*, 23(2): 235–41.

Fishbein, M., Triandis, H.C., Kanfer, F.H., Becker, M., Middlestadt, S.E. and Eichler, A. (2001) 'Factors influencing behaviour and behaviour change', in A. Baum, T.A. Revenson and J.E. Singer (eds), *Handbook of Health Psychology*. London: Lawrence Earlbaum Associates, pp. 3–17.

Fisher, C.B., Wallace, S.A. and Fenton, R.E. (2000) 'Discrimination distress during adolescence', *Journal of Youth and Adolescence*, 29(6): 679–95.

Flay, B.R., Hu, F.B. and Richardson, J. (1998) 'Psychosocial predictors of different stages of cigarette smoking among high school students', *Preventive Medicine*, 27(5pt2): A9–A18.

Formann-Hoffman, V., Riley, W. and Pici, M. (2005) 'Acute impact of the September 11 tragedy on smoking and early relapse rates among smokers attempting to quit', *Psychology of Addictive Behaviors*, 19(3): 277–83.

Franke, W.D., Collins, S.A. and Hinz, P.N. (1998) 'Cardiovascular disease morbidity in an Iowa law enforcement cohort, compared with the general Iowa population', *Journal of Occupational and Environmental Medicine*, 40(5): 441–4.

Galera, C., Fombonne, E., Chastang, J.-F. and Bouvard, M. (2005) 'Childhood hyperactivity–inattention symptoms and smoking in adolescence', *Drug and Alcohol Dependence*, 78(1): 101–8.

Gilbert, E. (2005) 'Contextualising the medical risks of cigarette smoking: Australian young women's perceptions of anti-smoking campaigns', *Health, Risk and Society*, 7(3): 227–45.

Glendinning, A. (2004) 'Self-esteem and smoking in youth – muddying the waters?', *Journal of Adolescence*, 25(4): 415–25.

Glendinning, A. and Inglis, D. (1999) 'Smoking behaviour in youth: The problem of low self-esteem?', *Journal of Adolescence*, 22(5): 673–82.

Glied, S. (2003) 'Is smoking delayed or averted?', *American Journal of Public Health*, 93(3): 412–16.

Gonzalez, J., Field, T., Yando, R., Gonzalez, K., Lasko, D. and Bendell, D. (1994) 'Adolescent perceptions of their risk-taking behaviour', *Adolescence*, 29(115): 701–9.

Goodwin, R.D., Lewinsohn, P.M. and Seeley, J.R. (2005) 'Cigarette smoking and panic attacks among young adults in the community: The role of parental smoking and anxiety disorders', *Biological Psychiatry*, 58(9): 686–93.

Gullone, E., Moore, S., Moss, S. and Boyd, C. (2000) 'The Adolescent Risk-Taking Questionnaire: Development and psychometric evaluation', *Journal of Adolescent Research*, 15(2): 231–50.

Guthrie, B.J., Young, A.M., Williams, D.R., Boyd, C.J. and Kintner, E.K. (2002) 'African American girls' smoking habits and day-to-day experiences with racial discrimination', *Nursing Research*, 51(3): 183–90.

Hall, S.M. (2004) '"History of depression and smoking cessation outcome: A meta-analysis": The Covey–Hitsman exchange', *Nicotine and Tobacco Research*, 6(4): 751–2.

Halpern-Felsher, B.L., Biehl, M., Kropp, R.Y. and Rubenstein, M.L. (2004) 'Perceived risks and benefits of smoking: Differences among adolescents with different smoking experiences and intentions', *Preventive Medicine*, 39(3): 559–67.

Hapke, U., Schumann, A., Rumpf, H.J., John, U., Konerding, U. and Meyer, C. (2005) 'Association of smoking and nicotine dependence with trauma and posttruamatic stress disorder in a general population sample', *Journal of Nervous and Mental Disease*, 193(12): 843–6.

Harakeh, Z., Engles, R.C.M.E., de Vries, J. and Scholte, R.H.J. (2005) 'Association between personality and adolescent smoking', *Addictive Behaviours*, 31(2): 232–45.

Henker, B., Whalen, C.K., Jamner, L.D. and Delfino, R.J. (2002) 'Anxiety, affect, and activity in teenagers: Monitoring daily life with electronic diaries', *Journal of the American Academy of Child and Adolescent Psychiatry*, 41(6): 660–70.

Hines, D., Fretz, A.C. and Nollen, N.L. (1999) 'Regular and occasional smoking by college students: Personality attributions of smokers and non-smokers', *Psychological Reports*, 83(3Pt2): 1299–306.

Holm, K., Kremers, S.P.J. and de Vries, H. (2003) 'Why do Danish adolescents take up smoking?', *European Journal of Public Health*, 13(1): 67–74.

Horn, K., Dino, G., Kalsekar, I., Massey, C.J., Manzo-Tennant, K. and McGloin, T. (2004) 'Exploring the relationship between mental health and smoking cessation: A study of rural teens', *Prevention Science*, 5(2): 113–26.

Hunt, Y. (2005) 'Generalized expectancies for negative mood regulation and patterns of substance use in adolescents', *Dissertation Abstracts International: Section B: The Sciences and Engineering*, 65(7-B): 3745.

Huver, R.M.E., Engels, R.C.M.E. and de Vries, H. (2006) 'Are anti-smoking parenting practices related to adolescent smoking cognition and behavior?', *Health Education Research*, 21(1): 66–77.

Islam, S.M.S. and Johnson, C.A. (2005) 'Influence of known psychosocial smoking risk factors of Egyptian adolescents' cigarette smoking behaviour', *Health Promotion International*, 20(2): 135–45.

Ismali, K., Blatchley, N., Hotopf, M., Hull, L., Palmer, I., Unwin, C. et al. (2000) 'Occupational risk factors for ill health in Gulf veterans of the United Kingdom', *Journal of Epidemiology and Community Health*, 54(11): 834–8.

Johnson, E.O. and Breslau, N. (2006) 'Is the association of smoking and depression a recent phenomenon?', *Nicotine and Tobacco Research*, 8(2): 257–62.

Jones, L.R. (2004) 'Gender and ethnic differences in perceived stress as a predictor of smoking behaviors in rural adolescents', *Dissertation Abstracts International: Section B: The Sciences and Engineering*, 65(4-B): 2082.

Karatzias, A., Power, K.G. and Swanson, V. (2001) 'Predicting use and maintenance of use of substances in Scottish adolescents', *Journal of Youth and Adolescence*, 30(4): 465–84.

Kashdan, T.B., Vetter, C.J. and Collins, R.L. (2005) 'Substance use in young adults: Associations with personality and gender', *Addictive Behaviours*, 30(2): 259–69.

Kawabata, T., Shimai, S., Cross, D. and Nishioka, N. (1999) 'Relationship between self-esteem and smoking behaviour among Japanese early adolescents: Initial results from a three-year study', *Journal of School Health*, 69(7): 280–4.

Kikuchi, Y., Masuda, M., Yoshimura, K., Inoue, T., Ito, M. and Watanabe, S. (1999) 'Health consciousness of young people in relation to their personality', *Journal of Epidemiology*, 9(2): 121–31.

Klevens, R.M., Giovino, G.A., Peddicord, J.P., Nelson, D.E., Mowery, P. and Grummer-Strawn, L. (1995) 'The association between veteran status and cigarette-smoking behaviors', *American Journal of Preventive Medicine*, 11(4): 245–50.

Knox, S., Barnes, A., Kiefe, C., Lewis, C.E., Iribarren, C., Matthews, K.A. et al. (2006) 'History of depression, race, and cardiovascular risk in CARDIA', *International Journal of Behavioral Medicine*, 13(1): 44–50.

Koenen, K.C., Hitsman, B., Lyons, M.J., Stroud, L., Niaura, R., McCaffery, J. et al. (2006) 'Posttraumatic Stress Disorder and late-onset smoking in the Vietnam era twin registy', *Journal of Consulting and Clinical Psychology*, 74(1): 186–90.

Kopstein, A.N., Martin, S.S., Crum, R.M. and Celentano, D.D. (2001) 'Sensation seeking needs among 8th and 11th graders: Characteristics associated with cigarette and marijuana use', *Drug and Alcohol Dependence*, 62(3): 192–203.

Kouvonen, A., Kivimaki, M., Virtanen, M., Pentti, J. and Vahtera, J. (2005) 'Work stress, smoking status, and smoking intensity: An observational study of 46,190 employees', *Journal of Epidemiology and Community Health*, 59(1): 63–9.

Koval, J.J., McGrady, G.A., Carvajal, S.C., Pederson, L.L. and Mills, C.A. (2001) 'Models of the relationship of stress, depression, and other psychosocial factors to smoking behaviour: A comparison of a cohort of students in grades 6 and 8', *Preventive Medicine*, 30(6): 463–77.

Koval, J.J., Pederson, L.L. and Chan, S.S.H. (2004) 'Psychosocial variables in a cohort of students in grades 8 and 11: A comparison of current and never smokers', *Preventive Medicine*, 39(5): 1017–25.

Koval, J.J., Pederson, L.L., Mills, C.A., McGrady, G.A. and Carvajal, S.C. (2000) 'Models of the relationship of stress, depression, and other psychosocial factors to smoking behavior: A comparison of a cohort of students in Grades 6 and 8', *Preventive Medicine*, 30(6): 463–77.

Kremers, S.P.J., Mudde, A.N. and de Vries, H. (2001) 'Subtypes within the precontemplation stage of adolescent smoking acquisition', *Addictive Behaviors*, 26(2): 237–51.

Leigh, J., Bowen, S. and Marlatt, G.A. (2005). Spirituality, mindfulness and substance abuse. *Addictive Behaviours*, 30(7): 1335–41.

Lejuez, C.W., Aklin, W.M., Bornovalova, M.A. and Moolchan, E.T. (2005) 'Differences in risk-taking propensity across inner-city adolescent ever- and never-smokers', *Nicotine and Tobacco Research*, 7(1): 71–9.

Lerman, C., Niaura, R., Collins, B.N., Wileyto, P., Audrain-McGovern, J., Pinto, A. et al. (2004) 'Effect of Bupropion on depression symptoms in a smoking cessation clinical trial', *Psychology of Addictive Behaviors*, 18(4): 362–6.

Li, Y., Unger, J., Gong, J., Chen, X., Chou, C. and Johnson, C.A. (2003) 'Stressful life events and smoking in adolescents in Wuhan, China', *Chinese Mental Health Journal*, 17(2): 113–16.

Liu, X. (2003) 'Cigarette smoking, life stress and behavioural problems in Chinese adolescents', *Journal of Adolescent Health*, 33(3): 189–92.

Ludtke, H.A. and Schneider, H.G. (1996) 'Habit-specific locus of control scales for drinking, smoking and eating', *Psychological Reports*, 78(2): 363–9.

Manning, B.K., Catley, D., Harris, K.J., Mayo, M.S. and Ahluwalia, J.S. (2005) 'Stress and quitting among African American smokers', *Journal of Behavioral Medicine*, 28(4): 325–33.

Markham, W.A., Aveyard, P., Thomas, H., Charlton, A., Lopez, M.L. and de Vries, H. (2004) 'What determines future smoking intentions of 12- to 13-year-old UK African-Caribbean, Indian, Pakistani and white young people?', *Health Education Research*, 19(1): 15–28.

Matarazzo, J.D. and Saslow, G. (1960) 'Psychological and related characteristics of smokers and non-smokers', *Psychological Bulletin*, 57(6): 493–513.

Mazanov, J. and Byrne, D.G. (2006a) 'A cusp catastrophe model analysis of changes in adolescent substance use: Assessment of behavioural intention as a bifurcation variable', *Nonlinear Dynamics, Psychology and Life Sciences*, 10(4): 445–70.

Mazanov, J. and Byrne, D.G. (2006b) 'An evaluation of the stability of perceptions and frequency of adolescent risk taking over time and across samples', *Personality and Individual Differences*, 40(4): 725–35.

Mazanov, J. and Byrne, D.G. (2007) 'Changes in adolescent smoking behaviour and knowledge of health consequences of smoking', *Australian Journal of Psychology*, 59(3): 176–80.

Mazanov, J. and Byrne, D.G. (2002) 'A comparison of predictors of the adolescent intention to smoke with adolescent current smoking using discriminant function analysis', *British Journal of Health Psychology*, 7(2): 185–201.

McCrae, R.R. and Costa, P.T. Jr. (1996) 'Toward a new generation of personality theories: Theoretical contexts for the five-factor model', in J.S. Wiggins (ed.), *The Five-Factor Model of Personality: Theoretical Perspectives*. New York: Guilford, pp. 51–87.

McGee, R., Williams, S. and Shymala, N.-R. (2005) 'Is cigarette smoking associated with suicidal ideation among young people?', *American Journal of Psychiatry*, 162(3): 619–20.

McKenna, H., Slater, P., McCance, T., Bunting, B., Spiers, A. and McElwee, G. (2003) 'The role of stress, peer influence and education levels on the smoking behaviour of nurses', *International Journal of Nursing Studies*, 40(4): 359–66.

Merrill, R.M., Folsom, J.A. and Christopherson, S.S. (2005) 'The influence of family religiosity on adolescent substance use according to religious preference', *Social Behaviour and Personality*, 33(8): 821–36.

Miller, T.Q. and Volk, R.J. (2002) 'Family relationships and adolescent cigarette smoking: Results from a national longitudinal survey', *Journal of Drug Issues*, 32(3): 945–72.

Moore, S., Laflin, M.T. and Weiss, D.L. (1996) 'The role of cultural norms in the self-esteem and drug use relationship', *Adolescence*, 31(123): 523–42.

Morissette, S.B., Brown, T.A., Kamholz, B.W. and Gulliver, S.B. (2006) 'Differences between smokers and nonsmokers with anxiety disorders', *Journal of Anxiety Disorders*, 20(5): 597–613.

Nebot, M., Valmayor, S., Lopez, M.J., Tomas, Z., Arizen, C. and Juarez, O. (2005) 'Factors associated with smoking onset: 3-year cohort study of schoolchildren', *Archivos de Bronconeumología*, 40(11): 495–501.

Nesbitt, P.D. (1973) 'Smoking, physiological arousal and emotional response', *Journal of Personality and Social Psychology*, 25(1): 137–44.

Nonnemaker, J.M., McNeely, C.A. and Blum, R.W. (2003) 'Public and private domains of religiosity and adolescent health risk behaviours: Evidence from the National Longitudinal Study of Adolescent Health', *Social Science and Medicine*, 57(11): 2049–54.

Norman, S.B., Norman, G.J., Rossi, J.S. and Prochaska, J.O. (2006) 'Identifying high- and low-success smoking cessation subgroups using signal detection analysis', *Addictive Behaviors*, 31(1): 31–41.

O'Callaghan, F. and Doyle, J. (2002) 'What is the role of impression management in adolescent cigarette smoking?', *Journal of Substance Abuse*, 13(4): 459–70.

O'Connell, M.L., Freeman, M., Jennings, G., Chan, W., Greci, L.S., Manta, I.D. et al. (2004) 'Smoking cessation for high school students: Impact evaluation of a novel program', *Behavior Modification*, 28(1): 133–46.

Olff, M., Meewisse, M.L., Kleber, R.J., van der Velden, P.G., Drogendijk, A.N., van Amsterdam, J.G. et al. (2006) 'Tobacco usage interacts with postdisaster psychopathology on circadian salivary cortisol', *International Journal of Psychophysiology*, 59(3): 251–8.

Op den Velde, W., Aarts, P.G.H., Falger, P.R.J., Hovens, J.E., van Duijn, H., de Groen, J.H.M. et al. (2002) 'Alcohol use, cigarette consumption and chronic post-traumatic stress disorder', *Alcohol and Alcoholism*, 37(4): 355–61.

Panter, A.T. and Reeve, B.B. (2002) 'Assessing tobacco beliefs among youth using item response theory models', *Drug and Alcohol Dependence*, 68(Suppl1): S21–S39.

Parrott, A.C. (1998) 'Nesbitt's Paradox resolved: Stress and arousal modulation during cigarette smoking', *Addiction*, 93(1): 27–40.

Peterson, A.V.J., Leroux, B.G., Bricker, J., Kealey, K.A., Marek, P.M., Sarason, I.G. et al. (2006) 'Nine-year prediction of adolescent smoking by number of smoking parents', *Addictive Behaviors*, 31(5): 788–801.

Piko, B. (2001) 'Smoking in adolescence. Does it matter?', *Addictive Behaviors*, 26: 201–17.

Piko, B.F. and Fitzpatrick, K.M. (2004) 'Substance use, religiosity, and other protective factors among Hungarian adolescents', *Addictive Behaviours*, 29(6): 1095–107.

Pirkle, E.C. and Richter, L. (2006) 'Personality, attitudinal and behavioural risk profiles of young female binge-drinkers and smokers', *Journal of Adolescent Health*, 38(1): 44–54.

Poikolainen, K., Tuulio-Henriksson, A., Lonnqvist, J., Aalot-Setala, T. and Martunnen, M. (2001) 'Predictors of somatic symptoms: A five year follow-up of adolescents', *Archives of Disease in Childhood*, 83(5): 388–92.

Prendergast, T.J., Preble, M.R. and Tennant, F.S. (1973) 'Drug use and its relation to alcohol and cigarette consumption in the military community of West Germany', *International Journal of the Addictions*, 8(5): 741–75.

Presson, C.C., Chassin, L. and Sherman, S.J. (2002) 'Psychosocial antecedents of tobacco chipping', *Health Psychology*, 21(4): 384–92.

Richmond, R.L., Wodak, A., Kehoe, L. and Heather, N. (1998) 'How healthy are the police? A survey of life-style factors', *Addiction*, 93(11): 1729–37.

Rose, J.S., Chassin, L., Presson, C.C. and Sherman, S.J. (1996) 'Prospective predictors of quit attempts and smoking cessation in young adults', *Health Psychology*, 15(4): 261–8.

Rotter, J.B. (1966) 'Generalized expectancies for internal versus external control of reinforcement', *Psychological Monographs*, 80(1): 1–28.

Sarafino, E.P. (2006) *Health Psychology: Biopsychosocial Interactions* (4th edn). New York: John Wiley & Sons.

Schachter, S., Silverstein, B., Kozlowski, L.T., Perlick, D., Herman, C.P. and Liebling, B. (1977) 'Studies of the interaction of psychological and pharmacological determinants of smoking', *Journal of Experimental Psychology: General*, 106(1): 3–4.

Schneider, H.G. and Busch, M.N. (1998) 'Habit control expectancy for drinking, smoking and eating', *Addictive Behaviours*, 23(5): 601–7.

Simon, A.E., Wardle, J., Jarvis, M.J., Steggles, N. and Cartwright, M. (2003) 'Examining the relationship between pubertal stage, adolescent health behaviours and stress', *Psychological Medicine*, 33(8): 1369–79.

Singleton, M.G. and Pope, M. (2000) 'A comparison of successful smoking cessation interventions for adults and adolescents', *Journal of Counseling and Development*, 78(4): 448–53.

Siqueira, L., Diab, M., Bodian, C. and Rolnitzky, L. (2000) 'Adolescents becoming smokers: The roles of stress and coping methods', *Journal of Adolescent Health*, 27(6): 399–408.

Smith, D.R., Devine, S., Laggat, P.A. and Ishitake, T. (2005) 'Alcohol and tobacco consumption among police officers', *Kurume Medical Journal*, 52(1–2): 63–5.

Soldz, S. and Cui, X. (2001) 'A Risk Factor Index predicting adolescent cigarettes smoking: A 7-year longitudinal study', *Psychology of Addictive Behaviours*, 15(1): 33–41.

Sperber, A.D., Schvartzman, P., Peleg, A. and Friger, M. (2001) 'Factors associated with daily smoking among Israeli adolescents: A prospective cohort study with a 3-year follow-up', *Preventive Medicine*, 33(2Pt1): 73–81.

Spigner, C., Shigaki, A. and Tu, S.-P. (2005) 'Perceptions of Asian American men about tobacco cigarette consumption: A social learning theory framework', *Journal of Immigrant Health*, 7(4): 293–303.

Stephens, S., Cellucci, T. and Gregory, J. (2004) 'Comparing stage of change measures in adolescent smokers', *Addictive Behaviours*, 29(4): 759–64.

Steptoe, A. and Wardle, J. (2001) 'Locus of control and health behaviour revisited: A multivariate analysis of young adults from 18 countries', *British Journal of Psychology*, 92(Pt4): 659–72.

Steptoe, A., Wardle, J., Cui, W., Baban, A., Glass, K., Tsuda, A. et al. (2002) 'An international comparison of tobacco smoking, beliefs and risk awareness in university students from 23 countries', *Addiction*, 97(12): 1561–71.

Steuber, T. and Banner, F. (2006) 'Adolescent smoking and depression: Which comes first?', *Addictive Behaviors*, 31(1): 133–6.

Straub, D.M., Hills, N.K., Thompson, P.J. and Moscicki, A.-B. (2003) 'Effects of pro- and anti-tobacco advertising on nonsmoking adolescents' intentions to smoke', *Journal of Adolescent Health*, 32(1): 36–43.

Stuart, K., Borland, R. and McMurray, N. (1994) 'Self-efficacy, health locus of control and smoking cessation', *Addictive Behaviours*, 19(11): 1–12.

Thomsson, H. (1997) 'Women's smoking behaviour – caught by a cigarette diary', *Health Education Research*, 12(2): 237–45.

Thorndike, F.P., Wernicke, R., Pearlman, M.Y. and Haaga, D.A. (2006) 'Nicotine dependence, PTSD symptoms, and depression proneness among male and female smokers', *Addictive Behaviors*, 31(2): 223–31.

Thornton, W., Douglas, G.A. and Houghton, S.J. (1999) 'Transition through stages of smoking: The effect of gender and self-concept on adolescent smoking behaviour', *Journal of Adolescent Health*, 25(4): 284–9.

Tilleczek, K.C. and Hine, D.W. (2006) 'The meaning of smoking as health and social risk in adolescence', *Journal of Adolescence*, 29(2): 273–87.

Timberlake, D.S., Rhee, S.H., Haberstick, B.C., Hopfer, C., Ehringer, M., Lessem, J. et al. (2006) 'The moderating effects of religiosity on the genetic and environmental determinants of smoking initiation', *Nicotine and Tobacco Research*, 8(1): 123–33.

Turner, L.R., Mermelstein, R., Berbaum, M.L. and Veldhuis, C.B. (2004) 'School-based smoking cessation programs for adolescents: What predicts attendance?', *Nicotine and Tobacco Research*, 6(3): 559–68.

Tyas, S.L. and Pederson, L.L. (1998) 'Psychosocial factors related to adolescent smoking: A critical review of the literature', *Tobacco Control*, 7(4): 409–20.

Udry, J.R., Li, R.M. and Hendrickson-Smith, J. (2003) 'Health and behavior risks of adolescents with mixed-race identity', *American Journal of Public Health*, 93(11): 1865–70.

Unger, J.B., Li, Y., Johnson, C.A., Gong, J., Chen, X., Li, C.Y. et al. (2001) 'Stressful life events among adolescents in Wuhan, China: Associations with smoking, alcohol use, and depressive symptoms', *International Journal of Behavioral Medicine*, 8(1): 1–18.

Unger, J.B., Rohrbach, L.A., Cruz, T.B., Baezconde-Garbanati, L., Howard, K.A., Palmer, P.H. et al. (2001) 'Ethnic variation in peer influences on adolescent smoking', *Nicotine and Tobacco Research*, 3(2): 167–76.

Van den Bree, M.B.M., Whitmer, M.D. and Pickworth, W.B. (2004) 'Predictors of smoking development in a population-based sample of adolescents: A prospective study', *Journal of Adolescent Health*, 35(3): 172–81.

Vink, J.M., Boomsma, D.I., Willemsen, G. and Engels, R.C.M.E. (2003) 'Smoking status of parents, siblings and friends: Predictors of regular smoking? Findings from a longitudinal twin-family study', *Twin Research*, 6(3): 209–17.

Vlahov, D., Galea, S., Resnick, H., Ahern, J., Boscarino, J.A., Bucuvalas, M. et al. (2002) 'Increased use of cigarettes, alcohol, and marijuana among Manhattan, New York, residents after the September 11th terrorist attacks', *American Journal of Epidemiology*, 155(11): 988–96.

Wallace, J.M., Brown, T.N., Bachman, J.G. and La Veist, T.A. (2003) 'The influence of race and religion on abstinence from alcohol, cigarettes and marijuana among adolescents', *Journal of Studies on Alcohol*, 64(6): 843–8.

Weinstein, N.D. (1993) 'Testing four competing theories of health-protective behaviour', *Health Psychology*, 12(4): 324–33.

Whalen, C.K., Jamner, L.D., Henker, B. and Delfino, R.J. (2001) 'Smoking and moods in adolescents with depressive and aggressive dispositions: Evidence from surveys and electronic diaries', *Health Psychology*, 20(2): 99–111.

White, H.R., Pandina, R.J. and Chen, P-H. (2002) 'Developmental trajectories of cigarettes use from early adolescent into young adulthood', *Drug and Alcohol Dependence*, 65(2): 167–78.

White, V., Hill, D. and Hopper, J. (1996) 'The outgoing, the rebellious and the anxious: Are adolescent personality dimensions related to the uptake of smoking?', *Psychology and Health*, 12(1): 73–85.

Whitlock, E.P., Ferry, L.H., Burchette, R.J. and Abbey, D. (1995) 'Smoking characteristics of female veterans', *Addictive Behaviors*, 20(4): 409–26.

Wills, T.A., Sandy, J.M. and Yaeger, A.M. (2002) 'Stress and smoking in adolescence: A test of directional hypotheses', *Health Psychology*, 21(2): 122–30.

Wills, T.A., Yaegar, A.M. and Sandy, J.M. (2003) 'Buffering effect of religiosity for adolescent substance use', *Psychology of Addictive Behaviours*, 17(10): 24–31.

Wynd, C.A. and Ryan-Wenger, N.A. (1998) 'The health and physical readiness of Army reservists: A current review of the literature and significant research questions', *Military Medicine*, 163(5): 283–7.

35

Personality Assessment in Organizations

Robert P. Tett and Neil D. Christiansen

The goal of this chapter is to summarize evidence and practices regarding personality assessment in organizations toward realizing the full potential of personality at work. Reviews in this area are emerging with increasing frequency, some focusing on particular questions (e.g. criterion validity; Barrick and Mount, 1991; Hogan and Holland, 2003), others broader in scope (e.g. Hough and Furnham, 2003; Rothstein and Goffin, 2006). Although most reviews encourage use of personality tests in organizations, a number of factors affecting personality-outcome linkages have been overlooked or underplayed, leading to gross underestimates of the potential of personality tests to contribute to organizational success. Failure to appreciate these factors puts the future of personality testing in work settings at risk (cf. Morgeson et al., 2007). In the current chapter, research findings in this area are considered within a theoretical framework emphasizing the conditions under which personality tests are most likely to prove useful in organizations and expanding their application beyond that of personnel selection. We begin by defining what most organizational researchers understand 'personality' to mean.

PERSONALITY TESTS AND WHAT THEY MEASURE

In organizational settings, personality is almost exclusively construed in terms of traits.[1] Building on person–situation interactionist traditions (e.g. Bowers, 1973; Weiss and Adler, 1984), Tett and Burnett define personality traits as 'intraindividual consistencies and interindividual uniquenesses in propensities to behave in identifiable ways in light of situational demands' (2003: 502). This definition meets the aims of personnel selection, as the consistencies allow prediction of future behavior, the uniquenesses allow one person to be hired over others, and situations provide the context for behavioral interpretation and prediction. The multiplicity of traits fitting this definition is reasonably managed by the five-factor model (FFM, aka 'Big Five'), the five factors consisting of extraversion (sociability, dominance),

agreeableness (empathy, generosity), conscientiousness (methodicalness, achievement),
neuroticism (anxiety, low self-sesteem), and
openness to experience (creativity, curiosity).
Notwithstanding valid criticisms of the FFM
(e.g. Block, 1995; Boyle, Vol. 1), it clearly
serves well as an organizing taxonomy,
which is how we use it here.

By far the most common type of personality test used by organizations is the self-
report inventory. Detailed review of the pros
and cons of specific measures is beyond the
scope of the current chapter. Instead, we
summarize meta-analytic evidence addressing the criterion validity[2] of personality tests
used in the workplace. In setting a foundation
for that summary, we offer the following
overview of meta-analytic methods.[3]

META-ANALYSIS: A BRIEF GUIDE

The goal of any single study is to estimate a
feature of a known population. Single-
sample studies are 'noisy' to the degree their
samples are small; that is, they have a high
'sampling error.' This is problematic as there
is no way to know which study of a given
relationship provides the most accurate estimate. Adding to the haze, findings are
affected by measurement properties (e.g. test
reliability) that vary between studies. A third
possibility is that a given predictor–criterion
relationship varies across studies for substantive reasons; for example, job family. As
shown below, such cases of 'situational
specificity' warrant close attention in studies
of personality at work.

Averaging results from similarly targeted
studies, meta-analysis resolves these issues
by offering two straightforward outputs. The
first, in the present context, is the *mean correlation* between a given trait and workplace
criterion (e.g. job performance). This mean is
weighted by sample size[4] and is often corrected for measurement limitations, including
unreliability[5] and range restriction,[6] yielding
the correlation expected if all participants

from all input studies were combined in one
big sample under ideal measurement conditions. It is thus a more pristine estimate of the
population correlation (ρ) than is any one of
the more fallible input values.

The second key meta-analytic output, one
often overlooked (e.g. Morgeson et al.,
2007), is the *credibility interval*, revealing
the effects of substantive variables on the targeted relationship.[7] An '80% interval' of 0.10
to 0.30 (around a mean of 0.20), for example,
specifies that 10% of ρ's fall below 0.10
(possibly into the negative range), and 10%
above 0.30. Both the mean correlation and
80% interval are important in meta-analysis:
the first summarizes the overall relationship
and the second identifies how generalizable
that overall value is across populations and
settings. A narrow interval implies that the
average correlation is a 'universal truth' applicable to all situations. A broad interval, conversely, demands that the conditions affecting
the correlation be identified so that con-
sumers can better estimate how a given trait
will predict a given outcome in a particular
work setting.

PERSONALITY AND JOB PERFORMANCE

Table 35.1 summarizes meta-analytic results
from several studies bearing on personality–
job performance relations organized by the
FFM. Several major points bear noting. First,
the mean correlations uncorrected for measurement artifacts are quite weak on the
whole. In 25 of the 35 cases (71%), mean
$r < 0.10$, and the strongest mean r of all 35
is 0.22. Given that these values reflect the
real-life predictive power of personality
trait measures, unadorned by corrections
for measurement limitations, the picture
looks rather bleak for personality measures.
The brightest spot is conscientiousness,
which accounts for six of the ten cases where
mean r is at or above $|0.10|$. The importance
of conscientiousness in predicting job

Table 35.1   Summary of meta-analytic results for the FFM traits in relations with job performance

Criterion/FFM trait	K	N_{tot}	Mean r	Mean ρ	80% Cred. Int. Lower	80% Cred. Int. Upper
Job proficiency[1]						
Extraversion	89	12,396	.06	.10	−.03	.23
Agreeableness	80	11,526	.04	.06	−.12	.24
Conscientiousness	92	12,893	.13	.23	.10	.36
Neuroticism	87	11,635	−.04	−.07	−.21	.07
Openness	55	9,454	−.02	−.03	−.08	.02
Performance ratings[2]						
Extraversion	22	2,799	.06	.14	−.09	.37
Agreeableness	19	2,574	.00	−.02	−.08	.04
Conscientiousness	18	2,241	.10	.26	.12	.40
Neuroticism	22	2,799	−.06	−.18	−.31	−.05
Openness	11	1,629	.00	.02	−.06	.10
Task performance[3]						
Extraversion	9	1,839	.04	.07	.04	.10
Agreeableness	9	1,754	.05	.08	−.04	.20
Conscientiousness	12	2,197	.10	.16	−.01	.33
Neuroticism	8	1,243	−.09	−.14	−.14	−.14
Openness	7	1,176	−.01	−.01	−.27	.25
Sales performance: ratings[4]						
Extraversion	27	3,112	.09	.18	.09	.25
Agreeableness	23	2,342	.03	.06	−.12	.23
Conscientiousness	19	2,186	.11	.21	.11	.34
Neuroticism	24	3,134	−.05	−.10	−.25	.07
Openness	8	804	.06	.11	.01	.23
Sales performance: objective[4]						
Extraversion	18	2,629	.12	.22	.13	.29
Agreeableness	12	918	−.02	−.03	−.15	.10
Conscientiousness	15	1,774	.17	.31	.19	.40
Neuroticism	14	2,157	.07	.12	−.09	.23
Openness	6	951	.03	.06	−.19	.20
Managerial performance ratings[5]						
Extraversion	379	108,607	.05	.09	−.14	.32
Agreeableness	99	42,218	.03	.04	−.13	.21
Conscientiousness	186	50,367	.07	.11	−.16	.38
Neuroticism	202	69,889	−.04	−.08	−.30	.14
Openness	110	46,614	.05	.08	−.12	.28
Leadership[6]						
Extraversion	60	11,705	.22	.31	.09	.53
Agreeableness	42	9,801	.06	.08	−.14	.30
Conscientiousness	35	7,510	.20	.28	.06	.50
Neuroticism	48	8,025	−.17	−.24	−.47	−.01
Openness	37	7,221	.16	.24	.10	.38

[1]From Barrick and Mount (1991)
[2]From Salgado (1997)
[3]From Hurtz and Donovan (2001)
[4]From Vinchur et al. (1998)
[5]From Hough et al. (1998)
[6]From Judge et al. (2002)

performance is hardly news at this point, given that Barrick and Mount's (1991) most famous finding was published over 16 years ago. There is more to the story, however, than that conveyed by the mean r's and their corrected counterparts, the ρ's.

Consider the 80% credibility intervals. In only one case (3%) is the interval of 0 width (neuroticism in predicting task performance), offering a 'universal truth' ($\rho = -0.14$) applicable to all work situations. In 28 cases (80%), the interval exceeds 0.20 correlation units in width, and in 12 cases (34%), the interval extends in both positive and negative directions by at least |0.10|. These intervals tell us that how well a given trait predicts job performance depends on the situation, and that under some conditions a trait can be moderately strongly related to job performance. Thus, despite offering mean ρ's ranging from 0.11 to 0.31 (depending on the criterion), conscientiousness yields $\rho > 0.33$ to 0.50 in 10% of work situations. By the same token, it yields ρ's below −0.16 to 0.19 in 10% of situations. More striking examples obtain for other dimensions. Agreeableness, in particular, shows 80% intervals at least 0.24 correlation units wide for six of the seven criteria, and in all six of those cases ρ exceeds |0.10| in both directions. Openness shows a similar pattern, where, for example, mean ρ hovers near 0 for task and sales performance, but ρ is notably positive in 10% of situations and notably negative in 10%.

PERSONALITY AND CONTEXTUAL WORK BEHAVIOR

Table 35.2 summarizes correlations between the FFM traits and a variety of contextual behaviors, including citizenship, altruism, effort, generalized compliance, job dedication, teamwork, interpersonal facilitation, and interaction with others. In general, the mean correlations are modest but useful, with conscientiousness predicting cross-contextual behaviors and agreeableness for behaviors

with increased interpersonal demands (e.g. teamwork). To a lesser extent, individuals lower in neuroticism are also more likely to engage in contextual behaviors with interpersonal demands. Personality has been claimed to be a better predictor of contextual performance than task performance (e.g. Borman et al., 2001; Ployhart et al., 2006), owing to the discretionary nature of contextual behaviors. Comparing results in Tables 35.1 and 35.2 offers some support for this, as means are generally stronger in the latter. Alternatively, the task/contextual distinction may be less one of discretion and motivation than one of trait-relevant behavioral content: regardless of how discretionary it is in a given job, contextual behavior may simply be more expressive of agreeableness and (low) neuroticism.

Results in Table 35.2 also warrant discussion with respect to the 80% intervals. Based on available results, the intervals are less than half as wide, on average, as those reported in Table 35.1 for more general performance (0.14 vs. 0.30, respectively). Correspondingly, intervals tend to fall more on one side of 0 or the other, as opposed to showing evidence of both positive and negative correlations. This supports an understanding of contextual behavior as more universally valued and task behavior as more job-specific (Borman and Motowidlo, 1997). Thus, task demands vary across jobs such that a given trait predicts task performance positively in some and negatively in others, whereas contextual demands are more uniformly met by being at one end of a given trait (e.g. high A).

PERSONALITY AND COUNTERPRODUCTIVE WORK BEHAVIOR

Costs associated with absenteeism, turnover, accidents, and theft make such counterproductive behaviors prime targets for prediction. Personality-based integrity tests have received considerable attention in this respect. Ones et al. (1993) reported a

Table 35.2   Summary of meta-analytic results for the FFM traits in relations with contextual performance

Criterion/FFM trait	K	N_{tot}	Mean r	Mean ρ	80%.Cred. Int Lower	Upper
Overall citizenship[1]						
Extraversion	7	1,728	.06	.09	–	–
Agreeableness	7	1,554	.13	.18	–	–
Conscientiousness	10	1,963	.19	.27	–	–
Altruism[2]						
Agreeableness	6	916	.10	.13	.06	.20
Conscientiousness	7	2,172	.16	.22	.15	.29
Effort[3]						
Extraversion	17	17,823	.16	–	–	–
Agreeableness	1	7,666	.15	–	–	–
Conscientiousness	15	40,938	.17	–	–	–
Neuroticism	15	9,562	–.16	–	–	–
Openness	1	667	.11	–	–	–
Generalized compliance[2]						
Agreeableness	6	916	.08	.11	.11	.11
Conscientiousness	7	1,231	.17	.23	.15	.31
Job dedication[4]						
Extraversion	16	3,130	.03	.05	–.09	.19
Agreeableness	17	3,197	.06	.08	–.04	.20
Conscientiousness	17	3,197	.12	.18	–.04	.40
Neuroticism	15	2,581	–.09	.13	.13	.13
Openness	14	2,514	.01	.01	–.13	.15
Teamwork[3]						
Extraversion	39	2,307	.08	–	–	–
Agreeableness	7	329	.17	–	–	–
Conscientiousness	28	1,573	.17	–	–	–
Neuroticism	31	2,067	–.13	–	–	–
Openness	1	667	.11	–	–	–
Interpersonal facilitation[4]						
Extraversion	21	4,155	.06	.10	–.04	.24
Agreeableness	23	4,301	.11	.17	.03	.31
Conscientiousness	23	4,301	.11	.16	.07	.25
Neuroticism	21	3,685	–.10	–.16	–.16	–.16
Openness	19	3,539	.03	.05	–.04	.14
Interactions with others[5]						
Extraversion	9	1,412	.09	.14	.14	.14
Agreeableness	10	1,491	.17	.23	.23	.23
Conscientiousness	10	1,491	.13	.20	.20	.20
Neuroticism	10	1,491	–.12	–.19	–.19	–.19
Openness	9	1,412	.06	.10	.10	.10

[1]From Borman et al. (2001); excludes self-report criteria.
[2]From Organ and Ryan (1995); excludes self-report criteria.
[3]From Hough (1992)
[4]From Hurtz and Donovan (2001)
[5]From Mount et al. (1998)

mean validity of 0.33 (0.47 corrected) in correlations with counterproductive behaviors. Interestingly, integrity tests were also found to predict supervisor ratings of job performance with a mean validity of 0.21 (0.35).

Interpretation has proven challenging because integrity tests are multidimensional, including antisocial behavior, socialization, positive outlook, and orderliness/diligence (Wanek et al., 2003). Construct validation has shown them most strongly related to conscientiousness, followed by agreeableness and neuroticism (Ones et al., 1993), the latter emerging primarily due to socialization and positive outlook (Wanek et al., 2003).

Research has also examined relationships between normal personality traits and counterproductive behaviors. Table 35.3 summarizes meta-analytic results. Hough (1992) found conscientiousness to be the strongest predictor of irresponsible behavior. Considering more specific behaviors, Salgado (2002) reported few reliable FFM trait correlates of absenteeism, tardiness, accidents, and injury. Relatively small correlations have been found for conscientiousness and agreeableness with

deviant behaviors such as theft. Most predictable has been turnover, with individuals higher in neuroticism and lower in conscientiousness being more likely to quit.

Also notable in Table 35.3 are several wide credibility intervals. Those for extraversion, in particular, show that being high on this trait contributes to or reduces counterproductive behaviors, depending on the work situation (except turnover, where ρ is more uniformly negative). A similar pattern is evident for neuroticism. Why these traits vary in value across studies is rarely discussed in the personality-at-work literature. We offer a framework for addressing this challenge in a later section.

Table 35.3 Summary of meta-analytic results for the FFM traits in relations with counterproductive behaviors

Criterion/FFM trait	K	N_{tot}	Mean r	Mean ρ	80% Cred. Int. Lower	Upper
Irresponsible behavior[1]						
Extraversion	15	39,245	−.06	−	−	−
Agreeableness	4	24,259	−.08	−	−	−
Conscientiousness	73	118,152	−.23	−	−	−
Neuroticism	9	21,431	.15	−	−	−
Openness	2	1,414	−.15	−	−	−
Absenteeism and tardiness[2]						
Extraversion	10	1,799	.05	.08	−.24	.40
Agreeableness	8	1,339	−.03	−.04	−.04	−.04
Conscientiousness	10	2,155	−.04	−.06	−.19	.07
Neuroticism	12	2,491	−.03	−.04	−.28	.20
Openness	8	1,399	.00	.00	.00	.00
Accidents and injury[2]						
Extraversion	7	2,341	−.02	−.04	−.30	.22
Agreeableness	4	1,540	.00	.06	.01	.11
Conscientiousness	6	2,094	−.03	−.06	−.19	.07
Neuroticism	5	2,121	−.04	−.08	−.27	.11
Openness	5	1,660	.05	.09	.00	.18
Turnover[2]						
Extraversion	4	554	−.14	−.20	−.32	−.08
Agreeableness	4	554	−.16	−.22	−.22	−.22
Conscientiousness	5	748	−.23	−.31	−.31	−.31
Neuroticism	4	554	.25	.35	.35	.35
Openness	4	554	−.11	−.14	−.14	−.14
Deviant behavior[2]						
Extraversion	12	2,383	.01	.01	−.22	.24
Agreeableness	9	1,299	−.13	−.20	−.23	−.17
Conscientiousness	13	6,276	−.16	−.26	−.30	−.22
Neuroticism	15	3,107	.04	.06	−.12	.24
Openness	8	1,421	.10	.14	−.04	.32

[1]From Hough (1992)
[2]From Salgado (2002)

SUMMARY OF PERSONALITY–WORK OUTCOME META-ANALYSES

Three general points emerge from the preceding review. First, as has often been noted, conscientiousness is an important positive contributor to a variety of workplace outcomes. Second, other traits show generalizable relationships with selected criteria. Neuroticism, for example, seems universally disruptive with respect to both turnover (Table 35.3) and general performance (Table 35.1). Third, the meta-analytic evidence strongly supports situational specificity in personality-outcome linkages. Specifically, (a) *all five* FFM traits predict workplace criteria under some conditions, and (b) a given trait can predict positively in some situations and negatively in others. The evidence for situational specificity, we suggest, rivals the dominance of conscientiousness as a universal predictor, as *any* personality trait can, under some conditions, be quite strongly related to relevant workplace outcomes. Even conscientiousness shows stronger relations under some conditions than others in 13 of 15 cases reported in Tables 35.1 to 35.3.

Logically, our next questions should be: Under what conditions are trait–outcome correlations stronger versus weaker and positive versus negative? Barrick and Mount (1991) considered the first question with respect to job family, comparing personality trait validities in professional, police, sales, managerial, and other jobs. As might be expected, ρ's were stronger for some traits in some jobs. Extraversion, for example, proved better for predicting performance in management (mean $\rho = 0.18$) and sales (mean $\rho = 0.15$). Even in those cases, however, the 80% intervals are wide: 0.01 to 0.35 for managerial jobs and −0.05 to 0.35 for sales. For conscientiousness in predicting police performance, the interval stretches from −0.04 to 0.48. Results in Table 35.1 for sales (Vinchur et al., 1998) and managerial jobs (Hough et al., 1998) show similar situational specificity in ρ for all FFM dimensions. Thus, job family is, at best, a weak moderator

of trait–performance linkages, prompting deeper consideration of how those linkages form.

BIDIRECTIONALITY

In their meta-analysis of personality–job performance relations, Tett et al. (1991) identified a number of cases where a given trait was meaningfully correlated with performance positively in some jobs and negatively in others. Such 'bidirectionality'[8] is problematic for standard meta-analysis as averaging true positive and true negative correlations yields a mean that understates the trait's importance. Bidirectionality is evident in Tables 35.1 to 35.3 in cases where the 80% interval extends in both directions. There are two reasonable responses to bidirectionality.[9] First, we need to understand better the conditions under which a given trait contributes positively versus negatively to organizational success. We address this in a later section. Second, determining the overall power of personality as a predictor of job performance requires separating correlation strength and direction in meta-analysis. This is accomplished through use of absolute values with appropriate corrections.[10] Employing such methods, Tett et al. (1999) reported a mean ρ of 0.26 for all traits combined. This compares to a corresponding mean ρ of 0.09, from Barrick and Mount (1991), who allowed true positive and true negative correlations to cancel each other out. The corresponding average from Salgado (1997), who also allowed such cancellation, is 0.12. Thus, meta-analyses ignoring bidirectionality in this area have substantially understated the value of personality at work.

Bidirectionality can also occur within jobs. From Table 35.1, for example, openness facilitates leadership (Judge et al., 2002), yet from Table 35.2, it is also linked positively to deviant behavior and accidents (Salgado, 2002). Agreeableness contributes to teamwork and interpersonal interactions, but it undermines effectiveness in some leadership, management, and sales positions. Further evidence comes from single-sample research. Gellatly and Irving (2001) found that agreeableness contributes positively to managers' contextual performance under autonomous conditions but negatively when autonomy is low. Combining all managers yielded very weak results. Tett et al. (2003) reported that openness facets of 'culture' and 'curiosity' predicted technical performance negatively and positively, respectively, yielding weak validity at the general level. Griffin and Hesketh (2004) found in multiple samples that openness to internal experience and openness to external experience correlate in opposite directions with distinct work-related criteria. Such within-job bidirectionality, like its between-job cousin, leads to underestimation of the value of personality through cancellation of positive and negative effects.

CONFIRMATORY VERSUS EXPLORATORY RESEARCH STRATEGIES

The noted situational specificity and bidirectionality of personality–outcome relationships call for careful thinking about personality at work. One way to document this at a general level is to compare results of validation studies adopting confirmatory versus exploratory research strategies. In the former, researchers select particular traits to be related to performance in the targeted job; for example, based on job analysis. Conversely, exploratory studies are those in which all scales on a personality test are correlated with performance in essentially a 'fishing expedition.' Follow-up analyses of Tett et al.'s (1991) data using refined meta-analytic methods yielded mean corrected absolute value correlations of 0.30 versus 0.16 for confirmatory and exploratory studies, respectively (Tett et al., 1999). The 0.30 mean is considerably stronger than the noted

means of 0.09 from Barrick and Mount (1991) and 0.12 from Salgado (1997), derived without concern for bidirectionality and the confirmatory/exploratory distinction. Combining both factors, mean ρ's reported by Barrick and Mount and Salgado underestimate the predictive value of personality tests by up to 70%![11] Further underestimation occurs from ignoring situational influences on validity strength: validity is stronger under some conditions than others, even within job families and using confirmatory strategies, and identifying those conditions promises even greater yields from personality testing.

BROAD VERSUS NARROW TRAIT MEASURES

The resurgence of personality testing in organizations in recent years can be traced in part to the identification of the FFM, which offers a convenient framework for organizing otherwise diverse specific traits. Despite its convenience, the FFM has come under scrutiny with respect to the relative merits of broad versus specific traits in linkages with assorted workplace criteria.

Rothstein and Goffin (2006) recently identified four trends in the literature on use of narrow versus broad personality measures. First, factor analytic evidence supports multidimensionality within the Big Five categories. Roberts et al. (2005), for example, identified six factors from 36 conscientiousness facets. Similar results are reported by Griffin and Hesketh (2004) regarding openness, and by Van Iddekinge et al. (2005) regarding integrity. Second, of 11 studies directly comparing the validity of narrow versus broad trait measures in the prediction of job performance, *all* have supported use of narrow measures. Third, the broad/narrow issue continues to drive research despite numerous meta-analyses supporting personality–performance linkages in terms of the FFM. Thus, researchers acknowledge that the FFM is useful as an organizing frame-work, but are looking to more specific facets to increase validity. Fourth, there is growing agreement that both narrow and broad measures may be useful.

It has often been suggested that trait–performance relations are strongest when trait breadth is matched to criterion breadth (e.g. Ones and Viswesvaran, 1996). This intu-itively plausible suggestion warrants critical review. Note that it refers only to construct breadth. A more important consideration is how well trait and performance measures are matched on *content*. Imagine that perform-ance in a given job includes facets A, B, and C and that personality is assessed broadly to include corresponding traits, such that per-formance facet A is linked to trait A, and so on. In this case, the trait and performance aggregates might correlate quite strongly. Now imagine the same job, combining performance facets A to C, but with a person-ality measure targeting traits D, E and F. Here, the predictor and criterion are perfectly matched on breadth, yet we should not expect a useful correlation between them. Moreover, in order to ascertain or deliber-ately create a match on content, even with the use of broad measures, we must identify the specific performance facets and personality traits being combined in their respective measures. Predictive accuracy improves when traits and performance dimensions are thematically linked (Bartram, 2005; Hogan and Holland, 2003; Tett et al., 1991), and specificity feeds this advantage by promoting refined conceptual linkages.

Several further points bear discussion. First, as a practical matter, researchers using facet measures can later average them to create a general score; but those using global measures, undifferentiated with respect to facets, preclude the advantage of specificity. Second, focusing on carefully selected trait facets, determined via confirmatory methods (e.g. trait-based job analysis), allows more time to assess those facets well (more reli-ably) by not wasting time on irrelevant facets, and is also likely to promote favorable

applicant reactions and legal accountability. On the downside, use of specific measures adds complexity to decision making (which is likely why broad measures are popular: they are simpler to use). In response, Tett et al. (2003) recommend use of canonical correlation, which extends well-known mul-tiple regression analysis, linking multiple predictors to a single criterion, to the case of multiple predictors and multiple criteria.

THE ROLE OF THEORY IN LINKING PERSONALITY TO WORK OUTCOMES

Personality traits capture simple and conven-ient summaries of individuals' behavioral tendencies. Equally important, however, are the situations in which a given trait is expressed. This is implicit in much of per-sonality–work outcome research, where sig-nificant results are typically explained along the lines of, 'work situation A demands behavior B, so workers with trait B, who are more inclined to engage in B behavior, are more successful.' Beyond such blanket inter-pretations, little theory has been offered to allow refinements in trait-based prediction and, moreover, to account for observed situ-ational specificity and bidirectionality. In any research domain, theory helps integrate otherwise disparate phenomena, promises better predictions, and provides a conceptual platform for further theoretical development.

Building on established interactionist prin-ciples linking personality and situations, Tett and Burnett (2003) offer a theory of 'trait activation' to explain how any given trait comes to be related to job performance. It works like this: (a) personality traits (e.g. ambition) are latent propensities to behave in some identifiable way (e.g. as expressing ambition); (b) traits are 'activated' by situa-tions providing trait expression opportunities or 'cues' operating at three levels: task (e.g. a challenging assignment), social (e.g. emergent leadership opportunity), and organizational (e.g. an aggressive organizational culture);

(c) trait expression becomes job performance when that expression is valued by others (e.g. when ambitious behavior is judged to contribute to success in challenging assignments, leadership, and competitive cultures); (d) workers experience intrinsic satisfaction when expressing their traits (ambitious people like expressing their ambition); and (e) workers experience extrinsic satisfaction when rewarded by others for good performance.

Combining (d) and (e), the ideal situation for any worker is one providing opportunities to express his or her traits (at the task, social, and/or organizational levels) such that trait expression is valued positively by others (bosses, peers, subordinates, customers). In short, *people want to work where they are rewarded for being themselves.* By the same token, a bad situation is one that either offers no cues for trait expression or, worse, offers such cues but invites negative reactions from others when those cues are acted upon. Tett and Burnett call such negative cues 'distracters' to distinguish them from 'demands,' responses to which are valued positively. Two other situational features relevant to trait expression are 'constraints,' which eliminate or weaken trait-expressive cues (e.g. making an assignment less challenging), and 'releasers,' which counteract constraints (e.g. enhancing the assignment's status). Constraints and releasers can operate on demands or distracters: constraining distracters will improve trait-based performance, whereas constraining demands will weaken performance unless those constraints are released.[12]

The idea that traits require appropriate situations for their expression is not new (e.g. Allport, 1937; Murray 1938; Woodworth, 1937).[13] More recently, Tett and Guterman (2000) found that self-report trait measures correlate with trait-expressive behavioral intentions more strongly in situations more relevant to the given trait and that behavioral intent is more consistent across situations higher in trait relevance. Haaland and Christiansen (2002) and Lievens et al. (2006) similarly showed that assessment center

dimensions (e.g. drive, influencing others) correlate more strongly across exercises (e.g. leaderless group discussion, role play) more similar in trait expression opportunities. Applying trait activation theory to work groups, Tett and Murphy (2002) asked whether people prefer working with those offering cues for trait expression and under what conditions such preferences are strongest. As expected, higher-order interactions showed that, for example, low-autonomous judges especially preferred dominant co-workers when the latter were expected to be in charge.

Trait activation offers insights into the noted situational specificity and bidirectionality involving personality tests at work. In particular, trait–performance relationships will be stronger (positive or negative) to the degree a given work situation (tasks, people, organization) offers cues for trait expression valued by performance judges. Correlations will be positive where trait expression is judged to meet work demands and negative where trait expression interferes with meeting those demands (i.e. as responses to distracters). Complications arise from cues in multiple levels operating in different directions. For example, ambition effectively engaged in completing a challenging task might run afoul of group norms stressing member equality or an organizational culture favoring cooperation over competition. With relevance to performance appraisal, a rater who feels threatened by a co-worker's ambition may rate that co-worker *lower* on task performance, in spite of the positive impact of ambition on the ratee's actual performance. Results in Table 35.1 suggest a similar example: subjective sales performance is predicted negatively, on average, by neuroticism (mean $\rho = -0.10$), whereas objective sales is predicted positively (mean $\rho = 0.12$). Neuroticism may contribute to objective sales by ego-related motives, such that those with low self-esteem look to a successful sale as an 'ego fix.' Subjective ratings, on the other hand, come out of group settings, where N is judged negatively, as per results for teamwork and related outcomes in Table 35.2.

Our main points here are that (1) personality tests stand to offer more to organizations than is suggested by the overall middling mean correlations from meta-analyses ignoring the problem of bidirectionality and the benefits of confirmatory research and narrow measures (e.g. Barrick and Mount, 1991), and (2) trait activation theory offers insights into those challenges as a basis for getting more out of personality tests than most test users deem possible.

PERSONALITY-ORIENTED JOB ANALYSIS

In recognition of the importance of situations to understanding trait–outcome linkages, personality-oriented job analysis (POJA) is receiving increasing attention from both researchers and practitioners. In an early investigation, Lopez et al. (1981) tested their 'threshold traits analysis' (TTA) targeting 33 personal characteristics, among them 18 personality traits (e.g. adaptability-change). Although validation was largely successful, the personality components were ignored in this effort. More recently, Sumer et al. (2001) applied POJA to leadership positions in the Turkish military. Their findings suggest that POJA may identify traits especially important for predicting job performance, but that proposition was not directly tested.

In the first attempt to develop a job analysis tool exclusively for personality, Raymark et al. (1997) introduced the Personality-Related Position Requirements Form (PPRF). Twelve traits linked to the FFM were distinguished meaningfully among 12 occupational groups. The trait of leadership, for example, was rated highest in management, education, and firefighting, and lowest in janitorial, customer service, and cashier jobs. Results suggest that the PPRF might help in identifying job-specific traits. Whether test validities are stronger for identified traits, however, was not assessed.

Several POJA instruments are available as companions to established personality tests. The NEO Job Profiler (Costa et al., 1995), for example, was designed for use with the NEO-PI; Hogan Assessment Systems developed the Performance Improvement Characteristics Job Analysis (Hogan and Rybicki, 1998) for use with the Hogan Personality Inventory; Personnel Decisions International offers a behavioral rating form for use with their Employment Inventory; the Institute for Personality and Ability Testing developed the Personal Requirements Survey for use with the 16PF; and the Position Classification Inventory (Gottfredson and Holland, 1994) is based on Holland's RIASEC model. Published research on the validity of these POJA tools is lacking.

Three peer-reviewed studies speak to the value of POJA in improving personality test validity. Tett et al. (1999) reported that, of 46 studies using confirmatory strategies to link personality with job performance, the 7 using job analysis yielded a mean corrected validity of 0.33 compared to 0.26 for the remaining 39 studies ($p = 0.056$). Jenkins and Griffith (2004) found that POJA successfully differentiated between traits showing stronger versus weaker validities in predicting accountant performance. Finally, Cucina et al. (2005) offered mixed support for POJA in identifying traits linked to freshman GPA.

POJA appears to hold promise as an aid in linking personality to workplace outcomes. In light of earlier discussion, however, it faces a number of challenges that, to date, have largely been ignored. First, with respect to bidirectionality, it is important to assess whether favorable outcomes are more likely in those higher or lower on the trait. Second, trait-relevant cues and trait value must be determined separately for work tasks, social networks (e.g. teams), and organizational culture, each level offering different demands and distracters. Third, regarding trait specificity, those completing POJA tools face greater demands with greater specificity, as traits increase in number and distinctions among them, in subtlety.

Addressing the noted challenges, Tett and Burnett (2003) offer an example of a POJA instrument targeting work demands, distracters, and constraints relevant to the trait of methodicalness, operating at multiple levels. How all such information might be integrated for use in personnel selection (e.g. in setting cutscores) is unclear. What *is* clear is that more research on POJA is needed. For example, how should trait information be gathered: by identifying trait-expressive work activities (e.g. 'reviews records for completeness' as a demand for methodicalness) or by identifying traits workers need to possess, using trait definitions? Does it matter whether those completing the POJA are job experts (incumbents, bosses) or trait experts (I/O psychologists), and can training offset limitations in expertise? In the trait activation framework, which level of analysis (task, social, organizational) has the strongest influence on test validity and does it matter if the criterion is matched to the level? Also, are demands the most powerful situational features, followed by distracters, constraints, and releasers? Answers to such questions represent the future of personality testing in organizations, paving the way for the full potential of personality tests to be realized in light of known situational specificity and bidirectionality.

SELECTED ISSUES IN PERSONALITY ASSESSMENT IN ORGANIZATIONS

Faking

Among the more controversial issues regarding personality assessment in organizations is the effect of faking (motivated distortion, socially desirable responding) on hiring and promotion decisions. The extent of the problem is unclear due to conflicting results from studies employing different methods (Peterson and Griffith, 2006). Two general strategies are: (a) partialing or correcting trait scores based on elevations on social desirability scales and (b) contrasting groups differing in motivation to distort.

Studies where personality test scores have been adjusted based on respondents' desirability levels have consistently found no improvement in validity (Barrick and Mount, 1996; Christiansen et al., 1994; Ones et al., 1996). Two limitations in such studies, however, bear review. First, desirability measures have been shown to be relatively insensitive to intentional distortion, with no more than 20% of variance on such measures being explained by applicant faking (Burns and Christiansen, 2006). Second, the approach is based on a suppression model where very little improvement is possible even under optimal conditions (Goffin and Christiansen, 2003; see also Conger and Jackson, 1972). Accordingly, this line of research is of limited value (Burns and Christiansen, 2006).

In contrast, research comparing individuals differing in motivation to distort typically *has* found important differences in test scores. Results from faking simulations (e.g. where students are instructed to fake good or bad) have been replicated in field research using actual job applicants. Mean effect sizes, summarized in Table 35.4, show that applicants fake about half as much, on average, as do those in simulated conditions who are instructed to fake good (Tett et al., 2006). It has also been shown that convergent and discriminant validities suffer when individuals are instructed to respond as applicants (e.g. Christiansen et al., 2005), with a similar pattern emerging when the construct validity of applicants' and non-applicants' scores is compared (Griffith, et al., in press; Rosse et al., 1998).

More disconcerting is that deterioration of criterion-related validity, found in faking simulations (e.g. Douglas et al., 1996; Jackson et al., 2000), has replicated in studies comparing incumbents' and applicants' scores (Hough, 1998). As shown in Table 35.5,

Table 35.4   Mean shift between groups differing in motivation to inflate personality test scores

FFM trait	Faking simulations			Incumbents vs. applicants		
	K	N_{TOT}	d	K	N_{TOT}	d
Extraversion	15	1,122	.63	3	28,337	.11
Agreeableness	17	1,009	.48	2	2,408	1.33
Conscientiousness	29	2,650	.60	5	43,889	.70
Neuroticism	17	1,357	.64	3	3,353	−.61
Openness	11	614	.65	4	29,292	−.01
All traits	89	6,752	.60	15	107,272	.35

Note: Summary of faking simulation results are derived from between-subject fake good designs in Viswesvaran and Ones (1999); comparisons between incumbent and applicant samples are from Tett et al. (2006). Averages across traits are sample-weighted.

studies using incumbents have yielded validities about twice as large as those using applicants, with agreeableness and neuroticism showing the largest differences.[14] Evidence from simulations shows that fakers accumulate disproportionately at the top end of personality score distributions and that validity in this region suffers the most (e.g. Douglas et al., 1996; Mueller-Hanson et al., 2003). This has also been observed in actual job applicants (Haaland et al., 1999).

We draw the following implications. First, concurrent validation targeting incumbents, who have little motivation to fake, should be followed up by predictive validation targeting applicants, results of which will be directly generalizable to hiring settings. Second, when personality inventories are given to a relatively large number of applicants, scores should be used to screen out those at the undesirable end of the distribution rather than to differentiate among those at the top. Those at the bottom were either not motivated to fake or incapable of concealing their undesirable tendencies; either way, low scores are predictive of poor performance. Third, in smaller applicant samples, self-report personality test scores should be supplemented by other sources. Logical choices include interviews and simulations for external applicants (see below) and multi-source ratings for internal candidates. Use of multiple assessments is advisable in any high-stakes testing situation, and experts agree that comparing results across methods is the best way to identify dishonest test takers (Robie et al., 2006).

Table 35.5   Mean validity coefficients from studies assessing job incumbents and applicants

FFM trait	Incumbents' scores				Applicants' scores			
	K	N_{TOT}	Avg. r	Avg. ρ	K	N_{TOT}	Avg. r	Avg. ρ
Extraversion	216	54,792	.09	.14	71	13,770	.07	.10
Agreeableness	69	14,684	.08	.16	18	7,412	.01	.01
Conscientiousness	115	37,119	.09	.16	47	10,486	.05	.07
Neuroticism	123	23,443	−.11	−.20	59	11,705	−.05	−.07
Openness	35	4,522	.05	.09	11	6,775	−.02	−.03
All traits	558	134,560	.09	.15	206	50,148	.04	.06

Note: Estimates of criterion-related validity adopted from Hough's (1998) summaries for job proficiency from concurrent and predictive studies. *K* = number of validity coefficients contributing to mean; N_{TOT} = total sample size; Avg. *r* = mean observed validity coefficient; *Avg. ρ* = mean corrected validity coefficient with incumbent and applicant estimates corrected for criterion unreliability based on .52 (Viswesvaran et al., 1996), and incumbent estimates also corrected for range restriction (from .81 for Emotional Stability to .86 for Extraversion, Salgado, 2003). Averages across traits are sample-weighted.

APPLICANT REACTIONS TO PERSONALITY TESTS

Over the past 20 years, personnel selection research has turned increasingly to consider the perspective of job applicants. Those who react negatively to the hiring process are less likely to accept employment offers and more likely to dissuade other applicants and to challenge the legality of the process (cf. Smither et al., 1993). The driving theoretical perspective in this area is that reactions are a function of *fairness evaluations*, captured within broader organizational justice theories (Gilliland, 1993; Ryan and Ployhart, 2000).

Personality tests tend to be viewed negatively by current employees (e.g. Smither et al., 1993) and job applicants (Rosse et al., 1998). Hausknecht et al. (2004) showed using meta-analysis that reactions to personality tests are more negative than reactions to cognitive tests, resumes, references, work samples, and interviews, and were only more favorable than honesty tests and graphology. Furthermore, adding work-related 'tags' to personality test items did not improve the favorability of these evaluations (Holtz et al., 2005).

Several explanations for these findings have been offered. For one, personality tests are usually administered in their entirety, rather than just the most job-related scales. As might be expected, the perceived job-relatedness of assessments correlates highly with evaluations of favorability (Hausknecht et al., 2004). In addition, most personality inventories include items referencing activities outside of work or involving respondents' thoughts or feelings. Such inquiries may be considered invasive. Finally, applicants may believe that the results of personality tests can be easily gerrymandered by less honest individuals such that candidness is essentially penalized.

INTERVIEW-BASED ASSESSMENT OF PERSONALITY

Job interviews, the most common personnel selection tools, are increasingly the focus of personality research. Content analysis has shown that about a third of all interview dimensions are related to basic personality tendencies, more than any other construct type, including knowledge, skills, or mental ability (Huffcutt et al., 2001). Consistent with previous research (Jackson et al., 1980, 1982), Van Iddekinge et al. (2005) found that interviewers are able to pick up interviewee traits reliably and distinctively. They also found that interviews are less susceptible to faking than are self-report inventories. Possible reasons include: (a) interviews involve increased cognitive demands (McFarland et al., 2003), (b) interviewee verbal and non-verbal behaviors reveal trait standing beyond response content (Lippa and Dietz, 2000), (c) interview ratings are not within interviewees' direct control, and (d) interview responses need to be constructed, whereas those in inventories require mere recognition.

Blackman (2002) reported greater accuracy in personality judgments from unstructured interviews relative to structured interviews, even though the latter included four times as many personality-based questions. Additional analyses suggested that job candidates talked more during the unstructured format, resulting in a broader range of cues available to judges. Barrick et al. (2000) had experienced assessors interview undergraduates in simulated applicant conditions. Interviewers' impressions of interviewee personality correlated 0.27, on average, with self-reports and 0.28 with peer ratings. Convergence was higher for some traits (e.g. extraversion) over others, likely due to higher observability (Funder, 1999).

Meta-analytic evidence from Huffcutt et al. (2001), bearing on the criterion-related validity of personality-oriented interviews, is summarized in Table 35.6. Correlations range in absolute magnitude from 0.16 for openness (0.30 corrected) to 0.28 for agreeableness (0.51), with an overall mean of 0.19 (0.36). Notably, all the corrected correlations are stronger than those reported by Barrick and Mount (1991) for self-report inventories. A possible explanation is that interview scores are more saturated with cognitive variance

Table 35.6 Validity of personality-based employment interviews

FFM trait	K	N	Job performance			Incremental validity	
			Avg. r	Avg. ρ	B&M (2003)	r_{sp}	$ρ_{sp}$
Extraversion	8	1,055	.18	.33	.12	.13	.23
Agreeableness	4	344	.28	.51	.07	.23	.40
Conscientiousness	22	3,532	.18	.33	.22	.14	.25
Neuroticism	6	917	−.26	−.47	−.12	−.21	−.37
Openness	2	527	.16	.30	.05	.15	.32
All traits	42	6,375	.19	.36	.12	.15	.27

Note: Results adapted from Huffcutt et al. (2001) unless otherwise noted. Avg. *r* = mean observed validity coefficient; Avg. *ρ* = mean corrected validity coefficients corrected for range restriction in the interview and unreliability in the criteria. Correlational estimates derived from Huffcutt et al. (2001) are based on ratings from dimensions related to each FFM trait, collapsed across low and high structure. Values from Barrick and Mount (2003) and Ackerman and Heggestad (1997) reflect correlations corrected for unreliability in both the predictors and criteria. Incremental validity refers to the semi-partial correlations (r_{sp} and $ρ_{sp}$) computed from mean *r* and *ρ* values, partialing the relationship between personality-based interview ratings and cognitive ability from predictor scores only; estimates of the relationship between cognitive ability and performance taken from Hunter and Hunter's (1984) results for medium complexity jobs.

(see Huffcutt et al., 1996). Table 35.6 also summarizes correlations between personality-based interview dimensions and performance after controlling for the variance attributable to general mental ability (*g*). As can be seen in the table, all of the corrected estimates of the incremental validity for personality-based interviews (beyond cognitive ability) are higher than the corrected validity estimates reported by Barrick and Mount (2001) for personality inventories. Overall, our results show that personality-based interviews explain about 5 times the amount of variance in performance than is explained by personality inventories and that only part of that advantage can be explained by the stronger correlations with cognitive ability generally observed for the interview method.

Looking beyond *g*, we believe structured personality-based job interviews are more likely to be tied to job content and focus on a subset of traits, whereas studies using personality inventories are more likely to include all subscales. Indeed, Huffcutt et al.'s (2001) results for interview-based personality assessment more closely resemble the confirmatory values reported by Tett et al. (1991, 1999) than they do those of Barrick and Mount (2001), which combine exploratory and confirmatory findings indiscriminately. In addition, employment interviews are more likely to inquire directly about work behaviors (either past or expected), whereas self-report

inventories tend to ask about behavior in general or in non-work domains. Providing a work frame of reference enhances prediction of work outcomes (Bing et al., 2004; Schmit and Ryan, 1993; Truxillo et al., 2002). Finally, verbal and non-verbal behavior elicited in interviews may be less susceptible to faking (Van Iddekinge et al., 2005).

ASSESSMENT CENTERS FOR USE IN PERSONALITY ASSESSMENT

Assessment centers (ACs), consisting of multiple work-related simulation exercises, have a rich history in I/O psychology (cf. Thornton and Byham, 1982). From the beginning, personality dimensions were a primary target of such methods.[15] In the 1950s, ACs adapted for use in business (Bray et al., 1974) shifted away from personality traits toward more performance-oriented dimensions. Recent research shows a return to personality traits in ACs. As noted above, both Haaland and Christiansen (2002) and Lievens et al. (2006) found that ratings on AC dimensions conceptually linked to personality traits (e.g. sensitivity, drive) correlated more strongly between exercises similar in trait-expressive opportunities. Craik et al. (2002) reported that two managerial stylistic dimensions derived from AC dimensions correlated appreciably and meaningfully with personality judgments of independent AC observers. *Strategic* style (e.g. fact-finding, planning), for example, correlated uniquely with ratings of 'insightful,' and 'organized', whereas *Interpersonal* style (e.g. initiative, energy level) correlated uniquely with ratings of 'enterprising', and 'outspoken'. Notably, the personality scores were derived from others' observations and not by self-descriptions, which have been shown to be weakly related to traditional AC dimensions (Goffin et al., 1996). Lievens et al. (2001) showed that AC assessors record personality trait terms in their evaluations of assesses even though explicitly instructed to avoid such terms. Moreover, recorded trait terms correlated meaningfully with overall AC-based candidate recommendations.

All told, ACs hold promise for measuring personality. A question prompted by trait activation theory is whether trait value varies across AC exercises, such that cross-exercise *performance* (as valued behavior) is made inconsistent by exercise demands for expression of opposite poles of a given trait. Performance in an exercise demanding careful planning, for example, might correlate poorly or even negatively with performance in an exercise demanding decisiveness in the face of uncertainty, as planning and decisiveness fall at opposite poles of conscientiousness. Combining realism and control of extraneous factors, ACs offer prime opportunity for assessing personality in light of work-related situational factors (Bray and Howard, 1983; Turnage and Muchinsky, 1984), and we encourage further research along those lines.

LEGAL ISSUES IN ORGANIZATIONAL PERSONALITY ASSESSMENT

Personality assessment for use in personnel decision making raises several legal issues.[16] First, although group differences in personality test scores are smaller than those typically observed for cognitive tests, self-report personality inventories have shown group mean differences, raising concerns of adverse impact. Women score approximately one-quarter of a standard deviation higher than men on measures of neuroticism and lower by about the same amount on openness (Hough, 1998). Race differences tend to be smaller, with the only appreciable difference emerging for openness, where Whites score higher than Blacks. It is noteworthy that larger Black–White differences are obtained when interviews are used to assess personality, possibly due to greater saturation with cognitive variance. In this case, Whites score higher than Blacks on agreeableness and conscientiousness and lower on neuroticism by approximately one-third of a standard deviation (Huffcutt et al., 2001).

Second, the Americans with Disabilities Act (ADA) allows medical examinations only after a conditional job offer has been made and personality assessments are sometimes considered a medical examination. A personality test recommended by the publisher for use in clinical diagnosis (e.g. MMPI) may be deemed a medical examination by the courts. In such cases, it may be illegal to use the test prior to a conditional offer because someone with a psychological disability might be negatively affected.

Finally, some personality tests contain questions dealing with religion and sexual practices, raising concerns about invasion of privacy. Because each question on a test may be scrutinized in a legal setting, enquiring directly about work behaviors seems most prudent. If questions are to focus on more general tendencies, it would be best to avoid potentially sensitive topics.

BEYOND SELECTION: UNTAPPED POTENTIAL OF PERSONALITY TESTS IN ORGANIZATIONS

Personality tests offer more to the prediction and understanding of work behavior and organizational effectiveness than is evident from traditional applications to personnel selection. Two such extensions are considered below, both prompted by trait activation theory.

Management and leadership

In addition to explaining known situational specificity and bidirectionality in personality–outcome linkages, trait activation also attempts to vitalize personality traits with motivational force, encouraging use of trait measures to assist in managing and leading workers. Once workers' traits are identified, we might ask: What does the job require (demand) a worker to do at the task, social, and organizational levels offering a chance to express one trait or another, what distractions and constraints are there, and what releasers are available? Workers whose traits are matched to meet demands and avoid or overcome distracters will perform better and tend to find the workplace more rewarding. We suggest that managers and leaders who take note of trait-relevant situational cues and actively match workers to those cues in productive ways will be more successful in those roles.

Team building

Personality is relevant to teamwork in several respects. The first is what might be called 'teaminess.' In general, teams tend to perform better when their members average higher on g, C, and A, and lower on N (Hurtz and Donovan, 2001).[17] Second, personality can contribute to team functioning with respect to team tasks. Sundstrom (1999) proposes six team task types, which appear to vary in trait relevance. Service teams, for example, seem more likely to succeed when composed of members above average on A, whereas production and management teams may place a premium on C. Team member roles are a third way that personality can contribute to team functioning. Belbin (1996)

identifies several such roles, including resource investigator, coordinator, monitor evaluator, and others. A given role is likely to come more naturally to some team members than others. The best team coordinator, for example, may be someone high in E (dominance) and C (organization). The role of resource investigator, on the other hand, might best be served by someone high in E (assertive) and O (investigative). Assembling a team of role players poses challenges as some roles call for otherwise undesirable traits. The devil's advocate (low on A), for instance, has a place in teamwork, even at the expense of less cordial team relations. In other cases, an effective role might conflict with team culture: creative or divergent (high-O) thinkers, for example, can inject fresh perspectives and make unusual connections, but risk rejection if the team values conformity to conventional wisdom, the party line, or the views of the senior member.

A fourth way that personality comes into play in teams is in terms of who works well with whom. Framed as mutual trait activation (Tett and Murphy, 2002), the ideal team is one whose members bring out the best in each other. For example, a dominant team member and a submissive (low autonomous) team member may work well together because each offers cues for the other to express their respective trait, and is appreciated by the other when that trait is expressed. Similarly, compatibility can arise between someone high in nurturance (who wants to help) and someone high in succorance (who wants to be helped; both are aspects of A).

Finally, in light of the above, it is important to consider both a team's *mean* trait level and the *heterogeneity* of trait levels among team members. Neuman et al. (1999) found higher performance in teams with overall elevations on C, A, and O; but, for E and N, what mattered was greater member dispersion (heterogeneity). Interestingly, no traits showed any advantage for member similarity. The authors suggest that elevation results have the clearest implications for initial selection for teamwork, whereas dispersion is best manipulated when assigning members to particular teams.

SUMMARY AND CONCLUSIONS

Organizations are increasingly turning to personality tests to aid in personnel selection. Ironically, meta-analytic findings driving this surge – most notably, those from Barrick and Mount (1991) – actually *understate* the value of personality tests in work settings by ignoring critical conditions favoring personality test use. The full potential of personality testing in organizations is most likely to be realized when (a) a formal POJA is conducted to identify traits relevant to valued outcomes, (b) predictive directional hypotheses specify which pole of a given trait is desirable in the given setting with respect to targeted criteria, (c) relevant traits are assessed at a level of specificity promoting meaningful conceptual alignment to similarly articulated outcomes, (d) multiple traits and multiple criteria are linked using canonical correlation, and (e) personality information is used not only in hiring, but for post-hire practices as well, such as worker motivation, team building, and promotion.

Juxtaposed to the advantages and potentials of personality testing in organizations is the challenge of motivated distortion (i.e. faking). Job applicants fake personality test responses, on average, about half as much as they are capable of faking, but actual faking nonetheless undermines selection decisions. Screening out those scoring at the low end of a (positively valued) trait scale is advisable; high scores are more ambiguous. Also challenging is the generally negative attitudes test takers have toward personality tests. POJA may promote more positive attitudes, as it seeks to identify job-relevant traits. Notably, job relevance cuts in opposite directions with respect to test-taker acceptance and faking: traits or items more obviously relevant to a given job may be more acceptable yet easier to fake. Job interviews and assessment centers are appealing in these regards as they can assess job-specific traits based on responses less easily faked.

In closing, we identify the following questions as top priorities in future research on the use of personality tests in organizations: (1) What accounts for the notable situational specificity and bidirectionality of personality–outcome relationships? Does trait activation theory offer sufficient explanation and direction for hypothesis testing? If not, then what other theory is up to the task? (2) How should personality-oriented job analysis be conducted with respect to (a) use of behavioral work demands tied a priori to specific traits versus use of generic trait and criterion definitions, (b) the type of information targeted (e.g. trait relevance, trait value; demands, distracters, etc.; all at multiple levels), (c) who the judges are (e.g. incumbents vs. psychologists), and (d) training? (3) How do applicant versus incumbent conditions affect personality test validity and norms, holding methods and criteria constant? (4) Can alternatives to self-report personality tests (e.g. interviews, assessment centers) meet the challenges of faking, applicant reactions, and legal accountability while retaining adequate validity or improving on it? (5) Can personality data be harnessed for purposes other than selection toward improving the fit between people and their work environments? All these questions are prompted by the present state of the literature and corresponding answers promise greater yields from personality assessment beyond those currently enjoyed by organizations.

NOTES

1 Review of other approaches to personality, such as psychodynamic, social learning, and cognitive perspectives, is best left until a greater body of literature has accumulated on those topics as applied to work settings.

2 'Criterion validity' is one of several types of evidence bearing on the validity of inferences drawn from test scores. It is emphasized here because it is the most common method of personality test

validation in organizations and speaks directly to the usefulness of such tests in workplace applications.

3 The following is based on procedures developed by Hunter and Schmidt (2004). Other approaches to meta-analysis (e.g. Hedges and Olkin, 2005) offer similar output. Hunter–Schmidt methods are covered here because they are the most commonly used for integrating personality–criterion relationships in organizational settings. Space constraints restrict us from considering key issues in meta-analysis, including the file-drawer problem, the role of judgment calls, and fixed versus random effects models. Interested readers are directed to Hunter and Schmidt (2004) as a starting point for discussion of these and related matters.

4 Larger samples garner greater certainty in their findings and, accordingly, warrant greater weight in averaging.

5 A correlation between two measures is weakened to the degree those measures are unreliable. Correcting for unreliability yields the correlation expected if the measures were perfectly reliable.

6 When respondents are less variable than what is expected in future uses of the test (or criterion measure), such 'range restriction' weakens the correlation. When respondents are more variable than expected, such 'range enhancement' yields an overly strong correlation. Either way, corrections give the correlation expected under normal conditions regarding variability among respondents.

7 Unreliability and range restriction not only have a general weakening effect on correlations; they also account for differences between studies in correlation strength. Meta-analysis removes such artificial variability. Any residual variability denotes 'situational specificity' due to theoretically meaningful 'substantive' factors (e.g. job type).

8 Not to be confused with the same term used to denote reverse causality in recursive path models.

9 Ones et al. (2005) offer other suggestions.

10 Folding a distribution of correlations at 0 causes inflation in the mean and deflation in the variance. Knowledge of the degrees of inflation and deflation expected under specific conditions allows precise corrections, yielding a distribution of correlations capturing strength independent of direction.

11 Derived from $(0.30 - 0.09)/0.30 = 70\%$ and $(0.30 - 0.12)/0.30 = 60\%$. In terms of proportion of variance explained, using ρ^2, the losses are even greater: $(0.30^2 - 0.09^2)/0.30^2 = 91\%$ and $(0.30^2 - 0.12^2)/0.30^2 = 84\%$. Unsquared values are emphasized here because the value of a test (i.e. its utility) is a linear function of such values, not their squared counterparts.

12 A fifth situational feature, 'facilitator', is proposed as an enhancer or multiplier of any of the other features.

13 See Tett and Guterman (2000: 399–400) for a synopsis of sources in support of trait-situation matching.

14 Conversely, Tett et al. (1999) report a stronger mean correlation for recruits (0.30) over incumbents (0.23) based on fewer studies ($K = 12$ and 83, respectively) and using absolute values with appropriate corrections. Primary studies directly comparing personality test validity under applicant versus incumbent conditions, in light of possible bidirectionality and holding methods and criteria constant, are needed to more fully address this issue.

15 Henry Murray, a major proponent of trait–situation interactional psychology (e.g. Murray, 1938), was a key contributor to ACs developed by the Office of Strategic Services during WWII for selecting spies.

16 It should be noted that the issues addressed in this section relate primarily to the laws of the United States and that legal systems and societal norms will make these more or less salient in other countries.

17 E contributes to team viability – staying together – but less so to team performance (Barrick et al., 1998).

REFERENCES

Ackerman, P.L. and Heggestad, E.D. (1997) 'Intelligence, personality, and interests: Evidence for overlapping traits', *Psychological Bulletin*, 121(2): 219–45.

Allport, G.W. (1937) *Personality: A Psychological Interpretation*. New York: Holt, Rinehart Winston.

Barrick, M.R. and Mount, M.K. (1991) 'The big five personality dimensions and job performance: A meta-analysis', *Personnel Psychology*, 44(1): 1–26.

Barrick, M.R. and Mount, M.K. (1996) 'Effects of impression management and self-deception on the predictive validity of personality constructs', *Journal of Applied Psychology*, 81(3): 261–72.

Barrick, M.R. and Mount, M.K. (2003) 'Impact of meta-analysis on understanding personality–performance relations', in K. Murphy (ed.), *Validity Generalization: A Critical Review*. Hillsdale, NJ: Lawrence Erlbaum, pp. 197–221.

Barrick, M.R., Patton, G.K. and Haugland, S.N. (2000) 'Accuracy of interviewer judgments of job applicant personality traits', *Personnel Psychology*, 53(4): 925–51.

Barrick, M.R., Stewart, G.L., Neubert, M. and Mount, M.K. (1998) 'Relating member ability and personality to work team processes and team effectiveness', *Journal of Applied Psychology*, 83(3): 377–91.

Bartram, D. (2005) 'The Great Eight competencies: A criterion-centric approach to validation', *Journal of Applied Psychology*, 90(6): 1185–203.

Belbin, R.M. (1996) 'Team roles and a self-perception inventory', in J. Billsberry (ed.), *The Effective Manager: Perspectives and Illustrations*. London: Open University Press.

Bing, M.N., Whanger, J.C., Davison, H.K. and VanHook, J.B. (2004) 'Incremental validity of the frame-of-reference effect in personality scale scores: A replication and extension', *Journal of Applied Psychology*, 89(1): 150–7.

Blackman, M.C. (2002) 'Personality judgment and the utility of the unstructured employment interview', *Basic and Applied Social Psychology*, 24(3): 241–50.

Block, J. (1995) 'A contrarian view of the five-factor approach to personality description', *Psychological Bulletin*, 117(2): 187–215.

Borman, W.C. and Motowidlo, S.J. (1997) 'Task performance and contextual performance: The meaning for personnel selection research', *Human Performance*, 10(2): 99–109.

Borman, W.C., Penner, L.A., Allen, T.D. and Motowidlo, S.J. (2001) 'Personality predictors of citizenship and performance', *International Journal of Selection and Assessment*, 9(1): 52–69.

Bowers, K.S. (1973) 'Situationism in psychology: An analysis and a critique', *Psychological Review*, 80(5): 307–36.

Boyle, G.J. (2007) 'Critique of the five-factor model of personality', in G.J. Boyle, G. Matthews and D.H. Saklofske (eds), *The Sage Handbook of Personality Theory and Assessment*. Los Angeles: Sage, pp. 291–308.

Bray, D.W., Campbell, R.J. and Grant, D.L. (1974) *Formative Years in Business: A Long-term AT&T Study of Managerial Lives*. New York: John Wiley & Sons.

Bray, D.W. and Howard, A. (1983) 'Personality and the assessment center method', in C.D. Spielberger and J.N. Butcher (eds), *Advances in Personality Assessment* (Vol. 3). Hillsdale, NJ: Lawrence Erlbaum.

Burns, G. and Christiansen, N.D. (2006) 'Sensitive or senseless: On the use of social desirability in correcting for motivated distortion', in R. Griffith (ed.), *A Closer Examination of Applicant Faking Behavior*. Greenwich, CT: Information Age Publishing.

Christiansen, N.D., Goffin, R.D., Johnston, N.G. and Rothstein, M.G. (1994) 'Correcting the 16PF for faking: Effects on criterion-related validity and individual hiring decisions', *Personnel Psychology*, 47(4): 847–60.

Christiansen, N.D., Wolcott-Burnam, S. and Janovics, J.E. (2005) 'The good judge revisited: Individual differences in the accuracy of personality judgments', *Human Performance*, 18(2): 123–49.

Conger, A.J. and Jackson, D.N. (1972) 'Suppressor variables, prediction, and the interpretation of psychological relationships', *Educational and Psychological Measurement*, 32(3): 579–99.

Costa, Jr., P.T., McCrae, R.R. and Kay, G.G. (1995) 'Persons, places, and personality: Career assessment using the revised NEO personality inventory', *Journal of Career Assessment*, 3(2): 123–9.

Craik, K.H., Ware, A.P., Kamp, J., O'Reilly, C., III, Staw, B. and Zedeck, S. (2002) 'Explorations of construct validity in a combined managerial and personality assessment programme', *Journal of Occupational and Organizational Psychology*, 75(2): 171–93.

Cucina, J.M., Vasilopoulos, N.L. and Sehgal, K.G. (2005) 'Personality-based job analysis and the self-serving bias', *Journal of Business and Psychology*, 20(2): 275–90.

Douglas, E.F., McDaniel, M.A. and Snell, A.F. (1996) 'The validity of non-cognitive measures decays when applicants fake', Paper presented at the Annual Conference of the Academy of Management, August, Cincinnati.

Funder, D.C. (1999) *Personality Judgment: A Realistic Approach to Person Perception*. San Diego: Academic Press.

Gellatly, I.R. and Irving, P.G. (2001) 'Personality, autonomy, and contextual performance of managers', *Human Performance*, 14(3): 231–45.

Gilliland, S.W. (1993) 'The perceived fairness of selection systems: An organizational justice perspective', *Academy of Management Review*, 18(4): 694–734.

Goffin, R.D. and Christiansen, N.D. (2003) 'Correcting personality tests for faking: A review of popular personality tests and initial survey of researchers', *International Journal of Selection and Assessment*, 11(4): 340–4.

Goffin, R.D., Rothstein, M.G. and Johnston, N.G. (1996) 'Personality testing and the assessment center: Incremental validity for managerial selection', *Journal of Applied Psychology*, 81(6): 746–56.

Gottfredson, G.D. and Holland, J.L. (1994) *Position Classification Inventory*. Odessa, FL: Psychological Assessment Resources.

Griffin, B. and Hesketh, B. (2004) 'Why openness to experience is not a good predictor of job performance', *International Journal of Selection and Assessment*, 12(3): 243–51.

Griffith, R.L., Chmielowski, T.S. and Yoshita, Y. (in press) 'Do applicants fake? An examination of the frequency of applicant faking behavior', *Personnel Review*, 36(3): 341–55.

Haaland, S. and Christiansen, N.D. (2002) 'Implications of trait-activation theory for evaluating the construct validity of assessment center ratings', *Personnel Psychology*, 55(1): 137–63.

Haaland, D., Christiansen, N.D. and Kaufman, G. (1999) 'Applicant distortion of personality measures in police selection: Reasons for optimism and caution', Paper presented at the Annual Conference of the Society for Industrial and Organizational Psychology, April, Atlanta.

Hausknecht, J.P., Day, D.V. and Thomas, S.C. (2004) 'Applicant reactions to selection procedures: An updated model and meta-analysis', *Personnel Psychology*, 57(3): 639–83.

Hedges, L.V. and Olkin, I. (2005) *Statistical Methods for Meta-Analysis* (2nd edn). Orlando: Academic Press.

Hogan, J. and Holland, H. (2003) 'Using theory to evaluate personality and job-performance relations: A socioanalytic perspective', *Journal of Applied Psychology*, 88(1): 100–112.

Hogan, J. and Rybicki, S. (1998) *Performance Improvement Characteristics Job Analysis Manual*. Tulsa, OK: Hogan Assessment Systems.

Holtz, B.C., Ployhart, R.E. and Dominguez, A. (2005) 'Testing the rules of justice: The effects of frame-of-reference and pre-test validity information on personality test responses and test perceptions', *International Journal of Selection and Assessment*, 13(1): 75–86.

Hough, L.M. (1992) 'The "big five" personality variables – construct confusion: Description versus prediction', *Human Performance*, 5(1): 139–55.

Hough, L.M. (1998) 'Personality at work: Issues and evidence', in M. Hakel (ed.), *Beyond Multiple Choice: Evaluating Alternatives to Traditional Testing for Selection*. Hillsdale, NJ: Lawrence Erlbaum.

Hough, L.M. and Furnham, A. (2003) 'Use of personality variables in work settings', in W.C. Borman, D.R. Ilgen and R.J. Klimoski (eds), *Handbook of Psychology (Vol. 12): Industrial and Organizational Psychology*. Wiley.

Hough, L.M., Ones, D.S. and Viswesvaran, C. (1998) 'Personality correlates of managerial performance constructs', Paper presented in Personality Determinants of Managerial Potential Performance, Progression and Ascendancy, R.C. Page (Chair), 13th Annual Conference of the Society for Industrial Organizational Psychology, April, Dallas.

Huffcutt, A.I., Conway, J.M., Roth, P.L. and Stone, N.J. (2001) 'Identification and meta-analytic assessment of psychological constructs measured in employment interviews', *Journal of Applied Psychology*, 86(5): 897–913.

Huffcutt, A.I., Roth, P.L. and McDaniel, M.A. (1996) 'A meta-analytic investigation of cognitive ability in employment interview evaluations: Moderating characteristics and implications for incremental validity', *Journal of Applied Psychology*, 81(5): 459–73.

Hunter, J.E. and Hunter, R.F. (1984) 'Validity and utility of alternative predictors of job performance', *Psychological Bulletin*, 96(1): 72–98.

Hunter, J.E. and Schmidt, F.L. (2004) *Methods of Meta-Analysis: Correcting for Error and Bias in Research Findings*. Thousand Oaks: Sage.

Hurtz, G.M. and Donovan, J.J. (2000) 'Personality and job performance: The Big Five revisited', *Journal of Applied Psychology*, 85(6): 869–79.

Jackson, D.N., Peacock, A.C. and Holden, R.R. (1982) Professional interviewers' trait inferential structures for diverse occupational groups', *Organizational Behavior and Human Performance*, 29(1): 1–20.

Jackson, D.N., Peacock, A.C. and Smith, J.P. (1980) 'Impressions of personality in the employment interview', *Journal of Personality and Social Psychology*, 39(2): 294–307.

Jackson, D.N., Wroblewski, V.R. and Ashton, M.C. (2000) 'The impact of faking on employment tests: Does forced choice offer a solution?', *Human Performance*, 13(4): 371–88.

Jenkins, M. and Griffith, R. (2004) 'Using personality constructs to predict performance: Narrow or broad bandwidth', *Journal of Business and Psychology*, 19(2): 255–69.

Judge, T.A., Bono, J.E., Ilies, R. and Gerhardt, M.W. (2002) 'Personality and leadership: A qualitative and quantitative review', *Journal of Applied Psychology*, 87(4): 765–80.

Lievens, F., De Fruyt, F.D. and Van Dam, K. (2001) 'Assessors' use of personality traits in descriptions of assessment centre candidates: A five-factor model perspective', *Journal of Occupational and Organizational Psychology*, 74(5): 623–36.

Lievens, F., Chasteen, C.S. and Day, E.A. (2006) 'Large-scale investigation of the role of trait activation theory for understanding assessment center convergent and discriminant validity', *Journal of Applied Psychology*, 91(2): 247–58.

Lippa, R.A. and Dietz, J.K. (2000) 'The relation of gender, personality, and intelligence to judges' accuracy in judging strangers' personality from brief video segments', *Journal of Nonverbal Behavior*, 24(1): 25–43.

Lopez, F.M., Kesselman, G.A. and Lopez, F.E. (1981) 'An empirical test of a trait-oriented job analysis technique', *Personnel Psychology*, 34(3): 479–502.

McFarland, L., Ryan, A.M. and Kriska, D.S. (2003) 'Impression management use and effectiveness across assessment methods', *Journal of Management*, 29(5): 641–61.

Morgeson, F.P., Campion, M.A., Dipboye, R.L., Hollenbeck, J.R., Murphy, K. and Schmitt, N. (2007) 'Reconsidering use of personality tests in personnel selection contexts', *Personnel Psychology*, 60(3): 683–729.

Mueller-Hanson, R. Heggestad, E.D. and Thornton, G.C. III. (2003) 'Faking and selection: considering the use of personality from select-in and select-out perspectives', *Journal of Applied Psychology*, 88(2): 348–55.

Murray, H. (1938) *Explorations in Personality*. New York: Oxford University Press.

Neuman, G.A., Wagner, S.H. and Christiansen, N.D. (1999) 'The relationship between work–team personality composition and the job performance of teams', *Group and Organization Management*, 24(1): 28–45.

Ones, D.S. and Viswesvaran, C. (1996) 'Bandwidth-fidelity dilemma in personality measurement for personnel selection', *Journal of Organizational Behavior*, 17(6): 609–26.

Ones, D.S., Viswesvaran, C. and Dilchert, S. (2005) 'Personality at work: Raising awareness and correcting misconceptions', *Human Performance*, 18(4): 389–404.

Ones, D.S., Viswesvaran, C. and Reiss, A.D. (1996) 'Role of social desirability in personality testing for personnel selection: The red herring', *Journal of Applied Psychology*, 81(6): 660–79.

Ones, D.S., Viswesvaran, C. and Schmidt, F.L. (1993) 'Comprehensive meta-analysis of integrity test validities: Findings and implications for personnel selection and theories of job performance', *Journal of Applied Psychology*, 78(4): 679–703.

Organ, D.W. and Ryan, K. (1995) 'A meta-analytic review of attitudinal and dispositional predictors of organizational citizenship behavior', *Personnel Psychology*, 48(4): 775–802.

Peterson, M.H. and Griffith, R.L. (2006) 'Faking and job performance: A multi-faceted issue', in R.L. Griffith and M.H. Peterson (eds), *A Closer Examination of Applicant Faking Behavior*. Greenwich, CT: Information Age Publishing.

Ployhart, R.E., Schneider, B. and Schmitt, N. (2006) *Staffing Organizations: Contemporary Practice and Theory*. Hillsdale, NJ: Lawrence Erlbaum.

Raymark, P.H., Schmit, M.J. and Guion, R.M. (1997) 'Identifying potentially useful personality constructs for employee selection', *Personnel Psychology*, 50(3): 723–36.

Roberts, B.W., Chernyshenko, O.S. and Stark, S. (2005) 'The structure of conscientiousness: An empirical investigation based on seven major personality questionnaires', *Personnel Psychology*, 58(1): 103–39.

Robie, C., Tuzinski, K.A. and Bly, P.R. (2006) 'A survey of assessor beliefs and practices related to faking', *Journal of Managerial Psychology*, 21(7): 669–81.

Rosse, J.G., Stecher, M.D., Miller, J.L. and Levin, R.A. (1998) 'The impact of response distortion on preemployment personality testing and hiring decisions', *Journal of Applied Psychology*, 83(4): 634–44.

Rothstein, M.G. and Goffin, R.D. (2006) 'The use of personality measures in personnel selection: What does current research support?', *Human Resource Management Review*, 16(2): 155–80.

Ryan, A.M. and Ployhart, R.E. (2000) 'Applicants' perceptions of selection procedures and decisions: A critical review and agenda for the future', *Journal of Management*, 26(3): 565–606.

Salgado, J.F. (1997) 'The five factor model of personality and job performance in the European community', *Journal of Applied Psychology*, 82(1): 30–43.

Salgado, J.F. (2002) 'The Big Five personality dimensions and counterproductive behaviors', *International Journal of Selection and Assessment*, 10(1): 117–25.

Schmit, M.J. and Ryan, A.M. (1993) 'The big five in personnel selection: Factor structure in applicant and nonapplicant populations', *Journal of Applied Psychology*, 78(6): 966–74.

Smither, J.W., Reilly, R.R., Millsap, R.E., Pearlman, K. and Stoffey, R.W. (1993) 'Reactions to selection procedures', *Personnel Psychology*, 46(1): 49–76.

Sümer, H.C., Sümer, N., Demirutku, K. and çifci, O.S. (2001) 'Using a personality-oriented job analysis to identify attributes to be assessed in officer selection', *Military Psychology*, 13(3): 129–46.

Sundstrom, E. (1999) 'The challenges of supporting work team effectiveness', in E. Sundstrom and Associates, *Supporting Work Team Effectiveness: Best Management Practices for Fostering High Team Performance*. San Francisco: Jossey-Bass, pp. 3–23.

Tett, R.P., Anderson, M.G., Ho, C.L., Yang, T.S., Huang, L. and Hanvongse, A. (2006) 'Seven nested questions about faking on personality tests: An overview and interactionist model of item-level response distortion', in R.L. Griffith and M.H. Peterson (eds), *A Closer Examination of Applicant Faking Behavior*. Greenwich, CT: Information Age Publishing, pp. 43–83.

Tett, R.P. and Burnett, D.B. (2003) 'A personality trait-based interactionist model of job performance', *Journal of Applied Psychology*, 88(3): 500–17.

Tett, R.P. and Guterman, H.A. (2000) 'Situation trait relevance, trait expression, and cross-situational consistency: Testing a principle of trait activation', *Journal of Research in Personality*, 34(4): 397–423.

Tett, R.P., Jackson, D.N. and Rothstein, M. (1991) 'Personality measures as predictors of job performance: A meta-analytic review', *Personnel Psychology*, 44(4): 703–42.

Tett, R.P., Jackson, D.N., Rothstein, M. and Reddon, J.R. (1999) 'Meta-analysis of bi-directional relations in personality–job

performance research', *Human Performance*, 12(1): 1–29.

Tett, R.P. and Murphy, P.J. (2002) 'Personality and situations in co-worker preference: Similarity and complementarity in co-worker compatibility', *Journal of Business and Psychology*, 17(2): 223–43.

Tett, R.P., Steele, J.R. and Beauregard, R.S. (2003) 'Broad and narrow measures on both sides of the personality–job performance relationship', *Journal of Organizational Behavior*, 24(3): 335–56.

Thornton, G.C. III. and Byham, W.C. (1982) *Assessment Centers and Managerial Performance*. New York: Academic Press.

Truxillo, D.M., Bauer, T.N., Campion, M.A. and Paronto, M.E. (2002) 'Selection fairness information and applicant reactions: A longitudinal field study', *Journal of Applied Psychology*, 87(6): 1020–31.

Turnage, J.J. and Muchinsky, P.M. (1984) 'A comparison of the predictive validity of assessment center evaluations versus traditional measures in forecasting supervisory job performance: Interpretive implications of criterion distortion for the assessment paradigm', *Journal of Applied Psychology*, 69(4): 595–602.

Van Iddekinge, C.H., Taylor, M.A. and Eidson, C.E. Jr. (2005) 'Broad versus narrow facets of integrity: Predictive validity and subgroup differences', *Human Performance*, 18(2): 151–77.

Vinchur, A.J., Schippmann, J.S., Switzer, F.S. and Roth, P.L. (1998) 'A meta-analytic review of job performance for salespeople', *Journal of Applied Psychology*, 83(4): 586–97.

Viswesvaran, C., Ones, D.S. and Schmidt, F.L. (1996) 'Comparative analysis of the reliability of job performance ratings', *Journal of Applied Psychology*, 81(5): 557–74.

Wanek, J.E., Sackett, P.R. and Ones, D.S. (2003) 'Towards an understanding of integrity test similarities and differences: An item-level analysis of seven tests', *Personnel Psychology*, 56(4): 873–94.

Weiss, H.M. and Adler, S. (1984) 'Personality and organizational behavior', in B.M. Staw and L.L. Cummings (eds), *Research in Organizational Behavior* (Vol. VI). Greenwich, CT: JAI Press, pp. 1–50.

Woodworth, R.S. (1937). *Psychology*. New York: Holt.

Subject Index

Name Index

Abbott, L. F. 248
Abed, A. S. 493
Abel, K. 408
Abercrombie, H. C. 685
Abernethy, A. D. 477
Abler, B. 248, 685
Abraham, A. 363
Abrams, D. 492
Achat, H. 643
Achenbach, T. M. 435
Acierno, R. 709
Ackerman, P. L. 545, 734
Ackerman, S. J. 582
Adalbjarnardottir, S. 701
Adamec, R. 317
Ader, R. 645
Adler, A. B. 706
Adler, S. 720
Affleck, G. 474, 476, 645
Af Klinteberg, B. 367
Aguilera, M. 683
Aiken, L. S. 232
Aish, A. M. 472
Al'Absi, M. 707
Alanazi, F. M. 491, 494
Albert, C. M. 641
Alder, M. D. 661
Aldwin, C. M. 511
Alemagno, S. A. 643
Allbutt, J. 403
Allen, A. 83, 202, 205
Allen, G. J. 428
Allen, J. J. B. 345
Allgeier, E. R. 184–5
Allik, J. 131, 273, 287, 299–300, 494
Allison, P. J. 473
Allport, G. W. 2, 4, 84, 90, 125, 175, 190–2, 194,
    196–7, 202, 204, 206, 295, 336, 729
Allsopp, J. 361
Alpert, R. 425
Aluja, A. 298, 336, 368, 386, 391
Aluja-Fabregat, A. 391

Amalric, M. 39
Ambwani, S. 219
Amelang, M. 41, 63, 578
Amen, D. G. 343
American Psychiatric Association (APA) 600–2, 605,
    623, 659, 705
Amey, C. H. 704
Amirkhan, J. H. 509, 511
Amos, A. 702, 710
Anda, R. 641
Andersen, S. M. 89, 472
Anderson, C. A. 337
Anderson, E. M. 493
Anderson, J. C. 646
Anderson, J. R. 525, 528
Anderson, R. 317
Andreasen, N. C. 400
Andreu, J. M. 337
Andrews, G. 508
Andrews, J. J. W. 12
Andrucci, G. L. 384
Andrue, J. M. 343
Angleitner, A. 298, 512
Ansell, E. B. 637
Antonovsky, A. 510
Appadurai, A. 126
Appels, A. 665
Applebaum, S. A. 582
Araujo, K. B. 508
Arbuthnott, G. W. 247
Archer, R. P. 277
Archer, T. 221, 316
Arijit, N. 706
Aristippus, 316
Arkin, R. 316
Armitage, C. J. 703
Armitage, K. 317
Armstrong-Stassen, M. 510
Arnau, R. C. 218
Arndt, S. 403
Arnett, J. J. 701
Arseneault, J. 72